A History of Chinese Political Thought

VOLUME ONE

A History of
Chinese Political Thought

VOLUME ONE: FROM THE BEGINNINGS
TO THE SIXTH CENTURY A.D.

By Kung-chuan Hsiao
Translated by F. W. Mote

PRINCETON UNIVERSITY PRESS,
PRINCETON, NEW JERSEY

Copyright © 1979 by Princeton University Press
Published by Princeton University Press, Princeton, New Jersey
In the United Kingdom: Princeton University Press, Guildford, Surrey

Library of Congress Cataloging in Publication Data will
be found on the last printed page of this book

This translation of *Chung-kuo cheng-chih ssu-hsiang-shih* is authorized by the author, and incorporates minor changes that he has made in the text of the work as originally published, in Chinese, in two volumes (Commercial Press, Chungking and Shanghai, 1945–1946) and in six volumes, (Taipei, 1954, and repeatedly since, by various publishers). Except in cases where such changes involve only typesetting errors, departures from the published versions are noted in the translation. F. W. M.

This book has been composed in Monotype Baskerville

Printed in the United States of America
by Princeton University Press, Princeton, New Jersey

Table of Contents

Fan-li—General Principles Governing the Composition of This Work

One: This work adopts the point of view of political science, and employs the methods of history in briefly narrating the general features of political thought through the twenty-five hundred years commencing with the late Chou era. It is intended as a reference work for students in the political science departments of [Chinese] colleges and universities. With regard to the period preceding the late Chou, noting the inadequacy of documentary evidence, we have adopted for the present Confucius' example in "putting aside the points of which one stands in doubt" [*Analects*, II/18/2]. Thus there is no chapter devoted specifically to the earlier political thought, although some references to that appear in the chapters on Confucius, on Mencius and Hsün Tzu, and elsewhere.

Two: This work is structured on the warp of chronology, and the woof of the various thinkers and schools; its content is drawn principally from those figures of the past whose writings possess theoretical value and importance. The presentation attempts to include those political discourses which are judged to have had the greatest influence, and omits all of those which are relevant to concrete issues limited in their significance to particular places and times.

Three: In relating the thought of the various thinkers, this work strives to achieve an attitude of objectivity. Where critical evaluations occasionally appear, the intent has been to elucidate the historical position of the ideas in question, and not to impose subjective censure or praise, nor to indulge in personal judgments on the worth of these ideas.

Four: The manuscript of Part Five of this work [Chapter Twenty-five; Bibliography of Principal Works Consulted; Index] was lost; those headings have been retained in the Table of Contents to indicate the scope and form of the original work.

Five: The author is conscious of the inadequacies of his own learning; moreover, this book was completed during the war years [1937–1945], when access to reference materials was often difficult or impossible. Not only have my researches been less than exhaustive, I also fear that errors may abound. Although having failed to seek fuller guidance from my superiors in learning, I can yet hope that they will not now deny me their criticisms and advice.

K. C. HSIAO
[Manuscript completed June 26, 1941
at Chengtu, Szechwan]

Author's Foreword

It has been said that the greatest compliment a scholar can confer on a writer is to translate his work into another language, making it accessible to a wider circle of readers. F. W. Mote has done me a great honor indeed in rendering my book on Chinese political thought into English. This arduous task has been accomplished with as much consummate skill and erudition as with meticulous care. I owe him a debt of gratitude and appreciation far beyond repayment.

The original editions, prepared under less than favorable conditions, contain many errors, grave or inconsiderable, that, due to circumstances beyond my control, were mostly allowed to stand in later editions. Professor Mote has given me ample opportunity and valuable help in removing them in the English edition. I must be held responsible and offer apologies for whatever faults may still remain.

K. C. HSIAO
Seattle, 1972

Translator's Preface

A brief account of how this translation came into existence may not be entirely out of place here. The author's name, of course, was well known to me when, as a graduate student, I at last had the opportunity of meeting him at the University of Washington in 1950. I attended K. C. Hsiao's lectures in Chinese political thought at that time, but did not have an opportunity to read the work translated here until it was reprinted in Taiwan in 1954, for the earlier printing, while not unknown in American collections, was not widely available.[1] I found the book difficult, by reason of its profound insights into Chinese civilization and the knowledge required to appreciate those insights, but immensely stimulating. The thought of translating it was in my mind from the first reading.

Yet the practical difficulties in putting so large and so tightly knit a work of original scholarship into English were quite forbidding. At first I thought of asking the author whether he might not undertake the task himself, but others among his colleagues at the University of Washington reported that he was deeply engaged in teaching and in other research; moreover, he was not drawn to the idea of engaging in a vast re-creation in another language of a work whose original creation in Chinese had occupied long years in the (then) recent past. While in no sense seeking to have his work translated he offered, however, to assist a translator, should one wish to undertake the task, by reading the translation and offering advice. George E. Taylor, then Director of the Far Eastern and Russian Institute (which in 1971 became the Institute for Comparative and Foreign Area Studies) of the University of Washington, became interested in the idea of having the work translated, and offered his encouragement. Several former graduate students who had studied under K. C. Hsiao decided to work as a team, each translating those chapters closest to his research interests. Through the mid-1950's this plan was discussed, but it produced no results. In 1958, Professor Taylor invited me to come back to Seattle to get the translation started on an experimental basis. Three or four chapters were translated, enough to make me the more fully aware of the difficulties and dangers in such work, but also enough to convince me that, with Professor Hsiao's guidance, the task could be done.

[1] Publication data: *Chung-kuo cheng-chih ssu-hsiang-shih*, Commercial Press two-volume edition, vol. one, first Chungking edition, April, 1945; first Shanghai edition, December, 1945; vol. two, first published October, 1946, in Shanghai. Four or more reprintings of both volumes were made in Shanghai before 1950. First Taiwan edition, in six volumes, August, 1954; several reprintings of this edition have since appeared.

In general, the work of translation has merited very little encouragement or assistance. Until recently, sources of research grants normally would not consider an application for support to translate a modern work of scholarship, on the grounds that "translation is not scholarship." That view is defensible, yet translation can be important to a field of scholarship, and it is very difficult to accomplish the task in odd moments and during brief vacations. This translation therefore lagged for a decade, little or no further progress ensuing. When in 1971 I determined to make it the first order of business, regardless of all else, I accepted employment at the University of Washington to further that cause by being close to Professor Hsiao, who was by that time professor emeritus and living adjacent to the university campus. The Far Eastern and Russian Institute generously offered various kinds of support. The National Endowment for the Humanities also granted research support, without which the translation and preparation of the manuscript would have required still longer. The conjunction of these several favorable circumstances allowed the work to commence again in earnest. All the earlier work was retranslated to achieve greater consistency in style and usage, retyped, read by Professor Hsiao, and again revised after his meticulous and untiring editing. In this manner, the first part, comprising Volume One of this edition, was completed by the end of 1971, and the remainder has since been translated, assuring that the task will at last be completed. I recount this experience in order to pay thanks to those who have patiently waited the matter through, especially those who have encouraged and supported the task from its inception. Above all, I wish to point out my many layers of indebtedness to Professor Hsiao himself for keeping faith with a translator who had dawdled for over a decade, and for yet giving him the benefit of his unfailing wit, wisdom, and limitless erudition.

Without the author's willingness to assist by editing and correcting the draft translation, this translator would have been unwilling to undertake the task, and unable to complete it. I have committed many errors in translating, yet with patience and precision Professor Hsiao has always offered the appropriate corrections, neatly inserted on slips of paper. The translation thus has become a joint effort in which the author's judgment has ruled. Also, many typesetter's errors and other minor inaccuracies in the original have been corrected (and, except where substantial, usually without noting those departures from the Chinese text). Thus this translation, despite continuing inadequacies of English style, nonetheless is authorized by Professor Hsiao to supersede the Chinese original, where discrepancies exist. Although in that limited sense the translation takes precedence over the original where specific discrepancies of content occur, the translator's purpose has been merely to bring the work to a wider audience, not to render the original work obsolete. The translation suffers all the shortcomings obvious in pedestrian academic English frequently interrupted by bracketed insertions. The original, in striking contrast, is one of the masterpieces of modern literary Chinese. It possesses immense richness of style and forceful clarity of expression, together with masterly subtlety and allusiveness ever varying in relation to the period and the subject under discussion. That dimension of the work has been lost in translation, and for those who have access to the original, it should by all means and in all circumstances take priority over the impoverished translation.

Finally, the work of translation has been for the translator a rigorous continuing course in classical Chinese in philosophy, in history, and in Western political concepts and methods. My original impulse to undertake the translation was totally selfish, motivated by the desire to receive precisely this training from the hand of this master; what student of China would not wish to have so stimulating, so profitable, and so profoundly pleasant an experience?

F. W. MOTE

Notes on the Principles Guiding Translation

The translator's intent has been to reproduce the original work, not to produce a new study of the subject taking into account the relevant scholarship now in existence. The author's original footnotes are extensive, and are adequate to sustain the text they accompany. Nevertheless, the work is written in an elegant and highly learned classical style for students assumed to possess considerable background knowledge of the Chinese cultural tradition. Unfortunately, with the passage of only twenty-five or thirty years, such readers are now unusual in China, and they have always been rare in the West. Therefore the translator has felt it necessary to insert some notes into the text to clarify the meaning of difficult or obscure passages. Also, many allusions to classical works have been identified. *All such additions to the original, both in the text and in the accompanying footnotes, have been enclosed in square brackets.* Parentheses have been used only as in the original. The insertion of words and occasionally of whole sentences in brackets creates the risk of destroying the continuity and readability of the original; therefore these have been reduced to a minimum, but they still may offend some readers.

The reader of Chinese familiar with the original will note several other departures from the original text. Single sentences in the original have often been divided into two or more English sentences, and paragraphs in the original have often been subdivided. Also, in translating the author's footnotes, the translator has adopted forms of citation standard in Western language bibliographies. Otherwise, the format and content of the original have been preserved. No portions have been omitted, except for a word or a line here and there, as noted in square brackets in all cases. Also, in the very few instances where a loose paraphrase has seemed preferable to a close translation, those have been noted. The use of quotation marks in the translation also varies slightly from that in the original, in the following way only: some words and phrases embodying well-known allusions in the original, in keeping with Chinese usage, are not enclosed in quotation marks there. In many such cases quotation marks have been added in the translation, in keeping with English usage, and for the convenience of the reader who might not recognize them as allusions. Otherwise, this is an integral, direct translation, as faithful to the original as possible.

In translating passages quoted from Chinese classical, historical, and scholarly works, the translator's purpose has been to find English equivalents expressing the sense in which the author has quoted those in the original. Therefore, alternate interpretations *usually have not* been indicated, but where they might contribute to the English reader's understanding, they have occasionally been noted. Standard English translations are cited where possible, in the version closest to the author's intent, but for the sake of consistency in handling recurring terms, modifications of wording have often been necessary, and in all cases have been noted. Eminent translations into other languages have in many cases been consulted, but have seldom been quoted, since the purpose is to produce an English equivalent of the book as it exists in Chinese, not to establish any issues in scholarship, nor to supply bibliographic guidance to the scholar who might wish to pursue further research interests of his own.

The following comments indicate in a general way the translations that have been most heavily drawn upon for quotations from the pre-Ch'in political thinkers: For the *Analects*, as for the Chinese canonical works, first reference has been made to the translations of James Legge (i.e., *The Chinese Classics*, 1895, in the University of Hong Kong's 1960 reprint in five volumes, and the *Li Chi*, or *Li Ki* in the *Sacred Books of the East*, edited by Max Müller). Arthur Waley's translation of *The Analects of Confucius* (1938) in some instances has been preferred to Legge, and sometimes the best features of both have been combined.

When the chapter on Mencius was first translated, W. A. C. H. Dobson's new translation (1963) and D. C. Lau's (1970), had not yet appeared; the Legge translation has been heavily drawn upon, but a few revisions based on others, e.g., W. T. Chan, have been introduced.

H. H. Dubs' *The Works of Hsüntze* (1928) and later studies by J. J. L. Duyvendak, Y. P. Mei, and *Hsün Tzu: Basic Writings*, translated by Burton Watson (1963), have been consulted.

Quotations from Mo Tzu have been translated following Y. P. Mei's *Motze* (1934) where possible, with frequent reference to Burton Watson's *Mo Tzu: Basic Writings* (1963), but several of the key terms have been standardized, following the versions in W. T. Chan's *Source Book in Chinese Philosophy* (1963).

The *Lao Tzu, or Tao Te Ching* and the *Chuang Tzu* have been the most difficult to handle. The range of interpretations is the broadest, and the number of English versions of the former is very great. It would be difficult to devise a new translation of any line of the *Lao Tzu* that would not, consciously or unconsciously, coincide in some degree with existing ones. My solution has been, nonetheless, in some cases to produce new translations, after consulting a dozen existing versions ranging from Legge's (1891) to W. T. Chan's (1963).

For the *Chuang Tzu*, a similar range of translations has been consulted, with W. T. Chan and Burton Watson's *Complete Works of Chuang Tzu* (1968) proving most useful, but not to the exclusion of Legge's and Giles' earlier versions.

The *Kuan Tzu* is a large and difficult work for which English versions are less complete or less satisfactory than for any of the other early political thinkers. The translations in Maverick's pioneering *The Kuan-tzu* (1954) are in many cases paraphrases. A. W. Rickett's translation of twelve chapters from the *Kuan Tzu* (1965) includes few of the portions of that book most pertinent to political thought. Therefore it has been necessary in almost all cases to produce new translations of the quoted passages.

The *Book of Lord Shang* has been brilliantly translated and annotated by J. J. L. Duyvendak (1928). The *Han Fei Tzu: Basic Writings* (1964), the partial translation by Burton Watson, is in its use of English somewhat more useable than the *Complete Works of Han Fei Tzu* translated by W. K. Liao (two volumes, 1939 and 1960), yet the latter also has been consulted, with much profit, throughout.

The model of Derk Bodde's superb translation of Fung Yu-lan, *History of Chinese Philosophy* (two volumes, 1937/1952 and 1953) has been clearly in the mind of the translator, who is indebted to it not only for the inspiration it provides but also for translations of many terms and passages. The present work should be read in conjunction with Bodde's translation of Fung in order to understand some of the relationships between philosophy and political thought.

W. T. Chan's *Source Book in Chinese Philosophy* has been indispensable as a reference tool, and as a standard for meticulous translation. His *The Way of Lao Tzu* (1963) supersedes the translation of the *Tao Te Ching* found in the *Source Book* and offers fuller supporting scholarship, but the latter has been cited, for convenience, as the source of passages quoted here. The translator's notes indicate the extent to which the *Source Book* has been drawn upon. In addition, it is a pleasure to acknowledge the helpful advice drawn from Professor Chan's careful reading of the first eight chapters of the translation.

A. C. Graham's *The Book of Lieh-tzu* (1960) is another good example of recent translation that has been useful to the translator here, particularly in Chapter XI. Unfortunately, a number of excellent translations relevant to the present task, such as D. C. Lau's *Mencius* and *Tao Te Ching*, Timotheus Pokora's *Hsin-lun* (*New Treatise*) *and Other Writings by Huan T'an*, Ch'i-yün Ch'en's *Hsün Yüeh*, to name but a few outstanding examples, appeared only after the chapters to which they are relevant had already been translated and put into final form, so the translator was unable to benefit from them.

Finally, this translator must acknowledge the help and pleasure he has found in the vast achievement of Arthur Waley, whose translations of the *Analects* and the *Lao Tzu* have been noted above, and whose brilliantly rendered selections from Mencius, Chuang Tzu, and Mo Tzu are found in *Three Ways of Thought in Ancient China* (1939).

F. W. MOTE

Part One

*The Political Thought of the Feudal World—
the Period of Creativity*

以仁心說以學心聽以公心辯

此荀卿子之名言也余往歲竊

取其意而為治學之座右銘曰

以學心讀以平心取以公心述

壬子初夏錄應

復禮教授吾兄雅屬

七十五叟　公權

Introduction

SECTION ONE
The Starting Point of China's Political Thought

CHINA'S history is a continuum extending through centuries from a remote past. Its distant origins can be traced back four thousand years or more. [The archaeological evidence of course extends an ever more clearly verifiable indigenous pre-history many millennia back beyond the beginning of recorded history.]* Yet one who would study the history of China's political thought must excise all that precedes a beginning no earlier than the late Chou period. The realities of the situation demand this; it does not signify a careless disregard for our origins. Prior to the Three Dynasties [i.e., Hsia, Shang, and Chou, the "Three Dynasties of Antiquity," the latter two comprising the fully historical part of the pre-imperial era], Chinese society had scarcely developed, and no written records exist to bear witness to it; obviously we cannot deal with that early period. Even in the ages of Hsia and Shang, intellectual and material civilization were still in their formative beginnings. Learning and thought [this translation of *hsüeh-shu ssu-hsiang* 學術思相 has been suggested by the author as the most suitable equivalent, in this context, of a much overused modern Chinese term] were at best only commencing to bud; they still had not assumed definite form. Without historical records, and with only inadequate literary documentation, even if speculative thought had existed, it would now be difficult to reconstruct. Confucius, living in the Spring and Autumn Age, even then had to note regretfully that the institutions of the two [dynasties of Hsia and Yin-Shang] could not be attested to.[1] Although the "Nine Regulations in the Great Plan" [*Hung Fan Chiu Ch'ou* 洪範九疇] may perhaps represent something of the "great law" of the Emperor Yü's government in the Hsia period, it is a very simple and brief text. Much of the "Documents of Shang" is authentic, yet these records too are scattered and fragmentary.[2] As for the texts of the oracle bone inscriptions from the Yin-hsü sites, although they may serve as the basis for a theoretical reconstruction of ancient institutions,[3] after all they are not records of learning and

*Square brackets indicate that the words enclosed were added by the translator.

[1] The *Analects*, III/9 [Legge, p. 158].

[2] In his *Ku-shih hsin-cheng*, Wang Kuo-wei [1877–1927] states the opinion that all of the section called "Documents of Shang" [in the *Book of Documents*, or *Shang Shu*], with the exception of the "T'ang Shih," is genuine, as is that called the "Documents of Chou," except for the "Hung Fan," which is doubtful.

[3] See Chou Ch'uan-ju, *Chia-ku wen-tzu yü Yin Shang chih-tu* and Kuo Mo-jo, *Chung-kuo ku-tai she-hui*.

thought. All these constitute important materials for the historian and the archaeologist, but, from the point of view of political science, one is forced to concede that they rarely contain anything of real usefulness. Hence, when we attempt today to make a systematic study of China's political thought, the Chou period must be taken as our starting point. The civilization of ancient China flowered in the Chou dynasty. While we need not accept Hsia Tseng-yu's statement that "The whole of China's religion, ritual forms, government and literature is the creation of the Chou people,"[4] nonetheless it is clearly a fact that formal learning and thought were the creation of Chou period persons.

The great flourishing of learning did not occur during the heyday of the Chou dynasty but instead came long after the capital was moved to the east [to Lo-yang in 770 B.C.], at the end of the Spring and Autumn Period and during the Warring States Period.[5] Political thought, too, saw a rapid and sudden development at this time, when Confucius assumed the role of teacher and established his teachings [literally "in the capacity of *shih-ju*," which the *Chou Li* defines as a "local teacher"] and the doctrines of the various other schools appeared in turn. "By the Warring States Period, writing and exposition had become specializations."[6] Well-reasoned political theories appeared in great profusion, presenting a grand spectacle. Although we today cannot adduce the historical facts that conclusively and fully explain this sudden flowering, nonetheless we can deduce a generally satisfactory explanation by referring to the main features of the historical environment and broadly applicable principles of cultural development. There are two chief reasons for the rise of political thought in the late Chou period: in simplest terms, they are the rapid changes underway in the structure of society, and the opportune appearance on that scene of some great thinkers.

The Chou house, from the end of the reign of King P'ing [720 B.C.], was headed for insignificance and impotence. The feudal nobles were growing great and powerful, "the states of Ch'in, Chin, Ch'i and Ch'u

---

[4] Hsia Tseng-yu, *Chung-kuo ku-tai shih*, p. 290. Confucius said: "Chou had the advantage of viewing the two past dynasties. How complete and elegant are its regulations! I follow Chou." [*Analects*, III/14; Legge, p. 160.] And further: "The Chou dynasty has followed the regulations of the Yin: wherein it took from or added to them may be known." [*Ibid.*, II/23/2; Legge, p. 153.] This shows that he did not regard the Chou as innovator.

[5] In the first year of King P'ing (770 B.C.) the capital was moved to Lo-yi [i.e., Lo-yang in modern Honan]. The Spring and Autumn Period commences with the First year of the reign of Duke Yin of Lu (the Forty-ninth year of the reign of King P'ing or 722 B.C.), and ends with the Fourteenth year of the reign of Duke Ai (481 B.C.). The date of the beginning of the Warring States Period still is not agreed upon; hence I shall take it to correspond with the 259-year period from the end of the Spring and Autumn Period until the unification under The First Emperor of Ch'in, i.e., from the Fourth year of King Ching until the Twenty-sixth year of The First Emperor (480–221 B.C.).

[6] Chang Hsüeh-ch'eng [1738–1801]: *Wen-shih-t'ung-yi, ch.* 1, "Shih chiao, shang."

in turn flourished,"⁷ thus producing the conditions that prevailed throughout the Spring and Autumn Period. The feudal political institutions were
beginning to collapse; simultaneously the social system and the way of
life of the feudal aristocracy were being transformed. ["Feudal" is used
throughout simply as the convenient and thoroughly standardized translation of "*feng-chien*"; the Chinese term means a system of enfieffing
vassals to build a loose structure of decentralized authority, but most
scholars regard Chinese "feudalism" as something significantly different
from both European and Japanese "true" feudalisms.] The dividing line
between aristocrat and commoner was gradually disappearing.⁸ Service
in government and the acquisition of learning, both privileges originally
limited to noble families, were now opened to commoners.⁹ The historians
tell about the displacement of the hereditary court officials, and not without foundation in fact. Moreover, a multiplicity of feudal states coexisted,
and contended with each other for supremacy. Clearly, uniformity of
learning and thought could not be maintained. Thought was freed, learning was unrestricted. Scholars without official responsibilities [i.e.,
"*ch'u-shih*," "recluses," but in the broadest sense, persons in non-official
and private capacities, free to say what they pleased], were able to
develop their views freely; "heterodoxies" thus could widely prevail.
Rulers of princedoms, intent upon self-aggrandizement, greatly valued
the services of talented scholars. Duke Wen of Wei [reign 446–397 B.C.]
and the T'ien family rulers in Ch'i who maintained the Chi-hsia¹⁰ Academy are the most striking examples of this in the Warring States Period.
At this time, when "throughout the world there is no *Tao*" [*Analects*,
xvi/2/1, "When bad government prevails in the empire," Legge, p. 310;

---

⁷ *Kuo Yü*, ch. 16, "Cheng Yü." The *Shih Chi*, ch. 4, "Chou pen-chi" contains the same
passage.

⁸ For example, the *Tso Chuan*, Third year of Duke Chao, states: "The Luan, the Ch'üeh,
the Yüan, the Hu, the Hsü, the Ch'ing and the Po, are reduced to the position of menials.
[Legge, p. 589. These names are those of the former great aristocratic clans of the state.]
Other examples are Ning Ch'i, who had herded cows, yet was appointed to service under
Duke Huan of Ch'i, and Pai-li Ch'i, who though poor and humble served Duke Mu of
Ch'in.

⁹ Confucius taught the *Odes* and the *Documents* and the Six Disciplines according to the
principle that "In teaching, there should be no distinction of classes" [*Analects*, xv/38;
Legge, p. 305], thereby establishing the practice of making education generally available.

¹⁰ Duke Wen of Wei came to the throne in the Twenty-third year of the Chou King
Chen-ting (446 B.C.). King Wei of Ch'i established the Chi-hsia Palace [as a place to house
"guest scholars"] and established the practice of offering emoluments to attract scholars;
this was probably at the beginning of his reign [357 B.C.]. During the reign of King Hsüan
[319–301 B.C.] Chi-hsia again flourished, having as many as "several hundreds or a
thousand persons" (*Shih Chi*, ch. 46, T'ien Ch'i shih-chia), [who] "took delight in discussing affairs of government" (Liu Hsiang, *Hsin Hsü*, ch. 2). During the reign of King Min
(300–284 B.C.) it was disbanded.

cf. *Mencius*, iv/i/7/1, and vii/i/42/1], during this transitional period of social metamorphosis, not only did strife and disorder persist, making the livelihood of the people ever more precarious, but also all of the customs and institutions that previously had united people's minds and preserved social order were shaken to the point of collapse, their former effectiveness dissipated. Men of profound thought and far vision inevitably were moved to make critical inquiries into the causes and influences of these great changes, and quite naturally voiced opposition or offered constructive proposals. In consequence, political thought suddenly flowered. All of the factors mentioned above were already incipient in the Spring and Autumn Period, and by the Warring States Period they had intensified.[11] Consequently, the development of thought also reached its most intense stage only in the Warring States Period.

The social environment, however, provides no more than the conditions for the budding of thought. Had there not been born into that special environment thinkers of intellectual capacity far beyond the ordinary, men such as Confucius, Mencius, Chuang Tzu, and Han Fei Tzu, how

---

[11] Ku Yen-wu [1613–1682]: *Jih-chih-lu*, *ch.* 13, under the heading "Chou-mo feng-su" states: "In the Spring and Autumn Period, protocol and good faith were still respected, but among the Seven States [of the Warring States Period] protocol and good faith were definitely no longer observed. In the Spring and Autumn Period the Chou King still commanded respect, but among the Seven States the King definitely was not even mentioned. In the Spring and Autumn Period the sacrifices were still rigorously performed, and importance was attached to ceremonial etiquette and rites, but among the Seven States such things no longer existed. In the Spring and Autumn Period they still attached importance to clan and family relationships, but among the Seven States there is no single reference to such matters. In the Spring and Autumn Period at banquets of state the *Odes* were still recited, but we hear nothing of this among the Seven States. In the Spring and Autumn Period announcements of celebrations and mournings still were properly made, but there were none among the Seven States. States had no stable diplomatic ties, and men had no constant overlord. All of these changes occurred during the one hundred thirty-three year period for which historical records are lacking, but about which men of later ages can make their own deduction." This sets forth with great clarity the transformation from the Spring and Autumn Period to that of the Warring States.

Liu Hsiang [first century B.C.] also states in his preface to the *Chan-kuo Ts'e* "After Chung-ni [i.e., Confucius] died, the T'ien family seized the State of Ch'i, and the six chief minister divided up the State of Chin. Morality largely fell into decline; superior and inferior lost their status. Duke Hsiao of Ch'in abandoned comity and prized warfare, he discarded benevolence and righteousness and employed trickery and deceit—solely in the quest for power. Usurpers came to be ranked with princes and nobles, treacherous and deceitful states waxed to the status of great powers. Then this came to be imitated, and those who followed took Ch'in as their model. Thereafter [the States] all undertook to swallow and annihilate one another, annexing large and small, engaging in violent war year after year, shedding blood through all the countryside. Fathers and sons failed to observe family bonds, brother could not trust brother, husbands and wives were separated, and no one could guarantee his own life. In chaos and confusion, morality was extinguished." Here we see the main features of late Chou society.

could that all-important "Golden Age" in China's intellectual history have come into being? Political thought, we must conclude, arose in the late Chou period as a result of circumstances that might occur but once in a thousand years. Thus we have the most natural of reasons for taking this period as the starting point of our researches.[12]

Section Two
The Periodization of the History of Chinese Political Thought— in Accordance with the Main Outlines of the Development of Thought

WESTERNERS discussing China's culture always remark on its tendency toward conservatism. Hence scholars might suspect that China's political thought has long remained stagnant, unchanging from antiquity to modern times. In fact, however, although the changes in political theory in China are not to be compared with those in Europe with respect to the speed and intensity with which they have occurred,[13] careful examina-

---

[12] See Liang Ch'i-ch'ao: *Lun Chung-kuo hsueh-shu ssu-hsiang pien-ch'ien chih ta-shih* and *P'ing Hu Shih Chung-kuo Che-hsüeh-shih Ta-kang*; Hu Shih: *Chung-kuo Che-hsüeh-shih Ta-kang*, Vol. I, Part II, chapter I; and Fung Yu-lan: *Chung-kuo che-hsüeh-shih* [tr. by D. Bodde as: *A History of Chinese Philosophy*], Chapter One, Section Two. The above all discuss the reasons for the rise of learning and thought in the pre-Ch'in period and may be referred to in this connection.

[13] See the author's *Chung-kuo cheng-chih ssu-hsiang shih ts'an-kao tzu-liao* (Reference materials for the history of Chinese political thought), Introduction, Section I, in which the similarities and differences of Chinese and Western political thought are discussed briefly. [This has been reprinted in the author's Collected Works, the *Chi-yüan wen-ts'un* 迹園文存, compiled by Dr. Wong Young-tsu, Taipei, 1970, pages 50–121. The relevant portions, found on pages 51–53, follow:

" . . . We affirm that China not only possesses its own political thought, also that that thought has undeniable value. Its points of distinctiveness from European and American political thought do not lie in its value *per se* but in its particular differences of character. Thus before we undertake a study of Chinese political thought we should first investigate the matter of what constitutes those special characteristics.

"A practical emphasis that does not esteem abstruse theorizing is the most obvious of the special characteristics of Chinese political thought. The great eighteenth-century German philosopher Leibnitz has compared the Chinese and Western cultures, concluding that the Chinese are stronger in practical matters while the Europeans are skilled in speculative pursuits. Thus the fields of logic, mathematics, and metaphysics were virtually the latter's provinces, while ethics and politics were the arena in which the former excelled. Although his view is not fully accurate it is in the main acceptable. The intent underlying Western thought and learning was to extend knowledge. Chinese thought and learning were based on the idea of practical application. The one whose purpose is to extend knowledge seeks truth, and no matter whether his methodology is inductive or is deductive, is that of

tion shows that Chinese political theory has nonetheless undergone some
very clearly discernible and highly important changes. Observing the
ebb and flow of these changes during the course of more than two thousand
years, we can see four main divisions in the history of thought in general:

---

analysis or that of synthesis, his argumentation must be free of contradiction and it must
take form in a system. Pressed to the limits, that cannot admit the restriction of being
applicable to a particular time or place, but seeks to establish general, universal principles. The one whose purpose lies in practical applications has implementation as his
objective, thus never pays much attention to abstract theories, the methods of thought,
logical consistency in his argument, or to similarities and differences among conceptualiza-
tions. When something worthwhile comes to mind, it is set forth in words; it need not find
its proof in argumentation, nor need one attempt to fit it into a system. Whether it is true
or false, availing or ineffective, is decided only by whether the theory can be implemented
and realized. What Hsün Tzu meant by speaking of "learning carried to the point of
implementation, there to stop," or, as Wang Yang-ming said: "Acting is the fulfillment of
knowing," although coming close to the standards of Western Pragmatism, is really the
closest to displaying the spirit of China's traditional learning. For more than two-thousand
years, therefore, eighty or ninety percent of the writings relevant to politics has discussed
methods of government. No more than ten or twenty percent has dealt with principles, or
represents investigations into pure science, pure philosophy. In the main, that is to say
that Chinese political thought belongs in large part to the realm of *Politik*, or the Art of
Politics, and only in small part to that of *Staatslehre*, political philosophy, or political science.

"The second special characteristic of Chinese political thought is that it is mostly conventional, in smaller part creative. The political thought of any people will always have its
historical conditions. Even the most fully transcendant utopianism still cannot help but
reflect actual government. This is true in China as elsewhere, but it has been particularly
true in China. Inasmuch as China's thought and learning have stressed application, it
inevitably has focussed on problems of the here and now, and has sought the courses to
their solutions. In its shifts and turns, thought consequently was restricted by realities and
novel theories transcending time and place naturally were not readily generated. If social
advance is very rapid, and political change is extreme, the setting thereby becoming ever
new, and its problems arising continuously, thought could be expected to change along
with those transformations, and it would be capable of being ever innovational, in keeping
with the times. Thus, although truths of enduring applicability would not necessarily be
obtained, a continuous progress could be achieved. But in China, with the exception of
those great transitions from Shang to Chou [in the twelfth century B.C.] and from Chou
to Ch'in [in the third century B.C.] in which first the previous tribal organization evolved
into the feudal [*feng-chien*], and then decentralization was transformed into unification,
during the more than two-thousand years from the Ch'in-Han epoch to the Ming-Ch'ing
[i.e., from the third century B.C. to the beginning of the present century], the imperial
order was unchanging and the social order evolved but little. In a milieu tending toward
the static, thought quite naturally was largely conventional. It had to await the opening
from the sea, bringing the simultaneous incursions of foreign aggressions and Western
learning, before the society was thrown into agitation, people's minds were stirred, incit-
ing the unprecedented changes in thought during the Ch'ing dynasty's final decades.
Compared with Europe, China's circumstances are of quite another kind. Western theorists on government have not focussed much attention on immediate issues and therefore
have been able the more readily to find lofty and remote foci, and new theories that rise
above immediate conditions. For example, the thought of Plato and Aristotle, even though
always set against the background of actual Greek government, was nonetheless not

1. The Period of Creativity—from the birth of Confucius (551 B.C.) to the unification of The First Emperor of the Ch'in (221 B.C.), a period of about three hundred years, including the latter part of the Spring and

wholly circumscribed by that. Later on the great figures such as Hobbes, Locke, and Rousseau also were able to seek general truths from among the specific facts of history. Precisely because they were not excessively concerned with direct application they could evade the faults of shortsightedness. Escaping the rut of stale phrasings they achieved knowledge in advance of their times. Add to that the fact that social and political change in Europe through more than two thousand years was both complex and rapid; in consequence of that, Europe's political thought, regardless of whether it was realistically attuned to the problems of the here and now, witnessed constant replacement of the old by the new, with innumerable shifts and changes. From ancient Greece to the present, in the struggles among the many national entities and the diversely emerging new theories, European history constitutes a veritable prolongation of [circumstances analogous to China's relatively brief] Warring States era [480–221 B.C.]. Compared with the mere two or three hundred years of that Pre-Ch'in Period during which China's "Various Masters and Hundred Schools" were active, one can readily see that the difference between transitory and enduring innovation [in thought paralleled the difference between brief and lengthy periods of political change]. To carry this a step further, China's monarchical political structure was brought into being during the Ch'in-Han period and terminated only with the closing of the Ming-Ch'ing period so that discourses on government through those more than two thousand years more or less turned on the central feature of the Way of the Ruler. The world offers no example of political theorizing on the authoritarian political system that, in precision and in comprehensiveness, surpasses the Chinese. Yet among all the imperial rulers during the more than twenty imperial dynasties, there were few indeed capable of realizing in practise the governing methods explored and developed by all those thinkers from Confucius and Mo Tzu onward. Valid theories were never implemented, yet the faith in them was perpetuated; erroneous theories also were never tried out, yet their weaknesses thereby remained concealed. Accordingly, the need for revising thought was necessarily diminished, and reverence for the past and conservative ways consequently were nourished. The alterations of the laws proposed by Wang An-shih [eleventh century A.D.] had to claim a derivation from the Six Offices as set forth in the [ancient] *Institutes of Chou*. K'ang Yu-wei's [died 1927] attempts to change the laws likewise appealed to [an ancient] authority, that of the *Spring and Autumn Annals* and its [*Kung-yang Commentary's* description of the] Three Ages. This shows how difficult it was to overcome the well-hardened practices of conventionalized thinking. Government in Europe from ancient Greece onward underwent successive changes of form from monarchy to democracy, minority rule to majority rule, all of them tried one after another by the fifth century B.C. When one developed faults, another form would arise, and political theory followed in approving this and repudiating that. There we see thought and institutions in mutual engagement and interlocked processes of change. Critics therefore could see that there were no institutions capable of remaining free of weaknesses for a hundred years, and consequently knew that the theory in support of any laws was inevitably subject to revision, or else to abandonment. This then must be counted one of the reasons for the manifold changes in Western political thought. And we can draw there a further contrast between China and Europe with the latter's intermeshing of ethnic entities, the complexity of their interrelationships and the proximity of its many nation states. These influences of the natural environment on political thought, impelling the generation of change at disparate rates of speed in the two cases, is a clear and obvious matter demanding no further comment."]

Autumn Period and the Period of the Warring States, which scholars call the "pre-Ch'in age."

2.   The Period of Continuation—from the Ch'in and Han to the Sung and Yuan dynasties (227 B.C. to A.D. 1367), a period of sixteen hundred years.

3.   The Period of Change—from the beginning to the Ming to the late Ch'ing (1368–1898), a period of about five hundred years.

4.   The Period of Fruition—from the establishment of the Three People's Principles until the present. (The *San-min Chu-yi* lectures were delivered in 1924. They were first formulated during Sun Yat-sen's two years of residence in England, between 1896 and 1898, following his kidnapping by the Chinese Embassy in London.)

That the pre-Ch'in age was a period of creativity is so obvious that it scarcely seems necessary to discuss the point further. Yet Confucius said of himself that he was "a transmitter and not a maker . . . ,"[14] and a disciple also said of him that he". . . handed down the doctrines of Yao and Shun [as ancestral teachings], and adhered to and showed forth clearly the laws of Wen and Wu [taking them as his model]."[15] Mo Tzu "applied the government of Hsia"[16] and in his sayings repeatedly praised Yao, Shun, Yü, T'ang, Wen, and Wu.[17] The Taoist and Legalist schools held the Yellow Emperor of antiquity in great reverence. In promoting their ideas the Legalists also at times cited the regulations on punishments previously promulgated by the various states.[18] Thus we see that the theories of all the schools of philosophy drew upon earlier origins and were not altogether new inventions of the minds of the times, theories simply spun out of the air. Indeed we may doubt the suitability of the word "creation," unless we understand it thus: creation not meaning to make something from nothing.

Since men of the pre-Spring and Autumn Age engaged in political life, must they not also have had political concepts? Concepts of the Mandate of Heaven and of the fundamental importance of the people, theories about rites and music, military affairs and punishments, as we see them in the earliest texts such as the *Odes* [*Shih*] and the *Documents* [*Shu*], all were drawn upon by all schools of the pre-Ch'in age, and they provided essential elements in China's political thought. However, these early con-

[14] The *Analects*, vii/1.

[15] *The Doctrine of the Mean*, xxx/1. [Modified from Legge, p. 427, following the gloss of Chu Hsi.]

[16] *Huai-nan Tzu, ch.* 21, "Yao-lüeh."

[17] See Wang Chung, *Shu hsüeh*, "Mo Tzu hou hsü."

[18] The "Journal of Literature," *Yi-wen chih* in the *Chin Shu* states: "The works on regulations commenced with Li K'uei, who compiled the laws of the various states and wrote the *Classic of Law (Fa Ching)* . . . Lord Shang used this wherewith to serve the State of Ch'in as prime minister."

cepts originally lacked systematization, and their implications were relatively simple and limited. We must make a distinction between their primitive stage and their subsequent development and synthesis at the hands of the great pre-Ch'in thinkers, by whom these concepts were extended and ordered. These became broader and more profound in their significance, developing into the distinctive theories of individual thinkers. This work of melting down the old so as to cast from it something new is no less than an act of creation. Workmen constructing a building, for example, must use wood and stone, brick and tile, which are in themselves finished products, but this does not prevent the construction of a building that is itself a new thing.

To come at this in another way, the "Journal of Literature" of the *Han Shu* sets forth the idea that the distinct schools of philosophy are all derived from the various offices of the royal court.[19] Confucius followed the Chou [institutes], and his teaching of the *Odes* and the *Documents* and the Six Disciplines was probably the closest to the earlier official studies that can be found among the various schools of philosophy. That is why Chang Hsüeh-ch'eng said: "The Six Classics all are governmental statutes of the former kings,"[20] and "Confucius studied and carried to its limits the *Tao* of the Duke of Chou."[21] Seen in this way, all the political thought of the pre-Ch'in age would seem already to have existed prior to the Spring and Autumn and Warring States Periods; the Confucian, Mohist, Taoist, and Legalist schools continued earlier traditions and were not new creations.[22] Even though such a view can be reasonably argued, it does not necessarily contradict our view set forth above. Let us illustrate the point with the Confucian school. Even though Confucius' political thought was based on the political institutions of King Ch'eng and the Duke of Chou, still it did not adhere slavishly to the old patterns. His teachings for later ages did not consist *merely* of the institutes of the former kings. Within the old political institutions he must have found new meaning whereby to establish his distinctive position in order for the "seventy disciples" to have been so wholeheartedly won over to his teachings, and to recognize in him the founder and master of a school. Let us suppose that he did no more than transmit the governmental institutes of the Duke

---

[19] Since the origins of the tenets of the various philosophers will be referred to below as they are discussed individually, they will not be dealt with here.

[20] *Wen-shih t'ung-yi*, *ch.* 1, "Yi-chiao," Part I.

[21] *Ibid.*, *ch.* 2, "Yuan-tao," Part I.

[22] E. g., Chiang Ch'üan, *Tu tzu chih-yen*, *ch.* 2, p. 28, states: "The teachings of Mo Tzu are derived from Shih Yi . . . Shih Yi wrote a book in two *chüan*, which is listed first among the Mohist works in the "Journal of Literature" in the *Han Shu*, where it states that he was a Chou official of the time of Kings Ch'eng and K'ang [1115–1052 B.C.]; hence from Shih Yi it was a period of several centuries until the time of Mo Tzu. Before Mo Tzu himself there already existed Mohist teachings."

of Chou, literally, without deviation, and departing from them in no respect. We must note, however, that the *Odes* and the *Documents* and the Six Disciplines at that time were still official works, and the records of the government of Kings Wen and Wu had not yet been burned by the Ch'in emperor. Confucius clearly was not the only one who had access to the records preserved by the Chou and Lu courts.[23] The *Tso Chuan* records many instances of nobles and officials of the Spring and Autumn Period who in conversation could quote from the *Odes* and the *Documents*. What, then, made it inevitable that the *Ju* school would take Confucius as its central figure? [That is to say, the mere act of transmitting alone would not have distinguished Confucius at that time.] If instead we say that Confucius used the established forms of Kings Wen and Wu, added to them creatively from his own thought, and drew upon this as the basis for his teaching, it would seem to be closer to the truth, and his achievement is more readily understandable.

Nonetheless, although we regard the pre-Ch'in age as one of creativity, there still remains one most important element in the situation that has not been mentioned in the above discussion and that must be noted. This is that, regardless of the origins of their theories, the different philosophers themselves were in actual fact "creating antiquity," laying down the main lines of development for future generations of their followers. Political thought, from the Ch'in and Han dynasties on through to the Sung and Yuan dynasties, while not devoid of new meaning and new content, nonetheless never succeeded in wholly transcending the boundaries set in the pre-Ch'in age, as far as fundamental concepts and basic principles are concerned. Not until the Ming and Ch'ing periods, with the opening of the sea routes and the introduction of Western learning, was thought susceptible to radical change. The student of Chinese political thought therefore, may well leave unmentioned the ages prior to the Spring and Autumn Period, but he must look upon the Spring and Autumn Period itself as the starting point of his entire study. Without laboring the point further, it is quite obvious how much importance must be attached to this period. In brief, pre-Ch'in thought, with respect to that which preceded it, was a melting of the old metal in order to cast something new from it. And with respect to the Ch'in and Han and following ages, it established the main lines and fixed the boundaries. Using the word "creativity," seen in this light, is then perhaps not far wrong.

The creativity of the pre-Ch'in age was not creation from nothing, lacking precedent and foundation. Similarly, all the continuation through

---

[23] *Tso Chuan*, Second year of Duke Chao, contains reference to the examination of the documents in the office of the Grand Historian by Han Hsüan-tzu of the State of Chin; he remarked "The institutes of Chou are all in Lu." [Legge, p. 583.]

the long period from Ch'in and Han to Sung and Yuan was not mere copying of fixed forms; it was not simply a step-by-step pursuit of antique learning without forward development and change. The First Emperor of Ch'in annexed the remaining Six States and in this transformation from the old feudal order to the new commandery-county system [*chün-hsien*] he brought into being the unified authoritarian polity that was to endure for two thousand years. Within a social environment that had become entirely different, the conditions allowing the competitive existence of the "Hundred Schools," each flourishing on its ability to create new doctrines, no longer existed.

Simultaneously, and precisely because of the changed environment, thinkers of the Ch'in and Han and later dynasties, while retaining the concepts of their forerunners and preserving their terminology, faced political realities that were strikingly different. Hence the content of these same concepts, and the implications of these same terms, obviously could not correspond entirely to the content and implications intended by men of earlier times. Strictly speaking, therefore, the political thought of the Han and later ages, though it did not necessarily change the ancient names, in fact altered the ancient realities. We look upon this period as far inferior to the pre-Ch'in age in the abundance of creative spirit, and we note that most of its thinkers lacked any intent to create. Hence we call it an era of "continuation." But this is not to say that throughout these sixteen hundred years political discourse wholly conformed to the late Chou models.

In this connection, moreover, it becomes significant that each of the pre-Ch'in philosophers established a distinct "school" [*men-hu*—often equivalent to a "factional following"], that disputation arose among the later followers of the schools, and that attack and counterattack among the schools raged fiercely. Mencius, for example, opposed Yang Chu and Mo Tzu,[24] Hsün Tzu pointed out the fallacies of the "Twelve Philosophers,"[25] Mo Tzu ridiculed the Confucians,[26] and Chuang Tzu criticized and evaluated all the philosophers according to their implementation of *Tao*.[27] These are but some of the more obvious examples. Although nominally at least their purpose was to uphold the teachings of their founders and to silence the suspect deviations, we witness in fact battling protagonists and antagonists, clashing predilections and prejudices. Each school had its fallibilities and suffered varying fortunes in the continuing battle of ideas. This battle of ideas for intellectual hegemony may be

[24] *Mencius*, III, "T'eng Wen Kung."
[25] *Hsün Tzu*, ch. 6, "Fei Shih-erh tzu."
[26] *Mo Tzu*, the chapters 14–16 "Chien-ai," 20–21 "Chieh yung," 25 "Chieh tsang," 26–28 "T'ien chih," and 31 "Ming kuei."
[27] *Chuang Tzu*, ch. 33 "T'ien hsia."

likened to a chase in which rival hunters, having hotly pursued the same deer, are unable to decide by whose hand it would be brought down. But by Ch'in and Han times, the contest among the followers of the various schools had long existed; contacts among them had become numerous, with resulting compromise and mutual accommodation. There appeared strong tendencies toward amalgamation and unification of thought and learning. Some who advocated this abandonment of the distinct "factions" or "schools" subsequently evolved the *Tsa-chia* School.[28] [See the *Han Shu*, "Journal of Literature," where it states that "the philosophers of the category *Tsa-chia* combined aspects of Confucianism and Mohism . . . together with elements from the School of Names and from Legalism." Hence this refers to a specific school, and not to eclectic philosophies in general.] Even those who firmly maintained the distinct school divisions, however, also dabbled occasionally in unorthodox deviations in the hope of bringing others into harmony with their master's teachings. The extent of such borrowing varied, with the result that the purity of these later teachings also varied. In consequence we can always see one of two possible situations in the thought of Ch'in-Han and later times: One is that the name of a school remains the same but the content of its teachings changes; the other is that, on the one hand, divergent lines develop within one school or, on the other hand, several schools merge and become one.[29]

From this time onward, where those pre-Ch'in era schools of thought survived, even though the formal identities of schools were rigorously defended, no more than the main motifs of the original teachings survived. In the most extreme cases of transformation, external features might remain apparently unchanged while the spirit of the teachings had become totally different. Yet the mutual attack and unremitting conflicts among intellectual camps persisted; the desire to triumph over rivals remained as strong as it had been in the pre-Ch'in age. After political unification, however, the authoritarian imperial power strove always to achieve a corresponding unification within the world of thought. The First Emperor of Ch'in "employed magistrates [who were followers of the Legalist school] as the teachers of men"; and Emperor Wu of Han granted the supreme place to Confucian doctrines. However, their "distinguishing as between black and white in fixing the one supreme [criterion of thought]" could not necessarily eliminate the spirit of rivalry between the schools and direct them away from factional contention toward more peaceful ac-

---

[28] The *Lü Shih Ch'un-ch'iu* is the most important representative of this. [See Chapter 10, below.]

[29] Yao Shun-ch'in: *Ch'in Han che-hsüeh-shih*, Chapter Two, states that the philosophies of the Ch'in and Han periods were agglomerations of mixed constituents; this is a very discerning observation.

commodation. Thus the period from the Ch'in and Han dynasties witnessed a harmonization and accommodation within the content of thought, but at the same time it was a period of decisive struggle between and among the schools as such. In the thousand and more years following the fall of Ch'in [207 B.C.] the various schools contended among themselves for supremacy, flourishing or subsiding in the wake of developments within the historical environment. Some schools were stronger at first and later declined;[30] others suffered decline only to be again revived;[31] some were extinguished, never to reappear.[32] A school might achieve sole dominance but subsequently prove unable to retain its monopoly,[33] or it might lose its place as the leading school but continue as the opposition of the main current.[34] Although the content of thought changed continuously with the movement of time, the main outlines remained identifiable with those laid down in the pre-Ch'in age. Wholly new elements were extremely rare.

In simplest terms, this flow and development of political thought lasting throughout the Period of Continuation can be looked upon as one extended internal war within Chinese thought and learning. The combat units deployed in this war were the schools of thought indigenous to ancient China. Its super weapons were the theories devised in the pre-Ch'in age. In sixteen hundred years the only exceptions to this were the additions to the battle of disputes raised by ideas from abroad, such as the conflict involving Buddhists and Taoists over such issues as the respect due emperors and fathers [i.e., against religious claims of supreme reverence to a diety or to a religious principle], distinctions to be maintained between "barbarian" and Chinese civilizations and peoples, and the like. However, these were of short duration, and they made no noteworthy contribution to thought's overall course of development. The result of this internal warfare in the world of thought was a near stagnation in political thought.

Meanwhile, we note in the imperial authoritarian forms of government only insignificant changes from the Ch'in and Han dynasties onward. Pre-Ch'in thought flourished suddenly, in a social environment of radical changes; it is indeed most natural that from the Ch'in and Han onward, when there was lessened change within the social environment, thought also should lack a corresponding degree of creativity. Indeed, this warrants

[30] E.g., the Legalists in the Ch'in and Han periods, the Confucians in the Han and Wei.

[31] E.g., the Taoists in the Wei and Chin periods.

[32] E.g., the Mohists in the Han period.

[33] E.g., the Confucians in the Han period.

[34] E.g., the Taoists and Legalists in the Han period and the Confucians in the Wei and Chin.

no surprise. And had it not been for the continuous process of cultural and military invasion from the West via sea routes during the Ming and Ch'ing dynasties, I fear that the Period of Continuation in political thought need not have ended with the Sung and Yuan dynasties and that the subsequent Period of Change might not have come as it did in the Ming and Ch'ing.

The direct cause of the changes in China's political thought was the stimulus of outside forces. Buddhism spread eastward and established a precedent for invasion by foreign cultural elements; the "Five Barbarian Nations" brought chaos to China, foretelling, as it were, further instances of foreign domination. [The period of the "Five Barbarian Nations" is a traditional way of referring to the invasions of the fourth and fifth centuries A.D.] Yet, although both of these events spurred disturbances and advances in all the fields of government, society, religion, and philosophy, they did not induce any transformation of political thought. For Buddhism is a religion and not a political philosophy. Its negative and other-worldly view of life has points of similarity with philosophical Taoism [*Lao-Chuang*—a development in Taoism in the Northern and Southern Dynasties Period; see below, Chapter Eleven]. Thus we could hardly expect it to make a great contribution to political thought. As for the non-Chinese peoples who invaded China during the Chin dynasty [A.D. 317–419], their cultural level was low, and, after they occupied the central plain of North China, their civilizations tended to give way before voluntary "adoption of Chinese ways to transform [their own] barbarian ways."[35] Their political concepts did not go beyond the old forms of proclaiming themselves rulers and establishing a new dynasty. Thus it would have been most difficult for them to have had any capacity for stimulating changes in China's political thought. China had to wait until the opening of the sea routes during the Ming and Ch'ing periods, when the knowledge of Europe's high-level civilization was disseminated within the land, in the wake of missionaries. On top of this, the conditions making for the "closed door" and defensive seclusion were shattered. In place of the unified "one world" of the past, China became merely one among the nation-states. Moreover, in a time of accumulated weaknesses, China suffered repeated invasion and humiliation. So profound was this vast misfortune that is inexorably aroused a revolution in thought. This must certainly be accounted the main cause of that Period of Change which has developed during the Ming-Ch'ing era.

To these reasons for change [in the later imperial era] can be added the factor of Mongol rule over China, lasting about a century [A.D. 1279–1368]. The Chinese nation suffered the widespread effects of an alien

[35] The *Chin Shu, ch.* 105, "Tsai-chi," 5, "Biography of Shih Lo," part two.

people's unjust and harsh rule. Confucian benevolence and righteousness, rites and music; Legalist reverence for the ruler, supremacy of the state, and rigidly maintained laws and regulations; Taoist "knowing the white yet clinging to the black," according with nature and observing inaction; and indeed all of the old political theories and practices that China previously had known, by these facts of history [i.e., the Yuan period Mongol rule and the subsequent conflicts with European powers] had been clearly demonstrated to be incapable of ensuring the nation's future. The extremity so realized induced conditions for far-reaching changes. Ming and Ch'ing political thought thereafter was forced to explore new paths and advance on new fronts.

Although the Period of Change includes the full five hundred years of the Ming and Ch'ing dynasties, only the beginnings of change are to be observed during the Ming and the early part of the Ch'ing. The great transformation of casting off the old and adopting the new did not really get under way until the end of the Ch'ing dynasty. In the first parts of the Ming and the Ch'ing dynasties, some recluse loyalists and "men of principle" [*chih shih*] developed ethnocentric thought as a form of protest against alien political domination, thereby bringing about a major departure from the traditional concept of "the great community" [*Ta-t'ung*]. From the mid-Ming onward the Wang Yang-ming school developed its concepts of freedom of thought in protest against the shackles of Sung and Ming rationalism [*li-hsüeh*]. This too was aimed at breaking free from the bonds and expunging the long-fixed habit of reverence for the past and preservation of the old. All these are of great significance and clearly indicate the direction that change eventually would have to take; yet the bases on which these developments were founded, and their very content, nonetheless came into being through a mere metamorphosis of the old thought and, in the last analysis, do not go beyond the bounds set by . men of the past. They give evidence that the old could be displaced, yet still do not signify the establishment of the new.

Subsequently, the T'aip'ing Rebellion burst into being, marking the first instance of something founded on [ideas as exotic as] Christian doctrine, to which elements of ethnocentric thought were added; that stimulated changes in thought unprecedented in China's history. Thereafter came, successively, the reform movement of 1898 and the revolution of 1911, and regardless of what their ideologies may have been, in fact both were directly influenced by Western thought; moreover, both were in opposition to more than two thousand years of traditional Chinese thought, so unintentionally they reinforced each other. We clearly cannot suspect that because the new thought also accepted some elements of the old thought system, it was therefore quite consonant with the "*Tao t'ung*" [i.e., the self-conscious Confucian tradition of the past two thousand years]. Rather, when the thinkers of the late Ch'ing reform and revolutionary movements utilized old concepts, they did so wholly in accordance with their own independent standards. A statement drawn from any particular philosopher might be used, not because it was the word of a former sage, but because the statement appeared to suit contemporary conditions. "The power of judgment lies with me; I take or reject as I wish."[36] The spirit of independent judgment in thought was thus reintroduced virtually for the first time since the pre-Ch'in age.

The Revolution of 1911 marks a final stage in the Period of Change in Chinese political thought, and opens a new Period of Fruition. Sun Yat-sen's theories of the Three People's Principles and of the Five Powers of Government combined elements both old and new, both Chinese and Western; they also included unique elements of his own and synthesized the main currents of an entire era. They not only established the theory on which the revolution was grounded, but also gave full form to guiding principles with which to build a new nation-state. Two thousand years of political thought thus approached a stage of fruition [anticipated by the radical departures in Sun's political thought, and not yet fully realized].

SECTION THREE

The Periodization of the History of Chinese Political Thought—in Accordance with the Historical Backgrounds of Thought

IN the preceding section, considering the main outlines of the overall development of thought through more than two thousand years has led us to divide that process into four periods. Such a division may not be wholly satisfactory, but neither, probably, is it altogether wrong. If however, we focus attention on the historical backgrounds of thought, we might make an alternative division into three periods, as follows:

[36] Among the thinkers of the 1898 Reform, K'ang Yu-wei seems to be an exception. In his advocacy of institutional change, he found support in the idea of the Three Ages in the *Spring and Autumn Annals*, and he claimed that Confucius established a standard for all time, which to be sure looks suspiciously like conservatism. However, in his *K'ung-tzu kai-chih k'ao* he states that the philosophers of the Hundred Schools of the pre-Ch'in age all represented new creative developments, and that Confucius too wrote the Six Classics advocating institutional changes for which precedent was sought in the past merely as a legitimizing device. Perhaps this is because K'ang himself also hoped to use the device of seeking authorization for institutional change in the past. Also, although the ideals of the *Ta-t'ung Shu* are drawn from the "Li Yün," it is in fact mostly inspired by Western ideas. [*Li Chi, ch.* 9; in many editions of the *Li Chi*, the "Li Yün" is *ch.* 7; throughout this translation the chapter numbers of the standard *Li Chi chi-shuo* are followed.]

1. The thought of the feudal world—including the Spring and Autumn and Warring States Periods, and coinciding with the Period of Creativity described in the preceding section. [*T'ien-hsia* "All under Heaven" is here and in some subsequent usages translated "the world" in order to convey the implied connotation of one all-embracing world of men. After the establishment of the Chinese Empire, *t'ien-hsia* became equivalent to "empire," or the central empire and the peripheral regions.]

2. The thought of the authoritarian empire—including the two thousand years from the Ch'in and Han through the Ming and Ch'ing, and corresponding in the main to the Period of Continuation and the Period of Change described in the preceding section.

3. The thought of the modern nation-state—including the late Ch'ing reform movement of 1898 and the revolution of 1911 and continuing to the present day, corresponding to the later portion of the Period of Change and the Period of Fruition described in the preceding section.

Between political thought and political systems there is always interaction. For this reason the history of political thought might just as appropriately take its periodization from the main outlines of the development of systems. From the Shang and Chou dynasties to the present, China's political system has undergone three major transformations. By the time of the transition from Shang to Chou, tribal society[37] had gradually advanced to the stage wherein a feudal world was established,[38] thus marking the first transformation. The First Emperor of Ch'in annexed the other Six States, divided his whole world into commanderies and counties, and firmly established the authoritarian imperial system, thus marking the second transformation. With the failure of government in the late Ch'ing period and the founding of a republic, two thousand years of imperial rule came to an end, thus marking the third transformation. These divisions are clearly discernible and have long been widely accepted. It would be most natural for us to use these dividing lines derived from the history of political institutions to mark our divisions in the history of political thought.

The political thought of the feudal world did not develop in the time of the Chou dynasty's greatest flourishing; rather it appeared later, only after the dynasty's decline, as has been briefly mentioned in the preceding section. Therefore, while all the thought of the pre-Ch'in age had the feudal world as its setting, it did not thereby always take the feudal

[37] Cf. Hsü Hsieh-chen, "Preface" to his *Yin-ch'i t'ung-shih*, where he states that the earlier part of the Yin period was one of "tribal society in breakdown," while the latter part was "tribal society organized under princely courts."

[38] For a general description of Chou feudalism reference may be made to the *Shih Chi* of Ssu-ma Ch'ien [ca. 145–90? B.C.], *chüan* 4, "Chou pen-chi" ["Annals of the Chou House"].

world as its subject of consideration, or as its ideal. This can be illustrated by reference to some of the more important philosophers. For example, Confucius "followed the Chou,"[39] and in his thought the feudal world served both as background and as ideal. Mencius' statements that "With a territory which is only a hundred *li* square, it is possible to attain to the royal dignity" and "[The empire] will be settled by being united under one sway,"[40] while failing to grant supremacy to the Chou dynasty, still did not deny the feudal ideal. Mo Tzu's "Condemnation of Offensive War" was actually a protest against the aggression and annexation carried on in the Warring States Period, and his theory of "agreement with the superior" sets forth the idea that the "head of the family" [*chia-chün*] and "ruler of the state" [*kuo-chün*] must make uniform their criteria [in judging what is beneficial].[41] All this, purely and completely, is thought of the feudal world. In this respect, however, the two schools of Taoism and Legalism differ considerably. Lao Tzu came close to the principle of *laissez faire*, Chuang Tzu approached anarchism, and the two both directed violent, negative criticism against the government of the late Chou and adduced an ideal of a free society of a kind that had never existed in history. Legalists, such as Shang Yang, and Han Fei Tzu, recognizing the harsh realities of the Warring States Period in which the Seven States vied fiercely for supremacy, produced their theories of enriching the state and strengthening its military forces, of exalting the ruler and rigorously enforcing his laws. The background of their thought was not that of the heyday of early Chou feudalism, and their ideal tended toward the authoritarianism achieved subsequently in the State of Ch'in. Thus among the various schools we find that the Confucians and the Mohists supported the already collapsing feudal world, the Legalists anticipated the practices of the forthcoming imperial unification, and the Taoists denied the validity of all the institutions in history.

The political thought of the authoritarian world had as its background the political institutions of the period from the Ch'in-Han dynasties to the Ming-Ch'ing. [In Chinese historical writing, it is customary to couple these pairs of dynasties to designate the larger periods.] With all the schools of philosophy that had existed from pre-Ch'in times, it was their ability to adapt to the new historical environment [of the imperial age] that determined their prosperity or decline. The Confucians' adaptability was greatest;[42] hence the transmission of their teachings continued longest,

[39] See *Analects* [iii/14; Legge, p. 24]; *The Doctrine of the Mean*, [xxviii/5; Legge, p. 288].

[40] *Mencius*, i, "King Hui of Liang" [i/i/5/2; Legge, p. 134, and i/i/6/2; Legge, p. 136].

[41] *Mo Tzu*, chs. 12 and 13 "Shang-t'ung," i.e. "On the Identification with the Superior," parts 2 and 3; [in the Y. P. Mei translation, *The Works of Motze*, pp. 59–77. Mei translates the two terms; "the emperor" and "the clan patriarch."]

[42] *Hsün Tzu*, ch. 8, "*Ju hsiao p'ien*," i.e. "The Model of the Great Confucians," describ-

and their real power and influence were strongest. No other school could compare with them in this respect. Legalist thought tended toward authoritarianism and was in fact the basis of Ch'in unification; hence that system would seem likely to have flourished greatly in an authoritarian world. However, when the theories of Shen Pu-hai and Han Fei Tzu were put into practice by Li Ssu, their main tenets—such as exaltation of law, emphasis on regulations, and the demand that actual performance correspond to designated responsibility [*fa*, "law"; *ling*, "regulations"; and *ming-shih*, "names and realities"; cryptic references to prominent legalist doctrines]—gradually emerged as governmental techniques in practical applications; and this halted further development in the realm of theory. Moreover, their chief doctrinal requirement that both ruler and official must observe the law, i.e., "the law is supreme over the emperor,"[43] was in fundamental conflict with the spirit of the autocratic age, and hence was particularly difficult for men of that age to accept. Therefore, from the Ch'in-Han onward, although Legalist doctrines were occasionally articulated, Legalism could never again attain the position of a school prominent enough to offer real opposition to the Confucians. Although the institutions of authoritarian government grew and developed with the aid of the pre-Ch'in Legalists, Legalism was nonetheless rejected and ignored thereafter and it therefore declined into obscurity and impotence—if not a case of authoritarianism's "cannibalism of its own mother" [referring to an old legend about an owl whose young devour their mother] at least one of "forgetting the fish trap after the fish are caught." [*Chuang Tzu*, *ch.* 26; Watson, p. 302.] If it is to be said that the authoritarian empire experienced much turbulence and little order, this conceivably offers part of the explanation. [That is to say, when the rulers, characteristically inept, abandoned the principle of governing by laws and acted on their whims, the empire suffered the consequences of bad government.]

Mohism originally, like Confucianism, was thought rooted in the feudal world, but it lacked Confucianism's facile ability to change. Also, as others said of it, "Such teaching is too barren;"[44] "It is as if burned and charred."[45] [Comments of Chuang Tzu and Hsün Tzu on its hard and unfeeling severity and its lack of human warmth and attractiveness.] Nor

---

ing the Confucian, says: " . . . in danger, his responses to changing situations are indirectly appropriate; at the right time he shifts his position, he bends and unbends with the world; through a thousand affairs and ten thousand changes, his way [*Tao*] is the same." [Modified from Dubs, tr., *The Works of Hsüntze*, p. 109.]

[43] *Kuan Tzu, ch.* 16, "Fa-fa."

[44] *Chuang Tzu, ch.* 33; "T'ien-hsia"; [cf. the Giles translation of chapter 33, "The Empire," pp. 437–54, especially pp. 440–43, and Watson's translation of the complete works of Chuang Tzu, pp. 364–67, where Mo Tzu's doctrines are criticized.].

[45] *Hsün Tzu, ch.* 10, "Fu Kuo." [Dubs, "A Rich Country"; the section criticizing Mo Tzu is omitted in the Dubs translation.]

did it have anything comparable to Confucianism's *Odes* and *Documents*,
Rites and *Music*, nor even such supplementary components as the Five
Agents and Three Systems, which at their best could "lead to refined
institutions and good government,"[46] and at least could serve to embellish
times of peace. [For the latter, a system of divination and magic; see Fung/
Bodde, Vol. 1, p. 27, particularly footnote 1.] It was for these reasons
that by Ch'in and Han times the influence of this school had ebbed and
vanished, and throughout the two thousand years of the authoritarian
world, Mohism remained completely dead as a school of thought.[47]

Taoism bent itself to the character of the times less than any other
philosophy. Its negativism remained largely the same from beginning to
end, undergoing no fundamental changes when the feudal world was
transformed into one of commanderies and counties. [I.e., the basic
institutional change marking the beginning of the imperial era, by which
a system wherein decentralized rule had been extended through semi-
independent fiefs became one wherein units of local government were
administered directly under the central government.] Hence, except for
one very short period when it was applied by the court and achieved a
position of exclusive supremacy,[48] the political thought of philosophic
Taoism remained the most thoroughgoing protest against the authoritarianism that characterized the long era of the autocratic empire. Opposing
Confucianism, it stood something like a party out of power with respect
to the party in power. In times of great prosperity and peace, or in times
verging on decline but not yet fallen into disorder, Confucianism always
waxed strong and Taoism waned. But when social order disintegrated
and the people suffered hardship, ideas of inaction and anarchism rose to
prominence in response to such conditions. This continued to be true
until, in the Sung and Yuan dynasties, the authoritarian system of
government reached its highest development. Then the expression of this
kind of opposition began to subside, and in political thought there was no
longer an independent Taoist school.

To summarize the above discussion, we can see that three trends
emerged in political thought during the period of the authoritarian world:
1. Confucianism changed from a position of supporting the feudal order

---

[46] *Ibid.*, *ch.* 6, "Fei shih-erh tzu." [The passage cited is omitted in the Dubs translation.]

[47] In the late Ch'ing, T'an Ssu-t'ung [1865–1898] wrote in the "Author's Preface"
or "tzu-hsü" to his *Jen-hsüeh* that Mo Tzu was one of the sources of his thought, but he has
never been looked upon as the restorer of Mohism to the status of an independent school
of thought. [The author has pointed out to the translator that his memory failed him at
this point. The reference should be to the fifth of the twenty-seven "*chieh-shuo*" (axioms, or
explanations) preceding the first chapter of the *Jen-hsüeh*.]

[48] From the first years of the former Han until the reign of the Emperor Wen [179–157
B.C.] *Huang-Lao* temporarily experienced considerable vogue. [For an explanation of this
variety of Taoism-as-statecraft, see below, Chapter 10, Section 2.]

to one of supporting the authoritarian political system, and maintained itself throughout the two thousand years as the orthodox school of learning.[49] 2. Confucianism's power and influence thrived while both Legalism and Mohism failed to survive. 3. Confucianism and Taoism, in response to the alternations of order and chaos in society, waxed and waned complementarily.[50]

The thought of the feudal age and that of the authoritarian age have one special characteristic in common: regardless of their content, they always were oriented toward "the world" [*t'ien-hsia*, or "all under heaven"]. The source of difference between them is that the feudal world had within it legally recognized regional divisions and controls, whereas the authoritarian world was one of absolute unification. The connotations of this "world" concept are somewhat similar to those of the early medieval concept of world empire in Europe. Ideally, its scope was to be unlimited. The saying of antiquity that "Under the wide heaven, all is the king's land; within the sea-boundaries of the land, all are the king's servants"[51] is the clearest expression of this concept. Consequently, all the political relationships of the period when this "world" concept prevailed, pertained exclusively to internal government, and no diplomatic relations between nations could exist. When the feudal system was

[49] Hsia Tseng-yu in his *Chung-kuo ku-tai shih*, p. 258, states in discussing the psychology of the authoriatarian ruler: "Summarizing the lives of the two rulers (i.e., The First Emperor of Ch'in and Emperor Wu of Han) their acts can be categorized under three headings: The first is honoring Confucian techniques; the second is believing in magicians; the third is fondness for military undertakings. . . . All of the above can be said to be but expressions of the authoritarian mind. Their honoring of Confucian techniques had nothing to do with any predilection for benevolence, righteousness, respect and frugality. Rather it was because of their conviction that Confucian practices and techniques were in fact those most beneficial to the cause of authoritarianism. The significance of their territorial expansion policies lay in their unwillingness that there should exist any rulers other than themselves; they could feel happy only when they had brought the whole world under the sway of one man. This was not similar to the nature of modern international competition. As for their search for immortality, this was because they already had attained the extremes of wealth and high position, and, having nothing more to seek after, could desire nothing further than to evade death so that they might go on enjoying this happiness forever." This is a most accurate observation on the relation between Confucian doctrine and authoritarianism.

[50] The Mencian tradition within Confucianism, with its emphasis on the doctrine of the fundamental importance of the people, stood in a relationship to the main Confucian tradition of Ch'in and Han times onward that somewhat resembled the relationship of Taoism to Confucianism. In periods when bad emperors ruled and national crisis impended, the Mencian views that killing an evil ruler was but "cutting off a common fellow" [and not regicide, cf. Legge, *Mencius*, p. 167] and "attainment of the imperial sway" through "the love and protection of the people" [*ibid.*, p. 138] always came to the fore, complementing the [Taoist] thought of inaction and anarchism.

[51] *The Odes*, "Hsiao-ya," the ode "Pei-shan" [Legge, p. 360].

replaced by autocracy, then even those relationships which appear to have been diplomatic in form, such as to dispatch missions of good will or condolence and the forming of leagues and alliances, disappeared completely. In Chou and Ch'in and later ages the "barbarians" on the four borders were occasionally looked upon as enemies; at times they even invaded China proper and "arrogated to themselves the prerogatives of the imperial position," thereby violating the "world" concept in deed. ["Imperial position," *shen-ch'i*, literally, the "divine vessel."] Nonetheless, from Han times onward people who discussed policies devised for the control of the barbarians continued to do so in such traditional locutions as "all within the four seas are one family," or "bring peace within and extend kindness to those who dwell afar."[52] The most fantastic and ludicrous manifestation of this attitude occurred when the English ambassador, Lord Macartney, came to China in 1793.[53] All boats and carts in which he traveled were ordered to fly pennants saying that England was submitting tribute; at his audiences he was forced to kneel in obeisance. The Emperor Kao-tsung's [the Ch'ien-lung Emperor] letter to the King of England contained such phrases as "incline your hearts toward us and take on our ways" and "navigate the seas in order to come [to seek audience] at our court," clear evidence of the fact that the Chinese had no concept of internationalism. When we seek the sources of this "political solipsism,"[54] we find that China's conception of a unitary world must bear at least partial responsibility.

In addition, the thought of the authoritarian world shows a strong tendency toward the "doctrine of the great community" (*Ta-t'ung chu-yi*). Little attention was given to ethnic distinctions but there was great emphasis on cultural identity or variance.[55] The result of this, throughout the

---

[52] The Kung-yang school is most representative of this attitude. Note, for example, in discussing the meeting at Chung-li in the Sixteenth year of Duke Ch'eng, where the *Kung-yang Commentary* states: "In the Spring and Autumn Period [the feudal rulers] looked upon their countries as 'the within' and upon all of the other Chinese states as 'that without'; or looked upon the Chinese states collectively as 'the within' and upon the barbarian nations as 'that without.' As a king desired to unify the world, why do we employ the terms 'within' and 'without' in our commentary? What we are saying is that he should commence with the nearer regions." [I.e., distance from the center, not ethnic or cultural difference or political division, should be the fact of importance.]

[53] With reference to the Macartney embassy, see *Ch'ing-ch'ao hsü wen-hsien t'ung-k'ao*, *chüan* 300, "ssu-i k'ao," 6, "Ying-chi-li" [England].

[54] "Political Solipsism." This term, which has been coined by the author for this phenomenon, is perhaps capable of conveying the spirit of one aspect of the *t'ien-hsia*, or "all under heaven" concept; [*t'ien-hsia* is translated here simply as "the world"].

[55] This also was originated by the Kung-yang school. Their criterion for advancing or degrading, for praising or censuring, was one of advancing a barbarian nation to consideration as "China" when they adopted Chinese ways, and censuring China by considering it "barbarian" when it took over any barbarian practice. Commenting on the meeting at

whole two-thousand-year period during which China's power remained great, was strong advocacy of the theory of the "adoption of Chinese ways to transform the barbarians." When foreign peoples invaded China, only to be mastered by her culture, this could assuage the pain of China's political submission to them. If the conquerors but practiced China's "Way of the former kings" and became culturally assimilated, then one could "face the north and declare himself a servitor." [Facing the north meant acknowledging the ruler, who ritually faced south.] Acknowledging the political authority of an alien ruler [in such circumstances] involved not the slightest humiliation. Nationalism [*min-tsu ssu-hsiang*; this term can also be translated "ethnic consciousness" or "racism" in some other contexts] was underdeveloped; this was another of the consequences of the thought of the autocratic empire.

All the above points can be summed up in the single statement that the concept of the modern nation-state was lacking. No absolute standard exists whereby to determine what constitutes the modern nation-state. But in terms of the political experience of the countries of the world, what we call the modern nation-state possesses at least the following characteristics:

(1) Political power is established through national self-determination;

(2) There is recognition of the coexistence of other nations and the maintenance of reciprocal diplomatic relations;

(3) Law is respected and political institutions are stressed; there is no one-sided reliance on social relationships and morals as means of governing.

Huang-ch'ih in the Thirteenth year of Duke Ai, the *Kung-yang Commentary* says: "Wu was a barbarian state, in which people cut their hair short and tattooed their bodies. [Its ruler now] wished, by means of the ceremonies of Lu and the power of Chin, to bring about the wearing of both cap and garments. He contributed also from the products of the State to do honor to the king approved by Heaven. Wu is here advanced." [Modified slightly from Legge, *The Chinese Classics*, Vol. v, *The Ch'un Ts'ew*, Part i, pp. 80–81.] This is an example of the former. In the thirty-second year of Duke Hsi, where the raid made by the State of Ch'in on the State of Cheng is recorded, the *Kung-yang Commentary* states: "What is it that the State of Ch'in should be called? It is to be called barbarian." This is an example of the latter. From Ch'in and Han times onward there were persons who, consciously or unconsciously, perpetuated this attitude. A few prominent examples are Wang T'ung [A.D. 583–616], who looked upon the Yuan Wei [alien] rulers as "recipients of the *Tao* of the kings of old" and acknowledged them as emperors [in fixing their place in history]. (Cf. his *Yuan ching*, "Shu shih."); Hsü Heng [A.D. 1209–1281], who assisted the Mongols in establishing a government based on the Confucian social and ethical principles (cf. *Lu-chai yi-shu*); Ling T'ing-k'an [1757–1809, see Hummel, pp. 514–15], who defended the alien invaders of China (cf. his *Chiao-li t'ang wen-chi* and *Chiao-li t'ang shih-chi*); K'ang Yu-wei proposed his plans for preserving the state through reform, in service of the Manchus. The Ch'ing Emperor Shih-tsung's [the Yung-cheng Emperor, reg. 1723–36] book, *Ta-yi chüeh-mi lu* [see Hummel, p. 749] employed this argument in condemning the racist [nationalist] thought of Lü Liu-liang [1629–1683, see Hummel, pp. 551–52], and Tseng Ching [1679–1736, see Hummel pp. 747–49].

These three characteristics were present, at least in general form, in the major European states by the fifteenth century. Their development was very rapid, and by the sixteenth and seventeenth centuries they had achieved considerable maturity. If we consider the eighteenth century and thereafter we also remark:

(4)   Ever wider popular participation in political power.
This too can be looked upon as one of the special characteristics of the modern nation-state.[56]

China totally lacked all four of these characteristics throughout the period of the authoritarian world empire; in the earlier period of the subdivided world of feudalism China had at best only traces of them, and even those traces were more seeming than real. Two thousand years of fermentation and agitation in political thought were incapable of giving birth to the modern nation-state concept. This, to be sure, was so because of limitations of the historical environment, and is not to be taken as something whereby to belittle the great men of the Chinese past. By comparison, the thinkers of Europe too were concerned only with the city-state in antiquity, and were intoxicated by the idea of empire throughout their medieval era; not until modern times were they capable of evolving the theory of the national state.

The development and growth of the modern nation-state in Europe was several centuries ahead of the same development in China. In time-span of national existence China is very old while the European nations still possess the strength of youth. In level of political development, however, Europe is very advanced while China has only lately reached maturity. When the two first confronted each other, their relative strengths became immediately evident. At the end of the Ming and the beginning of Ch'ing, even though missionaries came to the Orient, the Chinese were still bound to the long-fixed ways of the authoritarian empire, and the Western learning that the missionaries brought with them had no widespread influence. China had to experience the humiliations and territorial losses of the wars of 1841, 1860, 1894, and 1900 before people both in the government and throughout the country gradually realized that the old institutions of the authoritarian empire were inadequate to guarantee the nation's continued existence. Thereupon proposals for imitating the West, and modernizing through reform, appeared in profusion. Modern European and American nation-state concepts penetrated China, though the conflict between them and the traditional thought was only partially reconciled. The consequences of this confrontation were often curious, often dazzling; they constitute an imposing spectacle. First came the

---

[56] When Liang Ch'i-ch'ao said that in two thousand years of Chinese political discourse there is evidenced only an awareness of the imperial court and no awareness of the nation, that is what he meant. Cf. his *Shao-nien chung-kuo shuo.*

reform movement of 1898 and following that the revolution of 1911. In Sun Yat-sen many aspects of the whole process were brought to fruition, and in his time the third period in China's political thought truly begins.

We have assumed two different points of view in an attempt to devise two kinds of periodization. The results, in the final analysis, are essentially in agreement. This may provide adequate indication that while these periodizations are perhaps not perfect, still we can feel some assurance that neither are they too grossly in error. In this work these periodizations will be employed as the history of the political thought of more than two thousand years is discussed, stage by stage, in its chief features.

CHAPTER ONE

The Various Schools of Political Thought in the Pre-Ch'in Age

SECTION ONE
The Historical Background

PAST discussions of the thought and learning of the pre-Ch'in age have customarily employed the names "The Hundred Schools"[1] and "The Nine Categories.[2] In a discussion of political thought, however, only the Confucian, Mohist, Taoist, and Legalist schools are important enough to be called major schools. Not only did each of these four make its own particular discoveries and establish itself as a distinctive school, but the four together also represent all the important attitudes of thought of the late Chou period.

Let us speak first about attitudes of thought. Even at its best the feudal world of the Chou[3] had been incompletely unified.[4] The slackening of this unity initially permitted many separate, virtually autonomous, states to appear, and it ultimately led to one of those kings' establishing auto-

---

[1] Cf. *Hsün Tzu*, "Ch'eng hsiang" [*ch.* 25, omitted in the Dubs translation] and the *Han Shu, ch.* 6, "Wu-ti chi," "Annals of Emperor Wu." The *Shih Chi, ch.* 130, "T'ai-shih-kung tzu-hsü," contains an account of "the Six Schools."

[2] Cf. *Han Shu*, "Yi-wen chih" *ch.* 30, "Journal of Literature". Refer also: *Chuang Tzu, ch.* 33, "T'ien-hsia" [Giles tr., "The Empire," pp. 437–54; Watson tr. "The World," pp. 362–77]; *Hsün Tzu*, 6 "Fei Shih-erh tzu" "Against the Ten [sic] Philosophers" [Dubs tr. pp. 77–80]; *Han Fei Tzu, ch.* 50, "Hsien Hsüeh [Liao tr. vol. 2, pp. 300ff]; all discuss the groupings and school divisions in thought.

[3] For a general description of the Chou government, see Hsia Tseng-yu: *Chung-kuo ku-tai shih*, Part I, Chapter Two. Reference may also be made to Ch'ü T'ung-tsu, *Chung-kuo feng-chien she-hui* [Shanghai, 1937].

[4] Of scholars of the past who have discussed feudalism, Liu Tsung-yuan [A.D. 773–819] may particularly be considered to have grasped its real character. Liu said that both the Shang and Chou dynasties achieved supreme rule through their reliance on the strength of the various feudal nobles; after succeeding in establishing themselves, they were unable to do away with those nobles or alter their reliance upon them. Hence feudalism came about as the inevitable consequence of actual conditions. See *Liu Ho-tung chi*, "Feng-chien lun." We may note that, while records are lacking for Hsia and Shang-Yin and earlier times, it would appear from the *Shih Chi* that, from the Yellow Emperor to King Wu of Chou, military conquest of the empire was in most cases accomplished by one of the feudal lords who had gained the support of other lords and was thereby enabled to seize the position of the legitimate ruler. With The First Emperor of Ch'in we have the earliest example of one state relying on its own power to annex and annihilate all the other feudal states, creating the new situation of one unified world-empire. See *Shih Chi, chs.* 1 through 4.

cratic rule over all the rest. The Chou's political foundations were, in truth, extremely unstable. That the dynasty could endure for so long a time as several centuries finds its political explanation in the fact that the royal house was [at first] strong; thus it could wield control through the "rites and music" [li-yüeh] and "punitive campaigns" [cheng-fa].[5] It finds its social explanation in the "clan-law" [tsung-fa] class, in the landholding system, and in other such institutions.[6] During [the period of] the feudal

[5] The Son of Heaven controlled the feudal nobles merely by two chief methods: The royal tours of inspection [hsün-shou] and punitive campaigns [cheng-fa]. He also appointed certain of the larger and stronger nobles "fang-po" ["Earls of the Marches"]. [Legge tr. "chiefs of regions"; hegemon [pa] he translates as "presiding chief." See Chinese Classics, Vol. v, Part I, p. 114, for his discussion of this problem. "Po" also meant "chief among the feudal nobles."] These assumed special responsibility for punitive expeditions in order to protect the royal house. The assumption of governmental powers by the hegemons [pa-cheng] in the late Chou period developed through metamorphosis of this institution, so that formally it still required the granting of authority by the Son of Heaven. Notable examples are: Duke Huan of Ch'i, who was granted the title of po ["Earl"] in the Tenth year of King Hui [666 B.C.]; in his Seventeenth year King Hsiang [634 B.C.] conferred upon Duke Wen of Chin the [symbolic] gifts of a jade tally, a bow-case, a bow and an arrow, and appointed him po; in the Twenty-sixth year of King Hsien [343 B.C.] the Chou court granted the title of po to Duke Hsiao of Ch'in (for all the above see Shih Chi, ch. 4). Government by the hegemons was clear evidence that the feudal world was beginning to disintegrate; the next stage was that of the Warring States, contending among themselves for mastery. For the forms of court audience and tribute, see the Chou Li, chs. 9–10, "Ch'iu-kuan ssu-k'ou."

[6] The Tso Chuan, Seventh year of Duke Chao [534 B.C.], quotes the Ch'ien-yin [Legge incorrectly reads the words as "Woo—director;" it is a title of office] Wu-yü [admonishing his prince] saying: " . . . The dominion of the Son of Heaven extends everywhere; the princes of States have their own defined boundaries. This is the ancient rule;—within the State and the kingdom, what ground is there that is not the ruler's? What individual of all whom the ground supports is there that is not the ruler's subject? . . . The day has its ten divisions of time, and of men there are the ten classes; and so it is that inferiors serve their superiors, and that superiors perform their sacrifices to the spirits. Hence the king makes the duke [=the prince of a State] his servant; the duke, the great officer; the great officer, the [simple] officer; the officer, the lictor; the lictor, the crowd of underlings; the underling, the menials; the menial, the laborer; the laborer, the servant; the servant, the helper. There are also grooms for the horses, and shepherds for the cattle;—and thus there is provision for all things. [Legge, p. 616.] In this we can generally picture the system of feudal classes. (Reference may also be made to the Second year of Duke Huan 709 B.C., the words spoken by Shih-fu) [Sze-fuh; Legge, pp. 40–41]. All in the class of "officer" and "great officer" [shih ta-fu] and above were of the aristocracy; those below were commoners or were "mean people." The lines of division between them were firmly fixed and were not easily altered. Thus it is that in the Tso Chuan, in the ninth year of Duke Hsiang 563 B.C., Tzu-nang says: " . . . his merchants, craftsmen, and inferior employees know nothing of changing their hereditary employments." [Modified from Legge, p. 440]; and in the Kuo-yü, ch. 6, "Ch'i-yü," Kuan Chung [Kuan Tzu] says: "Officers' sons shall perpetually be officers," "Craftsmen's sons shall perpetually be craftsmen," "Merchants' sons shall perpetually be merchants," and "Farmers' sons shall perpetually be farmers." For a general description of clan-law [tsung-fa] see the Li Chi, ch. 15, "Sang-fu

world's great heyday, life was more or less ordered, and upper and lower classes maintained their status in peaceful relationship to each other. Hence it can with some reason be called an "age of great peace." But time passed and conditions changed. Both in government and in society, transformation was underway, and there was a general trend away from that peace and stability and toward unrest. Three Chou kings, Yi [894–879 B.C.], P'ing [770–720 B.C.], and Ching [519–476 B.C.], came to the throne only through reliance on the power of feudal princes. Chou prestige and power were declining, and the royal house experienced a succession of aggressions and humiliations. Thereafter a man of the State of Cheng shot an arrow wounding the Chou King in the shoulder, and the King of Ch'u asked [the ambassador of King Ting of Chou] about the [size and weight of the royal] tripods.[7] [These are not only examples of *lese majesté* and violations of ceremonial behavior, indicating the declining prestige of the Chou kings and the weakening regulative influence of traditional ceremonial behavior, but also of an actual threat of usurpation by the King of Ch'u.] Ultimately the feudal princes engaged in annexation of neighboring territories, and chief ministers seized the governments in the princely states.[8] Long before King Nan of Chou became a hostage in the State of Ch'in, the feudal government had disintegrated and all but ceased to function. [These events traditionally are seen as developments marking the disappearance of Chou's vestigial powers. King Nan, 314–255 B.C., was the last Chou King who reigned, the next to last before the extinction of the dynasty in name as well as in fact.]

Simultaneously, the chief support of feudal society, its system of social classes, was falling speedily into dissolution along with the government of the legitimate Chou kings. Aristocratic clans fell, their members becoming mere clerks and minor functionaries, subservient to superiors who in some instances had come from the lowest classes.[9] The "clan-law" and "well-

---

hsiao-chi" and *ch.* 16, "Ta-chuan". Whether or not the well-field [*ching-t'ien*] system was actually practiced during the Chou dynasty still remains to be conclusively demonstrated. For the main idea of it, see *Mencius*, III/i/3/13 ff. and v/ii/2; [Legge, p. 243 ff. and 373 ff.].

[7] See, respectively, *Tso Chuan*, the Fifth year of Duke Huan [Legge, p. 46] and the Third year of Duke Hsüan [Legge, pp. 292–93]. The events themselves took place in the Thirteenth year of King Huan [707 B.C.] and the First year of King Ting [606 B.C.].

[8] For example, the *Kung-yang Chuan*, for the Eighth year of Duke Ting states that Yang Hu controlled the Chi family, and the Chi family controlled the State of Lu.

[9] *Tso Chuan*, Third year of Duke Chao [538 B.C.], Shu-hsiang says: " . . . The people [feel], when they hear the Duke's commands, as if they must escape from robbers and enemies. The Luan, the Ch'üeh, the Hsü, the Yuan, the Hu, the Hsü, the Ch'ing, and the Po, are reduced to the position of menials. [Surnames of great clans of the State of Chin; "people" in the first sentence means in fact "the upper classes."] . . . 'The Ducal clans of Chin are at an end.' " [Legge, p. 589.] In the *Kuo-yü ch.* 9, "Chin-yü," Tou Ch'ou [*ta-fu*

field" institutions also were gradually obliterated.[10] All the old ceremonial behavior and customs that in the past had bound people together intellectually and spiritually lost their original significance. There was enough to unsettle men's minds even without the hardships of war and calamities. The conditions were such that the feudal world that Kings Wen and Wu had brought into being could hardly continue to exist much longer.

The Warring States Period was an era of unremitting competition, in

---

or Great Officer of the State of Chin] says: "The Fan and Chung-hang clans [leaders of a disastrous revolt in Chin in 493–489 B.C.] were not troubled by thought of the calamities they caused in their desire to seize control of the State of Chin, and their sons and grandsons are about to become plowmen in the State of Ch'i. Those who should have been conducting sacrifices before their ancestral altars [a prerogative of the aristocracy] are instead reduced to hard labor in the fields. When have there ever been such changes in [the status of] men?" These are examples of the fall and disappearance of aristocratic clans.

In the *Tso Chuan*, Tenth year of Duke Hsiang [562 B.C.], the steward of Wang-shu says: "When people who live in hovels, with wicker doors fitted to holes in the wall, encroach on their superiors [it is hard to be a man of superior rank]." [Modified from Legge, pp. 448–49.] And in the Eighth year of Duke Ting, Kung-sun Chia says: "If the State of Wei has had any misfortunes, the artisans and merchants have always [used the opportunity] to cause trouble." [Modified from Legge, p. 769.] These are examples of menial people infringing on the rights of their superiors. That the system of social classes bore a relationship to the problem of order versus disorder in the feudal world was perceived by some persons at the time. For example, the *Tso Chuan*, the Thirteenth year of Duke Hsiang [559 B.C.], quotes the words of the "superior man" [*chün-tzu*] saying: "In an age of good government, men in high stations prefer ability, and give place to those who are below them, and the lesser people labor vigorously at their husbandry. . . . But in an age of disorder, men in high stations proclaim their merit in order to impose their will on those who are below them, and the lesser people boast of their arts to encroach on their superiors." [Legge, p. 458.] Chang Ping-lin, in discussing the changes in the system of clan-law society in *Chang T'ai-yen wen lu, ch'u-pien, pieh-lu, chüan 2, "She-hui t'ung-ch'üan" shang-tui* [i.e., a Criticism of E. Jenks: *A History of Politics*], states: "Clan-law [society] was controlled by those whom it exalted, and its provisions applied to 'scholars of the first class' and above [i.e., *yüan-shih*, using Legge's translation of the term as it appears in his *Mencius*, p. 374]. Clan members' excess wealth and property reverted to the clan, and deficiencies were supplied from the clan. At the higher level were the hereditary chief ministers [*shih-ch'ing*] among whom the heirs of the clans [i.e., eldest lineal descendants, *tsung-tzu*] normally held the chief governmental powers. They relied on their governmental powers, by which they dispensed punishments and rewards, as the means of restraining those below them. From the time of the Seven States and onward [the Warring States Period, from ca. 480 B.C. to 221 B.C.], those who exercised political authority often came from the ranks of wandering political advisors and job-hunters, while the clan heirs fell and became clerks and lictors. Having lost their grasp on political power, they were unable to command those below themselves, and in consequence their control of the clans also vanished completely."

[10] The *Kung-yang Chuan*, Fifteenth year to Duke Hsüan [593 B.C.]: "For the first time taxes were levied per *mou* of land;" and *Kuo-yü, ch.* 5, "Lu-yü" Part 2: "Chi K'ang-tzu wished to impose a tax on cultivated land." From these we can deduce something about changes in the landholding system.

which all the resources of craft and force were employed. The effects of
this cleared the way for the First Emperor of Ch'in: The most significant
characteristic of government in the Warring States Period was the expanding power of the rulers. Because they held ever more extensive territories and ever greater power, most of the rulers of the Seven States had
by this time arrogated to themselves the title of king, ["*wang*"—technically
the exclusive prerogative of the Chou kings]. Those most capable of
vigorous action and ambitious undertakings succeeded in making their
states ever stronger, and themselves ever more autocratic rulers.[11] There
was no restraining authority from the legitimate king above and no
guiding or controlling influence exerted by the aristocracy below. Absolute power came to be held both in name and in fact. Enriching and
strengthening the state became the main element of state policy; and the
ruler became the focal point of the state's government. Liberated by the
disintegration of feudalism, the centrifugal forces that destroyed Chou
hegemony had by this time changed into centripetal forces hastening the
accomplishment of centralized authoritarianism. The First Emperor's
unification merely followed a course for which a definite trend was already
set; he simply replaced the centralization of authority within the separate
territories of the seven contending states with one all-encompassing
authoritarianism under a single ruler.[12] In the course of this transitional
period when the feudal world was being transformed into the authoritarian
empire, there were only three attitudes possible in political thought: (1)

---

[11] Among the most prominent examples is that of Duke Wen of Wei, who employed Li
K'uei's "doctrines about exploiting the land to the limit, so as to make the state rich and
powerful." (*Han Shu, ch.* 27, "Shih-huo Chih.") [Cf. Swann, *Food and Money in Ancient China,*
p. 136.] King Wei of Ch'i established the Chi-hsia Palace and assembled scholars there.
King Min [of Ch'i] and King Chao of Ch'in called themselves, respectively, Emperors of
the East and of the West (cf. *Shih Chi, ch.* 46, "T'ien Ching, Chung Wan shih-chia").
Duke Hsiao of Ch'in employed Lord Shang to " . . . alter the laws, and to enforce them
with penalties; at home, to give special attention to agriculture, and abroad, by a system
of rewards and punishments, to encourage people to fight to the death. . . . After five
years, the people of Ch'in were rich and strong, and the Son of Heaven sent a present of
sacrificial meat to Duke Hsiao, and all the feudal lords congratulated him." (*Shih Chi, ch.*
68, "Shang-chün lieh-chuan.") [Translation follows Duyvendak, *The Book of Lord Shang,*
p. 12, note 2, and p. 19.]

[12] Ku Yen-wu, *Jih chih lu, ch.* 22, "Chün-hsien" demonstrates with examples that the
commanderies and counties had already commenced to come into existence in the Spring
and Autumn and Warring States ages, and were not an invention of The First Emperor of
Ch'in; this is adequate to corroborate the point made here. The important changes in
society frequently develop through protracted period of fermentation. The person who at
the last carries the process to the point of completion then may thereby enjoy sole credit
for the accomplishment (or be charged with sole blame for it). This has been true for many
events, not only of The First Emperor and his transformation of the empire into one of
commanderies and counties.

expression of a lingering nostalgia for the disappearing old system, coupled with the endeavor to maintain or to reconstitute it; (2) recognition of current realities and, consciously or unconsciously, receptiveness to the trend of the future and justification of it; (3) annoyance and repugnance for all systems, old or new, and inclination toward individual self-sufficiency and individual freedom. In general terms, both the Confucianists and Mohists belong to the first of these categories; the various philosophers of the Legalist school all belong to the second; and the *Lao-Chuang* philosophers of Taoism, together with all the "individualist" thinkers—recluses cultivating their solitary virtue and the like—belonged to the third category. Carrying such analysis one step further, however, we note that, although both Confucianism and Mohism were sympathetic to feudalism and both were colored by restorationist or conservative thought, the Confucianists' "following the institutes of Chou" and their esteem for refinement [*shang wen*] displays a point of view close to that of the aristocracy, while Mo Tzu's "turning his back on the institutes of Chou"[13] and his prizing simplicity [*shang chih*] reveal a point of view wholly of the common people. [*Chih*, 質 the original substance, as opposed to *wen*, 文 "superficial refinement" or culture.] Thus, while Mohism was sympathetic to the political system of the feudal world, it was clearly dissatisfied with the class organization of clan-law society. Hence there are important differences between the attitudes of the two schools. Confucius may be called the Sage of clan-law society,[14] while Mohism is nothing less than a reaction against the system of hereditary position [in government and society]. Mencius and Hsün Tzu, because they lived in the Warring States Period, display somewhat less the element of "following the Chou" in their thought [than does Confucius]. Mencius is closer to Confucius, while Hsün Tzu is closer to the Legalists. The difference between the Legalists and the Taoists is still clearer. The former promoted reform from the standpoint of the ruler's interests; the latter advocated negativism with a view to liberating the individual. The one was the forerunner of the autocratic empire; the other voiced its protest against degenerate and chaotic government. The following table is designed to display an overall view of the attitudes of the four philosophies:

[13] The *Huai-nan Tzu, ch.* 21, "Yao lüeh hsün," says that Mo Tzu: "Turned his back on the Ways of Chou, and adopted the governmental institutions of the Hsia." Whether or not Mo Tzu actually used the Hsia is a matter that will be discussed in a following chapter, but there is no doubt about his rejection of the Chou.

[14] The phrase is Yen Fu's; see his *She-hui t'ung-ch'üan* [1904, Yen's translation of Jenks *A History of Politics*, 1900; cf. footnote 9 above]. Confucianism did not give unconditional support to the clan-law system of social classes. The statement made here is intended to apply only to a comparison of them with the Mohists. The following chapter discusses this more extensively.

Table One

	Sympathetic to the Decaying Feudalism	Acknowledging the Emergent Authoritarianism
Positive-Minded	Sympathetic to Clan-law Confucians—Aristocratic point of view Confucius—Mencius—Hsün Tzu	Rejecting Clan-law Legalists—The ruler's point of view
	Opposed to Clan-law Mohists—Common man point of view	
Negative-Minded	*Disgusted with all institutions*	
	Taoists—The individual's point of view	

However, to proceed a step further, Confucian thought may have had the Yin culture as its background.[15] Confucius was a descendant of the Yin people, as is well known and as he himself admitted.[16]

Po-ch'in [the son of the Duke of Chou, and nephew of King Wu, the Chou founder] was enfiefed in Lu, but the place had been the region of Shang-yen in the Yin dynasty, and its people were of the Six Clans of Yin.[17] Hence some scholars have concluded that Confucius' wearing the

[15] Cf. Fu Ssu-nien "Chou tung-feng yü Yin yi-min" and Hu Shih "Shuo ju"; both are to be found in *Hu Shih lun-hsüeh chin-chu, ti-i-chi*. Note also that according to the *Han Shu*, *ch*. 10 and *ch*. 67, the Emperor Ch'eng [reg. 32–7 B.C.], adopting the proposal of Mei Fu, enfiefed Confucius's descendants as "Marquis of Shao-chia in Yin," therein also acknowledging Confucius' descent from the Yin.

[16] In the *Li Chi*, "T'an-kung, Part I" [*ch*. 3], Confucius is quoted as saying: "The people of Yin bury their dead in the space between two pillars . . . and Ch'iu [i.e., "myself"] am a man of Yin. Last night I dreamed of sitting by the funeral offerings between two pillars . . . I feel I am soon to die. . . . " [See also Legge, *Li Chi*, or *Li Ki*, vol. I, pp. 138–39.]

[17] The *Tso Chuan*, Fourth year of Duke Ting, states: "To the Duke of Lu there were given . . . [the Heads of] six clans of the people of Yin,—the T'iao, the Hsü, the Hsiao, the So, the Chang-shuo, and the Wei-shuo, were ordered to lead the chiefs of their kindred, to collect their branches, the remote as well as the near, to conduct the multitude of their connexions, and to repair with them to Chou, and to receive the instructions and laws of the Duke of Chou. . . . The people of Shang-yen were also attached; and a charge was given to Po-ch'in [the son of the Duke of Chou, enfiefed in Lu] and the old capital of Shao-hao was assigned as the center of his State." [Legge, p. 754.] Refer also to the *Shih Chi*, *ch*. 33, "Lu Po-ch'in shih-chia." Also the *Tso Chuan*, Ninth year of Duke Chao, says: "The King then sent Huan-po of Chan to address the following remonstrance to Chin: —'. . . P'u-ku and Shang-yen were our territories in the East. . . .'" [Legge, p. 625.] The *Cheng-yi* [commentary] quotes Fu Ch'ien [scholar of the second century A.D. who

Yin headdress called *"chang-fu"* 章甫 when living in the State of Sung, and his observance of three years' mourning, were old institutions of the Yin dynasty.[18] Such evidence is adequate to prove that the "learning of the *ju*" had pre-Chou origins. On the other hand, however, it would be incorrect to rely on this to advance the argument that Confucius did not "follow the Chou." For Confucius' political thought clearly and un-equivocally acknowledges contemporary political authority, and main-tenance of the Chou system is its starting point. The literary and political doctrines that he taught did perhaps adhere to the former Yin forms at certain points; but their overall intent was to "elegantly display the regulations of [Kings] Wen and Wu," and they took the institutes of Chou as their source and standard for political institutions.[19] Further-more, the Chou "had the advantage of viewing the two past dynasties, [i.e., Hsia and Shang-Yin; cf. *Analects*, III/14; Legge, p. 24], and conformed to the ceremonies of Yin. Thus in the Chou institutions there are also elements of Yin institutions;[20] and thus, in "following the Chou," Con-fucius was not necessarily repudiating the ways of the Yin.

If we agree that Lu was then the home of the earlier Yin peoples, as Mo Tzu was also a man of Lu, he too may have had a Yin cultural back-ground. The Yin esteemed "simplicity" [*chih*] whereas the Chou esteemed "refinement" [*wen*]. The Mohists also esteemed simplicity, seeming in that to have inherited a Yin characteristic. They did not dare speak directly of "following the Yin," so they claimed to be applying the [way of] Hsia. It was probably fear of arousing the wrath of contemporary [Chou] rulers that made them camouflage their doctrine as that of earlier antiq-ity. [Hsia was neutral, since neither the Chou nor the Yin came directly from Hsia backgrounds; and it was revered by both Chou and Yin for its antiquity.] Their attacks on Confucianism's excessive refinement and superfluous ceremonial seem intended to project a purer approach to the Yin ways and a protest against the Chou government's mixing of elements from the two earlier dynasties.[21] Mohists also sought careers in govern-

---

specialized in the study of the *Ch'un-ch'iu*]: "P'u-ku was the State of Ch'i; Shang-yen the State of Lu."

[18] Mao Ch'i-ling's [1623–1716] *Ssu-shu sheng-yen, ch.* 3, states: "Duke Wen of T'eng asked [advice from] Mencius and only then fixed the mourning period at three years." [Cf. *Mencius*, III/i/2; Legge, pp. 235–239.] And his *Ssu-shu kai-ts'o, ch.* 9, also says: " . . . he fixed upon the three year period of mourning." For both, see *Mao Hsi-ho ho-chi.*

[19] For a detailed discussion of this see the following chapter.

[20] Lo Chen-yü, in the preface to his *Yin-hsü shu-ch'i k'ao-shih*, states that it is possible to deduce from the official titles found in the oracle bone inscriptions that "The Six Institutes of [the Duke of Chou], Chi Tan, were largely based on [those of] the Shang-Yin."

[21] If the three-year mourning period really was a Yin institution, then Mohists' attack on it would seem to be inconsistent with this view. In short, the thought of Confucius and Mo Tzu was not necessarily confined to the institutions of any one dynasty. It is appro-priate here merely to direct our attention to the general character of their thought.

ment, and sought them no less eagerly than did Confucians. Mohists, however, did not give up their lower-class occupations, while the Confucians' "four limbs are unaccustomed to toil" and they "eat without laboring."[22] Even when they were not employed in the government, the Confucians vigorously maintained their dignity and self-importance as scholar-officials [shih ta-fu]. This is one of the differences between the two schools.

Inasmuch as the Mohists' manner of life was quite different from that of the Confucians, their methods for emancipating the common people likewise differed very greatly. The Confucians acknowledged clan-law and sought merely to open to commoners a route to high public office beyond that which the traditional institution of hereditary rank and office provided [for the aristocracy]. The Mohists, on the other hand, openly attacked the great-clan upper classes [men-fa, 門閥 the great established clans and their followings]; they loudly proclaimed their equality-of-opportunity principle, which they called "elevating the worthy." From this we may say that Mohist thought, insofar as its sources can be traced to origins in the Yin people's esteem of simplicity [shang chih], was more archaic than Confucianism; but in its destructive attack on clan-law and its accommodation to the trend of developments in late Chou society, it was ahead of Confucianism.

The Taoists were perhaps like the Confucians and Mohists in also belonging to the Yin cultural system.[23] The Shih-Chi states that Wei Tzu, after censuring the tyrant King Chou and being ignored by him, went away and disappeared.[24] [The last ruler of Yin-Shang, King Chou was a symbol of the evil ruler. Wei Tzu, the Viscount of Wei, was his older brother.] Subsequently, after King Ch'eng [of Chou] (reg. 1114–1078 B.C.) had annihilated Wu-keng [the last Shang ruler, King Chou's 紂 son and heir-pretender, leader of an abortive revolt of the Yin people against the new Chou 周 dynasty] he enfiefed Wei Tzu in the State of Sung; "the former Yin people there bore him the greatest affection." It also tells about Chi Tzu ["The Viscount of Chi," uncle and preceptor to the last Yin king, who censured him in vain for his dissolute conduct], who on passing the "Wastes of Yin" was moved to compose his Song of the Verdant

---

[22] In the Analects [xviii/7/1,] the old man carrying a basket replies to Tzu-lu, seeking Confucius, who has asked him if he has seen "my master": "Your four limbs are unaccustomed to toil; you cannot distinguish the five kinds of grain:—who is your master?" [Legge, p. 335.] In the Mencius [vii/i/32,] Kung-sun Ch'ou asks Mencius: "It is said, in the Book of Poetry, 'He will not eat the bread of idleness.' How it is that we see superior men eating without laboring?" [Legge, p. 467.]

[23] Hu Shih, in his "Shuo ju" [see footnote 15 above], says that Lao Tzu, with his knowledge of the rites and in his retiring behavior, was conforming to the orthodox line of "ju" learning of the Yin descendants.

[24] Ch. 38, "Sung Wei-tzu shih-chia."

Grain; "the Yin people on hearing it all shed tears." [A song composed to express his grief on passing the ruins of the Yin capital, laid waste by the Chou dynasty conquerors. It blames the evil King Chou of Yin for the collapse of Yin rule.] The *Shih-Chi Chi-chieh* [commentary on the *Shih-Chi* by P'ei Yin, of the fourth century A.D.] quotes Tu Yü here: "The grave of Chi Tzu is in the region of Liang." [Tu Yü, A.D. 222–284, scholar of the Chin period famous for his study of the Commentary of *Tso* to the *Spring and Autumn Annals*.] Although this information may not be completely reliable, Sung and Liang were undoubtedly the regions in which the Yin people were concentrated. If Chuang Tzu was in truth a native of the State of Meng, then he too was born in the area of the Yin people, and it is even possible that he himself was of the Yin people. Although the State of Ch'u was not in close relationship to the Yin state, yet when we note that Chou T'ai-po and Chou Chung-yung fled to join the *man* barbarians in the Ching region, we can probably deduce that dissident elements under Yin rule looked upon the South as a paradise to which they could flee from the world. [The two were uncles of Chou Ch'ang, posthumously called King Wen of Chou. As dissident feudal lords under the last Yin rulers, they fled to the Ching region in the South to escape Yin rule. Ching loosely designates the Central Yangtze Valley, south of the Yin and later incorporated into the Chou territories.] Lao Tan [Lao Tzu] was born at Hu-hsien in Ch'u[25] and his background was probably also somewhat like Chuang Chou's at Meng in the State of Sung. The negative philosophy of Lao Tzu and Chuang Tzu, moreover, accords well with the frustrated psychology of the scattered peoples of fallen states. [Chuang Tzu and Taoism in general are often identified exclusively with the culture of the southern state of Ch'u, not however, necessarily with great accuracy. See below, Section Two.]

In view of the preceding discussion it would seem that all the three

---

[25] The *Odes*, "Shang sung" v., "Yin wu":
" 'Ye people' [said our king of Yin], 'of Ching Ch'u
Dwell in the southern part of my kingdom' " [in the Central Yangtze basin, comprising the area of the State of Ch'u]
and also says: [of the King of Yin]:
"And vigorously did he attack Ching Ch'u."
[Legge, pp. 643–44.]

The *Shih Chi*, ch. 40, "Ch'u shih-chia," states: "The final generations of the Yin house . . . were variously in the central state [*Chung-kuo*, i.e., "China," the central area of Chinese civilization] and among the *man* and *yi* barbarians" [the barbarians associated with the sourthern and eastern borders of the central Chinese culture area]. It is quite evident that Ch'u's relationship with Yin was somewhat distant. H'u-hsien [Lao Tan's reputed birthplace] originally was part of the State of Ch'en, and was the fief of the descendants of the Emperor Shun, hence also descended from Emperor Chuan-hsü, and thus it shared its distant ancestry with the State of Ch'u, and both Ch'en and Ch'u were outside the domain of Chou culture.

schools, Confucianism, Mohism, and Taoism, are alike in having as their background the descendants of the Yin dynasty. Since they differed in the attitudes they adopted toward the Chou institutions, their theories also developed along different lines and in divergent directions. If in consideration of this we designate all three schools as the "old" learning, then the thought of the Legalists, who were not heirs to the old Yin civilization, can be called the "new" learning. The works on penal laws and the penal tripods appeared in the States of Cheng and Chin respectively. [I.e., "*hsing shu*" and "*hsing ting*," penal regulations cast in bronze or on tripods and put in public view as a means of making the rule of law effective. See *Tso Chuan*, e.g., the Twenty-ninth year of Duke Chao; Legge, pp. 729, 732, where the casting of penal tripods in the State of Chin is commented upon.] Legalist techniques were most fully applied in the State of Ch'in and in the three states formed from Chin. [In about 403 B.C. the State of Chin was divided into the three states of Wei or Liang, Han, and Chao.] These all stood in comparatively intimate relationship to the Chou domain itself; they were not regions in which the former Yin clans had been re-enfiefed, as was the case in the States of Ch'i, Lu, Sung, and Wei. [This State of Wei 衛 is not to be confused with Wei, 魏 one of the successor states of Chin.][26] The occasional exceptions to this [associations of Legalism with non-Yin backgrounds], such as the *Kuan Tzu*, which claims origin in the State of Ch'i, or Shang Yang, who was born and reared in the State of Wei, represent only a small minority of cases. Hence Legalist thought, once divested of such attitudes as those of compromise on a "golden mean" [*chung-yung*], of flexible accommodation, of pacificism, and of humble withdrawal [all readily associable with Confucianism, Taoism, or Mohism, and, by implication, with the conquered Yin people] could then devote itself entirely to exalting the ruler and stressing the importance of the state, and to enriching and strengthening the state through ambitious schemes for its aggrandizement. In this connection we need not attempt to evaluate the content of Legalist theories; the point to be noted is that Legalism's attitude of positive optimism and its confident "new nation" mood are quite lacking in the

---

[26] King Ch'eng's younger brother, Shu-yü, was enfiefed at T'ang, which had been the former fief of Emperor Yao's descendants. Of the three families who divided the State of Chin, the ancestors of the Han were of the same surname as the Chou, and so was Pi-kung, the ancestor of the Wei. The Chao family were of the same ancestry as the rulers of Ch'in. Duke Huan of Cheng [of the Chou royal line, and whose name was] Yu, was enfiefed there only in the Twenty-second year of King Hsüan [805 B.C.], and he: "Assembled together the people of Chou; the Chou people were all made happy" [*Shih Chi, ch.* 42]. The State of Ch'in was far off on the western boundaries; its ancestry was traced from the distant descendants of the Emperor Chuan-hsü. See, respectively, in the *Shih Chi*, the "Shih-chia" chapters, 39 and 43–45, on the ducal houses of Chin, Cheng, Han, Chao, and Wei, and *chs.* 5–6, "Ch'in pen-chi."

other schools. The discussion above can be summarized and represented graphically as follows:

Table Two

	Positive Attitudes	Negative Attitudes
Thought having the vanquished Shang-Yin dynasty background	Confucians Acknowledge the Royal Chou Clan's political authority; Follow the Chou and Esteem Refinement	Non-cooperative with the Chou—seeking the liberation of the individual
	Reject the Chou and Esteem Simplicity Elevate the status of the common people Mohists	Taoists
Thought having the Late Chou—"New Nation" background	Legalists	
	Acknowledging the disintegration of the feudal world; Hastening the emergence of an authoritarian political order	

Turning to the content of the thought of the four schools, we find that each produced its own distinctive theories, each created something that had the effect of launching it as a separate school, and each thereby laid down a line of development for subsequent thought and learning. The first of these lines can be called "government of men"; to it belonged the Confucians and Mohists. Confucian government took the "superior man" as its essential element.[27] [*Chün-tzu* is customarily translated "the superior man," following Legge, who used this "for want of a better term;" cf. *Chinese Classics*, Vol. I, p. 3, notes. Although the inadequacy of this translation is generally recognized, perhaps no better solution exists.] The superior man was one who combined in one person both the perfection of his ethical nature [*te*] and the possession of office, and who in consequence could bring about beneficial results by cultivating [his person], regulating [his family], rightly governing his state, and making [the world] tranquil and happy. [So it is expressed in *The Great Learning;* see Legge, pp. 357 ff.] This was the ideal held by the Confucians. Mo Tzu, too, in discussions of government, emphasized the worthy man

[27] Liang Ch'i-ch'ao's *Hsien-ch'in cheng-chih ssu-hsiang-shih*, p. 311, states: "All government proceeded from the superior man [*chün-tzu*]; this was the unique hallmark of the Confucians. Evidence of it is to be found throughout all of the Confucian writings and it is a point that is undeniably correct."

[*hsien jen* 賢人, cf. Y. P. Mei, *The Ethical and Political Works of Motze*, p. 30, note 1, for a comment on this translation of the word "*hsien.*"] "Therefore [heaven] chose the worthy in the world and crowned him emperor,"[28] while appointments to all of the government also were to be made to those judged worthy. Whether order or disorder would prevail was seen to hinge upon the character of the persons who served in the government and did the governing. This is something that Mohists stressed and in which they agreed with the Confucians.

Nonetheless, here too there were differences between the Confucians and the Mohists. The Confucians' "superior man" has about him a great deal of the aristocrat; his value-standards incline markedly toward the ethics of clan-law society. The Mohists' "worthy men" mostly had the status of commoners and their value-standards were slanted toward the spirit of service and practical techniques.[29] The former stressed the motive behind the deed; the latter valued the effectiveness of an action. Hence, even though they coincided in looking upon man as the instrument of government, they differed in their theoretical conception of the man to whom they would entrust government.

The second main grouping can be called that of "government by laws," represented by the Legalists. Although Shen Pu-hai, Shang Yang, and Han Fei Tzu each displays his own views in the theories he set forth, without exception each held punishments and laws to be the essential element in the government, and thus they were directly opposed to the government of men advocated by Confucians and Mohists. The contribution of Legalist thought lay in the elucidation of the fact that a government of virtuous men cannot be depended upon, and need not be; that the soundest and most dependable government, on the contrary, is one of clearly articulated laws and rigid regulations, severe punishments, and heavy fines.[30] The Legalists are always criticized for their harsh stringency

[28] *Mo Tzu*, "Shang t'ung," Part I [*ch.* 11; following the translation of Y. P. Mei: *The Works of Motze from the Chinese*, p. 56].

[29] However we must note that Mo Tzu's disciples were mostly commoners, but there were some among them who harbored a feverish desire to enter officialdom; of those individuals about whom we know some concrete facts, almost all roamed about asking service with various feudal lords. The chapter "Kung Meng" tells [about a young man who became Mo Tzu's student in the hope of getting official position thereby]: "He studied for one year, after which he demanded that Mo Tzu find him a position." [Modified from Y. P. Mei, *ibid.*, p. 239.] This is particularly revealing of the psychology of Mo Tzu's followers. Of Confucius disciples, those who came from the hereditary aristocracy numbered no more than four or five; by far the greatest part of them were of the common people, and many of them, such as Yen Hui, Jan Keng, and others, lived in retirement, refusing to hold official position. See Sun Yi-jang: *Mo-hsüeh ch'uan-shou k'ao*, and *Shih Chi*, *ch.* 67, "Chung-ni ti-tzu lieh-chuan."

[30] Note that the thinking about the rule of law in ancient China was fundamentally different from European legalist thought; for a discussion of this, cf. below, Chapter Six.

and lack of mercy;—this was precisely because they had abandoned the principle of government founded on men, and relied solely on materialistically conceived instrumentalities. Both the believers in government by men and those of government by law were positive in their political thought.

Only the anarchists, of whom the Taoists are representative, took a negative attitude, and they were in opposition to both the groupings described above. Lao Tzu and Chuang Tzu ridiculed benevolence and righteousness [i.e., the symbolically Confucian virtues] and turned away

Table Three

	Polity	Principle	Ideal Governing Methods
Government of Men	Confucians—the "superior man" [chün-tzu]	Jen—"broadly extending succor to the masses"	Nourishing and teaching; [Rectification of names]
		"establishing others; advancing others"	All the realm turning to the benevolent ruler
	Mohists—the "worthy" [hsien-jen]	Universal love	Elevating the Worthy, Agreement with the Superior
		Mutual benefit	Condemnation of Offensive Warfare, Economy of Expenditure
			[Governing equable; people at peace]
Government of Law	Law	Laws, Methods, Power	Clearly articulated laws, strict regulations; Severe punishments, heavy penalities
			The state strong, the ruler supreme
Non-governing	The Tao	Non-action	Eradicate interference and anxiety Rely on spontaneous nature
			Small states with few people An age of "perfect virtue" [naturalness or spontaneity]

in disgust from laws and regulations; they renounced wisdom and advocated limitation of desires, they esteemed neither virtue nor ability, and held as their ideal a government of "the natural" [or "the spontaneous" *tzu-jan*] and of "inaction" [*wu-wei*]. The Table Three is designed to show these points of comparison:

Section Two
The Geographical Distribution

THE schools of thought of the pre-Ch'in era may also be classified according to the regions in which they originated. In both their natural and social backgrounds, the various feudal states were different and, as a consequence, the content of thought varied also. Liang Ch'i-ch'ao classified all the philosophers as belonging to either a Northern or a Southern School. He took Confucius as "founder of the main line of the Northern School," and representative of the States of Tsou and Lu. In addition to this major line there were Kuan Chung [Kuan Tzu] and Tsou Yen in Ch'i, the various Legalist philosophers in Ch'in and Chin, and the School of Names and the Mohists in Sung and Cheng. Lao Tzu he calls "founder of the main line of the Southern School," to which also belonged Chuang Tzu, Lieh Tzu, and Yang Chu. Both Hsü Hsing and Ch'ü Yuan are taken to represent branch lines from the Southern School.[31] Liang's view has in it much that can be accepted, although his distinction between main lines and branch lines does not seem to mean much. As for the places of birth of the various philosophers, there too some points need further study.[32] The following table has been made, mainly observing Liang's views, and bearing in mind the places where the Four Schools originated:[33]

A look at Table Four shows that the regions where the three schools of Confucianism, Mohism, and Taoism originated are all apparently smaller and more confined than that from which Legalism emerged. The State of Lu [Confucianism and Mohism] was merely one of the smaller northern states, lying somewhat east of the "center." Lao Tzu's and Chuang Tzu's Hu and Meng also were: the one, no more than a corner

---

[31] In "Lun Chung-kuo hsüeh-shu pien-ch'ien chih ta-shih," *Yin-ping-shih wen-chi*, VII. Yang Yu-chiung's *Chung-kuo cheng-chih ssu-hsiang-shih*, Chapter I, Section 3, apparently adopts his views, except that he calls Confucius "the chief of the Northern School" and Lao Tzu the "chief of the Southern School." He also departs from Liang's views in saying: "From the Taoists to the Diplomatists [*tsung-heng chia*] and the Legalists, each established a separate school," and also says that Mo Tzu was born in the State of Sung, " . . . hence his learning took from both the Northern and the Southern Schools."

[32] For example, his saying that Mo Tzu was a native of the State of Sung.

[33] Where geographic identification of a person is doubtful, or is known and should place the person in question elsewhere in the table, that person's name is placed in parentheses.

Table Four

States		Political Thinkers		Schools			
Lu		Confucius	(Mencius)	Confucianism			North
			(Hsün Tzu)				
		Mo Tzu		Mohism			
Ch'i		(Kuan Tzu)					
Wei		Lord Shang					
Cheng		Teng Hsi				Positive Thought	
		Shen Pu-hai		Legalism			
Chin	Wei	Li K'uei					
	Han	Han Fei					
	Chao	Shen Tao					
Ch'u (?)		(Lao Tan)		Taoism		Negative Thought	South
		(Chuang Tzu) (Sung?)					

of the State of Ch'u; the other, a village fief lying between Liang and Sung.[34] But the distribution of the states that produced the Legalist thinkers covered virtually the entire Yellow River drainage. Confucianism and Mohism, moreover, were produced in a rather special environment, and the area of their immediate influence, in consequence, could not become very extensive. Legalist thought, on the other hand, grew in response to conditions that were fairly general during the late Chou era. Hence, when it appeared, it struck a sympathetic note in other places as well and spread abroad extensively.

As for the negative thought of the Taoist thinkers, it was basically a kind of protest against the conditions of a degenerate age; hence it would

[34] Tentatively following the *Shih Chi, ch.* 63, "Lao, Chuang, Shen, Han lieh-chuan," and the explanations in the *Chi-chieh* and *So-yin* commentaries. Note that the *Han Shu, ch.* 30, "Yi-wen chih" or "Journal of Literature," under "*Tao-chia*" ["Taoists"] lists the *Kung Tzu Mou,* in four essays, [*p'ien*]; the note calls its author a man of the State of Wei. The *Tzu Hua Tzu* is also a representative of the Taoist school; the [commentary] *Shih-wen* to Chapter 28, "Jang Wang" of *Chuang Tzu* quotes Ssu-ma [Piao] in identifying its author as a man of the State of Wei. The *Shih Chi, ch.* 74, "Meng, Hsün lieh-chuan," calls T'ien P'ien a man of the State of Ch'i. Ch'eng Hsüan-ying's *Chuang Tzu Su* also refers to P'eng Meng as a native of Ch'i. Thus is it perhaps true that Taoists also came from the north?

not seem that its growth should have remained confined to one region. However, even though Lao Tan is generally recognized as its founding master, the dates and facts of his life are still elusive and uncertain. [Literally, "like a divine dragon, whose head and tail both remain unseen."] Whether or not the book, the *Lao Tzu* [i.e., the *Tao-te Ching*] is the work of the founder of the school and prime source of its tenets is still doubtful. Of other Taoists, and "notable worthies" who resembled the Taoists, such as Lieh Yü-k'ou [Lieh Tzu], Yang Tzu-chü [Yang Chu], and Tzu Hua Tzu, even their native states cannot be known with certainty. In the case of all the other recluses, and followers of the line of relativism [*ch'i-wu* 齊物] and egocentricity, such as P'eng Meng, T'ien P'ien, Shen Tao, Chieh Tzu, Huan Yüan, as well as Ch'en Chung Tzu, Ho K'uei ["the man carrying the straw basket"], Ch'u K'uang [Chieh Yü, the "madman of Ch'u"], Ch'ang Chü, and Chieh Ni,[35] they were in all the states of Chao, Ch'i, Wei, Ch'u, and Ts'ai. Their area, like that of the Legalists, is of great extent.

Today we are unable to determine the reasons why these philosophies appeared in different places; however, we may make some conjectures from the overall situation. Since the *Institutes of Chou [Chou-li]* were preserved in Lu, it is only natural that Lu should be the home of the *ju*. [It is customary to translate post-Confucian "*ju*" as "Confucianism," but here both the pre-Confucian *ju* learning and Confucianism are intended.] Mohism was influenced by Confucianism but was a reaction against the clan-law system; hence it too appeared in that same place. The State of Chin was apparently the center of the region from which Legalism emerged, while Wei and Cheng were of secondary importance in this process. In the State of Wei, K'ang-shu [younger brother of King Wu and of the Duke of Chou, founder of the ducal house of Wei] had first been enfiefed *ssu-k'ou* [minister of penal matters] of Chou. Not only was a background of the Chou institutes missing there, but emphasis on law also became the main element in the testamentary admonition [i.e., the *K'ang Kao*] given on the founding of the state.[36] Therefore that the

---

[35] See *Shih Chi*, *ch.* 47, "K'ung Tzu shih-chia" and *ch.* 74, "Meng, Hsün lieh-chuan" and the *Analects*, XIV, "Hsien-wen" and XVIII, "Wei-tzu."

[36] Note that, according to the *Shih Chi*, *ch.* 37, "Wei K'ang-shu shih-chia," K'ang-shu had been *ssu-k'ou* of Chou. The "K'ang Kao" in the "*Chou Shu*" [i.e., "Documents of Chou," a division of the *Documents*] is more than half devoted to setting forth the principle of "reverently seeking clear understanding in the application of punishments." [Modified from Legge, *Documents*, page 388.] This shows that in Wei from the very founding of the state there had existed this background of emphasis on law; this did not have to wait until the late Chou for Kung-sun Yang [i.e., Lord Shang] to invent it. The "K'ang Kao" also includes the passage: "I think of the virtue of the former wise kings of Yin, whereby they tranquilized and regulated the people." [Legge, pp. 395-96.] This is probably because

State of Wei should respond to the developments of the late Chou by producing the teachings of Shang Yang [Lord Shang] seems quite natural. The State of Cheng was wedged in between great states and, in practices aimed at its own self-preservation, penal administration was given precedence over benevolence and righteousness.[37] Tzu-ch'an made people "hide away their clothes and caps, and count their fields by fives." [Stern administrative measures adopted by Tzu-ch'an while he was chief minister of Cheng, ca. 543–22 B.C.] In this he came rather close to the practices of the Legalists. When he had the penal regulations cast in bronze in the Sixth year of Duke Chao [of Lu—i.e., 536 B.C.], he directly brought about the practice of relying primarily on laws. How natural, then, that within forty years Teng Hsi made his penal laws inscribed on bamboo,[38] and that a hundred years later the great master of the Legalists, Shen Pu-hai, was born in the same area as Duke Huan's original fief. The Three States of Chin also provided an environment that was particularly conducive to the development of Legalist thinking. Although the laws that T'ang-shu [founder of the ducal line of Chin] had received[39] [from the Chou king at the time of his enfieffment] were not necessarily penal regulations, yet in the Twenty-ninth year of Duke Chao [of Lu, i.e., 513 B.C., the *Tso Chuan* informs us that] tripods bearing penal regulations were cast there. This is enough to show that by the Spring and Autumn Period the practice of depending greatly on laws already existed in Chin,

---

Wei is the place where [the last Yin King] the tyrant Chou's son, Wu-keng, had been enfiefed over remnant Yin people; hence it was not governed solely according to the *Institutes of Chou*. [Wu-keng led a revolt against the new Chou rulers in the early part of King Ch'eng's reign; after its suppression Wei was given to K'ang-shu in fief.]

[37] The *Kuo-yü, ch.* 16, "Cheng-yü," quotes the words of Shih Po advising Duke Huan of Cheng [Duke Huan, by name Yu, was a younger brother of King Hsüan of Chou and first of the ducal line enfiefed, in 805 B.C. in Cheng. Shih Po, the Grand Recorder *T'ai shih* of the Chou court, was a senior official. Yu, who at that time held the office of *ssu-k'ou* at the Chou court, applied to him for advice about how a small state could maintain itself in the face of many difficulties. A portion of his advice, intended by Shih Po to apply to a region within Chou, was subsequently applied by Yu to Cheng when it was created out of that same region of Chou, and he was enfiefed there as its duke. Shih Po said: "Before lies the State of Hua [most commentaries agree that *hua* 華 is a mistake for *hsin* 莘, or designates *ying* 潁, the names of rivers, corresponding to the names of the other rivers mentioned; these together roughly bounded a central area somewhat analogous to that of Cheng] and behind is the Yellow River [on the right the Lo River and on the left the Chi River"; the foregoing phrase is perhaps inadvertently omitted in the original note]. "Sacrifice to Mt. P'i-kuei and drink from the Wei and Chen streams. Perfect the institutions and penal regulations wherewith to govern this area; in that way the difficulties can be made few." This subsequently became the national policy of the state of Cheng.

[38] For both the above instances, see the *Tso Chuan* [Legge, p. 558 and p. 772, respectively].

[39] See *Tso Chuan*, Twenty-ninth year of Duke Chao [Legge, p. 732].

as well as in Cheng. Moreover, Chin was rather distant from Lu, and adjacent to Cheng and Ch'in. The ceremonial rites and customs that prevailed along the Chu and the Ssu rivers [i.e., in Lu] naturally could not readily extend their influence to those states. Therefore as early as when Shih, the actor, was telling Li-chi how to slander Shen-sheng, the words "to promote benevolence is not the same as to promote the country's interests" already appear.[40] [An anecdote about the history of the ducal family in Chin in the middle of the seventh century B.C. Li-chi was the concubine of the Duke; Shen-sheng was the legitimate heir-apparent born of another mother. Li-chi plotted with her lover, the actor Shih, to disinherit Shen-sheng and permit her own son to succeed. The phrase quoted shows consciousness of the distinction between the values of humanistic ethics, stressed by the Confucians, and those of statism, stressed by the Legalists.] And again, Chi Cheng replied to Duke Wen's questions with such phrases as "constancy [*hsin*] in the matter of regulations" and "constancy in [the people's] doing of their work."[41] [Chi Cheng, a Great Officer at the court of Duke Wen of Chin, reg. 634–629 B.C., uses these phrases in advising his Duke on how to meet the unusual emergencies of government in a period of famine. They reveal some of the tone of Legalism.] At least some of the reasons for Chin's repeated attempts forcibly to establish hegemony over the other feudal lords can be found herein. Add to this the decline and disappearance of the ducal houses and families having hereditary official position that, as seen in the extant records, apparently took place with unusual rapidity in the State of Chin.[42] Then three noble clans divided Chin into the States of Han, Chao, and Wei; and these too entered into the struggle for supremacy that went on among all the feudal states. Wei had its Li K'uei, Han its Han Fei, and Shen Tao —whose learning combined Taoism and Legalism—was born in Chao. Kuan Chung, a man of Ch'i, served Duke Huan of Ch'i as chief minister, and secured for him his position as hegemon [i.e., *pa* "Lord Protector," "President," etc.] "And in Ch'i, the eager pursuit of accomplishment and profit [i.e., utilitarian ends, as opposed to Confucian righteousness], and delight in boasting and deceit became customary behavior; these practices

[40] *Kuo yü, ch.* 7, "Chin-yü" 1 [cf. *Tso Chuan*; Legge, pp. 114–15].

[41] *Kuo-yü, ch.* 10, "Chin-yü" 4. Note also the *Tso Chuan*, Second year of Duke Chao, when Han Hsüan Tzu [was sent from Chin] to Lu, where he looked at the documents in charge of the Grand Historiographer and for the first time saw the "Institutes of Chou" [*Chou Li*]. This is proof that the Confucian *Six Disciplines* were not widely disseminated throughout the Three States of Chin at that time. [539 B.C.; see Legge, p. 583.]

[42] Cf. items cited in note 9 above, and *Tso Chuan*, Twenty-fifth year of Duke Chuang: "Duke Hsien completely exterminated all the clan of Dukes Huan and Chuang"; and, Second year of Duke Hsüan: "In Chin, there were no branches of the ducal clan." [Cf. Legge, p. 291, whose translation differs]; and Third year of Duke Chao: "The ducal clans of Chin are at an end." [Legge, p. 589.]

were the outgrowth of government by hegemon."[43] [I.e., government by force, as opposed to kingly government, or government by moral suasion.] It is indeed quite possible that herein lie the beginnings of Legalist thought. There is merely the problem of the book *Kuan-tzu*, for it is not yet determined who its author may have been. If, however, it is indeed a false attribution [to Kuan Chung] by some writer of the Warring States Period, then it becomes very difficult to prove that Legalist thought first appeared in the State of Ch'i.

Of the reasons why the four schools arose in different places, those explaining the Taoist school's origins are the most difficult to discover. The native places of Lieh Tzu and Yang Chu and others are difficult to determine; but more about this shortly. "The climate of the South being mild, and its soil rich, life there is easy"; to take this as the explanation of why a whole school of thought should be produced that "venerated fantasy and advocated inaction"[44] seems to be faulty, as overly abstract. For although the State of Ch'u had its origins among the southern barbarians,[45] it nonetheless "pacified and brought order to the Southern Sea region [barbarian tribes lying further to the south, and bordering on the southeast coasts] and taught them to associate together with the Chinese states."[46] First, King Chuang [seventh century] of Ch'u asked about the tripods [see page 46 above], and later on King Ling [sixth century] schemed to make himself hegemon. [Both show Ch'u involvement in politics of the central Chinese states.]

Ch'u's national policies and the character of her government were certainly not radically different from those of the North China states. For example, for pleasure excursions there was the Tower of Chang-hua [a pleasure palace constructed to entertain visiting rulers and dignitaries from the northern states]; in matters of penal regulations they used the law of P'u-ou. [A law concerning fugitives made by King Wen of Ch'u, 688–676 B.C.] Shen Shu-shih, in discussing the education of the heir apparent, suggested that Confucian texts, historical records, "laws and penalties" be included in the curriculum.[47] In discussing the relationship between ruler and servitor, the Duke of Yün stressed the importance of

---

[43] Chu Hsi, *Lun-yü chi-chu*, VI/22, commentary on the line: "Ch'i, by one change, would come to the State of Lu." [Translation modified from Legge, p. 192.]

[44] Yang Yu-chiung, *Chung-kuo cheng-chih ssu-hsiang-shih*, p. 41.

[45] King Wu of Ch'u [reg. 703–689 B.C.] in making war against the State of Sui still referred to himself as a "*man-yi*"; cf. *Shih Chi*, ch. 40, "Ch'u shih-chia."

[46] *Kuo-yü, ch.* 17, "Ch'u-yü," 1; the words are those of Tzu Nang [younger brother of King Kung of Ch'u, reg. 589–559].

[47] *Ibid.*; for the law of P'u-ou see *Tso Chuan*, Seventh year of Duke Chao [Legge, p. 616]. Shen Shu-shih was "a worthy great officer of Ch'u." The Confucian texts he mentioned were the *Ch'un-ch'iu* and the *Odes*; "laws and penalties" were to be items in a supplementary course of instruction.

maintaining strict distinction between superior and inferior.[48] [Descendants of a collateral branch of the Ch'u royal house were enfiefed Dukes of Yün, and served in high position as chief ministers; the conversation referred to here probably occurred in the year 506 B.C.] In all of these there is some similarity to Confucianism or Legalism, but nothing whatsoever in common with Taoism's teachings of purity, quiescence, and pristine simplicity. And if we were to say that the philosophy of inaction is a reaction against harsh government, then "making laws and regulations more numerous and more prominent"[49] was done nowhere to a greater extent than in Ch'in and Chin, so why is it that these are not the native countries of Taoism? That the origins of Taoist thought are not to be found in this explanation would seem quite obvious.

Confucianism, Mohism, and Taoism may, all three, have in their backgrounds the descendants of the Yin people; this has already been discussed. Reasoning from this about the origins of Taoist thought, we can perhaps arrive at a fairly acceptable hypothesis. Lao Tzu and Chuang Tzu were born in the states of Ch'u and Sung and were perhaps themselves descendants of the Yin people; in addition to this, those others of the philosophers whose thought and lives are similar to the Taoists were in most cases born in places where the Yin descendants were settled. For example, in Ch'i there were P'eng Meng (?), T'ien P'ien, Chieh Tzu, and Ch'en Chung Tzu. In Wei there was Ho K'uei, in Ts'ai there were Ch'ang Chü and Chieh Ni. In Ch'u there were madman Chieh Yü and Huan Yüan. [See above p. 63; also footnote 35, for all these names.] Of the birthplace of Yang Chu nothing is known; but since he traveled about in Liang and Sung it was perhaps not far from the origins of Lao Tzu and Chuang Tzu. Those not within the bounds of this region are Lieh Yü-k'ou, who was perhaps a native of Cheng, and Tzu Hua Tzu, who may have been a native of Wei. Shen Tao's theories lie midway between Taoism and Legalism; he was born in Chao. On the basis of these incomplete historical data, it appears that the "egocentric" thinkers from the State of Wei were the more numerous, while those born in the States of Ch'u and Sung were the more important. The reasons why Ch'u and Sung should be the home of Lao Tzu and Chuang Tzu have already been speculated upon during our discussion of the backgrounds of the four schools. That Ch'i should produce so many Taoists is perhaps in part because of the psychology of the [conquered] Yin descendants, in part because of the in-

[48] *Ibid.*, *ch.* 18, "Ch'u-yü," 2.

[49] *Tao Te Ching*, Chapter 57. Cf. Ch'ien Mu, *Hsien-ch'in chu-tzu hsi-nien k'ao-pien*, pp. 208, 342, and 394, who states that *Huang-Lao* [Taoist political thought] arose in Ch'i as a reaction against the practical, this-worldly thought of Confucianism and Mohism. This is a novel view that may be considered in this connection.

fluences of the doctrines of Ch'i T'ai-kung. [I.e., T'ai-kung Wang, original name Lü Shang, advisor of Kings Wen and Wu and founder of the ducal house of Ch'i, where he was enfiefed by King Wu at the time the Chou state was founded. He had been a recluse before serving King Wen; the tradition about him reflects attitudes clearly associable with later Taoism.]

If the records in the chapters "Ch'i T'ai-kung shih-chia" and "Lu Po-ch'in shih-chia" [genealogical histories of the ducal houses of Ch'i and Lu] in the *Shih Chi* are to be believed, T'ai-kung governed Ch'i by "following their customs, and simplifying their institutions [*li*]," not forcibly altering the old practices of the Yin people; this method of managing his state differed radically from that of Po-ch'in in governing Lu, for he "transformed their customs, and replaced their institutions." Hence, that Ch'i should be the place where a philosophy of "inaction" originated is quite conceivable. And when in the past Taoism has been called the learning of the South, this was probably in reference only to Lao Tzu and Chuang Tzu. For, to be quite accurate, late Chou "egocentric" thought was not confined to that little corner comprising the districts of Hu and Meng.[50] Therefore Taoism, perhaps, as well as Confucianism and Mohism, also had as its background the descendants of the fallen Yin dynasty, but they differed among themselves because the government, the leading doctrines, the institutions and the practices of the different states in which they lived were different; as the thought of the philosophers was subjected to these differing influences, so the content of their theories also differed.

If, considering the political backgrounds, we classify the various states in which the philosophers lived as "Yin culture," "Chou culture," and "beyond the reach of culture," the geographical distribution of the pre-Ch'in age schools can be shown as follows:

The geographical distribution of the origins of the four schools is more or less as described above. Some aspects of their transmission and dissemination are also worth studying. After leaving Lu, Confucius traveled through Ch'i, Wei, Sung, Ch'en, Ts'ai, and Ch'u, but failed always to be accorded the reception by their rulers that he sought. Moreover, "among

[50] That the book *Kuan Tzu* is not from the hand of Kuan Chung is by now accepted as a certainty. However, from the fact that its content includes elements of Taoism and Legalism, it would seem to be in the tradition of T'ai-kung's manner of governing— "Following their customs and simplifying their institutions; opening up channels for the pursuit of crafts and commerce; and facilitating the flow of profits from fish and salt" —and thus it is perhaps quite in keeping with the prevailing ways in the State of Ch'i. Further, at the beginning of the Han there was one "Ho-kung of Chiao-hsi" [western part of Shantung peninsula, corresponding to the State of Ch'i] a profound student of *Huang-Lao* (cf. *Shih Chi*, ch. 54, "Ts'ao hsiang-kuo shih-chia"); this is additional evidence for a large number of Taoists in the State of Ch'i.

Table Five

The Yin (Shang-Yin) Culture

Political Backgrounds		Confucianism	Mohism	Taoism	Legalism
Ancient Shang-Yen area; the Six Clans of the Yin people	Lu	Confucius Tzeng Tzu Mencius	Mo Tzu		
Lu, a subordinate state of the Yin; (originally enfeoffed to the descendants of Chüan-hsü)	Tsou				
Ancient P'u-ku area; (The Rites derived from the customs here)	Ch'i			P'eng Meng T'ien P'ien Chien Tzu Ch'en Chung Tzu	Kuan Tzu
The Seven Clans of the Yin people; "The government of Yin and the standards of The Chou"	Wei 衛	Pu-shang (?)		The "old man with the basket"	(Wu Ch'i)? Lord Shang
Granted in fief to Wei Tzu, to continue sacrifices to Yin ancestors	Sung			Chuang Tzu	
After eliminating the line of Yin heir Wu-keng, granted in fief to [Chou descendant] Ts'ai Chung	Ts'ai			Chang Chü Chieh Ni	

Table Five

Chou Culture

Political backgrounds		Confucianism	Mohism	Taoism	Legalism
Chou King Hsüan's younger brother [Yu, enfeoffed] Duke Huan, "Gathered together the Chou people" here [in mid-eighth century B.C.]	Cheng			Lieh Yü-k'ou (?)	Teng Hsi Shen Pu-hai
(Chin) Descendants of Yao at the ancient Hsia site (The government of Hsia and the norms of the Jung barbarians) a. Descendants of Pi-kung	Wei 魏	(Wu Ch'i) (Li K'e) (Shih Chiao)		Tzu Hua Tzu	Li K'e Shih Chiao (?)
b. Of the (royal Chou) Chi surname, as also the State of Wei	Han				Han Fei Tzu
c. Same ancestry as the Ch'in ducal house	Chao	Hsün Tzu			(Hsün Tzu) Shen Tao

Beyond Culture

Descendants of Chuan-hsü, for many generations in contact with the northern barbarians	Ch'in				
Descendants of Chuan-hsü, for many generations in contact with the southern barbarians	Ch'u			Lao Tan Huan Yuan "Madman" Chieh-yü	Li Ssu

Confucius' immediate disciples, natives of Lu were most numerous; next were those of Wei, Ch'i and Sung, all of them neighboring states."[51] Of Confucius' later followers, those whose names are known and about whom information can be established were mostly natives of the states adjacent to Lu. Of those from more distant places, many were not pure Confucianists. To take as examples some of the better known of his disciples: Yen Hui, Min Sun, Jan Keng, Jan Ch'iu, Tsai Yü, Yen Yen, Yu Jo, Yuan Hsien, Tseng Shen, Fu Pu-ch'i, Nan-kung K'uo, Kung-hsi Ch'ih, and Tuan-sun Shih were all natives of Lu;[52] while Pu Shang, Tuan-mu Ssu, and Kao Ch'ai were natives of Wei;[53] and Kung-yeh Ch'ang and Fan Hsü were natives of Ch'i.[54] Ssu-ma Keng was from Sung, and Ch'i-tiao K'ai was from Ts'ai.[55] Among the more famous of his later followers, Mencius was from Tsou, and Hsün Tzu from Chao. Comparatively few of Mencius' disciples are known: Kung-sun Ch'ou was a native of Ch'i, and T'eng Keng was from T'eng; Po-kung Yi was from Wei, and Yueh-cheng K'e may have been a native of Lu.[56] All of these, with the single exception of Hsün Ch'ing, were born in states close to Tsou and Lu. Hsün Ch'ing's thought has points of similarity to that of the Legalists. Liang Ch'i-ch'ao has said that his learning belonged to the [thought] system of Tzu-yu and Tzu-hsia.[57] [I.e., Yen Yen and Pu Shang, two of Confucius' disciples, who traditionally are held to have emphasized the cultivation of literature in their transmission of Confucius' teachings.] Moreover, as both Han Fei and Li Ssu studied under Hsün Tzu, his own learning could certainly not have followed the original Lu traditions strictly. [Literally: "The tone prevailing in the region of the Chu and Ssu rivers."] Furthermore, Li K'e, a native of Wei who wrote legalistic

[51] Ts'ui Shu: *Chu-Ssu k'ao-hsin-lu*. Quoted on page 56 of Ch'ien Mu's *Hsien-ch'in chu-tzu hsi nien k'ao-pien*.

[52] This fact about Tseng Shen is based on *Chu-Ssu k'ao-hsin-lu*; that about Tuan-sun Shih is based on *Lü-shih ch'un-ch'iu*, 4, "Tsun shih"; all the rest are based on the *Chi-chieh*, *So-yin*, and *Cheng-yi* commentaries to the *Shih Chi. ch.* 67, "Chung-ni ti-tzu lieh-chuan." The "Chung-ni ti-tzu lieh-chuan" takes Yen Yen to have been a native of Wu, but Ts'ui Shu [author of *Chu-Ssu k'ao-hsin-lu*], on the basis of the *So-yin* commentary, determines that he was a native of Lu.

[53] In all these cases, the information is based on the above-cited *ch.* 67 of the *Shih Chi*, and the *Chi-chieh* and *So-yin* commentaries. In the case of Pu Shang, the sub-commentary [*shu*] to the chapters 3 and 4, "T'an Kung" [in the *Li Chi*], states that he was a native of Wei.

[54] The *Chi-chieh* and *Cheng-yi* commentaries to the above-cited *chüan* of the *Shih Chi* call them natives of Lu.

[55] *Ibid.* The *Cheng-yi* commentary states that Ch'i-tiao K'ai was a man of Lu.

[56] See *Meng Tzu chi-chu.* "Kung-sun Ch'ou," Part i; "Chin-hsin," Part i; "Wan-chang," Part ii; and "Liang Hui-wang," Part ii.

[57] *Ju-chia che-hsüeh* (*Yin-ping-shih ch'üan-chi*, 103). For the fact that Han and Li studied under Hsün Tzu, cf. *Shih Chi, ch.* 74, "Meng, Hsün lieh-chuan."

works advocating the greatest possible exploitation of natural resources [as a means of strengthening the state] was also a disciple of Tzu-hsia[58] and was also a Confucian who went into Legalism. If it is also true that Wu Ch'i of Wei was indeed a disciple of Tseng Tzu,[59] then he especially must be cited as a traitor to Confucianism more extreme than Hsün Ch'ing, who was "in the main, pure, but not without minor blemishes." [Said by Han Yü, ninth century, of Hsün Tzu and Yang Hsiung, to distinguish them from Mencius, who, in Han's view, represented the purest tradition of Confucian thought.] As for the Ch'u native, Ch'en Liang, about whose learning and its line of transmission we know nothing, "Pleased with the

[58] The *Han Shu*, *ch.* 30, "Yi-wen chih," or "Journal of Literature," lists under the category of "Confucians" the book of Li K'e [or K'o] in seven chapters. Pan Ku [the author of the *Han Shu*] adds the note that Li K'e was a disciple of Tzu-hsia. The "Shih-huo chih," or "Journal on Economy," *ch.* 24 of the *Han Shu*, says that Li K'uei taught the doctrines of exploiting natural resources to the fullest degree possible while in the service of Duke Wen of Wei. The *Shih Chi*, in both *ch.* 30, "P'ing-chun shu" and *ch.* 129, "Huo-chih lieh-chuan," states that Li K'e devoted himself to [principles of] exploiting natural resources to the fullest possible degree, but in *ch.* 74, "Meng, Hsün lieh-chuan," writes the name "Li K'uei." Ts'ui Shu, in his *Shih Chi t'an-yüan*, states "the characters 'K'uei' and 'K'e' represent variant forms with the same [ancient] pronunciation," and that the two men are in fact one and the same person. In addition it should be noted that not only Li K'e came from the school of Tzu-hsia, but among the later products of his school there was also Hsün K'uang [i.e., Hsün Ch'ing, or Hsün Tzu]. The *Analects*, VI/11, contains Confucius' warning to Tzu-hsia: "Do be a scholar after the style of the superior man, and not after that of the mean man." [Legge, p. 189.] This may indicate that Confucius knew that in Tzu-hsia's learning there was the tendency to transform the institutes and music [*li, yüeh*] into punishments and laws [*hsing, fa*], which would not be in keeping with the learning of the "scholars and great officers." Tuan-kan Mu, a native of Chin, and a man of lofty ideals who would not serve in office, was honored by Duke Wen of Wei and praised by Mencius; the *Lü-shih Ch'un-ch'iu*, *ch.* 21/2, "Ch'a-hsien," states that he had studied under Tzu-hsia, and if so he was of strikingly different character from Tzu-hsia's other disciples.

[59] Cf. *Lü-shih Ch'un-ch'iu*, *ch.* 2/4, "Tang jan" and *Shih Chi*, *ch.* 65, "Wu Ch'i lieh-chuan." This biography states: "[Wu] Ch'i, as chief minister in the State of Ch'u, clarified the laws and examined the regulations . . . ," and " . . . the crucial thing was the strengthening of the army." The *Lü-shih Ch'un-ch'iu*, 25/6, "Shen hsiao," tells that Wu Ch'i, while in official position in Wei, "commanded the people to overturn a pillar in order to make people trust his word," much in the manner of Shang Yang. [The anecdote tells that Wu Ch'i promised a very high office to the man who would overturn a pillar that had been erected outside the city gates; no one paid heed, feeling it to be too unreasonable to be true. One man, however, did it and was rewarded as promised. Consequently everyone believed implicitly his every word without considering whether or not it was reasonable. Obtaining such automatic response without judgment was a Legalist ideal in statecraft. Shang Yang employed a similar device to the same effect when he first took service under Duke Hsiao of Ch'in, about 356 B.C.; see Duyvendak, *The Book of Lord Shang*, pp. 15–16.] However, Liu Hsiang's *Pieh-lu* states that Wu Ch'i studied the *Tso Chuan* under Tseng Shen [申, a later figure; not Confucius' disciple Tseng Shen 参, or Tseng Tzu] and is therein at variance with the *Lü-shih Ch'un-ch'iu*.

doctrines of the Duke of Chou and of Confucius, he came northwards to the Middle Kingdom and studied them,"[60] it would appear that he exemplifies the southward extension of Confucian learning.

However Ch'en Liang, in order to study Confucianism, could not remain in the regions of Ching and Ying [southern regions, in the central Yangtze valley, i.e., the State of Ch'u] but was compelled to travel north. Thus it would seem that, even by the time of Mencius, Confucian learning had not yet come to flourish in the South, so that it was necessary to go abroad to study, so as to come into intimate contact with "the scholars of the Northern regions." And even to Ch'en Liang's disciples, Ch'en Hsiang and Ch'en Hsin, it was said that: ". . . you followed him some tens of years, and when your master died, you have forthwith turned from him, him, in order to follow Hsü Hsing, a 'shrike-tongued barbarian of the south.' " [The words of Mencius to them, berating them for abandoning their master's teachings. All of the quoted passages here follow Legge's *Mencius*, III/i/4/13 ff., pp. 254 ff.] In the eyes of the Confucians [extending Confucian learning to such men of the South] was in truth as useless as "dressing up a monkey" [to make it into a man], for in an instant they would turn away and abandon their learning. Moreover, this is evidence enough for the conjecture that Confucianism was northern learning that could not easily be transplanted to the southern regions.

In addition, from noting the places where Confucius' immediate disciples and later followers traveled about in order to take office, one can deduce something about the general spread of Confucianism. The *Shih Chi*, *ch.* 121, "Ju-lin lieh-chuan" i.e., "Biographies of Confucians," states: "Following the death of Confucius, his seventy disciples scattered and travelled about [in search of office in the various states of] the feudal rulers. The more important ones became teachers or chief ministers [to the lords], the lesser ones became friends and teachers of the knights and Great Officers, [*shih ta-fu*, cf. footnote 6 above], while in some cases they retired and were no longer seen." [Cf. Fung/Bodde, Vol. I, p. 106, where a longer portion of the same passage also is quoted. Bodde's translation has been somewhat modified here.] The passage that follows cites Tzu-lu, Tzu-chang, Tzu-yü, and Tzu-hsia, who lived, respectively, in Wei, Ch'en, Ch'u, and Hsi-ho. Most of the rest of the disciples are mentioned in "Chung-ni ti-tzu lieh-chuan" [the *Shih Chi*, *chüan* 67, "Biographies of Confucius' Disciples"]. If we examine the cases of those about whom the facts are to be found, those of "the seventy disciples" who became teachers or chief ministers to rulers of states, there were merely: "Tzu-hsia who became the teacher of Duke of Wei; Tzu-kung who served Lu and Ch'i as emissary to Wu and Yüeh; and Tsai Yü who served in Ch'i as a great

[60] *Mencius* III [III/i/4/12; modified from Legge, p. 254].

officer."[61] The vast majority of them "retired and were no longer seen"; evidence of their activities is most difficult to trace. For example, Yen Hui, Min Sun, Kung-hsi Ai, and their like probably in most cases lived out their lives in Lu. The others served in office but achieved no prominence, and many were "household servitors" [chia-ch'en] in the state of Lu. [Waley, Analects, p. 204, translates it "retainers of the Great Houses," i.e., officials in service of the great noble families, managing their family affairs, from which position they were often able to represent them in the affairs of the country. This was criticized by Confucius as aiding usurpers of legitimate authority.] For example, this was the case with Jan Ch'iu, who was steward to the Chi clan; Chung Yu, who was both steward to the Chi clan and governor of K'ung-k'uei; Yen Yen, who was governor of Wu-ch'eng; Fu Pu-ch'i, who was governor of Tan-fu; Kao Ch'ai, who was governor of Fei; and Pu Shang, who was governor of Chü-fu.[62] [The term tsai is translated here both "steward" and "governor"; where the town or district of which one served as "tsai" was the seat of a noble family, as was often the case, the functions of "steward of the household" and "magistrate of the district" merged. In either event, the appointments implied personal service to a noble family rather than public office.] Most prominent among those of the later followers of his school who achieved positions such as teachers or chief ministers to rulers were K'ung Chi [i.e. his grandson, Tzu-ssu], who became the teacher of Duke Mu [415–383 B.C.] of Lu, and Mencius who, though a scholar of Tsou, became a minister [ch'ing] to King Hsüan of Ch'i. Even if it is true that Hsün Tzu as a scholar at Chi-hsia in Ch'i served as libationer [at the great sacrifice], that still is to be distinguished from serving in office. [Cf. Dubs: Hsüntze, the Moulder of Ancient Confucianism, p. 27. To be chosen to offer the wine was equivalent to being regarded as the most eminent scholar in residence

---

[61] Shih Chi, ch. 121, "Ju-lin lieh-chuan," the So-yin commentary. However, it also should be noted that according to ch. 67, "Chung-ni ti-tzu lieh-chuan" of the same work, Tsai-wo became great-officer [ta-fu] of Lin-tzu.

[62] Information drawn from the Analects, passim, and the "Chung-ni ti-tzu lieh-chuan"; the latter's reference to Kung-hsi Ai records the comment: "Confucius said: 'The world has degenerated. Most men become household servitors, and serve in [such] office at the capital city.' " This shows the prevailing situation among the followers of Confucius. For at this time the Warring States Period custom of traveling about as a [political] advisor had not yet arisen, and cases of commoners intervening in the affairs of the ruler or of rising to the position of chief minister of state were still rare. Moreover, the Institutes of Chou were observed in Lu, with the result that it was particularly difficult to get into official service there [the Chou institutes reinforced the hereditary character of public office]; hence persons motivated by "desire for official emolument" had no choice but to lower their objectives and assume positions as "p'ei-ch'en" [i.e., servitor of a noble; Legge, Analects, p. 310, translates "p'ei-ch'en" as "subsidiary ministers of the great officers," and notes that they are the same as "chia-ch'en." Waley, Analects, p. 204, translates: "retainers of the great Houses"].

at the famous academy of Chi-hsia.] Nor did his office-holding in Ch'u bring him to eminent rank. [Hsün Tzu in later life served for some years as Magistrate of Lan-ling, originally part of Lu, but by that time annexed by Ch'u. Dubs, *op.cit.*, p. 37, states that this was for a period of eighteen years, ending in 237 B.C.] The *Han Fei Tzu, ch.* 38, "Nan-san," states that King K'uai of Yen looked upon Tzu-chih as a worthy man, but repudiated Hsün Tzu; perhaps therefore he at one time went to Yen and was not favorably received there. [Ch'ien Mu, *Hsien-ch'in chu-tzu hsi-nien k'ao-pien*, Appended Table III, p. 41, dates this event in the year 316 B.C. Tzu-chih was chief minister of Yen, to whom King Yen turned over the country. His rule was disastrous and contributed to the downfall of Yen.] The only exception is the statement in the "Ch'u Ts'e" [in the *Chan-kuo Ts'e*] that "Sun Tzu [i.e., Hsün Tzu] went to Chao; Chao employed him as a Superior Chief Minister." If this is to be believed, he thus perhaps reached high official position in his own native state at one time. Beyond these examples, there is little indeed that can be known. Therefore, from the places to which the "scholars traveling in search of office" journeyed, there is ample evidence for the statement that Confucianism was a northern school of learning, having the State of Lu as its center.[63] Those who went beyond the territory of Lu and Wei and achieved noble rank and official eminence, such as Li K'e and Wu Ch'i in the States of Wei and Ch'u, were in no instance pure Confucians. [I.e., Wei of the Three States of Chin.] The case of Pu Shang's [i.e., Tzu-hsia's] becoming teacher of Duke Wen of [the same] Wei is something of an exception, and as such is not enough to qualify the above conclusion.

The area through which Mohism was spread was apparently broader than that of Confucianism. Like Confucianism, Mohism was a northern school of learning. However, Confucianism was limited to the North; Mohism in contrast went southward, and it also went to more distant parts of the north. *Chuang Tzu, ch.* 33, "T'ien-hsia," cites "Mohists of the South such as K'u Huo, Chi Ch'ih, and Teng Ling Tzu," showing that it flourished there. [Cf. Watson, *Chuang Tzu*. p. 336.] Unfortunately nothing can be known of the majority of Mo Tzu's followers. Of those whose native states can be determined, in addition to the three mentioned above, Ch'ü Chiang Tzu likewise appears to have been a native of Ch'u.[64] Natives of Sung include Sung K'eng and T'ien Hsiang Tzu;[65]

---

[63] Cf. *Li Chi, ch.* 9, "Li Yün": "Confucius said: 'I observe that injury was done to the *Tao* of the Chou dynasty by Kings Yu and Li; were I to renounce Lu, where else could I go?' " Lu was not only the home of Confucian learning; it was also the citadel of the feudal order.

[64] Cf. Sun Yi-jang: *Mo-hsüeh ch'uan-shou k'ao.*

[65] *Mencius*, VI/ii/4/32, where Sung Hsing wants to persuade the Kings of Ch'in and Ch'u to desist from warfare [cf. *Mencius*, VI/ii/4/1; Legge, p. 428, where he is called Sung K'eng.

natives of Cheng include a man whose personal name was Ti [surname unknown];[66] natives of Ch'i include Kao Ho,[67] Hu Fei Tzu,[68] Hsien Tzu-shih,[69] and T'ien Chiu;[70] natives of Ch'in include T'ang Ku Kuo;[71] and the *Mo Tzu*, *ch.* 49, "Lu wen," lists the names of his disciples from Lu who had died in battle. Hence merely from the native states of Mo Tzu's disciples, we can see that Mohism was spread throughout a wider area than was Confucianism.

The area in which Mohists are known to have traveled and to seek or take public offices included the states of Ch'i, Wei, Sung, Ch'in, Tai, and Chung-shan in the North, and Ch'u and Yüeh in the South. Examples are Sheng Ch'o, who served Ch'i;[72] Hsiang Tzu-niu and Kao Shih Tzu, who served Wei;[73] Ts'ao Kung Tzu, who served Sung;[74] Hsieh Tzu, who was received in audience by the King of Ch'in;[75] T'ien Chiu, who traveled to Ch'in to seek office; and Fu T'un who dwelt in Ch'in.[76] The *Lü-shih Ch'un-ch'iu*, *ch.* 18/7, "Ying-yen," narrates that "Ssu-ma Hsi rebutted a Mohist teacher's denunciation of aggressive warfare before the King of Chung-shan," and the *Huai-nan Tzu*, *ch.* 18, "Jen-chien hsün" says that "The King of Tai adopted Mohism and [his state] was shattered." All of the above were Mohists in the North. Those who made an appearance in the South include T'ien Chiu, Keng Chu, and Meng Sheng, who held office in Ch'u;[77] and Kung-shang Kuo, who traveled to the State of Yüeh;[78] in number these appear to have been fewer than those in the North. However, they are sufficient evidence of Mohism's southward spread.

The curious thing, on the other hand, is that Mohism, which indeed

---

"K'eng" and "Hsing" were homophones in archaic Chinese]. *Hsün Tzu*, *ch.* 6, "Fei Shih-erh tzu," lists Mo Ti and Sung Hsing together. Sung Hsing probably was a Mohist. For T'ien Hsiang Tzu see *Lü-shih Ch'un-ch'iu*, *ch.* 19/3, "Shang Te."

[66] *Chuang Tzu*, *ch.* 32, "Lieh Yü-k'ou."

[67] *Lü-shih Ch'un-ch'iu*, *ch.* 4/3, "Tsun shih."

[68] Fang Shou-ch'u, *Mo-hsüeh yüan-liu*, p. 137, citing the opinion of Liang Yü-sheng.

[69] *Mo Tzu*, *ch.* 46, "Keng Chu;" *Lü-shih Ch'un-ch'iu*, *ch.* 4/3, "Tsun-shih."

[70] *Han Fei Tzu*, *ch.* 42, "Wen T'ien," and *ch.* 32, "Wai chu shuo, tso-shang"; *Lü-shih Ch'un-ch'iu*, *ch.* 14/3, "Shou-shih," and *Han Shu*, *ch.* 30, "Yi-wen chih."

[71] *Lü-shih Ch'un-ch'iu*, *ch.* 16/7, "Ch'ü-yu." Fang Shou-ch'u, *Mo-hsüeh yüan-liu*, p. 145, states that of those Mohists whose birthplaces are known, there are five from Ch'i, four from Ch'u, and one each from Sung, Ch'in, and Cheng.

[72] *Mo Tzu*, *ch.* 49, "Lu-wen."

[73] *Ibid.*, *ch.* 46, "Keng Chu."

[74] *Ibid.*, *ch.* 49, "Lu-wen."

[75] *Lü-shih Ch'un-ch'iu*, *ch.* 16/7, "Ch'ü-yu."

[76] *Ibid.*, *ch.* 1/5, "Ch'ü-ssu."

[77] See footnote 70, also *Mo Tzu*, *ch.* 46, "Keng Chu," and *Lü-shih Ch'un-ch'iu*, *ch.* 19/3, "Shang te."

[78] *Mo Tzu*, *ch.* 47, "Kuei-yi," and *ch.* 49, "Lu-wen."

may not have "filled the empire" as Mencius said it did [*Mencius*, III/ii/9/9; Legge, p. 282] but whose extent was indeed broader than that of Confucianism, appears not to have been widely current in Mo Tzu's own native State of Lu. If we seek explanation of this fact, may it not be that "Lu clung to the Institutes of Chou," and some carryover of the old feudal ways still persisted there? By the same token, then, would not Mohism, which turned its back on the Chou Institutes, be difficult for Lu people to respect, and therefore incapable of victory in any contest against Confucianism?[79]

It also can be said that, while the area through which Mohists traveled in search of office was greater, the political positions gained by them were in no case superior to those achieved by Confucians, and may even have been inferior. For example, when Kao Shih Tzu served in Wei, "the emolument given him by the Wei ruler was very great, and he was appointed to office as a Chief Minister, but his doctrines went unheeded"; yet, among Mo Tzu's followers, he apparently was the one who achieved the highest position. Kung-shang Kuo received the command of the King of Yüeh to invite Mo Tzu [to come and receive high office], but Mo Tzu rejected the invitation with the excuse that he did not wish to "sell his righteousness." [Cf. Y. P. Mei, *The Works of Motze*, p. 250.] There was Keng Chu Tzu, who served in Ch'u and sent ten *chin* of silver to Mo Tzu. [Cf. *ibid.*, p. 214. Mei explains *chin* as twenty taels of silver; the point of the anecdote is that, from the conflicting evidence, Mo Tzu himself did not know whether or not his disciple had achieved high position; hence the matter is obviously a doubtful one.] And, there was Sheng Ch'o, who accompanied Hsiang Tzu-niu three times on his invasions of Lu territory. [Cf. *ibid.*, p. 254.] None of these [disciples] seems to have achieved great power or high position. The others were even less worthy of mention, having no achievements at all. To summarize this situation: not only were they far inferior to [the Legalists] Shen Pu-hai, Kung-sun Yang, Li K'e, and Wu Ch'i, who gained the favor of rulers and were entrusted by them with important duties; they were not even to be compared with [the Confucians] Pu Shang, K'ung Chi, and Mencius, who were friends and teachers of rulers and chief ministers. This is most likely because of those Mohist doctrines which condemned aggressive warfare, exalted the virtuous, and the like—that is to say, which either repudiated the old

---

[79] Reference may be made to Ch'ien Mu's discussion of this on p. 170 of his *Hsien-ch'in chu-tzu hsi-nien k'ao-pien*. [He states] "Mo Tzu was a native of Lu; the states to which he traveled were the four: Ch'u, Sung, Wei, and Ch'i. Although Lu was his native state, just at that time Tseng Shen and Tzu-ssu were the recipients of high honors as the great Confucian teachers. And although Duke Wen of Wei patronized worthy men, Tzu-hsia, T'ien Tzu-fang, Tuan-kan Mu, Li K'e, and Wu Ch'i [leading recipients of his patronage] all were Confucianists. For this reason [the spread of] Mohist doctrines was blocked there." One can find explanations in this for the fact that Mohism was blocked in Wei, and it was perhaps not suited to the conditions in Lu.

clan-law social order, or could not be reconciled with the newly dominant national policies emphasizing agricultural production and military
strength. Thus Mohism lost its footing, being on all sides incompatible.
It had nothing to compare with Confucian doctrines of refined institutions
and good government, which would occasionally gain the ear of a ruler.
Hence, though it set forth lofty ideals, they were of a kind that made them
most difficult of acceptance and application. This was a matter of the
prevailing mood of the times and the conditions of the age; it had nothing
to do with limitations imposed by regional factors.

The region in which Legalism was spread, as seen from the places to
which its thinkers traveled to serve in office, had Ch'in as its center, and
Han and Wei second only in importance. [Two of the three states formed
from Chin.] Shen Pu-hai served as chief minister of state in Han, while
Shang Yang first served Wei and was later chief minister in Ch'in. Han
Fei went to Ch'in, but [died] before he could gain employment there.
Li Ssu, though a native of Ch'u, became chief minister of Ch'in. When
viewing Li K'e and Wu Ch'i both as Confucianists who inclined toward
the Legalists, one should also note that they both had served in Wei.[80]
These all are generally known historical facts, needing no critical examina-
tion.

However, it might well be looked upon as curious that, although Ch'in
made such great use of Legalists, not one of the Legalists was born in
Ch'in. This is probably because Ch'in's cultural development was comparatively late;[81] thought and learning had still not come to flourish
there by the Warring States Period. Not only were there no native
Legalist thinkers; neither was there any Confucian school. Hence Ch'in
was forced to look in the other states for people to employ. Moreover,
Ch'in lacked the practices and ways of clan-law aristocracy, while the
aristocracy of the three states of Chin had degenerated early. Wu Ch'i
was unable to achieve his purposes in Lu; Shen Pu-hai and Shang Yang
found freedom for drastic action in Han and Ch'in. This would seem to
be one of the chief reasons for the concentration of Legalists there.

The foregoing discussion has already mentioned that the facts of the
lives of the Taoists thinkers are very difficult to uncover. Since Taoist
thought was an outgrowth of the "attitude of diminution" [of the activities of government] its followers quite naturally were not so concerned
with finding employment in the world of affairs as were the Confucians,
Mohists, and Legalists. Therefore, Chuang Tzu rejected the appointment

[80] See footnotes 58 and 59.

[81] Ch'in for generations had maintained intercourse with the northern barbarians [yi-
ti], and it was not until the Thirteenth year of Duke Wen (the Fifty-eighth year of King
P'ing of Chou, 753 B.C.) that Ch'in: " . . . first had an official historian to keep a chronology of its affairs; its people in large number came to be transformed [i.e., civilized]."
Shih Chi, ch. 5, "Ch'in pen-chi."

as chief minister of state that King Wei of Ch'u offered him.[82] Lao Tan did indeed serve as keeper of the archives in Chou, but this was not an office that commanded authority or that was concerned with political responsibilities. Yang Chu's words "filled the Empire" [said by Mencius of Yang Chu and Mo Tzu; see page 58], but he never held office. Tzu Hua Tzu persuaded the states of Han and Wei not to fight over disputed territory.[83] P'eng Meng and T'ien P'ien both journeyed to Chi-hsia. [The famous academy maintained for scholars-in-residence in Ch'i.] T'o Hsiao and Wei Mou and their like show no evidence that they ever held office; and there is even less reason for thinking that others, the recluses and men of lofty ideals, would have done so. If we merely consider the places to which their travels took them, however, Taoism appears to have been present throughout all the North and South. Moreover, the chapters 20 and 21, "Chieh Lao" and "Yü Lao," in the *Han Fei Tzu* [explicating Lao Tzu's teachings] are more than sufficient evidence that, by the end of the Warring States Period, Taoist thought had penetrated deep into the citadel of Legalism. For Taoist thought, expressing aversion to the world, is by its nature least subject to limitations of time and place. There is nothing surprising in the relatively great extent of its spread.

Summing up, we might come to the following conclusions: Confucian thought drew heavily on the historical backgrounds of the State of Lu; of the four schools it was the one richest in local character. Legalist thought established its doctrines with a view to the immediate needs of the seven contending states; it is the richest in contemporary relevance. Taoism's self-centeredness transcends time and place. Mohism acknowledged feudal government, yet attacked the clan-law social classes; it vacillated irresolutely between the tides of the old and the new and was incompatible with both, making it difficult to apply in the world that confronted it,[84] so that within a short time it lacked transmitters to perpetuate it. Therefore the account of its successes and reverses is in no way comparable to that of Confucianism, which served as the imperial orthodoxy for two thousand years; or to Taoism, which was the enduring source of protest in times of national degeneration and harsh government; or to Legalism, which contributed to the unification of Ch'in, and so helped to launch the new age of authoritarian government which followed.[85]

---

[82] *Shih Chi, ch.* 63, "Lao, Chuang, Shen, Han lieh-chuan."

[83] *Lü-shih Ch'un-ch'iu, ch.* 2/2, "Kuei sheng."

[84] Mohism apparently was granted some favorable attention at that time; cf. *Huai-nan Tzu, ch.* 18, "Jen-chien hsün," cited above [on p. 57].

[85] This is intended merely to point out the general situation with regard to the adoption or rejection of the doctrines of the Four Schools; their success or failure in this regard does not necessarily imply any qualitative ranking of them.

The four schools discussed above represented the main currents of political thought in the pre-Ch'in age. In addition to these there also were Hsü Hsing's Agriculturist School and Tsou Yen's *Yin-Yang* School. The former promulgated the doctrine that even the ruler and his ministers should till the soil; their ideal of equality aimed at the abolition of class distinctions. The latter proclaimed their theories of the *Yin* and the *Yang* and the Five Agents and predicted the rise and fall of fortune according to the dominant cosmic influence of an age [*shih-yün* 世運]. The influence of this school on the thinkers of Ch'in and Han was especially great. Unfortunately, the texts and documents are lacking; in consequence, the content of these [theories] cannot be studied in detail. If we compare them with the other four schools, the Agriculturists are a reaction against aristocratic government and Confucian thought; their attitude is somewhat similar to that of the Mohists.[86]

The *Yin-Yang* thinkers, "starting from the time of the separation of Heaven and Earth, . . . made citations of the revolutions and transmutations of the Five Powers, arranging them until each found its proper place. . . ."[87] That which is called the "Five Powers" is the same as the "Five Elements [or "Agents"]." "The sequence of the Five Powers is acoording to the inability of one to conquer the next. Hence Yü was under the power of earth. Hsia of wood, Yin of metal, and Chou of fire.[88] [Fire conquers, melts metal; metal conquers, cuts wood; wood conquers, grows from earth, etc. Yü means the Emperor Shun, the ruler who was succeeded by the Hsia dynasty, etc. See also Fung/Bodde, Vol. I, note at bottom of page 163.] To express this in concrete terms, the transmutations of the Five Agents correspond to the rise and fall of political orders. As [Tsou Yen] said: "Governmental regulations and philosophic doctrines [may incline toward either] refinement or simplicity; hence it is said that there is a corrective [for the excesses of either]. When something is suited to the times, it can be used; when that time has passed, then it can be abandoned. When there is something that should be changed, then change it."[89] This shows clearly that Tsou Yen's teachings were a kind of philosophy of history, including everything from antiquity to the

---

[86] For Hsü Hsing's theories see *Mencius*, III, "T'eng Wen-kung," Part I. Ch'ien Mu, in his *Hsien-Ch'in chu-tzu hsi-nien k'ao-pien*, Number 113, states that Hsü Hsing and the Mohist Hsü Fan both studied under Ch'in Ku-li. Fang Shou-ch'u in his *Mo-hsüeh yuan-liu*, pp. 143–44, refutes this, stating, however, that Hsü Hsing was profoundly influenced by the Mohists.

[87] *Shih Chi*, ch. 74, "Meng, Hsün lieh-chuan." [Modified slightly from Fung/Bodde, Vol. I., p. 160, where the entire *Shih Chi* biography of Tsou Yen is translated; see also Chan, *Source Book*, pp. 244–50.]

[88] *Huai-nan Tzu*, ch. 11, "Ch'i-su hsün," the commentary of Kao Yu quoting Tsou Yen.

[89] *Han Shu*, ch. 64–B, "Yen An Chuan." ["Refinement" and "simplicity" are "*wen*" 文 and "*chih*" 質.]

present. His discourses on heaven and earth come close to cosmology and to geography. These all represent theories newly created toward the end of the Warring States Period, just on the eve of the unification.

However, the *Yin-Yang* philosophers appear to have some points in common with Confucianism. The *Shih Chi, ch.* 74, "Meng, Hsün lieh-chuan," in setting forth Tsou Yen's doctrines, says of them: "Yet if we reduce them to fundamentals, they all rested on the virtues of benevolence, righteousness, restraint, and frugality, and on the practice of the proper relations between ruler and servitor, of superior and inferior, and among the six relationships. . . ." [Modified from Fung/Bodde, I, 161.] This very obviously is close to Confucianism, while Tsou's theory about governmental regulations and philosophic doctrines alternating between refinement and simplicity, and using the one or abandoning it for the other, also seems close to the meaning of Confucius' "taking from or adding to" the institutions of the Hsia and Yin dynasties, and of "Chou having the advantage of viewing the two past dynasties."[90] Mencius said: "It is a rule that a true Imperial sovereign should arise in the course of five hundred years," and he also said: "A long time has elapsed since this world of men received its being and there has been, along its history, now a period of good order, and now a period of disorder."[91] This too is a kind of simple philosophy of history, which is more or less an antici-pation of Tsou Yen's later doctrines about "*chu yün*" ["the dominant cosmic influence"] affecting rise and fall [of dynasties]. ["*Chu yün*" 主運 is the name of one of the essays that Tsou Yen is said to have written; it means "The determining cosmic influence" among the five elemental influences.] Subsequently Hsün Tzu went so far as to say in his chapter, "Fei Shih-erh tzu," that the "Five Elements" theories were promulgated by Tzu-ssu and that Mencius had been in accord with them. [Tzu-ssu was an immediate disciple of Confucius, as well as being his grandson.] Although there is no proof for Hsün Tzu's statement, if we can base a conjecture on the fact that the *Yin-Yang* thinkers and the Confucians do indeed have points of similarity, then it probably is not wholly un-founded. The *Shih Chi* also says: "Tsou Yen saw that the rulers were becoming ever more dissolute and profligate; they were incapable of valuing virtue and of conforming to the great ethical pattern whereby to rectify their persons and extend [the benefits of their virtue] to the common people. Therefore he made a profound examination of the in-crease and decrease of *Yin* and *Yang* and wrote of their strange and vast transformations in the essays [entitled] "Chung-shih" and "Ta-sheng," which totaled more than one hundred thousand words." [Extensively

---

[90] *Analects*, II/23, and III/14; [Legge, pp. 153 and 160, respectively].
[91] *Mencius*, II/ii/13/3, and III/ii/9/2; [Legge, pp. 232 and 279, respectively].

modified from Fung/Bodde, I, 160, following Ku Chieh-kang punctuated edition 1936 of the *Shih Chi*, III, p. 136. Cf. Chan, *Source Book*, pp. 246–47, for another translation.] From this we can see that the basic tenets on which he built his theories were not greatly different from Confucianism.

The reason why Tsou Yen's doctrines were of necessity "grandiose and bizarre" was that he felt very profoundly that Confucius' and Mencius' teachings about benevolence and righteousness were incapable of holding their own against the competing doctrines about strengthening and enriching the state. Therefore he created his "Talk about Heaven," reducing the Confucians' [concept of the Nine] Regions of Yü to "*shen-chou*" ["the Divine Province"] and shrinking the cosmic destiny of the temporal ruler to that of but one Power [of the Five Powers; Tsou Yen said that "China" was not the major and central portion of the world but merely one-eightieth of the world; he called it *shen-chou*, the "divine province." The earlier Confucian concept of geography, in contrast, saw the Nine Divisions of the Empire established by the Great Emperor Yü as constituting the great center about which less important peripheral regions clung.] He made his hearer aware that the Empire [*t'ien-hsia*] is small and not worth taking delight in and that the destiny of a dynasty is brief and not worth relying upon; so that [the ruler] might better turn his efforts upon himself, cultivate his virtue, and rid himself completely of the evils of covetousness and violence that characterized the rulers of the Seven Contending States. The *Shih Chi* appends Tsou Yen's biography to that of Mencius and praises him with the words that, although his teachings were not orthodox, they might also have had the same purport as those of Yi Yin, who exploited his cooking pot to become Chief Minister to T'ang, or Po-li Hsi, who through herding oxen came to be Chief Minister in the State of Ch'in. [Two examples of worthy ministers who came to the attention of their rulers through unlikely circumstances; *Mencius* discusses them both in the chapter v, "*Wan Chang*," Part i; Legge, p. 360 ff, but denies that these persons devised unusual circumstances simply to attract their rulers' attention to themselves.] However, Tsou's doctrines were not carried out, being similar in that respect to those of Mencius.[92] Ssu-ma Ch'ien [in writing the *Shih Chi*] was probably

[92] The *Shih Chi*, ch. 74, "Meng, Hsün lieh-chuan," in discussing Mencius says: " . . . The feudal lords faced East in homage to Ch'i. The empire was then engaged in forming vertical [north-to-south] and horizontal [east-to-west] alliances [among the states], and held aggression and military campaigning to be something worthy, whereas Mencius was [intent on] transmitting the virtues of T'ang [i.e., Yao], Yü [i.e., Shun], and the Three Dynasties. The result was that wherever he went he did not meet accord [with his principles"; modified somewhat from Fung/Bodde, Vol. I, p. 107]. Discussing Tsou Tzu it says: "Kings, nobles and great officials, when they first encountered his doctrines, were struck with fear and gave thought to transforming themselves, but later were unable to put them into practice." [Modified somewhat from Fung/Bodde,

also hinting at the similarity of principle in Mencius and Tsou Yen and at his feelings of profound dismay that benevolence and righteousness are so difficult to apply. If this surmise is not in error, then it is quite possible to go on to the further conclusion that the Agriculturists may represent a metamorphosis of Mohism, and the *Yin-Yang* philosophers appear to be an offshoot from Confucius and Mencius. Hsü Hsing [the Agriculturist] opposed Confucianism, while Tsou Yen [the *Yin-Yang* theorist] wanted to broaden it.

Although the work the *Tsou Tzu* in forty-nine essays and Tsou Tzu's *Chung-shih wu-te* in fifty-six essays[93] are lost, from the fragments quoted in the *Shih Chi, Huai-nan Tzu* and the *Han Shu* it is possible to see something of the unbridled tone and the fantastic convolutions of his thought, which might have been useful as a corrective against the rigidity and banality of the later Confucians. The unfortunate thing is that rulers of his time were not capable of applying the ultimate principles on which he founded his theories, while his compatriots were to use his doctrines about the Five Powers to gain favor in Ch'in.[94] Then in the Ch'in-Han period Tsou Yen's school split into two branches. One was that of genii and immortals of the *fang-shih* [magician] type, who abandoned Tsou's governmental and philosophic teachings to dwell in the realm of imagination "beyond the Red Regions";[95] unbounded fantasy usurped the place of benevolence and righteousness. [Tsou Yen's "Divine Province," i.e., China was located

---

Vol. i, p. 161.] A following passage compares Tsou Yen's honors and eminence with the difficulties and frustrations that faced Confucius and Mencius, and that superficially seen appears to be critical of Tsou's willingness to flatter and beguile in order to gain favor. But in the end it uses the "ox cauldron" allusion, implying praise of him. [Ssu-ma Chen explains this allusion in his *So-yin* commentary thus: "The *Lü-shih Ch'un-ch'iu* says, 'A cauldron that holds an ox is not to be used for cooking a chicken.' "] The intent of this probably is to say, in Mencius' words, "Your aim is great, but your argument is not good." [Legge, *Mencius*, p. 429; Mencius says this to Sung K'eng, the Mohist.]

[93] *Han Shu, ch.* 30, "Yi-wen chih."

[94] The *Shih Chi, ch.* 26, "Feng-shan shu" states: "During the reigns of Kings Hsüan and Wei [357–301 B.C.; however, Ch'ien Mu, *Hsien-Ch'in chu-tzu hsi-nien k'ao-pien*, pp. 402–03, demonstrates that Tsou Yen was born about 300 B.C. or slightly earlier, hence was not yet active during the reigns of Kings Wei and Hsüan], persons like Tsou Tzu discoursed upon and wrote about the cyclic sequence of the dominant influence of the Five Powers. When the Ch'in [ruler] became Emperor [221 B.C.], men of Ch'i presented these to him; consequently The First Emperor adopted and applied them." [Cf. Fung/Bodde, p. 169, where this passage also appears.]

[95] The same chapter of the *Shih Chi* cited in note 94 says further: "Tsou Yen achieved eminence at the courts of the feudal rulers for his [theories about] *Yin* and *Yang* and about the determining cosmic influences [*chu-yün*] and the magicians who lived along the coast in Yen and Ch'i transmitted his doctrines without being able really to understand them. Nonetheless, this led to the rise of persons who employed fantastic theories, specious flattery and guile to seek favor, in numbers beyond reckoning." [Cf. also Fung/Bodde, p. 169, where the passage is translated.]

within a "Red Region."] The other branch became that of the Three Systems [*san-t'ung*] of the Kung-yang school, which abandoned [his theory of the alternating] increase and decrease [of *yin* and *yang*] for theories about interactions [*kan-ying*, between cosmic forces and human affairs], in which benevolence and righteousness were channeled into the course of deviously avoided taboos, and of obsessive apprehensions. By the time of the Han dynasty *Yin-Yang* philosophers, these teachings had become something close to superstition and retained little of their ethical foundations; they no longer bore any resemblance to the original form they had in Tsou Yen's "Talk about Heaven."[96]

The development of the Agriculturist and *Yin-Yang* schools is described above in general terms. The regions in which they were disseminated may also be roughly indicated. Tsou Yen was born in the State of Ch'i, and Hsü Hsing came from Ch'u. Therefore the *Yin-Yang* school was one of northern learning, while the Agriculturists belonged to the South. Hsü Hsing went to the State of T'eng, where Ch'en Hsiang and his brother studied under him, a case of southern learning moving northward. Tsou Yen was honored in Ch'i, Liang, Chao, and Yen;[97] thus it is an example of northern learning achieving prominence in the North. Beyond this, little further can be discovered about them.

SECTION THREE
Interacting Influences

THE pre-Ch'in philosophies established their own distinct school-followings [i.e., *men-hu*, literally "gates and doors," emphasizing the factional exclusiveness of schools and their followers]; these attacked and disparaged one another. Examples of this are the chapters "Anti-Confucianism" in the *Mo Tzu*, and the importance that Mencius attached to refutation of Yang Chu and Mo Tzu; Shen Pu-hai and Shang Yang discredited literary education and cultivation of the self; Lao Tzu and Chuang Tzu

[96] *Shih Chi, ch.* 130, "T'ai shih-kung tzu-hsü," discussing the main tenets of the Six Schools of Philosophy, states: "The practice of the arts of *Yin* and *Yang* greatly flourished, and the people came to observe taboos and prohibitions, causing men to feel restricted and subjecting them to many fears." Ch'ien Mu in his *Hsien-Ch'in chu-tzu hsi-nien k'ao-pien*, p. 404, expressed the suspicion that the "Three Systems" [*san t'ung*] theory of the K'ung-yang school was an outgrowth of the *Yin-yang* School, and cites as one corroboration of this the fact that the *Han Shu, ch.* 30, "Journal of Literature," lists a work "The Spring and Autumn Annals with Commentary by Tsou" (*Ch'un-ch'iu Tsou-shih chuan*). Ch'ien's view on this is very pertinent.

[97] *Han Fei Tzu, ch.* 15, "Wang Cheng," states: "Tsou Yen's service in the State of Yen was without meritorious achievement; moreover, the *Tao* of the country was severed" [i.e., the life of the dynasty was imperiled, its "fate sealed"]. For the other states [in which he served], see the *Shih Chi, ch.* 74, "Meng, Hsün lieh-chuan."

derided both [Confucian] benevolence and righteousness, and [Legalist] laws and political methods. Fiercely maintained factional identities would seem to preclude the possibility of mutual interactions. However, brief examination of the matter makes us aware that, since all the various pre-Ch'in philosophical theories emerged from historical environments of overall similarity, we could scarcely expect that they could have avoided influencing each other. Let us discuss this briefly, on the basis of those philosophers the origins of whose theories are comparatively accessible to research.

(1)   Mo Tzu was influenced by Confucian learning. *Huai-nan Tzu, ch.* 21, "Yao-lüeh hsün" states: "Mo Tzu received the education of a *ju*, and was taught the doctrines of Confucius; but he was displeased by the rites [*li*], which were to him complicated and troublesome; by the elaborate funerals, which were so costly that they impoverished the people; and by their extended periods of mourning, which are injurious to the health and which interfere with work. Therefore he turned his back on the Ways of the Chou and adopted the governmental institutions of the Hsia." Except for the doubtful points of whether or not Mo Tzu ever was an *immediate* disciple of Confucius and whether or not Mo Tzu did adopt what were in fact governmental practices of Hsia, this explanation in the *Huai-nan Tzu* sets forth in the best possible fashion the relationship between Confucianism and Mohism.[98]

(2)   A portion of Legalist thought probably was derived from Confucianism. Li K'e was a disciple of Pu Shang [i.e. Tzu-hsia, one of the immediate disciples of Confucius] and Shang Yang [Lord Shang] studied Li's *Classic of Law, [Fa-ching]*[99] while Han Fei and Li Ssu both studied under Hsün Tzu. Wu Ch'i while in office in the State of Wei, conducted government in a way that evidenced much of the spirit of the Legalists; yet the *Lü-shih Ch'un-ch'iu* states that he had studied under Tseng Tzu [i.e., Tseng Shen, one of the immediate disciples of Confucius, and traditionally held to be the author of the *Classic of Filial Piety*, or *Hsiao-ching*]. What the Confucians meant by their doctrine of the "rectification of names" [*cheng ming*] took form as rites [*li*] when applied to the aristocratic classes [*shih ta-fu*]; and when applied to the common people it became penal regulations. Then when clan-law fell into ineffectiveness, *li* lost its func-

[98]   *Han Fei Tzu, ch.* 50, "Hsien Hsüeh," states: "Confucius and Mo Tzu both talk about Yao and Shun, yet they differ in what they accept of them and what they discard." This also can serve as evidence of the similarity of the two schools. However, insofar as they differed in what they accepted and discarded, the Mohist school also possessed an element of creativeness.

[99]   See note 58; also, if the *Shih Chi, ch.* 68, in the biography of Shang Yang is not in error in saying that Shang Yang on first meeting Duke Hsiao of Ch'in talked about the emperors and kings of the Three Dynasties [i.e., Hsia, Shang, and Chou], then Shang Yang was also familiar with the Confucian arts.

tion, and the principle of the rectification of names consequently tended to be subverted by the trend toward punishments and laws. Thus a branch of the Confucian school first underwent change through Wu Ch'i and Li K'e, then was further transformed by Lord Shang and Han Fei. Hsün Tzu's thought, thus, represents transitional thought of this period of change.[100]

(3) The Legalists were also influenced by the Taoists. The *Han Fei Tzu* contains the chapters "Commentaries on Lao Tzu's Teaching" and "Illustrations of Lao Tzu's Teachings. [*Chs.* 20, 21; "Chieh Lao," and "Yü Lao."] In the *Kuan Tzu* the chapters "Straight Thinking" and "Pure Heart" [*chuan* 13, essays 36–38; "Hsin Shu" parts one and two, and "Pai Hsin"], are also clarifications of the Huang-Lao tenets.[101] Shen Tao gave primary emphasis to law, for which he was praised by Shen Pu-hai and Han Fei.[102] And chapter 33, "T'ien-hsia" of the *Chuang Tzu* classes P'eng Meng, T'ien P'ien, and Shen Tao together as belonging to the school of relativism [*ch'i-wu*]. The *Shih Chi, ch.* 74, "Meng, Hsün lieh-chuan," states that Shen Tao, Chieh Tzu, and Huan Yuan all studied the doctrines of the Yellow Emperor and of Lao Tzu, of the Way and of its Power. [Cf. Fung/Bodde, 1, p. 132, where this passage is translated.] Hence the learning of Shen Tzu [Shen Tao] combined Legalism and Taoism, somewhat as Wu Ch'i and Li K'e drew simultaneously on both Confucianism and Legalism. This also is proof that, although Huang-Lao is distinct as a school-faction from that of Shen Pu-hai and Han Fei, there existed nevertheless interpenetration between them on the level of thought.

(4) There probably also existed such interpenetration between Taoists and Mohists.[103] Sung K'eng may have been a follower of Mo Tzu, hence the *Mencius* in Book vi, "Kao Tzu" tells about his desire to speak against aggressive warfare, and in *Hsün Tzu*, chapter 6, "Against the Twelve Philosophers" cites him together with Mo Ti [Mo Tzu], criticizing them

---

[100] Ch'ien Mu in his *Hsien-Ch'in chu-tzu hsi-nien k'ao-pien*, pp. 211–12, states that Shang Yang, in his prime ministership in Ch'in, practised " . . . in large part the doctrines inherited from Li K'e and Wu Ch'i," and also states: "People say merely that Legalist origins are in *Tao* and *Te* [i.e., Taoist principles], apparently not aware that their origins in fact are in Confucianism. Their observance of law and sense of public justice are wholly in the spirit of Confucius' rectification of names and return to propriety, but transformed in accordance with the conditions of the age."

[101] Note that in the "Journal of Literature," *ch.* 30 of the *Han Shu*, the *Kuan Tzu* is listed among the Taoists; only with the "Journal of Writings" ("Ching-chi chih") of the *Sui Shu* is it first listed as a Legalist work. [Chapter titles are as translated in Lewis Maverick, *The Kuan Tzu*, p. ix.]

[102] Commentary on [*ch.* 30] the "Journal of Literature" of *Han Shu*.

[103] Liang Ch'i-ch'ao in his *Mo Tzu hsüeh-an*, p. 160, refers to Sung as being of the "orthodox line" [of Mohism].

both for "valuing utility, carrying austerity to excess, and holding [social] distinctions in contempt." However, in *Hsün Tzu*, chapter 17 "Concerning Heaven" says: "Sung Tzu [Sung K'eng] had insight regarding the [fact that human desires may be] few, but no insight regarding the [fact that they may be] many." The chapter 18, "On the Correction of Errors," says: "Master Sung Tzu says: 'Men's passions desire but little, but everyone supposes that his own passions desire much, which is an error.' "[104] It also says: "The teacher Sung Tzu says: 'To show clearly that to meet with insult is no disgrace will prevent people from fighting.' " *Han Fei Tzu, ch.* 50, "Hsien Hsüeh," states that he "Looked upon insult as no disgrace." *Chuang Tzu, ch.* 33, "T'ien-hsia," further praises them: "Not to be involved in the mundane, not to indulge in the specious, not to be overreaching with the individual, nor antagonistic to the public; but to desire the tranquility of the world in general with a view to prolonging life, to seek no more than sufficient for the requirements of oneself and others, and by such a course to purify the heart. . . ." All these passages are very close to the tenets of Taoism. Although we should not regard this as proof that the origins of Taoism are in Mohism,[105] still it appears quite possible that Sung Tzu bridged the two schools. For if one bases his conjectures simply on the content of the thought of Lao Tzu and Sung Tzu, it is possible to see how [Mo Tzu's] "Condemnation of Aggressive Warfare" turns into [Sung K'eng's] "no disgrace" [in insult], and then one can proceed still further to [Lao Tzu's] "cling to the female [i.e., the passive]." [Mo Tzu's] "economy of expenditures" can turn into [Lao Tzu's] "lessening of desires" and then proceed still further to [Lao Tzu's] "knowing contentment" and "divesting oneself of [knowledge and desires] day by day." This indeed seems to us to be a most natural sequence.

However, the point that we must note is that Taoist thought, by the late Chou period, was already split into more than one school. The main features of this are apparent in the distinctions observed in the *Chuang Tzu*, "T'ien-hsia," in listing P'eng Meng, Lao Tan, and Chuang Chou separately. The school of Chuang Tzu observed quite different critical criteria from Yang Chu, Tzu Hua Tzu, T'o Hsiao, Wei Mou, and others, yet all of them belong to the "egocentric" thought system. Sung Tzu carried his insistent clamor throughout the world, "doing too much for others, too little for himself." [*Chuang Tzu, ch.* 33.] The fundamental

---

[104] [*Hsün Tzu*], the chapter "Chieh Pi" [21], also states: "Sung Tzu was blinded by the problem of desire, and did not know the value of virtue." [Following the translation in Fung/Bodde, p. 149, drawn from Dubs.]

[105] Ch'ien Mu in his *Hsien-ch'in chu-tzu hsi-nien k'ao-pien*, p. 342, on the basis of the similarity between the thought of Sung K'eng and Lao Tzu comes to the decision that "Taoism originated in Mohism."

spirit of this in fact is that of the Mohists' "universal love" [chien-ai]. When this is compared with Chuang Chou's "unfettered roaming," they are poles apart, absolutely contradictory. [Fung/Bodde uses "The Happy Excursion," and Watson uses "Free and Happy Roaming," as a translation of this term," hsiao-yao," taken from the title of the first chapter of Chuang Tzu.] However, those doctrines which in the Han period were called "Huang-Lao," advocating quiescence, harmony, and peaceful rule, did not stress solely the ideals of individual happiness and freedom in enunciating their principles, so that aspects of these may well have reflected Sung Tzu's teaching.

(5) The Agriculturists were influenced by Mohism, and the Yin-Yang School appears to have been an off-shoot of Confucianism. This has been explained above and need not be discussed again here.

(6) Of all the possible relationships between the various philosophers, none is harder to ascertain than that of Confucius and Lao Tzu. The Shih Chi, ch. 47, "K'ung Tzu shih-chia," states that Confucius went to Chou to ask Lao Tzu about the rites, and "is said to have seen Lao Tzu," in ch. 63, "Lao, Chuang, Shen, Han, lieh-chuan," it says that he [went to Chou] "in order to inquire about the rites from Lao Tzu." [In some editions, the biography of Lao Tzu with the passage quoted are in chüan 61.] But whether this event ever occurred is something that remains indefinite, while the words of Lao Tzu that are recorded in this connection seem to have nothing in common with the learning of the ju. Only the remarks that Lao Tzu made in reply to Confucius' question about the rites when Confucius went with Lao Tan to aid neighbors at a burial, as recorded in the Li Chi, ch. 77, "Tseng Tzu wen," are of a character similar [to the ju traditions]. If one accepts this, then it could appear that Confucius was influenced by Lao Tan.

The main features of the transmission of the teachings of the various philosophers, and of their influences on each other can be summarized in the form of a table, as below (Table Six).

SECTION FOUR
Chronological Sequence

BEFORE concluding this chapter, we should discuss the chronological sequence in which the different philosophers appeared. The extant documentary materials are inadequate; here indeed is a problem of greatest difficulty. However, there are two courses that can be followed in determining the sequence of the various philosophic schools of the pre-Ch'in period. The one is to treat the chronological sequence in which they originated; the other, the sequence in which they became independently established. The former is the more difficult, the latter somewhat easier

Table Six

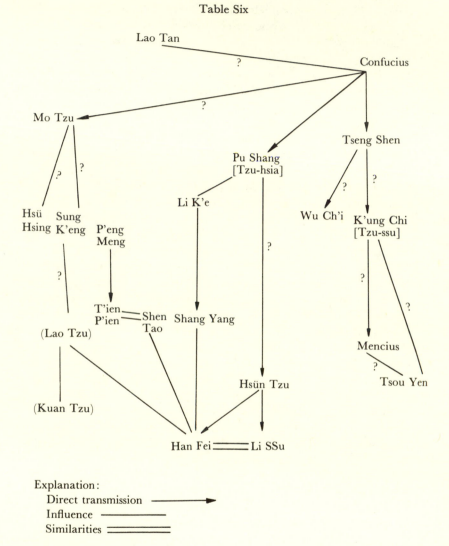

Explanation:
    Direct transmission ⟶
    Influence ⸻
    Similarities ⚌

to undertake. The origins and course of development of the various philosophic schools is something about which people of the Ch'in-Han period already lacked precise documentation. For example, in *Chuang Tzu*, the [final] chapter "T'ien-hsia" states that the various philosophers all inherited "the *tao shu* [ways and teachings] of antiquity"; and the *Han Shu, ch*. 30, "Journal of Literature," states that the different philosophies all developed from the duties of the officials of the kings, but neither says anything about their chronological sequence. There are further references, such as that in *Han Fei Tzu, ch*. 50, "Hsien Hsüeh" which says that Confucius and Mo Tzu "both talked about Yao and Shun" and in *Huai-nan Tzu, ch*. 21, "Yao-lüeh Hsün," where it says that Mo Tzu turned his back on Chou and employed Hsia. These statements too are unclear in their implications, and inadequate on which to base conclusions. As for the Taoists' claims that their origins went back to the Yellow Emperor, and Hsü Hsing's tracing his to the Divine Agriculturist [Shen-nung, the name of one of the legendary Emperors of earliest antiquity], these attributions inspire even less confidence, and border on the nonsensical. If we decide to put aside these traditional accounts and base an investigation solely on extant historical materials, then we find that the origins of Confucianism [*ju-hsüeh*] are apparently of the greatest antiquity, as well as being the most easily traced. The historical background of Confucius' political thought is the Chou feudal world. However, the records of the institutions of antiquity were perhaps not wholly lost by the Spring and Autumn Period, so that Confucius, with his "fondness for antiquity and eager quest for knowledge" [*Analects*, vii/19] perhaps had opportunities to see something of them, and hence was able to talk about the old institutes of Hsia and Yin and to know something of the continuity and change during the Three Dynasties. Moreover, the *Odes* and the *Documents* and the history of antiquity definitely embody political concepts and principles, which Confucius "ventured to adopt." [*Mencius*, iv/ii/21/3]. It becomes evident that the remote origins of Confucius' political thought can be traced back to the Three Dynasties, while more recently they are founded directly on the rites and institutions of the Chou. Although it may be difficult to find direct evidence for this, in general it cannot be far wrong.

For the origins of Legalism there also are clues that can be traced. Li K'e compiled and arranged the laws of all of the states and produced his *Fa-ching* [*Classic of Law*], which shows that the laws of the states were in fact the direct source of legalistic thinking. Of those examples whose names are still in existence, there are the Penal Tripods [*Hsing-ting*] of the State of Cheng, the "Penal Regulations" [*Hsing-shu*] of the State of Chin, the "Law of P'u-ou" of the State of Ch'u, and the "Code of Ta-fu" of the State of Wei.[106] These are products of the late Chou, not comparable in antiquity to the literary remains on which the Confucians based themselves. In the section above we have touched upon the fact that many of the Legalist thinkers had been educated in Confucian doctrines; this is particularly clear proof that the fundamentals of Legalist thought appeared only after Confucianism.

Mo Tzu, in turning his back on the Chou, must also clearly be post-Confucian. However, he is somewhat similar to the Confucians in the way he cites the *Odes* and *Documents* and praises [Emperors] Yao, Shun, Yü, and T'ang and [Kings] Wen and Wu. Although the two philosophies differ in what they take and what they discard from these sources, the foundations of their thought are in general the same. We are completely unable to demonstrate whether the literary works on which Mohism was based are the work of Mo Ti himself, or whether they were transmitted to him from Yin Yi.[107] It is also impossible to verify whether or not it came to him via the mediation of the Confucian school. Hence, as far as their origins are concerned, it is very difficult to determine the sequence of the Confucians and the Mohists.

The beginnings of Taoist thought are still more elusive. Ssu-ma Ch'ien says: "While the various schools of philosophers tell of the Yellow Emperor, their words are not authoritative and reasonable." [Watson's translation, *Ssu-ma Ch'ien, Grand Historian of China*, p. 183.] Another source says: "Taoists always make attributions to the Divine Agriculturalist and the Yellow Emperor."[108] This tendency to assign things metaphorically to antiquity is particularly strong in Lao Tzu and Chuang Tzu. When Confucians and Mohists speak about antiquity, they are perhaps somewhat more trustworthy; but when Taoists speak of the transmission of their own doctrines from the past, they merit scant belief. Add to this, the facts concerning the lives of the Taoist philosophers are in very few cases ascertainable. To draw on such materials with which to reconstruct the sources of their learning and thought would be most

---

[106] See, respectively, the *Tso Chuan*, the Sixth, Seventh, and Twenty-ninth year of Duke Chao, and the *Chan-kuo-ts'e*, "Wei Ts'e," 4. As for the "Code of Ta-fu," the Ming scholar Tung Yüeh, in his *Ch'i-kuo-k'ao*, maintains that it was a law that had been continuously in existence in the state of Wei even before the time of Li K'uei. The "five punishments" [*wu hsing*] of the "Yü Shu" in the *Documents* [Legge, p. 58] are not clearly of historical authenticity, nor do they indicate a reliance on law; they are not therefore to be regarded as the distant source of Legalism.

[107] The *Han Shu*, ch. 30, "Journal of Literature," lists the *Yin Yi*, in two parts, as the first work under the Mohists. The commentary states that Yin was a minister of the Chou dyansty in the time of Kings Ch'eng and K'ang [traditional reign dates 1115–1053 B.C.]. Chiang Ch'üan's *Tu tzu chih yen*, ch. 2, p. 28, adopts this.

[108] See respectively the *Shih Chi*, ch. 1, "Wu ti pen chi," and *Huai-nan Tzu*, ch. 19, "Hsiu-wu hsün."

difficult. If we make deductions based on the content of their thought, its formulations seem to have coalesced at the very latest by the late Spring and Autumn Period. In the *Analects*, "Hsien wen," there appears Confucius' rejection of "the principle that injury should be recompensed with kindness" [xiv/36; Legge, p. 288,] and in "T'ai-po" there are Tseng Tzu's disapproving words about "offended against and yet not protesting" [viii/5; altered slightly from Legge, p. 210]. These may represent comments upon Lao Tzu's doctrine that one should suffer humiliation without contesting. The *Kuo-yu*, in the second part of the chapter "Yüeh-yü," in the third year of the reign of Kou-chien, quotes Fan Li: "The *Tao* of Heaven fills but does not overflow, flourishes but does not grow proud, labors but does not seek recognition for its accomplishments." [Fan Li was a prominent minister under King Kou-chien of Yüeh in the early fifth century B.C.] This is close to the import of the *Tao Te Ching*. The *Li Chi*, *ch.* 4, "T'an-kung," tells of Confucius' friend Yuan-jang, who mounted the coffin and sang at the time of his mother's death. [Cf. *Li Chi*; Legge, *Li Ki*, Vol. i, pp. 198–99. Confucius sternly reproved Yuan Jang for such unbecoming conduct.] This strongly resembles the accounts in the *Chuang Tzu*, *ch.* 6, "Ta tsung-shih," of Meng-sun Ts'ai, who did not grieve on the death of his mother, and of Meng Tzu-fan and Tzu Ch'in Chang, who sang to observe mourning for their friend who had just died. [Fung Yu-lan: *Chuang Tzu*, p. 123 ff.; Watson, *Complete Works of Chuang Tzu*, pp. 86, 88.] *The Doctrine of the Mean* also records Confucius' reply to Tzu-lu, who had asked about energy: "To show forbearance and gentleness in teaching others; and not to revenge unreasonable conduct: —this is the energy of Southern regions . . . ," and in contrast to it: "To lie under arms; and meet death without regret: this is the energy of Northern regions." [Ch. 10/3–4, Legge, pp. 389–90.] From this it would appear that at that time the character of the South was quite in keeping with the teachings of Lao Tzu. If we further consider Lü Shang [i.e., Chiang T'ai-kung, first ducal lord of Ch'i, minister to the Chou kings Wen and Wu at the time of the founding of the dynasty], who appears in the *Shih Chi*, *ch.* 32, "Ch'i T'ai-kung Shih-chia," as one who followed the common practices and simplified ceremonial behavior, and the recluses Yü Chung and Yi-yi mentioned in the *Analects*, "Wei Tzu," as persons who: "While they hid themselves in seclusion, they gave a license to their words . . ." [xviii/8/4; Legge, *Analects*, p. 337] and look to them as perhaps being forerunners of Taoism, then the origins of Taoism are earlier than Confucianism. But of this too we can have no certain knowledge.

The *Shih Chi* records that Confucius inquired about the rites from Lao Tan, but this is inadequate evidence on which to base a judgment as to which of the two philosophies was the earlier. As to whether or not the event ever really took place, it is needless to engage in a discussion here. But even if we assume that it did, the concern for the rites was only one aspect of Confucius' teachings. Lao Tzu's words recorded in the "T'an-kung" [*chs.* 3–4 of the *Li Chi*] were all concerned merely with minutiae of ritual forms, and it would be difficult from this to prove that all of, or the general outlines of, Confucius' teachings had been influenced by Lao Tzu. [Cf. *Li Chi*, *ch.* 7, "Tseng Tzu Wen," pars. 16 and 33.] Even if we adopt the view advanced by recent scholars that Taoism and Con-fucianism both go back to the Yin people, this problem still may not yield to easy solution. Today it is difficult to make out what the content of the Yin people's thought may have been. What we do know is merely that they valued simplicity and honored spirits and gods. The Confucians stressed rites and music, and the Taoists spoke of Heaven's disinterested-ness; both would represent departures from the earlier Yin thought. Unless we have other means of access to this problem, we really cannot decide which of the two may have made its changes first and, thereby, whose origins are the earlier. That is to say, Confucius, in following the Institutes of Chou, may have wished to conform to the Chou rites in order to liberate the Yin people; Lao Tzu and Chuang Tzu adhered to humble submissiveness, perhaps hoping to escape the restraints of "Chou bond-age" and reach a state of individual contentment and freedom. They differed greatly in what they adopted and what they discarded, and the chronological sequence of it remains difficult to determine. In any event, a point that deserves our attention is that, in the case of all the various Taoist philosophers, if indeed their teachings have their origins in the unwillingness of conquered people to cooperate with the government of the Chou, we may see evidence of the intentional use of obscurity for the sake of self-concealment. We can then readily understand Lao Tzu's "lofty elusiveness" [literally, like a dragon," the description of Lao Tzu credited to Confucius in the *Shih Chi*] and Chuang Tzu's "metaphor" [literally "*yü-yen*," the name of Chapter 27 of the *Chuang Tzu*; the name has come to mean indirect expression or, technically, "metaphor"], as well as the difficulty we face in trying to uncover the actual facts regarding the lives of the other Taoist philosophers. This is in greatest contrast to the Mohists' and Confucians' quest for prominence and fame. Ssu-ma Ch'ien was relatively close to antiquity, yet with regard to Lao Tzu's character he was forced to resort to vague and purposely non-committal language.[109]

[109] The "K'ung-tzu shih-chia" [*Shih Chi*, *ch.* 47] says that Confucius "Went to Chou to inquire about the rites, where it is said he met Lao Tzu." In *ch.* 63, "Lao, Chuang, Shen, Han lieh chuan," it says that Lao Tzu, observing the decline of Chou, "thereupon went away and arrived at the Pass," where at the request of the Keeper of the Pass, Yin Hsi, he wrote his book of five thousand characters and went away, "and no one knows what became of him." It also states: "It is also said that Lao Lai Tzu also was a native of

Today documentary evidence is still more deficient; who can judge this puzzling ancient case?

If we abandon the attempt to determine origins, and concern ourselves with the sequence in which the schools became established, the problem is somewhat easier. Of the various schools, the Confucian was established by K'ung Ch'iu [the formal name of Confucius], the Mohist by Mo Ti, the Agriculturalist by Hsü Hsing, and the *Yin-Yang* by Tsou Yen. In these four cases, it was the intellectual force of one man that imparted to the school its enduring character, created the foundations of its thought and learning. We need but determine the birth and death dates of the founders in order to fix the sequence in the establishment of the schools. For the birth date of Confucius there are two dates, 552 and 551 B.C.[110] [i.e., respectively, the Twenty-first and Twenty-second years of the reign of Duke Hsiang of Lu]. The year of his death is 479 B.C. [i.e., the sixteenth year of the reign of Duke Ai of Lu]. For the birth date of Mo Ti the divergence of opinion is somewhat greater. Relatively reliable ones are (1) that he was born about ten years before the death of Confucius, and (2) that he was born about ten years after the death of Confucius.[111] Mo Tzu lived until the age of about ninety, and his death date can be reckoned therefrom. Hsü Hsing's birth and death dates cannot be determined, but he was a contemporary of Mencius. Tsou Yen lived after Mencius, his birth probably falling late in the reign of King Hsüan of Ch'i [reign 331–313 B.C.]. Hence in the establishment of these four schools, the Confucian is the first, the Mohist second, the Agriculturist next, and the *Yin-Yang* last. The Taoist and Legalist schools are somewhat more difficult to fix. This is because their establishment was not the work of one man, and the historical traces of their various philosophers are in many cases indistinct and blurred.

Among the Taoists, the writings of Lieh Yü-k'ou, Yang Chu, Tzu

---

Ch'u." This Lao Tzu was more than one hundred and sixty years old, or, also, "more than two hundred years old." It further states: "One hundred and twenty-nine years after the death of Confucius, the T'ai-shih of the State of Chou, Tan, met Duke Hsien of Ch'in," and "It is also said that Tan was Lao Tzu. It is also said that he was not. The world has no knowledge of whether or not it is so. Lao Tzu was a recluse gentleman." It further says "Lao Tzu's son's name was Tsung. Tsung was a general in the State of Wei, and was enfiefed at Tuan-kan. Tsung's son was Chu, Chu's son was Kung, and Kung's fourth generation descendant was Chia. Chia held office under the Han Emperor Hsiao-wen. . . ." Note that the Emperor [Hsiao] Wen reigned 179–157 B.C.

[110] The former view originated with the *Kung-yang* and *Ku-liang* commentaries to the *Spring and Autumn Annals*; the latter first appears in the *Shih Chi, ch.* 47, "K'ung Tzu shih-chia." Through two thousand years this problem has lacked a conclusive solution.

[111] The general import of Wang Chung's [1745–1794] "Preface to Mo Tzu" ["Mo Tzu hsü"] in his *Shu hsüeh* is conveyed in the former; the latter represents the import of Sun Yi-jang's [1848–1908] "Preface to the Chronological Biography of Mo Tzu" [Mo Tzu nien-piao hsü].

Hua Tzu, P'eng Meng, and others have been lost or falsified. In the transmission of the school to later ages, the outstanding exponents of its central tenets have in fact based themselves primarily on the *Lao Tzu* and the *Chuang Tzu*. If we take these two works to represent the establishment of Taoism, then Chuang Chou was slightly later than Mencius, and the composition of the *Lao Tzu* may have been subsequent to Confucius' visit inquiring about the rites, or may have been between the time when Chuang Tzu and Hsün Tzu wrote their discourses. Scholars debate the issue vigorously, and as yet there is no definitive view.[112] In fact the date that the two views propose differ by two hundred years. But even though there is no definitive solution, that has no great effect upon the task of studying the history of Chinese political thought. One could easily find reason in whichever view one adopted. In this work it has been decided to follow the older view with regard both to the origins of Taoism and to the question of dating Lao Tzu's birth, which will be presumed to have been earlier than Confucius; for the date of the composition of the book of Lao Tzu [the *Tao Te Ching*], we shall follow the opinion of the majority of scholars and assume that it belongs after Mencius.

The establishment of Legalism would seem to be properly credited to Shen Pu-hai's discussions of method [*shu*] and Kung-sun Yang's concern with law [*fa*]. Shen Pu-hai was chief minister to Duke Chao of Han, and was thus a contemporary of Mencius. Lord Shang [i.e., Kung-sun Yang] was chief minister to Duke Hsiao of Ch'in, and hence was also a contemporary of Mencius. If we take as our representative Han Fei Tzu, who accomplished the great synthesis of Legalism, then the establishment of Legalism must be set another century later, to the period just preceding the fourteenth year of the reign of The First Emperor of Ch'in [233 B.C.]. In the present work, the chapters that follow will set forth an account of pre-Ch'in political thought in the sequence: Confucianism, Mohism, Taoism, and Legalism; this follows more or less the sequence of their

---

[112] In the *Chu Tzu yü-lu* [of Chu Hsi, A.D. 1130–1200] it states: "Chuang Tzu was several years junior to Mencius," which appears to be accurate. The *Chuang Tzu's* quotations of Lao Tzu's words for the most part are not to be found in the extant *Tao Te Ching*. *Hsün Tzu*, ch. 17, "T'ien lun," contains criticisms of the *Lao Tzu*. Therefore we can deduce that the writing of the *Lao Tzu* was later than the *Chuang Tzu* and earlier than the *Hsün Tzu*. Moreover, the *Analects*, *Mo Tzu*, and *Mencius* all lack any explicit attack on Lao Tzu, and, although this is not proof that the *Lao Tzu* is late, it is worth noting. Most recent scholars have maintained that the *Lao Tzu* is a work of the Warring States Period; especially prominent among these are Ts'ui Shu [1740–1816] in his *Chu Ssu k'ao hsin lu* and Wang Chung [cf. note 111] in his *Shü hsueh*, "Lao Tzu k'ao-yi." Among modern scholars those who accept this view include Liang Ch'i-ch'ao, Fung Yu-lan, Ku Chieh-kang, Ch'ien Mu, and others. Hu Shih, however, stoutly maintains the view that the *Lao Tzu* is earlier than Confucius; see his *Chung-kuo che-hsüeh shih*, Vol. I, and his *Lun-hsüeh chin-chu*, pp. 103–34.

Table Seven

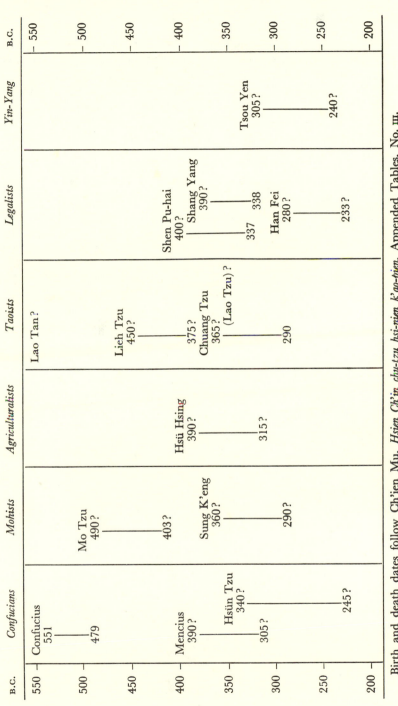

Birth and death dates follow Ch'ien Mu, *Hsien Ch'in chu-tzu hsi-nien k'ao-pien*, Appended Tables, No. III.

establishment, and simultaneously makes for convenience of discussion. It is not, however, the intention to make herein a precise and unalterable final judgment about the chronology of the various philosophers.

The chronology of establishment of the various political philosophies of the pre-Ch'in period is presented in table form, as above.

Author's note: The material presented in this chapter in large measure remains hypothetical and is offered to the reader merely for what reference he may wish to make to it.

CHAPTER TWO
Confucius (551–479 B.C.)

SECTION ONE
Confucius' Life and His Age

THE personal name of Master K'ung, or Confucius, was Ch'iu, and his formal name was Chung-ni. According to the accounts in ancient works, his ancestor, K'ung Fu-chia, was of the noble rank of *kung* [usually translated "duke"]* and had served the state of Sung as Ssu-ma, or Grand Marshall. His great-grandfather, [K'ung] Fang-shu, was forced to flee for his life to the State of Lu, where he became the *Fang Ta-fu*, or Great Officer of the city of Fang.[1] His father, whose name was [K'ung] Shu-liang Ho, was a Great Officer of the town of Tsou.[2] None of this is necessarily wholly accurate, yet we need not doubt that Confucius was a descendant of the fallen Yin dynasty aristocracy. Confucius lost his father while still very young, however, and in his youth he was poor and in humble circumstances.[3] What kind of education he received, we have no way of determining in detail. A Grand Minister praised him for his many accomplishments, and the villager from Ta-hsiang reported that he was a man of extensive learning.[4] The *Shih Chi* records that he "as a child playing games often set out the sacrificial vessels," and in his own time he himself had the reputation of being "expert in matters of ritual."[5] [Cf.

---

*Square brackets indicate that the words enclosed were added by the translator.

[1] Sun Hsing-yen, *K'ung Tzu chi-yü shih-p'u, shang,* quotes the commentary on the Preface to the "Sacrificial Odes of Shang" in the *Book of Odes,* which in turn quotes the *Shih-pen* as follows: "Duke Min of the State of Sung was the father of Fu-fu-ho, and that Fu-fu-ho was the father of Sung-fu, Sung-fu of Cheng-k'ao-fu, and Cheng-k'ao-fu of K'ung Fu-chia, who was Ssu-ma in the State of Sung. Hua Tu murdered him and extinguished the hereditary succession to nobility in the family; K'ung Fu-chia's son, Mu-chin-fu was degraded to the rank of knight [*shih* 士]. Mu-chin-fu was the father of Ch'i-fu, who was the father of Fang-shu, who was forced by the Hua clan to flee to the State of Lu. There he became Great Officer of Fang for which reason he is known as Fang-shu." [See Legge, *Analects,* "Prolegomena," pp. 56–58, for a fuller discussion of this geneology.]

[2] *Ibid.,* quoting the *Ch'ien fu lun, ch.* 35, "Chih shih hsing," which states: "Sung-fu was the father of Shih-tzu, and Shih-tzu of Cheng-k'ao-fu." It also states that Shu-liang Ho "was a Great Officer of Tsou." For the rest it more or less agrees with the *Shih-pen.*

[3] In the *Analects* [IX/6/3; Legge, p. 218, here modified from Waley, p. 139] Confucius says of himself "When I was young, my condition was low, and therefore I had many practical accomplishments, but in mean, everyday matters."

[4] *Shih Chi, ch.* 47, "K'ung Tzu shih-chia."

[5] *Analects,* III/15 [Legge, p. 160], "The Master, when he entered the grand temple, asked about everything. Someone said, 'Who will say that the son of the man of Tsou knows the rules of propriety.' " [Confucius' father was said to have been a Great Officer of

Analects, xv/1/1; Legge, p. 294.] The *Analects* [vii/26] also records that Confucius "fished with a line but not with a net; when fowling he did not aim at a roosting bird." When refusing to receive a call from Ju-pei he sang as he played the lute; after he returned to the State of Lu "the music was reformed." And as for the *Odes* and *Documents*, and the Six Disciplines, political administration, and the literary arts in which his students were trained,[6] these all must have been things in which Confucius himself was well versed. We must note carefully that although Confucius said of himself that he had "many practical accomplishments, but in mean, everyday matters," it is quite evident that the studies that he pursued were in fact all of those arts by which the *shih-ta-fu* maintained their positions and followed careers in the world of affairs. [In Confucius' time the term *shih-ta-fu* refered to the lower aristocracy, among whose prerogatives was government service.] Beyond these things he would not stoop to waste his time. It was for this reason that when Fan Ch'ih asked to be taught about farming, Confucius derided him as a small man.[7] And the "old man carrying a basket" in turn derided Confucius, saying: "Your four limbs are unaccustomed to toil; you cannot distinguish the five kinds of grain." [*Analects* xviii/7; following Legge, p. 335.] For in the Spring and Autumn Period, agricultural work was the occupation of the ordinary people; the *shih-ta-fu* did not engage in production. This more or less paralleled the situation of the aristocracy of Europe or of ancient Greece.

Thus even though Confucius as a youth was poor and in humble circumstances, he devoted his energy to "the learning of the superior man." Moreover, since he was a descendant of the ducal line in the State of Sung and of a Great Officer of Lu, this superior man's education which he achieved was not limited to what could be drawn from his own family's traditions, but because of his "great family" connections he was granted still wider opportunities for learning and reading. Confucius himself said that he could say something about the rituals of the Hsia and the Yin dynasties, but that he had gone to the States of Ch'i and Sung [which were supposed to be heirs to the traditions of Hsia and Yin] and he knew that their records and their learned men were inadequate [to prove him rigth or wrong].[8] From the fact that Confucius had gained access to the docu-

---

Tsou, a town in Lu. "Rules of propriety" is Legge's translation here of *li*, "rites."] It is evident from this that Confucius had a reputation for knowledge of the rites, yet some persons may have questioned his knowledge.

[6] See *Analects*, respectively: vii/26 [Legge, p. 203—here following Waley, p. 128]; xvii/20 [Legge, p. 327, here following Waley, p. 204]; ix/6/3 [Legge, p. 218, here modified from Waley, p. 139]; and xi/2 [Legge, p. 237].

[7] *Ibid.*, xiii/4/2 [Legge, p. 265; Waley, p. 172, translates it "Fan is no gentleman"].

[8] *Analects*, iii/9. [Legge, p. 158, Waley, p. 96; note discussions of difficulties in interpreting this passage; some scholars would prefer "their records and writings."]

ments of Ch'i and Sung, we can assume that he had also been able to see those of Chou and of Lu. Confucius also clearly stated that he "could still remember when a historiographer would leave a blank in his text"[9] [rather than fill in inaccurate details without foundation]; therefore perhaps those which Han Hsüan-tzu saw[10] were the same on which Confucius once cast his gaze. [The *Ch'un-ch'iu* and *Tso Commentary* record that the State of Chin sent Han to Lu in the year 539 to examine the records relevant to Chou Institutions; Han remarked on the fullness of Lu records.] In addition, such things as his entering the ancestral temple to observe the ritual vessels, and traveling to the State of Chou to ask about the rites,[11] all give ample evidence of the diligence with which he pursued his studies. Tzu-kung said of him: "From whom indeed did our Master *not* learn? But at the same time, what need had he of any fixed and regular teacher?"[12] This is the best statement of just how Confucius actually pursued learning.

The record of Confucius' lifelong activities shows just three major elements: service in government, teaching, and compiling texts. His life in government was of the briefest duration. In the beginning he probably took service because he was poor, and held posts of keeper of the stores and director of the public pastures.[13] Later he was Governor of Chung-tu, [a city in the State of Lu] and thereafter advanced to the post of Minister of Crime,[14] consequently joining the ranks of the Great Officers. While

---

[9] *Ibid.*, xv/25 [Legge, p. 301].

[10] *Tso Chuan*, Second year of Duke Chao [Legge, p. 583, paragraph 1].

[11] *Shih Chi*, ch. 47, "K'ung-tzu shih-chia"; *Hsün Tzu*, ch. 28, "Yu-tso"; *Huai-nan Tzu*, ch. 12, "Tao-ying hsün"; *Shuo-yüan*, ch. 10, "Ching-shen".

[12] *Analects*, xix/22 [here following Waley, p. 229].

[13] *Mencius*, v/ii/5/4 [Legge, pp. 383–84].

[14] *Ibid.*, vi/ii/6/6, states: "When Confucius was Chief Minister of Justice [*Ssu-k'ou*, or, "Minister of Crime"] in Lu, the prince came not to follow his counsels. Soon after there. was the solstitial sacrifice, and when a part of the flesh presented in sacrifice was not sent to him, he went away without even taking off his cap of ceremony." [Legge, pp. 434–35.] The *Shih Chi* states that from a minor official's [*li*] post he was made governor or chief officer [*tsai*] of the town of Chung-tu, then was promoted to that of Minister of Works [*Ssu-k'ung*], and subsequently was again promoted to the post of Minister of Crime [*Ta Ssu-k'ou*], in which capacity he concurrently assumed responsibilities as a chief officer of state (*she hsing hsiang shih*). [See notes, Kramers, *School Sayings of Confucius*, pp. 251 and 255.] Ma Su's *Yi-shih* argues against this, saying that the Minister of Works was one of the Three Ministers [*ch'ing*] of the State, and that the Three Descendants of Duke Huan [reign 711–694 B.C.; his three younger sons and their descendants, who were the heads of the all-powerful Three Families of Lu] headed these three ministries by hereditary privilege. The post of *Ssu-k'ou* was held by a man of the rank of Great Officer [lower than a Minister, *ch'ing*] and in ducal states like Lu the title was not prefixed by the word *Ta*. Chiang Yung's *Hsiang-tang t'u k'ao* argues that *she-hsiang*, "concurrently chief minister" in fact meant *hsiang-li*, "assisting at the rites," or "councillor for the rites." The post of *hsiang* "councillor" in Lu was, however, one of the Three Ministries, and the Chi family

in the office of Minister of Crime he at one time assisted Duke Ting [of Lu] at the meeting with the Duke [Ching] of Ch'i at Chia-ku, and through his skill with speech overcame Duke Ching. [This follows the account in the *Tso Chuan*; Legge, pp. 776–77. Cf. Kramers' *School Saying of Confucius*, pp. 202–04, for a still more elaborate version.] He also devised the fall of three cities with the object of weakening the power of the three great families of Meng, Shu, and Chi. Subsequently the Duke of Ch'i sent a gift of female musicians [to the Duke of Lu], and when his Duke did not send him a portion of the flesh [from the solstitial sacrifice], Confucius knew he would no longer be used there; so he left Lu and went to Wei. [This follows Mencius; see footnote 14.] After this he had no further occasion to participate in government.

Confucius' activities as a teacher appear to have commenced very early. Confucius said of himself: "At thirty, I stood firm." [*Analects* II/4; following Legge's translation, p. 146. The meaning of the line is that at thirty he was accomplished enough in learning on which he had set his heart from the age of fifteen, to maintain himself.] The *Tso Chuan*, under the Twentieth year of Duke Chao [521 B.C.] says that Confucius stopped [his disciple] Ch'in Chang from expressing condolence on the death of Tsung-lu. [This event is historically dated, and may be the earliest in which the student-teacher relationship between Confucius and one of his disciples is made explicit. See Legge, *Ch'un Tsew*, p. 682, end of paragraph 3.] Confucius was just thirty years old in that year. Perhaps it was at this time that he began to accept students.[15] The best of his disciples numbered about seventy. Of these, those who came from poor and humble backgrounds seem to be by far the largest number. As has been noted: "Yen Tzu's home was in a humble lane; when he died he had a coffin but no enclosure for it. [Evidence of his poverty; see the account of his funeral, *Analects* XI/7–10. For an explanation of the "enclosure," see Waley, *Analects*, additional notes, XI, 7, p. 246.] Tseng Tzu worked at cultivating the melon patch, and his mother wove cloth. Min Tzu-ch'ien wore clothing made of reeds, and drove the carriage for his father. Chung-kung's father was of very humble status. Tzu-kung engaged in commerce. Tzu-lu ate goose-foot [a poor man's food; see Kramers, *op.cit.*, pp. 236 and 332], carried loads of rice on his back, wore a cap of cock feathers and a waist-pendant of boar's teeth. [Rustic symbols of bravery.] Yu Tzu had served as a foot soldier. Yuan Ssu lived in a poor alley and was dressed in

---

was in control of government. [I.e., this post would have been in the hands of a member of this hereditary Ministers' i.e., *ch'ing* family, and not in that of a mere Great Officer *ta-fu*.] Thus is would seem that Mencius' statement on this is closer to the truth. [The foregoing all point out discrepancies in detail of the account of Confucius' career in office; the details about posts held are very dubious, and he may not have held them.]

[15] *Analects*, I, "Hsüeh erh"; Ch'ien Mu, *Hsien Ch'in chu-tzu hsi-nien k'ao pien*, page 3.

tattered gown and cap. Fan Ch'ih asked to be taught about farming. Kung-yeh Ch'ang had been imprisoned. Tzu-chang was of a petty family of Lu. Although this information may not be completely reliable, the essential fact becomes evident. Only Nan-kung Ching-shu[16] in Lu and Ssu-ma Niu from Sung came as members of the aristocracy to study; beyond these two there is no report of any other."[17] Because he "taught without distinction of classes,"[18] by no means all of Confucius' disciples observed such rituals as "not going on foot," or maintaining the manners of the *shih-ta-fu*. [Confucius, on the occasion of Yen Hui's funeral, explains that *li*, or ritual behavior, prevented a man of his rank from going on foot; see *Analects*, xɪ/7/2; Legge, p. 238.]

However, although Confucius' followers were of low status, their studies were chiefly concerned with the skills by means of which one could advance in office. Thus we find Yen Hui inquiring about the administering of the state, and of Jan Yung it is said that he was qualified to rule. [Loosely translated with reference to *Analects* xv/10 and vɪ/1. Cf. Legge, pp. 297–98 and 184.] The affairs of government were thus established as a special area of study; the questions and answers exchanged among the teacher and his followers were largely concerned with governmental problems. Even when Tzu-lu said: "There are the common people and officers; there are the altars of the spirits of the land and grain. Surely, 'learning consists in other things beside reading books,' " Confucius was unable to refute him and could say only: "It is remarks of that kind that make me hate glib people."[19] [Tzu-lu was defending his action in appointing a young man to an administrative post, taking him away from his formal studies before he had completed them.] The tone of the Confucian school can be inferred from this.

Confucius' activities in the authorship and exegesis of texts has long been the subject of scholars' widely varying views. We need not enter into a discussion of this. Confucius was "devoted to antiquity, and diligent in his study of it"; [*Analects* vɪɪ/19] he gained access to the documents in

---

[16] The *Tso Chuan*, Seventh year of Duke Chao, records that Meng Hsi Tzu, close to death (he died in the Twenty-fourth year of Duke Chao) commanded his sons Yi-tzu and Nan-kung Ching-shu to study under Confucius. [Legge, *Ch'un Ts'ew*, pp. 618–19, paragraph 6.]

[17] Ch'ien Mu, *op. cit.*, p. 77. In view of the fact that Confucius was himself a descendant of Yin aristocracy, there may well have been Yin descendants among his disciples. However the only one for whom explicit evidence to that effect can be adduced is Tuan-sun Shih [i.e., Tzu-chang]. The *Li Chi*, in *ch.* 3, "T'an Kung" states: "At the mourning for Tzu-chang, Kung-ming Yi made the ornaments of commemoration. There was a tent-like pall, made of plain silk of a carnation color, with clusters of ants painted at the four corners, for he was an officer of Yin." [Modified from Legge, *Li Ki*, p. 140.]

[18] *Analects*, xv/38 [Legge, p. 305].

[19] *Ibid.*, xɪ/24 [here following Waley, p. 159].

state archives, and worked at ordering and organizing them and at developing his own interpretations of their meaning. Moreover, he transmitted this to his disciples and later followers. The *Shih Chi*, ch. 47, states: "Confucius instructed his disciples in the *Odes* and the *Documents*, the *Rites* and the *Music*"; this much is a matter of fact and can be accepted as reliable. Moreover, one can even go further and say that the source of the items of instruction employed by the Confucians was not limited to such official documents. Confucius not only widely collected all the different existing exegeses, but also added to these his own original views. Confucius went to the State of Chou to investigate the rites, and went into the Ancestral Temple inquiring about everything there. When Kung-sun Chao of the State of Wei asked from whom Chung-ni [Confucius' formal name] had derived his learning, Tzu-kung replied: "The Way of the kings Wen and Wu has never yet utterly fallen to the ground. Among men, those of great understanding have recorded the major principles of this Way and those of less understanding have recorded the minor principles. So that there is no one who has not access to the Way of [the Chou founding Kings] Wen and Wu. From whom indeed did our Master *not* learn? But at the same time, what need had he of any fixed and regular teacher?" [*Analects* xix/22, following Waley's translation, pp. 228–29.] This amply illustrates that Confucius did not limit himself to drawing on the written records. Tzu-kung said: "Of our Master's views about Man's nature and the ways of Heaven, he will not tell us anything at all." And Confucius said: "My friends, I know you think that there is something I am keeping from you."[20] These remarks show that Confucius' instruction at times went beyond the recorded texts of the *History* and the *Odes*.

When we examine the concrete facts of the whole course of Confucius' life, his greatest achievement is not [as he had hoped] bringing order into the chaotic affairs of his time, but rather is establishing his teaching and instructing his followers. Chang Ping-lin [eminent "democratic classicist," 1868–1936] has stated: "Confucius was for China the fountainhead of the people's well-being as well as of their cultural advance." This view is well justified. Chang has also written: "The *hsiang-hsüeh* [local schools] as defined in the *Institutes of Chou* [*Chou Kuan*] were wholly occupied with the Six Disciplines [the basics of the Confucian education]. However, the great principles of ritual behavior still did not extend down to the common people. The governmental institutes of the time were in keeping of the royal Chou court; some evidence for this is to be found in the *Odes* and the *History*. The Masters of Instruction used them to teach the students of the royal academy [i.e., the *kuo-tzu*, "scions of the realm"],

---

[20] *Ibid.*, v/12 [modified from Waley, p. 110], and vii/23 [following Waley, p. 128].

but they were not given to the common people. For this reason, if the common people of the ordinary population wanted to become informed about affairs of the past, they found the way closed and no means whereby to receive such knowledge. Hence there has come down the references to 'officials who pursued studies under the Masters in Instruction'; and to the fact that 'official-scholars were among the Great Officers.' " [Cf. the *Li Chi*, i; Legge, pp. 63–64, paragraph 17; and xvIII/2/2, Legge, p. 168, paragraph 28.] It is clearly evident from this that if one were not of the noble officers or their official attendants, he had no way of learning about the body of practices that made up statecraft. But from the time Confucius read the documents [at the office] of the *Chu-hsia* [a reference to Confucius' visit to the royal Chou court to investigate the records of ritual in the archives there, presided over by Lao Tan, who held the office of *Chu-hsia-shih* 柱下史, i.e. archivist, as told in *Shih Chi*, ch. 47,] and 'transmitted what was taught him without making up anything of his own' [*Analects* vII/1, adapted from the Waley translation, p. 123], excised and corrected the wording of the Six Texts [i.e., the *Six Classics*, embodying the Six Disciplines], disseminating them among the people, people from that time onward knew about the revered texts of their tradition, and in private homes one could study the historical documents." Chang also wrote: "In the Spring and Autumn Period and earlier, office-holders were mostly hereditary ministers. A man who raised himself up from the ranks of fishermen and herdsmen did so by happening to meet with the favor of a prince, and using the propitious circumstances of the moment to advance. Normally it was impossible. This by no means proves that talent was not to be found in rustic surroundings. It was simply a case of such talent having no training in the texts on which government was based, of 'being remote and therefore bogged down' [*Analects*, xIx/4; cf. Legge, p. 341], inadequately equipped to match their talent against the hereditary ministers. The one or two who were raised up and employed were merely officials having specialized skills, and they were given posts of the nature of subsidiary positions. Subsequently, Confucius disseminated the written records, and trained his three thousand followers, and aided them to achieve prominence throughout the seventy-two states. They learned to study the people, to understand local conditions, and to be able to identify appropriate political measures. His followers and their descendants rose and strove to advance themselves, in open competition with the holders of political power. After the death of the Sage, it was less than a hundred years until the Six States arose and hereditary ministerships were abandoned. [The Six States are those which endured through the centuries of war and annexation, and which remained to the end of the Warring States Period.] If any commoner possessed skills, he was qualified to serve as a minister or a chancellor. In consequence, the system of social classes was broken down, and men of humble origins were permitted to rise. This has remained operative until the present day.''[21] This sets forth the achievement of Confucius in its most pertinent essentials.

That is, if Confucius is to be discussed in terms of his deeds, his greatest achievement lies in establishing a body of thought and learning, based on older traditions, by means of which the scholar "superior man" could advance in office, and which he could apply in practical fashion. Further, it lay in his instructing common people in this, and developing in that way a new ruling class founded upon intellectual and ethical qualities. Still, he was able to bring about such an achievement, in part to be sure because of his own earnest search for knowledge and his native intellectual endowment, but in part also because of the influence of the times. For if the moment had not been ripe for it, even had a person possessed the greatest wisdom and produced the wisest sayings, would there have been other persons able to grasp their significance and accept them?

Confucius was born in the Twenty-second year of Duke Hsiang of Lu (551 B.C.) and died in the Sixteenth year of Duke Ai (479 B.C.). This was just at the end of the Spring and Autumn Period, at the beginning of the period of transition from the era of the feudal world to that of the autocratic empire. The Institutes of Chou were in decline but had not yet completely disappeared; the old social classes were on the point of being destroyed but were still much in evidence. In his own personal experience Confucius had been steeped in the influences of the old social order; and yet he was able to discover wholly new meaning in the institutions of the old society. Thus he was led to the desire to use his discoveries as the instrument for reforming and restoring the old order. Yet the noble lords and hereditary ministers of his own time were not necessarily capable of accepting and applying his teachings, so he transmitted his skills to commoners, making it possible for the most accomplished of them to serve lords and ministers, thereby gaining the opportunity to apply what they had learned. Inevitably there existed then sons of commoners who were anxious to raise themselves up from the fields and the market places, but who had not yet discovered means for doing so. With the aid of the education that Confucius imparted to them, they eagerly pursued such careers.

The most important elements of the Confucian learning thus were governmental principles and administrative methods. The means for achieving its objectives was teaching. The goal was service in government.

---

[21] *T'ai-yen wen-lu, ch'u pien, ch.* 2, "Po chien-li K'ung-chiao yi" ["Refuting the Proposal to Establish Confucianism as a Religion"]. For the use made of the Six Disciplines and the Six Ritual Deportments by teachers of the national academy in teaching the students there, see the *Chou Li*, "Ti-kuan, Ssu-t'u."

His learning drew mainly upon the documents and historical records of the old aristocracy, but he established his teachings largely with sons of poor and humble people. When Chang Ping-lin writes about the effect of Confucius in breaking down the old system of social classes, he does not mean that the old aristocracy was pressed down to equality with lictors and clerks. Rather it was that some commoners were enabled to raise themselves to the level of the aristocracy. Seen in these terms, Confucius by no means failed to serve the old order as its loyal supporter; but at the same time he was the benefactor and friend of the common man. Confucius' followers were in large part men of humble origins; therein lies the important reason for so judging him.

Even though instructing people in the *Odes* and *History* and the Six Disciplines as an instrument for their advancement in public life came to be widely done only because of Confucius, it did not begin with Confucius. Chang Ping-lin has said: " '*Ju*' had three meanings." ". . . It was a generic name: all who were versed in specialized arts were called *ju*." ". . . It was a class name applied to [those of] the *ju* who had knowledge of rites, music, archery, charioteering, calligraphy, and mathematics. . . ." [I.e., the Six Disciplines.] "It was a proper name . . . [referring to those of] the *ju* who regarded Confucius as their Master."[22] [*Ju* is usually translated "Confucian" in post-Confucian times; Chang here emphasizes the pre-Confucius tradition as well as the post-Confucius sense of the word. In some contexts it may also be translated "literati."] From this it is evident that the name "*ju*" was not established by Confucius, but that the way of the *ju* was enlarged in its significance by him. Confucius himself maintained the distinction between "the *ju* of the superior man" and "the *ju* of the small man."[23] Confucius did not make explicit wherein the distinction between the two lay. However, from the fact that he criticized Fan Ch'ih as "a small man" for requesting instruction in farming, we can assume that the superior man was not supposed to concern himself with seeking material goods for his own use [but was to serve his fellow humans]. When we note that he ridiculed some of his followers for being "household servitors,"[24] we can be certain that the superior man was to be scrupulous about whether to serve or to withdraw into retirement.

"Superior man" [*chün-tzu*] in Confucius' mind was a term of ethical

---

[22] *Kuo-ku lun-heng, hsia,* "Yuan ju."

[23] *Analects,* VI/11.

[24] The *Shih Chi,* "Chung-ni ti-tzu lieh chuan," *ch.* 67, states: "Confucius said, 'The whole world lacks men of integrity; many are those who take posts as household servitors, and serve at the seats of the feudal lords. [I.e., they do not serve as courtiers of the legitimate dukes or the Chou Kings.] There is only Chi-tz'u [Kung-hsi Ai], who has never so served.' "

evaluation, as well as a designation of status. Simultaneously to possess both virtue and position was the highest standard toward which the "superior man" should strive. The intent of the Confucian school's teachings was that position should be achieved because of virtue. The man who was at once *ju* and a "small man"[25] was a flagrant violator of the chief tenet underlying his teachings. With this in mind, then, it can be said that Confucius had two objects: the first was to transform commoners who possessed neither virtue nor official position into superior men who possessed virtue but might lack a position; the second was to assure that virtuous gentlemen [men of status] lacking positions would become superior men who possessed both virtue and position. [The lack of an English word possessing all of the meanings of *chün-tzu* forces the translation "gentlemen" at some points, as contrasted with the translation "superior man" elsewhere; both appear in this sentence.] His ideal somewhat resembled Plato's "philosopher king."[26] The sad thing is that although Confucius set forth a very high ideal, so few among his disciples were capable of carrying it out with unflagging zeal. Those among the seventy disciples who gained something from the teachings of "virtuous action" in many cases became lofty-minded recluse-gentlemen. Those who gained something from the instructions on the arts of speech and on administration [cf. *Analects*, xi/2/2] were inevitably attracted to the pursuit of emolument and the means of rapid advance; but even so they seldom gained positions beyond the rank of household servitor or steward

[25] *Mo Tzu, ch.* 34, "Fei Ju," Part ii: "For [the Confucianist] in spring and summer begs for grains. When the five grains are all gathered in, he betakes himself off to the funerals. All the sons and grandsons are taken along and are filled to satiety with food and drink. It is sufficient for him to manage but a few funerals. He depends on other families for his wealth and on the products of others' fields to maintain his dignity. When a death takes place in a rich family, he will rejoice greatly; for it is his opportunity for clothing and food." [Modified slightly from Y. P. Mei, *The Works of Motze*, pp. 202–03.] *Hsün Tzu, ch.* 8, "Ju hsiao": "They have large clothes, wide girdles, and high hats; they sketchily follow the early Kings, but are satisfied with the teaching of a confused age; . . . they invoke the early Kings in order to cheat stupid people and seek for a living; if they get fed and accumulate enough to fill their mouths they are satisfied; they follow their master and they serve their talkative favorites and their upper class retainers; they are quite like life-long prisoners, not daring to have any other purposes—such are vulgar Confucians." [Modified from Dubs, *The Works of Hsüntze*, pp. 110–11.] *Mencius*, vii/ii/30, records that Mencius went to the State of T'eng, where the keeper of the place [where he and his party were lodged] suspected one of his followers of having pilfered a sandal, which shows clearly the lack of respect in which Confucians were held by the society at large. [Cf. Legge, *Mencius*, pp. 492–93.]

[26] *Plato: The Republic*, Book iv (Jowett, third edition 1888) 473: "Until philosophers are kings, or the kings and princes of this world have the spirit and power of philosophy, and political greatness and wisdom meet in one . . . cities will never have rest from their evils, —no, nor the human race. . . ." [Pp. 170–71.]

of a fief, in this being less successful than Confucius himself, who at one time reached the rank of a Great Officer.

The most obvious reason for this failure is the limitations of the historical environment. For the ducal house had declined into insignificance by Confucius' time, and the real political power in the State of Lu had shifted to the hands of the Great Officers and household servitors.[27] To expect them to break all precedent and bestow important positions on other men would indeed have been expecting too much. And when we note that Confucius himself repeatedly suffered slander and vilification,[28] we gain therein a glimpse of the real state of affairs of the time. For even though the hereditary ministers were, as a class, in decline, class concepts still existed. For a petty commoner who had tilled fields and practiced husbandry to achieve place among ministers and chief officials might not have been reconcilable with the fixed ways of the age. It had to wait until the spirit of the times had undergone a fundamental transformation before the status of the "superior-man *ju*" could gradually be raised. Tzu-hsia and Tzu-ssu were teachers and friends of the rulers of states; Mencius could feel contemptuous of a ministership in the State of Ch'i, and resign it. Here we see the ideal of Confucius being realized at least in part. But this practice of respecting the scholar-official was in fact instituted by Marquis Wen of Wei, who as a Great Officer was able to usurp the throne. Tzu-hsia, who had received from Confucius himself the warning against "practicing the *ju* of the small man," nonetheless accepted the honor and emolument of this ruler, an action manifestly contrary to the Master's teachings. Tzu-hsia's student, Li K'e, went even further in service to the same ruler in his program for "exploiting natural resources to the fullest degree" [this was a proto-Legalist approach to statecraft; see Chapter One, p. 3 and footnote 58,] and is still further

[27] In *Analects*, xvi/3 [Legge, p. 311], Confucius states: "The revenue of the State has left the ducal House now for five generations. The government has been in the hands of [*tai*] the Great Officers for four generations. On this account, the descendants of the three Huan are much reduced." [Legge's note on this passage explains that the Dukes of Lu had become mere pensioners of their Great Officers.] The *Chi-chu* [Commentary of Chu Hsi] states: "From the time that Duke Wen died [609 B.C.], and Duke [Chuang's son] Sui murdered [Duke Wen's son and heir] Tzu-ch'ih, and elevated Duke Hsüan, all the rulers, failed to govern properly, onward through the reigns of [Dukes] Ch'eng, Hsiang, Chao, and Ting, five Dukes in all. The word *tai* 逮 means *chi* 及 ["to come to"; Legge translates the word *tai* in the passage above, "the government *has been in the hands of . . .* "]. From the time when Wu Tzu of the Chi clan commenced to control the government by himself, onward through [his descendants] Tao, P'ing, Huan, his heirs [continued his control] for four generations, and then they came under the domination of their household servitor, Yang Hu." Refer also to Chapter One, footnote 8, above.

[28] Confucius suffered slanderous attacks on himself in the states of Ch'i, Lu, Wei, and Ch'u. See *Shih Chi*, *ch.* 47, "K'ung-tzu shih chia."

shadowed with disrepute for having "abetted a tyrant." [Literally, "supported King Chieh," in analogy to the somewhat legendary evils of the last ruler of the Hsia dynasty.] From this time onward, it tended to be true of commoners who reached the ranks of minister and premier that: "the lower down [their origins], the more they were like that." [*Mei hsia yü k'uang*, 每下愈况, cf. *Chuang Tzu*, XXII.] They not only were not "superior-men *ju*," but in most cases were anti-Confucian advocates of war and of rigid laws, and opportunistic promoters of the shifting "vertical" and "horizontal" alliances. These examples all reflect the changing tenor of life in this period of great change, which had developed a long way beyond the environment in which Confucius originally established his teachings. The doctrines of benevolence and righteousness could not readily be adapted to the conditions of the age of the seven martial chieftains [i.e., the seven ducal houses of the Age of the Warring States]. Thus in terms of merit for breaking down the old social class system, Confucius was no less an instigator of rebellion than were Ch'en She and Wu Kuang. [Ch'en She, or Ch'en Sheng and Wu Kuang, insurgent heroes whose rebellion against the Second Emperor of Ch'in, 210–206 B.C., opened the period of civil war out of which the Han dynasty emerged.] Yet, despite all, those who benefitted the most [were not men of Confucian ideal, but] were the ilk of Lord Shang and Han Fei, Su Ch'in, and Chang Yi, and other such promoters of "aberrant doctrines" and "heterodox theories." [Lord Shang and Han Fei were the two greatest exponents of Legalist thought and practice; Su Ch'in and Chang Yi were leading figures in the development of the amoral tactics of the Diplomatists; they typify the new mode in Warring States political life.]

To proceed one step further, Confucius' intent was to raise commoners to an equal footing with the nobles. Moreover, his thought represented a synthesis of the Way of the "Former Kings"; hence it regarded the feudal political institutions and clan-law society as necessary conditions for the successful realization of that Way. Thus the words and deeds of his whole life were forcefully directed toward the clear definition of privilege and status, restraining encroachment and impropriety, and emphasizing binding social relationships. He displayed this in planning the capture of the strongholds of the Three Families when their illicit power had become excessive, and in urging a punitive campaign against Ch'en Heng, who had murdered Duke Chien of Ch'i. [For these events see *Tso Chuan*, Legge, p. 781; and *Analects* XIV/22, Legge, p. 284.] And there are several other instances of his lending support to activities of this nature. However, "it passes on just like this." [*Analects* IX/16; following Legge, p. 222.] The movement of history could not be stopped. That feudal world that Confucius wanted to reform and preserve ultimately collapsed and disappeared very quickly. It was inevitable, under the conditions of that age, that those who practiced the *ju* of the superior man could not compete with the professional schemers of the utilitarian stamp.

If the foregoing inferences are not entirely wrong, then despite the fact that Confucius' political ideals were intended precisely for that late phase of the feudal age, they never encountered an opportunity for throughgoing realization. His ideal of "the superior-man *ju*" was surpassingly noble and magnificent. But at best it was incapable of elevating his disciples into the ranks of the aristocracy and of the great ministers. On a lesser level, it made them regard service in a private household [i.e., to be a "household servitor" of one of the great families that exercised real power without legitimate foundation] as a shameful compromise. Those Great Officers and their household servitors who usurped the powers of the ducal states and controlled their governments were the ones who in fact hastened the downfall of the great-clan aristocratic classes, and contributed to the emergence of ministers and premiers from the ranks of commoners.[29] Yet Confucius opposed and reproved them. The Son of Heaven, lord of the Chinese nation [i.e., the Chou King, nominal hegemon of the Chinese world] had been debased in prestige and deprived of power; he had long been an inadequate instrument with which to make the Way prevail. Yet Confucius defended and supported him. This spirit of the one who "knows it's no use, but keeps on doing it"[30] is both the reason for Confucius' greatness, and the reason for his failure. For the real-life achievements of the "uncrowned king" were in fact of far less consequence than the eventual impact of his wise teachings. In modern academic terms, Confucius was a great political thinker but a failure as

[29] Duke Wen of Wei and King Wei of Ch'i both were Great Officers who usurped the thrones in their states (King Wei, who first usurped that royal title, was the grandson of T'ien Ho). [T'ien Ho, who was responsible for the actual usurpation, died in 384 B.C.; his grandson, King Wei, came to the throne of Ch'i in 377.] Duke Wen [of Wei] was famous among all the feudal states for his courteous treatment of worthy men of talent, and started the custom of maintaining scholars at the State's expense. Both Wu Ch'i and Li K'e were employed by him. King Wei [of Ch'i] established the Palace of Chi-hsia, to which he invited scholars; here talent gathered in great abundance, and it became the center of thought and learning during the Period of the Warring States. (Note that Hsü Kan's [third century A.D.] *Chung Lun*, "Wang kuo p'ien" states: "Duke Huan of Ch'i established the Palace of Chi-hsia;" this would mean that it was T'ien Ho's son [not grandson] who was responsible for it.) Later on Shen Pu-hai was chief minister to Duke Chao of Han (Duke Ching when a Great Officer usurped the dukedom of Han [in 402 B.C.]; Duke Chao was the fifth generation descendant from him.) Hui Shih and Chang Yi were employed in the State of Wei (by King Hui), and Su Ch'in "hung at his belt the seals of office of chief minister in six states." The practice of commoners' becoming ministers and premiers thus became very widespread.

[30] *Analects*, xiv/41 [Waley, p. 190]; the words are those used by the gate-keeper at Shih-men [on the border of Lu] in describing Confucius.

a political reformer. His stature is greater than that of Yao and Shun because even though he lacked the position that Yao and Shun had acquired he was able to establish a body of teachings the likes of which Yao and Shun never attained. [Symbolically, Yao and Shun were the greatest of Chinese rulers. This is an allusion to Tsai Yü's appraisal of Confucius in *Mencius* II/i/2/26; Legge, p. 195.]

The rulers and the ministers of the later authoritarian era, although honoring Confucius and upholding Confucian learning, in fact did so in a selective and distorted fashion, and to serve their own private ends. [Literally *tuan chang ch'ü-yi*, "breaking the passage to pluck out an idea," or distorting the original intent by ignoring the original context.] They preserved terms such as benevolence and righteousness, but ignored their feudal age implications. They could forget the basic tenet of levelling social classes, and overlook the significance of his instruction to be the "*ju* of the superior man." Did not "Confucian ministers" who rose in officialdom unabashedly and brazenly imitate Tzu-chang in his avid pursuit of official emolument? [For which Confucius criticized him; see *Analects* II/18; cf. Legge, p. 151.] Did they not frequently even adopt methods similar to the boring of holes and climbing through gaps [like the sneaking methods of thieves; Confucius used the comparison, see *Analects* XVII/12; Waley, p. 213] and become "vulgar Confucians" who "declaimed about the Former Kings to deceive the foolish, for the sake of material gain?" [Literally "to get clothing and food"; taken from a description of "vulgar Confucians" in the *Hsün Tzu*; see footnote 25.] Those who were capable of being "refined Confucians" and who practiced neither trickery nor deception were but a handful of the best. Confucius wanted to transform the common man *ju* into the superior-man *ju*; men of later ages often "took over [the forms of] benevolence and righteousness, and used them to commit thievery" [an allusion to *Chuang Tzu*, x, cf. Watson, *Complete Chuang Tzu*, p. 110], adopting the "superior man" appellation in order to carry out their "small man" purposes. To designate the Confucians of Han and later ages "Hsüntzian Confucians"[31] would seem to be exaggerated praise.[32]

[31] T'an Ssu-t'ung, [1865–98, in his] *Jen-hsüeh*, "*hsia*" [does so, intending thereby to deprecate].

[32] For more on the events of Confucius' life see *Shih Chi, ch.* 47, "K'ung-tzu shih chia," and *K'ung-tzu chia-yü* [translated in part by R. P. Kramers as *The School Sayings of Confucius*]. Recent scholars consider these sources to be in large part falsified and unreliable. There are chronological biographies (*nien-p'u*) by Cheng Huan, Chiang Yung, Ts'ai K'ung-hsin, and Hsia Hung-chi. Ts'ui Shu, in his *Chu-ssu k'ao hsin lu*, has made many corrections and emendations of the older scholarship on the subject. In addition to these there are many other relevant items, too numerous to list exhaustively. [In western languages, the most influential work in recent years is H. G. Creel's *Confucius, The Man and the Myth*, N.Y., 1949, also published in paperback as *Confucius and the Chinese Way*, N.Y., 1960. This book, while

SECTION TWO
"Following Chou" and the "Rectification of Names"

CONFUCIUS' "following the Chou" has been briefly discussed in the preceding chapter. This was in truth the starting point of his political thought; hence it is necessary to return to it for a somewhat more detailed discussion. Confucius said: "I may describe the rites of the Hsia dynasty, but Ch'i cannot sufficiently attest my words. I have learned the rites of the Yin dynasty, and in Sung they still continue. I have learned the rites of Chou, which are now used, and I follow Chou." He also said: "Chou had the advantage of viewing the two past dynasties. How complete and elegant are its regulations! I follow Chou."[33] Beyond these there are the passages in which Duke Ai of Lu asked him about government, and he referred to the records on wood and bamboo tablets of the reigns of Kings Wen and Wu [father and son, the founders of the Chou dynasty, whose records "*fang ts'e*" 方策 then were still in existence] and the one in which he sighed bitterly because his affairs were in such a state of decay that for long he had not had the auspicious experience of seeing the Duke of Chou in a dream.[34] [Son of King Wen and younger brother of King Wu; in Confucian eyes, the great man of early Chou times.] From this it would seem to be beyond doubt that Confucius held up the political institutions of Chou as his standard and model. Yet, inasmuch as Confucius was "a man of Yin," were there not elements of "the rites of Yin" in his thought, or did he draw exclusively on the Chou rites? [*Li* is customarily translated "rites" or "ceremonies," but the scope of these was so broad that the translation "*The Institutes of Chou*" is often used for the title of the work known as the *Chou Li* or the *Chou Kuan*. It is in this broader sense that the word "rites" is used in the following passages.]

From the incomplete documentary evidence that exists today, we can conclude that in all places where Confucius' political thought touches upon questions of institutions there are extremely few elements of the Yin rites. It is possible that his motive in promoting ideas leading to the breakdown of rigid social classes [i.e., the aristocracy established by the

---

deservedly popular as a detailed biographical and historical study, adopts much of the extreme skepticism characteristic of Chinese scholarship fifty years ago, but since largely rejected as overly skeptical.]

[33] See, respectively, *The Chung-yung*, ch. 28 [Legge, p. 424] and *Analects*, III/14 [Legge, p. 160].

[34] See, respectively, *The Chung-yung*, ch. 20 [Legge, p. 405] and *Analects*, VII/5 [Legge, p. 196]. The comments of his immediate followers and disciples also agree in this with Confucius' own remarks. An example is Tzu-kung's testimony that the Master's learning was of the Way of Kings Wen and Wu, see Chapter one, footnote 12, above.

Chou following their conquest of the Yin] may have been to liberate the
Yin descendants. Anything beyond this is difficult to conceive of. There
are three reasons for this conclusion: (1) The civilization of Yin apparently
had reached only a very low level of development. Modern scholars have
in some cases concluded that it was still in the stone age,[35] in others that
it already used bronze.[36] In the degree to which it still clung to the
"substance" [as opposed to Chou "refinement"], it was in any event still
crude and simple, incompatible with the *ju* ideal. (2) Even if the level of
the Yin-Shang culture had been very high and the Chou had accepted the
Yin rites, still, Confucius in following the Chou, was only indirectly adopting the rites of Yin. He was not simultaneously drawing on two distinct
institutional systems and working out their synthesis. For the fall of the
Yin dynasty was already an event six hundred years in the past. Not only
was there no hope of re-establishing that state; most of its descendants
by this time surely tended to be culturally assimilated. We can prove this
by several items of evidence: The State of Sung had been the fief given to
Wei Tzu; it was commanded to carry on the sacrifices to the Yin royal
ancestors; this should have enabled it to preserve something of the Yin
rites. [Wei Tzu was of the Yin royal family; he had rebelled against the
last Yin king before the Chou conquest.] Yet according to the account
in the "Genealogical Table of the House of Sung Wei-tzu" in the *Shih
Chi, ch.* 38, the succession passed from Wei Tzu, named Ch'i, to his younger
brother Wei-chung. From Wei-chung it passed to his son Chi. From Chi
it passed to Duke Ting, named Shen; and from Duke Ting, named Shen,
it passed to Duke Min, named Kung; and from Kung to his younger
brother, Duke Yang, named Hsi. The names "Min" and "Hsi" are
posthumous honorific names. After this there followed in succession Dukes
Li, Li, Hui, and Ai. Thus we see that after four reigns from the founding
of the State of Sung it had already adopted the Chou culture's system of
posthumous honorific names.[37] Is this not evidence of cultural assimilation?
The "Genealogical Table of the House of Lu Po-ch'in" in the *Shih Chi, ch.*
33, also records: "Duke Po-ch'in of Lu when first enfiefed went to Lu,
and only three years later came to report on his governing. [Po-ch'in,
the first Duke of Lu, was a son of the Duke of Chou, and thus a grandson
of King Wen.] The Duke of Chou asked: 'Why is it so slow?' Po-ch'in

---

[35] See "Introduction," footnote 37, above. [Archaeological opinion in the last thirty
years has fully verified the view that the Yin civilization should be designated "Bronze
Age culture"; the subject has undergone rapid change as new archaeological finds are
reported and studied.]

[36] Ma Heng, *Chung-kuo chih t'ung-ch'i shih-tai* and Kuo Mo-jo *Chung-kuo ku-tai she-hui
yen-chiu.*

[37] *Li Chi, ch.* 3, "T'an Kung," Part I, "The posthumous honorific is a practice of the
Chou." [See also Legge, *Li Ki,* Vol. 1, p. 144, paragraph 33; his translation is worded
differently.]

replied: 'I am changing their customs and reforming their rites; only after three years have I been able to uproot them.' " This fully shows that the State of Lu exerted itself in the task of transforming the Yin people there to the Chou pattern; it reflects a policy quite different from the *laissez-faire* policy of Duke T'ai in Ch'i, who said: "Let the rites be conducted in accordance with their customs." [Ch'i T'ai-kung Wang, unlike Po-ch'in who was enfeoffed in Lu, was not a member of the Chou royal house.] Confucius said: "A single change could bring Ch'i to the level of Lu; and a single change would bring Lu to the Way." [I.e., the Way of the Former Kings, especially the Chou Founders, Kings Wen and Wu.]³⁸ The old commentaries on this passage say that the State of Ch'i, whose customs were fostered under a hegemonic state naturally would be inferior to those in the State of Lu. [I.e., *Pa-kuo*, hegemonic state, or one which imposed its authority by force, referring to Ch'i under the Duke Huan, 684–642 B.C.] Actually, however, the Yin-derived practices in the State of Ch'i remained more deeply entrenched, and Ch'i's accommodation to the standards of Chou was relatively superficial, therefore it was said to be farther from "the Way." That the rites of Chou were to be found above all in the State of Lu was universally acknowledged. After the Way of the Chou had suffered the setbacks inflicted during the reigns of King Yu [781–771 B.C.] and Li [878–842 B.C.], Confucius was all the more faced with the fact that if he abandoned Lu, with all its shortcomings, still there was no better place to which he could go.³⁹ Confucius was born in this state which was the center of the old Chou culture, where his grandfather, like his father, apparently, had served it as Great Officers. And Confucius himself was quite obviously assimilated into the Chou culture. That he was heart and soul dedicated to the Chou rites and institutions is wholly consonant with the nature of

³⁸ *Analects*, vi/22 [modified slightly from Waley, p. 120]. Refer also to the *Tso Chuan*, Fourth year of Duke Ting, the passage cited in Chapter One, footnote 17, of the present work. Also, *Analects*, xiii/7 [modified from Legge, p. 266], where Confucius is quoted as saying: "In government, Lu and Wei are brothers." And in the *Tso Chuan* passage cited above, after describing separately the enfiefment of Po-ch'in in the State of Lu and of K'ang-shu in the State of Wei, it remarks: "Both in Wei and in Lu they were to commence their government according to the principles of Shang, but their boundaries were defined according to the rules of Chou." [Legge, p. 754.] (Commentary of Tu Yi, the word *suo* 索 means *fa* 法) [Legge translates it "rules"]. Confucius' meaning [in the line from the *Analects* above] is probably that the governments of the two states both represented inheritances from the Shang that were transformed according to the Chou model, and not merely that their founders were in fact brothers.

³⁹ *Li Chi, ch.* 9, "Li Yün": Confucius said, "Ah! Alas! I observe that the Way of Chou was greatly corrupted in the time of Kings Yu and Li. But were I to leave Lu, where should I go [to find it better preserved]? The border sacrifice of Lu [performed as an] offering to the royal ancestors [of Chou] is contrary to the rites. How the [Great Way of the] Duke of Chou has fallen into decay." [Modified from Legge, *Li Ki*, Vol. i, p. 372.]

the situation. (3) Confucius was not entirely consistent in the way he
accepted or rejected the rites and cultural practices of the Yin. Yet it
seems that those aspects which he adopted were in all cases minor matters
relating only to private life or to social life, and having no direct or important bearing on government. An example appears in Chapter 41,
"Ju Hsing," of the *Li Chi*, where it tells that Confucius replied to Duke
Ai's inquiry about the dress of the *ju*, saying: "When I was young, I lived
in Lu, and wore the garment with large sleeves; when I was grown up
I lived in Sung and was then capped with the *chang-fu* cap [of Yin]."
Ch. 4, "T'an-kung," Part II, states: "Under the Yin, the tablet was put
in its place on the change of the mourning at the end of twelve months;
under the Chou, when the [continuous] wailing was over. Confucius
approved the practice of Yin." [Cf. Legge, *Li Ki*, Vol. II, p. 402, and
Vol. I, p. 172.] Book 15, "Wei Ling Kung," of the *Analects* contains Yen
Yuan's question about the governing of the state, and Confucius' reply,
which included the remark that the ruler should ride in the state carriage
of Yin. [*Analects* xv/10; following Legge, p. 295.] These are examples of
his following the Yin.[40] When K'ang-shu was enfiefed in the State of Wei,
the Duke of Chou issued his "Proclamation on Wine," containing ample
evidence that excessive drinking was one of the bad customs of the Yin
people. [K'ang-shu was a younger brother of King Wu, and was enfiefed
in the Yin stronghold of Wei in order to oversee and govern the conquered
Yin population there; he issued the "Chiu Kao," cf. *Shoo King*, i.e., *Documents*, "The Book of Chow," x, Legge, p. 399.] In the *Analects*, IX/15,
Confucius says of himself: "Nor have I ever been overcome with wine,"
and again, in x/8 he states that [although no limit is to be laid down]
"one must not drink wine to the point of becoming disorderly." *Ch.* 32,
"Piao Chi," in the *Li Chi* comments that "The Yin people honor spirits."
The oracle bones found at the Wastes of Yin still further display the Yin
people's shamanistic practices of consulting spirits. The *Analects*, xi/11,
contains Confucius' reply to Tzu-lu's question about how one should
serve spirits: "Till you have learnt to serve men, how can you serve
spirits?" And, the philosopher Mo Tzu, in denouncing the Confucians,
made much of the point that they did not believe in spirits and gods.

---

[40] *Ibid.*, *ch.* 3, "T'an Kung," Part I, "The people of Chou buried those who died between sixteen and nineteen in the coffins of Yin; those who died between twelve and
fifteen or between eight and eleven in the brick enclosures of Hsia; and those who died
[still younger], for whom no mourning is worn, in the earthenware enclosures of the time
of the lord of Yü." "Under the sovereigns of the Hsia dynasty, they used [at burials]
mock-vessles. . . . Under the Yin they used the [ordinary] sacrificial vessels. . . . Under
the Chou we use both." [Modified from Legge, *Li Ki*, pp. 125 and 151.] These clearly
show that the Chou institutions basically included a mixture of elements adopted from
Hsia and Shang. Confucius' statement that Chou "had the advantage of viewing the two
earlier dynasties" is thus correct, and can be demonstrated to be so.

[In the above quotations from the *Analects*, ix/15, x/8 and xi/11, Waley pp. 142, 149, 155, has been followed, with minor modifications.] "T'an-kung" [Part ii, *ch.* 4, of the *Li Chi*] records: "Under the Yin, they presented condolences immediately at the grave; under the Chou, when the son had returned and was wailing." Confucius commented: "Yin was too blunt; I follow Chou." [Legge, *Li Ki*, Vol. i, p. 170.] These are examples of his rejecting the Yin. However none of these examples, either of following or of rejecting, is adequate evidence for concluding that Confucius adopted any political institutions of the Yin.[41]

If we go one step further and infer something from the environment of Confucius' thought, we can discover more compelling reasons for concluding that he followed the political institutions of Chou. Although Confucius was conscious that he was a man of Yin, in his own service to the State of Lu he had acknowledged Chou political authority. In order not to "follow the Chou" he would have to abandon all the institutions of Kings Wen and Wu and to create something different in their place. Would that really have been possible? Moreover, Chou itself took over the Yin rites, whose regulations were at that time still "complete and elegant." Chou's rites and ordinances, its ceremonies and their appurtenances, were not necessarily opposite to those of the Yin; but they were merely more splendid and more elaborate. The records and the wise men of the States of Ch'i and Sung [identified most directly with the maintenance of Yin traditions] were inadequate; so that even had Confucius wanted to restore the institutions of the past, given that lack of evidence about the Yin rites, he would have had the greatest difficulty in finding anything on which to base any convincing claims. By that time there were already no longer any more of the "recalcitrant people" of Yin about; who was there to follow Confucius in a rebellious movement of resistance to the Chou? Confucius once remarked: "Let a man who is ignorant be fond of using his own judgment; let a man without rank be fond of assuming a directing power to himself; let a man who is living in the present age go back to the ways of antiquity;—on the persons of all who act thus calamities will be sure to come."[42] [For a slightly different translation, essentially the same in meaning, see Creel, *Confucius and the Chinese Way*, p. 219. Creel argues strongly against the possibility of this chapter of the *Chung Yung* (*Doctrine of the Mean*) being truly Confucian, but his arguments are inconclusive, particularly as regards the lines

---

[41] Hu Shih, in his "*Shuo Ju*," has stated that to be "assistant at the rites" *hsiang-li* was a professional task assigned to the Yin descendants, and that Confucius transformed the weak and compliant manner of the *ju* of Yin into the self-reliant and strong-willed attitude of the Confucian *ju*. This is a strikingly distinctive interpretation of the matter. Unfortunately, he did not also offer there a discussion of Confucius' political point of view.

[42] *The Doctrine of the Mean*, or *Chung Yung*, ch. 28 [Legge, p. 423].

quoted here.] This clearly demonstrates that Confucius' political attitude was that of a compliant Chou subject, and that his political views were conservative. Herein too lies an important reason for the favor that Confucian doctrines found in the eyes of later autocratic emperors.

The starting point of Confucius' political thought was to "follow the Chou," and his concrete proposal for carrying it out was the rectification of names. Explained in modern terms, what he called the rectification of names meant readjusting the powers and duties of ruler and minister, superior and inferior, according to the institutions of the Chou feudal world's most flourishing period. Confucius was born after the decline of the Chou, when feudal government and clan-law society had both degenerated; he himself witnessed the chaos that had upset the order of the world. Seeking the reasons for this, he could see only that the blame lay in abandoning the Chou institutions. Thus the words and deeds of his entire life were directed toward bringing about the veneration of the Chou royal house and reverence for the ruler, toward limiting the excesses and encroachments of the nobility, and toward curbing the usurpations and illicit appropriations of authority committed by ministers and subordinates. He was not unsparing in the standard he set for other men, and he was no less strict in the demands he placed on himself. Some examples may be given, such as his use in the *Spring and Autumn Annals* of the phrase: "The King's first, or correct [*cheng*] month." [*Spring and Autumn Annals*, First Year of Duke Yin; cf. Legge, *Ts'un-chew* discussion on page 4. This simply reiterated in the annals for each year the fact that, in principle, all the states acknowledged the royal Chou prerogatives in the ordering of the calendar.] In the *Analects*, xvi/2, he is recorded as saying: "When the Way prevails under Heaven all orders concerning ritual, music and punitive expeditions are issued by the Son of Heaven himself." x/1 records his reverential and cautious demeanor when in the ruler's hall of audi-

---

[43] [The position of the number indicating this footnote in the original text has been corrected here.] *Analects*, see respectively iii/1 [Legge, p. 154] and xiii/14 [Legge, p. 268]. Other examples of this [insistence on correct correspondence of name with reality] are to be found through the work, which should be examined in its entirety with this in mind. [Creel rejects the doctrine of the rectification of names, *cheng-ming*, as a later Legalist interpolation, incompatible with the spirit of Confucius. He does so, however, entirely in terms of the credibility of one sentence in the *Analects*, rather than in terms of the significance of the concept in the total system of Confucius' thought. By rejecting the one sentence in which the term appears, he feels he has proved its non-Confucian origin; but he has disregarded its presence as a functional concept throughout the *Analects*. Although the present work appeared in Chinese several years before Creel's, Creel has not responded to any of the points of view presented herein with regard to the doctrine of the rectification of names, among others; hence this note by the translator to call attention to the somewhat narrow view adopted in Creel's deservedly influential and in its way extremely valuable work. See specifically *Confucius and the Chinese Way*, p. 221; p. 313, note 11; and pp. 321–22, note 13.]

ence. ix/11 tells how he sighed sadly at the pretense of having retainers
when he in fact had none. [A pretense designed by Tzu-lu, who told the
disciples to conduct themselves, as retainers to Confucius, to display their
reverence for him when he was in his last illness. To have retainers was a
prerogative of royalty and the higher nobility only. The above three
passages drawing on the *Analects*, follow Waley's translation, pp. 204,
146, 140.] When the head of the Chi family employed eight teams of
dancers, Confucius denounced him saying: "How can he be endured."
[Only the King could employ eight teams; the head of the Chi family was
merely a usurper of the power legitimately exercised by the Duke of Lu,
and should have used no more than four teams.] When talking with Jan
Ch'iu about his coming back from attendance at the court, he insisted on
the distinction that it could not have been "affairs of state" [with which
the court had been occupied].[43] [Cf. Waley, p. 174.] Examples of this
kind are too numerous all to be cited. From these one can see that the
rectification of names was no incidental concern of Confucius. Thus when
Tzu Lu asked what was the first task of government, Confucius' answer
was: "What is necessary is to rectify names." When Duke Ching of Ch'i
asked about government, he also admonished: "Let the prince be a prince,
the minister a minister, the father a father and the son a son."[44] To set
forth more what Confucius intended by this passage, if persons who were
rulers or ministers, fathers or sons, would consider these words and reflect
on their significance, in each case fulfilling to the limit the responsibilities
attendant upon their designated position in society, and employing only
those material things which were properly to be used by them, then order
would be perfectly achieved, thereafter all manner of commerce could
be conducted, and all the people could live together in peace. For when
cornered vessels no longer have corners,[45] the state is no longer a state.

---

[44] *Ibid.*, respectively, xiii/3 [Legge, p. 263] and xii/11 [here following Waley, p. 166;
Legge, p. 256, is essentially the same]. In the latter place, Duke Ching, on hearing Confucius' reply, sighed and said: "How true! For indeed when the prince is not a prince, the
minister not a minister, the father not a father, the son not a son, one may have a dish of
millet in front of one and yet not know if one will live to eat it." [Legge translates the last
line: "Although I have my revenue, can I enjoy it?"]

[45] *Ibid.*, vi/23 [Legge, p. 192]: "The Master said, 'A cornered vessel without corners—
A strange cornered vessel! A strange cornered vessel.'" The [Chu Hsi commentary]
Chi-chu comments: "Ku [i.e., a cornered vessel] means of roof ridge corner, or it may also
mean a wine vessel, or also a strip of wood; all of these are items which have corners."
It further states: "Master Ch'eng [Yi] says that a *ku* vessel that lacks its own form is not
then a *ku*. (Lines omitted) Similarly a ruler who lacks the proper Way of a ruler is not then
a ruler. If a minister fails in the responsibilities of his office, then his position is in fact an
empty one." The passages in the *Six Classics* that make clear and explicit the doctrine of
rectifying names and submitting to the rites are very numerous. The issue emerges very
clearly for example, in the [*Li Chi, ch.* 9] "Li Yün," Section One, where it states: "The
border sacrifice of Lu performed as an offering to the royal ancestors of Chou is contrary

[Following Legge's translation; other explanations of Ku, "the four-cornered vessel," have long been debated, but they do not affect the sense of the passage. Cf. Waley, *Analects*, p. 120, n. 5.] Thus it becomes evident that the rectification of names is indeed the indispensable condition for all government.

The rectification of names demands reliance upon a concrete standard. The standard that Confucius took as his basis was the institutional system of the Chou's flourishing period. [I.e., the first reigns of the dynasty, especially those of Kings Ch'eng and K'ang, traditional dates 1114–1052 B.C., or more loosely, the period before the disorders of A.D. 770 that forced the abandonment of the Western Capital.] In the narrowest sense of specific political institutions, it means those [recorded on] "wood and bamboo tablets" of the reigns of Kings Wen and Wu. It means to rectify the names according to the government of Kings Wen and Wu; hence it is said [Confucius] "elegantly displayed the regulations of Wen and Wu." [Cf. *Doctrine of the Mean*, ch. 30, following Legge's translation, p. 427.] In the broader sense of political systems, it meant the "Institutes of Chou": to use the regulations and ordinances of the Duke of Chou as the basis for rectifying names. Hence he said: "I have learned the rites of Chou." And what Confucius referred here to as "rites" *li* were of course not limited to the details of ceremonial acts and the ritual forms of the capping ceremony, of marriage, of burial, and of sacrifice and the like. The rites were in fact the whole corpus of the society's institutions; and if man could "overcome himself and submit to the rites," then "everything under Heaven would be restored to benevolence [*jen*]." [*Analects*, xii/1.] If Confucius' rectification of names could but be carried out, then government, which had fallen into the hands of the Great Officers, would be returned to the ducal courts, and those rulers of states who waged wars [against one another] would cease to do so and conduct punitive expeditions only at the command of the celestial king. The decline and disorder of the Spring and Autumn Period would be restored to the Age of Great Peace of the reigns of Kings Ch'eng and K'ang. The Warring States era would never arise, and The First Emperor would have no opportunity to accomplish his unification. Seen in these terms, "the place of Confucius' political thought in the late Chou period was somewhat analogous to that of Socrates' follower Isocrates in Athens. Although Isocrates produced no profound and comprehensive thought comparable to that of Confucius, yet in advocating a restoration of the ancestral polity devised by Solon, he was somewhat similar to Confucius' exposition of the theme of follow-

---

to the rites" . . . to the end of the chapter where it says "We have that condition which may be described as 'an infirm state.' ". . . [For fuller evidence, refer to this work.] [Cf. footnote 39 above; the passages referred to are found in Legge, *Li Ki*, pp. 372–76.]

ing the Chou.''[46] The intimacy of the relationship between Confucius' thought and the feudal world can be glimpsed herein.[47]

SECTION THREE
Jen (Benevolence)

"FOLLOWING Chou" and the "rectification of names" constitute the starting point of Confucius' political thought, and also constitute his specific advocacy of a political system. If Confucius' learning had stopped with this, he would have been nothing more than a rear-guard defender of feudalism, a compliant subject to the Chou pattern, a loyal member of the conservative camp; nothing there explains how he ultimately gained a status described as "more worthy than Yao and Shun." [See above, p. 155.] Confucius could follow the Chou, without being limited to the "tablets of wood and bamboo." He could acknowledge the political authority of the rulers of his time, but he was by no means satisfied with contemporary conditions. Within the Chou institutional system Confucius discovered profound and far-reaching significance and purpose; consequently the institutions of the rulers of his age tended to be regarded as transcending the age, and therein becoming idealized. The heart of this discovery was the concept of "*jen*." [Legge translates *jen* variously as "per-"perfect virtue" and as "benevolence," Waley as "Goodness," Creel as "virtue," Fung Yu-lan in his *Short History* as "human-heartedness," following Bodde, etc. W. T. Chan prefers "humanity"; that is perhaps the closest equivalent semantically, but it is awkward to use. Here *jen*

---

[46] See my *Reference Materials for the Study of Chinese Political Thought*, "Introduction," Section one. Isocrates (436–338 B.C.): *Areopagiticus*, "patrios politeia" (Ancestral Polity); Barker: *Greek Political Theory*, pp. 101 ff.

[47] Ho Hsiu, and other such persons, in the Han dynasty said that Confucius "regarded the Chou as the new [regime] and the Sung state as [representing] the old [the defunct Yin dynasty], and the *Spring and Autumn Annals* as [depicting the regime of] a new king." He further said that there were "Three Ages" in the Spring and Autumn Period, and that "The age that [Confucius] saw directly" (the reigns of Dukes Chao, Ting, and Ai) were "resplendently governed as an era of Great Peace." The Ch'ing scholar K'ang Yu-wei and others cited and further developed these ideas, stating that Confucius created a pattern for all ages. All such interpretations are incompatible with the purport of "following the Chou," and appear on the other hand to conform to the later Kung-yang scholars' theory that Confucius sought justification in antiquity for institutional reform. There is no reason to believe that these interpretations have any foundation in historical fact whatsoever. The author has already dealt with this in his review of Wu K'ang's "Les trois theories du Tch'ouen Ts'ieou, interpretées par Tong Tsong-chou d'apres les principes de l'école de Kong-yang" [*Tsing Hua Journal*, Vol. 8, No. 1, reprinted in K. C. Hsiao, *Chi-yuan Wen-ts'un*, pp. 191–95]. The subject will also be taken up again in this chapter, below, in connection with the discussion of "Great Community and Lesser Tranquility" [Section 6, below.]

and the translation "benevolence" will be used interchangeably.] Liang Ch'i-ch'ao has said: "Whenever Confucians have spoken of ethics and of government, they have always taken *jen* as their basis." [*Hsien Ch'in cheng-chih ssu-hsiang shih*, p. 67, in *Yin-ping-shih ho-chi, chuan-chi*, Vol. 13.] This is a definitive conclusion.

The implications of the word *jen* are extremely complex. If one simply looks at all of the quotations of Confucius in the *Analects*, the content of the term is rather diverse.[48] Here we need not engage in a detailed discussion of this. If we speak merely of how relevant it is for political thought, then what Confucius called *jen* is an enlargement of self-respect, extended to become an attitude of love or concern for others. Hence when Fan Ch'ih inquired about *jen*, Confucius said: "It is to love *all* men." [*Analects*, XII/22/1; Legge, p. 260.] Chung-kung asked about *jen* and the Master said: "Do not do to others what you would not like yourself."[49] Tzu-kung asked about *jen*, and Confucius said: "Now the man of benevolence [*jen*] wishing to be established himself, seeks also to establish others; wishing to be enlarged himself, he seeks also to enlarge others. To be able to judge of others by what is nigh in ourselves;—this may be called the way of benevolence."[50] Thus the achievement of *jen* has its beginnings in subjective emotions but in the end lies in objective deeds.

The whole of social and political life, as Confucius saw it, was in fact but an arena for the manifestation of benevolent [*jen*] conduct. The man of *jen* first cultivated his own subjective benevolent mind [*jen hsin*],[51] then extended his objective benevolent conduct from the nearer to the more distant, according to the limits of his own ability. This began in filial piety and fraternal submission in the family,[52] and ended in the "extensive dispensation of succor to the masses" ["*po shih chi chung,*" 博施濟衆 cf. *Analects* VI/28; Legge, p. 194], so that "everything under Heaven would revert to benevolence." ["*T'ien-hsia kuei jen,*" cf. *Analects* XII/1; Legge, p. 250; both Legge and Waley construe this differently.][53]

[48] Ts'ai Yuan-p'ei has remarked that *jen* is "a term that comprehensively pervades all the virtues, and perfects the human character" (*Chung-kuo lun-li-hsüeh shih*). This statement most adequately expresses the complexity of meaning that it connotes. [Cf. Chan, *Source Book*, pp. 788–89.]

[49] *Analects*, XII/2 [Waley, p. 162].

[50] *Ibid.*, VI/28 [modified from Legge, p. 194]. Refer also to *The Great Learning, Commentary*, Chapter X, "The principle with which, as with a measuring-square, [the ruler] may regulate his conduct." [Legge, p. 373.]

[51] Among Confucius' disciples, Yen Yüan's achievement [in *jen*] was the greatest. Thus it was said of him "Such was Hui [Yen Yüan's formal name] that for three months there would be nothing in his mind contrary to perfect virtue [*jen*]. The others may attain to this on some days or in some months, but nothing more." *Analects*, VI/28 [Legge, p. 186].

[52] *Analects*, I/2/2, "Filial piety and fraternal submission!—are they not the root of all benevolent actions?" [Legge, pp. 138–39.]

[53] *Ibid.*, VI/28/1, "Tzu-kung said, 'Suppose the case of a man extensively dispensing

In the *Great Learning* there is the passage: "Their persons being cultivated, their families were regulated. Their families being regulated, their States were rightly governed. Their States being rightly governed, the whole kingdom was made tranquil and happy." [Legge, p. 359.] This is an adequate explanation of the process of growth and far-reaching extension that would stem from the benevolent mind and benevolent action. Thus, in terms of personal cultivation, *jen* is a matter of one's individual ethics. But in terms of practice, *jen* is additionally both social ethics and political principle. When Confucius spoke about *jen* he was in fact smelting the ore of ethics, social relationships, and politics together in one crucible; he was bringing others, the self, the family, and the state into alignment through the development of "one all-pervading" concept. [The metaphor in the last clause refers to *Analects* IV/15; Legge, p. 169.]

The relationship of the world and the self, [literally *wu*, 物 i.e., all the myriad things of the phenomenal world; and *wo*, 我 the subjective ego], while conditioned by distinctions of proximity and of priority, was not a distinction of the internal versus the external or of the unimportant versus the important. If we were to attempt a comparison of Confucius' understanding of *jen* with European theories, then we would have to note that this concept is on the one hand different from that of emphasis on groups and the de-emphasis of the individual as encountered in collectivism, and simultaneously is dissimilar to the aggrandizement of the self and the restraining of the state in individualism. For both of these acknowledge the antithesis of the individual and society, whereas Confucius obliterated such boundaries and effected a unity of mankind with the self. To carry this a step further, in the feudal world both the legitimate king and the feudal lords could coexist, exemplifying the idea of unity in subdivision. And in clan-law society it was scions of the

---

succor to the masses, and able to assist all, what would you say of him? Might he be called perfectly virtuous [*jen*]?' The Master said, 'Why call him only a man of perfect virtue? He would without a doubt be a Sage. Even Yao and Shun were still solicitous about this.' " [Modified from Legge, p. 194; Waley's interpretation, p. 122, is quite different.] The [Chu Hsi commentary], *Chi-chu* quotes Ch'eng [Yi] on this, "Extensively dispensing succor to the masses is the great accomplishment of the Sage." And further, "For is not 'extensively dispensing' that which the Sage is desirous of doing? However one must be fifty before he wears silk, and seventy before he eats meat. [A reference to *Mencius*, I/i/3/4; Legge, pp. 131–32.] The Sage-mind does not seek to prevent younger people as well from dressing in silk and eating meat. But he observes that, as he nourishes the people, there are some to whom he cannot give. Thus he is concerned that his dispensing is not more extensive. Is not succoring the masses what the Sage desires? However his governing can extend only throughout the Nine Divisions. [*Chiu chou*, an early term for the geographical components of the Chinese Empire.] The Sage does not desire to bar those beyond the Four Seas from also being succored at the same time. But he observes that there are some beyond the reach of his governing. Thus he is concerned that his succor is not of massive proportions."

[ruling] clan who became the hereditary ministers, thus bringing about a mingling between family matters and the affairs of the state. Both of these, having gained a basis in the theory of *jen*, subsequently lost their original faults of inequality and of ethical inadequacy, and were transformed into a noble, idealized system. In Han and T'ang and later ages, Confucianists always praised the government of the feudal world. However, what they were praising was not the actual historical feudalism but a feudalism humanized and idealized by Confucius.

The possible sources of Confucius' understanding of *jen* could not lie beyond: (1) the contemporary learning of the royal Chou; (2) the ancient learning from the Yin-Shang dynasty; and (3) new elements created by Confucius. To base an estimate on the extant documentary record, it would appear that the elements of the first category are relatively few, while those of the second two categories are more numerous. The relatively more reliable among extant early documents in which the government of the Chou is recorded very rarely speak of *jen* and *yi*, benevolence and righteousness. For example, in the *Ya* and *Sung* [containing texts of the more formal ritual songs and chants] sections of the *Book of Odes*, where the virtue of the Former Kings of Chou is praised, there is no single instance of the use of the word *jen*. The various chapters of the "New Text" portions [whose historical authenticity is better established] of the *Classic of History* also do not refer to *jen*. In the "Old Text" portions it is occasionally encountered, but even there it is used only four or five times.[54] If we examine the matter on the basis of the *Chou Shu* ["The

[54] For example, in the *Book of Odes*, "The Greater Odes of the Kingdom" or *Ta Ya*, the Ode "Sheng-Min" [Legge, p. 465 ff.] praises Hou Chi for causing agriculture to prosper; the Ode "Kung Liu" [Legge, p. 483 ff.] praises Kung Liu for causing the people to multiply; the Ode "Mien" [Legge, p. 437] praises the ancient duke T'an-fu, for giving the people houses; the Ode "Huang yi" [Legge, p. 452 ff.] praises King Wen for his campaign against the [insubordinate] people of Mi; the Ode "Ling-t'ai" [Legge, p. 456] praises the building of the tower; the Ode "Wen wang yu sheng" [Legge, p. 460] praises [King Wen] for overthrowing the city of Ch'ung and for fixing his residence in the capital of Hao; but none of these touch on the subjects of benevolence [*jen*] or righteousness [*yi*]. In the *Book of Documents*, the "Documents of Chou" of the "Old Text" portions, there are not more than two or three examples of the use of the word *jen* such as that in [T'ai shih] "The Great Declaration," Part II, "Although he has his nearest relatives with him, they are not like my virtuous [*jen*] men" [Legge, p. 292]. Furthermore, in the "New Text" portions of the "Documents of Chou," where the political events of the Chou are recorded, the emphasis in most cases is on the subjugation of the Yin people, and on the establishing of government and the clarification of punishment regulations and the like. For example, the "Hung fan" (governmental structure), the "Ta Kao" (campaign to exterminate the rebellion of Wu-keng), the "K'ang kao" (command to K'ang-shu as prince in Wei to maintain carefully the punishments), the "Chiu kao" (command to K'ang-shu to forbid the people to drink wine), the "To shih" (admonishing the Yin people), the "To fang" (announcing to all the parts of the realm the extinction of the State of Yen), the "Li Cheng" (establishing the offices of government and appointing persons to them)—none

Documents of Chou," thirty-two chapters of the *Book of Documents* purporting to be documents of the Western Chou period, 1122–770 B.C.]
and the *Chou Li* [*The Institutes of Chou*], that which the Chou people most
emphasized and at which they were best were such things as their system
of officialdom, their rites and music, punishments and regulations,
agriculture, and education. Their institutions, their regulations, and
their material accouterments of feudal-age rule were resplendent in
their completeness. This of course need not all be taken as representing
their own new creation, yet in the completeness and detailed working out
of the system it went well beyond everything the previous dynasty had
known. In its contribution to ancient political systems the Chou can
indeed be called the Roman Empire of ancient China.

As for Hsia and Shang and all earlier times, the records are even less
adequate and references to *jen* and *yi*, which might supply us today with
some solid evidence, are rarely seen. However, the idea that the government of the Yin-Shang dynasty was lenient and simple is one that had
already become a tradition in antiquity. In the *Book of Documents*, in the
"*Shun Tien*" it says that when the primal ancestor of the Yin [i.e., the
Shang Kings], Hsieh, was Minister of Education to the Emperor Shun,
"he reverently spread the Five Teachings, following a policy of leniency;"
["The Canon of Shun"; Legge, *Documents*, p. 44, uses "gentleness"] and,
in the "Charge to Wei-tzu" it also says: "Your ancestor T'ang the Perfector watched over the people with leniency." [Wei-tzu was a Yin
descendant enfiefed by the Chou after their conquest of Yin; in the
"Charge" to him on his enfiefment he is reminded of the exploits of his
ancestor, King T'ang the Perfector, the founder of the Shang-Yin dynasty.
Cf. Legge's translation, *Documents*, p. 378.] The "Annals of Yin," *ch.* 3,
in the *Shih Chi* records the story about King T'ang, who went into the
countryside and on seeing hunting nets spread out on all four sides,
ordered them removed on three sides. His prayer for the success of the
hunt was: "Let those who want to run to the left go to the left; let those
who want to run to the right go to the right. Those who choose to disobey,

---

of these ever mentions the word *jen*. Liang Ch'i-ch'ao, on page 19 of his *Ju-chia che-hsüeh*, or
"*Confucian philosophy*," has already made this point. Juan Yüan, *Yen-ching-shih chi* (in
Huang Ch'ing ching-chieh, ch. 1072, pp. 9a-b), has written: "The word *jen* does not appear
in the portions of the *Book of Documents* known as the "Book of Yü-hsia" and the "Book of
Shang," or in the *Ya* and *Sung* portions of the *Book of Odes*, or in the *Book of Changes* in the
texts of the oracles or of the *yao* [explanations]. [I.e., the word *jen* does not appear in the
earliest portions of any of the earliest classics.] Thus the appearance of the word *jen* in the
chapter "Ta Ssu-t'u" of the *Chou Li* "[For teaching the myriad people and elevating some
among them to public service, there are, first,] the Six Virtues, which are wisdom, benevolence [*jen*], understanding, judgment, moderation, and compatibility." This is the first
extant appearance of the word *jen*." Thus, Juan adds: "This word [*jen*] clearly originated
with the Chou people . . . not with Confucius." [Sentence added at author's suggestion.]

they then shall fall into my nets." [This incident became a famous symbol of benevolence in government; for a full translation and commentary, see E. Chavannes, *Les mémoires historiques de Se-ma Ts'ien*, Vol. I, p. 180, where the last sentence of T'ang's prayer is rendered: *"que ceux qui en ont assez de la vie entrent dans mon filet."* That agrees with the same incident as given in a slightly different form by Liu Hsiang, 77–6 B.C., in his *Hsin hsü, ch. 5.*] Although this story may well be somewhat legendary, it too provides ample evidence that already in antiquity there existed a tradition about the leniency of Yin government. Also, the Chou people placed the blame on the last Shang King, the tyrant Chou, for the use of such punishments as broiling people alive, but Tzu-kung has said of him: "The tyrant Chou cannot really have been as wicked as all this!"[55] And Wei-tzu, in describing the bad government of the tyrant Chou, further says of him that he did not establish the bonds and restraints, and that his fault was leniency.[56] These make it evident that the violence and oppressiveness of the tyrant King Chou's government may have been "intensified in the telling" by the Chou people in their exaggeration of his crimes. And, in the war between the States of Sung and Ch'u, Duke Hsiang of Sung, leading "the descendants of the vanquished state" [as the people of Sung, descendants of the vanquished Yin dynasty, were designated] and adhering firmly to the principle that "the superior man does not again wound an enemy who has already been wounded, and does not take captive those whose hair is graying," was heavily defeated at the battle of Hung, and yet did not regret his conduct of the battle.[57] Later men ridiculed him for practicing *jen* to the point of bringing defeat on himself; he was probably but displaying the lingering spirit of the vanquished Yin dynasty in so doing.[58] Since Confucius was a Yin descendant and

[55] *Analects*, XIX/20. [Waley, p. 228. A description of his wickedness is given in *Shih Chi, ch. 3*, "The Annals of Yin."]

[56] The *Book of Documents*, "*Wei Tzu*": "The Viscount of Wei spoke to the following effect:—(lines omitted)—'The people of Yin, small and great, are given to highway robberies, villainies and treachery. The nobles and officers imitate one another in violating the laws; and, for criminals, there is no certainty that they will be apprehended. The lesser people consequently rise up, and make violent outrages on one another.' . . ." And; "The Grand Tutor made the following reply:—'King's son, Heaven in anger is sending down calamities, and wasting the country of Yin, which even now is in that lost and maddened condition because of wine-drinking.'" [Modified slightly from Legge, *Documents*, pp. 275 and 276.] Also, the *Book of Odes*, in the Ode "Tang" in the "Greater Odes of the Kingdom" [*Ta Ya*], King Wen recounts the crimes of the Shang-Yin under seven headings, noting that they did not use strict punishments and severe laws; this also can be adduced as corroboration. [Legge, pp. 505–10, especially p. 509.]

[57] *Tso Chuan*, Twenty-second year of Duke Hsi. The account in the *Shih Chi, ch. 39*, "Sung Wei Tzu shih-chia," is more or less the same.

[58] The Yin nation apparently were more naively attached to the simple and unsophisticated virtues than were the Chou people. The stories about simple-minded people in

furthermore was "devoted to antiquity and diligent in his study of it" [*Analects* VII/19] he must of necessity have been profoundly aware of the traditional view that the Yin government had been lenient and magnanimous. The government of Chou emphasized refinement, and, despite the completeness of its institutional system, it had not proved capable of perpetuating itself forever; by the Spring and Autumn Period it was already inclined toward dissolution. Confucius may have perceptively observed the principle that "laws alone cannot carry themselves into practice," and while adopting the completeness and detailed development of the Chou system, had the ideal of yet supplementing it to make it viable. [Cf. *Mencius*, IV/i/1/3; following Legge's translation, *Mencius*, p. 289.] Therefore he discovered, in the lenient and simple government of the Yin, a principle of benevolence and love, which he combined with the rites and institutes of the Chou, making thereby a system that possessed both ethical foundations and the capacity for practical application. With this, his advocacy of following the Chou now took on profound and far-reaching significance; therein, also, was established the ultimate goal, the final stage, toward which Confucius' whole corpus of political thought pointed. This ultimate goal of *jen* was in fact devised and established by Confucius, who nonetheless told how it had been derived from the Way of Yin; this explains why the discussion of *jen* begins to assume large proportions only among the followers of Confucius.

Since Confucius derived the beginnings of his doctrine of *jen* from the Yin government, why did he not openly explain it as something originally proclaimed by "the former wise kings of Yin"? There are two possible reasons for this: (1) Confucius had explicitly said that a man who lived in the present but attempted to return to the ways of the past, would bring down disaster upon his head. [See p. 97, footnote 42.] Even had he held aloft the superiority of the defunct dynasty in the attempt to convince the present rulers, perhaps feeling safe to do so because the former Yin state had been vanquished so long ago that there was no longer a need to maintain customary taboos on speaking well of it, even so, to speak from the point of view of a "Great Officer of the vanquished state" could scarcely have been expected to arouse much confidence among his contemporaries. Therefore whenever Confucius' discussion goes beyond the scope of the institutes of Chou, he usually finds his precedents in Yao, Shun, and Yü, [semi-legendary rulers of pre-Shang times,] and rarely touches upon Hsieh or King T'ang. [Hsieh was the distant ancestor of the

---

ancient records like that about sitting by the tree waiting for a [second] rabbit [to run into it accidentally and stun itself], or pulling on the grain sprouts to hasten the growth, are mostly told about natives of the State of Sung, and may reflect this fact. [For the former see *Han Fei Tzu*, ch. 49; Liao, Vol. II, p. 276, and for the latter see *Mencius*, II/i/2/16; Legge, pp. 190–91.]

Shang royal line, and T'ang was its first reigning monarch.] (2) Confucius "handed down the doctrines of Yao and Shun as if they had been his ancestors, and elegantly displayed the regulations of Wen and Wu, taking them as his model." [*Doctrine of the Mean*, xxx/1, following Legge's translation, p. 427.] Although the political institutions of Yao and Shun may well have been no longer extant [in any documentary form], the governmental principles attributed to Yao and Shun might have been passed on in some form of oral tradition or written record. Though nothing else may have been known of them, at least it can be stated conclusively that they were still more lenient and simple, cruder and more elemental, than those of the Yin period. Therefore Confucius' praise of Yao was phrased: "There is no greatness like that of heaven, and only Yao could copy it. How vast was his virtue! The people could find no name for it." And his praise of Shun was: "Among those who ruled well without exerting themselves, surely Shun may be counted. For what did he do? He did nothing but gravely and reverently occupy his royal seat; that was all."[59] The virtues that Confucius extols here are precisely those which could correct the Chou people's predilection for complex rites and institutions and toward burdensome government. Hence his "elegantly displaying the regulations of Wen and Wu" sought to preserve their precise and detailed development [i.e., as representing the Chou government at its best], while his "handing down the doctrines of Yao and Shun as if they had been his ancestors" sought to promote their liberal and generous spirit. If our inferences are not fundamentally in error, then Confucius in following the Chou can be said to have been conservative, and in his advocacy of *jen* he can be said to have sought a return to antiquity. But were we to adopt the terminology of the Kung-yang scholars [see below p. 124 ff.] and say that he "claimed ancient precedents in order to reform institutions," that too would be correct.

SECTION FOUR
Virtue, Rites, Politics, and Punishments

THE chief tenets of Confucius' political thought are more or less as set forth in the preceding section. Having made clear those chief tenets, we can then proceed to a discussion of Confucius' techniques of governing. Reduced to the simplest terms, the techniques of government that Confucius proposed are three: (1) to nourish; (2) to teach; and (3) to govern. The instruments with which to nourish and to teach are "virtue" [*te*]

---

[59] See, respectively, *Analects*, viii/19 [modified from Legge, p. 214, and Waley, p. 136]; and xv/4 [modified from Legge, p. 295, see especially his note no. 4; and Waley, page 193, see especially his note no. 7].

and the rites [*li*], while the instruments with which to govern are "politics" [*cheng*] and punishments [*hsing*]. Virtue and rites are major; politics and punishments are auxiliary. The central policy that Confucius most emphasized was that of transforming through teaching.

Confucius looked upon providing for the people's nourishment as an essential duty; that is one manifestation of his concept of benevolence and love [*jen ai*]. Thus he looked upon "the extensive dispensation of succor to the masses" as the achievement of the Sage. [See page 169, and footnote 53.] Moreover, the ranking of all those who served in government past and present should depend on their success or failure in nourishing the people. For example, there is Confucius' praise "of Tzu-ch'an, that in him were to be found four of the virtues that belong to the superior man"; one of these was "in nourishing the people, he was abundantly kind." And he denounced Jan Ch'iu, saying: "He is no follower of mine," precisely because as collector of revenue for the Chi family he worked hardships upon the people.[60] The significance of this is obvious so we need not go more deeply into it.

As for the course to be followed in nourishing the people, Confucius is also simple and direct; in the main it does not go beyond enriching the people's livelihood, keeping taxes and imposts light, limiting labor service exactions, and restricting fiscal expenditures.[61] One thing we must note in particular is that all Confucius had to say about nourishing the people was concerned with providing amply for their own livelihood. Anything beyond this, as, for example, the policies that emerged in the Warring States Period aimed at enriching and strengthening the state, were something he could have neither imagined nor approved of. For Confucius was advocating simply the self-sufficiency of the people, and not increase of the state's revenues. His views on fiscal policy were more or less similar to those of Aristotle in ancient Greece.[62] Moreover, the standard of plenty, as Confucius saw it, apparently had nothing to do with the absolute quantity of production, but merely with relative equality of distribution.

[60] See, respectively, *Analects*, v/15 [modified from Legge, p. 178, and Waley, pp. 110–11]; and xi/16 [Legge, p. 243].

[61] *Ibid.*, xiii/9/1–3, "When the Master went to Wei, Jan Yu acted as driver of his carriage. The Master observed, 'How numerous are the people!' Jan Yu said, 'Since they are thus numerous, what more shall be done for them?' 'Enrich them,' was the reply." [Legge, p. 266.] i/5: "The Master said, 'To rule a country of a thousand chariots, there must be reverent attention to business, and sincerity; economy in expenditure, and love for men; and the employment of the people at the proper seasons.'" [Legge, p. 140.] The *Great Learning*, Commentary, *ch.* x/19: "There is a great course also for the production of wealth. Let the producers be many and the consumers few. Let there be activity in the production, and economy in the expenditure. Then the wealth will always be sufficient." [Legge, p. 379.]

[62] Aristotle, *Politics*, book i, passim.

Confucius once said: "Concerning the head of a State or Family I have heard the saying:

'He is not concerned lest his people should be poor,
But only lest what they have should be ill-apportioned.
He is not concerned lest they should be few,
But only lest they should be discontented.'

And indeed, if all is well-apportioned, there will be no poverty; if they are not divided against one another, there will be no lack of men, and if there is contentment there will be no upheavals."[63] This spirit is in striking contrast with that of "exploiting natural resources to the fullest degree possible" and all similar [statist] policies.

Nourishing the people was one of the state's indispensable policies, but it is not its highest policy. For the objectives of the state are not merely that the people should enjoy plenty with regard to food and clothing, rather that they should be noble and virtuous in character and in deed. Therefore in discussing the people of the State of Wei, Confucius said that when they were already enriched, they could then be taught [*Analects*, xiii/9/4; Legge, pl. 267]; and in reply to Tzu-kung's inquiry about government he advocated foregoing the people's food but retaining their trust [if forced to select between these alternatives].[64] And when it comes to his views on transforming through teaching, he sets them forth again and again, and with greatest care and attention. If we seek the reason for Confucius' emphasis on transformation through teaching, we will find the source of it in his doctrine of *jen*. "The man of benevolence, wishing to be established himself, seeks also to establish others; wishing to be enlarged himself, he seeks also to enlarge others." [*Analects*, vi/28; modified from Legge's translation, p. 194.] The cultivation of the self and the establishment of virtuous practices are ultimately responsibilities upon the self; therefore it follows inevitably that one must proceed to a concern for the perfection of others, so that all men, starting with those nearer and reaching beyond to those more distant, all will be encompassed in a transformation, bringing them to "rest in the highest excellence" [*Great Learning*, 1; Legge, pp. 356 and 363] and "revert to benevolence." [*Analects*, xii/1, where most translators take the ambiguous passage to mean "ascribe perfect virtue to the ruler." See Legge, pp. 250–51. Waley,

---

[63] *Analects*, xvi/1/10 [modified slightly from Waley, p. 203].

[64] *Ibid.*, xii/7, "Tzu-kung asked about government. The Master said, 'The requisites of government are that there be sufficiency of food, sufficiency of military equipment, and the confidence of the people in their ruler.' Tzu-kung said, 'If it cannot be helped, and one of these must be dispensed with, which of the three should be forgone first?' 'The military equipment,' said the Master. Tzu-kung again asked, 'If it cannot be helped, and one of the remaining two must be dispensed with, which of them should be forgone?' The Master answered, 'Part with the food. From of old, death has been the lot of all men; but if the people have no faith in their rulers, there is no standing for the State.' " [Legge, p. 254.]

p. 162, has "everyone under Heaven would respond to his, i.e. the ruler's, Goodness." See also p. 169, above.] Seen in this way, transformation through teaching is not merely one of the techniques of governing, but is in fact the central element in Confucius' political policy.

The methods with which to achieve the transformation through teaching are two: (1) to be a model in one's person; and (2) to instruct others in the Way. Confucius attached particular importance to the former. This is because all the aspects of government are included in the practice of *jen*, and the practice of *jen* as a means of governing finds its starting point in personal cultivation, as has been explained in the preceding section. If a person who is not himself a man of *jen* occupies high position, governing lacks its starting point. Even if he should be a man of vigorous action, he would in all likelihood only create more disorder and confusion the more he applied himself, and would end up having accomplished nothing beneficial for all the labor expended. When Chi K'ang [head of the Chi family, the most powerful of the Three Families of Lu, and real holder of power in the State of Lu] asked Confucius about government, Confucius replied: "To govern means to rectify. ["To rectify," *cheng* 正 is the root of the word *cheng* 政 "to govern."] If you lead the people with rectitude, who would dare to be lacking in rectitude?" [English, unfortunately, does not convey the semantic relationships as clearly as the Chinese. See *Analects*, xii/17.] And he also once said: "Once a man has contrived to put himself aright [*cheng*], he will find no difficulty at all in filling any government post. But if he cannot put himself aright, how can he hope to succeed in putting others right?" And he also said: "If a superior love propriety, the people will not dare not be reverent. If he love righteousness, the people will not dare not to submit to his example. If he love good faith, the people will not dare not to be sincere." Carrying this further, Confucius created an analogy to clarify his meaning; he said: "The character of the superior man is like that of the wind; the character of the small people is like that of grass. When there is a wind over the grass, it cannot choose but bend."[65] Therefore, as Confucius looked upon it, the cultivation of the self for the sake of rectifying [*cheng*, or "putting aright"] others was in fact a technique of governing [*cheng*] that was in itself most simple, in producing results most speedy, and in its ultimate achievement most grand. If one could but employ this technique, then "his government

[65] See, respectively, *Analects*, xiii/13 and xiii/4 [Waley, p. 174, and Legge, p. 265]; and xii/19. The doctrine of being a model for others in one's own self is also to be encountered in the *Book of Odes*, for example in the "Minor Odes of the Kingdom" [*Hsiao Ya*], the Ode "Chiao kung," "What you teach, the people all imitate." [Legge, p. 405]; and in the "Greater Odes of the Kingdom" [*Ta Ya*], the Ode "Yi," "When there is upright virtuous conduct, all in the four corners of the state will conform to it." [Modified from Legge, p. 511.]

is effective without the issuing of orders," and he could "rule well without exerting himself."[66] A date could be envisaged when government would be reduced and punishments no longer used.[67] The ideal of "everything under Heaven reverting to benevolence" could be attained in this way. [See, p. 110, the comment on *Analects* xii/1.]

As for those other elements of his teachings, such as the *Odes* and the *Documents*, rites and music, filial and fraternal submission, loyalty and good faith, these too were the frequent themes of "the master's discourse" [cf. *Analects*, vii/17; following Legge's translation, p. 200], even though their effectiveness was not so profound or so far-reaching as that of self-cultivation. Generally speaking, the larger portion of Confucius' instruction of his disciples seems to have focused upon methods of transforming the people and inculcating good ways among them. A most striking example of this is to be seen in the case of Tzu-yu, who served [ably] as governor of the city of Wu; in the city, consequently, there could be heard the sounds of stringed instruments and singing [evidence that the people's ways had been made harmonious].[68] The thing we must particularly note, however, is that Confucius' political policy of transforming through teaching had as its objective to nurture the individual's integrity; it did not lay great stress on knowledge or specialized skills. As for the arts of archery and charioteering and the like, they too were intended to have a moulding influence on a man's character; they were not training to improve one's physical health or to prepare one for earning his livelihood. This of course simply reflects the overall force of Confucius' concept that government is based on *jen*, and it is therefore by no means surprising.

When all of the foregoing is taken into consideration, it becomes evident that "politics" [or governing, i.e., *cheng*] in the thought of Confucius is not merely different from politics as discussed by modern scholars, but is also somewhat distinct from that encountered in Plato's theories in ancient Greece. The applications of politics as discussed by modern

[66] *Ibid.*, xiii/6, "The Master said, 'When a prince's personal conduct is correct [*cheng*], his government is effective without the issuing of orders. If his personal conduct is not correct, he may issue orders, but they will not be followed.' " [Legge, p. 266]; also xv/4, "The Master said, 'Among those who ruled well without exerting himself, surely Shun may be taken as an example. For what action did he take? He merely gravely and reverently occupied his royal seat, and that is all.' " [Modified from Waley, p. 192; cf. also Legge, p. 295.]

[67] *Ibid.*, xiii/10–12; "The Master said, 'If there were any [of the princes] who would employ me, in the course of twelve months, I should have done something considerable. In three years, the government would be perfected.' " And he also said: "If good men were to govern a country in succession for a hundred years, they would be able to transform the violently bad, and dispense with capital punishments." And further: "If a truly kingly ruler were to arise, it would still require a generation; and then virtue would prevail." [Modified slightly from Legge, p. 267.]

[68] *Analects*, xvii/4.

scholars do not go beyond the two spheres of governing people and dealing with affairs. Confucius, however, held the principle that "politics is to rectify," perceiving that the transformation of people is the principal work of government. [The phrase is: *cheng che cheng yeh* 政者正也; the translation could be alternatively worded: "to govern is to set aright" or "to make upright."] The principal task was not *per se* to rule over the people, much less was it to manage affairs. Thus, politics and education had similar results; the ruler and the preceptor shared the same duties of office. Although the state also had such other educational institutions as the village schools, local schools, the higher schools, and the specialized schools, the entire corpus of government and society in themselves was nothing more than a vast organization for the nurturing of men's character. [The ancient names for the four kinds of schools are: *hsiang, hsü, hsüeh,* and *hsiao;* see *Mencius,* iii/i/3/10; Legge, p. 242, and note, for some of the explanations of these.] In the chapter "T'ai-Shih," or "The Great Declaration" of the *Documents,* it says: "Now Heaven, to protect the people below, made for them rulers, and made for them preceptors." [Legge, *Documents,* p. 286, slightly modified.] This already clearly manifests a tendency for such a situation [stressing teaching as an adjunct to governing] to develop.

Plato also regarded ethics as the highest aspect of the state's existence, and his "philosopher King" ideal is close to Confucius' advocacy of the idea that governing and teaching are inseparable, and that the roles of ruler and preceptor must be combined. However, Plato's philosopher-king was to be a philosopher who valued knowledge above all,[69] while Confucius' ruler-preceptor was a man of *jen* who valued ethics above all. The ruler-preceptor was to employ ethics wherewith to transform the people, whereas the philosopher-king was to employ knowledge wherewith to rule the country. Both as men and in their modes of action they are different.

The third of Confucius' techniques of government is conveyed by the terms "politics" and "punishments." This technique does not lie within the scope of ethics or of education, but is government in the narrower sense. In simplest terms, what Confucius called politics and punishments included all regulations and constitutions, laws and ordinances, all of the things referred to in the records of the government of Kings Wen and Wu, all that is recorded in the Institutes of Chou—the institutionalized organs and capacities of the state and which have as their purpose to govern people and to handle affairs. Since Confucius believed that transformation through teaching could produce the effect of ruling well without action,

[69] The philosopher king, in addition to his knowledge and skill in political affairs, music, and the dance, had also to be versed in astronomy, mathematics, "dialectic," principles of philosophy, and the like; see [Plato] *The Republic,* Book vi.

why then did he also approve of political action and the act of punishing?
This is because even though Confucius held the ideal of everything under
Heaven being restored to benevolence [*jen*], he was clearly aware that
men differ in their native capacities. Thus [Confucius noted] there are
some who are born with wisdom, and some who are dull and will not
learn; there are those whose talents are above average, with whom one
can discuss the highest subjects; [he also made the striking observation]
that only the wisest and the most stupid cannot be changed.[70] The
people in the world who, on being exposed to education, are not brought
under moral influence thereby, probably are not a minority. So the logic
of this one fact forces one to accept the principle that the state cannot
eliminate laws and regulations, punishments and rewards.

However, the application of politics and punishments has limits: They
can do no more than supplement in those areas which transformation
through teaching fails to reach. Therefore whenever Confucius mentions
politics and punishments he invariably exposes his dissatisfaction with
them. For example, in reply to Chi K'ang's inquiry about government
he asks: "Why should you use capital punishment at all?" [Cf. *Analects*,
xii/19; Legge, p. 258.] And in discussing hearing litigations, he remarks:
"It is necessary to bring about the conditions where there will be no
litigations." And he sets this concept forth even more explicitly in the
passage where he says: "Govern the people by regulations, keep order
among them by chastisements, and they will flee from you, and lose all
self-respect. Govern them by moral force, keep order among them by
ritual, and they will keep their self-respect and come to you of their own
accord."[71]

From this it can be seen that in Confucius' techniques of governing
there is a tendency toward enlarging the scope of transformation through
teaching, and reducing the scope of politics and punishments. His attitude
toward ethics is positive to the extreme, while his attitude toward politics
borders almost on the negative.[72] If we proceed a step further to locate
the reasons for this, we can see a few relevant facts in the historical
background. In Section Three of this chapter we have said that, in his

[70] *Analects*, vi/19 [Legge, p. 191], xvi/9 [Legge, pp. 313–14], and xvii/3 [Legge, p.
318].

[71] *Ibid.*, xii/13 [modified slightly from Legge, p. 257]; and ii/3 [Waley, p. 88].

[72] In this, Confucius' view is something like Thomas Paine's. Paine distinguishes between social and political life, stating: "Society is produced by our wants, and government
by our wickedness; the former promotes our happiness *positively*, by uniting our affections;
the latter *negatively*, by restraining our vices. . . . The first is a patron, the last a punisher."
And further, "Society in every state is a blessing, but government, even in its best state, is
but a necessary evil." *Common Sense*, from the first two paragraphs. P'u Hsüeh-feng [Dison
Poe], *Hsi-yang chin-tai cheng-chih ssu-ch'ao*, "Currents of Modern Western Political Thought,"
p. 465. Thomas Paine (1757–1809), *Common Sense*, 1776.

concern with *jen*, Confucius may have received some insight from the lax and permissive government of the Yin dynasty. To base a deduction on this, Confucius' de-emphasis of politics and punishments may well represent a reaction against Chou governing modes and an attempt to improve them. The Chou dynasty placed high value on refinement; its institutional forms sought both completeness and detailed perfection. However, the pursuit of that refinement could easily have led to a reliance on mere forms. Confucius is known to have commented: "Ritual, ritual! Does it mean no more than presents of jade and silk? Music, music! Does it mean no more than bells and drums?" And again, "If a man lack *jen*, what can the rites mean to him? If a man lack *jen*, what can music mean to him?"[73] These appear to be responses to just such a condition, for the fault of over-refinement [as contrasted with simplicity, or basic substance,] unavoidably would be "laws and orders made prominent" [Lao Tzu, *Tao Te Ching*, p. 57; cf. Chan, *Source Book*, p. 166] and the trend toward this is abundantly evident in the Chou government. The *Institutes of Chou* in the section concerned with the Six Chief Officers[74] sets forth the details of a system of great complexity. In the chapter "Ta Ssu-k'ou" there is described the act of hanging up the penal regulations at the Hsiang-wei gate-tower [see *Ch'un-ch'iu*, Second year of Duke Ting, 507 B.C.; Legge, p. 746]; this practice comes very close to unlimited reliance on law. When one examines all of the details recorded in the texts of the *Li Chi* and the *Yi Li* [works on rituals of the Chou] one truly has the feeling that the Chou rites were of burdensome complexity. When one reads the "Ta kao," "Tuo shih," "Tuo fang," "K'ang kao," and the "Chiu kao" chapters of the *Documents*, one is impressed all the more with

---

[73] *Analects*, xvii/11 [following Waley, p. 212]; and iii/3. Further, when Tzu-hsia asked about one of the *Odes*, Confucius replied: "The painting comes after the plain ground-work," and he praised Tzu-hsia for interpreting this to mean that "ritual comes afterwards" [i.e., ritual belongs to a secondary stage of importance; other more personal values are primary]. This also displays the intent to correct the fault of over-refinement. Refer also to the *Li Chi*, ch. 32, "Piao chi": "Under the Chou dynasty, they honored the ceremonial usages, and set a high value on bestowing [favors]; they served the *manes* and respected Spiritual Beings, yet keeping them at a distance; they brought the people near, and made them loyal; in rewarding and punishing they used the various distinctions and arrangements of rank; showing affection [for the people], but not giving them honor. The bad effects on the people were that they became fond of gain and crafty, stressed refinement at the expense of a sense of shame; injured one another, and had their moral sense obscured." [Modified slightly from Legge, *Li Ki*, Vol. ii, p. 342.]

[74] See *Chou Li*, "Ta Ssu-k'ou." The *Book of Documents*, "The Declaration on Wine" ["Chiu Kao"], states: "If you are told that there are companies who drink together, do not fail to apprehend them all, and send them here to Chou, where I may put them to death." [Legge, p. 411.] The custom of applying the death penalty to enforce the prohibition against the Yin people's gathering in groups to drink may well be regarded as one example of relying on severe laws in establishing the penal regulations of the new state.

the feeling that in the mood of the early Chou dynasty, awe of ruthless power is more evident than the virtue of leniency and generosity. The records are now lost and incomplete, so that we cannot determine the precise situation of the Chou people's rule over the Yin population; but if we base an inference on the usual situation that prevails when a conqueror forces an oppressive rule on the survivors of a fallen state, then it is well within the realm of possibility that the early Chou carried out a policy of "relying on heavy regulations in establishing the penal laws of the new state." [Cf. the *Chou-li*, under "Ta Ssu-k'ou."] Whether or not the men of Chou had a worthy and compelling aim in so doing, their methods of "by force, subduing men" appeared to the Yin people purely and simply as oppressive government, and could not make men "submit in their hearts." [Cf. *Mencius*, ii/1/3/2; Legge, p. 196.] The Yin people clung to the recollections of their former dynasty, feeling all the more that it had been generous in spirit, and loved by the people. Whether it was actually generous in spirit, we cannot determine, but there undoubtedly existed a tradition that the government of Yin had been lenient and large-spirited. Even though Confucius had no intent to repudiate the Chou and follow the Yin, still his program of emphasizing rites and virtue in order to effect a transformation through teaching, and of de-emphasizing the supervisory and control tasks of politics and punishments, may well have reflected this historical background. He honored and acknowledged the institutions of the rulers of his own time; he contracted the scope of their application; he augmented their ethical significance; and he incorporated progressive reform into a program that none the less had as its core concept the preservation of the past. That more or less sums up Confucius' techniques of governing, in their main outlines.

Section Five
The Superior Man

If we are to say that "governing through benevolence" [*jen chih* 仁治] is the primary focus in Confucius' reform of the Chou government, then "government by men" [*jen chih* 人治] is its second important principle, and the "superior man" about which he so frequently spoke represents the crystallization of all his thought on the subject of a government by men.

The term "superior man" [*chün-tzu*] is to be found in the *Odes* and the *Documents*; it was by no means an invention of Confucius. It is encountered in the "Documents of Chou" five or six times, and in the "Odes of the States," and the "Minor and Greater Odes of the Kingdom" more than one hundred and fifty times. This is ample evidence that it was a highly current term in Chou usage. However, in the *Odes* and the *Documents*, the term refers to a social position and not to the individual's moral character. Even where it in part implies something about a man's character, it simultaneously indicates his status. Use of it with implications for character only, irrespective of status, are totally lacking.[75] Confucius' use of the term

[75] The "Books of Shang" portions of the *Documents* do not contain the term *chün-tzu*. It is found six times in the "Books of Chou" portions: "T'ai shih," "Oh! my valiant men [*chün-tzu*] of the West" [Legge, p. 294]; "Lü Ao," "When a prince treats superior men [*chün-tzu*] with [contemptuous] familiarity, he cannot get them to give all their hearts; when he so treats inferior men [*hsiao-jen*], he cannot get them to put forth all their strength" [Legge, p. 348]; "Chiu kao," ". . . all ye high officers, ye assistants, and all ye noble chiefs [*chün-tzu*]" [Legge, p. 404]; "Shao kao," ". . . with the king's heretofore hostile people, with all his officers [*chün-tzu*] and his loyal friendly people . . ." [Legge, p. 432]; "Wu yi," "The superior man [*chün-tzu*] rests in this,—that he will have no luxurious ease. He first understands the painful toil of sowing and reaping, how it conducts to ease, and thus he understands the law of the support of the inferior people [*hsiao-jen*]" [Legge, p. 464]; and "Chou kuan," "Oh, all ye men of virtue [*chün-tzu*], my occupiers of office . . ." [Legge, p. 531]. [Legge's translations are followed throughout, although in the first and the last of the six examples the translation inaccurately reflects the later Confucian ideal of virtue coupled with high position.] All of these instances of the use of *chün-tzu* exclusively indicate status. None of the three "Sacrificial Odes" sections of the *Book of Odes* contains the term *chün-tzu*. Most of the uses of the term *chün-tzu* in the two [Minor and Greater] "Odes of the Kingdom" sections and the "Odes of the States" sections also refer exclusively to status. Some examples are: from the "Minor Odes of the Kingdom," the Ode "Ts'ai wei," "The four steeds are yoked,/The four steeds, eager and strong;—/The confidence of the officer [*chün-tzu*],/The protection of the men [*hsiao-jen*]." [Modified slightly from Legge, pp. 260–61]; [the Chinese text includes here a philological note, discussed also in part in Legge's notes, pp. 260–61, according to which the last two lines might be translated "The officer rides in the chariot; the ordinary men follow on foot." This makes the status identification of *chün-tzu* still clearer; but it is omitted from the translation as an unnecessary complication for the reader of English]: the Ode "Nan shan yu t'ai," "To be rejoiced in are ye, noble men [*chün-tzu*],/Parents of the people." ["*Chün-tzu*" occurs in almost every couplet of this poem; only one example is selected for illustration here. The same is true of several of the other poems cited here; Legge, p. 273]; in the Ode. "Ssu kan," "Here will our noble lord [*chün-tzu*] repose." "Sons shall be born to him . . . ," "The [future] king, the princes of the land." [Legge, pp. 305–306]; the Ode "Ch'iao yen," "A very grand ancestral temple;—/A true sovereign [*chün-tzu*] made it." [Legge, p. 341.] There are instances of its simultaneous reference to both status and character, such as, in the "Minor Odes of the Kingdom," in the Ode "Chan lu," "Distinguished and true are my noble ·guests [*chün-tzu*], . . ." and "Happy and self-possessed are my noble guests [*chün-tzu*]" [Legge, p. 276]; in the Ode "Ku chung," "Of the virtuous sovereigns [*chün-tzu*] of old,/The virtue was without a flaw." [Legge, p. 367]; and in the Ode "Chiao kung," "If the sovereign [*chün-tzu*] have good ways, . . ." [Legge, p. 406]. And in the "Greater Odes of the Kingdom," in the Ode "Chüan ah," "Oh, happy and courteous sovereign [*chün-tzu*],/You are a pattern to the four quarters [of the kingdom]." [Legge, p. 493.] The term *chün-tzu* was a general term for persons of status. Therefore it could be applied at the highest level to the Son of Heaven (as in the "Greater Odes of the Kingdom," the Ode "Chia Lo," "Of [our] admirable, amiable sovereign [*chün-tzu*]/Most illustrious is the excellent virture/He orders rightly the people, orders rightly the officers,/ And receives his dignity from Heaven." [Legge, p. 481]; at the lowest it can be used to

chün-tzu in the *Analects* includes exclusive references to status, exclusive references to character, and uses in which the reference is to character and status simultaneously. For example, Confucius said: "Superior men [*chün-tzu*], and yet not men of *jen*, there have been, alas! But there has never been a mean man who was a man of *jen*," and "A man in a superior station [*chün-tzu*], having valour without righteousness, will be guilty of insubordination; one of the lower people, having valour without right-eousness, will commit robbery."[76] [Legge's translation clearly brings out the point, translating *chün-tzu* here as "a man in a superior station, and *hsiao-jen* as "one of the lower people."]

In each of these instances "superior man" [*chün-tzu*] clearly designates the Knights and Great Officers of noble rank, while "mean man" [*hsiao-jen*] designates the common people of the countryside and the market place; they are purely references to social position, and have nothing to do with character. Confucius, however, also said: "The superior man dislikes the thought of his name not being mentioned after his death," and "The superior man may indeed have to endure want, but the mean man, when he is in want, gives way to unbridled license."[77] These refer exclusively to a man's character, and do not indicate anything about his social status. Uses of these terms which simultaneously have both mean-ings, however, also exist, such as: "The Master said of Tzu-ch'an that he had four of the characteristics of the superior man:—in his conduct of himself, he was humble; in serving his superiors, he was respectful; in nourishing the people, he was abundantly kind; in ordering the people, he was just." And again, "Tzu-lu asked what constituted the superior man. The Master said: 'The cultivation of himself in reverential care-fulness.' 'And this is all?' said Tzu-lu. 'He cultivates himself so as to ease the lot of other people.' Tzu-lu said: 'Can he not go further than that?' The Master said: 'He cultivates himself so as to be able to ease the lot of all the people! He cultivates himself so as to be able to ease the lot of all the people! Even Yao and Shun had to worry themselves about that.' "[78] It may be inferred that the first of Confucius' meanings in his use of the term "superior man" completely follows that encountered in the

---

refer to servitors [*ch'en-hsia*] (as in the "Greater Odes," the Ode "Yün han," "My great officers and excellent men [*chün-tzu*], [Legge, p. 534]. But their status probably was in any event always above that of the "common knights" *shu shih* 庶士 [not the "common man" we talk of in history].

[76] See [*Analects*], respectively, xiv/7 [modified from Legge, p. 277] and xvii/23 [Legge, p. 329].

[77] For both of these see *Analects*, xv/19 [Legge, p. 300] and xv/1 [Legge, p. 294].

[78] *Ibid.*, respectively, v/15 [slightly modified from Legge, p. 178], and xiv/45 [modified from Waley, pp. 191–92].

Odes and the *Documents*, while his second meaning must have been his own invention, and the third meaning follows the old usage but slightly alters its import. The old meaning of the word contains the general implication that the man who possessed rank should cultivate his virtue, while Confucius tended toward an emphasis on the cultivation of virtue in order to acquire rank. Thus Nan-kung Kuo [himself a member of the hereditary aristocracy] asked of Confucius: "Yi was a mighty archer, and Ao shook the boat, yet both of them came to a bad end. [Legendary exploits of heroes—Waley explains the latter, saying Ao shook his enemies out of the boat, in a great battle that he won.] Whereas Yü and Chi, who devoted themselves to agriculture, came into possession of all that is under Heaven."[79] [Yü the Great was the semi-legendary Emperor who succeeded Shun; Chi was the founding ancestor of the Chou royal line.] Confucius was deeply pleased that Nan-kung Kuo had apprehended his idea of acquiring position by virtue, and praised him as a "superior man" and one who "esteemed virtue."

Confucius' repeated references to the "superior man" apparently sprang from two different intents. The one was to rescue from the decline that had befallen it the clan-law hereditary ministership, and the second was to overcome the faults induced in Chou government by the over-emphasis on refinement. In fact, however, the two were in many ways related issues. In the Spring and Autumn Period, feudal clan-law was already in a state of decline. The clan heads, in their capacities as hereditary ministers, were already incapable of maintaining their exclusive control over affairs of state. Power counted far more than great family background; physical force could suppress the exercise of clan privilege. This was all the more true when men of high status [*chün-tzu*] could be in fact other than benevolent [*jen*], and when the nobles were so frequently licentious and unbridled. The loss of authority was thus partly due to their own fault. As the old great-family ruling class was gradually drifting toward extinction, the issue of into whose hands actual political power should pass had of necessity become a very serious problem, because the traditional standard for determining this issue had become inoperative. If the clashing of forces and contesting of wits of those "pursuing the stag"

---

[79] See [*Analects*], xiv/7 [modified from Waley, pp. 180–81, with reference also to Legge, p. 277]. The [Chu Hsi commentary] *Chi-chu* states: "Nan-kung's intention apparently is to compare Yi and Ao to the powerful men of his own time, and to compare Yü and Chi to Confucius." This is entirely correct. We should note that Confucius was extremely displeased with the political figures of his own time. Therefore when Tzu-kung asked: " 'Of what sort are those of the present day, who engage in government?' The Master said, 'Pooh! they are so many pecks and hampers, not worth being taken into account.' " See *Analects*, xiii/20 [Legge, p. 272].

[an early Chinese idiom meaning "contesting for mastery of the state"]
were to be allowed to decide that issue, there inevitably must follow a
dissolution of order, and unending chaos. Confucius must have observed
this, and in consequence he set up his doctrine that rank and position
should be acquired in recognition of virtue. Accordingly, he taught his
disciples the techniques for bringing about order and peace, thus qualifying
them for office and enabling them to put his teachings into practice,
assuming control of government in the place of the hereditary ministers.
Confucius' ideal superior man was therefore a man complete in virtue
and elevated in status. He was not a clan head whose only resource was
aristocratic hereditary privilege; much less was he a power-wielding
minister who relied only on naked force. The former was legitimate but
did not conform to the ideal; the latter was as much a violation of the
ideal as of legitimacy. [At author's suggestion, one sentence in the original
is left out here.] Were we to say that in this Confucius wanted to reconstitute completely a ruling class for the feudal world, it would seem to be
not far from the truth.

To carry this a step further, it could be said that, although Confucius
had in fact already recognized the failure of clan-law society, he had not
openly attacked it. For the failure Confucius recognized was merely that
of the system of clan-law social classes. He without any doubt still acknowledged and still clung to the basic principle that family and state should
comprise one entity.[80] The reason why Confucius continued to use the old
term "superior man" [here a more literal translation of *chün-tzu*, bringing
out its original feudal meaning of "son of a noble" would convey the intent
of this sentence better] seemingly is that without openly repudiating the
traditional system he still had scope to carry out his desired program of
political reform. He took the old designation for clan-law social status and
added the new meaning of cultivating one's virtue in order to acquire
rank and position. It can be compared to grafting a flower on an old
tree; his skill was amazingly deft, and he devoted the most intense effort
of mind and spirit to the task. It is to be regretted that even as hereditary
ministers were indeed infrequently men of virtue, so were men of *jen* hard
put to it to get high office. The Chi family [of hereditary ministers who
had usurped ducal authority in Lu] was "richer than the Duke of Chou"
[*Analects*, xi/16] and Yen Yüan [Confucius' favorite disciple] died poor

---

[80] Cf. "Section Three" of this chapter. See also *Analects*, ii/21: "Someone addressed
Confucius, saying, 'Sir, why are you not serving in government.' The Master said, 'The
Book of Documents says, be filial, only be filial and friendly towards your brothers, and in
that way contribute towards government. This is also serving the government; why must
one think that everyone should be in the government service?' " The import of this passage
is very clear [i.e., family responsibilities and political responsibilities are part of one set of
responsibilities, and they are inseparable].

in a humble lane. The Son of Heaven did not "promote" him or "raise him up," and "Confucius did not obtain the throne."[81] Confucius' new ruling class still had not emerged by the end of his life. His highest ideal, of the superior man possessing both virtue and office, had to be diminished, becoming a principle of preserving one's personal integrity by practicing the Way when suitably employed, and simply becoming a recluse when not so employed. [Cf. *Analects*, vii/10.] Of Ch'ü Po-yü he said: "When good government prevails in his State, he is to be found in office. When bad government prevails, he can roll his principles up, and keep them in his breast."[82] And Confucius also praised him as a "superior man"; this is quite different in tone and meaning from his reasons for praising Tzu-ch'an as a "superior man." [See above, page 118.]

We may also add a comment on the relationship between the individual and government as seen in Confucius' thought. Since the Sung dynasty Confucians have maintained that the minister-servitor had the absolute duty of total loyalty to sovereign and dynasty and claimed that their view on this was derived directly from Confucius himself. When we carefully review this matter, we discover that Confucius taught no such thing. The essence of all Confucius' discourse on the ruler-servitor relationship is contained in the passage: "[What is called a great minister] is one who serves his prince according to what is right, and when he finds he cannot do so, retires."[83] For the superior man, in the spirit of loving the people, implements government of *jen*. This is the proper objective in soliciting the ruler for official appointment. When conditions permit conforming to this standard and one yet refuses to take public office—that is to abandon the "high principle of ruler-servitor." [Cf. *Analects* xviii/7/5; Legge, p. 336.] When conditions do not permit adherence to this standard and one yet strives for high position—that is to "be concerned chiefly about emolument," or "to have one's thought fixed on the rewards of office." [Cf. *Analects*, ii/18/1; Legge, p. 151, and viii/12; cf. Legge's note, p. 212. This passage is taken in the sense that Waley, *Analects*, p. 135, adopts.] Both were things of which Confucius could not approve. Thus Confucius

[81] *Mencius*, v/i/7/3, "In the case of a private individual obtaining the throne, there must be in him virtue equal to that of Shun or Yü; and moreover there must be the presenting of him to Heaven by the preceding sovereign. It was on this account that Confucius did not obtain the throne." [Legge, pp. 359–60.] Refer also to Section One of this chapter where Confucius' objectives in establishing his teachings are discussed.

[82] See, *Analects*, respectively, vii/10 [cf. Legge, p. 197]; and xv/6/2 [Legge, p. 296].

[83] *Ibid.*, xi/23/3–6; "Chi Tzu-jan asked whether Chung Yu and Jan Ch'iu could be called great ministers. The Master said, '. . . what is called a great minister, is one who serves his prince according to what is right, and when he finds he cannot do so, retires. Now, as to [Chung] Yu and [Jan] Ch'iu, they may be called ordinary ministers.' Tzu-jan said, 'Then they will always follow their chief;—will they?' The Master said, 'In an act of parricide or regicide, they would not follow him.' " [Legge, pp. 245–46.]

scorned the old recluse carrying a basket as one who "to maintain his own integrity" did not hesitate "to subvert the Great Relationship." [Cf. *Analects*, xviii/7/5; Waley, pp. 220–21.] But he also noted sadly that those who took office as retainers of Great Households [instead of at the court of the legitimate rulers] lacked the sense of shame. Confucius [in a context concerning when to take office] said of himself that "I have no 'thou shall' or 'thou shall not.' "[84] This shows unequivocally that Confucius did not hold unalterably either to the view that one must serve in office or to the view that one must be a recluse; rather one must consider only whether or not he can act "according to what is right" [i.e., *hsing Tao*; following Legge, as in note 83. A more literal translation might be "to practice the Way"] as his standard for deciding whether to serve or to retire. Since the standard for deciding whether to serve or to retire is simply that of acting according to the Way, the implication clearly is that a man has no absolute duty toward the ruler or the state *per se*, and the statement that "There is no escaping the great and high principle of ruler-servitor anywhere in Heaven or earth" is a misguided one. [In fact, the phrase is from the *Chuang Tzu*, where it is used to ridicule Confucians.] Confucius himself, although he tried with all his energy throughout a lifetime to find a ruler to whom to offer his services, and because of this sometimes suffered taunts and ridicule,[85] wanted only to seek the one-in-ten-thousand chance to practice his Way. He was not thereby debasing himself to the level of the unscrupulous man of learning. [See above, page 188, and footnote 25.] We observe that he often had praise for those who fled the world to follow the noble path of the recluse,[86] and was totally unforgiving of those who served in office but without righteousness, and from this we can see wherein lay his real feelings on this issue. But there is more evidence than just this. Confucius, in saying that the servitor-official should not acknowledge the ruler's unworthy commands, explicitly denied the duty of absolute obedience. In leaving Lu to seek official appointment in the State of Wei, Confucius clearly did not establish any

[84] *Ibid.*, xviii/8/5 [Waley, p. 222; see also Legge, p. 337]. Refer also to viii/13/2–3, where Confucius says: "When right principles of government prevail in the kingdom, he [the superior man] will show himself; when they are prostrated, he will keep concealed. When a country is well-governed, poverty and a mean condition are things to be ashamed of. When a country is ill-governed, riches and honor are things to be ashamed of." ["Well-governed," literally *yu tao*, "has the Way," opposed to *wu tao*, "lacking the Way," or "ill-governed"; Legge, p. 212.] Also, xvi/11/2, where Confucius says: " 'It is by dwelling in seclusion that they seek the fulfillment of their aims; it is by deeds of righteousness that they extend the influence of their Way.' I have heard this saying, but I have never seen such men." [Waley, p. 207.]

[85] Such as that of the Madman of Ch'u, the old man shouldering a basket, Ch'ang Chü and Chieh Ni. [Cf. *Analects*, xviii/5/6 and 7.] The *Shih Chi*, ch. 47, "K'ung-tzu shih-chia," records that a man in the State of Cheng said of Confucius that he "had a downcast and forelorn appearance like a dog that has lost its home."

[86] Such as Wei-tzu, Po-i, Shu-ch'i and others mentioned in the *Analects*, xviii/1/8.

"binding principle" of not serving two rulers. Man of later ages discoursed on the Confucius of the feudal world from the point of view of their authoritarian world-empire. This is like putting one man's hat on another man's head; it does grave disservice to the men of antiquity.

The second objective of Confucius' very frequent references to the "superior man" was to overcome the faults of Chou government engendered by over-emphasis on refinement. This directly manifests his thinking on the subject of "government by men." The Chou government had a tendency toward "laws and order made prominent," as has been briefly described in the preceding section [page 187]. The complete and detailed perfection of the Institutes of Chou, plus the evidence that several hundred years of putting them into practice had not averted decline of the sovereign and degeneration of government, together led to the clear and unavoidable conclusion: for its governing, the state could not rely solely on a complete and perfect set of institutions. Since Confucius had profoundly considered the ancient learning and was thoroughly knowledgeable about the Chou Institutes, he must have had a completely clear view of their bearing on Chou prosperity and decline. Precisely because of that Confucius established his doctrine of "benevolent government" [*jen chih*], taking as the starting point of all politics a belief that no individual's mind can be set against *jen*. The *Great Learning* presents a dictum of the Confucian school: "From the Son of Heaven down to the mass of the people, all must consider the cultivation of the person the root of everything." [Modified slightly from Legge, *Great Learning*, p. 359.] It becomes quite evident that the idea of "government by men" [*jen chih*] in fact is inseparable from the idea of "government of benevolence" [*jen chih*]. [Refer to page 116; the two words "*jen*" are of course semantically related.]

The clearest of all the expositions of Confucius' government-by-men philosophy is to be found in the opening passage of Chapter xx in *The Doctrine of the Mean*: "The Duke Ai asked about government. The Master said, 'The government of Wen and Wu is displayed in the records,—the tablets of wood and bamboo. Let there be the men and their government will flourish; but without the men, then government decays and ceases. With the right men the growth of government is rapid, just as vegetation is rapid in the earth; and moreover their government might be called an easily growing rush. Therefore the administration of government lies in getting proper men. Such men are to be got by means of the ruler's own character. That character is to be cultivated by his treading in the ways of duty. And the treading those ways of duty is to be cultivated by the cherishing of benevolence [*jen*].' " [*The Doctrine of the Mean*, Legge, pp. 404–05.] These words are very clear; there is no need to explain or analyze them further. However we should note that although, Confucius says that the administration of government lies in getting the proper men, that is not to say that government does not need institutions. Confucius wanted to overcome the faults in Chou government; he had no desire to destroy it or abandon it together with the records of wood and bamboo tablets [on which it was based]. Considering the entire body of his political thought, we can say that his two-part program of "following Chou" and elevating *jen* meant that the two were mutually supportive; neither one could be abandoned. We can believe that Confucius': "How complete and elegant are its regulations!" was said in sincere admiration of Chou government; and his statement that he followed the Chou was made in complete sincerity. It was not done to deceive his times and mislead the ignorant. [The word that Legge here translates "regulations" is *wen*, the same word that throughout this chapter has been most frequently translated "refinement," as in the expression "*shang wen*," "to esteem, or over-emphasize refinement." Both meanings are included, and are obviously related. "Refinement" is prior; "regulations" are an expression of Chou emphasis on refinement. "Literature" *wen* is an extension of "regulations," which were written, and which represented the increasingly important literary aspect of Chou "culture"—also *wen*.] Yet, he regretted deeply the decline of the Way of the Chou, and therefore he hoped that "government-by-men" might overcome the faults inherent in [government-by-] regulations. Therefore Confucius' stress on the "superior man" was not intended to substitute a government by men for government by laws, but rather to implant the concept of government by men within a system of government by law. The two, like a carriage and its wheel aids, depend on one another; they are as interdependent in their functioning as the mind and the body.[87] [The "carriage and its wheel aids" 輔車之相依 refers to an ancient saying describing mutual dependence; see *Tso Chuan*, Legge, *Chiun Ts'ew*, p. 145, paragraph 9. For "wheel aids" see Legge's note in the *She King*, p. 319.] Later men held up government of men and government by laws as opposites, as if they are two necessarily mutually exclusive methods, and in this way claimed that Confucius repudiated institutions and relied solely on the functioning of humanistic ethics and morality. Such a view is inaccurate.

Section Six
Great Community, Lesser Tranquility, and the Theory of the Three Ages

THE essential elements of Confucius' political thought are more or less as presented in the five preceding sections. However, there still remain to be discussed the two concepts stressed by Kung-yang scholars. [*Kung-yang*

---

[87] This principle has been set forth most clearly by Hsün Tzu; the following chapter will discuss it in more detail.

chia, scholars specializing in the study of the *Kung-yang Commentary* on the *Spring and Autumn Annals*.] Those are the concepts of the "Great Community" [*ta-t'ung* 大同] and the "Three Ages" [*san shih* 三世]. A discussion of these is appended here to form a final section of this chapter.

The words Great Community and Lesser Tranquility are found in Chapter Nine, "The Evolution of Rites" in the *Li Chi, incipit*: "Chung-ni [Confucius] was present as one of the guests at the Cha sacrifice." When the ceremony had ended, Confucius was overcome with sighs [about the sad state of the world as evidenced in certain ritual improprieties in Lu] and replied to Yen Yen's question about his sighs. This reply was, in part: "When the Great Way was in practice, a public and common spirit ruled everything under Heaven; men of talent, virtue, and ability were selected; sincerity was emphasized and harmonious relationships were cultivated. Thus men did not love only their own parents, nor did they treat as children only their own children. A competent provision was secured for the aged till their death, employment was given to the able-bodied, and a means was provided for the upbringing of the young. Kindness and compassion were shown to widows, orphans, childless men, and those who were disabled by disease, so that they all were sufficiently maintained. Men had their proper work and women had their homes. They hated to see the wealth of natural resources unused [so they developed it, but] not for their own use. They hated not to exert themselves [so they worked, but] not for their own profit. In this way selfish schemings were thwarted and did not develop. Bandits and thieves, rebels and trouble-makers did not show themselves. Hence the outer doors of houses never had to be closed. This was called the Great Community."

"Now the Great Way has fallen into obscurity, and everything under Heaven exists for the family [or, for one family, i.e., the inheritance of the Sons of Heaven. Both this meaning and that of society existing in separate family units instead of in one common whole are included in the concept of *chia t'ien-hsia* 家天下]. Each one separately loves his own parents; each looks upon his own children only as his children. People take the wealth of natural resources and the fruits of their own labors as their own. The great among men consider hereditary privilege to be but an aspect of ritual propriety. Castle walls and outer defenses, moats and ditches, are made strong and secure. Rites and the sense of righteousness are regarded as the bonds by which the ruler-servitor relationship is kept correct, the father-son relationship is kept intense, the elder and younger brother relationship is kept harmonious, and the husband-wife relationship is kept considerate. In accordance with [rites and the sense of righteousness], forms [i.e., physical forms as well as institutional systems] are established and measurements are prescribed, fields and hamlets are laid out, the worthy men of valour and knowledge are judged, and merit is accrued to men's personal advantage. Thus the schemers can use these to carry out their schemes, and warfare finds herein its cause for erupting. Yü, T'ang, Wen and Wu, King Ch'eng and the Duke of Chou obtained their distinction because of these. (Passage omitted.) This is called the Lesser Tranquility."[88]

We must note that the authenticity of the "Li Yün" chapter has been doubted by some persons since the Sung dynasty. For example, Huang Chen of the Sung said: "The ideas developed in the opening section [i.e., referring to the section translated above] seem somewhat to resemble those of Lao Tzu." Yao Chi-heng of the Ch'ing dynasty was of the opinion that it was written by followers of Lao Tzu and Chuang Tzu during the period of transition from Chou to Ch'in [third century B.C.]. Lu K'uei-hsün went still further in concluding that it was a forgery artfully contrived of various elements by Tai [Sheng, the early Han scholar credited with having compiled the *Li Chi*] and attributed to Confucius to make it more acceptable to the early Han age when attitudes of reverence for the Huang-Lao theories were dominant.[89] [Huang-Lao was an early Han movement in political theory, of Taoist derivation; see below Chapter Ten, Section Two.] In view of its content, Yao also stated that the comment about loving not only one's own parents and regarding not only one's own children as his children was Mohist doctrine. The modern scholar, Ch'ien Mu, basing upon the evidence from the *Shih Chi* to the effect that Tzu-yu [i.e. Yen Yen] was forty-five years younger than Confucius,[90] and further drawing upon the relevant scholarship of [the Ch'ing scholars] Chiang Yung and Ts'ui Shu, has reasoned that when Confucius served in the post of Minister of Crime and participated officially in the Cha sacrifices, Tzu-yu was only six years old and thus scarcely an appropriate person with whom to discourse upon the meaning of the Great Community and the Lesser Tranquility.[91] None of these arguments is wholly groundless. Therefore it has virtually become a final conclusion that one must regard the "Li Yün" with suspicion and cannot take it as representing Confucian

[88] Also to be found in the *K'ung tzu chia-yü*, where the wording is slightly different. [The translation of this long quotation from the "Li Yün" chapter has been based on that in Legge, *Li Ki*, Vol. I, pp. 364–67, and reference has also been made to that in Fung/Bodde, Vol. I, pp. 377–78, but it departs from both in several places.]

[89] The *Hsü Li Chi chi-shuo* quoting the *Huang Shih jih ch'ao*, the *Ku-chin wei-shu k'ao* and the *Tai chi hsü-yen*.

[90] *Shih Chi*, ch. 67, "Chung-ni ti-tzu lieh chuan." It should be noted that the *Shih Chi*, neither in ch. 47, "K'ung-tzu shih-chia," nor in this chapter, records the fact of Confucius having served as attendant at the winter sacrifices [referred to as the occasion when he discoursed with Tzu-yu on the Great Unity and the Lesser Tranquility]. If the "Li Yün" is in truth a forgery of the Han period, it may thus date from after the time of Ssu-ma Ch'ien [who wrote the *Shih Chi*].

[91] Ch'ien Mu, *Hsien Ch'in chu-tzu hsi-nien k'ao-pien*, p. 66.

theory. However the concept of the Great Community has a nobility that excites admiration, and, although lying somewhat beyond the scope of Confucius' usual subjects of discourse, it still is not in contradiction with the basic tenets of Confucian theory. For example, the statement about a common and public spirit ruling everything under Heaven, or the complaint that hereditary privilege was regarded as but an aspect of ritual propriety, can be seen simply as extensions of the doctrine that official position should be acquired through virtue. To love not only one's own parents and to look upon not only one's own children with paternal regard could be simply a metamorphosis of Confucius' statements about a broad and encompassing love for mankind. The Great Community appears to be but another term for the Way of *jen*, and the Lesser Tranquility has much in common with the purport of "following the Chou." Although Confucius' more frequently encountered expressions and this passage from the "Li Yün" differ somewhat in degree, there is no fundamental difference of kind between them. If we can lay aside the extremely circumspect attitude of those "skeptics of antiquity" and recognize in the Great Community an ideal of Confucius, we probably would not be falling into truly serious error. [*Yi-ku*, "to doubt antiquity," is an attitude that dominated much of Chinese scholarship in the period after 1920, and that became a formal movement in critical scholarship in the 1920's and 1930's; later it was felt by some of its leading participants to have carried skepticism too far.]

But the *Spring and Autumn Annals* "Three Ages" is something quite distinct again. This theory arose in the Han dynasty; the representative figures in connection with it are Tung Chung-shu [ca. 179–104 B.C.] and Ho Hsiu [A.D. 129–182]. Tung's "Three Systems" [*san t'ung*] and "Five Agents" [*wu hsing*] are clearly and very obviously terms taken over from the *Yin-Yang* School.[92] There is no need to go into a thorough examination of this point. Ho Hsiu's theory of the Three Ages,[93] having undergone extensive elaboration at the hands of more recent Kung-yang scholars, is, however, a somewhat more complex issue. Ho Hsiu stated that Confucius, "during the age which he knew through transmitted records, made manifest the order arising from the midst of decay and chaos," while "in the age which he knew through oral testimony, he made manifest the order prevailing in Approaching Peace," and in "the age in which he himself experienced," he "exhibited clearly the order reigning in Great Peace." K'ang Yu-wei, in the Ch'ing dynasty, regarded the Approaching Peace age in the *Spring and Autumn Annals* as identical with the Lesser Tranquility of the "Li Yün,"[94] and he said that of those who looked upon the empire

[92] Tung Chung-shu, *Ch'un-ch'iu fan-lu*, "San-tai kai-chih chih-wen."

[93] Ho Hsiu, *Ch'un-ch'iu Kung-yang chieh-ku*, "First year of Duke Yin," under the line: "Kung tzu yi shih tzu."

[94] *K'ang Nan-hai wen-ch'ao*, "Li-yün chu."

as their family property [i.e., the basic characteristic of government in
the Lesser Traquility age], none were as good as King Wen, who through
civilization overcame the wild barbarians, and was a sovereign who
combatted chaos to bring about Approaching Peace. And in the age when
the world was common to all [the Age of Great Community], there were
none as good as "Emperors Yao and Shun, who selected worthy men of
ability and transmitted the throne to them; this was the democracy of
Great Peace of the Age of Great Community."[95] K'ang also maintained
that "Mencius' teachings had been transmitted through Tzu-yu and Tzu-
ssu from Confucius." Thus the doctrine of the importance of the people and
the unimportance of the ruler was "Confucius' own teaching about the Age
of Approaching Peace. In addition Confucius also had his [still more
ideal] Way of the Great Community, 'when all the dragons would be
without a leader' (cf. Wilhelm-Baynes, *The I Ching*, Vol. ii, p. 7: "There appears a flight of dragons without heads"], meaning that when the world had
achieved perfect order, even the rulers could be abolished; is this not more
than simply regarding the ruler as unimportant!"[96] He thus went still
further, to equate the Age of Great Peace and Great Community with one
of anarchy, yet "even Yao and Shun had to worry themselves about [the
popular welfare." *Analects* vi/28 and xiv/45; Yao and Shun, the great
emperors of antiquity who ruled without exerting themselves], so, there
was nothing to do but downgrade that [ideal state in Mencius in which the
ruler was merely unimportant, and take it to be equivalent] to the Lesser
Tranquility of Approaching Peace. K'ang Yu-wei further extended his
theory, saying: "Within one age there are the three ages, hence one can
develop from this a sequence of nine ages or, yet further, a sequence of
eighty-one ages, and so on to infinity."[97] Since Confucius is responsible
for the establishment of "the extraordinarily novel and strange theory"
that "the new was the Chou, and the past was the Sung [the Chou period
State of Sung, representing the Yin dynasty's fate in this sequence of
alternations], so that in the Ch'un-ch'iu era there should emerge a new
king," he also "comprehended the Three Systems" and "set forth [the
doctrine of] the Three Ages" as a basis for adapting and perfecting the
constitutions of states for all future time.[98] Therefore, from K'ang's point
of view, in expounding the political thought of Confucius, if we do not

[95] K'ang's *Meng Tzu wei*, the section headed "K'ang Wen-kung wei shih-tzu."
[96] *Ibid.*, "Introduction." In the section headed "Min wei kuei," K'ang has also commented: "This is where Mencius establishes the democratic system of government, the
institutions of the Age of Great Peace."
[97] *Ibid.*, under the heading "Chün-tzu chih yü wu yeh."
[98] Essay written on the publication of *Ch'un-ch'iu pi-hsüeh ta-i wei-yen k'ao*. This is based
on Ho Hsiu's *Chieh-Ku*, Fourteenth year of Duke Ai, where it says that Confucius' "fore-
knowledge of things to come had no limits."

base everything on the *Kung-yang Commentary* appended to the *Spring and Autumn Annals*,[99] but instead regard it merely as a work relevant only to the feudal world, we are simply guilty of underestimating the Sage.

If we wish to demonstrate the fact that the Kung-yang scholars' theory of the Three Ages is spurious, we need merely to observe the single issue of Ho Hsiu's own inconsistencies. Ho's comment on the Sixth year of Duke Ting says: "The language used throughout the [*Kung-yang Commentary* on] the two reigns of Dukes Ting and Ai conveys [the existence of] Great Peace, for [Confucius] wants to make it evident that the Kingly rule is established, so there is nothing further to condemn. There is only the matter of the two-word name [improperly used by one man, i.e., the fault of *erh-ming* 二名, a relatively unimportant technical error in usage, for which reproach is expressed] and for this alone there is condemnation." This seems to show ignorance of the fact that elsewhere Ho Hsiu has already written in commentary on the First year of Duke Ting that the *Spring and Autumn Annals* condemns "Duke Ting who had a king and yet [whose reign] lacked [the King's] first month; [see Legge, *Ch'un-Ts'ew, Prolegomena*, p. 54–76, specimen translations of the *Kung-yang Commentary*, for Kung-yang views on the importance of "the Duke's first year, the King's first month"] who did not devote himself to the affairs of the ducal house, and who wasted away the treasure of the State." Ho says further "Duke Ting was so happy to gain the throne that he forgot about the shame of his father's having been branded and banished from the state." Later on Ho comments on the Seventh year of Duke Ai that the *Spring and Autumn Annals* reproaches the State of Lu for having "violated and plundered the State of Chu-lou repeatedly and unceasingly, and for again having invaded [its capital] and captured its [duke];" and under the Twelfth year of Duke Ai, Lu is again condemned: "Duke Ai in external affairs admired the power of the State of Wu, and he exhausted the reserves of the State." All these condemnations are far more serious than that about the two-word name. Yet Ho's commentary says that other than the reproach about the two-word name, there are no further condemnations. How could such a work merit any credence!

Another example is to be found in the statement in the *Kung-yang Commentary* that "In the Annals of Dukes Ting and Ai there are many

[99] K'ang said that the *Analects* represented Tseng Tzu's ". . . individual views, and not the whole of the Confucian school's heritage"; "Introduction" to his *Lun-yü chu*. However K'ang also placed high value on the *Great Learning* and the *Doctrine of the Mean*; he wrote: "Sageliness within and kingliness without, a statement both well-reasoned and well-expressed, simple in language and yet complete in its meaning. Seeking it among the writings left by Confucius, we find it only in the *Great Learning*." And he also wrote: "Of all Confucius' teaching's, none is more excellent than Tzu-ssu's *Doctrine of the Mean*." [K'ang accepted the tradition that this essay was transmitted by Tzu-ssu, the grandson of Confucius.] See his Introductions to his *Ta-hsüeh chu* and *Chung-yung chu*.

subtle expressions." Tung Chung-shu explained this saying that the closer in time [to Confucius, who was regarded as the author] the more careful the language, for the sake of maintaining his [Confucius'] personal safety. Ho Hsiu also says of this: "Confucius feared the rulers of his own time, therefore at best, he concealed [the misdeeds of] those of high status and magnified their graciousness, and at least he could thereby avoid harm and protect his person."[100] Are we to believe then that the principle underlying the writing of the reigns of Dukes Ting and Ai in the *Spring and Autumn Annals* was "The language conveys the Great Peace," or was it instead "When bad government prevails, actions may be lofty and bold, but the language may be with some reserve?" [*Analects*, xiv/4; Legge, p. 276.] Here again his statements are mutually contradictory.

As a man of our times would see it, what the Kung-yang scholars would call "subtle language" comes very close to intentional deception. What they call "Great Peace" was but a term designed to find favor with their own times [i.e., the Han dynasty]. Thus when in the Fourteenth year of Duke Ai there is recorded that some hunters in the West captured a unicorn, the *Kung-yang Commentary* says that Confucius wept, saying: "My Way has run its course." Ho Hsiu here gives himself over to unrestrained commentary, saying that Confucius throughout was guided by the Heavenly Plan [*T'u-lu*, see Fung/Bodde, Vol. ii, pp. 88–91,] and knew that a commoner by the name of Liu Chi [better known as Liu Pang, a rebel leader who became the Founding Emperor of the Han] was supposed to succeed the Chou. Noting that a fuel gatherer had captured the unicorn, Confucius knew that it had appeared for him [Liu Chi]. What is the explanation of all that? The unicorn represented the essence of the element wood. The fuel gatherer stood for a commoner starting a fire. This meant that a Red Emperor would succeed the Chou rulers and occupy their place; hence the unicorn was captured by a fuel gatherer. The fact that a hunter in the West had captured it meant that the royal power would spread from the east to the west. The character *mao* symbolizes the east,

---

[100] See, respectively, Tung Chung-shu's *Ch'un-ch'iu fan-lu*, under the heading "Ch'u Chuang-wang," and Ho Hsiu's *Kung-yang chieh-ku*, under the First year of Duke Ting. For *The Spring and Autumn Annals* refusal to call the ruler's of the State of Lu *wang*, i.e., "king" out of deference for the honor of the Chou Kings, refer to the *Kung-yang's* comments on the phrases "*Ch'un, wang cheng yüeh*" [translated in Legge, *Ch'un-ts'ew*, "Prolegomena," pp. 54–55] and "*Chai-po lai*" under the First year of Duke Yin; "*K'ao Chung-tzu chih kung*" under the Fifth year of Duke Yin; "*Wei-hou Shuo ju yü Wei*" under the Sixth year of Duke Chuang; "*Shih-shih wu huai*" under the Thirteenth year of Duke Wen; "*Ssu-pu chiao*" under the Thirty-first year of Duke Hsi; "*Chao Ch'uan ch'in Liu*" under the First year of Duke Hsüan; "*Ch'u chih Ch'ing Feng*" under the Fourth year of Duke Chao; "*T'ien-wang chü yu Ti-ch'üan*" under the Twenty-third year of Duke Chao; "*Chü chung chiang chu Chi-shih*" under the Twenty-fifth year of Duke Chao; and the passages cited in footnotes 102 through 105 of this chapter.

as the character *chin* symbolizes the west. The word "to capture" is an
expression denoting warfare. This forms the words: "The Han dynasty
will be of the surname *mao, chin, and tao.* Through warfare it will gain the
empire." [The three elements, 卯, 金, 刀 together compose the surname
Liu 劉, the surname of the Han founder. The third of these elements,
tao "blade," indicates weapons or warfare. This appears to be a garbled
application of Tsou Yen's theory of the Five Elements or Powers, dating
from the fourth century B.C. "In Tsou Tzu's cycle of the Five Powers,
each one follows that one which it cannot overcome. The power of earth
is followed by the power of wood. The power of metal follows next; that
of fire follows next; and that of water follows next." That is Li Shan's
statement, A.D. seventh century, quoted in Fung/Bodde, Vol. I, p. 162.
Ho Hsiu apparently identified the Chou dynasty with the "power of wood"
and the Han with the "power of fire," hence, "red emperor." The short-
lived Ch'in dynasty was not included in the sequence.]

The *Kung-yang Commentary* took "to overcome the chaos of the age, and
to restore it to correctness" as the central theme of the *Spring and Autumn
Annals.* Ho Hsiu however went on to speak of: "words written in blood,
then turning white" to become the work known as the *Yen K'ung T'u,*
". . . and in it are delineated charts for instituting laws. Confucius, looking
aloft inferred Heaven's decree, and, looking down, he examined the
changes underway at that time, observing the future as well, and com-
manding limitless knowledge of things to come. He knew that the Han
dynasty was destined to follow after a period of great disorder; hence he
devised the method of overcoming chaos to instruct the Han." [Ho Hsiu
here draws on some of the fantastic anecdotes in the Han apocrypha;
see discussion of this in Fung/Bodde, Vol. II, pp. 129–30, and in K. C.
Hsiao, *A Modern China and a New World,* pp. 106–07. Ho's comments are
to the first line under the Fourteenth year of Duke Ai in the *Kung-yang
Commentary.* The "charts" refer to the *Yen K'ung t'u,* "Expository Charts
on Confucius," in the *Ch'un-ch'iu wei,* or "Apocryphal Treatise on the
Spring and Autumn Annals". See Fung/Bodde, Vol. II, pp. 129–30.]

Thus Confucius has been transformed into a sorcerer, and we are
expected to believe that the *Spring and Autumn Annals* were written entirely
with the Han dynasty in mind. Rather than discourse on learning in such
a fashion, it would indeed "be better to be without *Documents*" at all.
[Mencius' phrase; cf. *Mencius* VII/ii/3/1; Legge, p. 479; in this use of the
phrase, it might be taken in a more general sense, to mean "it would be
better to have no books or documents at all."] Having shown Ho Hsiu's
interpretations to be worthless, we feel there is no point in preparing an
argument about the views of K'ang Yu-wei and such persons. For whenever one discards clear and explicit statements in the ancient records and
sets up an interpretation based on "linguistic subtleties" to support some

hypothesis of one's own, then, after the requisite amount of forcing and twisting, a perfect case can always be built—to show, if one wishes, that Confucius was a member of the Party for the Preservation of the Emperor, or of the Revolutionary Party, or of the Nihilist Party—nothing is then impossible. [Shortly after the collapse of the Reform Movement of 1898 K'ang Yu-wei organized the Party for the Preservation of the Emperor, in opposition to the Empress Dowager who had seized control of the Imperial government.] However, that is something less than a strictly scholarly undertaking, and should not be credited as anything else.

Mencius said: "Confucius completed the *Spring and Autumn Annals*, and rebellious ministers and villainous sons were struck with terror," and Chuang Tzu wrote: "The *Spring and Autumn Annals* defines names and duties."[101] Both regarded the *Spring and Autumn Annals* as a work into which Confucius emplaced his ideas conveying "the rectification of names," and this indeed offers the most accurate view of the matter. For Confucius sought to make use of this text from the historiographers of Lu to preserve the Institutes of Chou, and to deter all encroachment upon and license against them. Therefore, though the feudal lords all had come to be addressed by titles of prince and duke, the *Spring and Autumn Annals* writes their original rank;[102] the Chou house had long since declined into insignificance, yet the text of this classic accords it the greatest honor and deference.[103] Other examples also can be cited, such as when ministers murdered their rulers or Great Officers usurped control of states, and here too condemnation of them is clearly recorded.[104]

---

[101] *Mencius*, iii/ii/9/11 [Legge, p. 283] and *Chuang Tzu*, ch. 33, "T'ien-hsia."

[102] For example, in the *Analects* there already appears the title "Duke Huan," while the *Ch'un-ch'iu* calls the same ruler "the Marquis of Ch'i." The ruler of Ch'u took the title of "king" in the First year of Duke Huan of Lu [710 B.C.], yet the *Ch'un-ch'iu* writes of him always as "viscount."

[103] For example, in the Twenty-eighth year of Duke Hsi, Duke Wen of Chin summoned King Hsiang [of Chou] to his court [at Ho-yang], yet [to give the opposite impression] the event is recorded: "The King [by] Heaven's [grace] held a court of reception in Ho-yang." [Legge, p. 207.]

[104] For example, under the Fourth year of Duke Yin, where the Duke's son Hui—because he is later to murder Duke Yin—is here shorn of his title "*kung-tzu*" ["Duke's son"]. Under the Sixteenth year of Duke Hsiang is recorded Lu's conference with the other feudal lords at Ch'ou-liang, yet it is recorded as ". . . their Great Officers made a covenant" [to expose the unfortunate fact that the states were under the illicit control of Great Officers rather than of their legitimate rulers]. For further examples, reference may be made to the author's compilation *Reference Materials for the Study of the History of Chinese Political Thought*, Appendix ii, 5. Note that the Sung scholar Su Shih in his *Tung-p'o hsü-chi*, ch. 8, has an essay entitled "*Ch'un-ch'iu pien Chou*" in which he argues that the *Kung-yang* commentary does not abandon the Chou dynasty in its point of view, so that Ho Hsiu, seen in this light, has perpetrated a crime against the *Kung-yang* commentary [in arguing that Confucius had done so].

The import of all of these cases of "defining names and duties" is seldom exposed and developed in the *Tso Commentary*, whereas in the *Kung-yang* and *Ku-liang Commentaries* these are delineated in great detail. Moreover the *Kung-yang Commentary* stresses and explicates the doctrine of honoring the Chou kings, paralleling and reinforcing Confucius' statement that: ". . . ceremonies, music and punitive military expeditions [should] proceed from the Son of Heaven." [The *Analects*, xvi/2; Legge, p. 310.] For example, under the Fifth year of Duke Huan the *Spring and Autumn Annals* records: "In autumn, an army of Ts'ai, an army of Wei, and an army of Ch'en followed the king and invaded Cheng." [Legge, p. 45.] The *Tso Commentary* merely narrates the event. The *Ku-liang* states that this was intended to conceal the impropriety of a Chou attack on a state whose rulers were of the same clan as the Chou kings. The *Kung-yang*, however, states: "What is the meaning of the statement that they followed the king in the attack on the State of Cheng? It means that to follow the king is correct." Another example is that in the First year of Duke Ch'eng, where the *Spring and Autumn Annals* states: "In autumn, the king's army was disgracefully defeated by the Mao-jung." [Legge, p. 336.] The *Tso Commentary* merely records the sequence of events, and the *Ku-liang* states that it does not mention doing battle, for no one dared oppose [the King]. The *Kung-yang* also states: "The king has no enemies, for no one dares oppose him." And, again, in the Thirteenth year of Duke Chao the *Spring and Autumn Annals* records: "Lu, Marquis of Ts'ai, returned to [the rule of] Ts'ai, and Wu, Marquis of Ch'en to [the rule of] Ch'en." [Legge, p. 647.] The *Tso Commentary* says: ". . . which was proper." [Legge, p. 652.] The *Ku-liang* comments: ". . . to indicate disapprobation of their conquest by the State of Ch'u." [Ch'u had murdered their fathers and kept these two sons and heirs prisoners.] But here the *Kung-yang* states: "These were both extinguished states. [Ch'u had extinguished them, and now the Ch'u ruler was restoring them, but, in so doing, arrogating to himself as a mere feudal lord a prerogative of the Chou kings.] Why does it say that [the two Marquises] *returned* [instead of saying they were restored to their fiefs?]. Because it is not granted to the feudal lords the right to enfief a ruler." There are still other examples of this kind, such as [the *Kung-yang*] writing under the First year of Duke Yin: "[Why does it (so) mention the king's first month?]. To magnify the union of the kingdom (under the dynasty of Chou)" [following Legge, "Specimens of the Commentaries of Kung-yang and Kuh-lëang, in his *Ch'un Ts'ew*, p. 55]; and, "There is nothing external to the King"; and, under the Twenty-third year of Duke Chao, "Making manifest that there is the Son of Heaven." All of these convey the desire to employ the "rectification of names" method of writing history, long after the feudal government has degenerated into chaos, to maintain, nonetheless, the forms of the

Chou rites and institutions. "Tzu-kung wished to do away with the offering of a sheep connected with the inauguration of the first day of each month. The Master said, 'Tz'u, you love the sheep; I love the ceremony.' "[105]

If we put aside all preconceived ideas and simply examine the text of the *Kung-yang Commentary* itself [without the explications later provided by Han scholars], we can perceive that the larger significance of the *Spring and Autumn Annals* [with its three *Commentaries*] lies in their constituting another expression in the same vein as Confucius' "loving the ceremony." The "extraordinary novel and strange theories" not only are not to be found in the three *Commentaries*, much less are they present in the *Ch'un-ch'iu* text itself; rather, they are entirely baseless fabrications by which men of the Han period [notably, Ho Hsiu and Tung Chung-shu,] sought authority for their views.

To carry the discussion a step further, Confucius completed the *Spring and Autumn Annals* in the desire to rectify names so as to straighten out real situations; this did not mean that he merely looked on as the system of royal powers and prerogatives fell apart but ignored the situation, or that he denied the existence of that situation. Confucius undoubtedly realized that the Institutes of Chou could not be completely restored overnight. Hence he consistently sought the next best thing. Any deed that was beneficial to the feudal system, even though not in conformity with the highest standards, was granted his relative approval. Thus, when the feudal lords proclaimed themselves Lord Protectors [*pa*] or when Great Officers controlled the affairs of a state [but did not openly usurp the legitimate ruler's position and displace him], such too were covered by his expression: "*shih yü*" 實與, or "the actualities allow this." [In this and in the following quotation, Legge's interpretation is slightly modified; the word "shih" is taken to mean both the statement in the *Ch'un-ch'iu* to which the commentary applies and the actual events to which they refer, hence the translation "actualities" to include both.] An example of this is found under the Second year of Duke Hsi, where the *Ch'un-ch'iu* records: "In spring, in the king's first month, we (aided in the walling) of Ch'u-ch'iu." [Legge, *Ch'un Ts'ew*, p. 136.] The *Kung-yang* explicates this as follows: "Why does it not say that it was Duke Huan [of the State of Ch'i] which walled it? Because it is not allowed to the feudal lords to arrogate to themselves the right of granting investiture. [The restitution of the recently demolished state of Wei, and the "walling" of its new capital at Ch'u-ch'iu, was tantamount to investiture of the state; Duke Huan of Ch'i did this in his unofficial capacity as Lord Protector, in the name of the Chou King, but actually usurping the authority of the King in this de-

---

[105] *Analects*, III/17. [Legge, p. 161. Cf. Legge's notes on this passage.]

cision.] In what sense is it disallowed? The actualities allow it, but the style [of the expression recording the event] does not allow it. Why does the style not allow it? According to the right idea of a feudal lord, he cannot arrogate it to himself to grant investiture. . . . What is meant by saying that the actualities allow it? Above there was no Son of Heaven; on a lower level, there were no Chiefs of Regions. [I.e. *Fang-po*, who were chief regional leaders appointed by the early Chou kings from among their kinsmen, to buttress the Chou authority in strategic areas. The institution had fallen into disuse, making necessary the *ad hoc* arrangement of the *pa*, or Lord Protectors, which emerged at this time. See Legge, *op.cit.*, p. 114. Saying that "Above there was no Son of Heaven" of course means merely that, no longer in a position to wield his authority, the Son of Heaven had virtually become nonexistent.] All of the feudal lords were engaged in exterminating each other, and when force could save the situation, then it was permissible to save it that way." And again, under the Eleventh year of Duke Hsüan, the *Ch'un-ch'iu* records: "In winter, in the tenth month, the people of Ch'u put to death Hsia Chen-shu of Ch'en." The *Kung-yang* says: "Why does it say 'the men' [of Ch'u put to death Hsia Cheng-shu]? It is to express reproach. Why is this to be reproached? Because it is not allowed for the outer states [i.e., other than royal Chou] to carry out punitive campaigns. . . . What is meant by saying it is not allowed? The actualities allowed it, but the style does not allow it. Why does the style not allow it? According to the right idea of a feudal lord, he cannot arrogate it to himself to make punitive campaigns. . . . What is meant by saying that the actualities allow it? Above there was no Son of Heaven, and on a lower level there were no Chiefs of Regions. All of the feudal lords were active in deed but deficient in the Way. Ministers were guilty of regicide, and sons of parricide. If force was necessary to effect a campaign to punish this, then it was permissible to punish it in that way."[106] The concept that the *Kung-yang* develops and makes explicit tallies perfectly with Confucius' praise of Duke Huan

[106] Under the First year of Duke Ting it is recorded that Wei-shu of the State of Chin seized Chung-chi of the State of Sung because he refused to help with re-building the walls of the Chou capital at Ch'eng-chou, and the *Kung-yang* states that the Great Officers here arrogated to themselves the right to seize them, commenting: "The actualities allowed it, but the style does not allow it." [I.e., the situation really demanded this action but the language of the *Ch'un-ch'iu* cannot openly admit it as it was carried out by Great Officers who did not have legitimate authority to take such action.] The *Ku-liang Commentary*, remarking on similar incidents, praises the action as "an innovation which is nonetheless correct." Examples of this [in the *Ku-liang*] are to be found: under the Fifth year of Duke Hsi, when Duke Huan of Ch'i had a meeting with the other feudal lords at Shou-tai [Shou-chih]; under the Twenty-ninth year, when the various Great Officers walled the capital city of Ch'i; and under the Thirty-second year of Duke Chao when the various Great Officers walled the capital of Chou.

and his petitioning for a campaign to punish Ch'en Heng [in *Analects* xiv/18 and 22].

K'ang Yu-wei felt that the *Spring and Autumn Annals* presented the whole Confucius, while the *Analects* shows only one facet of him. As we would see it, however, the *Analects* covers the entire range of his essential concepts, from benevolence and altruism, loyalty and faith, rites and music, to politics and punishments, whereas the *Spring and Autumn Annals* sets forth merely the single aspect of the rectification of names. It requires no profound investigation to determine which work specializes on one aspect and which embodies the whole. K'ang's view is virtually a complete reversal of the actual facts. Hence to accept his view is to hold up the idea of the Great Community and derogate the Lesser Tranquility; it is to support the *Kung-yang Commentary's* interpretation of the *Spring and Autumn Annals* in order to depreciate the whole body of canonical writings and the other commentaries; it is to cling to the extraordinary import of subtle expressions in order to suppress the clear and direct language of the ancient documents. When one, on the other hand, adopts the view that we present here, Confucius' Way achieves an all-pervading unity, and the import of all the classics becomes intelligible. The only things that one is thus forced to abandon are the distorted doctrines of Tung Chung-shu and Ho Hsiu, and K'ang Yu-wei's efforts "to borrow [the authority of] the past" [in order to lend plausibility to his own views].

Inasmuch as the writings of the *Kung-yang* scholars [i.e., not the *Kung-yang Commentary* itself, but the writings of later Kung-yang theorists who based themselves on it] are shown to be groundless, we would do well, then, to recognize in Confucius' political thought a very clear and manifest contemporaneity. That is to say, since his thought was based on the historical environment of feudal clan-law society, it is inseparable from that environment, although at the same time its content is not restricted to it. But to put oneself apart from the late-Chou historical background when discussing Confucius' political thought leads one into the danger of what Han Fei called "both citing Yao and Shun," or what Chuang Tzu referred to as "each has his right and wrong." [The former is an abridged quotation from the *Han Fei Tzu*, *ch*. 50: "Confucius and Mo Tzu both cited Yao and Shun; they differed in matters of acceptance and rejection." Modified from Liao, Vol. 2, p. 298. The second is an abbreviated reference to a passage in the *Chuang Tzu*, *ch*. 2, which may be freely rendered (following Kuo Hsiang's commentary): "The one regards himself as right and the other as wrong; the other also regards himself as right and his opposite as wrong." Cf. Legge, *Sacred Books*, Vol. 12, p. 91, and Giles, *Chuang Tzu*, p. 18.] Such a procedure would contribute nothing to our efforts in "ascending to consider the men of antiquity." [An abridged quotation from *Mencius*, v/ii/2: "he (a scholar) proceeds to ascend to consider the men of antiquity. He recites their poems, and reads their books. But as he feels that he should have knowledge of what they were as men, he accordingly considers the times and circumstances in which they lived." Modified from Legge, p. 392.]

Ho Hsiu's *Chieh-Ku* [his commentary on the *Kung-yang*] also contains the idea that in the Age of Approaching Peace there still would exist the condition of "having the various tribes of Hsia [*chu-hsia*, 諸夏, i.e., the peoples within the Chinese culture group] within, and keeping the *Yi* and *Ti* barbarians out," whereas in the Age of Great Peace "The *Yi* and *Ti* barbarians will come in and receive titles of nobility, and throughout the world the far and the near, the great and the small, shall be as one." This view is somewhat better founded; it is not entirely his fabrication, spun from nothing. There are two possible bases on which to separate nations: racial, and ethnic [i.e., cultural]. The places in Chinese ancient writings that touch upon the issue of nation, mostly fasten their attention on cultural distinctions. Those which use the racial concept to distinguish the barbarians from the Chinese are a distinct minority, such as the example in the *Tso Chuan*: "If he is not of our race, he is sure to have a different mind" [modified from Legge, p. 355, under the Fourth year of Duke Ch'eng; Legge takes this in the narrow sense of "kin"] and that in the "Chou Yü": "[As for the Jung and Ti barbarians . . .] they do not govern their passions; they are like the birds and beasts." [Under the Twenty-fourth year of King Hsiang, *ch.* 2 of the "Chou Yü" section of the *Kuo Yu.*]

Confucius' comments on the barbarians, *Yi*, and the Chinese, *Hsia*, abandon that racial standard and employ a cultural one as the basis for his distinction. To look more closely at this issue as it appears in the *Analects*, Confucius apparently had four different views on the subject. Tzu-kung remarked that Kuan Chung was not a man of benevolence [*jen*]. [Kuan Chung was an eminent statesman of pre-Confucian times, seventh century B.C., who assisted Duke Huan of Ch'i to make his state powerful; he is sometimes regarded as a proto-legalist. He led Ch'i in driving back the invasions of the *Ti* barbarians, who wore their hair loose and fastened their garments on the left.] Confucius replied: "But for Kuan Chung, we should now be wearing our hair unbound, and fastening our garments on the left side." This clearly evidences the attitude that the Chinese are superior to and distinct from the barbarians. "The Master was wishing to go and live among the nine wild tribes of the east. Someone said, "They are rude. How can you do such a thing?" The Master said, "If a superior man dwelt among them, what rudeness would then be?" This implicitly conveys the idea that the barbarians could be culturally assimilated. "Fan Ch'ih asked about benevolence. The Master said, "It is, in retirement, to be sedately grave; in the management of affairs, to be reverently attentive; in intercourse with others, to be strictly sincere. Though a man go among rude, uncultivated tribes, these qualities may not be neglected." "Tzu-chang asked how a man should conduct himself. The Master said, 'Let his words be sincere and truthful, and his actions honorable and careful;—such conduct may be practiced among the rude tribes of the South or the North.' " This recognizes that although the barbarians and the Chinese live apart, the same principles apply among them. "The Master said, 'The barbarians of the East and the North have retained their princes. They are not in such a state of decay as are we in China."[107] This states that in their conduct the barbarians were occasionally superior to the Chinese.

The references to the *Yi* and *Ti* barbarians in the *Ch'un-ch'iu* more or less corroborate these citations. The principle of having the Chinese within and keeping the barbarians out is to be seen in the two Commentaries [i.e., the *Kung-yang* and *Ku-liang*] in such examples as those under the Seventh year of Duke Yin, where the *Jung* barbarians attacked the Earl of Fan; the Tenth year of Duke Chuang, where King Ching [of the *man* barbarians] defeated the army of Ts'ai; the Twenty-first year of Duke Hsi, where the viscount of Ch'u seized the Duke of Sung; and the Twenty-seventh year, where a man of Ch'u [and others] laid siege to the capital of Sung; and the Fifteenth year of Duke Ch'eng, the meeting with the State of Wu at Chung-li. All these are instances of barbarian encroachments on the Chinese, and they all draw expressions of condemnation.[108] [See Legge, *Ch'un Ts'ew*, respectively pp. 22, 85–86, 179–80, 201, and 377–78.] The *Kung-yang* says of the covenant at Shao-ling in the Fourth year of Duke Hsi: "It is to be rejoiced at that Ch'u submitted. [The State of Ch'u was regarded at this time as a barbarian state. Cf. also Legge, *Tso Chuan*, p. 141, paragraph 3.] . . . They are barbarians and have been a severe plague on China. . . . Duke Huan [of Ch'i] was rescuing China and driving back the barbarians, in the end forcing the Ching [a name for the barbarians of Ch'u] to submit. This is a matter of the king's business." The purport of this is very close to that of "But for Kuan Chung, we should now be wearing our hair unbound, and fastening our garments on the left side."

As for the principles of using Chinese ways to transform the barbarians, and that China had lost the Way, these are to be seen in the two Com-

---

[107] See, respectively, *Analects*, xiv/18/2; ix/13 [Legge, p. 221]; xiii/19 [modified from Legge, p. 271]; xv/5 [modified from Legge, p. 295]; and iii/5 [Waley, pp. 94–95].

[108] The *Kung-yang* comments on the meeting with Wu at Chung-li: "The *Ch'un-ch'iu* regards its own State [of Lu] as the inner and the other Chinese states as the outer; it takes the Chinese states as the inner and the barbarians as the outer. The king desires to unify the world; why therefore are the terms inner and outer employed? This expresses the idea that it must start with those who are nearer."

mentaries in such examples as that under the Fourth year of Duke Ting, where the Marquis of Wu rescued the State of Ts'ai. The *Kung-yang* says: "Why is the ruler of Wu called 'Viscount.' It is because even though barbarian [Wu] is [here] concerned about China."[109] And again, under the Thirteenth year of Duke Ai, where the Duke of Lu held a meeting with the rulers of Chin and Wu. The *Ku-liang* says: "Is not the Viscount of Wu advanced at this meeting in Huang-ch'ih? Here it is that he is [styled] viscount. Wu was a barbarian state, where they cut their hair short and tattooed their bodies. [Its ruler now] wished, by means of the ceremonies [*li*] of Lu and the power of Chin, to bring about the wearing of both cap and garment. He contributed [also] of the products of the State to do honor to the king approved by Heaven. Wu is here advanced." [Legge, *Ch'un Ts'ew*, "Prolegomena," p. 81.] This is a case of "The *Yi* and *Ti* barbarians will come in and receive titles of nobility," to be culturally assimilated by China. Under the Seventh year of Duke Yin, when the *Jung* barbarians attacked the Earl of Fan, the *Ku-liang* says: "These *Jung* [barbarians] were [in fact the forces of] Wei [a Chinese state]. Designating Wei as *Jung* is to demote them for having attacked the emissary of the Son of Heaven [an act unworthy of a Chinese state but befitting to barbarians]; hence it is called *Jung*." [Legge, following another interpretation, regards these as real barbarians, see his *Ch'un Ts'ew*, p. 23, paragraph 7. The *Ku-liang*'s point is that the Chinese were *acting like* barbarians.] This is an example of what Confucius meant in lamenting that the barbarians, in some cases have "retained their princes," not being in such a sad state of decay as were the Chinese themselves. And under the Fourth year of Duke Ting there is the example of the State of Wu invading Ch'u. Both the *Kung-yang* and the *Ku-liang* record that the men of Wu invaded Ch'u and committed acts of unrestrained violence and licentiousness, reverting therein to the ways of barbarians. Therefore these commentaries deprive the head of the Wu state of his noble title, and "label it barbarian" again. [This was in 483 B.C. Under the Thirteenth year of Duke Ai, 505 B.C., the passage cited above, and in footnote 109, Wu previously had been "advanced" and its ruler was called viscount.] And again, under the Twenty-third year of Duke Chao, on the day *wu-ch'en*, when Wu defeated the armies of Tun Hu, Shen, Ts'ai, Ch'en, and Hsü, the *Kung-yang*, comments: "This was a battle of fixed positions. Why is it described in terms appropriate to a sudden attack?[110] This is

---

[109] The *Ku-liang* explains the reason for referring to the ruler of Wu as "viscount" as follows: "Wu kept faith with China and repelled the barbarians; Wu is here to be advanced."

[110] A note reads: "[In recording] a *cha-chan* 詐戰 ("sudden attack") the day [on which it took place] is given; [in recording] a *p'ien-chan* 偏戰 ("battle of fixed positions") the month [in which it took place] is given."

because it is not allowed for the barbarians to have mastery over China. However, why is China not then caused to hold the mastery of this situation? It is because China is also here newly barbarized." [A battle of fixed positions is one in which the rules of etiquette are observed among the participants; here the initiative is with Wu, a barbarian state. If this were recognized, it would be tantamount to a barbarian state imposing its mastery of the situation on the Chinese participants. Yet Wu's actual mastery cannot be concealed by pretending that the Chinese states were imposing their mastery on the situation, because their behavior was unworthy of the Chinese cultural tradition. Hence the historian had to avoid the issue by describing the battle in terms with no broader implications.] This also clearly shows that the distinction between the barbarians and the Chinese is determined according to their behavior. When their behavior [in respects relevant to cultural standards] varied over time, then the separation between "barbarian" and "Chinese" also came to have no fixed boundaries.

Of greatest interest to us, however, is the fact that Confucius used a cultural standard in deciding who was a barbarian and who a Chinese. In this, his intent was to bring about the transformation of the barbarians by having them adopt Chinese ways. Since the distinction between them was not one of any fixed line, but one that fluctuated according to rising or falling cultural levels, it therefore entirely lost its racial significance and became a purely cultural term. Therefore, when Confucius called something "*yi-ti*" (barbarian), its connotations were more or less like those of the modern usage of the word "wild man," and not like "Ainu" or "Malay." [I.e., specific racial designations.] What he intended by the term *chu hsia*, i.e., "the various peoples of Hsia," was also simply something like the modern usage of the term "civilized country." It did not denote "the descendants of the Yellow Emperor" or "the Chinese race." If our explanation is not here in error, then, strictly speaking, there is in Confucius' thought nothing like the modern concept of nationalism [i.e., of the racial basis of the state].

Seeking the reasons for this, we probably can find them in the body of Confucius' thought itself, as well as in its historical backgrounds. The races and the cultures of ancient China apparently achieved a mixing and blending at a comparatively early stage of their development. Among the various states of the Chou period there are many cases of states that were originally of the central cultural area [*chung kuo*] yet that moved toward the barbarian world or that fell for a time into an intermediary situation between the barbarian and the Chinese worlds, later to return to the Chinese fold. The states of Wu, Yüeh, Ch'in, and Ch'u are all examples of this.[111] The State of Chin "commenced its government ac-

---

[111] The *Shih Chi, ch.* 31, "Wu T'ai-po shih-chia," tells that T'ai-po and Chung-yung,

cording to the rules of Hsia, and defined its boundaries by the rules of the *Jung* [barbarians]." Its people were of the clans of the surname *Huai*, and its territory centered on the former capital of the Hsia dynasty.[112] Here we see very clearly the background of cultural mixing. As for the Chou culture itself, it too retained a great deal drawn from the Hsia and Yin dynasties' older institutions. The Hsia and Yin were relatively under-developed; the Chou, by comparison, was a more fully evolved culture. Statesmen of the early Chou seem to have hoped, by employing their system of "reflecting on the two past dynasties" [*Analects*, III/14] to assimilate on all sides the remnant peoples from earlier dynasties, and in this they had at least partial success. And in any event, in racial terms, all of the various peoples of the Nine Divisions of the world were similar in having yellow skins and black hair. [An early geographical concept, embracing most of the world as the Chinese saw it.] Since they were already racially mixed, it was difficult to maintain any distinctions among them on a physical basis; in contrast, culturally the variations among them —degree of civilization or wildness—made for very obvious and readily established distinctions between those nearer and those farther away. Thus it was that the distinction between barbarian and Chinese gradually shifted to the cultural standard, and it was purely the degree of their assimilation that decided the issue. Thus King Wu of [the border] State of Ch'u, although claiming descent from the Yellow Emperor, called himself a Southern barbarian [*man-yi*], while the Sage Emperor Shun and King Wen of Chou, representing respectively the Eastern and Western

---

sons of the T'ai-wang of Chou [grandfather of King Wen] fled to the region of the *Ching* and *Man* barbarians of the South, "who tatooed their bodies and cut short their hair and called themselves the [State of] Kou-wu." *Ch.* 41, "Yüeh wang kou-chien shih-chia" tells that King Kou-chien of Yüeh was a descendant of King Yü [of the Hsia Dynasty] and when his clan were enfiefed at K'uai-chi they "tatooed their bodies and cut short their hair, wore capes of woven grass and established their state there." *Ch.* 40, "Ch'u shih chia" records that the Kings of Ch'u were descendants of the Yellow Emperor's grandson Chuan-hsü. By the end of the Yin dynasty they were: "at times in the Middle Kingdom, and at times among the barbarians." In the thirty-fifth year of his reign [705 B.C.] when King Wu of Ch'u made war against the State of Sui, he still said of himself, "I am a Southern barbarian [*man-yi*]." *Ch.* 5, "Ch'in pen-chi" states that the Ch'in ruling house, descendants of Chuan-hsü, lived in the Western border regions, "at times in the Middle Kingdom, and at times among the barbarians." *Ch.* 44, "Wei shih chia" states that Kao, the Duke of Pi, of the [royal clan] surname Chi, was enfiefed at Pi, and that his descendants were disinherited and became commoners, living "at times in the Middle Kingdom, and at times among the barbarians." The ancient documents also record examples of inter-marriage between the Chinese and the barbarians.

[112] The *Tso Chuan*, Fourth year of Duke Ting [Legge, *Ch'un Ts'ew*, p. 754]. Of the three families [that divided the State of Chin into three separate kingdoms], the Chao rulers were of the same surname as the rulers of the State of Ch'in. The Wei apparently were of mixed Chinese and barbarian blood; see footnote 111. The Han were of the [royal Chou] surname Chi, and perhaps of somewhat purer lineage; see *Shih Chi, ch.* 45, "Han shih-chia."

border barbarians, yet carried their high principles into practice in the Middle Kingdom.[113]

These events were all brought about because the racial distinction had been abandoned in favor of the cultural one. Confucius' concept of barbarian versus Chinese took form amid this kind of historical conditions. Even if we were to ignore that historical background in discussing the content of Confucius' thought, his theory that the man of *jen* "loves all men, and extensively dispenses succor to the masses" in itself embodies the potential to break down ethnic boundaries. "The superior man cultivates himself in reverential carefulness" [see footnote 78 above] and after that "He is affectionate to his parents, and lovingly disposed to people generally. He is lovingly disposed to people generally, and kind to creatures."[114] If he is kind even to animal creatures, how much more so must he be to barbarians, who are, after all, of the same human race? Therefore, the ideal of "uniting and harmonizing the myriad states" so that "the barbarous tribes shall lead one another on to make their submission"[115] was undoubtedly one of which Confucius approved. However, the barbarians and the Chinese differed in that some were nearer and some were farther away, and also in the practice of benevolence, for some had been at it longer than the others. The *Kung-yang* says that the *Spring and Autumn Annals* uses the words "outer" and "inner" for the barbarians and the Chinese, making clear that the king is to unify the whole world, but that "it starts with those who are nearer." This indeed shows a grasp of Confucius' original intent; and in that respect it is much simpler and more direct, and closer to the truth, than is Ho Hsiu.[116]

---

[113] *Mencius*, iv/ii/1/1 and 2 [Legge, p. 316].

[114] *Ibid.*, vii/i/45 [Legge, p. 476].

[115] *Documents*, "*Yao tien*" [Legge, p. 17] and "*Shun tien*" [Legge, p. 42].

[116] The *Spring and Autumn Annals*, in its rectification of names, displays in different places four different attitudes: (1) It rigidly maintains the principle that all ". . . ceremonies, music, and punitive military expeditions proceed from the Son of Heaven" [*Analects*, xvi/2/1; Legge, p. 310] and uses condemnatory expressions for all matters that are not in accordance with rites and institutes, or that disregarded or confused of the prerogatives of legitimate status. (2) With respect to all "ceremonies, music, and punitive military expeditions that proceed from the feudal lords" in the course of government by the Lord Protectors, it allows a certain degree of approbation. (3) Those among the Great Officers who arrogate to themselves the rights of governing but who do so in the spirit of the Lords Protector, in order to maintain the feudal order, are also granted approval. (4) When barbarians accord with the ways of the Chinese and carry out actions in the spirit of government by the Lord Protectors, they are advanced to noble title and rank. This, then, also affords an example of the intimacy of the relationship between Confucius' thought and the feudal world.

CHAPTER THREE
Mencius and Hsün Tzu

SECTION ONE
The Lives and the Times of Mencius and Hsün Tzu

THE *Analects* records that Confucius' teachings were of four divisions [or subject-classes]* and the *Han Fei Tzu* states that "the *ju* learning had divided into eight branches"; the *Shih Chi* also has said that the Confucian school "had seventy-seven followers who received his instruction and became deeply versed in it."[1] Something of the flourishing condition of the Confucian thought and learning can be learned from these statements. However, not everyone who underwent training in consequence of which he was able to find employment in government necessarily also founded an independent line of teachings that could become prominent in its own right, and even those who did write books or establish their own theories were not all successful in having these transmitted to later ages. Among Confucius' later followers, of those whose political thought merits consideration as a distinct intellectual position and for which there are documentary remains that attest it, we have only the two figures, Mencius and Hsün Tzu.[2]

---

*Square brackets indicate that the words enclosed were added by the translator.

[1] *Analects*, XI, "Hsien chin" "Distinguished for their achievement in virtuous principles and practice, there were Yen Yuan, Min Tzu-ch'ien, Jan Po-niu, and Chung-kung. In language and speaking there were Tsai Wo and Tzu-kung. In affairs of government, there were Jan Yu and Chi Lu. In the study of literature, there were Tzu-yu and Tzu-hsia. [These are the "four divisions" of Confucius' teachings. Modified from Legge, pp. 237–38.] The *Han Fei Tzu, ch.* 50, "Hsien hsüeh": "Since the death of Confucius, there have appeared the School of Tzu-chang, the School of Tzu-ssu, the School of the Yen Clan, the School of the Meng Clan, the School of the Ch'i-tiao Clan, the School of the Chung Liang Clan, the School of the Sun Clan, and the School of the Yo-cheng Clan. [These led to the "eight branches" of the School. W. K. Liao translation, *Han Fei Tzu*, Vol. 2, p. 298.] The *Shih Chi, ch.* 67, "Chung-ni ti-tzu lieh chuan" briefly records the words and deeds of the seventy disciples. [See Legge, *Analects*, "Prolegomena," pp. 112–27 for a useful compendium of traditional information about Confucius' followers.]

[2] The *Han Shu, ch.* 30, "Journal of Literature" under the heading "Ju chia" ["Confucian School"] includes such writings as: *Tzu-ssu*, twenty-three chapters (*p'ien*); *Tseng Tzu*, eighteen chapters; *Ch'i-tiao Tzu*, thirteen chapters; *Mi Tzu* [also read "*Fu Tzu*"], sixteen chapters, etc. Except for the *Mencius* and the *Hsün Tzu*, none of these is extant, except that the teachings of Tzu-ssu may perhaps be evident in the "Chung-yung," *ch.* 28, and the "Piao chi," *ch.* 29, of the *Li Chi*, and Tseng Tzu's teachings may likewise be evident in the "Tseng Tzu li-shih," the "Pen hsiao," and other such sections of the *Ta-tai Li Chi*. Even if all the views of Han period persons about the transmission of the canon by the disciples were wholly reliable, they still would provide insufficient evidence to reconstruct the thought of the seventy disciples.

Mencius and Hsün Tzu both were transmitters of the Confucian teachings. Because the historical environments in which they found themselves were different from that of Confucius, the content of their thought also evidences some slight changes and differences. Confucius lived in the last years of the Spring and Autumn Era; Mencius and Hsün Tzu lived in the later part of the Warring States Period. The institutions and the values of the feudal world in the former time still partially existed, had not yet wholly vanished; but by the latter age they had been eradicated without leaving any lingering traces. The *Shih Chi* writes, of the background of Mencius' times: "During this time, the State of Ch'in, employing Lord Shang [eminent proponent of Legalist theories and methods; see below, Chapter Seven], enriched the state and strengthened its military power. The States of Ch'u and Wei employing Wu Ch'i" [professional minister who served both states, emphasizing laws and strict methods; see below, footnote 104], defeated their weaker neighbors in warfare. Kings Wei and Hsüan in the State of Ch'i, employed the followers of Sun Tzu and T'ien Chi [military theorists and strategists], and all the feudal princes looked eastward to pay court to Ch'i. The whole world was concerned primarily with joining the vertical alliance or associating with the horizontal alliance, regarding attacks and field campaigns as the most worthy undertakings. Yet Mencius was setting forth the virtues of the Sage Emperors Yao and Shun and of the Three Dynasties of Antiquity. Thus it was that he could not get along with the persons [in power] whom he encountered, so he retired and, with men like Wan Chang, devoted himself to explaining the *Odes* and *Documents*, and setting forth the ideas of Confucius; and thus he wrote the *Mencius* in seven books."[3]

Hsün Tzu's environment was similar to this. The difference between the two lay simply in the fact that the earlier rivalry between Ch'i and Chin for seizure of dominant power among the states had given way by the later time to one in which Chao had displaced the power of Ch'i, and Ch'in had developed even greater strength and influence, preparing for the time, now near at hand, when it would annex the other six states. [This sentence is somewhat paraphrased in translation.] The precise dates of the birth and death of both Mencius and Hsün Tzu still remain unverified today. The events of their lives, too, have been preserved only in bare outline.

Meng K'o [Mencius is a latinization based on his surname, Meng; his given name is K'o, also spelled K'e] was a man of the State of Tsou, who studied under a follower of Tzu-ssu, [i.e., K'ung Chi, Confucius' grandson, and one of the principal transmitters of the Confucian teachings].

---

[3] *Shih Chi*, ch. 74, "Meng, Hsün lieh chuan." Refer also to the "Introduction" and to footnote 11 of Chapter One of the present work. [The passage cited is also translated in Fung/Bodde, Vol. I, p. 107.]

If we accept the findings of Chou Kuang-yeh in his *Meng Tzu ssu k'ao*, Mencius was born in the Seventeenth year of King Ai [of Chou] and died in the Twelfth or the Thirteenth year of King Nan [the last Chou King].[4] Throughout his whole life he travelled to the States of Sung, Hsüeh, T'eng, Lu, Liang [Wei], and Ch'i, his reputation ever growing, and his way of life ever more opulent. "The carriages in his train numbered several dozens, and his followers numbered several hundred, as he travelled about living off one after another of the feudal princes." [Cf. *Mencius*, III/ii/4; Legge, pp. 269–70.] Not only Yen Hui and Yuan Hsien [two of Confucius' best disciples, noted both for their retiring behavior and for their poverty] would not have been able [to approach close enough] so much as to glimpse him; even Confucius with his single cart drawn by two horses presented an appearance that is by no means in a class with Mencius. P'eng Keng wondered if Mencius were not too extravagant;[5] and this doubt was in truth not without some ground. However, though Mencius' fame grew to great proportions, his actual accomplishments in government were quite meager. During the reign of King Hsüan he served as a minister [*ch'ing*] in the State of Ch'i, receiving an emolument as great as ten thousand *chung*,[6] far greater in its prestige and prominence than the office of Minister of Crime in Lu that Confucius held. [The interpretation of this amount is difficult; see note in Legge, *Mencius*, "Prolegomena," p. 28.] Yet in the end his doctrines of benevolence and righteousness were unavailing; they did not change the current emphasis on strengthening and enriching the state. After a short time he resigned his office and left Ch'i, and thereafter probably never again held office.

Hsün K'uang's courtesy name was Ch'ing. He was a man of the State of Chao. Wang Chung [1745–1794] has concluded that Hsün Tzu lived

---

[4] These dates would correspond with the years 385–303 or 302 B.C. of the Western calendar. The old view is that he was born in the Fourth year of King Lieh and died in the Twentieth year of King Nan (372–289 B.C.); see Ch'eng Fu-hsin, *Meng Tzu nien-p'u*. In addition, reference may be made to: Yen Jo-chü, *Meng Tzu sheng-tsu-nien-yüeh k'ao*; Ti Tzu-ch'i, *Meng Tzu pien-nien*; Jen Chao-lin, *Meng Tzu shih-shih-lüeh* (in *Hsin-chai shih chung*); Lin Ch'un-p'u, *K'ung Meng nien-piao*; *Meng Tzu lieh-chuan tsuan* (in *Chu-po Shan-fang shih-wu chung*); Ts'ui Shu, *Meng Tzu shih-shih lu*; Wei Yuan, *Meng Tzu nien piao k'ao* (in *Ku-wei-t'ang wai-chi*), etc.

[5] *Mencius*, "T'eng wen-kung," Part II [III/ii/4; Legge, p. 269].

[6] Wang Chung's *Ching-yi hsin-chih chi* states that Mencius ". . . occupied the position of guest-teacher and was respected for his knowledge of the Way." Ts'ui Shu's *Meng Tzu shih-shih-lu* [see footnote 4 above] states: "Mencius held the office of minister [*ch'ing*] in the State of Ch'i, that is, he served as a guest-minister (*k'e ch'ing*), and as such was not the same as those who held office and bore responsibility for official duties." Ti Tzu-ch'i's *Meng Tzu pien-nien* [see footnote 4 above] states: "When Mencius was in the State of Ch'i he first served as a guest-teacher; therefore he received the Duke's gift of subsistence income, but did not receive a salary of office. Subsequently he served as a minister, and received a salary of one hundred thousand [*chung*] of grain."

roughly between the Seventeenth year of King Nan and the Ninth year of the First Emperor[7] [298–238 B.C.], which seems to be close to the truth. As a youth, he went to study at Chi-hsia [the great academy maintained by the Dukes of Ch'i], and on one occasion discussed the problem of safety and danger in international affairs with the chief minister of Ch'i.[8] Finding no employment at the court of Ch'i, however, he left during the reign of King Min [312–282 B.C.] of Ch'i and went to the State of Ch'u, where he became the magistrate of Lan-ling.[9] In addition he appears to have visited the State of Yen, where he failed to be

[7] Wang Chung's *Hsün Tzu nien-piao* (in *Shü-hsueh nei-wai p'ien*). This corresponds to the years 298–238 B.C. of the Western calendar. Ch'ien Mu's *Hsien Ch'in chu-tzu hsi-nien k'ao-pien*, Section 103, states that Hsün Ch'ing was born before the Thirtieth year of the Chou King Hsien (i.e., before 340 B.C. by the Western calendar); this significantly supplements Wang's view. Also, the problem of Hsün Tzu's teacher and the line of transmission that he represented has never been established by scholarship. Liang Ch'i-ch'ao's view (in *Ju-chia che-hsüeh*) that Hsün Tzu's learning stems from the line of transmission through [Confucius' disciples] Yu Tzu [i.e., Jan-ch'iu] and Tzu-yu [i.e., Yen Yen] and Tzu-hsia [i.e., Pu Shang] may be inadequately supported by facts, particularly in view of the fact that Hsün Tzu, in his essay, ch. 6, "Fei shih-erh tzu," i.e., "Denunciation of the Twelve Philosophers" classes Tzu-kung [i.e., Chung-kung, or Jan Yung] together with Confucius himself, and denounces Tzu-chang, Tzu-hsia, and Tzu-yu as unworthy Confucians.

[8] For his conversation with the chief minister of Ch'i, see *Hsün Tzu ch.* 16, "Ch'iang kuo p'ien." In brief, he said that when Ch'u (lying on Ch'i's south and east), Yen (to the north), and Wei (to the west) plotted together, "Ch'i would be certain to be broken up into quarters," and that only by cultivating the rites and deferring to men of loyalty and trust could the country become firm in itself. As to Hsün Tzu's first coming to Chi-hsia, there are two versions of the account, the one that he was fifty at the time, and the other that he was fifteen. The former is recorded in the *Shih Chi, ch.* 74, "Meng, Hsün lieh chuan," and in Liu Hsiang, *Sun Ch'ing shu lu hsü.* The latter stems from Ying Shao's *Feng-su t'ung, ch.* 7, "Ch'iung t'ung p'ien."

[9] His reason for leaving Ch'i and going to Ch'u has traditionally been explained in two ways: that he was slandered, and that the State of Ch'i was imperiled. His biography in *ch.* 74 of the *Shih Chi* says: "Someone in the State of Ch'i slandered Hsün Ch'ing; at any rate Hsün Ch'ing went to Ch'u, where the Lord of Ch'un-shen made him magistrate of Lan-ling." [This more or less follows Dubs' translation of the *Shih Chi* biography, in his *Hsüntze, the Moulder of Ancient Confucianism*, pp. 26–28.] The accounts in the *Feng su-t'ung* and Liu Hsiang's [*Sun Ch'ing shu lu*] *Hsü* say roughly the same thing. The chapter "Lun Ju" in Huan K'uan's *Yen-t'ieh lun* says: "King Min of Ch'i struggled vigorously to carry on [Ch'i's success in war] for a second generation [following the successes of his father, King Hsüan] . . . and sought glory incessantly. The common people could bear no more. [Adding two characters missing from the quoted passage.] All the scholars remonstrated, but were not heeded, so they all scattered. Shen Tao and Chieh Tzu departed; T'ien P'ien went to the State of Hsüeh; and Sun [i.e., Hsün] Ch'ing went to the State of Ch'u." If Hsün Tzu went to Ch'u in the last year of King Min's reign [282 B.C.] then he must have been about fifty-six years old before the year 284 B.C. In the year 262 B.C., the Lord of Ch'un-shen was chief minister to King K'ao-lieh of Ch'u. By that year Hsün Tzu would have to have been nearly eighty years of age. Ch'ien Mu, in his *Hsien Ch'in chu-tzu hsi-nien k'ao-pien*, number 140, observes that the *Shih Chi* account is in error.

appointed to office.[10] During the reign of King Hsiang [281–264 B.C.], he again lived for a time in Ch'i, and at Chi-hsia "was the most eminent senior teacher."[11] After that he again left Ch'i, visited the State of Ch'in, and returned to his native Chao. While in Ch'in he replied to King Chao's question about the usefulness of the Confucian teachings, and discussed the political measures of Ch'in with the Marquis of Ying, on which occasions he greatly stressed the doctrines of filial and fraternal submission, of right-eousness and of good faith.[12] [The Marquis of Ying was the title borne by the political strategist Fan Chü, also read Fan Sui, who served as Chief Minister, *hsiang*, in the State of Ch'in at this time.] In the State of Chao he held the office of Chief Minister [*shang ch'ing*], and joined with the Lord of Lin-wu in submitting proposals on military affairs to King Hsiao-ch'eng.[13] If the *Shih Chi* is reliable in recording that his death and burial both took place at Lan-ling, then it would seem that, in his last years, he must have again taken up residence in Ch'u.

No more than twenty or thirty years after Hsün Tzu's death, the First Emperor completed his unification of the empire.[14] Although the doc-trines to which Hsün Tzu adhered all his life were not always in complete

---

[10] *Han Fei Tzu, ch.* 38, "Nan san," "King K'uai of Yen held Tzu-chih to be a worthy counsellor, and rejected Hsün Ch'ing; as a consequence he was murdered and became the butt of the world's scorn." [Tzu-chih was the inept prime minister to the muddle-headed King K'uai; between them their policies brought about the destruction of Yen by Ch'i. This passage appears on pages 179–80 of W. K. Liao's translation of *Han Fei Tzu*; the translation here departs from that.] Ch'i's war against Yen took place in the year 314 B.C. If Hsün Tzu did indeed visit Yen, it must have been in his youth when he was living in Ch'i.

[11] The accounts in the *Shih Chi* and in Liu Hsiang's [*Sun Ch'ing shu lu*] *Hsü* agree on this, except that they do not say that he went again to Ch'i. This follows Ch'ien Mu's view; see his *Hsien Ch'in chu-tzu hsi-nien k'ao pien*, number 143.

[12] See *Hsün Tzu, ch.* 8, "Ju hsiao," and *ch.* 16, "Ch'iang kuo."

[13] *Chan kuo ts'e*, "Ch'u ts'e, 4," Sun [Hsün] Tzu left and went to the State of Chao; in Chao he was made a Chief Minister." [Hsün Tzu's name is variously written Sun in many early works; "Chief Minister" does not mean an actual premier, but a minister accorded the highest honor and dignity.] Chapter Seven of the *Feng su t'ung* says that while Hsün Tzu was in office as magistrate of Lan-ling, someone slandered him, so "The Lord of Ch'un-shen dismissed him. Sun [Hsün] Ch'ing went to the State of Chao, and accepted an appointment to office in the State of Ch'in." *Hsün Tzu, ch.* 15, "Yi ping p'ien," records Hsün Tzu's proposals made together with the Lord of Lin-wu before King Hsiao-ch'eng of Chao. King Hsiao-ch'eng reigned between the years 265 and 245 B.C., when Hsün Tzu's age may have been over eighty.

[14] Ch'ien Mu regards as unreliable the lines in *ch.* 18, "Hui hsüeh pien," in the *Yen T'ieh lun*, which say: "Li Ssu held the prime ministership in Ch'in [from 221 B.C.] be-cause the First Emperor relied on him, and no other minister could be compared with him. Because of it, Hsün Ch'ing refused to eat [and died]." Instead, he tentatively concludes that Hsün Tzu died about the second year of the First Emperor's reign. [I.e., 244 B.C.] See *Hsien Ch'in chu-tzu hsi-nien k'ao pien*, number 156.

conformity with those of Confucius and Mencius, nonetheless, from the evidence of them, and that of his desire to employ the teachings about the rites and righteousness with which to modify the methods of government, removing their use of brute force and deceit, and in his insistent drumming away at the theme, consistently maintaining his principles, he is quite worthy of being regarded as a forceful contributor to the later Confucian school. Yet Hsün Tzu lived just on the eve of the establishment of the authoritarian empire. He travelled about through all the states during his entire life, from early manhood to old age. "The rulers were kept apart and would not be seen; worthy men were estranged and not granted office."[15] He was not so successful as were his followers Han Fei and Li Ssu in having his doctrines carried out,[16] or in serving in a chief ministerial position. So, in the frustrating circumstances that beset his life, he was no different from Confucius and Mencius.

SECTION TWO
The Importance of the People

CONFUCIUS centered his discussions of government on benevolence or *jen* as its primary element. Mencius accepted this doctrine and further developed it into his theories of "the benevolent mind" *jen hsin* and "benevolent government" *jen cheng*, which he subsequently worked out fully and in great detail. The point of origin of the benevolent mind is in the fundamental goodness of human nature. Mencius believed that the four virtues—benevolence, righteousness, propriety, and wisdom—all came into being as extensions and developments of every human being's innate sense of commiseration, of shame, of respect, and of right and wrong.[17] Therefore, "All men can be Yaos and Shuns,"[18] and the be-

---

[15] See, *Hsün Tzu*, *ch*. 32, "Yao wen p'ien." The preceding passage is: "Sun Ch'ing [i.e., Hsün Tzu], pressed by the chaotic conditions of his time, tended to rely on harsh punishments. There had long been no worthy overlords, and ahead lay only the tyrannical State of Ch'in. Propriety and righteousness were not observed, moral suasion through teaching could not be realized, the benevolent suffered. The world was dark and foreboding."

[16] The *Shih Chi*, *ch*. 63, "Lao, Chuang, Shen, Han lieh chuan" says: "[Han] Fei and Li Ssu both studied under Hsün Ch'ing; *ch*. 87, "Li Ssu lieh chuan" states: "[Li Ssu] became a student of Hsün Ch'ing in the study of the methods of emperors and kings."

[17] *Mencius*, "Kao Tzu," Part 1; Mencius, replying to Kung-tu Tzu's question about human nature, says: "The feeling of commiseration belongs to all men; so does that of shame and dislike; and that of reverence and respect, and that of right and wrong. The feeling of commiseration springs from benevolence [*jen*]; that of shame and dislike from righteousness [*yi*]; and that of reverence and respect from propriety [*li*]; and that of right and wrong from wisdom [*chih*]. [Modified from Legge, *Mencius*, vi/i/6/7, p. 402.] Also, in "Kung-sun Ch'ou," Part 1: "Mencius said, 'All men have a mind that cannot bear to see the sufferings of others. The ancient kings had this commiserating mind, and as a matter

nevolent mind is something common to all men.[19] Sages and worthies are different from other men in their ability to nourish and expand the goodness of their original natures. The superior man differs from the small and mean man in his ability to enlarge the scope of that which he "cannot endure" [*pu jen* 不忍, "cannot endure the sufferings of others"; "compassion"]. When the benevolent mind develops and manifests itself in actions, that becomes "the realization in deeds of one's kindness of heart."[20] A benevolent government is one that, by applying the mind that cannot bear [the sufferings of others], succeeds in realizing in deeds that kindness of the heart. On a smaller scale it can be achieved in one state; on a larger scale it can extend throughout the world. It commences in being affec-

---

of course they had a commiserating government. When with a commiserating mind was practiced a commiserating government, to rule the kingdom was as easy a matter as to make something roll around in the palm of one's hand.' " He also said: "The commiserating mind is the beginning of benevolence. The shamed and revulsed mind is the beginning of righteousness. The humble and deferring mind is the beginning of propriety. And the mind that distinguishes right from wrong is the beginning of wisdom. . . . Since all men have these four beginnings in themselves, let them know how to give them all their development and completion. It is like a fire starting to burn, or a spring starting to flow." [*Mencius*, II/i/6/1–2 and 7, wording considerably modified from Legge, pp. 201 and 203. With the extension of its meaning, the word "*li*" or "ritual" often, as here, must be translated "propriety," or "a sense of the ritually, or socially, appropriate." Note that the word "*jen*," below, in the term "*pu jen*" or "compassion" bears no relation to "*jen*" or "benevolence."]

[18] "Kao Tzu," Part II, "Chiao of Ts'ao asked Mencius, saying, 'It is said, "All men may be Yaos and Shuns." Is it so?' Mencius replied, 'It is.' " It should be noted [in contrast], that on the subject of man's nature, Confucius: ". . . will not tell us anything at all." [*Analects*, v/12; Waley, p. 110.] The few incidentally relevant passages in the *Analects*, such as: ". . . the very stupidest . . . cannot change" [*Analects*, XVII/3, Waley, p. 209]; and, "to those who are below mediocrity, the highest subjects cannot be announced" [*Analects*, VI/19; Legge, p. 191]; or the statement that "By nature, men are nearly alike; by practice, they get wide apart" [*Analects*, XVII/2; Legge, p. 318]—all these vary somewhat from Mencius' theory of the goodness of human nature.

[19] "Kao Tzu," Part I, Mencius said: "Benevolence [*jen*] is man's mind." [*Mencius*, VI/i/11/1; Legge, p. 414.]

[20] In *The Mencius*, I, "Liang Hui-wang," Part I, Mencius says to King Hsüan of Ch'i, "Treat with the reverence due to age the elders in your own family, so that the elders in the families of others shall be similarly treated; treat with the kindness due to youth the young in your own family, so that the young in the families of others shall be similarly treated. Do this, and the kingdom may be made to go around in your palm. It is said in the *Book of Odes*: 'His example affected his wife. It reached to his brothers, and both his family and his State were governed by it.' The language shows how King Wen simply took his kindly heart, and exercised it toward those parties. Therefore, a prince's carrying out his kindness of heart will suffice for the love and protection of all within the four seas. And if he does not carry it out, he will not be able to protect his wife and children. The way in which the ancients came greatly to surpass other men was no other than this: Simply they knew well how to carry out, so as to affect others, what they themselves did." [*Mencius*, I/i/7/12; modified from Legge, pp. 143–44.]

tionate to one's parents, and reaches its limits in being kind to creatures.[21] All of these pronouncements are in fact based squarely on Confucius. They are more detailed in their expression, but in no sense do they differ in their basic meaning.

The benevolent government must have its concrete forms through which to be practiced. Mencius' statements on this would all seem to be more or less summed up under the headings: to teach and to nourish. Moreover, his theory of nurturing the people is especially penetrating, and quite precisely delineated; there is nothing comparable to it in all the pre-Ch'in philosophies [i.e., in all the philosophies of the Golden Age of Chinese philosophy, sixth to third centuries B.C., prior to the unification of the Empire under the Ch'in dynasty in 221 B.C.]. Throughout the Seven Books of the *Mencius*, Mencius focuses his concern on enriching the people's livelihood, decreasing taxes and imposts, bringing wars to an end, and correcting boundaries.[22] In addition to these, Mencius also proposed the

[21] *The Mencius*, VII, "Chin hsin," Part I, "[The superior man is] . . . affectionate to his parents, and lovingly disposed to people generally. He is lovingly disposed to people generally, and kind to creatures." [*Mencius*, VII/i/45; Legge, p. 476.]

[22] The essentials of Mencius' view on enriching the people's livelihood can be seen in *The Mencius*, I, "Liang Hui-wang," Part I, in his remarks addressed to King Hui. He said, in part: "If the seasons of husbandry are not interfered with [i.e., if the government does not divert the peasants from their essential agricultural labors at these seasons of the year when they must devote their full energy to them], the grain will be more than can be eaten. If close nets are not allowed in the pools and ponds, the fishes and turtles will be more than can be consumed. If axes and bills enter the hills and forests only at the proper time, the wood will be more than can be used. When the grain and fish and turtles are more than can be eaten, and there is more wood than can be used, this enables the people to nourish their living and mourn for their dead, without any dissatisfactions or regrets. This condition in which the people nourish their living and bury their dead, without any dissatisfactions or regrets, is the first step toward kingly government. Let mulberry trees be planted about the homesteads in the five *mou* of land allotted for the dwelling [one *mou* was about one-sixth of an acre] and persons of fifty years of age may be clothed with silk. In keeping fowls, pigs, dogs, and swine, let not their times of breeding he neglected, and persons of seventy years may eat flesh. Let there not be taken away the time that is proper for the cultivation of the farm with its one hundred *mou*, and the family of several mouths that is supported by it shall not suffer from hunger." [*Mencius*, I/i/3/3–4, modified slightly from Legge, pp. 130–31.] His views on light taxation are briefly set forth in "T'eng Wen-kung," Part II, where he speaks of "Levying taxes of one-tenth only, and doing away with the duties charged at the customs barriers and in the markets" [*Mencius*, III/ii/8/1; modified slightly from Legge, p. 278]. Also, in "Chin hsin," Part II: "There are the exactions of hempen cloth and silk, of grain, and of personal service. The prince demands but one of these at a time, deferring the other two" [*Mencius*, VII/ii/26/1, modified slightly from Legge, p. 491]. Also, in "Kung-sun Ch'ou," Part I: "[The ruler should] . . . in the market place of his capital, levy a ground rent on the shops, but not tax the goods, or, enforce the proper regulations but not even levy a ground rent. . . . At his frontier passes, there should be an inspection of persons, but no taxes charged. . . . He should require the farmers to give their mutual aid to cultivate the public field, and exact no

idea that [the ruler] should "let the people share the same pleasures as his own." His reply to the question put to him in the Snow Palace by King Hsüan of Ch'i was: "When a ruler rejoices in the joy of his people, they also rejoice in his joy; when he grieves in the sorrow of his people, they also grieve at his sorrow. A common bond of joy will pervade the kingdom; a common bond of sorrow will do the same."[23] His meaning is set forth here with remarkable clarity and aptness, profound and far-reaching in its import; nothing Confucius ever said, in fact, matches it. To eat well and live in comfort and peace are things that all men enjoy. People would not live in earth-floored huts and under straw roofs unless compelled to do so; since that would be contrary to human nature, it definitely should not be done. [Mo Tzu and other early writers ascribe such austerities to Yao and other sages of antiquity.] But if the ruler were capable of applying the governmental technique of carrying out in deeds the kindness of one's heart, the whole nation would overflow with joy and the ultimate limits of benevolent government could be achieved.

---

other taxes from them;" and "From the shop-keepers in his market place he should not exact the fine of the individual idler, or of the hamlet's quota of cloth" [*Mencius*, II/i/5/1–5, modified slightly from Legge, pp. 199–200; who found the meaning obscure; see his note, p. 200. Cf. the translation of passages concerning the economy, including this one, in Dobson, *Mencius*, pp. 178 ff.]. However, Mencius rejected Po Kuei's suggestion that he should levy a tax of only one-twentieth; see "Kao Tzu," Part II [VI/ii/10/1; Legge, pp. 441–42]. On the subject of stopping wars, see "Kao Tzu," Part II, where Mencius tells Shen Tzu that the State of Lu is already larger than one hundred *li* square, which was its original size and says: "Though by a single battle you should subdue Ch'i, and get possession of Nan-yang, the thing ought not to be done." [*Mencius*, VI/ii/8; Legge, pp. 438–30.] There is also the example in "Liang Hui-wang," Part II, where Mencius urges Duke Wen of T'eng to model his actions on those of King T'ai, who left the area of Pin, adopting a policy of non-resistance to the *Ti* barbarians [who were continually attacking it; I/ii/14, Legge, p. 174].

Other examples illustrating these points are numerous; it is not necessary to cite all of them.

On the matter of correcting the boundaries, see "T'eng Wen-kung," Part I, "Now, the first thing toward a benevolent government is to lay down the boundaries. . . . I would ask you, in the remoter districts, observing the nine-squares division, to reserve one division to be cultivated on the system of mutual aid, and in the more central parts of the kingdom, to make the people pay for themselves a tenth part of their produce." And, "a square *li* covers nine squares of land [more literally, "A square *li* makes one well-[field]," or *ching* 井, i.e. 田], which nine squares contain nine hundred *mou*. The central square is the public field, and eight families, each having its private hundred *mou*, cultivate in common the public field."

[23] "Liang Hui-wang," Part II [*Mencius*, I/ii/4/3; slightly modified from Legge, p. 158]. The tone of the comments is the same in three other relevant passages: in the same chapter, where Mencius answers Chung Pao's question about King Hui's love of music [I/ii/1/1]; where King Hsüan of Ch'i asks Mencius about the size of King Wen's palace park [I/ii/2]; and in "Liang Hui-wang," Part I, where Mencius responded to King Hui's question asked at the edge of the pond [I/i/2].

Mencius, placing so much stress on the people's livelihood, consequently was extemely harsh in condemning the princes and ministers of his own time who were guilty of the failure to nourish the people fully, never willing to forgive them on this count. For example, he condemned King Hui of Liang, saying that he was guilty of "leading on beasts to devour the people"; and to Duke Mu of Tsou he said that "the superiors in your State have been negligent, and cruel to their inferiors." He denounced those given to warfare, saying that they should "suffer the highest punishment," and he accused the promoters of the policies of strengthening and enriching the state of being what the ancients called "robbers of the people."[24] The *Documents* contains the phrase: "The people are the root of a country"[25] [the following line is: "The root firm, the country is tranquil," Legge, p. 158]; certainly Mencius was the one who most ably expounded and illuminated the significance of this concept.

On the essentials of his concept of nourishing the people, Mencius tirelessly reiterated and expanded his views. But he usually treated the subject of teaching the people as something subsidiary to it, and set that forth only in its larger outlines. Therefore, replying to King Hui of Liang's question about how to wipe out the disgrace of Chin [i.e. Liang] having been defeated, Mencius said: "being sparing in the use of punishments and fines, and making the taxes and levies light, so causing that the fields shall be plowed deep, and the weeding of them be carefully attended to, and that the strong-bodied, during their days of leisure, shall cultivate their filial piety, fraternal respectfulness, sincerity and truthfulness, serving thereby at home their fathers and elder brothers, and abroad their elders and superiors. . . ."[26] [If he did thus, Mencius assured the king, his people, without proper arms, would be more than a match for the legions of enemy states.] When Duke Wen of T'eng asked him about the proper way of governing a country, after discussing landholding, taxes, and imposts, Mencius said to him: "Establish *hsiang, hsü, hsüeh* and *hsiao* [four traditional categories of schools; see above, Chapter Two, p. 184] for the instruction of the people," and "The object of them all is to illustrate the human relations."[27] Discussions of the meaning of education throughout the whole Seven Books of the *Mencius* go no further than just this. Compared with Confucius' attitude that good faith [between ruler and people] is fundamental, while food is merely the last item in impor-

[24] See, respectively, "Liang Hui-wang," Part I [I/i/4; Legge, pp. 132–34]; Part II [I/ii/12/2; Legge, p. 173]; "Li Lou," Part I [IV/i/14/3; Legge, p. 305]; and "Kao Tzu," Part II [VI/ii/9/1; Legge, p. 440]. [All of the above quotations are slightly modified from Legge's wording of the same passages.]

[25] [*Shang Shu* or *Documents*], "Documents of Hsia," "Wu tzu chih ko" [Legge, p. 158].

[26] "Liang Hui-wang," Part I [*Mencius*, I/i/5/3; Legge, p. 135].

[27] "T'eng Wen-kung," Part I [*Mencius*, III/i/3/10; Legge, p. 242].

tance, we see here a very apparent discrepancy in emphasis. [This refers to the ranking, in their importance to the well-being of the state, of faith, weapons, and food; see *Analects*, xii/7, and Chapter Two above, note 64.]

Seeking an explanation of this, one encounters two facts that seem to be relevent: First, Mencius appears to have been heavily influenced by the idea that only when food and clothing are adequately supplied can one meaningfully maintain distinctions between honor and disgrace [This alludes to a passage in the *Kuan Tzu*, i, "Mu Min," which has been translated: "When garment and food suffice for their needs, they will distinguish between honor and shame." Lewis Maverick, *The Kuan-Tzu*, p. 31], recognizing therein that an abundant material life is a prerequisite condition for morality. Thus he said: "The Way [i.e., *Tao*, which here might also be translated "ethical orientation"] of the people is this:—if they have a constant livelihood, they will have constant hearts; if they have not a constant livelihood, they have not constant hearts. If they have not constant hearts, there is nothing they will not do in the way of self-abandonment, of moral deflection, of depravity, and of wild license." He also said: ". . . an intelligent ruler will regulate the livelihood of the people, so as to make sure that, for those above them, they shall have sufficient wherewith to serve their parents, and, for those below them, sufficient wherewith to support their wives and children; that in good years they shall always be abundantly satisfied and in bad years they shall escape the danger of perishing. After this he may urge them, and they will proceed to what is good, for in this case the people will follow after with ease. Nowadays the livelihood of the people is so regulated, that, above, they have not sufficient wherewith to serve their parents, and, below, they have not sufficient wherewith to support their wives and children. Notwithstanding good years, their lives are continually embittered, and, in bad years, they do not escape perishing. In such circumstances they only try to save themselves from death, and are afraid they will not succeed. What leisure have they to cultivate propriety and righteousness?"[28]

Second, Mencius once said: ". . . never was there a time when the sufferings of the people from tyrannical government were more intense than the present."[29] We may refer to the slaughter of populations in warfare as one proof of his statement. The "Liu kuo piao" or "Table of Events in the Period of the Warring States," *ch.* 15, in the *Shih Chi* records that, in the Fifth year of King Hsien [363 B.C.] at the battle between the forces of Ch'in and Wei at Shih-men, sixty thousand heads were taken; in the Fourth year of King Shen-ching [316 B.C.] when Ch'in defeated

[28] See, respectively, "Teng Wen-kung," Part i [iii/i/3/3; modified from Legge, pp. 239–40]; and "Liang Hui-wang," Part i [i/i/7/21–22; modified slightly from Legge, p. 148].
[29] "Kung-sun Ch'ou," Part i [ii/i/2/11; Legge, p. 184].

Chao and Han, eighty thousand heads were taken; in the Third year
of King Nan [311 B.C.] when Ch'in attacked the armies of Ch'u, eighty
thousand heads were taken; and in the Eighth year [306 B.C.] when
Ch'in captured the stronghold at Yi-yang, eighty thousand heads were
taken. All these events took place during Mencius' lifetime.[30] Although
the numbers of heads cut off may not be entirely reliable, yet when compared with the accounts of warfare in the Spring and Autumn Period as
the *Tso Chuan* records them, one truly has the feeling that the earlier age
was better than this one. So Mencius said: "When contentions about
territory are the ground on which they fight, they slaughter men until
the fields are filled with them. When some struggle for a city is the ground
on which they fight, they slaughter men until the city is filled with them."[31]
And indeed, these words are neither forced nor without foundation in
fact. Mencius, appealing to the compassion of the human heart, wanted
to overcome the faults of the tyrannical government of his time. Thus he
repeatedly directed his remarks to the distress of the common people, and
from this produced his theory of the need to "protect the people," *pao min*.
In this he was undoubtedly much affected by the influences of his own age;
it does not signify in him any conscious desire on his part to alter the
teachings of Confucius.

We can go a step further and say that, although Mencius was stimulated
by his historical environment to advocate policies of regulating agricultural
production to assure abundance for the people,[32] he made no compromise
with the prevailing current of the time that would have led him to accept
its utilitarianism [*kung-li* 功利]. For, proceeding from his theory of the

[30] When, in the Twenty-second year of King Nan [292 B.C.], Po Chi [commanding the
armies of Ch'in] defeated the State of Han and took two hundred and forty thousand
heads, Mencius was dead, so he did not know of this occasion. [Figures for battle casualties
for this period were recorded as "heads cut off"; whether to take the phrase literally has
been much debated by scholars.]

[31] "Li Lou," Part I [IV/i/14/2; Legge, p. 305].

[32] "Chin hsin," Part I, "Mencius said, Let it be seen to that their fields of grain and
hemp are well cultivated, and make the taxes on them light; so the people may be made
rich. Let it be seen to that the people use their resources of food seasonably, and expend
their wealth only on the prescribed ceremonies; so their wealth will be more than can be
consumed. The people cannot live without water and fire, yet if you knock at a man's
door in the dusk of the evening and ask for water and fire, there is no man who will not
give them, such is the abundance of these things. A sage governs the kingdom so as to cause
pulse and grain to be as abundant as water and fire. When pulse and grain are as abundant as water and fire, where shall there be found a man who is not a benevolent *jen*
person?" [VII/i/23; modified slightly from Legge, pp. 462–630.] This passage displays an
apparent heavy emphasis on production. In that sense it is somewhat at variance with
Confucius, who said [of the ruler of the state] ". . . He is not concerned lest his people
should be poor, but only lest what they have should be ill-apportioned," displaying a
heavy emphasis on the problem of distribution. [Cf. Chapter Two, p. 110 and note 63.]

basic goodness of human nature, Mencius was not merely concerned with the results of actions; he also stressed simultaneously their motivation. Thus on his first meeting with King Hui of Liang, he said: "Why must your Majesty use that word 'profit' [*li* 利]?" And when he heard that Sung K'eng hoped to dissuade the rulers of Ch'in and Ch'u from going to war on the grounds that it would be unprofitable to them to do so, Mencius was quick to reply: "Master [your aim is great], but your argument is not good."[33] [Sung K'eng was a philosopher of the time whose ideas seem somewhat Mohist; see below, Chapter Four, Section Seven.] Indeed, profiting the country should be an urgent duty, and forestalling a war is a most noble activity. In terms of the results, the ideas of enriching the people and stopping wars, ideas about which Mencius customarily talked so much, were not far removed from the objectives of King Hui of Liang and Sung K'eng. Yet Mencius condemned both of them because both talked about the "profit" of their proposed actions. Their policies did not spring from the compassion of the benevolent mind, but rather contributed to cold-blooded selfishness. When this fault is extended to its limits, it must bring about the ruler's selfishness with respect to his own state, the individual's selfishness with respect to his own person, and a struggle between those above and those below for selfish advantage, to the peril of the nation. If, on the other hand, one pursues the opposite course to achieve the same ends [of benefiting the state and ending wars], applying the mind that cannot bear the sufferings of others to devising a compassionate way of governing, then one gains benefits without having sought profit for its own sake.[34] When this is compared with the conscious pursuit of profit, which can only bring about its opposite through the harmful consequences that must ensue, the relative merits of the two courses are incommensurable.

Since nourishing the people is to be regarded as the first principle of government, Mencius had only to proceed one step further to arrive at his theory of the importance of the people [*min kuei lun* 民貴論]. We must take note of the facts that during Mencius' lifetime the state of Wei and Ch'i were contesting for the role of hegemon, while the power of the State of Ch'in was just beginning to wax great. [*Pa*, or "hegemon," is often somewhat more formally translated "Lord Protector," or, in Legge, "Presiding chief," and "chief among the Princes."] The state was becoming stronger and the ruler more majestic; the first buds of authoritarianism were beginning to put forth leaves. The followers of Lord Shang and of

---

[33] See, respectively, "Liang Hui-wang," Part I [I/i/1/3; Legge, p. 126], and "Kao Tzu," Part II [VI/ii/4; Legge, pp. 428–29].

[34] Mencius, speaking to King Hui of Liang, said: "There never has been a benevolent man who neglected his parents. There never has been a righteous man who gave only secondary consideration to his sovereign." [I/i/1/5; modified from Legge, p. 127.]

Shen Pu-hai were just coming into positions as chief ministers of state, and were vigorously promoting theories of the necessity for heavy regulations [over the people] and increased dignity of the ruler. The prevailing current of the time certainly favored augmenting the importance of the ruler and diminishing that of the people. Yet Mencius forcefully countered all the other opinions, and openly proclaimed to the world: "The people are the most important element in a nation; the spirits of the land and grain are next; the sovereign is the lightest. Therefore to gain the peasantry is the way to become sovereign [*T'ien-tzu*, "The Son of Heaven"]; to gain the sovereign is the way to become a Prince of a State [*chu-hou*, a feudal lord]; to gain the Prince of a State is the way to become a Great Officer. When a Prince endangers the altars of the spirits of the land and grain, he is changed, and another is appointed in his place. [The "Spirits of the land and grain," *she-chi*, were symbolic of the national survival.] When the sacrificial victims have been perfect, the millet in its vessels all pure, and the sacrifices offered at their proper seasons, if yet there ensue drought, or the waters overflow, the spirits of the land and grain are changed, and others appointed in their place."[35] Here the ruler is seen as gaining his position from the peasantry, and the feudal princes as well as the altars of the state as subject to removal and replacement. The only thing in a state that continues forever and that cannot be moved or displaced is the people. Herein Mencius looks upon the people not only as the objective toward which government is directed, but also as the chief element of the state.

Such ideas expressed by him were not only beyond the comprehension of the average person of his own time; they were also beyond anything that Confucius had set forth in his discourses. For, according to Confucius, "The people may be made to follow a path of action, but they may not be made to understand it."[36] His statement implies a certain slighting of the importance of the people. Moreover, Confucius' ideal was that of the ruler who carries benevolence into practice, from the nearer first, and ultimately extends it also to those far away; that further tends toward the acceptance of the ruler and the people as one entity. Mencius first hints at the idea of the ruler and the people being in opposition, and makes most explicit the view that the people are the masters and the ruler is their servant, and that the people were the essence [*t'i*] and the state merely the function [*yung*].

The *Mencius* states this in the clearest possible terms, for example: "Mencius said to King Hsüan of Ch'i, 'Suppose that one of your majesty's ministers were to entrust his wife and children to the care of his friend, while he himself went into Ch'u to travel, and that, on his return, he should

---

[35] "Chin hsin," Part II [vii/ii/14; Legge, pp. 483–84].
[36] *Analects*, "T'ai-po," Book 8 [viii/9; Legge, p. 211].

find that the friend had let his wife and children suffer from cold and hunger;—how ought he to deal with him?' The King said, 'He should cast him off.' Mencius proceeded, 'Suppose that the chief criminal judge could not regulate the officers under him, how would you deal with him?' The King said, 'Dismiss him.' Mencius again said, 'If within the four borders of your kingdom there is not good government, what is to be done?' The King looked to the right and left, and spoke of other matters." This clearly implies that the ruler has duties of his office similar to those of all the other officials of state, and that those who fail in these duties should be dismissed.[37] And, again, Mencius replied to King Hsüan of Ch'i's question about King T'ang's having driven out the tyrant Chieh and King Wu's having punished the tyrant Chou, saying: "He who outrages the benevolence proper to his nature is called a robber; he who outrages righteousness is called a ruffian. The robber and the ruffian we call a mere fellow. I have heard of the cutting off of the fellow Chou, but I have not heard of the putting a sovereign to death, in his case."[38] [His examples refer to the military campaigns that led to the downfall of the Hsia and Shang dyansties, and their displacement by the Shang and Chou dynasties; in these cases the tyrant last rulers were deposed, banished, or killed.] This clearly expresses the view that it is proper to kill a tyrannical ruler.

Mencius regarded the people as important; hence he attached extreme importance to the people's opinions, and felt that the people's acceptance or repudiation should be the ultimate standard for determining a change of political power, or the adoption or abandonment of any item of governmental policy. To gain the peasantry is the way to become a sovereign, and those who lose the people's hearts lose thereby the empire.[39] Yao,

[37] "Liang Hui-wang," Part II [1/ii/6; Legge, pp. 164–65]. Mencius, discussing the arrangement of dignities and emoluments of the Chou court, said: "The Son of Heaven constituted one dignity; the dukes one; the marquises one; the earls one; the viscounts and the barons each one of equal rank, altogether making five degrees of rank. The Ruler again constituted one dignity; the Chief Minister one; the Great Officer one; the Scholars of the First Class one; those of the middle class one; and those of the lowest class one, altogether making six degrees of dignity." See, "Wan Chang," Part II [v/ii/2/3; modified from Legge, p. 373]. This also manifests the idea that the ruler and his servitors were of one class of person, and is quite different from the concept of the authoritarian age, when ruler and servitor came to be separated by a vast gulf.

[38] "Liang Hui-wang," Part II [1/ii/8/3; Legge, p. 167].

[39] "Li Lou," Part I, "Mencius said, 'Chieh and Chou's losing the throne, arose from their losing the people; [Chieh and Chou were the infamous tyrannical rulers whose reigns ended the Hsia and Shang-Yin dynasties, respectively] and to lose the people means to lose their hearts. There is a way to get the kingdom: get the people and the kingdom is gotten. There is a way to get the people: get their hearts and the people are gotten. There is a way to get their hearts: it is simply to collect for them what they like, and not to lay on them what they dislike.' " [Mencius, IV/i/9/1; Legge, pp. 299–300.]

Shun, Yü, and T'ang, in gaining the empire did so variously—through the succession being decided by merit, or through the succession passing to the son and heir, or through abdicating voluntarily in favor of a chosen successor, or through military force and punishment of the former ruler. In all these cases, though "granted by Heaven" the succession in fact depended on "the people's voluntary acceptance."[40]

To explain this in modern terminology, we should say Mencius believed that the ultimate sovereignty lay with the people. Therefore, not solely in times of dynastic changeover could the people indicate the choice of a successor by resisting or accepting him, but also in ordinary times the major policies of government should reflect popular opinion. For example, Mencius admonished King Hsüan of Ch'i, when he sought to depart from procedures and promote men on the basis of talent and virtue [regardless of social rank], "When all the people say, 'This is a man of talents and virtue' . . ." then only should he examine further into the case, and [if appropriate,] appoint him. And in deciding criminal cases, it must be a case of: "When the people all say, 'This man deserves death,' . . . only then can he examine the case further and [if necessary] put him to death."[41] This kind of government by "Consulting the grass and firewood-gatherers" [an expression used by a Great Officer of early Chou times, in the Ode "Pan," *Shih Ching*, "Ta-ya," Legge, pp. 499–504, where it is described as "a saying of the ancients" about the proper conduct of government; hence it tends to lend support to the view that the Mencian theory of government had ancient precedents], although perhaps a heritage from antiquity[42] and not something invented by Mencius, is none-

[40] In "Wan Chang," Part I, Mencius, discussing the Sage Emperors Shun and Yü quotes from "The Great Declaration" ["T'ai Shih"] the lines: "Heaven sees as my people see; Heaven hears as my people hear." [The translation here follows Legge, *Shoo King*, or *Documents*, p. 292, instead of Legge's *Mencius*, v/i/5/8, p. 357.] The import of this is roughly that of "*vox populi vox dei.*" Also relevant in this connection is the passage in "Liang Hui-wang," Part II, where Mencius discusses what the State of Ch'i should do, having invaded and punished the State of Yen, and says: "If the people of Yen will be pleased with your taking possession of it, then do so. If the people of Yen will not be pleased with your taking possession of it, then do not do so." [*Mencius*, I/i/10/3; Legge, p. 169.]

[41] "Liang Hui-wang," Part II [*Mencius*, I/ii/7/3–5; Legge, pp. 165–66].

[42] The *Chou Li* [*ch.* 9, "Ch'iu-kuan ssu-k'ou," 5, *incipit*,] "Hsiao ssu-k'ou": "The first is to consult [the people] in times of national peril; the second is to consult on the occasion of transferring the capital; the third is to consult on the matter of [an unclear] royal succession." This institution of consulting the people was still occasionally employed in the Spring and Autumn Period, but by that time it was no longer common. Examples are recorded as follows: *Tso Chuan*, Thirty-first year of Duke Hsiang [541 B.C.], "A man of Cheng rambled into a village school, and fell discoursing about the conduct of the government. . . ." Tzu-ch'an [the chief minister of Cheng, on being advised to destroy the schools to prevent their becoming hot-beds of criticism] replied: ". . . I will do what they approve of, and I will alter what they condemn—they are my teachers." [Legge, *Ch'un*

theless something that was developed and proclaimed abroad only by Mencius.

In addition, Mencius, in placing authority with the people, thereby recognized that the government had the absolute duty of nourishing the people and maintaining peace and stability in the country, while the people did not have any absolute duty of obedience to the government. If the government should fail in its responsibilities, then the people need not be loyal to it. Mencius replied to the question of Duke Mu of Tsou: "The superiors in your State have been negligent, and cruel to their inferiors"; in this situation the people could "pay him back" by not loving their ruler and superiors and not dying for their officers. "What proceeds [from you,] will return to you again";[43] injury will be recompensed by injury. ["Injury," *yüan*, 怨 is Legge's translation of the word in the famous passage, *Analects*, XIV/36, see Legge, p. 288; Waley, p. 189, translates it "resentment."] The ruler's relation to the people becomes in the last analysis one of equality. [That is, possessing the right to respond in kind to the ruler's treatment of themselves, the people stand, in this way, on the same footing with him.]

The doctrine that it is the people who are important and the ruler unimportant, it should be noted, was in fact already established before the time of Mencius. There are, for example, instances like that of Chi Liang [in the year 705 B.C.], who stopped the Marquis of Sui from pursuing the armies of Ch'u [and included in his arguments the] comment: "When the

---

Ts'ew, pp. 565–66, paragraph 3.] In the Twenty-fourth year of Duke Chao [517 B.C.], at the time of the troubles in connection with Prince Chao, the late King's son. [In the royal Chou domain, the emissary of Chin, ". . . Shih-po] took his position by the Kan-Ts'ai gate, and questioned a great multitude of the people [about what to do]." [Modified from Legge, p. 702, paragraph 2.] In the Eighth year of Duke Ting [501 B.C.], when Duke Ling of Wei, about to revolt against the State of Chin, gave audience to the people, he asked them: "If Wei revolt from Chin, and Chin five times attack us, how would you bear the distress? They all replied, 'Though it should five times attack us, we should still be able to fight.' So he said 'Then let us revolt.' " [This passage shows some typographical errors; the punctuation has been corrected by moving the quotation marks. Otherwise it is translated as it appears, thereby differing in wording but not in meaning from the version given in Legge, pp. 767 and 769, paragraph 10.] In the First year of Duke Ai [494 B.C.], it tells that when the forces of Wu invaded the State of Ch'u, the Marquis of Wu summoned Duke Huai of Ch'en to join him in the conquest, and "Duke Huai assembled the people of his state to ask their opinion, and said, 'Let those who wish to side with Ch'u go to the right, and those who wish to side with Wu go to the left.' " Refer also to *Kuo Yü*, ch. 1, "Chou Yü," the comment on King Li [reign 877–827 B.C.], who sought out and executed his critics among the people; and, under the Twenty-seventh year of Duke Chao [514 B.C.] in the *Tso Chuan*, where it discusses the actions of the chief minister of Ch'u, Yin Tzu-ch'ang, who killed dissenters in the effort to stop their criticisms of his government. [Legge, p. 723, paragraph 2.]

43 "Liang Hui-wang," Part II [*Mencius*, I/ii/12/2–3; Legge, pp. 173–74].

ruler thinks only of benefiting the people, that is loyal loving of them."
Or the occasion when Duke Wen of Chu consulted the oracle about
changing his capital to the city of Yi, remarking: "My appointment [from
heaven to be Duke of Chu] is for the nourishing of the people." And there
is that incident in which the Musicmaster K'uang was asked by the
Marquis of Chin [in 558 B.C.] if the people of Wei had not done a bad
thing in expelling their ruler, and he replied: "Now, the ruler is the host
of the spirits, and the hope of the people. If he make the life of the people
to be straitened, and the spirits to want their sacrifices, then the hope of
the people is cut off, and the altars are without a host;—of what use is
he, and what should they do but send him away?"[44] And similarly, P'an-
keng proclaimed to the people of Yin ". . . of old time my royal predecessors cherished every one and above everything a respectful care of the
people . . ."[45] [P'an-keng was a king of Yin traditionally said to have
reigned in the middle of the fourteenth century B.C.], and the passage in
the "Great Declaration," the "T'ai-shih," about heaven seeing and
hearing as the people see and hear puts the origins of this concept still
farther back into antiquity. [The *Documents* "T'ai-shih," part ii, 7; Legge,
p. 292; the "T'ai-shih" dates from the earliest years of Chou history.]
However, despite Confucius' sage-like stature, he had expressed such
ideas as "the people may be made to follow" and "there will be no
discussions [of government policy] among the common people."[46]

From this, it is clearly evident, the ancient concept that the people
were of primary importance had, by Mencius' time, long since been
submerged and lost sight of, and had virtually ceased to be a continuing
element of current learning. Mencius' contribution lay not in having
created this doctrine through his own original intellectual activity, but in
having again brought into prominence a doctrine that had dropped out
of sight, and having done so in the late Chou era of dictatorial rulers and
tyrannical governments. In consequence of this, Mencius' political thought
became for all future time the protest directed precisely against the evils
of tyranny. Although the conditions of his age prevented his thought from
having been accepted and practiced by the rulers of his own time, throughout the succeeding two thousand years, every time conditions deteriorated
and the age became disorderly and violent, Mencius' ideas experienced

[44] See, respectively: *Tso Chuan*, Sixth year of Duke Huan [Legge, p. 48]; Thirteenth
year of Duke Wen [Legge, p. 264]; and Fourteenth year of Duke Hsiang [Legge, p. 466].
Refer also to *Kuo Yü, ch.* 4, "Lu Yü," where the murder of Duke Li of Chin by the people
of Chin is discussed.

[45] *Shang Shu* [*Documents*], "The Documents of Shang," "P'an Keng," Part II [Legge,
Shoo King, p. 234].

[46] *Analects*: "T'ai-po," Book 8 [VIII/9, Legge, p. 211]; and "Chi-shih" Book 16 [XVI/2/3,
Legge, p. 310].

a new revival, in a kind of mutal interplay with the anarchist thought of Lao Tzu and Chuang Tzu. Hence, in terms of his influence, the Confucian learning of Mencius was not merely distinct in some ways from that of Hsün Tzu, but also was quite different in certain respects from the teachings of Confucius himself. This is because Mencius adopted the point of view of the people in discussing government, whereas Confucius and Hsün Tzu tended more toward the viewpoint of the sovereign.

Nonetheless, Mencius' theory of the importance of the people differed from modern democracy; the two should not be confused. In simplest terms, democratic thought must contain all the three concepts of "for the people," "of the people," and "by the people." For, not only must the people be the objective toward which government is directed, and the chief element of the state, but they must also necessarily have the right voluntarily to participate in the authority of government. Weighed in this balance, Mencius' "importance of the people" merely commences with the idea of "for the people," and proceeds toward that of "of the people." Both the principle of "by the people," and the institutions necessary to it, were things of which he had never heard. Therefore, in the thought of Mencius, the opinion of the people was capable only of passive manifestation, while the political authority was to be wholly exercised by the class that "worked with their minds." It was necessary to wait for heaven's agent to appear before the tyrannical sovereign could be punished.[47] Thus the people, other than adopting the passive resistance as expressed in not loving their ruler and superiors and not dying for their officers, had no further right to overthrow tyrannous government through rebellious action. All these aspects of Mencius' thought reflect the limitations imposed by the contemporary environment. When we note that in Europe in the sixteenth and seventeenth centuries theories favoring violent death to tyrants were still rampant,[48] and that not until the eighteenth century and later did the theory and the institutions of popular rule begin to be developed and become widespread, then we can look back at Mencius, who advocated the importance of the people and the

---

[47] "Those who labor with their minds govern others; those who labor with their strength are governed by others." [*Mencius*, III/i/4/6; Legge, pp. 249–50]; see, "T'eng Wen-kung," Part I [III/i/4/4–5], where words are spoken by Mencius to Ch'en Hsiang. See also, in the same chapter, where Mencius replies to Pi Chan: "If there were no superior men, there would be none to rule the rude men. If there were no rude men, there would be none to provide the sustenance of the superior men." [III/i/3/14, modified slightly from Legge, p. 244.] It is evident from these passages that Mencius had no concept of political equality. For the term "heaven's agent," *t'ien li* 天吏 see "Kung-sun Ch'ou," Part II [II/ii/8/2; Legge, p. 223, and note, p. 201; Dobson, p. 24, translates it: "He who is appointed by Heaven to do so."]

[48] Among the more prominent of these are: Duplessis-Mornay (?), *Vindiciae contra Tyrannos* (1579); Juan Mariana (1536–1624), *De rege et regis institutione*.

relative insignificance of the ruler already in the fourth century B.C., and conclude that one may "find no flaw in him" there. [Cf. *Analects* VIII/21.]

Mencius, proceeding from his basic tenet of the importance of the people, went on to discuss the responsibilities in office of the servitor-officials, and concluded that they were the public servants of the nation, bearing the sovereign's charge to nourish the people, and not the private retainers of the sovereign himself. Thus he told the governor of P'ing-lu that, if he could not fulfill his responsibilities, he should resign. In answer to the question of King Hsüan of Ch'i about high ministers who are noble and are relatives of the prince, he replied: "If the prince have great faults, they ought to remonstrate with him, and if he do not listen to them after they have done so again and again, they ought to dethrone him." To his question about high officers of a different surname from the prince, Mencius said: "If the prince has faults, they ought to remonstrate with him; and if he do not listen to them after they have done this again and again, they ought to leave the State."[49] This, while adding more extensive exposition, is not fundamentally different from the purport of Confucius' [definition of the great minister as one who] "serves his prince according to what is right, [and when he finds he cannot do so, retires, *Analects*, XI/23/3; Legge, p. 245]. But we can go further in this comparison. Confucius' attitude in his statement [that one should maintain] "The full observance of the rules of propriety in serving one's prince . . ." is one of respectful humility. [*Mencius*, III/18; Legge, p. 161.] Mencius, on the other hand, raised to a higher level the position of the servitor, establishing the ideal of "the servitor who cannot be summoned," and further holding up age and virtue to counter the noble rank of the court.[50] Consequently, between ruler and servitor there existed the basis for honor and dignity of each. The servitor could judge the noble-mindedness or meanness of his ruler's treatment of him and adjust his repayment of that treatment accordingly. Grace and injury were clearly distinguished; one could come into service or retire from it freely and easily.[51]

---

[49] See, respectively, "Kung-sun Ch'ou," Part II [II/ii/4; Legge, pp. 217–18] and "Wan Chang," Part II [v/ii/9; Legge, pp. 392–93].

[50] "Kung-sun Ch'ou," Part II, Mencius, speaking to Ching Tzu, says: "In this world there are three things universally acknowledged to be honorable. Noble rank is one of them; age is one of them; virtue is one of them. In the court, noble rank holds the first place of the three; in villages, age holds the first place; and for helping one's generation and presiding over the people, the other two are not equal to virtue. How can [the King of Ch'i], possessing only one of these, presume to despise one who possesses the other two?" [*Mencius*, II/ii/2/6; modified from Legge, pp. 213–14.]

[51] "Wan Chang," Part II, Mencius replied to the question of Wan Chang about the scholar who does not go to see the princes, saying: "The Son of Heaven would not summon a teacher. How much less should a prince do so!" [v/ii/7/3; modified from Legge, p. 388;

The theory developed subsequently in the authoritarian age that the loyal servitor would not serve another ruler [other than one belonging to the dynasty, or surname, which he first served] was something of which Mencius in no case could have approved. Although in this too he shared the same stand as Confucius, Confucius' ideal was one of a ruler who acted in the capacity of a teacher, whereas Mencius wanted to be the ruler's teacher. Confucius hoped that the superior man would gain rank and status in recognition of his virtue, whereas Mencius wanted him to use his virtue to resist the prerogatives of status. These differences between the two philosophers are also no doubt to be explained as consequences of their times. The late Chou practice of maintaining scholars and honoring men of talent and ability was inaugurated at Hsi-ho in the State of Wei [Duke Wen of Wei, last quarter of fifth century, B.C., was famous for his patronage of scholars from all over China] and reached its most flourishing development at the Chi-hsia [Academy] in the State of Ch'i. [See above, Chapter Three, Section One, where Hsün Tzu's association with the Academy is discussed. These developments were post-Confucian and pre-Mencian.] Confucius did not live to see either of these developments. Moreover, with Confucius' ideal of the superior man who possessed both virtue and status clearly impossible of attainment, it was most natural that Mencius, caught up in the currents of the Warring States Era, further developed that ideal into the theory that virtue could serve as a counter to status.[52]

---

the following passage is from the same chapter, Legge, p. 389.] He also cites the case of Tzu-ssu, who was displeased at the Duke's suggestion that he was a friend of Duke Mou, and who said: "With regard to our stations, you are sovereign and I am servitor. How can I presume to be on terms of friendship with my sovereign? With regard to our virtue, you ought to make me your master. How can you be on terms of friendship with me?" And in the "Li Lou," Part II, "Mencius said to King Hsüan of Ch'i, 'When the prince regards his ministers as his hands and feet, his ministers regard their prince as their belly and heart. When he regards them as his dogs and horses, they regard him as any other man. When he regards them as the earth or the grass, they regard him as a robber and an enemy.' " In the "Kao Tzu," Part II, Mencius replies to Ch'en Tzu's question about the principles that determined when [the wise men of antiquity] took office, saying: "There were three cases in which they accepted office, and three in which they left it," and the general purport of it all is that the conditions for taking office are that the servitor must be able to carry the Way into practice, and that the rites must be properly observed. [*Mencius*, VI/ii/ 14; Legge, pp. 445–46.] In the "Wan Chang," Part II, where Mencius says of Confucius that he took office when "the practice of his doctrines was likely," or "when his reception was proper" or "when he was supported by the state," his intention is the same as in the foregoing examples. [*Mencius*, V/ii/4/6; Legge, pp. 382–83.]

[52] However Mencius' view already existed in the Spring and Autumn Period. Refer to the *Tso Chuan*, under the Twenty-fifth year of Duke Hsiang [547 B.C.], where it narrates that Yen Ying refused to commit suicide at the time his Duke Chuang of Ch'i was murdered and explained his stand, saying: "Is it the business of the ruler of the people merely to be above them? The altars of the State should be his chief care. Is it the business of the

We may also at this point discuss Mencius' views on the issue of whether or not the individual should serve in government. The book *Mencius* contains expressions of three distinct attitudes toward this. (One) Mencius praised Confucius as "the one among the sages who acted according to the time." ["*Sheng chih shih che* 聖之時者;" *Mencius*, v/ii/1/5. Legge, p. 372, translates this difficult phrase using a word coined for the occasion, "the timeous one," meaning, "that Confucius did at every *time* what the circumstances of it required."] This was because Confucius always judged whether or not he would be listened to in deciding whether to carry his Way into practice or to withdraw into concealment. When he could take office he did so; when it was better to give up office he did so. In this he differed both from the standard of "purity" [*ch'ing* 清] upheld by Po-yi [the recluse who could not serve the new Chou out of loyalty to the old Shang, and starved in the wilds, even though he recognized the legitimacy of the new dynasty] and from the "sense of duty" of Yi-yin. [Yi-yin felt a duty, *jen* 任, to serve the ruler, for he felt the charge to serve nobly and well was the heaviest duty on everyone who was prepared for office, and he would thus accommodate himself to the conditions of office, though without compromising his principles. "*Jen*" here is not the same word *jen* as that translated elsewhere as "benevolence," nor is it the same as that in the phrase "*pu jen*"—"unable to bear."] It was all the more different from Hui of Liu-hsia, who was "wanting in self-respect." [Hui of Liu-hsia was honest and upright, but by serving any kind of a prince he endangered his principles.][53] Hence Confucius alone was regarded by Mencius as worthy of being the model for his own behavior.

---

minister of a ruler merely to be concerned about his support? The nourishment of the altars should be his object. Therefore when a ruler dies or goes into exile for the altars, the minister should die or go into exile with him. If he dies or goes into exile for his seeking his own ends, who, excepting his private associates, would presume to bear the consequences with him?" [Legge, p. 514. Duke Chuang was murdered as a consequence of his licentious behavior, in the boudoir belonging to the beautiful wife of one of his chief officers.]

[53] See, respectively, "Wan Chang," Part II [*Mencius*, v/ii/1/5; Legge, pp. 371–72] and "Kung-sun Ch'ou," Part I [II/i/9; Legge, pp. 206–08]. In "Chin hsin," Part I, Mencius tells Sung Kou-chien: "When the men of antiquity realized their wishes, benefits were conferred by them on the people. [The Chinese phrase is "*te chih* 得志," "to realize their ambitions," by implication, to have successful careers in office.] If they did not realize their wishes, they cultivated their personal character, and became illustrious in the world. If poor, they attended to their own virtue in solitude; if advanced to dignity, they made the whole kingdom virtuous as well." [*Mencius*, VII/i/9/6; Legge, p. 453.] This passage further develops the same meaning. There is also the passage in "Kao Tzu," Part I, "The men of antiquity cultivated their nobility of Heaven [i.e., their natural or innate capacity to be noble men] and the nobility of man [i.e., high social status] came to them in its train." [VI/i/16/2; Legge, p. 419.] This also matches very well the idea of Confucius' words that ". . . learning may incidentally lead to high pay." [*Analects*, xv/31; the context of this passage leads Waley, whose version is used here, to add the word "incidentally." Out of context, as it is usually quoted, it suggests the opposite idea.]

(Two) Mencius at times abandoned this view, and admitted the individual's duty to serve. For example, he replied to the question Chou Hsiao asked about serving in government by saying: "The Record says, 'If Confucius was three months without being employed by some ruler, he looked anxious and unhappy. . . .' Kung-ming Yi said, 'Among the ancients, if an officer was three months unemployed by a ruler, he was condoled with.'" Mencius explained these lines saying: "The loss of his place to an officer is like the loss of his State to a prince," and: "An officer's being in office is like the plowing of a husbandman."[54]

(Three) However, the attitude that Mencius repeatedly stressed and that seems to be that which he tended to regard the most seriously, is of cultivating the self for the sake of one's personal ethical attainment. Carrying the Way into practice and achieving merit thereby, on the contrary, was but the last duty incumbent upon one. Thus, in one place he says: "Shun would have regarded abandoning the kingdom as throwing away a worn-out sandal." And in another: "Wide territory and a numerous people are desired by the superior man, but what he delights in is not here. To stand in the center of the kingdom, and tranquilize the people within the four seas;—the superior man delights in this, but the highest enjoyment of his nature is not here."[55] The attitude exposed in these statements differs from that of Confucius, both in the latter's "knowing that it's no use, but keeping on doing it," and in his "unwillingness to set aside the duties that should be observed between sovereign and minister."[56]

If we attempt to ascertain why Mencius frequently varied his statements on this subject, the explanation seems to lie in the fact that each of his statements was made in response to a specific situation, that each has its particular significance [in relation to that], and that the different statements do not necessarily conflict with each other. Those which emulate the attitude of Confucius derive from Confucius' basic doctrines about the benevolent mind leading naturally to benevolent government, and were apparently addressed to the problems of governing an age when hereditary ministerships were already extinct [and when the decision about under what conditions a man might serve had become more subjective]. His statements that the officers' being employed in office resembles the husbandman's ploughing, suggesting that service in govern-

[54] "T'eng Wen-kung," Part II [III/ii/3; Legge, pp. 266–67].

[55] Both quotations are to be found in "Chin hsin," Part I [VII/i/35/6; Legge, p. 470, and VII/i/21/1–2; Legge, p. 459].

[56] See, respectively, Analects, "Hsien wen," Book XIV [XIV/41] and "Wei-tzu," Book XVIII [XVIII/7; Legge, p. 336]. However, Confucius also now and then is found to be in agreement with the attitude Mencius later upheld. For example, in "Hsien chin," Book XI, where he has his disciples tell their ambitions, he does not comment approvingly on the ambitions of Tzu-lu, Jan-yu, and Kung-hsi Ch'ih to govern the state. He approves only of Tseng Tien's ". . . I would wash in the Yi River, enjoy the breeze among the rain altars, and return home singing." [Analects, XI/25; Legge, pp. 246–49.]

ment is a responsibility that could not be abdicated, apparently bear on the situation in earlier antiquity, when clan-chief hereditary ministers and aristocrats with hereditary clan privileges alone enjoyed the right to serve in government, and bore exclusive responsibility for the maintenance of the state. When, on the other hand, he said that the empire could be looked upon as a worn-out sandal, he recognized the fact that, while the hereditary ministerships could not be restored, yet persons who held high rank often were not suited to it and that, rather than lower one's purpose and humble one's person, it would be better [uncompromisingly, if out of office] to honor virtue and find delight in righteousness. This attitude seems to be directed specifically against the practice, quite prevalent by the Warring States Age, of wandering about, discoursing [amorally] on political theories in search of material gain.

Mencius' purpose, then, in promoting self-cultivation, was to urge that by such achievement one might yet make one's mark in the world. His was thus a different objective from that of the recluses [who also stressed self-cultivation but] who preferred to follow the "noble and solitary path." For when one [by self-cultivation] secured emolument of office he could [with honor] give up the labor of husbandry,[57]—one could even receive the highest emolument of office, and still need have no position or duties.[58] This also displays practices common by the Period of the Six States [i.e., the Warring States Period], and of which Confucius could never have imagined. Even though Mencius himself said that he regarded it a shameful thing for a mean fellow to monopolize a market and become wealthy thereby,[59] at the same time he would have a hard time totally escaping the condemnation directed at the philosopher T'ien P'ien for "refusing to hold office" [while gaining great wealth irresponsibly].[60]

[57] "Chin hsin," Part I [vii/i/32; Legge, pp. 467–68]. Refer also to "T'eng Wen-kung," Part II, "For the scholar to perform no service and receive support notwithstanding [is improper]." [iii/ii/4/2; modified from Legge, p. 269.]

[58] "Kung-sun Ch'ou," Part II, Mencius here says of himself that while he was a guest-teacher in the State of Ch'i and being supported by the state: ". . . I am in charge of no Office; on me devolves no duty of speaking out my opinion." [ii/ii/5/5; Legge, p. 219.]

[59] "Kung-sun Ch'ou," Part II [ii/ii/10/9–7; Legge, pp. 226–28]; Mencius says this to Ch'en Tzu about his declining the one hundred thousand chung emolument offered him by the King of Ch'i.

[60] Chan-kuo ts'e, ch. 11, "Ch'i ts'e," no. 4, "A man of Ch'i on meeting T'ien P'ien said, 'I have heard that your noble doctrine is that you plan not to take office and are willing to perform hard labor.' T'ien P'ien said, 'What then have you heard?' The man replied, 'I have heard about the daughter of a neighbor.' T'ien P'ien said, 'What is said of her?' He replied, 'My neighbor's daughter plans not to marry. She is now thirty years old, and she has seven children. If she doesn't want to marry, it is of course all right for her not to marry but this is more excessive than if she were married. Now you plan not to take office. Yet you draw an income for your support amounting to a thousand chung and you maintain a hundred retainers. For you not to take office is all right in itself, but this is more

SECTION THREE
"Stability in Unity"

KING Hsiang of Liang asked how the kingdom could be settled, and Mencius replied: "It will be settled by being united under one sway" [i.e., *ting yü i* 定於一, or "stabilized in unity"].[61] This is one of the most significant differences between the political thought of Confucius and Mencius, and it must be discussed in somewhat fuller fashion. We have already stated in Chapter Two that Confucius' idea in rectifying names and in following the Chou was to improve and also to restore feudal institutions, with the condition that Chou political authority must continue to be acknowledged. By the time of Mencius, Chou had further declined and was on the verge of annihilation, while the various feudal princes were growing ever stronger. "The lands within the four seas include nine states, each as large as a thousand *li* square" [*Mencius*, 1/i/7/17; cf. Legge, p. 146; Mencius emphasizes the great power and size of the few remaining states]; of these, Ch'u, Wei, Ch'i, and Ch'in had become especially large states, each having the power to try to conquer the whole world by force. For this reason, Confucius' insistence on respecting the primacy of the Chou no longer held any real meaning. Mencius had made penetrating observation of the changes transforming his world, and he was urgently concerned to bring relief to the suffering people. He lodged his hope not in a restoration of Chou dynasty power, but in the conclusive emergence of a new king. What he referred to as "settling the kingdom by its being united under one sway" is an expression of this hope.

Although Confucius "elegantly handed down the doctrines of Kings Wen and Wu" and "dreamed that he saw the Duke of Chou," his references to King Wu's conquest of the kingdom are few indeed. [The Chou *t'ien-hsia* may be variously translated "the world" and "the kingdom."] Yet he bestowed his most extreme expressions of approval on T'ai-po for having thrice declined the kingdom when offered to him, though the people had no chance to praise him for it [because they could not know the details of it], and on King Wen, who possessed two-thirds of the world and yet used it to "serve the Yin dynasty."[62] He praised both men as

---

excessive than if you were in office.' Master T'ien said nothing and left." This ridicules the scholars of the Chi-hsia Academy who "were all granted titles and honors equivalent to the chief great officers, but they did not govern and just engaged in discourse." (*Shih Chi*, ch. 46, "T'ien Ch'i shih chia.") Although Mencius may never have gone to Chi-hsia (Ch'ien Mu, *Hsien Ch'in chu-tzu hsi-nien k'ao-pien*, number 76), yet in his becoming very wealthy without having taken office, he is somewhat the same as Master T'ien.

[61] "Liang Hui-wang," Part I [*Mencius*, 1/i/6/2; Legge, p. 136].

[62] *Analects*, "T'ai-po," Book VIII [VIII/i; Legge, p. 207, and VIII/20/4; Legge, p. 215].

"having reached the highest point of virtue." Although this is, to be sure, the attitude that a Yin descendant might be expected to have held, it also shows that Confucius' political thought tended toward the recognition of established authority. He did not approve of the Chou house's seizure of the kingdom, yet he approved of their governing the kingdom.

Mencius, when appearing before King Hsüan of Ch'i and King Hui of Liang,[63] frequently discussed Kings T'ang and Wu [the martial conquerors who established the Shang and Chou dynasties]. With regard to T'ang, Mencius said he started from a small state of only seventy *li* in size, used virtue and practiced benevolence, carried out his campaign to execute [Heaven's] justice [the euphemism used for the military conquest by Heaven's appointed agent] throughout the four quarters of the realms, and "exercised his government throughout the kingdom." Of King Wu, Mencius said that he "by one display of his anger, gave repose to all the people of the kingdom" and that, when he punished Yin and executed justice on the tyrant King Chou, all the common people were happy.[64] Throughout the *Mencius* the citations of King Wen are especially numerous. When we examine the reasons for his being praised there, we find that it is not because he served the Yin dynasty and reached the highest point of virtue in so doing, for which Confucius singled him out, but rather because he started with a small state one hundred *li* in size, practiced benevolence, and consequently came to govern the whole kingdom.[65] King Wen's great achievement, therefore, is not different from

---

The Chu Hsi commentary says: "In view of his virtue, at the time of the transition from Shang to Chou, T'ai-po certainly could have assembled all of the feudal lords at his court, and taken over the kingdom. But he cast it aside and would not take it; further he concealed all traces of his actions. From this can be known how extreme and complete was his virtue! His heart was [as loyal as] the hearts of Po Yi and Shu Ch'i when they grasped [King Wu's] bridle [to restrain him from engaging in the campaign against Shang], and the affair itself was one of still greater distress. Thus it fully warranted Confucius' deeply moved sigh, and his expression of great praise and admiration." Chu also quotes Fan [unidentified]: "King Wen's virtue was enough to warrant his displacing the Shang dynasty. Heaven approved of him and the people all turned to him. But he did not take the kingdom. Instead, he submissively served it; therein he achieved the highest point of virtue. Confucius, following his words about King Wu, then continues on to the subject of King Wen's virtue, and praised both him and T'ai-po as having reached the highest point of virtue; his intent is subtly profound."

[63] "Liang Hui-wang," Part II [*Mencius*, I/ii/8; Legge, p. 167; etc.]; "Kung-sun Ch'ou," Part I [II/i/3/1; Legge, p. 196]; and "T'eng Wen-kung," Part II [III/ii/5; Legge, pp. 273–74].

[64] "Liang Hui-wang," Part II [*Mencius*, I/ii/11/1; Legge, p. 170 and I/ii/3/7; Legge, pp. 156–57]; "T'eng Wen-kung," Part II [III/ii/9/6; Legge, p. 281].

[65] "Li Lou," Part I [*Mencius*, IV/i/7/4–6; Legge, pp. 297–98]; "Kung-sun Ch'ou," Part I [II/i/1/8; Legge, pp. 182–83]; "Liang Hui-wang," Part II [I/ii/3/6; Legge, p. 156, and I/ii/5/3; Legge, pp. 161–62, and I/ii/10/3; Legge, p. 169].

that of Kings T'ang and Wu. Here we have one evidence that Mencius
did not feel obligated to the Chou dynasty, but hoped for the rise of a
new king. Mencius went about, accepting the support of one after another
of the feudal princes, and constantly urging them to practice kingly
government. At that time the kings of Wei and Ch'i were engaged in a
struggle to see which would become the chief among the princes. The
struggle was just at its most intense in these years, and apparently Mencius
followed it with greatest attention. Consequently he urged the essence of
his thought upon King Hui of Liang [i.e., Wei]; Mencius urged him to
believe that kingly government could be established even in a small state
of only one hundred *li*, and that the benevolent ruler will have no opponent
who can stand up to him. Even King Hsiang [who succeeded King Hui
in Wei in 319 B.C., and], who "didn't have the appearance of a sovereign"
[I/i/6; Legge, p. 136], was introduced to the theory of stabilizing the world
by unifying it. This indicates that Mencius hoped Liang [i.e., the State of
Wei] would gain control of the whole realm. When talking to King
Hsüan of Ch'i [about how to attain the royal sway], he said: "The love
and protection of the people; with this there is no power that can prevent
a ruler from attaining it." He urged the king to model himself on Kings
Wen and Wu, who "by one display of their anger, gave repose to all the
people of the kingdom," and set forth for him the principles of King Wen's
government in the [ancient] State of Ch'i 岐.[66] Back and forth he went
over the details of this principle, displaying his thought in most complete
and explicit fashion. This shows that Mencius hoped [King Hsüan's
State of] Ch'i 齊 would accomplish the unification. Finding his models
in King T'ang the Perfector and in King Wen, he firmly believed that:
"With a territory that is only a hundred *li* square, it is possible to attain
to the royal dignity." Hence, even before the ruler of a state representing
an accumulation of weaknesses, like that of Sung, Mencius still urged that
the government of King T'ang be applied, telling him that no one in the
world would dare be his enemy if he did so, and that the great States of
Ch'i and Ch'u were nothing to be afraid of. Even to the ruler of a tiny
state like T'eng, Mencius still "always made laudatory references to Yao
and Shun," and spoke to its Duke about taking King Wen as his teacher.[67]

[66] For these passages, see "Liang Hui-wang," Parts I and II [I/i/7/3; Legge, p. 138;
I/ii/3/5 and 7; Legge, pp. 156 and 157; I/ii/5/3; Legge, pp. 161–62]. In "Kung-sun
Ch'ou," Part II [II/ii/22/5], Mencius, after leaving Ch'i, said: "If the king were to use me,
would it bring about merely the happiness of the people of Ch'i? All the people of the
whole kingdom [i.e., "world"] would be made happy!" [Legge, p. 231] His meaning
is here made quite clear.

[67] See, respectively, "T'eng Wen-kung," Part I and Part II. [III/i/1–2–4; Legge, pp. 234
and 235; III/ii/5/7; Legge, p. 274.] Also, Mencius said to Duke Wen of T'eng, "The *Book
of Odes* says 'Although Chou was an old country, it received a new destiny.' That is said
with reference to King Wen. If you will but practice those same things with vigour, you

These passages show that he even had hopes that Sung or T'eng might gain mastery of the world! These are further proof that Mencius did not acknowledge the Chou dynasty, and that he hoped for a new king to emerge.

The differences between Confucius and Mencius can also be seen in their attitudes toward kingly government [*wang cheng*] and power government [*pa cheng*. The *pa* were hegemons who achieved their positions by reason of their real power; hence the term came to stand for government by force instead of government by the Confucian kingly ideal of moral suasion]. Although Confucius said: "When bad government prevails in the empire, ceremonies, music, and punitive military expeditions proceed from the princes" [*Analects*, xvi/2/1; Legge, p. 310]; yet he had high praise for the achievements of Duke Huan [of Ch'i] and [his chief minister], Kuan Tzu. [Duke Huan, 683–642 b.c., was the first of the *pa*, or hegemons.] It was Mencius who first so venerated the kingly way and denounced the rule of force that he would say: "There were none of the disciples of Confucius who spoke about the affairs of Dukes Huan and Wen."[68] [Duke Wen of Chin, 634–627 b.c., was the second of the great *pa* of the Spring and Autumn Era.] The function of their "government by hegemon," at that time when the feudal institutions were already in a process of dissolution but had not yet collapsed, was to support the Son of Heaven in imposing his commands on the feudal lords, thereby maintaining some order in the midst of threatening chaos. But by the time when the heads of the seven warring states were all struggling for supremacy, support of the Son of Heaven was already pointless, and enforcing his commands on the feudal princes was out of the question. Even had Dukes Huan and Wen reappeared at this time, they would not have

---

also can by them make new your kingdom." [*Mencius*, iii/i/3/12; modified from Legge, p. 243; cf. Dobson, *Mencius*, p. 198, and note 1.32.] When Mencius urged people to "Take King Wen as their teacher," he always had this thought in mind.

[68] "Liang Hui-wang," Part i [i/i/7/2]. Mencius did not always have the same standard in mind in discussing the distinction between kingly government and rule by force. Sometimes it depended on whether the manifestations of benevolence and righteousness were true or false: ("Chin hsin," Part i "[Benevolence and righteousness] were natural to Yao and Shun. T'ang and Wu made them their own. The five chiefs of the princes [*pa*] feigned them." [vii/i/30/i; Legge, p. 466.] This became the authority for the distinction between the kingly government and rule by force based on the working of the mind, which was maintained by Sung dynasty Neo-Confucian rationalist philosophers.) Sometimes the standard was that of the opposite methods of effecting action: ("Kung-sun Ch'ou," Part i, "He who, using force, makes a pretence to benevolence is the leader of the princes" [*pa*], and "He who, using virtue, practices benevolence is the sovereign [*wang*] of the kingdom.") [ii/i/3/i; Legge, p. 196.] Sometimes it depended on the status of the person who was carrying it out: ("Kao Tzu," Part ii, "The sovereign commands punishment but does not inflict it; the princes inflict punishment but do not command it." [vi/ii/7/2; modified from Legge, p. 436.]

been able to convene again a meeting of all the feudal rulers, observing all the old proprieties. [Paraphrasing the original, which says literally to convene "a meeting with jade and silk, official head gear and court robes," referring to the old meetings of the feudal princes at which the earlier *pa* had presided in the name of the Chou Kings.] Hence Confucius' attitude was different from that of Mencius, and in fact the attitude of each reflected the historical environments of their times. Moreover, as Mencius saw it, force was both an unworthy alternative and an uncertain means of success, while the kingly way was both nearer the ideal, and easier for success. Therefore he said: "He who, using force, makes a pretence to benevolence, is the leader of the princes [i.e., is the *pa*]. A leader of the princes requires a large kingdom. He who, using virtue, practices benevolence is the sovereign of the kingdom [i.e., is the *wang*]. To become the sovereign of the kingdom, a prince need not wait for a large kingdom." [II/i/3/i; Legge, p. 196.] And he also said: ". . . never was there a time farther removed than the present from the rise of a true sovereign; never was there a time when the sufferings of the people from tyrannical government were more intense than the present. The hungry readily partake of any food, and the thirsty of any drink."[69] This shows clearly why Mencius felt compelled to hammer away at the theme of benevolence and righteousness whenever he had the ear of any ruler of his time, not because he really wanted to submerge the personal ambitions of such sovereigns to master the world, but rather because he wanted precisely to teach them how to avoid the difficult course and follow the easier one in hastening the day when they would achieve their great ambitions. The sad thing about it all is that the benevolent government that Mencius imagined to have been employed by Kings T'ang and Wu was not adopted by these rulers, while his "stability in unification" ideal was in fact implemented by "tyrannous Ch'in." He succeeded merely in leaving behind a theoretical problem of kingly government versus power government to serve as the subject of debate among Confucians ever after.

In the Sung period Chu Hsi and Ch'en Liang exchanged a correspondence on the subject running to tens of thousands of words, the crux of their argument being the [highly abstract] problem of distinguishing between Heaven's principles and man's desires,[70] which ignores the fact that

---

[69] "Kung-sun Ch'ou," Part i [*Mencius*, II/i/1/11; Legge, p. 184].

[70] *Chu-tzu wen-chi* ["The Collected Works of Chu Hsi"], "Ta Ch'en T'ung-fu shu" ("Three Letters) [in reply to Ch'en Liang"]; and *Lung-ch'uan wen-chi* ["Collected Writings of Ch'en Liang"], "Chia-ch'en ta Chu Yüan-hui pi shu" ["A Reply to Chu Hsi's Private Letter, 1184"], and "Yü Chu Yuan-hui shu, yu shu" ["A Letter to Chu Hsi, and a Further Letter"] (Spring, 1185). [Chu Hsi's letters to Ch'en Liang are translated in part and discussed in Fung/Bodde, Vol. II, pp. 563–66.]

Mencius' doctrines honoring the kingly way and denouncing rule by force had real meaning both as history and as political theory. Their discussion indeed displays the error of not having known how to read their *Mencius*.

If the discussions and the conclusions drawn above are not seriously wrong, then Mencius' denunciation of rule by force was meant to honor the king and hasten the success of his unification. However, the one he honored was not the collapsing Chou king. It was to be a new king who had not as yet emerged, and the unification whose success he hoped to hasten was not the authoritarian one of the Ch'in dynasty, but a pre-Ch'in unification of the feudal world type. In brief, Mencius' intent was to help establish a new political authority that would restore the old political institutions. His sentiments of lingering regard for feudal government, and his advocacy of supporting and preserving feudal government, were in both cases more or less identical with those of Confucius. The two differed only with respect to the courses they laid down for pursuing these objectives. Confucius wanted to preserve the Chou house in order to restore feudalism, while Mencius had the hope that, after a change of dynasty and under a new ruling house, the world would again experience a glorious age when "ceremonies, music, and punitive military expeditions proceed from the Son of Heaven." Hence, in terms of his views on political institutions, Mencius also displays a tendency toward archaism.

Mencius' institutional return-to-the-past can be demonstrated by reference to his comments on taking the ancient kings as models. Mencius profoundly believed that the institutions established by the kings and sages of antiquity were perfect, and should serve as models to all time. All rulers of later ages must accept them as their own standard. Therefore he said: "Virtue alone is not sufficient for the exercise of government; laws alone cannot carry themselves into practice." And further, "It is said in the *Book of Odes*,

'Without transgression, without forgetfulness,
Following the ancient statutes.'

Never has anyone fallen into error, who followed the laws of the ancient kings."[71] Examination shows that of the methods of the ancient kings that Mencius praised, the three principal ones apparently are the well-field [system of land tenure], hereditary emolument of office, and the *hsiang-hsü* schools. All these institutions Mencius believed to have been in practice throughout all the Three Dynasties of Antiquity [i.e., Hsia, Shang, and Chou]; he was not one with Confucius in having special reverence for the Institutes of Chou. For example, Mencius believed that the agricultural tax of one-tenth of production had been a method devised by Yao and Shun—which had then been carried into practice through the Hsia,

---

[71] "Li Lou," Part I [*Mencius*, IV/i/1/3–4; Legge, p. 289].

Shang, and Chou periods. The well-field system, Mencius thought, had had its origins in the Yin [Shang] "seventy *mou* allotment, and the system of mutual aid." [The *mou* is a unit of land measure, in modern times roughly one-sixth of an English acre.] The Chou rulers had slightly altered it, enacting "the hundred *mou* allotment, and the share system." But none of these, he felt, repudiated the principle of the one-tenth tax. Mencius also had been known to urge the rulers of his time to take King Wen as their teacher. The plan of government practiced [by King Wen] in [his ancient] State of Ch'i 岐, as Mencius referred to it, was: "The husbandman cultivated for the government one-ninth of the land; the descendants of officers were salaried; at the passes and in the markets, strangers were inspected but goods were not taxed; there were no prohibitions respecting the ponds and wiers; the wives and children of criminals were not involved in their guilt." In discussing educational institutions he said: "Establish *hsiang, hsü, hsüeh,* and *hsiao*—all those educational institutions—for the instruction of the people. [Four types of schools; see above, Chapter Three, Section Two, p. 271 and Chapter Two, Section Four, p. 184.] The name *hsiang* indicates nourishing as its object; *hsiao* indicates teaching; and *hsü* indicates archery. By the Hsia dynasty the name *hsiao* was used; by the Yin, that of *hsü*; and by the Chou, that of *hsiang*. As to the *hsüeh*, they belonged to all three dynasties, and by that name. The object of them all is to illustrate human relations.""[72] In all the Seven Books of the *Mencius* the discussions by Mencius that are in any way relevant to institutions in no case go beyond the scope of these few items. And it is the well-field system and that of hereditary salaries to which Mencius seems to have granted special importance. Hence, in talking with King Hsüan [of Ch'i], he told him that what is called an ancient kingdom is one that has "ministers sprung from families that have been noted in it for generations." And to Duke Wen [of T'eng] he said that benevolent government found its first step in "laying down the boundaries" [i.e., boundaries of the fields, in the well-field system], while "As to the system of hereditary salaries, that is already observed in T'eng." The well-field system and that of hereditary salaries were main elements of the feudal institutions; thus Mencius' program for stability through unity was not a forerunner's announcement anticipating the coming unification under the First Emperor of Ch'in; rather, it was a long look back at the feudal world. Of this there cannot be the slightest doubt. If the ruler of Liang or of Ch'i had been able to put his ideas into practice and gain mastery of the world thereby, then the royal tours of inspection,

[72] See, respectively, "Kao Tzu," Part II [VI/ii/10/7; Legge, p. 442], where Mencius is speaking to Pai Kuei; "T'eng Wen-kung," Part I [III/i/3/6, Legge, pp. 240–41], speaking to Duke Wen; and "Liang Hui-wang," Part II [I/ii/5/3; Legge, pp. 161–62], where Mencius is addressing King Hsüan.

the appearances at court of the feudal lords, the congratulatory announcements and bestowals of royal rewards, the punitive campaigns and executions of the kings' punishments,[73] might even have reappeared long after
the Way of the Chou had fallen into disuse.

However we may still have two kinds of questions about the foregoing.
Why is it that: (1) Confucius exclusively "followed the Chou" while
Mencius spoke very generally about the ancient kings; and (2) Confucius
established the doctrine of gaining official position through the possession
of virtue, whereas Mencius set up the idea that "the descendants of
officers of government should be salaried"? Let us seek first the explanation of the former.

In the preceding chapter we have already discussed Confucius' reasons
for following the Chou. Confucius was closer to antiquity; in his time not
only were the records still in existence, but the traditions of Kings Wen
and Wu were still carried on. The Chou dynasty's institutions were still
impressively accessible for study and corroboration. Even though the
Chou royal house still carried on its political powers more in name than
in fact, still there was no unmistakable evidence that it was doomed to
destruction. Confucius followed the Chou, apparently much influenced
by such historical facts. Mencius was farther away from that antiquity,
having lived through the final stage of the Chou dynasty's collapse. When
we note his reply to Pei-kung Yi's question about the dignities and
emoluments of the Chou court: "The particulars of that arrangement

---

[73] "Kao Tzu," Part II, "Mencius said, 'The five chiefs of the princes [*pa*] were sinners
against the three kings.' '. . . When the sovereign visited the princes, it was called "a tour
of inspection." When the princes attended at the court of the sovereign, it was called
"giving a report of office." It was a custom in the spring to examine the plowing and
supply any deficiency of seed; and in autumn to examine the reaping, and assist where
there was a deficiency of the crop. When the sovereign entered the boundary of a state,
if the new ground was being reclaimed, and the old fields well cultivated; if the old were
nourished and the worthy honored; and if men of distinguished talents were placed in
office: then the prince was rewarded—rewarded with an addition to his territory. On the
other hand, if, on entering a state the ground was found left wild or overrun with weeds;
if the old were neglected and the worthy unhonored, and if the offices were filled with hard
tax-gatherers: then the prince was reprimanded. If a prince once omitted his attendance at
court, he was punished by degradation of rank; if he did so a second time, he was deprived
of a portion of his territory; if he did so a third time, the royal forces were set in motion,
and he was removed from his government. Thus the sovereign commanded the punishment, but did not himself inflict it, while the princes inflicted the punishment, but did
not command it. The five chiefs, however, dragged the princes to punish other princes;
and hence I say they were sinners against the three kings.' " [*Mencius*, VI/ii/7/1–2; Legge,
pp. 435–37.] This expands and develops Confucius' theory that "When good government prevails in the empire, ceremonies, music, and primitive military expeditions proceed from the son of Heaven." [*Analects*, XVI/2/1; Legge, p. 310.]

cannot be learned,"[74] we can correctly infer that by Mencius' time the Institutes of Chou were already no longer adequately attested, in that similar to those of Hsia and Yin [in the time of Confucius]. What Confucius praised as the "complete and elegant regulations" [of Chou] had become things of which Mencius could no longer gain full knowledge. Thus, even if Mencius had wished to follow the Chou, this was something that conditions would have precluded; hence he found it expedient to relinquish the Institutes of Chou and talk more broadly about the ancient kings. His desire was that the various regulations and institutions of Yao and Shun and the Three Dynasties, as he idealized these, could be made to serve as the prototype of the new state that the King of Ch'i or of Liang would bring into being through rebellion against the present one. And we might go further at this point to ask how Mencius, who could not even learn the particulars of the Chou institutions, was able to attest so fully the details of the government of Yao and Shun and the Three Dynasties. Mencius said: "It would be better to be without the *Book of History* than to give entire credence to it."[75] It is evident that what he called the methods [*fa*] of the former kings were no more than the general outlines of some ancient institutions to which he added ideal elements of his own creation; they were thus mixed and amalgamated formulations, not necessarily entirely based upon historical foundations. We note that Confucius, in discussing the rites of the Three Dynasties, indicated that each had done its own adding and subtracting, perpetuating some features and discarding others; Mencius, on the other hand, in establishing the institutions intended to stabilize the Warring States world through a new unification, looked upon Yao and Shun and Kings Wen and Wu as the eternally valid standard that could always serve to instruct later ages in correct methods. This discrepancy between the two philosophers results from the earlier man's having a greater regard for historical facts, whereas the later one was more subjective. It does not result from their having different basic attitudes toward the issue of protecting and preserving feudal government as such.

Likewise, Mencius' reasons for advocating hereditary salaries for officials should also be sought in the historical environment of the Warring States Period. With the degeneration and relaxation of clan-law society, the rulers as well as the leading officials of the various feudal states had gradually come to represent the old established clans less and less. For commoners to rival the fame of princes and feudal lords, and to achieve the highest positions as ministers and premiers, was becoming common-

---

[74] "Wan Chang," Part II [v/ii/2/1–2; Legge, p. 373].
[75] "Chin-hsin," Part II [vii/ii/3/1; Legge, p. 479].

place. The worst aspect of this situation, the tendency for it to engender an unprincipled race for the spoils of success, was rapidly becoming its dominant characteristic. High officials in public service no longer identified themselves with a particular ruler [in loyal constancy], and their policy formulations often were nothing more than unprincipled deceptions. At the worst, this led to the misfortunes of ever more widespread warfare and a cruelly ravaged populace, and, at the least, it entailed a lust for power and a struggle for high position that brought personal disasters and the destruction of families. Su Ch'in and Chang Yi [two famous strategy specialists of the time] promoted their policies of vertical alliance versus horizontal entente, while wandering from state to state serving as chief ministers; they are most representative of the "opportunistic elements" of that age. [See *Shih Chi*, *ch*s. 69 and 70.] These persons were contemporaries of Mencius, and he undoubtedly knew of them or came into contact with them. Confucius had regretted that the hereditary ministers were so seldom men of virtue, and hence, in order to correct that weakness, had established his doctrine that rank and position should be achieved through virtue. But the commoner ministers and premiers also in many cases went the same way; they too displayed the long-standing fault of possessing high position though lacking virtue, to which they added the social insecurity attendant upon their unrestrained pursuit of wealth and power.[76] This, in truth, was a situation that Confucius had not anticipated. And thus Mencius wanted to reinstitute the old system of families having a tradition of public service through successive generations, and the associated system of hereditary salaries.

When we note that Mencius, in discussing the defect of the state that lacked such hereditary officials, said: "Those whom you advanced yesterday are gone today, and you do not know it" [said to King Hsüan of Ch'i; *Mencius*, 1/ii/7/1; Legge, p. 165], it becomes very obvious that his purpose was to focus on the evil of men like Su Ch'in and Chang Yi, who characteristically were "in the service of Ch'in at dawn, and in the service of Ch'u by sunset." For, in the recruitment and employment of men, talent and virtue are unquestionably the ideal standards to be observed. But if it becomes impossible to maintain the respect for virtue, then, as Mencius saw it, it would be better to maintain the hereditary

---

[76] "T'eng Wen-kung," Part II, "Ching Ch'un said to Mencius 'Are not Kung-sun Yen and Chang Yi really great men? [These men were wandering scholars of the day, famous for their skill in involving the princes of the time in trouble-making schemes.] Let them once be angry, and all the princes are afraid. Let them live quietly, and the flames of trouble are extinguished throughout the kingdom.' [Mencius replied: 'How can such be great men?' " He goes on to define the great man as one of high ethical principles. III/ii/2/1–2; Legge, pp. 264–65.] Mencius denounced their practices as "the way of wives and concubines," [i.e., the way of women.]

principle as an aspect of ritual propriety. "Even if it did not guarantee talent and ability, it at least assured the maintenance of law and system,"[77] and it avoided the danger of leading society into confusion and disorder.

SECTION FOUR
Alternating Order and Chaos

CONFUCIUS had said: "Chou had the advantage of viewing the two past dynasties. How complete and elegant are its regulations." [*Analects*, III/ 14; Legge, p. 160.] The import of this is an indirect suggestion that the regulations and institutions of Kings Wen and Wu were the result of political progress. And even though he said that "we can foretell what the successors of Chou will be like, even supposing they do not appear till a hundred generations from now" [meaning that institutional change would be very gradual; see *Analects*, II/23; Waley, p. 93], Confucius nonetheless spoke of institutions in terms of selectively perpetuating or discarding their main features. He probably did not believe that, after the refined age of the Chou, it would ever be possible to revert to the cruder and simpler usages of Hsia and [Shang-] Yin. But in Mencius, since he regarded the ways of the ancient kings as immutable standards for all time, and since he further invented a theory of history as "alternating order and chaos," Confucius' hint at political progress was obscured or even obliterated. The consequence was that a theory of cyclic political changes came to be the most compelling thesis present throughout the subsequent two thousand years. This, together with the importance of the people and the concept of stability through unification, also constitutes an important contribution of Mencius, and as such merits some further discussion.

Mencius' view that order and chaos alternate was set forth in response to his disciple Kung-tu's question about whether or not Mencius was fond. of disputing. [His answer was: "I am not fond of disputing, but I am compelled to do it." Then he went on to discuss his view of history, showing that the disorders of his own age forced upon him the duty of refuting bad doctrines being spread abroad by others. *Mencius*, III/ii/9/1; Legge, p. 279.] In part, he said: "A long time has elapsed since this world of men received its being, and there has been along its history, now a period of good order, and now a period of confusion. In the time of Yao, the waters, flowing out of their channels, inundated the Middle Kingdom. Snakes and dragons occupied it, and the people had no place where they could

---

[77] Here the phrase [of the T'ang statesman] Han Yü is borrowed from his "Tui Yü wen," where he discusses the Sage Emperor Yü's having passed the throne on to his son [thereby establishing the principle of hereditary succession instead of that of succession to the most worthy man, by which latter principle Yü himself had come to the throne].

settle themselves. In the low ground they made nests for themselves on the trees or raised platforms, and in the high ground they made caves. It is said in the *Documents*, 'The waters in their wild course warned me.' Those 'waters in their wild course' were the waters of the great inundation." This represented one period of chaos. "Shun employed Yü to reduce the waters to order. Yü dug open their obstructed channels and conducted them to the sea. He drove away the snakes and dragons and forced them into the grassy marshes. On this, the waters pursued their course through the country, even the waters of the Chiang, the Huai, the Ho, and the Han; and the dangers and obstructions that they had occasioned were removed. The birds and beasts that had injured the people also disappeared; and after this men found the plains available for them, and occupied them." This was to be one period of order. "After the deaths of Yao and Shun, the principles that marked the sages fell into decay. Oppressive sovereigns arose one after another, pulling down houses to make ponds and lakes, so that the people knew not where they could rest in quiet. They threw fields out of cultivation to form gardens and parks, so that the people could not get clothes and food. Afterwards, corrupt speaking and oppressive deeds became more rife; gardens and parks, ponds and lakes, thickets and marshes, became more numerous, and birds and beasts swarmed. By the time of the tyrant Chou, the kingdom was again in a state of great confusion." This constituted another period of chaos. "The Duke of Chou assisted King Wu, and destroyed the tyrant King Chou. He smote Yen, and after three years put its sovereign to death. He drove Fei-lien into a corner by the sea, and slew him. The states that he extinguished amounted to fifty. He drove away also the tigers, leopards, rhinoceroses, and elephants;—and all the people was greatly delighted." This became another period of order. "Again the world fell into decay, and principles faded away. Perverse speakings and oppressive deeds waxed rife again. There were instances of ministers who murdered their sovereigns, and of sons who murdered their fathers."[78] This was a new age of chaos.

The cycle of alternating order and chaos is indeed not something manifest only in the history of the Three Dynasties; it has consistently characterized the two thousand years of imperial history, starting with the Ch'in and Han dynasties as well. This thesis of Mencius in truth embodies a sound observation. However, inasmuch as Mencius regarded the ways devised by the ancient kings as the acme of human social principle, and also said if one does good, among his descendants in after generations there would be one who would attain the royal dignity,[79] then Yao and

[78] "T'eng Wen-kung," Part II [III/ii/9/2–7; modified slightly from Legge, pp. 279–81].
[79] "Liang Hui-wang," Part II, addressed to Duke Wen of T'eng [I/ii/14/3; Legge, p. 175].

Shun, Yü and T'ang, Wen and Wu, all had the benefit simultaneously of the most perfect of sage-ordained institutions and perfect records for good accomplishments, why was it that they could not maintain a long-lasting era of order and peace? Although Confucius said nothing specifically directed to this question, it can be inferred from the content of his thought that "heaven's will" might possibly have been his reply. [Confucius used the expression "*t'ien ming*," translatable in some contexts as "The Mandate of Heaven"; in some others it is often called "fate," although in that sense it remains a difficult concept to express in English. See Chan, *Source Book*, pp. 78–79, "comment."] Even though Confucius did not talk about the Way of heaven [*t'ien tao*], yet it appears that he had a firm belief in heaven's will. Thus he said: "Heaven produced the virtue that is in me," and: "If heaven had wished to let this cause of truth perish. . . ."[80] Mencius was being true to this same idea when he said: "My not finding in the prince of Lu a ruler who would confide in me, and put my counsels into practice, is from heaven." Again, he said: "But heaven does not yet wish that the kingdom should enjoy tranquility and good order. If it wished this, who is there beside me to bring it about?"[81] In discussing fate, however, Confucius apparently limited its application to the personal successes and failures of individuals. Mencius, on the other hand, employs it when discussing changes in the sphere of political authority. For example, Kings Yao and Shun selected their successors on the basis of worthiness, while Yü named his son his successor. Mencius explained all these events in terms of heaven's intention, saying: "When heaven gave the kingdom to the worthiest, it was given to the worthiest. When heaven gave it to the son of the preceding sovereign, it was given to the son."[82] Although "Heaven sees according as my people see . . . ," and the people's will thus was in actual practice to be the ultimate standard of political authority, yet in theory heaven's will unquestionably remained the highest arbiter of the affairs of all creatures. This view also is something that Mencius had not himself devised, but had in fact drawn from ancient doctrines. More than one passage in the *Documents* has the same purport as these sayings of Mencius. For example, Tsu-chi instructs the king with the words: "Heaven reflects the [mind of] the ordinary people." [Tsu-

[80] The *Analects*, "Shu erh," Book Seven [vii/22; Legge, p. 202] and "Tzu han," Book Nine [ix/5/3; Legge, p. 218]. Also, in "Hsien wen," Book Fourteen, Confucius refers to the issue of whether the Way will prevail or will perish as "a matter of fate." [xiv/38/2, Waley, pp. 189–90, where "*ming*" is translated "heaven's will."] In "Chi-shih," Book xvi, he says that "the superior man stands in awe of heaven's will." [xvi/8; Legge, p. 313, translates *t'ien ming* here as "the ordinances of Heaven"; Waley, p. 206, as "the will of Heaven"; Chan, *Source Book*, p. 45, as "the Mandate of Heaven."]

[81] "Liang Hui-wang," Part ii, speaking to Yüeh-cheng Tzu [i/ii/16/3; Legge, p. 179]; and "Kung-sun Ch'ou," Part ii, speaking to Ch'ung Yü [ii/ii/14/5; Legge, p. 232].

[82] "Wan Chang," Part i [v/i/6/1; Legge, p. 358].

chi was a worthy minister of King Wu-ting of Shang-Yin, whose tradi-
tional dates place his reign in the middle of the thirteenth century B.C.]
The proclamation made by the Duke of Shao [a brother of King Wu of
Chou, active in the affairs of the dynasty at its beginning] says: "August
Heaven, the Supreme ruler above, has changed his decree in favor of our
[Chou] ruler." And King Ch'eng, in his address to the officers of the
"Numerous Regions" [of his newly-conquered realm], said: "Heaven at
this time sought a true lord for the people."[83] [King Ch'eng was the son
of King Wu of Chou, and his successor.] Moreover, the line that Mencius
quoted about heaven hearing and seeing as the people hear and see, also
is from "The Great Declaration," or "T'ai-shih," in the *Documents*.
[Legge, *Documents Shoo King*, p. 292. In the foregoing section, the language
of the Legge translation of the *Documents* has been consistently altered to
suit the context in which quoted passages appear. However, Legge's
predilection for seeing the Chinese *t'ien*, "heaven" as a kind of *Old Testa-
ment* Jehovah cannot be totally eradicated; moreover, the necessity to
specify person and number, and other requirements of English grammar,
further contribute to distortion of meaning in translation.]

"The Master seldom spoke about . . . the appointments of heaven."
[*Analects* IX/1, speaking of Confucius; following Legge's translation, p. 216,
of the word *ming* in this context; Waley, p. 138, translates it simply as
"fate."] He did not discuss such things as apparitions and spirits at all,
and alongside his respect for heaven he reveals a degree of skepticims. In
the case of Mencius, however, the element of religious belief is somewhat
stronger. When we note that Hsün Tzu in denouncing the theorists of the
Five Elements and of mysterious spiritual forces, included Tzu-ssu and
Mencius among his examples,[84] we can readily bring something of this to
mind. Reverencing heaven and worshipping spirits, establishing religious
practices directed toward the incomprehensible ways of spiritual forces—
these were all things common to the society of antiquity. They are what
the *Li Chi*, *ch.* 29, "Piao Chi," refers to in saying: "Under the Yin dynasty,
they honored Spiritual Beings [and led the people on to serve them . . .
etc.]." [Following Legge, *Li Ki*, Vol. 2, p. 342.] Hsün Tzu's comments

---

[83] See, respectively [*Documents*, Legge, *Shoo King*], "The Documents of Shang," "Kao-
tsung t'ung-jih," paragraph 3 [modified from Legge, p. 264]; and "The Documents of
Chou," "Shao Kao," paragraph 9 [modified from Legge, p. 425]; and "To fang,"
paragraph 6 [modified from Legge, p. 497]. The appendix to Liang Ch'i-ch'ao's *Hsien
Ch'in cheng-chih ssu-hsiang shih*, containing many passages from the *Shang Shu* mentioning
the "Will of Heaven" *t'ien ming*, makes most convenient reference to these, and may be
read in this connection. [Liang's book has been published in an English translation,
albeit of inadequate quality, by L. T. Ch'en, under the title *History of Chinese Political
Thought during the Early Tsin Period*, London, 1930.]

[84] *Hsün Tzu*, *ch.* 6, "Fei shih-erh tzu." For a more detailed discussion of this, see Section
Seven of this chapter.

[about Mencius] are certainly not without foundation in fact. Hence, too, it can be said that, in so frequently turning to the subject of heaven's will, Mencius displays but another aspect of the archaism of his thought and simultaneously of not adhering to the Way of the Chou.[85]

Mencius also presents a theory of a five-hundred-year cycle of order and chaos, something that the records of the past had not conveyed to him, and that may well be of his own creation. In answer to Ch'ung Yü's question he replied: "It is a rule that a true sovereign should arise in the course of five hundred years, and that during that time there should be men illustrious in their generation." And, on another occasion, he brought forward historical facts to corroborate this view, saying: "From Yao and Shun down to T'ang were five hundred years and more. As to Yü and Kao Yao, they saw those earliest sages, and so knew their doctrines, while T'ang heard their doctrines as transmitted, and so knew them. From T'ang to King Wen were five hundred years and more. As to Yi Yin and Lai Chu, they saw T'ang and knew his doctrines, while King Wen heard them as transmitted, and so knew them. From King Wen to Confucius were five hundred years and more. As to T'ai-kung Wang and San Yi-sheng, they saw King Wen and so knew his doctrines, while Confucius heard them as transmitted, and so knew them."[86] This clearly is talking about alternations of order and chaos as a complete, orderly, and definitely fixed cyclic movement. Calculating this movement according to the number of years in a cycle, one can know the ups and downs of a hundred generations in advance, so that one can forestall mistakes. The reason why Mencius so confidently took "bringing peace and order into the world" as his responsibility, and vigorously urged others to "protect the people and in that way become the true sovereign" was precisely because he already nourished in his breast the faith that this cyclic movement was due to bring about an age of order. He knew all too well that seven hundred or more years had elapsed since King Wen, and that the reckoned time was overdue, but that the conditions of the time were appropriate to such a development. [Cf. note 86.] Although Mencius' view in this instance is not wholly in harmony with historical fact, it

[85] The "Piao Chi" further says: "Under the Chou dynasty, they honored the ceremonial usages [li], and set a high value on bestowing [favors]; they served the manes and respected Spritual Beings, yet keeping them at a distance." [Legge, Li Ki, Vol. 2, p. 342.] In the light of this, Confucius' "Respecting Spiritual Beings, but keeping aloof from them" [Analects, vi/20, Legge, p. 191], was also a matter of following the Chou.

[86] See, respectively "Kung-sun Ch'ou," Part ii [Mencius, ii/ii/13/3; Legge, p. 232] and "Chin hsin," Part ii [vii/ii/38/1–3; Legge, pp. 501–02]. "Kung-sun Ch'ou," Part ii, further says: "From the commencement of the Chou dynasty till now, more than seven hundred years have elapsed. Judging numerically, the date is past. Examining the character of the present time, we might expect the rise of such individuals in it." [Legge, p. 232.]

nonetheless constitutes a most fascinating philosophy of history. The Sung period philosopher Shao Yung [1011–1077] with his system of "cyclic convergence in the cosmic epicycles"[87] must in truth credit Mencius as his distant forerunner.

SECTION FIVE
Li (The Rites)

CONFUCIUS' discourses on politics established his two major tenets— the practice of benevolence and the rectification of names. The former was greatly augmented through the efforts of Mencius; the latter was given its more complete and thorough working out by Hsün Tzu. Were we to state that all of the theorizing about the rites [*li* 禮] of the pre-Ch'in era was drawn together and brought to the fullest development in Hsün Tzu, we would be essentially correct.

The *Li Chi, ch.* 29, "Piao Chi," states: "Under the Chou dynasty, they honored the ceremonical usages [*li*], and set a high value on bestowing [favors]." [Legge, *Li Ki*, Vol. II, p. 342.] Both Confucius and Hsün Tzu, in their statements on the rites, thus followed the way of the Chou; they were not in this respect opening the way to a basically new philosophical view. An examination of the ancient texts makes it evident that discussions of the rites by men of the Spring and Autumn Period embody two different conceptions, one broader and one narrower. In the narrower one, the word *li* denotes the forms of ceremonial acts and their accouterments [which Legge translates "deportment"], while in the broader usage it indicates all regulations and institutions [which Legge translates "propriety"]. Under the Fifth year of Duke Chao [536 B.C.] the *Tso Chuan* records: "The Duke went to Chin; and from his reception in the suburbs to the presentation of gifts at his departure, he did not fail in any point of ceremony [*li*]. The Marquis of Chin said to Ju Shu-ch'i, 'Is not the Marquis of Lu good at propriety [*li*]?' . . ." He replied: "That was deportment [*yi* 儀] . . . and should not be called propriety. Propriety is that by which [a ruler] maintains his state, carries out his governmental orders, and does not lose his people."[88] This points out the distinction between the

---

[87] Shao Yung, *Huang chi ching-shih shu* [translated in part in Chan, *Source Book*, pp. 484–94]. However, Shao Yung was deeply influenced by Taoism, and his ideas are not drawn exclusively from Mencius. We should note also that Confucius believed in the will of heaven [or, fate], but he had no theory of a five-hundred-year cyclic reappearance of order. Hence he said: "If good men were to govern a country in succession for a hundred years, they would be able to transform the violently bad, and dispense with capital punishments. . . . If a truly royal ruler were to arise, it would still require a generation, and then virtue would prevail." *Analects*, "Tzu-lu," Book XIII [XIII/11–12; Legge, p. 267].

[88] Refer also to *Tso Chuan*, Twenty-third year of Duke Chuang, ". . . the Duke went to Ch'i to see [the service at] the altar to the Spirits of the Land. This was contrary to

two meanings of *li* in the clearest and simplest fashion. That to which the Confucians attached great importance and which they sought to develop and clarify is the broader conception of the rites; they did not restrict themselves to the narrower subject of capping and marriage rites, burial and sacrificial ceremonial, bowing and deferring, greeting and entertaining, and other such formal usages.[89] Hsün Tzu's political thought has its base in this broader sense of *li*; this he combined with his theory that human nature is evil, and from the two he produced an extensive development of his own thought.

Hsün Tzu advanced the view that human nature is evil; among the Confucians of the pre-Ch'in era, this is an original view and a most extraordinary one. Confucius had said: "By nature, men are nearly alike; by practice, they get to be wide apart." [*Analects*, xvii/2; Legge, p. 318.] This clearly displays the opinion that in their native endowment men are without any difference as to good or evil nature, and that the worthy and the unworthy are the products of environmental influences. He also said: "There are only the wise of the highest class and the stupid of the lowest class who cannot be changed." [*Analects*, xvii/3; Legge, p. 318.] This acknowledges, however, that human nature is of different qualities, some higher and some lower, some of which are difficult to transform despite all moulding influences. Mencius went on to create the theory that human nature is good, levelling this difference between the higher and lower quality of human nature by saying: "All men may be Yaos and Shuns." [I.e., sages representing the perfection of all human

---

propriety [*li*]. Ts'ao Kuei remonstrated with him, saying, 'This cannot be. Propriety is that by which the people are rectified [*cheng min*]. Hence there are meetings of the princes at the royal court, to inculcate the duties severally incumbent on the high and low, and to lay down the amount of contributions which are to be severally made. There are court visits, to rectify the true position of the different ranks of nobility, and to arrange the precedence of older and younger. There are punitive expeditions to punish those who are not in accord [with these rules of propriety].' " [Modified from Legge, p. 105.] See also the *Kuo Yü*, *ch.* 4, "Lu Yü," Part i, where the wording differs slightly. "*Cheng min*," 整民 here is to be taken in the sense of "*cheng min*" 正民 ["rectify the people"]. In the *Li Chi* the broader sense of the *li* is set forth in great detail; the relevant passages cannot all be quoted here.

[89] Yet the Confucians also were thoroughly familiar with the minutiae of ceremonial forms, as one can know from reading the accounts of these in the *Yi Li* and the *Li Chi*. Confucius himself was noted as a man who knew the rites. *Mo Tzu*, *ch.* 39, "Fei Ju," says that the Confucian: "Elaborates the ceremonials and music to make man extravagant." [Modified slightly from Y. P. Mei, *Motze*, p. 212.] These examples show that indeed the Confucians also maintained the ritual proprieties. Confucius' contribution lay in his broadening the scope of the rites and deepening their significance, so that they became the essential means for rectifying the people and governing the state. It was in this attitude toward the *li* that he said: "Ritual, ritual! Does it mean no more than presents of jade and silk?" [*Analects*, xvii/11; Waley, p. 212.]

qualities; *Mencius*, vi/ii/1; Legge, p. 424.] This doctrine goes beyond the scope encompassed by Confucius' views.

Subsequently, Hsün Tzu attacked Mencius precisely to refute this view, but at the same time he also expressed ideas that do not conform to those of Confucius. In his essay, *ch.* 23, "Hsing O," i.e., "That the Nature is Evil," he states: "The nature of man is evil; his good qualities are artificial." [They are "artificial" in the sense that they are acquired training, accomplished through the laudable artifice of human civilization, and not as an expression of the innate human character. This chapter of the *Hsün Tzu* is translated by Legge, *Mencius*, Prolegomena, pp. 79–88; Dubs, pp. 301–17; Watson pp. 157–71; and Chan, *Source Book*, pp. 128–35. See also Fung/Bodde, Vol. i, pp. 297–99.] For Hsün Tzu believed that man from birth is fond of personal gain, anxious to avoid everything unpleasant, and addicted to the desires of ear and eye, of sound and color. If these predilections are allowed to grow naturally and are not subjected to restraints and controls, they will lead him to contentions and robberies, violence and injuries, and excessive and disorderly conduct of all kinds; and a social life of "rectitude, order, and good government" would be impossible to achieve. Once such a theory of man's evil nature is established, then without much detailed analysis it is obvious that the rites and usages of propriety become indispensable. His *ch.* 19, "Treatise on Rites," says: "What is the origin of the rites? Men are born with desires. When they do not get what they desire, they must seek means of obtaining it. When this seeking is without standard, measured, and distinct limits, then it can produce only contention. Contention leads to disorder, and disorder to exhaustion [of material resources]. The former kings hated this disorder, hence devised rites [*li*] and righteousness [*yi* 義] to maintain the necessary distinctions, to nurture people's [proper] desires, and to assure the supply of things that people seek." [*Yi* here is a different word from that translated above as "deportment." The translation "righteousness" is retained here for consistency, to show the continuity and development of the word through Confucius and Mencius. It is also often translated "justice," a term that may suggest some of the codification of standards for its application, toward which Hsün Tzu's thought inclined. For a somewhat different translation of these lines, see Watson, *Hsün Tzu*, p. 89, where *li-yi* is taken as one noun meaning "ritual principles."] "For bending came into existence because there was crooked wood; the carpenter's square and ruler came into existence because things are not straight; and the authority to rule is instituted and propriety [the rites] and righteousness are made clear because man's nature is evil." [*Hsün Tzu*, ch. 23, Chan, *Source Book*, p. 132; cf. Watson, pp. 163–64.] This makes most clearly manifest that what Hsün Tzu referred to as the rites was the good but bitter medicine for the evil nature of mankind, and at the same time was the basic condition for man's social life. One advocating the goodness of human nature would logically have to favor the unrestrained expression of that nature; thus Mencius emphasized benevolence [*jen*]. One avowing that human nature is evil would be constrained to teach the regulation of that nature; thus Hsün Tzu stressed the rites [*li*]. In both cases, these characteristics are determined by theoretical and logical necessity; each was able to expand and round out his theory, making a complete philosophical system of it.

There is, however, one point of which we should take careful note: Hsün Tzu developed his theory of *li* as something by which desire is to be limited and restricted, not by which people shall abolish desire. The real objective of the rites was to employ the method of restricting men's desires in order to permit the needs of material existence to be satisfied as generously as possible for all mankind. Although as a method this bordered on the negative, its results were manifestly positive. Hsün Tzu had clearly acknowledged the principle that "human life is impossible without the social group," that people must be cooperative and effect a division of labor before they can hope to survive. Since man's nature is evil, however, there inevitably arise in the life of the social group two serious difficulties: The one is that, when the individual's rights are not definitely fixed, he will struggle to gain greater material well-being; the other is that, when the individual's duties are not clearly fixed, he will become indolent in his work. The only means of solving these difficulties is to devise *li*, which make clear the social distinctions, so that everyone's rights and duties are both definite and universally known.[90] Then society will be orderly and stable, and people will be prosperous and happy.

As Hsün Tzu set forth his ideal of government by *li*: "Virtue must be commensurate with position, position must be commensurate with emolument, and emolument must be commensurate with the uses [it provides for]." "At court there must be none whose positions were gained fortuitously; among the people there must be none whose livelihood is gained

---

[90] *Ch.* 10, "Fu kuo," i.e., "The Rich Country": "People desire and hate the same things. Their desires are many but things are few. Since they are few, there will inevitably be strife. What a hundred workmen accomplish contributes to nourishing each individual. Yet an able person cannot be skilled in more than one line; one man cannot simultaneously perform two functions. If people leave their positions and do not serve each other, there will be poverty; if the masses [comprising the whole social group] are without social divisions, there will be strife. Poverty is an affliction, strife a calamity. To eliminate affliction and avert calamity, there is no method so good as clarifying social distinctions, thereby causing people to form a social group. . . . Work is what people dislike; gain and profit is what they like. When duties of office and the tasks of the occupations lack the distinctions, in such a situation people will find it difficult to carry on their work, and will be beset by strife over the profit and gain therefrom. . . . Therefore wise men have introduced social distinctions." [Modified from Dubs, *Works of Hsüntze*, pp. 152–53.]

fortuitously."[91] "Thus when a man of benevolence is at the top, the farmers will exert their strength to make the most from their fields, the merchants will exert their circumspection to make the most from their wealth, the various craftsmen will all employ their arts to make the most from their vessels and tools; and from the scholars and great officers all the way up through the dukes and marquises, there shall be none who do not use benevolence and a generous spirit, knowledge and ability to achieve the utmost in their official capacities. This is what is called the absolute equity [*chih p'ing* 至平]. Then even in the case of the one whose income is the revenues of the whole empire [i.e., the Son of Heaven], that is not excessive; and even those who are mere door-keepers and guest-greeters, gate-guards and night-watchmen, will not feel themselves to be deprived. Hence the saying: 'Uneven and yet uniform, crooked and yet conforming, different and yet made one'—thus the human relationships."[92] [Hsün Tzu introduces an old saying to describe the individual diversities harmonized and ordered under one set of comprehensive principles.] In this society of "absolute equity," men would not be led to pursue desires that could not be gratified; wealth and material goods would be regulated, and made obtainable. Such goods would be weighed and calculated to satisfy needs and desires; "those two [goods and desires] should sustain each other and increase." Therefore he said: "It is the rites that nurture".[93]

---

[91] *Ibid.*

[92] *Ch.* 4, "Jung ju," i.e., "Glory and Shame."

[93] *Ch.* 19, "Li Lun," i.e., "Treatise on Rites." Hsün Tzu at times judges whether a government has achieved order or chaos according to whether or not the people are properly nurtured. For example, *ch.* 11, "Wang-pa," "King, or Hegemon," says "Men's feelings are such that the eye desires the limit of color and the ear desires the limit of sound, the mouth desires the limit of flavor, the nose desires the limit of fragrance, and the mind desires the limit of ease. These five limits [of possible satisfaction] are things that man's feelings demand he should not forego. The means exist whereby to sustain these five limits. But if the means are not provided, then the five limits cannot be realized. A state of ten thousand chariots [measuring the resources of a country by the size of its army] can be said to be broad and vast, rich and abundant. Add to [such resources] the principle by which government is made firm, and it is possible then to be peaceful and happy, with no troubles or sorrows. And then the means for sustaining the five limits can be said to be complete. So it is said: 'All happiness is defined as being born in a well-ordered state. Grief and anxiety can be defined as being born in a chaotic state.' " The *Li Chi* also repeatedly develops the idea that the rites are in basic accord with man's feelings and nature. For example, in *ch.* 30, "Fang Chi," it says: "The rites, complying with men's feelings provide regulatory patterns, thereby setting bounds for the people." In *ch.* 9, "Li yün," it says: "The rites accord with Heaven's seasons, are supplied by earth's abundance, follow the ways of the dead and the spirits, accord with men's hearts, and bring order to all things." And *ch.* 49, "Sang-fu ssu-chih," states: "The general outlines of the rites are that they embody the conditions of heaven and earth, are modeled upon the four seasons, observe the standard of *Yin* and *Yang*, and comply with human nature and feelings; thus they are called *li* [the rites]." One should note that throughout all of the

The ultimate purpose of the rites is to nurture. [I.e., *yang* 養; Dubs translates this "to educate and nourish." Confucius declared that to nourish was the first task of government; see, Chapter Two, Section Four, p. 109 above. Mencius also attached great importance to it; see, Chapter Three, Section Two, p. 153 above.] Therefore the *Hsün Tzu* discusses the matter of enriching the state in great detail and with an intensity that equals and at times even surpasses Mencius. The principles that he advanced for insuring the state's material sufficiency embody the two aspects: "Regulate consumption through the rites, and keep the people in plenty through administrative measures."[94] And what he refers to as keeping the people in plenty through administrative measures does not go beyond "lightly taxing plowed fields and open lands, making uniform the imposts collected at customs barriers and markets, lessening the numbers of merchants and traders, only rarely bringing about the need for labor corvee, and never encroaching on the seasonal demands of agriculture." These are all fairly close to the ideas of Mencius.

The most striking departure in his thought from issues marked out by Mencius undoubtedly is his theory concerning the circulation of money and goods. Hsün Tzu erected the ideal of economic cooperation, encouraging exchange of all the world's products, so that, using what one has, one could acquire whatever one lacks, effecting thereby a mutual supplying of needs. "For men of the marshlands then will have sufficient timber, and men of the mountains sufficient fish. Farmers need neither chop and cut, nor work as potters, nor smelt ores to have sufficient implements to use. Craftsmen and traders need not till the fields to have sufficient cereal grains." In consequence, "all within the four seas can be like one family," and all the people can obtain the wherewithall of their nurture, and enjoy contentment.[95] We should note even more particularly that, despite his pessimistic view of human nature, he was optimistic about economic life. Hsün Tzu believed that a policy of guaranteeing plenty to the people could cause unlimited growth of material production. Therefore the crux of the problem of enriching the state lay not in lowering demands but in expanding supply. The sage in instituting rites should weigh and calculate goods

---

chapters of the *Li Chi* [in the versions] of both the elder and the younger Tai [Tai Te and his nephew Tai Sheng, who edited versions of the *Li Chi* during the Han period], there is to be found great similarity to the content of Hsün Tzu's writings. No doubt portions [of the *Li Chi* as it took form in Han times] are derived from the system of thought of Hsün Tzu's school.

[94] *Ch.* 10, "Fu kuo."

[95] *Ch.* 9, "Wang chih," or "Kingly Ordinances." Note that Hsün Tzu looked upon society as an organization based on division of labor and on cooperation. The import of this is rather close to Mencius' denunciation of Hsü Hsing's ideal of a society in which all the members engage in agricultural production together. However, Mencius did not develop this line of his thought extensively or in detail.

in order to give men what they desire. And such desire is a motive force for production, so the regulation of consumption through the rites should cease whenever possible. If constantly and repeatedly damaged, the motive to produce eventually will disappear. Even [an austere policy] "like something scorched, like something burned" [Hsün Tzu so described the austerity of Mo Tzu's doctrines],[96] would be unavailing in bringing the world to a condition of plenty and, on the contrary, contained within it the danger of hastening the trend toward impoverishment and dearth. This concept, which Hsün Tzu up-held, has points of great similarity to the ideas of some modern Western thinkers. It is not only very different from those of the Mohists [Hsün Tzu presents his economic ideas as a refutation of those], but also displays considerable advance over Mencius' ideal of making the cereal grains as plentiful as water and fire. [*Mencius*, vii/i/23/3; Legge, pp. 462–63.]

The purpose of the rites, then, is to nurture; the means of bringing this about is to "fix distinctions" [*pieh* 別]. These distinctions are what he refers to as: "Noble and humble status have their rankings, elder and younger maintain their disparity, the richer and the poorer, and persons of greater and lesser importance, all have what is appropriate to them."[97] The concrete manifestations of these distinctions are all the state's institutions establishing the differences of rank and degree. Hence he says:

[96] *Hsün Tzu, ch.* 10, "Fu kuo": "Mo Tzu, whether master of the whole empire or merely ruler of a single state, would grimly enforce the wearing of coarse clothing and the eating of bad food. People would be sad and music would be banned. In this way [people] become deprived. Deprived people cannot satisfy their desires. When desires cannot be satisfied, the system of rewards for merit cannot be made effective. Mo Tzu, whether master of the whole empire or merely ruler of a single state, would dispense with apprenticeship [of trainees following an official in government] and would eliminate offices and ranks. Those in high positions would have to engage in toil and drudgery, having to share in the same kind of work as the masses, and equal with them in the rewards gained. In such a situation there would be no awe of the superior, and without awe the penal regulations could not be enforced. When rewards are not effective there would be no means by which the worthy can be advanced for merit. When penal regulations are not enforced there would be no means by which the perverse can be effectively restrained. There would be no way to judge the capable and the incompetent, and give [the former] office. In such circumstances all things would lose their proper balance; and the process of events would go awry. Above, there would be confusion of heaven's seasons; below, there would be confusion of earth's provenance; in between [among men], there would be a failure of peoples' harmonious relations. The realm would be in suffering, as if burned and scorched. Even though Mo Tzu were to wear the coarsest clothing and tie a rope around his waist for a belt, nibble at rough grains, and drink only water, it could scarcely avail. For the foundations would have been undercut, the source would have been exhausted, and the whole world would become as if parched."

[97] *Ch.* 19, "Li lun" and *ch.* 10, "Fu kuo" both contain this passage. [The translation of the passage in the former, Dubs, p. 214, has not been used; cf. also, Watson, *Hsün Tzu*, p. 90.]

"The rites put wealth and goods to their uses, mark outwardly noble and humble status, by [effecting variations in] abundance and paucity create differences, and by greater elaborateness or diminished simplicity achieve what is appropriate."[98] Once the institutions based on the rites are achieved in practice, people will then be content with their lot; belligerence and disorder, dissolute and slothful conduct, will have no further cause to arise. Such a state can be achieved solely by applying distinctions to vary sameness, by replacing equality with differentiation, by substituting restraint for freedom. However, the distinctions derived from the rites, and the inequalities of these distinctions, are not arrived at wilfully or arbitrarily; they must be determined wholly in accordance with the concerned individuals' character and ability. *Ch.* 9, "Wang chih," says: "Those who lack virtue shall not be ennobled, those who lack ability shall not be given office, those without merit shall not be rewarded, and those without guilt shall not be punished. At court there must be none whose positions were gained fortuitously; among the people there must be none whose livelihood is gained fortuitously." [See also Dubs, *The Works of Hsüntze*, pp. 131–32, for another translation.] And it also says: "Though a man be the descendant of princes, nobles, knights, or great officers, if he cannot be subservient to the rites and to righteousness, he should become a commoner. And though a man may be the descendant of commoners, if he accumulates refinement and learning, and exemplifies them in his person and in his deeds, having the capacity to be ruled by the rites and by righteousness, then he should become a chief minister, knight, or great officer." The tenor of this is very high-minded, and the principle involved is very reasonable; within the inequality of it there is an implicit element of equality. It is heir to the Confucian ideal of position through virtue, and it helped create the new Ch'in-Han era of chief ministers and great officials who came from the ranks of the commoners. As compared with Mencius' advocacy of hereditary emolument, Hsün Tzu here displays a greater ability to escape the lingering influences from the feudal world and to advance toward the new social order.

That the thought and learning of Hsün Tzu belong to the age just before the dawn of the authoritarian world-empire is further evident in his attitude of reverence for the ruler. Mencius, in his theory that the

---

[98] *Ch.* 19, "Li lun." [Dubs' translation, p. 226, has not been used, but is perhaps also a justifiable rendering; cf. also, Watson, p. 96.] The *Li Chi, ch.* 30, "Fang chi," also says: "The Master said, 'It is by the rules of ceremony that what is doubtful is displayed, and what is minute is distinguished, so that they may serve as dykes for the people. Thus it is that there are the grades of the noble and the mean, the distinctions of dress, the different places at court; and so the people [are taught to] give place to one another.'" [Legge, Vol. II, p. 285; see his note on page 284 on "dykes."] Also *ch.* 10, "Li ch'i," which discusses the ritual institutions in considerable detail, can also be referred to here.

people are of prime importance and the ruler relatively unimportant, was indeed—when viewed against the background of the prevailing tendencies of the Warring States Period—open to the charge of "living in the present age yet going back to the way of antiquity." [This critical phrase is attributed to Confucius; see *The Doctrine of the Mean*, xxvIII/1; Legge, p. 423.] Confucius did not slight the importance of the ruler, but, on the other hand, neither did he make any statements explicitly affirming the ruler's absolute powers.[99] When it comes to Hsün Tzu, the idea of the elevation of the ruler is vigorously proclaimed and supported. In *ch.* 8, "Ju hsiao," it says: "The Confucians model their doctrines on the Former Kings, magnify the rites and righteousness, are circumspect as ministers and as sons, and honor their superiors to the fullest extent." [Dubs, *The Works of Hsüntze*, pp. 93–94, offers a slightly different translation.] This implies that the elevation of the ruler is one of the important aspects of Confucian doctrine. *Ch.* 14, "Chih shih" says: "The ruler is the eminence of the state; the father is the eminence of the family. Single eminence results in order, double in chaos." This is not significantly different from the old idea that "heaven does not have two suns." [*Mencius*, v/i/4/1; Legge, p. 352, where this is credited to Confucius. The same line also appears several times in the *Li Chi*; one example is quoted in note 99.] In the *ch.* 18, "Cheng lun," he states: "The Son of Heaven is one whose power and position are high to the extreme—he is without a peer in the world. . . . He assumes his southward-facing position, giving audience to the world-empire, and there are none among the world's living men who are not stirred and made submissive, transformed so that they conform to his will. In all the empire there are then no scholar-officers who conceal themselves away; there are no good men who are neglected and lost. All that is one with him is right, and all that diverges is wrong." [See also Dubs, *The Works of Hsüntze*, p. 198.] The purport of this is remarkably close to the ideas of the Legalist school, and strikingly different from the doctrines of Mencius. To draw some inferences about Hsün Tzu's reasons for believing in the exaltation of the ruler, we can find one such reason in environmental conditions, and three belonging to the realm of theory. To comment first on the environmental factor, Mencius and Hsün Tzu both lived in the age of large states and of rulers who occupied positions of awe and power. Mencius elaborated on antique ideas in order to resist this trend; Hsün Tzu accepted the condition of the age in order to

[99] However, the *Li Chi*, *ch.* 30, "Fang chi," states: "The Master said, 'There are not two suns in the sky, nor two kings in a territory, nor two masters in a family, nor two superiors of equal honor; and the people are shown how the distinctions between ruler and subject should be maintained. [Legge, *Li Ki*, Vol. II, p. 285.] This is merely to manifest the idea that the ruler's position is a supremely exalted one; it does not necessarily mean that the ruler's power is absolute. That distinction should be clearly noted.

establish his theories. The environments of the two were more or less the same, but the response of the two to their environment was very different.

In terms of the content of their thought, Hsün Tzu focused upon the rites with a view to emphasizing the differences of noble and humble status, to stressing the distinctions between superiors and inferiors, and to differentiating between ruler and servitor, as the essentials of the matter. If he did not elevate the ruler, it would then be impossible to gain the functioning of these distinctions. Therefore there could not be two [competing] rulers, for his power and effectiveness depended on his being alone in eminence. This point is an obvious one. *Ch.* 9, "Wang chih," says: "If the social distinctions are equalized, then there will not be enough to go around. If powers are shared evenly, then there can be no unity. If the masses are all uniform, they cannot then be directed." And further: "That two persons of noble status cannot serve each other and two persons of humble status cannot direct each other, is simply in the nature of things." [I.e., *"t'ien shu,"* 天數 or "the inherent nature of things"; this expression is sometimes translated less naturalistically, i.e., "heaven-ordained principle." Dubs, *Works of Hsüntze,* p. 124, translates it "—this is a law of nature."] The purport of this passage is abundantly clear. So much for the first of Hsün Tzu's theoretical necessities for the exaltation of the ruler.

The ruler occupies a position of extreme importance in Hsün Tzu's thought-system. In one place Hsün Tzu has said: "Heaven and earth constitute the beginning from which comes life. The rites and righteousness constitute the beginning from which comes order. The ruler constitutes the beginning from which come the rites and righteousness." And further: "It is the ruler whose skills bring into being the social group."[100] "The strength of all the 'hundred clans' needs [the ruler] in order to accomplish anything; the social group composed of all the 'hundred clans' need him in order to be harmonious; the wealth and goods of all the 'hundred clans' depends upon him in order to be accumulated; the situation of all the 'hundred clans' depends on him in order to be secure; the life-span of all the persons of the 'hundred clans' depends on him in order to reach high longevity."[101] [*"Po hsing"* or "the hundred clans" originally meant the upper strata of society, which alone had surnames; during the Chou period it came to mean "the people" as clan institutions and the possession of surnames came to include the whole society. In the *Hsün Tzu* the broader meaning is usually more appropriate.] "Now suppose we try to remove the authority of the ruler, and be without the reforming influences of the rites and of righteousness; suppose we try to remove the order gained through laws and governmental measures and to be without the restrain-

[100] *Ch.* 9, "Wang chih" [see also Dubs, p. 137, especially note 2].
[101] *Ch.* 10, "Fu kuo."

ing influences of punishments. Let us then stand by and observe how the people of the world would treat each other. In this situation, the strong would do injury to the weak and despoil them; the many would inflict violence on the few and tear them to shreds; the world would be plunged into chaos and destruction in the shortest time."[102] Thus governmental organization depends on the ruler of sage-like wisdom in order to come into existence, and political life also depends on a perpetuating monarchical institution for its continuing existence. The issue of order versus chaos is bound up with one man, so the honor and glory accruing to him must be of another kind than that which might attach to the broad masses of men. Herein lies the second of Hsün Tzu's theoretical necessities for the exaltation of the ruler.

Furthermore: "The ruler of men is the essential agency for controlling the allotments and assignments [*fen* 分, in society]."[103] Therefore it follows that the ruler's responsibilities of office are to determine clearly the powers and duties of all the servitors and common people of the entire nation and to supervise them in these. Should the ruler occupy something less than the most elevated of positions, and possess less than the greatest authority, then his important responsibilities would be difficult of execution. And this is an additional reason for Hsün Tzu's elevation of the ruler.

Because of these several reasons, Hsün Tzu somewhat altered the doctrines of Confucius and Mencius, and drew closer to those of Shen Pu-hai and Han Fei [as representatives of Legalism]. Confucians of the T'ang and Sung dynasties regarded Mencius as the heir to the orthodox line of Confucian thought, and designated Hsün Tzu's theories a "minor blemish" [*hsiao tz'u* 小疵]. When one considers his two tenets, that human nature is evil, and that the ruler should be exaltated, there is indeed a basis for such criticism. But we can carry this still a step further. For in the benevolence-based political thought of Confucius and Mencius, despite an all-pervading consistency between personal ethics and political life, the inner and the outer lives could still be separated. When the *Tao* prevails, come forth; when the *Tao* is lacking, then withdraw into concealment. [*Analects*, VIII/13/2.] When able to achieve prominence and success, extend benefits to all; when frustrated by ill-fortune, then cultivate one's own person. [*Mencius*, VII/i/9/6.] Even when the world was enveloped in general disorder, one could still flee the world's demands and be a man of noble worth in private and seclusion. Thus beyond political life the individual could still maintain his personal ethical life. Hsün Tzu wanted, through the ruler's and the elite's ritual forms [*li*] and concept of righteousness [*yi*], to overcome the predilection for evil inherent in man's nature. If the ruler were deficient in *Tao*, violence and

---

[102] *Ch.* 23, "Hsing o" [modified slightly from Dubs, p. 308].
[103] *Ch.* 10, "Fu kuo."

disorder would be the consequence. In such circumstances of life-and-death urgency for all, could the individual stand aside in the deluded hope of maintaining his own perfection? Therefore, before good government is established there is no possibility of cultivating the self; and beyond political life there can be no area of personal ethical life. Although Hsün Tzu did not explicitly affirm that the individual has an absolute political duty, he in fact implies something like the Legalists' views about the importance of the state as compared with the relative unimportance of the individual. History records that Han Fei Tzu and Li Ssu both studied under Hsün Tzu, and it is precisely in those aspects of his thought which diverge from the Confucian tradition that he can be regarded as a predecessor of the Legalist school.[104]

Nonetheless, in his exaltation of the ruler, Hsün Tzu still clearly displays fundamental points of difference from the Legalists. The Legalists lean toward the concept of the ruler as the principal element of government, whereas Hsün Tzu did not abandon the ideal that the people are of paramount importance. For Hsün Tzu's principal reason for elevating the ruler was that the ruler had important responsibilities and duties. In modern terminology the ruler was, in Hsün Tzu's conception of him, a high and mighty, majestic and dignified, public servant; he was by no means the possessor of the vast earth and the masses of its people. Whenever he failed to fulfill responsibilities incumbent upon him, by the nature of his office [t'ien chih 天職] he thereby lost his lofty majesty, and he could be dethroned or could be executed. Hsün Tzu has stated that "It is not for the sake of the ruler that heaven brings forth the people. Rather, it is for the sake of the people that heaven establishes the ruler." And, further: "When a servitor slays his ruler, or an inferior assassinates his superior, surrenders his ruler's cities to the enemy, violates his obligation of loyal service, and fails to serve faithfully unto death, there is no other cause than that the ruler has brought it upon himself by misgovernment." And also: "The one to whom the world voluntarily turns is to be called a king; if the world rejects him, it is called the demise [of the state]. Thus Chieh

---

[104] It should be noted that before Hsün Tzu there were two persons among the Confucian school, i.e., Wu Ch'i [d. 381 B.C.] and Li K'e [fl. fourth century B.C.] whose thought was close to that of the Legalists. It is unfortunate that their works are not extant and their theories cannot be studied in detail. Moreover, though Hsün Tzu stressed the state, he by no means denied the necessity for the ethical cultivation of the self; refer in this connection to The Hsün Tzu, ch. 2, "Hsiu Shen," and ch. 3, "Pu kou." Yet it can be said that Hsün Tzu tended toward the encouragement of hypocrisy in maintaining the semblance of virtue. For example in ch. 4, "Jung ju," he says: "Filial and fraternal piety spring from vigorous attention to the control of one's own conduct, alacrity in responding punctiliously and cautiously in all one's affairs, and not daring to indulge in carelessness or disrespect. It is in this way that the ordinary man insures that he will dress warmly and eat his fill, to preserve life and extend longevity, and to evade corporal punishment and death."

and Chou were not really the possessors of kingdoms, and T'ang and Wu were not guilty of regicide."[105] [The former were bad last rulers of the Hsia and Shang dynasties, who no longer deserved their thrones; the latter were the glorious founders of the succeeding Shang and Chou dynasties, who killed and succeeded Kings Chieh and Chou.] The meaning of these passages is the same as Mencius' statement about "cutting off a common fellow." [Mencius' way of referring to the death of the tyrant King Chou; see Section Two of this chapter, and footnote 38.] They constitute full proof that Hsün Tzu is correctly to be regarded as an important further development within the Confucian tradition.

Section Six
The Methods of Governing and the Men Who Govern

Hsün Tzu's theories, at certain points, come very close to those of the Legalists, as has been briefly indicated in the preceding section. The boundary line separating rites [li] from law [fa] is a delicate and by no means easily distinguished one that defies too ready a definition. Just as the rites, so too has law [fa] both narrower and broader meanings. The narrower meaning of it is that of articulated regulations governing the conduct of lawsuits and the adjudication of cases. In its broader definition it includes the institutions by which government is constituted and civil order maintained. If we examine the issue with reference solely to the narrower definition, the distinction between the rites and the law is an obvious one, but if we take the broader definitions of both, the two may be readily confused. We may note that in feudal clan-law society, all relationships derived from personal factors; institutions therefore gave prime importance to the rites. Capping, marriage, mourning and sacrifice, the rural archery contests and wine-drinking ceremonies, court audiences,

---

[105] See respectively, ch. 27, "Ta lüeh," ch. 10, "Fu kuo," and ch. 18, "Cheng lun." [For the latter, refer Dubs, p. 105.] Also, ch. 9, "Wang chih": "When the horses are fearful of the carriage-traces the master [chün-tzu] cannot ride in safety; when the common people are fearful of government the prince [chün-tzu] cannot be secure in his position. When horses fear the carriage traces, nothing serves so well as to calm them; when the common people fear government nothing serves so well as to favor them. Select worthy and able [for office], appoint the sincere and attentive, promote the filial and fraternal piety, take in orphans and widows, assist the poor and deprived, and in this way the common people can be made to feel secure in their government. When the common people feel secure in government the prince then can be secure in his position. There is a traditional saying that: 'The prince [chün] is a boat; the common people are the water. The water can sustain the boat; the water can overturn the boat.' This is what is meant. [Cf. Watson's Hsün Tzu, pp. 36–37, for a slightly different translation of this passage.] And ch. 11, "Wang pa," discussing the tyrannous ruler, says: "The people despise him like the plague-ridden, hate him like a demon. Their constant desire is to find an opportunity that will allow them to band together, trample on him, drive him out."

ceremonial visits and offerings, and all of the written regulations for these, were in themselves adequate to maintain social order and ensure a well-governed society. Then when the clan-law system degenerated, the relationships deriving from the personal element gradually gave way to those deriving from place and status, and those in control of governments were compelled to establish new policies that "gave honor and privilege to the nobly placed" [*kuei kuei* 貴貴] and that replaced the older ones that "treated relatives with familial regard" [*ch'in ch'in* 親親]. But the old names of the rites had long been in use, and were not always abandoned and displaced as this transition occurred. Thus the newly developing institutions might still utilize the terminology associated with the old rites, though their content gradually became more broadly inclusive than formerly, and their meaning came to be merged with that of law in the broader sense.[106] Hsün Tzu's ideas about governing through the rites also apparently manifest this transition period trend. Thus he stressed *li* but not as the purest Confucian would; he ventured close to Legalism, yet did not end up in the same camp with Shen Pu-hai and Lord Shang.

In his elevation of the ruler, Hsün Tzu acknowledged "the one who sat facing the south and gave audience to the problems of government" [the Son of Heaven] to be the single pivot on which the issue of order or chaos in the state was balanced. This certainly is a concept that is not present in the older *li*. For in the earlier times when clan-law reigned supreme, the nobles and hereditary ministers had the privilege of participation in government, the great clans could not be affronted, and the ruler could not arrogate powers to himself alone. Here Hsün Tzu's alteration of the ancient institutions is clearly evident. When we examine his statements describing the content of the rites, we find the antique and the contemporary meanings of them juxtaposed and intermixed;[107] and in the ideas set forth throughout the thirty-two essays [comprising *The Hsün Tzu*] the contemporary meaning seems to predominate. Thus, in terms of the

---

[106] The book known as the *Chou Li* is not regarded by modern scholars as being directly descriptive of early Chou institutions (e.g., Ch'en Li, in his *Tung-shu tu-shu-chi*). Hence it is thought that it was gradually added to and altered, becoming the book we know today, having been composed by persons of the Warring States Period who based it only loosely on ancient institutions (Ch'ien Mu, "Chou kuan chu-tso shih-tai k'ao," based on [the eminent scholar of the later Han period] Ho Hsiu; see, *Yen-ching hsüeh-pao*, number 11). Thus its content would be precisely representative of just this metamorphosis. Be that as it may, even if the *Chou Li* was composed at the end of the Chou period, the tendency evident in it to transform the rites *li* into laws *fa* goes back perhaps to the beginning of Chou. For it is probable that Chou feudalism was itself a development marking a kind of transformation from the pure clan-law system of the Shang people's tribal organization.

[107] For example, the *ch.* 19, "Li lun," except for the opening section, in general sets forth the antique concept, while *ch.* 11, "Wang pa," and *ch.* 10, "Fu kuo," and other chapters in large part embody the new ideas.

whole, it is chiefly the new meaning that he is concerned to explain and uphold. And if we speak generally, in terms of the whole body of thought, the focus of Hsün Tzu's concern is not the ancient rites of the feudal world; rather, it is the "methods of governing" [*chih fa* 治法] in which the old and the new are combined. [The word "*fa*," although designating the polar opposite from *li*, or institutions based on ritual propriety, also contains the idea of "regular methods," and in some places must be translated "method" instead of "law."] Here we shall take up a few of the more important aspects of this and discuss them briefly.

One: The method of employing persons. Hsün Tzu felt that the ruler should possess full authority, yet could not rule by himself. He must have "persons possessing his full confidence in intimate attendance" in order to "see afar and gather in all that influences the people"; and he must have chief ministers and advisors to serve as "essential aids," persons who would be "adequate to the task of making his will known and resolving undecided matters in distant places" to be dispatched to the courts of the neighboring feudal lords.[108] In this way, both at the court and in the provinces, in external relations and in domestic affairs, the right personnel would be available, and the ruler could achieve good government without undue labor and toil. Hsün Tzu clearly had a profound belief in the division of labor between ruler and servitor, each having his own duties and responsibilities. The superior's meddling with the inferior, or the inferior's encroaching upon the superior, were both to be avoided. The various officials each had their specific offices and functions, and the ruler, on the other hand, showed his competence in assigning specific functions to these officials." "For should one person now try to administer to the whole realm, he might persist for a long time but would still be unable to accomplish all the tasks of governing. So he has others act in his behalf. Whether in the whole realm or in the single state of a feudal ruler, if the ruler insists on doing all himself before he can be satisfied, then he will merely be subjecting himself to the greatest possible toil, and drudgery, and wasted pains." But if the ruler is capable of "judging good qualities and deputing the able and so bestowing office"; if he can command his "scholars and great officers to assume separate duties and administer, establish his state on the rulers of the feudal principalities, each with its territory and its responsibilities, with the Three Dukes in command of the Marches and submitting their advice, then the ruler can well fold his hands and relax."[109]

---

[108] *Hsun Tzü, ch.* 12 "Chün tao," i.e., "The Way of the Ruler". Hsün Tzu also divided human talent into three ranks: 1. The talent appropriate to local officials and minor staff personnel; 2. The talent appropriate to Great Officers and court officials; 3. The talent appropriate to chief ministers and advisors to the ruler.

[109] *Ch.* 11, "Wang pa."

The essence of Hsün Tzu's discussions on appointing people to office can be summed up in a few statements. In *ch.* 12, "Chün Tao," he says: "The way (*tao*) of selecting men is to assess them according to the *li* [rites, propriety]; the rule [*fa*] for employing men is to restrict them according to [a system of] ranks. Keep them within the boundaries of propriety as they take action to achieve righteous government; evaluate them according to their actual achievement as they consider alternatives to adopt or reject. As time passes by, compare their accumulated merit and promote them accordingly. Then the inferior ones will not reach exalted positions; the light will not be expected to counter-balance the heavy; the stupid will not direct the intelligent. And thus in all circumstances there will be no serious errors."

However, in the above passage, where it states that "the inferior ones will not reach exalted positions," it means that there is a system of ranks and steps within the officialdom indicative of merit in office. That is not to say that within the highest ranks there should be no men of humble background, or that office and emolument should be hereditary. For what Hsün Tzu advocated was the destruction of the powerful great clans in favor of a civil bureaucracy in which the standard should be that of individual talent and ability. Thus he said: "Even though a man be the son or grandson of a prince, duke, knight, or great officer, if he cannot be classed as a man of propriety and righteousness, then he is to be counted a commoner. Even though a man be the son or grandson of a commoner, if he has acquired learning, and observes right behavior, and can be classed as a man of propriety and righteousness, then he should be counted as one of the chief ministers, knights or great officers." [See above, p. 320.] This is precisely the opposite of the hereditary emolument system; its purport is abundantly clear and no further comment is needed. So we may note that Hsün Tzu's chief principle in granting office to a person is that an open system must be established in order to avoid misuse of position for private ends. And the references in the foregoing passage to "assessing according to *li*, restricting according to ranks," and "evaluating their actual accomplishments and promoting them according to merit," are all extensions of that idea. For the private ends that can be served by giving persons office are in most cases those of the ruler himself. Therefore the establishment of open or public institutions of office was intended to forestall the ruler's private dealings. Hsün Tzu has discussed the calamities caused by permitting private interests to prevail. "An enlightened ruler may give gold, gems, and valuables to someone to whom he is personally attached and wishes to show personal affection; he should never grant him office and rank, nor assign him government functions to perform. Why is that? Because it is not in his own interest or that of the recipient. If the latter is incompetent and the ruler employs him, then the ruler is muddle-headed. If the servitor is incompetent, and he makes pretence of competence, then the servitor is treacherous. When the ruler overhead is muddle-headed and the servitor is treacherous, the end is at hand; that is the way of the great disaster."[110]

The essential features of Hsün Tzu's rules for employing persons are more or less complete in the foregoing. We should remember that, by the end of the Warring States Period, the hereditary chief ministership was already a vanished institution; yet the person of ability still had no certain path to office. At the lower level the roaming political advisors were establishing the pattern of quick rise to high office. Men like Su Ch'in and Chang Yi are the most prominent examples of the type. [They were famous "smooth talking" political strategists who manipulated the power alliances of the late fourth century. See above, p. 302.] On the top, rulers were increasing their arbitrary power, elevating favorites and favoring sycophants. Such examples as a Tsang Ts'ang's stopping his ruler [from going to call on Mencius; *Mencius*, I/ii/16; Legge, pp. 177–79. Tsang Ts'ang was of the house that had earned Confucius' criticism in an earlier age, see, *Analects*, XIV/15; Legge, p. 281], and a Tzu-chih receiving the throne [of Yen; the muddle-headed King K'uai, reigned 319–311 B.C., who tried to abdicate in favor of his sycophant minister, Tzu-chih] all illustrate what happened when such favorites were employed. Hsün Tzu's rules for employing persons must have been aimed at this kind of practice, in the hope of correcting its evils.

Two: The method of exhorting and prohibiting. In this area Hsün Tzu had relatively little to say that was new. In *ch.* 24, "Chün-tzu," he says: "In antiquity, punishment did not exceed the crime, and noble rank did not exceed its recipient's virtues. Hence there are cases of executing a father and appointing the son to office, or of executing an elder brother and having the younger brother as one's servitor. Punishments and penalties were not in excess of the crime, while rank and rewards were not in excess of the recipient's virtues. Clearly and distinctly each person was advanced according to his loyalty and devotion. In this way those who did good deeds were exhorted to continue, and those who did evil were stopped. Punishments and penalties were used with extreme infrequency, yet the respect for authority was everywhere present. Governmental regulations were abundantly clear, and they were made effective as if by magic." What Hsün Tzu advocated, by and large, did not go beyond the scope of the Confucian school's stress on cautious use of punishments;[111] it is unnecessary to extend this discussion.

---

[110] *Ch.* 12, "Chün tao."

[111] In *ch.* 18, "Cheng lun," Hsün Tzu argues that in antiquity there had existed no symbolic punishments. [I.e., "*hsiang hsing*," described as the punishment of wearing garments indicative of the crime, to humiliate the criminal, or otherwise marking him in public as an offender. Whether such a system really existed in antiquity was much debated

Three: The method of rectifying names. His *ch.* 22, "Cheng Ming," says: "When sage-kings instituted names, the names were fixed and actualities distinguished. The sage-kings' principles were carried out and their wills understood. Then the people were carefully led and unified. Therefore, the practice of splitting terms and arbitrarily creating names to confuse correct names, thus causing much doubt in people's minds and bringing about much litigation, was called great wickedness. It was a crime that was punished like private manufacturing of credentials and measurements, and therefore the people dared not rely on strange terms created to confuse correct names. Hence the people were honest. Being honest, they were easily employed. Being easily employed, they achieved results. Since the people dared not rely on strange terms created to confuse correct names, they singlemindedly followed the law and carefully obeyed orders. In this way, the traces of their accomplishments spread. The spreading of traces and the achievement of results are the highest point of good government. This is the result of careful abiding by the conventional meaning of names." And he says further: "Thus the people can be easily united in the Way [*Tao*], although they cannot be given all the reasons for things. Hence the wise ruler deals with the people by authority and guides them on the Way; he orders things by his decrees, explains things by his proclamations, and restrains them by punishments. Thus his people are turned into the Way as by magic. Why should he use dialectic?"[112] Confucius had said that "commoners do not discuss public

throughout later history.] He says, in part: "The basis of corporal punishment is that it prohibits violence and causes the despicable to be despised; and it is a preventive against what might otherwise come to pass." He also says: "For it can be said that ennoblement and rank, official status and appointment, rewards and good fortune, punishments and penalties, all are compensation reflecting the circumstances from which they derive." This seems to go beyond anything said by Confucius and Mencius.

[112] [The translation of the first quoted passage follows Chan, *Source Book*, p. 124; the second follows Bodde, Fung/Bodde, Vol. I, p. 311.] The same Chapter [22] also says: " 'It is no disgrace to be insulted'; 'the sage does not love himself'; 'to kill a robber is not to kill a man' "; and says that "these are examples of the fallacy of so using names as to confuse names." It also cites: " 'Mountains are on the same level as marshes'; 'The desires seek to be few'; 'Tender meat adds nothing to sweet taste, and the great bell adds nothing to music' "; commenting that "These are examples of the fallacy of using actualities to confuse names." And of: " '*Fei-erh-yeh*,' '*ying-yu-niu*'; 'a [white] horse is not a horse' " that "These are examples of the fallacy of so using names as to confuse actualities." [The six untranslated words, like the other propositions discussed, are cited from the paradoxes of the sophists. Most scholars believe these six words to have been garbled in transmission because no reasonable translation of them seems possible. For a discussion of Hsün Tzu on sophistry, see Fung/Bodde, Vol. I, pp. 308–11.] These three taken together are called the "Three Fallacies" [*san huo*] and he wanted to forbid them all. That is to say, Hsün Tzu would have attached the crime of confusing the names on the followers of Sung K'eng, of Chuang Tzu, of Mo Tzu, and of Kung-sun Lung and of all the schools of thought except the Confucian, and would have had the state use its laws and regulations to prohibit them. [Translations cited above follow Chan, *Source Book*, p. 127.]

affairs" and that they "cannot be made to understand." [*Analects*, xvi/2; Waley, p. 204, and viii/9; Waley, p. 134.] The essential foundations of Hsün Tzu's rectification of names is thus derived from Confucius. However, Confucius took benevolence and love as the basis of all government. Hence even though he was somewhat scornful of the people's intelligence, no one practicing his manner of government would fail to maintain a benevolent despotism. Hsün Tzu strung together the concepts of the rectification of names, of the evil nature of man, and of government according to the rites, and lost something of Confucius' warm-hearted and generous-spirited doctrine. Li Ssu took these concepts and applied them in office as the First Emperor's chief minister, further adding to and developing them so that they could take form in the policy of "distinguishing black from white and fixing a single standard." [Quoting *Shih Chi*, ch. 6, "Basic Annals of the Ch'in dynasty," where the First Emperor's absolute and arbitrary policies are described.] Thus we can see that Hsün Tzu's rectification of names and Li Ssu's keeping the people ignorant are not far apart. Moreover, this is not the only place wherein we can see that Hsün Tzu was not purely Confucian.

Mencius too had on some occasions taken upon himself the duty of defending the doctrines of the former sages, yet where Mencius felt compelled "to oppose Yang Chu and Mo Tzu, and . . . drive away their licentious expressions" [*Mencius*, iii/ii/10; Legge, p. 283], he was merely setting his own voice against those of opponents, and for it he had been somewhat derisively labelled a disputatious person. When we examine carefully his responses to the Kings of Ch'i and Liang we cannot find that he ever revealed any intent to use the arm of the state to put an end to "perverse teachings." Though Mencius was courageous in rushing to the defense of the Way, he never failed to display what in the West is considered to be the enlightened attitude that pits theory against theory, attacks discourse with discourse. To come to Hsün Tzu, in setting up for the rulers the methods of rectifying names and prohibiting fallacies, it is not too much to say that he was in a sense the initiator of a development that was to have evil consequences [literally, "was as the person who first made burial figurines"; cf. *Mencius*, i/i/4/6; Legge, p. 133], in the subsequent burning of the books by the First Emperor. His actual intent may have been no different from that of Mencius, but the methods he was willing to employ were indeed different!

Nevertheless, in urgently promoting his methods of governing, despite some impurity of content, Hsün Tzu looked solely to the Sage Kings of the ancient Three Dynasties, and sought his models there. Confucius said of himself that he followed the Chou; he repudiated those who, living in the present, would go back to outworn ways of antiquity. [See *Chung Yung* 28/1; Legge, *Doctrine of the Mean*, p. 423.] Hsün Tzu, taking up this point, developed his theories about "emulating the later kings." He wrote: "If one would observe the traces of the Sage Kings [the text has "former kings," amended here to agree with standard editions], he might best do so where they are most clear. The later kings are so. Those later kings were the rulers of the whole realm [*t'ien hsia*]. To abandon these later kings and talk about earlier antiquity is to be compared with abandoning one's own ruler and serving someone else's."[113] Mencius extolled "the sages [by whom] the human relations are perfectly exhibited," and urged people to imitate the former kings. [*Mencius*, IV/i/2/1; Legge, p. 292.] Hsün Tzu also said: "One who speaks of flavors will cite Yi-ya, and one who speaks of sounds will cite Master K'uang. [Two gentlemen mentioned in the *Spring and Autumn Annals* as experts on cooking and music, respectively. Mencius also cited them in a somewhat similar passage; see *Mencius*, VI/i/7/5 and 6; Legge, pp. 405–06.] One who speaks of good government will cite the Three Kings [of antiquity; the founders of the Three Dynasties, including the founder of the Chou dynasty]. Since the Three Kings have already prescribed laws and standards and instituted rites and music, and transmitted these, if one were to fail to employ them, and were to change to others of his own making, how different would that be from altering the recipes of Yi-ya and changing the pitches of Master K'uang?"[114] It would appear from this that, in discussing institutions, Hsün Tzu was not far different from Confucius and Mencius.

If we were to ask wherein the methods he would employ are different, the answer would be in two parts: One: As we attempt to distinguish the discrepancies in Confucius' and Hsün Tzu's governing methods, we should focus on their content, and should not merely observe their terminology. Hsün Tzu said: "From among the Five Emperors [of very early antiquity, prior to the Chou dynasty], no governmental institutions have been passed down to us. . . . Some of the institutions of the Great Yü and King T'ang have been transmitted, but they are not so ascertainable as those of the Chou," as if those [still later Chou] institutions of King Wu, the Duke of Chou, were indeed so clear and accessible to reference, and there were points of difference between them and those of the earlier kings. But in discussing the thought of Mencius we have already pointed out that insofar as possible, the feudal lords had by that time made away with the records of the Chou court relevant to the regulations about dignities and emoluments. [See above, p. 300; also, *Mencius*, V/ii/2/1–2 and ff.; Legge, p. 373. Mencius says the later feudal princes did so to conceal the extent of their own usurpations.] From this we can deduce that the bamboo tablet records of the time of Kings Wen and Wu [by

[113] *Ch.* 5, "Fei hsiang." [also translated in Fung/Bodde, p. 282.]
[114] *Ch.* 27, "Ta Lüeh."

Mencius' time] were long since fragmentary and incomplete. Hsün Tzu lived still later than Mencius, so there can be no doubt that he was even less able to set his eyes on the complete *Institutes of Chou*. Hence what he refers to as the "clear traces of the later kings" need not, in fact, be taken literally. Hsün Tzu said: "If you want to know about earlier ages, then examine the Chou ways; if you want to know the Chou ways then examine the rulers whom they honored."[115] The import of this is more or less evident. Nonetheless, what Hsün Tzu knew as the "later kings" certainly were [still more recent. historical rulers, and] not what Confucius had in mind when he referred to Kings Wen and Wu [as "later kings"]. Two: We can find still further evidence in the examples Hsün Tzu gives of the methods of governing. In the several foregoing discussions of various methods of governing, we have already discussed those points which were at variance with antique institutions and antique principles. And Hsün Tzu said: "All music that is lacking in classical elegance should be abandoned; all decorations that do not follow old patterns should be given up; all vessels and trappings that are not like those of earlier times should be discarded. This is what is called reviving the old."[116] Despite this, the content of his methods of ruling shows in many places the admixture of elements of Warring States Period provenance. Hence in his self-proclaimed "reviving antiquity," Hsün Tzu violated his own prohibition against "using names to confuse realities," and his proclamation that he was "reviving antiquity" is not sufficient to prove that he really did follow Confucius' models.

Hsün Tzu's theories truly do show points of continuity with the spirit of Confucius, but these are notably not to be found in his discussions of the methods of governing; rather, they are to be found in his corollary emphasis on the persons who should do the governing. In short, Hsün Tzu's political thought held law to be non-essential, and regarded the human element as basic. Thus, where he seems close to Shen Pu-hai and Lord Shang [i.e., representatives of the origins of Legalist theory], it is in those more superficial things; but in the essentials of his system he is quite in line with Confucius and Mencius.

In his statements on the men who should do the governing, Hsün Tzu is most explicit in his essay *ch.* 12, "Chün Tao," or, "The Way of the Ruler." His views take as their starting point the idea that with the right men government flourishes, but without the right men government decays and ceases [paraphrasing the *Doctrine of the Mean*, xx/2; see Legge, p. 405], and he developes this theme further. His statement begins: "There

---

[115] *Ch.* 5, "Fei hsiang." The annotation of Yang Liang [a ninth-century annotator of the text of the *Hsün Tzu*] states: "This refers to their [i.e., the Chou people's] own rulers." [Cf. Fung/Bodde, p. 282, where the passage is translated in a different sense.]

[116] *Ch.* 9, "Wang chih." [Following the translation of Watson, p. 42.]

are chaos-producing rulers but there are no [innately] chaotic states; there are order-inducing men but there are no [of themselves] order-inducing methods of governing. Yi's [i.e., the great mythological archer of antiquity] methods have not been lost, but Yi's do not score bullseyes in every generation; Yü's [the great legendary King Yü, founder of the Hsia dynasty, whose mastery of hydraulic engineering won him the throne] methods are still preserved, but the Hsia dynasty does not reign on, generation after generation. Thus we can say that methods and laws cannot stand by themselves; precedents cannot realize themselves in practice. Get the right men and the methods can be employed; lose the right men and all is lost. For the methods are the beginnings of government, but the superior man is the source of the methods. Therefore, when one has superior men, even though the fixed methods [or laws] be incomplete, there will be sufficient [resource] to extend [to all needs]. Without superior men, however, even though the methods [or laws] are complete, they will not be employed with judgment; and they will not be adjusted to changing conditions, and this will be enough to cause chaos." We may note that in this discussion, Hsün Tzu seems to have dual and complementary meanings. The one is that laws alone are incapable of being effective, and the second is that the superior man is enough to carry on government. In his *ch.* 9, "Wang Chih," he says: "For if there be laws and methods but [men enforcing them] do not discuss and revise them, then matters for which they do not provide will certainly be left untended. When there be duties and offices but incumbents are not thoroughly understanding men, then whatever the office fails to provide for will fall into neglect. [Watson's translation, p. 35, is slightly different, as is Dubs's; p. 123.] And "Chün Tao" says further: "Matching the halves of tallies and separating the parts of a contract are things done to insure good faith. If the ruler lusts for power and engages in plotting, then his ministers and officials, and deceiving, scheming people, will take advantage of that fact, so that cheating will ensue. Drawing lots and casting for shares are done to be fair to all [the precise identification of this means of drawing lots is uncertain, but the general meaning of the passage is clear]: If the ruler plays false for his own selfish ends, then his ministers and officials will take advantage of that fact, and, in consequence, inequity will ensue. Balance-weights and scales are used to achieve even measure: If the ruler is given to upsetting the balance, then then his ministers and officials will take advantage of this and peril will ensue. Pecks and bushels and grain measures are used to obtain accuracy: If the ruler pursues personal advantage, then his ministers and officials will take advantage of this, and debasement will ensue. There will be generous taking and parsimonious giving, and unlimited exactions on the people. Therefore, it is evident that implements and devices are but the trappings of good government, not the source of good government." These passages all are to make clear the idea that laws and methods cannot function of themselves.

Again in *Chün Tao*, Hsün Tzu says further: "Someone asked about the administration of the state. I replied, 'I know something about the cultivation of one's person; I am not informed about the administration of the state. The ruler may be likened to the standard, and the people, its shadow.'" And "If the ruler is devoted to propriety and righteousness, honors the worthy and employs the able, and is free of the pursuit of personal advantage, then his assistants will also practice unselfishness and self-effacement wholeheartedly. They will be wholly loyal and trustworthy, and will diligently carry out their roles as servitors. In such circumstances, then, even among the humble people there will be good faith even without matching tallies and separating of the parts of a contract. There will be fairness without drawing lots and casting shares. There will be even measure without using balance-weights and scales. And, there would be accuracy without using pecks and bushels and measures of grain. In that way, rewards will not need to be used and the people will yet be persuaded [to be upright]; penalties will not need to be used and the people will yet be compliant. The offices of government will not need to toil, yet things will be orderly. Governing will not need to become burdensome, yet customs will nonetheless be admirable." This passage displays the idea that the superior man is sufficient resource with which to accomplish good government.

All the foregoing statements are quite compatible with the thought of Confucius, and they are more than adequate to manifest the fundamental difference between Hsün Tzu and the Legalists: The Legalists lodged the authoritarian power of the ruler within trappings and devices [of office], whereas Hsün Tzu wanted the personal stature of the ruler to be manifested above and beyond the legal institutions of government.[117] The former lay sole stress on the methods of governing, whereas the latter seeks governors to put into practice the methods of governing. Hsün Tzu's is a theory of government concurrently of men and of laws and methods, and in truth it is directly heir to the teachings of Confucius,[118] not some new creation of Hsün Tzu's. Nonetheless, we cannot suppress a certain feeling about

[117] *Ch.* 18, "Cheng lun," says: "The common run of sophists say: 'The way of the ruler benefits from secrecy.' This is not so: the ruler is the guide of the people; the superior is the model for the inferior. They must listen for the guide and respond, watch their model and react. If the guide is silent, the people have no way of responding; if the model is concealed, then the inferior has no way of reacting to it. With no responding and no reacting, superior and inferior have nothing wherein they are mutually dependent, and that would be the same as if there were no superior. Of all inauspicious portents, that would be the most serious."

[118] See, the last paragraph of Section Five, Chapter Two, above.

this issue. Confucius and Mencius emphasized the morality of the ruler and deemphasized his power, whereas Shen Pu-hai and Lord Shang emphasized the the ruler's power and did not heed the issue of his morality. Hsün Tzu was concerned with both. Drawing all the elements together and retaining all the good features [of both], his theory would seem to achieve the best possible solution. When we examine the facts, however, we find that the rulers of his time, or at least those that he may have encountered, included: in the State of Ch'i, Kings Wei, Hsüan, and Min; in the State of Yen, Prince Tzu-k'uai; in the State of Ch'u, King Ch'ing-hsiang; in the State of Chao, King Hsiao-ch'eng; and in Ch'in, King Chao-hsiang. Among this collection of rulers there was not one who could serve as the basis for Hsün Tzu's ideal of the ruler of men. And in the period from Ch'in and Han and thereafter, Confucians distorting their school's teachings appropriated Hsün Tzu's idea about the exaltation of the ruler, added to it the ideal concept of who should govern men, and with that flattered rulers, venerating [emperors] to the highest limits. This current grew and spread to the point where rulers who might be incompetent, muddle-headed, violent tyrants not only came to wield the most enormous powers but also bore the most extravagantly flattering of titles and descriptions. Such confusing of realities with names contributed to subsequent harm of no insignificant degree. Even though this was something Hsün Tzu had no way of foreseeing, his theoretical formulation was faulty to begin with, as this line of reasoning indicates. In this respect he was inferior to Confucius and Mencius, who placed their dominant emphasis on the ruler's virtues, hoping to overcome some of the shortcomings of the feudal order, or even to Shen Pu-hai and Lord Shang in their sole reliance on laws and methods whereby possibly to forestall some of authoritarianism's evils. In the more than two thousand years that followed, if we were to seek even the quality of government that Hsün Tzu saw when he visited the [authoritarian] State of Ch'in, we would not find many eras when government could even measure up to that.[119] Thus

---

[119] *Ch.* 16, "Ch'iang kuo," or "Strengthening the State," says: "The Duke of Ying [Fan Chü, Chief Minister in Ch'in when Hsün Tzu visited that state], asked Hsün Tzu, 'what have you observed since coming into the State of Ch'in?' Hsün Tzu replied: 'It is favored by topography, with firm natural defenses, and has fine hills and forests, streams and valleys. Its natural endowment provides many benefits. This is the excellence of its situation. Coming within its borders, I have observed its ways and customs. Its common people live simply; the sounds of their music display no tendencies toward the licentious. Their dress is not fanciful. They are greatly in awe of the officials and are obedient. They are as the people of antiquity. And coming to the towns with their government offices, [I note that] the staffs of officials are decorous and respectful; there are none among them who are not reverential and temperate, earnest and sincere, loyal, trustworthy and not rude. They are as the officials of antiquity. Entering the capital, I have observed the scholars and great officers on leaving their own gates and entering the offices

we might say that Hsün Tzu, in seeking to preserve both ideals, in fact destroyed both of them.

SECTION SEVEN
The Distinction between Heaven and Man

IN the China of the Spring and Autumn Period there still persisted some remnants of the ancient religious practices honoring gods and spirits. The examples of superstitious belief recorded in the *Tso Chuan* are by no means rare. A typical case is that of King Ch'eng of Ch'u, commenting on the fate of the fugitive Prince Ch'ung-erh of Chin, saying: "When Heaven intends to prosper a man, who can stop him?" And another is that of Wang-sun Man, replying to the King of Ch'u's [grossly inappropriate] question about the [royal Chou] tripods with the comment: "Though the virtue of Chou is decayed, the decree of Heaven has not yet changed."[120] These are examples of the belief that the rise and fall of states was determined by the Will of Heaven. A further example is found in Shih Wen-po's statement to the Marquis of Chin, explaining a solar eclipse: "When there is not good government in a state, and good men are not employed, it brings reproof to itself from the calamity of the sun and moon." And Duke Min of Sung, replying to the Duke of Lu's messenger who brought condolences on the flood in Sung, said: "I must confess my want of reverence, for which heaven has sent down this plague."[121] These are examples of the belief that natural calamaties were caused by bad government. In a further example, King Hui of Chou asked a certain Kuo, "the Historiographer of the Interior," why a spirit had descended in the region called Hsin, eliciting the reply: "When a

---

of government, and on emerging from the offices of government to enter again into their own homes. They were involved in no private matters; they are not partisan and cabalistic; they do not form cliques or factions. Dignified in manner, none among them are not intelligent and understanding and equitable in their actions. They are as the scholars and great officers of antiquity. Observing the court, [I note that] in the administering and judging of government business, all matters are disposed of readily and quietly, as if there were no governmental business there at all. It is like a royal court of antiquity. . . . And yet, there is something frightening about it. [You have] exhaustively combined all the methods and devices into one [system], yet when all of this [imposing array] is weighed in the balance of the [True] King's capacity and fame, then it is gravely apparent that he comes far from equaling it." [That is to say, the ruler is not up to the demands of the complex system within which he functions. Hsün Tzu goes on to comment that the reason the person and personality of the ruler fail to assume their proper role is that there are no Confucian advisors to the throne in Ch'in.]

[120] See, respectively, Twenty-third year of Duke Hsi [636 B.C.; Legge, p. 187] and Third year of Duke Hsüan [605 B.C.; Legge, p. 293].

[121] See, respectively, Seventh year of Duke Chao [534 B.C.; Legge, p. 617] and Eleventh year of Duke Chuang [682 B.C.; Legge, p. 88].

state is about to flourish, intelligent Spirits descend in it, to survey its virtue. When it is going to perish, Spirits also descend in it, to behold its wickedness. Thus there have been instances of states flourishing from Spirits appearing, and also of states perishing. . . ."[122] This is an example of the belief that ghosts and spirits portend by their actions the rise and decline of states. Other examples, like the ghosts of P'eng-sheng [*Tso Chuan*, Eighth year of Duke Chuang; Legge, p. 82] and Po-yu [cf. Seventh year of Duke Chao; Legge, p. 618; cf. Chan, *Source Book*, p. 12, for this and similar anecdotes, also, p. 445, below,] or prodigies like the talking stone [cf. Eighth year of Duke Chao; Legge, p. 622] and the duelling snakes [cf. Fourteenth year of Duke Chuang; Legge, p. 92] and such extraordinary events would be all the more difficult to cite fully. But this is enough to demonstrate that right down to the late Chou, the practices referred to in the statement "the Yin people honor spirits" [*Li Chi, ch.* 32, "Piao Chi," paragraph 19] were still not wholly eradicated. The Chou people, on the other hand, were said to "serve spirits and reverence gods, but keep aloof from them" [*Li Chi, ch.* 32, "Piao Chi," paragraph 11], and the influence of the Chou policies and doctrines [in lessening the role of the irrational] seems to have been of some significance. In the Spring and Autumn Period there occasionally appeared some individuals capable of casting off superstition. Tzu-ch'an of the State of Cheng refused to believe in spirits. When Pei-tsao told him that a certain comet portended a conflagration, he replied: "The way of heaven is distant, while the way of man is near. We cannot reach to the former; what means have we of knowing it?"[123] His statement is quite penetrating and perceptive. Although Confucius' attitude was not so thoroughgoing as Tzu-ch'an's, yet from his reply to Tzu-lu's question about serving spirits, "While you are not able to serve men, how can you serve their spirits," and from his reply to Fan Ch'ih's question about what constitutes wisdom, ". . . while respecting spiritual beings, to keep aloof from them . . ."[124]—from these it is perfectly clear that in this Confucius accepted the Way of the Chou people. But as a Sung descendant Confucius may not have totally cast off those teachings of the Yin people's which stressed veneration of the spirits.[125] If the *Doctrine of the Mean* was written by [Confucius' grandson]

---

[122] See, Thirty-second year of Duke Chuang [661 B.C.; Legge, p. 120]. This also is found in the *Kuo Yü, ch.* 1, "Chou yü, Part one," where the wording differs slightly.

[123] *Tso Chuan*, Eighteenth year of Duke Chao [523 B.C.; Legge, p. 671]. See also in the Nineteenth year where Tzu-ch'an refuses sacrifices to a dragon [Legge, p. 675]. The import is more or less the same.

[124] See *Analects*, respectively, Book XI, "Hsien chin" [XI/11; Legge, p. 240] and Book VI, "Yung yeh" [VI/20; Legge, p. 191].

[125] Confucius' faith in the Will of Heaven has already been pointed out in footnote 87 of this chapter.

Tzu-ssu, then the various places in it where it speaks of ghosts and spirits,[126] if not representing the "true mind" ["*hsin fa*," 心法] of the Confucian school, still might possibly reflect the grandfather's and his grandson's family tradition. Mencius spoke much about heaven's will; his thought at this point also seems somewhat close to the views of antiquity. Coming to Hsün Tzu, we note that he spoke exhaustively about the distinction between heaven and man, wholly adopting the Chou doctrine, and looking in the direction of Tzu-ch'an, thus opposing Tzu-ssu and Mencius.

Hsün Tzu argued most forcefully that the will of heaven, [or of nature, i.e., *t'ien ming*, the same term that as a specific political concept, is translated "The Mandate of Heaven"], calamities and freakish phenomena bore no relationship to government and human affairs; his expositions of this are extremely clear and vigorous. In *ch.* 17, "T'ien lun," he says: "Nature [*t'ien*, heaven] operates with constant regularity. It does not exist for the sake of [sage-emperor] Yao nor does it cease to exist because of [wicked king] Chieh." And further: "Are order and chaos due to heaven? I say: the sun, the moon, the stars, planets, and auspicious periods of the calendar were the same in the time of [sage-king] Yü as in that of [wicked king] Chieh. Yet Yü brought about order while Chieh brought about chaos. Order and chaos are not due to heaven." [The two quotations follow Chan, *Source Book*, pp. 116, 118. See also Fung/Bodde, p. 285.] That is, since order and chaos are not the will of heaven, it can only be that heaven and man do not intervene in each other's affairs. "Man has

---

[126] The *Doctrine of the Mean*, Ch. xvi, "The Master said, 'How abundantly do spiritual beings display the powers that belong to them! We look for them, but do not see them; we listen to, but do not hear them; yet they enter into all things, and there is nothing without them . . .'" [Legge, p. 397]; Ch. xxiv: "It is characteristic of the most entire sincerity to be able to foreknow. When a nation or family is about to flourish, there are sure to be happy omens; and when it is about to perish, there are sure to be unlucky omens. *Such events are* seen in the milfoil and tortoise, and effect the movements of the four limbs. When calamity or happiness is about to come, the good shall certainly be foreknown by him, and the evil also. Therefore the individual possessed of the most complete sincerity is like a spirit." [Legge, pp. 417–18]; Ch. xxix/4. "His [the ruler's] presenting himself with *his institutions* before spiritual beings without any doubts arising about them, shows that he knows Heaven." [Legge, p. 426.]

We should note that in the *Analects* it states: "The Master never talked of prodigies, feats of strength, disorders or spirits (vii/20) [Waley, p. 127; Waley's original note: "Disorders of nature; such as snow in summer, owls hooting by day, or the like"]; "The Master seldom spoke of profit or fate or Goodness" (ix/1) [Waley, p. 138]; and [Confucius' disciple] Tzu-kung also said of him, [of] "our Master's views . . . about man's nature and the ways of Heaven he will not tell us anything at all" (v/12) [Waley, p. 110]; Confucius apparently taught his disciples [as seen in the *Analects*] according to the Way of the Chou, and transmitted the Way of the Yin people [as seen in the *Doctrine of the Mean*] as a family teaching only.

his government" [*Hsün Tzu*, ch. 17, Chan, *Source Book*, p. 117]; his whole attention is devoted to this. Man's orderings can overcome heaven [or nature]; he has no reason for concern or fear. "If the foundations of living (i.e., agriculture and sericulture) are strengthened and are economically used, then nature cannot bring impoverishment. If people's nourishment is sufficient and their labor in keeping with the seasons, then nature cannot inflict sickness. If the Way is cultivated without deviation, then nature cannot cause misfortune. Therefore flood and drought cannot cause a famine, extreme cold or heat cannot cause illness, and evil spiritual beings cannot cause misfortune." Thus Hsün Tzu says: ". . . one who understands the distinctive functions of heaven and man may be called a perfect man," and further, "The Sage, however, does not seek to know heaven." [All three passage follow, with minor changes, the translation of Chan, *Source Book*, pp. 117–18. Chan uses "Nature" interchangeably with "Heaven" for *t'ien*; all other translators merely use "Heaven." Here we use "heaven," "nature," etc.]

Hsün Tzu went a step further and explained why calamities and unusual phenomena need not give rise to fear, in terms that are fully reasonable and realistic, capable of dispelling obsessions and correcting fallacious thinking. He created exchanges of questions and answers [one of which] follows: "When stars fall or trees make a [strange] noise, all people in the state are afraid and ask 'Why?' I reply: There is no need to ask why. These are changes of heaven and earth, the transformation of *Yin* and *Yang*, and rare occurrences. It is all right to marvel at them, but wrong to fear them. For there has been no age that has not had the experiences of eclipses of the sun and moon, unreasonable rain or wind, or occasional appearances of strange stars. If the ruler is enlightened and the government peaceful, even if all these things happen at the same time, they would do no harm. If the ruler is unenlightened and the government follows a dangerous course, even if not a single one of them occurs, it would· do no good." [Translation slightly modified from Chan, *Source Book*, p. 120.] However, we should note especially that Hsün Tzu's sole interest was in dispelling superstition; he was not seeking to alter customs and practices. Hence his statement: "When people pray for rain, it rains. Why? I say: There is no need to ask why. It is the same as when it rains when no one prays for it. When people try to save the sun or moon from being eclipsed, or when they pray for rain in a drought, or when they decide an important affair only after divination, they do so not because they believe they will get what they are after, but to use them as ornament [*wen* 文] to governmental measures. Hence the ruler intends them to be an ornament, but the common people think they are supernatural. It is good fortune to regard them as ornamental but it is evil fortune to regard them as supernatural."[127] [Translation is that of Chan, *Source Book*, p. 121; see also his "Comment" there.]

Beliefs involving the will of heaven, spiritual beings, and the like are deeply imbedded in men's minds. Even a sage like Confucius was unable wholly to escape their compelling force. For Hsün Tzu to have been able to elaborate on the ideas of Tzu-ch'an and develop from them a political view that denied fate and negated spiritual forces, demands that we acknowledge him as a great and bold figure. The unfortunate thing is that established customs are very difficult to get rid of. His words did not, in fact, gain a major following, and in Hsün Tzu's lifetime the followers of Tsou Yen [d. ca. 240 B.C.] were achieving conspicuous successes with the kings of the time by employing their theories about the Five Agents [or Elements] and the Heavenly Cycles. Subsequently, during the Han dynasty, men like Tung Chung-shu and Han Ying further promoted the ideas about the correlative interaction of heaven and man. In that time also, men like Yi Feng and Ching Fang were making even more extended use of theories about the *Yin* and the *Yang*, and the relationship between governmental affairs and the occurrences of calamities and prodigies. During the reign of the Han Emperors Yuan and Ch'eng [48–7 B.C.] there also flourished a movement employing the "River Chart" and the "Prognostication Texts." [I.e., *ho-t'u* and *ch'an-shu*; see Fung/Bodde, especially Vol. II, p. 88 ff.] These things all represent abstruse, fantastic, groundless, or eccentric developments, beyond explicit description. Compared with pre-Ch'in theories, these [Han and later] developments appear still more excessive and extreme. Subsequently, there appeared Wang Yen, who defied ghosts, and Huan T'an, who repudiated the prognostication texts. [See Chapter Eleven, Section One, below, on the late-third-century thinker Wang Yen, and Chapter Nine, Section Five, below, on

---

[127] In the opening passage of *ch.* 5, "Fei hsiang," i.e., "Against Physiognomers," Hsün Tzu says: "Physiognomers did not exist among the ancients; learned men made no mention of them. In antiquity there was a man called Ku-pu Tzu-ch'ing, and in recent times there is T'ang Chü of the State of Liang; they physiognomize people by the shape and form, color and appearance, of their facial features and know from that their good luck or bad, the foresigns of ill or happy fortune. It is common practice in our times to praise them. But among the ancients there was no such thing; learned men made no mention of it. Thus we may say that doing physiognomy by the facial features is not as worthwhile as talking about the inner man, and judging the inner man is not to be compared with choosing the [proper] methods. Features cannot prevail over the inner man, and the inner man cannot prevail over the [proper] methods. When the methods are upright, the inner man complies with them. In such a case, if the inner man and his methods are good, even if the physiognomy is inauspicious, that cannot prevent him from being a superior man. And if the inner man and his methods are evil, even though his physiognomy be good, that cannot prevent him from being a petty man. What the superior man regards as auspicious, the petty man considers to be inauspicious." This is another example of Hsün Tzu's rejection of common practice.

the early-first-century thinker Huan T'an.] These also were attempts to eradicate superstition; they are worthy of being designated heirs to Hsün Tzu's long-since discontinued line of thought, and, in their solitary but noteworthy achievements, they again display some resemblence to Hsün Tzu's earlier example.

Yet one area of doubt about this issue persists. Prior to the Spring and Autumn Era in China, the ruler was not an authoritarian despot. Clearly, there were certain limitations upon the employment of the ruler's authority. Among the restricting influences, the aristocracy and the hereditary ministerships, the powerful retainers and the great clans, all imposed direct limitations on the ruler's power. Beyond those, there were indirect limitations in the support or opposition of the common people, the concept of the bestowal and withdrawal of the Heavenly Mandate, the rewards and penalties stemming from spiritual beings, the auspicious or inauspicious portents of the diviners.[128] The theories about the will of heaven and about the basic importance of the people developed by Mohists, Confucians, *Yin-Yang* thinkers, and the other schools had the function of placing implicit restrictions upon the ruler's power. Although the Legalists rejected these devices altogether, nonetheless a certain type of limitation is provided by their own ideal: "The law is something that the ruler and his servitors must jointly maintain." Theories of Han dynasty thinkers about the Five Agents, calamities, and prodigies in fact were heir to the ancient learning, and had as their purpose to limit the ruler; it would seem impossible to deny that altogether. Now, as we observe, Hsün Tzu repudiated the will of heaven, and demolished the superstitious beliefs in calamities and curious phenomena. In so much as this represented an attack on one of the important theoretical means by which the ancients had limited the ruler, and at the same time his thought

---

[128] The *Book of Documents*, "Hung Fan," i.e., "The Great Plan" [discussing how the ruler resolves doubts], says: "If you have any doubt about important matters, consult with your own conscience [four characters added to the passage as quoted], consult with your ministers and officers, consult with the common people, and consult the tortoise shells and stalks. If you, the tortoise shells, the stalks, the ministers and officers, and the common people all agree, this is called a great concord. There will be welfare to your own person and prosperity to your descendants. The result will be auspicious. If you, the tortoise shells, and the stalks agree, but the ministers and officers and the common people oppose, the result will be auspicious. If the ministers and officers, the tortoise shells, and the stalks agree, but you and the common people oppose, the result will be auspicious. If the common people, the tortoise shells, and the stalks agree but you and the ministers and the officers oppose, the result will be auspicious. If you and the tortoise shells agree but the stalks, ministers and officers, and the common people oppose, the internal operations will be auspicious but external operations will be unlucky. If both the tortoise shells and the stalks oppose the views of men, inactivity will be auspicious but active operations will be unlucky." [Chan, *Source Book*, p. 10; see also Legge, pp. 337–38.] This shows that the ruler did not make arbitrary decisions by himself alone.

lacked anything analogous to Shen Pu-hai's and Han Fei's unequivocal laws and respect for the integrity of institutions [with which to limit imperial whim], there must be some serious flaw in his thought that was destined to have undesirable effects in later times. Yet whether he was right or wrong, a constructive or a negative force, is a most difficult question.

We might suggest the following explanation: If we wish to assess the strengths and weaknesses of Hsün Tzu's thought, it would seem that we should first discuss the actual effectiveness of concepts like that of the will of heaven, and of portents revealed through calamities and unnatural phenomena. We must note that when a government establishes religious observances of the ways of spiritual beings, that may indeed achieve a temporary effectiveness. Yet when practiced over a long time, the rulers will ultimately see through the device, and it then will have lost all its original effectiveness. The events of the Han period offer ample evidence that this is indeed so. Such evidence would include the Emperor Wen's issuing a decree blaming himself on the occasion of a solar eclipse,[129] and the Emperor Ai's issuing a decree dismissing his chief minister on the occasion of some natural disturbances.[130] Tung Chung-shu remonstrated with the Emperor Wu, using the phrase "Heaven and man respond to each other,"[131] and Wang Mang listed a series of auspicious omens to support his usurpation of the Han throne.[132] Pan Piao used the theory of the Destiny of Kings to intimidate Wei Hsiao,[133] and Kung-sun Shu used references to the River Chart and Prognostication Texts in support of his seizure of the Province of Shu. [All the foregoing are events of Han history displaying cynical use of the device of heavenly portents to justify political action.] Thereafter, in the Wei and Chin and Six Dynasties periods there was no usurpation or illicit seizure that did not use the doctrine of the Heavenly Mandate as an elaborate cover. The ancient faith in the awe-inspiring heavenly might was totally dissipated, but this was not all: The misappropriation of the Heavenly Mandate doctrine to facilitate usurpations, regicides, violence, and brutality may well be taken to prove that the doctrine—which Hsün Tzu had attacked, hoping to eradicate it—may not in fact have had any constructive political value anyway. Therefore in all fairness we may conclude that Hsün Tzu's "Discourse on Heaven" probably did not cost his civilization anything,

---

[129] *Han Shu, ch.* 4, "Basic Annals of the Emperor Wen." [See Dubs' translation, Volume One; see also Watson, *Shih Chi,* Vol. I, pp. 351–52; and de Bary, *Sources,* p. 229.]

[130] *Han Shu, ch.* 81, "Biography of K'ung Kuang."

[131] *Ibid., ch.* 56, "Biography of Tung Chung-shu."

[132] *Ibid., ch.* 99, "Biography of Wang Mang." [Translated in de Bary, *Sources,* pp. 196–98.]

[133] *Ibid., ch.* 100, Part One. [Translated in part in de Bary, *Sources,* pp. 192–97.]

even though it also does not appear to have gained much for it. [Paraphrasing the original loosely.[134] On the term "T'ien lun," "Discourses on Nature, or Heaven," this also is the name of *ch.* 17 of the *Hsün Tzu*, translated by Chan, *Source Book*, pp. 116–24, as "On Nature," and by others, e.g., Watson, *Hsün Tzu*, pp, 77–89, as "A Discussion of Heaven."]

[134] *Hou Han Shu, ch.* 43, "Biography of Kung-sun Shu."

CHAPTER FOUR
Mo Tzu (ca. 490–403 B.C.)

SECTION ONE
Mo Tzu's Life and His Times

Mo Tzu's surname was Mo, his given name was Ti, and he was a native of the State of Lu.[1] Both his birth and death date are difficult to ascertain. Various scholars have offered quite different conclusions, but the most

[1] The *Shih Chi* does not contain Mo Tzu's biography; it merely adds a statement of twenty-four characters' length to *ch.* 74, "Meng Tzu, Hsün Ch'ing lieh-chuan," "Biographies of Mencius and Hsün Tzu," saying: "Mo Ti apparently was a Great Officer of the State of Sung. He was skilled at military defense, and advocated economy of expenditures. By some it is said that he was a contemporary of Confucius; by some that he lived after him." Sun Yi-jang [A.D. 1848–1908] in his "Mo Tzu chuan lüeh" ["Brief biography of Mo Tzu"; this and other items by Sun are appended to Sun's *Mo Tzu chien-ku*] says that Ssu-ma Ch'ien [the author of the *Shih Chi*] ". . . venerated Confucianism while being fundamentally a Taoist, hence Mohism was not something he cared for!" Fang Shou-ch'u, in his *Mo-hsüeh yüan-liu*, p. 201, states that some portions of the *Shih Chi* biography probably are missing, and that the text [of it in the *Shih Chi* today] is not that which Ssu-ma Ch'ien originally wrote. As for Mo Tzu's surname and given name, there were no variant views in antiquity. It was not until the Yuan period [thirteenth and fourteenth centuries A.D.] that Yi Shih-chen, in his *Lang-huan chi*, first said that Mo Tzu's surname was Chai [翟 the same character, when used as his given name, is read "Ti"], and his given name Wu 烏. Chou Liang-kung [1612–1672] of the Ch'ing dynasty in his *Yin-shu-wu shu-ying* and the recent scholar Chiang Ch'üan, in his *Tu-tzu chih-yen*, accept this view, both saying that Mo was not his surname but was a cognomen. Ch'ien Mu, on the other hand, advances the view that "Mo Ti was not surnamed Mo; 'mo' designating persons on whom punishment had been afflicted." ["*Mo*" being the name used for branding or tattooing a mark on the face, the lightest of the five corporal punishments.] Fang Shou-ch'u, in Part One, Chapter Two of his *Mo-hsüeh yuan-liu*, refutes this view in exhaustive detail. Here, the early view is accepted. In the past there have been three places, i.e., the States of Sung, Ch'u, and Lu, given as Mo Tzu's birthplace. The *Shih Chi* contains the statement that [Mo] Ti "was a Great Officer of Sung." Men of later times have sometimes suspected that he may have been a native of Sung. (E.g.: Ko Hung [A.D. c.277–c.357], in his *Shen-hsien chuan*, as quoted in the *Wen-hsüan, ch.* 18, "Ch'ang-ti fu" [by Ma Jung], in the commentary of Li Shan [d. 689]; and the *Hsün Tzu, ch.* 2, "Hsiu-shen," in the commentary of Yang [Liang, ninth century].) But the commentary of Kao Yu [fl. A.D. 205] on *ch.* II/4, "Tang jan," and *ch.* xv/1, "Shen Ta," in the *Lü-shih Ch'un-ch'iu*, says that he was a native of Lu. Pi Yüan [1730–1797] in his "Mo Tzu chu hsü" and Wu Yi [1745–1799] in his "Pa Mo Tzu," because they believe that the Lu referred to as his native place means the district of Lu-yang, which in the Ch'un-ch'iu Period belonged to the State of Ch'u, therefore state that Mo Tzu was a man of Ch'u. The Sun Yi-jang "Chuan lüeh," or "Brief Biography," concludes that he was a native of the State of Lu. Chang Ch'un-yi's "Mo Tzu Lu-jen shuo," i.e., "That Mo Tzu was a native of Lu" accepts Sun's view and expands upon it, citing passages in *chs.* 17–19, "Fei kung," *ch.* 47, "Kuei-yi," *ch.* 49, "Lu Wen," and *ch.* 56, "Pei T'i" as evidence. Sun's view is accepted in the present work.

reliable view seems to be that he was born about the Thirtieth year of the reign of the Chou King Ching [490 B.C.]* and died about the Twenty-third year of King Wei-lieh [403 B.C.].² As for the events of his life, we know next to nothing, because of the lack of documentary evidence. Mo Tzu's ancestors may have been Yin dynasty descendants.³ While Confucius' ancestors are known to have been [Yin descendants] among the nobility of the State of Sung, and hence became Great Officers in the State of Lu, nothing can be learned of Mo Tzu's family background, and he himself was a "mean person" [*chien jen* 賤人; the term designates a social group of the lowest standing]. Hence Mu Ho suspected that his book "was the doings of a mean person, and thus could not be used."⁴ Hui Tzu [the philosopher Hui Shih, a contemporary of Chuang Tzu] praised Mo Tzu for his great skill seen in the way he could fashion a carriage yoke.⁵ When we read the things recorded in the *ch.* 50, "Kung-shu," and *ch.* 52, "Pei ch'eng-men," and other such chapters of the Mohist canon, it becomes evident that the line of work that Mo Tzu followed was in all probability neither that of the farmer nor that of the merchant, but that he was a craftsman, skilled in the use of tools.

In the Spring and Autumn Age learning was still not universal. Since Mo Tzu was of the mean people, the matter of the teacher from whom he gained his learning remains a great unresolved question. The chapter "Tang Jan" [II/4] in the *Lü-shih Ch'un-ch'iu* says: "Duke Hui of Lu [reigned second quarter of the eighth century, B.C.] sent Tsai-jang to get permission from the Son of Heaven to conduct the ceremonies of the suburban temple [the Grand Temple of Heaven]. King Huan [of Chou] despatched the archivist Chiao. Duke Hui retained him there; his descendants continued to live in Lu, and Mo Tzu studied under them." This is one of the ac-

---

*Square brackets indicate that the words enclosed were added by the translator.

² Wang Chung's [A.D. 1745–1794] *Shu Hsüeh, Nei P'ien, san*, "Mo Tzu hsü," or "Preface to *Mo Tzu*," says that Mo Ti actually could have known Confucius. Fang Shou-ch'u accepts this, and concludes that Mo Ti was born in the Thirtieth year of King Ching [490 B.C.] and died before the Twenty-third year of King [Wei-] Lieh [403]. Sun Yi-jang's "Nien piao" ["Chronological Table" appended to his *Mo Tzu chien-ku*] starts with the First year of King Ting and runs to the Twenty-sixth year of King An (468–368). Liang Ch'i-ch'ao, in his *Mo Tzu hsüeh-an*, revises Sun's statements, saying that Mo Ti was born between the First and Tenth years of King Ting [468–59], and died between the Twelfth and the Twentieth years of King An [389–381]. Ch'ien Mu, in his "Chu tzu sheng-tsu nien-shih-yueh shu piao" [in the work cited immediately below], concludes that he was born in 480 and died in 390. (See also Ch'ien's *Hsien Ch'in chu-tzu hsi-nien k'ao-pien*, no. 31, and footnote 111 to Chapter One of the present book.)

³ Yü Cheng-hsieh [1775–1840], in his *Kuei-ssu lei-kao, ch.* 14, states: "Mo Tzu, as a descendant of the Yin people was much affected by resentful feelings; he would not accept the Chou model, but found his models in antiquity."

⁴ *Mo Tzu, ch.* 47, "Kuei-yi" [cf. Fung/Bodde, vol. I, p. 79].

⁵ *Han Fei Tzu, ch.* 32, "Wai chu-shuo, tso, shang."

counts.[6] *Huai-nan Tzu, ch.* 21, "Yao lüeh hsün," says: "Mo Tzu received
the training of a *ju* and was educated in the doctrines of Confucius, but
he was displeased by their rites [*li*], which were to him complicated and
troublesome; by their elaborate funerals, which were so costly that they
impoverished people; and by their extended periods of mourning, which
were injurious to the health and which interfered with work. Therefore
he repudiated the Way of Chou, and adopted the governmental institutions of the Hsia." This is another version.[7] Although these two versions
are different, they are not necessarily mutually irreconcilable. And, from
the evidence they convey, it is very clear that Mo Tzu's teachings were
deeply influenced by Confucian doctrine. Thus the account in the *Huai-
nan Tzu* would seem to have best grasped the actual facts about the sources
of Mo Tzu's learning.[8]

However, if Mo Tzu was born about the Thirtieth year of King Ching
[ca. 490], at the time of Confucius' death [479] he still would not have
come to the age of a grown boy, and could not possibly have received
instruction from him in person. If his education in the Confucian learning
was not directly from the master, it must have been transmitted to him
by one of the immediate disciples. Since Mo Tzu was said to have been
a "scholar of talent," that he is not ranked among the seventy immediate
disciples may well be for this reason, and not merely because he later
"denounced the Confucians," repudiated the Chou, and established his
own independent line, thereby making his teachings a heterodoxy in the
eyes of Confucians. The thing we should especially note, however, is that,
although Mo Tzu may have been educated by a descendant of the archivist Chiao and by disciples of Confucius, his doctrines were an alloy
of ancient principles and concepts, adapted to the needs of his time; with
them he independently created a new school of thought that became
therein something of his own, not something that can be fitted within the
bounds of his predecessors' thought. *Chuang Tzu, ch.* 33, "T'ien-hsia p'ien,"
says that Mo Tzu practiced the way of the Great Emperor Yü [semi-
legendary founder of the Hsia dynasty], and the *Huai-nan Tzu, ch.* 21,
"Yao lüeh hsün," says Mo Tzu adopted the governmental institutions of
the Hsia. Neither of these statements adequately suggests the whole corpus

---

[6] The *Han Shu, ch.* 30, "Journal of Literature," states that the Mohist school derived
from the attendants of the *Ancestral Temple* [*Ch'ing Miao*], which roughly agrees with this.
Wang Chung's *Mo Tzu hsü* accepts this, and further discusses the idea that Mo Tzu's
learning derived from that of the ancient archivists, citing as evidence the fact that the
Journal also lists the work *Shih Yi*, i.e., "The Historian Yi," in two chapters, as the first
work under the heading of the Mohists.

[7] Sun Hsing-yen [1753–1818], in his "Mo Tzu chu hou-hsü," accepts this view.

[8] Sun Yi-jang, in his "Mo Tzu chuan-lüeh" or "Brief Biography," rejects as incorrect
this statement in the *Huai-nan Tzu.*

of Mohist learning. In his "Mo Tzu hou hsü," Wang Chung says that Mo Tzu "studied them, but made his own way," and that, in his writings, "discussions of Yao, Shun, Yü, T'ang, Wen, and Wu [i.e., all the sage rulers from legendary antiquity to early Chou] occur in six places; discussions of Yü, T'ang, Wen, and Wu occur in four other places; and discussions of King Wen occur in still three more; and in no place has he ever discussed Yü alone." This comment is entirely correct. Mo Tzu must have observed the chaotic late Chou age, and sought validity in the past for new doctrines of his own invention, with the intent of setting aright and reforming his evil times. Moreover, in the urgency with which he sought to bring about the application of his methods, he was in the main no different from Confucius.

As a youth Mo Tzu lived chiefly in the State of Lu, and frequently engaged in debate with the Confucian scholars of Lu, and he also on one occasion engaged the Duke of Lu in questions and answers.[9] But because his doctrines were not adopted in his native state, he sought opportunities to test them in practice in other states. At the time Kung-shu Pan (also written Kung-shu P'an) [the facts of this famous craftsman's life cannot be established] was building "cloud ladders" [yün-t'i, a wall-scaling device used in offensive warfare] for Ch'u to use in an attack on Sung. Mo Tzu heard of it and, starting from Lu, traveled ten days and ten nights until he reached Ying [the capital of Ch'u], persuaded the King of Ch'u, and succeeded in having him call off the campaign.[10]

We should note that if Mo Tzu was a Yin descendant he had a special relationship with the State of Sung. [Sung was originally founded as a Chou fief to give Yin descendants place of residence.] His theory opposing offensive warfare was somewhat akin to the efforts of [the Sung statesmen] Hua Yuan and Hsiang Hsü to stop wars. [See Tso Chuan, Twenty-seventh year of Duke Hsiang; Legge, pp. 532-34 for the account of Hsiang Hsü's efforts to negotiate an end to warfare.][11] Now, in addition, he saved Sung from aggression. It would seem that Mohist doctrine should have been widely practiced in Sung. Older accounts claim that Mo Tzu served in office as a Great Officer in Sung. Liang Ch'i-ch'ao has argued that this is not correct.[12] When we note that Mo Tzu, after stopping Ch'u's attack,

[9] See, respectively, Mo Tzu, ch. 7, "San Pien," ch. 46, "Keng chu," ch. 48, "Kung Meng," and ch. 49, "Lu Wen."

[10] Mo Tzu, ch. 50, "Kung-shu."

[11] Yü Cheng-hsieh has said: "Universal love and the condemnation of offensive warfare appear to have been general characteristics of the Sung people." Hua and Hsiang tried to stop wars, but Mo Tzu initiated the study of methods of defense and of repelling attack.

[12] Mo Tzu hsüeh-an, p. 3. The general import is that Mo Tzu would not have compromised his principles for personal gain [i.e., yi yi t'iao 以義糶; Y. P. Mei, Works, p. 251, translates the term "sell his righteousness"], and that his efforts to rescue the State of Sung were not undertaken in the interests of gaining official position there.

passed through Sung on his return to the north and was refused shelter
from the rain by the keeper of the pass,[13] we must conclude that this
scarcely could have happened had Mo Tzu already achieved eminence
there as a public official. Moreover the *Shih Chi*, *ch.* 83, "Tsou Yang lieh-
chuan," "Sung placed its faith in the stratagem of Tzu-han, and imprisoned
Mo Ti." So it may be that his theories antagonized some powerful minister, and he suffered personal hardship in consequence. We can go further,
and note that of Mo Tzu's disciples, those about whom we can ascertain
biographical facts today include extremely few natives of Sung. And as
for taking service in Sung, we count only Ts'ao Kung Tzu, who had only
a very superficial belief in Mo Tzu's teachings.[14] So we must conclude
that Mohist doctrine, after all, was not greatly put into practice in the
country of Wei Tzu. [Wei Tzu was a member of the Yin royal family who
turned to the Chou at the time of the conquest, and was enfiefed the first
Duke of Sung.] Noting the way Mo Tzu valued integrity and scorned
salary, we may well ask how he could have consented to take office in Sung.
Liang Ch'i-ch'ao concludes that he spent his whole life as a commoner;
this is indeed the inevitable conclusion. Mo Tzu also once travelled to the
State of Wei, where he spoke with Kung-liang Huan Tzu, and urged
him to build up his army to prepare for difficulties. [See *Mo Tzu*, *ch.*
47, "Kuei yi"; Y. P. Mei, *Works*, p. 227.] He also had his disciple Kao
Shih Tzu appointed to office in Wei. [*Mo Tzu*, *ch.* 46, "Keng Chu";
Y. P. Mei, *Works*, p. 217.] Although Wei "ranked him among the ministers," in the end he left because his words went unheeded, and travelled
to Ch'i. This is a case of Mohist doctrine again failing to be accepted and
practiced, although in a place that originally had been settled by the
seven clans of the Yin people. [Yin nobility from the seven great Yin
clans had been settled in Wei by the Chou conqueror.]

Among the places to which Mo Tzu's travels took him in the north of
China, the State of Ch'i still must be named. At one time or another he
discoursed on his theory against aggressive warfare with Hsiang Tzu-niu
and T'ien Ho [who later reigned as] King T'ai [of Ch'i; T'ien Ho was the
head of the T'ien family which usurped the throne of Ch'i in 390 B.C.;
although he was confirmed by the Chou court as Marquis in 385, he
reigned as king. Hsiang Tzu-niu was a chief minister of Ch'i]. By that time
Mo Tzu was not only greatly advanced in age; he was prominent for his

---

[13] *Ch.* 50, "Kung-shu." Also, in *ch.* 47, "Kuei-yi," it tells that when Mo Tzu travelled
to the State of Wei, he said of himself: "Above, I have no responsibilities of service to a
prince"; this may be taken as further evidence.

[14] Refer to Sun Yi-jang's "Mo-hsüeh ch'uan-shou k'ao" [appended to his *Mo Tzu chien-
ku*] and Fang Shou-ch'u's "Mo Tzu ch'uan-shou piao" (in his *Mo-hsüeh yüan-liu*, pp. 136–
42). One Great Master [chü-tzu] after Meng Sheng, by name T'ien Hsiang Tzu, was a
native of Sung. However, he was a later follower, not one of the immediate disciples.

thought and learning. In consequence, a very large number of Mohists were natives of Ch'i. And Mo Tzu sent his disciple Sheng Ch'o to serve Hsiang Tzu-niu, subsequently having to "request him to withdraw from this service" because Sheng Ch'o three times participated in Ch'i's invasions of Lu. [*Mo Tzu, ch.* 49, "Lu Wen"; Y. P. Mei, *Works,* p. 254.] So it may well be that his reputation in Ch'i was much greater than it had been when he was in Sung and Wei.[15]

Mo Tzu's travels to the south took him as far as the State of Ch'u. While still young he had gone to Ch'u, where he discussed "grappling hooks and ramming prows" [for use in naval warfare] with Kung-shu Pan.[16] Later on he again went to [the Ch'u capital] Ying, to stop Ch'u from attacking Sung. And, in the later years of the reign of King Hui [reign 487–430], Mo Tzu again travelled to Ch'u to submit a letter. The king, although prizing its ideas, was however unable to adopt them.[17] While in Ch'u he repeatedly urged his theories against aggressive warfare on Lord Wen of Lu-yang. His disciple Keng Chu took service in Ch'u. A later follower, T'ien Chiu, was a general in the service of Ch'u. The Great Master of the Mohists, Meng Sheng, was a friend of the Lord of Yang-ch'eng [in Ch'u].[18] The *Chuang Tzu, ch.* 33, "T'ien-hsia p'ien," says that among the Mohists in the south there were also K'u-huo, Chi-ch'ih, and Teng Ling Tzu; if all three were natives of Ch'u,[19] that would offer sufficient proof that the Mohist movement spread southward. As for Yüeh in the southeast, and Ch'in in the northwest, even though Mohist teachings at one time reached both, Mo Tzu himself apparently never travelled to either.[20]

---

[15] For all these facts, see *ch.* 49, "Lu Wen." *Ch.* 47, "Kuei-yi," says: "Mo Tzu travelled northward, to the State of Ch'i . . . , not long thereafter he returned." It also says: "Mo Tzu travelled from Lu to Ch'i, where he met an old acquaintance." And, *ch.* 46, "Keng Chu," says: "Kao Shih Tzu left Wei and went to Ch'i, where he met Mo Tzu." This demonstrates that Mo Tzu repeatedly visited Ch'i.

[16] *Ch.* 49, "Lu wen."

[17] *Ch.* 47, "Kuei-yi." Ch'ien Mu's *Hsien Ch'in chu-tzu hsi-nien k'ao-pien,* No. 42, says that the submission of this letter and halting the attack on Sung were events of the same time; this view is also possible.

[18] *Ch.* 46, "Keng Chu" and *ch.* 49, "Lu Wen." For T'ien Chiu see *Lü-shih Ch'un-ch'iu,* xiv/3 "Shou shih." For Meng Sheng see the same work, xix/3 "Shang te."

[19] Sun Yi-jang, "Mo-hsüeh ch'uan-shou k'ao" [cf. footnote 14].

[20] *Ch.* 49, "Lu wen," states that Mo Tzu sent Kung-shang Kuo to the State of Yüeh. Kung-shang Kuo urged his doctrines upon the King of Yüeh. The King of Yüeh was greatly pleased, had fifty wagons made ready to go and bring Mo Tzu and offered to enfief him with five hundred *li* of the former territory of the State of Wu. Mo Tzu, considering that the king would not be able to accept and heed his teachings, was unwilling to "sell his righteousness," and rejected the offer. The *Lü-shih Ch'un-ch'iu,* xiv/3, "Shou shih" records that T'ien Chiu visited the State of Ch'in. The same book, in i/5 "Ch'ü ssu" says that the Great Master of the Mohists, Fu-t'un, resided in Ch'in. His son killed someone

Mencius said that "The doctrines of Yang Chu and Mo Tzu are over-flowing the world." [*Mencius*, III/ii/9/9.] The area into which Mohists went as travelling scholars was extremely broad; Mencius' comment is by no means a baseless fabrication. And yet, there remains one curious question about this. Confucius was a Great Officer in Lu; Mencius held the rank of a Minister in Ch'i; Hsün Tzu too held a post as Governor, at Lan-ling. The Confucians could support themselves without engaging in the productive labor of farming because their emolument of office could take the place of the income from farming. But now we come to Mo Tzu, who "above, has no responsibilities of service to a ruler, and below, knows none of the hardships of the man who tills the soil." [Mo Tzu is said to have so described himself; see footnote 11, above.] He travelled abroad throughout the various states, and his situation was no longer like that of his youth when he may have lived in a shop as a craftsman. So what, then, was it on which Mo Tzu relied for his living? The *ch.* 46, "Keng Chu," says: "Mo Tzu recommended [his follower] Keng Chu Tzu to Ch'u. Some [other] pupils visited him. They were given only three *sheng* of grain at a meal, and were not generously entertained. The pupils returned and reported to Mo Tzu, saying: 'Keng Chu Tzu has not profited by serving Ch'u. When we visited him we were given only three *sheng* each meal and we were not generously entertained.' Mo Tzu said: 'You cannot tell.' Shortly after, Keng Chu Tzu sent Mo Tzu ten catties of silver, saying: 'Your junior, unworthy disciple sends herewith ten catties of silver, which I hope you will use.' Mo Tzu said: 'So, indeed we cannot tell.' " Thus we can know that after the Mohist teachings had achieved prominence, even though he did not receive support from the state, or official salary, he nonetheless in fact drew money from his disciples, who traveled to the various states to serve in office. He did not have to keep himself busy at hard labor all his life, then, in order to assure himself food and clothing.[21]

---

and, "in accordance with the law of the Mohists"; he was executed. In the *Huai-nan Tzu*, *ch.* 19, "Hsiu-wu hsün," there is also mentioned a Mohist in Ch'in called T'ang Ku-liang (who appears in the *Lü-shih Ch'un-ch'iu*, xvi/7, "Ch'ü-yu," as T'ang Ku-kuo).

[21] However, Mo Tzu did not because of this abandon his doctrine, saying "if a man does not exert his strength he cannot live," *ch.* 32, "Fei yüeh, shang" [see footnotes 69 and 88, below]. Yet Mo Tzu evidently recognized that the establishment of society demanded a division of labor, and that not everyone had to engage directly in argicultural labor to supply his own needs. Thus he said: "Those with the ability to discuss and debate should discuss and debate; those who can narrate should narrate; those who have the ability to engage in work should engage in work—then righteous acts should be established." (*ch.* 47, "Kuei-yi.") It is apparent that Mo Tzu's views were quite far removed from Hsü Hsing's doctrine that all members of society alike should engage in agricultural produc-tion. Wu Lü, a rustic from the south of Lu, made pottery in winter and farmed in summer, and Mo Tzu criticized him on the grounds that the strength of one man, when devoted to

That Confucius and Mo Tzu represent quite distinct philosophies is a generally recognized fact. Yet that is, after all, but a very superficial view. As we examine the accounts of their lives, it is apparent that the two truly had many points of similarity. Both set forth the learning of antiquity in order to open up the basic tenets of his own school. Both sought to establish methods of governing in order to overcome the evils of their age. Both travelled about among the different states, yet, to the end, met no opportunity to try out their methods. So they both instructed large groups of followers in the hope that these would carry their teachings into practice and transmit their learning to later generations. In all of these things Confucius and Mo Tzu were similar. They differed in that: the one held office and the other did not;[22] the former started life in hum-

---

farming or weaving, can supply only an inconsequential portion of the people's needs, hence: "none of these [productive activities] is as good as to familiarize myself with the *Tao* of the ancient sage kings, and discover their principles, and to understand the words on the pages and be clear about their expressions; and with these to persuade the rulers and then the common people and the pedestrians. When the rulers adopt my principles, their states will be orderly. When the common people and the pedestrians adopt my principles, their conduct will be regulated. Therefore I think though I do not plow and feed the hungry or weave and clothe the cold, I have greater merit than those who plow and feed, and weave and clothe." [*Ch.* 49, "Lu Wen," following the translation of Y. P. Mei, *Works*, p. 249.] This is roughly the same in its purport as Mencius' reply to Kung-sun Ch'ou's question about "eating the bread of idleness." (*Mencius*, VII/i/32; Legge, p. 467.)

[22] Mo Tzu did not have an official career, but simply because the circumstances did not permit; he had not set up any principle of remaining aloof and detached from the mundane world. His principles governing when to serve in office and when to withdraw are in fact similar to those established by Confucius. For example, in declining the support of King Hui of Ch'u, Mo Tzu said: "I have heard that when the worthy man is offered advancement to high office, he will refuse to accept emolument if his Way is not put into practice, and he will not take his place at a court where his standard of righteousness goes unheeded. The letter that I submitted [conveying my governmental principles] is not about to be applied; therefore I request permission to leave." ("Kuei-yi") [*ch.* 47; these lines are not included in Y. P. Mei's translation, as they are reconstructed from another source]. And again, in rejecting the appointment to office proffered by the king of the State of Yüeh: "If the King of Yüeh will listen to my words and adopt my Way, I shall come, asking only for food according to the capacity of my stomach, and clothing according to the stature of my body. I shall just be one of the ministers. What is the use of any commission? On the other hand, if the King of Yüeh will not listen to my words and adopt my Way and I should go nevertheless, I should then be selling my righteousness." ("Lu Wen") [*ch.* 49; Y. P. Mei, *Works*, pp. 250–51]. And again, when Kao Shih Tzu held office in the State of Wei and resigned because his words were not heeded, he suspected that the ruler of Wei would think he was crazy [for abandoning a good post carrying large salary and high honors], but Mo Tzu commented on this: "If you left for the sake of the Way, what does it matter even if you are accused of being crazy?" [*Ch.* 50, "Keng Chu"; cf. Y. P. Mei, *Works*, p. 217.] All of these examples display a principle in common with that of Confucius. In addition, it can be noted that the Mohist followers in seeking office display a similarity with the disciples of Confucius. Mo Tzu, in sending his followers [to various states] to seek office, displayed a manner of acting that was derived from the Confucian

ble status, but worked his way up to the ranks of Great Officers, while the latter chose to remain a humble man all his life, wearing his haircloth clothing and straw sandals, clinging to this manner even in his advanced old age. As we seek to establish the reasons for these similarities and differences, it seems inevitable that Confucius and Mo Tzu should display some similarities in their careers as in their thought, for both their historical times and political surroundings were roughly identical, to which must be added the fact that Mo Tzu perhaps had come under the influences of Confucian instruction. There is this one point of difference; Confucius was the descendant of the old Yin aristocracy, while Mo Tzu's family was of no eminence. His forefathers may have been descendants of Yin commoners, and his lifelong advocacy of toil and hardship, his willingness to practice the "way of the laborer," probably was something that sprang from the influence of his own home and family life. We may well feel that, in very general terms, Mo Tzu was a common-man Confucius, and the Mohist doctrines are common-man Confucianism. The words and deeds of the two differ in degree, but each aspect of the basic spirit of the two men can be matched, the one to the other. Mencius denounced Mo Tzu's way as that of birds and beasts, while Hsün Tzu ridiculed it as that of a common laborer.[23] This is precisely what Han Yü [A.D. 768–824] called: "Disputes arising among late followers of a school."[24] It is not to be regarded as evidence that Confucius and Mo Tzu really were diametrically opposed to each other.

school. One example of this is Confucius' hoping to send Ch'i-tiao K'ai off to take office. [But Confucius was pleased when Ch'i-tiao K'ai said he was not yet ready; see *Analects*, v/5; Legge, p. 174.] Mo Tzu was even more energetic in working toward this end: he, for example, sent Keng Chu to hold office in Ch'u, and Kao Shih to Wei (*ch.* 46, "Keng Chu"); Kung-shang Kuo to Yüeh (*ch.* 49, "Lu Wen"); Ts'ao Kung Tzu to Sung and Sheng Ch'o to Ch'i ("Lu Wen"); all of these are examples for which the evidence is available. Moreover, also among the Mohists [as among Confucius' less worthy followers] there were some who were concerned primarily with salary and rank. For example *ch.* 48, "Kung Meng," records the case of one who entered the Mohist school, and after a year of study demanded that Mo Tzu get him an official appointment. This person, moreover, seems not to have been the equal of Tzu-chang in praiseworthy qualities. [The follower of Confucius who, although generally praiseworthy, was criticized by the Master for being too concerned with rank and salary; see *Analects*, ii/18; Legge, p. 151.] If Fang Shou-ch'u in his *Mo-hsüeh yüan-liu* (pp. 207–08) is correct in his account of Mohist sycophants at the court in Ch'in, then it was not merely those "small-man Confucians" who were guilty of distorting their school's doctrines in the pursuit of worldly advantage.

[23] See, respectively, *Mencius*, "T'eng wen-kung," Part i [iii/i/4/8] and *Hsün Tzu*, ch. 11, "Wang pa."

[24] Han Yü, "Ch'ang-li wen-chi ["Collected Writings," ch. 12 in the *Chu Wen-kung chiao Ch'ang-li Hsien-sheng Chi*, *SPTK* ed.], "Tu Mo Tzu" i.e., "On Reading the Mo Tzu." The more detailed discussion of the similarities and differences of Confucius' and Mo Tzu's doctrines is set forth in subsequent portions of this chapter. Further, it can be noted that precisely because the Confucian and Mohist teachings were fundamentally so similar,

The histories claim that Confucius' disciples numbered three thousand, of whom some seventy were able and worthy. When we examine the relevant data in ancient records, we find that the Mohist followers were of comparable numbers. Mo Tzu, in persuading the King of Ch'u, said: "My followers Ch'in Ku-li and others, numbering three hundred, are already armed with my implements of defense, waiting on the city wall of Sung to repel the attack by Ch'u." The *Huai-nan Tzu* says: "Mo Tzu's followers number one hundred and eighty men, all of whom will obey his command to go through fire or tread on sword-blades, and who will die without turning away." The *Lü-shih Ch'un-ch'iu* also records that when the Mohist Great Master, Meng Sheng, died defending the Lord of Yang-ch'eng, ". . . the followers who died there numbered one hundred and three."[25] The large numbers of the Mohist followers can be deduced from these accounts; it is much to be regretted that the documents are so incomplete that their learning and activities cannot be made more clearly known. Of all his disciples and later followers, the names of no more than forty can be recovered today.

All of the writings of the Mohists are lost except for the fifty-three chapters of the book *The Mo Tzu* itself.[26] If we examine the matter from the extant writing only, it would appear that the content of none of the

---

the Mohists were forced to attack Confucian doctrines in the effort to establish themselves as a separate school, stressing the points of difference and covering over the similarities. And in this they resembled Aristotle of ancient Greece, who, in establishing his own theories and in teaching his followers, had to attack the views maintained by his teacher Plato and his school.

[25] See, respectively, *Mo Tzu, ch.* 49, "Lu Wen" [cf. Fung/Bodde, p. 81]; *Huai-nan Tzu, ch.* 19, "T'ai-tsu hsün"; and *Lü-shih Ch'un-ch'iu,* XIX/3, "Shang-te." For the names of Mohists that can be ascertained, see above, footnote 14.

[26] The *Han Shu, ch.* 30, "Journal of Literature," lists a *Mo Tzu* in seventy-one chapters. [Critical editions of the *Mo Tzu* edited in the Ch'ing period usually contain a "Table of Contents" listing seventy-one chapters, of which eighteen are missing, although titles of eight missing chapters are known. See Sun Yi-jang, *Mo Tzu chien-ku.*] The book probably was not written by Mo Tzu himself, but was in large part recorded by his immediate disciples and later followers (see Fang Shou-ch'u, *Mo-hsüeh yüan-liu,* Part I, chapter 3). Of the extant fifty-three chapters, *ch.* 1, 2, 3, "Ch'in shih," "Hsiu-shen," and "So-jan" appear not to be from the hands of Mohists (see Liang Ch'i-ch'ao, *Mo Tzu hsüeh-an*). And the eleven [extant] chapters starting with *ch.* 52, "Pei ch'eng-men" [i.e., number 52, 53, 56, 58, 61–63, and 68–71] are perhaps entirely false attributions from the Han dynasty (see Ch'ien Mu, *Mo Tzu,* quoting Chu Hsi-tsu), or the first seven of those may be works of the Warring States Period (see Fang Shou-ch'u). The *Yin-yi* in two chapters, *T'ien Ch'iu Tzu* in three chapters, *Wo Tzu* in one chapter, *Sui Fei Tzu* in six chapters, *Hu Fei Tzu* in three chapters—that is to say, all of the other Mohist works listed in the *Han Shu* "Journal"—are no longer extant. Ma Kuo-han, in his *Yü-han-shan-fang chi-yi-shu,* presents collected extant fragments of the *T'ien Ch'iu Tzu* and the three following items. Sun Yi-jang, in his "Mo-chia chu-tzu kou-ch'en" (appended to his *Mo Tzu chien-ku*) adds some items that Ma's compilation overlooked.

Mohist political theories that are mentioned, or quoted elsewhere in order to be refuted by other writers, goes beyond the scope of the *Mo Tzu* book itself. If the *ch.* 40–45, "Mohist Canon," in six books was indeed written by the "Later Mohists" [*pieh Mo*],[27] then the most important advances in Mohist thought after the death of Mo Tzu were in the fields of logical theory [*ming hsüeh* 名學] and science.[28] The Mohist followers' further contributions to political thought probably were no more than to fill out and revise somewhat the major tenets already delineated by Mo Tzu; there is no reason to assume that they expanded and developed their master's teachings, in the manner of Mencius and Hsün Tzu, to the point that they became independent teachings in their own right. Thus even though all of those other Mohist writings have been lost, still the main outlines of Mohist political thought have not disappeared with them, and this must be regarded as one fortunate circumstance in the midst of the misfortune of those other losses.[29]

[27] Pi Yüan (in his *Mo Tzu chu*), Liang Ch'i-ch'ao (in his *Mo-ching chiao-shih*), and others support the view that the so-called "Mohist Canon" [*ch.* 40–45] is the work of Mo Tzu himself. Wang Chung (in his *Mo Tzu hsü*), Sun Yi-jang (in his *Mo Tzu chien-ku*), Hu Shih (in his *Chung-kuo che-hsüeh-shih*, "History of Chinese Philosophy," pp. 185 ff.), Fang Shou-ch'u (*op.cit.*, p. 43), and others state that it was written by later Mohists [i.e., *pieh Mo* 別墨].

[28] Fang Shou-ch'u, *op.cit.*, Part I, pp. 159–85. [See also A. C. Graham, "The Logic of the Mohist *Hsiao-ch'ü*," *T'oung Pao*, 51, 1964, pp. 1–54.]

[29] From ancient times to the present, scholars, without perhaps consciously intending to do so, have often stressed the differences between the manner of Confucians' and Mohists' lives, and have disregarded their similarities. That careers of Confucius and Mo Tzu themselves were somewhat similar has been alluded to above. Among the followers of the two masters also there are many instances of similar deeds and similar sayings. Among the Confucian students, "those whose studies were distinguished then served in office" [*Analects*, XIX/13] and the Mohists also followed official careers at the courts of the feudal princes. Most of Confucius' immediate followers were poor and of humble status, and among Mo Tzu's, too, there were few members of the aristocracy. Tzu-kung had engaged in commerce, and Tzu-lu wanted to share his well-fed horses and luxurious clothing with his friends, but [others among Confucius' immediate disciples], such as Yen Hui and Yuan Hsien, lived lives fully as poverty-stricken as any of Mo Tzu's followers. It has also been much said that the Confucians were usually bookish weaklings, while the Mohists honored martial knights. This too is not entirely correct. Hu Fei Tzu [a Mohist follower and teacher] so well confuted one Ch'ü Chiang Tzu, who had called upon him "bearing a sword and wearing a soldiers' hat," that the latter lay aside his sword and hat and asked to become his follower. (Sun Yi-jang, "Mo-hsüeh ch'uan-shou k'ao" quoting the *T'ai-p'ing yü-lan*.) This incident is remarkably similar to Tzu-lu's first meeting with Confucius. [See Legge, *Analects*, "Prolegomena," pp. 114–15.] Moreover, the Confucians also esteemed the kingly virtues. Tseng Tzu spoke of: "The man to whom one could with equal confidence entrust an orphan not yet fully grown or the sovereignty of a whole State, whom the advent of no emergency however great could upset." [*Analects*, VIII/6; following Waley, p. 134.] Tzu-chang said: "A knight who confronted with danger is ready to lay down his life . . . [such a one is all that can be desired]." [*Analects*, XIX/1; Waley, p. 224.]

SECTION TWO
Universal Love and Mutual Benefit

THE Ch'ing scholar Chang Hui-yen [A.D. 1761–1802], in his postface to a work on Mo Tzu, "Shu Mo Tzu 'ching-shuo chieh' hou" [i.e., 'Postface' to his commentary on *ch*. 42–43 of the *Mo Tzu*], wrote: "Universal love is the basic element of Mohism," and added: "Reverence for

---

This theory of the knightly virtue represents a development and expansion of the idea expressed by Confucius in saying that the [knight who has the heart of a knight] will [never] seek life at the expense of Goodness [*jen*]. [*Analects*, xv/8; Waley, p. 195.] Ch'i-tiao K'ai represented one of the eight schools of Confucians; Mo Tzu said: "Ch'i-tiao had a ferocious appearance," ("Fei ju") [*ch*. 39; Y. P. Mei, *Works*, p. 211], and the *Han Fei Tzu* says: "According to the theory of Ch'i-tiao, a man should not change his facial color before others, nor should he blink even in the face of danger; if he acts wrongly, he should give way to bondmen and bondwomen; and if he acts aright, he should assert himself even before the feudal lords. ("Hsien-hsüeh") [*ch*. 50; W. K. Liao, *Han Fei Tzu*, vol. 2, p. 300]. This is also similar in its meaning to what [the Mohist] *Hu Fei Tzu* calls "The bravery of the superior man." And [Confucius' follower] Tzu-lu, who died calmly after re-tying the strings of his cap [which had been cut by the dagger of his assailant], faithful in service to Duke Ch'u [of Wei]. (*Shih Chi, ch*. 67) is a perfect match for the story of Meng Sheng's defense to the death in the service of the lord of Yang-ch'eng. (*Lü-shih Ch'un-ch'iu*, xix/3, "Shang te." However, it is true that among the schools during the pre-Ch'in period, the Confucians placed somewhat greater emphasis on literary cultivation, whereas the Mohists tended more toward stress on the knight-errant's virtues. Then, through Ch'in and Han and subsequent ages, after the Mohist knights had vanished completely, the Confucians gradually acquired the faults of excessive refinement associable with a degenerated movement; its rhapsodists of the virtues of the former kings mostly came to be men whose arms lacked enough strength to fight off a chicken.

The two schools also had much in common in the relationship they cultivated between masters and disciples. Mohists on going out to hold public office mostly did so in obedience to the commands of the master, and thus Mo Tzu had his pupils serving in office in the various states. If they violated his teachings and sought personal advantage, he would order them to withdraw from their office (as in the case of Sheng Ch'o, who served Hsiang-tzu Niu in the State of Ch'i; see *ch*. 49, "Lu Wen") [cf. Y. P. Mei, *Works*, p. 254]. However, Keng Chu Tzu, who served in the State of Ch'u, may have been incapable of carrying out Mo Tzu's Way there. He sent Mo Tzu a gift of ten catties of silver, yet Mo Tzu said of him "One really can't tell [how he may be getting along there]." But we have no evidence that Mo Tzu ever ordered him to withdraw. Kao Shih Tzu, who resigned his post as a minister in Wei, apparently did so of his own volition, not in response to the Master's command (*ch*. 46, "Keng Chu.") Confucius also once sent Ch'i-tiao K'ai out to take office. He also criticized Jan Ch'iu for assisting the head of the Chi clan in collecting excessive taxes, saying: "He is no disciple of mine. My little ones, you may beat the drum and set upon him. I give you leave." (*Analects*, "Hsien chin") [xi/16/2; Waley, pp. 156–57]. Here we have an example of Confucius also overseeing the careers of his followers.

The Mohists had the institution of their *chü-tzu* 鉅子, i.e., "Great Master" (*Chuang Tzu, ch*. 33, "T'ien-hsia": "The Great Master was regarded as a Sage; all of the followers willingly looked upon him as their master and guide, and aspired to be his successor." The

heaven, proving the existence of spirits, identification with the superior, and economy of expenditures are its branches. Anti-fatalism, anti-music, and simplicity in funerals are merely other issues upon which circumstances provoked him to take such stands."[30] Chang's view is most perceptive and accurate.

Mo Tzu was born at the beginning of the Warring States Period. All

---

Lü-shih Ch'un-ch'iu, xix/3, "Shang te," states that when ". . . the Mohist's Great Master Meng Sheng . . ." was about to die, he charged T'ien Hsiang Tzu of Sung to succeed him as Great Master). This is an institution that the Confucians seem to have lacked, yet Mencius said: "Formerly, when Confucius died, after three years had elapsed. . . . Tzu-hsia, Tzu-chang, and Tzu-yu, thinking that Yu Jo resembled the sage, wished to render to him the same observances that they had rendered to Confucius. They tried to prevail upon Tseng Tzu to join them in this, but he would not give it his approval." ("T'eng wen-kung," Part i) [*Mencius*, iii/i/4/13; Legge, pp. 254–55]. Although because of Tseng Tzu's disapproval they did not succeed in establishing him, still their intent apparently was to establish one person who would fulfill functions like those of the Mohist's Great Master. However, the Mohist followers seem to have split into three camps after the death of their Master (*Han Fei Tzu*, ch. 50, "Hsien-hsueh") and the "separatist Mohists disputed among each other constantly about their differences of interpretation" (*Chuang Tzu*, ch. 33, "T'ien hsia"). Thus, it seems that although the Great Master was designated by his predecessor, he faced the problem of maintaining the effective leadership of the whole body of Mohists. We might speculate that each of the various schools of Mohists had its own Great Master, and that each different school need not have felt bound to respect the commands of another. This is a doubtful issue, and one that we have no possibility of clarifying. Also, the *Lü-shih Ch'un-ch'iu*, i/5, "Ch'ü-ssu," records that when the son of the Great Master Fu-t'un killed someone, King Hui of Ch'in had found an excuse whereby to pardon him, but Fu-t'un said: "According to the laws of the Mohists, he who has killed a man must die, and he who has wounded a man must suffer corporal punishment." [Cf. Fung/Bodde, Vol. i, p. 84.] As a consequence, he was executed. Thus we can see that the Mohists were an organized community in which the Great Masters held the power to execute and to punish. That is something that the Confucians never had. (Refer also to Fang Shou-ch'u, *Mo-hsüeh yüan-liu*, Part i, Chapter vi.)

[30] *Ming-k'e wen-pien*, among the appendices to Sun Yi-jang's *Mo Tzu chien-ku*. Liang Ch'i-ch'ao, in his *Mo Tzu hsüeh-an*, accepts this view. Fang Shou-ch'u, in his *Mo-hsüeh yüan-liu*, Part i, p. 75, states that this is so in terms of logical system, but that if one speaks of the sequence in which the concepts developed, the condemnation of offensive wafare is the first principle. His view is also reasonable. Also, ch. 49, "Lu Wen," contains Mo Tzu's statement, as follows: "Upon entering a country one should locate the need and work on that. If the country is upset and in confusion, teach them with the doctrines of the Elevation of the Worthy and the Agreement with the Superior. If the country is in poverty, teach them with Economy of Expenditures and Simplicity in Funerals. If the country is indulging in music and wine, teach them with the Condemnation of Music and Anti-fatalism. If the country is insolent and without propriety, teach them to reverence heaven and worship the spirits. If the country is engaged in conquest and oppression, teach them with Universal Love and the Condemnation of Offensive War." [Following, with slight modificatons, the translation of Y. P. Mei, *Works*, p. 251. The words in capitals are also names of chapters in the *Mo Tzu*.] According to this, although Mo Tzu wanted to decide what was most appropriate in terms of local conditions, and teach according to the men to be taught, universal love still served as his teachings' central concept.

the states were involved ever more constantly in usurpations and murders, aggression, and punitive campaigns, from which disastrous consequences multiplied. Wu was annihilated by Yüeh, Ch'u eradicated Ts'ai and Ch'i, while other small states, such as Tai, T'eng, T'an and Chü, all were annexed, one after another, by the more powerful ones. Within the states quarrels and strife, regicide, and forceful seizures of power were so frequent as to no longer be unusual. Such instances as the murder of Duke Ai in Cheng ["by the people of the state," in 454 B.C.], the break-up of Chin by the three powerful families [gradually completed by 402 B.C.], the take-over of power by the T'ien clan [improperly active for decades before they completed their usurpation in 390–385] in Ch'i are but the most prominent ones. All of these occurred during "the times personally witnessed" by Mo Tzu; he must have been profoundly con-scious of the bitter suffering and disastrous calamities that they induced. Seeking their cause, Mo Tzu concluded that all of the world's disorders resulted from man's own selfishness. In *ch.* 14, "Chien ai," or "Universal Love," Part One, he states: "Suppose we try to locate the cause of dis-order, we shall find it lies in the want of mutual love. What is called dis-order is just the lack of filial piety on the part of the minister and the son towards the ruler and the father. As he loves himself and not his father, the son benefits himself to the disadvantage of his father. As he loves himself and not his elder brother, the younger brother benefits himself to the disadvantage of his elder brother. As he loves himself and not his ruler, the minister benefits himself to the disadvantage of his ruler. And these are what is called disorder. When the father shows no affection to the son, when the elder brother shows no affection to the younger brother, and when the ruler shows no affection to the minister, this too is what the world knows as disorder. When the father loves only himself and not the son, he benefits himself to the disadvantage of the son. When the elder brother loves only himself and not his younger brother, he benefits himself to the disadvantage of the younger brother. When the ruler loves only himself and not his minister, he benefits himself to the disadvantage of his minister. And why does this come about? It all arises from the want of mutual love. It is true, moreover, throughout all the world, even among robbers and thieves. As he loves only his own family and not other families, the thief steals from other families to profit his own family. As he loves only his own person and not others, the robber does violence to others to profit himself. And why does this come about? It all arises from the want of mutual love. It is true, moreover, even among Great Officers who upset each others' families, and to the feudal princes who commit ag-gression against each others' countries. As the Great Officer loves only his own house and does not love other houses, he upsets other houses to benefit his own. As he loves only his own state and does not love the other states, the feudal prince attacks the other to benefit his own. This sums up all of the world's disorders. When we seek the reason for all of this coming about, we find it all arises from the want of mutual love."

Onee we know that all of the world's disorders find their origins in man's selfishness and want of mutual love, the method for stopping disorders lies in eliminating man's selfishness and in causing men to practice mutual love. This line of reasoning becomes absolutely clear. Mo Tzu explains it as follows: "Suppose everyone in the world loves universally, loving others as one's self. Will there yet be any unfilial individual? When everyone regards his father, elder brother, and emperor as himself, whereto can he direct any unfilial feeling? Will there still be any unaffectionate individual? When everyone regards his younger brother, son, and minister as himself, whereto can he direct any unkindness? Therefore, there will not be any unfilial feeling or unkindness. Will there then be any thieves and robbers? When everyone regards other families as his own family, who will steal? When everyone regards other persons as his own person, who will rob? Therefore there will not be any thieves or robbers. Will there be upsetting of each other's houses by the Great Officers, and attacks on each other's countries by the feudal princes? When everyone regards the houses of others as his own, who will do the upsetting? When everyone regards other states as one's own, who will commit aggression? Therefore there will be neither disturbances among the houses of the Great Officers nor aggression among the states of the feudal princes. If everyone in the world will love universally, states not attacking each other, houses not upsetting each other, thievery and robbery ceasing to exist, rulers and ministers, fathers and sons, all being affectionate and filial—if all this comes to pass the world will be orderly. Therefore, how can the sagelike man who devotes himself to the governing of the world fail to restrain hate and encourage love?"

However, since in Mo Tzu's time the world not only did not practice mutual love but was sunk in chaos, promoting the doctrine of universal love was anything but easy. Hence Mo Tzu set up a series of hypothetical objections and replied to them one by one, to prove that his proposed method would really work. One of these is that the "six ancient sage-kings" had personally practiced it; also, the Great Emperor Yü's controlling the floods had benefited the whole world; and King Wen's rule in the state of Ch'i [in the northwest, where he developed the forerunner of the subsequent Chou government] had brought well-being to all the people.[31] All of these could be taken as standards for the present. Another

---

[31] See, respectively, *ch.* 15 and 16, "Chien ai" Part II and III. [Y. P. Mei, *Works*, pp. 85 and 92 ff.] Furthermore, this [appeal to historical precedents] constitutes what Mo Tzu called the "basis" [*pen* 本] among the "three standards" [*san piao* 三表] of any good

is that "The ruler liked it; therefore the ministers did it."[32] King Ling liked slender waists; therefore his courtiers all ate only one meal a day. King Kou-chien liked bravery; therefore his servitors were all willing to walk into fire for him. [Incidents cited in "Chien-ai," Part III, ch. 16; see Watson, *Mo Tzu*, pp. 47–48.] How much more would they be willing mutually to love and to benefit each other. A third is: " 'Every word has its answer; every good deed has its recompense. . . . When one throws to me a peach, I return to him a plum.' [These lines are from the *Book of Odes*, the ode "Yi," in "Major Odes of the Kingdom," Legge, pp. 515–16.] This is to say that whoever loves others will be loved, and whoever hates others will be hated."[33] Since the benefits of universal love are as great as this, one can declare conclusively that it is sure to be accepted as a norm and put into practice by people.

Mo Tzu's fundamental doctrine of universal love is more or less as set forth above. Is his doctrine, then, the same as Confucius' statements about

---

measure]. *Ch.* 35, "Fei ming," Part I says: "Therefore for any doctrine there must be the three standards. What are the three standards? Mo Tzu said, [1] There must be a basis or foundation. [2] There must be an examination. [3] And there must be practical application. [1] Where to find the basis? Find it in the [will of Heaven and the spirits and] the experiences of the ancient sage-kings above. [2] How is it to be examined? It is to be examined by inquiring into the actual experience of the eyes and ears of the people below. [3] How to apply it? Put it into law and governmental measures and see if they bring about benefits to the state and the people. These are called the three standards." [Translation is that of Chan, *Source Book*, p. 222. See his notes on difficult passages. Square brackets are used above as in Chan.] Part II [of the three "Fei ming" chapters, in analogous passages] uses the term "three methods" [*san fa* 法] in place of "three standards" [*san piao* 表], and it explains the meaning of the ideas of "the basis" and "the examination" of a doctrine in slightly different fashion. [Both Y. P. Mei, *Works* and Chan, *op.cit.*, translate both "*san piao*" and "*san fa*" with the same English terms, i.e., "tests" and "standards," which is reasonable in the overall sense of these chapters. Cf. their footnotes.]

[32] *Ch.* 15, "Chien ai," Part II. The tenor of Part III is roughly the same, as it refers to this point. This constitutes the standard of "examination" [*yuan* 原] of the "three standards." ["Universal Love" in three *chüan*, nos. 14–16, is like several of the portions of the *Mo Tzu* in being synoptic, or presented in three successive *chüan* that are more or less repetitive; Part II is translated in Chan, *Source Book*, and Part III in both de Bary, *Sources* and Watson, *Mo Tzu*. Mei, *Motze*, offers both II and III.]

[33] *Ch.* 16, "Chien ai," Part III. Part II says: "Those who love others will be loved by others. Those who benefit others will be benefited by others. Those who hate others will be hated by others. And those who harm others will be harmed by others." [Chan, *Source Book*, p. 214.] This is the standard of "practical application" [*yung* 用] among the "three standards." *Ch.* 16, Part III, also establishes the terms "universal [*chien*] man" and "partial [*pieh*] man" [i.e., who practices partiality], also "universal ruler" and "partial ruler," and further concludes that in selecting a friend or a ruler one must select the "universal" and reject the "partial." This again appears to be in accord with his standards of "examination" and "application" of a doctrine.

overflowing love and extensively conferred benefits, carrying out one's own [good will] so that it reached others, [cf. *Analects*: 1/6, vi/28; *Mencius*, 1/i/7/12] or is it different? Han Yü wrote: "Mo Tzu must have drawn on Confucius;" Confucius also advocated universal love. [See footnote 24.] The Ch'ing scholar Wang Chung said [on the other hand, in his "Mo Tzu hou hsü"] that Mo Tzu "Studied [the learning of the past] but went on to evolve his own doctrines." [See footnote 2.] The recent scholar, Fang Shou-ch'u agreed with Wang and added: "There was no Mohist doctrine before Mo Tzu."[34] If, however, we accept the statement in the *Huai-nan Tzu* [that Mo Tzu "was educated in the doctrines of Confucius," etc.], and go on to discuss the content of the concept of universal love, it then becomes evident that Han Yü's conclusion must be very close to the truth, and that Mo Tzu's "love" [*ai*] was formulated in the wake of Confucius' benevolence [*jen*] with only minor changes.

Briefly, there are four kinds of evidence for this: (1) The two terms, *jen* and *ai*, have the same semantic denotation. The *Analects* records Fan Ch'ih's question about the word *jen*, and Confucius' reply that it meant "to love [*ai*] people." [*Analects*, xii/22; Legge, p. 260.] Mencius also said that "The commiserating mind is the beginning of benevolence." [*Mencius*, ii/i/6/5; cf. Legge, p. 212.] *Mo Tzu*, ch. 40, "Ching," Part i, says: "Benevolence [*jen*]—its essential is love [*ai*]." Since *jen* and *ai* have the same definition, it is scarcely possible that they should have conflicting philosophical implications. (2) Overflowing love [*fan ai* 泛愛, the Confucian term] and universal love [*chien ai* 兼愛] in their main purport are the same. Chung Kung asked about *jen*, and Confucius replied that it is ". . . not to do to others as you would not wish done to yourself." [*Analects*, xii/2; also cf. xv/23.] And when Tzu-kung asked about *jen*, Confucius said "[The man of *jen*], wishing to be established himself, seeks also to establish others; wishing to turn his own merits to account, helps others to turn theirs to account." [*Analects*, vi/28; Legge, p. 194, Waley, p. 122.] Mo Tzu, explaining universal love, said: "Others are regarded the same as one's self."[35] Although the wording differs, the meaning of these sayings is without significant difference. (3) The Mohists' denunciations of the Confucians refer to many issues. The Confucians accept fate, but do not believe in spirits; they have lavish funerals, and extended periods of mourning; their ritual behavior becomes involved and complex, and they embellish it with music; they revere antiquity and evade work.[36] All these features of their strongest attacks on Confucianism are side issues involving the character and behavior of Confucianists. In no instance have their attacks on the Confucian school drawn on the issue of universal love.

[34] Fang's *Mo-hsüeh yüan-liu*, Part i, p. 73.
[35] *Ch.* 16, "Chien ai," Part iii [slightly modified from Y. P. Mei, p. 88].
[36] See *ch.* 39, "Fei ju," Part ii and *ch.* 48, "Kung Meng."

If the two schools, at this point in their doctrines, are not derived from a common source, how can one explain the lack of any discussion whatsoever [of their apparent convergence] in the entire book of *Mo Tzu*? On the other hand, in *ch.* 48, "Kung Meng," it says: "In a discussion with Ch'eng Tzu, Mo Tzu cited Confucius. Ch'eng Tzu inquired, since he condemned Confucianism, why he had cited Confucius. Mo Tzu said: 'In those things in which I have cited Confucius, he is right, and what is right is inalterably so.'" This clearly indicates that there were things that Mo Tzu had gained from Confucius. It is greatly to be regretted that this passage does not make clear what it was that Mo Tzu had cited; we have no way of determining whether or not it might have been relevant to benevolence [*jen*] and love [*ai*].[37] (4) No Confucianist attacked Mo Tzu more vehemently than did Mencius; he went so far as to label his universal love a doctrine expecting people to act "as if without fathers," and be therefore "like the birds and the beasts." [*Mencius*, III/ii/9/9; Legge, p. 282.] The Ch'ing scholar Wang Chung has already demonstrated that Mencius was being unfair in that view. It is precisely what Han Yü labelled disputes arising among late followers of a school, in the effort to promote one's own teacher's views. Such denunciations are insufficient evidence for determining the strengths and weaknesses, the similarities and differences, of the two schools.

To draw an inference about why Mencius did not condemn other aspects of Mohist doctrine but concentrated solely on universal love, it must be because he was quite aware that on this issue the two schools were the closest. He was disturbed that in this the Mohists rivalled the Confucians on their own ground [literally, he "hated purple because it stole from crimson"]; he felt compelled to resist them precisely at this point. If we take Mencius' statements on benevolence [*jen*] and righteousness [*yi*] and hold them up against Mo Tzu's love [*ai*] and benefit [*li* 利], examining both quite objectively, we must feel that they are in basic accord, not at all in conflict with each other. [*Li* may also be translated "profit," as in Legge's translation of the opening lines of the *Mencius*, and sometimes in Mohist contexts, "utility."] Mencius valued "righteousness" [*yi*] above all, and condemned "benefit" [*li*], but one can assume that in this he was utilizing the terms benevolence and righteousness to characterize graphically a government that realizes in practice the ruler's kindness of heart, and the ruler's inability to bear the suffering of others. At the same time he used the term benefit [*li*—as "profit"] to characterize

---

[37] It may also be that later followers of the Mohist school disliked the fact that such passages damaged their own position, hence removed them from the text. Might this not explain why the quotations throughout the book from the *History* and the *Odes* are the same as those used by Confucians, yet there is not a single passage in which the words of Confucius himself are quoted?

selfish and "snatching" activities.[38] He did not say that the benevolent persons managing the state need have only minds that could not bear suffering, or that they need not carry out governmental measures that would benefit [li] the people. And Mo Tzu's advocacy of "universality in order to overcome partiality" was to define as universality [chien] loving others as one's self, and as partiality [pieh], harming others to profit one's self. He did that precisely in order to establish the public good versus the private good as the standard for distinguishing between righteousness and [selfish] "profit." It was not as if he had some other method of government in mind that should displace benevolence and righteousness. Hence ch. 27, "T'ien chih," Part II, records Mo Tzu's words saying that the sage rulers of the Three Dynasties of antiquity practiced universality and eradicated partiality, extending the benefits of this to Heaven and man, gaining praise for their "benevolence and righteousness." Ch. 40, "Ching," Part I, says: "Righteousness is benefit." Ch. 42, "Ching shuo," Part I, explains this, saying: "Righteousness means having the great intent to love the world and the ability to bring great benefits to it; it is not necessary that it already exist in application [in order to be called righteousness]." [The translation of this difficult passage follows the Sun Yi-jang commentary.] Here it is clear that what are called love and benefit agree completely with the Confucian principle of extensively dispensing succor to the masses. [Analects, VI/28, where this is described as the acme of jen.] What Mencius denounced as "benefit" [li] was precisely what the Mohists rejected as "partiality" [pieh]. They differed in their use of terms, but there is in fact no great difference between the principles they were establishing.

However, there do appear to exist some differences between Confucian and Mohist statements about love, with respect to the gradations in its application and the sources from which it comes into existence. These discrepancies must be clearly distinguished. Let us first discuss the grades of the application of love. Although Confucians held up as the highest ideal to "be benevolent to all men and lovingly concerned about all creatures," thereby "bringing the whole world to goodness" [Mencius, VII/i/45 and VII/i/9/6] as the highest ideal in the practice of benevolence,

---

[38] "Liang Hui-wang," Part I [Mencius, I/i]: "Mencius went to see King Hui of Liang. The King said, 'Venerable sir, since you have not counted it far to come here, a distance of a thousand li [miles], may I presume that you are likewise provided with counsels to profit [li] my kingdom?' Mencius replied, 'Why must your Majesty use that word 'profit?' What I am 'likewise' provided with, are counsels to benevolence and righteousness, and these are my only topics. If your Majesty say, 'What is to be done to profit my kingdom?' the Great Officers will say, 'What is to be done to profit our families?' and the inferior officers and the common people will say 'What is to be done to profit our persons?' Superiors and inferiors will try to snatch this profit the one from the other, and the kingdom will be endangered.' " [Slightly modified from Legge, pp. 125–26.]

yet they consistently and firmly upheld the principle that one's beneficence should be extended to others in degrees of intensity and in a priority sequence determined by family relationship, and by distance. Thus it was said: "When one's family has been regulated, then the state will be rightly governed." [*Great Learning*, paragraph 5, modified from Legge, p. 359.] And further: "Treat with reverence due to age the elders in your own family, so that the elders in the families of others shall be similarly treated; treat with the kindness due to youth the young in your own family, so that the young in the families of others shall be similarly treated." [*Mencius*, 1/i/7/12; Legge, p. 143.] The clan-law society background, from which the thought of Confucius and Mencius never detached itself, inevitably was reflected in the ranks and grades of "all-embracing love." Mo Tzu, however, was a humble man who had neither the personal associations with the clan-law system, nor any sympathetic nostalgia for it. Thus his theory of universal love, while not denying the family and its social bonds,[39] was relatively more concerned with universalizing love and material benefits.

Mencius' statements in refuting the philosopher Yi Chih are probably the best illustration of the two schools' divergence on this. [Yi Chih was a Mohist.] Yi Chih said: "According to the teachings of the Confucians, the ancients acted toward the people 'as if they were watching over an infant.' What does this expression mean? To me it sounds that we are to love all without difference of degree; but the manifestation of love must begin with our parents." Mencius refuted this saying: "Now, does Yi really think that a man's affection for the child of his brother is *merely* like his affection for the infant of a neighbor?"[40] Each person feels closest to his own family, and feels parental regard toward his own children; that is indeed a natural tendency of all humankind. The Confucians made use of this as the foundation of their extensive love; the Mohists, on the other hand, transcended it in the hope of directly achieving the Great Community. We can observe herein that Mo Tzu began by accepting the Confucian teachings about benevolence and righteousness, but ended up by

[39] Throughout the *Mo Tzu* one encounters in many places comments touching on the father-son, elder-younger brother, and husband-wife relationships. And *ch.* 14, "Chien ai," Part 1 also uses such terms as "filial" [*hsiao*] and "affection"or "kindliness" [*tz'u*]. *Ch.* 40, "Ching," Part 1 states: "To be filial is to profit one's parents." *Ch.* 42, "Ching shuo," Part 1 [which is an exposition of *ch.* 40], states: "To be filial is to regard one's parents with love and to have the capacity to profit one's parents, and not necessarily thereby to gain their approval." *Ch.* 11, 12, 13, "Shang t'ung," discussing the methods of elevating and identifying with the superior, speaks of first accomplishing this in the family, then extending it to the country and finally to the whole world, the sequence here being the same as that of the Confucians.

[40] *Mencius*, "T'eng wen-kung," Part 1 [III/i/5/3; Legge, pp. 257–58; Chan, *Source Book*, pp. 70–71].

having to diverge from them, altering his objective in raising aloft his own banner of universal love.

Discussing the sources of benevolence and love, moreover, they again display a discrepancy. In talking about benevolence, Confucius saw its point of origin in the benevolent mind of each individual. Mencius discussed benevolence as something incipient in the commiserating mind of man. [Cf. *Mencius*, II/i/6 and VI/i/6/7; "The incipient state," or *tuan* 端, is sometimes translated as the bud, or the tender shoot, of the innate capacity for virtue.] Both called attention to subjective feelings; they did not regard the objective consequences as essential to the quality of benevolence and love. Mo Tzu, however, no longer attached such importance to the individual's character, and tended toward adopting a standard for loving or hating things that directly reflected their material benefit or harm. Therefore throughout the three parts of his essay on universal love [*ch.* 14–16] one finds mostly a careful weighing of the greater rewards paid by universality as contrasted with partiality, and absolute silence on the matter of the subjective feelings of benevolence and love.

And that is not all. Mencius declared his belief in the goodness of human nature. Therefore he spoke of the benevolent mind and benevolent government, both of which he saw as founded in man's natural feelings. The *Mo Tzu* repeatedly hints that human nature is evil.[41] That which he describes in *ch.* 11, "Shang t'ung," Part I, as "In the beginning of human life when there was yet no law and government . . . everyone worked for the disadvantage of others with water, fire, and poisons" is in truth essentially the same as the situation Hsün Tzu sets forth in his essay presenting his view that human nature is fundamentally evil. [The quotation follows the translation of Y. P. Mei, *Works*, p. 55.] Hence Mo Tzu sought to establish universality and abolish partiality, not because he considered mutual love to be the natural temper of mankind, but rather because he hoped by his theory of mutual benefits to overcome man's natural predilection for selfishness and for harming others. If this explanation is not

---

[41] Mo Tzu's thought contains an element of utilitarianism, and his observations on human nature somewhat resemble those of the English philosopher Jeremy Bentham. *Ch.* 40, "Ching," Part I states: "Profit is something that delights one who obtains it. . . . Injury is something hated by the person who receives it." This is very close in meaning to the passage on page one of *An Introduction to the Principles of Morals and Legislation*: "P. 1, iii, by utility is meant that property in any object, whereby it tends to produce benefit, advantage, pleasure, good, or happiness (all this in the present case comes to the same thing), or (what comes again to the same thing) to prevent the happening of mischief, pain, evil, or unhappiness to the party whose interest is considered: if that party be the community in general, then the happiness of the community; if a particular individual, then the happiness of that individual." Also it should be noted that Hsün Tzu, who held the view that man's nature is evil, was later than Mo Tzu. In the *Hsün Tzu*, Mo Tzu is denounced for such ideas as economy of expenditure, simplicity in funerals, condemnation of music, esteem for utilitarian values, and the breakdown of social ranks and classes, but he never touches on Mo Tzu's universal love, in this greatly at variance with Mencius.

seriously wrong, then on the basis of it we may conclude that although the Confucians and the Mohists were one in preaching benevolence and love, yet in so doing their points of departure were a vast distance apart. The essential element in the problem of their similarities and differences would seem to lie right here.

SECTION THREE
Agreement with the Superior

IN the past the English philosopher Jeremy Bentham said that "utility" was the force that guided all of man's actions, and that the application of utility depended on the sanctions imposed by government, morality and religion.[42] Mo Tzu's political thought found its starting point in the choice between benefit and harm, and went on to establish the doctrines of agreement with the superior, of the will of Heaven, and of the proof of the existence of spirits, to insure the practice of universal love. Agreement with the superior may be regarded as Mo Tzu's political sanction, while the will of Heaven and the existence of spirits became his religious sanctions. ["Identification with one's superior" is another standard translation of the term shang t'ung 尚同; both meanings are included in it.]

The principal reason why universal love must [in practice] depend on the agreement with the superior is that man's nature is basically evil. When one gains advantage he is happy; when he suffers harm he is displeased. To seek advantage and avoid harm is simply an expression of man's own nature. If this is not subjected to some external restrictive force, it will inevitably carry man to utter disorder. Therefore there must be erected one political authority for all the world in common, to supply the standards for everyone's conduct, thereby to cause the individual to rid himself of selfishness and to devote his efforts to the common good. What Mo Tzu referred to as the agreement with the superior [shang t'ung] is little more than just this. We may well cite ch. 11, "Shang t'ung," Part I, to illustrate this. "Mo Tzu said: 'In the beginning of human life, when there was yet no law and government, the custom was: Everyone according to his own idea. Accordingly, each man had his own idea, two men had two different ideas, and ten men had ten different ideas—the more people the more different notions.[43] And as everyone approved of his own

[42] An Introduction to the Principles of Morals and Legislation, Chapter Three. See also A Fragment on Government.

[43] Note that ch. 40, "Ching," Part I, defines: "Righteousness is profit." What the passage quoted refers to as "everyone according to his own idea" probably does not refer exclusively to theoretical issues of what is true and what is false but applies to differing opinions about profit and injury. This can be seen by reading the whole of this chapter [ch. 11] plus chs. 12 and 13, "Shang t'ung," Parts II and III.

view and disapproved the views of others, so arose mutual disapproval among men. As a result, father and son, and elder and younger brothers, became enemies and were estranged from each other, since they were unable to reach any agreement. Everyone worked for the disadvantage of others with water, fire, and poison. Surplus energy was not spent for mutual aid; surplus goods were allowed to rot without sharing; the good ways were kept secret and not revealed. The disorder of the human world could be compared to that among birds and beasts. Yet all this disorder was due to the want of a ruler. Therefore [Heaven] (chose) the most virtuous in the world and established him as the Son of Heaven. [See Y. P. Mei, *Works*, p. 56, for his reasons for inserting "Heaven" as subject in this sentence. This agrees with the author's views, as expressed near the end of this section, and in Section Two of this chapter.] Once established, the Son of Heaven felt his strength inadequate, so he selected the most virtuous men in the world and installed them as his Three Senior Lords. When the Son of Heaven and the Three Senior Lords were installed, seeing the vastness of the world and the difficulty of attending to matters of right and wrong and benefit and harm among peoples of far countries, they divided the world into the myriad states and established in them the feudal lords and rulers. These feudal lords and rulers of states once installed, they felt their strength inadequate, and made a further selection of the virtuous of their states and installed them as officials [*cheng chang* 正長]. When these officials were all installed, the Son of Heaven issued a rescript to all the people, saying: 'Upon hearing good or evil, everyone shall report it to a superior. What the superior thinks to be right, all shall think to be right; what the superior thinks to be wrong, all shall think to be wrong. When the superior is at fault, there shall be corrective counsel; when the subordinates show virtue, they shall be sought out and recommended for service.' To identify one's self with [or agree with] the superior and not to unite one's self with the inferiors—this is what deserves encouragement from above and praise from below. On the other hand, if upon hearing good or evil one should fail to report to a superior; if what the superior has decided to be right one thinks not to be right; if what the superior has decided to be wrong one thinks not to be wrong; if when the superior was at fault there should be no corrective counsel; if when inferiors showed virtue there should be no seeking out and recommending for service; if people should make common cause with inferiors and not agree with the superior—this is what deserves punishment from above and condemnation from below.' "[44]

[44] [Translation follows that of Y. P. Mei, *Works*, pp. 55–56, with minor changes. See also Watson, *Mo Tzu*, pp. 34–36.] Note that Mo Tzu, in addition to his rewards and punishments, which served as his "political sanctions," also always referred to the condemnation and praise of the people at large, which operated as a "social sanction." This passage offers one example of that.

The erection of a political system started with the selection of a Son of Heaven; this was done from above and imposed on those below. However, the work of achieving agreement with the superior was carried out from each hamlet and each household; it was done from below, and it reached all the way to the top. Mo Tzu said: "For this reason, the neighborhood headman [*li-chang*] was the most benevolent [*jen*] man of the neighborhood. He notified the people of the neighborhood, saying: 'Upon hearing good or evil you shall report it to the head of the village [*hsiang chang*]. What the head of the village thinks to be right, all shall think to be right. What he thinks to be wrong, all shall think to be wrong. Put away from your speech that which is not good and learn his good speech. Remove from your conduct that which is not good and learn his good conduct. How can there then be disorder in the village?' Now, how was order brought about in the village? There was order in the village because the head could unify the ideas in the village. The village head was the most benevolent man in the village. He notified the people of the village, saying: 'Upon hearing good or evil, you shall report it to the ruler of the state. What the ruler thinks to be right, all shall think to be right; what he thinks to be wrong, all shall think to be wrong. Remove from your speech that which is not good and learn his good speech. Take away from your conduct that which is not good and learn his good conduct. How then can there be disorder in the state?' Now, how was order brought about in the state. There was order in the feudal state because the ruler could unify the ideas in the state. The ruler of the state was the most benevolent man in the state. He instructed the people of the state, saying: 'Upon hearing good or evil, you shall report it to the Son of Heaven. What the Son of Heaven thinks to be right, all shall think to be right; what the Son of Heaven thinks to be wrong, all shall think to be wrong. Take away from your speech that which is not good and learn his good speech. Remove from your conduct that which is not good and learn his good conduct. How then can there be disorder in the world?' Now, how was order brought about in the world? There was order in the world because the Son of Heaven could unify the ideas of the world."

These are the words of Mo Tzu as recorded in *ch*. 11, "Shang t'ung," Part I. *Ch*. 12, Part II, says more or less the same thing. *Ch*. 13, Part III, does not mention the neighborhood and village, but says: "Let the clan-head issue laws and proclaim to the clan saying; 'Whoever discovers someone who loves and benefits the clan must report it; whoever discovers one who hates and hurts the clan also must report it. Whoever sees someone who loves and benefits the clan and reports it is himself to be regarded as one who loves and benefits the clan. Learning about it, the superior shall reward him; hearing of it, all the people will praise him.' " And it also says: "Once the clan is ordered, is the way of the state then complete in this or not? It is not. The number of clans comprising the state is great indeed. They all approve of their own clan and disapprove of other clans, in consequence of which there is chaos among the strong clans and struggle among the weak. Therefore, it is necessary further to have the clan heads to bring together the ideas of the clan and identify all of these with the superior in the person of the ruler of the state." [The foregoing quotations are modified somewhat from Y. P. Mei, *Works*, pp. 55–58 and 73.] And the ruler of the [feudal] state in turn issues laws and synthesizes ideas, and identifies with the superior in the person of the Son of Heaven. In this way the world is brought to peace and order. And after laws and government have been thus established, the rulers and superiors hover above, while the system of rewards and punishments, condemnations and praise, drives on all below, so that even where the people of the world might want not to love universally and mutually benefit each other, they would be able to find no way of getting around it.

The significance of this agreement with the superior is easily grasped; there is no need to illustrate it or expatiate further on it. However, we should note that although Mo Tzu stressed political sanctions, yet he was not like the various Legalist thinkers in their tendency to favor monarchic despotism. In simplest terms, the Mohists' agreement with the superior was in fact a transformed version of the theory of government for the people. For, the reason the ruler was able to maintain his rule over the people was that he could firmly sustain the goal of the common good, taking that as his standard for agreement with the superior. If the ruler did not fulfill this fundamental obligation, he lost the basis of his personal rulership, and had no means of ruling.

Ch. 12, Part II, sets up some questions and answers to clarify this point, saying: "People might then ask: At the present time rulers are not absent from the world, why then is there disorder in it? Mo Tzu said: The officials of government of the present day are quite different from those of old. . . . Thus we see in ancient times the installing of government officials was so that they would then govern well the people. They may be compared to the skein on which the floss is wound, or the drawstring on a fishing net; in the same way the official is to draw together all of the unbridled and violent ones in the world and unify their ideas by making them agree [with the superior]. . . . But the princes and lords and great men of our time are just the opposite of that in their maintenance of laws and government. Government is done by flattery. Fathers and brothers and other relatives and friends are placed at the right and left and appointed officials. The people know that these officials are placed there by the ruler, not for the sake of governing the people well; therefore they all remain distant and aloof, and will not agree with the superior in the person of such a ruler. In consequence, the ideas of superior and inferior cannot be unified. And whenever the ideas of superior and inferior cannot be unified, rewards and praise are not enough to encourage the people to do good, while punishments and fines are not adequate to dissuade them from evil. How do we know that this is so? In governing the country, the ruler proclaims: 'Whoever deserves reward I will reward.' Suppose the ideas of the superior and the inferiors are different, whoever is rewarded by the superior will be condemned by the public. That would be 'to dwell amidst the people and be condemned by the masses.' Though there is reward from the superior, it will not serve to encourage them. In governing the country, again, the ruler proclaims: 'Whoever deserves punishment, I will punish.' But if the ideas of the superior and the inferiors are different, the one punished by the superior may be applauded by the masses. That would be to dwell amidst the people and be praised by the masses. Though there is punishment from the superior, it will not serve to dissuade them. Now in establishing a government for the country and installing officials over the people, if rewards cannot induce people to do good and punishments cannot restrain them from doing evil, is this not just the same as in the beginning of human life when there were no rulers?" [The foregoing is slightly modified from the translation of Y. P. Mei, *Works*, pp. 66–67.]

Here we find that Mo Tzu has both said: "What the superior thinks to be right, all shall think to be right; what the superior thinks to be wrong, all shall think to be wrong," and also: "Whoever is rewarded by the superior may be condemned by the masses, and whoever is punished by the superior may be applauded by the masses." Is not Mo Tzu here contradicting himself? Mo Tzu seems to have acknowledged that the public good was the ultimate standard by which to unify ideas, and that both rulers and people should hold the benefiting of the whole society to be their common objective. If the rulers always could carry out their political sanctions according to this public good, then the rulers' ideas, as the embodiment of the public good, would serve as the focus of the whole group in their agreeing with and identifying with the superior. It was not as if the ruler personally possessed the overawing power to decide as he wished what was right and what was wrong. If the ruler did not comprehend this basic principle of group responsibility for governing the people, then the ruler's "ideas" would be nothing more than "one man having his own ideas"; in that case, how could he hope to gain the masses' agreement with the superior?[45]

---

[45] The *Mo Tzu* contains no doctrine of the right to kill a tyrannical ruler, and thus Mo Tzu's philosophic conviction that the people are of fundamental importance seems far less strikingly evident than in the case of Mencius. Fung Yu-lan, in his *History of Chinese Philosophy*, Chapter Five, Section Eight [Fung/Bodde, Vol. i, pp. 100 ff.], observes that the theory of the agreement [or identification] with the superior much resembles the thought of the English philosopher Hobbes (Thomas Hobbes, *Leviathan*, pt. i, ch. 17;

And we may go still further: Not only was Mo Tzu's ideal form of political institutions not that of absolute despotism; it also was not that of a single unified authoritarian system. Mo Tzu lived in the early years of the Warring States Era, still a long time off from the subsequent unification of the realm effected by the First Emperor of Ch'in. Although he was unwilling to go along with Confucius' support of the Chou dynasty, he also was unable to pin his hope, as [later] Mencius would, on the emergence of a new royal power. This was quite natural to those circumstances, in no sense surprising. Hence his theory about agreement with the superior of necessity looked to a world divided into fiefs, upholding ideas the feudal rulers were agreed upon. If this concept had been carried into practice, and had been applied in conjunction with Mo Tzu's universal love and his disapproval of offensive warfare and other methods of governing, then the Son of Heaven would have sat on his throne, and feudal rulers would have governed in their separate states. The feudal states all would have been preserved, and the seven final contestants [for total hegemony] would never have appeared. The Western Chou system in that way might again have re-emerged, long after King P'ing's transfer of the capital to the east. [The designation "Western Chou" denotes the early centuries of Chou rule, when its capital was in the West, near modern Sian, prior to the disastrous collapse of Chou power and the flight of King P'ing in 769 B.C., after which the capital was at Lo-yang.] Mo Tzu's ideal of the agreement with the superior was in fact a reflection of the same feudal-age political circumstances as Confucius' ideal, expressed in his statement that [when the kingdom is well-governed], ". . . ceremonies, music and punitive military expeditions proceed from the Son of Heaven." [*Analects*, XVI/2.] Mo Tzu's ideal does not embody any fundamentally different, original conceptions.

---

pt. II, ch. 29). This observation is not lacking in perception. However, we should note that Hobbes denies religion's authority, and accepts the social contract, while Mo Tzu acknowledges the will of Heaven and lacks the concept of the social contract. *Ch.* 40, "Ching," Part I, states, "The ruler, the minister, the people are embraced within an agreement," which someone might take to be the same as the social contract of Western philosophers. However, Sun Yi-jang's commentary explains this as "to be in agreement and embraced within [the different ranks of society], there are only these three terms [to convey the meaning of the whole]." Thus it explains further, "ruler is to be taken as a term." Although this interpretation [i.e., to regard the passage as part of a discussion of the logic of terminology], may not be wholly certain, it would seem to be less forced and far-fetched than to explain it as a reference to the social contract. For there simply is no possibility of such a concept's having being produced in the Spring and Autumn and Warring States Periods. Moreover, if Mo Tzu had produced a new theory of this kind, he certainly would have enlarged upon and developed it, and would not have left it to a few incidental words in passing. That such an interpretation would be arbitrary and unfounded should be quite obvious.

Before we conclude this section, there still remain two important questions that we must attempt to explicate. The first is that Mo Tzu has declared that when law and government first arose, it was by selection of a virtuous person to be the Son of Heaven. By whose hand was this selection of the Son of Heaven accomplished? Recently some scholars have argued that Mo Tzu expressed support for a popular election system.[46] We should note that in the absence of any explicit statement about popular elections in the *Mo Tzu*, and with no possibility that the concept of popular elections could have developed out of those historical backgrounds or within Mo Tzu's thought system itself, arbitrarily to impose an interpretation concluding that such meaning must be there, undoubtedly makes one guilty of seriously traducing Mo Tzu. At a time before any law and government yet existed and [according to Mo Tzu] people all had their divergent ideas, contending with and doing injury to each other, who could believe that such people, "as disorderly as the birds and beasts," would be able to consult among each other and arrive at a common opinion about the selection of a virtuous person whom all could support? Therefore we declare: the concept of popular elections is not consonant with Mo Tzu's thought [either as Mo Tzu's idealized explanation of how ancient man acquired his rulers, or as a proposal for Mo Tzu's own time].

Among China's ancient legends is that of the Sage Emperors, who passed the royal succession to the most virtuous and worthy man who could be found, instead of to their own eldest sons. But there is absolutely no suggestion anywhere of election by the people of their ruler. This is even so of Mencius, with his strong views about the importance of the people. He developed the idea that the way to become the Son of Heaven was to gain the peasantry [*Mencius*, vii/ii/14/2; Legge, pp. 483–84]. Yet when we look more carefully into the truth of it, he no more than acknowledged that after selection of a sovereign had been decided, either through transmission to the most worthy or transmission to the eldest son; the people still had the opportunity to express whether or not they would give their voluntary support to the new ruler. He did not mean that the people could directly select the most worthy and most suitable candidate, much less did he imply that even before governmental leaders had been instituted, could the people cautiously weigh the merits of all the possible

[46] Fang Shou-ch'u in his *Mo-hsüeh yüan-liu*, Part i, p. 85, states that the Son of Heaven "is responsible to the people . . . hence that which selected him must also have been the people." He also states that the textual references to this selection "may have been altered by later Mohist followers in revising Mo Tzu's theories so that selected by Heaven became selected by the people." Yang Yu-chiung, *Chung-kuo cheng-chih ssu-hsiang shih*, i.e., "History of Chinese Political Thought," p. 123, basing himself directly on the text of *ch.* 11, "Shang t'ung," Part i, writes: "Mo Tzu went still further and talked about the way political institutions could actually be established; that is, they were to be generated by a systematic and well-organized institution of popular elections." [!]

selections from among the countless masses of the people and settle on one who would thereby be confirmed in the position of chief leader of the world. We have said, therefore, that the popular election interpretation of this aspect of Mohism is something that the historical background does not allow. If we abandon all such fanciful hypotheses and confine ourselves to the overall character of Mo Tzu's thought to draw our inference, that then will be that instituting a Son of Heaven must have expressed the will of Heaven [*t'ien chih* 天志], not that it was an act of popular selection. For convenience in presentation, the discussion of this will be reserved for the following section.

Our second problematical issue is that the function of agreeing with the superior was to establish concrete institutions of government that would guarantee the realization of universal love. Therefore, in Mo Tzu's thought, the relationship between the agreement with the superior and universal love is somewhat analogous to that between the rectification of terms and the practice of benevolence in the thought of Confucius. However, Confucius' rectification of terms was done in the name of following the Chou, while Mo Tzu's agreement with the superior did not advocate the supremacy of any particular past dynasty, to the exclusion of others. Why was this? Our hypothesis is that Mo Tzu's historical background as a low-status descendant of the Yin people might be one possible reason. Confucius was born in the State of Lu and he served Lu as an official. Even though he was the descendant of an aristocratic clan of the State of Sung [identifying him with the descendants of the Shang-Yin dynasty], he nonetheless could not have escaped being profoundly affected by the *Institutes of Chou*. Mo Tzu, on the other hand, had no possibility of establishing close connections either with the Chou tradition or with the State of Lu, so that his lack of sympathy for the *Institutes of Chou* is only what we might expect that situation to have produced.

Confucius, moreover, was completely immersed in antiquarian lore, and quite clear about the continuity and change in the transmission of institutions from one dynasty to the next, and of the sources of the governmental forms in the various feudal states. He himself had a basis for picking and choosing among these, and consequently went along with the State of Lu in following the Chou models. Hence his discussions of institutions are usually quite rich in historical and regional import. Mo Tzu, on the other hand, stressed actual practice, and may not have devoted himself in that same way to the "fondness for antiquity and diligence in pursuing it" through scholarly activity. Although his statements often cite the former kings, his intent is merely to seek authority in antiquity for his own teachings. He did not really want to put ancient institutions into practice.

Finally, Mo Tzu was himself a man of lowest social status; he had thus no nostalgia for the old Yin dynasty, and all the less was he prepared to follow the Chou system. Nor did he show a particular predilection for the institutions and doctrines of any of the feudal states of his own time. Hence his teachings are relatively lacking in historical and regional character, and display a somewhat more universal coloring.

SECTION FOUR
The Will of Heaven and the Existence of Spirits

Mo Tzu, having established the agreement [or identification] with the superior as a political sanction, still felt that to be inadequate; he thus proceeded to promote theories of the will of Heaven, and about the existence of spirits, in order to have religious sanctions as well. Thus he says in *ch.* 11, "Shang t'ung," Part I: "If, however, the people all identify themselves with the Son of Heaven but not with Heaven itself, then the disaster is still unremoved. Now, the frequent visitations of hurricanes and torrents are just the punishments from Heaven upon the people for their not identifying their standards with the will of Heaven." [Cf. Y. P. Mei's translation, *Works*, p. 58.]

Mo Tzu's theory of the will of Heaven appears to rest on three foundations. (1) Mo Tzu held that: "To accomplish anything whatsoever, one must have standards." Square and compass, carpenter's chalk-line and pendulum, serve the artisans as standards. Ruler, teacher, and parents similarly serve the people as standards. However, the rulers, teachers, and parents in the world are countless, while "benevolent ones are very few." If they are to be taken as standards, "this could be to emulate the non-benevolent." Thus, since ruler, teacher, and parents are not reliable models, the only thing left to serve as a standard is Heaven. For "Heaven is all-inclusive and impartial in its activities, abundant and impartial in its blessings, lasting and unfailing in its guidance. Hence, the Sage Kings modeled themselves upon it."[47] (2) Heaven is the master over the whole race; its rewards and punishments are rigorously and clearly bestowed on all alike, and are inescapable. It is not like offending the head of one's clan or the head of one's state, when one can still flee to refuge in a neighboring household or a neighboring state. Therefore men cannot but adopt an attitude of absolute subservience toward Heaven.[48] (3) Heaven possesses awesome powers of control over mankind, and not even the Son of Heaven can evade its dispensation of rewards and punishments. Therefore, "Mo Tzu said: 'Those gentlemen in the world who want to practice benevolence and righteousness, cannot but examine the origin of righteousness. Since we want to examine the origin of righteousness, where

[47] *Ch.* 4, "Fa yi" [modified from Y. P. Mei, *Works*, p. 14].
[48] *Ch.* 26, "T'ien-chih," Part I.

then does it originate?' Mo Tzu said: 'Righteousness does not originate with those both stupid and lowly, but with those both honorable and wise. ["Honorable" in the sense of "possessing noble status," the opposite of "lowly."] How do we know it does not originate with the stupid and lowly but with the honorable and wise? For, righteousness is the standard. How do we know righteousness is the standard? For with righteousness the world will be orderly, and without it the world will be disorderly. Therefore, righteousness is known to be the standard. As the stupid and the lowly cannot make the standard, and only the wise and honorable can, therefore I know righteousness does not come from the stupid and lowly, but from the honorable and wise. Now who is honorable, and who is wise? Heaven is honorable, Heaven is wise. So, then, righteousness must originate with Heaven.' People in the world say, 'That the Son of Heaven is more honorable than the feudal lords and the feudal lords more honorable than their Great Officers, we clearly see. But that Heaven is more honorable and more wise than the Son of Heaven, we do not see.' Mo Tzu said, 'I have a reason for knowing that Heaven is more honorable and wise than the Son of Heaven: When the Son of Heaven practices virtue, Heaven rewards him; when the Son of Heaven does evil, Heaven punishes him. When there are disease and calamity, the Son of Heaven will purify and bathe himself and prepare clean cakes and wine to do sacrifice and libation to Heaven and the spirits. And then Heaven can remove those evils. But I have never heard of Heaven invoking the Son of Heaven for blessing. So I know Heaven is more honorable and wise than the Son of Heaven. And this is not all. We also learn of this from the book of the ancient kings which teaches us of the vast and ineffable Way [Tao] of Heaven. It says: Brilliant and perspicacious Heaven on High, which descends and is sovereign over the earth below. [For Legge's rendering of similar lines from the *Book of Odes* as it now exists, see his *She King*, p. 363. Mei's note and translation, *Works*, p. 142, give the erroneous impression that Mo Tzu quotes these lines as they now appear in the *Book of Odes*.] This shows Heaven is both more honorable and wiser than the Son of Heaven. But is there yet anything more honorable and wiser than the Son of Heaven? Heaven is really the most honorable and the wisest. Therefore, righteousness surely comes from Heaven.' "[49]

Since this says ". . . descends and is sovereign over the world below," Heaven's control over the Son of Heaven is like the Son of Heaven's control over the Three Senior Lords and the feudal princes, and the control of the rulers of states and heads of families over the common people and the sons or younger brothers in the family.[50] Hence the whole political

[49] *Ch.* 27, "T'ien-chih," Part II [modified somewhat from Y. P. Mei, *Works*, pp. 140–42].

[50] *Ch.* 26, "T'ien-chih," Part I.

structure that Mo Tzu envisaged was much like the layered structure of a pagoda. The Will of Heaven was the finial atop its highest point, and going downward from this one encountered the Son of Heaven, the Three Senior Lords [*san kung*], the rulers of the feudal states [*kuo chün*], generals [*chiang-chün*], great officers [*ta-fu*], the ordinary knights [*shih*], through all of these ranks until one came to the base-layer, the common people.

Moreover, as the Son of Heaven experienced the controlling power of Heaven, it was no vague and distant, baseless sort of empty talk. Mo Tzu believed that the ancient Sage Kings Yao, Shun, Yü, T'ang, Wen, and Wu had all gained their reward directly as a result of having conformed to Heaven's intents, whereas all of the tyrants like Kings Chieh, Chou, Yu, and Li had suffered their punishments as the consequence of having rebelled against Heaven's intents. [Chieh and Chou are well-known as the bad last Kings of Hsia and Shang-Yin; Mo Tzu also adds the two Kings of the later Western Chou period whose behavior was held responsible for disastrous events.] "The virtuous were promoted and exalted; the vicious were kept back and banished."[51] Good and evil are clearly distinguished, and they brought the expected retribution. The hearts of the people may incline toward or away from them, may accept their leadership or reject it, but only by expressing this in criticisms or praise of their ruler after Heaven's will [*t'ien chih*] has already been made known; they have no capacity for deciding such issues or guiding their outcome before the event.[52] If one but notes that the banishing or installing of rulers and relevant issues of succession to the throne were determined

---

[51] *Ch.* 9, "Shang hsien," Part II [following Y. P. Mei, *Works*, p. 44]; *ch.* 26, "T'ien-chih," Part I, contains a parallel passage with slight difference of wording.

[52] *Ch.* 9, "Shang hsien," Part II: "Now, who were those that, possessing wealth and position, still strove after virtue and were rewarded (by Heaven)? They were the sage-kings of the Three Dynasties, namely, Yao, Shun, Yü, T'ang, Wen, and Wu. How were they rewarded? When they governed the empire, they loved all the people universally and benefited them, and led them in doing honour to Heaven and service to the spirits. As they loved and benefited the people, Heaven and the spirits rewarded them, appointing them to be the Sons of Heaven, and parents of the people. And, thereupon people praised them, calling them Sage Kings even unto this day. These, then, were those that, possessing wealth and position, still strove after virtues and were rewarded. Now, who were those that, possessing wealth and position, yet practiced evil and were punished? They were the wicked kings of the Three Dynasties, namely, Chieh, Chou, Yu, and Li. How do we know they were those? When they governed the empire they hated all the people and oppressed them and led them to curse Heaven and the spirits. Oppressing and destroying the people, they were punished by Heaven and the spirits; their corpses were mangled and lacerated; their children and grand-children were scattered and dispersed; their family hearths were extinguished and their descendants exterminated. And all the people revile them, calling them wicked kings, even unto this day. These, then, are those that, possessing wealth and position, yet practiced evil and were punished." [Slightly modified from Y. P. Mei, *Works*, pp. 44–45.]

by Heaven and not decided by the people, then all the more it should be self-evident that, in the beginning before law and government existed, the selection of the Son of Heaven also must have been regarded as an act of Heaven and not an act of the people.[53] In the preceding chapter we have discussed Mencius' doctrine of the importance of the people, noting that he quoted in this connection from the old-text *Book of History* the lines: "Heaven sees as my people see; heaven hears as my people hear." This is adequate proof that his doctrine was built on the belief that "heaven's approval" was granted to that which "the people accepted." Now as we examine Mo Tzu's will of Heaven, we find its fundamental import to be diametrically opposed to Mencius' view, for it binds man's acceptance to that which Heaven has approved. Thus Mo Tzu's thought, in modern terminology, must be considered purely a doctrine of celestial-right (or divine right), having nothing whatsoever in common with the theory of popular right [or the people's will].

Beyond that, in addition to his doctrine of the will of Heaven, Mo Tzu also held a concurrent faith in the existence of spirits; he believed that ghosts and spiritual beings in their rewarding and punishing of good and evil, thereby controlling both the ruler and the people, were one with the will of Heaven. Moreover, he repeatedly cited stories of ghosts and spirits from the past as proof that this was so, and to rebut the view that there were no spirits. For Mo Tzu was profoundly convinced that the chaos in the world and among the people was the result of ". . . doubt of the existence of the ghosts and spirits, and ignorance of their being able to reward virtue and punish vice."[54] This again is completely different from the Confucian attitude of remaining aloof from spiritual beings.

Mo Tzu's reason for promoting this reverence for Heaven and for spirits clearly is that he wanted to use divine authority as a force to strengthen his own theories. Therefore all of those doctrines which Mo Tzu constantly went about promoting, such as universal love, anti-aggression, austerity in consumption, and the like, were declared to be the

---

[53] *Ch.* 13, "Shang t'ung," Part III: "Thereupon Heaven wished to unify the standards in the world. The virtuous was selected and made the Son of Heaven . . ." [modified slightly from Y. P. Mei, *Works*, p. 71]. Sun Yi-jang suspects that the first "*T'ien-hsia*," i.e., "the world," in this passage should be simply the word "*T'ien*," "Heaven." [Mei has translated the passage in this way.] Basing himself on this passage, Fang Shou-ch'u, in his *Mo-hsüeh yüan-liu*, Part I, p. 84, says: "The selector is Heaven; this therefore expresses the doctrine that royal authority is divinely (i.e., celestially) conferred." It might well seem more accurate and more appropriate to base this conclusion on the entire system of Mohist doctrine. [The term "heaven" or *t'ien* usually is not capitalized in this translation of K. C. Hsiao's work, except where it is capitalized in other English translations of early Chinese writings that are quoted verbatim. In quotations from the *Mo Tzu*, however, "Heaven" is capitalized here, to suggest the special quality of Mo Tzu's conception.]

[54] *Ch.* 31, "Ming kuei," Part III [Y. P. Mei, *Works*, p. 160]. (Parts I and II are no longer extant.)

things that Heaven and the spirits liked, while anything running counter to them was said to be that which they abominated.[55] Consequently those who practiced the Mohist doctrines were sure to be the recipients of the good fortune dispensed by Heaven and the spirits; their rewards were not merely to be the granting of rank and wealth by the ruler and his officials, or the praise of the community, or the recompense from other persons. However, even if by "establishing his doctrines according to the Way of the spirits" he was able to convince people and transform their ways, did it in fact contribute positively toward the preservation and effective realization of Mohist doctrine? In view of the actual facts of the case, we can conclude that it did not necessarily do so. For example, the incidents involving heaven and spirits recorded in the *Tso Chuan* are numerous. Evil spirits like the ghosts of P'eng-sheng and Po-yu were particularly effective in bringing about retribution that was both un-equivocal and speedy. [For P'eng-sheng, i.e., P'ang-sang, see *Tso Chuan*, under Eighth year of Duke Chuang; Legge, p. 82. For Po-yu, i.e., Pih-yëw, see under Seventh year of Duke Chao; Legge, p. 618.] Yet the rulers of the Spring and Autumn Period, although credulous and fearful, still never were so affected by these incidents that they gave up their lascivious and unrestrained conduct to be transformed into better men. So it is also obvious that tales of ghosts and spirits were not enough to threaten or effectively warn the recalcitrant offender. Moreover, to establish doctrines according to the Way of the spirits, although an inevitable phenomenon in primitive societies, is something that loses its effectiveness the more a people's knowledge begins to expand, so that once their pristine naïveté has been shattered, they may not again revert to the state of willing belief that Heaven [i.e., in the specifically religious conception of Mo Tzu] and spirits must be real. On the basis of the evidence recorded in *ch.* 48, "Kung Meng," even among his disciples there were some who expressed doubts about his statements that ghosts and spirits really could command evil and good fortune.[56] In upholding this view in debate against the

[55] *Ch.* 27, "T'ien-chih," Part II, and *ch.* 31, "Ming kuei," Part III.

[56] *Ch.* 48, "Kung Meng": "A man visited Mo Tzu's school and said to Mo Tzu: 'Sir, you teach that the ghosts and spirits are intelligent and can bring calamity and blessing to man, bringing blessings to the good and harm to the evil. Now, I have served you for a long time, yet no blessing has come? Can it be that your teaching is not entirely correct, and that the ghosts and spirits are not intelligent? Else why don't I obtain any blessing?' " And, "Mo Tzu was sick. T'ieh-pi came and inquired: 'Sir, you have taught that the ghosts and spirits are intelligent and are in control of calamity and blessing, bringing reward to the good and punishing the evil. Now you are a sage. Why is it that you can be ill? Can it be that your teaching was not entirely correct, that the ghosts and spirits are, after all, unintelligent?' " [Modified slightly from Y. P. Mei, *Works*, p. 240.] Moreover, Mo Tzu's insistence on the existence of ghosts and spirits did not necessarily imply his own belief in spirits. *Ch.* 31, "Ming kuei," Part III, says that even if there really are not any ghosts and spirits, the wine and food offerings to them still are useful for [the post-sacrificial] celebrations in which all took part. [Cf. Y. P. Mei, *Works*, p. 173.]

Confucians, hoping to change ways and alter customs so as to lead the world into an era of Great Peace, Mo Tzu was engaging in unavailing efforts. It may be that Mo Tzu, having in mind the common "humble people" as the recipients of his teachings, adopted the superstitions of the common people to reinforce his doctrines. His tactics were quite different from those of Confucius, who established his doctrines from the [upper class] point of view of the knight and Great Officer [*shih ta-fu*] group.[57]

The religious thought of the Mohists was somewhat crudely and loosely conceived and does not warrant profound examination. However, their doctrine of "anti-fatalism" [*fei ming*] possessed the ability to induce self-reliance and clarity of thought; the Confucianists had nothing exactly comparable in this respect. Mo Tzu said: "The fatalists say: 'When fate [*ming*] decrees that a man shall be wealthy, he will be wealthy; when it decrees poverty, he will be poor; when it decrees a large population, it will be large; when it decrees a small population, it will be small; if order is decreed, there will be order; if chaos, there will be chaos. If fate decrees longevity, there will be longevity; if untimely death, there will be untimely death. Even if a man sets himself against his fate, what is the use?' Above, the rulers are persuaded to act in accordance with this in administering the affairs of the government, while below it is applied to block the common people from pursuing their tasks. Hence those who uphold this doctrine of fatalism are not benevolent men."[58]

Mo Tzu explains this further, saying: "Now the rulers go to court early and retire late, hearing lawsuits and attending to government, and meting out justice for the whole day, and dare not be negligent. Why do they do this? They think diligence will bring about order, and negligence chaos; diligence will produce safety, and negligence danger. Therefore

---

[57] Mo Tzu's doctrines about Heaven and spirits may have another source. *Huai-nan Tzu*, ch. 21, "Yao lüeh hsün," states that Mo Tzu repudiated the Way of the Chou and adopted the governmental institutions of the Hsia dynasty. We may note that the *Li Chi*, ch. 29, "Piao chi," says [paragraph 30]: " 'Under the Hsia dynasty it was the way to give honor to the nature [*ming*] conferred on men; they served the manes of the departed, and respected Spiritual Beings [*kuei-shen*], keeping them at a distance. . . . Under the Yin dynasty, they honored Spiritual Beings, and led the people on to serve them; they put first the service of their manes [*shen*], and last the usages of ceremony [*li*]. . . .' " [Quoting Confucius; the translation follows Legge, the *Li Ki*, pp. 341–42.] According to this, Mo Tzu both repudiated the Chou and failed to adopt the ways of the Hsia. May he not have perhaps adopted the Yin dynasty's practice of revering the spirits and giving prime honors to ghosts, however, as a means of countering the Confucians' policy of respecting ghosts and spirits but keeping aloof from them? We may also note that if Mo Tzu in fact studied under the descendants of the archivist Chiao, and that in antiquity the "*wu*" ["sorcerer," or "shaman"] and "*shih*" ["archivist"] were the same persons performing two different functions, may not his doctrines of the will of Heaven and of the existence of spirits be perhaps derived from some remnant of the earlier [Yin] royal ancestral shrine rites?

[58] Ch. 35, "Fei ming," Part I [slightly modified from Y. P. Mei, *Works*, p. 182].

they dare not be negligent. The Ministers and Great Officers exhaust the energy in their limbs and stretch the wisdom of their minds, within to look after the court and without to collect taxes at the passes and markets, on the products of mountain, wood, pond, and field to fill the treasury. They dare not be negligent. Why do they do this? They think diligence will procure honor and negligence dishonor; diligence will procure glory and negligence disgrace. Therefore they dare not be negligent." And so on, all the way down to the farmer, who feels compelled to be diligent in his labors in field and grove, and to the women, who must be similarly diligent in their spinning and weaving; with them too the reason is that they can enjoy wealth if they force themselves to work energetically, but must suffer privation if they are negligent and lax. "Now, if they should believe in fate and behave accordingly, the rulers would be negligent in hearing lawsuits and attending to government; the Ministers and Great Officers would be negligent in attending to court; the farmers would be negligent in sowing their fields and tending their groves; the women would be negligent in weaving and spinning."[59]

Mo Tzu, having shown that belief in fate was not beneficial to society, further uses his "three tests" [san piao] to prove that fate could not possibly exist.[60] In the main, his statements on this are not faulty. Nonetheless, even though Mo Tzu's anti-fatalism, when used to denounce the tyrants of antiquity, is something we might accept,[61] we should note that when used to attack the Confucians, there is an element of injustice in it. For though Confucius and Mencius both held that there was something called fate, neither one ever taught that men should for that reason simply "heed heaven and acquiesce in one's fate." Confucius was a man who "knows it's no use, but keeps on doing it" [Analects, xiv/41; Waley, p. 190], while Mencius urged people on with the phrase: "Work forcefully to accomplish what is good." [Mencius, I/ii/14/3; "forcefully," ch'iang, implies "overcoming resistance."] From this we can see that the fate believed in by Confucius and Mencius was totally different from that which Mo Tzu repudiated. Coming to Hsün Tzu, his concept of "the separation of [the spheres of] heaven and man," is, in the spirit in which he developed this doctrine, not greatly different from that of Mo Tzu when he said: "In ancient times the confusion of the tyrant Chieh was reduced to order by the Sage King

---

[59] Ch. 37, "Fei ming," Part III [following Y. P. Mei, Works, pp. 198–99].

[60] Ch. 36, "Fei ming," Part II [cf. Y. P. Mei, Works, p. 189].

[61] The Book of Documents, in the "Speech of T'ang," quotes King Chieh [the tyrannical last ruler of the Hsia dynasty, confidently], saying: "Why should my fate expire?" (This follows the interpretation of Hsia Tseng-yu, according to whom "hours and days" [in the original] means "the hours and days of my life," or "fate.") And in "The Chief of the West's Conquest of Li," King Chou [the evil last King of the Shang] says: "Oh! Is not my life secured by the Decree [ming] of Heaven?" [Legge, pp. 271–72.]

T'ang, and that of the tyrant Chou by King Wu. Now the times did not change and the people did not alter. Yet when the superior changed a regime the subordiaates modified their conduct. Under T'ang and Wu it was orderly, but under Chieh and Chou it was disorderly. Hence peace and danger, order and disorder, all depend on the government of the superior. How can it be said everything is according to fate?" [Modified slightly from the translation of Y. P. Mei, *Works*, p. 190.] Thus, in relation to the thought of Confucius, Mencius, and Hsün Tzu, it would appear that to attack the Confucians using Mo Tzu's anti-fatalism is virtually to fire without a target.[62]

SECTION FIVE
Elevating the Worthy

CONFUCIUS and Mo Tzu both lived when the late Chou system of hereditary ministerships had degenerated but had still not totally disappeared; it was an age when government in the hands of all powerful officials was just coming into prominence and tending toward still fuller development.[63] In consequence, Confucius revered virtue i.e., *te*, and Mo Tzu elevated the worthy i.e., *hsien* [or "the man of useful virtues"; "*shang*

[62] That which Mo Tzu condemned may well have been the practices of the vulgar Confucians [*su-ju* 俗儒]. We should note that the Confucians in general acknowledge that good should beget reward and evil should bring punishment; however, deeds and their recompense may not always correspond, and the individual must make the most of his own possibilities, "and if he succeeds, it is heaven's doing." This view, as compared with Mo Tzu's [correcting "Confucius" in the text to read "Mo Tzu"] theory of Heaven and the spirits, by which good is certain to be rewarded and evil is certain to be punished, is somewhat less difficult to maintain. For, in fact, the good are not necessarily rich and noble, and evil men are not necessarily poor and lowly.

[63] Refer also to Chapter One, footnotes 6 through 9, and Chapter Two, Sections One and Five. Additional evidence of the partial persistence of clan law into the Spring and Autumn Period is to be seen the exclusive controls over the government of the State of Lu maintained by the three houses of the Huan clan and the fact that even a man like Confucius was unable to satisfy his ambitions. [The three branches of the Huan clan owed their position to the fact that they were collateral branches of the ducal house; Confucius' political ambitions were somewhat blocked by his lack of higher status and more imposing clan connections.] In the State of Sung also the Huan clan enjoyed great power, its junior members filling all the leading posts in the Six Offices of administration (*Tso Chuan*, Fifteenth year of Duke Ch'eng) [575 B.C.; Legge, pp. 388–89]. And in the case of Hsien, Viscount of Shan, who cast out his relatives to employ a Lord Protector but was assassinated (*ibid.*, Seventh year of Duke Chao) [534 B.C.; Legge, p. 619], and that of Wu Ch'i, who as chief minister of Ch'u abolished aristocratic clans and reduced hereditary ranks but suffered death [381 B.C.] by dismemberment (*Shih Chi*, ch. 65, Wu Ch'i's biography; also *Han Fei Tzu*, ch. 13, "Ho shih p'ien," and *Huai-nan Tzu*, ch. 19, "T'ai-tzu hsün."). These cases in particular offer full evidence that the nobility, although in decline, still exercised great power.

hsien" is here translated "Elevating the Worthy," following W. T. Chan. Cf. Y. P. Mei, who translates it "Exaltation of the Worthy." See his note, *Works*, p. 30, on the inadequacy of the word "virtue" to express the meaning of "*hsien*." Waley translates Confucian "*te*" as "moral force." "*Hsien*" may be thought of as implying a high standard of virtue in that sense, plus the talents and skills that enabled a man to serve society]. Although they differed somewhat in the way they conceptualized these doctrines, they had the same objective of wanting to correct the more serious faults that marred their times.

"The unrighteous will not be enriched, the unrighteous will not be honored, the unrighteous will not be favored, the unrighteous will not be drawn close. . . . Therefore, ranks should be conferred according to virtue [*te*], tasks assigned according to office, and rewards given according to labor spent. When emolument is distributed in proportion to achievement, officials need not remain forever ennobled, or common people forever in humble status."[64] The basic import of Mo Tzu's elevating the worthy is wholly indicated by these few words. Mo Tzu's meaning is that ruling the country and nourishing its people was a task of vast difficulty and scope. Only those both worthy and able could meet the great demands of the task. Therefore the man in high position must be possessed of extraordinary abilities, so elevating the worthy became "the basis of government."[65] To accept this principle could bring order; to reject it led to chaos. From antiquity to the present there was only this one principle; Heaven and man both were subject to the same Way [*Tao*];[66] there never had been an exception to this.

With regard to the method of employing the right persons, Mo Tzu also laid down simplest and most appropriate principles. In *ch.* 8, "Elevating the Worthy," Part I, it says: "Therefore in administering the government, the ancient sage kings ranked the morally excellent [*te*] high and

[64] *Ch.* 8, "Shang hsien," Part I [cf. Watson, *Mo Tzu*, p. 20].

[65] In *ch.* 9, "Shang hsien," Part II, Mo Tzu says: "When those both noble and wise act as governors over those both stupid and humble there is order; when those both stupid and humble act as governors over those both noble and wise, there is chaos. Hence we know that elevating the worthy is the basis of government."

[66] *Ch.* 8, 9, and 10, Parts I, II, and III [on "Elevating the Worthy"] all cite real historical events in corroboration. Part II further says: "For Heaven too shows no discrimination between rich and poor, eminent and humble, near and far, the closely and the distantly related. It promotes and honors the worthy, and demotes and rejects the unworthy." [Watson, *Mo Tzu*, page 30.] Thus it was that [the sage kings] Yao and Shun, Yü and T'ang, Wen and Wu, "when rich and noble, acted worthily" and Heaven rewarded them. [The bad kings] Chieh and Chou, Yu and Li, "when rich and noble, acted violently" and Heaven punished them. Lord Kun, "though closely related [to the ruler], failed to do good" so Heaven punished him. Yet the [eminent servitors of the Emperor Shun], Yü, Chi, and Kao-yao were capable, and Heaven employed them. [Cf. Watson, *Mo Tzu*, pp. 30–31.]

exalted the virtuous [*hsien*]. If capable, even a farmer or an artisan would be employed—commisioned with high rank, remunerated with liberal emolument, trusted with important charges, and empowered to issue final orders. For, if one's rank is not high, people will not respect him; if his emolument is not liberal, people will not have confidence in him; if his orders are not final, people will not stand in awe before him. To bestow these three things upon the virtuous is not done to reward his virtue, but to enable him to be successful in the performance of his work." *Ch.* 9, Part II, also says: "The ancient sage kings said: 'He who is too ambitious in government will not share his tasks with others. He who over-values material wealth will not share it to give emolument to others.' When tasks are not given out and emolument not properly divided, let me ask,—whence come the virtuous and worthy men of the world to the side of the king and the rulers?" [The two passages quoted above follow with minor modifications the translation of Y. P. Mei, *Works*, pp. 32–33 and 40.] However, the one who practiced elevating the worthy would of course have to employ such virtuous persons in positions of great importance, and would also have to [assign responsibilities] according to their particular abilities. "To make those incapable of ruling a thousand men rule ten thousand is to increase their duty tenfold. The business of government comes daily. It is to be attended to every day, yet the day cannot be lengthened tenfold. To govern, again, requires knowledge. When knowledge is not increased by ten times even though a tenfold task is assigned, the result obviously will be one attended to and nine neglected." ". . . Those capable of governing the country were made to govern the country; those capable of being senior officials [of the court] were made senior officials; those capable of governing a district were made governors of districts." The one who "advances the virtuous" must "listen to what he says [and act on it], observe his conduct, ascertain his capabilities and carefully assign them their offices."[67] In this way he would be virtually free of serious error.

Mo Tzu's essential ideas in connection with elevating the worthy are roughly as outlined above. Their significance is obvious without further explanation. However, there still are a few points that can readily lead to misunderstanding, and we must take special note of them.

One: Mo Tzu's elevating the worthy was not only in opposition to [the old ideal of] hereditary office-holding and hereditary emolument; in reality it was also an attack on [the current reality of] all-powerful ministers and court sycophants improperly occupying positions. Therefore in his analysis of what causes the government of a state to degenerate into disorder and confusion, he especially mentions the employment of relatives

[67] *Ch.* 9, "Shang hsien," Part Two.

by the king and his lords, and further denounces the employment of persons who have done nothing to merit the wealth and high status that they possess, and of those who merely have handsome faces.[68] Those whom he designates the undeserving rich and noble, and the pretty of face, must be those power-wielding officials like Yang Hu of the State of Lu, and those royal favorites like Tzu-tu and Tzu-chih. [Yang Hu is the household servitor who in the time of Confucius usurped the already illicit power of the leading Chi clan at the court of Lu. Tzu-chih and Tzu-tu were good-looking nonentities who served as favorites of the states of Yen and Cheng; see *Mencius*, II/ii/8 and VI/i/7/7.] These cases, however, have no implications for the issue of hereditary ministerships or that of royal relatives in government as such.

Two: Mo Tzu's elevating the worthy, in its overall significance, fits the new principle of equality of opportunity into the old institutions of the feudal era's last stages. It does not imply a levelling of classes, or the humbling of the aristocracy with a concurrent raising up of the lower classes. The political organization envisaged in Mo Tzu's thought is still that composed of all the social strata, from the Son of Heaven to the feudal princes, Ministers, Great Officers, knights, and commoners. The superiors issued their commands to their inferiors, and inferiors obeyed their superiors. Distinctions of status were clearly indicated; they could not be blurred or levelled. Although Hsü Hsing [a contemporary of Mencius, regarded as a Mohist] promoted the theory that even the ruler and his ministers should all engage in farming like everyone else; Mo Tzu himself accepted the division of labor concept.[69] Although all are human beings, the ignorant and worthless among men should be "men of low status" who would labor at farming and crafts, while the wise and able ones among men should be officials enjoying high rank and generous emolument. The thing that Mo Tzu especially stressed was equality of opportunity by which officials need not be forever in high status nor the people forever low. What he proposed was a rational standard for deter-

[68] *Ch.* 9, "Shang hsien," Part II. In *ch.* 10, Part III, it says: "Princes and dukes and [other] eminent personages are [merely] the blood relations of the ruler who have gained wealth and nobility for no reason, or because they have handsome faces." The preceding chapter [Part I, *ch.* 8] also contrasts the rich and noble relative of rulers with worthy persons.

[69] See footnote 21 to this chapter. Also, *ch.* 32, "The Condemnation of Music," Part II, says that because birds and animals have feathers and fur they need not wear clothing, and because they have water and grass they need not plow and spin, ". . . But man is different from such creatures. If a man exerts his strength he may live, but if he does not exert his strength, he cannot live. If the gentlemen do not diligently attend to affairs of state, the government will fall into disorder, and if humble men do not diligently pursue their tasks, there will not be enough wealth and goods." [Modified slightly from Watson, *Mo Tzu*, pp. 113–114.]

mining status according to qualifications of talent and ability. What he wished to eradicate was nothing more than the non-rational policies favoring relatives and personal favorites. As for the social boundary indicated in the saying [more or less as quoted by Mencius in refuting the theories of Hsü Hsing; *Mencius*, iii/i/4/6] that those who labor with their minds govern others, while those who labor with their strength serve the others, he not only acknowledged that division but wanted to maintain it. We may observe that many of Mo Tzu's immediate disciples devoted themselves to official careers, and they gained high office and accepted emolument therefrom just like anyone else. Most prominent examples of this are Kao Shih Tzu, who served the State of Wei, and Keng Chu Tzu, who served the State of Ch'u. From this we can see the real meaning Mo Tzu intended to convey with elevation of the worthy. Hsün Tzu, in his denunciations of Mo Tzu, comments [on his political theory] in one place: "Whether it be [the ruler] grandly possessing the empire or [the feudal lord merely] having one small domain, if they must do everything themselves before it is properly done, then no greater toil or burden can be imagined. If that were to be the case, the lowliest servants would not trade their places for the power and position of the Son of Heaven." And in another, "They [i.e., Mo Tzu and Sung K'eng, discussed together in this passage] did not understand the instruments for uniting the empire and building up the state. They honor utility and exalt economy, but they disregard distinctions of rank and class. Thus there is possible no discernment of difference, and no separation of rulers and servitors." According to [these charges] it might indeed appear that Mo Tzu was one who "lacked all insight into [natural] differences" [i.e., non-uniformities in personal capacities, in social roles, and the like],[70] thereby totally rejecting the distinctions of high and low status.

That, however, is grave slander of Mo Tzu. Like Mencius' denunciation of him for "doing away with fathers," it too is without foundation, we can be virtually certain. For Mo Tzu, in advocating economy of expenditures, took as his ideal sovereigns [the ancient Sage Kings] Yao and Shun and the Great Yü, who had belabored their bodies and lived simply. Hsün Tzu distorts his intent by removing the context in which the remarks were

---

[70] See: *Hsün Tzu*, ch. 11, "Wang pa"; *ch.* 6, "Fei shih-erh tzu"; and *ch.* 17, "T'ien lun." [The latter two quotations are modified from Dubs, p. 78 and pp. 184–85.] Liang Ch'i-ch'ao, in his *Mo Tzu hsüeh-an*, p. 156, has said: "In as much as he both advocates the principle of equality and also argues in favor of agreeing with the superior and not conforming to the [socially] inferior, this is a point of contradiction." This displays a failure to have grasped the true meaning of "agreeing with the superior" [*shang t'ung*] and "elevating the worthy" [*shang hsien*]. There are some other points of mutual contradiction between Mo Tzu's "elevating the worthy" and his "economy of expenditure" theories, for which see [Section Six] below.

presented, and proceeds to denounce Mo Tzu for them. It is as if he did not know that Confucius too had praised Yü for having used coarse food and poor garments, and having lived in a low mean house! [*Analects*, VIII/21; Legge, p. 215.] Mo Tzu is accused of having disregarded the distinctions of rank and class; did Confucius, then, also disregard such distinctions? Furthermore, Mencius argued for the ideal that ruler and people should share the same pleasures. Now Mo Tzu advances the idea of economy of expenditure, which can be interpreted to mean that superior and inferior should undergo the same hardships together. If sharing the same pleasures is not to disregard the distinctions that should separate the ranks and classes, is sharing the same hardships then to disregard those same distinctions? That Hsün Tzu's criticisms failed to be fair and just becomes abundantly evident here.

Three: Mo Tzu's exaltation of the virtuous, although a repudiation of the Chou system, was not a repudiation of the *ju* teachings. [In post-Confucian usage, "*ju*" is normally interchangeable with "Confucian"; here, however, it is best to keep the word *ju* in the broader sense. See Chapter Two, Section One, above.] "Hereditary transmission" of noble rank and income was a phenomenon necessary to the existence of the Chou dynasty's clan-law social order. Confucius and Mo Tzu both held the ideal of "ministers and premiers of commoner origin," and referred to it repeatedly. Mo Tzu's denunciations of the *ju* teachings in no instance used his "elevating the worthy" concept as the basis of attack on Confucius.[71] That furnishes enough evidence that the two philosophers were in agreement on this point. The Confucians, to be sure, placed great emphasis on the family and clan, but their purpose in so doing was to use the ethical principles implicit in filial and fraternal relationships as the foundation on which to build self-cultivation and the establishment of good government. Their purpose was by no means to allow the treatment appropriate to relatives within the clan to displace the elevation of the worthy in government. Therefore Yao and Shun, in transmitting the throne on the [non-family] principle of merit, and the Duke of Chou, who declared that [a higher principle of integrity] supersedes family relationships, were all praised for these attitudes by the Confucian school. Among Confucius' immediate disciples of humble background there were many who studied

[71] It is, to be sure, true that the opening section of "Fei ju," i.e., "Condemnation of Confucians" *ch.* 39, Part III, says: "The Confucians say: 'There are precise ways of treating relatives as relatives, as there are rankings in elevating the worthy.'" [Cf. Watson, *Mo Tzu*, p. 125.] The following lines go on to attack the foolishness and error of the Confucian teachings about marriage, burials, and other rituals. Pi Yuan [see footnote 1, above] however has said this chapter represents later Mohist followers' "extension of their Master's teachings for the purpose of refuting Confucians" and is not one of Mo Ti's own writings. One should also note that the attacks all are on relatively minor aspects of ritual and deportment, and are not relevant to issues of government.

the methods of rulership at the highest levels. This offers further proof of Confucius' profound belief that the system of hereditary ministerships should be corrected and reformed. Analyzed in the light of these facts, Confucius' thought was, to be sure, not wholly consistent on the issue of following the Chou.[72]

Coming to the thought of Hsün Tzu, we find it even closer to the "elevation of the worthy" doctrine. In his *ch*. 12, "Chün tao," i.e., "The Way of the Ruler," Hsün Tzu says: "Though they be the sons and grandsons of princes, dukes, knights, or Great Officers, those who cannot be made subject to propriety and righteousness should be given the status of commoners. Though they be the sons and grandsons of commoners, those who acquire refined learning and embody it in deed and are capable of being subject to propriety and righteousness should then be given the status of ministers, knights, and Great Officers."[73] The basic concept of this is in complete agreement with Mo Tzu's saying that officials need not be forever noble, and commoners need not be to the ends of their lives always in humble status; the two views could have come from the same mouth.[74]

Nonetheless, between Confucians and Mohists there still remains an issue of wide discrepancy. The Confucians wanted the "superior man" to succeed to the perogatives of the hereditary minister; his ideal superior man need not be of aristocratic background, but he must have cultivated his person and have established his virtue, to serve as teacher and model to the common people below him. Thus the Confucians in their elevation of the worthy used not merely the standard of meritorious achievement in the world of affairs, but concurrently demanded a high standard of personal ethics. Mo Tzu also talks again and again about the worthy man's effectiveness. In *ch*. 9, "Elevating the Worthy," Part II, it says: "When the worthy rules the country, he starts the day early and retires late, hearing lawsuits and attending to the government. As a result, the country is well governed and laws are justly administered. When the worthy administers the court, he retires late and wakes up early, collecting taxes at markets and customs barriers on products from mountains, woods, waters, and bridges, to fill the court. As a result the court is filled and wealth is not wasted. When the worthy governs a district, he goes out before sunrise and comes back after sunset [to supervise] plowing and sowing, planting and cultivating,

[72] Refer to Chapter Two, Section Five, above.

[73] Mencius on occasion defended hereditary emoluments, in disagreement with the Mohist position. See the final part of Chapter Three, Section Two, above.

[74] Hsia Tseng-yu has stated: "Confucius stressed treating relatives as relatives, while Mo Tzu taught the elevation of the worthy." He then goes on to list eight other matters, leading him to conclude that Mo Tzu "in no instance was not diametrically opposed to Confucius." (This is cited in Fang Shou-ch'u, *Mo-hsueh yuan-liu* [see footnote 1], Part I, page 111.) This view would seem to be incorrect.

and gathering harvests of grains. As a result, grains are in plenty and people are sufficiently supplied with food." [Following, with minor modifications, the translation by Y. P. Mei, *Works*, p. 37.] Every point alluded to here is wholly and exclusively relevant to material benefits. That is to say, what Mo Tzu called the worthy [or the virtuous] man, from the point of view of the Confucians, is nothing more than a man possessing a specific talent or technical ability, who devotedly labors at his assigned tasks and serves his ruler. But he in no sense could be said to have achieved that highest point of virtue manifested in transforming the peoples' ways and perfecting their social practices. Hsün Tzu criticized Mo Tzu as one "whose fault was his concern for utility, and who had no comprehension of refinement." This may be taken as but one more proof that the Mohist teachings were Confucian doctrines recast to suit the level of the common people.

Section Six
Economy of Expenditure

Mo Tzu valued frugality; this is one of the special characteristics of his thought, and it has been much criticized by the other schools. We may note that Mo Tzu's high esteem for frugality embodied three ideas: (1) economy of expenditures, (2) simplicity in funerals, and (3) the condemnation of music. [This is to adopt Y. P. Mei's translation of these terms, which are also chapter titles in the *Mo Tzu*.] Economy of expenditure is the major tenet, while simplicity in funerals and the condemnation of music are particularized extensions of it.

The immediate objective of economy in expenditures is more amply to fulfill the needs of the people's livelihood; its ultimate objective is to realize in practice universal love and mutual benefit. Thus Mo Tzu said that the Sage Kings of antiquity "loved the people loyally and benefited the people generously," in consequence establishing the ways of economizing in expenditures.[75] However, we should note that Mo Tzu advocated not merely frugality in expenditures and costs as a matter of principle, but in fact stressed particularly the eradication of non-profitable consumption. In *ch*. 20, "Economy of Expenditure," Part I, it says: "When a Sage governs a state, [the benefits to] it can be doubled. When on a vaster scale he governs the world [the benefits to] it can be doubled. This doubling does not mean seizing more territory outside; it is accomplished because the state does away with useless expenditures, and that is sufficient to double [the benefits to] it." [Cf. the translation of this chapter in Watson, *Mo Tzu*, pp. 62–64.]

---

[75] *Ch*. 21, "Chieh yung," i.e., "Economy of Expenditures," Part II.

In *ch.* 21, "Economy of Expenditures," Part ii, the concrete measures for economizing on expenditures are set forth and discussed: "[The Sage Kings] said: 'All you artisans and workers—carpenters and tanners, potters and smiths—do what each of you has the skill to do. Stop whenever you have adequately supplied the people's needs.' Whatever caused extra expense but adds no benefit to the people the Sage Kings would not undertake." According to this standard there were definite limitations on food and drink, clothing, dwellings and houses, implements, and other objects. "Stop when there is enough that hunger is satisfied, the breathing is sustained, limbs are strengthened, and the eyes and ears become sharp. There is no need of perfecting the balance of the five flavors or harmonizing the sweet fragrances. There is no need to procure exotic and rare delicacies from far lands." This was the regulation on food and drink. " 'In winter be satisfied with clothes of blue or grey silk [the commonest textile in ancient China] that are light and warm, and in summer with clothes of flax-linen that are light and cool.' Whatever caused extra expenditure but does not add benefits to the people the Sage Kings would not undertake." This was the regulation on clothing. "Just so that on the sides it can keep off wind and cold, on top can keep off snow, frost, rain, and dew, within it is clean enough for the sacrificial purposes, and that in a dwelling the partition is high enough to separate the men from the women—that is enough. Whatever caused extra expenditure but did not add any benefit to the people, the Sage Kings would not undertake." This was the regulation on dwellings. "In ancient times the Sage Kings noted that great streams and broad valleys could not be crossed, so for the advantage in it they made boats and oars, but they went no further than to accomplish that, and then ceased. Even though it was a superior such as the Three Senior Lords or the feudal princes who came, the boats and oars were not exchanged and the boatmen were not adorned." [Translation of this and the previous four quoted passages somewhat modified from Y. P. Mei, *Works*, pp. 120–22.] This was the regulation concerning implements and other objects.

Building on this principle that nothing should be done that did not increase the people's benefits, Mo Tzu also erected his doctrines of economy in funerals and the condemnation of music, which were used against the Confucians. Mo Tzu's only reason for opposing elaborate funerals and long mourning periods was that those who adopted these practices could not thereby enrich the poor, multiply the few, overcome peril, or bring order into chaos. For, as Mo Tzu looked at it, funerals and mourning, to begin with, were simply things that could not be avoided and that produced no particular benefits, so that the more one expended on them the greater was the loss involved. Hence in *ch.* 25, "Simplicity in Funerals," Part iii, he says: "So, then, in elaborate funerals much wealth is buried, and in extended mourning abstention from work is prolonged. Wealth already produced is carried away into the grave. Child-bearing is postponed. To seek wealth in this way is like seeking a harvest by prohibiting farming." [Following the translation by Y. P. Mei, *Works*, p. 126.] Moreover, the damage caused by elaborate funerals and prolonged mourning does not stop with this. People who cannot enjoy wealth lack food and clothing; they will then resent their fathers and elder brothers, and their rulers, and will engage in unrestrained and violent acts toward each other, leading thereby to chaos. If the people do not engage in their work [because extended mourning forbids useful work], supplies will not be stored up, inner and outer walls of cities will not be kept in repair, superiors and inferiors will not be harmonious to each other. If a larger state attacks, the state will be incapable of defending itself, leading thereby to its annihilation. If the people are thus impoverished and the state brought to disorder, the sacrifices will not be properly attended to, leading thereby to punishments imposed by Heaven and the spirits. Mo Tzu therefore regarded elaborate funerals and prolonged mourning as constituting one of the "four policies" by which Confucians brought disaster into the world.[76] Consequently he devised the regulations for simple funerals and brief mourning in order to change the Confucian practice.

The sense of his condemnation of music was roughly the same. His comments on it do not go beyond the following six points: (1) Performance of music demands musical instruments. Musical instruments cannot "be produced as easily as by scooping up water or digging into the earth. Inevitably, heavy-taxes have to be collected from the people . . . [it can only] deprive the people of their means of providing food and clothing for themselves." (2) "There are three things that afflict the people, namely, those who are hungry can obtain no food, those who are cold can obtain no clothing, and those who are fatigued from labor can obtain no rest. These three are what plague the people. Now suppose we strike the big bell, beat the sounding drum, play the *ch'in* and the *seh*, and blow the *yü* and the *sheng*, perform ceremonial dances [this phase, omitted in Y. P. Mei's translation, *Works*, p. 176, seems to be an allusion to the *Book of Odes*, "Greater Odes of the Kingdom," "Kung Liu," 1, Legge, p. 484; but it may be incorrectly placed in the *Mo Tzu* due to accident in transmission of the text], where are the resources for supplying the people with food and clothing to come from? As for this, I think it may well not be possible at all." (3) Performing music does not contribute to the prevention of violence or the ending of disorder, hence adds nothing of use in the accomplishment of tasks. (4) Performing music demands the services of musicians, and to become a musician it is necessary to abandon the

---

[76] *Ch.* 48, "Kung Meng."

productive work of field and grove, of the spinning wheel and the loom. (5) Persons listening to music will be made inattentive to their work: "If gentlemen listen to music, it will prevent them attending to their work." (6) The Sage Kings of antiquity did not have music.[77] Moreover, Mo Tzu's condemnation of music was not just limited to times when the country was impoverished and in difficult straits. "Kung Meng Tzu said: 'When the country is in chaos it should be put in order; when it is in order, rites [li] and music may be pursued. When the country is poor, work should be attended to; when it is rich, rites and music may be pursued.' Mo Tzu [correcting his view,] said: 'A country may be orderly. But it is because it is being well governed that it is orderly. As soon as good administration is abandoned, order disappears also. A country may be rich. But it is because work is being attended to that it is rich. As soon as work is abandoned, wealth disappears also. Therefore although a country is orderly, it is necessary to encourage unceasing attention to administration.' "[78]

We must note that Mo Tzu's doctrine esteeming frugality, although expressed as if aimed at the whole social order, seems to indicate by its content that he particularly hoped for the kings and great lords to accept and practice it. Thus, in praising the virtue of austerity, he cites Yao's and Shun's having eaten coarse food and worn rough clothing.[79] His condemnation of extravagant ways says that "the rulers of today . . . exhaust wealth and waste labor, and in the end it is all for no use."[80] It thus becomes evident that Mo Tzu's intent in elevating the worthy was to raise the status of the humble man up to a level with that of the gentleman, while through the results induced by honoring frugality he intended to lower the princes' and rulers' living standard to that of the common people. Some of the things that the Confucians specially stressed, such as exaggerating the significance of status, and using impressive ceremonial forms and their elaborately refined accouterments, Mo Tzu apparently spurned completely. His ideal society, expressed in modern terms, seems to have been a kind of work organization in which there were tasks, but no enjoyment of pleasure, and that emphasized duties but de-emphasized rights.

Although Mo Tzu rigorously maintained those principles, which [his Confucian and Taoist critics said] were "as if scorched, as if parched" [Hsün Tzu, ch. 10] and which "caused people anxiety, and caused people

---

[77] Ch. 32, "Fei yüeh," i.e., "Condemnation of Music," Part i. Ch. 33 and 34, Parts ii and iii, are no longer extant. [The translations of quoted lines follow Y. P. Mei, Works, pp. 126, 176–78.]

[78] Ch. 48, "Kung Meng."

[79] Ch. 32, "Chieh yung," Part ii, and Han Fei Tzu, ch. 49, "Wu Tu."

[80] Ch. 6, "Tz'u kuo" [modified from Mei, Works, p. 24].

sadness" [*Chuang Tzu, ch.* 33], it was not without reason. A great number of the rulers of states and members of the aristocracy in the late Chou period were given to unbridled luxury and debauchery, showing no concern about the people's wasted energies. Examples of this abound; they turn up on every hand. In the State of Chin [Duke P'ing, died 531 B.C.] constructed the Palace of T'ung-ti, and in Ch'u there was the Chang-hua Terrace [built in 534 B.C.]. "Po-yu in the State of Cheng made an underground hall and held nocturnal drinking parties there." [*Tso Chuan,* Thirtieth Year of Duke Hsiang, 542 B.C.; Legge, p. 557.] People in Ch'i sent Duke Ai [of Lu] a present of female musicians [in 517 B.C.] and Duke Ai stopped attending his court's early morning meetings. [*Analects,* XVIII/4; Legge, p. 332.] [The extravagant] King Ching of Chou [died 519 B.C.] had cast the bronze bell called *Wu-yeh.* Duke Yi of Wei [in 659 B.C.; *Tso Chuan,* Legge, p. 129] raised storks that were driven about in carriages [like aristocrats]. In the State of Ch'i [a straitforward advisor told its Duke]: "Your palaces and mansions are daily changed. You do not shun licentious pleasures. The favorite concubines in your harem send forth and carry things away from the markets; your favorite officers abroad issue false orders in the borders."[81] Mencius said: "In your kitchen there is fat meat; in your stables there are fat horses. But your people have the look of hunger, and on the wilds there are those who have died of famine." [*Mencius,* I/i/4/4; Legge, p. 133.] These things, about which Mencius later was moved to sigh so sadly, earlier had been witnessed by Mo Tzu also. Thus his doctrines of economy of expenditure and condemnation of music were formulated for a purpose, were uttered in response to compelling stimuli. For this reason they accurately struck home at the ills of the times and were wholly sincere views of someone who understood the situation. Indeed, it is quite unjustified to denounce them [as did Hsün Tzu, *ch.* 21] as nothing more than the specious doctrine of one "blinded by utility and ignorant of refinement."

Nonetheless, if we can put aside the special environment of the Warring States Period, and concern ourselves exclusively with evaluating the doctrine of austerity itself, then it will probably become apparent to us that Mo Tzu was guilty of over-correction, and of the error of one-sidedness. To summarize, he has committed three errors: First, he denies human nature. Human beings, after satisfying the minimal livelihood needs, inevitably will want to go further and enlarge their demands. The higher a society's level of civilization, the greater its productive capacity, and, simultaneously, the broader grows the scope of its enjoyment of luxury. Consequently, what has previously been regarded as extravagant luxury, without conscious awareness of the change, will come generally

---

[81] *Tso Chuan,* Twentieth year of Duke Chao [521 B.C.; Legge, p. 683].

to be regarded as mere necessity. One of the most obvious differences between men and animals is just this: men are capable of limitlessly expanding their desires, while animals lack such capacity. And one of the differences between savages and civilized man lies in the ability of the latter to realize the greatest possible enlargement of his capacity for consumption, while the former cannot. To be sure, it cannot be said that Mo Tzu's views on limitation of consumption reduced men to the condition of animals, but there is no doubt that they tended to stand in the way of civilization's advance.[82]

And, beyond that, men must have some rest and recreation in the time over and beyond that used for work, in order to maintain health and balance. In *ch.* 7, "San Pien," or "Threefold Argument," there is recorded Ch'eng Fan's objections to Mo Tzu's views, as follows: "Sir, you say the Sage Kings did not have music. But anciently when the feudal lords were fatigued from attending the government, they found recreation in music of bells and drums. When the knights and Great Officers were tired from attending to the duties of office, they found recreation in the music of pipes and strings. And the farmers would plough in spring, weed in summer, reap in autumn, and store away their products for the winter, and then they would enjoy the music of strumming on jars and vases. Sir, you say the Sage Kings did not have music. This would be comparing them to the horse under yoke that is never set free; or the bow drawn taut that is never released. Is this not impossible for ordinary human beings?" [Modified slightly from Y. P. Mei, *Works*, p. 28. "Ordinary human beings" is his translation of "*yu hsüeh ch'i che*" 有血氣者 or "those having the physical passions."] This is in truth a most appropriate and fair question, and Mo Tzu was unable to find the words to rebutt it.

Human beings, moreover, by nature possess a spirit of playfulness; not all their actions need be "purposeful." All pleasures and all art are developments springing from this basic fact.[83] *Ch.* 48, "Kung Meng," records that Mo Tzu: "Asked a Confucian, 'Why do the Confucians pursue music?' He replied, 'Music is pursued for music's sake.' [Modified slightly from Y. P. Mei, *Works*, p. 236. The reply: "Music is for music's sake" utilizes a play on words, since "music," *yueh*, can also be read "*lo*," or "pleasure."] Mo Tzu said: 'You have not answered me. Suppose I

---

[82] Hsün Tzu's theory about "cultivating the five extremes" [or the "five limits" of possible satisfaction; *ch.* 11; see also Chapter Three, footnote 93 above] comes close to this idea. Among recent scholars, T'an Ssu-t'ung [1865–1898], in his *Jen-hsüeh*, appears to have most fully developed the theories about extending use and enjoyment [of civilization's material elements] to their furthest limits.

[83] Liang Ch'i-ch'ao, in his *Yin-ping-shih wen-chi*, number 39, has an essay entitled "Hsüeh-wen chih ch'ü-wei," or "The fascinations of scholarship," which sets forth this point with great clarity.

asked why one builds houses, and you answered that it is to keep off cold in winter, and the heat in summer, and to separate men from women. Then you would have told me the reason for building houses. Now I am asking why you pursue music, and you answer that music is pursued for music's sake. This is comparable to replying to the question about why houses are built by saying they are built for houses' sake.' " From the Mohists' point of view, this is an incomparably marvelous argument, enough to leave Confucians speechless. They did not understand that the building of houses and the pursuit of music cannot be discussed in the same terms. And, by putting the argument in this way, Mo Tzu exposes his inadequacy. He could only understand the motive for building houses, but could not comprehend the psychology of one who pursues music. Chuang Tzu said: "His Way is too harsh. . . . If he teaches others in this manner, I fear he has no love for them. And if he practices it himself, he surely has no regard for himself." Chuang Tzu added that "It is contrary to the heart of the world, and the world cannot endure it. Though Mo Tzu himself may have been capable of enduring it, could anyone else in the world do so?"[84] This comment truly hits the mark.

The second error in Mo Tzu's stress on austerity is that it is contrary to the principles of ruling. We can explain this point best by comparing some points of the Confucian and the Mohist theories. Mo Tzu's sole reason for denouncing rites and music, and disregarding the usual social ranks [that ritual propriety reinforced], was that rites and music had no utility. But, as the Confucians saw it, for maintaining peace above and keeping order among the people, there is nothing as effective as the rites, while for transforming customs and changing the people's practices there is nothing better than music.[85] Thus the great needs of the world are all to be served in this way. Which, then, of the two schools holds the more accurate view here? Putting aside all our preconceptions and attempting to judge the matter objectively, we must acknowledge the incontrovertible fact that rites and music [as the Chinese defined them] do serve some purpose. A cursory exploration of the matter, in all parts of the world and in all ages, provides evidence that this is indeed a quite general truth. Mo Tzu's extreme demands for austerity declared war, as it were, on this widespread fact. That it should encounter difficulties, then, is no more than we would expect.

Mo Tzu's doctrine of the economy of expenditures included high praise for the Sage King Yao for paying no heed to the taste of the food he ate, yet at the same time his theory about elevating the worthy included granting high rank and generous salary to persons employed in office.

[84] *Chuang Tzu, ch.* 33, "T'ien-hsia."

[85] See: the *Li Chi, ch.* 19, "Yüeh chi"; and *Hsün Tzu,* the chapters 19 and 20, "Li lun" and "Yüeh lun."

These two points imply mutual contradiction, and conflict of attitude. Were economy of expenditure practiced, then one would "dress in rough cloth, use a rope for a belt, eat coarse grain, and drink water."[86] When life becomes so barren that desires cannot be satisfied, then ". . . let me ask, whence come the virtuous and worthy men of the world to the side of the king and the rulers?"[87] And we may note that even among Mo Tzu's disciples there were those who took public office and received very large salaries for doing so. Moreover, when Keng Chu held office in Ch'u, ". . . some other pupils visited him. They were given only three *sheng* of grain each meal and were not generously entertained." [Translation follows Y. P. Mei, *Works*, ch. 46, "Keng Chu," p. 214.] This aroused the critical comment from the other pupils [when they returned and reported it to Mo Tzu] that Keng Chu was not being profited by serving Ch'u. Mo Tzu did not thereupon instruct them in the proper teachings by referring to the Sage Emperor Yao, who ate only one kind of millet and used only coarse earthenware bowls [as the *Mo Tzu* describes his austerities; ch. 21, "Economy of Expenditure," Part II; Y. P. Mei, *Works*, p. 121], but merely remarked: "You cannot tell." From these facts we must assume

---

[86] *Hsün Tzu, ch.* 10, "Fu Kuo." Hsün Tzu says there: "Mo Tzu's words, with insistent clarity, convey his deep concern about the insufficiencies [of material things] in the world. As a matter of fact those insufficiencies are not the common worry of the world but are peculiar to Mo Tzu in his excessive calculations about his private worries. . . . I take the position that Mo Tzu's 'condemnation of music' could induce poverty throughout the world. It is not as if he intended to work harm, but his theories could well bring down [those hardships] inescapably upon us. Mo Tzu, whether [indicating he who] grandly possesses the whole empire or merely referring to one small state, would have even the rulers rigorously limited to wearing rough clothing and eating coarse food. All would be sad and grim, yet music would be forbidden to them. How barren life would be, and in its barrenness it would fail to satisfy men's desires. Not able to satisfy desires, rewards could not be carried out. Mo Tzu, whether [indicating he who] grandly possesses the empire or merely one small state, would reduce the number of people and eliminate offices in government. The superiors [in society] would have to labor and toil, participating in the same tasks with the common people, equally sharing their labor and its rewards. In that way they would possess no authority, and, having no authority, they could not mete out punishments. When rewards cannot be carried out, there is no way the worthy can be advanced in office. When punishments cannot be meted out, there is no way the unworthy can be eliminated from office. When the worthy cannot be advanced and the unworthy eliminated, then no individual's competence and incompetence can be assessed for filling offices. By that process, all things will fail to harmonize, all events will fail to interact appropriately. Above, there will be failure to meet with heaven's time; below, failure to gain earth's benefits' and, in between, failure to achieve men's accord. The world will take on a burned appearance, as if scorched, as if parched. Even though Mo Tzu may dress in rough clothing, use a rope for a belt, eat coarse grain and drink water, how can that produce a sufficiency?" The following passage goes on to present Hsün Tzu's positive proposals [for enriching the nation], and merits note.

[87] *Ch.* 9, "Shang hsien," Part II; following the translation of Y. P. Mei, *Works*, p. 40].

that the views on economy of expenditure represent but an extreme outburst, for not even Mohists were capable of fully practicing it.

We may go even further, and conclude that another shortcoming of Mo Tzu's doctrine of the economy of expenditure was that it concentrated on the negative policy of reducing consumption, and never explored the positive methods of expanding production. Mo Tzu recognized that human beings could not, like birds and beasts, rely solely on what the natural environment supplied them to maintain their livelihood, and he was also deeply conscious that human labor was the basic productive force. He therefore advocated early marriage for the sake of increasing the population.[88] But with regard to the general problem of producing wealth, he was virtually lacking in all proposals and plans, except for such empty and meaningless principles as: "When many produce and few consume [then there can be no bad year]."[89] He was not in this respect up to Mencius and Hsün Tzu, whose discussions of how to amplify the people's livelihood and enrich the state are thoughtful and orderly. Hsün Tzu said that the problem of material insufficiencies was "peculiar to Mo Tzu in his excessive calculations about his private worries" [see footnote 86, above]. Insofar as the Mohists failed to concern themselves with methods of developing the sources of wealth, this is by no means a baseless criticism.

Section Seven
Condemnation of Offensive Warfare

WE have just discussed the shortcomings of Mo Tzu's ideas on economy of expenditure, noting that they display merely a concern for the satisfaction of people's basic needs, and display no attempt to seek out basic principles concerning the production of wealth. But when we come to his condemnation of offensive warfare we find, in addition to a theoretical statement of clarity and perception, that superior techniques of defensive warfare are also provided. Hence it can be said that, for its practical value in application, nothing in Mohism exceeds this achievement.

Confucius refused to reply to questions about tactics put to him by

---

[88] *Ch.* 32, "Fei yüeh," Part I, states: "But man is different from these (birds and animals). If a man exerts his strength, he may live, but if he does not exert his strength, he cannot live." [See footnote 69, above.] *Ch.* 20, "Chieh yung," i.e., "Economy of Expenditures," Part I, says: "What, then, is it difficult to double the number of? It is difficult to double the number of people. And yet it can be done. In ancient times, the sage kings made a law saying: 'No man of twenty shall dare to be without his own household; no woman of fifteen shall dare to be without a husband.' " [Slightly modified from Watson, *Mo Tzu*, p. 63.]

[89] *Ch.* 5, "Ch'i huan," i.e., "Seven Calamities" [following Y. P. Mei, *Works*, p. 19].

Duke Ling of Wei. [*Analects*, xv/1.] Mencius said that those skilled in warfare should be dealt the most severe punishments. [*Mencius*, iv/i/14/3.] Since the Confucians all along had opposed all aggressive military action, the condemnation of offensive warfare certainly was no new idea created by Mo Tzu. But the Confucians, although able to denounce aggression, were incapable of devising defenses against attack, and their views on war thus lacked much practical effectiveness. Mo Tzu not only firmly maintained his theory, debating it energetically and unremittingly; he also was most skilled in devising defensive tactics, and was expert in the manufacture of defensive weapons.[90] Moreover, he personally led his disciples in the defense of states where aggression threatened, and in preventing the outbreak of war's misfortunes. His rescue of the State of Sung became an event much admired by later ages.[91] Chuang Tzu praised him as "One of the world's best men," and this is not superfluous praise. [The author has suggested this slight change in the sense of this line.]

The theoretical aspects of Mo Tzu's condemnation of offensive warfare also display some points of difference with that of the Confucian school. Sung K'eng [a Mohist] wanted to present the argument of its "unprofitableness" to prevent the threatened war between the States of Ch'in and Ch'u, and Mencius [although admitting the greatness of his aim] criticized him saying: "Your argument, sir, is not good."[92] Mo Tzu's condemnation

[90] In the extant text of the *Mo Tzu*, the eleven chapters starting with *ch.* 52, "Pei ch'eng-men," i.e., "Preparing Walls and Gates," all are devoted to discussions of defensive weapons and tactics. Among them quite possibly are portions dating from the Ch'in and Han dynasties that are falsely attributed to Mo Tzu, but in general they probably all represent enlargements of the Master's original teachings as developed by later Mohists. The "Mohist defense" [meaning, by extension, the stubborn defense of the virtually indefensible, especially in rhetoric and debate] came by Han times to be an item of common knowledge, therefore Ho Hsiu [A.D. 129–182] used the term in the title of his book [*Kung-yang Mo-shou* or "An unyielding defense of the *Kung-yang Commentary*"].

[91] *Ch.* 50, "Kung-shu," records the event. It tells, in part: "Kung-shu Pan [famous as a skilled artisan] was constructing scaling ladder machines for the State of Ch'u. They were ready, and were about to be used in an attack on Sung. Mo Tzu heard about the matter in [far off] Ch'i, and started off, travelling continuously for ten days and ten nights until he reached Ying [the Ch'u capital], where he went to see Kung-shu Pan." Then he proceeded to use his arguments against aggressive warfare to dissuade the King of Ch'u and Kung-shu Pan from their intention, but the King of Ch'u still could not quite set aside his fascination with the scaling ladders. Mo Tzu ". . . then went to see Kung-shu Pan. Mo Tzu untied his belt and laid out a city with it, and used small sticks to represent the various military installations. Kung-shu Pan nine times set up offensive stratagems, and Mo Tzu nine times repulsed them. Kung-shu Pan exhausted all his attack devices, while Mo Tzu still had further defensive means in reserve. Kung-shu Pan in defeat said: 'I know how to stop you. I will not say how.' Mo Tzu also spoke: 'And I know how you plan to stop me. I will not say how.' The King of Ch'u asked what was meant. Mo Tzu replied: 'Master Kung-shu's intent is merely to have me murdered. If I

of aggressive warfare, however, on all occasions in all places, harked constantly back to the theme of "unprofitableness." For, as Mo Tzu saw it, aggressive campaigns mostly were undertaken because the aggressor regarded war as profitable.[93] Thus he had first to refute this erroneous evaluation of it before his anti-aggression theories could prevail. But in fact the disaster of war in many cases sprang from the martial ambitions and vast schemes of individual rulers. So his arguments about the unprofitableness of aggressive warfare also, in the main, fasten on the person of the ruler himself, aiming to arouse his awareness and alert him to the personal consequences, to prevent him from embarking on a course of danger and self-destruction. This so-called "ignoble argument, lacking loftiness of ideals" [echoing Mencius' criticism], must have been in fact far more realistic and more convincing than any preaching about benevolence and righteousness.

All of Mo Tzu's arguments on the unprofitableness of offensive war can be summarized under three headings: (1) As for a war of aggression ". . . when we consider the victory as such, there is nothing useful about it. When we consider the possessions obtained through it, it does not even make up for the loss." [Mo Tzu, ch. 18, "Condemnation of Offensive War," Part II; Y. P. Mei, Works, p. 102.] If now a city of only three li is attacked, or a walled area of only seven li, many persons must be slaughtered, and victory will be uncertain; even if one succeeds in capturing it, it will have become a useless "waste city." (2) Aggressors hold the mistaken view that through attack they can annex territory and make the state richer and stronger. They unfortunately fail to see that the victor in one war of aggression may become the victim of another,—the mantis catching a locust may be unaware that a meadow lark is watching from behind. [Using the metaphor of an anecdote about the King of Wu, in Shuo Yuan, ch. 9, SPTK, p. 3b.] The State of Wu, under Kings Ho-lü and Fu-ch'ai, fought wars for [so-called] righteousness, and became the strongest nation in the world, yet in the end could not stave off defeat

---

have been killed, Sung then will have no way of defending itself, and you can attack it. However, my followers Ch'in Ku-li and others numbering three hundred are already armed with my implements of defense, waiting on the city wall of Sung to repel the attack by Ch'u. Even if you kill me, that would not be able to terminate [their resistance]! The King of Ch'u said: 'Well spoken. I shall command that we not attack Sung, then.' " [Cf. also Fung/Bodde, Vol. I, p. 81.]

[92] Mencius, "Kao Tzu," Part II [VI/ii/4/2; Legge, p. 429. See also Waley, Three Ways of Thought, pp. 135–36, for a slightly different translation].

[93] Ch. 18, "Fei kung," Part II, says: "The state promulgates its governmental measures, takes away the things the people use, destroys things of benefit to the people, committing such acts in very great number; yet why is it that it does these things? [Its rulers] say: I do these things seeking the glory that comes from winning victory in a campaign, and for the benefits accruing from that. That is why I do it."

at the hands of King Kou-chien [of the State of Yüeh]. Chih-po was the most powerful of the six generals of the State of Chin, and he devoted his energies entirely to wars of aggrandizement, yet in the end was defeated at the hands of the three clans [which held power within his own state].[94] All of these examples among our predecessors should serve to warn us that the course of aggression is in fact unprofitable. (3) Furthermore, the disaster resulting from aggressive warfare is not limited to its effects on ruler and nation. Mo Tzu said: "If the people of Heaven are deployed to attack the towns of Heaven, this would be to murder the men of Heaven [for all people, towns, men, etc., belong to Heaven], to dispossess the spirits of their altars, to overthrow their state, and to wantonly kill off their sacrificial animals. That would in no way profit Heaven on high. Is it intended, then, to profit the spirits? But if the men of Heaven are murdered, the spirits are thereby deprived of their sacrifices, the former kings are neglected, the multitudes are caused to suffer loss and mistreatment, and the people scattered. That, then, would prove to be of no profit to the spirits in the middle. Is it intended, then, to profit men? To kill people must be of very meagre profit to those people! And when we calculate the expenses involved, these are found to be destructive of the very basis of life, and they exhaust the wealth and livelihood of innumerable masses of the world's people. Thus neither is it of profit to the people of the world below."[95] [This reflects Mo Tzu's belief in three spheres of the world—that of Heaven on high, of the spirits in between, and of men below. War is seen as destructive and unprofitable to the inhabitants of all three spheres.]

Mo Tzu recognized that the desire for fame also functioned as a primary motive for aggression, thus directs his arguments to this as well, to demonstrate that offensive wars by no means are to be undertaken. In *ch.* 28, "The Will of Heaven," Part III, it says: "For, the rulers of large states say in warlike fashion, 'Being a big state, if I do not attack small states, in what way am I to be considered big?' Therefore they muster their warriors, deploy their boat and chariot forces, and attack some

[94] *Ch.* 18, "Fei kung," Part II. *Ch.*20, "Fei kung," Part III develops the point further through the device of setting up the questions of a person challenging Mo Tzu's position. He says that the States of Ch'u, Yüeh, Ch'i, and Chin, each starting out as a small state a few hundred *li* in extent have through aggressive warfare reached the point where the four can divide the world among themselves." Is this not to be judged a benefit [*li*]? Mo Tzu responds to this saying: "In ancient times the Son of Heaven enfoeffed over ten thousand feudal lords. And yet now, because of the annexation of one state by another, these ten thousand domains have all disappeared and only the four remain. But it is rather like the case of a doctor who administers medicine to over ten thousand patients but succeeds in curing only four. He cannot be said to be a very skilled physician." [Following Watson, *Mo Tzu*, p. 59.]

[95] *Ch.* 20, "Fei kung," Part III [following Y. P. Mei, *Works*, pp. 108–09. Cf. Watson, *Mo Tzu*, pp. 53–54, and W. T. Chan, *Source Book*, p. 227].

innocent state. They break into its borders, plunder its fields and farms and fell its trees, despoil its city's walls and fill up moats and ditches, burn its ancestral temples and kill off its sacrificial animals. The strong among the people are killed and the weak are enslaved and brought back with the returning armies, where the men are made to serve as servants and grooms and captive slaves and the women become household attendants. And such warlike rulers do not even understand that this is neither benevolent nor righteous. They send announcements to all the rulers of neighboring states saying, 'I have attacked a state, defeated an army, and killed so-many generals.' And the rulers of neighboring states do not even know that this is neither benevolent nor righteous. They send envoys, complete with furs and silks, to convey their congratulations. And the warlike rulers are still further ignorant of the unbenevolent and unrighteous nature of this, for they also record it on bamboo and silk and preserve the records in the archives of the state, so that their descendants might be led to emulate these deeds of their forebears, saying: 'Why don't we open up our state archives and look upon the model and standard of our ancestors?' " All the world's people are unaware of the unrighteousness of invasions and aggressive wars, ". . . so attacks and assaults go on generation after generation without end." [Following the translation of Y. P. Mei, *Works*, pp. 157–58.]

Mo Tzu directs straightforward comment to clarification of this unawareness: "If someone now should enter another's garden or orchard, and take someone else's peaches and plums, melons and ginger, the superiors will catch and punish him, and all the people hearing of it will denounce him. And why is that so? It is because he did not share the toil, yet takes of its fruits, that he is denounced for having taken the things." How much more so should it be so in the case of aggressive assaults and annexation of territory, when what is seized is "many thousands and tens of thousands" times as much. Mo Tzu says further: "If a man now should enter another's garden or yard, and take his peaches and plums, all the people hearing of it will denounce him, and the superiors in the government will catch and punish him. Why is this so? Because he injures others to profit himself. As to seizing dogs, swine, chickens, and young pigs from another, that is even more unrighteous than to enter someone's garden or yard and steal peaches and plums. Why is this so? Because the injury to others is still greater, so its non-benevolence is greatly increased and the wrong is made thereby the more serious." Then how much more, in a case of aggressive attack and annexation of territory where the injury to others for the sake of profiting oneself is still more than hundreds of times greater than in a case of stealing peoples' belongings.[96]

To summarize, the ruler who indulges in aggressive warfare is misled

---

[96] *Ch.* 17, "Fei kung," Part I [following the translation of Y. P. Mei, *Works*, p. 98].

to covet unrighteous profit or hopes to cover himself in military glory; his fault is his failure to recognize that his personal selfishness becomes the public disaster. If judged according to the standard of universal love [*chien-ai*], then of those who are guilty of "leading on the land to devour human flesh" it can truly be said that: "death is not enough for such a crime."[97] Much less do they deserve praise and fame for it.

Since aggressive warfare is never to be undertaken, all countries should seek methods of self-defense and self-preservation and nothing more than that [in the sphere of military activity]. That Mo Tzu was himself an expert at defensive tactics has been alluded to above. Apparently Mo Tzu realized that aggressive warfare could not be completely brought to a halt; hence he advocated self-defense against aggression in order to quench the ambitions of the powerful; his intent here can be likened to what the modern world calls armed peace. Thus he said: "Preparation is most important to the state, food supplies are most precious to the state. Soldiers are the state's claws, and walls are its self-defense." He also said: "The reason in all cases that large states do not attack small states is that the latter's supplies have been accumulated in quantity and their inner and outer walls are in good repair, and superiors and inferiors are in harmonious accord with each other. It is for these reasons that large states have no taste for attacking them."[98]

Moreover, Mo Tzu not only taught people to go no further than to defend themselves, he also advocated diplomatic methods, such as aiding the weak and keeping neighboring states peaceful, to enlarge the scope of the armed peace and to insure that the powerful states would be in circumstances that would bring about their defeat. In his own words: "For the world has long been in turmoil and war, and it is as weary as the little boy after playing horse [i.e., pointlessly wearied]. If only there were someone who would first profit all the other princely states in good faith! When some large state acts unrighteously, he would join in the sorrow; when some large state attacks some smaller one, he would join

---

[97] *Mencius*, "Li Lou" Part i [iv/i/14/2; Legge, p. 305]. Mo Tzu also had said: "If someone kills one man, he is condemned as unrighteous and must pay for his crime with his own life. According to this reasoning, if someone kills ten men, then he is ten times as unrighteous and should pay for his crime with ten lives, or if he kills a hundred men he is a hundred times as unrighteous and should pay for his crime with a hundred lives. Now all the gentlemen in the world know enough to condemn such crimes and brand them as unrighteous. And yet when it comes to the even greater unrighteousness of offensive warfare against other states, they do not know enough to condemn it. On the contrary, they praise it and call it righteousness. Truly they do not know what unrighteousness is." See *ch.* 17, "Fei kung," Part i [following Watson, *Mo Tzu*, p. 51].

[98] See, respectively, *ch.* 5, "Ch'i huan," and *ch.* 25, "Chieh tsang," Part iii. Also, *ch.* 47, "Kuei yi," urges the ruler of Wei to maintain a force of knights; his intent there is the same.

in rescuing it. When the outer and inner city walls in some small state are in ruin, he would join in their re-building. When supplies of cloth and grain are exhausted, he would contribute some. When money and negotiable wealth are inadequate, he would supply them. Were the large states befriended in this way (then the rulers of large states would be made happy, and if small states were befriended in this way) [parentheses in the original, showing reconstruction of a lost passage], the rulers of small states would be made happy. When the others are hard at work and one's self at ease, then one's own armor and weapons would be stronger. When with kindness and mercy people's needs are alleviated, such people will be won over. When good government is substituted for aggressive warfare, the benefits that must ensue will be manifold. When the expenses of maintaining one's own military forces are applied to overcoming the shortcomings of the princely states, then it shall be possible to gain and enjoy the benefits. Let the control of the army be upright and its cause righteous. If one will then be lenient with his people, and place confidence in his army, and in this way meets the armies of the princely states, he need fear no enemy in the world."[99]

All the points of this discussion, generally speaking, are penetrating and appropriate, and cannot easily be faulted. However, were we to conclude that Mo Tzu was unique in having conceived such a theory of armed peace, we would be in error. Confucius said: "The requisites of government are that there should be sufficiency of food, sufficiency of military equipment . . ." and further: "Let a good man teach the people seven years, and they may [only] then likewise be employed in war."[100] Hsün Tzu said: "Cultivate the rites so as to make orderly the court, correct the regulations so as to make orderly the offices of government, implement the governing equally so as to make orderly the population. Subsequently the ordinances shall be observed in orderly fashion at the court, all matters shall become orderly in the office of government, and the masses of the common people shall become orderly below. In this way the nearer shall be made respectfully close, and the distant shall come from afar to submit themselves in willingness [to such a government]. Above and below shall be of one mind, and the three armies [i.e., all the state's armed forces] shall be united in strength. [Such a ruler's] name and fame shall be as resplendent as the sun, as bright as flame. His majesty and power shall be adequate to induce compliance; he can direct affairs with his hands

[99] *Ch.* 19, "Fei kung," Part III [following with slight changes the translation of Y. P. Mei, *Works*, pp. 114–15]. Note that the metaphor of the small boy playing horse comes from *ch.* 46, "Keng Chu": "A small boy playing horse uses his legs until he is worn out."

[100] *Analects*, "Yen Yüan" Book XII [XII/7/1; Legge, p. 254] and "Tzu-lu" Book XIII [XIII/29; Legge, p. 275; the following sentence is: "To lead an uninstructed people to war is to throw them away."

folded. Moreover all violent and aggressive states will fall back and yield; it will be like a midget inflicting a beating on a giant."[101]

These statements of Confucius and Hsün Tzu are in their basic sense somewhat similar to Mo Tzu's. This is but another point at which these two schools show closely similar ideas. Mo Tzu, in explaining the Sage Emperor Yü's expedition against the Miao aborigines, King T'ang's campaign against the tyrant Chieh, and King Wu's against the tyrant Chou, holds that: "These are not what is called offensive war, they are what should be called punitive action."[102] His words, and those of Mencius when he spoke of "cutting off an ordinary fellow" and "being Heaven's agent,"[103] as well as those of Hsün Tzu in talking about ". . . preventing violence and eliminating harm . . . ," and ". . . armies of benevolence and righteousness. . . ,"[104] appear indeed to have been uttered from the same mouth. It may well be that Mo Tzu's concept of the condemnation of offensive war, though formulated with the particular evils of his own age in mind, also was something that he took over from the Confucian teachings, but expanded and elaborated upon to the point of full development.

[101] *Hsun Tzu, ch.* 10, "Fu kuo."
[102] *Ch.* 19, "Fei kung," Part III.
[103] *Mencius,* "Liang Hui-wang" Part II [I/ii/8/3] and "Kung-sun Ch'ou" Part II [II/ii/8/2].
[104] *Hsün Tzu, ch.* 15, "Yi ping," i.e., "Debating Military Affairs" [translated in full by Watson, *Hsün Tzu,* pp. 56–78].

CHAPTER FIVE

Lao Tzu and Chuang Tzu

SECTION ONE
The Lives and Times of Lao Tzu and Chuang Tzu

OF the great thinkers who appeared during the pre-Chin period, biographical facts are in no other case so difficult to ascertain as are those concerning Lao Tzu and Chuang Tzu, and of the two, that is especially so of Lao Tzu. Not merely are the events of his life shrouded in obscurity, even his surname, his given name, his birth, and his death are the subjects of many widely variant views, and no one can honestly say any of them is correct. The *Shih Chi, ch.* 63, in its biography of Lao Tzu, offers merely a vague and sketchy account of only about three hundred characters in length. Moreover, the account of his admonitions to Confucius, and Confucius' laudatory comment on him, comprise virtually half of the entire biography. When it comes to the account of Lao Tzu's life and career, the statements are extremely terse and incomplete, and full of expressions of uncertainty.[1] If the historian Ssu-ma Ch'ien [the first

---

[1] *Shih Chi, ch.* 63 [in some editions, e.g., that of Ku Chieh-kang and Hsü Wen-shan, Peiping, 1936, it is located in *ch.* 61], says: "The person [known as] Lao Tzu was a native of Ch'ü-jen Hamlet in Li Ward of H'u Hsien district in the State of Ch'u. His surname was Li, his given name was Erh, his courtesy name was Po-yang, and his posthumous honorific was Tan 冉, 聃. He was keeper of the Archives at the Chou court. Confucius traveled to Chou, intending to consult Lao Tzu on the rites. Lao Tzu said [replying to his questions]: 'Those matters of which you speak, sir, the persons and even their bones have long since crumbled away; only their words remain. Moreover, the gentleman who meets the proper time can go about in a carriage, but when the times are inappropriate, he must conceal himself and slink away. I have heard it said that an able merchant, though possessing full warehouses, appears as though they were empty; and that a gentleman, though filled with virtues, displays the countenance of one who is ignorant. You should strive to put aside your proud bearing and your numerous desires, your lusts and your excessive ambitions. They are of no benefit to your physical being [your person, yourself]. Whatever I could tell you is as this, and nothing more.' . . . Lao Tzu cultivated the Way and its Powers, making it the urgent purpose of his learning to conceal himself and to remain nameless [obscure]. After long residing in Chou, he observed that the Chou [Mandate] was in decline, so he left and traveled westward to the Pass. The Keeper of the Pass, Yin Hsi, said to him: 'You intend to withdraw into seclusion. Won't you make the effort to compose a book for me [before you may leave]!' Thereupon Lao Tzu composed a book in two parts, setting forth the meaning of the Way and its Powers [*Tao Te*] in five thousand and more characters, after which he departed. His end is wholly unknown. But it also is said that Lao Lai Tzu also was a man of the State of Ch'u, who wrote a book comprising fifteen essays telling about the applications of the Taoist School teachings. He was a contemporary of Confucius, it is said. Moreover, it would seem that Lao Tzu lived to the age of one hundred and sixty, or perhaps, as it is said, to over two

century B.C. author of the *Shih Chi*],* who was relatively close in time to that antiquity, was already unable to ascertain more fully and conclusively the facts needed to make up a reliable historical account, then for men of post-Han times, when the documentary sources were even scarcer, to attempt to supplement and correct that account was indeed a difficult undertaking. In truth, we may well feel that they merely spent their labor in vain. And we now are faced with the sole course of examining the various efforts of all the scholars of past and present to select the facts that seem the most nearly reasonable and consistent, and to adjust these to each other as best we can. Thus, inferentially, we may arrive at a general outline of the life of this founding master of Taoism; we can do no more than this.

Lao Tzu was of the surname Li, his formal name was Erh, and his courtesy name was Tan. His forebears were natives of the State of Sung, and of the surname Tzu 子, the sound of which shifted to that of the character *li* 李. Or, Lao 老 may have been the clan name.[2] Commoners

---

hundred. He did that by cultivating the Way to increase longevity. Two hundred and twenty-nine years after Confucius' death, history records that Tan, Grand Historian of the Chou court, met Duke Hsien [reigned 383–361 B.C.] of the State of Ch'in. . . . It is also said that [this] Tan 儋 was Lao Tzu. But is also said that that is not so. In this time, no one knows whether it is so or not. Lao Tzu was an [elusively] recluse gentleman."

Also, in *ch.* 47, "The Family History of Confucius," it states: "Nan-kung Ching-shu [of Lu] said to the ruler of Lu, 'Please allow me to travel with Confucius to Chou.' The ruler of Lu granted Confucius one carriage, two horses, and an attendant, and they travelled together to Chou to inquire about the rites. There, it is said, he encountered Lao Tan 耼 [some texts say Lao Tzu]. As he took his departure, Lao Tzu bade him leave, saying: '. . . One who is intelligent and profoundly perceptive brings himself close to death, when he is given to criticizing people. One who is so profusely and limitlessly eloquent endangers his own life, when he exposes the evil deeds of people. As a son, do not act considering yourself. As a servitor [of the ruler], do not act considering yourself.' "
In addition to these, the ancient works that mention Confucius' having visited Lao Tzu are the *Chuang Tzu*, and the *Li Chi. ch.* 7, "Tseng Tzu wen." We should note that Lao Tzu and Chuang Tzu both lived in concealment, withdrawn from the world, circumstances making it inevitable that their lives should leave no traces and their deeds not be recorded for transmission. Confucius' sigh that Lao Tzu was like a dragon [i.e., noble and secretive, seldom seen in the mundane world], and Ssu-ma Ch'ien in the *Shih Chi* stating that nothing is known of the end of his life, in truth make the most appropriate comments on Lao Tzu's life history. What can men of later times do, despite a wish to ascertain the details of his life, in face of this fundamental lack of documentary evidence?

*Square brackets indicate that the words enclosed were added by the translator.

[2] Yao Nai [1732–1815], "Lao Tzu chang-yi hsü." Ma Hsü-lun [born in 1884], in his *Lao Tzu ho-ku*, also states: "Lao Tzu was a native of Sung, and his surname was Tzu." Hu Shih, in his *Chung-kuo che-hsueh shih* [*ta-kang*], Part I [published 1919], says that Li was the surname, Lao the courtesy name, and Tan the formal name. Lao Tan, i.e., referring to him by formal and courtesy names simultaneously, reflects a standard practice among persons of the Spring and Autumn Period, other examples of which we see in the cases of [Confucius' ancestors] K'ung Fu-chia and Shu-liang Ho, and in Meng Shih-she, Meng Ming-shih, and the like. Kao Heng in his *Lao Tzu cheng-ku* [revised edition 1943, pp. 156–

in antiquity had no clan surnames; therefore Lao Tzu probably was a descendant of someone in the knightly class [*shih* ±] of the fallen Yin dynasty who had moved his place of residence to Hu-hsien [in modern southern Honan Province].[3] Because of his complete mastery of the ancient rites he was appointed keeper of the archives of the Chou court. He was senior in age to Confucius,[4] and on one occasion discussed the rites with him; Confucius cited him in laudatory terms.[5] However, Lao Tzu, a descendant of a fallen dynasty, was fully aware that his own chaotic age was not one in which to attempt positive actions; hence he devoted himself to the study of the Way [*Tao*] and its Powers [*Te*], "making it his urgent purpose to conceal himself and to remain nameless." [See footnote 1.] He resigned his official post and withdrew from the world, and nothing is known of the end of his life. The *Shih Chi* claims that he composed his book for the keeper of the [Han-ku] Pass, a man named Yin Hsi. Many recent scholars have doubted that the *Tao Te Ching* was written by Lao Tan.[6] We may note that inasmuch as Lao Tzu withdrew from the world to conceal himself, he probably would not have written

---

160] states that Lao Tzu's surname was Lao, the pronunciation of which subsequently shifted to Li. He cites two points in evidence: (1) in the Spring and Autumn Period there was the surname Lao, but no surname Li, e.g., a man who held the office of Ssu-ma [Marshall] in Sung named Lao Tso, and one who served as Ssu-t'u [Director of Works] in Lu called Lao Ch'i; (2) all of the philosophers of the Chou and Ch'in periods are called by their surnames.

   [3] According to the *So-yin* Commentary on the *Shih Chi*, Hu-hsien originally belonged to the State of Ch'en, until Ch'u destroyed the State of Ch'en (in the Forty-second year of the Chou King Ching) [477 B.C.], at which time it became part of Ch'u. Noting that Ch'en shared a boundary with the southern edge of Sung, that Lao Tzu's ancestors may have moved there from Sung, is a most likely possibility. Furthermore, Ch'en was a weak state, repeatedly suffering encroachments and humiliations. When Ch'en was destroyed Lao Tzu may already have been dead.

   [4] Hu Shih, drawing on Yen Jo-chü [1636–1704], demonstrates that Lao Tzu was at most twenty years older than Confucius, and probably was born in the First year of King Ling (571 B.C.). Recent scholars have been very skeptical that the incident of Confucius consulting Lao Tzu about the rites may be a fabrication; e.g., Wang Chung [1745–1794] in his *Lao Tzu k'ao-yi* and Ts'ui Shu [1740–1816] in his *Chu-ssu k'ao-hsin lu*.

   [5] Of the ancient works that carry the reference to Confucius' having met Lao Tzu, in addition to the *Shih Chi*, where it appears both in his "Shih-chia," i.e., "Family History," *ch.* 47, and in the biography of Lao Tzu; *ch.* 63, the most important are the *Li Chi*, *ch.* 7, "Tseng Tzu wen," which records that Confucius and Lao Tzu discussed mourning rites (Confucius was assisting at a funeral in a village) and where Confucius quoted Lao Tzu [as his authority] when explaining that there should be no empty spirit shrines within the Seven Ancestral Shrines [of the royal line], and in explaining the rites for the death of a child of seven to ten years, or building the brick enclosure around the coffin, or burial within the garden area [for minors], etc. The references to their meeting in various chapters of the *Chuang Tzu*, however, may be metaphorical and should not be cited in evidence.

   [6] Ts'ui Shu, *Chu-ssu k'ao-hsin-lu*; Wang Chung, *Lao Tzu k'ao-yi*; Ch'ien Mu, *Hsien-Ch'in chu-tzu hsi-nien k'ao pien*, Number 72.

a book to reveal himself; in that case, may not "the five-thousand character book" [the *Tao Te Ching*] be the work of his later follower, the senior
archivist Tan? [i.e., the T'ai-shih Tan 太史儋, forth century B.C.].[7]

Chuang Tzu "lived without leaving any traces; engaged in activities
that were not recorded for preservation." In this he somewhat resembles
Lao Tzu. The *Shih Chi*, ch. 63, says: "The man called Chuang Tzu was a
native of the State of Meng. His given name was Chou. Chuang Chou
at one time served as an administrative official [*li*] at Ch'i-yuan [the
"lacquer garden"; usually identified as a town in modern Shantung,
Anhwei or Honan Province].[8] He was a contemporary of Kings Hui of
Liang and Hsüan of Ch'i.[9] He made himself well-acquainted with all the
learning of his time, but the essentials of his own thought were derived
from the words of Lao Tzu. Therefore he wrote essays totalling more then
one hundred thousand characters, in the main consisting of allegorical
illustrations. He wrote "Yü-fu," "The Old Fisherman," "Tao Chih,"
"Robber Chih," and "Ch'ü ch'ieh," "Rifling Trunks," to satirize and
rebuke that fellow Confucius, and to clarify the methods of Lao Tzu.
Names such as "The Wastes of Wei-lei" [or "The Hill of Wei-lei," "The
Mountains of Zigzag," in *ch.* 23, "Keng-sang Ch'u"] and "The Master
K'ang-sang," are all invented locutions having no relation to reality.
Yet, he was a most skillful writer and user of phrases; he could point to
instances that had analogical import. He employed these to excoriate
Confucians and Mohists, and not even the most profoundly learned of
his time could deflect or evade [his wit]. His writings sparkle and glisten,

[7] Wang Chung, *Lao Tzu k'ao-yi*. The Sung dynasty scholar, Yeh Shih, in his *Hsi-hsüeh
chi yen*, was first to make this point, but the basis of his argument differs somewhat. Yeh
bases his opinion on the content of the thought, whereas Wang infer it from biographical
information. Even if the "five-thousand character book" [the *Tao Te Ching*] was not
written by the Lao Tzu of the Spring and Autumn Period, its content in general must be
regarded as adequately representative of his thought.

[8] The *So-yin* Commentary on the *Shih Chi*, citing the *Pieh-lu* [by Liu Hsiang of the Han
dynasty], states that Meng belonged to the State of Sung. The "Yi-wen chih," or "Journal
of Literature," *ch.* 30 of the *Han Shu*, says Chuang Tzu was a native of Sung.

[9] King Hui reigned from 370 to 319 B.C., King Hsüan from 319 to 301. King Wei
reigned from 339 to 329. Liang Ch'i-ch'ao deduces that Chuang Tzu's birth and death
dates were the Thirty-fourth year of King Hsien and the Fortieth year of King Nan
(335–275 B.C.). Ma Hsü-lun, in his *Chuang Tzu nien piao* ("Chronological table of Chuang
Tzu's life") (in *T'ien-ma shan-fang ts'ung-shu*), commences [the chronological record of
Chuang Tzu's life] with the Seventh year of King Lieh and goes to the Twenty-ninth
year of King Nan (369–286 B.C.). Ch'ien Mu's *Hsien Ch'in chu-tzu hsi-nien k'ao-pien*, Number
88, fixes Chuang Tzu's birth between the First and Tenth years of King Hsien and his
death between the Twenty-sixth and Thirty-sixth years of King Nan, and offers the tentative birth dates of the Fourth year of King Hsien and death date of the Twenty-fifth
year of King Nan (365–290 B.C.). If we accept Ch'ien's view, Chuang Tzu was about ten
years younger than Mencius.

flowing spontaneously in perfect expression of himself. Therefore Princes and Lords and the great and mighty men were unable to make use of him. King Wei of Ch'u [see footnote 9] heard about Chuang Chou's worthy qualities and sent an emissary bearing valuable gifts to bring him [to court], offering to appoint him chief minister of state. Chuang Chou laughed, and said to the Ch'u emissary: 'A thousand ounces of gold is indeed a great reward, and the office of chief minister is truly an elevated position. But have you, sir, not seen the sacrificial ox awaiting the sacrifices at the royal shrine of state? It is well cared for and fed for a few years, caparisoned with rich brocades, so that it will be ready to be led into the Great Temple. At that moment, even though it would gladly change places with any solitary pig, can it do so? So, quick and be off with you! Don't sully me. I would far rather roam and idle about in a muddy ditch, at my own amusement, than to be put under the restraints that the ruler would impose. I will never take any official service, and thereby I will [be free to] satisfy my own purposes.' "[10]

Although extremely few facts about the lives of Lao Tzu and Chuang Tzu have been preserved, it none the less is quite obvious that both of them had some connections with the State of Sung. Sung, anciently, had been established as the fief of Wei Tzu, and thus it was the ancestral state of the conquered Yin people.[11] [Wei Tzu was the older brother of the tyrant, the last reigning king of the Shang or Yin dynasty; the Chou founder admired his character and enfieffed him at Sung, where the majority of the conquered Yin people were told to reside under his rule, and where Wei Tzu could carry on the sacrifices to the Shang-Yin royal ancestors.] The thought of Lao Tzu and Chuang Tzu apparently stemmed from the Yin cultural background, in this being analogous to Confucianism and Mohism. However, Confucius and Mo Tzu, living at a time of the Chou dynasty's decline, attempted to employ their positive governmental methods based on benevolence and righteousness in the one case, and on love and profit in the other, to overcome disorder and restore things to their proper functioning. Their attitudes were comparatively optimistic. Lao Tzu and Chuang Tzu, however, tended toward negativism, offering the methods of withdrawal and quiescence whereby the individual could preserve his own safety and be at ease with himself. Their attitudes were pessimistic to the extreme. For in very ancient times there had already existed a line of thought that advocated "assuming the stance of

---

[10] *Chuang Tzu, ch.* 17, "Ch'iu-shui," i.e. "Autumn Floods," also contains reference to his rejecting an offer of official appointment in Ch'u, but it uses the story about a sacred tortoise to illustrate his reasons. [Chapter titles throughout are as translated in Burton Watson, *The Complete Works of Chuang Tzu.*]

[11] See, Chapters One and Two of the present work.

weakness and submissiveness" as the way to act,[12] and it was known to both Confucius and Lao Tzu. Lao Tzu accepted this doctrine of yielding compliance and humility and developed it further, whereas Confucius transformed its soft submissiveness into [the Confucian *shih* 土 who is] a man "both great and strong."[13] In consequence, Confucius and Lao Tzu became the founders of two distinct schools of thought and learning. The inscription on the tripod [in the ancestral shrine] of Cheng K'ao-fu says: "When he received his first appointement to office, he walked with his head bowed down. When he got the second, with his shoulders bent. When he got the third [he walked] with his whole body bent. In this way he hurried along the walls [saying to himself], 'Thus no one will presume to despise me.' "[14]

Thus the K'ung [i.e., Confucius'] clan's own ancestral instruction was profoundly consonant with the Taoist tenet of humble compliance. Confucius said: "When the Way does not prevail, be bold in action but conciliatory in speech." He also said: "Some men of worth retire from the

---

[12] Ma Hsü-lun, in his *Lao Tzu ho-ku*, states: "The Lao P'eng of the *Analects* is Lao Tzu." He notes that Confucius said of himself: ". . . A transmitter and not a maker, believing in and loving the ancients, [I venture to compare myself with Lao P'eng; see *Analects*, vii/1; Legge, p. 195] thus in fact [Ma believes] Confucius did find the source of his teaching in the learning of Lao Tzu, and it was not a new creation of his own. Ma adduces four further items of evidence for this: (1) The four sentences in Chapter Six of the *Tao Te Ching*, commencing: "The valley spirit does not die" [*ku shen pu ssu*] are false [attributions to Lao Tzu]; The *Lieh Tzu* quotes them as the words of the Yellow Emperor. Although the Yellow Emperor may very well not have written any book, this passage definitely expresses an idea of great antiquity, and as such it is quoted in both the *Lü-shih Ch'un ch'iu* [third century B.C.], and in Chia Yi's *Hsin Shu* [second century B.C.]. (2) In Chapter Thirty-six there is a line: "In order to grasp, it is necessary first to give" [*chiang yü to chih, pi ku yü chih*], which [he states] is identical with a line in the *Book of Documents*, "Chou Shu" [not found in the existing text, but quoted as a line from the "Chou Shu" in *Han Fei Tzu, ch.* 22, and in *Chan Kuo Ts'e, ch.* 22]. (3) The line in Chapter Forty-two: "Those who use force and violence do not die a proper death" [*ch'iang-liang che pu te ch'i ssu*] comes from an inscription on a bronze statue in the royal Chou ancestral temple. (4) The line in Chapter Seventy-nine: "The Way of Nature displays no partiality; it is always on the side of the good man" [*T'ien tao wu ch'in, ch'ang yü shan jen*] is from a lost portion of the *Book of Changes*. [The foregoing may be taken simply as evidence that ideas logically antecedent to those in the *Lao Tzu* had long existed in pre-sixth century B.C. Chou China.]

We may also note that Fan Li's words in his discussion on the Tao of Nature [*t'ien tao*], recorded in the *Kuo Yü*, "Yüeh yü" [Part Two; *ch.* 21] under the Third year of King Kou-chien (494 B.C.) also can serve as evidence that before Lao Tzu there already existed the ideal of "having the capacity to hold yet never over-flowing" [*ying erh pu yi*; i.e., keeping what one has by not striving for excess, cf. *Tao Te Ching*, Chapters Nine and Fifteen, where similar wording appears].

[13] Hu Shih, *Lun hsüeh chin chu*, First Collection [1936], pages 68, 74–75. [Cf. *Analects*, viii/7, for the allusion to the Confucian *shih*.]

[14] *Tso Chuan*, Seventh year of Duke Chao [534 B.C.; translation modified slightly from Legge, p. 619. Cheng K'ao-fu was an ancestor of Confucius; see Chapter Two, footnote 1.]

world," and further: "He who recompenses injury with kindness is a man who is careful about his personal safety."[15] His disciple Tseng Tzu also said: "Gifted with ability, and yet putting questions to those who were not so; possessed of much, and yet putting questions to those possessed of little; having, as though he had not; full, and yet counting himself as empty; offended against, and yet entering into no altercation: formerly I had a friend who pursued this style of conduct."[16] These all make it clear that both the master and his disciples, in the Confucian school, had also heard of the doctrines of yielding compliance for the sake of preserving one's life. And that passage in the *Doctrine of the Mean, ch.* x, which quotes Confucius' reply to [his disciple] Tzu-lu's question about strength, saying: "To be genial and gentle in teaching others, and not to revenge unreasonable conduct—this is the strength of the people of the South. The superior man lives by it." [Chan, *Source Book*, pages 99–100]. This would be all the more appropriate as a description of Lao Tzu himself.

Although Confucius accepted some aspects of that doctrine of gentleness and compliance, in general, however, his thought adopts the ideal of being "great and strong" [as in *Analects*, viii/7] with which to counterbalance the compliant attitude, leading ultimately to a median between extremes [as in the *Doctrine of the Mean*]. Therefore Confucius, in setting forth his views, repeatedly expressed himself on overcoming the cautiously reserved and superficial [even hypocritical] correctness of the countryside [*Analects*, xvii/13], and stirring people up to more vigorous attitudes. When asked about the principle that injury should be recompensed with kindness, he replied: "With what then will you recompense kindness?" And discussing the determined scholar and the man of benevolence, he said that they should be willing to sacrifice their lives to preserve their virtue complete.[17] The point most important to note here is that Confucius' objective in disseminating his teachings was not to achieve the safety of the individual, but that his concern was directed toward the common welfare of the whole world. This is precisely the point at which the spirit of Confucius is fundamentally different from that of Lao Tzu and Chuang Tzu, and it would not do to lose this distinction in observing the fact that both [Confucius and the two Taoists] emerged from among the Yin descendants. For, although political thought cannot be produced apart

[15] See, respectively, *Analects*, "Hsien wen" Book xiv [xiv/4, following Waley, p. 180, and xiv/39/1, following Legge, p. 290], and *Li Chi*, "Piao chi" [*ch.* 32; cf. *Analects* xiv/36, and Legge's note, p. 288].

[16] *Analects*, "Tai-po," Book viii [viii/5, Legge, p. 210]; [Chu Hsi's commentary], the *Chi-chu*, states: "Ma [Jung, of the Han dynasty] regards this as a reference to Yen Yuan; that is correct."

[17] See, respectively, *Analects*: "Hsien wen" Book xiv [xiv/36, Legge, p. 288] and "Wei Ling-kung" Book xv [xv/8, Legge, p. 210].

from its environment, yet not all of the thought within the same historical environment need be of the same mold. Individual character and temperament, family life, influences of teachers and friends—all of these can cause different individuals to respond differently to the same environment, and lead to divergences in their thought. The doctrines of Confucius and of Lao Tzu serve as an example of this. It is to be regretted that there remains so little information about [Lao Tzu's and Chuang Tzu's] lives that we are unable to ascertain in greater detail the concrete reasons that would clarify how the two schools, having emerged from one source, yet followed such different courses, and we are able to offer only very general deductions about the formation of Lao Tzu's thought.

Lao Tzu was a little older than Confucius. The world that confronted him also was that of the Late Chou kingdom in which the Way [*Tao*] had ceased to prevail. All of those instances which could be cited of all of the feudal states engaging in aggression, usurpation, and slaughter; of the aristocracy's excessive ways and their predilection for disorderliness; of oppressive government "more to be feared than fierce tigers" [see below, p. 295]; of "laws and regulations more numerous than the hairs of an ox" [said by the eighth-century poet Tu Fu of the laws of Ch'in]—all of these things witnessed by Confucius and Mo Tzu must also have been profoundly familiar to Lao Tzu. Confucius, though a descendant of the Yin aristocracy in the State of Sung, had personally known the persuasive influences of the Chou rites and moreover had served the State of Lu as an official in residence there; thus his methods for overcoming disorder and restoring things to their proper functioning display a mixing of Yin and Chou elements, using the rectification of names to correct the faults into which an excessive refinement could degenerate, and the practice of benevolence to restore some content to the emptiness of over-ritualization. Mo Tzu followed him, somewhat changing his doctrines, but like him also proposing to use the world's ways to rescue the world, and from the first never entertaining any doubts about the efficacy of political means and of transforming people through cultural means.

Lao Tzu was born into a family of Yin descendants who had moved to the State of Ch'en. [A small state of Chou times in what would be modern southeastern Honan, also populated largely by Yin descendants.] Although history does not record the reasons for their having left their native state, it may well have been for reasons similar to those that forced [Confucius' great-grand-father] Fang-shu to flee to the state of Lu. And Ch'en was a small state that not only suffered repeated invasions but also was subject to much internal disorder. Although the fief of the descendants of the Sage Emperor Shun, it was like the State of Sung in being populated by "descendants of a fallen dynasty," and as compared with the State of Lu, which above all others preserved the Chou rites, it was one in which the ways [of the previous age] that prevailed at the beginning of the dynasty still persisted, hence his situation there was quite different. Lao Tzu probably had never experienced the influence of the Chou rites, to which Confucius was subject. Therefore the one met the Duke of Chou in his dreams [see *Analects*, vii/5], while the other felt the Chou government to be burdensome and oppressive;[18] the one hoped for the restoration of the age of peace, while the other lived in a chaos-ridden state and harbored many fears. That their thought should have taken different directions may find here one of its explanations.

Beyond this, the thought and learning of Confucius and Lao Tzu focused upon somewhat different subject matter, and this may be another reason for the differences between the two bodies of thought. Confucius described himself as fond of antiquity and zealous in his pursuit of it, but the records on wood tablets and on bamboo of Kings Wen and Wu seem to have been the main body of material to which this pursuit led him. For if the records preserved in the States of Ch'i and Sung were inadequate to attest [the institutions of earlier times; Confucius himself made this statement; cf. *Chung Yung*, xxviii/5, and *Analects*, iii/9], it is unlikely that there was available to him much of the record of still more ancient times. Lao Tzu was keeper of the archives of the Chou court, and thus what he had access to, bearing on the study of antiquity, may have been still more ancient than anything known to Confucius. Moreover Lao Tzu, having unrestricted access to the archival records, could make a more thorough study of the facts of history, and thus could have come to know very clearly the falseness of the traditions that exaggerated the nobility and superiority of the past, permitting him to gain a different insight. Thus Confucius proclaimed himself a follower of the Chou while transforming ancient institutions, further seeking in the breadth and simplicity of the Yin ways to find a corrective for the faults of Chou over-refinement. Lao Tzu, however, was firmly convinced that the causes of disorder in the world lay, not in the shortcomings of specific institutions, but rather in the fact that institutions themselves were an unsatisfactory method of achieving order. Therefore problems of what to retain and what to abolish, what institutional elements to diminish and what to increase, were more or less vain expenditures of one's efforts. Benevolence and righteousness, rites and music, could only add to the disorder. The Yin had failed in this respect,[19] and the Chou had not been able to do much

---

[18] A situation in which "laws and orders are made prominent" [*Tao Te Ching*, Chapter 57] was one of the faults produced by the extremes of cultural refinement to which the government of the Chou tended; see Chapter Two, Section Four, of the present work.

[19] From antiquity, however, there had existed the tradition about the breadth of spirit and simplicity of Yin government. Although Lao Tzu did not say of himself that he followed the Yin, it may be that unconsciously with him it was a case of "The actualities

better. All the way back to the Sage Kings Yao, Shun, Yü, and Chi
[i.e., the Chou ancestral founder], which of them had ever been able to
devise a method that guaranteed enduring peace and order? All of the
praise of enlightened rulers and able ministers was no more than empty
phrases to shield persons who in fact were plunderers of the nation and
voracious seekers for power. The consequence [of such discoveries] must
have been that all mankind's hopes and all its bright dreams about human
society dispersed and vanished, leaving nothing behind. Chuang Tzu
then took those ideas established by Lao Tzu and greatly developed them,
clarified their implications, and extended them to their logical limits.
Thus a political philosophy of "inaction" [*wu-wei*, or, of taking no purposive action] was developed by men of deep concern, but men who had
lost all hope; it proceeded to become at once the subtlest and the most
telling of protests against tyrannical rulers and oppressive governments.[20]

The political thought of Lao Tzu and Chuang Tzu, nonetheless, is not
completely negative; it also has positive elements. Lao Tzu and Chuang
Tzu were skeptical about the efficacy of government and affirmed the
value of the individual. All of the delusions about society could be swept
aside, but the existence of the individual and his wish to preserve his life,
free from frustration or contortion, were realities that could not be denied.
If social institutions were detrimental to the individual's personal well-
being or the unhampered expression of his nature they should be abolished or reduced to prevent, as it were, the branches and leaves from
injuring the trunk and roots. Thus the preservation of life and the free
expression of man's nature became the ultimate goals of Lao Tzu's and
Chuang Tzu's political philosophy. Mencius said: "Yang Chu's principle
is 'each man for himself.' " [In the *Mencius*, Yang Chu is the prototype
of the Taoist against whom Mencius levels his criticisms of Taoism.
Mencius, III/ii/9/9; Legge, p. 282. See also VII/i/26; p. 464. The term used,
wei wo 爲我, may mean both "egocentric" and "individualistic." The
latter sometimes implies an overly aggressive character, out of keeping
with philosophical Taoism; hence "egocentric" is used here.]

The thought of Lao Tzu and Chuang Tzu indeed offers the purest

---

allowed it, but the style does not allow it." [A phrase much used in the *Kung-yang Commentary*, meaning "In reality it was so, but the record could not say so." See above, Chapter
Two, Section Six.] For "non-action" would be the most natural thing for a conquered
people to hope for from government, while yielding softness would also be the safest of
attitudes for a conquered people to maintain toward their government. This may be a
point at which Lao Tzu's background as a Yin descendant displays itself.

[20] Huang Chen [thirteenth century], in his [*Huang-shih*] *Jih ch'ao*, says: "The book
The Lao Tzu must have been written by a recluse scholar who resented the chaotic state
of the world and longed for peace and order." He thus is prior in offering this interpretation.

and most freely extended as well as the most systematic example of egocentric thought of the pre-Ch'in era.[21]

SECTION TWO
"Reversal is the Movement of Tao"

Chuang Tzu, ch. 33, "T'ien-hsia," discusses Lao Tzu's method in applying the Tao as follows: "[He said]: 'He who knows the male but clings to the female [as active and passive modes] becomes the ravine [recipient] of the world. He who knows the white [prominence] yet clings to the black

---

[21] The Late Chou egocentric thought was a strongly developed and influential school of thought. Lao Tzu and Chuang Tzu are the two representatives of it whose thought is relatively systematic and whose works have been preserved in the largest quantity. The *Han Shu, ch.* 30, "Journal of Literature," records other writings, such as the *Wen Tzu, Chüan Tzu, Kuan Yin Tzu, Lieh Tzu, Kung Tzu Mou, T'ien Tzu, Lao Lai Tzu,* and *Ch'ien Lou Tzu,* none of which is extant. (The extant *Wen Tzu* and *Lieh Tzu* were forged by later persons.) Still others either did not write anything, or their writings were already lost by Han times; therefore we discuss here only Lao Tzu and Chuang Tzu. See also Chapter One, Section Two, of the present work. Note that in the pre-Ch'in period, egocentric thought seems to have had a northern branch and a southern branch. The State of Ch'i was the center of the northern branch, where P'eng Meng (?), T'ien P'ien, Chieh Tzu, Ch'en Chung Tzu (and the author of the *Kuan Tzu*) belonged to it. Its doctrines tended to emphasize detachment, quiescence, and non-action as political methods. In the early part of the Han dynasty, the "Huang-Lao" school seems to have been the heir to this line, while Duke T'ai's policies of going along with the ways of Ch'i provided its background. [T'ai-kung Wang, first Duke in Ch'i at the founding of the Chou dynasty; he adopted a *laissez-faire* policy with regard to local ways and customs. See above, Chapter One, Section Two.] The southern branch had its center in Sung and Ch'u, where Lao Tan, Chuang Chou, Huan Yuan, Chieh Yü, and others belonged to it. Its doctrines tended to emphasize somewhat more the preservation of life and the freedom of the individual to follow his own nature. The Chin [third and fourth centuries A.D.] dynasty's "Lao Chuang" school developed its doctrines from this source. Fung Yu-lan, in his *Chung-kuo che-hsueh-shih,* Part I, Chapter Seven, page 179, says: "Lao Tzu's philosophy, then, is that of Yang Chu advanced one step forward; while that of Chuang Tzu is Yang Chu's philosophy pushed yet another step forward." [Fung Yu-lan, *A History of Chinese Philosophy,* translated by Derk Bodde, Vol. I, p. 143. Fung's *Short History of Chinese Philosophy,* published some fifteen years afterward in 1948, says on pages 93–94 that he now feels the date of the *Lao Tzu* to be still later than he had assumed when writing the earlier work, though his reasons are not developed. The author of the present work, in accepting the primacy of a figure who has come to be called Lao Tzu, and the priority of the *Lao Tzu* in the history of philosophical Taoism, presents his own well-ordered view of the development of the school, while also reflecting one that has been more important in the academic life of contemporary China than Western language works have usually indicated. In the West it has often been mistakenly assumed that only pre-modern authorities consider the *Lao Tzu* to be earlier than the *Chuang Tzu.* One other contemporary scholar writing in English who shares K. C. Hsiao's view is Wing-tsit Chan; see the introductory essays in his *The Way of Lao Tzu,* 1963, for a review of the issues.]

[obscurity], becomes the valley of the world.'[22] Others all rushed to the fore; he alone took to the rear, saying: 'I will receive what the world casts off.' . . . Others all strove for good fortune; he alone bended and yielded, thereby keeping himself whole, saying: 'By any means at hand, avoid calamities.' He took the most profound as his base, and he took simplicity as his standard, saying: 'That which grows firm and unyielding then gets destroyed; that which is sharp then gets blunted.' He was always considerate and deferent toward things, and he never encroached on or took from people. That can be called 'reaching the extreme' [of personal achievement]."

This indeed is the simplest and most accurate explanation of Lao Tzu's principles, and it also fully demonstrates that "yielding softness and humility," generous accommodation to others, and non-assertive withdrawal were the basic tenets of Lao Tzu's thought.

The ancient practice of the *Way* also had originally included a distinct tradition of yielding softness and of seeking to preserve life; we have already touched upon this in the preceding section. Lao Tzu "heard of it and was delighted with it" [according to *Chuang Tzu, ch.* 33]; hence his own doctrines do not represent a new creation. Yet Lao Tzu not only extended and proclaimed these basic tenets, he also drew upon his own observations of the Way of Nature [*t'ien tao*] and the affairs of men, formulating theoretical foundations for that practice of the Way, enabling it to become a well-founded and reasonable thought system. This, then, is Lao Tzu's contribution, and the reason for his having acquired the title of founding Master of Taoism.

That the Way, or *Tao* of Nature, displays cyclical movement, and that things and their principles fall into complementary opposites [or, into dialectical pairs], forms one of the basic principles of Lao Tzu's thought. In commentary portions of the *Book of Changes* we find: "There is no going not followed by a return"; "a new beginning follows every ending"; "When the sun stands at midday, it begins to set; when the moon is full, it begins to wane."[23] Lao Tzu's own observations are quite consonant with these statements. Thus he says: "Being and non-being produce each other, the difficult and the easy complement each other, being long and being short give meaning to each other, the high and the low expose each other, sounds and reverberations accord with each other, the foremost and the

---

[22] Also see the *Lao Tzu*, Chapter Twenty-eight, where the wording differs slightly. [Chuang Tzu's term is *Tao-shu* 道術, the "methods of the Way" or the "Art of *Tao*."]

[23] See respectively: The hexagram "T'ai," in the text of the "image," or *hsiang*; the hexagram "Ku," in the text of the "judgment," or *t'uan*; and the hexagram "Feng" [correcting a misprint in the text saying "Fu"], in the text of "judgment" [for all of the above, see the Wilhelm/Baynes translation of the *I Ching*, or *Book of Changes*, third edition, 1967, pp. 50, 477, and 670.]

last follow each other." He also says: "Bad fortune is that whereupon good fortune leans; good fortune is that wherein bad fortune lies resting." And further: "Things in some cases may gain by losing, or in other cases may lose by gaining."[24] Lao Tzu, thus, even more called attention to a principle of things in nature that, to summarize it, is stated: "Reversal is the action of *Tao*."[25] [Also translated "Reversal is the movement of Tao."] This principle of "reversal," when applied to preserving life and handling one's affairs, leads to the following five practices or methods:

The first is yielding softness [*no-jo* 懦弱]. The ordinary man's view invariably is that the methods of strength and firmness lead to victory, whereas the stance of yielding softness can invite only humiliation. Consequently, one should apply himself to becoming courageous and strong, and enter vigorously into the competition for mastery. But the ultimate result of this, it eventually will be discovered, in virtually all cases will be inevitable defeat, and, as Lao Tzu saw it, this displayed a failure to understand the way of "reversal." For "weakness is the function of Tao."[26] When we examine for ourselves the phenomena of the natural world, we discover that maturity and fullness are but the forerunner of decline and insignificance, that firmness and strength are the prelude to extinction and disappearance from existence. "Men are soft and weak at their birth, rigid and tough in death. All the plants and trees are yielding and tender in life, and stiff and brittle in death. Hence unyielding strength is the companion of death, while yielding softness is the companion of life."[27] Hence, not only is it true that "things [objects] in their prime then become old."[28] This is true not only of all living beings; even the Way of Nature inevitably follows such a course.

"Thus, the windstorms will not last a whole morning; the pounding rain will not last a whole day. What does these things? It is heaven and earth [i.e., Nature] that does them. If heaven and earth cannot make them long endure, how much less can man?"[29] And if one seeks the proof of this principle in the affairs of man, then "the one whose courage leads him to take risks shall die violently" and "those who use force and violence do not die a proper death."[30] That rigidity and force are injurious becomes quite clear and obvious. When, on the other hand, we observe

---

[24] See, respectively, Chapters Two, Fifty-eight, and Forty-two.

[25] Chapter Forty. Chapter Seventy-eight says: "Straight words seem to be their opposite." [W. T. Chan, *Source Book*, p. 175.]

[26] Chapter Forty. [Chan, *Source Book*, p. 160.]

[27] Chapter Seventy-six.

[28] See also Chapters Thirty and Fifty-five. "After things reach their prime, they begin to grow old, which means being contrary to the Tao. Whatever is contrary to Tao will soon perish." [Chan, *Source Book*, p. 155.]

[29] Chapter Twenty-three.

[30] Chapters Seventy-three and Forty-two.

softness and compliance, we discover that their usefulness is very great. "The Way of Nature is not to contend, yet always to gain the victory"; this is to say that nature conquers through softness. "In all the world there is nothing softer than water, yet as it attacks the unyielding and the firm, nothing can prevail against it";[31] this is to say that water conquers through softness. For weakness and softness can insure self-preservation, while the firm and the strong must be broken; not to contend can lead to victory, while those that lack this *Tao* are quickly used up: Thus "softness and weakness conquer firmness and strength."[32] This indeed is an ultimate and unvarying principle, the essential art in dealing with life's problems.

The second is humility [*ch'ien-hsia* 謙下]. Humility is also one of the manifestations of yielding compliance. In the principles of things there is nothing that can demonstrate its usefulness so well as the principle of rivers and seas. "The rivers and seas can rule over all the upland streams, because they skillfully remain below them; thus it is that they rule over all those streams." In the affairs of men, that which best fits the principle of humility should be the form of titles that kings and lords give themselves. "People most of all hate to be the orphaned, or be bereaved, or be the unworthy, yet kings and lords use these names for themselves."[33] [*Ku, kua* and *pu ku*. All were conventional terms of humility used by kings and lords as euphemisms for the royal "We."] Were humility applied to the affairs of government, it would bring order within and peace without, and in both areas would become the talisman of invariable success. For "Those skilled in employing people are humble toward them"; therefore "Thus it is that if one wants to rule over the people, he must say he is below them; if one wants to be at the fore of the people, he must place himself after them. Thus it is that the Sage can occupy the highest place, yet the people do not feel his weight; he can occupy the foremost place, yet the people are not envious of [or distressed by] him. Thus it is that the world joyfully supports him and does not weary of that. It is precisely because he does not compete that the world cannot compete

---

[31] Chapters Seventy-three and Eighteen. Chapter Thirty-six says: "In order to contract, it is necessary first to expand. In order to weaken, it is necessary first to strengthen. In order to destroy, it is necessary first to promote. In order to grasp, it is necessary first to give. This is called subtle light." [Chan, *Source Book*, p. 157.]

[32] Chapter Thirty-six. Chapter Forty-three also says: "The softest things in the world course freely over the hardest things in the world."

[33] Chapters Sixty-six and Forty-two. Chapter Eight says: "The highest good is to be like water. Water skillfully brings benefits to all things and does not contend with them. It places itself in the lowest settings that all others disdain. That is how it comes so to being like *Tao*." Here the meaning is the same.

with him."[34] This is the effect produced when humility is used in domestic affairs of state. When applied to external affairs, its benefits are also of the largest scope and with the most realistic consequences. For international conflicts arise from large countries' using their power to encroach against smaller ones, and the weaker countries' arousing a spirit of resistance to the stronger. If each could but adopt a mode of deference toward the other, then the difficulties would be dispersed and the conflicts resolved; they could exist in mutual accord and be trouble-free. Lao Tzu explained this, saying: "A great country can be compared to the lower drainage of a river. It is where the world converges; it is the female of the world. The female, by its quiescence, always overcomes the male. By quiescence it assumes the lower place. Thus it is that a great state, by condescending to small states, gains them for itself; and that small states, by abasing themselves to a great state, win it over to them. In the one case, the abasement leads to gaining adherents; in the other case, to procuring favor. Large states want merely to annex and accumulate people, while small states want merely to be brought in and given services to perform [as in the feudal-type relationship among states]. Both, indeed, can gain their objectives, so the large state should assume the more lowly place."[35]

The third is generous accommodation of others [k'uan jung 寬容]. Arbitrariness and stubborn prejudice, forcing others to give in to one's self—these too can be the causes of political disorder. Wanting to correct these faults, Lao Tzu established the doctrine of generous accommodation of others, saying: "The Sage has no fixed mind; the mind of the common people becomes his mind. I treat the good with goodness; the bad I also treat with goodness. So, goodness is attained. I keep trust with those who are trustworthy; with the untrustworthy I also keep trust. So, trust is attained. The Sage, in [ordering the affairs of] the world, blithely accepts the whole world as one, indistinct within his own [undifferentiating] mind."[36] Should the ruler, in presiding over the world and wielding the power of government, be incapable of "separating white from black" [i.e., to make arbitrary distinctions] and fix upon a single, highest standard, and remain blithely undifferentiating, his mind free of ruling

[34] Chapters Sixty-eight and Sixty-six [the latter modified from Chan, *Source Book*, p. 171].

[35] Chapter Sixty-one. Kuo Hsiang's [d. A.D. 312] Commentary adds: " ' Taking over a small state' means that the small state will make itself subsidiary to [the large state that accommodates] it; and 'taking over a large state' means that the large state will contribute to [the small state that adopts an accommodating attitude toward] it."

[36] Chapter Forty-nine. Kuo Hsiang's Commentary explains: "[The word translated] 'blithely' means that the mind is subject to no ruling attitude of judgment, and 'accepts the whole world as one, indistinct within his own mind' means to be without predilections or prejudices." [Cf. *Analects* IV/10.]

judgments, he would seem to have failed to carry out the functions of rulership. However, as Lao Tzu saw it, "the foremost and the last follow each other," and the true and the false are relative to each other. This is an inexorable principle of the Way of Nature, and of all things. If one fails to understand this principle, and sets up standards of name and reality against which to judge things, not merely will that force the one who grasps "this" then to lose "that," but the arbitrary separation of the high from the low also will be the source of troubles and disputes. That would turn out far worse than if the ruler should blithely assume the undifferentiating attitude of mind, in order to let conflicts and struggles subside, thereby ensuring the preservation and utilization of things. Thus the *Lao Tzu* says: "Do not exalt the worthy, and the people will not contend." And it also says: "The Sage is always ready to rescue people, therefore no people are cast off; he is always ready to rescue things, therefore no things are abandoned. This is called 'following the light' [of Nature's Way]."[37]

Yet the ruler's most difficult achievement is not merely always to use a generously accommodating attitude in his overall relations with the common people. The ruler truly able to carry the generous accommodation of all others to the fullest degree is the one who can, in the blithely detached and disinterested spirit, approach even those matters involving his private favor and antipathy, likes and dislikes, benefits and obligations, wholly without calculation. Then he can "recompense injury with kindness," and can "hold the [humbler] left-hand half of the tally, and not charge others with the performance of duties."[38] This, then, is the most

[37] See, respectively, Chapters Three and Twenty-seven. In a note on "following the light," Ma Hsü-lun, in his *Lao Tzu ho-ku*, states that *hsi* 襲, "following" in ancient usage was interchangeable with *hsi* 習, "normal practice." However, the Kuo Hsiang Commentary on Chapter Twenty-seven develops the concept of going along with people's wishes, according to which "following the light" should mean "following the light of the people's natural tendencies without imposing one's [the ruler's] attitudes upon them." Ma's interpretation would appear to be incorrect. [See also Chan, *Source Book*, p. 153, note 71.]

[38] See, respectively, Chapters Sixty-three and Seventy-nine. Kuo Hsiang's Commentary: "To hold the left-side of the tally is to guard against the quarter from which resentments develop." Note that in the *Li Chi*, ch. 1, "Ch'ü li," Part One, it says: "The one offering grain holds the right-hand half of the tally." The sub-commentary [*su*] on this line reads: "The [two sides of] the tally are symbolic of relative dignity. The right half signifies the higher dignity." The *Chan-kuo ts'e*, ch. 28, "Han ts'e," 3, says: "Some one said to Chung-kung . . . The lord of An-ch'eng is highly regarded in the State of Wei on the east, and highly esteemed in the State of Ch'in on the west. He holds the right side of the tally and charges the rulers of Ch'in and Wei with responsibilities on behalf of his Duke." From these it appears that "the left-hand side of the tally" should be taken to mean "the humbler one, not empowered to hold others to the performance of duties" [especially, the payment of obligations].

difficult achievement, and at the same time is the ultimate in the practice of *Tao*.

The fourth method is contentment [*chih tsu* 知足]. Once we know that the Way of Nature is cyclical, and that good and bad fortune are latent in and relevant to each other, then knowing how to be contented is the supreme art of relating oneself to the world around one. That is, to occupy the lofty place is to place oneself in peril; to be anxious for gain is to expose oneself to loss. Hence Lao Tzu said: "To grasp and be filled to overflowing is not as good as stopping in time. To temper steel until it is the keenest makes it impossible to keep it sharp. A house overfilled with gold and jade cannot be long preserved. Fortune and high place bring arrogance, which induces its own downfall. Withdraw from the scene when your tasks are completed, for that is the Way of Nature [*t'ien tao*]." And elsewhere, "Intense fondnesses inevitably lead to profligate expenditures; vast hoarding invariably leads to great losses. He who knows contentment will not be disgraced; he who knows when to stop will not be imperiled. Such a one will long endure." The advantages of contentment being so great as this, "The sage therefore discards all intensities, discards all profligacies, discards all superfluities."[39]

The fifth is to perceive the subtle [*chien wei* 見微]. In the foregoing we have already set forth the general outlines of Lao Tzu's doctrines about preserving life and relating to the world about one. There remains, however, a further point not yet touched upon. We may indeed understand that things at their limit must reverse themselves, that when one's tasks have been successfully completed one should then withdraw. But if we are not able to continue on, or to halt, when the proper moment is at hand, then the art of knowing contentment becomes most difficult to apply; good and bad fortune are latent in each other, and the approach of either can be virtually imperceptible. Both the beginning of success and the first stages of failure are extremely minute and inconspicuous. One who has the capacity to perceive the subtle signs and comprehend the delicate springs of movement can then control their incipient manifestations, and bring them to fruition, forestalling incipient failure. Lao Tzu said: "Seek the difficult where it is still easy; accomplish the great where it is still small." He further said: "That which is at rest is easily kept hold of; before a thing has given indications of its presence, it is easy to take measures against it; that which is brittle is easily broken; that which is very small is easily dispersed. Action should be taken before

---

[39] See, respectively, Chapters Nine, Forty-four, and Twenty-nine. Chapter Sixty-seven says: "I have three treasures; cling to them and maintain them: The first is a tender concern; the second is frugal restraint; and the third is never daring to place myself foremost in the world." This summarizes the four practices of yielding weakness, humility, generous accommodation of others, and knowing contentment.

a thing has made its appearance; order should be secured before disorder has begun."[40] Once this art is made clear, then the course toward safety and the evasion of injury becomes all the more full and perfect in its completeness.

In the conclusion of the preceding section we have said that Lao Tzu held a low evaluation of society but a high one of the individual, and in that way he lodged the positive in the negative. That is to speak of the final objectives of his thought. The five practices listed in this section, although formulated and advocated principally in keeping with the idea that "weakness is the *Tao* in application," and functionally seeming to incline toward the negative, yet when examined for their practical meaning, reveal that indeed they have lodged positive attitudes within the negative. For if "reversal is the movement of *Tao*," then the one who moves in the reverse direction does so with positive intent; he does not reverse himself for the sake of going backwards. Accepting this line of argument, one can then say that the one who "keeps to the female" [i.e., retains the passive mode] does so precisely with the desire "to be the settling basin [for the streams] of the whole world." The one who is yielding and soft wants thereby to prevail over the strong and the firm. The one who speaks as though he were below the people desires to preside over them. The one who neither contends nor attacks wants to gain thereby the kind of success so that nothing in the world will be able to contend with him. In short, in all those things of which Lao Tzu said: "straight words seem to be their opposite," his purpose was to advance by retreating; it was not limited to knowing contentment and finding lasting safety. Therefore, to say that Lao Tzu's theories are wholly nihilistic is indeed to misunderstand them.

Implicit also in Lao Tzu's Way of yielding compliance and humility is another significant tendency that we have not yet mentioned. Lao Tzu said: "The Sage has no fixed mind; the mind of the common people becomes his mind," and, further: "He does not dare to become the foremost in the world." He also said: ". . . wanting to rule over the people, he must say that he is below them; wanting to be at the fore of the people, he must place himself after them." If those who rule the country and preside over the people were really capable of carrying into practice all of these methods, one by one, then all of the people of the whole world would do what they are supposed to do and would pursue peaceful and happy lives. The restrictions practiced by government would be extremely few.

[40] Chapters Sixty-three and Sixty-four [following Legge]. It should be noted that this concept does not appear in the description of Lao Tan's way of practicing the *Tao* given in *Chuang Tzu, ch.* 33, "T'ien-hsia"; it is possible that this does not represent the thought of Lao Tzu and could be the interpolation from a later hand; therefore I retain a measure of skepticism about this item.

Moreover, they would be designed to accord with the wishes previously indicated by the common people, in their expressions of opinion, and by their actions; they would not emerge from the ruler's despotic personal decisions as stringent regulations forced upon the people. This theory is vastly different from those held by the Confucians, the Mohists, or the Legalists. Mo Tzu said: "Whatever the superiors approve of the inferiors must all approve of; whatever the superiors disapprove of the inferiors must all disapprove of." Hsün Tzu, discussing the way the people should follow their ruler, said that those who agreed with him were right, and those who differed with him were wrong. Han Fei Tzu said that: "The ruler of men must be so clear-minded that he understands how to achieve orderly government, and so rigorous that his governing will be carried out. Then even when he runs counter to the people's wishes, his governing will be effected." And even Confucius, despite his stress on benevolence and virtue, nonetheless said: "The people may be made to follow a path of action, but they may not be made to understand it."[41] Insofar as he would have one man's mind necessarily dominant over all men, he is indeed no different from Lord Shang and Han Fei Tzu [the leading figures of Legalism]. To express this in modern terminology, Confucius and Mo Tzu and all the others were close to the concept of monarchic despotism, while Lao Tzu alone inclined toward what we would call popular government under a "figurehead monarch." The thing to be regretted is that in ancient times China had no actual institutions of popular rule, like those which appeared in ancient Greece, that could have enabled Lao Tzu to use them as the basis on which to erect a positive and practical democratic philosophy. As it was, his methods of compliance and humility were able to develop into nothing more than negative political protest. This, however, is because the historical setting imposed its limitations, and thus should not be used to fault Lao Tzu himself.

Section Three
"Taking No Action, Yet Leaving Nothing Undone"

In the thought of Lao Tzu we encounter two basic concepts: the one is "reversal," *fan* 反; the other is "nothing," *wu* 無. The important aspects of his political philosophy are based on the latter; hence it in particular deserves our attention.[42]

---

[41] See, respectively, *Mo Tzu, ch.* 11, "Shang t'ung"; *Hsün Tzu, ch.* 18, "Cheng lun"; *Shang Tzu, The Book of Lord Shang, ch.* 17, "Shang hsing"; *Han Fei Tzu, ch.* 18, "Nan mien" [cf. Liao, vol. I, pp. 154–55, and Watson, *Han Fei Tzu*, p. 94] and *Analects*, "T'ai-po" [VIII/9; Legge, p. 211].

[42] To express this in simple terms, "nothing" is the essence of *Tao*; "reversal" is the application of *Tao*. "No form" is the basic principle underlying the production of living

Lao Tzu made profound observations of the universe, leading him to conclude that heaven and earth and all the things within it were produced from spontaneous Nature [*Tao*].[43] Hence all those which have form came from "no form" [*wu hsing*]; the mystery and emptiness was the root from which sprang the concrete substance.[44] If we observe the sequence through which "being is born from nothing," we discover that: the formation of the universe proceeds from void to reality; that starting with quiescence there is then produced movement; that first there is simplicity but subsequently there comes complexity.[45] Moreover, the *Tao* produces [or, gives birth to] all things in a most natural manner, accomplishing that quite purposelessly;[46] it definitely is not a conscious, intentional act of creation. Were we to say that the great Way exists of itself, and that all things produce themselves, this too would be by no means inappropriate. Having clarified this principle [of what exists and how it comes to exist, or] of being and non-being, Lao Tzu then proceeded to conclude that the subsequent "that which is" should take as its model and example the prior "nothing." [It is, to be sure, misleading to translate *yu* 有 and *wu* as "being" and "non-being," although that is often done, for these abstractions have more complex meaning for contemporary readers, as also for Chinese of the imperial period, than they seem to have had for Lao Tzu and Chuang Tzu. But there seems to be no other convenient solution.] For to require the subsequently emergent to model itself on the preexistent was, in fact, no different from causing that which has gone on to reverse itself and return to its beginnings. Therefore, this matter of

---

things, and "reverse action" is the transforming process involving everything "having form." Philosophically speaking, "nothing" is more important than "reversal."

[43] Chapter Twenty-five says: "There was something undifferentiated and yet undefined, which existed before heaven and earth. Soundless and formless, it depends on nothing and does not change. It operates everywhere and is free from danger. It may be considered the mother of the universe. I do not know its name; I call it *Tao*. Forced to name it, one could call it 'Great.' . . . Man models himself on earth, earth models itself on heaven, heaven models itself on *Tao*. *Tao* models itself on the 'Spontaneous' [or, 'Nature']." [Modified from Chan, *Source Book*, p. 153.]

[44] Chapter Forty: "All the myriad things of the world emerged from being; being emerged from non-being."

[45] Chapter Forty-two: "Tao produced one; one produced two; two produced three; three produced all things." Kao Heng's *Lao Tzu cheng-ku* says that ["one" is the undifferentiated matter of heaven and earth], "two" means heaven and earth, while "three" means the *Yin* force, the *Yang* force, and the combined force of the two, *ho ch'i*, or harmony.

[46] Chapter Ten: "It gives birth to but does not possess; it serves but does not make claims; it presides over all but does not command. This is called its mysterious power." Chapter Fifty-one contains similar wording. Chapter Thirty-four says: "The great *Tao* flows everywhere; it is there on the left and on the right. All things emerge from it and are sustained by it, but it does not take charge over them. It completes its tasks but does not take possession; it spreads itself over all but does not make itself the master."

modelling after the prior, Lao Tzu called "seeing the return," or "returning to what is destined," or "keeping to the mother," or "holding steadily to the Way of the past."[47] To speak more concretely, "returning to what is destined" meant "to return again to the absence of things," which means nothing more or less than the meticulous preservation of the pristine natural *Tao*[48]. However, we should note that although Lao Tzu taught that people should return to the root, and should value emptiness and nothingness, serenity and unity, and spontaneous nature, yet he never wanted to eradicate all of the myriad things possessing bodily form in order to return to the primeval state of "no forms." For "nothing" in giving birth to "being" is simply expressing the spontaneous nature of Tao. And although that act is not equal to absolute serenity and quiescence, still it differs from intentional and purposeful action. Nature, in giving birth to all the myriad forms of existence, displays merely that "*Tao* invariably takes no action, and yet there is nothing left undone."[49] Although the myriad things certainly are not to be equated with *Tao*, still the *Tao* omnipresently exists in all things. "For an illustration, *Tao's* presence throughout the universe is like all the streams and rivulets running into the rivers and seas."[50] Hence this act of returning to what is destined is not a matter of giving up all of the myriad things that are presently in existence in order to revert back to that indistinct and undefined state out of which things come into being. Rather, it seeks to preserve some of the power [*te*] of the quiescent void here in the midst of the world of things, so that one will not again be found "pulling on the rice shoots to help them grow faster," or, acting contrary to the fundamentals of nature. [Refers to an anecdote about a simple-minded farmer of the State of Sung, used by Chuang Tzu to illustrate the folly of interfering with nature.] Therefore Lao Tzu's statement: "When once it [*Tao*] was given

[47] Chapter Sixteen: "Attain complete vacuity; keep to steadfast quietude. All things simultaneously emerge into existence; I see therein their return. For as all things flourish, each one returns again to its root. Returning to the root is called quiescence; it can be called returning to what is destined. To return to what is destined is called the eternal [*Tao*]. To know the eternal is called enlightenment. Not to know the eternal is to act blindly, and that results in disaster." Chapter Fifty-two: "The universe has its beginning; that can be taken as the mother of the universe. Having found the mother, one then recognizes her children. Having recognized the children, then proceed to keep to the mother, and be free from peril to the end of your life." Chapter Fourteen: "Hold steadily to the Way of the past and master the things of today. When one is able to recognize the ancient beginnings [of Nature's process, he understands] what is called the true character of the *Tao*."

[48] This is somewhat similar in import to the eighteenth-century European "return to nature." The early writings of Rousseau represent one example of it.

[49] Chapter Thirty-seven.

[50] Chapter Thirty-two.

a name, names then came into existence [to distinguish things]. At that point, one must know that it is time to stop, for by knowing when to stop [in this process of imposing artifice on nature], one can remain free from danger."[51]

To take this principle of returning to the fundamental, and turning back to what is destined, and to apply it to government, leads to a detached and quiescent governing through non-action. Lao Tzu said: "By purity and quiescence one becomes the world's leader." And, elsewhere: "By doing it without taking action, there is nothing that is not well-governed." Further: "The sage manages affairs through the course of taking no action, and spreads the teachings that are not put in words." He also said: "In carrying out the Tao, diminish day by day, and after diminishing continue still further to diminish, in that way to achieve the state of taking no action, [for with the state of no action, there will be nothing left undone]."[52]

As he urges [rulers] to diminish, and then diminish still more, the first principle of non-action is to decrease the things done by government, and to reduce the scope of governmental activity to the very lowest levels and smallest degrees possible. As for handling all of the affairs of the world, the common people themselves are permitted to do as they wish, then superior and inferior can live together in peace, each achieving what is most appropriate to him. But if one forcibly intervenes, and launches numerous activities, it will inevitably lead to a still greater confusion of the affairs of government, mislead people, and produce disturbance and trouble. This is not an extremist pronouncement designed just to startle the hearer, but is something he corroborated by referring to all the experience of mankind. "The more artificial taboos and restrictions there are in the world, the more the people are impoverished; the more useful implements the people possess, the more the state becomes disorderly; the more artifices and clever skills men acquire, the more harmful things they will produce. The more that laws and regulations are given prominence, the more thieves and robbers there will be."[53] This passage refers to the evil harvest that an activist government must reap. However, this assumes that activism does not involve oppressive government [the effects of which should be much worse than the consequences of a meddlesome administration]. In point of fact, those rulers who induce the eras of great

[51] Chapter Thirty-two.

[52] See, respectively, Chapters Forty-five, Three, Two, and Forty-eight.

[53] Chapter Fifty-seven. Also, Chapter Fifty-two says: "Stop up their apertures, close their doors and gates, and they will have lifelong freedom from afflictions. Open up their apertures, assist in all their affairs, and they will suffer a lifelong plague." ["Apertures" may refer both to the eyes, ears, mouth, nose, etc., i.e., the avenues of sensory perception, and to the openings through which pass communication and travel.]

chaos are not merely those who meddle and disturb, but inevitably are those who also inflict all kinds of violent oppression on the people.

The most severe aspects of such truly oppressive government, those most injurious to the people, are three: excessive taxation, harsh punishments, and frequent warfare. "The people hunger because their superiors consume an excess in taxation. That is why they go hungry." And: "The royal courts are extremely ornate; the fields are extremely weedy [and untended]; the granaries are extremely empty. Garments are embroidered and ornamented, keen swords hang at the waist; food and drink are consumed to satiety, while goods and treasure are possessed in excess."[54] These describe the harm done by heavy taxation, which takes from those who have not enough and gives to those who have an excess. "The people do not fear death; what use, then, to threaten them with death?"[55] This is the counter-reaction produced by harsh punishments and heavy fines. "When the Way does not prevail, war horses are bred even in the suburbs." "Where armies have been stationed, thorns and brambles grow. After a great war, harsh years of famine are sure to follow."[56] These describe the evil results of exhausting wars and excessive reliance on military action. To govern the realm in this way can indeed be described as not merely non-beneficial, but actually destructive; it is worse than no governing at all.

"Oppressive government is fiercer than tigers." [*Li Chi, ch.* 4, "T'an-kung," Part Two, quoting Confucius.] This troubled not only Lao Tzu; Confucius too gave deep thought to how this problem could be corrected. But the Confucians sought cure for it in the virtues of benevolence and righteousness, loyalty and filial submission, and through the civilizing refinements of rites and music, regulations and institutions. From Lao Tzu's point of view, all of these measures depended upon purposive action, and hence could accomplish nothing that would help. For, "When the great *Tao* declined [the doctrine of] benevolence and righteousness arose. When knowledge and cleverness appeared, there emerged great hypocrisy. When the six family relationships are not in harmony, there will be [the advocacy of] filial piety and parental love. When a country is in disorder, there will be [the praise of] loyal ministers." Moreover, "Only when the *Tao* is lost does the doctrine of Virtue arise. When Virtue is lost, only

[54] Chapters Seventy-five and Fifty-three. Also, Chapter Seventy-seven: "Is not the *Tao* of Nature like drawing a bow? It brings down the higher part, and raises the lower part. It lessens the redundant [convex part] and fills up the insufficient [concave] part [to draw the bowstring back on the arrow]. Nature's Way is to take away where there is excess, and to supplement where there is deficiency. The way of man is not thus; rather, it is to take away where there is too little and offer up where there already is excess." This also appears to be a condemnation of heavy taxation.

[55] Chapter Seventy-four.

[56] Chapters Forty-six and Thirty.

then does the doctrine of benevolence arise. When benevolence is lost, only then does the doctrine of righteousness arise. When righteousness is lost, only then does the doctrine of ritual propriety arise. Now, propriety is a superficial expression of loyalty and good faith, and the beginning of disorder."[57] Since benevolence and righteousness, the rites and the forms of propriety, all totally repudiate the fundamentals of nature, to employ them in the attempt to overcome disorder is then as pointless an effort as [in the words of an ancient saying] stirring hot water to keep the pot from boiling over. On the other hand, to eradicate oppressive government and bring an end to violent tyranny, the only course is to "restrain it with that simplicity which has no name." ["Simplicity" is, literally, the "uncarved block," *p'u* 樸, Lao Tzu's favorite symbol of pristine simplicity; the un-named refers to the state before the proliferation of names and distinctions, i.e., before the descent into civilization.] Or to "support all things in their natural state, and dare to undertake no action," in order to await the world's "stabilizing itself" and nothing more. "Therefore the Sage says: I take no action yet the people transform themselves, I favor quiescence and the people right themselves, I take no action and the people enrich themselves, I am without desires and the people are themselves pristine."[58]

"Ruling a large country is like frying a small fish";[59] this statement of Lao Tzu's has been admired throughout the Chinese world for its marvelous aptness in conveying the idea of detached and simple government. [I.e., do not fuss with it or it will fall apart and be spoiled.] However, the real import of non-action goes beyond just this. The Tao produces all the myriad things, but does so purposelessly, intending nothing. Therefore "no action" [*wu-wei*] can also be defined as action undertaken with no particular purpose in mind. That is, people's personal intentions and purposes are also one of the major causes of chaotic misrule. Acts of personal strife and extravagant consumption, oppressive and meddlesome government, all can arise from such [intentions and purposes]. Therefore only by eliminating all private purposes and intentions can one bring about the return to Nature's non-action. "That is why the Sage puts himself at the rear yet is at the fore, puts himself outside [the action] and preserves himself." "[That is why the sage] manages affairs through the course of taking no action, and spreads the teachings that are not put into words. All things arise [in the process of nature] and he does not turn away from them. He produces them but does not take possession of them. He acts, but does not expect a reward for the results. He accomplishes his task but does not claim credit for it." In this way [the enlightened sagelike rulers]

---

[57] Chapters Eighteen and Thirty-eight [slightly modified from Chan, *Source Book*, pp. 148 and 158].

[58] Chapters Thirty-seven, Sixty-four, and Fifty-seven.

"accomplish their tasks so that all affairs go their way, and the people all say 'We just follow Nature's Way.' "[60] In consequence, the world is well-governed.

Nonetheless, the desire to acquire things and possess more is common to all mankind,[61] while the avarice and deceit through which men satisfy such desires always spring from knowledge and cleverness of mind.[62] The Sage, therefore, in practicing his rule through non-action, must further "always cause the people to be without knowledge or desires." For, "Not exalting the virtuous causes the people to have no contentions. Not valuing goods that are difficult to procure causes the people not to become robbers. Not displaying objects of desire causes the people's minds to be untroubled."[63] These passages describe the method of limiting desires. "The one who knows does not speak, the one who speaks does not know. Stop up their aperatures, close their doors and gates. [See also foot note 53.] Blunt their sharpness, set loose their entanglements. Share their light, and tread in their dust." [Elsewhere, he says] "Common folks are indeed brilliant; I alone seem to be in the dark. Common folks see differences and are clear-cut; I alone make no distinctions."[64] This conveys Lao Tzu's advocacy of abandoning knowledge. When desires are few and knowledge has been cast aside, then mankind can "be as full of virtue [te] as a new-born infant."[65] [Some translators prefer always to take te in the more positive and specific sense of the "power imparted by the Tao."] Then, how could the world ever again be afflicted by disorders stemming from strife and robbery, from man's deception and rapacity?

We must note in particular that although Lao Tzu's doctrine here may

[59] Chapter Sixty.

[60] Chapters Seven, Two, and Seventeen.

[61] Chapter Forty-six says: "No disaster is greater than not to know what is enough. No fault is greater than the desire to acquire." [Following Duyvendak.]

[62] Chapter Sixty-five says: "Those of old who knew best how to make the Tao prevail did so not by enlightening the people, but by keeping them ignorant. The people become difficult to govern when they know too many things. Thus, he who spreads such knowledge to rule the state becomes the despoiler of the state, while he who does not spread knowledge in order to rule brings good fortune to the state."

[63] Chapter Three. Chapter Nineteen says: "Exhibit plainness and embrace simplicity; lessen self-interest and keep desires few." Chapter Thirty-seven says: "Lacking desires brings tranquility, and the world that way will stabilize itself." All these present the same basic idea.

[64] Chapters Fifty-six and Twenty [the latter following Chan, Source Book, p. 150]. Chapter Nineteen says: "Cast off the sages and abandon knowledge, and the people will benefit a hundred fold. Cast off benevolence and abandon righteousness, and the people will resume filial and parental love. Cast off cleverness and abandon gains, and robbers and thieves will be no more." ["Cleverness" means skills in making intricate objects, and "gains" means the profits from trading in those.]

[65] Chapter Fifty-five.

seem to limit and diminish the individual, its objective is to bring about
his happiness through knowing contentment. Hence, limiting desires and
casting off knowledge are for the purpose of ridding the individual's life
of all unnecessary distractions and demands on his energies, and to adjust
his life to the scope of what is natural. Its purpose was not to suppress
or to diminish the natural life of man *per se*. However, the question
remains: where lie the boundaries of the natural? Lao Tzu said: "The
five colors make men's eyes go blind. The five sounds make men's ears
go deaf. The five flavors dull men's appetites. Speeding carriages, and
chases across the open fields [in the hunt] cause men's minds lose all judgment. Goods that are difficult to procure entangle man's conduct. That
is why the Sage acts for the belly and not for the eye. Therefore he
dispenses with all those things, and clings to this [essential *Tao*]." And
further: "The Sage rules the people by emptying their minds, filling
their bellies, weakening their ambitions, and toughening their bones."[66]
This makes it clear that "the natural," which Lao Tzu favored, represented the lowest level of human life. All of the comforts produced
by civilization were included in his rejection. To seek non-action in this
way is in truth wondrously effective, like taking the fuel from under the
pot. [The fundamental method of keeping the pot from boiling over, as
opposed to the pointless way of stirring the hot water.] It is quite different
from the methods of rites and music, benevolence and righteousness, for
pursuing those is tantamount to forgetting about the basic issue while
trying to clear up the superficial ones.

We should note, however, that while Lao Tzu's political philosophy of
inaction bears some resemblance to the most thoroughgoing of European
laissez faire doctrines,[67] in the last analysis it differs from anarchism. For
Lao Tzu felt that, in the study of the *Tao* as in governing the country,
the highest plateau is reached when one can "take no action yet leave
nothing undone."[68] This is indeed because the Tao's giving birth to all
the myriad things is to proceed from being to non-being. For "when the
uncarved block [pristine nature] is fragmented and dispersed, one then
makes implements. The Sage uses those [instruments of civilization]; he
establishes officials and rulers."[69] Just as it is natural that things acquire
physical forms [in the process of nature], so, in the same way, non-action
in government need not destroy and cast aside the ruler-servitor institu-

[66] Chapters Twelve and Three. Kuo Hsiang's Commentary says: "Acting for the belly
means using material things to nourish oneself; acting for the eye means letting material
things enslave oneself." It further says: "The mind cherishes knowledge and the belly
cherishes nourishment . . . the bones support us without knowledge; ambition gives rise
to affairs that lead to chaos."

[67] It is also somewhat similar to what [T. H.] Huxley called "administrative nihilism."

[68] Chapters Thirty-seven and Forty-eight.

[69] Chapter Twenty-eight.

tion, and return to the total lack of restraints that exists among birds and beasts. The only thing that should be scrupulously avoided and never allowed to come into practice is that misgovernment induced by purposive action. For, in theoretical terms, what Lao Tzu attacked was not government in and of itself, but was any kind of governing which did not conform to "Taoistic" standards. [I.e., the standards of the *Tao* and its spontaneous workings, or "*te*"; the term used here, "*Tao-te*," came to mean "ethics" or "the ethical," only in later Chinese usage.] Lao Tzu on one occasion listed several kinds of government and ranked them from good to bad, to establish a standard by which to judge governments. "The very best [rulers are those where] the ruled are simply conscious [that the ruler] exists." This results from governing by taking no action. "The next best [are those rulers] who are loved and praised. Next are those who are feared." These represent governing through benevolence and righteousness, or through punishments and penal regulations. "Next are those who are scorned."[70] These represent the failing, collapsing government by tyrannous oppression.

Lao Tzu also set forth the content of an ideal form of political organization, as follows: "Let there be a small country with few people. Though there be ample arms for squads and companies of soldiers, let them not be used. Let the people value their lives highly and not migrate far. Even if there be ships and carts, none will ride in them. Even if there be armor and weapons, none will display them. Let the people revert to the use of knotted cords [a method of recording used before writing was invented]. They savor their own food, admire their own clothing, are content with their own homes, and take delight in their own customs. Though a neighboring state is within sight, so that they hear each other's cocks crowing and dogs barking, yet the people will grow old and die without ever visiting one another."[71]

Such were Lao Tzu's political ideals. If we compare them with the various governments that existed in the late Chou period, we find that virtually no element of his ideal is not contrary to the real conditions of his time. The skills of a Kung-shu [famed military engineer, carpenter, and builder of the implements for offensive warfare; see Chapter Four, p. 217, and footnote 91, p. 266, above] were highly valued in that age; thus it was not one in which weapons and implements were not used, or boats and carts were not ridden in. Among the various states of the time aggressive campaigns and warlike alliances fill the pages of their histories; hence it was by no means an age in which arms and armor were

[70] Chapter Seventeen.
[71] Chapter Eighty [following Yü Yüeh]. Note that the references to savoring their food, admiring their clothing, and the like intend that the people shall know contentment; this is not to say that they should strive to make those things more enjoyable and beautiful.

not displayed or in which people grew old and died without ever having travelled. Moreover, the Chou overlordship had in reality ceased, though in name the Chou rulers still existed. Ch'i and Ch'in and some of the other states had grown to vast extent and large population, thus were particularly out of keeping with the ideal of the small country and the sparse population. In consideration of these facts, Lao Tzu's attack bears not only upon [conditions subsequently realized in] the unified authoritarian empire that came into existence after the Warring States Period; even the feudal world of the Spring and Autumn Period and earlier must also have failed to merit his approval. Of all the political systems of antiquity, the only ones that seem somewhat closer to his ideal are those of the early Yin, and of the pre-Yin primitive tribal cultures of a still earlier stage of civilization. And the primitive tribe, strictly speaking, is not really a political organization. Thus, were we to say that Lao Tzu was opposed to all of the political institutions that came into existence from Western Chou and later, it would seem to be a fair statement.[72]

SECTION FOUR
Equalizing Things and Transcending Life

THE thought both of Lao Tzu and of Chuang Tzu clearly elucidates an "egocentric" [wei-wo] doctrine. Lao Tzu developed his yielding softness, humility, and the other practices in order to ensure the individual's personal existence. He further established the doctrine of taking no action in order to guarantee a social environment appropriate to the individual's continued existence. But Lao Tzu's objective in seeking to ensure the individual "enduring safety" and "freedom from peril" was, in practice, most difficult to achieve. Human affairs are confused and complex, subject to unforeseeable developments. The individual, situated in this midst, trying to devise a means of achieving safety reliable under any circumstance that might ever occur, had no real hope of success.[73] Moreover, the more urgent becomes the mood of valuing life and valuing the self, the more overwhelming become the obsessions with safety and

[72] Lao Tzu's repudiation of the Chou, and reversion to an earlier antiquity was even more extreme than Mo Tzu's. But Lao Tzu did not advocate revolution. His pronouncements attacking government are merely expression of protest containing absolutely no element of "direct action."

[73] Chuang Tzu, ch. 20, "Shan mu": "However, given the nature of all the myriad things, and the traditions governing men's relations with each other, it cannot be so [with men as it is in nature]. Those which are united get separated, things completed are destroyed, the upright are injured, the noble are disparaged. Those who are active in doing things suffer losses, while those who are worthy are plotted against, and the unworthy are despised. How then, can any one be sure of anything?" [Chuang Tzu goes on to say that one can be sure of the Way and its Power.]

danger, life and death. Even if an individual should luckily succeed in living out a long life, he could scarcely avoid the morass of anxieties and worries about it, so that even as he lived he would be incapable of enjoying life's pleasures.

Chuang Tzu seems to have been aware of this weakness in Lao Tzu's doctrines;[74] hence he cut through the rigorously maintained egocentric element in Lao Tzu's thought and developed in its place his own theories about the relativity of things [ch'i-wu 齊物] and of transcending life [wai-sheng 外生].[75] In consequence, "heavenly happiness" [t'ien lo 天樂] [i.e., heaven in the Taoist sense of Nature; this means to take delight in the Way of heaven, or the Tao of Nature, and is a naturalistic concept, not that of a supernatural or divine Heaven beyond this world] and the "unfettered bliss" [hsiao-yao 逍遙] became the highest level of human existence, while "enduring safety" and "freedom from peril" were demoted to a secondary order of importance.

Chuang Tzu's equalizing of things and transcendence of life were theories derived from the concept of the Tao, or Way of Nature [t'ien tao]. Chuang Tzu acknowledged that all the myriad things were produced from the formless Tao,[76] and that the Tao was omnipresent, in all things.[77]

---

[74] Tao Te Ching, Chapter Thirteen: "The reason that I am subject to great afflictions is that I have my body. If I had no body, what could afflict me?" This also displays the idea of transcending life.

[75] "Transcending life" is encountered in ch. 6, "Ta Tsung shih," where Nü-yü tells about instructing Pu-liang Yi in the way to become a sage. "After three days he was able to detach himself from this world." Then, "After seven days he was able to detach himself from things." And "After nine days he was able to detach himself from life." [Although "wai" is usually translated "to transcend," it means "to be outside of," not "to be above," or "super-natural."] Refer to Fung Yu-lan's Chung-kuo-che-hsueh-shih, Part I, pages 179 and 305 [cf. Fung/Bodde, vol. I, pp. 238–39]. It should be noted that Chuang Tzu did not after all entirely eliminate the doctrine of preserving life. Ch. 4, "Jen chien shih," contains many elaborations on Lao Tzu's methods of "keeping to the black" [shou hei, i.e., identifying with negative values to seek safety]; the allegorical anecdotes about the great oak tree and about crippled Shu are examples of this. [See Watson, Complete Works of Chuang Tzu, pp. 63–65 and 66; for "shou hei" see Tao Te Ching, Chapter 28.]

[76] Ch. 12, "T'ien-ti": "In the great beginning there was non-being; it had no existence, no name. From it, the one arose; the one existed, but it had no physical form. Things, obtaining it, emerged and so called it te [i.e., the power that obtains]. The not-yet-formed became differentiated [into the dual modes Yin and Yang], but without separation; that is called 'what is destined.' Now quiescent, now active, they produced all things. Things produced assumed patterns; those are called 'physical forms.' Physical forms embody spirits, so each has its own manner and standard; that is called its 'nature' [hsing, 性, or, its specific character]." [Cf. Watson, Complete Works, pp. 131–32; Chan, Source Book, p. 202; and Fung/Bodde, p. 224.]

[77] Chuang Tzu, ch. 22, "Chih pei yu": "Tung Kuo Tzu asked about Chuang Tzu: 'This thing called Tao, just where is it?' Chuang Tzu replied: 'There is not a place that it is not present.'"

In view of their all having emerged from the same *Tao*, it becomes very difficult to mark a dividing line between "things" and "the self." "Heaven and earth coexist with me; all the myriad things and I are one."[78] But in terms of their individual nature's each having its own "*virtus*" [*te*, in the sense of a thing's intrinsic and distinctive character], all the myriad classes of things are different from each other, each having a nature appropriate to itself. "Each thing has its [distinct] reason for being as it is; each thing has its [individual] appropriateness. There are no things that are not so; there are no things that are not appropriate."[79] This principle once established, all distinctions of things and the self [that is, "I" and "not-I"], of true and false, of noble and humble, then lose their absolute boundaries, and all the inequalities of things bring themselves into positions of relative equality and unity. Chuang Tzu puts these words into the mouth of one Pei-hai Jo [or, "The Spirit of the North Sea"]. "From the point of view of Tao, material things have no qualities of noble or humble. From the point of view of those things, however, they ennoble themselves and regard each other with scorn. From the common man's point of view, to be noble or humble does not lie with himself. From the point of view of differences among things, if we grant bigness to a thing because of some quality of bigness it possesses, then there is nothing among the myriad material things that is not [in some way] big. If we bestow smallness on a thing because of some quality of smallness it possesses, then there is nothing among the myriad material things that is not [in some way] small. When we understand that heaven and earth are but as tiny grains of rice, or that the tip of a hair is as a hill or a mountain, then all the rankings and distinctions have become equal. From the point of view of its accomplishments, if we regard a thing as having merit in view of some usefulness that it has, then among the myriad material things there is none that does not possess that. And if we judge that it is lacking in that, then there is none among the myriad material things that is not so lacking. When we recognize that east and west are relative opposites, and that neither can exist except in relation to the other, then their separate shares of achievement can be established. From the point of view of people's interests and tastes, if we say a thing is right because it has some aspect that gains approval, then there is no thing that is not right. If we say it is wrong because of some aspect that draws disapproval, then there is no thing that is not wrong. When we understand that [the sage] Yao and [the tyrant] Chieh each approved of himself and disapproved of the other, then we have observed how interests and tastes

[78] *Ch.* 2, "Ch'i-wu lun." *Ch.* 5, "Te ch'ung fu" also says: "Seen in the light of their shared feature, all the myriad things are one."

[79] *Ch.* 2, "Ch'i-wu lun."

are [subjectively] applied."[80] Thus his theory that all the true and the false, the noble and the humble, are equatable. In *ch.* 21 "T'ien Tzu-fang," he creates a scene in which he has Lao Tan say [to Confucius]: "It is precisely the world itself in which all the myriad things have their oneness. When a person obtains [an understanding] that all things are one, his limbs and body will all be but as the dust of the earth, and, life and death, beginning and end, will be as the alternation of day and night, and cannot destroy his peace of mind." In *ch.* 6 "Ta-tsung-shih," he imputes to Confucius a discussion of [persons who] "wander beyond the world" in which Confucius says: "They are companions of the maker of things [i.e., Nature], and they wander freely within the unifying breath of heaven and earth. Life, to them, is a useless appendage, like a swollen sore, and death they look upon as the cutting off of an abscess. To such persons, what could living and dying, precedings and followings, matter? It is as though they had borrowed some strange object, lodged their life in a shared body; they are oblivious to their liver and gall [the seat of passions] and have put aside their ears and eyes [sensory perception]. They come and go, start and stop, unaware of beginnings and endings." And in the same chapter he has [the physically deformed] Tzu-yü discuss "release from bondage" ["*hsuan-hsieh*" 縣, 懸解, meaning a release of the spirit, permitting one to "wander in unfettered bliss," *hsiao-yao yu*, in the imagination]: "I can suppose that my left arm has been transformed into a cock, with which I can announce the dawn. I can imagine that my right arm has become a sling, with which I can go hunt for a pigeon to roast. I can suppose that my buttocks have changed into wheels, and my spirit into a horse; riding with these, what need have I of a carriage?"[81] Thus his way of describing how things and the self are equalized.

[80] *Ch.* 17, "Ch'iu shui"; cf. Watson, *Complete Works*, p. 179; Chan, *Source Book*, pp. 205–07.] *Ch.* 2, "Ch'i wu lun" also puts words into the mouth of Wang Ni [or Yi; reputedly an ancient worthy] to explain, in brief, that man and the beasts each have their own peculiar ideas of the appropriate with regard to dwelling places, food, beauty, and the like, and that there is no absolute "correct." It also has one Ch'ang-wu Tzu [a fictitious character] argue that in any debate between you and me it becomes impossible to decide who is right. If a third person is called in to judge, then regardless of whether his opinion agrees with yours or with mine, he still will be unable to establish a standard of what is true and what is false. [Cf. the complete translations of *ch.* 2 in Chan, *Source Book*, pp. 179–91, in Watson, *Complete Works of Chuang Tzu*, pp. 36–49, etc.]

[81] At the end of *ch.* 2, "Ch'i-wu lun," there is the allegory of Chuang Tzu's dreaming he is a butterfly, which says: "I do not know whether Chuang Chou dreams he is a butterfly, or whether a butterfly dreams he is Chuang Chou." This also is a description of the same state of mind. Note that all of those states of mind which Chuang Tzu describes, calling them "the fasting of the mind" [*hsin chai*, 心齋, see *ch.* 5, "Jen-chien shih"] and "heavenly happiness" [*t'ien lo*, see *ch.* 13, "T'ien tao"] and the like, may be what William

Lao Tzu had said, "If I had no body, what could afflict me?" But after things are equalized and life is transcended, then "the world is stored [or kept] in the world itself" and one can "wander where nothing succeeds in escaping, but where all things are preserved."[82] Then, there no longer are such things as past and present, and life and death have become one. "Content with whatever occurs in the course of time, and compliant with it, then sadness and joy cannot take effect." There is no greater beauty and goodness in the individual's life than this. Lao Tzu had also said "Reversal is the action of *Tao*"; now Chuang Tzu urges people to place themselves beyond life in order to gain the life of ultimate peace and ultimate happiness. Lao Tzu could not have found a more apt or felicitous pupil than he. For we must take note of the point that what Chuang Tzu called transcending life [*wai-sheng*] was not a state of pure quiescence and solitary nothingness, or the extinction of the self; rather, it meant fully complying with nature and doing away with obsessive concerns [especially that with life and death]. It neither forced others to become as one's self, nor relinquished the self to conform with others. Each person followed his own nature's lead, and that never led him to anything that was not "unfettered bliss" [*hsiao yao*]. Thus he said: "The truly right person does not fail to maintain his life's destined nature. Therefore, for him webbed toes are not abnormally joined, and the extra finger is not a superfluous appendage; what is [by nature] long is not too long and what is [by nature] short is not too short."[83] So it is clear that what is called transcending life has as its basic tenet to accord with life's innermost nature, while the equalizing of things functions in letting things be as disparate as it is in their natures to be. Were one to cling stubbornly to one standard against which to equalize things, their natural reality [*t'ien chen* 天眞] would perish; those things and the self both would suffer therein. "For horses and oxen to have four legs is called Nature [or *t'ien*, "heaven"]; to put a halter on a horse's head or a ring in an ox's nose—that is called man."[84] "A duck's neck, to be sure, is short, but to stretch it out long would make it suffer, a heron's legs are indeed long, but to cut them off short would cause it grief."[85] The sea-gull died

---

James called "pure experience." (Fung Yu-lan, *Chung-kuo che-hsueh shih*, Part I, p. 298.) [Fung/Bodde, Vol. I, pp. 241–42.] However, it is also possible to interpret Chuang Tzu's thought system on a shallower and more immediate level. *Ch.* 9, "Ma t'i" says: "The common people have a constant nature; they spin and are clothed, till and are fed. This is called the [natural] capacity that all alike possess." This passage clearly indicates that *Tao* is to be found in normal, daily natural living, and that when the artificial [i.e., man's artifices] do not obliterate the natural, man can be in accord with the *Tao*.

[82] *Ch.* 6, "Ta tsung-shih" describing Tzu-yü's "release from bondage."

[83] *Ch.* 8, "P'ien mu."

[84] *Ch.* 17, "Ch'iu shui."

[85] *Ch.* 8, "P'ien mu."

from the [lavish human] treatment accorded it by the Duke of Lu;[86] Hun-t'un died from Pei-hu's borings;[87] all of these are cases of forcing others to be like one's self, of "using man to destroy heaven."[88] The doer's own life does not necessarily follow its natural course thereby, and the nature of the things so dealt with is certain to be overcome. "Two fellows, Tsang and Ku [children of bondservants], were herding sheep together, and each lost his sheep. When Tsang was asked what he had been doing, he said he had taken along a book [on bamboo strips] and was studying. When Ku was asked what he had been doing, he said he had been throwing dice for diversion. The occupations of the two were dissimilar [the one activity respectable, the other frivolous], but they were identical in each having lost his sheep. [The eminent worthy] Po-yi died for honor at Mount Shou-yang, while [the brigand] Chih died for cupidity on the Easter Range. The reasons for the two men's deaths are different, but they are the same in having destroyed their lives and done violence to their natures."[89]

And as for the petty man who dies seeking profit, the scholar who dies for fame, the Great Officer who dies for family, or even the sage who dies for the world, "the likes of Hu Pu-chieh, Wu Kuang, Po-yi, Shu-ch'i, Chi Tzu, Hsü Yü, Chi-t'o, and Shen T'u-ti, all of them enslaved themselves to the interests of others. They followed courses of interest to others, and did not pursue their own interests."[90] [Persons, some clearly historical and some perhaps legendary, who died nobly observing some moral principle, mostly that of loyalty to a vanquished superior.] The nature of the other person did not necessarily gain thereby, and their own lives were lost. Thus, in the search to preserve both the other and the self, the only way is to cause both the other and the self to be unconcerned with each other. If this method can be put into practice, then, with the exception of one's own ego's natural predilections, there is virtually no matter and no thing in the whole world that is to be regarded as having value. Moreover, all of the sanctions and institutions of government, as also the proprieties and conventions of society, become nothing but restrictions and restraints having no usefulness at all. In Chuang Tzu's thought, the political ideas of "non action" [*wu wei*] thus inevitably offer the ultimate resolution.

---

[86] *Ch.* 18, "Chih lo."

[87] *Ch.* 7, "Ying ti wang." [Pei-hu bored holes in Hun-t'un so he would have mouth, nostrils, etc., like those of a human, which he was not.] The opening passages of *ch.* 9, "Ma t'i," also presents this principle in the references to Po Lo's handling of horses, and to the potter and the carpenter in their skills with clay and wood.

[88] *Ch.* 17, "Ch'iu shui."

[89] *Ch.* 8, "P'ien-mu."

[90] *Ch.* 6, "Ta tsung-shih." [Cf. Chan, *Source Book*, p. 192.]

SECTION FIVE
Letting People Alone

CHUANG TZU said: "Heaven and earth were born together with me; all the myriad things and I are one." [See footnote 78] Seen superficially, the meaning of this expression looks much like the Confucian statements about "regarding heaven and earth and all things as being of one body."[91] However, the Confucians' unity of the self and the world was to cause men to feel that the self and the world share a common set of joys and concerns, while Chuang Tzu's unity of self and the world has as its purpose to effect a severing of all connections between the world and the self. Thus the dominant principles underlying the thought of the two schools are diametrically opposed. For Confucianism took the practice of benevolence toward others to be its central tenet, while Chuang Tzu's doctrines pushed egocentrism to the extreme limit. Egocentrism, extended to its limits, inevitably must eliminate the distinction between the world and the self. Transcending life and equalizing things are but ingenious paths to the realization of this objective. Chuang Tzu's eliminating the distinction between the world and the self embodies two principles: One is not to belabor oneself for the good of the world; that is to say, I will not interfere with others. The second is that each person should pursue his own predilections; that is to say, others shall not interfere with me. By expanding these principles, asserting that the world and the self should not interfere with or impose upon each other, one is led to the ideal of non-governing, and to the political method of "letting the world alone." [Tsai yu 在宥; this is Fung Yu-lan's apt translation of tsai yu, in his Short History of Chinese Philosophy, p. 106. Legge used "letting be"; Giles used "letting alone." Traditional explanations of the term, which Chuang Tzu created and which displays his personal and creative use of language, say that it means a complete and measured liberality of judgment about all the affairs of one's self and of all others.]

The Lieh Tzu quotes words attributed to Yang Chu, saying: "If everyone would refuse to take the world as a gain, then the world would be in perfect order."[92] Chuang Tzu's ideal of no governing may represent a continuation of the thought of Yang Chu. If the individual wants to preserve his own person and experience the heavenly happiness, he will

[91] These are the words of [the Ming Confucian idealist] Wang Shou-jen [1472–1529]. See the Yang-ming chi-yao "Collection of Essential Writings of Wang Yang-ming," "Li Hsüeh chi," ch. 2, "Ta-hsüeh wen," or, "Inquiry on the Great Learning" [see W. T. Chan, Source Book, pp. 659 ff., and his Instructions for Practical Living, p. 272.]

[92] Ch. 7, Lieh Tzu, "Yang Chu" [following the translation in Fung Yu-lan, Short History of Chinese Philosophy, p. 63. Cf. A. C. Graham, Lieh Tzu, p. 148].

not allow himself to assume any responsibilities toward society. The *Chuang Tzu* repeatedly sets forth this idea. For example, *ch.* 17, "Ch'iu shui" includes an anecdote: "Chuang Tzu was fishing on the P'u River. The King of Ch'u sent two officials there to say [for him]: 'I would like you to assume responsibility for the affairs of my entire realm.' Chuang Tzu, holding his fishing pole and not turning his head to them, said: 'I have heard that the State of Ch'u possesses a divine turtle, now already three thousand years dead, which your King keeps stored away in the Ancestral Shrine, in a carefully wrapped box. Now, would this turtle rather be dead, with its bones preserved and venerated, or would it prefer to be alive, dragging its tail in the mud?' The two officials said: 'It would rather be alive and dragging its tail in the mud.' Chuang Tzu said: 'Then be off with you! I shall drag my tail in the mud.' "[93] And *ch.* 7, "Ying ti-wang," says: "T'ien Ken was wandering along the southern slopes of Mount Yin. As he reached the Liao River he encountered a nameless person, of whom he asked the question: 'May I ask your opinion on how the world can be ruled?' The nameless man said: 'Go away! You are a boorish fellow! What tiresome questions you ask. I am about to join in company with the maker of things [i.e., Nature], and should we get bored, we may then soar away on a far-flying bird, beyond the six directions, and wander in the zone of nothing-at-all, to take my place in the vast reaches of limitless expanse. How can you come with these questions about ruling the world and disturb my mind?!' " If no one were to disturb his mind about how to rule the world, or assume responsibility for the affairs of the realm, then all the doings of rulers and their ministers would grow dim and fade from notice, and all of what we today know as political and social life also would vanish into [Taoist cosmogony's primordial] formlessness. "And so it is that in an age when the *te* [i.e., the Tao in application] perfectly prevails, the people's step will be slow and sure, the people's gaze will be straight and pure. In that age, there will be no paths or roads through the mountains, there will be no boats or bridges on the waters. All the myriad natural things will burgeon, in endless extension from one place to the next. Birds and beasts will multiply in their flocks and herds; grasses and plants will all grow and flourish. Then it will be that people can lead birds and beasts around with leashes [without their feeling any constraint] and can bend down the branches to peer into magpies' nests. For in the age when the *te* perfectly prevails men shall live together with the birds and beasts, and shall be joined in existence with all other living things. And who will know any-

[93] *Ch.* 1, "Hsiao-yao yu" tells that when the Emperor Yao offered him the empire, Hsü Yu declined it saying: "If I were in charge of the empire, there is nothing that I would do." The sense of this is slightly different.

thing about the distinctions of 'superior man' and 'common fellow' then?"[94] Under such circumstances, even though rulers might exist, there would in fact be no governing. All men would follow their own individual natures, each doing what was appropriate for him. Even though they might live in groups residing at one place, they would still be totally free of organization and restraints. In modern terms, this ideal of no governing would mean the disappearance of duties, the end of authority; it really would be a state of absolute freedom. The pre-Ch'in period produced no development of egocentric thought more thoroughgoing and complete than this.

However, there remains one question that must be raised. Since this perfect world [described as if it had once existed] had no government, what then was the need for a ruler? To have a ruler but no governing—is that not something of a contradiction? Yet an examination of Chuang Tzu's own words show repeated implications that his antique ideal world included a king.[95] What is the reason for this? Since Chuang Tzu himself

---

[94] *Ch.* 9, "Ma t'i."

[95] *Ch.* 7, "Ying ti-wang," contains a passage purporting to offer the words of one P'u Yi Tzu, saying: "Yu-yü [i.e., the sage-emperor Shun] was not as good as T'ai [i.e., the mythical ruler of still earlier antiquity, Fu-hsi]. For Yu-yü still maintained benevolence *jen*, with which to draw men to him. Yet, though he did get men that way, he never succeeded in getting beyond [the awareness of what is] not of man. T'ai, however, took his repose in leisurely tranquility, and spent his waking hours in satisfied contentment. Sometimes he thought of himself as a horse, at other times as an ox. His knowledge was unfailingly true, and his powers [of spirit] were intensely genuine. And he never fell into the [awareness of what is] not of man." [That is, benevolence is a humane standard that limits one to the narrower world of man; T'ai was oblivious to this distinction, quite able to imagine himself an animal, or other form of existence.] *Ch.* 10, "Ch'ü-ch'ieh," says: "In the past [during the reigns of] Jung-ch'eng, Ta-t'ing, Po-huang, Chung-yang, Li-lu, Li-hsü, Hsien-yüan, Ho-hsü, Tsun-lu, Chu-jung, Fu-hsi, Shen-nung [all mythical rulers of a distant antiquity]—in those times men knotted ropes and used that [in place of writing], enjoyed their food, thought their [rude] clothing beautiful, took pleasure in their daily ways, and dwelt in contentment. Neighboring countries could gaze back and forth upon each other, and the sounds of the chickens and the dogs could be heard from the one to the other [so small and close were they], yet their people throughout a whole lifetime would never go back and forth among them." [Cf. the same idea in the *Lao Tzu*, Ch. 80, quoted in footnote 71.] *Ch.* 12, "T'ien-ti," says: "During the age when *te* perfectly prevailed, the worthy were not honored and the capable were not employed in office. The rulers are like the branches on tall trees [i.e., occupying a high position naturally without doing anything], and the people are like the wild deer [i.e., uninhibited and lacking self-consciousness]. All are upright without knowing about righteousness; all have concern for each other without knowing about benevolence. They are genuine without knowing about loyalty, reliable without knowing about trustworthiness. They display vigor and energy as they work for each other but do so without the air of conferring favors. Thus actions occurred but were not recorded, events took place but there was no purpose in transmitting any accounts of them." All of these display the idea of conditions under which there is no governing yet there is a ruler. *Ch.* 4, "Jen-chien shih," says: "The minister's service to

is not explicit on the matter, it would be difficult to impose an explanation arbitrarily. But it may be that the result of equalizing things and transcending life was to emphasize the issue of freedom, and not to stress social equality. If only the imposition of the real means of control could be avoided, it would no longer matter about the nominal designations of noble and humble. If there could be achieved the complete natural freedom and lack of imposed restrictions so that "the people are like wild deer," then one could tolerate the existence of "rulers like the branches of tall trees" and forget about them. Chuang Tzu's intent may have been thus.

A man will not serve the ruler, and the ruler shall not implement any governing: such was Chuang Tzu's ultimate ideal. Yet if an individual should unavoidably occupy the position of the ruler, he should seek methods of ruling well. No method of governing will exist, however, except that of governing by non-governing. "Should a superior man find that he had no choice but to preside over the empire, nothing would serve as well as to take no action. For after he has followed the course of taking no action, he can preserve his inner nature in tranquility."[96]

The term "taking no action," *wu-wei*, was one already made current by Lao Tzu; Chuang Tzu wanted to greatly broaden the spirit of this *laissez-faire* principle. Thus he established the additional concept of "letting people alone," *tsai yu*, about which he said: "I have heard of letting mankind alone, but not of governing mankind. Letting alone springs from the fear that otherwise people will pollute their innate nature and set aside their *te*. [*Te*, i.e., the powers native to beings and things.] When people do not pollute their innate nature and set aside their *te*, then is there any need to govern mankind?"[97] It would thus appear that Chuang Tzu's reason for advocating *laissez faire* was his certainty that the people of the world did not need to be controlled or supervised. "The common people have a constant nature; they spin and are clothed, till and are fed. This is called 'the natural capacity, *te*, which they all alike possess.' They are as one in this, and not so because of conscious inclination; it is what may be called their 'natural freedom.' "[98] These people of natural freedom [*t'ien fang* 天放] were born and died of themselves,

---

his ruler is a matter of duty. There is no place where his ruler's interests do not extend. There is no escaping it in heaven or earth." This all the more clearly and explicitly expresses the idea of the existence of rulers.

[96] *Ch.* 11, "Tsai yu." *Ch.* 12, "T'ien-ti," also says: "The rulers of remote antiquity took no action in ruling the empire; it was done by natural *te* [i.e., *t'ien te*, or "the force of Nature"] and nothing else."

[97] *Ch.* 11, "Tsai Yu" [slightly modified from Fung Yu-lan, *Short History of Chinese Philosophy*, p. 106].

[98] *Ch.* 9, "Ma-t'i."

knew neither restrictions nor restraints, lacked knowledge and wisdom, were neither contentious nor disorderly. Were the person who ruled over them to establish rites and music, punishments and laws, with which to govern them, it would indeed be no different from stretching the short legs of the duck and trimming off the long legs of the heron, cutting into the uncarved block, or haltering a horse; that would not merely be of no benefit, it would work harm. The world, therefore, does not simply not need governing; in fact it should not be governed. And once the principle of equalizing things had been made clear, then to set up a standard, according to one man's notions of right and wrong, which all the masses of the people must either conform to or defy, is obviously most unreasonable. Yet the Confucians and the Mohists, with their doctrines of esteeming virtue and elevating the worthy, aspire to unify the people's minds through the upright man whom all will follow. The cause of their having been led into such "error," we find, probably is that their views about the right and the wrong of their own and others' ideas have powerful hold on their minds, and thus prevent them from being able to let people alone. Chuang Tzu developed his principle of the equality of things to condemn governmental methods that "press too harshly."[99] The *ch.* 11, "Tsai yu," says: "The ordinary sort of person always is happy to find others like himself, and dislikes people who are different from himself. The reason that he wants people to be like himself and does not want people to be different from himself is that he longs to be outstanding. But if the desire is to be outstanding, how can one ever stand out in this way? Follow the crowd and be content therein, for no individual's knowledge can surpass the group of talents within the crowd. Likewise, the man who would like to assume rule [e.g., as an advisor] in someone's country: he would like to take over all the benefits enjoyed by the Three Kings of antiquity without having perceived all their troubles. This is to subject another man's state to mere chance; how often has mere chance ruled and the state not lost thereby?" And *ch.* 7, "Ying ti-wang," has Chieh-yü [the "madman of Ch'u," who appears also in the *Analects* xvii/5 as a critic of Confucius] expatiate upon this idea: "Chien-wu went to call on the madman Chieh-yü. Chieh-yü asked: 'What was it that Jih Chung-shih told you?' Chien-wu replied: 'He told me that a person who would rule over others should set himself up as the standard, apply justice, and pass judgment on people, then who would dare not heed him and be transformed by that?' Chieh-yü said: 'That would destroy the workings of *te*. To govern the empire in that way would be like trying to walk across the ocean, dig through a river, or make a mosquito carry a mountain on its back.'"

[99] The phrase is found in *ch.* 4, "Jen-chien shih."

We may go further, and say that making others the same as one's self is something at which not only the ordinary man must fail; even the outstanding man of virtue and wisdom has no hope of accomplishing it. For the *p'eng* bird and the cicada fly differently. [The first chapter of the *Chuang Tzu* develops the contrast between the vast *p'eng* bird's conception of flying and that of the tiny cicada.] The wise and the ignorant are concerned with different things. To force them into sameness is to counter their natures and induce disaster. Therefore: "[It is asked] 'Couldn't one follow what is correct and avoid what is false, follow order and avoid disorder?' . . . [No] . . . for that would be [as self-deluding] as to follow heaven but ignore earth, to follow *Yin* but ignore *Yang*. That quite obviously cannot be done."[100] Chuang Tzu provided a further fable to clarify this point: "In the past [Sage King] Yao once questioned [his designated successor, the sage] Shun: 'I have a strong desire to send a punitive campaign against the States of Tsung, Kuei and Hsü-ao. Since coming to the throne I have felt ill at ease about this matter. Why should that be?' Shun replied: 'But those three kings still remain in the most primitive circumstances. Why should you retain any uneasy feelings about them? In the past when ten suns shone simultaneously, all the things in the world were brightly illuminated, yet how much more even than the suns is *te* [luminous]!' "[101] Thus, even though I may be virtuous and wise, I should merely find my own satisfaction in this virtue and wisdom. If it is someone else's nature to be doltish and ignorant, one should also let him go on in his doltishness and ignorance. "[Therefore, the former sages] did not expect the same capacities in all, and did not try to make them all do the same things. Names should not go beyond realities, and principles should be designed to correspond with natural tendencies."[102] When the world and the self become oblivious to each other, each is transformed by the Tao. This is taking no action yet having the world well-ordered.

The second obstacle to letting people alone is the erroneous belief that those practices such as benevolence and righteousness, rites and music, punishments and laws, can be used to achieve good order. Chuang Tzu expands on Lao Tzu's tenet "When the great *Tao* is abandoned, then

[100] *Ch.* 17, "Ch'iu shui."

[101] *Ch.* 2, "Ch'i-wu lun." Kuo Hsiang's [d. A.D. 312] Commentary says: "In this case, wanting to eradicate the backward preferences of those still living in primitive circumstances and make them accept one's leadership, is hardly the way to enlarge the *Tao*! Hence the feelings of being ill at ease distracted [Shun's] spirit. May all things be allowed to express their inner natures, and be content in that which pleases themselves. With no distinctions of where or what, let all beings do as they please, each to the limits of its own capacities. Then they will all be satisfied, and we also will have nothing to mar our happiness."

[102] *Ch.* 18, "Chih lo."

we have benevolence and righteousness"; time and time again he argues
that all governing through positive action [*yu wei*] must fail to bring about
order. The various methods of managing the state all have as their
purpose to end disorder. However, men's minds can be deceitful and
tricky, and they may well use these means of ending disorder to create
disorder. The *ch.* 10, "Ch'ü ch'ieh," sets this forth the most clearly and
unequivocally: "In the past, in the State of Ch'i, neighboring towns
could gaze upon each other, and the sounds of the chickens and the dogs
could be heard from the one to the other. Its nets and seines when all
spread out, and its plows and harrows when all turning the earth, filled
more than two-thousand square *li* [so large and prosperous a country was
it]. Within its four boundaries the ancestral shrines and the altars of the
state were set up, its towns and villages, its households and lanes, streets
and hamlets, all were properly laid out; were they in any feature not
modelled on those of the ancient sages? Yet one day along came T'ien
Ch'eng Tzu, who murdered the ruler of Ch'i and stole his state. Nor did
he merely steal the state; he stole that along with all its sagelike knowledge
as embodied in its laws and institutions. Thereby, T'ien Ch'eng Tzu,
possessing the name and reputation of a bandit and thief, nonetheless
could safely enjoy the personal satisfactions of a Yao or a Shun. Smaller
states dared not denounce him, and larger states dared not punish him.
Twelve successive generations [of the T'ien clan] have possessed the
state. Is not this, then, a case of stealing the State of Ch'i together with
the sagelike knowledge in its laws, and using those to maintain the thieves
themselves? . . . Provide pecks and bushels to measure with, and people
will steal by the peck and the bushel. Provide scales and steelyards to
weigh with, and people will steal by the scales and the steelyards. Provide
tallies and seals to guarantee things, and people will use tallies and seals
to steal with. Provide benevolence and righteousness to rectify the people,
and they will steal by benevolence and righteousness. . . . So it is that
the great brigands pursue all these things, are elevated into the nobility,
steal benevolence and righteousness, together with all the profits to be
gained through using pecks and bushels, scales and steelyards, tallies and
seals. Though there exist the rewards of carriages and coronets, they
cannot be enticed [to be ethical]; though there are the punishments of
ax and sword, they cannot be intimidated." Thus, that laws and institutions cannot bring order into the world, but on the contrary only contribute to disorder, is made clear beyond all doubt.[103] As for such virtues as

---

[103] *Ch.* 14, "T'ien yün," compares the Ways of the Former Kings upheld by Confucius,
to straw dogs [made for sacrificial use] that have already been displayed [and are now to
be discarded]; discussing this it adds: "Rites, righteousness, laws, and institutions are
things that change with the times." This then indicates that Chuang Tzu was not opposed
to laws and institutions *per se.*

benevolence and righteousness, wisdom and trust, which the Confucians held aloft and with which they hoped to transform the people to achieve good government, as Chuang Tzu saw it, these too were as useless as the laws and institutions and all other machinery of government. "Ever since [the Sage Ruler] Shun started promoting benevolence and right-eousness to stir up the world, the whole world has been in a life-and-death chase after benevolence and righteousness."[104] "Nowadays [however] such is the state of things that [one may see the] people stretch their necks and stand on tiptoes, while they say: 'In such and such a place there is a great worthy.' Putting provisions in their packs, off they will go; at home, they will abandon their families, and, beyond their homes, they will disregard obligations to their rulers. Their footprints go all the way to the next state's boundaries; their carriage tracks form trails leading a thousand li away."[105] This is to be ignorant that the common people have a constant nature. If one does not "permit them to follow freely the course of their natures"[106] but tries to "work on peoples' minds" by means of benevolence, righteousness, and knowledge, then one's desire to bring order into the world can only lead it into chaos. "Long ago the Yellow Emperor started working on people's minds with benevolence and righteousness. Then Yao and Shun came along, laboring until the fuzz was worn off their thighs, and their shins had no more hair on them, trying to nourish all the bodies in the empire. They hurt their five viscera in the effort to achieve benevolence and righteousness. They strained their blood and breath trying to apply laws and institutions. Yet they still could not succeed. Yao then had to banish Huan Tou to Mount Ch'ung; he also drove the three tribes of the Miao all the way to San-wei, and exiled Kung-kung to the far north. By this he showed that he could not master the empire. Then the three dynasties followed, and the empire was in great commotion. Among the worst there were villains like [the tyrant] Chieh and [the brigand] Chih, while at best there were worthy men like [Confucius' disciple] Tseng Tzu and Shih Yü [an honest minister in Wei]. Then, finally, the Confucian and the Mohist schools arose. Consequently, the pleased and the angered grew suspicious of each other. The foolish and the wise cheated each other. The good and the bad denounced each other. The mendacious and the honest reviled each other. The world thereupon started into decline. The great te disintegrated; men's natures crumbled and weakened. The world became avid for knowledge, which the common people pursued to the limits of their strength. Consequently, axes and saws cut and formed things, line and chalk marked things, hammers and drills bored things, and the empire

[104] *Ch.* 8, "P'ien mu."
[105] *Ch.* 10, "Ch'ü ch'ieh."
[106] *Ch.* 8, "P'ien mu."

was thrown into a great turmoil [of cutting and destroying nature]. The blame for it all must be put on working on people's minds."[107]

Once we know the cause of disorder in the world is that the sages employ [the devices of] man to eliminate Nature; that is, they foolishly establish benevolence and righteousness, laws and institutions. Then the only way to repair the damage is to revert to the real, to return to the pristine simplicity—to let the world alone. So, Chuang Tzu said: "Cast off the sages and abandon knowledge and the great brigandage will cease. Smash the jade and destroy the jewels, and the petty banditry will not arise. Burn the tallies and destroy the seals, and the people will again be rustic and simple. Shatter the peck-measures and demolish the scales, and the people will not have quarrels. Obliterate all the traces of all the world's sagelike methods and then again it will be possible to talk sensibly with the people."[108]

We should note that although Chuang Tzu maintained an extremely pessimistic attitude toward government, he had a most optimistic attitude about human nature. The point that Chuang Tzu consistently and firmly upheld was that the natures of all people and all things all have their own distinctive aptness. In all cases where this stemmed from Nature it was perfectly and wholly good, but whatever resulted from artifice or corrective influences would lead to calamity and chaos. Mencius argued that human nature is basically good, while Hsün Tzu maintained that the nature is evil. Weighed in this balance, Chuang Tzu is closer to Mencius.[109] Yet Mencius said that the nature has within it the beginnings of goodness, not that it is wholly good; hence he wanted to use the transforming power of teaching to bring it to perfect development. Hsün Tzu said that the nature has within it the beginnings of evil and tends toward violence and disorder; hence he wanted to apply rites and righteousness as corrective forces to make men accept peace and order. Chuang Tzu alone felt human nature to be naturally perfect in goodness; what was needed was freedom in society, with no necessity for the superior man's transforming through teaching. For "in the age when *te* perfectly prevailed" all the virtues naturally exist. "All men will be [or were] upright without knowing about righteousness, all have concern for each other without knowing about benevolence, they are genuine without knowing about loyalty, reliable without knowing about trustworthiness."[110] Seen in terms of the innermost nature's spontaneous manifestations, then to take as an example the affections that exist between fathers

[107] *Ch.* 11, "Tsai yu."

[108] *Ch.* 10, "Ch'ü ch'ieh."

[109] Chuang Tzu did not explicitly state that the nature is good, but that his thought demands this assumption is beyond question.

[110] *Ch.* 12, "T'ien ti" [cf. footnote 95].

and sons, even "Tigers and wolves are benevolent."[111] So how could a
natural ethical sense be lacking in humans? Thus when Mencius argued
for the goodness of human nature yet wanted to "radiantly exemplify
proper human relations" [*Mencius*, III/i/3/10] it was analogous to pulling
on the rice shoots to help them grow faster. Hsün Tzu maintained that
human nature is evil and even more urgently wanted to "transform the
nature and promote the growth of culture"; the insanity of this is close
to that of trimming off the feet to make shoes fit. Lao Tzu said: "The man
of superior spiritual powers [*te*] does not act according to 'virtue' [*te*], and
thereby his spiritual power is effective."[112] Chuang Tzu added: "I feel
my own inadequacy in the face of the *Tao* and its *te* [or, the Way and its
Power]; therefore, at my best, I do not dare insist on the practice of benevolence and righteousness, and, at my worst, I dare not allow myself to
practice licentiousness or perversity."[113] Chuang Tzu's basic concept
here is in fact also derived from Lao Tzu before him. He uses the hypothesis of the absolute perfection of Nature [*t'ien hsing* i.e., "heavenly nature,"
or the natural character of beings] as his basis for advocating man's
absolute freedom; in terms of pure theory, his views are indeed quite
logical.

There is still another aspect of the thought of Chuang Tzu that merits
our notice. Although Chuang Tzu's ideas are expressed in a form that is
profoundly persuasive and transcendently original to the extreme, his
objective in producing his writings was by no means to overwhelm the
world as he found it, and to transform all the ordinary people into "true
men" [*chen-jen*, one of several Taoist terms, used more or less interchangeably to designate the enlightened Taoist]. For, in light of the theory about
the equality of all things, among the masses of good and simple people
there is no single one who does not possess his absolute value; thus there is
no single one who is not already, in his own right, a "true man." These
common people have their constant nature; they spin and are clothed,
they till and are fed. The here and the now is where the ultimate Tao
resides. Their constant nature, which leads them to spin and to till, is
precisely the reason why one should grant the people the right "to be let
alone" [*tsai yu*]. *Ch*. 12, "T'ien-ti," says: "When those above take no
action, those below also will take no action; that is when the same *te* is
found below and above." Where in the *Chuang Tzu* is found any advocacy
of all the people in the world flocking to observe a way of ritualized
behavior based on the attributes of a mystic ruler-figure? [paraphrased]

---

[111] *Ch*. 14, "T'ien yun."

[112] *Lao Tzu*, Chapter Thirty-eight. [This difficult passage can be translated in many
ways; see Chiang Hsi-ch'ang, *Lao Tzu chiao-ku*, pp. 243–45.]

[113] *Chuang Tzu, ch.* 8, "P'ien-mu." Note that it is evident here that Chuang Tzu
opposed government, but was not opposed to ethics.

Ch. 11, "Tsai-Yu," says: "The humble of status who yet must be permitted to go their own ways—those are the common people." When did Chuang Tzu ever expect that all the people of the world must be transformed by the *Tao* [to a state of enlightment like the immortals], and ignore the affairs of the mundane world, and only then be able to govern by letting people alone?"[114] Such things as the age of T'ai, [i.e., the legendary Sage Emperor Fu-hsi; see footnote 95], the people of Ho-hsü [a legendary Sage Ruler], travelling about [like Lieh Tzu], by riding on the wind, and [Chuang Tzu's] dream of being transformed into a butterfly[115]—all such are but Chuang Tzu's metaphors. If we expect to find the "heavenly happiness" some place beyond the six directions, at the beginning of primordial time, then we have been dazzled out of our perception by the fantastically rich imagery of his style to have lost sight of Chuang Tzu's real meaning, and, I fear, have set ourselves in the footsteps of those who "have become submerged into obscurities, so that one cannot engage them in straightforward conversation." [See *ch.* 33, "T'ien-hsia," *Chuang Tzu*, explaining why Chuang Tzu adopted his own fanciful style.]

Given the ordinary, common people, practice the method of just letting them alone: when put in this way, Chuang Tzu's political thought is indeed to be regarded as the most thoroughgoing of all individualisms, ancient and modern, Chinese and foreign, and it is also the most extreme of libertarian philosophies, ancient and modern, Chinese and foreign. However this may be, there is still one issue to be resolved. Europe's individualisms and liberalisms have often been expanded and developed into revolutionary currents in protest against authoritarianism, or have tended to develop into democratic thought movements supporting republicanism. Inasmuch as Chuang Tzu's thought was, like Lao Tzu's, a voice of protest in the degenerate age of late Chou, why did it not develop into something of revolutionary democratic import? If we seek the solution of this problem in the content of Lao Tzu's and Chuang Tzu's thought, it may not be so difficult to find. For an individualism to develop into a revolutionary democratic thought system, it must possess an attitude not only positive with regard to the individual, but also *not* negative with regard to society and government. That against which it is in protest cannot be all institutions as such, but only those institutions at the time confronting it which fail to satisfy people. Its reason for advocating revolution is the hope that through its ideal new institutions, it can

---

[114] These rhetorical questions refer to explications of Chuang Tzu's theories that we have encountered. As to whether or not Chuang Tzu's actual view here discussed is reasonable, and whether or not it could be realized in practice, these are distinct problems which need not be taken up here.

[115] See, respectively, *ch.* 7, "Ying ti wang"; *ch.* 10, "Ch'ü ch'ieh"; *ch.* 1, "Hsiao-yao yu"; and *ch.* 2, "Ch'i-wu lun."

then guarantee the well-being of the individual. When revolutionaries have not lost faith in government, they always have as their objectives such institutions as constitutional government, or democracy, or the like. But if revolutionaries have lost all hope in government as such, they then hold as their ideal some "anarchistic" form of social organization. All of these situations display a lack of thoroughgoing optimism about human nature and a failure to believe that mankind can be permitted to enjoy absolute freedom; hence they continue to look upon organization as a necessity. "He gazed upon it and was distressed by the world's ills." [*Ch*. 8, "P'ien mu," *Chuang Tzu*, says this of the "man of benevolence," i.e., one believing in political and social organization.] Persons so agitated will always want to use extreme measures to achieve their ambition of reconstructing society. Chuang Tzu's theories display unconditional confidence in the individual, but they hold unconditional contempt for organization. For no matter whether they are good or bad, institutions and systems can contribute nothing to the individual's freedom. "Rather than praise the Sage King Yao and condemn the tyrant Chieh, it would be better simply to forget both [praising and condemning] and follow the transformations of *Tao*."[116] Chuang Tzu lived in the last stages of the decline of the feudal world, and certainly never had any concept of democratic government. Even if he had acquired such a concept, he would not necessarily have wanted to see it established in place of monarchy, and give up his fishing pole there beside the P'u River [see p. 511 and footnote 93] to unfurl the banner of revolution.

Seen from another point of view, however, Chuang Tzu's attitude toward the individual may appear more negative than that of some European liberals. For example, John Stuart Mill's call for liberty had as one of its most important bases the idea that the individual's knowledge and capacities are to be developed and expanded.[117] Lao Tzu and Chuang Tzu, on the other hand, firmly maintained that man's natural character was of great value, and they were opposed to all education and development assimilated from the cultural environment. European liberals wanted government to "day by day diminish in pursuit of the Way" [slightly altering the sense of the line in *Tao Te Ching*, ch. 48; cf. p. 547 above] in order to make possible the individual's "day by day increasing his own learning." But Lao Tzu and Chuang Tzu thought that the individual should abandon knowledge and make few his desires, seek self-contained contentment and not seek individual advancement, sharing accord with ruler and superiors about the way [of simplifying life] through diminishing. Hence the political method of letting people alone

[116] *Ch*. 6, "Ta tsung-shih."

[117] See J. S. Mill, *On Liberty*. Refer also to P'u Hsüeh-feng, *Hsi-yang chin-tai cheng-chih ssu-ch'ao*, i.e., "Currents in Modern Western Political Thought," Volume ii, pp. 775–81.

did not demand "popular knowledge" and did not demand social
equality. Except for the single matter of "interfering with others," everyone could do entirely as he pleased. In consequence, the individual becomes the only value, and freedom is not a means for guaranteeing the
growth of knowledge and human capacities, but becomes in itself the
ultimate goal. Thus Chuang Tzu's "letting people alone" is the most
thoroughgoing of libertarian philosophies, and indeed is the purest of all
liberal philosophies as well. We must not make the mistake of assuming,
simply because he did not explicitly call for the abolition of the ruler,
that he acknowledged the necessity of restraints or controls.[118] If we grant
this, then, it would not be inaccurate to call Chuang Tzu's thought the
most radical of all anarchisms.[119]

[118] European thought relatively close to that of Lao Tzu and Chuang Tzu is to be found
in the Cyrenaic and Epicurean schools of ancient Greece. The former are especially close
to the *Tzu Hua Tzu*. If one also considers the single point of the denial of the necessity for
social organization, then the Cynics could also be included. These three schools also somewhat resemble Lao Tzu and Chuang Tzu in not advocating revolution. See Barker,
Greek Political Theory, chapters 3–5, and McIlwain, *The Growth of Political Thought in the
West*, Chapters 1 and 4.

[119] European anarchisms have inclined toward the abolition of political sanctions but
the retention of social restrictions. Therefore they are not as thoroughgoing in theory as is
Chuang Tzu's concept of letting people alone [*tsai yu*]. Perhaps the only one who is
somewhat closer to Chuang Tzu is Max Stirner (Kaspar Schmidt), 1806–1856, who
wrote *The Ego and His Own* [*Der Einzige und sein Eigenthum*] (original German, 1844).

CHAPTER SIX
Kuan Tzu

SECTION ONE
Kuan Tzu's Life and Times

KUAN TZU's formal name was Yi-wu, and his courtesy name was Chung;
he was a native of Ying-shan district in the State of Ch'i.[1] In his youth,
poor and of humble status, he became a close friend of a man called Pao
Shu [or, Pao Shu-ya].* "Later, Pao Shu served Hsiao-po, a son of the
Duke of Ch'i, and Kuan Chung served [another son, named] Chiu.
Subsequently, when Hsiao-po succeeded to the ducal throne as Duke
Huan, the Duke's son Chiu died, and Kuan Chung was imprisoned.
[This account conceals the unseemly rivalry between Duke's sons over the
succession. Chiu was put to death on the order of his brother, Duke Huan,
and Kuan Chung, in exile in the State of Lu with Chiu, was to have been
executed with him. Instead of dying he took service with Duke Huan,
for which he was much discussed in later times. See, *Analects*, XIV/10/2–3,
and Legge's notes, pp. 279, 281.] Pao Shu subsequently brought about
Kuan Chung's appointment to office.[2] Once thus employed, Kuan Chung
assumed full responsibilities of government in Ch'i. Duke Huan of Ch'i
became the Hegemon. Assembling all the feudal lords together, imposing
order on the world,—all that was brought about by the stratagems of
Kuan Chung."[3] After serving as Duke Huan's chief minister for forty
years, he died;[4] thereafter the government of Ch'i deteriorated. Although
his *Shih Chi* biography does not say explicitly that he wrote a book [its
author] Ssu-ma Ch'ien does remark: "I have read the "Mu min,"

*Square brackets indicate that the words enclosed were added by the translator.

[1] Chang Shou-chieh in his *Shih Chi cheng-yi* [pref. date A.D. 736] quotes Wei Chao
[A.D. 204–273]: "Kuan Chung was descended from the [royal Chou] Chi clan; he was the
son of Kuan Yen [and his name was] Ching-chung." [I.e., posthumously known as Kuan
Ching-chung; other sources usually say T. Chung, Pth. Ching.]

[2] For the accounts of Kuan Chung's career as chief minister in Ch'i, and his stratagems
to make the Duke of Ch'i the Hegemon [i.e., *pa*, or chief among the Chou King's nominally
subordinate vassals], see: in the *Tso Chuan*, the various references under the reigns of
Dukes Chuang and Hsi; in the *Kuo Yü*, ch. 6, "Ch'i yü"; in the *Shih Chi*, ch. 32, "Ch'i T'ai-
kung shih-chia"; and in the *Kuan Tzu*, ch. 18, 19, 20, "Ta k'uang," "Chung k'uang,"
and "Hsiao k'uang."

[3] *Shih Chi*, ch. 62, "Kuan, Yen lieh chuan."

[4] *Shih Chi*, ch. 32, "Ch'i T'ai-kung shih chia." The year of his death corresponds to the
year 645 B.C.; the year of his birth cannot be ascertained. He first took service as chief
minister [*hsiang*] to Duke Huan in 685 B.C. [In the Spring and Autumn Period, the title
"*hsiang*" meant a "second" or supporting official to the ruler; in Kuang Chung's case it
was tantamount to prime ministership.]

319

"Shan kao," "Ch'eng ma," "Ch'ing chung," and "Chiu fu" [apparently all the titles of treatises on government; some correspond to chapter titles in the extant *Kuan Tzu*] by Mr. Kuan, and the *Yen Tzu ch'un-ch'iu*; how detailed and complete are their discourses. . . ." And, he adds, "his writings abound in our times."[5] Thus, by Han times, there actually did exist a book, the *Kuan Tzu*. Ever since the Chin [third-fourth centuries A.D.] and T'ang dynasties, many scholars have doubted that the *Kuan Tzu* was written by Kuan Chung, feeling that it was all or in part a forged compilation, or a false attribution, or a work with interpolations from the hands of later persons.[6] That the *Kuan Tzu* was put together as a compila-

---

[5] *Shih Chi*, ch. 62, the "Encomium" to the *Kuan, Yen lieh-chuan*, i.e., "Biographies of Kuan Chung and Yen Ying." P'ei Yin's [fifth century A.D.] *Chi-chieh* Commentary quotes Liu Hsiang's [first century B.C.] *Ch'i-lueh*: "The work 'Chiu-fu' is no longer extant among the people. 'Shan kao' is also known by the title 'Hsing shih.' All of these are titles of essays among the works written by Kuan Chung." Chang Shou-chieh's *Shih Chi Cheng-yi* also quotes the *Ch'i-lüeh*: "The *Kuan-tzu*, consisting of eighteen essays, belongs to the category of the Legalists." The *Han Fei Tzu*, ch. 49, "Wu Tu," says: ". . . everyone has a copy of the *Laws* of Shang Yang and Kuan Chung in his house." Thus in pre-Han times the work was already very widely circulated.

[6] The opinions of scholars past and present who have studied this work critically are many and varied; they can be summarized as: (1) It is not from the hand of Kuan Chung himself, but it is not spurious; (2) it is a work that later persons have put together and to which they have made additions; hence it represents a mixture of real and false elements; (3) it is purely a work of forgery. Yen K'e-chün [1762–1843], in his *T'ieh-ch'iao man-kao*, says: "The works of all of the philosophers of the pre-Ch'in age were composed and put into their final form by their immediate disciples, or the followers in that school's traditions, or by their invited staff-associates, or by their sons and grandsons, and need not have come from the hand of the man himself." Chang Hsüeh-ch'eng in his *Wen-shih t'ung-yi*, ch. 2, "Shih chiao" Part I, says: "In the Spring and Autumn Period there already existed a book, the *Kuan Tzu*. However, it was an account of the institutions and regulations of government of the time, in that sense analogous to there having existed the Duke of Chou's official work on the rites and institutions. [I.e., the *Chou kuan*, or *Chou li*.] It recorded the words and deeds of Kuan Tzu; that is, it was a compilation put together by someone thoroughly familiar with Kuan's regulations and methods [of government], and not something actually written by Kuan Chung himself. . . . Among the men of antiquity there was no such thing as private authorship; in all cases their works were compiled and arranged by later men." These represent the first of the three opinions.

Fu Hsüan's [died A.D. 278] *Fu Tzu*, ch. 30, says: "The book the *Kuan Tzu* consists in the larger part of additions made by over-zealous persons of a later time." Chu Hsi [1130–1200], in the *Chu-tzu yü-lu*, says: "The *Kuan Tzu* was not written by Kuan Chung. Chung in his time was responsible for the very numerous affairs of government in the State of Ch'i, and during whatever leisure that allowed him, he indulged his obsession for the *san kuei*. [See, *Analects* III/22. Confucius mentioned this criticism of Kuan Chung. Interpretations vary; Legge refused to translate it. Chu Hsi thought it the name of a pleasure pavilion to which he was addicted. The point is that Kuan Tzu had other activities than the writing of books to which he was said to have devoted his limited leisure.] He definitely was not the sort of man who used his leisure to write books. Persons who wrote books were not among those employed by the state. The book, I suppose, was just put together

tion of materials has indeed come to be the accepted conclusion. However, we cannot say because of this that its content has no relationship whatsoever to the man Kuan Yi-wu [i.e., Kuan Chung, or Kuan Tzu]. Moreover, when we carefully examine the political thought embodied in the entire book, we perceive that a very great part of it is directly relevant to the historical backgrounds of the Spring and Autumn Period,[7] and thus differs in very significant fashion from the works of Lord Shang and Han Fei Tzu and others whose thought reflects the later Warring States Period backgrounds. Thus, the actual writers may have included later persons from the time of the Six States [i.e., the Warring States Period], its view may now and then display influence of the concepts current on the eve of the authoritarian world empire's emergence, and yet its thought in the main is perhaps of a character that could not have continued to exist after the "three houses" divided the State of Chin, or after the T'ien family assumed control of the State in Ch'i [events of the years roughly 402 B.C. and 385 B.C., respectively]. But we should also be aware that there are some among contemporary scholars of note who regard the concept of government by law as a product only of the late Warring States Period, hence not one that Kuan Tzu could have held, from this concluding that the *Kuan Tzu* is purely a forgery.[8] That view, however, ignores the fact that although the *Kuan Tzu* advocates a government of laws, neither in point of view nor in substance is it closely analogous to the works of Shen Pu-hai, Kung-sun Yang [Lord Shang], Han Fei Tzu and Li Ssu. [The leading theoreticians and practitioners of Legalism.]

---

by persons of the Warring States Period who assembled topically the accounts of deeds and statements from Kuan Chung's lifetime, to which were added other writings." These represent the second opinion.

Huang Chen [thirteenth century], in his *Huang-shih Jih-ch'ao*, says: "It is not known who compiled the book, the *Kuan Tzu*, but it is of vast bulk and, is mixed and repetitious, apparently not the work of one man." Lo Ken-tse, in his *Kuan Tzu t'an-yüan* [published 1931], has gone still further and deduced estimates of the dates of each of the essays comprising the *Kuan Tzu*, concluding that the earliest are from the Warring States Period, and the latest from the Ch'in and Han dynasties. These represent the third opinion.

We should note that both the first and the second opinions hold that the *Kuan Tzu's* content bears some relationship with the man Kuan Chung.

[7] The most striking of these are: (1) What the book discusses as *pa-cheng* [rule by the Hegemons, or the institution of the Lords' Protector who in the Spring and Autumn Period still possessed some validity as upholders of Chou power, and had not yet become the evil symbols of government by force, as Mencius saw them] is still a variant form of feudal government; (2) the *Kuan Tzu* consistently expresses an attitude of high regard for the family and clan-law institutions; (3) the *Kuan Tzu* does not repudiate government of men; moreover it stresses the rites and proprieties; (4) the *Kuan Tzu* elevates the ruler but does not abandon the concept of following the people's wishes. For more detailed discussion of these points see this chapter, Section Three and following.

[8] Hu Shih, *Chung-kuo che-hsüeh shih*, Part One.

When measured against the standard of Lord Shang and Han Fei Tzu, the *Kuan Tzu's* legalism surely would arouse the sigh that it "was largely correct despite many minor faults" [as Han Yü, died A.D. 824, said in rejecting Hsün Tzu]. The "Journal of Literature" in the *Han Shu* [of the first century A.D.] lists it among the "Taoist" works; that in the *Sui Shu* [written in the seventh century A.D.] first changes it to the head of the category of "Legalist" works. From these differing classifications of it we can sense something of the inconsistent and impure nature of its content. We probably are not seriously wrong to state that the *Kuan Tzu*, while a forerunner of the thought and learning of Lord Shang and Han Fei Tzu, surely is not to be looked upon as the authoritative canon that founded the Legalist School. The question of whether the book was in fact written by Kuan Chung, or whether it embodies posthumous transmissions of his doctrines from the time when Ch'i became the Hegemon, is, then, a matter of only secondary importance.

Section Two
Elevating the Ruler and Following the People's Wishes

AMONG the various thinkers of the pre-Ch'in period, similar political ideas are often encountered, and at some points boundaries become difficult to establish among them. For example, the Confucianists in their rectification of names and punctilious observance of the rites seem indistinct from the Legalists in their rigid fixing of status and their stress on law. Nonetheless, to distinguish between the Confucians and the Legalists one can always apply the one clearly evident and natural criterion: that is the relative weight accorded "the ruler" and "the people" in their thought. The Confucians stress the importance of the people; the Legalists elevate the position of the ruler. The Confucians take the people to be the basic element in government; the Legalists regard the ruler as the basic element in government. If we look at the differences between the two schools in terms of this standard, they are as the rivers Ching and Wei, whose waters differ so that anyone can see it. [The two rivers flow together in Shensi Province, where they then become a tributary of the Yellow River. They symbolize things difficult to distinguish when apart, readily distinguished when they come together. The Wei's waters are clear, as indeed the Ching's waters appear, until they are seen to muddy the Wei's waters at the point of confluence.] Among the thinkers of the Confucian school, Mencius best expressed the doctrine of the importance of the people. Although Hsün Tzu did, to be sure, hold the opinion that the ruler must occupy an elevated position, when we carefully seek his real intent, we find that he would elevate the ruler only as a means of better providing for the people's welfare, and not as a political goal in itself.[9] Hence Mencius stressed the importance of the people and devalued the ruler, while Hsün Tzu elevated the ruler in order to ensure the people's interests. Thus, in modern terms, all Confucian thought embodies the principles of "for the people" and "of the people." This comparison of Mencius and Hsün Tzu thus reveals no more than differences of degree, but no differences in their essential character. Coming to Lord Shang and Han Fei Tzu and their like, we find the ruler-people relationship completely reversed. The ruler is elevated to the highest extreme, and the people are then regarded as merely the resource from which the state can be enriched and strengthened, in their persons no longer possessing any absolute value. The most extreme among them regard the people as being as stupid and as stubborn as beasts that can be made tractable only by the use of the ruler's whips and spurs. Such views are so precisely the opposite of Confucian thought that there is no possibility of reconciling the two. If an explanation of why the two schools disagree so widely on this issue is to be sought, it probably must be found in the ever-changing historical environment. Confucian thought, in which the people are the basic element, more or less acknowledged and accepted what was still left of clan-law feudal society, while Legalist thought, accepting the ruler as the basic element in the state, is a product of the age following the decline and disappearance of clan-law feudal institutions. In the clan-law system, the ruler and his aristocratic kin shared a divided authority, permitting no one person to be elevated far above the others, while the knights and the people bore the valued relationship of subsidiary clans, and were not truly debased.[10] Add to this the fact that the feudal world was jointly held together by the mutually sustaining King and his feudal nobles; that early Chou situation of co-existing states had achieved a more or less general security and stability. Hence, at that time the common practice of annexing the smaller and attacking the weaker, not yet having developed, it was not necessary to enrich the state and

---

[9] For the discussion of this point, see in Chapter Three the last part of Section Five. Mo Tzu's discussion of the ruler-people relationship is fairly close to Hsün Tzu's. Also, Fung Yu-lan, in his *Chung-kuo che-hsüeh-shih*, vol. I, p. 383 [Fung/Bodde, *History of Chinese Philosophy*, vol. I, p. 312], says that the Confucians, Mohists, Lao Tzu, and Chuang Tzu all "agreed in discussing government primarily from the point of view of the people," but that the Legalists "discussed government wholly from the point of view of the ruler or the state"; Fung thus is prior in expressing this idea.

[10] Slaves, of course, were an exception [but they were few]. *Mencius*, "Wan-chang," Part II: "The knights of the lowest class, and such of the common people as were in office had the same emolument. [Modified from Legge, *Mencius*, v/ii/2/7, p. 375; Legge translates *shih* "scholar," which is good enough for Mencius' time and thereafter, but in general descriptions of the Chou institutions it is better translated "knight."] This statement may well have some foundation in fact, and it shows that the common people were not wholly debased [but might rise into the ranks of petty office-holding].

strengthen it militarily to ensure its continued existence. Governments had in fact no tasks more demanding than providing for the people's livelihood. The people still *could* be held important; the conditions for that clearly obtained. But with the dissolution of clan-law institutions, and the aristocracy's disappearance from the scene, the positions of ruler and people gradually tended toward total separation. Nothing lent importance to the people [in these new conditions], while the ruler's position constantly grew more elevated. All the masses of the ordinary common folk lost the support inherent in their status as subsidiary clans; they were reduced to that of the monarch's mere subjects. Their position in society was for them to achieve according to their personal qualities of intelligence and adaptability, or the lack of those, while their status *vis-á-vis* the government was for the ruler to determine by rewarding and bestowing, or by ordering punishment and deprivation of rank. Thus, in an undefined and gradual process, the ruler and the state were identified with one another as a single entity, while the people were transformed into the object of the monarch's control. Moreover, as feudal government accompanied clan-law society along their common path to ultimate dissolution, the rulers of the states warred mightily and the vanquished became ever more numerous. The state that was not rich and strong lacked the means to respond to a changing world, and the ruler who was not despotic and arbitrary lacked the means to implement enriching and strengthening measures. Simply assuring that the people could supply their own needs of food and clothing could no longer be regarded as government's principal task. For the people's labor and the people's wealth had become the material resources that the state must utilize to become rich and powerful; they no longer could be left to the individual's unrestricted uses. Conditions were changing in ways that inevitably called for the rulers' elevation to ever greater heights and powers. In truth, the thought of the two schools, the Confucian and the Legalist, reflect this important historical change; their differences are not merely a matter of stubbornly clinging to basically irreconcilable intellectual positions.

Having made clear the fundamental difference between the Confucian and Legalist schools, we can then procede to decide to which school the *Kuan Tzu* belongs. [Here, as throughout this chapter, the man Kuan Chung and the book the *Kuan Tzu* may be referred to interchangeably, unless specifically stated otherwise, regardless of the historical accuracy of this, as explained in Section One of this chapter.] The *Kuan Tzu*, on the one hand, in its discussions of politics, adopts the Legalist's point of view that the ruler is the fundamental element in the state; yet, on the other hand, it is not completely divorced from the influences of the feudal and clan-law historical background.

Hsün Tzu felt that the responsibility of the ruler lay in his being "the essential agency for controlling the allotments and assignments" [*fen* 分, in society]; hence his position could not be other than elevated, or his power less than massive. Kuan Tzu, in discussing the Way of the sovereign, more or less agrees. *Ch.* 45, "Jen fa," says: "The producer of laws is the ruler." In *chs.* 31 and 32, "Chün ch'en," Parts One and Two, we find: "Morality, rewards, and punishments issue from the ruler." The person of the ruler thus is the crucial element in deciding whether order or disorder shall prevail throughout the state; therefore: "In elevating the ruler lie peace and stability for the state."[11] What is here meant by elevating the ruler is that he is granted the highest possible authority and status, with dictatorial powers of decision, subject to no unsettling forces. For: "That whereby the ruler is the ruler is his power."[12] So it follows: "If commands are not from on high they will not be carried out; if not exclusive, they will not be heeded."[13] The method to assure that power be secure and that commands be obeyed lies in [having the ruler] *alone* occupy the supreme position from which to exercise absolute control over rewards and punishments. "Therefore, those [handles of authority] which the enlightened ruler holds are six: to grant life, to kill, to enrich, to impoverish, to ennoble, to debase. It is these six handles which the ruler holds. The [positions of authority] that the ruler occupies are four: the first is called the civil; the second is called the military; the third is called majestic sternness; the fourth is called gracious kindness. These four positions are those which the ruler holds. To rely on others to employ that which he should exercise,—that is called usurping the handles of authority. To rely on others to fulfill that which he should assume,—that is called forfeiting the position of authority. When the handles of authority have been usurped and the positions of authority have been forfeited, seeking to have one's commands carried out is to seek the impossible."[14] If the ruler can remain in sole possession of his power position, then "a second majesty must not be established, and a second door from which governmental measures might issue must not exist. To govern the state by laws then would be as simple and easy as to lift up [something] by hand and to put it down again; [there would be no ado at all]."[15]

[11] *Ch.* 15, "Chung ling." [Unless otherwise noted, footnotes that follow in this chapter are to chapters in the *Kuan Tzu.*]

[12] *Ch.* 16, "Fa fa." ["Power" is *shih* 勢, sometimes translated as "the compelling force of circumstances," implying position as well as force. See discussion of this concept in Chapter Seven.]

[13] *Ch.* 23, "Pa yen."

[14] *Ch.* 45, "Jen fa." *Ch.* 53, "Chin ts'ang" says "To reward and to punish are as the civil and the military" [i.e., as the two complementary components of government].

[15] *Ch.* 46, "Ming fa." And, in *ch.* 52, "Ch'i ch'en ch'i chu," it states: "Power and authority are things that the ruler of men keeps in his exclusive possession." *Ch.* 23, "Pa yen," says: "The ruler is elevated and the servitors are lowly; the superior possesses

Moreover, we should note that in terms of his legally defined position, the ruler was to be exalted because of the office that he filled. His personal character and morality had not the slightest direct bearing on the matter. Thus Chapter Twenty, "Hsiao k'uang," records Duke Huan's having said of himself that he possessed the "three major depravities" of avarice for land, addiction to wine, and lust for women, yet Kuan Tzu replied to him: "Bad things these are, indeed! Yet they are not crucial faults." And in Chapter Sixteen, "Fa fa," it says: "In any ruler's conduct and demeanor he may not as an individual be more worthy than other men. But he is titled the ruler of men; therefore we accept his leadership and elevate him, and do not dare to indulge in opinions about the quality of his conduct." [Cf. Rickett, *Kuan-tzu*, p. 101, where this passage is taken in quite a different sense.] This statement most clearly presents the essence of what the elevation of the ruler signified; it is one of the special characteristics of Legalist thought, and it also is in implicit accord with more recent European concepts of sovereignty.

Kuan Tzu's discourses on the techniques of the ruler, however, are not in complete accord with those of Lord Shang and Han Fei Tzu. Hsün Tzu condemned the theory that "The way of the ruler benefits from secrecy." [See Chapter Three, footnote 117.] This is an inescapable point of conflict between the Confucian and Legalist schools, the one with its theory of a government of men and the other with its theory of a government by laws. The Confucians, drawing on their clan-law backgrounds in devising their political ideals, wanted the ruler to be a model in his own person, to transform all the people into upright ways. Therefore, if the ruler's virtue was not manifest, it would fail to provide a suitable image on which the people could fix their vision. The Legalists rejected clan-law society and set up the quite distinct ideal of authoritarianism. Their only fear was that the ruler, by interjecting his personal ideas, would throw the laws into confusion, creating a situation that treacherous ministers could manipulate to their own advantage. Hence they not only did not seek to manifest the personal virtue of the ruler, they wanted him to conceal his private feelings and reveal no personal wishes, so that he could not be surreptitiously found out and made vulnerable. The *Kuan Tzu*, while early in advocating the Warring States kind of full reliance on law, yet still did not display complete freedom from feudal and clan-law influences. Consequently we find mixed together in it elements of the government of men and the government of laws, even to the point of

---

majesty and the inferiors display respect; commands are issued and the people submit to them;—this is perfect order. Were the empire to have two Sons of Heaven, the empire could not be put in order. If one state were to have two rulers, that one state could not be put in order. If one family had two fathers, that one family could not be put in order."

internal inconsistency in its arguments. It says: "He is titled the ruler of men; therefore we accept his leadership and elevate him, and do not dare to indulge in opinions about the good or bad quality of his conduct." This conveys the theory of the government by laws, as in Lord Shang or Han Fei Tzu. Yet it also says: "The ruler in the capital of his state is like the mind in the body. When morality is established overhead, then the common people below will be transformed. Similarly, when the mind forms its concerns within, the countenance will be moved without."[16] This conveys the theory of a government of men, as in Mencius or Hsün Tzu. From Chin [fourth century A.D.] and T'ang [seventh century] times onward scholars have often doubted that the *Kuan Tzu* could be from one hand, because of the disorderly and inconsistent nature of its content. These passages offer one example of the sort of thing that has given rise to such doubts.

If we look only at the one feature of "elevating the ruler," Kuan Tzu and Hsün Tzu do not appear to be strikingly different. But when we examine this feature of their thought in relation to the *Kuan Tzu's* various discussions of the people, then the evidence that the two diverged sharply in their attitudes becomes immediately apparent. We have remarked previously that Hsün Tzu's government of rites had as its ultimate goal a satisfying standard of life for the entire body of the people. Therefore the state was to be well-governed for the sake of nourishing the people, and the ruler's place in the state was merely that of an instrument with which to achieve that objective. The political objectives set forth in the *Kuan Tzu* are quite different. For example, there is this statement: "All shepherds of the people [a traditional metaphor for governors and kings,] wish to

---

[16] *Ch.* 31, "Chün-ch'en" Part Two. *Ch.* 52, "Ch'i ch'en ch'i chu," says: "So it is that the order or chaos of one person stems from his mind. A state's survival or destruction stems from its ruler. The world's gains and losses all procede from one man. If the ruler stresses the essential [i.e., agriculture] the people will open new uncultivated areas to agriculture. If the ruler likes money and goods, then the people will peddle goods and attend markets. If the ruler is fond of palaces and dwellings, then there will be clever builders and craftsmen. If the ruler is addicted to patterns and colors, then there will be many women doing fine work. Thus, the King of Ch'u was fond of slender waists and women all ate less, the King of Wu was addicted to swordsmanship and all the knights of the country became casual about dying. To die and to forego eating are things that normally would be universally hated. So why is it that people willingly seek to do them? It is because in so doing they comply with the wishes of their ruler." The import of this is very close to that of the Confucians' saying that "The grass must bend, when the wind blows across it." [*Analects*, XII/19, Legge, p. 259.] Note also that Kuan Tzu, in rejecting any concern with the ruler's personal morality, may have been considering only his legal position. The ruler's becoming upright in his own person thereby to transform his people, however, speaks exclusively to the ruler's political function. If we explain the discrepancy in this fashion, it might be possible to force a kind of compatability on the two otherwise apparently contradictory concepts.

govern a people who can be driven."[17] And further: "I conclude that the reason the ruler loves the people is that he uses them; therefore he loves them."[18] For the indispensable support of all enriching and strengthening measures is a people whose minds are set to obey commands and whose physical strength is conscientiously expended. Only when the people are so utilized by the ruler can his projects be carried to fruition. *Ch.* 16, "Fa fa," explains this as follows: "The rulers of large countries are esteemed; the rulers of small countries are demeaned. Why is it that the ruler of a large country is esteemed? It is because those whom he uses are of a vast number. Why is it that the ruler of a small country is demeaned? It is because those whom he uses are few. Thus it is that when the ruler can make use of many people he can be esteemed, and when he has only a few to make use of he will be demeaned. So, how can a ruler of men not desire that the masses of the people will not be put to use by himself?" [Cf. Rickett, *Kuan-tzu*, p. 96.] Such being the function of the people, then "he who would contest for the world must first contest for people."[19] And contesting for people is not alone to contest for numbers of them. "When the people are of great number but are not well ordered, that is what is called 'overwhelmed with people.' " Even if it has been made possible for all to obtain plentiful food and clothing and yet they cannot be utilized by the ruler and his state, and are not willing to "charge bared steel, withstand assault from arrows and slings, and go through fire and water in obedience to their superior's command,"[20] what good are they to ruler and state?

Once we realize that concern for the people is a means and not an end, then we need not be misled on encountering all of the places in the *Kuan Tzu* where concern for the people's livelihood is stressed, and will know better than to class him with Mencius and Hsün Tzu. For example, there is the reply to Duke Huan's question about the foundations underlying the Hegemon's government: "Kuan Tzu replied saying, 'The common people of the State of Ch'i are your Lordship's foundation. The people are fraught with anxiety about hunger, yet the taxes and imports are severe; the people are terrified of death, yet your administration of corporal punishments is inordinate; the people are grievously overworked, yet you launch your projects at improper times. [I.e., public works and military efforts, for which the people were commandeered, were undertaken at times that interfere with their essential agricultural work, instead of on their slack seasons.] If your Lordship will lighten their taxes, the

---

[17] *Ch.* 3, "Ch'üan hsiu."
[18] *Ch.* 16, "Fa fa." [Cf. Rickett, *Kuan-tzu*, p. 96.]
[19] *Ch.* 23, "Pa yen."
[20] *Ch.* 16, "Fa fa."

people will not be anxious about hunger; temper their punishments, and they will not be in terror of dying; undertake your projects at suitable times, and they will not suffer overwork.' "[21] The practices advocated here sound much like Mencius' saying that the ruler should "be sparing in the use of punishments and fines and make taxes and levies light," and "should not rob them of their time at the wrong seasons." [Cf. *Mencius*, 1/i/5/3–4; Legge, p. 135.] Yet the motive is entirely different.

Since the people are but tools to be used by the ruler, the ideal relationship exists between ruler and people when the ruler issues his commands and the people unfailingly obey. In other words, when Kuan Tzu's methods are put into practice, then within the structure of government the ruler's will possesses absolute authority, while the people's will does not have the slightest force. Because if the popular will should by chance intrude into the affairs of government, then "When a command is issued from above, should there be inferiors who discuss whether or not to obey it, it signifies that the ruler's majesty is contingent on [the will of] the populace below. When that majesty is so linked to the populace below, the ruler simply cannot be free from peril."[22] Therefore, "When there is an enlightened ruler in the highest place, the people will not dare to arrogate to themselves the self-importance of expressing personal opinions," and "stubbornly independent persons who would alter commands, establish other standards, devise methods and propose policies should all be severely punished."[23] Moreover, were the ruler arbitrarily to put his policies into effect, even though they run entirely counter to the people's will, if they but benefit the state they should be rigorously pursued without any feelings of regret. "For the one who is most skilled in using the people can kill them, imperil them, work them, exhaust them, cause them to suffer hunger and thirst; indeed, the one who [knows how to] utilize the people may achieve these extremes, yet among the people will be no one plotting harm to the ruler. When there is an enlightened ruler overhead whose ways and whose laws are implemented throughout the state, the people will all forego their own desires and do that which they hate to do." After that has been achieved, "when they are led to work, the people will no longer dare to evade the labor, and when they are pushed off to battle, the people will no longer dare to worry about dying. When they do not dare to evade labor, there can be great accomplishment; when they do not dare to worry about dying, they will be invincible. . . . Therefore the benevolent one, the knowing one, the one who understands the Way, will not deliberate with the people

---

[21] *Ch.* 22, "Pa hsing."
[22] *Ch.* 15, "Chung ling."
[23] *Ch.* 16, "Fa fa." [Cf. Rickett, *Kuan-tzu*, p. 92.]

in initiating an action."[24] And elsewhere it says: "The one who heads the state must counter the people's natures, after which he can then be friendly with the people."[25] To pursue the issue of why the people's will is not worth heeding, it is because the people's minds are accustomed to easy solutions, and ignorant about where their own true interests lie; they understand men's selfish concerns, yet are incapable of governing themselves. For "the people submit to intimidation [by the ruler's majesty]. Kill, and then they will obey; show them where their interests lie, and then they can be used; impose rule upon them and then they will become upright; when they have gained a sense of security, then they will be upright."[26] [Some versions say: "then they will be quiescent."]

The *Kuan Tzu* also offers a theory about "following the people's wishes" [*shun min* 順民], which might seem to contradict what has just been discussed, but which in fact wholly complements it. *Ch.* 1, "Mu min," says: "It is acting in accord with the people's wishes that causes governments to prosper; it is acting contrary to people's minds that causes them to fail. The people dislike anxiety and toil; I can give them ease and happiness. The people dislike poverty and humble status; I can enrich and ennoble them. The people dislike peril and collapse; I can give them security and preserve them. The people dislike death and extinction; I can give them life and nurture. When one has the capacity to give them ease and happiness, the people will bear anxiety and toil for him; when one can enrich and ennoble them, the people will bear poverty and humble status for him; when one can make them secure and preserve them, the people will bear peril and collapse for him; when he can assure them life and nurture, the people will bear death and extinction for him." In *ch.* 64, "Hsing shih chieh," we also find: "The reason that when the ruler commands something it is done, and prohibits something and it ceases, is that his commands must have accorded with the people's likes, and his prohibitions with the people's dislikes. It is the nature of the people that none do not wish to live, or dislike dying; none do not wish for advantage, and dislike harm. Therefore when the superior's commands help the people to live and to gain advantage, they are carried out. When his prohibitions are to stop killings and harm, then what he prohibits will cease. The reason why commands are carried out is that the people must be pleased with their [ruler's] governing." [Cf. the slightly different

---

[24] All are to be found in *Ch.* 16, "Fa fa." [Cf. Rickett, pp. 96–97, where a somewhat different sense is offered.]

[25] *Ch.* 35, "Ch'ih mi." The next line reads: "The people like to be idle so they should be taught to labor diligently; the people want to live so they should be taught to die. When the doctrine of labor is established, the state will grow rich; when the doctrine of dying [for the ruler] is established, his majestic influence will prevail."

[26] *Ch.* 47, "Cheng shih."

translation of this passage, in the context of the entire chapter, Rickett, *Kuan-tzu*, p. 125.]

Kuan Tzu's intention undoubtedly is to say that the people have certain basic interests; when they gain them, the people's livelihood is assured and the strength of the state increases. Blinded always by minor advantages of a temporary nature, the people cannot perceive the real advantages that are crucial to themselves. However, the one who acts as the ruler of men should, through his administrative commands, his supervision, and his prohibitions, cause the people to gain those fundamental, those true advantages. Whenever a command has just been issued, the people are certain to feel that the monarch has deprived them of a minor advantage, and be displeased. From that point of view, he has acted "contrary to the people's nature." But when the matter has been brought to its conclusion, the people will have gained their true advantage and they will be happy. In view of this, he has then "followed the people's wishes."[27] Therefore "the people cannot share with [the ruler] the deliberations prior to inaugurating an undertaking, but they can rejoice with [him] on its successful completion."[28]

Further, with respect to their true advantage, the people not only can perceive after the commands have been carried out and the deeds accomplished, but also from the consensus of the multitude. *Ch.* 30, "Chün ch'en," Part I, says: "When the people are listened to individually they are foolish, but when they are listened to collectively they are sagacious. Even if the ruler has the virtues of a [sage king like] T'ang or Wu, he still will be in agreement with what men in the street say. Thus the wise ruler acts in accord with the people's minds, is at ease with their natures, and procedes from the common objects of the masses. In this way commands issued are not hindered [in their implementation]; punishments are established but need not be applied. The former kings were skilled at being as one with the people. When the ruler is as one with the people, the whole nation serves to maintain the nation, the whole people to preserve the people. And then the people will not find it expedient to do wrong." If, on the contrary, the ruler, in promulgating his administrative measures and issuing his commands, acts seriously against the true advantage of the people and, simultaneously, gives no attention to whether in their hearts they accept or reject his government, then his power will pass to others and his commands will be blocked; then his overthrow and destruction can be expected. "Even if it be the Son of Heaven or the feudal lords, if the people all know their reputation and are repelled, then they will give up their lands and leave. Therefore the

---

[27] This somewhat resembles Rousseau's theories of the "public advantage," the "general will," and the "particular will." See, his *Social Contract*.

[28] *Ch.* 1, "Mu min."

Former Kings feared the people."[29] Yet inasmuch as the *Kuan Tzu* advocated prohibiting the people's private expressions of opinion, how were they expected to express their acceptance or rejection? In *ch.* 56, "Huan Kung wen," it says that Kuan Tzu urged Duke Huan to establish an "assembly hall of consultation" so that relying on it he could "find out what the people dislike in order to be cautioned by that knowledge"; his purpose must have been to establish a public expression of opinion to function in place of private opinion, something like the "village school" of the man of the State of Cheng.[30] This, moreover, was a measure designed to support his basic theory about the elevated status of the ruler; it did not conflict with that. For, in heeding their expressions of opinion, acting in accord with their mind, and pursuing their advantage, his sole objective was to ensure the people's usefulness to the ruler. It was not because of love or concern for the people themselves. Therefore this saying: "Knowing that to give is for the purpose of being able to take is the gem of political wisdom."[31] Confucius said: "The people may be made to follow a path of action, but they may not be made to understand it." He also said: "When right principles prevail in the kingdom, there will be no expressions of opinion among the common people."[32] Mencius said: "To gain the peasantry is the way to become sovereign."[33] Hsün Tzu

---

[29] *Ch.* 32, "Hsiao ch'eng."

[30] *Tso Chuan*, Thirty-first year of Duke Hsiang [Legge, p. 565]. Liang Ch'i-ch'ao, *Kuan Tzu chuan* (in his *Yin-ping shih, chuan-chi*, number 28), p. 25, says that the "assembly hall" (*chi shih*) "was very much like the national assemblies of the modern world," and was "an institution through which the people supervised government." We should note that this assembly hall at the very most could have been no more than something resembling modern advisory or consultative organs. Whether any opinions expressed there would ever be adopted was entirely in the hands of the ruler to decide. That differed totally from the balloting on proposed legislation in a national assembly. This essay of Liang's was written in 1909 and was written for a specific purpose; that is why he was willing to indulge in such a forced interpretation, one which we need grant no credence.

[31] *Ch.* 1, "Mu min." Note that "following the people's wishes" need not necessarily be in conflict with authoritarianism. The monkey-keeper's three [chestnuts, or acorns] in the morning and four in the evening, or alternatively four in the morning and three in the evening, did not fail to accord with the monkey's will, but nonetheless one cannot say that the monkey-keeper was not authoritarian. [Refers to famous anecdote in the *Chuang-tzu, ch.* 2, Legge, 2/1/2/4, p. 185; or Watson, *The Complete Works of Chuang Tzu*, p. 41.] Among all the most authoritarian governments of past and present, both Chinese and foreign, there are none that have not depended for their continued existence on the support and submission of the majority of their people. The concrete distinction between democracy and authoritarianism lies in whether or not the people possess the legally established right to supervise and control government, and in nothing else.

[32] *Analects*, respectively, "T'ai-po" VIII/9 [Legge, p. 211] and "Chi-shih" XVI/2/3 [modified from Legge, p. 310].

[33] *Mencius*, "Chin hsin" Part II [VII/ii/14/2, Legge, p. 483].

said: ". . . he whom the empire abandons is called doomed."[34] Were it not that the *Kuan Tzu* in its discussions of government displays fundamentally different goals from those of the Confucians, one might well isolate these views on according with or acting contrary to the people, and conclude that Kuan Tzu is indistinguishable from the [Confucian] proponents of "benevolence and righteousness." Mencius said: "The five hegemons all feigned [benevolence and righteousness],"[35] and this may be regarded as the ultimate comment on Kuan Tzu's doctrines. However, "consulting the people" was in any event one of the common practices of feudal government, as we have previously mentioned.[36] Kuan Tzu, taking as his basic doctrine the elevation of the ruler, while also advocating the tactic of heeding the people's wishes, is in truth both the heir to the lingering ideas of feudalism before him, and a presentiment of things to come in Lord Shang and Han Fei Tzu. Its content is indeed mixed and inconsistent, displaying therein a standard quite characteristic of transitional thought, albeit one that is particularly evident in this work. Moreover, that the Hegemons all should have "feigned" [their benevolence and righteousness] of course also has historical causes; it is no mere coincidence.

Section Three
Governing by Law

AUTHORITARIAN rule by the sovereign alone [or, autocratic despotism], is the national polity that the *Kuan Tzu* would establish. With that polity made clear, we may proceed to a consideration of Kuan Tzu's governing methods. *Ch.* 46, "Ming fa," says: "A second majesty [or awe, as a political attribute of the autocrat] must not be established, and a second door from which governmental measures might issue must not exist. To govern the state by laws would then be [as simple and easy] as to lift up [something] by hand and to put it down again; [there would be no ado at all]." This "governing by law" is the central element in Kuan Tzu's methods of governing.

At the beginning of the preceding section we have said that the two terms, rites [*li*] and law [*fa*], are used in overlapping and non-distinctive senses. For rites and law have both their broad and their strict definitions. The narrower definition of rites is the proprieties [*yi* 儀, or ceremonial forms]; the stricter definition of law is penal regulations [*hsing* 刑,

---

[34] *Ch.* 18, "Cheng lun" [translation is from Bodde, vol. I, p. 301, where the context of the passage is given more fully].

[35] *Mencius*, "Chin hsin," Part I [VII/i/30/1; cf. Legge's translation, p. 466].

[36] For a more detailed discussion of this, see Chapter Three, footnote 42, of the present work.

especially those involving corporal punishments]. By the broader definitions of both rites and law, each comprises the sum total of all social and
political institutions. To use the doctrines of ceremonial forms and their
refined accouterments together with social ranks and classes, as the chief
means of maintaining institutions, and to use corporal punishments and
penalties as supplementary aids, is to carry on "governing by rites"
[li-chih]. To use the intimidation of corporal punishments and penalties
as the chief means of maintaining institutions, and to use ceremonial
forms and all the rest as mere aids, is to carry on "governing by law"
[fa chih]. Thus there is no absolute line of demarcation between rites and
law. Government of rites does not necessarily have to abolish punishments
and laws; government by law does not necessarily have to eradicate rites
and ceremonial usages. The thought of the two philosophers, Hsün Tzu
and Kuan Tzu, provides us with specific corroboration of this point.[37]
Hsün Tzu repeatedly advocated well-defined penal measures, yet he is
correctly seen as the representative of the later development within
Confucianism. Kuan Tzu at times sets forth principles of the rites, yet he
may be regarded as the forerunner of Legalism. The point is again evident
in that.

The definitions of "law" that the *Kuan Tzu* establishes are not fully
consistent. Yet, despite the fact that their implications are not the same in
all cases, a comprehensive overview reveals that law undoubtedly is used
as the general term for all political institutions. To cite some of the more
important examples: "Law is that by which one makes the people
uniform and commands the empire";[38] "Law is that by which meritorious
achievement is induced and violence is intimidated";[39] "Law is the model
for the empire, that by which uncertainties are resolved and right and
wrong are made manifest";[40] "Foot and inch measures, string and black
powder [the Chinese version of the carpenter's chalk line], compass and
square, balance and weights, peck and bushel, horn measure and bulk
measure, these are called laws";[41] "Law once promulgated is not subject
to discussion"; "Death penalties are not to be remitted"; "Rank and
emolument are not to be granted on false grounds"; "When these three

---

[37] Confucius wanted to achieve a state in which the people would have no litigations,
thereby evidencing the ultimate ideal of the government of rites. Lord Shang regarded
rites and music as among the "six kinds of lice," displaying in that judgment the extreme
form of legalist policy. ["Lice" are parasites on the body politic. See; Duyvendak, *Book of
Lord Shang*, p. 256; elsewhere the "six kinds of lice" are variously identified, e.g., *op.cit.*,
p. 197.]

[38] *Ch.* 45, "Jen fa."
[39] *Ch.* 50, "Ch'i ch'en ch'i chu."
[40] *Ch.* 53, "Chin ts'ang."
[41] *Ch.* 6, "Ch'i fa."

principles are guarded by officialdom, they together constitute law."[42] All of these describe the content and the functions of law. In addition, there are the four terms: regulations [*lü* 律], commands [*ling* 令], punishments [or penal regulations, *hsing* 刑] and administrative measures [*cheng* 政], different in name from law [*fa*] but similar in function, and more or less included within the scope of the word "law." For, "Regulations [*lü*] are that with which to determine status and stop disputes; commands [*ling*] are that with which to command people and supervise affairs."[43] "To legislate and define the five corporal punishments so that each is appropriate to its name, so that the criminal will have no resentment, and the good man need not be fearful,—this is called punishments [*hsing*]."[44] "To correct them, to make them subservient, to prevail over them, to assign them tasks, commands must be made strict, and the people will conform to them—this is called governing [*cheng*]."[45] Since we know that law [*fa*] is his general term for all institutions, it is then clear that what Kuan Tzu calls "governing the state by law" is in fact no different than to say the ruler of a state must establish clearly-defined and stable institutions; that would not permit the monarch to impose arbitrary decisions according to his personal whims whenever he chooses. Hence he says: "If laws are not observed there can be no constancy in affairs." [*Ch.* 16, "Fa fa"; cf. Rickett, p. 90.]

Governing the state demands reliance on institutions; the Confucians were no less understanding of this point and Hsün Tzu discussed it with particular care and depth. The *Kuan Tzu's* discussions of why political institutions are necessary are not as detailed or penetrating as in Hsün Tzu. But its methods for the application of law even go beyond Lord Shang and Han Fei Tzu in some instances.

Kuan Tzu establishes the fact that interdictions and organization are those means by which the state is constituted. Thus, in *ch.* 31, "Chün ch'en," Part II, it says: "In antiquity there was no distinction of ruler and

---

[42] *Ch.* 14, "Fa chin." The *Yin-wen Tzu, ch.* 1, "Ta Tao," says: "Law has four courses. . . ." "The first of these is the unvarying law; it is that of ruler and servitor, of superior and inferior. The second is the law that makes uniform everyday customs; it applies to the able and the incompetent, to differences and similarities. The third is the law that keeps order among the masses of the people; it applies to felicitations and rewards, corporal punishments and penalties. The fourth is the law of weights and measures; it applies to pitchpipes and footrules, balance weights and measuring vessels." This supplements and clarifies the other passages quoted.

[43] *Ch.* 52, "Ch'i ch'en ch'i chu."

[44] *Ch.* 43, "Cheng." This is law in the strict sense. *Ch.* 36, "Hsin shu" Part I, says: "That which discerns even the smallest of deviations from the Way and executes, interdicts, and punishes, is what is called the law." [Translation of this probably corrupt passage is tentative; cf. Rickett, *Kuan-tzu,* paragraph 1b11, p. 175.]

[45] *Ch.* 43, "Cheng."

servitor, superior and inferior, there did not exist the union of husband and wife, man and mate. People dwelt like beasts and lived in herds, using their strength to attack each other. Consequently the clever tricked the stupid and the strong encroached on the weak. The aged and the young, fatherless children and childless old people, orphans and those left alone, were given no adequate provision for their needs. Therefore men of wisdom used the strength of the group to prohibit the depredations of the strong, and violence against people ceased. They promoted benefit and expunged harm to the people, correcting the people's sense of virtue so that the people followed their guidance. That is how moral ways and virtuous conduct came to proceed from men of superior worthiness. The people accepted righteousness and adhered to order; as these took form in men's minds, the people turned to right ways. Because in forms and distinctions they might behave contrary to right and wrong, rewards and punishments were implemented. Superior and inferior status were instituted, the people assumed their [social] forms, and the national capital was established. Thus we can say: What makes the state a state is that the people assume a social form; what makes the ruler a ruler is that he applies rewards and punishments."[46]

The state has its regularly established and maintained institutions, and the ruler carries on the rewarding and punishing according to those institutions; the principle of governing by law is no more than this. However, in order to achieve rule by law, two methods must be put into use. The first is called the method of establishing laws, and the second is called the method of administering the laws. With regard to the former in particular, Kuan Tzu offers many highly original views. Kuan Tzu once said: "The producer of laws is the ruler."[47] However, although the ruler produces the laws, he does not do so with reference only to his personal ideas, arbitrarily, but must take both human nature and the principle in Nature [*t'ien tse* 天則] as his standard. *Ch.* 6, "Ch'i fa" says: "Rooted in the matter of heaven and earth, in the harmony of cold and heat [i.e., the seasons], in the nature of water and soil; all the living forms of men, of birds and beasts, plants and trees, all possess this quality, though not in great amount, and it is forever unchanging,—that is what is called the principle [*tse*]. "... To be unclear about the principle and yet to desire to issue orders and commands is like being from dawn to dusk on a revolving potter's wheel, holding a bamboo pole outward and trying to keep its tip-end steady." The manifestation of this natural principle in man is mankind's innate capacity for liking and disliking. These likes and dislikes

---

[46] The commentary says: "Noble and humble status are realized in ritual forms; only then can the state come into being." In other words, there then exists political organization.

[47] *Ch.* 45, "Jen fa."

of human nature are thus an important standard in legislating. *Ch.* 64, "Hsing shih chieh," says: "The reason that when the ruler commands something it is done, and prohibits something and it ceases, is that his commands must have accorded with the people's likes and dislikes. It is the nature of the people that none do not wish to live, or dislike dying; none do not wish for advantage, and dislike harm. Therefore when the superior's commands help the people to live, and to gain advantages, they are carried out. When his prohibitions are to stop killings and harm, then what he prohibits will cease."

Furthermore, the people's capacities have definite limits, to which the legislator also must give his attention. *Ch.* 2, "Hsing shih," says: "Do not force beyond capacities." *Ch.* 64, "Hsing shih chieh," explains this as follows: "The enlightened ruler calculates how much human strength can do, and only then assigns tasks. For, when commands accord with people's capacities for performance, then commands will be carried out; when assignments accord with people's abilities, then things get done. The chaotic ruler does not calculate people's strengths; he commands people beyond their capacities for performance, thus his commands are ineffective; he assigns people to tasks beyond their abilities, thus his undertakings all fail. . . . Therefore it is said: 'do not force beyond capacities.'" *Ch.* 5, "Ch'eng ma," also says: "What the wise understands but the dull does not comprehend, cannot be used to teach the people. . . . Unless it be within every man's capacities, no great accomplishment could be achieved."

In addition, the people also have natural limits to their obedience to laws and commands, and the legislator must be particularly careful not to unthinkingly exceed these. Thus *ch.* 16, "Fa fa," says: "The one who seeks much will get little; the one who prohibits much will succeed in stopping little; the one whose commands are many will have few of them carried out." And *ch.* 47, "Cheng shih," says: "In governing, nothing is more to be valued than achieving a balance. If the controls imposed over the people are too demanding, the people will feel pressed. When the people feel pressed, then they lose the sense of security in their livelihood.[48] But if they are too lax, they will be unrestrained, and if unrestrained, they will commit excesses, and in such excesses they will pursue private interests, and when pursuing private interests they will become estranged from the public concerns, and when estranged from the public concerns, it will be difficult to make use of them." All of these passages deal with the influence of human nature in legislating.

Since mankind is one entity within nature, the one who establishes the laws also must make a study of "heavenly timeliness and earthly advan-

[48] [Philological notes; translation omitted here, as the passage quoted is translated according to the suggestions contained in this note.]

tages" as a basis for devising his laws. Kuan Tzu said: "Commands have their proper times . . . the Sage King strives so adjust to time, and to relate his governmental measures to it."[49] Spring, summer, autumn, and winter, each has its activities which should be done at those times.[50] "When man and heaven are in accord, only then can the perfection of heaven and earth come into being."[51] When commands and orders are not appropriate to the season, then "things undertaken will not get accomplished, and there is sure to be a great calamity."[52]

Kuan Tzu also established the idea that man's innate nature varies in accordance with local geographical and climatic conditions.

"The waters of Ch'i flow impetuously and in torturous courses; hence its people incline to be covetous, coarse, and daring.
The waters of Ch'u are gentle and clear; hence its people act swiftly and decisively, and tend to be wicked.

[49] *Ch.* 40, "Ssu shih."

[50] *Ch.* 52, "Chin ts'ang," raises the issue of administrative measures corresponding to the needs of the four seasons, and says: "When the four seasons are provided for, the people's accomplishments will increase hundredfold." *Ch.* 40, "Ssu-shih," lists five administrative measures for spring, summer, autumn and winter each. [Translated in Maverick, *Kuan-tzu*, pp. 88 ff.] *Ch.* 41, "Wu hsing," says that in one year five sets of commands are issued, each being in force for seventy-two days and then terminating. *Ch.* 8, "Yu kuan," and *ch.* 9, "Yu kuan t'u," relate the affairs of government to the four seasons and the five directional locations [i.e., east, south, west, north, and center. *Ch.* 8 is translated in Maverick, *Kuan-tzu*, p. 57 ff.]

[51] *Ch.* 41, "Wu hsing."

[52] *Ch.* 40, "Ssu shih." [Cf. Fung/Bodde, vol. I, pp. 166–67.] It may be noted that all of these theories and statements are roughly similar to the chapter on the "Monthly Commands," i.e., *Yüeh ling* in the *Li Chi, ch.* 4, and the *Lü-shih Ch'un-ch'iu* [Section 1 of Books 1–12]. Lo Ken-tse, in his *Kuan Tzu t'an-yuan* [1931], says that the *ch.* 40, "Ssu shih," i.e., "On the Four Seasons," and *ch.* 41, "Wu hsing" i.e., "On the Five Agents," were written by men of the *Yin-yang* School of philosophy at the end of the Warring States Period, and he may be correct in this. However, we should also note that although the *Kuan Tzu* contains references to theories of "heaven and man," the "*Yin* and *Yang*," the "five agents," and the "four seasons," yet it does not touch upon the ideas of the sequence of the agents and their manifestations in disasters and omens, nor on the cyclic ascendancy of the [five] powers, nor on the greater and smaller Nine Regions and the like; therefore its author would seem to have lived before the time of Tsou Yen [ca. 305–240 B.C.]. Furthermore, in the theory about "commands having their proper time" in the *Kuan Tzu* there are also elements quite in keeping with the practical relationships of Nature and man; for example, the spring commands include repairing ditches and dykes, prohibiting hunting across the fields, and the autumn commands include urging people to gather the harvest, to repair that which is broken and plug that which is breached. Thus they preserve the flavor of agrarian society. Is it not possible that Kuan Chung may originally have devised some system of applying administrative measures according to the seasons, and some later persons "augmented his statements," producing these passages which were thus made to appear more like the tenets of the later *Yin-yang* School than had been their original purport?

The waters of Yüeh are heavy and turbid, and overflow the banks; hence
its people are stupid, unclean, and irritable.

The waters of Ch'in are thick, stagnant, and impure; hence its people
are greedy, perverse and untruthful, and incline to meddle in other
people's affairs.

The waters of Chin trickle in small streams but with ease; hence its people
tend to be flattering, cunning, and profit-loving.

The waters of Yen flow downward with a weak current, and yet they are
muddy and impure; hence its people are ignorant and simple, have a
liking for divination, act impetuously, and sacrifice their lives easily.

The waters of Sung are light, strong, and pure; hence its people are
leisurely and at ease, and strive to be correct."

"Thus the Sage in his ordering of the world, need not proclaim his
views person-by-person, or try to prevail household-by-household, for the
determining factor is the waters."[53] Should this be so, what methods must
the legislator use and what institutions should he establish to overcome
the faults related to these rivers, and to bring about the desired results?
Unfortunately, the *Kuan Tzu* contains no single word of advice to the
reader on this problem.

There are three major aspects to the technique of applying the laws:
the first is the advance preparation; the second is the attitude with which
they are carried out; the third is the force by means of which they are
promoted. Kuan Tzu advocated giving preparatory guidance to the
people before putting the laws into operation, so that they would know
about the laws and observe them. To punish those who have never been
instructed is something of which he disapproved. *Ch.* 3, "Ch'üan-hsiu,"
says: "Be generous in concern and benefits [to the people] and they can
be won close; manifest wisdom and propriety and they can be taught. The
ruler must himself adhere to [the laws] in order for others to follow; he
must carefully calculate the measures by which they are applied in order
to establish restrictive bounds. In the districts, governors must be appointed in order to exhort and guide the people. Only thereafter can the
regulations and laws be instituted. They must be encouraged by rewards,
and warned by punishments. Then the common people will all joyfully
do good, while violent and disorderly conduct will have no cause to
appear." However, merely to offer preparatory guidance is still not
enough to win the people's confidence [in the laws]. "For this reason, the
enlightened ruler, knowing that the people will take their superior's
mind as their own, therefore establishes laws in order to keep himself in
order, erects norms so that he can keep himself upright. For if the ruler

---

[53] *Ch.* 39, "Shui ti" [although the import is clear enough, this passage presents numerous textual problems; the translation is quoted in major part from Maverick, *The Kuan-tzu*,
pp. 87–88].

himself does not [abide by these norms] in practice, the people will not follow them. And if the people do not submit to the laws, and if they would [not when necessary] die for the regulations, the state is sure to lapse into chaos. It is for this reason that the capable and wise ruler in carrying out his laws and setting up his institutions himself submits to them, even before the people."[54]

Instructional guidance, and taking the lead in submitting [to the laws], are psychological preparations, but the effective operation of the laws commences only when their texts have been publicly revealed. *Ch.* 16, "Fa fa," discusses this in the clearest possible manner: "Before a command has been promulgated, should the people happen to act in accordance with it, and be rewarded for having observed it, that is a case of the ruler's rewarding foolishly. . . . If a command has not yet been promulgated and penalty is meted out, that is a case of the ruler's chastising foolishly. . . . After a command has been promulgated if rewards do not follow, that is a case of leading the people to ignore exhortation, not to observe regulations, and be unwilling to die for principle. . . . After a command has been promulgated and penalties do not follow, that is to teach the people disobedience." Since "promulgation" is so important as all this, the procedures of promulgation should be undertaken with greatest care.[55]

---

[54] *Ch.* 16, "Fa fa."

[55] The Section "Shou hsien" of *ch.* 4, "Li cheng," says: "On the first day of the first month of the year, all of the officials are present at court. The ruler on this occasion issues his commands, promulgating his ordinances throughout the state. The Governors of the Five Provinces, and the Five Great Officers subordinate to them, receive the ordinances from the Grand Archivist. On the day of the court's great audience, the Governors of the Five Provinces and the Five Great Officers subordinate to them study the ordinances before the ruler himself. Then the Grand Archivist promulgates the ordinances and brings their texts from the Royal Treasury, and distributes the texts of the ordinances in the ruler's presence. The Governors of the Five Provinces go out from the court, and all receive the ordinances, from the provincial officers to the subordinates of the province, even to the chiefs of the hamlets. When the ordinances have been so promulgated, they then return to report their commands to the ruler. And only after that may they return to their own residences. . . . The subordinate Five Great Officers all go the court in chariots, and upon leaving the court must hasten off without going to their residences; on the day they arrive at the capitals (of the Five Provinces) they immediately assemble their subordinate clerks in the Shrine, so that they can all receive the ordinances. When the ordinances have all been so promulgated, they then despatch messengers reporting the day and the time of day of promulgating the ordinances. When the ordinances have been so promulgated and the messengers so sent, only then does [the Great Officer] dare to go to his residence. . . . After the ordinances have been so promulgated, failure to carry them out is called 'disobeying the command' and is a crime for which the death penalty cannot be remitted. Investigation of the ordinances, indicating discrepancy between them and the texts deposited in the Royal Treasury, is called 'arbitrary enactment' in cases where it exceeds the original text, and 'voided command' in cases where it falls short of it; there are crimes for which the death penalty cannot be remitted." [Cf. the quite differently worded partial translation in Maverick, *Kuan-tzu*, p. 44.]

Three attitudes toward the laws must exist if they are to be practically effective: the people must believe that they are unfailingly certain, that they are unvaryingly constant, and that they are impersonally applied. "Display administrative measures that are imperative, and establish penalties that are indefeasible, then the people will know to what they must adhere, and know what they must avoid. . . . Thus the laws will not be burdensome, and the officials will not be overworked; the people will not transgress the interdicts, nor will the common people resent their superiors."[56] Thus his theory of unfailingly certain laws.

"When commands and orders have already been issued and one changes them; when rites and principles of righteousness are already in practice and one discontinues them; when weights and measures are already fixed and one varies them; when punishments and penal codes are already in operation and one modifies them,—if one does these things, then even though rewards are lavish, the people will not be subject to suasion; though killings and executions are commonplace, the people will not be intimidated. Thus it is said that when above there is no fixed purpose, below there will be doubts; when the state has no constant canons, the people's strength is sure to be exhausted. This is in the nature of things."[57] Thus his explanation of unvaryingly constant laws.

However, "constancy" as used here means that there cannot be "commands of the morning, changed by the evening." That is not to say that laws and institutions once established should never again be changed. For "laws are not perdurable. . . . The so-called 'enlightened ruler' of antiquity was not just one ruler. The rewards that they instituted ranged from the niggardly to the generous, and the prohibitions that they ordained could bring either slight or severe punishment. Their actual deeds were not necessarily uniform, but [that was] not merely to be contrary. All of them adjusted to the needs of their times, responding to different conditions among their common people."[58]

In implementing laws, nothing is more difficult than to achieve their impersonal functioning. Moreover, nothing can damage the law's workings more seriously than the interference of private interests. "It is private interests that bring the world to chaos."[59] For the members of officialdom will always be trying to upset the workings of the law in order to gain their personal ends. "If he who is above all men dispenses with the law to advance his private interests, then his servitors will elevate the private to consideration as public interest."[60] Therefore: "To depart from the law and heed servitors of noble status,—this is what is called being in awe of

[56] *Ch.* 52, "Ch'i ch'en ch'i chu."
[57] *Ch.* 47, "Cheng shih."
[58] *Ch.* 37, "Hsin shu," Part II.
[59]
[60] *Ch.* 30, "Chün ch'en," Part I.

the nobility. If rich men gain entry to their ruler's service by offering him gold and gems, and the ruler departs from the law to heed them,—this is what is called appointments made because of wealth. If lowly persons come humbly and in self-abasement, and respectfully and piteously make charges against their masters, and the ruler departs from the law to heed them,—this is what is called being in the employ of the lowly. If those in close relationship use their closeness and affection to plead with their ruler, and the ruler departs from the law to heed them,—this is what is called giving in to affection for those who are close. If beautiful persons employ artful speech and their physical attractions in making requests of their ruler and the ruler departs from the law and heeds them,—this is what is called being debauched by beauty. . . . If these five errors are not avoided by the ruler himself, then all of the officials and the common people will come with their personal causes, seeking the favor of the ruler. If through such favor they gain their objectives, the ruler will be encroached upon daily, and if, despite his favor they do not gain their objectives, resentments will arise daily."[61] Under such conditions the ruler would be in grave peril. To carry this further, one notes that twisting the law to serve personal ends is, in the majority of cases, done by those officials of high station who are close to the ruler. However, "For commands to be carried out, it is necessary first that they prevail over those close to the ruler and only then will they be carried out. For when interdicts are not binding on the near and the noble, and penalties do not apply to attendants and favorites, when interdicts and laws bring no punishments for serious violations [at hand] but work harm on those far away, and when rewards are not extended to the lowly, and yet to expect that commands will unfailingly be carried out, is to expect the impossible."[62] The enlightened ruler's governing, therefore, must regard the eradication of private interest as a necessary task. "Heaven does not deviate from its times for the sake of any being; the enlightened ruler and the sage also will not deviate from their laws for the sake of any being."[63] "Without considering whether related or remote, close or distant, of high rank or low, of attractive appearance or repellent, judge all by the standard measures, then when the ruler executes people, it will not arouse resentment, and when he rewards people they will not feel personally beholden to him."[64] Within the officialdom and among the people certainly there existed persons worthy of being loved. But the enlightened ruler has but one standard in the law, and there are none for whom he

[61] *Ch.* 45, "Jen fa."

[62] *Ch.* 15, "Chung ling." [The passage containing the words here translated as "the lowly," appears to be corrupt; translation tentative.]

[63] *Ch.* 38, "Pai hsin."

[64] *Ch.* 45, "Jen fa."

can have special concern, for he has another object of his love and concern. The ruler's high status is the result of the awe that the state inspires, and the awe of the state comes from his commands being obeyed. "Hence he would not impair his imperium [*ming* 命] even for valuable treasure, so it is said that commands are worth more than treasure. He would not imperil the altars of the earth and grain even for cherished family members, so it is said that the altars of the earth and grain are closer than kin. He would not deviate from his law even for a beloved person, so it is said that the law is more to be loved than persons. He would not discount [or, fritter away] the awe invested in him even for [persons enjoying] highest rank and emolument, so it is said that the royal awe is more important than noble rank and emolument."[65] If the ruler of men can but comprehend this principle, then "no single move he makes can be contrary to the law,"[66] and "Like a clod of earth, he never loses the Way."[67] "Govern men as one governs streams and freshets; nourish men as one nourishes the six domestic animals; employ men as one employs grass and plants." This is the extreme to which eliminating personal interest could be carried. And, we should also note: "All private interests arise only because the sovereign has nurtured them."[68] When the servitors or other people intrude their personal interests, in all cases it is because they have taken advantage of the ruler's personal interests, in the wake of which their own could be pursued. Thus the ultimate key to rule by law lies in the ruler's himself observing the law. Kuan Tzu was profoundly aware of this principle, and did not hesitate repeatedly to state it in unequivocal terms. For example, *ch.* 16, "Fa fa" says that the enlightened ruler "establishes laws in order to keep himself in order; erects norms so that he can keep himself upright." He says, again, "He does not alter his commands for the sake of the ruler's wishes, for the commands are more to be looked up to than the ruler himself." *Ch.* 45, "Jen fa," says: "Ruler and servitor, superior and inferior, noble and lowly, all obey the laws; this is called the Great Order."[69]

The third essential in carrying the laws into practice is the force to implement them. In other words, this means using rewards to stimulate their observance, and penalties to inhibit violations. *Ch.* 16, "Fa fa," says: "When laws exist but are not observed, it indicates that he who prepared the mandates [establishing them] lacked judgment. If he has, however, been judicious, yet they still are not observed, then rewards and penalties are too light. If they are heavy, yet the laws are not observed,

---

[65] *Ch.* 6, "Ch'i fa."

[66] *Ch.* 46, "Ming fa."

[67] *Chuang Tzu, ch.* 33, "T'ien hsia," discussing P'eng Meng, T'ien P'ien, and Shen Tao.

[68] *Ch.* 52, "Ch'i ch'en ch'i chu."

[69] *Ch.* 52, "Ch'i ch'en ch'i chu" also says: "The law is that which the ruler and the ministers jointly establish."

then it is because there is no [confidence in the] certainty of rewards and penalties." *Ch.* 6, "Ch'i fa," also says: "When correct pronouncements cannot be established [as law or policy]; when incorrect pronouncements cannot be expunged; when those having accomplishments cannot be rewarded, and those guilty of crimes cannot be punished;—for these things to be so, and an orderly governing of the people yet to exist, is something that has never happened." That implementing law should depend on rewards and penalties, and that rewards and penalties can function as the force to implement rule by law, is because within human nature exists the inborn capacity for liking and disliking. "The nature of all men is such that, seeing advantage, there are none who will not seize it, and seeing harm, there are none who will not avoid it."[70] If the ruler carefully judges where advantage and harm lie in devising his rewards and penalties, then the people will conform to his will in those things which they seize and those which they avoid. However, rewards and penalties must be heavy, and they must be certain, in order to be efficacious. "If rewards are niggardly the people will see no advantage in them, and if interdictions are light, perverse people will not be intimidated."[71] Therefore it is best for rewards and penalties to be heavy. Display only administrative measures that are imperative, and establish penalties that are inexorable, then the people will know to what they must adhere, and know what they must avoid."[72] Hence, in rewards and penalties, it is their certainty which is important.

Once the rule by law is implemented, how effective will it be? *Ch.* 30, "Chün ch'en," Part One, says: "The wise ruler has at the top the Five Officials to shepherd the people, thus the masses of people will not dare to act in ways that go beyond the norm. Below them there are the Five Investigators [*wu heng* 五横] to survey the offices of government, thus those in office will not dare to depart from the laws in performing their duties. The court has its fixed systems and correct forms by which the royal status is elevated; coats and robes, decorations and mourning garments all have their regulations and models,—thus the ruler is established on his throne in complete conformity to the law. The ruler issues commands in accordance with the law; those in office receive their commissions and carry on their work; the common people comply with their

[70] *Ch.* 53, "Chin ts'ang."

[71] *Ch.* 47, "Cheng shih."

[72] *Ch.* 52, "Ch'i ch'en ch'i chu." *Ch.* 55, "Chiu shou," says: "In using rewards, it is their reliability which is important, and in using punishments it is their inexorability which is important." *Ch.* 7, "Pan fa," says: "When the laws and institutions are correct and upright, a crime punishable by death is not to be remitted. The death penalty must be of unfailing certainty, so that the people will be intimidated by their fear of it." *Ch.* 16, "Fa fa," says: "In all cases the remission of guilt produces but small benefits and works great harm." All of the above passages offer further elucidations of this principle.

superior and their compliance becomes a custom. Firmly maintained for a long time, it [i.e., the custom of compliance] becomes normal and unvarying, so that those who violate the accustomed way and depart from the instructions are regarded as malefactors by the multitude, and thus the superior is left in unconcerned ease." *Ch.* 38, "Pai hsin," also says: "When the terms are correct [i.e., correctly matched to realities] and the laws complete, the Sage ruler has nothing to do." This then is "governing without taking action [*wu-wei*]," which is the ultimate result of governing by law.

Kuan Tzu's ideal of governing by law possesses many acceptable features, yet is not something that we should class together with European thought on the rule of law. The real significance of European legal thought lies in its looking upon the law as the highest authority within the political organization. Although the ruler is elevated, he is merely the highest public servant in the maintenance of the law, and no more. Therefore the authority of the law is above the authority of the monarch, and the monarch is subject to the restrictions of the law. These theories began to emerge in the Middle Ages.[73] Thereafter the aristocracy and common people in England and France and other countries repeatedly had recourse to law in resisting the power of the monarch.[74] In modern democratic states, constitutional thought has further developed it as a bulwark against despotic tendencies in government.[75] Among very recent scholars one may encounter views granting law extremely high importance, even going so far as to feel that the formation of the state must be subsequent to the formulation of its laws.[76] All these conceptions of law

---

[73] Such as Hincmar of Rheims, *De Regis Persona*, vi; or Sedulius Scotus, *De Rectoribus Christianis*, viii; both are ninth-century men. Refer to R. W. Carlyle and A. J. Carlyle, *A History of Medieval Political Theory in the West*, Vol. iii.

[74] England's *Magna Carta* of 1215 was ratified by King John under pressure from the barons. Subsequently, in a series of incidents and difficulties, the authority of the law in England grew ever more firmly established, while the royal power was continuously limited, and in the end England became the forerunner among modern democracies. George B. Adams, *The Origin of the English Constitution* [1912], and William Stubbs, *The Constitutional History of England* [1874].

[75] The concept of a written constitution in the American Revolution is a concrete expression of legalist thought; Thomas Paine's saying that constitutions are produced before governments, and governments come into being through the agency of constitutions, as he developed that concept throughout *The Rights of Man*, Part Two, (1792), especially Chapters One and Two, is very expressive of this spirit. The French Revolution was influenced by the American, and witnessed several times the demand for a constitution. Refer to P'u Hsüeh-feng, *Hsi-yang chin-tai cheng-chih ssu-ch'ao*, i.e., "Currents in modern Western political thought," vol. ii, Chapter Five.

[76] Such as Leon Duguit, Hugo Krabbe, and others. The latter's *Modern Ideas of the State* [1915] exists in the translation of Wang Chien under the title: *Chin-tai kuo-chia kuan-nien.*

as the basic element of the state, regardless of all specific differences in the content of laws, are at the polar extreme from all of China's pre-Ch'in thought concerning "government by laws," which regarded the monarch as the basic element of the state and the law as a mere instrument.[77] Therefore, strictly speaking, the *Kuan Tzu's* "governing by law" is but one further variety of the "government of men" kind of thought, not in this respect fundamentally different from that of Confucius, Mo Tzu, Mencius, and Hsün Tzu, all of whom regarded the monarch as the highest wielder of political authority. The point at which these Chinese thinkers do differ among themselves is that the Confucians and Mohists held as their goal a more attractive and satisfying life for all the people, while Kuan Tzu sought the elevation of the ruler; Mencius and Hsün Tzu accepted benevolence and righteousness, rites and music, as techniques of governing, whereas Kuan Tzu would rely on the laws. If we consider methods of governing only, and acknowledge the fact that the *Kuan Tzu* represents the school of thought that seeks to govern by law, as an aid to our distinguishing it from the Confucians' rule by virtue and rule by the rites, this would not be unacceptable. But the methods that it proposes are vastly different from those of European legalist thought, which places the authority of the law above the authority of the monarch.

However, we must not disparage Kuan Tzu for this. European thought —venerating the law—was long in gestation, very gradual in its development, and the beneficiary of many contributing factors from the historical environment. Democratic political forms had already existed in Western antiquity, and in the Middle Ages the limitation of monarchical powers already came to be acknowledged in fact and in deed.[78] Regarding the people as the basic element of the state and using the law to resist the overriding powers of the state—these two things complemented each other, and the rule-of-law concept consequently came to be established in thought.[79]

[77] The pre-Ch'in monarchic concept among Legalist thinkers somewhat resembles that of legalistic thinkers of the Roman Empire. For example, Ulpian (170–228) declared that the monarch was not subject to legal restrictions (*princeps legibus solutus est*).

[78] The matter of limitations on the powers of the king appeared among the Germanic people. The legal restrictions to which their kings were subject were three: (1) customary law; (2) Roman law; (3) laws ratified with the agreement of officials and people. See R. W. and A. J. Carlyle, *op.cit.*, vol. I, p. 235.

[79] From the view of historical fact, the rule of law and democracy have existed in an inseparable relationship. The Rule of Law cannot be established without democracy, and democracy cannot be assured without the Rule of Law. Whether the laws in an authoritarian government are effective or not, hinges on the wishes of the sovereign. Although the *Kuan Tzu* says many times that commands are to be venerated more than the ruler, it offers no method for guaranteeing that the ruler would not violate the laws. Democracy without law inevitably must evolve into what the ancient Greeks knew as "mob rule," and its evils are probably no less than those of despotism. Thus all states in which there is

The political background of China in the pre-Ch'in period, however, was vastly different. To speak of the major trends: in each of the states there existed in the beginning of the period a division of powers between ruler and aristocracy. Subsequently the aristocracy encroached upon the rulers and brought the states to disorder. By the end, powerful ministers had usurped the powers of state, the aristocracy had declined and disappeared, and the old monarchical system was superseded. At the time of the aristocracy's ascendancy [in the Spring and Autumn era], it was found necessary to revere the ruler [as Confucius and then Hsün Tzu did]; after the fall of the aristocracy [in the Warring States era], the elevation of the ruler was inevitable [a trend that Mencius sought to attenuate by his doctrines of the "importance of the people" and of "hereditary ministers"]. The political methods stressing full reliance on laws also flourished just at this juncture. "In modern constitutional nations, what is spoken of as the Rule of Law always means to limit the powers of the monarch, yet when Kuan Tzu spoke of governing by law his purpose was always to seek the enlargement of the monarch's powers."[80] Nor is this to be wondered at.

SECTION FOUR
Regulating Customs

KUAN TZU regarded the elevation of the ruler as the purpose in establishing a government. Therefore in discussing how to govern the people, he seeks to achieve, negatively, that they will not be disorderly, and

---

to be found Rule of Law must be democracies, and authoritarian governments have no choice but to approve "government of men."

[80] Liang Ch'i-ch'ao, *Kuan Tzu chuan*, i.e., "Biography of Kuan Tzu" p. 20. Liang also says: "In Kuan Tzu's time the powers of the ruler were not yet positively and clearly established" (page 5). That his own background was humble, and that he wanted to give full play to the laws, and elevate the ruler thereby, so as to hold down the aristocracy, also is within the realm of possibility. If this argument is correct, Kuan Tzu then employed legal curtailments to restrict the aristocracy in the State of Ch'i, while Confucius used ritual curtailments to restrict the aristocracy in the State of Lu, the two men's purposes being more or less the same although their techniques differed. Even though the *Kuan Tzu* was not written by Kuan Chung, in view of this argument its content here again displays the response to conditions prevalent in the historical environment of the Spring and Autumn Era. Its author[s] may have lived later than Confucius, but that they must have been earlier than Lord Shang and Han Fei Tzu would seem to be beyond question. For Lord Shang and Han Fei Tzu were no longer concerned about the aristocracy's encroachments against the ruler (they were concerned about powerful ministers and favorites of the ruler usurping his powers and reducing the state to chaos), while the *Kuan Tzu*, throughout the book, acknowledges the existence of the powers of the aristocracy; nor is this merely that his legalistic thinking is less thoroughgoing and complete than that of the two Legalist philosophers. The following portions of this chapter have more to say about this.

positively that they can be utilized. His principal method is "governing by law." Therefore he wanted to establish regularly functioning institutions, and to exhibit invariably certain rewards and punishments, so that all of the people of the whole country would be induced to obey any command without hesitation, and to display uniformity in all their behavior. In the preceding section we have already discussed in general outline his methods for accomplishing this. In this section and the following two sections we shall proceed to discuss the foundations on which [he felt] government should be erected. *Ch.* 15, "Chung ling," says: "At the court there is a well-regulated bureaucracy [*ching ch'en* 經臣], throughout the state there are well-regulated customs [*ching su* 經俗], and among the people there is well-regulated livelihood [*ching ch'an* 經產]." These three constituted the principal conditions for achieving the complete government by laws.

"What is referred to as the state's regulated customs? In what [the people] like or dislike they will not contradict the ruler's interests; in what they prize or scorn they will not contradict his commands. No one shall do anything that conflicts with the ruler above; no one shall be allowed to give expression to partisan views below. There shall be no lavish consumption, and no exceeding of rank in dress. There shall be circumspect conduct within the village community, and nothing that contravenes the present government's undertakings. This constitutes the state's regulated customs."[81]

Governing by laws anticipated that officials and people all would peacefully accept their ordained lives and obey commands. Although rigorously maintained and clearly defined rewards and punishments could bring this to pass, it could do so only with time and habituation, as the expected behavior became second nature to people. Only then would the effects of governing by law become pervasive and unshakeable. What Kuan Tzu speaks of as regulated customs in fact comprises the psychological basis for governing by law, while nurturing well-regulated customs into full growth depended on appropriate educational policies. Kuan Tzu acknowledged that mankind's political organization demanded morality to sustain it. The four elements of political morality indispensable to the establishment of the state, Kuan Tzu labelled the "four cords" [*ssu wei*, 四維]. Of these four cords: "The first is ritual propriety [*li*]; the second is righteousness [*yi*]; the third is integrity [*lien*]; and the fourth is the sense of shame [*ch'ih*]. With propriety, the social boundaries are not infringed; with righteousness there is no selfaggrandizement; with integrity there is no concealed wrong-doing; and with a sense of shame there is no recourse to deviousness."[82]

---

[81] *Ch.* 15, "Chung ling."
[82] *Ch.* 1, "Mu min."

The *Kuan Tzu* speaks of propriety and righteousness in particular detail, almost to the point of outdoing Hsün Tzu [to whose thought they are central], and the import is in many respects close to Hsün Tzu's thought. *Ch*. 36, "Hsin shu," Part I, says: "Going up to and coming down from [a shrine or hall], bowing and deferring, the rankings of nobler and humbler status, the distinctions of the nearer and more distant relationships,—these are called the rites." This is the narrow sense of *li*. *Ch*. 10, "Wu fu," says: "Superior and inferior status embody righteousness; noble and humble ranks maintain the distinctions, senior and junior convey the principles of precedence, while poverty and wealth reflect standards. These eight things comprise the 'warp' of ritual propriety." This is *li* in the broader sense. Propriety and righteousness differ as to specific content, but they reinforce each other functionally. [The same chapter also says:] "Righteousness has its seven forms [*t'i*, 體 or "embodiments"]. What are these seven forms? There is that of filial and fraternal submission and of affection and kindness, by which the family is sustained. There is that of respect and reverence, loyalty and good faith, by which service is rendered to the ruler. There is that of moderation and uprightness, and adherence to appropriate standards, by which conduct is kept within the bounds of propriety and restraint. There is that of uniform observance of the restraints and taboos, by which penalties and punishments are avoided. There is that of prudent frugality and economy of expenditures, by which provision is made against famine. There is that of generous sincerity and steadfast purity, by which disorder and trouble are prevented. There is that of harmonious cooperation and friendly association, by which defenses are maintained against banditry and attack."[83] When all the officers and common people throughout all the

---

[83] *Ch*. 31, "Hsin shu," Part one, says: "The rites follow from man's nature, and relate to the principle of righteousness [or justice; the same chapter defines "*yi*," righteousness" as "each getting what is inherently appropriate"]; these restraints receive elegant form [to emerge as the ritual proprieties]. Thus the rites are said to embody principles. These principles are the clearly defined social positions and attendant responsibilities, exemplifying the meaning of righteousness. Thus it is that the rites emerge from righteousness, and their principles follow from what is inherently appropriate." And, further: "Ruler and servitor, father and son, the stuff of human existence,—this is called righteousness." *Ch*. 4, "Li cheng," says: "Stipulate [men's] dress according to noble rank, control their expenditures according to their official emolument; set limits on food and drink, regulate standards for items of clothing; there should be regulations for palaces and dwellings; there should be fixed numbers of domestic animals and servants; and there should be prohibitions governing the use of boats, carriages, and ceremonial vessels. While living, the distinctions apply to men's carriages and coronets, costumes and class-rankings, as to their incomes, dwellings and lands, and in death the regulations govern their coffins and shrouds, graves, and tombs. Though a person may possess worthy qualities and personal excellence, if he does not possess the rank he dare not wear that costume; though he be of wealthy family and have vast means, if he does not have the official emolument he dare not

ranks of society strictly observed these teachings on propriety and right-eousness, the government's awe-inspiring powers needed not be brought into play to achieve upright and orderly behaviour and general good government.

Extending the four cords [of public morality] depended on education. Thus in *ch*. 3, "Ch'üan-hsiu," it says: "The shepherd of the people shall see to it that none of the men [*shih* 士] be guilty of improper conduct and none of the women of lascivious acts. For the men to be free of improper conduct is a matter of education [*chiao* 教]; for the women to be free of lascivious acts is a matter of admonition [*hsün* 訓]. When through educa-tion and admonition, people's customs have been perfected, punishments and penalties can be diminished." However, such perfecting of customs through education and admonition cannot be expected to show results in a matter of months. It must await the gradual nurture and growth of habits and practices.[84] Before such transformation of customs is complete, government must at all times be prepared to supervise and monitor, encourage and intimidate, lending support to the effort of teaching and admonishing. Hence the *Kuan Tzu* demands that local chiefs and the Great Officers in the Five Regions of administration assume responsibility for reporting good behavior and citing faults, causing both the talented and worthy to be promoted into service, and the bad being punished. After customs have been perfected, however, the people's ways and habits should maintain themselves in rectitude. "Immoral men will lose their status, and immoral women will lose their homes. Men who three times divorce their wives will be driven out of the country, while women who [are cast out] and marry three times will be sentenced to the grain mills. This will make all the people struggle to be good persons."[85]

Kuan Tzu also felt that the social system itself served educational purposes; hence he directed much attention to it. He wanted to make use of two existing organizational contexts, the family and the neighborhood. "Ruler and servitor, father and son, the stuff of human existence—this is called righteousness," while ". . . filial and fraternal submission,

---

so use his money." In all of these points, the *Kuan Tzu* is close to Hsün Tzu's ideas. In the *Analects*, Book Three, "Pa yi," Confucius comments on Kuan Tzu as "a man of very narrow capacities." [Waley, *Analects*, p. 99; the passage goes on to criticize Kuan Tzu's failure to observe the rites punctiliously.] Because of this his knowledge of the rites has been doubted. Yet Kuan Tzu held the view that the State of Ch'i could be governed by the rites, and though the extant work, the *Kuan Tzu*, is not from his hand, it is in fact heir to these same concepts [as the foregoing detailed descriptions of the ritually ordered society demonstrate].

[84] *Ch*. 6, "Chi fa," says: "Inculcation, compliance, submission, persistence, practice, habituation,—these are called transforming."

[85] *Ch*. 20, "Hsiao k'uang." [Labor at husking grains was a standard punishment for immorality in women.]

affection and kindness, by which the family is sustained . . ." is defined as one of the forms comprising righteousness. Therefore [Kuan Tzu is quoted advising Duke Huan]: "Let the Duke put the ducal clan in order, and let each household keep its own clan in order; have their members join in their activities, and assist each other financially; and in that way the people will all treat each other kindly."[86] Once the doctrines of filial and fraternal submission were established, then the people's leaders should also "display respect at their ancestral shrines, and have reverence for the patriarchal heritage." For, ". . . if they do not respect their ancestral shrine, the people will emulate their superiors [in disrespect]; if they do not reverence the patriarchal heritage, the people also will be lacking in filial and fraternal submission."[87] In those circumstances, the people's transformation into the ways of propriety and righteousness would encounter hindrances and become difficult to accomplish.

In discussing the neighborhood organization, too, Kuan Tzu's ideas are particularly full and detailed. All of the important administrative tasks, such as public safety, social morality, rewarding merit and punishing crime, levying taxes and service obligations, and the like, were to be entrusted to the village organizations of the Tens and the Fives [variously explained as groupings of households].[88] Furthermore, the categories of people were all to reside apart, separated according to their occupations, and not permitted to live mixed together. *Ch.* 20, "Hsiao k'uang," explains his intent: "Officers [i.e., *shih*, in earlier times "knights," gradually becoming scholar-officials, and in imperial history usually translatable as "scholars"], farmers, craftsmen, and merchants; these four categories of people, are the state's "bedrock people." [Literally *"shih-min,"* 石民, which a commentary explains: "As the base-stone is to the columns, so are these four categories of people to the structure of the state."] They cannot be permitted to live together in one place, for if mixed together in one place they will be noisily quarrelsome, and their work will be disordered. So it is that the Sage Kings of antiquity in locating the officers, provided that they dwell amidst peace and quiet, and in locating farmers, provided that they be amidst their fields and wilds, and in locating craftsmen, provided that they be adjacent to government and court, and in locating merchants, provided that they be in the town market squares." In this way, then: "While still young they became accustomed to that,

[86] *Ch.* 20, "Hsiao k'uang."

[87] *Ch.* 1, "Mu min." *Ch.* 24, "Wen," also says: "One must not allow any disorder in maintaining the ancestral shrine, so that the people will have that guiding influence to which to relate." [The translation paraphrases a double meaning of the word *"tsung"*; i.e., both "ancestral" and "that which people turn to as a guiding principle."]

[88] *Ch.* 4, "Li cheng," *ch.* 5, "Ch'eng ma," *ch.* 20, "Hsiao k'uang," and *ch.* 57, "Tu ti," in their discussions of the systems of local responsibility, are quite inconsistent in detail, thereby offering convincing evidence that the *Kuan Tzu* does not come from one hand.

and their minds were content in that; they did not see strange things to which their minds would turn. Thereby the teachings could be imparted by fathers and elder brothers without severe measures, while the skills could be gained by sons and younger brothers without toilsome exertion. Because of this, the sons of officers always became officers . . . the sons of farmers always became farmers . . . the sons of craftsmen always became craftsmen . . . the sons of merchants always became merchants."[89] The four categories of people thus having fixed places of residence and their perpetual vocations, all people could then devote themselves entirely to fulfilling their duties and making the most of their allotment. "Thereby it will be so, that those who are not honest merchants will not be able to gain their livelihood as merchants, and those who are not honest craftsmen will not be able to gain their livelihood as craftsmen, and those who are not honest farmers will not be able to gain their livelihood as farmers, and those who are not reliable scholars will not be able to stand at court."[90] That kind who "in their persons lacked vocations, and in their families lacked property and a regular means of livelihood"[91] were to be banned by law.

Confucius said: "If the people be led by governmental measures, and uniformity sought to be given them by punishments, they will try to avoid punishments, but have no sense of shame. If they be led by virtue, and uniformity sought to be given them by the rules of propriety, they will have the sense of shame, and moreover will become good."[92] Kuan Tzu regarded the precise methods of "achieving regulated customs" as the very foundation upon which the government of laws rested. His view on this is quite close to that of Confucius. However, if we make an attempt to probe a little more deeply, we shall discover that on this matter too the two thinkers are in fundamental disagreement at some points. The Confucians, in utilizing teaching in their governing, had as their objective the comprehensive betterment of the world, to make it possible that every person have opportunity to "become a whole person." In other words, the Confucians looked upon the individual's ethical development as the highest ideal of government. Thus, even though their methods of governing included rites and righteousness as well as penalties and laws, rites and righteousness were principal. The objective of Kuan Tzu's education, however, was not to complete the individual's ethical development;

---

[89] The same chapter also says: "To manage the state divide it into twenty-one *hsiang* [units of two thousand households each], of which six shall be for commerce and crafts, and fifteen for agriculture." The *Kuo yü*, *ch*. 6, "Ch'i yü," varies somewhat in its wording of this description [of the ideal system Kuan Tzu reputedly set forth for Duke Huan].

[90] *Ch*. 5, "Ch'eng ma."

[91] *Ch*. 14, "Fa chin." [The interpretation of this passage, here and in note 93 is somewhat tentative; see the extensive commentaries.]

[92] *Analects*, Book Two, "Wei cheng" [II/3; slightly modified from Legge, p. 146].

rather, it was to ensure the people's obedient submission in serving ruler and state. Therefore he says in *ch.* 4, "Li cheng": "Appoint the time and they come, charge them with tasks and they go; the common people should give up their own interests and take the mind of their ruler as their own mind,—that is what teaching should accomplish. [The ruler's command] starts out imperceptibly [as it takes form in his mind] but ends up having outrivalled all: one man commands and all men obey,—that is what admonition should accomplish. Before any command is issued, the action is underway; before persons must be sent, they will already have left [to do what is required]; the superior issues no exhortations, yet the people on their own exert their energies to the limit,—that is what the customs are expected to accomplish." And *ch.* 14, "Fa chin," says: "Of old, the sages in governing did not value men for the breadth of their learning; they desired rather that people obey commands in harmonious uniformity." Since the desire was for harmonious uniformity in obeying commands, all violations of customary behavior, and all individualistic, variant conduct would have had to be prohibited.[93]

Persons whose conduct varied from custom as regulated by the state were "people who could not be shepherded," and "people who cannot be shepherded are beyond the standard [literally, the marking line]; those beyond the standard are to be punished."[94] Confucius said: "The 'honest villager' [representing conventional morality] spoils true virtue," and, "If I cannot get men who steer a middle course to associate with, I would far rather have the zealous and the scrupulous. For the zealous at any rate assert themselves; and the scrupulous have this at least to be said for them, that there are things they leave undone." And further: "[A great minister is one who will only] serve his prince while he can do so without infringement of the Way, and as soon as that is impossible, resigns." And also: "When the Way prevails in the land, be bold in speech and bold in action."[95] These show that his teachings clearly were far removed from

---

[93] Within the chapter called "Fa chin" [*ch.* 14, "Legal Interdicts"] there are some twenty items listed as "prohibited by the Sage Kings." Among these items, many are of a kind that particularly limit the individual's personal development, such as: "being personally unwilling to enter the ruler's service"; "differing from the age in conduct, disagreeing with the ruler to achieve notoriety, continually opposing the ruler's laws and governing to assemble a faction within the state"; "in their persons lacking vocations, and in their families lacking poverty and a regular means of livelihood, placing themselves between the overlords and the underlings and expressing opinions in order to become known" [see note 91]; "subverting customs and varying the ritual proprieties, loudly proclaiming their views and getting people to emulate their ways, refuting [the ruler's] actions and arrogantly undertaking their own."

[94] *Ch.* 16, "Fa fa" [cf. Rickett, *Kuan-tzu*, p. 93].

[95] *Analects*, "Yang Huo," Book 17, and "Tzu-lu," Book 13. "Hsien chin," Book xi, and "Hsien wen," Book xiv. [xvii/13, xiii/21, xi/23, xiv/4, following Waley, *Analects*, pp. 213, 177, with modifications based on Legge, pp. 158 and 180.]

Kuan Tzu's. As for Confucius' actions, such as: avidly acquiring his extensive learning and vast knowledge; or assembling his followers to discuss the Way, or ridiculing the men serving in government with: "Ugh! They are a set of peck-measures [not worth taking into account]"; his making "obeisance below the dais," not hesitating to oppose the common practice in so doing;[96]—if he were to be measured against the standard of the "regulated customs," he undoubtedly would have been castigated as one of those "who cannot be shepherded." Seen from this point of view, it becomes very obvious that *Kuan Tzu* was no "Confucian" [*ju*]. Confucius looked upon teaching as governing. Kuan Tzu utilized teaching to implement the laws.[97] The two, in their methods, also are diametrically opposed here.

Furthermore, Kuan Tzu's concept of governing by law also differs from that of Lord Shang and Han Fei Tzu. Lord Shang and Han Fei Tzu advocated total reliance on law, and abandonment of all efforts to transform the people through the teachings of benevolence and virtue, the rites and righteousness. Kuan Tzu, on the other hand, still thought it desirable to utilize the teachings of propriety as a means of achieving the rule of law. This is one of their points of difference. Lord Shang and Han Fei Tzu inclined toward reliance on the state's laws and the ruler's awe and majesty as the only forces that could control the people, whereas Kuan Tzu still granted importance to the network of relationships deriving from family and from human relations. This constitutes a second point of difference. From these we can infer that the background of Kuan Tzu's thought ante-dated the Six States [i.e., the Warring States] Period, and corresponded to a time before feudal influences had completely vanished. The lingering traces of feudal ideas in the book are numerous.[98] For example, the system of the four categories of people with their fixed places of residence and perpetuating vocations is not one that a man of the Six States [i.e., Warring States] Period would have been able to advocate. The *Yi-chou-shu* [which purports to be a chronicle dating from the Spring and Autumn Era] says: "The Knights and Great Officers are not to mix together with the craftsmen and merchants. . . . If craftsmen do not dwell together, they will be insufficient to provide for the official clans; if their residence quarter is not separate [from that of others], they will not be able to provide their benefits.[99] In the *Tso Chuan* it says: [Of the

---

[96] *Analects*, "Tzu-lu," Book xiii, and "Tzu-han," Book ix. [xiii/20 and ix/3/2, following Waley, pp. 176 and 138.]

[97] The *Kuan Tzu*, ch. 45, "Jen fa," says: "Those things called benevolence, righteousness, rites and music [i.e., the institutions valued by the Confucians] all are products of the laws."

[98] See Section Two of this Chapter, and footnote 7 in Section One.

[99] Chu Yu-tseng [mid-nineteenth century] in his *Yi-chou-shu chi-hsün chiao-shih* (*Hsü*

ruler of Chin] ". . . His officers vigorously obey their instructions, his common people attend diligently to their husbandry; his merchants, mechanics, and inferior employees know nothing of changing their hereditary employments."[100] Yen Tzu also said [explaining to the Duke of Ch'i how a state can be governed so as to become stable]: "The people must not move about; the farmers must not change their work, craftsmen and merchants must not shift their professions, and the officers must not exceed their proper roles."[101] All of these are close to the general sense of the *Kuan Tzu* [on the regulation of society]. Thus, even though the *Kuan Tzu* was compiled and assembled by later persons, its content is by no means all groundless fabrication. Here we find one further type of evidence to support that view.

Section Five
Regulated Livelihood

One further foundation on which the government of laws is erected is "among the people there is a regulated livelihood." "What is called the people's regulated livelihood? In animal husbandry and horticulture special care must be paid to the seasonal requirements. In growing the cereal grains effort must be devoted to plowing, cultivating, and weeding. To pursue the superficial activities [other than basic production] must be forbidden. That constitutes the people's regulated livelihood."[102]

Mencius said that "if the people do not have a constant livelihood they cannot have constant minds" [*Mencius*, 1/i/7/20]. In his concern for regulating the productive aspects of the economy Kuan Tzu had a somewhat similar intent. Thus he said: "When the granaries and storage bins are full, then the people will be aware of propriety and restraint; when their clothing and food are adequate, then they will understand honor and shame." And also, "When the people do not have enough, the commands will not be respected. When the people suffer hardship and

---

ch'ing ching-chieh, ch. 151), under "Ch'eng-tien chieh," *ch.* 12. See also in "Tso Lo chieh," *ch.* 48, under the heading "Nung chü t'u." Although scholars have expressed doubts about the *Yi-chou-shu*, in his preface to his commentary on it Chu concludes: "An essential point is that [while it may be of doubtful attribution], neither is it something that a person of [as late as] Warring States times, or of the Ch'in-Han period, could have forged." This would seem to be correct.

100 "Ninth Year of Duke Hsiang" [i.e., B.C. 563; modified slightly from Legge, *Ch'un Ts'ew*, p. 440].

101 *Tso Chuan*, "Twenty-Sixth Year of Duke Chao" [524 B.C.; Legge, *Ch'un Ts'ew*, p. 718, has a somewhat differently worded translation]. The wording of the corresponding passage in the *Yen Tzu ch'un-ch'iu*, "Wai p'ien," *ch.* 7, section 15, is slightly different.

102 *Ch.* 15, "Chung ling,"; discussions of economic, fiscal, and related matters occupy about one-fourth of the entire book, the *Kuan Tzu*.

calamity, the commands cannot be implemented."[103] Kuan Tzu clearly understood that ensuring the people's livelihood constitutes one of the essential elements of government. Plenty or deficiency can be the issue determining whether government will be stable or shaky. There are two major reasons for this: One is the psychological reason; the other is the material reason. "For the people must obtain those things which they want, and after that they will be heedful of their superiors; after they have become heedful of their superiors governing can be well carried out."[104] Moreover: "When the people are prosperous, they will be content with their rural communities and value highly their homes. Satisfied with their communities and valuing their homes will make them respect superiors and be fearful of committing crimes. When they are respectful toward superiors and fearful of committing crimes, they are easy to govern. When people are poor, they create uneasy conditions in the countryside and show scant concern for their homes. When the countryside is uneasy and people are not concerned about their homes, they will dare to disrespect superiors and violate the interdicts. When they disrespect superiors and violate interdicts, they are difficult to govern. Thus it is that well-ordered states are always prosperous while disorderly states always are poor. Therefore those skilled in ruling will first enrich the people, and thereafter impose their governing on them."[105] This sets forth the psychological reason.

"Calculate the extent of the rural countryside in relation to the numbers of the people. When weed-grown fields are numerous and cleared fields are few, though there be no floods or drouths, it is the rural countryside of a famine-plagued state. In such circumstances, where people are few, then they will not be sufficient to defend the region. In such circumstances, where the people are many, then the state will be poor and the people famine-plagued, for in such circumstances, when flood or drouth occurs, the people will scatter and cannot be reassembled. In the other circumstances, where the people are too few to defend the region, the cities will not be secure; where the people are hungry they cannot be made to fight and when the people have scattered and cannot be reassembled, the state will become a wasteland."[106] This describes the material reason [for governments being stable or not].

[103] See, respectively, *ch.* 1, "Mu min," and *ch.* 7, "Pan fa."
[104] *Ch.* 10, "Wu fu."
[105] *Ch.* 48, "Chih kuo." [Cf. Maverick, *Kuan-tzu*, p. 93.] Also, in *ch.* 4, "Li cheng," it says: "If the people do not cherish their property, the state is in peril." *Ch.* 35, "Ch'ih mi," says: "Provide adequately for their wants, supply their desires, and then [the people] can be made use. Should they now be made to wear skins for clothing and fashion hats of horn, eat the wild grasses and drink the raw waters, who could employ them?" A commentary explains: "This sentence says that if the people lack adequate clothing and food the ruler will get no use from them."

Kuan Tzu establishes methods for regulating the productive factors, among which the policy of emphasizing agriculture is central, and the supporting methods are those of limiting consumption, keeping goods in circulation, and providing relief in difficult times. His policy of emphasizing agriculture displays few differences from that of other thinkers. For example, *ch.* 1, "Mu min," says: "To accumulate in never-empty granaries, much effort must be devoted to producing the five cereal grains. To store away in inexhaustible warehouses, silk and hemp and the six domestic animals must be raised." *Ch.* 48, "Chih kuo," says: "When the people devote themselves to farming the fields will be cultivated; when fields are cultivated the grains will be plentiful; when grains are plentiful the state is rich." These express the view that agricultural production is the source of wealth.[107]

The principal devices for stimulating agriculture do not go beyond simply assuring farmers all convenience in pursuing their agricultural tasks, and encouraging them to engage in agriculture as the basic activity, and to refrain from pursuing the "superficial" activities [especially commerce]. Therefore, we find that the "Minister of Works" [*ssu-k'ung*] was to keep hydraulic works in repair; the "Field Supervisor" [*yu t'ien* 由田] was to supervise work on the land, and the "District Preceptor" [*hsiang shih* 鄉師] was to encourage diligence in the work.[108] Yet the profits from commerce and craftsmanship were greater than those from farming, and if the government did not intervene, the farmers would abandon that "basic" activity to pursue the "superficial." "Therefore the former kings provided that farmers, scholars, merchants, and craftsmen, the four categories of people, exchanged skills and traded the products of their work, so that the profits of their year-long labors did not allow any one [of the four categories] to gain unfair advantage over the others. Thereby the people's labors were combined and they all gained equitable benefits from it."[109]

Kuan Tzu's views on limiting consumption also set forth few novel

---

[106] *Ch.* 13, "Pa kuan." A commentary explains: " 'Wei' 猥 means 'the mass of the people.' Calculate how wide the rural [or open] countryside, *yeh* 野 is in relation to how many persons constitute its population."

[107] *Ch.* 13, "Pa kuan," says: "If the seasonal products are not forthcoming, though gold and gems be numerous, it is to be called a poor country." A commentary adds: "the seasonal products are grains and textiles and animal products."

[108] *Ch.* 4, "Li cheng." [Cf. the translation in Maverick, *Kuan-tzu*, p. 45.]

[109] *Ch.* 48, "Chih kuo." Note that the commentary would seem to be incorrect in saying that the phrase translated as "exchanged skills and traded the products of their work" should be interpreted as "this is to say that even the scholars also were skilled at farming, and even the farmers acquired knowledge of the scholars' professions." On the contrary, this should be taken to mean that they integrated their labors and exchanged their services, or what in modern times is called "the division of labor."

ideas. *Ch.* 13, "Pa kuan," says: "When the state is extravagant, it will be wasteful in consumption. Wasteful consumption impoverishes the people. When the people are impoverished, sly minds emerge. When sly minds emerge, devious artifice is undertaken." However, what this passage refers to as extravagance designates activities that are wastefully destructive of materials and goods without returning any benefits to the enterprise. When expenditures are necessary, Kuan Tzu would not be penurious. Thus he says: "To stint is to harm the enterprise; to be lavish harms [only] goods."[110] There is a section in *ch.* 10, "Wu fu," which sets forth a theory of "the six policies" [*hsing* 興] that includes more or less all the positive aspects of Kuan Tzu's policies on regulating production. It says: "What are the six policies? Clear lands for cultivation, give aid in building houses, improve horticulture, exhort officers and people, encourage diligence in farming, repair walls and houses,—this is called enriching the people's livelihood. Develop unused sources of wealth, transport stored accumulations, repair roads and paths, make customs stations and markets function more conveniently, extend care to the start-ings and stoppings [of goods in transit],—this is called circulating the people's wealth. Canalize the flooding streams, repair ponds and ditches, cut channels into backwashes, dredge out silted riverbeds, open up blocked waters, give care to crossings and bridges,—this is called bestowing benefits on the people. Lessen the imposts, lighten tax levies, relax punish-ments and penalties, grant amnesties for criminals, remit minor infrac-tions,[111]—this is called liberalizing government measures. Provide support for the aged, care for the young and orphaned, and give aid to the bereaved and widowed, investigate illnesses, and commemorate the victims of disasters,—this is called assisting people in distress. Clothe the cold, feed the starving, aid the impoverished, relieve victims of emer-gencies, and supply material needs where resources are exhausted,—this is called giving relief to the impoverished. . . . When these six [sets of measures] have been put into practice, then none of the people's desires will be beyond their attaining."

Yet we should note that Kuan Tzu's intent in perfecting the functioning of regulated production was to enrich the state, not to enrich the people. The people must enjoy plentiful food and clothing, but private individuals were not permitted to accumulate large amounts of goods and wealth. Were private individuals to accumulate material wealth, a disparity would come to exist between the poor and the rich, and when such a disparity widens it can produce crises. Thus the *ch.* 10, "Wu fu," says: "When wealth and poverty are not moderated by standards, the people

---

[110] *Ch.* 5, "Ch'eng ma."

[111] This point is inconsistent with the statements made in *ch.* 7, "Pan fa," *ch.* 16, "Fa fa" and elsewhere, saying that no amnesties or remissions of punishment should be granted.

will act without restraint." *Ch*. 35, "Ch'ih-mi," also says: "The extremely rich cannot be made to serve; the extremely poor are not subject to shame."[112] *Ch*. 73, "Kuo hsü" explains this: "Persons who are rich cannot be induced by the emolument of office to take service, and those who are poor cannot be intimidated by penalties. The failure of commands to be carried out, as well as the failure to bring order over the ten-thousands of people, all derive from the unevenness in wealth and poverty."

The methods that can be used to balance out wealth and poverty do not go beyond simply equalizing the profits from farming and land, and equalizing the profits from crafts and commerce. In the *Kuan Tzu* we find a theory about "One square *li* constitutes the fields of nine farmers," apparently advocating something in the nature of the well-field system of land holding. [See Chapter Three, Section Three.] Yet if land is so distributed and market prices are uneven, then among the farming population excessive disparities of wealth and poverty still could develop. Kuan Tzu therefore advocated nationalizing the major portion of the profits from crafts and commerce. His chief methods with which to accomplish this were: (1) The government should use its currency to manipulate market prices;[113] (2) [profits of] the mountains and seas [especially iron mining and salt] should be put under official control;[114] (3) the govern-

---

[112] *Ch*. 5, "Ch'eng ma."

[113] *Ch*. 73, "Kuo hsü," says: "There are bountiful and lean harvest years, hence so are there high and low grain prices. Seasonal demands [following Maverick, *Kuan-tzu*, p. 116 and note 6] may be slow or brisk; hence things may be cheap or expensive. If the ruler cannot govern these situations, that will permit the hoarding merchants to speculate in the market, take advantage of the people's shortages to earn profits of a hundred-fold. Though the land be evenly distributed, it is the strong who will be able to retain their holdings. Though material goods be evenly distributed, it is the clever who will be able to acquire more. . . . In such circumstances, though the ruler enjoin the people to engage in the basic work [i.e., farming], and goad them to their tilling, and though he mint coins continually and unceasingly, he will only be helping the people to be forced into the service of others [i.e., the rich speculators]; how then can he bring about orderly governing?"
The methods to redeem this situation are as follows: "When the people have a surplus of anything, they value it lightly; therefore the ruler levies imposts when things are cheap. When the people have deficiency of anything, they value it highly; therefore the ruler distributes what has grown expensive. Collect and accumulate when things are cheap; distribute into circulation when things are expensive. Thereby the ruler is sure to gain a ten-fold profit, and an increase in the supply of goods will be attained that will level prices." The chapter *ch*. 76, "Shan chih shu," says: "When money is high goods are low; when goods are high money is low. . . . The ruler should manipulate the values of grains and money and gold, and the empire can thereby be stabilized."

[114] *Ch*. 72, "Hai wang," says: "Duke Huan inquired of Kuan Tzu: 'I would like to impose a tax on buildings. Would that do?' Kuan Tzu replied: 'That would bring ruin to existing buildings.' 'I would like to impose a tax on trees.' Kuan Tzu said: 'That would be tantamount to cutting down the living trees.' 'I would like to put a tax on the six domestic animals.' Kuan Tzu answered: 'That would lead to killing off the living animals.' 'I

ment should supply basic needs of the agrarian sector.[115] By these means the greater profits would all revert to the state, the rich and powerful would be without that resource [of their economic power], and the government, by controlling the sources of wealth, would become able to supply its own needs.[116]

---

would like to impose a tax on people. How would that be?' Kuan Tzu replied: 'That would lead to concealing the truth.' Duke Huan asked: 'Well, then, how should I manage this state?' Kuan Tzu replied: 'The only feasible way is to place the mountains and the seas under official control.' Duke Huan asked: 'What is meant by putting the mountains and seas under official control?' Kuan Tzu replied: 'The ruler of a maritime state [such as the State of Ch'i, located on the Shantung Peninsula] should carefully levy a tax on salt.' " Further on the same chapter speaks of an "iron official" who determined the amount of tax on iron implements according to their weight. In *ch.* 81, "Ch'ing chung," Part Two, there is also reference to the profits gained from mountain iron [as mining was associated with mountainous regions]; it says: "Let the people [who produce iron] set its price high, and calculate the earnings from it, the people getting ten (presumably an error for "seven") parts of that and the ruler taking three." Other mines than those so supervised, moreover, were to be "carefully closed and their operation forbidden." ("Ti shu," *ch.* 77). Forests also were to be taxed on the basis of the size of the timbers cut from them. ("Shan kuo kuei," *ch.* 75).

[115] Kuan Tzu advocated releasing the poor from debt obligations to the rich and powerful by having the government supply farmers with capital and implements. Ch. 83, "Ch'ing chung," Part Four, tells that Pao Shu [a high official and friend of Kuan Chung] and others were commanded to go out into all parts of the state to make an investigation of debtor households and the total amount of indebtedness. Duke Huan then [called all the creditors into his presence and insisted upon] presenting "*chü-chih lan-ku*" [probably a type of ceremonial bell or drum] to them in repayment of the people's debts [at an exorbitant rate of exchange that forced losses upon the creditors] so that the indebted people "would no longer be under any contracted obligation" to them. [See translation of the anecdote in Maverick, *Kuan-tzu*, pp. 191–93.] Ch. 74, "Shan kuo kuei," says that "In mid-spring, . . . mid-summer . . . mid-autumn . . . mid-winter: . . . These are the times when the prices of goods fluctuate; these are the times when the people take advantage of each other to extend their properties by acquiring others.' . . . To all households without means . . . should be loaned, [at interest,] tools and implements [from the government], . . . and clothing from the government . . . so that labor supplied by the people will become of use to the ruler." The chapter *ch.* 73, "Kuo hsü," says: "Plows and harrows, tools and implements, seeds, food and provisions, all should be supplied by the ruler, so that the great merchants and hoarders will not be allowed to plunder our common people."

[116] Kuan Tzu did not advocate increasing taxes. The passage quoted above in Note 114, from *ch.* 72, "Hai wang," is sufficient to corroborate that. Ch. 73, "Kuo hsü," says: "Taxes on craftsmen and merchants are collected upon demand. Taxes on the farmers are requested after careful consideration. The ruler who would preside over all the others will do away with those taxes collected on demand, and abolish those carefully considered taxes, and the world will gladly follow his leadership." [A philological note is omitted; the sense of it is reflected in the translation.] This, however, does not mean that all taxes are entirely abolished. Ch. 74, "Shan kuo kuei," says: "Do away with taxes on field lands by levying taxes on [the products of] the mountains [e.g., mining]. Great households that bury their dead with heavy expenditures shall pay a heavy tax; petty households that

Among the eighty-six chapters of the *Kuan Tzu*, the passages devoted to discussions of managing the economy constitute approximately one-fourth of the book. These include many brilliant ideas, and qualify the work for being designated an important compendium of ancient economic thought.[117] Despite this, men such as Fu Hsüan [A.D. 217–278] have said that: "The various chapters on '*ch'ing-chung*' [i.e., on prices and money, chapters 68–86] are of particularly low quality and unrefined." Yeh Shih [1150–1223; see Chapter Fourteen, Section Five] said that the "especially erroneous and specious chapters of the work are above all those on '*ch'ing-chung*.'" And, Huang Chen [of the late Sung] doubted whether the man Kuan Tzu could have been so trivial-minded in his "multifarous methods" as the "*ch'ing-chung*" chapters would indicate.[118] These comments all reflect the suspicions induced by Confucians' subjective standards, and they do not merit our confidence.

When we investigate Kuan Tzu's historical backgrounds, we come to realize that the economic policies set forth in the book are not necessarily later persons' groundless concoctions. The *Shih Chi*, in its chapter 32 on the ruling house in the State of Ch'i [i.e., "Ch'i T'ai-kung shih-chia"], tells that: "Duke T'ai [the first Duke, enfieffed at the end of the twelfth century B.C.], on arriving at the state, and in devising its governing, followed its local customs, simplified the rites, opened up the activities of commerce and crafts, and facilitated the pursuit of profits from fish and salt. Thus many people were drawn to Ch'i."[119] From this it can be seen that initially the State of Ch'i had adopted *laissez-faire* policies favoring commerce. Coming to Kuan Tzu's time, in the aftermath almost four hundred years later, the faults that had resulted apparently were those of an excessive growth in craft industry and commerce, allowing private individuals to amass vast wealth.[120] Kuan Tzu, wishing to bring about

bury their dead meagerly shall pay a small tax. Great households that embellish their palaces and residences shall pay a heavy tax; small households that dwell in huts shall pay a small tax." (Quoted with emendations from Liang Ch'i-ch'ao's *Biography of Kuan Tzu*; i.e., *Kuan Tzu chuan*, p. 69.)

[117] Chapter Eleven, "Kuan Tzu's Economic Policies," in Liang Ch'i-ch'ao's *Biography of Kuan Tzu*, although occasionally displaying faults of forced interpretation, offers many valuable insights, and is worth consulting.

[118] See, respectively: Fu Hsüan's *Fu Tzu*, *ch*. 30; Yeh Shih's *Hsi-hsüeh chi-yen*; and Huang Chen's *Huang-shih Jih-ch'ao*; all of the passages are quoted from Chang Hsin-ch'eng's *Wei-shu t'ung-k'ao* [1939], vol. 2, pp. 763–65.

[119] The *Shih Chi*, *ch*. 129, "Huo-chih lieh-chuan" [has a similar statement].

[120] As for the actual situation, it is difficult now to say. However, the wealth of Lin-tzu [the capital city in Ch'i] was frequently referred to in antiquity. One example is found in the *Chan-kuo ts'e*, *ch*. 8, "Ch'i ts'e," 1, where Su Ch'in [the eminent strategist, died 317 B.C.], in trying to persuade King Hsüan of Ch'i to join the State of Chao in the Vertical Alliance [against Ch'in, reminds the King of the extent of Ch'i's wealth and strength, saying, in part]: "Lin-tzu is exceedingly rich and solid. Its people all play flutes and

Ch'i's hegemony over the other feudal princes, saw a necessity to forcibly curb two faults: on the one hand, he stressed agriculture and austerity in consumption; on the other, he suppressed the rich and powerful and put an end to their extensive landholding. By bringing profits [from various entrepeneurial activities] to the state and by assuring that the common people would not suffer distress and deprivation, he garnered the consequences for the state in the form of wealth and power.

All the families of great wealth, moreover, were families of the aristocracy. *Ch.* 83, "Ch'ing-chung," Part Four, says that in the eastern part of Ch'i "The creditor clans include the Ting, the Hui, the Kao, and the Kuo." The Kao-tzu and the Kuo-tzu [titles of high office, from which the surnames Kao and Kuo derived] were leading [hereditary] officials at that time; [Ting and Hui probably also were leading clans in the Ch'i aristocracy]. As the financial strength of these great clans was extended, the awe and power of the ruler was correspondingly diminished. Kuan Tzu was of humble birth; moreover he had himself once been a petty trader.[121] He must have had very full knowledge about the long and the short of conditions among the people. The ways of using money also would have been totally familiar to him. That he should completely alter the *lassez-faire* policies on which the state had been founded and institute instead centralized, interventionist policies is both natural under those circumstances, and quite believable. It is indeed difficult to understand what could provide grounds for calling the book trivial minded in its concern with multifarious methods, and on those grounds, doubting its authenticity.[122]

SECTION SIX
A Regulated Officialdom

THE state depended on its ruler to establish its institutions, and on its people to supply the means whereby it could become rich and strong. To aid the ruler by keeping the people well-ordered there were the officials

---

strum zithers, pluck guitars and strum lutes, go to cock fights and dog races, know all the gambling games and play kick-ball [a team sport used for military training]. In the streets of Lin-tzu, the hubs of carts' and carriages' bump against each other, while the shoulders of people rub together [so numerous are they]. The gowns [of the crowds] merge together like a curtain; when they raise their arms their sleeves appear like one vast drapery. When they all brush aside their perspiration it produces a rain shower. The families are harmonious and prosperous; they display the attitudes of self-confidence and success." Although this is not free of hyperbole, it nonetheless quite adequately conveys the sense of Lin-tzu's size and prosperity.

[121] *Shih Chi*, *ch.* 62, "Biography of Kuan Tzu and Yen Ying," where: "Kuan Tzu said, 'In the beginning when I was in difficult straits, Pao Shu and I were for a time peddlars.'"

[122] Although the book undoubtedly was not directly written by Kuan Tzu, we are merely making the point here that its content has a basis in fact.

of all the various ranks. Regulating these officials, therefore constituted, along with regulated customs and regulated livelihood, one of the indispensable conditions for the government by law.

"What is known as the court's regulated officials? They accept appointments according to clear knowledge of their own abilities—perpetrating no deception on the ruler; they apply the laws carefully and scrupulously to maintain order—showing no partiality or favoritism; they exercise all their skills—without thought of personal gain; they face difficulties and brave dangers—willing to die when necessary; the emolument they receive does not exceed their accomplishments and the positions they occupy do not outstrip their abilities—never receiving anything which they do not deserve; these are the court's regulated officials."[123]

To gain such regulated officials there must be correct methods for employing people. What Kuan Tzu advocated in this respect is covered in the one phrase: "Apply the laws in selecting men. . . . Should now the ruler dispense with the laws and promote those of ability on the basis of favorable reputations, then the officials will turn from the ruler above and form covert associations among themselves below. Should he advance persons into office on the basis of their factional identifications, then the people will devote all their attention to forming personal alliances, and not strive to merit employment. . . . Persons forming covert associations connive together to conceal the truth, abandon their ruler in supporting to the death their personal allies, in order to promote their own favorable reputations [within their cliques]. That is why those who have formed a mass of personal alliances have the biggest reputations. Outside and inside the court such factional groupings can include major evildoers, and yet keep the ruler screened from knowledge of many things. That is why loyal officials may die for crimes they have not committed and treacherous officials may advance for merit they have not achieved; their deaths are for falsely attributed crimes and their advancements for falsely claimed merit. As officials come to value highly their personal interests and take lightly their public responsibilities, for ten trips to a private associate's door not one is made to the ruler's court; for a hundred worries over their own family concerns not one thought is given to the state. Although their numbers may be many, the elevation of the ruler gains nothing from that. Although all the offices of government be filled, the state's interests are not tended to by that. This is what is known as the state's wanting for men."[124] In such straits, how can a regulated officialdom be obtained?

Selecting men to serve by applying the laws thus has consequences all so serious, yet the matter is not all that difficult to begin with. Stated concretely, it means merely these two principal measures:—to employ

[123] *Ch.* 15, "Chung ling."
[124] *Ch.* 46, "Ming fa."

people according to a clear-cut, fixed standard and through clear-cut, fixed procedures. The single sentence: "Rank and emolument shall not be conferred on any who does not deserve them,"[125] effectively sums up the standard Kuan Tzu established for this. The intention here is roughly the same as Hsün Tzu's in saying [that the ruler must be competent in] "judging good qualities and deputing the able and so bestowing office." However, Hsün Tzu insisted that in employing persons the only consideration should be to assess their personal qualities and abilities, without regard for their social status. The *Kuan Tzu* makes no explicit statements on this subject. But when we note how he erected a system under which the four categories of people [i.e.; officers, or scholar-officials; farmers; craftsmen; merchants] were to have their fixed places of abode in separation from each other, he would seem not to have subscribed to any doctrines favoring a levelling of the social classes. Moreover, his method of having the Kuo-tzu and the Kao-tzu [heads of the senior aristocratic clans; see above, final paragraph of Section Five] share the headship of certain districts with Duke Huan in governing the state, appears all the more clearly to reflect the heritage of the hereditary chief minister concept from the feudal age; this is distinctly at variance with Hsün Tzu's thought.

The *Kuan Tzu* speaks of a procedure for selecting officials through investigation and nomination in the districts and the villages; this too is something the like of which Hsün Tzu never spoke.[126] *Ch.* 4, "Li cheng," says: "Persons who are filial and fraternal, loyal and trustworthy, of worthy character and outstanding ability, whether they be in the senior branch of a clan or related through collateral branches and junior lines, or through household servitors or concubines, or servants or guests [those persons should be brought to the head of the clan, and from the head of the clan they] should report to the Heads of the Five- and Ten-household Groups, who shall report them to the leader of the Neighborhood [*yu tsung* 游宗]; the Leader of the Neighborhood shall report them to the Hamlet Chief [*li wei* 里尉]; the Hamlet Chief shall report them to the Prefect [*chou chang* 州長]; the Prefect shall render an account of them to

---

[125] *Ch.* 14, "Fa ching." *Ch.* 4, "Li cheng" also says: "The ruler carefully assesses three things: One is virtue not commensurate with status; the second is achievement not commensurate with emolument; the third is capacity not commensurate with official position. These three [kinds of deficiency] are the source of disorder. Therefore, when there exist virtuous and righteous persons in the state who have not yet made those qualities evident to the court, they cannot be granted elevated status; when their meritorious achievement to the state has not yet been manifested, they cannot be granted heavy emolument; when in the conduct of affairs they do not arouse the confidence of the people, they cannot be appointed to high office." It says further: "In all cases promote the worthy no higher than the level [of their worthiness]; assign the capable to no concurrent appointments."

[126] See, Chapter Three, footnote 109.

the Governor [*hsiang shih* 鄉師], who shall then have them put on record with the Preceptor of Officers [*shih shih* 士師]." This describes the system of nomination and recruitment in the districts and villages. *Ch.* 20, "Hsiao k'uang," says that during the First Lunar Month the governors of the provinces [*hsiang chang* 鄉長] with their five subordinate Great Officers were to present themselves at the ducal court to report, at which time the ruler would in person inquire of them about the virtuous and capable [potential] officers in their Districts. If they reported any, those would be granted audience by the Duke in person, and in order to bestow official appointments, "the chief of the officials meeting with them to write up their accomplishments and report [to the throne]." The ruler thereupon "had broad inquiries made throughout their home districts, to see whether their reported qualities stood up to investigation. He then summoned them into his presence and sat with them, carefully assessing their qualities, studying the facts of their achievements and successes. When found qualified for appointment, they were asked hypothetical questions about difficulties that the state might encounter. [Cf. parallel passage in the *Kuo yü*, *ch.* 6, "Ch'i yü," on the basis of which the translation has been made; the author's parenthetical note at this point is therefore omitted]. Afterward, investigations were made in their home districts to find out about their abilities, and whether they had committed any grave faults. Then they were entered into official service as assistants to the chief ministers. This was known by the name of the threefold selection." By such a system the ruler was to investigate persons for appointment.

To have a regulated officialdom, it was necessary to select for appointment according to the laws. After the selection, it was further necessary to employ them according to the laws. Kuan Tzu turned his special attention to the demarcation of authority and duties between ruler and servitor. For, "The producer of the laws is the ruler; the upholders of the laws are the servitors."[127] "That is why the ruler defines [laws] and the chief ministers observe them; the chief ministers define [matters] and the officials carry them out. . . . Assessing qualities, measuring abilities, understanding their virtues, and appointing [his servitors] is the Way of the sovereign. Focusing the mind, being wholeheartedly observant of responsibilities of office, and never minding the toil is the mission of the servitors. If the ruler should extend his actions down into the functions of his officials, then the functionaries would shirk their responsibilities; if the servitors participate in the ruler's decision-making above, then the lord of men would lose his majesty. . . . The man above clearly manifests his Way; the men below restrict themselves to their duties; above and below are divided in their differing responsibilities but united in one

---

[127] *Ch.* 45, "Jen fa."

corpus [of government]." In this way the ruler does not toil in person, while the servitors must exert all their strength, and all the business of the state is attended to.[128]

The *Kuan Tzu* also frequently discusses the structure of central and local governments. These passages are not always completely consistent, but there is no need to discuss that here. There are, however, two aspects of this issue that we should note. The first is the attention directed toward local government. *Ch.* 3, "Ch'üan hsiu," says: "The provinces and the court compete in governing," and "the court does not govern the population as a whole, for the governors severally govern the provinces." And further, it says: "If the provinces are not well-governed, can one expect the state to be?" Since Kuan Tzu attached the degree of importance to local government that these comments indicate, he therefore established a quite complex set of local official titles, and assigned heavy governing responsibilities to those offices. They show that the polity he was erecting was that of a monarchic authoritarianism, and not that of administrative centralization. Beyond that, although Kuan Tzu may have "desired to use his native state to make it the overlord of all within the realm,"[129] yet

---

[128] *Ch.* 30, "Chün ch'en," Part One. Further, *ch.* 31, "Chün ch'en," Part Two, says: "For the ruler may have major faults, and servitors may commit great crimes. . . . When the ruler has a fault and he does not correct it, that is called 'collapse,' and when servitors commit crimes for which they are not punished, that is called 'chaos.' " The ruler, as this indicates, holds authority but no responsibility for administration; therefore "faults" may be ascribed to him, but he does not commit "crimes."

[129] Liang Ch'i-ch'ao, *Biography of Kuan Tzu*, i.e., *Kuan Tzu chuan*, p. 5. We should note that Kuan Tzu, as chief minister to Duke Huan, did hold the Chou Son of Heaven in his power, and through him issued commands to all the other feudal lords [i.e., Kuan Tzu brought Duke Huan into the role of *pa*, or Hegemon], but seemingly with no intent to displace or supplant the Chou dynastic authority. When we observe how he prevailed upon Duke Huan, insisting that he must kneel to receive gifts of sacrificial wine and meat for use in conducting sacrifices to [the Chou founders] Kings Wen and Wu, along with gifts of ceremonial bow and arrows, and a carriage, which the Chou King Hsiang once sent to him (*Shih Chi, ch.* 32, "Ch'i T'ai-kung shih-chia"), one can see that there was a great contrast between this submission and the arrogance, with which Duke Wen of Chin [who succeeded Duke Huan as the second Hegemon, in the years 634–27 B.C.] summoned the Chou King to meet him at Ho-yang. [This event in 629 B.C., in its rudeness on the part of a feudal lord toward the Chou King, later so shocked Confucius as he read the historical annals, that he is said to have used a euphemism to record the event in the *Spring and Autumn Annals*.] How can it be inferred that Kuan Tzu harbored any intent to "inquire about the weight of the tripods?" [In 605, the fifth Hegemon, King Chuang of Ch'u went so far as to commit this act of *lèse-majesté*; his asking the Chou King's envoy about the Chou royal ceremonial tripods implied an intent to move them, i.e., to dismantle the Chou royal shrine, thereby to end the dynasty. See, *Tso Chuan*, "Third Year of Duke Hsüan"; Legge, *Ch'un Ts'ew*, p. 293.] When in the *Kuan Tzu* we encounter phrases about "prevailing as king over the world," these can be taken as evidence that the book was not written by Kuan Tzu himself [and includes some materials extraneous to the tradition associated with him].

his ideal still was that of the feudal world's overlord, and not that of having an emperor over a unified state. In *ch.* 30, "Chün ch'en," Part One, it says: "The Son of Heaven issues his commands to the realm [*t'ien-hsia*]; the feudal lords accept the commands of the Son of Heaven." *Ch.* 57, "Tu ti," says: "In the realm there are ten thousand feudal lords, among whom are dukes, earls, marquises, barons, and knights. The Son of Heaven, from the center, places all these [in their proper fiefs]." This is indeed but slightly different from Confucius' statement: "When good government prevails in the empire, ceremonies, music, and punitive military expeditions proceed from the Son of Heaven." [*Analects*, xvi/2/1; Legge, p. 310]; it also serves to corroborate that the content of Kuan Tzu's thought fully reveals the historical backgrounds of the Spring and Autumn Period.

CHAPTER SEVEN
Lord Shang and Han Fei Tzu

SECTION ONE
Lord Shang's and Han Fei Tzu's Lives and Times

ADOPTING the sequence in which the schools were established, we have already designated the political thought of the Legalist school the last of the Pre-Ch'in era's four major schools.[1] The book called the *Kuan Tzu*, without doubt, does not come from the hand of Kuan Chung [even though its name attributes it to the famous statesman of the seventh century B.C. in the State of Ch'i; see Chapter Six above].* Moreover, a study of its content shows it to be, in large measure, a mixture of varied and inconsistent components; therefore it cannot be accepted as adequately representative of a new tradition. Other than Kuan Chung, there is also Teng Hsi, who, as a man of the Spring and Autumn Period, also had some connection with Legalism. In the *Tso Chuan*, Ninth year of Duke Ting, it tells that Ssu Chuan [chief minister in Cheng] had Teng Hsi put to death but adopted his *Bamboo Penal Code*.[2] The *Commentary* of Tu Yü [A.D. 222–284] says that he "wanted to alter Cheng's existing regulations of government, which had been cast [on iron tripods]; without having been so commanded by the ruler, he privately produced a penal code. This was written on bamboo slips, hence was called the *Bamboo Penal Code* [*chu hsing*]."[3] This shows that Teng Hsi was a man profoundly versed in the works on law; the *Lü-shih Ch'un-ch'iu*, ch. 18/4, "Li wei," adds: "When Tzu-ch'an [as chief minister] governed in the State of Cheng, Teng Hsi made a point of opposing him. He had agreed with the populace that in law suits his fee for a major law case was to be one coat, and, for a minor

---

*Square brackets indicate that the words enclosed were added by the translator.

[1] See above, last paragraph of Chapter One, Section Four. The *Ju* or Confucians, the Mohists, and the followers of Yang Chu, i.e., the Taoists, all attacked each other with extreme acerbity, yet failed to mention the Legalists; this can be taken as further corroboration of the late emergence of the Legalist school.

[2] The *Hsün Tzu*, ch. 28, "Yu tso," the *Lieh Tzu*, ch. 6, "Li ming," and the *Lü-shih Ch'un-ch'iu*, ch. 18/4, "Li wei," all say it was Tzu-ch'an who killed Teng Hsi. However, the *Han Shu*, ch. 30, "Journal of Literature," in the commentary of Yen Shih-ku, offers conclusive argument that Tzu-ch'an died in the Twentieth year of Duke Chao, thereby making more credible the view that Teng Hsi was killed by Ssu Chuan. The Twentieth year of Duke Chao corresponds with the year 522 B.C., the Ninth year of Duke Ting with the year 501 B.C.

[3] *Tso Chuan*, Sixth year of Duke Chao (536 B.C.) records that Tzu-ch'an had his penal code [*hsing shu*] cast in metal. [Duyvendak explains this as "engraved on iron tripods"; The *Book of Lord Shang*, p. 70. Cf. Legge, *Ch'un Ts'ew*, p. 609.]

case, one pair of trousers. The number of persons who presented him with coats and trousers in order to be instructed by him in litigations was beyond counting. He could make the false to be true, and the true to be false. The standard of true and false ceased to exist, so that the permissible and the non-permissible fluctuated from day to day. Those whom he wished to win their cases won, and those whom he wished to lose lost. The State of Cheng was thrown into chaos, and from the people's mouths poured forth dispute and contention."[4] This indicates that Teng Hsi's practices were much like those of the professional litigants of a later age. If we piece together these two items of information about Teng Hsi—that he privately produced his own laws and that he manipulated the letter of the law so that it was thrown into confusion—it would appear that Teng Hsi's arts were quite contradictory in spirit to Lord Shang's and Han Fei Tzu's principles of "*ting-fa*" 定法 or "clearly establishing the law" and "*yi-min*" 一民 or "unifying the people." Moreover, the *Bamboo Penal Code* is no longer extant, and in the "Journal of Literature" of the *Han Shu* the work known as the *Teng Hsi* in two chapters is classed with the School of Names [*ming chia*],[5] so that, even if genuine, it would appear to have nothing to do with legalistic political ideas. Therefore Teng Hsi does not fulfill the qualifications to be considered the founding figure of Legalism; in that respect he is no different from Kuan Tzu.

Li K'uei, Shen Tao, Shih Chiao, Shen Pu-hai, Shang Yang, Han Fei, and Li Ssu all were men of the Warring States Period. Li Ssu, who was chief minister to the First Emperor following the unification [of Ch'in, in 221 B.C.], was purely a practitioner in the realm of government; hence he can be set aside without further discussion.

---

[4] The same chapter further states: "In the State of Cheng it was a common practice to put up anonymous pronouncements [on matters involving the laws as a means] to carry on disputes. Tzu-ch'an issued an order forbidding people to put up such pronouncements. Teng Hsi then sent him anonymous letters. Tzu-ch'an ordered that there be no more such letters sent to him. Teng Hsi found devious ways to continue sending them. Commands were issued inexhaustibly [against him], and Teng Hsi's resources to those likewise were inexhaustible. [Interpretation of this passage based on Wang Ch'i-hsiang's *Teng Hsi Tzu Chiao-ch'üan*, "Appendix."]

[5] Liu Hsiang's [d. 6 B.C.] "Preface" [on submitting an emended text of the work to the throne] states: "There are variant versions of his essay on 'No Magnaminity' ['Wu hou'], but, in any case, it belongs to the same category as [the School of Names work] the *Kung-sun Lung Tzu*." The *Hsün Tzu*, ch. 3, "Pu kou," says of the various arguments about "equating mountains and canyons, equalizing heaven and earth" [and other such seemingly indefensible statements] that "Hui Shih and Teng Hsi were skilled in arguing them." The same work's *ch*. 6, "Fei shih-erh tzu," also names Hui Shih and Teng Hsi together, thereby corroborating the *Han Shu*, "Journal of Literature," in so associating them. Ch. 1, "Wu hou" in the extant work [called the *Teng Hsi Tzu*], presents ideas distinct from those of Hui Shih as described in *Chuang Tzu*, ch. 33, "T'ien hsia," confirming that the extant *Teng Hsi Tzu* is spurious.

Li K'uei 李悝 ". . . as chief minister to Marquis Wen of Wei enriched
the state and strenghthened its military forces."⁶ Moreover, there once
was a work known as the *Li Tzu* [or, "The Book of Master Li"] in
thirty-two chapters; that might qualify him to be regarded as the forerunner of the Legalist school. Unfortunately, however, since the book is
no longer extant, there is no way of studying his thought.

Shen Tzu [i.e. Shen Tao 慎到] was a native of the State of Chao. Like
T'ien P'ien, Chieh Tzu, Huan Yuan ". . . they all studied the political
methods of Huang-Lao [Taoist political doctrines] and of the Way and its
Power [or, of the *Tao Te Ching*]. . . . They all served as masters at the
Chi-hsia Academy [in the State of Ch'i]. . . . Shen Tao composed twelve
chapters of discourses."⁷ "His learning revered the law but lacked [the
substance of] law"; ". . . he was blinded by the idea of law and lacked
awareness of worthy human capacities"; ". . . he had insight about being
a follower, but no insight about leading."⁸ He "discarded knowledge and
renounced the self, and accepted involvement only where he could not
evade it. He was indifferent to all things. Thus he constituted his principles." Along with P'eng Meng and T'ien P'ien, he shared the way
described as "open-minded and non-partisan, equable and selfless,
neither arbitrary nor prejudiced."⁹ Ch. 30, "Journal of Literature," of the
Han Shu, records his book, in forty-two chapters, and lists it among the
works of the Legalist school. By Sung times, however, it was almost
entirely lost, and the work that goes by his name today is a hodgepodge of
fragments and spurious elements, clearly inadequate to serve as the basis
[for study of his thought].¹⁰ The thought of this great Warring States
Period master of "Huang-Lao" concepts, thus, is preserved only in
fragments. Fortunately the main outlines of his discussions on the concept
of power [*shih* 勢, or, the compelling force of circumstances] can still be
seen as preserved in the writings of Han Fei Tzu. [For discussion of how
best to translate "*shih*," see: Duyvendak, *Lord Shang*, pp. 98 ff; Fung/
Bodde, vol. I, pp. 318 ff., and Liao, *Han Fei Tzu*, vol. II, p. 199.]

⁶ The *Han Shu*, "Journal of Literature," lists the *Li Tzu* in thirty-two chapters as the
first title under the heading of Legalists, and the sentence quoted here appears there as
commentary. Duke Wen of Wei reigned from 446 B.C. to 397. It should be added that Li's
learning also partook of Confucianism; see footnote 58 to Chapter One of the present work
[referring to "Li K'e," whose name is also written "K'uei"].

⁷ *Shih Chi, ch.* 74, "Biography of Mencius and Hsün Ch'ing."

⁸ See, *Hsün Tzu:* respectively, *ch.* 6, "Fei Shih-erh tzu"; *ch.* 21, "Chih pi"; and *ch.* 17,
"T'ien lun."

⁹ *Chuang Tzu, ch.* 33, "T'ien-hsia."

¹⁰ Among current editions there are: (1) that reconstructed and edited by Yen K'e-
chün [1762–1843] (in the *Shou-shan-ko ts'ung-shu*); (2) that with textual emendation by
Shen Mou-shang [late Ming] (in the *Ssu-pu ts'ung-k'an*); (3) that with textual emendation
by Ch'ien Hsi-tso [1801–1844] (in the *Chu tzu chi-ch'eng*); etc.

Shih Chiao 尸佼, a native of the State of Chin, was a "guest" of Wei Yang, chief minister in the State of Ch'in. [Lord Shang was of the ducal house of Wei, hence also is called Wei Yang.] "Lord Shang never failed to square his ideas with [Shih] Chiao when he was planning activities, devising tactics, establishing laws, or regulating the people. When Lord Shang was executed, it was feared that Chiao would be executed along with him, but he escaped and fled into Shu. His writings consist of twenty chapters, but they too are no longer extant."[11]

Shen Pu-hai 申不害: ". . . was a lowly servitor of the former State of Cheng. He studied political methods [*shu* 術] and thereby gained the attention of Marquis Chao of Han. Marquis Chao employed him as a chief minister. Within, he put in order the governing and its doctrines, while without he parried with the rulers of the other states for fifteen years. . . . Master Shen's learning was based upon Huang-Lao and [yet it] emphasized *hsing* 刑, actualities, and *ming* 名, names [or, terminological distinctions]. He wrote a book in two chapters called the *Shen Tzu*."[12] This work has long been lost. The main outlines of his doctrines concerning political methods also can be seen in the *Han Fei Tzu*.

The thought trends in the pre-Ch'in era, which centered on respect for the authority of the ruler and reliance upon laws and methods, took more or less concrete form with the appearance of Li K'uei, Shih Chiao, Shen Pu-hai, and Shen Tao. But a more rigorously developed legalist thought-system had to wait for Shang Yang before it finally emerged. Han Fei Tzu then drew all the parts together, thereby formulating the comprehensive synthesis of the Legalist school's thought and learning. These two men are remarkable not only for the content of their thought; the extant corpus of their writings also is of impressive scope and richness. Hence in our wish to set forth the political thought of the Legalists, we have no alternative but to focus attention primarily on Lord Shang and Han Fei Tzu.

"The Lord of Shang was one of the descendants, by a concubine, of the

---

[11] *Shih Chi, ch.* 74: "In the State of Ch'u there was Master Shih." For this line the *Chi-chieh* commentary cites Liu Hsiang's *pieh lu*, as quoted. The *Han Shu*, "Journal of Literature," classes the work among the Tsa-chia [see "Introduction," p. 12, above]. The commentary at that place says: "He was a native of Lu, and served as a chief minister in Ch'in; Lord Shang was his follower." In this connection it should be noted that the date of Lord Shang's execution was the first year of King Hui-wen of Ch'in (338 B.C.). The work known as the *Shih Tzu* exists today in the edition reconstructed by Wang Chi-p'ei in two chapters, plus one chapter of "doubtful passages" (in the *Hu-hai-lou ts'ung-shu*).

[12] *Shih Chi, ch.* 63, "Biographies of Lao Tzu, Chuang Tzu, Shen Pu-hai, and Han Fei Tzu." Shen Pu-hai served as a chief minister to Marquis Chao of Han between the eighth and twenty-second years of his reign, which corresponds to the period 351–337 B.C. The *Han Shu*, "Journal of Literature," lists a work, *Shen Tzu* in six chapters, among the Legalists. It is no longer extant. In his *Yü-han shan-fang chi-yi-shu* Ma Kuo-han [1794–1857] has collected some fragments of it. [Duyvendak translates *hsing-ming* together as "criminal law." See Chan, *Source Book*, pp. 787–88 for an important discussion of this term.]

[ducal] family of Wei. His given name was Yang, and his family name was Kung-sun. His ancestors had, originally, the [royal Chou] surname of Chi. In his youth, he was fond of the study of criminal law; he served Kung-shu Tso, the Minister of Wei, and became a *chung-shu-tzu* [i.e., charged with the education of the sons from the princely families]." After Kung-shu Tso's death, Shang Yang went to the State of Ch'in where [eventually] he greatly pleased Duke Hsiao of Ch'in, and [in 556 B.C.] was appointed by him to the office of *tso-shu-chang* [a councillor of the tenth rank]. Shang Yang ". . . enacted an ordinance to alter the institutions. He ordered the people to be organized into groups of fives and tens, mutually to control one another and to share in one another's punishments. Whoever did not denounce a culprit would be cut in two; whoever denounced a culprit would receive the same reward as he who decapitated an enemy; whoever concealed a culprit would receive the same punishment as he who surrendered to an enemy. Households that had two or more sons, and did not divide into separate households, had to pay double taxes. Those who had military merit all received titles from the ruler, according to a hierarchic ladder. Those who had private quarrels were punished according to the severity of their offence. Great and small had to occupy themselves, with united force, with the fundamental occupations of tilling and weaving, and those who produced a large quantity of grain or silk were exempted from forced labor. Those who occupied themselves with secondary sources of profit, and those who were poor through laziness, were taken on as slaves. Those of the princely family who had no military merit could not be regarded as belonging to the princely clan. He made clear the distinctions between high and low, and between the various ranks and degrees, each according to its place in the hierarchy. He apportioned fields, houses, servants, concubines, and clothes, all differently, according to the families. Those who had merit were distinguished by honors, while those who had no merit, though they might be rich, had no glory whatever. When the ordinances were already drawn up but still unpublished, fearing that the people would not believe it, he had a thirty-foot pole erected near the south gate of the capital, and, having summoned the people, said that he would give ten ounces of gold to anyone who could remove it to the north gate. The people found that strange; there was no one who dared move it. Thereupon he said he would give fifty ounces to anyone who would remove it. There was one man who removed it, and forthwith he gave him the fifty ounces of gold, to make it clear that he deceived no one. Finally the ordinances were published. When they had been enforced upon the people for the term of a year, the people of Ch'in who came to the capital and at first said that the laws were not appropriate could be counted by the thousands. Then the Crown Prince infringed the law. Wei Yang said: 'It is owing to the

infringements by the highly-placed that the law is not carried out. We shall apply the law to the Crown Prince; as, however, he is His Highness' heir, we cannot subject him to capital punishment. Let his tutor, Prince Ch'ien, be punished and his teacher, Kung-sun Chia, be branded.' The following day the people of Ch'in all hastened into the path of the law. When it had been in force for ten years, the people of Ch'in greatly rejoinced: belongings accidentally dropped on the road were not picked up [by others]; in the mountains there were no robbers; families were self-supporting, and people had plenty; they were brave in public warfare and timid in private quarrels; and great order prevailed throughout the countryside and in the towns. From among those of the people of Ch'in who had at first said that the mandates were inappropriate, some now came forth to say that the mandates were appropriate. Wei Yang said: 'Such as these are all trouble-making people.' So he had them all banished to the frontiers, and thereafter none of the people dared to discuss the ordinances. Then [in 352 B.C.] Yang was appointed *Ta-liang-tsao* [a high military rank]."

Subsequently he persuaded Duke Hsiao to [let him] defeat the State of Wei, whereupon ". . . he was awarded fifteen cities in Shang, as fief, and was called the Lord of Shang." When Duke Hsiao died, the Crown Prince ascended the throne as King Hui-wen [in 338 B.C.]. The partisans of Prince Ch'ien [who had been punished by Lord Shang for breaking his new laws] accused Lord Shang of plotting rebellion. He fled, but did not escape in time [and fell back to his own fiefdom, where he raised troops to resist capture]. Ch'in sent an army against him that captured and killed him. His corpse was torn apart by being attached to chariots [driven in opposite directions] as an exemplary punishment of warning to the people; his family line was exterminated.[13]

Lord Shang was a practicing statesman; whether he ever wrote any books is a matter of real doubt.[14] Yet Ssu-ma Ch'ien [the first century B.C. author of the great history, the *Shih Chi*] has stated: "I have read the books on 'Opening and Debarring' [the name of the present Chapter Seven] and on 'Agriculture and War' [similar to the name of Chapter Two]."[15] Han Fei Tzu remarked: "In every family there are kept copies of the *Laws* of Lord Shang and of Kuan Tzu."[16] The "Journal of Litera-

---

[13] *Shih Chi, ch.* 68, "Biography of Lord Shang." Lord Shang died in the Twenty-fourth year of the reign of Duke Hsiao, or in the year 338 B.C. Note further that if the statement in Huan T'an's *Hsin Lun* is to be believed, Shang Tzu's learning was derived from Li K'uei's *Classic of Law*, or *Fa ching*. [This translation of Lord Shang's biography follows with minor modification that of Duyvendak, in his *Book of Lord* Shang, pp. 8–31.]

[14] *SKTY* [see also the discussion in Duyvendak, *Lord Shang*, Chapter IV].

[15] *Shih Chi, ch.* 68, "Encomium" ["*Tsan*"].

[16] *Ch.* 49, "Wu Tu" [Liao, vol. II, p. 290].

ture" in the *Han Shu* records that the *Book of Lord Shang* [as known in the first century A.D.] had as many as twenty-nine chapters. The extant work, containing twenty-four chapters, has many references to events that post-date Lord Shang's death. "For, it would appear, the *Book of Lord Shang* is like the *Kuan Tzu* in that both come from the hands of those who transmitted their doctrines."[17] Although the book may not have been written by Wei Yang himself, its content need not be looked upon as altogether spurious.

"Han Fei Tzu was a scion of the ducal house in the State of Han. He delighted in the study of *"hsing-ming"* or "actuality and name" and of political methods, and his doctrines derived ultimately from Huang-Lao [i.e., Taoist-derived statecraft] studies. . . . Along with Li Ssu, he had studied under Hsün Tzu." King An of the State of Han did not give him official appointment. "He therefore wrote his essays entitled 'Solitary Indignation' ['Ku fen,' *ch.* 11], 'Five Vermin' ['Wu Tu,' *ch.* 49], 'Inner and Outer Congeries' ['Nei-wai chu shuo,' *chs.* 30–35], 'Collected Persuasions' ['Shuo-lin,' *chs.* 22–23], 'Refutations' ['Shuo-nan,' *ch.* 12], and other writings totalling more than one-hundred-thousand words." In the fifth year of King An's reign,[18] Ch'in attacked Han, and the State of Han sent Han Fei Tzu as envoy to Ch'in; subsequently he was detained there. Li Ssu [at this time a chief minister in Ch'in] and Yao Ku [also a high official in Ch'in] slandered him, and he was sent to prison, where he died. That was during the fourteenth year of the First Emperor's reign.[19] It was merely twelve or thirteen years before the extinction of the Six States and the unification of the empire [under the First Emperor of Ch'in]. The currently extant *Book of Han Fei Tzu* contains fifty-five chapters, the same number as recorded for it in the "Journal of Literature" in the *Han Shu*. Although it may include interpolations and additions by later persons,[20] in the main it is to be considered genuine.

The deaths of Lord Shang and Han Fei Tzu were separated by a century. Yet in the thought of both are developed, to an extreme degree, ideas elevating the ruler and giving primacy to the state. They reflect the historical circumstances existing just as the authoritarian world empire was about to emerge. In that they quite obviously display the distance separating them from the era of Kuan Tzu, in which elements of the feudal age still persisted. The thought of the pre-Ch'in Legalists was not

[17] [The contemporary Scholar] Ku Shih's *Han-shu yi-wen-chih chiang-shu*, quoted in Chang Hsin-ch'eng, *Wei-shu t'ung-k'ao, hsia*, p. 770.

[18] *Shih Chi, ch.* 45, "Han shih-chia." The fifth year of King An's reign corresponds to 234 B.C.

[19] *Shih Chi, chs.* 6 and 63. The fourteenth year of the reign of the First Emperor corresponds to 233 B.C.

[20] *SKTY*; Hu Shih, *Chung-kuo che-hsüeh-shih ta-kang*; Chang Hsin-ch'eng, *Wei-shu t'ung-k'ao, hsia*, pp. 781–82.

one man's creation; much less was it the product of a single period. The phases of its development from its earliest origins, nonetheless, can be traced in a general way. That is, it is roughly comparable to the Confucian School's first having had a Confucius, who established his teachings on the basis of ancient learning, and subsequently had its Mencius and its Hsün Tzu, who accepted the Confucian teachings but altered the body of Confucian learning. There are differences between the two schools in the circumstances affecting their development, but they are quite similar in revealing the evidence of such further development. Han Fei Tzu is the last figure in Legalism's development, and he in fact brought all the earlier contributors to that development together into a grand synthesis. "Law," i.e., *fa*, "political methods," i.e., *shu*, and "power," i.e., *shih*, the three principal concepts in his thought-system, all were the products of historical circumstances; they were conceived, given birth, and nurtured; then, coming to Han Fei Tzu, they took on the form of their ultimate maturity.

The historical circumstances that conceived, gave birth to, and nurtured those concepts were, in a word, simply those various social and political realities attendant upon the process through which the old feudal world disintegrated and collapsed. To speak of the political realities, the direct consequence of feudalism's collapse was the weakening of the [Royal Chou King, the] Son of Heaven, and the strengthening of the feudal lords. However those newly powerful feudal lords were not the same as the ancient enfieffed hereditary noble families [dating from the Chou conquest in the twelfth century B.C.], but were in virtually all cases powerful ministers who had usurped their previous overlords' positions. The few rulers who had been so lucky as to maintain their positions in most cases retained only the name but had lost the reality [of ruling power], creating conditions of "the governing is in the hands of Ning Shih, but the ancestral sacrifices will be conducted by Ourself" [as said by Duke Hsien of the State of Wei, proposing a compromise with the Ning clan, which had usurped the powers of his rule; see, *Tso Chuan*, Twenty-sixth year of Duke Hsiang, or 546 B.C., Legge, p. 523]. At first, the Ministers and Great Officers infringed the prerogatives of the rulers they served; subsequently the Household Servitors were aggressive against their masters [who were already illegitimate usurpers of ducal and princely powers].[21] Thus the bonds and the proprieties that in ancient

[21] Those usurpers of thrones included the T'ien clan in the State of Ch'i and the Three Clans of the State of Chin [which partitioned it into Han, Wei, and Chao]. Those who illicitly dominated the rightful rulers of states were the Three Branches of the Huan clan in the State of Lu [of the time of Confucius; see Analects xvi/3, etc.] and Yuan Hsüan in the State of Wei [at the end of the seventh century B.C.]. One [household servitor] who aggressed against his superior was Yang Hu [also a contemporary of Confucius, sometimes identified with Yang Huo, *Analects*, xvii/1]. These are but some of the more prominent examples.

times had held the social order together gradually had lost their effectiveness. Moreover, the strengthening of the feudal lords [or princes of the states, at the expense of the Chou sovereigns] in itself was, simultaneously a prior condition to and a direct consequence of the aggressive wars and annexations among the states. Those which became larger and stronger in that process devoted all their energies toward further annexations, and, having succeeded in annexing other territories, they became all the stronger and larger. Both aggression and self-defense were dependent on success in enriching the state and increasing its military capacity. Because of this, the enhanced power of the sovereign also became, simultaneously, both a political necessity and the goal of politics; political thought likewise rushed along the path of elevating ruler and state while giving full reign to laws and political methods.

To make a somewhat more specific analysis: the body of thought concerning government by laws has the most archaic origins and had a relatively early development. That of elevating the ruler arose in its wake, and dates from about the same time. Both first came into existence during the Spring and Autumn Period. The thought centering on governing through political methods [or "statecraft," *shu-chih* 術治] achieved currency the latest, commencing to flourish only in the Warring States Period. The government of the royal Chi clan of the Chou dynasty, from its beginnings [in the twelfth century B.C.], displayed a tendency to rely on laws; we have discussed this above.[22] Yet the principles underlying early Chou royal government were not necessarily fully realized throughout all the feudal states. Its legalistic spirit, moreover, had merged with the customs prevailing throughout feudal society. When we hold the government of that earlier age up for comparison with the elevation of the ruler, the disappearance of social class distinctions, and the stress on instruments [of war and of punishments] and on calculations [with productivity statistics] that characterize Legalist governing, it becomes obvious that there are indeed significant differences. Then, as clan law largely decayed, elite and commoners became mixed together, individuals achieved freedoms, and "rites" [*li*] lost their effectiveness. States such as Cheng and Chin, lying within what we designate the "Chou culture" area,[23] were particularly early in coming under those influences, and one after another adopted legalist policies. Beyond those states, the feudal order had relatively shallow foundations in the State of Ch'u, and in consequence it already also possessed well-established works on penal law in the Spring and Autumn Period.[24] However, during the Spring and

[22] See Chapter Two, Sections Three and Four.
[23] See Chapter One, Table Five.
[24] See *Tso Chuan*, under the Twenty-seventh year of Duke Hsi (633 B.C.), where Duke Wen of the State of Chin makes the law promulgated [at the time of a hunt] at P'i-lu.

Autumn Era, although in point of fact government by laws had already become a necessity, conservatives could not, psychologically, grant it their acceptance. Thus, when Tzu-ch'an as chief minister in the State of Cheng compiled his work on penal law, Shu Hsiang [a contemporary statesman in the State of Chin] wrote to him criticizing the act, saying, in part: "When the people know there is this code, they will have no respect for superiors. Moreover, they will come to have contentious minds

---

The content of that law is unknown, yet under the Sixth year of Duke Wen (corresponding to the Seventh year of Duke Hsiang of Chin, or 621 B.C.) the *Tso Chuan* says: "Hsüan Tzu (i.e., Chao Tun) began to administer the government of the State [of Chin]. He established regular rules for the conduct of government affairs, adjusted the laws and the [definitions of] crimes, codified penal matters, had persons fleeing punishments brought under supervision, ordered the use of securities and bonds, reorganized the long-accumulated confusion [of statutes], restored to their original form the distinctions of rank, and renewed the functions of offices that had fallen into disuse [omitted in text], and brought back to office persons whose careers had been improperly blocked. When all these regulations were completed, he delivered them to the Grand Assistant Yang and to the Grand Master Chia T'o, so that they might be carried into practice throughout the State of Chin, and to serve as its regular laws." [Modified from Legge, pp. 243–44.] This represents the first beginnings of the trend toward primary reliance on laws. Subsequently, Duke Ching of Chin [reigned 598–580 B.C.] again: "collated and assembled all the old regulations, and the statutes governing social forms, from the Three Dynasties [of Hsia, Shang, and Chou], and proceeded to draw up administrative standards which could be used as the laws of Chin." The commentary explains: "When Duke Wen of Chin ordered the hunt at P'i-lu, he made the law of administrative standards. Since the time of Duke Ling, [reigned 619–606] those have become incomplete, and have not been kept in use." (From the *Kuo Yü*, ch. 2, "Chou Yü, Part Two." Note that the law reform referred to under Duke Ling must have occurred between the years 599 and 586 B.C.). During the reign of Duke Ch'ing, the tripods bearing the penal laws were cast, following the penal code [previously] created by Fan Hsüan Tzu [in 621 B.C.; see above, this note]. (See *Tso Chuan*, Twenty-ninth year of Duke Chao, corresponding with the year 513 B.C.) [Legge, pp. 731–32]. This now greatly increased the tendency to rely on laws. Tzu-ch'an, in the State of Cheng, had ordered the casting of penal tripods during the Sixth year of Duke Chao (536 B.C.). After that, Teng Hsi Tzu had created his "Bamboo Penal Code," and [the chief minister] Ssu Chuan had Teng executed yet adopted his Bamboo Penal Code (see *Tso Chuan*, Ninth year of Duke Ting, or 501 B.C.). Compared with the earlier penal laws [cast on the tripods], the Bamboo Penal Code apparently was more extensive and precise, hence its adoption. The *Tso Chuan*, under the Seventh year of Duke Chao, says that the State of Ch'u had the Law of P'u-ou [dating from the reign of the Ch'u King Wen, reigned 688–676 B.C.; see Legge, p. 616]. To come to the time of the six states [i.e., the Warring States Period, after 479 B.C.], the compilation and promulgation of legal codes was ever more frequent. King Chuang of the State of Ch'u (reigned 613–591 B.C.) had his Law of Mao-men, or "Law of the Inner Gate" (*Han Fei Tzu*, ch. 34, "Yu chu shuo, shang"). Also, King Huai of Ch'u instructed Ch'ü Yuan to draw up laws (*Shih Chi*, ch. 84). [See D. Hawkes, *Ch'u Tz'u*, pp. 11–15, translation of the *Shih Chi* biography.] In the State of Wei there was the Ta-fu Statute (*Chan Kuo Ts'e*, ch. 25, "Wei ts'e, Part Four"). After that Li K'uei, drawing on the laws of all the states, wrote the *Fa Ching*, or "Classic of Law." Still other examples in addition to these exist, but need not all be listed here.

and in disputes will appeal to the letter of the code, hoping thereby to gain fortuitous victories in their disputes." [See, *Tso Chuan*, Sixth year of Duke Chao, Legge, p. 609.] When the penal tripods were cast in the State of Chin, Confucius also condemned it, saying: "Chin should adhere to the laws and standards that T'ang-shu [progenitor of Chin's ducal house, who lived at the time of the Chou conquest in the twelfth century B.C.] received for the regulation of his people, and by which the Ministers and Great Officers are kept in their proper ranks. The people, because of [those laws and standards], can be led to respect their superiors, and those superiors, because of them, are enabled to retain their inheritances. When the distinction between noble and humble is not blurred, that is what is called having a standard. . . . Now that standard is abandoned, and penal tripods are made. How can respect for superiors be ensured? And how can superiors retain any inheritance? When there are no rankings of noble and humble, how can the state be maintained?" [*Tso Chuan*, Twenty-ninth year of Duke Chao; modified from Legge, p. 732.]

Seen from these remarks made by Shu Hsiang and Confucius, in establishing the state, having laws is, to be sure, quite appropriate, but if the laws and standards are openly proclaimed to the people, then the nobles lose their former positions of authority, and the foundations of the feudal order are, in consequence, shaken.[25]

There were some thinkers at the time who observed the vast and unprecedented transformations underway in society and who tried to devise positive responses; these we can divide into two groups: The one regretted the feudal order's collapse and wanted to rescue it; the other group observed that the feudal order was not worth saving and was ready to let it wither away. Confucius was the most prominent representative of the former. His doctrines of rectifying terms and restoring the rites were, in fact, intended to place strict limits on the willful and excessive behavior of aristocrats and thereby bring about their self-preservation. By that method he would bring security and stability to society. Lord Shang, on the other hand, was in the line of such persons as Tzu-ch'an and Chao Tun [see footnote 24], but he both altered their methods in fundamental ways, and intensified them. He is the most extreme proponent of the second group's views. Hsün Tzu's and Kuan Tzu's learning combined

---

[25] Ch'ien Mu, in his *Hsien Ch'in chu-tzu hsi-nien k'ao-pien*, p. 17, has said in his discussion of Teng Hsi Tzu: "From the time when punishments came to be regularized by statutes, the rewards and punishments meted out to the common people were no longer totally dependent on the pleasure and anger of the aristocrats, but now were provided with a reference point on the basis of which challenges could be made. Teng Hsi Tzu's Bamboo Penal Code appears to have served as the instrument for instructing the people how to make such challenges, and those in high position at that time had no choice but to appropriate that [instrument] by which such challenges arose, and employ it in their own governing. This constituted the crux of one of that age's great changes."

aspects of the [old] rites and the [new] laws, and they represent transitional thought lying between those two. If we should set aside all considerations of origins, and if we regard the penal codes and penal tripods as mere initial manifestations of legalistic political thought, then we may say that the waning of the rites, relative to the waxing of the laws, occupied the period of approximately two hundred years, from the end of the sixth century to the end of the fourth century, B.C.

Governing by means of power [*shih-chih* 勢治] had its origins in the elevation of the ruler. In the heyday of the feudal order, the rulers and their aristocratic hereditary officials shared powers and maintained each other's status; from above and from below they supported each other, each within the fixed boundaries of his own status. The ruler undoubtedly had no idea of being solely elevated above all others. But gradually the powerful ministers took over the states, their rulers becoming weaker and more insignificant. For one example, in the State of Lu, "at the time of Duke Tao, the Three [usurping] Families of the Huan clan were triumphant; the Dukedom of Lu was like a petty marquisate conferred by consent among the three Huan clans."[26] There is no need to mention all the other cases of regicide and usurpation. Those who defended the feudal order arose in the face of these conditions to try and put down the usurping ministers and to prop up the declining rulers. Confucius, who "served his ruler according to the full prescriptions of the rites" [*Analects* III/18], brought telling censure to bear on "rebellious ministers and villainous sons" [*Mencius*, III/ii/9/2]. In fact, in so doing he implicitly launched the theories justifying elevation and veneration of the ruler that were subsequently developed with great clarity by Hsün Tzu. Nonetheless, the Confucians' motive in elevating the ruler was to correct the evils committed by too-powerful servitors; it was not to find in the sublime ruler an objective of government *per se*. As powerful ministers assumed illicit authority, the states gradually grew rich and militarily strong, while the ducal houses and the hereditary servitors [of the old aristocracy] declined into virtual disappearance. By the time the newly centralized authority had become reality, the ruler's elevation to new heights inevitably followed, just from the force of those circumstances. The Legalists not only recognized the logic of this new historical reality, they also added their explanations of it. Theories of authority and power consequently took form. Shen Tao, with his phrases about flying dragons and soaring serpents [metaphors suggesting the sovereign's *shih*, or power] can be looked upon as the representative figure in the emergence of these theories.

Governing by "methods" [*shu chih*] took form with Shen Pu-hai. It is also related to the elevation of the ruler, but in particular it was a response

---

[26] *Shih Chi*, ch. 33, "Lu Chou-kung shih-chia." [Duke Tao reigned 466–430 B.C.]

to political needs following the collapse and abandonment of the system of hereditary officialdom. During the Spring and Autumn Period cases of regicide and of illicit take-over of powers by ministers were frequent enough; in the Warring States Period that followed, such behavior grew worse, witnessing outright seizures of states and usurpations of thrones as well. Analysts tracing the causes could lay the blame only on rulers' lack of methods in handling their servitors. But, of course, in the earlier period, when the feudal order had not yet disintegrated, when officials were appointed and responsibilities were allocated, the existence of class rankings and of clan law provided a standard to follow. The ruler could not advance and demote at will, and he seldom assumed the responsibility to assess talent and select persons according to demonstrated capacities. Following the age when Confucius and Mo Tzu, trying to correct the faults of their times, had proposed the levelling of social classes, the states subsequently came to have very few hereditary officials; [rulers were forced to] "cast aside relatives and employ strangers."[27] Anyone who possessed a single talent or special skill might gain appointment and advancement, without reference to his state of origin or any aristocratic affiliations. Remnants of aristocratic classes could sometimes rise up to resist these developments, as when Wu Ch'i was murdered in Ch'u,[28] or when misfortune befell Lord Shang in Ch'in. Yet both of them had been able to assume full powers of government in states where they were outsider-officials [i.e., originally from other states]. Not only did they represent violations of Kuan Tzu's dictum: "Do not appoint men from other states to office"; they also had failed to observe Mencius' warning: "Do not arouse the resentment of the great clans." [*Mencius*, IV/i/6.] Once the custom got started, the wandering persuaders who brandished their talents became more numerous day by day. Rulers who commanded no political methods by which to distinguish those of ability from the rest experienced great difficulties in employing people. Moreover, persons who were drawn by the advantages of association with power usually could not be trusted. If [the prospective employer] lacked methods for controlling and using these sometimes loyal, sometimes treacherous, individuals, their states would be in peril and their thrones might totter.

---

[27] *Tso Chuan*, "Seventh Year of Duke Chao," in the account of Hsien, Viscount of Shan, being killed. [Legge, p. 619.]

[28] *Shih Chi*, *ch.* 65, "Sun Tzu, Wu Ch'i lieh chuan," says that Wu Ch'i, "as chief minister in Ch'u, made the laws clear and definite, and revised the statutes. He abolished unnecessary offices and disinherited the ruler's distant clansmen, in order to [use the money so saved] to support the country's fighting men. As a consequence all Ch'u's aristocrats and royal relatives wanted to murder Wu Ch'i. When King Tao died, the royal clansmen and high officers rebelled and attacked Wu Ch'i." The *Han Fei Tzu*, *ch.* 13, "Ho shih," says that Wu Ch'i instructed King Tao: "confiscate the ranks and incomes of all descendants of vassals after three generations." [Cf. Liao, *Han Fei Tzu*, vol. I, pp. 114–15.]

Because of these various kinds of need, specialists on the art of ruling eventually began to produce theories about governing by methods. This group's most eminent representative is Shen Pu-hai.[29]

Shen Tao clarified the subject of power [*shih*], "Shen Pu-hai discoursed on methods [*shu*], and Kung-sun Yang [Lord Shang] applied himself to laws [*fa*]."[30] Han Fei Tzu synthesized the three bodies of thought, taking the ruler's power as the basic substance, and regarding laws and methods as its functions [or applications]. He made further additions by drawing on Huang-Lao doctrines for the concept of "taking no action" [*wu-wei*]. From these elements he created and brought to completion the most comprehensive system of Legalist thought.

Section Two
Power

THE Legalist elevation of the ruler is not a matter of venerating the person of the ruler, but is to raise the authority and status of his position. The *Kuan Tzu* in *ch.* 16, "Fa fa," states: "That by which the ruler is a ruler is power." This term "power," or *shih*, is consistently employed by the Legalist writers to designate in a general way the ruler's status and authority. The *Kuan Tzu* develops the idea briefly.[31] Then, when Han Fei Tzu took up Shen Tao's theories, the concept came to be fully worked out. "Shen Tao said, 'A flying dragon rides on the clouds, and a soaring serpent strolls through the mists [both are auspicious symbols of the ruler]. When the clouds disperse and the mists clear away, the dragon and the serpent are then no different from mere earthworms or ants, for they have lost that on which they were conveyed. When worthy men are held subject to the unworthy, it is because their authority is slight and their status is low. When the unworthy can hold the worthy in their service,

---

[29] Ch'ien Mu, in his *Hsien Ch'in chu-tzu hsi-nien k'ao-pien*, p. 223, discusses some events in Shen Pu-hai's life. He has commented: "The essentials of his theories can be summed up: using methods to select servitors. This was in a wholly different category from those earlier figures such as Wu Ch'i and Lord Shang, who changed the laws in order to make the state more powerful. The reason why Shen Pu-hai did as he did is that wandering men of learning had gradually become so numerous, all struggling to find favor with a ruler so that they then could get their hands on power. The rulers had no recourse except to respond to them with clearly worked-out political methods." This view is quite correct. The explanation found in the *Huai-nan Tzu*, *ch.* 21, "Yao lüeh hsün," would seem not to be wholly correct. [At the end of this chapter, the author characterizes the various schools in terms of factors stimulating their emergence. He explains Shen Pu-hai's ideas in relation to the geographical, political, and cultural conditions of that part of modern Shansi then comprising the Chin successor state of Han, where Shen Pu-hai had served in office. See also below, Chapter Ten, Section Four, on the *Huai-nan Tzu*.]

[30] *Han Fei Tzu*, *ch.* 43, "Ting fa."

[31] See Chapter Six, Section Two.

it is because their authority is great and their positions are high. When the [sage emperor] Yao was still just a common man, he could not keep three persons in good order, while [the incompetent tyrant] Chieh, in the role of Son of Heaven, could bring chaos to the whole empire. From this I know that power and status are dependable supports, while worthy qualities and knowledge are scarcely worth one's respect.' "[32] An argument from so extreme a position could not fail to arouse doubts. So *Han Fei Tzu* devises what are offered as the words of an opponent in debate, who says: "True, the flying dragon rides on the clouds and the rising serpent strolls through the mists. The dependence of the dragon and the serpent on the circumstances [*shih*] of the clouds and the mists I never deny. However, if you cast worthiness aside and trust to position [*shih*] entirely, is it sufficient to attain political order? No such instance have I ever been able to witness. Indeed, if the dragon and the serpent, when having the circumstances of clouds and mist, can ride on and stroll through them, it is because their talents are excellent. Now, though the clouds are thick, the earthworm cannot ride on them; though the mists are deep, the ant cannot stroll through them. Indeed, if the earthworm and the ant, when having the circumstances of thick clouds and deep mists, cannot ride on and stroll through them, it is because their talents are feeble. That brings us to [the incompetent tyrants] Chieh and Chou, who faced the south [the ritual position of the ruler] and held sway over the empire; though the Son of Heaven's inherent awesomeness provided them with their clouds and mists, even so the empire could not escape utter chaos. Is that not because the talents of Chieh and Chou were so shallow?"[33] Han Fei Tzu's counter to that argument is expressed in a passage for which the text has become corrupt and incomplete; the meaning of it is not entirely clear. But if we speak in terms of the overall thrust of his thought, it would appear that he would not grant the ruler's own capacity to achieve effective governing, but would see that as dependent on his legally established authority and on his real sources of strength.[34] Moreover, the

---

[32] *Han Fei Tzu*, ch. 40, "Nan Shih." *Ch.* 28, "Kung ming," also says: "The person who has talent but lacks power, even though worthy will not be able to impose his rule over the unworthy. To illustrate, set up a foot-long piece of timber·on top a high mountain and it can then overlook the valleys a thousand rods below it. That is not because the timber is long, but because its position is lofty. Chieh as Son of Heaven was able to impose his rule over the empire, not because he was worthy but because his power was great. Yao as a common fellow could not straighten out the affairs of three families, not because he was unworthy but because his status was low."

[33] The text is corrupt; the alteration here follows Wang Hsien-shen's emendation, [and clearly borrows from Liao's translation].

[34] Note number 32 quotes the passage beginning "Chieh as Son of Heaven," etc., from "Kung ming," *ch.* 28, which appears to be indicating what modern usage would designate legally defined authority. "Jen chu," *ch.* 52, says: "The reason horses can bear

capacity to wield that authority and force is further dependent on the position that the ruler occupies. The people recognize the ruler's position and obey him; the ruler relies on that position in order to command the people. All of these variously relevant elements constitute what Han Fei Tzu called power. The individual's ethical qualities and talents bear no direct relationship to that. For the reason why the people carry out the commands of a ruler who relies on his position in issuing those is not because they issued from a sage or a worthy, but because they issued from a ruler. Were the people to assess the ethical qualities of the one issuing commands in order to decide whether or not to obey those, then the commands themselves would have lost all force of authority. To push that argument to its limits, there then would exist only ethical sanctions in society, and there would be no political decrees. "Chieh [the incompetent tyrant], in the role of Son of Heaven, could impose his rule on the whole empire." The reason is that Chieh possessed what all the people in common recognized as authority and force. "Yao [who subsequently became a great sage ruler], while still a common man, could not keep three persons in good order." The underlying reason is that morality does not constitute a political decree. European political thinkers have often expressed this principle. In China, those who first elucidated it were Kuan Tzu, Shen Tao, and Han Fei Tzu.

The debating opponent [supplied by Han Fei Tzu in the chapter quoted] says that [the tyrants] Chieh and Chou, utilizing their royal power, were able to throw the world into chaos; his skepticism centers on the inadequacy of power to achieve good government. Han Fei Tzu again responds with an explanation whose central idea is that governing by power assumes one condition: that most rulers will have mediocre talents. Thus even if one cannot prevent inferior talents from occasionally creating chaos, neither need the world wait for the highly exceptional, superior talent to come along before there can be good government. He says: "Yao and Shun [sage rulers] as well as Chieh and Chou [tyrants and incompetents] appear only once in a thousand generations; the other types, different from [those extreme cases], are produced in shoulder-to-shoulder, toe-to-heel profusion. Those ruling in this world have formed a continuous sequence of middling talents. These mediocre persons cannot compare with Yao and Shun at the top; yet neither do they become Chiehs and Chous at the bottom. When they embrace the laws and assume their place of power, good governing results. When they turn their backs on the laws and abandon their power, chaos ensues. Now to reject power

heavy burdens and pull loads long distances is the strength of their muscles. The lord over [a state possessing] ten-thousand war chariots, or the ruler having a thousand war chariots, can impose rule on the empire and send campaigns to subdue the feudal princes because of his awesomeness and power. That awe and power are the ruler's muscular strength."

and repudiate the laws while waiting for a Yao or a Shun to appear, so that with the Yao or the Shun there will be good government, is to go through a thousand reigns of chaos to achieve one of good order. To embrace the laws and assume the power while waiting for a Chieh or a Chou to emerge, even though with the Chieh or the Chou there will be chaos, is to have a thousand reigns of good order and only one of chaos." Moreover, what he calls "not waiting for a Yao or a Shun" means that we can obtain good governing with rulers of only middling talents by utilizing the power of the position; it does not imply any willingness to bestow that royal power on a Chieh or a Chou. The critic of his argument raises the alternatives of the sage ruler and the mad man, so casts doubts on the rule by power. For, if one "in discussing governing, should use the cases of Yao and Shun, or else insist upon the chaos induced by Chieh and Chou, it is as if flavors had to be categorized either with sweet gluten and honey, or with bitter-greens and sour-parsley. In short, it is a forced argument composed of contentious wordiness, unreasoning, and unskilled, a false dilemma of extremes."[35]

Nonetheless, if the one exercising power, *shih*, should be of inferior talent and, like Chieh and Chou, bring the world to chaos, what should be done? Here, too, Han Fei Tzu firmly maintains his elevation-of-the-ruler doctrine. He believed that servitors and common people alike must display loyalty even to a vicious overlord, and opposed Mencius' statement [that a king so unkingly as those symbolic tyrants] "is but a common fellow who can be killed." [*Mencius*, 1/ii/8/3; this could also be expressed: "Tyrannicide is not regicide."] Therefore Han Fei Tzu wrote: "Yao, Shun, T'ang [the Shang Founder], and Wu [who effected the Chou conquest, i.e., all paragons], each at some time or another violated the principles of the ruler-servitor relationship and in so doing are guilty of confusing the teachings of later ages. Yao while the ruler made a servitor the ruler. Shun while a servitor made the ruler a servitor. T'ang and Wu while servitors slew their rulers and applied mutilating punishments to their corpses. Yet the whole world has lauded them. It is for such reasons that the world still, to this day, does not have orderly government."

Han Fei Tzu no doubt felt that the constant norm for the world was: "Servitors serve their ruler; sons serve their fathers; wives serve their husbands." Rulers and fathers enjoyed the exercise of absolute authority; servitors and sons must fulfill unlimited obligations and duties. "Even though the ruler is unworthy, the servitor dares not infringe his interests." Servitors and sons, no matter how worthy, can be employed only by rulers and fathers. "The reason why a father hopes for a worthy son is that, if the family is poor, he may enrich it; if the father is in distress, he

---

[35] *Ch.* 40, "Nan shih."

may bring joy to him. The reason why a ruler hopes to have worthy servitors is that, when the country is in disorder, they may bring about order; should the ruler be insignificant, they may bring about his eminence. Now, should there be worthy sons who do not work for their father's interests, the father will experience difficulties in managing his household. Should there be worthy servitors who do not strive for their ruler's interests, the ruler will face peril in his royal position. In those situations for fathers to have worthy sons and rulers to have worthy servitors is quite enough to constitute a disadvantage; how could they gain any benefits from that?" That is to say, going one step further, that not only can servitors and sons not be permitted to take any advantages away from rulers and fathers, even to engage in indirect evaluation of them is something their status does not allow. "For, should a son be always praising other person's parents, saying 'so-and-so's parents go to bed late and get up early, work very hard to earn more so they can take care of sons and grandsons and keep men and women servants,' so to speak is to slander one's parents. And should a servitor always be extolling the former kings for their great virtues, and wish that their likes might again appear, he is slandering his own ruler. . . . Therefore, it is the servitor who never praises Yao's and Shun's worthy qualities, who never praises the conquests of T'ang and Wu, who never speaks of noble heroes' loftiness, but who exerts all of his own strength to maintaining the laws, and devotes his whole mind to the service of his ruler, who is the loyal servitor."[36]

The Confucians have high praise for the great merit of turning thrones over to the most worthy successors [instead of to sons], and of suppressing tyrants. They also detested the regicide and the usurpation committed by rebellious ministers and villainous sons. For the Confucians held the people to be the objective of politics, and regarded ethics as the standard of life. Therefore they could charge rulers with failures of ritual proprieties, and could blame servitors for failures of loyalty, hold fathers guilty for failures of loving concern, and sons guilty for failures of filial submission. Rulers had no absolute authority, while superior and inferior [in all social relationships] had mutual responsibilities. Although sons had no justification for rebelling against fathers, servitors had the obligation to correct their rulers. Whether servitors and people should serve and obey depended on the factor of whether or not the ruler was ethical.

Han Fei Tzu's elevation of the ruler was wholly different from that. According to his theories about rule by power, the servitors and the people were charged with the duty of absolute obedience, regardless of the ruler's personal conduct. Thus the ruler in his own person became the ultimate

---

[36] *Ch.* 51, "Chung hsiao."

objective of politics, and its sole standard. Likewise, this governing by power became the most logical theory for monarchic despotism. The Confucians merged ethics and politics into one in their discourses, retaining some of the coloring of ancient thought. As Han Fei Tzu discussed power, he set ethics completely outside the realm of politics, and established a wholly political kind of political thought, having thereby a modern flavor.[37] Regardless of whether its content is appropriate and acceptable, it has a very significant place in history. Confucians of Sung and Ming times [the Neo-Confucian formative era] did not realize that although Confucianism and Legalism both elevate the ruler, their principles in so doing are fundamentally different. They loudly proclaimed the teachings about the "three bonds" [i.e., those binding ruler and servitor, father and son, and husband and wife] and declared themselves the transmitters of Confucius' and Mencius' teachings. In fact they were unknowingly serving Shen Tao and Han Fei Tzu, "acknowledging a bandit to be their father" [to use an appropriate Chinese saying]. Moreover, they failed to maintain rigorously their own school's standards; along with the subtle significance of the teachings about prizing virtue and valuing the common people, they also interpolated authoritarian theories. In consequence, when one on the lowest level of talent took over the imperial power, he too would claim the noble name of a Yao or a Shun, and, uninhibited by any restraints, could inflict evils on the people many times more severe than those of Chieh and Chou. Thus we must note that the unfortunate consequences of that subsequently confused identity [literally: "neither ass nor horse"] were not felt only on the level of theory.[38]

We should also note that Han Fei Tzu not only placed ethics beyond the scope of politics, but he also regarded personal ethics and political needs as mutually incompatible, and attacked the former. The Confucians attached an extreme degree of importance to family and clan, to the point that when duties to family and to the state were in conflict they advocated foregoing the state in the interests of the family.[39] Han Fei Tzu

[37] Students of European political thought history customarily regard Niccolo Machiavelli, 1469–1527, as the forerunner of modern thought. One reason for that is that Machiavelli's Il Principe clearly sets ethics beyond the scope of politics.

[38] Reference may be made to the last portion of Section Six in Chapter Three of the present work. Also, Chang Ping-lin [1868–1936] in his T'ai-yen wen-lu, ch. 1, in the essay "Shih Tai," discussing the calamitous consequences of "relying primarily on laws yet mixing in elements of [the ethical teaching of] Ch'eng-Chu School Neo-Confucianism," in the Ming dynasty, also offers views that are relevant to this point.

[39] Analects, "Tzu-lu," Book Thirteen: "The Duke of Sheh said to Confucius: 'In my country there is a man called honest Kung. His father took a sheep and his son gave evidence against him.' Confucius said: 'In my country the upright men are of quite another sort. A father will screen his son, and a son his father—which does involve a kind of

completely reversed that principle. Therefore we read in *ch.* 49, "Wu Tu": "In the State of Ch'u there once was an honest man named Kung whose father stole a sheep, and who reported that to the local official. The magistrate said: 'Put him to death,' regarding the son as honest toward his ruler but treacherous toward his father. So the man [Kung] was punished. Looked at this way, the ruler's honest servitor may be the son who subjects his father to violence. There was a man in Lu who accompanied his Duke into war. In three battles he fled three times. Confucius asked him why he had done that. He replied: 'I have an old father, and if I am killed there will be no one to care for him.' Confucius looked upon him as [nobly] filial, and commended him highly. Looked at this way, the father's filial son is the ruler's treacherous servitor. Of course, after the magistrate ordered the execution [of honest Kung], no more crimes were reported in Ch'u, and, after Confucius' praise, the people of Lu were very apt to surrender or flee in battle. Thus are the interests of superior and inferior different."

Private ethical standards, moreover, are especially apt to be in conflict with the state's interests. *Ch.* 47, "Pa Shuo," says: "To perform a private favor for an old friend is called being faithful in friendship. Using public funds to make gifts to the poor is called being benevolent. To disdain income but preserve one's personal standards is called being a superior man. To subvert the laws in order to protect one's family is called having principles. Not to support the officials in order to favor a crony is called displaying a knightly sense of justice. To detach oneself from mundane interests and foresake one's responsibilities toward superiors is called being highminded. To take up disputes and disobey the ordinances is called showing unswerving spirit. To pass out favors and gain a mass following is called winning the people." *Ch.* 46, "Liu fan," also says: "One who fears death and avoids difficulties is a person who would surrender or retreat, yet the world will honor him as a gentleman who reveres life. One who studies the ways [of antiquity] and proposes his own solutions to problems is a person who would discredit the laws, yet the world will honor him as a gentleman of refined learning. One who dwells in idleness and enjoys lavish support is a person who [in effect] steals his food, yet the world will honor him as a gentleman of talent. One who twists words and pretends

---

uprightness.' " [Modified from Waley, *Analects*, xiii/18, pp. 175–76.] The *Mencius*, "Chinhsin, Part One," also has: "'T'ao Ying asked: 'Shun being sovereign, and Kao-yao chief minister of justice, if [Shun's father] Ku-sou had murdered a man, what would have been done in the case?' Mencius said: 'Shun would have regarded giving up his kingdom as throwing away a worn-out sandal. He would privately have taken his father on his back, and retired into concealment, living somewhere along the sea-coast. There he would have lived out his life, happy and cheerful, forgetting the kingdom.' " [*Mencius*, vii/i/35; slightly modified from Legge, pp. 469–70.]

to great knowledge is a person who would lie and cheat, yet the world will honor him as a gentleman of discriminating intelligence. One who wields a sword, attacks people, and commits murders is a person who lives by violence and arrogance, yet the world will honor him as a gentleman of upright courage. One who rescues robbers and shelters evil-doers is a person who merits death, yet the world will honor him as a gentleman of knightly virtues."[40]

Han Fei Tzu's purpose in destroying the concept of personal ethics is, quite obviously, to eliminate the private for the benefit of the public. To state that differently: all aspects of moral conduct and good reputation that are not beneficial to ruler and state are rejected by him. To extend his theory to its limits: government and society should leave virtually no room for the individual's private life. The Confucians believed that when in extremity the individual should preserve his virtue in solitude, retire from public life in order to maintain his standards, that constituting one of the varieties of the noble life. As Han Fei Tzu saw the matter, such behavior should not be tolerated by the nation's laws. Thus he cited the example of T'ai-kung Wang's [Duke of the State of Ch'i] telling the Duke of Chou why he had put to death two recluses [who would not render service in his state], saying: "Their refusal to serve the Son of Heaven was evidence that I would not be able to govern over them. That they would not associate with the feudal lords was evidence that I would not be able to command them. They tilled for food, dug a well for drink, and sought nothing of other men. That was evidence that I would not be able to encourage or intimidate them with rewards and punishments. Moreover, their refusal to accept any title from above indicated that, despite their learning, I would not be able to employ them. They had no desire for emolument from the ruler, indicating that, despite their worthy qualities, they would not perform any tasks for me. In not serving, they were ungovernable; in not holding office, they were disloyal."[41] If such as these were not to be executed, who should be?

---

[40] The same passage continues: "One who rushes into dangers and is a martyr to honor is a person who would die rather than lose virtue, yet the world will demean him as a fellow whose calculations have gone awry. One of simple learning who obeys commands is a person who will observe all the laws, yet the world will demean him as a simple-minded fellow. One who toils to eat is a person who will be productive, yet the world will demean him as a fellow of no skills. One who is generous and pure-minded is a person of upright goodness, yet the world will demean him as a mindlessly foolish fellow. One who seriously accepts orders and meticulously deals with public affairs is one who will respect his superiors, yet the world will demean him as a cowardly fellow. One who resists robbers and stops evil-doers is one who will uphold the instructions received from above, yet the world will demean him as a flattering troublemaker." Also, *ch.* 45, "Kuei shih," has a passage of similar wording and intent.

[41] *Ch.* 34, "Wai chu shuo, yu shang." See also *Mencius*, "T'eng Wen-kung, Part Two,"

Han Fei Tzu's elevation of the ruler and suppression of the people must be said to have reached the extremes. The historical factors influencing that have been discussed above, and those points need not be restated here. The theoretical bases of that, however, demand careful note. Hsün Tzu said that man's nature is evil, but that man can do good. The various Legalist thinkers all went one step beyond him in declaring that man's nature is evil and that he is incapable of good. Therefore their harsh and ruthless policies, and sole reliance on awesome power, constituted but the theoretically inescapable consequences of that view. Han Fei Tzu had decided that selfishness is the basic nature of humans, and that it prevails even over interests of family, and of flesh and blood kinship. "The attitude of fathers and mothers toward their children is such that when a baby boy is born, there are mutual congratulations, yet when a baby girl is born they disregard [some interpretations say "kill"] her. Both are produced from the parents themselves, yet boys are loved and rejoiced over while girls are cast aside [or "killed"]. That is because the parents are concerned about the later advantages and are calculating the long-range benefits. So, it is apparent, even fathers and mothers adjust their attitudes toward their own children according to the calculating mind; how much more does that prevail when that element of parental affection is lacking?"[42]

Humans, moreover, not only are deficient in the deeper feelings of benevolence and generosity, still more are they lacking in far-sighted judgment and perceptions. "The intelligence of the common people is worthless, just as is the mind of an infant. If an infant's head does not get shaved [i.e., the popular hygienic practice], the pains will recur, and if his sores are not lanced, they will get larger. When his head is being shaved or his boil is being lanced, nonetheless, he must be held in someone's embrace while the loving mother performs the task, and even so he will scream and cry continuously. For the infant does not realize that thus causing him a small discomfort will bring him great benefit. . . . Long ago [the great Emperor] Yü channeled the Yangtze and deepened the Yellow River [to drain flooded lands], yet the people gathered tiles and

---

where he grants that Wu-ling Chung Tzu is to be regarded as one of the great and worthy personages in the State of Ch'i [although he was unwilling to associate with any persons, including family members, who served the state]. *Chan-kuo ts'e*, "Ch'i ts'e, Part Four," there is the anecdote in which the Duchess Wei of the State of Chao asks the envoy from Ch'i: "Is Wu-ling Chung Tzu still alive? It is this man's principle that he will not serve his king above, nor assume his family duties below, and in between [those two social levels] he will have no association with the feudal lords. He leads the people into ways that are useless. Why have you still not put him to death?" This story and that in the *Han Fei Tzu* can be seen as elucidating each other. Hsün Tzu also implied that there was no private life beyond the scope of politics; see the final paragraphs in Chapter Three, Section Five, of the present work.

[42] *Ch.* 46, "Liu fan." [Cf. W. K. Liao, *Han Fei Tzu*, vol. II, p. 239.]

stones [to throw at him]. Likewise, Tzu-ch'an cleared fields and planted mulberry trees, but the people of Cheng slandered and reviled him. Yü benefitted the world, and Tzu-ch'an preserved Cheng [through his rigorous administrative measures], yet the both of them were vilified. Thus it is very clear that the people's intelligence is not worth relying on."[43] Since human nature is so churlish and uncharitable, so senseless and benighted as all this, then men cannot be transformed by kindness and good will and benevolent teachings. Truly, only the political devices of authoritarianism and overwhelming monarchic awe can bring about a well-governed people. Therefore Han Fei Tzu wrote: "It is the nature of the people that they are quite submissive to power, but how rare it is that they truly cherish righteousness." For, despite Confucius' sageliness, he was able to bring about the submission to his will of no more than his seventy immediate followers, while so mediocre an individual as was Duke Ai of the State of Lu [who reigned 494–465 B.C., and who drove Confucius to frustration] could impose his commands on an entire state. [See *ch*. 49, where this comparison is more fully developed.]

"Take the case of a boy lacking good qualities. Though his parents become angry with him, he will not change his ways. Though the villagers scold him, he will be unmoved. Though his teachers and elders instruct him, he will not be transformed. . . . But should the county magistrate call in the soldiers to enforce the laws, and to seek out evil-doers, then he will be shaken for fear, reform his standards and alter his conduct."[44] The Confucians are fond of saying that after the family is regulated, then the state can achieve good government. [*The Great Learning*; cf. Legge, p. 359.] This statement from Han Fei Tzu, on the contrary, virtually says that only when the state is under proper government can the family become regulated. This not only runs contrary to Confucian views, but also is obviously quite different from the *Kuan Tzu's* view that the family can serve as a tool to help achieve good government.

The Confucians also repeatedly express their belief that the customs of high antiquity were pure and admirable, and should be taken as a model by the present age. Han Fei Tzu demolished that theory, stating: "In early antiquity people strove to attain virtue; in the middle era they aspired to be wise; and in these present times they fight to be strong. In

---

[43] *Ch*. 50, "Hsien hsüeh." [Cf. Liao, *op.cit*., pp. 309 and 310.] See the *Tso Chuan*, Thirtieth year of Duke Hsiang [542 B.C.], where it is recorded that when Tzu-ch'an first applied his rigorous measures, the people gave vent to their hatred of him in a ditty the last two lines of which read: "Who will kill Tzu-ch'an?/I shall be with him." However, three years later, hatred turned into admiration, and the people sang him praise: "Should Tzu-ch'an ever die,/Who possibly could succeed him?" [English note added by K. C. Hsiao for this translation.]

[44] *Ch*. 49, "Wu tu," or "Five Vermin of the State." [Modified from Watson, p. 103.]

early antiquity problems were few and things were simple; life was crude and rustic, with many things wanting. Thus they used clam shells for hoes, and men pushed carts. In early antiquity, people were few, and were kind to each other; material things were plentiful, so people were unconcerned about advantage, and willing to defer to each other. That is why at that time there were examples of bowing in deference to others and in that manner transferring the succession to the throne."[45] "In early antiquity, men did not till, for the fruits and grains of the trees and grasses supplied enough to eat. Women did not weave, for the skins of animals supplied enough to make clothing. Without engaging in labor there was enough to supply men's needs. People were few and goods were abundant; therefore the people did not quarrel and fight. That is why generous rewards were not given out, why severe punishments were not employed; yet the people kept themselves in good order. Now, in the present times, when people have five sons it is not regarded as many, and as their sons each have five sons, a grandfather will have twenty-five grandsons by the time he dies. So people have become numerous, and goods scarce. People labor intensively and yet the supply of men's needs remains insufficient. Therefore people quarrel and fight. Even though rewards are doubled and punishments are made more severe, disorder is not prevented. . . . Thus when people of antiquity were casual about the material goods, it was not because they were benevolent, but because goods were plentiful. When men today fight and plunder, it is not that they are base, but that the material goods are scarce."[46]

Thus we see the pure customs of early antiquity could not conceal that human nature is basically evil. The fighting and plundering of later ages fully demonstrate that man lacks the capacity for good. Monarchic despotism truly is the form of government required to bring peace and order to a disorderly world. Moreover, while Han Fei Tzu admitted that men of early antiquity possessed a capacity for self-government, Lord Shang denied that. His *ch*. 7, "K'ai se," says: "During the time when heaven and earth were first established and the people were produced, people knew their mothers but not their fathers. Their way was to love their relatives and to be fond of what was their own. From loving their relatives came discrimination, and from fondness of what was their own, insecurity. As the people increased and were preoccupied with discrimination and insecurity, they fell into disorder. At that time, people were intent on excelling others, and subjugated each other by means of force; the former led to quarrels and the latter to disputes. If in disputes there

---

[45] *Ch*. 47, "Pa shuo." [A philological note, the import of which has been conveyed by the translation, is omitted.]

[46] *Ch*. 49, "Wu tu."

were no justice, no one would be satisfied; therefore men of talent established equity and justice and instituted unselfishness, so that people began to talk of [or, to rejoice in] moral virtue. At that time, the idea of loving one's relatives began to disappear, and that of honoring the worthy arose. In general, virtuous men are concerned with the fondness for one's own things; likewise, the way of worthy men is to outvie one another. As people increased and were not restrained and had for long been in the way of outvying one another, there was again disorder. Therefore, a sage took over, made distinctions of land and property, and of men and women [i.e., allotting property, rights and duties]. Distinctions having been established, it was necessary to have restraining measures, so he instituted prohibitions. Prohibitions being instituted, it was necessary to have those who could enforce them, so he established officials. Officials having been established, it was necessary to have someone to unify them, so he set up a prince. Once a prince had been set up, the idea of elevating the worthy disappeared, and that of prizing honor arose. Thus in early antiquity, people loved their relatives and were fond of what was their own; in the middle era, they elevated the worthy and talked of moral virtue; and in later ages, they prized honor and venerated office. . . . Loving one's relatives means making selfishness one's guiding principle, but the idea of equity and justice is to prevent selfishness from holding the field. . . . Elevating the worthy means outvying one another with doctrines, but setting up a prince means relegating the worthy to unemployment."[47]

Lord Shang and Han Fei Tzu held views such as these about the development of society.[48] In their repudiation of Confucian views, such as

[47] *Shang-chün shu, ch.* 7, "K'ai Se." The same chapter also says: "Of old, people lived densely together and all dwelt in disorder, so they desired that there should be a ruler." [The translation follows, with slight modification, that of Duyvendak, in his *Book of Lord Shang,* pp. 225–27, 232.]

[48] Fung Yu-lan, in his *Chung-kuo che-hsüeh shih* ["History of Chinese Philosophy"], Volume One, p. 387, has said: "Though this division into three ages of 'early antiquity,' 'the middle era,' and 'the recent age' may not be wholly appropriate from the view of anthropology and sociology, when we apply it to the history of the Spring and Autumn and the Warring States Periods, we find that segment of history can indeed be divided into three such periods." The early portion of the Spring and Autumn Period was a period of aristocratic government, and it was an age when: "in early antiquity, people loved their relatives and were fond of what was their own." Subsequently, as men from the commoner class could obtain power, the Confucians and the Mohists both advocated "elevating the worthy and employing the capable" [*Mo Tzu*] and that one should "overflow in love to all, and cultivate the friendship of the good [*jen*]." [*Analects* 1/6; Legge, p. 140.] Thus it was an age when "in the middle era they elevated the worthy and talked of benevolence [*jen*]." Because rulers of states or one or two noble families began elevating the worthy, gaining thereby the assistance of worthy and capable persons, they could eliminate views differing from their own and establish one single pre-eminent standard; then the worthy commenced competing for dominance, using the tools of talent and knowledge, in short:

transforming through virtue, and that the people are the fundamental value, as also in their insistence on a polity relying exclusively on monarchic power to achieve order, their logic, at least, cannot be faulted.

SECTION THREE
Agriculture and War

ONCE the ruler assumes the position of full authority and wields power [*shih*] by which to control his servitors and people, the most important of the political and social conditions are fulfilled. But all the other states lie in waiting on all sides, from time to time making aggressive incursions; the state that lacks the force derived from agricultural wealth and military strength will not have the means to survive. Lord Shang said: ". . . that through which the county is important, and that through which the ruler is honored, is strength."[49] Han Fei Tzu also said: "When one's strength is great, others come to pay court; when one's strength is weak, one must pay court to others. Therefore the enlightened ruler devotes his efforts toward acquiring strength."[50] The means of acquiring strength are those whereby the people are made to devote their lives to two activities: agriculture and war. Anything else, whether it merely fails to contribute to those two, or positively detracts from them, must be suppressed. For diligent application to farming can build up economic strength, while training in warfare can build up military strength; these are clear and self-evident principles.[51] Nor were they original ideas with Lord Shang and

---

"outvying each other with doctrines." But after a long period of "outvying each other with doctrines, there was again disorder," so that rulers and princes came to detest all that, and again imposed controls and restrictions on it. The final phase of the Warring States Period was one when: ". . . in later ages they prized honor and venerated office." Setting up a prince means relegating the worthy [who had become specialists in manipulating competing doctrines in order to gain power as chief ministers] to unemployment"; this "came as a reaction to the evils inherent in the preceding period of honoring the talented. This tendency toward the concentration of power was the basis upon which the governments of the latter part of the Warring States Period rested." Fung's views here are in the main quite correct. This amply reveals that the Legalists represented renovating thought trends at that time, adapting to the tide of developments. Also, Legalists like Han Fei Tzu were highly conscious of historical facts in working out their theories, for in support of each separate concept they drew on actual human events of past and present as precedents and proofs. In this, their methods also somewhat resembled those of Machiavelli. [See Fung/Bodde, p. 316, for the translation of the full argument.]

[49] *Ch.* 25, "Shen fa." [Duyvendak, *Lord Shang*, p. 325.]

[50] *Ch.* 50, "Hsien hsüeh."

[51] Lord Shang, in his *ch.* 6, "Suan ti," says: "Indeed, having a large territory and not cultivating it is like having no territory; having a numerous population but not employing it is like having no population." [Duyvendak, *Lord Shang*, p. 216.]

Han Fei Tzu.[52] Yet it was these two men whose stress on agriculture and war went so far that they would have liked virtually to destroy and expunge all of a nation's thought, learning, and culture, and to make of the government and society a Spartan type of fighting organization. Herein lies the uniqueness of their views; in this they are unmatched in all of Chinese antiquity.

To encourage the people in agriculture and warfare, it is first of all necessary to get rid of the wandering scholars who traveled about in search of employment, peddling their theories. The *Book of Lord Shang*, says: "If there are a thousand people engaged in agriculture and war, and only one in the *Odes* and the *History* and in clever sophistry, then those thousand will all be remiss in agriculture and war; if there are a hundred people engaged in agriculture and war and only one in the arts and crafts, then those hundred will all be remiss in agriculture and war. The country depends on agriculture and warfare for its security; and likewise the ruler depends on agriculture and warfare for his eminence. If indeed the people are not engaged in agriculture and warfare, it means that the ruler is fond of words [i.e., of theories and philosophical views] and that the officials have failed in their regular duties."[53]

The *Han Fei Tzu* also says: "Erudite and polished, discerning and knowledgeable as were Confucius and Mo Tzu, neither Confucius nor Mo Tzu tilled and cultivated, so what did the state gain from them? Cultivated in filial piety, austere in controlling desires as were Tseng Tzu and Shih Ch'iu [the former being the respected author of the *Hsiao Ching*, the latter, also known to Confucius as Shih Yü, served nobly in Wei], neither Tseng nor Shih could go into battle or join in an attack, so what did the state gain from them?"[54] Moreover, those who positively hurt agriculture and warfare were not limited to those "who practice correctness and faithfulness" [and who thereby become known as the worthy men of their time], or to those purveyors of "subtle and unfathomable doctrines" [by which men come to be known as wise]. For even those who devote their discourses to practical and applied learning, yet do not

[52] Kuan Tzu earlier had discussed the importance of agricultural wealth and military strength [*fu-ch'iang*], but with less thoroughness than Lord Shang and Han Fei Tzu. It should be noted the Confucius also had replied "sufficiency of food, sufficiency of military equipment" to Tzu-kung's question about the requisites of government (*Analects*, "Yen Yuan" xii/7). Hsün Tzu's writings also include chapters on such subjects as *ch*. 10, "On Enriching the State" and *ch*. 15, "On Military Matters." The Confucians also attached importance to military and agricultural affairs. But their objective was not to enlarge the ruler's power; in that they were in distinct contrast to Lord Shang and Han Fei Tzu, and this point should be kept in mind.

[53] *Ch*. 3, "Nung chan"; also, "Shen fa," *ch*. 25 expresses more or less identical ideas. [Translation slightly modified from Duyvendak, *Lord Shang*, p. 189.]

[54] *Ch*. 47, "Pa shuo" [Cf. Liao, *Han Fei Tzu*, p. 251.]

in person participate in military and agricultural tasks, also are detrimental to good government. "Nowadays everyone under the sun talks about problems of governing, and in every family there are kept copies of the *Laws* of Lord Shang and of Kuan Tzu, and the state grows ever poorer. For flocks of people talk about tillage, but few indeed set their hands to a plow. Everyone in the realm talks about military matters, and in every family there are kept copies of the treatises [on warfare] of Sun Tzu and of Wu Ch'i, and the armies grow weaker and weaker. Those who talk about warfare are numerous, but few indeed even don armor."[55]

Lord Shang and Han Fei Tzu propose rather similar ideas about how to induce better performance in agriculture and in war. The basic outline of their policies is expressed in the sentence: "The soldiers should have full benefit of the profits on the frontiers, and farmers should have full benefit from the profits of the market."[56] Han Fei Tzu's concrete methods for carrying out this policy do not go beyond what is set forth in *ch.* 49, "Wu tu," where it says: "In the state of the enlightened ruler there is no literature written on bamboo slips, but the laws serve as the teaching. There are no sayings of the ancient kings; magistrates act as teachers. And there is no valor through private swords; instead, courage will be demonstrated by those who decapitate the enemy in battle. Consequently, among the people within the borders of the state, whoever talks must follow the law, whoever acts must aim at accomplishment, and whoever shows courage must do so exclusively in the army. Thus the state will be rich when at peace and the army will be strong when things happen." [Largely following W. T. Chan, *Source Book*, p. 260.]

What Lord Shang called his laws for "unifying rewards" and for "unifying teachings"[57] were intended to make sure that ". . . the gate to

---

[55] *Ch.* 49, "Wu tu." Also, in *ch.* 32, "Wai chu shuo, tso shang," where Li Tz'u reports back to the Sovereign Father of the King of Chao on conditions in the State of Chung-shan, saying that because the ruler there is fond of favoring recluses living in grottoes and caves, the common people have grown lax in agriculture and warfare; therefore the state is susceptible to successful attack.

[56] *Book of Lord Shang*, *ch.* 22, "Nei wai." It says, further: "If one wishes to enrich the country through agriculture, then within the borders grain prices must be high, taxes on those who are not farmers must be many, and dues on market-profit must be heavy [with the result that people are forced to have land]." Also, *ch.* 6, "Suan ti" says: "If profits come from the soil, then people will use their strength to the full; if fame results from war, then they will fight to the death." [Translations follow, with slight modification, those of Duyvendak, *Lord Shang*, pp. 313 and 219.]

[57] *Ch.* 17, "Shang hsing," says: "What I mean by unifying rewards is that profits and emoluments, office and rank, should be determined exclusively by military merit, and that there should be no other reasons for distributing them." And: "What I mean by unifying teachings is that all those proponents of wide scholarship, sophistry, cleverness, good faith, integrity, rites and music, and moral culture, whether their reputations are unsullied or foul, should not for any reasons [deriving from association with those doc-

riches and noble status has its approach in soldiering; then, when people hear of war, they congratulate each other and whether at work or at rest, at times of drinking or eating, they will sing songs of war."[58] Lord Shang, moreover, not only worked to implement a national military education for the people; he also advocated the idea that every subject of the state should be available for military service. His *ch.* 12, "Ping shou," says that: ". . . one army should be formed of able-bodied men, one of able-bodied women, and one the old and feeble men and women. These are called the three armies. Cause the army of able-bodied men, with abundant provisions and sharp weapons, to marshall themselves, and to await the enemy. Cause the able-bodied women, with abundant provisions and ramparts at their backs, to marshall themselves and to await orders, so at the approach of the invading force they can dig earthworks, form obstructions and pitfalls, pull out bridge timbers and tear down buildings, . . . so that the invaders will acquire nothing that could assist their attack. Cause the army of the old and feeble to guard the oxen, horses, sheep and swine, and to collect all consumable products of earth and water in order to feed people, thereby obtaining food for the able-bodied men and women." [Modified from Duyvendak, *Lord Shang*, pp. 250–51.] These practices persisted so that in the [subsequent] Han period throughout all the commanderies of the Kuan-hsi region [i.e., the region comprising the former State of Ch'in in modern Shensi and the further northwest] "the women still carry spears and halberds, or have bows at their sides and arrows on their backs."[59] This bears witness to Lord Shang's success in unifying rewards and unifying teachings.

However, this extreme position in stressing war was not adopted by Han Fei Tzu. His view was: "Lord Shang's *Laws* say: 'For cutting off one head [in battle], a person is to be promoted one grade in rank, and if

---

trines] be allowed to become rich or acquire noble status. Neither can they be allowed to discuss punishments, nor compose their private views independently and memorialize their superiors about them. The strong should be broken and the sharp should be blunted. Although one may be called a sage, or wise, or clever, or eloquent, or liberal, or simple, yet none who lack merit may monopolize the ruler's favors, but the gate to riches and noble status should lie in war and in nothing else." [Following, with minor modifications, the translation of Duyvendak, *Lord Shang*, pp. 275 and 282.]

[58] *Ch.* 17, "Shang hsing" [Duyvendak, *Lord Shang*, p. 283].

[59] *Hou Han Shu, ch.* 100, "Cheng T'ai chuan." Also, in Ch'iao Chou's *Ku-shih k'ao* (the text reconstructed by Sun Hsing-yen, included in the *P'ing-chin-kuan ts'ung-shu*), it says: "The State of Ch'in adopted Shang Yang's [i.e., Lord Shang's] plan and established twenty ranks of nobility, according to which heads taken in battle were counted to calculate the noble rank to be bestowed. Thus it came to be that the people of Ch'in were victorious in all battles, that even the old and feeble, and women and children were all among the dead, and that when merit was calculated the numbers of those receiving rewards ran into the thousands." This provides evidence that the system of the three armies was put into actual practice.

the person wishes to be an official, he is to be granted a post earning fifty piculs [of grain as salary]. For cutting off two heads, a person is to be promoted two grades in rank, and if the person wishes to be an official, he is to be granted a post earning one hundred piculs.' Appointment to office and promotion in rank are thereby made equivalent to success in taking heads. Supposing we were to have a law now that said that persons who cut off heads in battle were to be appointed physicians or carpenters, houses would never get built and diseases would not be brought to halt. For carpenters have special skills of the hand, and physicians know about preparing medicines. To make persons do these things in recognition of their success in taking heads would not be appropriate to their demonstrated skills. Governmental office demands knowledge and skills. Taking heads in battle is a matter to which courage and strength contribute. Because of achievement utilizing courage and strength, to make a person an official needing knowledge and skill, is as if one appointed men physicians and carpenters because they have succeeded in cutting of heads."[60]

Section Four
Law

HAN FEI TZU said: "All the great matters of the ruler of men are matters either of law *fa*, or of methods *shu*. The laws are compiled in documents, ensconced in government offices, and promulgated among all the people. The methods are concealed within the breast, are deployed to meet all contingencies in government, and to control covertly the servitors. Thus the law works best of all when clearly revealed, while methods should not be obvious."[61] He also said: "Shen Pu-hai advocated methods and Shang Yang advocated law. Methods involve appointing officials according to individual capacities, demanding that actual performance

---

[60] *Ch.* 43, "Ting fa." Note that *The Book of Lord Shang, ch.* 19, "Ching nei," says: "If a person succeeds in cutting off one head of a person of rank, he is awarded one degree of rank, granted one *ch'ing* [or one hundred *mou*] of fields, and nine *mou* of household land, and one attendant will be appointed to him." [Cf. translation and discussion in Duyvendak, *Lord Shang*, pp. 299–300.] This shows that merit in warfare brought one both wealth and noble status. The *Han Fei Tzu* does not criticize this system for enlarging landholdings, perhaps considering it irrelevant to political issues. However, the *T'ung tien* [governmental encyclopedia dating from the late eighth century] quotes one Mr. Wu, commenting: "It was the Ch'in system that if one took in battle the head of an armed man his fields and household lands would be increased, and if the heads of five armed men were taken he would be given five households into his service. The evils of tenancy and landlordism emerged from this." Tung Chung-shu and Pan Ku of the Han dynasty (*Han shu, ch.* 24, "Shih-huo chih") both comment on the Ch'in system as having induced such faults.
[61] *Ch.* 38, "Nan san."

correspond to the titles [of offices they occupy], exercising the power of life and death, and rating the abilities of all servitors. These are powers held by the ruler. By law is meant statutes and mandates that are made manifest in offices of government, and penalties and fines that are felt in the people's minds to be inescapable. Rewards belong to those who are meticulous in observing the laws, while punishments are meted out to those who violate orders. These are things the servitors must heed. On the higher level, if the ruler is deficient in methods he will be ruined. On the lower level, if the servitors are deficient with respect to laws, there will be chaos. Neither of these can be dispensed with. They are the tools of emperors and kings."[62] Although Shen Pu-hai and Lord Shang both are famed experts on "the great matters," yet "with respect to law and methods, the two both failed to achieve perfection." [*Ch*. 43, final comment of Han Fei Tzu about them.] Moreover, to specialize in the use of only one of those tools may indeed accomplish something, but it can not produce an achievement of great scope.[63] So Han Fei Tzu thus joined the achievements of the two men, applying the methods to maintain the ruler's security while controlling his servitors, and establishing the laws to keep the people in order while stabilizing the state. The two tools of government mutually reinforced each other in application, and only thereby could their effectiveness achieve vast scope.

The fundamental significance of rule by law has been set forth in connection with our discussion of Kuan Tzu. [See p. 333–47 above.] Lord Shang and Han Fei Tzu developed no new and original views on that, but in their discourses on the ways of implementing laws they indeed went far beyond the scope of the *Kuan Tzu*. Here we may take up some of the more important aspects of that.

The first is disseminating knowledge of the laws. Making known the texts of regulations and orders to all the people is something that in fact got its start with the promulgation of the penal codes and the casting of penal tripods. In the book the *Kuan Tzu* also, we find statements about announcing the regulations and spreading instruction about them. Lord Shang and Han Fei Tzu accepted that and produced more detailed explanations of it; in the *Book of Lord Shang* these become especially complete and full. Lord Shang's principle for establishing order lay in making sure that none of the officials or common people throughout the realm

---

[62] *Ch*. 43, "Ting fa" [wording modified from Chan, *Source Book*, p. 255].

[63] *Ch*. 43, "Ting fa" states that when laws and controls are inconsistent [i.e., lacking unity]: ". . . even though Shen Pu-hai ten times advised Marquis Chao of the State of Han to use methods, yet the treacherous servitors still found excuses to twist his words. . . . Whenever there was a victory in war, the chief servitors gained prestige; whenever territories were enlarged, unauthorized fiefs were created, all because the ruler lacked methods for detecting treachery. Even though Lord Shang improved his laws ten times, the servitors simply turned them to their personal advantage." [Cf. Liao, *Han Fei Tzu*, vol. II, pp. 213 and 214.]

would be ignorant of the laws. Since the officials well knew that the people had knowledge of the laws and orders, ". . . they dare not treat the people contrary to the law, nor dare the people transgress the law, as they would come into conflict with the law officers." For when ". . . the law is clear and easy to know," then when "the ten thousands of people all know what to avoid and what to strive for, they will avoid calamity and strive for happiness, and so govern themselves." The system that Lord Shang devised was extremely close-knit. Its most eminent feature was the establishment of law officers [*fa kuan* 法官] and law-enforcing officials [*fa-li* 法吏], who were "to be the teachers of the empire." Then: "The Son of Heaven shall set up three law officers. . . . In the various prefectures and sub-prefectures of the feudal lords shall be instituted one law officer, together with government officials [*li* 吏]. . . . And moreover the aforementioned government officials and people who are desirous of knowing what the law stipulates shall all address their inquiries to these law officers, and they shall in all such cases clearly tell them about the laws and mandates about which they wish to inquire." Anyone who tampers with the text of a law or who does not answer what is asked was to be punished according to the provisions of the law under inquiry. Furthermore, all questions and answers had to be recorded under the precise date, along with the name of the responsible official, on a tally, the left half of which went to the inquirer, and the right half to be kept by the official.[64] The intent in this also is to prevent malfeasance and trickery. Han Fei Tzu spoke of "the law working best when clearly revealed," and of "[the law-enforcing] officials being the teachers."[65] Although his statement of the issue is simple and brief, his intent is identical.[66]

The second aspect is rewards and punishments serving as sanctions. That the implementation of law depends on rewards and punishments is a clearly evident principle.[67] The special feature of Lord Shang's and

[64] *Ch.* 26, "Ting fen" [Wording somewhat modified from Duyvendak, *Lord Shang*, pp. 327, 330, and 335.]

[65] *Ch.* 49, "Wu tu."

[66] In the *Shih Chi*, *ch.* 6, "Shih-huang-ti pen-chi," there is mention of the Erudit Ch'un-yü Yüeh, who urged that the ancient feudal system be adopted as model, and [the Chief Minister of Ch'in] Li Ssu, submitting the [counter] proposal to have all the books [of such old lore and learning] burned; ". . . for if there are persons who should wish to study the laws, the officials [*li*] shall be their teachers." The imperial action was to approve his proposal; that represented the implementation of Han Fei Tzu's policy.

[67] *Book of Lord Shang*, *ch.* 9, "Ts'o fa," says: "Now, the nature of man is to like titles and emoluments, and to dislike punishments and penalties. A prince institutes these two in order to guide men's wills, and to obtain what he desires [of them. Duyvendak, *Lord Shang*, pp. 241–42, modified]. *Han Fei Tzu*, *ch.* 48, "Pa ching," says: "Human feelings include likes and dislikes, therefore making it possible to apply rewards and punishments. Because rewards and punishments can be applied, prohibitions and commands can be established, and therein the course of government takes form."

Han Fei Tzu's thought is their advocacy of heavy rewards and severe penalties, not necessarily in keeping with the merit or crime to which they were applied. Lord Shang's theory about penalizing evil actions but not rewarding the good ones seems particularly extreme and unreasonable. Han Fei Tzu acknowledged that: "When rewards are generous then what [the ruler] desires to achieve will be speedily achieved; when penalties are severe, then what he desires to prohibit will be speedily achieved." His critics usually pointed out with some skepticism that generous rewards waste [the state's] wealth, while severe penalties harm the people. Such critics simply fail to observe that: "Generous rewards not only recompense the meritorious recipient but simultaneously exert a guiding influence on the entire nation." As for severe penalties, likewise: "a penalty falls severely upon one evil-doer and simultaneously brings to an end all the wrong-doing within the state," for when robbers and thieves are punished, fear strikes at the hearts of all the law-abiding people. Moreover, "What is stopped by heavy penalties would not in all cases be stopped by light penalties; whereas what is stopped by light penalties would in all cases also be prevented by severe penalties. Therefore, where the ruler establishes severe penalties all wrong-doing ceases. If all wrong-doing ceases, how can the people suffer any harm [either from the penalties of from criminal misdeeds]?"[68] Lord Shang's theoretical justifications for heavy punishments are quite similar.[69] In governing the State of Ch'in his actual administrative measures in fact corresponded closely to his theories.[70]

　　Whereas Han Fei Tzu advocated both heavy rewards and heavy penalties, Lord Shang said that: "In an orderly country, punishments

---

[68] *Ch.* 46, "Liu fan."

[69] *Lord Shang*, ch. 5, "Shou min," says: ". . . in the application of punishments, light offenses should be regarded as serious; if light offenses do not occur, serious ones have no chance of coming about. . . . If in the application of punishments, serious offenses are regarded as serious, and light offenses as light, light offenses will not cease and in consequence there will be no means of stopping the serious ones." [Changing *chih*, "to come about," to *chih*, "to stop," in the last clause. The translation follows Duyvendak, *Lord Shang*, p. 209.]

[70] *Shih Chi*, ch. 68, "Encomium" ["Tsan"] to the "Biography of Lord Shang," where the *Chi-chieh* commentary quotes [Liu Hsiang's] *Hsin Hsü* [a mid-Han dynasty work], saying: ". . . Wei Yang [i.e., *Lord Shang*, when in power in Ch'in] in the interior made a cruel use of the punishments by sword and saw, and abroad he was deeply steeped in killing by means of the war-axe. Whosoever used paces more than six feet long [i.e., as in measuring land] was punished, and whosoever threw ashes on the street incurred corporal punishment. One day he sentenced criminals, more than seven hundred men, on the brink of the Wei river, so that the water of the Wei became entirely red, and the sound of crying and weeping stirred heaven and earth." [Following Duyvendak, *Lord Shang*, pp. 6 and 7, with minor modification; the entire comment from the *Chi-chieh* commentary is translated on pp. 3–7.]

are numerous and rewards are rare," and "Therefore a good ruler punishes the bad people, but does not reward the virtuous ones."[71] The reason for Lord Shang's advocacy of this extreme position is his profound conviction that human nature lacks the capacity for good, and that government's direct function is to maintain order, and not to promote morality. To be sure, distinctions must be drawn in political life between good and evil, but the basis for such a standard must be the law, and not ethics. Those whose conduct conforms to the law are good, and those whose conduct does not conform are evil. Since keeping the law is the inescapable responsibility of every person, evil-doing then is criminal action, while doing good is merely the basic responsibility of all citizens. Arguing from this position, then ". . . rewarding the virtuous is not permissible because it is like giving rewards for not stealing." Moreover, "When punishments are heavy, people dare not transgress, and therefore there will be no punishments; because none of the people will dare to do wrong, everyone in the whole country will be virtuous, so that without rewards the people will be virtuous."[72] However, Lord Shang did not say that rewards never could be used. What he opposed was ". . . rewards bestowed for people having done what was properly to be expected of them," and he favored rewards bestowed for reporting the wrong-doings of others." Lord Shang explained this as follows: "There is no greater benefit for the people in the empire than to have order, and there is no firmer order to be obtained than by establishing a prince. For establishing a prince, there is no more comprehensive method than making law supreme. For making law supreme, there is no more urgent task than banishing wrong-doing; and for banishing wrong-doing, there is no more pervasive way than severe punishments. Therefore one whose rule prevails restrains by rewards and encourages by punishments, seeks out offenses and not virtues, and relies on punishments to make them unnecessary."[73]

Even though Lord Shang's and Han Fei Tzu's positions on severe penalties can be faulted as unreasonable and extreme views, the two thinkers' theories nonetheless are roughly compatible with modern principles in respect to equality before the law. Lord Shang proposed

[71] See respectively, ch. 7, "K'ai se," and ch. 18, "Hua ts'e" [Duyvendak, Lord Shang, pp. 230 and 288].

[72] Ch. 18, "Hua ts'e" [Duyvendak, p. 288].

[73] Ch. 7, "K'ai se" [modified from Duyvendak, pp. 232–33]. Shih Chi, ch. 68, says: "He ordered the people to be organized into groups of fives and tens mutually to control one another and to share one another's punishments. Whoever did not denounce a culprit would be cut in two; whoever denounced a culprit would receive the same reward as he who decapitated an enemy. Whoever concealed a culprit would receive the same punishment as he who surrendered to an enemy." These measures no doubt are to be regarded as part of the effort to "use rewards to maintain prohibitions, and to use punishments to effect a guiding influence."

"unifying punishments", the similarity there is especially obvious. "What I mean by the unification of punishments is that punishments should know no degree or grade, but that from ministers of state and generals down to great officers and ordinary folk, whoever does not obey the king's commands violates the interdicts of the state, or rebels against the statutes fixed by the ruler, should be guilty of death and should not be pardoned. Merit acquired in the past should not cause a decrease in the punishment for demerit later, nor should good behavior in the past cause any derogation of the law for wrong done later."[74] This is wholly at variance with feudal law, which took into consideration issues such as kinships, friendship, individual worthiness, abilities, merit and noble status in relaxing or decreasing punishments and fines.[75] The histories praise Lord Shang's governing in Ch'in: ". . . his laws and orders were enacted rigorously; in the capital he did not flatter nobles and favorites, and in the provinces he was impartial toward those who were distant, with the result that when his orders were issued, forbidden actions stopped; when his laws were published, crime ceased."[76] Even when the heir-apparent broke a law, his tutor suffered corporal punishment.[77] Thus one can say that Lord Shang had gained the basic principles in implementing laws.

Yet we must note that Kuan Tzu had made the profound observation: "When law is not implemented, it is because of violations at the top." Therefore he too wanted to correct things at the essential point, purify the source, and make the ruler personally obey the laws. It is to be regretted that Kuan Tzu failed to establish law that could be imposed on

[74] *Ch.* 17, "Shang hsing" [Duyvendak, *Lord Shang*, pp. 278–79].

[75] The *Chou Li*, *ch.* 9, "Hsiao ssu-k'ou." Also, the *Li Chi*, *ch.* 1, "Ch'ü li," says: "The rites do not extend down to the common people; the punishments are not applied upwards as far as the Great Officers." The inequality [of feudal law] is made quite obvious here.

[76] *Shih Chi*, *ch.* 68, where the *Chi-chieh* commentary quotes from the *Hsin Hsü*. In the *Chan-kuo ts'e*, *ch.* 3, "Ch'in ts'e, Part I," there is a passage of similar wording. [Cf. note 70, references to Duyvendak's translation of the *Hsin Hsü* quotation; Duyvendak also has translated the parallel passage from the *Chan-kuo ts'e*, *op.cit.*, pp. 31–32.]

[77] *Han Fei Tzu*, *ch.* 34, "Wai chu shuo, yu shang," says: "King Chuang of Ching (613–591 B.C.) once issued the Law of the Inner Gate [*Mao-men chih fa*] to the effect that 'When any Ministers, High Officers, and Princes enter the court, if the hoofs of anyone's horse walk upon the gutters, the court guard should sever his carriage-shaft with an axe and execute his coachman.' Subsequently the heir-apparent entered the court. His horses stepped onto the gutter. The guard severed his carriage-shaft and executed the driver. The heir-apparent, angry, entered and pled, weeping, to the King: 'Have that guard killed for me.' The King said, 'It is by the law that the ancestral shrine is paid reverence, that the altars of the state are venerated. It is one who can maintain the law, obey the commands, and venerate the altars of the state who is the loyal servitor of the state. Why should such a one be killed?' " This is relevant to the point at hand. [Cf. Liao, *Han Fei Tzu*, vol. II, pp. 108–09.]

the ruler, so there is still a considerable gap between his thought and European thought on the subject of rule of law. To come to Lord Shang's and Han Fei Tzu's discussions of law, the ruler there is seen as occupying a status that is above law. Whether or not be personally obeys the laws is no longer an issue, and the effort has shifted to holding imperial relatives and nobles obedient to the law. With this development the theory of monarchic authoritarianism attains maturity, and the pre-Ch'in thought centering on "rule by law" gets further and further from anything approaching modern concepts of rule of law.[78]

The third aspect is sole reliance on laws, and on laws being unaffected by private views or good conduct records. Having magistrates in the role of the people's teachers leading the way, and the sanctions of rewards and punishments bringing up the rear, there was a general expectation that the laws could be fully implemented. But if there was not exclusive reliance on those laws, though laws might be implemented, they could not long prevail; therefore both Lord Shang and Han Fei Tzu insisted that the laws and orders should be the sole standard for all of political life. Beyond the laws and commands, all private judgments and moralistic statements must be totally excluded from consideration. The reason why private opinions should be abolished is that when statements flew back and forth, filling the court, there would come to be no absolute standard of right and wrong; and once arguments had begun to confuse the issues, the objectivity of rule by law would be shaken. Lord Shang explained this as follows: "Those who are engaged in governing in this world mostly dismiss the law and place reliance on private appraisal, and this is what brings disorder in a state. The early kings hung up scales with standard weights, and fixed the length of feet and inches, and to the present day these are followed as models, because their divisions were clear. Now dismissing standard scales and yet deciding weight, or abolishing feet and inches and yet forming an opinion about length, even if carefully done, is something merchants would not adopt, because that would lack definiteness. Now if the back is turned on models and measures, and reliance is placed on private opinion, that would in all cases produce uncertainty. . . . Therefore the ancient kings understood that no reliance should be placed on individual opinions or private approval, so they set up models and made the distinctions clear. Those who fulfilled the standard were rewarded; those who harmed the public interest were punished. The application of rewards and punishments did not deviate [from the established standards];

[78] From Ch'in and Han times onward, the authoritarian polity also developed, approaching maturity; with the exception of extremely few somewhat more enlightened rulers, the implementation of rewards and punishments was always interfered with by imperial relatives and persons of high status, so that even Lord Shang's and Han Fei Tzu's intention was abandoned.

therefore people did not dispute them."[79] Han Fei Tzu also said: "In the
state of an enlightened ruler, his orders are what are most authoritative
among men's statements, and the laws are the most suitable to [men's]
affairs. Statements cannot include two of [equal] authority; laws cannot
include two of [equal] suitability. Therefore words and deeds not conforming to the laws and commands must be prohibited. Should anyone
not acting expressly on law or command attempt to deal with unexpected
happenings, respond to events, produce benefits or control affairs [i.e.,
all of the circumstances in which the professional advisors hoped to be
called upon], the ruler must, on the basis of their words, hold them
responsible for all discrepancies with the [subsequently emerging]
realities. Where their words are appropriate to those, they may be granted
large rewards, but where not appropriate they must receive severe punishment. Then foolish people fearing the punishment will not dare speak out,
and the intelligent ones will have no quarrels among themselves."[80] In
this way the laws and commands can be fully implemented; moreover,
the confusion arising from ". . . words having no definite meaning and
conduct having no constant standard"[81] simply would not arise. Moralistic
expressions and exemplary conduct tend to be especially dazzling and
misleading to people's minds, and were deeply detested by Lord Shang and
Han Fei Tzu. The *Book of Lord Shang* says: "Once the law is fixed, one
should not damage it with moralistic talk." And, further: "Once the law
is fixed, the ruler given to employing the six parasites will perish. . . .
The six parasites are the *Rites* and *Music*, *Odes* and *History*, moral culture
and virtue, filial piety and brotherly love, sincerity and faith, chastity
and integrity, benevolence and righteousness, anti-militarism, and being
ashamed to make war."[82] Han Fei Tzu's discussions on this subject are
still more penetrating. In *ch.* 47, "Pa shuo," he says: "Laws are enacted in
order to lead the people, but when literary learning also is revered, it
only arouses doubts among the people about being led by the law. Granting rewards for merit is to encourage the people, but when exemplary
conduct also is venerated, it only makes the people lazy about producing
wealth." And in *ch.* 48, "Pa ching," he says: "When righteous conduct is
publicized, the ruler's awe is divided; when tender benevolence is heeded,
the laws and statutes are destroyed. . . . The way of the enlightened ruler
is that servitors are not permitted to gain glory for righteous conduct, or

---

[79] *Ch.* 14, "Hsiu ch'üan." [Slightly modified from Duyvendak, *Lord Shang*, pp. 261–62.]

[80] *Ch.* 41, "Wen Pien." [Cf. slightly different versions in Fung/Bodde, p. 323 and Liao, *Han Fei Tzu*, vol. ii, p. 207.]

[81] *Ch.* 50, "Hsien hsüeh." The *Shih Chi, ch.* 6, tells that in the Thirty-fourth year [213 B.C.] of the First Emperor's reign [his chief minister] Li Ssu proposed "as if distinguishing black from white, to establish one supreme standard," expressing this same idea.

[82] *Ch.* 13, "Chin ling" [modified from Duyvendak, *Lord Shang*, pp. 252, 256]. [Cf. *ch.* 20, "Jo min," where the "six parasites" are defined otherwise, under six headings.]

to accomplish merit through benefitting his family. Merit and glory shall be produced only through laws of government. Anything lying beyond what is specified in the laws, though it be conduct involving difficulties, shall not bring one eminence."[83] For, ". . . any action by the chief ministers should work to elevate the ruler; any merit among the people should work to profit the ruler" [ch. 48].

To pursue this a step further, Han Fei Tzu felt that not only were virtuous acts beyond those specified in the laws, when performed by servitors and people, apt to be detrimental to the laws, even if the ruler himself should perform such acts it inevitably would produce evil consequences. "To bestow upon the poor and the distressed is what this world calls benevolence and righteousness; to take pity on the common people, and to be so compassionate that one cannot punish [the guilty], is what this world calls graciousness and love. Yet to bestow such on the poor and distressed means that persons having gained no merit shall receive rewards. To be unable to bear punishing means that violence and disorder will not be stopped."[84] These actions are not the way to achieve good order. Nonetheless, to eschew grace and benevolence, because that would throw the laws into confusion, is not to say that violent and tyrannous government can be adopted. "When a benevolent man is on the throne, those below him will be unrestrained, and will not hesitate to violate the prohibitions in the laws, hoping for fortuitous advantage and expecting favor from above. When a violent man is on the throne, the laws and commands will be irrational, and ruler and servitors will be in conflict; the people will be resentful, and rebellious thoughts will lurk in their minds. Therefore it is said: 'Benevolence and violence both are destroyers of the state.' "[85]

---

[83] "Wai chu shuo, yu hsia," ch. 35, also says: "King Chao of Ch'in was ill. The common people in every hamlet bought an ox [for sacrifice] and every household held prayers for the king. Kung-sun Shu went out and observed this, then went to the court and offered congratulations. . . . The king said: 'Fine them, every person to pay two sets of armor. To be sure, their offering prayers without having been commanded to do so shows that they love Us, and because they love Us, We shall have to alter the laws to follow their wishes, and that will disestablish the laws. To disestablish the laws is to embark upon the course of chaos and collapse.' "

[84] "Chien, chieh, shih ch'en," ch. 14. "Wai chu shuo, yu hsia," ch. 35, tells: "There was a great famine in Ch'in, and Marquis Ying petitioned: 'The plants, vegetables, nuts, dates, and chestnuts in the five imperial parks would be sufficient to keep the starving people alive; I petition to have those distributed [to the people].' King Chao-hsiang replied: 'According to our Ch'in laws, the people are to be rewarded for merit, and punished for crime. Were I now to distribute the vegetables and plants of the five parks, it would be to reward both those among the people who have achieved some merit and those who have not. To reward both those who have merit and those who do not is to embark on the course to chaos.' "

[85] Ch. 47, "Pa shuo."

Benevolence and righteousness damage the law, and therefore could not be employed. If benevolence and righteousness [and the entire complex of Confucian ethical concepts] in themselves actually were effective when applied to governing, then the ruler might as well have relaxed his laws and restraints so as to apply them. But from Han Fei Tzu's point of view, benevolence and righteousness were nothing more than glittering words; they had no practical significance. The Confucians deprecated administrative measures and penal regulations, saying that they merely made people "evasive and shameless." [*Analects*, II/3.] They failed to realize that such measures and regulations provided the only governing means that worked in practice, and that the slogan which they were so fond of repeating about "all the world will respond to benevolence" [*Analects*, XII/1] was nothing more than vague and unattainable illusion. As has been stated, Legalists held human nature to be not good. Other than enticement and intimidation, there were no means of controlling people. "Expose trifling articles in some out-of-the-way place, and even [the moral paragons] Tseng Tzu and Shih Ch'iu [i.e., Shih Yü] might be suspected [of stealing them]; hang a hundred pieces of gold up in a market-place and even a great robber will not take them."[86] As this would have it, when there are no penal laws, then even those noted as superior men may develop the minds of petty men, but when penal laws are in force, then even petty men will conduct themselves like superior men. Moreover, in any state, the number of persons who can be considered superior men will indeed be very small! That is why: "When a sage rules the state, he does not depend on people's doing good of themselves; he sees to it that they are not allowed to do what is bad. If he depends on people's doing good of themselves, then within his borders he will not find enough instances to count in tens. But if he sees to it that they are not allowed to do what is bad, then the whole state can be made uniform [in orderliness]. Those who rule must use generally effective measures and abandon the standard of the minority. That is why they devote themselves not to virtue but to law."[87] Seen in this light, benevolence and righteousness, which the Confucians value so greatly, are in truth but useless, empty terms. "Nowadays when the shamans pronounce charms for people they say such things as: 'May you live a thousand autumns, or

[86] *Han Fei Tzu*, ch. 46, "Liu fan." The *Book of Lord Shang*, ch. 18, "Hua ts'e," also says: "Therefore, a good ruler succeeds in making a man like [the brigand] Chih trustworthy, how much more, then, a man like [the righteous] Po Yi; an incapable ruler makes a man like Po Yi untrustworthy, how much more a man like Chih. If conditions are such that one cannot commit crimes, then even a man like Chih will be trustworthy; but if conditions are such that it is possible to commit crimes, then even a man like Po Yi will be untrustworthy." [Modified from Duyvendak, *Lord Shang*, p. 288.]

[87] *Han Fei Tzu*, ch. 50, "Hsien-hsüeh" [modified slightly from Watson, *Han Fei Tzu*, p. 125].

ten-thousand years.' How the sounds of 'those thousand autumns' and 'ten-thousand years' strike the ears! Yet there is no proof that anyone ever lived so much as one day longer because of them. That is the reason why people have scorn and ridicule for shamans. The Confucians of our time urge their ideas upon rulers, not by discussing the ways of achieving orderly government in our time, but talking only about long past successes in governing. They do not examine real political and institutional issues, nor do they inform themselves on matters of evil-doing and treachery; the Confucians all talk incessantly about the models transmitted from earliest times, and praise the former kings for their achievements. The Confucians try to make their views more attractive by saying: 'If you listen to my advice I will make you a hegemonic lord or a kingly ruler. They are the shamans among our professional advisors, and no ruler with any standards of judgment would heed them."[88]

The *Teng Hsi Tzu* says: "The people should be brought to one standard by their ruler; all matters should be decided by the laws." The *Book of Lord Shang* says: "The intelligent ruler is conscientiously painstaking with regard to laws and regulations; he does not hearken to words that are not in accordance with the law; he does not exalt actions that are not in accordance with the law; he does not perform deeds that are not in accordance with the law."[89] The *Han Fei Tzu* says: "Order and strength come from the law; weakness and chaos come from flattering courtiers [who twist the law]. The ruler who understands this will uphold rewards and punishments, and will not employ benevolence toward his inferiors. Rank and salary come from merit; punishments and penalties come from wrong-doing. Servitors who understand this will exert the last ounce of their strength [to serve the state], yet will not be linked to their ruler by [the sentiment of] loyalty. When the ruler is not conscious of benevolence and the servitors are not conscious of loyalty, the royal sway can be realized."[90] If the laws were to be implemented to such a degree, that indeed could be called perfection, beyond all further criticism.

We must note, however, that the laws should constitute a firmly established and clearly precise institution, but they are not to be an eternally unchanging one. The various Legalist thinkers were profoundly

---

[88] *Ch.* 50, "Hsien-hsüeh." The preceding lines are: "To value the beauty of a Mao-ch'iang or a Hsi-shih [two fabled beauties of antiquity] delivers no benefits to one's own face. Using creams and ointments, rouge and paint, may make a person twice as good-looking as before. Talking about the benevolence and righteousness of former kings brings no improvement to one's governing. But if one makes his laws and regulations clear and makes his rewards and punishments definite, that is as if one had found creams and ointments, rouge and paint, for the state."

[89] *Ch.* 23, "Chün-ch'en" [wording slightly modified from Duyvendak, *Lord Shang*, p. 317].

[90] *Ch.* 35, "Wai chu shuo, yu hsia." [Cf. Liao, *Han Fei Tzu*, vol. ii, p. 117.]

conscious of social development; thus their political philosophy lacked any trace of conservatism. Kuan Tzu displayed this quality; with Lord Shang and Han Fei Tzu it is still more evident. The *Book of Lord Shang* says: "The sage's way, therefore, of organizing a country, is not to imitate antiquity, nor to follow the present, but to govern in accordance with the needs of the times, and to make laws that take into account customs."[91] The *Han Fei Tzu* says: "When times change and the laws do not change, chaos will ensue. As people's skills grow more numerous, if prohibitions do not change [the state] will be fragmented. Therefore, in the sage's governing, laws change with the times, and prohibitions are adjusted as the people's skills change."[92] And the same work also says: "For the sage does not try to practice the ways of antiquity or to abide by a fixed standard, but examines the affairs of the age and prepares to deal with them."[93]

The reasoning underlying all of those statements is entirely clear and convincing, making detailed discussion and explanation here quite unnecessary. However, Confucius also had said that a person who, living in the present age, goes back to the ways of antiquity is sure to be overtaken by calamity.[94] This shows that Confucius was not necessarily unsympathetic to the idea of establishing institutions in accord with the times. He also observed how it can be known that, throughout the Three Dynasties of Antiquity, each took from or added to the ritual institutions of each preceding age.[95] This demonstrates that Confucius did not fail to perceive that institutions should change. Han Fei Tzu nonetheless said that Confucius and Mo Tzu, "in claiming to adhere to doctrines of Yao and Shun of three thousand years ago," were "either fools or frauds."[96] That would seem to be something less than a totally fair criticism.

[91] *Ch.* 8, "Yi yen" [following Duyvendak, *Lord Shang*, p. 238]. Also, *Ch.* 1, "Keng fa" "On Changing the Laws" is devoted entirely to proposals concerning changes in laws; it is also relevant here.

[92] *Ch.* 54, "Hsin tu."

[93] *Ch.* 49, "Wu tu." *Ch.* 18, "Nan mien," says: "Those who have no understanding of government always tell you, 'Never change old ways; never depart from established custom!' But the sage cares nothing about changing or not changing; his only concern is to rule properly. Whether or not he changes old ways, whether or not he departs from established customs, depends solely upon whether such old ways and customs are effective, or not." [Following Watson, *Han Fei Tzu*, pp. 96–97 and 93.]

[94] *The Doctrine of the Mean*, ch. 28 [Legge, p. 423].

[95] *Analects*, ii/23/2 [Legge, p. 153].

[96] *Ch.* 50, "Hsien-hsüeh." The *Chuang Tzu*, *ch.* 33, "T'ien-hsia," compares Confucius' Way with the "straw dogs" that are to be cast aside after having been used in religious ceremonies, and adds: "Rites, proprieties, laws, and institutions are things that change in response to the times." It is thus in accord with Han Fei Tzu's point of view. Confucius, while recognizing that institutions could change, never relinquished his belief in the basic principles of feudal government, thereby holding a position difficult to reconcile with that of Chuang Tzu, Han Fei Tzu, and those others who willingly rejected the feudal order. Thus it can be said that in their attacks on Confucius, Chuang Tzu, Han Fei Tzu, and the others were not "firing off their arrows without a target."

Section Five
Methods

Han Fei Tzu said: "The enlightened ruler governs his officials; he does not govern the people."[97] This is at once a natural conclusion for authoritarian thought to have reached, and an inevitable tendency in political growth and development. In the earlier situation of the many feudal lords, the nobles and the ruler jointly governed the people; ruler and people were in direct contact, and the people themselves were the sole object of all governing measures. The contributing factor of clan law was not alone in bringing this about; the realities of small states and sparse population also helped to induce such a situation. Then, the small states were absorbed into large countries of ten thousand war chariots [this item of armament being a standard measure of a state's size and resources], and the aristocracy was eliminated, along with the virtual eradication of hereditary ministerships. The ruler's power situation became such that he could no longer function as chief of his clan and of his people. His servitors and subordinates gradually lost their position as co-governors; they sank to the status of administrative assistants, intermediate between ruler and people, subservient to the superior, and in control over their inferiors. In their persons they then became the objectives of the governing measures. Throughout the two thousand years [of the imperial era], from the Ch'in and Han dynasties onward, the political relationships were essentially thus. The beginnings of that development are incipient from the final phase of the Chou period, and the sentence quoted above from the *Han Fei Tzu* is its reflection in the realm of political theory.

As the law governs the people, so also does it govern officials. Han Fei Tzu's discussions about the laws for appointing to office and governing the officials do not, in the main, go beyond the scope of Hsün Tzu.[98] The *Han Fei Tzu* says: "The enlightened ruler applies the laws whereby to select persons; he does not elevate them on his own judgment. He applies the laws in assessing merit; he does not judge the matter on his own."[99]

---

[97] *Ch.* 35, "Wai chu shuo, yu hsia."

[98] Refer to Chapter Three, Section Six, of the present work.

[99] *Ch.* 6, "Yu tu." "Yung jen," *ch.* 27 says: "The minister who serves in a well-ordered state achieves merit in the service of the state so as to earn his position, manifests his ability in office in order to gain assignments, exerts his full energy to make measured judgments so that he can shoulder the responsibility of managing affairs. . . . The intelligent ruler allows no functions to impinge on each other, wherefore no disputes can arise; no official to hold concurrent posts, wherefore special skills have full play; and no one to share the same services with another, wherefore no rivalry can ensue." [Borrowing from Liao, pp. 269–70.]

And, again, "The intelligent ruler makes sure that none of his ministers shall let his expectations wander beyond the law's provisions, nor dispense personal favors even within the laws' provisions, that no single act shall be contrary to the laws."[100] Further, "The ruler should make sure that not even his wise and able servitors can ignore the laws and act on their own authority; that not even his worthy and exemplary servitors shall exceed the roles to which their merit has entitled them, or assume priority on account of their services; that not even those who have demonstrated loyalty and trustworthiness shall relax the laws and fail to observe the prohibitions."[101] Also, "The servitors set forth their statements, and, on the basis of their words, the ruler bestows assignments on them, then solely on their performance holds them responsible that their accomplishment [match their prior words]. When their accomplishment has matched the task assigned, and the task has matched their prior statements about it, they are to be rewarded. When their accomplishment has not matched the assigned task, and the task has not matched their statements about it, they are to be penalized. . . . Once in the past, Marquis Chao of the State of Han [who employed Shen Pu-hai as his chief minister] got drunk and fell asleep. The steward of the crowns saw that his ruler was exposed to a chill, so he took a cloak and covered him. When the Marquis awoke he was pleased at that, and asked his attendants: 'Who put the cloak over me?' The attendants replied: 'The steward of the crowns.' The ruler thereupon both punished the steward of the garments and executed the steward of the crowns. Punishing the steward of the garments was for failing in his responsibilities. Punishing the steward of the crowns was for exceeding his responsibilities. It was not that he did not hate catching a chill, but that he regarded the evil consequences of one official trespassing [on another's assigned duties] as more serious than a chill."[102] All of the above are evidence of Han Fei Tzu's having inherited the views of his teacher, [Hsün Tzu]; they also are consonant with Lord Shang's doctrines.

The Confucians maintained that "laws alone cannot carry themselves into practice." Han Fei Tzu also took over something from this concept. Thus, in commenting on Lord Shang's sole reliance on the laws, he said: "Although the laws were rigorously implemented by the officials, the ruler at the apex lacked methods."[103] In consequence, he drew upon Shen Pu-hai's "methods" [shu] to supplement the inadequacies of law, in order to strengthen the ruler's position and to prevent officials from encroaching on it, so that with the foundation of the state thus stabilized, the rule by law could then materialize. For methods are "that which the ruler wields"

---

[100] *Ch.* 6, "Yu tu."
[101] *Ch.* 18, "Nan mien."
[102] *Ch.* 7, "Erh ping" [cf. Watson, *Han Fei Tzu*, p. 32].
[103] *Ch.* 43, "Ting fa."

in order "covertly to control the body of his servitors" and to maintain all authority and power in his own person.

The distinctions between methods and law are three: The first is that laws are directed toward the people, while methods are directed toward the servitors and attendants. The second is that the laws are to be observed in common by ruler and servitors, while the methods are to be employed solely by the ruler. The third is that the laws are written regulations publicly promulgated to be understood by all, while the methods consist of tactical wisdom to be retained in the ruler's mind and to be secretely employed.

The historical factors bringing about the emergence of government by methods have been touched upon in the final portion of Section One of this Chapter. Han Fei Tzu apparently took up the strands of this development, which persisted after Shen Pu-hai's time, but supplemented and improved those. It was Han Fei Tzu's premise that no mutual benevolence, love, trust, or righteousness could exist between ruler and servitor. The ruler's position of authority was coveted by the servitors. The servitors harbored persistent designs to invade and usurp that authority, while the ruler with similarly unremitting determination sought to protect and maintain his authority. Therefore Han Fei Tzu's comment that: "Between superior and inferior there are each day a hundred battles."[104] And, further: "He who understands that ruler and servitor have quite different interests will be able to hold sway over all. He who thinks they have the same interests will suffer usurpation. He who administers affairs jointly [with his servitors] will die violently."[105] One who would rule must be aware of all his servitors' possibilities for infringing his interests, and deploy methods by which he can covertly waylay them. Should he rely on laws, regulations, and institutional structures alone, he would be in peril of treacherous ministers who might well evade or manipulate the laws in order to accomplish their evil-doing; he then would be plundered by the peck and the bushel, by the very scales and measures [which his laws had provided for, as *Chuang Tzu, ch.* 10, had cynically observed. Cf. Chapter Five, Section Five, p. 312 above].

Han Fei Tzu's discussions of the ways to employ methods are quite detailed; we need not review each of those here. His two most important points are detecting treachery among the servitors and underlings, and eradicating whatever personal power might be possessed by any other individual. The former was a matter of fundamentally guarding against all infringements and seizures of authority, while the latter required striking directly at all authority-wielding high ministers. Han Fei Tzu said: "That which brings the ruler to personal peril and the state to collapse is

[104] *Ch.* 8, "Yang ch'üan."
[105] *Ch.* 48, "Pa ching."

great officials being too high and court attendants too mighty."[106] There-fore, for the safety of the throne, the ruler should: ". . . prune his trees from time to time, and not let them grow too thick."[107] The direct method for pruning the trees is one that can only be used at a time before the power of his servitors has grown large. Otherwise the pruning would turn out like Duke Ai [reign 493–467 B.C.] of Lu's attempt to suppress the Three Huan Clans, or Duke Ch'u [reign 473–456 B.C.] of Chin's futile plan to eliminate the three great clans [that divided Chin into the States of Han, Wei and Chao].[108] Not only were those attempts not carried to successful conclusions, but the rulers themselves became subject to their underlings' control. Thus, the methods for pruning the trees must be carried out at an early time. The most suitable and reliable method is to prevent the emer-gence of an authority-wielding servitor. With this in mind, Han Fei Tzu analyzed the causes permitting ministers to wax great in illicit authority, and devised his theory of the "five obstructions." As he phrased it: "The ruler may encounter five kinds of obstructions. When the servitor is heedless of the ruler, that is an obstruction. When the servitor controls wealth and profits, that is an obstruction. When the servitor issues com-mands without authority to do so, that is an obstruction. When the ser-vitor can dispense favors, that is an obstruction. When the servitor can establish his own following, that is an obstruction."[109] There is no other method by which to remove these obstructions than that of ferreting out all treacherous underlings, and firmly grasping the handle [of the ruler's power].

There probably never has been in this world a ruler who gladly suffered usurpation, yet the principal reasons why so many have ultimately been the victims of usurpation are that the ruler's mind had grown benighted; he has cultivated personal favorites and heeded only certain advisors. Then, his servitors have taken advantage of this, to nurture their own power. Of the two, the damage that personal favorites can wreak is the greater; moreover, they frequently are the reason for his coming to heed only certain advisors. Han Fei Tzu thus feels compelled to go back and forth across this subject, examining it in great detail. For example, he has a discourse on the servitors' "eight methods" for accomplishing villainy, among which he lists "using bedfellows," "making use of attendants,"

---

[106] *Ch.* 52, "Jen chu." "Pa shuo," *ch.* 47 says: "In the state of the intelligent ruler there are ennobled servitors but there are no important servitors. Ennobled servitors are those whose noble rank is lofty and whose official position is great. Important servitors are those whose words are heeded and whose power is great."

[107] *Ch.* 8, "Yang ch'üan" [following Watson, *Han Fei Tzu*, p. 41].

[108] *Ch.* 33, *Shih Chi*, "Lu Chou-kung shih-chia," and *ch.* 39, "Chin shih-chia."

[109] *Ch.* 5, "Chu tao."

"making use of uncles and brothers," and "encouraging calamities";[110] all of these analyze situations in which sycophants and favorites gain access to rulers and thereby induce disorderly government and infringements of authority. He also offers a discussion of "ruler-manipulating servitors" in which he says: "Treacherous ministers will always try to agree with the ruler's wishes so as to grasp the power that goes with being a close favorite. That is why when a ruler reveals a like, the servitor will agree with him and praise it also; when the ruler makes known a dislike, the servitor will agree with him and discredit it also."[111] With respect to all such common tricks practiced by sycophant servitors in their quest for favor, Han Fei Tzu offers a most comprehensive exposé. Moreover, he shows that, in the beginnings of their careers in quest for such favor, if such treacherous servitors can make compliance and agreement be taken for ability in the management of affairs, their malevolent influence will not be readily discerned. By the time they have gained favor and have become the persons solely relied upon, the ruler's mind will become day-by-day more benighted, and his majestic awe will be day-by-day supplanted [by the illicit power of the servitor]. Though he desire to regain that and again act vigorously in his own right, it will be too late. When one servitor manipulates his ruler, his ears and eyes are thereby totally

[110] *Ch.* 9, "Pa chien": "What is meant by 'making use of [the ruler's] bedfellows?' It means tha trulers are readily disconcerted by their infatuations for elegant ladies or beguiling youths, by fawning favorites who arouse their lusts . . ." [so ministers manipulate these "bedfellows" in order to delude and control the ruler]. ". . . What is meant by 'making use of attendants?' It means . . . actors, jesters, and dwarfs, attendants, and personal favorites; these persons always ready to say 'Aye, aye' before he has even uttered a command, who will always shout 'Yes, yes!' before he has told them what to do, guessing his intentions before they are expressed, observing the ruler's facial expression to presume what the ruler wishes . . ." [these attendants too can become the instruments by which scheming ministers can influence a ruler]. ". . . What is called 'making use of uncles and brothers?' The ruler will have special affection for the sons in collateral branches of his clan. Moreover, in fixing his policies he will consult with the chief ministers and court officials. These will all urge their interests upon him with their utmost strength, and the ruler will be unable to disregard them. . . ." [The scheming ministers therefore may try to win over these relatives and senior advisors in order to further their own interests.] ". . . What is meant by 'encouraging calamities?' It means that the ruler may seek to delight himself with beautiful palaces, pavilions and terraces and ponds, and to have handsomely adorned attendants, dogs, horses, and the like. Such things bring only calamity to the ruler . . ." [because scheming ministers may exhaust the treasuries in order to supply them so as to gain influence over the ruler]. Treacherous servitors may utilize the special status of the first three, and also may play upon the ruler's passions and interests, and "establish their personal advantage thereby," rarely failing to get their way by such means. [Cf. the complete translation of this chapter in Watson, *Han Fei Tzu*, pp. 42–48.]

[111] *Ch.* 14, "Chien, chieh, shih ch'en."

lost.[112] The "dogs of the state" [i.e., officials whose fierce manner terrorizes associates and people] and the "rats of the shrine" [i.e., courtiers who gnaw away at the material substance of the state] are both hindrances and destroyers.[113] Therefore Han Fei Tzu says: "Do not trust only one man and lose thereby your state."[114]

To avoid trusting only one man, the negative method is to trust no one, and deny all servitors any opportunity to use positions of favor and proximity to spy out the ruler's secrets and act on them. The positive method, however, is for the ruler to make decisions alone, by himself, and thereby not permit his servitors any opportunities to arrogate authority and usurp powers. The *Han Fei Tzu* says: "The danger to a ruler lies in his trusting others, for by trusting others he becomes controlled by others. The servitors' relationship to their rulers is not as that of flesh-and-blood kin; they are bound by his power and have no alternative to serving him. Therefore the servitors spy and pry to learn the secrets of their ruler's mind, without a single moment's ceasing, and if the ruler occupies his

---

[112] *Ch.* 30, "Nei chu shuo, shang": "During the reign of Duke Ling in Wei, Mi Tzu-hsia was the recipient of his special favor, and in sole control over the governing of the state of Wei. On one occasion the court dwarf, appearing before the Duke, said to him: 'My dream has materialized.' The Duke asked: 'What dream?' The reply was: 'I dreamed that I saw a cookstove when I looked at your highness.' The Duke, angry, replied: 'I have always heard that a person dreaming of his ruler dreams that he sees the sun; how could you dream of seeing me and see a cookstove?' The dwarf explained: 'The sun, to be sure, shines over the whole world and no thing can deflect it; the ruler of men casts his radiance over the whole state and no man can obstruct that. Thus when one dreams of his ruler he dreams he sees the sun. But a cookstove—if one man stands in front of it, others standing behind him will not be able to see it. Now if a person should be standing in front of you, might it not be possible to dream of the ruler and to see only a stove?'" Note in this connection that "Ku fen," *ch.* 11, in discussing how high servitors can obstruct the will of their rulers, says: "When an administrator of government improperly exercises personal control over essential matters, then both foreign and court affairs will be manipulated to his uses. In such cases, even the heads of other states must adhere to his wishes or their business will not get taken care of. That may lead even enemy states to praise [and flatter] him. The officials of government all must adhere to his wishes or their advancement will not occur. That may lead to all the servitors' becoming his tools. Courtiers must adhere to his wishes or they will have no opportunities to come into the ruler's presence. That may lead to all the ruler's attendants' joining in concealing the truth from the ruler. The learned advisors must adhere to his wishes, or their salaries will be reduced and their dignities lowered. That may lead to the learned advisors' all speaking favorably of him. When the ruler cannot reach beyond these four aids [to villainy utilized by the manipulative minister, as described above] and luminously perceive the true character of his servitors, the ruler will grow ever more benighted and the chief ministers will grow ever more important." [Cf. the differently worded translation in W. K. Liao, *Han Fei Tzu*, vol. I, p. 98.]

[113] *Ch.* 34, "Wai chu shuo, yu shang."

[114] *Ch.* 8, "Yang ch'üan."

place over them indolently or in careless arrogance, that is what produces the usurpations and regicides of our times."[115]

Since servitors cannot be trusted, the ruler must employ the "seven methods" to control them. The seven methods are: "One, all the various possibilities must be known and compared; two, invariable punishments to maintain the sovereign's intimidating awe; three, rewards granted reliably so that all will exhaust their capacities for service; four, listen to everyone, and hold all responsible for what they say; five, issue unfathomable orders and make deceptive assignments; six, conceal one's knowledge when pursuing inquiries; seven, speak in opposites and act by contraries."[116] Numbers Two and Three are quite within the scope of governing by laws, thus require no further discussion. Of the others, numbers One, Five, Six, and Seven are among the essential doctrines of governing through methods. "Chang Yi [professional advisor on tactics] wanted to deploy the combined power of Ch'in, Han, and Wei to attack the States of Ch'i and Ching, while Hui Shih [the sophist] wanted to use the forces of Ch'i and Ching to stop the fighting. The two debated the issue. The assembled officials and attendants all spoke in favor of Chang Yi. . . . Hui Shih said: 'Any plan is susceptible to some doubts. When the doubters have honest doubts, those who favor a plan may number about half and those opposing it may number about half. In this instance the whole state favors the plan, which means that Your Majesty has lost half [your servitors]. Rulers who suffer usurpation are precisely those who have lost half [their servitors].'" This anecdote is to explain "knowing and comparing all the possibilities."

"The Chief Minister of Shang ordered a subaltern to go to the marketplace, look around, and return, upon which he inquired of him: 'What did you see?' [He first replied that he had observed nothing worth mentioning, but when pressed for details] he replied: 'Outside the south gate of the market there are so many oxcarts that I could scarcely get through.' The Chief Minister commanded the subaltern not to mention to anyone the matter on which he had been questioned. Then he called for the Prefect of the Market-Place, and accused him of dereliction, saying: 'Why is there so much ox dung accumulated outside the market gate?' The Market-Place Prefect was amazed that the Chief Minister had such rapid information, and thus came to tremble in fear of his omniscience." This anecdote is to explain what he meant by "unfathomable orders and deceptive assignments."

"Marquis Chao of the State of Han once clutched his fingernails into his fist and pretended he had lost a fingernail, hunting for it with great

---

[115] *Ch.* 17, "Pei nei."
[116] *Ch.* 30, "Nei chu shuo, shang."

anxiety. An attendant thereupon cut off his own nail and pretended it was [the lost nail of the Marquis]. Marquis Chao thereby gained the knowledge that his attendants were insincere." This anecdote is to explain what is meant by "concealing one's knowledge while pursuing inquiries."

"Once there were persons making charges against each other in a litigation. Tzu-ch'an [the Chief Minister in Cheng] separated them, and prevented them from having any communication with each other. He told to each the opposite of what the other had told him, and in that way came into full knowledge of the matter. Once Duke Ssu of Wei had some persons pose as travelers and pass through his customs barriers; the barrier officials made difficulties for them. Therefore [on the Duke's instructions] they gave some gold to employees of the customs barrier to bribe the barrier officials, who then let them go on their way. Duke Ssu later spoke to the officials, saying, 'On a certain date some travelers wanted to pass your customs barrier, and they paid you some gold so that you would let them go on.' The customs barrier officials were overtaken by great fear, and concluded that Duke Ssu must be a person able to find out everything."[117] These anecdotes are to explain "speaking in opposites and acting by contraries."

Employing only these seven methods, however, still would not be enough to maintain control over one's servitors. Even though the ruler employs his devious methods to spy on his servitors, the servitors also, in their anxieties and uncertainties, will be observing their ruler [waiting for opportunities to benefit themselves]; therefore the ruler must find ways to prevent his servitors from spying and prying. Han Fei Tzu said: "The enlightened ruler strives to maintain impenetrable secrecy."[118] Shen Pu-hai said: "If the ruler's enlightened nature is manifest, people will take precautions against it. If his benighted nature is obvious, people will deceive him. If his intelligence is displayed, people will embellish their acts. If his ignorance is made known, people will conceal their acts. If his lack of lusts is manifested, people will spy on him [to find his weaknesses]. If his lusts are made obvious, people will bait traps for him."[119] The *Han Fei Tzu* says: "Hence the saying: 'Do away with all [display of] likes and dislikes, and then the servitors will show their plain selves. When the servitors show their plain selves, then the great ruler will never grow benighted.' "[120] [I.e., his "radiant perception" will never become "clouded over" and obscured.]

Once the factor leading the ruler toward that benighted state has been eliminated, then the only further action that the ruler need bother to

[117] For all the foregoing, see *ch*. 30, "Nei chu shuo."
[118] *Ch*. 30, "Nei chu shuo, shang."
[119] *Ch*. 34, "Wai chu shuo, yu shang" [where this passage is attributed to Shen Pu-hai].
[120] *Ch*. 7, "Erh ping."

undertake with great care is the single matter of acting dictatorially and despotically. The *Lao Tzu* says: "Fish cannot be separated from the deep water; the sharp instruments of the state cannot be turned over to others."[121] Han Fei Tzu explains this passage according to his doctrine of the elevation of the ruler, saying: "The position of great power is the ruler's 'deep water.' To rule over people [his] power among the servitors must be overwhelming. If it is lost, it cannot be regained. . . . Rewards and punishments are the 'sharp instruments of the state.' If they are held by the ruler, he then can control his servitors. If they are held by the servitors, they then can prevail over the ruler."[122] Although this is a perfectly obvious idea that anyone could readily understand, yet the ruler in governing his state has no choice but to employ officials to govern the people. Whenever he inadvertently relaxes his caution, his great power gradually erodes away, and falls into the hands of the treacherous and evil servitors about him. Han Fei Tzu recounts some examples to clarify this point, such as: "Ssu-ch'eng Tzu-han said to the ruler of Sung: 'Rewards and gifts are welcomed by the people. You should confer those in person. Penalties and executions are hated by the people. Allow me to bear responsibility for those.' Thereafter whenever executing a commoner or inflicting corporal punishment on a high official, the ruler would say: 'Turn this matter over to Tzu-han for decision.' After a year, people all knew that decisions to execute persons were under the control of Tzu-han; consequently the whole country turned to him. Thereby was Tzu-han enabled to usurp the authority of the ruler of Sung and seize control of his government [his own power now] being beyond suppressing."[123] Once the ruler is aware of the peril in "delegating authority to underlings,"[124] then his only alternative is to practice an absolute authoritarianism, wielding all authority alone, personally doing all the giving and all the taking.[125] "The people uniformly subservient to the ruler, affairs

[121] *Ch.* 36, *Tao te ching*. [Translation based on Kao Heng's commentary, in his *Lao Tzu cheng-ku*.]

[122] *Han Fei Tzu, Ch.* 21, "Yü Lao."

[123] *Ch.* 34, "Wai chu shuo, yu shang." The same chapter also cites the cases of T'ien Ch'eng-tzu, who dispensed favors to the people in the State of Ch'i [preparing to usurp the throne there], and of Confucius' preventing [his disciple] Tzu-lu from privately providing provisions for men called up in service to the state.

[124] *Ch.* 31, "Nei chu shuo, hsia."

[125] *Ch.* 47, "Pa shuo," says: "If [the ruler's] own mouth does not make the judgments about sour and sweet, salty and flat, but leaves these to be judged by the head chef, then all the ordinary cooks will despise the ruler and revere the head chef. If his own ear does not make the judgments about sharp and flat, high or low, but leaves these to be judged by the chief musician, then all the blind players [i.e., ordinary musicians who, traditionally, were often blind men] will despise the ruler and revere the chief musician. If right and wrong in governing the state are not determined according to the ruler's methods [*shu*] but are decided by the ruler's favorites, then all the servitors will despise the ruler and revere his favorites."

all decided according to the laws."[126] Thus all the servitors become the ruler's servants; expel them and they go, hail them and they come. Let them live or have them die, ennoble them or humble them—all depend on the ruler's wishes. Then, what capacity for usurping his authority can they possibly possess?

The foregoing encompasses the main outlines of Han Fei Tzu's "governing by methods." From a modern point of view, there is not much that can be said for it. But at the end of the Warring States Period, when authoritarian rulership was just on the rise, Han Fei Tzu examined the body of historical experience, revised and brought up-to-date all the earlier theories, and produced a virtually comprehensive review of all the faults inherent in an authoritarian polity. His theoretical formulations, such as those he entitled "The Six Subleties" [ch. 31, "Liu wei"] "The Seven Methods" [ch. 30, "Ch'i shu"], "The Eight Villainies," [ch. 9, "Pa chien"], and "The Ten Faults" [ch. 10, "Shih kuo"] might almost be taken as a prophecy outlining all the failures of government that were to be committed by all the muddle-headed rulers of the two-thousand-year imperial era commencing with the Ch'in and Han dynasties. It is not excessive praise to label Han Fei Tzu's formulation of "governing by methods" traditional China's most complete and comprehensive theory of authoritarianism.

Also, we might note, the Confucians said that laws alone cannot carry themselves into implementation. Lord Shang had observed: "All states have law, but there are no laws that guarantee that the laws are practiced." [127] Han Fei Tzu, adopting Shen Pu-hai's concept of methods, and combining that with Lord Shang's ideas of law, apparently intended to supplement the deficiencies of law. In other words, Han Fei Tzu's learning in fact compounded the elements of the two schools of thought, that stressing government by laws and that advocating government of men. Even so, early China's legalistic thought, measured by modern standards, was but one variety of the government-of-men school of thought. For among the pre-Ch'in thinkers who stressed law, all alike looked upon the laws as an administrative instrument for achieving the elevation of the ruler; none conceived of law as something in itself possessing the authority and awe to bring the head of state and his officials under restraint. Yet, before the era when authoritarian rulership had grown to its fullest extent, theoreticians of the laws still proposed that the laws should be something that the ruler and his servitors observed in common, therein coming closer to modern conceptions of the rule of law. To make an inference about why that was so: it probably was because those early theorizers could envisage real results being achieved only by a government of laws as a product of ruler

---

[126] *Teng Hsi Tzu, ch.* 2, "Chuan tz'u."
[127] *The Book of Lord Shang, ch.* 18, "Hua ts'e" [following Duyvendak, p. 287].

and servitors jointly upholding the laws. They had not yet come to the stage where they could anticipate that rulers would be elevated to the highest extremes of authority and that thereafter they would brook no restraints whatsoever upon themselves. Subsequently, by Han Fei Tzu's time, both the authoritarianism actually realized by the rulers and the authoritarian thought of the Legalist thinkers were approaching full maturity. In that context, law and political methods were both quite clearly degraded to the level of mere tools of authoritarian rule. The ruler's authority and status subsequently rose far above ministers, people, laws, and institutions and totally denied limitations. Thus, Han Fei Tzu's learning, to describe it in terms of modern concepts of the rule of law, cannot escape being called a regression into "atavism." At the same time, in terms of the pre-Ch'in historical setting, it represents the highest stage of development of Legalist thought. It is indeed difficult to deny the significance of its place [in the history of thought].

We may now procede to comment on the achievements and the failings of Lord Shang's and Han Fei Tzu's thought. Inasmuch as their thought is that of absolute authoritarianism, any decision on the utility of the whole body of their thought, or the lack of that, must be made with respect to whether it could be accepted as useful to the ruler under conditions of absolute authoritarianism. Han Fei Tzu, in discussing the concept of power, said that to achieve a well-ordered state it was not necessary to await the emergence of the extraordinary capacities of a Yao or a Shun; rather, a mediocre ruler could perform adequately. That the governing by laws need not depend on a Yao or a Shun is indubitable. Yet when it comes to Han Fei Tzu's so-called mediocre ruler, if we examine all the various aspects of his governing-by-methods, it becomes apparent that his methods would have required a ruler of unusual talent and wisdom. For he would have to be a person occupying the most elevated position possible, in whose hands lay the highest authority possible, and who could with luminous perception ferret out all the innumerable villainies, who could fully control the many officials of state, who would never lapse into gratification of his private tastes, who would not be taken in by close associates and sycophants, who would be collected and imperturbable, who would remain unflustered by opinions and judgments, who would never display his likes and dislikes, who would never be unaware of advantages and disadvantages—rulers of this description, or even those slightly resembling this description, were few and far between in the two thousand years of imperial history. We could count them on the fingers of one hand. In difficulty of achieving these standards as in the honor those few have deserved, they are perhaps in no way inferior to Yao and Shun.

The Confucians established an ideal of the sagelike ruler, and when the sage ruler failed to materialize, then their benevolence and righteousness, ritual propriety and music, could not be realized. Han Fei Tzu deprecated benevolence and righteousness as nothing more than empty chatter, yet failed to realize that his laws and methods, in the extreme difficulty facing their practical implementation, were in fact in precisely the same category. One need merely observe that following the reigns of Duke Hsiao [under whom Lord Shang served] and the First Emperor [at whose court Han Fei Tzu appeared], the rule by law never thereafter succeeded in being thoroughly implemented. This shows that our argument in not unfair [in charging Legalist theory with having possessed practical shortcomings].

In antiquity Plato, in his theories of government, first erected the ideal of the absolute rule by a philosopher king, but subsequently discovered that this was a practical impossibility, and changed his views to support of a legalist polity. His intent was to replace the impractical ideal of the enlightened ruler with that of good laws capable of being enforced. Thereafter, having gone through successive developments, this concept has at last splendidly emerged as the modern theory and practice of constitutional government. Lord Shang and Han Fei Tzu recognized the inutility of righteousness and benevolence, yet failed to realize how difficult it is to have an enlightened monarch. Therefore they developed their ruler-centered Legalist political thought, and succeeded only in opening the door for subsequent monstrous rulers and oppressive officials. Even so, they were unable to compete for acceptance with Confucius and Mencius. In terms of this point, they were inferior in percipience to Plato.

Before concluding this chapter, we need to consider still another issue that is of an importance to warrant our serious attention, and that we must touch upon at least briefly. Among the various Legalist thinkers, Shen Tao, as well as P'eng Meng and T'ien P'ien, studied the doctrines of Huang-Lao [i.e., Taoist political theory; see below, Chapter Ten, Section Two]. In the *Kuan Tzu* there are numerous instances of Taoist terms and usages. The *Han Fei Tzu* also contains chapters called "Explaining Lao Tzu," i.e., "Chieh Lao," *ch.* 20, and "Clarifying Tzu," i.e., "Yü Lao," *ch.* 21. What then, in the final analysis, is the relationship between the Legalist school and Taoist political theory?

If we discard all consideration of historical origins and discuss the matter solely in terms of the content of their thought, then we must conclude that any resemblances between Taoist and Legalist thought are merely superficial, and in their fundamentals they are extremely dissimilar. The basic point of Huang-Lao [or Taoist political thought in general] in its discussions of politics does not go beyond pure quiescence and non-action [or taking no purposive action]. The various Legalist thinkers, to be sure, do on occasion express this idea. Shen Pu-hai, in discussing the

Way of the Ruler, says: "Drums have nothing to do with the five tones, yet they are the masters of the five tones."[128] And, elsewhere, "Only by taking no action can I regulate [or, keep watch over, the affairs of government]."[129] Han Fei Tzu said: "Therefore [the ruler], although possessing intelligence, still does not feel concern, but lets all things decide their own proper place; worthiness though he has, he does not display it in action, but only observes what motivates his servitors; courage though he possesses, he does not display anger, but allows his ministers to exercise their prowess to the fullest extent"; and, "so it is that in an age of total peace, the laws are like the morning dew, pure and pristine, and not dispersed. Minds hold no resentments and mouths utter no quarrelsome words."[130] The *Kuan Tzu* also says: "The vacuous and formless are called the Tao," and "When terms are rectified and laws complete, the sage ruler will have no matters to concern him."[131] Any of these sentences might be placed in the *Tao te ching* and would not be felt to be out of place. Yet we need merely undertake the slightest analysis to discover that Taoism and Legalism have at least three quite readily discerned and major points of difference.

The first is that although the ideals of taking no action yet achieving good government are somewhat similar in the two doctrines, the courses to be followed in achieving this are opposite from each other. The *Lao Tzu* says: "Decrease [action] and further decrease it, until one reaches the point of taking no action."[132] Although [Taoism argues] benevolence, righteousness, filial piety, and parental love are of no use, "laws and commands made prominent"[133] are even less to be tolerated. The ruler should take as his own mind the mind of the people,[134] allow the empire to exist spontaneously, and in that way the empire is well governed. Shen Pu-hai and Han Fei Tzu would achieve non-action by means of explicit laws and commands, heavy punishments, and unified doctrines, ultimately reaching a state wherein "an enlightened ruler presides above in non-action, while all the servitors tremble in fear below him."[135] These techniques of ruling are precisely what the *Lao Tzu* speaks of as: "The

---

[128] Ma Kuo-han [1794–1857], in his *Yü-han shan-fang chi-yi-shu* [containing a reconstruction of the lost text of Shen Pu-hai's works], quoting [the T'ang dynasty compilation], the *Yi-lin.*

[129] *Han Fei Tzu*, *ch.* 34, "Wai chu shuo, yu shang."

[130] See, respectively, *ch.* 5, "Chu tao," and *ch.* 29, "Ta t'i" [Cf. translations of these passages in context, in W. K. Liao, *Han Fei Tzu*, vol. I, pp. 31 and 279; for the former, Watson, *Han Fei Tzu*, pp. 17–18.]

[131] The *Kuan Tzu*, *ch.* 36, "Hsin shu," and *ch.* 38, "Pai hsin," respectively.

[132] *Tao te ching*, *ch.* 48 [following W. T. Chan, *Source Book*, p. 162].

[133] *Ibid.*, *ch.* 57.

[134] *Ibid.*, *ch.* 49.

[135] *Han Fei Tzu*, *ch.* 5, "Chu tao."

next best [government] is that which is feared,"[136] which describes the third class of governments, in rank still below that of the Confucian government of benevolence. Lao Tzu would achieve non-action through laissez-faire; Shen Pu-hai and Han Fei Tzu would achieve non-action through authoritarian control. Thus we have said that the courses that the two schools would have governments follow are the opposite from each other.

The second point of difference is that, even as the methods employed are different, so also the goals that the two upheld are particularly dissimilar. The *Lao Tzu* speaks of such things as: "A small country having few people . . . letting the people so value their lives that they will not risk traveling afar. Even though they have armor and weapons they will not display them. . . . Let them delight in their food, regard their [simple] clothing as beautiful, be content with their dwellings, and find happiness in their customs."[137] For the non-action of Taoist political thought had as its objective to set up pure and quiescent rule that would preserve the people's natural pursuit of happiness. The Legalist thinkers advised rulers to carry out laws and methods of non-action as a means for strengthening the ruler's authority and status, and to create the basis for enriching the state and strengthening its military force. When their methods were implemented, then: "the servitors have their labors; the ruler gains the results. . . . When there are achievements, the ruler gets the credit as the worthy one; when there are mistakes, the servitors get the blame as the wrong-doers."[138] Thus Shen Pu-hai's and Han Fei Tzu's advocacy of non-action had the negative function of guarding against the infringement of powerful ministers, and, as its positive function, to guard the ruler's authoritarian control. Its purposes were, therefore, wholly opposite from Taoist political thought where, negatively, non-action was intended to reduce the activities and powers of government, and positively it was to increase the people's freedoms.

The third point of major difference is that, in as much as non-action's objectives differ in the two cases, the positions of those implementing the methods also differ. We have said that Lao Tzu's ideas of non-action imply a tendency toward democratic government.[139] "The Sage has no constant mind of his own, but takes as his mind the mind of the people." In a situation of extreme laissez-faire and generous accommodation, the ruler's position is as if established for nothing; awe and power have no reasons to be utilized. Therefore it is said: "The best government is one

---

[136] *Tao te ching, ch.* 17. *Ch.* 74 says: "When the people no longer fear death, of what use is it to try and intimidate them with threats of death?"

[137] *Tao te ching, ch.* 80.

[138] *Han Fei Tzu, ch.* 5, "Chu tao."

[139] See, Chapter Five of the present work, the last portion of Section Two.

where the people merely know it exists."[140] In Taoist political thought, the ruler's position is probably to be seen as far inferior even to the importance and the respect that the ruler of a petty feudal state might have enjoyed; perhaps the only comparison that can be devised would be to a tribal chieftain in earliest antiquity.[141] The ruler who emerges in the thought of Shen Pu-hai and Han Fei Tzu is the authoritarian leader of a large state, on the eve of the First Emperor's unification of the empire, who represented a concentration of majesty and power in one person and who dispensed rewards and punishments to the masses. He pressed for agricultural production wherewith to sustain his war-making; his commands were uniform and his laws were standardized. All his policies were the complete opposite of Taoist political thought's concept of non-action. It was only when rule-by-law and rule-by-methods were in force that the ideal of non-action was then established. And when we examine the actual facts of the matter, the ultimate ideal of rule by law is "when terms are rectified and laws complete, the sage ruler will have no matters to concern him," and the hoped for consequence of rule by methods is "an enlightened ruler presides above in non-action, while all the servitors tremble in fear below him." Thus it is clear that what Legalism designated non-action was really just another name for "being secretive in imposing punishments, and concealing one's knowledge." It should not be mentioned in the same breath with: the ruler's "mind forms a harmonious whole with that of all his people."[142] When ruler and servitor engage every day in a hundred battles, the ruler's mind encounters in a day ten thousand schemes. The ruler who must within that mind seek means to "meet all contingencies," and "control his servitors," and who adopts the methods of "unfathomable edicts and deceptive assignments," would have to be an inexhaustibly alert and perceptive person engaging in extremes of purposive activity. Thus for a ruler to meet the standards of Shen Pu-hai and Han Fei Tzu, he would have to be the likes of a Marquis Chao of Han [who employed Shen Pu-hai as chief minister] or a First Emperor of Ch'in, or an Emperor Wu of the Wei dynasty [i.e., Ts'ao Ts'ao]; else he would be unequal to the task. The likes of an Emperor Wen of the Han dynasty [reigned 179–157 B.C.], who to some slight degree at least conforms to the Huang-Lao type, would not have been able to "decline the honor" [of being that kind of ruler] fast enough.

We have already discussed the way Confucians and Legalists in their use of the words "rites" and "laws" have tended to blur the definitions of these. The fundamental distinction between those two schools of thought is in the one placing primary value in the people and the other advocating

---

[140] *Tao te ching*, ch. 17.

[141] See, Chapter Five of the present work, the last portion of Section Three.

[142] *Tao te ching*, ch. 49.

the elevation of the ruler. Taoism and Legalism, in both using the term "non-action," also blur its definition, but if we adopt the criteria of "egocentrism" and "the elevation of the ruler" in assessing them, then the fundamental difference between these two schools immediately becomes apparent. The *Shih Chi* says that Shen Pu-hai and Han Fei Tzu drew their thought from Lao Tzu and Chuang Tzu, while the *Han Shu* lists the *Kuan Tzu* among the Taoist writings. On the basis of the extant writings, these judgments all display the fault of ignoring the fundamentals while matching up the superificialities, of accepting external features while overlooking the organic nature. These cannot be accepted as definitive judgments.

Part Two

*The Political Thought of the Authoritarian Empire (One)—
the Period of Continuity*

CHAPTER EIGHT

Mohists and Legalists in the Ch'in and Han Periods

Section One
The Decline of Mohist Learning

When the State of Ch'in eliminated the Six States it brought about a profound and unprecedented change in China's political history. Political institutions underwent the change from feudal decentralization to the commandery-county system of unification, while a polity of delegated powers exercised separately by members of an aristocracy was transformed into a monarchical authoritarianism.[1] Political thought, responding to this

---

[1] In the twenty-sixth year of his reign (221 B.C.) the First Emperor of Ch'in conquered the State of Ch'i, the last of the Six States to be eliminated; the empire was divided into thirty-six commanderies [administrative regions analogous to provinces]. Although monarchical authoritarianism and the commandery-county system had already begun to develop somewhat earlier, it was at that time that the systems were definitively imposed. The more aggressive ones among the rulers of the Six States' all had harbored ambitions to become the supreme ruler; although they all had failed, their powers and positions each "had all the constituents, but in smaller proportions" [*Mencius*, II/i/2/20] than the First Emperor. In the first year of his reign [249 B.C.] King Chuang-hsiang of Ch'in attacked the State of Han, and established [from seized territory] the San-ch'uan Commandery (see *Shih Chi*, ch. 88, "Biography of Meng T'ien"). King Hui of Ch'u in the tenth year of his reign [476 B.C.] conquered the State of Ch'en and made its territory into a county (*Shih Chi*, ch. 40, "Ch'u shih-chia"). And, during the reign of King K'ao-lieh [of Ch'u, reigned 261–237 B.C., his chief minister, the Lord of Ch'un-shen, named] Huang Hsieh petitioned that his fief, comprising twelve counties in the Huai-pei region, be reconstituted as a commandery. During the Twelfth year [513 B.C.] of Duke Ch'in in the State of Chin, when the six chief ministers exterminated the ducal clan, they divided its fiefs up to constitute counties (*Shih Chi*, ch. 39, "Chin shih-chia"). The State of Han included an area called Yi-yang, of which the chief minister in Ch'in, Kan Mao, said: "It is designated a county but in fact it is a commandery" (*Shih Chi*, ch. 71, "Kan Mao chuan"). King Wu-ling of Chao [reigned 325–299 B.C.] established the commanderies of Yün-chung, Yen-men and Tai (*Shih Chi*, ch. 110, "Hsiung-nu chuan"). The State of Wei established a commandery called Upper Ho-hsi (*Shih Chi, ibid.*). King Chao of Yen [reigned 310–278 B.C.] ordered his minister Yüeh Yi, who had captured more than seventy cities in the State of Ch'i, to make commanderies and counties of their territories (*Shih Chi*, ch. 80, "Yüeh Yi chuan"). All of the above are examples [of the prior existence of commanderies and counties]. Furthermore, the Ch'in-Han era was also a period of social transformation. Chao Yi [1727–1814] in his *Erh-shih-erh-shih cha-chi*, ch. 2, under the heading "Han-ch'u pu-yi ch'ing-hsiang chih chü" ["commoner chief ministers at the beginning of Han"] states: "The Ch'in-Han period was one in which the world underwent profound change. From antiquity there had always been the feudal overlords, each the master of his own state, and the chief ministers and Great Officers each holding his

vast change, likewise entered a new stage. The "Introduction" has discussed this situation in general terms. This and the several following chapters will deal separately with the general features of the principal pre-Ch'in schools of thought, through the Ch'in and Han and subsequent periods.

The decline of Mohism is a most noteworthy development in the history of Ch'in-Han thought. Sun Yi-jang [1848–1908] has said: "The school of Mo Tzu died out by the end of the Ch'in period. That is why the facts of Mo Tzu's life could not be known in detail already in the Western [Former] Han."[2] Huan K'uan [first century B.C.] said: "Formerly the State of Ch'in by means of military force swallowed up the whole empire; Li Ssu and Chao Kao [ministers of Ch'in] further compounded the disaster by using the baleful and the pernicious. Ancient methods were abolished and the old rites were destroyed. Punishments and laws were solely employed, and Confucians and Mohists lost their place."[3] Although there still were some Mohist followers in existence when the Prince of Huai-nan [d. 122 B.C.] had his book [The *Huai-nan Tzu*] compiled,[4] and Ssu-ma Ch'ien [d. ca. 90 B.C.] still could "read widely through the writings of former Confucians

---

hereditary office." But during the Spring and Autumn and Warring States Periods those established ways gradually changed. Fan Chü, Ts'ai Tse, Su Ch'in, Chang Yi, Sun Pin, Po Ch'i, Yüeh Yi, Lien P'o, and Wang Chien [all of the Warring States Period] were commoners who became generals or chief ministers. At the beginning of Han among the leading officials, except for Chang Liang, who was the son of a chief minister in the State of Han, and Chang Ts'ang, Hsiao Ho, and a few others who had been officials under the Ch'in, Ch'en P'ing, Wang Ling, Lu Chia, and Li Shang, and others all had been mere commoners. Fan K'uai, who had been a dog butcher; "Chou Po, who had earned his living by weaving baskets for raising silk worms"; Kuan Ying, who had been a silk peddlar, and Lou Ching, who had been a carter, had emerged from particularly humble circumstances. We should note also that Liu Chi [the Han Founder] had risen from the status of a police bailiff [*t'ing-chang*] to master the empire, and in so doing also created the precedent for commoners becoming emperors in later ages.

   [2] *Mo-hsüeh ch'uan-shou k'ao.*

   [3] *Yen-t'ieh lun, ch.* 24, "Lun fei."

   [4] *Op.cit., ch.* 8, "Ch'ao Ts'o," says: "In the past, the [Prince of] Huai-nan and [his younger brother, the Prince of] Heng-shan, engaged in the study of literature; summoning the itinerant scholars from all sides, all the Confucians and Mohists from the East of the Mountains [*shan-tung*] gathered in the region between the Yangtze and the Huai Rivers, to discuss their views and assemble their discourses, composing a book of several tens of essays." However, the extant *Huai-nan Tzu* not only contains extremely little in the way of Mohist statements; at many points it ridicules Mohists. (For one example, in *ch.* 2, "Ch'u-chen hsün," it says: "The followers of Confucius and Mo Tzu all apply their doctrines of benevolence and righteousness to teach and guide the world, yet they do not fail to exhaust themselves without yet having realized their own doctrines, much less teaching them. Why is that so? It is because they have abandoned the Way.") It may be that the Mohists already had become so obscure that they could offer no opposition to the other schools.

and Mohists,"[5] nonetheless the Mohists' status as a "prominent school"[6] had virtually been lost by the reign of the Emperor Wu [140–87 B.C.]. Thus when the chief minister Wei Wan, in 140 B.C., proposed that all candidates for office, nominated by the various administrative divisions of the empire, if specialists in the doctrines of Shen Pu-hai, Lord Shang, Han Fei Tzu, Su Ch'in, and Chang Yi, should be dismissed,[7] he did not mention Mohists. Throughout the early decades of the Han dynasty, Confucians, Taoists, and Legalists all struggled for supremacy under conditions of intense competition, but there were no Mohist contenders in that struggle.[8] Thereafter the school's presence grew ever more insignificant, and was virtually extinguished.[9]

[5] *Shih Chi, ch.* 130, "Tzu hsü." It may be noted that the *Shih Chi* appends an account of Mo Tzu to the biographies of Mencius and Hsün Tzu, and that account consists of no more than twenty-four characters. The sense of that account is incomplete, so it may well have suffered partial loss or excision.

[6] *Han Fei Tzu, ch.* 50, "Hsien hsüeh." The *Lü-shih Ch'un-ch'iu, ch.* 2/4, "Tang jan," also notes that Confucius and Mo Tzu ". . . both have long been dead. Their followers are legion, their disciples are flourishing; they overflow the world." [Both works date from the late third century B.C.]

[7] *Ch'ien Han Shu, ch.* 6, "Wu-ti chi." Tung Chung-shu's response to the throne included elevating the Six Arts [i.e., the study of the Six Canons comprising the core of Confucian education] and eliminating [posts for scholars from] the "Hundred Schools"; this is dated 134 B.C. (*Ch'ien Han Shu, ch.* 6), or 136 B.C. (see, Ch'i Shao-nan, *Han Shu k'ao-cheng*) and thus was several years after Wei Wan's memorial.

[8] Wang Ch'ung's *Lun Heng,* no. 67, "Po tsang" says: "Nowadays the Mohists contradict the Confucians and the Confucians deny the Mohists." This seems to be a reference to points of disagreement between the content of the thought of the two schools, and not necessarily a reference to a balance of actual authority between Mohists and Confucians of the time. Therefore the same section also states: "Mo Tzu would have people ignore their minds [hearts] and give precedence to material things, and credence to whatever one hears and sees. . . . Although this gives the foolish what they want, it does not accord with the mind of a knowledgeable person. . . . It is for such reasons, no doubt, that Mohism has not survived." From this is would appear that by Wang Ch'ung's time [A.D. 27-*c.* 100] Mohism had already ceased to exist [as an actively transmitted school]. Also, some have said that the "knights errant" [*yu hsia*] continued to uphold Mo Tzu's ideal of bringing practical benefits to all. The knights errant, however, did not set forth any doctrines and in that respect thus cannot be considered the perpetuators of the Mohist tradition.

[9] During the reign of Emperor Hui of the Chin dynasty (reigned A.D. 290–306) Lu Sheng produced his *Mo pien chu,* i.e., "Commentary on the Mohist Debates". The book is no longer extant, but the preface is preserved in the *Chin Shu, ch.* 94, "Yin-yi chuan," i.e., "Biographies of Recluses". Yüeh T'ai of the T'ang dynasty wrote a *Mo Tzu chu,* i.e., "Commentary on Mo Tzu" recorded by title in the *T'ung tien,* "Yi-wen lüeh," but this work also has failed to survive. During the Ch'ien-lung and Chia-ch'ing reigns, 1736–1820, of the Ch'ing dynasty, students of the *Mo Tzu* gradually became quite numerous, but those studies all were in the fields of philology and textual criticism and made no additions to any further development of Mohist thought.

That a prominent school whose doctrines "filled the world" [*Mencius*, III/ii/9/9] could, within the course of a hundred years, come so to falter as to display no activity, is in truth something to be wondered at. Scholars seeking the reasons for this have offered varying explanations. Those can be summarized under three principal headings: attacks from the other schools, changes in the setting, difficulties inherent in the Mohist thought itself. The latter two would seem to have greater significance. Attacks by the schools upon each other were an inevitable phenomenon, common to the situation of all the schools; success or failure [in their struggle to survive] need not be linked to the vehemence of the attacks upon them. The First Emperor of Ch'in employed Legalism and suppressed all the other schools, yet the Confucians and Taoists were not destroyed. Emperor Wu of the Han recruited Confucians and expelled from service persons belonging to all the other schools, yet Taoism and Legalism continued to exist. Only the Mohist schools went into decline; thus it seems quite evident that attacks from the other schools should not be held responsible.[10]

If we want to ascertain somewhat more accurately the causes for Mohism's decline, we must seek those in the historical setting and in the content of its thought. The *Chuang Tzu, ch.* 33, "T'ien-hsia," states: "His way is too harsh. . . . It is contrary to the heart of the world, and the world cannot endure it. Though Mo Tzu himself may have been capable of enduring it, could anyone else in the world do so?"[11] Wang Ch'ung also said of it: "Mo Tzu's arguments [supporting the existence of spirits] did not apply the mind to explain things, loosely believing in whatever was seen or heard. . . . Although that obtain what the ignorant desire, it does not agree with the minds of the knowing."[12] He also said: "The doctrines of the Confucian Way are transmitted while those of the Mohist methods decline; that is because the Way of the Confucian teachings can be practiced, and the Mohist methods are difficult to follow. How can that be demonstrated? The Mohists would have shabby funerals yet honor the spirits [of the deceased]; these teachings are unreasonable and contradictory. . . . Now the Mohist followers tell us that the spirit represents the essence of a person. To be generous toward the essence yet treat the corpse shabbily, that is to be generous to the spirit yet miserly toward the body. . . . It is human nature to desire the generous treatment and hate the miserly; the mind of spirits should also be that way. Using the Mohists' methods of serving spirits in order to obtain good fortune, fortune might be

---

[10] Hu Shih, *Chung-kuo che-hsüeh shih ta-kang*, or "Outline History of Chinese Philosophy," 1919 p. 250, [also published in English as *The Development of the Logical Method in Ancient China*, Shanghai, 1922], gives the opposition from Confucianism as the first among reasons for the decline of Mohism.

[11] See, Chapter Four, Section Six, p. 469 of the present work.

[12] Wang Ch'ung, *Lun Heng*, no. 67, "Po tsang." [Cf. Fung/Bodde, Vol. II, p. 160.]

expected to come infrequently, and misfortune to appear regularly. This single example reveals all, for the methods advanced by the Mohists all are of that kind. That they should be abandoned and fail to be transmitted is for good reason."[13] These statements all seek the reasons for Mohism's decline entirely in the body of the Mohist teachings themselves; these arguments are more or less fair, and display no particular factional prejudice.

One can go still further and state that in the content of Confucian and Mohist thought there are in fact many basically similar features.[14] Han dynasty writers often mention the Confucians and the Mohists together and occasionally even confuse aspects of the two schools' teachings.[15] However, the Confucians discussed government in terms encompassing all of past and present, with profound learning and broadly inclusive views. They possessed the capacity to "Combine cultural patterns and to be thoroughly versed in governing."[16] They succeeded in drawing the attention of rulers and scholar-officials; their doctrines displayed none of the Mohists' shallow simplicity, which, at best, could only "satisfy the ignorant's desires." Moreover, the Confucians "adjusted to the times, raised and lowered their gaze with the age."[17] In this they were still less to be compared with the Mohists, who clung narrowly to their Master's teachings, quite unwilling to go along with any perceptive adjustments. Therefore some essential Mohist doctrines, such as universal love and elevating the worthy, tended to be absorbed into the stream of Confucian thought and thereby to be preserved, while the school itself, because of its highly particular common-people qualities, was extinguished.

Nevertheless the principal reason for the decline and disappearance of Mohism seems to lie in the transformation of the setting, and in the fact that the Mohist followers were unable to adjust the Master's teachings in response to the changes. The Ch'in royal house unified what had been the separately enfeoffed states, transforming them into commanderies and

---

[13] *Ibid.*, no. 83, "An shu." Hsia Tseng-yu defends Mohism: "Inasmuch as Mo Tzu desired to simplify burial practices he had just to establish the existence of spirits. When ghosts and spirits exist, then when the body dies there will still be that immortal entity, continuing to exist, and burial observances then can be minimized. There is not one among the world's religions that teaches the existence of spirits, whether it be Buddhism, Christianity, or Islam, that does not have very simple funeral observance." (*Chung-kuo ku-tai shih*, "History of Ancient China," p. 90.) This view, however, comes very close to constituting a partisan argument, and it is unacceptable as evidence.

[14] Chapter Four, above, has discussed this.

[15] The "Li Yün" [Chapter of the *Li Chi*] is a conspicuous example.

[16] *Hsün Tzu*, *ch.* 6, "Fei shih-erh tzu" [where Hsün Tzu states that others, probably meaning the Taoists, were incapable of this].

[17] *Hsün Tzu*, *ch.* 8, "Ju hsiao."

counties.[18] The feudal lords all were eliminated, leaving the Emperor to be solely venerated. The weapons of the entire realm were smelted down, the metal used to cast bells and statues. Under these new circumstances, the doctrines of opposing aggressive warfare and of agreeing with the superior no longer applied. The First Emperor of Ch'in "whenever over-coming one of the feudal lords had diagrams made of their palaces accord-ing to which copies of them were erected on the northern slope overlooking [his capital city] Hsien-yang. On the south, close to the banks of the Wei, they extended from the Yung Gate eastward all the way to the Ching and Wei rivers; mansions and palaces lined the roads, while walls and pavilions faced each other. Fair women, the drums and the bells, captured from the various feudal lords, were placed in these to furnish them."[19] He "excavated and built [his tomb at] Mount Li," which "was lined with bronze, for his coffin to be placed there. There were palatial chambers and shrines, with places for all the court officials to stand in attendance; curious implements and rare treasures to fill it were taken and stored there."[20] Thus economy of expenditure, condemnation of elaborate funerals, condemnation of wasteful music [and other such austere doc-trines] could not be carried into practice. Clan law had long fallen into

---

[18] For this point, see the final portion of Section One, Chapter Four, above.

[19] *Shih Chi*, ch. 6, "Ch'in Shih-huang pen-chi." Also, *ibid.*, ch. 87, "Li Ssu lieh chuan," tells that the Second Emperor, when plotting with Chao Kao, said: "Now I am the master of the realm. I want to enjoy to the full all the pleasures of eye and ear, exhaust all the joys of my heart's desires." Also, he criticized Li Ssu, saying: "Why would the one person who is the most elevated being in the realm want to belabor his body and weary his spirit, his body resting in a travelers' inn, his mouth fed with a gatekeeper's rations, his hands engaged in the tasks of a servitor or bondsman? An incompetent person might force himself to do that, but a worthy man would not devote himself to such things. When a worthy man possesses the realm, he will exclusively exploit the realm in order to give full rein to his desires, and nothing else." Li Ssu, to curry favor with him, submitted a memo-rial quoting the philosopher Shen Pu-hai: "To possess the empire and yet not to freely indulge one's desires is what is called making shackles of the empire." Although the Second Emperor was by no means a "worthy ruler," his words in fact express very well the attitudes of the vast majority of rulers throughout the two thousand years of imperial history. Moreover, that self-indulgent attitude toward their world has been something from which not even the most outstanding emperors were free. Thus, Liu Chi [the Han Founder] "happened to have an opportunity to see the First Emperor of Ch'in. When he saw him he sighed and said, "Ah, this is the way a great man should be." (*Shih Chi*, ch. 8, "The Basic Annals of Emperor Kao-tsu.") [Translation follows B. Watson, *Record of the Grand Historian of China*, Vol. i, p. 78.] Huang Tsung-hsi [1610–1695] in his *Ming-yi tai-fang lu* ["A Plan for the Prince"], in the chapter called "Yuan chün" ["On the Prince," partial translation in W. T. de Bary, *Sources*, pp. 532–33] discusses how all the rulers from the Ch'in and Han dynasties onward regarded the empire as their personal property, and used it to sustain their private demands; indeed, his views are wholly correct, and require no restatement.

[20] *Shih Chi*, ch. 6.

abeyance, and hereditary ministerial posts had vanished from the scene. High lords and chief ministers had come from the lowliest huts, and a mere police bailiff had become the Son of Heaven. Thus to advocate levelling the hereditary social class structure by elevating the worthy into high office was passé [literally: as one of the previously used and now cast-off "straw dogs"]. Spirits and genies, magicians and manipulators of the Five Agents and the *Yin-yang* doctrines, fortune-telling, interpreters of prodigies, and portents and other superstitions were rampant; such theories were elaborately developed and persuasive.[21] Thus the doctrines about the will of Heaven, proving the existence of spirits and religious practices based on the way of the spiritual beings, might well have been scorned for being too simple and crude. Mohist political thought had been produced in specific response to real conditions of the late Chou historical setting. That they should lack impact and appeal in the unified empire of the authoritarian age was made inevitable by the new circumstances. Yet the intrinsic quality of thought is quite another matter, and one that is not at all to be judged by success or failure to survive.[22]

[21] For a detailed discussion of this, consult the following chapter.

[22] In his *Mo-hsüeh yuan-liu, ch.* 1, pp. 205–210 [the recent scholar] Fang Shou-ch'u lists four reasons for the demise of Mohism: (1) Mohist learning had internal inconsistencies; (2) its ideals were excessively lofty; (3) its organization had been destroyed; (4) it was under suspicion of having supported the Ch'in dynasty. The first two of these reasons display the same fault that Fang charges Liang Ch'i-ch'ao with having committed in seeking the reasons within the body of Mohist doctrines themselves: "If these are genuine reasons, then Mo Tzu's doctrines should have ceased to exist when he died; how could it subsequently have become one of the prominent schools; and only have been extinguished two hundred years later?" The third reason seems to be somewhat forced. The fourth point is strikingly novel. Yet the proof for it relies solely on the conjecture that the line in the *Lun Heng*, no. 20, "Fu-hsü p'ien" shows that the [corresponding] passage in [the *Mo Tzu, ch.* 31] "Ming-kuei" Part III, was altered to read "Duke Mu of Cheng" instead of [as originally intended] "Duke Mu of Ch'in"; that remains at best insubstantial. [For the corresponding line in the *Mo Tzu*, see Burton Watson, *Mo Tzu: Basic Writings*, p. 96, especially footnote 4. Fang's argument is that the Han work, the *Lun Heng*, preserves the original Mohist intent to flatter the ruler's of Ch'in.] On p. 209, Fang states: "Mohism was originally a development in response to the collapse of the old aristocratic society. During the transitional stages, its tenets, while provocative, nonetheless served to sustain activity. After that process of social transformation had been completed, however, and the political order had been stabilized, this anti-ruling class philosophical faction was no longer suited to the circumstances." Except for his use of the term "anti-ruling class," which too readily gives rise to misunderstanding, Fang's discussion otherwise is quite accurate. Generally speaking, the reasons given for the demise of Mohism in such writings as Fang's "P'ing Hu Shih *Chung-kuo che-hsüeh-shih ta-kang,*" Liang Ch'i-ch'ao's "P'ing Hu Shih *Chung-kuo che-hsüeh-shih ta-kang,*" Li Chi's *Hu Shih Chung-kuo che-hsüeh-shih p'i-p'an* (p. 174) [the foregoing are critiques of Hu Shih's "Outline History of Chinese Philosophy," first published in 1919], and Kuo Mo-jo's *Chung-kuo ku-tai she-hui yen-chiu* ["Studies on Ancient China's Society," published 1930], (first edition, pp. 72–73), all are more or less acceptable.

Section Two
Li Ssu (ca. 280–208 b.c.)

Legalist thought provided the foundation stone on which Ch'in government stood. The techniques were extensively applied by Lord Shang, and the theory was fully developed by Han Fei Tzu. Under Li Ssu it reached the apogee, then went into decline; thereafter, sharing the Ch'in dynasty's fate, Legalist government also came to an end.

"Li Ssu was a man of Shang-ts'ai in the State of Ch'u. As a young man he served as a clerk in the local government." Shortly thereafter, "he became a pupil of Hsün Tzu, under whom he studied the governing methods of emperors and kings."[23] Knowing that there was little hope for accomplishing anything in the Six States, he went off to the [seventh] State of Ch'in and, at the behest of Lü Pu-wei [chief minister in Ch'in between 250 and 237 b.c.], he presented his arguments to the [future] First Emperor. Throughout more than twenty years he served in posts from that of Senior Scribe [*chang shih*] to that of Minister of Justice [*t'ing-wei*]. After the unification of the empire [in 221 b.c.], Li Ssu received an imperial command to advise the throne on the subject of feudal investiture. Alone in opposing the consensus, he presented the arguments [eventually accepted] that the commandery-county system [of direct administration] was the method for achieving enduring stability and peace. Subsequently, when Li Ssu had become Grand Councillor [*ch'eng-hsiang*], he proposed the burning of the books. When the First Emperor had succeeded in unifying the [territories of the former] Six States, he "made the systems of writing uniform, built palaces and villas, and travelled widely throughout the realm. . . . On the frontiers he drove back the four [nations of] barbarian peoples. To all of these things, Li Ssu contributed forcefully."[24] In the thirty-seventh year of his reign (210 b.c.) the First Emperor died at Sha-ch'iu. Li Ssu and [the chief eunuch] Chao Kao plotted together to have [Hu-hai, a younger son] ascend the throne as The Second Emperor, and to put [the eldest son and heir] Fu-su to death. The Second Emperor entrusted Chao Kao with the responsibilities, gave rein to his passions, and indulged himself in pleasures, while also making penalties for crimes

---

[23] *Shih Chi*, ch. 87, "Biography of Li Ssu." [Derk Bodde's *China's First Unifier*, 1938, containing a translation of this chapter of the *Shih Chi*, as well as of supporting texts, has been heavily drawn upon here and in the following quotations from the *Shih Chi*.]

[24] *Shih Chi*, ch. 6, "Ch'in Shih-huang pen-chi," i.e., "Basic Annals of the First Emperor". The year in which Li Ssu entered the State of Ch'in corresponds to the third year of the reign of King Chuang-hsiang (247 b.c.). He became Minister of Justice and expressed his views on feudal investiture in the Twenty-sixth year of the First Emperor's reign (221 b.c.).

more severe, and executing many persons. Li Ssu feared plots against himself, therefore toadied to the Emperor's wishes; he submitted a memorial, nonetheless, urging the Emperor to put into practice the methods of supervising [officials] and holding them responsible [for their performance in office, in an effort to re-impose systematic Legalist government]. Chao Kao, however, finally succeeded in charging Li Ssu with plotting to rebel, for which he was thrown into prison and forced to plead guilty, then executed by being cut in two at the waist, in the market-place of Hsien-yang [the capital city]. That happened in the seventh moon of the second year in the Second Emperor's reign.[25] It was less than two years later that the Ch'in dynasty came to an end. The years of his life work and career thus, in point of actual fact, correspond to the period of the Ch'in dynasty's existence.

Li Ssu left no writings, yet his political doctrines are evident in his policies as implemented by the First Emperor, and in the debates and discourses he issued [in support of those]. The essentials of his political thought can be summarized under four headings.

The first is the elevation of the ruler, [*tsun-chün* 尊君]. In the twenty-sixth year of his reign, just after completing the consolidation of the empire, the First Emperor commanded his Grand Councillors and Chief Minister to submit proposals concerning the imperial title. Li Ssu, who was then Minister of Justice, submitted a discourse on this jointly with Wang Kuan and Feng Chieh, which said, in part: "Of old, the territory of the Five Emperors constituted a square of [only] one thousand *li*. Beyond this were the domains of the feudal lords and of the barbarians. Some of the feudal lords came to court to do homage, and some did not; the Son of Heaven was unable to keep control over them. But now Your Majesty has raised his armies of righteousness and put to death oppressors and brigands. You have pacified the world and have laid out all within the seas into commanderies and counties. Laws and ordinances emanate from one center. Such a thing has never existed from high antiquity until now; it is something the Five Emperors did not attain to. We, your ministers, having carefully deliberated with the Scholars of Wide Learning, would say: Of old there were the Celestial Sovereign *t'ien-huang*, the Terrestrial Sovereign *ti-huang*, and the Great Sovereign, *t'ai-huang*. The Great Sovereign possessed the most noble status. We, your ministers, at the risk of death for our words, would propose as a venerable appellation that the King be called the Great Sovereign, that mandates be called decrees [*chih* 制] and that ordinances be called edicts [*chao* 詔]. And let the Son of Heaven

---

[25] *Shih Chi*, ch. 87. The year of Li Ssu's death was 208 B.C. Ch'ien Mu in his *Hsien Ch'in chu-tzu hsi-nien k'ao-pien*, Section 156, hypothesizes that Li Ssu was in his thirties when he went to the State of Ch'in, and therefore must have been born about 280 B.C.

apply to himself [the Imperial pronoun] *chen* 朕.''²⁶ Although the First Emperor slightly changed the title, calling himself "Huang-ti" 皇帝, from this time onward all of the polite titles that had been used by kings and feudal lords throughout the pre-Ch'in period were abolished, and the Emperor henceforth was the highest and most venerated of all human beings. Inasmuch as the historical account, in addition to mentioning the Grand Councillors and Chief Minister, makes special point of mentioning the Minister of Justice, it seems probable that the proposal was put forth principally by Li Ssu.

Second is the centralization of authority [*chi-ch'üan* 集權]. The First Emperor, on receiving a petition from the Grand Councillor Wang Kuan asking that he install his sons as princes in order to impose control over the territories of the newly vanquished Six States, turned their proposal over to the court officials for deliberation. Li Ssu responded: "Kings Wen and Wu of the Chou dynasty granted numerous fiefs to their sons and younger brothers and other members of their clan. But as time passed these near relatives became estranged and divided; they attacked each other the same as enemies would. More and more these feudal lords warred among themselves, and the Chou Son of Heaven was unable to stop that. Now, owing to Your Majesty's divine powers, everything within the four seas has been unified, and has all been divided into commanderies and counties. The sons of the imperial family and the meritorious ministers have been amply rewarded with ducal titles and revenues from the taxes. This adequately provides for ease of governing. Let there be no contrary opinions about this within the realm. That is the method by which to achieve stability and peace. To invest feudal lords would not be advantageous."²⁷ The First Emperor adopted his view, and in consequence the commandery-county [directly administered] pattern for the empire took the definitive form it was to retain for the next two thousand years.

The third is the prohibition of private learning [*chin ssu-hsüeh* 禁私學]. In the thirty-fourth year of the First Emperor's reign [213 B.C.], a man of the [former State of] Ch'i named Ch'un-yü Yüeh again aroused the debate over feudal investiture; he said: "One has not heard of any matter which was not in accord with ancient models and which yet endured." Li Ssu submitted a discourse that argued: "In antiquity the realm was divided and disorderly; incapable of being united. Because of that the feudal lords all became active. In their speech they always drew on the

---

²⁶ *Shih Chi*, ch. 6. [Slightly modified from D. Bodde, *China's First Unifier*, pp. 77–78.]
²⁷ *Shih Chi*, ch. 6. [Modified from Bodde, *op.cit.*, pp. 78–79.] This was the first of the debates on the relative merits of feudal investiture and the commandery-county system [i.e., directly administered regional and local government] in the two-thousand-year period of the imperial era.

past in order to bring confusion into the present; they dissembled with meaningless terms in order to confuse reality. People admired their private learning, using it to contradict what the ruler had ordained. Today, Your Majesty, possessing the whole empire, has established his sole eminence by declaring unambiguous distinctions of right and wrong. Yet still there are some who draw on private learning whereby to contradict your decreed laws and teachings. Hearing that an ordinance has been issued, men argue about it in the light of their private learning. At court they retain their mental reservations, and away from court they express their own views in the streets. They gain fame by disagreeing with the ruler, and are looked up to for being of different mind. They lead the people to fabricate distortions. If this is not prohibited, the ruler's power over all will diminish, while factions underneath will come into being. It would be advantageous to forbid that.

"Your servant requests that all persons possessing works of literature, the *Odes*, the *Documents*, and the discourses of the hundred schools, should avoid penalty by getting rid of those. Those who have not destroyed all such within thirty days shall be branded and sent to do forced labor. Those which need not be so destroyed shall include works on medicine and pharmacy, on divination by tortoise and milfoil, and on agriculture and horticulture. As for persons who wish to study, let them take the [local] officials as their teachers."[28] The First Emperor approved this proposal; in consequence, the book burning policy that has so stirred all the ages was brought forth.

During the feudal age's most flourishing period, thought and learning had been the sole possession of the aristocracy. Private individuals had not

---

[28] *Shih Chi, ch.* 87 [drawing heavily on Bodde, *op.cit.*, pp. 23–24; cf. de Bary, *Sources*, p. 154–55]. *Ch.* 6, The First Emperor's "Basic Annals," has a slightly different wording. After "Your servant requests," it continues: "that all books in the bureau of history except the records of Ch'in be burned; that all persons in the empire, save those appointed as official Scholars of Wide Learning, [Erudits,] who dare to keep the *Odes*, the *Documents*, or the discourses of the hundred schools, shall send all of those writings to local authorities for burning. Anyone daring to discuss the *Odes* and the *Documents* among themselves shall be executed and their corpses exposed in the market place. Those who use the past to criticize the present shall be put to death, together with their entire families. Officials who observe or learn about [such infractions] and do not report them shall suffer the same penalties. Those who have not burned [all such forbidden writings] within thirty days are to be branded and sent to do forced labor. Those which need not be so destroyed shall include works on medicine and pharmacy, on divination by tortoise and milfoil, and on agriculture and horticulture. As for persons who wish to study laws and ordinances, let them take the [local] officials as their teachers." Here the enforcement is somewhat more rigorous. It should be noted that in the text of this "Basic Annals" version, some phrases are out of place: for owning books to be sent to do forced labor; for discussing among themselves to be executed and exposed in the market place; these would seem to be incongruities. One suspects that the text is corrupt.

written books; therefore there had been no need for prohibitions to prevent the existence of private learning. From the Spring and Autumn Period onward, however, learning gradually was extended to the common people. Confucianism and Mohism especially proliferated. Because Confucius "taught without distinction of classes" [*Analects*, xv/38], his achievement in broadly expanding knowledge and in hastening the advance of thought was particularly remarkable. Even though the shortcomings of the followers often led to conflicting "heterodoxies," and to confusing juxtapositions of true and false, yet from the standpoint of cultural history we cannot but look upon the disorderly competition among philosophic views that characterized the late Chou era as an advance. When the Ch'in dynasty, adopting Li Ssu's statements, prohibited all private learning, the free-thinking mode suffered a severe setback. Thereafter, most rulers continued to apply the insight previously gained by the First Emperor, "consistently extolling so-and-so while deprecating so-and-so, in a spirit of conformity."[29] Although this was the inevitable policy of authoritarian government, and Li Ssu was merely applying the doctrines of his teacher,[30] the responsibility therefore not lying with him as an individual, the consequences for Chinese thought and learning have been so pervasive and so profound as to be virtually incalculable. Later scholars have failed to mark this aspect of the matter, only concerning themselves to prove meticulously that the books the First Emperor burned were private writings and not official works.[31] How deficient in discernment that is!

[29] Liang Ch'i-ch'ao, *Ch'ing-tai hsüeh-shu kai-lun*, p. 144 [translated by Immanuel Hsü as *Intellectual Trends in the Ch'ing Period*, 1959; cf. p. 126].

[30] *Hsün Tzu, ch.* 22, "Cheng ming" says: "It is easy to unify the people by means of the Way, though they cannot share in the understanding of it. Therefore the enlightened ruler presides over them with power, guides them by the Way, leads them on by commands, and manifests standards to them with the models [of behavior], and restricts them by the punishments. His people therefore are transformed into the Way as if by spiritual forces. What need has he of arguments and persuasion?"

[31] For example, in K'ang Yu-wei's *Wei-ching k'ao, ch.* 1, where it states, under the heading: "A Study of the Fact that the Ch'in Burning of the Six Classics Did Not Actually Eliminate Them," that the First Emperor had ordered copies of the *Odes* and the *Documents* owned by the people burned, but the copies kept by the court's Erudits, i.e., *po-shih*, continued to exist. That view had already been previously expressed by Liu Ta-k'uei, [his collected prose writings,] *Hai-feng Wen-chi*, in an essay called "On the Burning of the Books" ["Fen shu pien"], stated that the loss of the Six Classics was not caused by the First Emperor, but that they were in fact lost during the Han period. His point is that when Hsiao Ho [an associate of the Han Founder in the civil war at the fall of the Ch'in] on reaching Hsien-yang [the Ch'in capital] took over the books on laws and regulations in the offices of the Grand Councillor, but did not extend that care to the books preserved by the Ch'in Erudits. Then, when Hsiang Yü [leader of the civil war enemy forces] entered the pass [leading to the capital], the Ch'in palaces were set afire, whereupon all

The fourth is implementing systems of supervision and of fixing responsibility [*hsing tu-tse* 行督責]. The Second Emperor put this searching question to Li Ssu: "I want to give uninhibited expression to my will and indulge my desires to the broadest extent. I hope long to enjoy the fruits of empire, and to suffer no harm. Why should I not do this?"

Li Ssu replied to this in a memorial. His words constitute the clearest and most extreme statement on the theory of authoritarianism in all the two thousand years of Chinese imperial history. He wrote: "Shen Tzu [the Legalist thinker Shen Pu-hai, died 337 B.C.] has said: 'To possess the empire, and yet not throw off all restraints, is called making shackles for oneself of the empire.' There is no reason for that to happen other than [a ruler's] failure to supervise [his underlings] and hold them responsible; when however his responsibilities must extend to belaboring his own body in service to the people of his empire in the manner of [the Sage Kings] Yao and Yü, [the empire] indeed is to be called his shackles.

"If one is unable to implement the intelligent methods [*shu*] of Shen Pu-hai and Han Fei Tzu, carrying out their means of supervising and holding others responsible, and devote oneself solely to using the empire for one's own interests, and if instead one has to belabor his body and weary his spirit by his personal services to the common people, then he is but a servant to the black-headed masses. He is not husbanding the realm. What is there about that which gives one eminence? For, when one is served by others, he is eminent and those others are base; when one serves others, those others are made eminent and one's self becomes debased. Therefore servants are base, and those they serve are the eminent ones. From antiquity to the present, it has always been thus."[32]

We have noted earlier that the special characteristic of Legalist thought is to take the person of the ruler as the objective of all governing. This discourse from Li Ssu not only expressed that central element in the theories of Lord Shang and Han Fei Tzu; it also exposes the secret yearnings of the authoritarian ruler. The clarity and frankness of this piece would have put even Lord Shang and Han Fei Tzu to shame. Li Ssu also discusses the ways by which the ruler can indulge his passions: "When abstemious, disciplined, benevolent, and righteous men stand in the court, then the wild and unrestrained revels cease. When remonstrating, dissuading servitors who talk of reason are to be heard from close by, then one's straying, expansive wishes will be set aside. When the deeds of

---

of the ancient books and records were totally destroyed by fire. Liu Ta-k'uei lived during the K'ang-hsi and Ch'ien-lung eras [died 1779]. *Ts'ui Shih* [1851-1924] in his *Shih-chi t'an-yuan*, *ch.* 3, also stated that the First Emperor burned books owned by the people and forbade private teaching, but allowed people to go to the Erudits for instruction in such learning.

[32] *Shih Chi, ch.* 87.

noble heroes who die for their principles attract the attention of the age, then all dissolute pleasures must be abolished from one's thoughts. Therefore the perceptive ruler is able to transcend these three [restrictive influences], to maintain his sole control over the methods of ruling; thereby he commands compliant and obedient servitors, and keeps his clear laws in operation. In that way, his person is elevated and his power [shih] is great. Any able ruler must have the capacity to shake off the world's standards and shape his practices, to discard what he dislikes and to institute what he desires. In that way, living he will possess awesome and overwhelming power, and in death he will be granted posthumous titles denoting his illustrious and worthy qualities. That is why the intelligent ruler decides matters solely on his own; hence authority does not lie with his servitors. Only then can he eliminate the [competing] course of benevolence and righteousness, stop up the mouths of eloquent persuaders, bar the deeds of noble heroes, block the wise ones and screen off the knowing ones, so that within [his palace] he can alone observe and listen. Thereby, from outside [his court] he will not be undermined by the deeds of benevolent and righteous heroes, and from within it he will not be preempted by the arguments of remonstrating, dissuading debaters. And so he will be able to indulge fully the dictates of his own mind, in solitary splendor, and no one shall dare oppose him. When he has achieved this, he can be said to have succeeded in grasping the methods [shu] of Shen Pu-hai and Han Fei Tzu, and in realizing the laws [fa] of Lord Shang. When those methods and the laws have been so grasped and realized, it is unheard of that the empire could know disorders."

When the ruler can exercise sole power of decision, he then can follow freely all his own desires. Yet if he does not employ severe penalties to keep his servitors and underlings intimidated and compliant, his methods will still be defective. Li Ssu also quotes: "Han Fei Tzu has said, 'It is the doting mother who has the prodigal son, while in a strictly run household there are no stubborn, bad tempered servants.' What does that mean? It means that one must not hesitate to increase penalties. Therefore, according to the laws of Lord Shang, there was corporal punishment for those who scattered ashes in the streets. Now, scattering ashes is a very slight offense, and corporal punishment is a heavy penalty. Only one who is capable of maintaining far-reaching supervision over slight offenses can be considered an intelligent ruler. For, when supervision is far-reaching even for slight offenses, how much more so will it be for serious offenses! And thus the people will not dare commit violations. . . . When such a condition exists, then it can be said that supervision and holding people responsible have become realities. Then the servitors will be free of bad conduct, and when the servitors are free of bad conduct, the empire is secure. When the empire is secure, the ruler is awesome and elevated.

When the ruler is awesome and elevated, then supervision and fixing responsibility are certain. When supervision and fixing responsibility are made certain, what is sought will be obtained. When what is sought can be obtained, the state will be prosperous. When the state is prosperous, then the ruler's pleasures will abound. Therefore, when the methods of supervision and fixing responsibility have been put into operation, then nothing that is desired will be beyond obtaining. Servitors and common people alike do not have enough time to save themselves from punishment. What resistance would they dare to plot?...."[33] All the references to methods to "sole power of decision," "supervising, and fixing responsibility," and "far-reaching supervision over slight offenses," are, according to Li Ssu's own statement, based on the doctrines of Lord Shang and Han Fei Tzu. Indeed, they are among the essential elements of Lord Shang's and Han Fei Tzu's thought. Although we may blame Li Ssu for giving such advice to so unworthy a person [as the Second Emperor], we cannot say that he had grossly misconstrued those predecessors.

Nonetheless, one question must arise in our minds. The methods of elevating the ruler and making penalties severe as employed by Lord Shang when he was chief minister to Duke Hsiao brought the State of Ch'in to wealth and power. They were used by Li Ssu in assisting the First Emperor to conquer the empire. The "Memorial on Supervision, and on Fixing Responsibility" in setting its ideas forth also, to be sure, refers to these as methods practiced by the earlier [Ch'in] rulers. Yet, the Second Emperor employed such methods for only a few years before he was assassinated and his dynasty had fallen. Must one assume that these methods were such that "only an intelligent ruler could practice them," and Hu-hai [the Second Emperor] simply was incapable of that? Or, is there a grave defect in Legalist thought itself, making it incapable of maintaining an enduring government?

The Second Emperor, as a person in his own right, was a muddle-headed incompetent, given to arrogant and unrestrained ways. It would be difficult to find one more subject to those faults among the kings and emperors of all past history. The *History of the [Former] Han Dynasty*, in its "Table of Past and Present Personages" [ch. 20] assigns him to the category of "Lower middle" [eighth of nine categories], erring somewhat on the side of generosity. Given such a ruler, occupying a position of authoritarian powers, no matter what political theories or policies he might adopt, his overthrow and collapse might be difficult to avoid. From this point of view, Hu-hai must be charged with responsibility for the Ch'in

---

[33] *Shih Chi*, ch. 87. Also, the *So-yin* [*Commentary*, on that passage], adduces the explanation: "Supervision means to investigate. On investigating someone's offense, that person is then made responsible for his actions by the use of corporal punishments and penalties."

collapse. Yet, to conclude that the political doctrines of Lord Shang and Han Fei Tzu nonetheless can provide a sound basis for government, is still incorrect.

Pre-Ch'in "Legalist" thought is in fact a misnomer for authoritarian theory. Its methods ostensibly emphasize laws, but implicitly elevate the ruler. Thus as its theories become the more fully developed, the latent impulse to elevate the ruler becomes the clearer, while stress on law grows correspondingly weaker. The *Kuan Tzu* lays great importance on the ruler's establishing laws that are binding upon himself, and also repeatedly speaks of [the ruler's] accepting remonstrance, limiting his desires, and the like. Therefore, though the ruler's authority is elevated, it is still subject to many limitations. Han Fei Tzu, however, no longer upholds the theory that "the regulations are more to be honored than the ruler," therein moving further from the concept of the government of laws [or, the rule of law] and closer to that of authoritarianism. Still, the chapter *ch.* 10, "Shih Kuo," or "Ten Faults," condemns such things as "not serious about attending to governmental affairs and being fond of music," "giving oneself to women and pleasure and being inattentive to governing the state," "travelling about far from the capital and being heedless of remonstrating officials," and "committing faults about which the advice of loyal servitors goes unheeded, while solely pursuing his own purposes." Han Fei Tzu's purpose is to restrict the ruler, not to allow him to indulge his passions. Therefore, even though Han Fei Tzu's authoritarianism has progressed beyond that of the *Kuan Tzu*, it still has not reached the ultimate limits.

Coming to Li Ssu, however, we find him, as the First Emperor's advisor, aiding him in building palaces, urging him to reject remonstrance, accompanying him on his distant travels. As chief minister to the Second Emperor, Li Ssu responded positively to his wish to indulge his passions, and supported that in his "Memorial on Supervision, and Fixing Responsibilities." Consequently, all those limitations [on the ruler's behavior] that Han Fei Tzu had established were totally abandoned. Thereupon the absolute monarchical authoritarianism, in theory and in fact, in which the ruler "alone ruled the empire, and was ruled by no one,"[34] came into glaring view on the Chinese scene.

Unlimited authority readily degenerates into excessive misuse. Successors in an imperial line are mostly incompetent and stupid, rarely outstanding and intelligent. These two norms are indisputably evident in all of mankind's political life. The great danger present in authoritarian theory is that it concentrates great powers in one person, yet is incapable of assuring that the ruler will possess superior qualities. The Second Em-

[34] A phrase from the "Memorial on Supervision, and on Fixing Responsibility."

peror is not worth considering, but even if the First Emperor had not died in the thirty-seventh year of his reign [210 B.C.], it seems unlikely that he would have been able to long maintain a stable government. When we observe his efforts to achieve immortality [through alchemy and magic], his devotion to sensual pleasures, the important posts in which he used [the nefarious eunuch] Chao Kao, his estrangement from his [vigorous and able eldest son,] Fu-su, and all such matters, it becomes obvious that he was a ruler of no more than mediocre abilities who gained mastery of the empire because he was heir to the achievements of Duke Hsiao [reigned 361–338 B.C., whom Lord Shang had served]. Measured against the standards for rulership that Han Fei Tzu sets up in his *ch.* 29, "Ta t'i," the First Emperor must, in truth, be seen as "a thousand *li* off the mark." Nonetheless, the First Emperor managed to employ Li Ssu, and General Meng T'ien, so he apparently possessed some ability in judging human capacities. His "self-indulgence" also was subject to at least some self-imposed limits. And, whenever important issues of government arose, he always referred them to his court officials for deliberation. In these things, the First Emperor's authoritarianism still retained traces of Han Fei Tzu's influence, and, compared with the absolute authoritarianism manifested in Li Ssu's "Memorial on Supervising, and on Fixing Responsibility," it is a shade paler. Thus it may be not without reason that the general outbreak of rebellion in the Kuan-tung region [which brought the Ch'in dynasty's downfall during the Second Emperor's reign] did not occur while the First Emperor was still on the throne.

Traditionally, and in the present, the assessments of Ch'in dynasty government have either ridiculed it for having failed through the excessive reliance on corporal punishments, or regretted that its efforts to rule through law did not endure. If the foregoing discussion is not erroneous, however, the Ch'in dynasty came to its rapid demise because of the inherent failings of authoritarianism; its collapse had very little to do at all with implementing a government of laws. The distinction between a government of laws and authoritarian government lies in the former's granting the highest authority to the law, which ruler and servitors must alike obey. In the latter, the ruler possesses supreme authority, and can alter the laws at will. To use this as a defining criterion, there was no true "government of law" political thought in the pre-Ch'in era, and still less was there any government actually practicing the government of law. The State of Ch'in, from the reign of Duke Hsiao [reigned 361–338 B.C.] onward, adopted the laws of Lord Shang and of Han Fei Tzu. When we analyze these, their most important articles do not go beyond: (1) elevating the ruler and emphasizing the state; (2) encouraging agriculture and pursuing warfare; (3) applying rigorous corporal punishments and making penalties certain; (4) clarifying the laws and openly promulgating the regulations. No single item among these can be acknowledged as embodying the essential tenet of government of laws. The first two items listed need not be discussed. The third, "applying rigorous corporal punishments," and the fourth, "clarifying the laws," appear to be relevant to the government of laws. However, both the "rigorous corporal punishments" discussed by Lord Shang and Han Fei Tzu, as also the "far-reaching supervision" discussed by Li Ssu, alike lacked the equity of law, and would not be acceptable to modern concepts of the government of laws. Clarifying laws and openly promulgating regulations, formulating definitive wording of the laws, and openly promulgating these to the people, are simply administrative actions that no government of whatever form could dispense with. If that is taken to signify government of law, then all governments are governments of law, and the Ch'in cannot claim any particular distinction in that regard. [The translation "government by laws" for *fa-chih* is used in Chapter Seven and elsewhere of the present work in describing Legalist governments in Chinese history, in the effort to distinguish them from "the Rule of Law."] Chang Ping-lin [1868–1936] has stated that China during the past two thousand years has not known government of law, "except only in the Ch'in system, based on Lord Shang's doctrines, where the rulers through successive generations observed the laws."[35] The reasons for Chang's having been led into that error would seem to be his own failure to comprehend the true significance of a government of law,[36] as well as his interest in praising the First Emperor while disparaging the rulers of the Han and T'ang dynasties. When we examine the events recorded in history with objectivity, we see then how many of the governmental acts in which the First Emperor and Li Ssu participated come very close to what Chang Ping-lin himself calls "being arbitrary," and we fail to discover any traces of their having "heeded the law."

We should go still one step further and state that although Lord Shang's and Han Fei Tzu's authoritarian thought and the State of Ch'in's authoritarian government bear some superficial resemblances to government of law, they are in fact fundamentally incompatible with government of law. Authoritarianism is a system of thought that takes the ruler as its standard [or basic element], but Rule-of-Law thought has law as its standard; this point has been repeatedly referred to in the present work. Inasmuch as authoritarianism employs the ruler's intentions as its ultimate

[35] *Chang T'ai-yen Wen-lu, ch.* 1, "Ch'in cheng-chi."

[36] Chang Ping-lin nonetheless wrote with great clarity on the distinction between government of men and government of laws. In his *T'ai-yen Wen-lu, ch.* 1, "*Fei huang,*" he wrote: "All government should shun arbitrariness. The distinction between being arbitrary or not is precisely that marked by either heeding the law or elevating worthy men." [In Chang's mind, the former characterized Legalism and the latter Confucianism.]

criterion, laws are then nothing more than instruments used in the tasks of governing. The ruler can alter their provisions at will, and the laws in consequence lack the power to restrict the ruler. "Chao Kao had previously instructed Hu-hai in writing, as well as in matters of litigation, regulations, ordinances and laws."[37] This makes it evident that the Second Emperor [Hu-hai] was not lacking knowledge of the laws. Yet not long after he had ascended to the throne, on Chao Kao's urgings, he "made laws and regulations anew," in accord with his private wish to indulge his own whims.[38] Thus, law in the authoritarian polity possesses a character very close to that of a mere written record of the ruler's wishes; it cannot transcend those interests and still take effect. Even should a ruler prove able to abide by his own laws, that would be in consequence of the ruler's personal choice and not of the binding power of the laws themselves. The government of law takes the law as its highest standard, and the ruler is an agency for implementing the law. Thus the constitutional monarch not merely has no power to alter the laws at will, neither is he permitted any actions that violate the laws.[39] [A short passage in the original text is omitted here, at the suggestion of the author who deems it of dubious validity.]

[37] *Shih Chi*, *ch.* 6.
[38] *Shih Chi*, *ch.* 87.
[39] The Rule of Law can be realized only under two conditions. The one is that of aristocratic government, and the other is that of a constitutional government. When an aristocracy possesses the real power whereby to resist the ruler, law also can serve as a sharp weapon for limiting the monarch's will. The aristocracy can utilize law as a protection of its own interests, and governments of law have taken advantage of that circumstance to come into being. Constitutional governments depend on the laws for all the definitions of official responsibilities and powers (even where there are no explicit written regulations there will exist demarcations embodied in custom and precedent). Not only is the constitutional law superior to all else, it will not even be possible for the government to violate the ordinary legal regulations at will. Modern constitutional government is the highest form of government of law; aristocratic government of law as a means of resisting monarchical power is its immature phase of development. English constitutional history provides an outstanding example of the progressive development of government of law, from the stage of aristocratic resistance to the monarch to that of constitutional monarchy. In antiquity China lacked government of law, probably because of fortuitous historical circumstances. In the clan-law society prior to the Spring and Autumn Era [before the eighth century B.C.], the *li*, i.e., rites, served to maintain the system, and it bore some superficial resemblances to a government of law. During the Spring and Autumn Era [eighth to fifth centuries] the *li* was transformed into laws, *fa*, and the aristocracy still existed; there appeared to be some possibility for a government of law to develop. Unfortunately, that aristocracy was largely incompetent and undisciplined, and powerful ministers characteristically usurped the powers of the monarch, producing thereby a greater need to elevate the rulers than to limit their powers. Therefore Confucius and Hsün Tzu stressed the *li*, while Kuan Tzu and Lord Shang emphasized laws, all sharing the concern about how to hold aristocrats and powerful ministers in check. Consequently,

To summarize, it is evident that authoritarianism and the government of law are quite opposite kinds of polities,[40] and the Ch'in government, as brought into being in accord with Legalist thought, was an authoritarian polity and not a government of law. Moreover, it should be clear that Ch'in's collapse was a failure of authoritarianism, not a defeat for government of law. For Ch'in's reliance upon its laws was by no means an example of the government of law. And even that policy of reliance upon laws was rejected by all the subsequent dynasties, from the Han and T'ang to the Ming and Ch'ing. Thus, throughout the two thousand years of China's imperial history, when did there ever appear a single instance of a government embodying the Rule of Law?

SECTION THREE
Continuing Strands of Legalist Thought

ON the basis of the existing literary material it can be concluded that Han Fei Tzu was the last important contributor to the development of Legalist theory; while Li Ssu was the ultimate practitioner of Legalist governing methods. After the fall of the Ch'in, and among all the rulers and ministers thereafter, there never again was one who attempted to

---

laws became the instrument for elevating monarchs. Later, when the social class distinctions were obliterated, the common people lacked power to resist their rulers, and the concept of using laws was transformed into a body of purely authoritarian thought. Thus ancient China's only chance to realize a government of law vanished during the Spring and Autumn Era. By the time of the First Emperor [third century B.C.] there long had existed a milieu that would not allow any further approaches to government of law. See Chapter Six, footnotes 74–79, of the present work.

[40] Liang Ch'i-ch'ao, in Chapter Thirteen of his *Hsien Ch'in cheng-chih ssu-hsiang shih* ["History of Pre-Ch'in Political Thought," translated by L. T. Ch'en as *History of Chinese Thought during the Early Tsin Period*, London, 1930], describes Legalist thought as "the doctrine of government by laws." Chapter Fourteen also describes "government by power" [*shih chih*] as "authoritarianism," and says that "government by methods" was "one variety of government of men," and considers all [of those elements of Legalism] to have been contradictory to government of law. (In Liang's *Yin-ping-shih, Chuan-chi* edition, pp. 138–39.) It appears that Liang used "reliance on laws" and "government of law" interchangeably. In Chapter Sixteen he states: "The Legalist school's greatest fault was that its legislative authority was incapable of achieving a radical reform," but could only allow the laws to be defined according to the will of the ruler. "In order to justify calling it a government of law, minimally it also must have something corresponding to what in modern times is called a constitutional form of government proceding from it" (pp. 148–49). This is in general terms correct. But his ridicule of Legalism as "taking Taoism's moribund, quiescent, mechanistic, materialistic philosophy of life as its starting point" (p. 154) not only displays a misunderstanding of the relationship between Taoism and Legalism; it also shows a failure to understand the true significance of [ancient China's] thought concerning reliance on laws.

carry into practice a purely Legalist government,[41] and likewise the learning of Lord Shang and Han Fei Tzu marked the end of all further advances in the realm of theory. There were indeed many of their immediate followers and their more distant disciples during the Han period, such as Lord Wu, the Prefect of Ho-nan, Chang Shu, Ch'ao Ts'o, Fan Yeh, Chou Yü, Yang Ch'iu, and others, all of whose studies were within a known line of transmission [from a Legalist master].[42] Beyond these, there is a still greater number of persons whose words and deeds display conformity with the doctrines of elevating the ruler, employing severe punishments, and the other distinctive tenets of the school. Yet these all

[41] Although the Emperor Wen [179–157 B.C.] "personally valued the Legalist [*hsing-ming*] doctrines" (*Shih Chi*, ch. 121, "Ju-lin chuan") [cf. Watson, vol. II, p. 398], in his governing he employed mainly the Huang-Lao [Taoist] teachings. The Emperor Hsüan [73–49 B.C.] managed to "make rewards dependable and punishments certain, and to examine and confront names with realities," (*Han Shu*, ch. 8, "Encomium" to the "Basic Annals of Emperor Hsüan"), [following Dubs, *Han Shu* vol. II, p. 265]. "He mainly employed Legalist officials with their multitude of statutes, and restricted his subjects according to their 'actualities and names,' [*hsing-ming*]." Yet, in response to the heir apparent's remonstrance against that, he said: "The Han dynasty has its own institutes and laws, combining various elements from the Lords Protector and the [sage] kings. How could we rely solely upon moral suasion, or upon Chou dynasty governmental ways?" (*Han Shu*, ch. 9, "Basic Annals of Emperor Yuan".) [Cf. the somewhat different translation in Dubs, vol. II, *Han Shu* 9, pp. 299–301, for the context of these remarks, and a slightly different translation. E.g., Dubs translates *hsing-ming* as "the principles of circumstances and names," referring to Fung/Bodde, vol. I, pp. 192, 323–25; cf. Chapter Eight, footnote 12, above. Although that is elsewhere justifiable, here "*hsing-ming*" is used as a general designation for Legalist governing principles.] This indicates that not even Emperor Hsüan relied purely on Legalist doctrines. From that time onward, the governmental methods that came closest to Legalism were those employed by Emperor Wu of the Wei dynasty [i.e., Ts'ao Ts'ao, A.D. 155–220] and of the Prime Minister of the State of Shu, Chu-ko Liang [A.D. 181–234]. Yet, when compared with the governing of the First Emperor of Ch'in and of Li Ssu, their methods again were different.

[42] Lord Wu, who lived during the reign of Emperor Wen [179–157 B.C.], "previously had lived in the same city as Li Ssu, and had once studied under him." (*Shih Chi*, ch. 84, "Biography of Chia Yi".) [Cf. Watson, *Shih Chi*, vol. I, p. 508.] Chang Shu, "Active during the reign of the Emperor Wen, he was appointed to serve the heir apparent because of his knowledge of the Legalist [*hsing-ming*; see footnote 41, above] doctrines." (*Shih Chi*, ch. 103, "Biography of Chang Shu.") [Cf. Watson, *Shih Chi*, vol. I, p. 554.] Ch'ao Ts'o "studied the Legalist doctrines of Shen Pu-hai and Lord Shang at the school of Master Chang Hui in Chih." (*Shih Chi*, ch. 101, "Biography of Yüan Ang and Ch'ao Ts'o.") [Cf. Watson, *Shih Chi*, vol. I, p. 527.] Fan Yeh lived during the time of the Emperor Kuang-wu [reigned A.D. 25–57]; "His conduct of government was severe and harsh, and he was predisposed to favor the Laws of Shen Pu-hai and Han Fei." (*Hou Han Shu*, ch. 107, "Biographies of Harsh Officials.") Chou Yü was active during the reign of Emperor Ho [reigned A.D. 89–105]; "as a person he was exacting and vindictive, lacking in mercy; he was devoted to the methods [in government] of Han Fei" (*ibid.*). Yang Ch'iu lived during the time of the Emperor Ling [reigned A.D. 168–188]; "by nature severe and cruel, he favored the doctrines of Shen Pu-hai and Han Fei" (*ibid.*).

merely continued the doctrines of their predecessors in response to the practical needs of their own times. They no longer devoted themselves to writing books,[43] nor can they be credited with any new and creative ideas. Although their power and influence was great and on the one hand they gained imperial favor, while on the other they competed with Confucian learning, vastly exceeding the Mohist school that had so suddenly lapsed into somnolent decline, yet from the standpoint of the history of thought, the school of *hsing-ming* [i.e., Legalist statecraft] during the Han dynasty was no more than a ripple from the teachings of Shen Pu-hai and Han Fei Tzu; their influences had not been terminated, yet neither was there any capacity to restore the flow of what once had been deep currents. [paraphrased] Comparing Legalism with Mohism, the one retreated fifty paces, the other one hundred, [but they were equally defective in that. Refers to the anecdote in Mencius 1/i/3/2; Legge, p. 130].

Among the later followers of Shen Pu-hai and Han Fei Tzu in the Han dynasty, there appear to have been several distinct groups, each stressing reliance on the laws, or severe punishments, or favoring authoritarian government, or devising means to make the state rich and militarily powerful. Chao Yü "closely followed the laws and applied them impartially."[44] During the reign of Emperor Wu, he who had once been a mere clerk advanced in office to the post of imperial secretary. He worked with Chang T'ang in deliberating on and devising many laws and statutes.[45]

[43] The exception is the item listed as *The Book of Ch'ao Ts'o* in thirty-one sections, under the heading "Legalists" in the "Journal of Literature" in the *Han Shu*; unfortunately, this work has not been preserved. However, an examination of the existing quotations from Ch'ao Ts'o's pronouncements and discourses indicates that neither are those purely Legalist nor do they contain any new ideas.

[44] *Shih Chi, ch.* 122, "Encomium" [*tsan*] to the "Biographies of Harsh Officials"; the *Han Shu, ch.* 90, has the same wording.

[45] The laws and statutes underwent successive enlargement and revision during the early Han, becoming progressively more minutely detailed. When Kao-tsu [the Founder] entered the Pass [i.e., the Han-ku Pass, within which lay the heartland of the Ch'in state], he reduced all the laws to Three Articles [see, Watson, *Shih Chi*, vol. I, p. 90]; that marked the first beginnings of the Han law code. While Hsiao Ho was prime minister [196–193 B.C.], he "gathered together the laws of the Ch'in dynasty [and choosing those which were suitable for those times] he made the Statutes in Nine Sections." (*Han Shu, ch.* 23, "Treatise on Punishments".) [Hulsewé, *Remnants of Han Law*, vol. I, p. 333.] Shu-sun T'ung [died *ca.* 190 B.C.] further expanded the law code to supplement it in areas it did not cover, making the "Sections Beside (the Laws)" in Eighteen Sections. (*Chin Shu, ch.* 30, "Treatise on Punishments".) [Follows the translation given in Hulsewé, *op.cit.*, p. 40.] During the reign of the Emperor Wu [140–87 B.C.], "there were called to the court people like Chang T'ang and Chao Yü to establish the laws and ordinances in paragraphs; they made the law of the (collateral punishment of) administrative chiefs being cognizant of and wittingly condoning (the commission of crimes by their subordinates or subjects)." [Following Hulsewé, *op.cit.*, p. 337.] Subsequently, "the net of prohibitions became continually tighter. The Statutes and Ordinances (contained) in all

This inaugurated the practice of applying laws with stringency and rigor. As a person he was honest and fair; he "prevented friends and visitors from coming to him [for favors]." When other officials strove to apply the laws with excessive sternness, Chao Yü, who had become Privy Treasurer, now became more lenient in his conduct of government and sought to achieve equity in the laws.[46] An overall assessment of Chao Yü's career suggests that he may be taken as a model of the statesman who relies fully on laws [*jen fa* 任法].

There were others. For example, Chih Tu, who held the office of Military Commander of the Capital during the reign of Emperor Ching [156–141 B.C.]. "When it came to applying the letter of the law he made no exception even for the emperor's in-laws. The feudal lords and members of the imperial family all eyed him askance and nicknamed him 'The Green Hawk.' " Ning Ch'eng succeeded Chih Tu as Commandant, and emulated his methods in governing. Yi Tsung, who served as Magistrate of Ch'ang-an during the reign of Emperor Wu, "applied the laws with honesty and directness and made no exceptions even for the emperor's in-laws."[47] Tung Hsüan was Magistrate of Lo-yang during the reign of Emperor Kuang-wu [A.D. 25–57]. He applied the law strictly in meting out punishment to a household slave belonging to the Princess Hu-yang who had killed a person. The Princess reported the matter to [her brother,] the Emperor, demanding Tung's death. Tung Hsüan said: "Your majesty's sagelike virtue has brought about this mid-point restoration [of the Han dynasty, after the interregnum of A.D. 9–24]. Should you now give licence to a slave to commit murder, how shall you in the future bring order to the empire?"[48] Each of these persons, in performing these govern-

---

three hundred and fifty-nine sections." (*Han Shu*, ch. 23) [following Hulsewé, *op.cit.*, p. 338]. These all represent the compilation of legal statutes for practical application. Their character was more or less that of the penal codes and penal tripods of the Spring . and Autumn Period, and not that of academic thought and learning.

[46] *Shih Chi*, ch. 122; also *Han Shu*, ch. 59, "Biography of Chang T'ang," and ch. 90, "Biographies of Harsh Officials." [Cf. Watson, *Shih Chi*, vol. II, p. 437, for the full account.]

[47] *Shih Chi*, ch. 122, and *Han Shu*, ch. 90. [Translation follows Watson, *Shih Chi*, vol. II, pp. 421–22 and 437.]

[48] *Hou Han Shu*, ch. 107, "Biographies of Harsh Officials." Emperor Kuang-wu, inasmuch as he had not punished Tung Hsüan, ordered Tung to apologize to the Princess. Tung was unwilling. The Emperor ordered underlings to force Tung, but he remained stubbornly unwilling to submit. The Princess said: " 'When you [i.e., the Emperor] were still a commoner you frequently concealed persons fleeing punishment and no official dared to enter your home [to arrest them]. Today you are the Emperor, yet is your authority now inadequate to prevail over a mere magistrate?' The Emperor laughed and said: 'The Emperor is not the same as a commoner.' Thereupon he commanded the stubborn magistrate to leave." Thereafter, Tung Hsüan laid the law so heavily on the rich and mighty that there were none of those who did not tremble with fright. In the capital, he was known by the sobriquet "the waiting tiger." [Literally, "the lying-in-wait tiger."]

mental acts, displays his deep indebtedness to Lord Shang's dictum
"There can be no distinctions of status in imposing punishments."
Furthermore, Tung Hsüan's words to the Emperor Kuang-wu are especially close to the spirit of Kuan Tzu's statement: "For commands to be
carried out, it is necessary first that they prevail over those close to the
ruler." [See Chapter Six, p. 342.]

Chang Shih-chih, who was active during the reign of the Emperor Wen
[179–157 b.c.], was opposed to the oppressiveness of Ch'in rule, and his
thought clearly diverged from that of Lord Shang and Han Fei. Nonetheless, while serving as Commandant of Equipage, he placed charges against
the heir apparent and [his brother,] the Prince of Liang for having violated
regulations in failing to dismount from their carriage at the Marshall's
Gate of the palace. In so doing, his intent was quite similar to that of Han
Fei in recording that a guard at the court of King Chuang of Ch'u had
once sternly corrected the behavior of the heir apparent for violating the
"Law of the Inner Gate." [See Chapter Seven, footnotes 24 and 77.]
Subsequently, Chang Shih-chih served as Commandant of Justice, in
which post he again denied Emperor Wen's demands that the laws be
exceeded so as to execute a man who had violated an order to clear the
roads when the imperial entourage was crossing a bridge on the Wei
River, and again in the case of a felon who stole jade rings from the doors
of the Han Founder's mortuary temple. He was, in the last analysis,
implementing Kuan Tzu's ideal of "[The servitor who] does not alter his
commands for the sake of the ruler's wishes, for the commands are more
to be looked up to than the ruler himself." [See Chapter Six, p. 343.]
In his reply to Emperor Wen [when the Emperor protested that the man
on the bridge deserved execution], Chang said: "The law must be upheld
by the Son of Heaven and by everyone in the empire alike. The law at
present stipulates this, and were we to increase the penalty [over what is
prescribed], the people would cease to have any faith in the laws."[49]
This expresses the central meaning of full reliance upon the law [*jen fa*].
It is an idea long since lost to view as a consequence of Li Ssu's having
allowed authoritarian rule to throw the laws into disorder. Curiously,
Chang Shih-chih's learning was not derived from Shen Pu-hai and Han
Fei, yet he was capable of giving so clear an expression to that idea.

During the Han period there were more statesmen who practiced Lord
Shang's views on "heavy penalties for light crimes" than there were who
upheld Kuan Tzu's teachings about observing the laws. Most of those
persons included in the "Biographies of Harsh Officials" [*Shih Chi*, ch. 122;

---

[49] *Shih Chi*, ch. 102, "Biography of Chang Shih-chih"; *Han Shu*, ch. 50, has the same
wording. [Modifying Watson, *Shih Chi*, vol. i, pp. 536–37; Watson offers a complete translation of the biography, pp. 533–39.]

Han Shu, ch. 90; *Hou Han Shu, ch.* 107] were of the same persuasion as Lord Shang. Among the more prominent examples there is Yi Tsung, who, in the post of Governor of Ting Hsiang, once executed more than four hundred persons in a single day, and "though the season was warm, the entire province shivered and trembled."[50] When Wang Wen-shu was Governor of Ho-nei, he executed persons until "the blood flowed for more than ten *li* around. . . . Within the prefectural city no one dared utter a sound; no one dared go out at night, and no thief in the night ever set the dogs barking."[51] While serving as Governor of Ho-nan, Yen Yen-nien pronounced sentences of death on prisoners in the jails until: "blood flowed for many miles about, and his nickname in Ho-nan was 'chief butcher.' Whenever he issued an order forbidding something, the whole province was free of that."[52] "When Wang Chi served as Governor in P'ei, whenever a criminal was executed, the corpse was exposed to view on a cart; the crime was posted on it, and it was displayed in each county within the province. During the summers the corpses would rot, so it became necessary to tie the bones together with ropes until they could be carted throughout the entire province. Viewers would be struck with terror. During five years in the post he executed more than ten thousand persons."[53] These all are outstanding examples among the Harsh Officials; they even surpassed the achievement of Lord Shang, who made the waters of the Wei River become entirely red [with the blood of criminals executed on its banks; see Chapter Seven, footnote 70].

Such "harsh officials" as we have already seen offer us no justification for speaking about a government of law;[54] moreover, it was precisely

[50] *Shih Chi, ch.* 122 [following Watson, *Shih Chi*, vol. II, p. 439]; the *Han Shu, ch.* 90, has the same wording.

[51] *Shih Chi, ch.* 122; *Han Shu, ch.* 90. Both Yi Tsung and Wang Wen-shu were active during the reign of Emperor Wu [140–87 B.C.].

[52] *Han Shu, ch.* 90; Yen Yen-nien served during the reign of Emperor Hsüan [73–49 B.C.].

[53] *Hou Han Shu, ch.* 107. Wang Chi served during the reign of Emperor Ling [A.D. 168–188].

[54] In the preface to its *ch.* 107 of "Biographies of Harsh Officials," the *Hou Han Shu* says: "The Han dynasty was heir to the residual poison generated during the age of the Warring States; there were many power-minded and treacherous people. Among those, some engaged in expansion of their property to the point that they came to overawe and intimidate whole countries. Some were bullies who made themselves the masters of their villages. Moreover, the provincial governors were few and far between, while the population was vast. Therefore those governing directly over the people engaged primarily in establishing a decisive authority. They would punish by exterminating whole clans of bandits and evil-doers. They would carry out these punishments first, and report them to the court later." This suggests that the harsh officials really were responding to the needs of their setting; [what they did], however, had nothing to do with Legalist principles of rule. Another point to consider is that the harsh officials were especially prominent during

those who were anxious to elevate the ruler and support authoritarian rule who openly relied fully on the laws [*jen fa*] while privately misusing the law. Chang T'ang and Tu Chou appear to have been the worst offenders in this regard. Tu Chou served as Commandant of Justice at the court of Emperor Wu. "He was skilled in attending the Emperor. If there was someone the Emperor wanted out of the way, he would manage to entrap him. When the Emperor wanted someone let off, Tu Chou would keep that person tied up in continuing investigations for a long time while allowing hints gradually to emerge that he had been unjustly accused. Once a guest asked him: 'You dispense justice for the Son of Heaven, yet you do not follow the statutes as they appear in the books; you simply indicate verdicts according to the ruler's wishes. Is that truly the way a justiciar should act?' Tu Chou replied: 'What is the source of the statutes in the books? Whatever previous rulers thought appropriate, they had written down as laws. Whatever subsequent rulers thought to be right, they added as ordinances. Whatever suits the moment is correct; what do the laws of the past matter?' "[55] Chang T'ang's acts were quite in keeping with that view. "Chang T'ang, as Commandant of Justice, when deciding cases, . . . he would always defer to the imperial wish. . . . If he knew the emperor wanted to have a certain person condemned, he would turn the case over to the harshest and most vindictive secretaries. When the emperor wanted to see someone go free, he would turn that case over to mild and just secretaries." All such behavior was, perhaps unwittingly, entirely in the style of Li Ssu's past arts of pleasing his ruler. It is precisely the opposite of Chao Yü's and Chang Shih-chih's and those others' maintenance of the law, with no favoritism or sycophancy. In fact, Chang T'ang's deeds were considerably more serious than those of Tu Chou. The histories record that: "Chao Yü's intent was to serve the public cause and keep himself free from influences, while Chang T'ang manipulated his learning in order to control others." Chang T'ang took good care of his relatives' and friends' interests; "he kept up social relations with guests and visitors . . . in making calls on all the prominent, he was not deterred by the hottest or the coldest weather. . . . The harshest and cruelest functionaries were in many cases employed by him to serve as his 'talons and fangs,' yet he cultivated the company of the scholarly men of refinement."

---

the reign of Emperor Wu; both [the Founding Emperor] Kao-tsu and Emperor Wen favored more generous-spirited and simpler means. Fan Yeh's preface [to Chapter Ninety of the *Hou Han Shu*, quoted above] gives the impression that during the early reigns of the Han dynasty there had already developed the mode of establishing the government's authority through intimidation; that might well introduce misunderstanding, hence should be corrected.

[55] *Shih Chi*, ch. 122; Tu Chou's biography in *ch.* 60 of the *Han Shu* contains the same passage.

He sought a good reputation while carrying on his private manipulations; he built his power while seeking to gain imperial favor. During the time that he was Imperial Secretary, "The Prime Minister was chosen just to have the vacancy filled; all the affairs of the empire were decided by Chang T'ang."[56] This is precisely the kind of situation Han Fei had in mind when he spoke of "ruler-manipulating servitors" who will always "agree with the ruler's wishes so as to grasp the power that goes with being a close favorite";[57] he felt that the enlightened ruler should execute such a person. In this manner of supporting authoritarianism, Chang T'ang also was completely different from Lord Shang in his service as prime minister to the State of Ch'in; there, Lord Shang acted primarily with the real interests of ruler and state at heart.[58] Nevertheless, the Han era did not altogether lack loyal officials who met the Legalist standard for elevating the ruler. Such, for example, was Chih Tu, who executed the high and the mighty and who did nothing to serve his own private interests. He once remarked: " 'I have turned my back on my family and have become an official; it is quite proper that I should fulfill my duties, until I die in office.' And to the end of his life he gave scant attention to his own wife and children."[59] This represents a standard that Tu Chou and Chang T'ang never attained.[60]

[56] Quoted passages all are from Chang T'ang's biography in *Han Shu*, *ch.* 59; the wording of parallel passages in *Shih Chi*, *ch.* 122, is more or less the same. [See biography translated in full in Watson, *Shih Chi*, vol. II, pp. 425–37.]

[57] *Han Fei Tzu*, *ch.* 14, "Chien, chieh, shih ch'en." [See Chapter Seven, above, p. 774, and footnote 111.]

[58] In his private manipulations, Chang T'ang's purpose was wholly to build up his own power. Tu Chou flattered and yielded to the ruler, with an interest in enhancing both his status and his wealth. Thus after Chang T'ang's death his family fortune amounted to no more than five hundred pieces of gold, while Tu Chou, "when first appointed a secretary in the office of the Commandant of Justice, had only one horse and even that was lame. But after holding office for a long time and having reached the ranks of the Three Lords [i.e., senior officials], his sons and grandsons all held high office and his family property was valued in the millions." [*Shih Chi*, *ch.* 122.]

[59] *Shih Chi*, *ch.* 122; identical passage in *Han Shu*, *ch.* 90.

[60] In an essay entitled "Yuan fa," included in his *Chien lun*, *san*, citing Huan Fan's *Shih-yao Lun*, the chapter "Pien Neng P'ien," Chang Ping-lin [1868–1936] has briefly noted that in giving full rein to "actualities and names" [i.e., *hsing-ming*; cf. footnote 41, above], Lord Shang and Han Fei had grievously transgressed against [the standards established by the ideal models for assistants to rulers] Yi Yin and the Duke of Chou. In their unrestrained executions and in making themselves subservient to their rulers' desires [the Han period "harsh officials"] Ning Ch'eng and Chih Tu may also be said to have grievously transgressed against the standards of Lord Shang and Han Fei. Yet they nonetheless merit commendation insofar as they were able to suppress the powerful, support their ruler, set aside all self-interest to work for the public good. "In recent centuries those [statesmen] considered to have had ability have violated the society's laws and have turned toward the acquisition of private power." Such statesmen, then, may also

Of Han dynasty figures who discoursed on the agricultural and military
means to wealth and power, there was Ch'ao Ts'o during the reign of
Emperor Wen. Later, during the reign of Emperor Wu, he was succeeded
by Chang T'ang, Sang Hung-yang, and others. Ch'ao Ts'o declared that
in order for "the state to be rich and the law be upheld," it is necessary
"to make the people devote themselves to farming. . . . If one desires to
make the people devote themselves to farming, it is necessary to enhance
the value of grain. The way of enhancing the value of grain lies in causing
the people to be able to use grain for obtaining rewards and for commut-
ing penalties. There should now be a general call to all under Heaven that
whosoever sends grain to the central government shall obtain the bestowal
of honorary rank, and/or pardon for crimes, . . . " At first the grain
received was to be sent to the frontiers to sustain the border defenses;
then, when frontier grain supplies were adequate for five years, grain
should be sent to the provinces to benefit the people. The Emperor Wen
followed his advice, with the consequence that the state was greatly
enriched.[61] Ch'ao Ts'o also devised a plan for Emperor Wen of defending
against the Hsiung-nu by the use of military colonies. He said: "The
people who dwell along the frontier [toil yet] gain little; they cannot
be expected to remain permanently in a region of grave peril." Therefore
it would be advisable to recruit felons, bondsmen, and ordinary people,
through the offer of high rank and generous rewards, and move them to
the border zone, using them to strike back at the barbarians. Moreover,
cities should be built and walled, fields laid out and houses built, so that
"when the settlers arrive they will have places to live, and there will be
necessities for their use in what they do." There would be established a
system of five hamlets joining to form a village with its own self-government organization, to instruct the people in warfare and to maintain
harmony among them.[62] These ideas apparently reflect to some extent,
but with practical modifications, Kuan Tzu's system for organizing rural
villages and hamlets [see Chapter Six, p. 351, and footnote 88] as well as
Lord Shang's law that the farmers should benefit from the profits of the
market, and the soldiers should benefit from the profits on the frontiers.
[See Chapter Seven, p. 395 and footnote 56.]

In their discussions of "profit," statesmen of Chang T'ang's and Sang

---

be looked upon as having grievously transgressed against the standards of Lord Shang,
Han Fei, Ning Ch'eng, and Chih Tu. That charge might appropriately be used as well
as the judgment on Tu Chou and Chang T'ang.

[61] *Han Shu*, ch. 24, Part one, "Treatise on Food and Money, Part One." [Translation
slightly modified from Nancy Lee Swann, *Food and Money in Ancient China*, pp. 166–67,
et.seq.]

[62] *Han Shu*, ch. 49, "Biography of Ch'ao Ts'o."

Hung-yang's type placed their emphasis on fiscal management, their views being close to Kuan Tzu's concept of *ch'ing-chung* [i.e., "prices and money"], and [in this respect] quite different from the doctrines of Lord Shang. Chang T'ang "proposed minting white metal coins and five-*shu* cash, and that a monopoly should control all the salt and iron in the empire. He advised taking steps against rich merchants and large-scale traders, and proclaimed regulations for confiscating accumulated capital [of newly rich merchants], and for eradicating powerful families which accumulated extensive land-holdings; he manipulated the letter of the law and artfully devised charges in the support of his laws."[63] Sang Hung-yang proposed that in all commanderies and counties there should be established offices of *chün-shu* ["equal distribution"] and offices for salt and iron. "Let orders be given that, in all places far distant, those products which merchants and traders buy up and transport for resale when prices are high, should be transported to the capital in lieu of taxes. In the capital there should be established an office of *p'ing-chun* ["standardization of prices"] which shall receive all the goods submitted from throughout the realm. Call upon the office for artisans to manufacture carts and all kinds of equipment; for all of the above the Ministry of Agriculture shall provide the means. Let the Ministry of Agriculture through these various offices achieve a total monopoly on all the money and goods of the empire. When prices are high, it shall sell; when goods are cheap, it shall buy. In this way rich merchants and great traders shall have no access to vast profits; the people will return to the 'fundamental pursuit' [agriculture], and the prices of goods will no longer rise wildly. In this way commodities throughout the realm will be held down in price; the name for this system shall be *p'ing-chun*."[64] The expenses of Emperor Wu's efforts to extend the Chinese borders [into Inner Asia] and establish his authority there were amply provided for; Sang Hung-yang's contributions to that thus constitute an enduring record of achievement.

[63] *Han Shu, ch.* 59, "Biography of Chang T'ang." [For the *Shih Chi* biography, which varies significantly, see the translation in Watson, *Shih Chi*, vol. II, pp. 425–37, especially p. 430. This understanding of regulations restricting merchants follows Nancy Lee Swann, *op.cit.*, in footnote 61, above, *passim*, especially pp. 275–89, and p. 304, footnote 593.]

[64] *Shih Chi, ch.* 30, "P'ing-chun Shu." Sang Hung-yang also advocated that donations of grain be accepted in return for the conferring of ranks and titles, and in remission of penalties for crimes. [Translation borrowed from Nancy Lee Swann, *op.cit.*, pp. 314–16, where the largely similar parallel passage in *Han Shu, ch.* 24-b, is translated, and from Watson, *Shih Chi*, vol. II, p. 103. Watson prefers "the balanced standard" as translation for "*p'ing chun.*"

SECTION FOUR

The Struggle for Supremacy between Legalism
and Confucianism, and Their Subsequent Convergence

IN the foregoing, we have stated that the Legalism of the Han dynasty ceased all further development of thought and learning, yet persisted in a struggle for supremacy with the Confucians. Documentation extant in our time is not plentiful, making it difficult to reconstruct the circumstances in detail. A general outline can nonetheless be perceived in the early records, at least in some measure. The *Shih Chi, ch.* 121, records that a certain Master Huang and Master Yuan Ku debated on the careers of [the Shang Founder,] T'ang and [the Chou Founder,] Wu before the Emperor Ching [reigned 156–141 B.C.]. Yuan Ku, drawing on the Ch'i tradition of the *Book of Odes* argued that Kings T'ang and Wu had won the hearts of the people, for which the Mandate was bestowed upon them. Master Huang however stated: "T'ang and Wu had no Mandate; they simply murdered their overlords and that is all there is to it!" The point is that the relationship between ruler and servitor should never be confused or disturbed. "Even a worn-out hat must be put on the head, while shoes, no matter how new, must be relegated to the feet. Why is that? It is simply the distinction that applies to high and low. Now in this instance, although Kings Chieh and Chou failed in proper conduct, still they were kings and overlords. Even though T'ang and Wu were sages, yet they were servitors and underlings. When the ruler commits failures of conduct, his servitors are unable to rectify his misdeeds by means of straight words of advice with a view to restoring the Son of Heaven's nobility, but on the contrary kill him for his faults and set themselves up in his royal position, —if they are not the assassins of their overlords, what are they?"[65] We should note that the idea about [dynastic Founders having righteously] taken up arms and having executed [the bad last rulers] was upheld by all the Confucians. Even Hsün Tzu, although stressing the elevation of the ruler, still acknowledged that [Kings] "Chieh and Chou did not [rightfully] possess the empire, and T'ang and Wu did not, therefore, assassinate their rulers."[66] Master Huang's argument here, moreover, is in basic accord with Han Fei Tzu's statement: "It may be said that [the Sage Kings] Yao, Shun, T'ang and Wu were guilty of violating the principle

---

[65] *Han Shu, ch.* 88, "Biographies of Confucians," contains the same passage. Yen Shih-ku's commentary states that the two sentences about hats and shoes are from [the ancient work on military matters] the *Liu T'ao*. [Cf. Watson, *Records of the Grand Historian*, vol. II, pp. 403–404.]

[66] *Hsün Tzu, ch.* 18, "Cheng lun."

governing the relationship of ruler and servitor."[67] Without any doubt, thus, we can take the debate between Huang and Yuan Ku as an example of the conflict between Legalist and Confucian thought.

There is no record of the Han dynasty's conflicts between Confucians and Legalists, however, which can surpass the detailed information recorded in Huan K'uan's "Debates on Salt and Iron," i.e., *Yen t'ieh lun.*[68] Huan K'uan was a Confucian, a specialist in the study of the *Kung-yang Commentary* to the *Spring and Autumn Annals* who, during the subsequent reign of the Emperor Hsüan, compiled a narrative record of the debates held at the court of the Emperor Chao in the sixth year of the reign-period Shih-yuan [i.e., 81 B.C.].[69] Inasmuch as it is not a verbatim record made at the time,[70] and moreover favors the Confucian participants, the account lacks fairness and objectivity.[71] Nonetheless, the proposals concerning salt and iron are a matter of historical fact, and the content of the arguments on the two sides, as recorded in the book, does indeed represent the head-on conflict between Legalist and Confucian thought during the

---

[67] *Han Fei Tzu, ch.* 51, "Chung hsiao."

[68] For a general account of the entire salt and iron issue, the reader can refer to the article by Ou Tsung-yu, "Yen-t'ieh chün-shu chih yu-lai chi hsing-chih" (Chung-shan University, *Li-shih yü-yen yen-chiu-so chou-k'an,* 1/7) and that by Chang Ch'un-ming, "Yen-t'ieh-lun chih cheng-chih pei-ching" (Nankai University, *Ching-chi chi-k'an,* 1/2). The passages quoted in this chapter all have been emended according to Wang Hsien-ch'ien's *Yen-t'ieh-lun,* "Chiao-k'an hsiao-chih."

[69] Corresponding to 81 B.C. The Emperor Hsüan reigned from 73–49 B.C.

[70] *Han Shu, ch.* 66, in the "Encomium" to the "Biography of Ch'e Ch'ien-ch'iu," says: "The so-called policy discussions on salt and iron were initiated during the Shih-yuan reign-period [86–81 B.C.]; learned and upright worthies were summoned and asked about the causes of good government and disorder. They all responded that they favored abolition throughout all the provinces of the controls over salt, iron, and wine, and the [system of controlled] equitable marketing." The Imperial Secretary [Sang] Hung-yang regarded those as the means of pacifying the borders and controlling the four barbarians; they represented a great enterprise of the state, and could not be abolished. The argument and mutual refutation that went on at the time produced quantities of written views. Later, during the reign of the Emperor Hsüan [73–49 B.C.], Huan K'uan of Ju-nan [Commandery]: "Expanded the discourses concerning salt and iron, added to and enlarged the number of sections comprising it, and set forth the strongest arguments possible against the measures, composing thereby a text of several tens of thousands of words, seeking also to make his own investigation of the causes of order and disorder and produce thereby a distinctive system of his own."

[71] The *Han Shu, ch.* 30, "Treatise on Literature" classifies this under the heading of "Confucian writings". The whole book contains sixty chapters. Numbers 1 through 41 comprise the debate itself, the consequence of which was the utter defeat of the Secretary [Sang] and his group. Numbers 42 through 59 contain the rebuttals of the proposal to abolish [the monopoly and control measures], and the result again is the defeat of the high officials. In Number 60, Huan K'uan uses the device "a stranger remarked" as the means for setting forth his own views repudiating Legalism and upholding Confucianism.

middle of the Western Han period. For, although the issues in dispute in the *Debates on Salt and Iron* have been subjected to Huan K'uan's additions and deletions in the re-telling, the participants in the debates still are in some measure otherwise known and corroborated. Also, Huan K'uan himself was writing at a time not far removed from the *shih-yuan* reign-period, so it is scarcely possible that he could have perpetrated a gross fabrication to misrepresent recently deceased men of the past.[72]

The discussions in this book of such matters as the [state-administered monopolies for] salt and iron, touching on governing principles as they do, are debated back and forth more than a hundred times. The statements are not summaries of essential points only; in manner of expression they are highly repetitious. There also are numerous junctures at which the discussions become illogical. A full summary of the principal content would not go beyond these headings: (1) civil cultivation versus military achievement; (2) agriculture as the basic activity versus crafts and commerce; (3) benevolence and righteousness versus utilitarian advantage; (4) penal measures versus ethics. The views advocated by the two sides in no place go beyond the scope of pre-Ch'in Confucian and Legalist thought. We shall briefly review here their arguments on these separate issues.

The Confucian literati first proposed abolition of all the measures inspiring state monopolies in the production and distribution of salt, iron, and wine, and those enforcing equalization of commodity prices [*chün shu* 均輸]. The Imperial Secretary [i.e., Sang Hung-yang, speaking for the government] replied that these all were necessary for meeting the expenses of military preparations against the Hsiung-nu, and that their abolition would be inexpedient. The literati responded: "In antiquity to accomplish things by virtue was the honored way, while employing military means was despised. Confucius said: 'If remoter people are not submissive, all the influences of civil culture and virtue are to be cultivated to attract them to be so; and when they have been so attracted, they must be made contented and tranquil.' [*Analects*, xvi/1/11; Legge, pp. 308–09.] Now we are abandoning ethics and relying on military force, raising up armies to attack them, placing garrison forces on the borders to defend

[72] According to the *Han Shu* and the *Debates*, those representing the government's views included the Chancellor (Ch'e Ch'ien-ch'iu) and the Imperial Secretary, i.e., Yü-shih ta-fu (Sang Hung-yang, usually referred to simply as the Ta-fu), Chancellery secretaries, and assistant court secretaries. The Imperial Secretary's statements are the most numerous, while the Chancellor [Ch'e] remains silent from the beginning to the end. More than sixty of the Confucian literati express opinions; among these are Master T'ang of Mao-ling, Master Wan of the State of Lu, Liu Tzu-yung of Chung-shan, and Master Chu of Chiu-chiang. Sang Hung-yang was executed in the first year of the Emperor Chao's Yuan-feng reign-period (80 B.C.). Among those Confucian literati who participated in the debates, some must still have been alive at the time Huan K'uan was active.

against them. We expose our soldiers to dangers, station armies off in the wilds, and maintain these for long periods. The transport of provisions for them will be unending. Without, we make our soldiers on the frontiers endure hunger and cold, while within the country the common people must toil and suffer. We have established salt and iron monopolies that have now enlarged the profit [to the state], and the offices of government use that to sustain [the military]; that is not a good policy."[73]

Such an ideal position as this, that "[the ruler of a state] who loves benevolence . . . will have no enemy" [*Mencius*, vii/ii/4/2], was one the Legalists could never accept. Therefore Sang Hung-yang rebutted it, saying: "Of old, King Yen of Hsü practiced righteousness and was vanquished; he was devoted to the Confucian teachings [his ideals were similar to those later espoused by Confucius, i.e., in the name of benevolence he refused to employ military measures], yet he was conquered."[74] "The Chou royal house maintained the Rites and favored the civil arts, yet the Chou state was reduced and weakened and was unable to preserve itself. . . . The ruler of Ch'in, after having conquered the whole empire, in the East went on to cross the P'ei River [in Liao-tung] and to destroy the Chao-hsien State [Korea]; in the South he seized Lu-liang [the barbarian region comprising modern Kwangtung and Kwangsi]; in the North he drove back the Hu and the Ti [barbarians]; in the West he smote the Ti and the Ch'iang [barbarians]. He instituted the [grandiose] title of 'Emperor' and summoned to his audiences all the barbarians of the four directions. Wherever boats and carts could go, as far as the tracks of men's feet extend, there were none who did not come to his court. These were not submissive to his virtue, they were in fear of his awesome majesty. 'When one's strength is great others come to pay court; when one's strength is weak, one must pay court to others.' "[75] At this point, the literati were notably lacking in ingenious refutations; they were able only to point out that the Ch'in dynasty had known but a brief existence, thereby corroborating their opposing view that: "The ruler who governs by ritual and yielding will endure as inexhaustibly as the currents of the River and the Sea." [Referring to *Analects*, iv/13.]

The Imperial Secretary Sang Hung-yang, seeing that arguments from the military situation would not settle the issue, turned to the economic situation to demonstrate the need for his policies. "In former times the

[73] *Yen-t'ieh-lun, ch.* 1, "Pen yi".

[74] *Ibid., ch.* 48, "Ho ch'in". [The reference is to the Viscount of Hsü, who assumed the title of king during the reign of King Mu of Chou, reigned 1000–946 B.C.]

[75] *Ibid., ch.* 44, "Chu Ch'in". See also: *ch.* 50, "Hsien ku"; *ch.* 38, "Pei hu"; *ch.* 16, "Ti kuang"; and *ch.* 43, "Chieh ho". The two sentences starting with "When one's strength is great . . ." are from *Han Fei Tzu, ch.* 50, "Hsien hsüeh". [See above, Chapter Seven, Section Three, p. 393.]

founders of states opened up the ways to both the primary [agriculture] and the accessory [crafts and commerce] occupations, and thereby achieved interchange between places where things are and those where they are lacking. . . . Thus where the crafts do not emerge, the agricultural needs are hampered, and where commerce does not emerge, the exchange of valuable goods is prevented. . . . The salt and iron monopolies and the system of commodity price equalization are the means by which to achieve the flow of accumulated wealth and adjust the balance between sufficiency and urgent need."[76] This represents the first advantage: benefiting the people.

"The [wise] ruler stops the flow of natural wealth, interdicts [its movement through] customs barriers and markets, maintains regulations and enforces time requirements, and uses price management to control the people. In a year of plentiful crops when the harvests are collected, he accumulates stores in preparation against shortages; in a bad year of poor harvests he administers the sale of commodities and transports goods from places of excess to adjust deficiencies. . . . In the past when money and goods were insufficient, the soldiers might not receive their pay. Now [under the managed economy], should Shantung suffer a disaster or famine appear in Ch'i or Chao, we can depend on the equalized distribution from stores and the accumulations in our warehouses and granaries; the soldiers thus receive their pay, and starving people thus are given aid. Therefore, the goods subject to equalized distribution, like the wealth accumulated in treasuries and warehouses, do not represent profiteering at the common people's expense for the sole purpose of supporting the army, they also are the means for bringing aid to the distressed and the improverished, and are a preparation against disasters of flood and drouth."[77] This presents the second advantage: succoring the people.

"One who is skilled in directing the affairs of government will value highly that to which the people attach a low value, and treat as important what the people regard as of little weight; he will use the secondary [crafts and commerce] with which to bring about exchange of the primary [agricultural production]; he will employ the superficial [trade items] to stimulate circulation of the substantial [basic products]. Nowadays the wealth of mountains and marshes [the exploitation of whose mining, salt production and other kinds of wealth the Confucians opposed], and the equalized distribution of accumulated stores have become the means by which we manage prices and values, and impose [economic] obligations upon all of the regional lords. The gold [mined from the mountains] of Ju and Han states, like other [domestic] tribute of fine and precious manu-

[76] *Ibid.*, *ch.* 1, "Pen yi".
[77] *Ibid.*, *ch.* 2, "Li keng".

factures, provide the means by which we entice the outer states [to engage in commerce with us] and draw in the treasures of the Ch'iang and the Hu [barbarians]."[78] This describes the third advantage: enriching the state.

"The cities of Cho and Chi in the State of Yen, Han-tan in the State of Chao, Wen and Chih in the State of Wei, Hsing-yang in the State of Han, Lin-tzu in the State of Ch'i, Wan-ch'en in the State of Ch'u, and Yang-ti in the State of Cheng, and the two Chou cities in the San-ch'uan [Commandery] are the richest places in all the empire; all are famous capitals of the realm. [They are such not because] there are people who help the inhabitants to plow their wilds or to turn their lands into fields; it is because they are situated along those busy crossroads of the nobles and lie astride the main thoroughfares. Thus, it is where goods are plentiful that the people burgeon; it is in those residences nearest the market places where the rich families are found. Wealth lies in the techniques of management, not in physical toil. Advantage derives from strategic locations, not from arduous ploughing." This indicates that the state need not devote its energies to agriculture, yet can become rich, nor need it practice frugality in order to be nobly virtuous. "In ancient times there were standards for palaces and residences; norms applied to the use of garments and carriages. The rough-hewn timbers and the hut with untrimmed thatch, [contrary to some Confucian traditions] are not the models ordained by the ancient kings. The superior man limits extravagance yet disparages frugality, for 'Frugality leads to meanness.' " [Analects, vii/35.][79] This presents the fourth advantage: having crafts and commerce.

"When money is in unrestricted circulation but the common people's needs are not supplied, it is because goods are being amassed. When one calculates the basic production and measures the reserves, but there are starving people, it is because grain is being hoarded. Intelligent persons in those ways acquire the results of a hundred men's efforts, while stupid persons do not gain enough to repay their own labors. If the ruler of men does not adjust [such imbalances], there will be instances of one person's wealth harming other people. This is how it comes about that some may amass a hundred years' excesses while others may lack even enough chaff and husks to subsist upon. People who are very rich cannot be made to serve by offering them salaries; the very powerful cannot be intimidated by legal penalties. Unless there is a means of distributing and gathering which equalizes the benefits, there can be no balance [ch'i 齊]."[80] More-

---

[78] Ibid., ch. 2, "Li keng".

[79] Both quotations are from Yen-t'ieh lun, ch. 3, "T'ung yu".

[80] Ibid., ch. 4, "Ts'o pi". The sentence beginning "People who are very rich" appears to be based on the Kuan Tzu, ch. 35, "Ch'ih-mi": "The extremely rich cannot be made to serve." [See above, Chapter Six, especially pp. 359–362.]

over, "When a family possesses a precious vessel, it will be kept stored away in a protective covering; how much more should the ruler of men do so with his mountains [i.e., mines] and marshes [i.e., salt-making resources]. For, the places from which power and profit are drawn invariably are located in the deepest mountains and most inaccessible marshes. None but powerful persons have the capacity to draw out their profits. In other times, before salt and iron were subject to the [state's] monopolies, there were such as (Mr.) Ping of [Lin-] Ch'ü [see Nancy Lee Swann, *Food and Money*, pp. 454–55, #13] among common people, and the King of Wu [the rebel King Liu P'i, 213–154 B.C.; see Swann, pp. 394–95] among rulers who were the earliest to advocate [their own private exploitation of] salt and iron [and misuse the profits]. . . . Duke T'ai [the first of the Ducal line in Ch'i, in the late twelfth century B.C.] said: 'One family may harm a hundred families, a hundred families may harm the feudal lord, the feudal lord may harm the entire realm; the King's laws [therefore] prohibit that.' Now today should we give reign to the people to pursue power and profit, abolish the monopolies in order to aid their violent and unbridled actions, allowing them to pursue their avarice? The depraved will all flock together, and the powerful families will form factions; then, as these power-wielding ones are left uncontrolled, within a short span of time groups treacherously pursuing self-aggrandizement will be formed."[81] Thus it becomes quite essential to establish the standardization of prices [*p'ing-chun* 平準], and "monopolize the profits from the whole realm's salt and iron in order to eliminate the rich merchants and great traders."[82] "Thereafter, prohibitions were laid on [the resouces of] the mountains and the seas so the people would not be subverted; noble and base were equalized so the people would have no uncertainties."[83] This is the fifth advantage: achieving economic balance among the people.

In response to these various lines of argument, the literati offered their point-by-point rebuttals. In the main their arguments rested on the traditional thinking that stressed the fundamental character of agriculture, and acknowledged agricultural pursuits to be the sole source of wealth. To relieve the distress induced by floods and drouths, likewise, there was no other method than to till more arduously, fill the granaries, limit desires, and reduce consumption. The valuable trinkets from distant places were of no use in allaying hunger, and therefore would not be sought by the superior man.[84] As for schemes by which economic balance could be achieved

---

[81] *Ibid.*, *ch.* 5, "Chin keng". This also derives from the *Kuan Tzu's* concept of putting the [wealth of] mountains and seas [i.e., metal mining and salt production] under government control thereby to suppress the rich and powerful.

[82] *Ibid.*, *ch.* 14, "Ch'ing chung."

[83] *Ibid.*, *ch.* 5, "Chin keng."

[84] These points are based on *ch.* 1, "Pen yi", *ch.* 2, "Li keng," and *ch.* 3, "T'ung yu".

among the people, to the state's advantage, those too were apparently plausible but actually were false. "The Son of Heaven holds in his stores everything within the seas"; therefore, there should be no need to impose prohibitions on mountains and seas. Moreover, "In the regions of Ch'in, Ch'u, Yen and Ch'i, the physical strength of people may vary; in some regions they are stronger, and in others weaker, presenting quite different conditions. The need may be for larger or smaller implements, circumstances may demand here one shape, there another; localities vary and practices change, and in each particular situation, each implement has its advantages. As the government imposes a single standard for all, iron implements are deprived of their specific aptness, and the farmers lose thereby the particular advantages of each."[85] "Unify the source, standardize the price; implements [of iron] are mostly hard and brittle, so there is no choice at all between the good and the bad. The government clerks frequently are not present, making the implements [whose production and sale they control] difficult to obtain. The farming households cannot stock up a large supply [of implements], as they rust in long storage. If they must abandon their work at the best growing times and go far off to buy their farming implements, they will have missed the best time. When salt and iron are expensive, that works disadvantages on the people. The poor sometimes have to plow with wooden plows and do the weeding by hand, farm primitively, and do without salt in their food. Iron monopoly officials, unable to sell their implements, sometimes allot them to the people [in that way forcing the people to buy them].[86]

All the foregoing make it amply evident that the policy of putting [the resources of] mountains and seas under official management brought troubles to the people, and was not necessarily of advantage to the state. Yet the basic objection of the literati and others to the various monopoly policies for salt, iron, and the like did not hinge on the issue of whether their implementation brought advantages; it stemmed, instead, from their denial that utilitarian advantage constituted an aim of government. The Imperial Secretary Sang Hung-yang said: "The State of Ch'in employed Lord Shang, whereby the state grew rich and powerful."[87] This

---

[85] *Ibid.*, ch. 5, "Ching keng".

[86] *Ibid.*, ch. 36, "Shui han". The *Han Shu*, ch. 24-b, "Treatise on Food and Money, Part Two," records that when Pu Shih was appointed Imperial Secretary [in 111 B.C.], he: ". . . saw that in the provinces and the fiefs [the people] in many respects found it inconvenient that the county magistrates made salt and iron implements, complaining bitterly that they were inferior and were overpriced, and that at times the people were forced to buy them." [Cf. Nancy Lee Swann, *Food and Money*, p. 311.] (*Han Shu*, ch. 58, "Biography of Pu Shih", contains more or less the same statement.) This is clear evidence that what is criticized here is precisely what the memorials to the throne from great nobles and leading ministers denounced as "ignoble acts of district magistrates."

[87] *Ibid.*, ch. 7, "Fei Yang."

represents the extreme of utilitarianism. The literati, at the very beginning of their statement of principles, said: "We have heard that the way to govern men is to prevent evil and error at their source, to broaden the beginnings of morality, to discourage secondary occupations, and open the way for the exercise of humanity and righteousness. Never should material profit appear as a motive of government. Only then can transformation through moral teaching prevail, and can the customs of the people be reformed." For, "When the people are led by virtue, they will revert to good practices; hold up crass advantage to them and their ways will grow mean."[88] From this, it becomes evident that: "Propriety and righteousness are the foundations of the state, while power and profit are the destroyers of government."[89] "Therefore, the Son of Heaven does not speak of 'more and less'; and the feudal lords do not speak of 'benefit and harm'; the great officers do not speak of 'gain and loss.' "[90] Benevolence and righteousness are sufficient to transform the people, so what need is there to employ the Imperial Secretary Sang Hung-yang to "painstakingly calculate and plan the state's material needs"?

The rebuttals and counter-rebuttals in the debate between those two sides turned on still a further issue: penalties and laws versus ethical teachings. The Imperial Secretary had abundant praise for Lord Shang's governing in Ch'in: "He established laws and standards, rigorously imposed corporal punishments and penalties; the treacherous and the false were simply not tolerated."[91] Presumably because: "the people are made impudent by love but pay heed to punishments" [his policies were appropriate and efficacious]. Therefore the ruler of men will not preserve an evil man, just as a farmer will not preserve useless seedlings . . . hoe out one bane and all the seedlings will grow; punish one evildoer and all the people will rejoice." The literati [in reply] did not deny that penal laws should exist, but believed they did not need to be used. Therefore, they said: "The ancients taught fervently in order to guide the people, clarified the avoidances so as to make the punishments proper. Punishments bear a relationship to governing like that of the whip to driving.

---

[88] *Ibid.*, *ch.* 1, "Pen yi." [In part following, with modification, the translation in de Bary *et al.*, *Sources*, pp. 236–37.]

[89] *Ibid.*, *ch.* 14, "Ch'ing chung."

[90] *Ibid.*, *ch.* 1, "Pen yi."

[91] *Ibid.*, *ch.* 7, "Fei Yang." *Ch.* 59, "Ta lun," also says: "Governing the people is comparable to the cutting strokes of a master artisan; it is carried out with an axe, and when that cuts to the chalk-line's mark, then it stops." The passage that follows praises the governing of Imperial Secretary Tu (Chou) and of the Commandant of the Palace Wang (Wen-shu), and expresses the judgment: "The one who achieves good rule relies on the laws." [For Tu and Wang, both "Harsh Officials" of the reign of Emperor Wu, see biographies from *Shih Chi*, *ch.* 122, translated by Burton Watson, *Records of the Grand Historian of China*, Vol. ii, pp. 448–50 and 440–47.]

The best charioteer would not drive without a whip, but, having a whip, he has no need to use it. The Sage uses the laws to carry out his teachings, but when his teachings are complete, the punishments need not be employed." The one who presides over the people should first make his own person upright; he should not charge the people with their failings. "For when the people are disorderly, that reflects the person [of the ruler]. When his person is upright, the realm will be stabilized."[92]

Whether this theory could be realized in practice, however, depended entirely on whether the people could be induced to accept teachings and be transformed to the good. The Imperial Secretary held the view that people's characters are fixed by natural endowment and cannot be altered. Therefore he denied absolutely the efficacy of transformation through teaching.[93] For: "The worthy and the unrighteousness differ in their substance, and avarice and baseness are matters of innate character. The superior man can be pure in his own heart yet incapable of purifying others by teaching them." Even such sages and worthies as the Duke of Chou and Tzu-ch'an were yet unable to transform the evil and specious characters of a Kuan [Shu-hsien] and a Ts'ai [Shu-tu, i.e., the rebellious younger brothers of King Wu and the Duke of Chou, ca. 1100 B.C.] or a Teng Hsi [see Chapter Seven, Section One, p. 368, above]. How could the officials be held responsible for the infractions committed by each and every one of the common people? The literati appear to have no satisfactory reply to this. They are able merely to reiterate tenaciously their argument: "The superior's transforming influence on those below is like the wind bending the grass" [cf. *Analects*, xii/19]; they fell back on the idea of "punishing one to set a hundred straight" in order to explain the [Confucian-approved] punishments meted out to Kuan, Ts'ai and Teng Hsi.[94]

The Imperial Secretary Sang Hung-yang, perpetuating one of Lord Shang's doctrines, also advocated rigorous punishments. His statement says: "Commands are that whereby the people are taught; laws are that

---

[92] *Ibid.*, ch. 34, "Hou hsing."

[93] *Ibid.*, ch. 18, "Hui hsüeh," says: "Master Ssu-ma said: 'Hustling and bustling, all the world goes after profit. Girls of Chao do not choose between handsome and ugly [husbands, so long as they are wealthy]; matrons of Cheng show no preference for [mates who dwell] nearby or far away [so long as they are well-heeled]; merchants are not ashamed of disgraceful [conduct, if it brings them lucre]; soldiers are ready to die, strong men disregard family attachment, servitors share the calamities of their lords—all have an eye on profit and remuneration.'" This implies subtly that man's "nature is evil." [The foregoing translation was supplied by the author.]

[94] *Ibid.*, ch. 33, "Chi t'an." *Ch.* 21, "Shu lu," says: "Among human temperaments there are the firm and the pliant; among physical forms there are the beautiful and the ugly. The sage is one who can accommodate to such; he cannot alter them." This also denies the function of transforming through teaching.

with which supervision is maintained over the evil. When commands are strict the people become circumspect; when laws are established evil is barred. When the net is loose, the trapped animal is lost; when the laws are loose, the guilty get away. When the guilty can get away, the people become demoralized, and lightly violate the prohibitions. Therefore, when prohibitions lack certitude, the ordinarily law-abiding fellow begins to trust his luck. When stark punishment can be relied upon, not even [the infamous bandits] Chih and [Chuang] Chiao will break the laws." Such a policy was particularly difficult for the literati to accept. Their reasons for opposing it were: "When laws and commands are many, the people become uncertain about which [forbidden action] they should be avoiding." Their evidence to support this was: "The laws of Ch'in were as profuse as autumn tendrils and their network was as thick as congealed tallow. Yet higher and lower were alike in evading them, so treachery and deceit burgeoned. . . . Now, today, the regulations and commands run to over a hundred articles; their text is voluminous, and the crimes they define carry heavy penalties. The way the provinces and constituent states apply them gives rise to doubt and uncertainty; whether transgressions shall be considered slight or serious is up to the officials. Even those versed in their meanings do not know how to apply them, and all the less so do the simple people. The texts of the regulations and commands lie gathering dust and being eaten by bookworms on the office shelves. The officials cannot read them all, and all the less can the simple people do so. This is why law suits grow ever more numerous and why infractions committed by the people are ever more manifold."[95]

In all the exchanges of arguments related above, the statements are made with reference to the context of the existing prohibitions. Sang Hung-yang, however, also argued from the needs of the age to justify a Legalist position: "For he who is skilled in governing sees a fault and amends it, sees a break and closes it. That is how Wu Tzu [i.e., Wu Ch'i, died 378 B.C.] employed laws to govern in Ch'u and Wei, and how Shen Pu-hai and Lord Shang employed laws to strengthen Han and Ch'in."[96] He further set forth the circumstances under which governments might be lenient or harsh; "Different ages each must adopt their own measures." He also noted: "When the prevailing customs are not those of [the glorious antique ages of the Sage rulers] Yao and Shun, and the times are not like that when [the exemplary ancient worthy] Hsü Yu's people lived, yet to wish to govern by dispensing with laws is a bit like trying to force twisted wood, or to straighten crooked wood, without using clamps or adzes."[97] The literati went on to rebut that view, determining that Shen

[95] *Ibid.*, *ch.* 55, "Hsing te."
[96] *Ibid.*, *ch.* 56, "Shen, Han."
[97] *Ibid.*, *ch.* 59, "Ta lun."

Pu-hai's and Lord Shang's governing were those of: "After turbulence [had appeared], they undertook to stop it; after agitation [had started], they undertook to still it. Both the ruler and the ruled were belabored and troubled, and the disorders multiplied." Instead of solving the immediate problems of governing, they undermined the foundations of government. Therefore, the concepts of Shen Pu-hai and Lord Shang definitely must not be adopted; instead, the ancient sages must be emulated. "The Sages devoted themselves to what had not yet come to pass, therefore the sources of disorder had no chance of coming into existence."[98] With ethical teachings well established, what faults then would ever have to be corrected?

Observing the struggle that went on between Confucians and Legalists during the Han dynasty, as set forth in the *Debates on Salt and Iron,* one gathers that their conflict was not merely in the realm of thought; personal feelings also were brought to the point of rupture. Thus, those offering their views on the issues also indulged in defamation of each other's character,[99] and attacked the founding teachers of each other's philosophical traditions.[100] Each side seems to have moved toward extreme positions, ruling out all possibility of harmonious accommodation. Yet as we examine the facts in the matter, that is not entirely so. The government throughout the Han dynasty concurrently employed both Confucians and Legalists. The strength of the two schools alternately rose and subsided, without either being abandoned or terminated. Such was the disposition of the government based in the imperial court; therefore scholar-officials ambitious for advancement in their political careers also had simultaneously to adopt both kinds of methods in order to enhance their employability. An outstanding example is that of [the Legalist minded, anti-Confucian chief minister] ". . . Chang T'ang, who decided that when he was passing judgment in important cases, it would be well to buttress his decisions with citations from the classics. He therefore asked some of the court Erudits, [*po-shih*] and their students who specialized in the study of the *Book of Documents* and the *Spring and Autumn Annals* to act as his secretaries in the offices of the Commandant of Justice and to help in deciding doubtful points at law."[101] This is an example of being

[98] See, respectively, *ch.* 56, "Shen, Han" and *ch.* 59, "Ta lun."

[99] Refer to *ch.* 19, "Pao hsien," and *ch.* 20, "Hsiang tz'u."

[100] Such as *ch.* 11, "Lun ju," and *ch.* 7, "Fei Yang."

[101] *Shih Chi, ch.* 122 [following, with slight modification, Burton Watson, *Records of the Grand Historian of China,* Vol. II, p. 428]. The wording in the *Han Shu, ch.* 59, is identical. *Shih Chi, ch.* 112, "Biography of Kung-sun Hung," tells that when young he had served as a minor official in the courts, and only after the age of forty commenced to study the *Spring and Autumn Annals* and various academic traditions. "He became skilled in writing, the laws, and bureaucratic affairs, and further adorned it all with the semblance of Confucian ways." He would seem to have been in the same category as Chang T'ang.

fully Legalist yet adorning it all with Confucian learning. Tung Chung-shu [see Chapter Nine, Section Three, below] employed citations from the Confucian classics in deciding cases at law, and wrote a work called *The Spring and Autumn Annals as Reference in Deciding Lawsuits* [*Ch'un-ch'iu chüeh shih pi*].[102] This is an example of Confucian methods being employed in implementing punishments and laws. As for persons such as Chia Yi and Ch'ao Ts'o, they were educated in both the Confucian-Mencian learning and that of Shen and Lord Shang,[103] thereby constituting particularly clear proof of Legalism's and Confucianism's convergence. Both schools, in fact, represent applied learning, and it is a quite natural and by no means surprising consequence of their existence within the authoritarian empire that they should present this heterogeneous appearance.

[102] This work has long been lost. Ch'en Li's [1809–1869] *Kung-yang Yi-shu*, under the Seventeenth year of Duke Wen, in his commentary on the line: "His wife, Chiang-shih, married in Ch'i," cites one case [from Tung's book of legal precedents] quoting from the *T'ai-p'ing Yü-lan* [late tenth century], as follows: "A's husband B is on board a ship that encounters gales at sea; the ship sinks, and he is drowned, lost at sea, and could not be given burial. During the fourth moon A's mother C marries off A. What laws apply to these matters? It may be said that since A's husband has not been given burial, the law cannot permit her to marry. Should she become his wife without being properly married, she would merit punishment of death. Opinion: Although your servant is ignorant, he takes it as the meaning of the *Spring and Autumn*, since it states that the wife married in Ch'i, and states that her husband had died and she had no son, that it is in accord with principle she should re-marry. Married women have no right to act arbitrarily or capriciously, and should obey and be compliant. One who has been married reverts to her husband. A, moreover, was re-married by order of a superior [i.e., her mother], she had no lascivious motives, and did not become some one's wife without authorization. This example makes it clear that in deciding such a case, all are without fault, and should not be charged with any crime."

[103] *Shih Chi*, ch. 130: "Chia Yi and Ch'ao Ts'o expounded the doctrines of Shen Pu-hai and Lord Shang," Chia Yi's *Hsin Shu* is listed in the *Han Shu*, ch. 30, "Treatise on Literature," as a Confucian work. Ch'ao Ts'o was a student of Shen's and Lord Shang's *hsing-ming* doctrines, but also received instruction in the *Book of Documents* from Fu Sheng (*Han Shu*, ch. 49). His statements and views as recorded in his biography and in the "Treatise on Food and Money," Part I (*Han Shu*, ch. 24-a) clearly display a mixture of Confucianism and Legalism. Because these convey no original theories, he is not discussed here.

CHAPTER NINE

From Chia Yi
to Chung-ch'ang T'ung

SECTION ONE
The Revival of Confucian Learning

DURING the Han dynasty, Confucian thought gained the position of the orthodox school of thought. This is widely known; it demands no further discussion. Yet were we merely to accept all those time-honored assertions that the Ch'in dynasty extinguished the ancient learning but, that, coming to the Han, it suddenly flourished anew, we would not be entirely faithful to the facts. Hsia Tseng-yu has stated that the Ch'in and the Han dynasties together constitute "the standard of Chinese culture,"[1] thereby noting that there were numerous elements of continuity in the Han institutions, and that there were similarities in the cultural policies they adopted. Ever since Hsün Tzu [died ca. 238 B.C.] commented that its utter reliance on laws and lack of Confucians constituted the Ch'in State's shortcomings,[2] later persons have accepted that as the definitive view, uncritically passing it on without modification. In fact, however, after completing his unification of the empire [in 221 B.C.], the First Emperor neither implemented a truly Legalist government nor wholly excluded Confucian methods. In the twenty-eighth year of his rule [219 B.C.], in implementing the system of commanderies and counties, he "consulted with the various Confucian scholars of [the former State of] Lu about inscribing a stone with a eulogy to the virtues of Ch'in; he also consulted with them about the *Feng* and *Shan* sacrifices and about the *Wang* sacrifices to mountains and rivers." In the Thirty-fourth year [A.D. 213], he "had wine prepared at the Hsien-yang Palace, to entertain seventy Scholars of Wide Learning [*po-shih* or "Erudits"] who came forward to express wishes for his longevity." Although not all of those learned scholars were Confucians, from [his son, Prince] Fu-su's remonstrance against his act of burying alive the scholars at Hsien-yang, which says "they all praised and emulated Confucius,"[3] it can be seen that the First Emperor must have had more than a few Confucians in his employment. Moreover, Shu-sun T'ung "during the Ch'in dynasty had been summoned to the court because of his literary learning, and served as Erudit for drafting edicts." When the Second Emperor learned of Ch'en

---

[1] Hsia Tseng-yu [died 1924], *Chung-kuo ku-tai-shih*, p. 226.
[2] *Hsün Tzu, ch.* 16, "Ch'iang Kuo." [Cf. Chapter Three, footnote 119.]
[3] *Shih Chi, ch.* 6, "Annals of the First Emperor."

Sheng's rebellion, he summoned his Erudits and a number of Confucian scholars to ask their advice, and Shu-sun T'ung was among those consulted.[4] This provides evidence that when he buried the Confucians alive, he merely executed some four hundred or more scholars at Hsien-yang who had committed infractions of his interdicts; he did not slaughter all Confucians, nor did he wholly forbid their teachings. Even clearer proof that the First Emperor employed Confucians is found in the inscriptions that he had put on stone when he travelled to K'uai-chi and other places; embodying the concepts of the unified empire with its now standardized script [and other cultural features], those inscriptions speak of how to set bounds of propriety for the people and make the practices of their daily lives more upright.[5] The act of burning the books was motivated solely by the fear that private learning would introduce confusion into [the state's] official teachings;[6] it was not intended to eradicate Confucian learning as such.

We should note that the State of Ch'in's policies of full reliance on the laws and abolition of Confucian learning were in point of fact confined to the period of Duke Hsiao's reign [361–338 B.C.] and Lord Shang's ministership. Dukes [after 324 B.C. called "King"] Hui and Chao devoted all their energies to aggressive warfare and continued the state's strategic policy, which gave primacy to agriculture and war. Lü Pu-wei [died 235 B.C.], as chief minister to Kings Chuang and Hsiang, summoned into service guest scholars, and had a book compiled [i.e., the *Lü-shih Ch'un-ch'iu; vide* Chapter Ten]. He initiated a clear repudiation of Lord Shang's earlier doctrines; he welcomed many peripatetic specialists on the *Odes* and the *Documents*. Subsequently, by the time the First Emperor had annexed and eliminated the Six States and established his unified, authoritarian government, he understood well that "Confucian learning is, of all doctrines, the most suited to authoritarianism."[7] Consequently he adopted it as a decoration for his governing, but he forbade private learning and charged his Erudits with responsibility for monopolizing and controlling all the learning of the realm. Therefore the First Emperor's government came to use Legalists and Confucians concurrently. In so doing, he both disavowed the prior institutions of Duke Hsiao, and anticipated agreement with the later Emperor Wu [of the Han dynasty]. Those two differed in this respect: the First Emperor held the reliance upon the laws to be his

---

[4] *Shih Chi, ch.* 99, "Biography of Shu-sun T'ung." [Translation in Watson, *Shih Chi,* Vol. I, pp. 291–98.] *Han Shu, ch.* 34, has identical wording.

[5] For the texts [of those inscriptions, with their elements of Confucian ethical tone], see *Shih Chi, ch.* 6. The argument advanced here is that of Ku Yen-wu [1613–1682]; see his *Jih-chih-lu, ch.* 13.

[6] Discussed in detail in Chapter Eight, footnote 31, above.

[7] Hsia Tseng-yu, *op.cit.* note 1, p. 256.

major principle, and ranked Confucianism as one among the many schools; the Emperor Wu acknowledged Confucius as the authoritative teacher [*tsung-shih* 宗師] and adopted the tenets of Kuan Tzu and Lord Shang to serve merely as supplementary aids in governing.

Nonetheless, because of the First Emperor's prohibition against all private learning, and the subsequent burning of the official book collections at Hsien-yang by Hsiang Yü [in 206 B.C., during the civil war between the Ch'in and the Han periods], the pre-Ch'in thought and learning indeed fell into a state of premature decline. It is fortunate that among the writings and the followers of the Hundred Schools, some survived. When Ch'en She proclaimed himself King [in 208 B.C., as rebel against Ch'in], a group of Confucians from the State of Lu went to announce their fealty to him, bearing ritual vessels that had belonged to Confucius, and K'ung Chia [eighth-generation descendant of Confucius] was appointed Erudit by him.[8] Shu-sun T'ung, who had served as Erudit under the Ch'in, subsequently held posts in succession under Hsiang Liang, King Huai [of Ch'u], Hsiang Yü, and the Han Founder.[9] Others such as Li Yi-chi and Lu Chia, former Confucian servitors of the Ch'in, aided the Han Founder in the founding of his dynasty.[10] In the fourth year of the reign of the Emperor Hui [191 B.C.] the [former Ch'in] law against privately owned books was formally rescinded,[11] thereby overturning the Ch'in dynasty's negative control policy, and gradually there developed the era of positive sponsorship. During the reigns of Emperors Wen and Ching [179–141 B.C.] Master Han and Master Yuan Ku, as specialists in the *Book of Odes*, were appointed Erudits. Tung Chung-shu and Master Hu-mu served the Emperor Ching as Erudits specializing in study of the *Spring and Autumn Annals*. Emperor Wen ordered Ch'ao Ts'o to go to receive instruction in the *Book of Documents* from the former Ch'in Erudit Master Fu Sheng.[12] The influence of Confucian learning clearly had already begun to make great advances through the first fifty years of the Han dynasty. Coming, then, to the reign of Emperor Wu, he adopted the proposal of the chief minister Wei Wan, [in 140 B.C.], to abolish the study of Shen Pu-hai's and Han Fei's, Su Ch'in's and Chang Yi's teachings, as a qualification for recommendation to office. In the fifth year of the Chien-yuan reign period [136 B.C., the Emperor Wu] established the offices

---

[8] *Shih Chi*, ch. 121, "Biographies of Confucian Scholars," [Watson, *Shih Chi*, Vol. II, p. 397]; *Han Shu*, ch. 88, contains a roughly similar account.

[9] *Shih Chi*, ch. 99, "Biography of Shu-sun T'ung"; [translated in Watson, *Shih Chi*, Vol. I, pp. 291–98].

[10] *Shih Chi*, ch. 97, "Biography of Lu Chia," [Watson, *op.cit.*, pp. 269–83].

[11] *Han Shu*, ch. 2, "Annals of the Emperor Hui."

[12] *Shih Chi*, ch. 121.

of Erudits of the Five Classics.[13] Kung-sun Hung, who specialized in the study of the *Spring and Autumn Annals* and as a commoner [after the age of seventy was appointed to office and], became one of the Emperor's Three Lords [or highest officials], and was granted the title Marquis of P'ing-chin. The scholars of the empire all flocked to emulate his style [of gaining success].[14] With the Five Classics instituted as the official learning, there were no longer any restrictions on their study among the people. The *Odes* and the *Documents* could bring material advantage and honor; classical studies were sufficient to qualify one for the official career. In consequence of these many kinds of encouragement and stimulus, Confucian studies attained unprecedented prosperity.

Confucian learning in the Han period more or less continued along the lines inherited from the pre-Ch'in era, yet it was not altogether unchanged or unchanging. Confucian political thought throughout the four hundred years of the dynasty in its two phases [of Former Han with its capital at Ch'ang-an and Later Han with its capital at Lo-yang] might be divided into three periods according to the major features of its changing content, as follows: The first period roughly comprises the four reigns of the Emperors Kao-tsu, Hui, Wen, and Ching [206–141 B.C.]. During these sixty years Huang-Lao doctrines flourished. The Confucians too were subject to their inevitable influences, and they therefore included the doctrine of *wu-wei*, or "taking no action" within their values. Chia Yi is this period's most prominent representative. The second period extends from the reign of Emperor Wu to the time of [the usurper] Wang Mang, [140 B.C. to A.D. 9], a period of about one-hundred sixty years. Although by this time Confucians had thrown off the bridle of Huang-Lao, and were in sole possession of the age's esteem, the content of their learning was no longer that of pre-Ch'in pristine Confucianism and also had diverged significantly from the thought of Mencius and Hsün Tzu. In the beginning it absorbed elements of *Yin-yang* and Five Agents ideas, and by the end of that period it had taken in the superstitions of the prognostication theories and the apocrypha. Tung Chung-shu is the great master of widest repute in this period. The third period is roughly equivalent to the two hundred years of the Later Han. Throughout this period the court continued to place its faith in the apocrypha and in portents, yet a certain number of the Confucians developed strong antipathies to all that, eventually repudiating all supernatural doctrines and crediting only the tangible and the practical. Thus even though the core doctrines still conveyed man's and heaven's interactions, their essential focus now was upon human affairs. By the

[13] *Han Shu, ch.* 6. [Shen and Han represent Legalism; Chang Yi and Su Ch'in were Diplomatists, or *Tsung-heng chia*, famous for their persuasive powers during the Warring States Period. The Five Classics represented the core of Confucian learning.]

[14] *Shih Chi, ch.* 121; the text in *Han Shu, ch.* 88, varies slightly.

time that Confucian learning reached this point, however, its influence had sharply waned, like a once-powerful bow whose force is spent; evidences of Confucian vitality had become rare. Those who discussed the arts of governing were mainly concerned with correcting the faults of their times, and they gradually grew pessimistic about authoritarian rule. The most prominent representatives of this period appeared in its latter half; they are Wang Fu, Hsün Yüeh, and Chung-ch'ang T'ung. Other Confucianists such as Shu-sun T'ung, Kung-sun Hung, and their ilk were nothing more than debasers of their learning who sought through sycophancy to achieve eminence.[15] Within the Confucian school they must be counted petty-minded Confucians concerned with self-aggrandizement, about whom it is unwarranted to speak of any thought and learning.

SECTION TWO
Chia Yi (200–168 B.C.)

THE Ch'in state mastered the world by applying harsh punishments and by audaciously utilizing its great military power, yet enjoyed its supremacy for less than forty years. The men of the early Han used that experience as a warning, always considering how to correct those faults. As specific prescription against the abuses of harsh and oppressive controls, they implemented an inaction doctrine derived from Huang-Lao teachings. As specific prescription against the abuses of harsh punishments and killings, they proclaimed Confucian benevolence and righteousness. To suggest a quite general characterization, the sixty years of early Han political thought constitute a period of reaction against the political failure of Lord Shang and Li Ssu. Chia Yi lived within this period, and he became the distinctive thinker in the field of harmonizing Confucian and Mencian thought with that of the Huang-Lao school. Chia Yi was a native of Lo-

---

[15] Shu-sun T'ung had been an Erudit under the Ch'in dynasty. During the reign of the Second Emperor [209–206 B.C.] when rebellions broke out in Shan-tung, Shu-sun T'ung responded [to the Emperor's questions about the rebellion] only to say what would please him, then fled [after receiving valuable rewards] to save his own life. Thereafter he served in succession many rulers, "all of whom he flattered to their faces in order to gain trust and high status." Later he served the Han Founder for whom he devised the ritual of the court. His followers, numbering more than one hundred, all gained appointments as palace attendants, and were rewarded with gifts of gold. Delighted, they all said: "Master Shu-sun is truly a sage; he understands the important needs of the times." (*Shih Chi, ch.* 99, "Biography of Shu-sun T'ung.") "As an expert on the *Spring and Autumn Annals* Kung-sun Hung was not the equal of Tung Chung-shu, but by anticipating the interests of the times and doing what was useful to the ruler, he reached the highest positions in the government. Tung Chung-shu scorned Kung-sun Hung as an obsequious sycophant, and so Kung-sun Hung hated him." He repeatedly slandered and harmed Tung. (*Shih Chi, ch.* 121.)

yang, as a youth deeply schooled in the writings of various philosophers and the Hundred Schools. Introduced to the court by Lord Wu [Governor of Ho-nan; see Chapter Seven, footnote 41], the Emperor Wen summoned him for appointment as Erudit. Within a year he had advanced to the high post of palace counselor. He frequently submitted plans and proposals, and also urged institutional changes, intended thoroughly to revise the Ch'in ways in governing. As he was opposed by [senior officials] such as Chou Po, Kuan Ying, Chang Hsiang-ju, and Feng Ching, he was barred from important service, and was sent out from the court to become tutor to the Prince of Ch'ang-sha and then to Prince Huai of Liang; he died in despondency and frustration. That was in the twelfth year of Emperor Wen's reign [168 B.C.], when Chia Yi was in his thirty-second year.[16] His writings total thirty-eight pieces [p'ien][17] which are listed in the Han Shu's "Journal on Literature" under the heading of the Confucian School. The Shih Chi contains the sentence: "Master Chia and Ch'ao Ts'o were versed in the writings of Shen Pu-hai and Lord Shang."[18] Further, because he was highly regarded by Lord Wu, there were those later on who on that basis classified him as a Legalist.[19] On examining his statements and writings, we can see that Chia Yi's political thought drew upon Confucius and Mencius for its central elements but drew as well on aspects of Huang-Lao teachings. Despite his occasionally drawing close to Legalist and Yin-yang doctrines, those never supply the foundations for his major tenets. The historical record clearly states that he was deeply schooled in the writings of the Hundred Schools. Therefore, strictly speaking, his learning might best be classified under the School of Eclectics [tsa-chia],[20] but he should in no case be classed with Ch'ao Ts'o and Sang Hung-yang.

[16] Shih Chi, ch. 84, "Biographies of Ch'ü Yuan and Master Chia," the Han Shu, ch. 48, contains roughly similar language. Wang Chung [1745–94], in his [collected works, entitled] Shu Hsüeh, "Nei p'ien," ch. 3, deduces that Chia Yi was born in the seventh year of the reign of the Han Founder [i.e., 200 B.C.].

[17] His extant works number fifty-six p'ien; the "Journal of Literature" of the New T'ang History [eleventh century] is the earliest record in which Chia Yi's writings are given the title Hsin Shu, or "New Writings." From Sung times onward many persons have expressed doubts about these writings. Yao Nai [1732–1815] condemned the collection as "the spurious doings of a preposterous person." The Ssu-k'u ch'üan-shu tsung-mu t'i-yao ["abstracts of works in the catalog of the Ch'ing imperial library"] assumes it to be the compilation of some later person, saying: "This work is not wholly genuine, nor is it wholly spurious." The recent scholar Yü Chia-hsi in his study [of that catalog], Ssu-k'u t'i-yao pien-cheng [published in 1932] partially modifies and supplements that view, and appears to come somewhat closer to the truth. Cf. also Chang Hsin-ch'eng's Wei-shu t'ung-k'ao, hsia, pp. 634–37.

[18] Shih Chi, ch. 130, "Tzu hsü."

[19] E.g., Yao Shun-ch'in, Ch'in-Han che-hsüeh-shih, Vol. One, Chapter Three.

[20] The "Journal of Literature" in the Sung Shih is the earliest work [thirteenth century] in which Chia Yi's writings are classified under the "School of Eclectics."

Chia Yi's discourses on government hold that the people are its ultimate objective, and regard the *Tao* as its highest principle. In his essay "Ta cheng, hsia," he says: "The people are the basis [for having] the feudal lords. Instructing them is the basis of governing. The *Tao* is the basis of instructing." The importance of the people [*min pen*] is something that really harks back as far as Mencius. As restated and developed by Chia Yi, its significance becomes even more striking. His essay "Ta cheng, shang" expresses this with the greatest force and clarity. It says, in part: "It is said of government that it possesses no aspect of which the people are not the basis. The state finds in them its basis, the ruler finds in them his basis, the officials find in them their basis. For that reason, the state is secure or in peril depending on its people; the ruler's grandeur or disgrace rest with the people; officials' high status or mean come from the people." The responsibility of government, thus, is to provide that well-being and happiness for its people, while the safety or peril for ruler and state depend entirely on whether, in their hearts and minds, the people uphold or reject them. "For the people are in the possession of the ruler; to be a servitor is to assist the ruler in tending them. So it is that the servitor gains merit by making the people prosperous and happy, and is to be condemned if they are impoverished and distressed. So it is that the ruler is declared enlightened if he can recognize worthy servitors; officials are declared loyal if they have concern for the people." When the ruler is enlightened and his servitors are loyal, the people's hearts will incline to them. When ruler and servitor do not perform their duties to the full, the masses of the people inevitably will desert them.

That indicates that the people are not merely the ultimate objective of governing; they also constitute the ultimate political authority. The ruler, in his own person, possesses no absolute dignity. "For [the tyrant] Chou called himself the Celestial King, and [the tyrant] Chieh called himself the Son of Heaven. Yet after they had been destroyed, the people among themselves all vilified them. From this one can see that position is not in itself sufficient to bestow dignity, and titles in themself are inadequate to impart grandeur. Thus the dignity of the ruler derives from the people's having dignified him, and for that he is said to possess dignity. Thus the wealth of the ruler comes from the people's being content with him, and for that he is said to possess wealth." In other words, the people's power to reward or punish clearly is not limited to granting or abrogating titles, but also includes the control over preserving or ruining the dynasty. "The people are a mighty clan . . . possessing force for which there is no match. . . . From ancient times to the present, if one establishes enmity with the people, whether sooner or later, the people always will triumph over him. . . . Thus it can be said of calamity and blessing that there is no destruction sent by heaven; rather, it indubitably lies with the people. The people being of such grave importance, there is no alternative to seeking their approval."[21] The ruler is declared enlightened if he can recognize [and employ] worthy servitors, and there is no more certain way of recognizing their worth than to heed the people. "For even though the people may be ignorant they also are percipient. Where the ruler selects officials he must gain the people's consent. So it is that if the people praise someone, the enlightened ruler then will investigate, and if what he finds agrees, he will appoint the man. And so it is when the people complain about someone, the enlightened ruler then will investigate, and if what he finds is wrong, he will get rid of the man. Thus it is said that when the ruler is not unwise in his selection of officials, it will cause the people to sing, after which he can respond in harmony with them. [Less literally: 'There will be a responsive spirit of cooperation between ruler and people.'] Thus it can be said that the people are the test through which the officials must be measured."[22]

In all of Chia Yi's statements quoted above concerning the people as the basic element in government he has used Mencius as his source; nothing there is his original thought. Yet for Chia Yi to have set Mencius' tenets forth with such clarity during those first years of the Western [Former] Han epoch is a matter of very great historical consequence. The fundamental distinction between Confucianism and Legalism lies in the issue of whether the people are held to be the important factor or whether the ruler is to be elevated. Thought favoring the elevation of the ruler had become embodied in practice since the time of Shen Pu-hai and Lord Shang, and with the advent of the Ch'in dynasty it had been distorted into a still more oppressive form; that swept the empire, having deeply influential impact. Simultaneously, theories centering on the people's primary importance became virtually extinct. At this time, after a lapse of a century, that Chia Yi should bring them forward again attests the depth and intensity of the reactions in thought aroused by the antipathy to the fallen Ch'in regime.

Quite apart from that, however, the doctrines of Lord Shang and Han Fei claimed to give full rein to the laws, while in fact they promoted authoritarianism. The basis of their theories was precisely the opposite from what Mencius called "gaining the hearts [and minds; i.e., *hsin*] of the people." Chia Yi hoped for "the people to sing and the ruler to respond in harmony"; this amply displays his antipathy toward the defunct Ch'in dynasty's authoritarianism. Mencius said: "Those who are fleeing from Yang Chu's [erroneous theories] must finally turn to Confucianism." [*Mencius*, VII/ii/26/1.] Speaking in terms of political thought, to flee from Han Fei's ruler supreme in an authoritarian system, and to

---

[21] All of the foregoing quotations are from Chia Yi's *Hsin Shu*, *SPTK* edition. Ch. 9, "Ta cheng, shang."

[22] *Ibid.*, "Ta cheng, hsia."

arrive finally at Mencius' regard for the people as the element of basic importance, is something which the circumstances of the time made almost inevitable.[23]

In his discussions of the forms of government, [*cheng t'i* 政體] Chia Yi wholly followed the Confucians. His discussions of governing methods [*chih shu* 治術], however, borrow simultaneously from Huang-Lao doctrines. He said that "*Tao*" is the basis both of governing and of [philosophical] teaching. "The *Tao* is what one follows in order to meet with all things [*chieh wu* 接物, i.e., "to deal with realities"]. Its basis can be called 'the vacuous' [*hsü* 虛]; its extension [into application] can be called 'methods' [*shu* 術]. 'Vacuous' is a way of describing its essential subtlety which, in its flatness and plainness, is beyond all purposive application. 'Methods' are those ways by which one controls all things [*chih wu* 制物]; it is the key [*shu* 數] to action and quiescence." To state that concept in other words, the vacuous [*Tao*] is pure and quiescent, and engages in no action, whereas its methods are that by which virtue transforms, and governing is made upright. "The enlightened ruler is he who faces the south and is upright, who is pure and vacuous and quiescent; he lets his rules be manifest of themselves, and allows affairs to be settled of themselves. . . . This is how the vacuous meets things. . . . The ruler of men is benevolent and all within the boundaries responds harmoniously, thereby none of his people will fail to have close and kindly feelings toward him. The ruler of men is righteous and all within the boundaries become orderly, thereby none of his people will fail to be compliant. The ruler of men has propriety [ritual correctness] and all within the boundaries become decorous, thereby none of his people will fail to be respectful. The ruler of men merits trust and all within the boundaries become pure and blameless [*chen* 貞], thereby none of his people will fail to be trustworthy. The ruler of men is just [*kung* 公] and all within the boundaries willingly submit, thereby none of his people will fail to uphold him. The ruler of men observes the law [*fa*] and all within the boundaries become regulated [*kuei* 軌], thereby none of his people will fail to assist and maintain [*fu* 輔] him."[24]

"This is how with methods one deals with realities" [paraphrased]. The "vacuous" takes no purposive action while its "methods" are active; those two concepts appear to be somewhat contradictory. Just how they

---

[23] From this also it should become all the more clear that Chia Yi should not be classified as a Legalist.

[24] Chia Yi's *Hsin Shu, ch.* 8, "Tao shu." [The quoted passages use a number of terms, e.g., *shu* 術, *shu* 數, *chen* 貞, *fa* 法, etc., that have specific application in various schools of thought; their use here for Confucian political ends displays the range of Chia Yi's eclecticism, and also makes for great difficulties in translation. The renderings given here should be considered tentative.]

relate to each other is something that Master Chia unfortunately has failed to explicate. If we attempt to seek an answer to that by examining the content of all the fifty-eight items comprising his collected works, we find that the greater portion of all his arguments concerning the methods of governing fall within the scope of Confucian thought.[25] In this too it is apparent that he charges the Ch'in dynasty with having erred in giving rein to its laws, and therefore he desires to counter its ways in order to achieve proper governance.

Chia Yi explicitly established distinct methods for gaining the empire and for governing it. The men of Ch'in had extended their means of gaining the empire to application for governing it; therefore in a matter of only thirteen years Ch'in was overthrown and destroyed. "Lord Shang parted with propriety and righteousness, cast off benevolence and mercy, concentrating all energies on aggressive expansion. He practiced that for two years, and Ch'in's customs steadily deteriorated."[26] "The King of Ch'in harbored his own relentless mind and exercised his own self-satisfied cleverness. He placed no trust in his meritorious servitors. He dispensed with the Kingly Way and in its stead he instituted his personal preferences. He burned documents and writings and made penalties and laws harsh. He put premium on trickery, and had no use for benevolence and righteousness. He employed violence and cruelty to launch his sovereign epoch. . . . If only the Second Emperor had been capable of even a mediocre ruler's deeds and had employed loyal and worthy servitors, if servitors and ruler could have been of one mind and have shown concern for the misfortunes afflicting the realm, while in the period of mourning [for the deceased First Emperor] they could have corrected the former Emperor's faults. . . . If all the people throughout the realm had been enabled to make a new beginning, to change the norms and observe standards of conduct, each person could then exert prudence in his personal life. By fulfilling the hope of all the people, he could have bestowed a vast grace upon the realm, and the world would have had a respite."[27] Once we understand that the methods by which Ch'in gained

---

[25] The "Fu-niao fu" ["Fu on the owl," translated in full in Watson, *Shih Chi*, vol. 1, pp. 512–15], contains statements such as "the Perfect Man abandons all things," which are close in meaning to Chuang Tzu. That piece, however, is not a political discourse. When it comes to the political actions that he urged Emperor Wen to undertake, such as "to alter the month upon which the year began, change the color of the vestments, put its administrative code in order, fix the titles of officials, and encourage the spread of rites and music . . . honor the color yellow and the number five . . ." (*Shih Chi*, ch. 84, "Biography . . .") [following Watson, *op.cit.*, p. 509], these are virtually identical with the arts of government subsequently instituted by Tung Chung-shu.

[26] *Han Shu*, ch. 48, "Biography of Chia Yi." The corresponding texts in the *Hsin Shu* frequently display minor discrepancies and contain faulty passages.

[27] *Hsin Shu*, *SPTK* edition, ch. 1, "Kuo Ch'in, hsia."

its success were precisely the causes of its failure, then, without further explanation, it becomes obvious what the way of governing should comprise. Chia Yi's ideal was to: "Change the prevailing modes and alter the common practices, causing the world thereby to turn back its mind, and to look to the *Tao*."[28] The common run of officials [the likes of whom administered the laws and governed the people under the Ch'in] "are not aware of the great essence," and do not understand how to employ propriety and righteousness, punishments and penalties; they give their utmost to the brush-pens and scrapers, the papers and the files. "Propriety [i.e., the Rites] is a thing that interdicts actions prior to their occurrence; the laws' interdictions fall only after the event. It is for that reason that the effects of using laws are easily seen, but the results produced by propriety are difficult to know. Nonetheless, "one who governs with propriety and righteousness accumulates propriety and righteousness; one who governs with punishments and penalties accumulates punishments and penalties. When punishments and penalties accumulate, the people turn away in resentment; when propriety and righteousness accumulate, the people draw close in harmony. . . . When they are guided by ethical teachings, and as those ethical teachings pervade, the atmosphere among the people is lighthearted. When they are bludgeoned with laws and commands, and as the application of laws and commands reaches the point of saturation, the prevailing mood among the people is one of sadness. Feelings of lightheartedness or of sadness are responses to the blessings and calamities [of government]."[29]

The ordinary people all can distinguish between bitterness and joy, between poverty and plenty, but by themselves they are unable to progress to the virtues of benevolence and righteousness, wisdom and trust. For the ruler to sponsor teaching is therefore a necessary task of government. "The word 'people' [*min* 民] means 'unseeing' [*ming* 瞑, in some texts 暝]; the word 'masses' [*meng* 氓] means 'blind' [*meng* 盲, in some texts 萌]. Therefore, only when the ruler provides them his support and guidance are they at all susceptible to transformation." For although the people are characterized by "accumulated ignorance," they are never incapable of being governed. The crucial element in that is the ruler's own uprightness. "If only the ruler is devoted to something, those below him will always be transformed to that [standard]."[30] "Thus, when the ruler is capable of

---

[28] *Ibid.*, *ch.* 3, "Su chi."

[29] *Han Shu*, *ch.* 48, "Biography of Chia Yi."

[30] *Hsin Shu*, *ch.* 9, "Ta cheng, hsia." *Ch.* 8, "Liu shu," takes benevolence, righteousness, propriety, wisdom, trust, and joy to be the "six qualities" of human nature. However, "All these are beyond the reach of ordinary people by themselves, and for that reason they must obtain the teachings of the Former Kings before they can know how to go about their affairs."

doing what is good, his officials most certainly also will be capable of doing the good. When the officials are capable of doing good, the people most certainly also will be capable of doing good. So it is that when the people are not good, the officials are to bear the blame. When the officials are not good, it is a fault of the ruler."[31] Mencius had said: "If the ruler be benevolent, all will be benevolent; if the ruler be righteous, all will be righteous. . . . Once rectify the ruler, and the state will be stabilized." [*Mencius*, iv/i/20.] Chia Yi's statements on this point are, to be sure, derived from the learning of the past. Mencius, however, repeatedly stated that security and peril [for the state] were linked directly to the person of the ruler, yet never turned his attention to guaranteeing that the ruler would be personally upright. Chia Yi would make good this deficiency, proposing that educating the heir apparent is the way to provide a good ruler; the Confucian theories about a government of men were brought by this closer to comprehensive formulation.[32] He commented on this subject: "The fate of the realm hangs on the heir apparent: the heir apparent's capacity for good is a matter of his early admonition and education and in the selection of his associates. Before his mind has overextended itself, if he is first admonished and taught, his transformation can be readily accomplished. If he develops in understanding of the meaning of *Tao* and the methods, of wisdom and righteousness, that is the achievement of his teaching. If, however, he adopts other practices and acquires other habits, it is simply because of his associates."[33] With regard to the teaching materials in which the heir apparent and the people were to be instructed, those, in the main, were to draw upon [the standard Confucian doctrines of] 'cultivating one's person and regulating one's family,' filial and fraternal submission, and moral social behavior, as their chief elements. Chia Yi was deeply troubled by those Ch'in measures which destroyed the ethical foundations of family and clan, and he judged Lord Shang to be the guilty party in that. "Among the people of Ch'in, if a family was rich and the sons mature, they would leave the family home, taking a share of its property. If a family was poor and the sons mature, they would leave the family to live in the homes of their wives. They

---

[31] "Ta cheng, hsia."

[32] Plato proposed employing educational methods by which to nurture and to select philosopher kings; that also is one plan for guaranteeing the rule of men. His theory was never tested in practice. In that instance in the city-state of Syracuse, whose tyrant-king, Dionysius II [fl. 367 B.C.] received the tutelage of the philosopher, it was an experience that ended in painful failure. One might argue that it was because the education of the ruler was not begun early enough and because he was not provided with selected assistants.

[33] *Han Shu*, *ch.* 48. The wording in the *Hsin Shu*, *ch.* 5, "Pao fu," varies slightly; on the methods of instruction, see also in *ch.* 5, "Fu chih," "Lien yü"; in *ch.* 6, "Jung ching"; and in *ch.* 10, "T'ai chiao."

would lend their harrows and hoes to their fathers with the concern [for the objects] but with the self-satisfied expressions of having been generous. If their mothers were to borrow a dust-pan or a broom, they would be quick to complain at them for that. A mother, while holding her child to nurse it might assume arrogant manners toward her father-in-law. If a wife and her mother-in-law were displeased with each other they might show angry looks and scheme against each other. Except that parents loved their children, and that people all had their human greed, there were otherwise few points of difference between them and the birds and beasts." All of this resulted by the time Lord Shang had been prime minister in Ch'in for only two years.[34] Chia Yi wanted to correct such practices, and to restore a form of political life centering on the family. Therefore he proclaimed: "The Way to serve one's ruler does not go beyond the standards for serving one's father. . . . The Way to serve a senior does not go beyond the standard for serving an older brother. . . . The Way of directing the empire is no different from dealing with a younger brother; the Way of showing a kindly concern for the people is no different from loving one's children. . . . The Way of serving in office is no different than holding a place in one's family."[35] This entire discussion setting forth the view that one principle governs both family and state is all too familiar to us; there is no need to explain it in lengthy detail.

None the less, we must carefully avoid the error of assuming that, because Chia Yi focused his emphasis upon the government-of-men ideal, in which governing and teaching were combined, he thereby believed institutions and punishments to be unnecessary. Confucius rectified names, Hsün Tzu adhered to the rites; their intent in that was fully subscribed to by Chia Yi. He stated: "When status and rank are clearly prescribed, inferiors will have no uncertainties; when authority and power are distinctly circumscribed, servitors will develop no deviant ambitions." Therefore those who govern states should assure that "rankings will exist for the noble and the humble, status will be evident in dress and assigned place. Once status and rank are established, each will remain within his limits, everyone will comply with the statutes. Any who irresponsibly fail to perform their duties should be reproved; any who usurp the prerogatives of a superior should be executed. Install laws [models] to regularize their behavior; establish offices to shepherd them. . . . When the honored and the humble are made known, when superior and inferior are distinguished, then social relations will have their models."[36] When throughout

---

[34] Same as footnote 26, above. [The evil practices cited all show violations of the family-centered proprieties and their ethical bases.]

[35] "Ta cheng, hsia."

[36] *Hsin Shu*, *ch*. 1, "Fu yi"; see also *ch*. 6, "Li."

the state ruler and servitors alike observe the ritual proprieties and comply with the statutes, there quite obviously would be no source from which disorders might arise. In addition to that, Chia Yi not only wanted to distinguish clearly the status of ruler and servitors; he also wanted to revamp the Chou dynasty's organization of social classes. Between the Son of Heaven and the ordinary people: "There should be, in the court the [Three] Lords and [Nine] Chief Ministers, the Knights and the Great Officers, while out [in the provinces] there should be the Dukes, Marquises, Earls, Viscounts and Barons."[37] In antiquity, the rites were not extended down to the common people, and the punishments were not extended upwards to the Superior Men. Therefore high officials should not be subject to physical punishment and humiliation, while the punishments and penalties should be limited to the common people. Lord Shang had said: "Punishments should know no degree or grade." [See Chapter Seven, above, p. 758.] Now Chia Yi, coming along after the social classes [of classical antiquity] have been completely levelled, nourished the thought of restoring them. This must be counted another manifestation of his desire to correct the faults that had marked the vanquished Ch'in dynasty's government.

And still further, Chia Yi could not agree with the [direct administrative] system of Commanderies and Counties that the First Emperor had implemented. The First Emperor had abolished the enfieffment of noble retainers, and he did not place any trust in his meritorious servitors; his errors in this respect were too obvious to merit recounting. If the Second Emperor had been able "to divide his territories and parcel out the people so as to enfief the descendants of the meritorious officials, establishing states and installing the ruler so that the rites prevailed throughout the realm,"[38] how could one common fellow's disturbance then have brought about the utter collapse of the dynasty? [Refers to Ch'en She, who rebelled in 209 B.C., provoking the widespread disorders that brought about the fall of Ch'in.] The Han system used Commanderies and Feudatories simultaneously; that was based on the idea of overcoming the weakness in the Ch'in system. It, however, adopted subdivisions that were too large and granted powers that were too great, so that already during the Han Founder's reign there were numerous instances of rebellion, while in the reign of Emperor Wen serious perils to the dynasty were encountered. Chia Yi's proposal was for all the enfieffed Kings to subdivide their fiefs among their sons and grandsons; with the passage of generations these states would naturally become reduced in size. His plan probably was a proposal for ensuring security, "for which nothing is

---

[37] *Ibid.*, *ch.* 2, "Chieh chi."
[38] *Ibid.*, *ch.* 1, "Kuo Ch'in, hsia."

so effective as enfieffing more feudal lords and decreasing their strength thereby. When their strength is small, they become more readily responsive to righteousness; when a feudatory is small it will have no evil thoughts."[39] Then it would become possible for the ruler to assume his position facing south, while all the Commanderies and Feudatories would join in mutual support, "and all the strength within the seas would be as that of the arms at the service of the body, or the fingers at the service of the arms, never failing to respond to control."[40] These views of Chia Yi, favoring the simultaneous use of both Commanderies and Feudatories so as to gain the best features of both, apparently were formulated with the actual experience of the Han dynasty in mind, and were not purely conceived as correctives to the faults of Ch'in.[41]

[39] *Ibid.*, *ch.* 1, "Fan ch'iang."

[40] *Ibid.*, *ch.* 2, "Wu mei." In addition to the essays cited, for Chia Yi's discussions of the feudal [*feng-chien*] system, see also his essays "Tsung shou," "Fan shang," "Ta tu," "Teng ch'i," "Yi jang," "Ch'üan chung," and "Shen wei." It should be noted that although in the essay "Chih pu ting" he uses the metaphor "When it comes to the hip bones and the thighs [i.e., the most powerful limbs of the body politic] one must use either a hatchet or an axe [i.e., as much force as one can, to deal with rebellion from these quarters], Chia Yi's motive in advocating the method of subdividing so as to enfieff more persons is really one of "benevolence and righteousness, mercy and generosity"; his proposal is in that quite different from Ch'ao Ts'o's plan to abolish all the Feudatories and strengthen the Commanderies.

[41] Roughly contemporaneous with Chia Yi, there was also Lu Chia, a "follower of the Han Founder as a guest [i.e., advisor] in his entourage during the founding of the dynasty" and whose thought was close to that of Chia Yi. When Lu Chia spoke favorably of the *Odes* and the *Documents* to Kao-tsu [the Han Founder], the Emperor rebuked him with the comment: "Whatever I possess I gained on horseback; why should I bother with the *Odes* and *Documents*?" Lu Chi replied: "It was gained on horseback, but can it be governed from horseback?" (This is identical to Chia Yi's idea that methods of conquering the empire were different from those of keeping it.) He was commanded to write a book [on government, which took form] in twelve chapters. This dealt with the reasons for the collapse of the Ch'in and the rise of the Han, and was called the *New Discourse, Hsin Yü* (see his biography in *Shih Chi, ch.* 97 and *Han Shu, ch.* 47). [*Cf.* Watson, *Shih Chi*, vol. I, pp. 275–80.] This title, but having twenty-three chapters, is listed in the *Han Shu, Journal of Literature*, under the category of "Confucian writings." The extant work has twelve chapters, and scholarly opinion on its authenticity is about evenly divided (see Chang Hsin-ch'eng, *Wei-shu t'ung-k'ao, hsia*, pp. 628–33). The content of this work is very much in harmony with Chia Yi's thought. Chapter Four, "*Wu-wei*," says: "The *Tao* is at its greatest in non-action [*wu-wei*]"; this corresponds to what Chia Yi refers to as vacuity [*hsü*]. It also says: "The First Emperor of Ch'in [had to go to extremes of cruelty, such as to] punish people with the execution of being torn apart by chariots, in order to restrain villains and lawbreakers"; and: "The more complex grows the conduct of affairs, the greater the disorder throughout the empire; the more detailed grow the laws, the more intense the villainies." And, further: "Laws and ordinances are a means to punish the wicked; they are not a means for encouraging the good." Chapter One, "Tao chi," says: "When tyranny is practiced, resentments accumulate; when benevolent rule prevails,

SECTION THREE
Tung Chung-shu (179–104 B.C.)

THE concept of heaven's and man's interaction found expression already in early antiquity, prior to Spring and Autumn times.[42] Tzu-ssu [Confucius' grandson] and Mencius carried on that line of thought, and eventually it developed into the theories about the Five Agents, and auspicious and inauspicious omens.[43] Hsün Tzu repudiated all that, strongly arguing that the sage had no need to seek knowledge of heaven. Tsou Yen's *Chung-shih wu-te* [in 56 *chüan*, no longer extant, but known to have discussed the transmutations of the Five Agents and their influence on the cosmos] established a school of thought distinct from the Confucians, yet its tenets clearly had much in common with them.[44] The Ch'in dynasty adopted ideas from the Yin-yang School, "and seriously calculated the Five [Agents'] power to overcome one another, [claiming it had itself gained the auspicious power of water]."[45] The "White Snake" and the "Red Emperor" images were used by [the Han Founder] Liu Pang as auspicious portents for the establishment of his dynastic power.[46] No such concepts existed before the Warring States Period, but by Ch'in and Han times they were widely current; they gradually assumed full development

---

meritorious conduct flourishes." All of these statements show agreement with Chia Yi's doctrines stressing the teaching of ethical norms and denying utility to punishments and killing. Chapter One, "Tao chi," also speaks of the "Early Sage-rulers," who "in making objects" were "guided by their images" [attributes of the culture heroes of earliest antiquity, according to the *Yi Ching*, "Hsi-tz'u chuan," Part I, no. 10, Wilhelm-Baynes, ed. 1950, p. 337], who promoted things advantageous and eliminated the harmful, after which came the "middle era sage-rulers," who established teachings and caused virtue to flourish, and then the "later sage-rulers," who cultivated the arts and defined the canonical works. These are ideas of which Chia Yi is not known to have spoken. Nonetheless, these concepts are close in character to those set forth in *ch.* 8, "Liu shu," of Chia Yi's *Hsin Shu*. Inasmuch as these two thinkers were so similar in their thought, the treatment of Lu Chia is appended in this note, in the interest of brevity.

[42] See: Fung Yu-lan, *History of Chinese Philosophy*, Vol. I, pp. 46–65 [in Derk Bodde's translation, pp. 22–42]; and Ku Chieh-kang, "Wu-te-chung-shih shuo hsia ti cheng-chih ho li-shih," (*Ch'ing-hua hsüeh-pao*, Vol. VI, no. 1, June, 1930, pp. 71–268).

[43] This assumes that the *Chung-yung* is a work emanating from the school of Tzu-ssu, and also accepts the view set forth in *Hsün Tzu*, *ch.* 6, "Fei shih-erh tzu."

[44] See the final paragraphs of Chapter One, Section Two [pp. 61–65], of the present work. Note that the chapter "Hung fan" in the *Documents* and the chapter "Yüeh ling" in the *Li Chi* display elements in common with pronouncements of the Yin-yang School. [*Cf.* Fung/Bodde, Vol. I, p. 163.]

[45] *Shih Chi*, *ch.* 26, "Li shu"; *cf.* also *ch.* 6, "Shih-huang pen-chi," under the twenty-sixth year.

[46] *Shih Chi*, *ch.* 8, "Kao-tsu pen-chi." [See Watson, *Shih Chi*, Vol. I, p. 80.]

and were openly acknowledged by the imperial court as articles of political faith. If one were to cite all of the ways of calculating recorded in the *Shih Chi*'s "Treatises" on the pitch-pipes [*Lü, ch.* 25], on the calendar [*Li, ch.* 26], on heavenly bodies [*T'ien-kuan, ch.* 27] and the Han Shu's "Treatises" on astronomy [*T'ien-wen, ch.* 26], the five agents [*Wu-hsing, ch.* 27], etc., as well as those used by all the various "numerology diviners" [*shu-shu-chia* 數術家],[47] the techniques employed would be seen to vary, but all would be seen to hold a common basis in the belief that heaven and man interacted.

The reason why divination rose so suddenly to prominence would seem in part to be that the age had needs that it served. Doctrines of the Heavenly Mandate, *t'ien-ming*, and of the powers of spiritual beings had flourished quite early in antiquity, then lapsed into a decline during the closing phase of the Chou era [twelfth to third centuries B.C.]. Observing Mo Tzu's strenuous efforts to promote the ideas of Heaven's will and of spiritual beings, one can see that kings and nobles and the elite of society had long since abandoned their belief in such. However, during the Warring States period [fifth to third centuries] the power of rulers greatly expanded, tending toward the emergence of authoritarian rule. Tsou Yen's "talk about heaven," explaining the Five Agents and the Nine Regions, had as its purpose precisely to frighten the rulers of his time with bizarre pronouncements, reminding them that the dominant cosmic influence could shift, and that they had only an unreliable grasp on their majestic power.

Han Confucianists in delineating Ch'in's faults in its excercise of despotic power tended to follow more or less the same principle, hoping to restrain and intimidate the ruler with ominous interpretations of calamities, prodigies, and heavenly portents; their intent was to constrain the ruler through fear, so that he would no longer dare indulge in unrestrained, despotic acts. All these efforts attempted to interpose heaven's authority as a restriction on the ruler's authority, and thereby to erect a defense against the festering evils inherent in monarchic authoritari-

---

[47] *Han Shu, ch.* 30, "Treatise on Literature," lists six categories of "Shu-shu" writings, including those on "astronomy," "the Five Elements," etc. "Those who practice astronomy arrange in order the twenty-eight constellations, and measure the five planets and the sun and moon, in recording the omens of the auspicious and the calamitous. The Sage Kings draw upon this in their governing. . . . For, observations of shadows as used to draw warning about the forms [which have cast them], that is something that only the most enlightened king is capable of heeding. . . . The Five Agents are the formative element of the Five Powers. The system has its origin in the cyclic sequence of the Five Powers [*Wu-te chung-shih*, also the name of a book attributed to Tsou Yen]. When the [relationships implicit in this system] are extended to their limits, there is nothing beyond their reach. However, the petty diviners also follow this in making the prognostications which they spread through the world, and which are in such confusing contradiction with each other."

anism.[48] All those who, in speaking of heaven's and man's interaction, laid their stress on the withdrawal of the mandate [*ko-ming* 革命], were of this strain.

However, this heavenly mandate concept, which could be used to explain the previous dynasty's fall from power, also could be invoked to show how the present ruler had gained his position. Ch'in, though a mere feudal state in the western borders, had eliminated the eight-hundred-year-long dominance of Chou and had terminated the overlordship of the Six Kingdoms [i.e., the Warring States]. Ch'in's mastery was imposed by force. The Ch'in rule possessed but scant elements of any psychological or theoretical foundation. Thus when Ch'en She arose in rebellion [against Ch'in], all the rebels appearing on the scene competed in claims representing themselves as legitimate heirs to the Six Kingdoms, as a means of pressing their offensives against Ch'in. Liu Pang rose to leadership from the humble status of a minor functionary; the foundations on which his political power rested included nothing that made him appear vastly superior to the First Emperor. Eventually, therefore it was Confucians, wishing to demonstrate their loyal service to him who, drawing on the Five Agents and the Heavenly Mandate concepts, with forced interpretations and gross fabrications and appeals to religious beliefs, supplied such support for the long-since established regime. All those who expatiated on heaven's and man's interaction to emphasize "receiving the Mandate" [*shou-ming* 受命] were of this strain.

On the basis of existing materials, it would appear that throughout the early Han up to the reign of the Emperor Yuan [48–33 B.C.] the withdrawal-of-the-Mandate current was in the ascendancy. But as the Han dynastic power declined, the ruler became insignificant in comparison with officials who exercised great power, so the idea that there was need to limit imperial authority became less tenable.[49] Subsequently the Mandate concept degenerated into a matter of divine patents and the occult apocrypha, while the [formerly intimidating] reports of calamities and

[48] See, the final paragraphs [pp. 211–13 above] of Section Seven in Chapter Three of this work. The reign of the Emperor Yüan [48–33 B.C.] is the period when theories about heaven-man interaction in support of the Mandate's withdrawal were rampant. For a period of more than ten years, every time there was a natural calamity or prodigy, the Emperor without fail issued an edict assuming the blame and soliciting opinions. Furthermore, in the year A.D. 46 he commanded that: "The Chancellor [*ch'eng-hsiang*] and the Imperial Secretaries [*yü-shih*] shall each select three persons from throughout the realm who are well versed in *Yin-yang* learning, and in calamitous and prodigious portents, for appointment to the court." Subsequently, "There were crowds of advisors; of those selected to be admitted into audience, each and every one was sure he had gained the imperial favor." (*Han Shu, ch.* 9, "Basic Annals of the Emperor Yüan.")

[49] See, footnotes numbered 129 through 134 of Chapter Three of this work.

prodigies became mere formulaic statements.[50] Instead, it is the auspicious auguries of protecting stars and felicitous clouds, of yellow dragons and red phoenixes, which repeatedly appear in the memorials submitted to the court. In lesser instances these were merely the means by which vulgar Confucians curried favor; in the more important instances they could provide the excuses for treacherous power-holders to commit usurpation and rebellion. To speak of the entire Ch'in-Han period, the reign of the usurper Wang Mang [A.D. 9–22] may be considered the ultimate outcome of that degenerated [i.e., sycophantic] heaven-man interaction school of thought. Tung Chung-shu, on the other hand, is the one who greatly expanded the concept of heaven's authority so as to impose restrictions upon the ruler, and he became the dominant figure among Confucians of the Western [Former] Han period.

In his youth Tung Chung-shu specialized in the study of both the *Kung-yang Commentary* and the *Spring and Autumn Annals*; he was appointed Erudit [for the latter] during the reign of Emperor Ching [156–141 B.C.], and was held in great esteem by scholars. During the reign of Emperor Wu, recommended as a Man of Wisdom and Virtue [*Hsien-liang*], he participated in an examination at the court, in the course of which he expressed veneration for Confucius, and explained heaven's and man's interaction. He was appointed Prime Minister to Yi, the Prince of Chiang-tu. "Prince Yi, the elder brother of the Emperor, had always been arrogant and bold. Tung Chung-shu corrected his behavior, using the principles of propriety and righteousness. The Prince respected and valued him. . . . In governing that state, Tung Chung-shu took the calamitous and extraordinary incidents recorded in the *Spring and Autumn Annals* as the basis for calculating the interactions of *Yin* and *Yang*." Later on while living at his home he composed a discourse on the calamity [a fire] that befell the mortuary temple of the Han Founder. Chu-fu Yen [his enemy at court] had the draft of this study stolen and submitted it to the court. "The Emperor called a number of Confucian scholars to look at it. Tung Chung-shu's student, Lü Pu-shu, not knowing that it was the work of his teacher, pronounced it 'very foolish.' Consequently Tung Chung-shu was placed in custody and condemned to die, but was pardoned by imperial edict. Thereafter Tung Chung-shu no longer dared to discourse on calamities and extraordinary phenomena." He died at home in his old age.[51] His

---

[50] The "Treatises on the Five Agents," or "Wu-hsing chih," in the various dynastic histories constitute examples of this.

[51] *Han Shu, ch.* 50, "Biography of Tung Chung-shu." Tung's birth and death dates are not known. The "Chronological Record of Tung Chung-shu" in *Ch'un-ch'iu fan-lu yi-cheng* by Su Yü [died 1914] commences with the first year of the reign of Emperor Wen and ends with the first year of the T'ai-ch'u reign period of the Emperor Wu (179–104 B.C.). Those dates probably come close to being correct. [A largely similar biographical sketch from *Shih Chi, ch.* 121, is translated in Watson, *Shih Chi*, Vol. II, pp. 409–12.]

writings, according to the listing in the "Treatise on Literature" of the *Han Shu*, are *The Works of Tung Chung-shu* in 123 chapters and the *Kung-yang Tung Chung-shu chih-yü* in 16 chapters. The extant version of his *Ch'un-ch'iu fan-lu* ["Luxuriant Dew of the Spring and Autumn Annals"] in 82 chapters, while not necessarily spurious, most certainly is not a work put in its present form by the hand of Tung Chung-shu.[52]

In order to clarify Tung Chung-shu's political thought, it is necessary first to set forth in brief his philosophical thought. He wrote: "The *Yüan* [元 "origin"] is the root of all things."[53] Also, "what is called the single *Yüan* is the great beginning [大始 *ta-shih*]."[54] The general import is that all things [i.e., affairs, events, relationships, and objects] have a point of origin. The origin of men and servitors is in the father and ruler.[55] Yet fathers and rulers do not produce themselves; traced back to their great beginnings, heaven is the origin [*yüan*] of rulers and fathers.[56] But within the bounds of the visible world everything that assumes shapes and has form is produced by heaven-and-earth [*t'ien-ti*]. Therefore heaven-and-earth is the origin of all things.[57] Thus, origin and heaven-and-earth in fact are the same thing designated by two names. When referring to it as abstract principle it is called origin [*yüan*].[58] When referring to its

[52] In his [critical work on bibliography] *Ssu-pu cheng-o*, Hu Ying-lin [1551–1602] has stated that the extant eighty-two chapter [*p'ien*] work represents what remains of the one-hundred and twenty-three chapter work listed in the *Han Shu* "Treatise," and that later persons have tampered with it, adding in the *Kung-yang . . . chih-yü* in sixteen chapters, while also putting onto it the *Fan-lu* title taken from Pan Ku's record of the work [in the "Treatise on Literature" in Pan's *Han Shu*]. Those views are largely acceptable. For other views see Chang Hsin-ch'eng, *Wei-shu t'ung-k'ao, shang ts'e*, pp. 412–16.

[53] *Ch'un-ch'iu fan-lu, ch.* 13, "Ch'ung-cheng." [*Cf.*, Fung/Bodde, Vol. II, p. 20.]

[54] *Ibid., ch.* 4, "Yü ying." [*Cf.*, Fung/Bodde, p. 19.]

[55] *Ibid., ch.* 6, "Wang tao," states: "The King is the beginning of man." *Ch.* 19, "Li yuan shen," states: "The ruler is the origin, *yuan*, of the state." [For the former, see Chan, *Source Book*, pp. 284–85; in the present translation, however, a formal distinction is maintained in consistently translating "*shih*" as "beginning" and "*yuan*" as "origin." For *ch.* 19, see de Bary, *Sources*, pp. 178–79.]

[56] *Ibid., ch.* 25, "Yao Shun pu shan yi; T'ang Wu pu chuan sha" states: "The King is also the son of heaven." *Ch.* 70, "Shun ming," states: "A father is heaven to the son; heaven is heaven to the father. To be produced [born] without heaven is something which has never occurred." *Ch.* 41, "Wei jen-che t'ien" states: "What produces [man] cannot [itself] be man, for the creator of man is heaven. The fact that men are men derives from heaven. Heaven, indeed, is man's supreme ancestor." [The latter follows Bodde, Fung/Bodde, vol. II, p. 32.]

[57] *Ibid., ch.* 33, "Kuan te," states: "Heaven and earth are the basis of all things; they are that from which our primal ancestors emerged." *Ch.* 70, "Shun ming," also states: "Heaven is the ancestor of all things; were it not for heaven, the myriad things would not be produced."

[58] Yao Shun-ch'in's *Ch'in-Han che-hsüeh shih* [date?], p. 120, quotes the view of Ho Hsiu [A.D. 129–182] that the origin, *yuan*, is the basis [source] of heaven and earth; this

concrete functioning it is called heaven-and-earth. "The material forces [*ch'i* 氣, or ethers, i.e., *Yin* and *Yang*] of heaven and earth combine and are one."[59] Heaven, thus can impose a mastery over earth; heaven is in reality the primal source of all the myriad things.

"Man is endowed with *ming* [命, "purposeful life"] by heaven; he is therefore supremely distinct from all other forms of life."[60] Therefore, within all the relationships among all the myriad things, that of heaven and man is the most intimate. Moreover, heaven, being man's "supreme ancestor" [literally: "great grandfather"], man's physical body, nature, and temperament all "correspond to heaven above," while "heaven's counterpart is found in man."[61] Thus man is produced by heaven and furthermore is the image of heaven; it follows then that man must reverence heaven on high and take it as his norm for the conduct of affairs. Tung Chung-shu thus states: "Heaven is the great source from which right principles [*Tao*] proceed."[62] Nonetheless, the heavenly *Tao* is high and far away; it is not something that ordinary men can attain. They therefore must look to the instruction and guidance of the ruler. Consequently, the Son of Heaven becomes the intermediary between heaven and man. "Only the Son of Heaven receives the Mandate [*ming*] of heaven, and all the empire [in turn then] accepts the mandates of the Son of Heaven."[63] "For this reason, the *Spring and Autumn Annals* decrees that

---

would appear to be incorrect. See Fung Yu-lan, *History of Chinese Philosophy*, Volume II, Chapter II, p. 504 [in the Bodde translation, Vol. II, pp. 19–20]: "*Yüan* or Origin thus exists before the physical Heaven designated by the phrase, 'Heaven and Earth.' " This refers to the "physical heaven" only and not "the entire natural universe."

[59] *Ch'un-ch'iu fan-lu*, *ch.* 58, "Wu-hsing hsiang-sheng."

[60] *Han Shu*, *ch.* 56, "Tui ts'e [Examination Essay] Number Three." The *Ch'un-ch'iu fan-lu*, *ch.* 14, "Chih fu hsiang," says: "Heaven and earth produce the myriad things in order to nourish man." [*Cf.* Fung/Bodde, p. 45, for a somewhat different translation; *ming*, also "Mandate" as granted to the ruler, is taken to mean more than just "life" as bestowed upon man, hence the translation "purposeful life."]

[61] *Ch'un-ch'iu fan-lu*, *ch.* 41, "Wei jen-che t'ien." It also says: "Man's physical body is given form through the transforming influence of the numerical [categories] of heaven. Man's vigor is directed to live [*jen*] through the transforming influence of heaven's will [*chih*]. Man's virtuous conduct is expressed in righteousness [*yi*] through the transforming influence of heaven's orderly principle [*li*]. Man's likes and dislikes are influenced by heaven's warmth and coldness. Man's joy and anger are influenced by heaven's cold and heat. Man's life endowment is influenced by heaven's four seasons." [Translation modified from Bodde, Fung/Bodde, vol. II, p. 32.] *Ch.* 56, "Jen fu t'ien shu" says: "Man has three-hundred-sixty joints" etc., etc., further extending and developing this theory [of the correspondence of man with the numerical categories of heaven. For a full translation of *ch.* 56, see Chan, *Source Book*, pp. 280–82.]

[62] *Han Shu*, *ch.* 56, "Examination Essay Number Three." [Following Bodde, Fung/Bodde, Vol. II, pp. 62–63.]

[63] *Ch'un-ch'iu fan-lu*, *ch.* 41, "Wei jen-che t'ien."

mankind follow the ruler and that the ruler follow heaven."[64] Its reasoning all follows from that.

If the explanation offered in the foregoing account is not erroneous, then Tung Chung-shu's theory on the relationship of heaven and man is, more precisely, a theory of the relationship between heaven and the ruler. One of its central tenets is that [rulers must] take heaven as their model [*fa t'ien*]. Tung Chung-shu wrote: "The one who is the ruler of men, in [establishing] his models [*fa*] draws patterns [*hsiang* 象] from heaven."[65] And he also wrote: "A king conducts affairs in accord with heaven's intent. . . . When desiring to accomplish something, it is appropriate to seek a point of departure in heaven."[66] The pattern of heaven's intent was by no means vague or uncertain. "The forces [*ch'i*] of heaven and earth unite and are one; they divide and are the *Yin* and the *Yang*; those part and are the four seasons; they [further] separate and are the Five Agents."[67] They display their pattern [*hsiang*] in the sun and the moon, the stars and the constellations, in the wind and the rain. They display the Mandate in the birds and beasts, insects and fishes, plants and trees. The one who takes heaven as the model [i.e., the ruler] observes these various phenomena in seeking heaven's principles [*t'ien tao*], and allows human affairs to follow along. To cite an example: "The King, in instituting his officials, has his three highest ministers [*san kung*], nine lower ministers [*chiu ch'ing*], twenty-seven great officers [*ta fu*], and eighty-one first-class officers [*yüan shih*], a total of one hundred twenty persons, with which his hierarchy of ministers is made complete." The quotas for these are not simply decided upon by whim. "That three men constitute the first selection [of officials] is modeled on the fact that three months constitute one season. And that four such selections are made and no more, is modeled on the fact that with the four seasons [the year] is brought to its conclusion. The three highest ministers are the men by whom the king supports himself. Heaven completes itself by three, and the king supports himself by three. When this complete number is established and [the process of selection] is multiplied four times, there can be no error."[68] Here the system of official posts is determined according to the pattern of heaven's seasons.

The east is wood [i.e., plant growth]; it is presided over by the Minister of Agriculture [*Ssu-nung*], who favors benevolence. [He sees to it that]

---

[64] *Ibid.*, *ch.* 2, "Yü pei."
[65] *Ibid.*, *ch.* 78, "T'ien-ti chih hsing."
[66] *Han Shu*, *ch.* 56, "Examination Essay Number One."
[67] *Ch'un-ch'iu fan-lu*, *ch.* 58, "Wu-hsing hsiang-sheng."
[68] *Ibid.*, *ch.* 24, "Kuan-chih hsiang-t'ien." The passage that follows extends the discussion to numerous elaborations of the theme which need not be quoted in full. [The translation follows Bodde, Fung/Bodde, Vol. ii, pp. 50–51, where more of the context is quoted.]

the basic agricultural activities are wholeheartedly pursued and food and clothing are sufficient. When the granaries and warehouses are filled, then [the next in sequence,] "the Minister of War eats grain." The Minister of War is fire; "therefore it is said that wood produces fire." The south is fire. It is presided over by the Minister of War [*Ssu-ma*], who favors intelligence. "Clear-mindedly, he alone perceives the subtle potentialities for survival or downfall," and therein serves his ruler by stabilizing the realm. "When the realm has been made peaceful, that which keeps ruler and officers of state secure is the Minister of Works [*Ssu-ying* 司營]. Therefore it is said that fire produces earth." The center is earth. It is presided over by the Minister of Works, who favors good faith [*hsin* 信]. "Perceptively observing [the causes of] success and failure, he subtly remonstrates, urging the good, while guarding against and eradicating evils." [Next:] "Responding to heaven and following the seasons in their changes, deterring the violent and oppressive by dint of awesome might thereby to achieve great order, such is the Minister of Instruction [*Ssu-t'u* 司徒]. The Minister of Instruction is metal. Therefore it is said that earth produces metal." The west is metal. It is presided over by the Minister of Instruction, who favors righteousness [*yi* 義]. [He instructs so that] "the servitor will die for his ruler and people will die for their fathers; distinctions of senior and junior [generations] among kin and of superior and inferior among social positions will exist; individuals will be ready to die for their duty and in their service they will transgress no bounds; [and, finally,] those who, holding appropriate authority, conduct punitive measures [against the unjust and the unruly] will not seek inequitable military victories nor will they take [objects of conquest] improperly gained, and will proceed only when righteousness dictates." Thus will the common people be attached to and affectionate toward [their ruler], the borders will be secure and peaceful, bandits and rebels will not appear, villages will be free of disputes and litigations, and the one who keeps the people affectionate and peaceful, and assures that the laws and regulations are all observed, is the Minister of Justice [*Ssu-k'ou* 司寇]. The Minister of Justice is water. "Therefore it can be said that metal produces water." The north is water. It is presided over by the Minister of Justice, who favors propriety [*li* 禮]. When rule by propriety has been established, superior and inferior will assume their ordered places. "The hundred artisans will get all of the implements made by the appointed time. When the tools and implements have been finished, those will be turned over to the Minister of Agriculture." The Minister of Agriculture is wood; "therefore it is said that water produces wood."[69]

---

[69] *Ibid.*, *ch.* 58, "Wu-hsing hsiang-sheng" 五行相生. What relationship this system of the five officials was supposed to hold to that of the three highest ministers [*san-kung*] mentioned above is not explained in his writings.

But should these five officials fail in their duties, the Five Agents will then be thrown out of their proper sequence, and the [normal] process of one generating the next will be deflected into that [abnormality] of the one overcoming the other. Should the Minister of Agriculture commit misdeeds, the farming people will rise up in rebellion. Then the Minister of Works will rise up in rebellion. Then the Minister of Instruction will inflict punishment, a situation of metal overcoming wood. Should the Minister of War be guilty of misrepresentation, trying to confuse and mislead the ruler, the Minister of Justice then will inflict punishment, a situation of water overcoming fire. Should the Minister of Works fail in his duties, there will be profligacy above and rebellion below. The people will commit regicide. This is a situation of wood overcoming earth. If the Minister of Instruction commits crime and is unable to control the masses, the Minister of War will then punish him, a situation of fire overcoming metal. Should the Minister of Justice commit irregularities, indulging in favoritism and injustice, the Minister of Works will then punish him, a situation of earth overcoming water.[70] Here we find a system of official posts determined according to the pattern of heaven's Five Agents.

Tung Chung-shu also said: "The forces [*ch'i*] of heaven and earth are part *Yin* and part *Yang*." The basic organization of human society and government takes its models entirely from the *Yin* and *Yang*. "All things must have their complement. . . . *Yin* is the complement to *Yang*, the wife is the complement to the husband, the son is the complement to the father, the servitor is the complement to the ruler. . . . The principles of ruler-servitor, father-son and husband-wife all are drawn from *Yin-Yang*."[71] The *Yang* is noble and the *Yin* is humble, "therefore it is that the ruler faces south, assuming his position from the *Yang* [i.e., the side on which the sun shines]."[72]

The institutions of government are patterned on heaven; administrative actions therefore must also correspond to and be responsive to the *Yin* and *Yang* and the Five Agents. "In heaven's course, spring with its warmth germinates, summer with its heat nourishes, autumn with its coolness destroys, and winter with its cold hibernates. Warmth, heat, coolness, and coldness are different forces, but their work is identical, all being instruments whereby heaven brings the year to completion. The sage, in his conduct of government, duplicates the movements of heaven. Thus with his beneficence he duplicates warmth and accords with spring, with his conferring of rewards he duplicates heat and accords with summer, with

---

[70] *Ibid.*, *ch.* 59, "Wu-hsing hsiang-sheng" 五行相勝. From a modern point of view, all this is meaningless. It is set forth here to display the special qualities of Tung's thought.

[71] *Ibid.*, *ch.* 53, "Chi yi." The following sentence is: "These three bonds [*san-kang*] of the Kingly Way can be sought in heaven."

[72] *Ibid.*, *ch.* 46, "T'ien-pien tsai jen."

his penalties he duplicates coolness and accords with autumn, and with his corporal punishments he duplicates coldness and accords with winter. His beneficence, rewards, penalties, and punishments are different in kind, but their work is identical, all being instruments whereby the king completes his virtue. Beneficence, rewards, penalties, and corporal punishments match spring, summer, autumn, and winter, respectively, like the fitting together [of the two parts] of a tally. . . . These four ways of government must not be allowed to interfere with each other, just as the four seasons cannot interfere with each other. The four ways of government cannot be shifted from their places, just as the four seasons cannot be shifted from their places."[73]

Nonetheless, beneficence, rewards, penalties, and corporal punishments can vary in degree. "The greatest aspect of heaven's way is found in *Yin* and *Yang*. *Yang* promotes virtue; *Yin* supplies punishments. Punishments preside over death, and virtue presides over birth. That is why *Yang* always occupies the vast summer and devotes itself to matters of birth, growth, and nurture. *Yin* always occupies the vast winter and accumulates in the vacant and unused places. From this it can be seen that heaven relies on virtue and does not rely on punishments. . . . The King is he who accepts heaven's intent in the conduct of his affairs; therefore he relies on virtue and instruction and does not rely on punishments. Punishments are incapable of bringing about an orderly age, just as it is not possible to rely on *Yin* to complete the year."[74]

The *Doctrine of the Mean* says of the sage that: "able to assist the transforming and nourishing powers of heaven and earth, he may with heaven and earth form a trinity." Tung Chung-shu found this highly compatible with his ideal of emulating heaven. Thus, he said: "The Way of the sage

---

[73] *Ibid.*, *ch.* 55, "Ssu-shih chih fu." [The translation, with minor modification, follows Bodde, Fung/Bodde, Vol. II, p. 48.] Note in this connection, from *ch.* 44, "Wang tao t'ung san,": "The ruler of men, with his likes and dislikes, joy and anger, transforms the habits and customs [of men], just as heaven, with its warmth, coolness, cold and heat, exercises a transforming influence upon plants and trees. When the joy and anger [of the ruler] are seasonable and proper, the year is fine; when they are unseasonable and improper, it is bad. Heaven, earth and the ruler of men are one." [Translation follows Bodde, *op.cit.*, p. 48; a somewhat different translation is found in de Bary, *Sources*, p. 181.] Also, *ch.* 42, "Wu-hsing chih yi," states: "Thus wood occupies the eastern quarter, where it rules over the forces, *ch'i*, of spring; fire occupies the southern quarter, where it rules over the forces of summer; metal occupies the western quarter, where it rules over the forces of autumn; water occupies the northern quarter, where it rules over the forces of winter. For this reason wood rules over the production of life, while metal rules over its destruction; fire rules over heat, while water rules over cold." [Follows Bodde, *op.cit.*, p. 21.] This indicates how the Five Agents correspond to the four seasons.

[74] *Han Shu*, *ch.* 56, "Examination Essay Number One." Note also that in *Tso Chuan*, Twenty-fifth year of Duke Chao [516 B.C.], where Tzu-t'ai-shu relates Tzu-ch'an's discourse on propriety [*li*] it is suggestive of quite similar ideas. [Legge, p. 708.]

is in union with heaven and earth."[75] [And] "The ruler of men holds a position of life or death [over men], and shares with heaven its transforming power. . . . Heaven, earth and the ruler of men are one."[76] The elevation of the ruler's position can be said to have reached the extreme. Yet the ruler was to "serve heaven and his father with the same ritual,"[77] to take heaven as the model and to carry out heaven's will in ruling over men; therefore his authority in fact was derived from heaven's will, and therein was subject to a limitation.

The limitations that heaven's authority places upon the ruler's authority are two: the first is that it can take away the dynasty's tenure; the second is that it oversees governmental actions. The former involves the theories about withdrawing the Mandate and receiving the Mandate. The latter involves the theory about the portents revealed through calamities and prodigies [or "anomalies"].

First the Ch'in dynasty and then the Han both came to power through the use of military force. From one point of view it would seem that political power was transferred [from one dynasty to the next] by human means, and that the ruler in his own person was quite capable of establishing his command over the realm all by himself. Tung Chung-shu's theory about the Heavenly Mandate seems designed to break up this potential for sustaining the concept of absolute authoritarianism. His "Examination Essay" states: "Your servitor has heard that in heaven's great conferring of responsibilities on the king there is something that human powers of themselves could not achieve, but that comes of itself. This is the sign that the Mandate has been granted. The people of the empire with one heart all turn to him as they would turn to their own fathers and mothers. Thus it is that heaven's auspicious signs respond to [the people's] sincerity and come forth. In the *Documents* it says: 'A white fish entered into the King's boat, and there was a big ball of fire which flew back to the King's house, transforming itself into a crow.' These surely were signs of the receiving of the Mandate."[78] When one received the sign from heaven that

---

[75] *Ch'un-ch'iu fan-lu*, ch. 53, "Chi yi." [For the quotation from the *Doctrine of the Mean*, see Legge, p. 416.]

[76] *Ibid.*, ch. 44, "Wang tao t'ung san." [Following Bodde, *op.cit.*, pp. 47–48.]

[77] *Ibid.*, ch. 25, "Yao Shun pu shan yi, T'ang Wu pu chuan sha."

[78] *Han Shu*, ch. 56, "Examination Essay Number One." [The "white fish" and other incidents appear in the "Appendix to the Great Declaration," in the *Documents*; see Legge, *Shoo King*, p. 298; cf. the similar account in *Shih Chi*, ch. 4, "Chou pen chi." They are presented as confirmations of the bestowal of the Mandate on King Wu at the time of the Chou conquest.] It should be noted that Tung Chung-shu makes no reference to the stories about the Han Founder's having killed the White Snake, and having been called the Red Emperor and the like; this shows clearly that Tung's purpose was to warn the rulers of his time, and is thus quite different from Ho Hsiu's sycophancy toward the Han Founder.

the Mandate was being bestowed, and subsequently gained the empire, his gaining it occurred because it was heaven's intent; he therefore could not fail to alter institutions, "in order to signify the manifestation [of heaven's intent] to him."[79] Therefore when emperors T'ang and Wu [founders of the Shang and Chou dynasties] received the Mandate, each interrupted the succession and changed the dynastic name, so that the one era is discontinuous from the other. This shows clearly that heaven's intent is variable and virtue is [the ruler's] only recourse.[80] That is to say, heaven's producing the people is not for the sake of the King, but heaven has established Kings for the sake of the people. Therefore if his virtue is sufficient for him to provide security and happiness for the people, heaven will grant [kingship] to him; but if his evil talent is sufficient only for him to plunder the people and bring harm to them, heaven will take [his kingship] away. The *Odes* contain the lines:

"The officers of Yin, admirable and alert,
Assist at the libations in [our] capital;
They became subject to Chou.
The Mandate of Heaven is not constant."

[Modified from Legge, *She King*, p. 430, where the lines appear in a different sequence.]

This tells that heaven grants, and takes away, without constancy. Heaven's giving and taking away are done through the agency of men. "Therefore, the Hsia dynasty grew tyrannical and the Yin smote it; the Yin grew tyrannical and the Chou smote it; the Chou grew tyrannical and Ch'in smote it; Ch'in grew tyrannical and the Han smote it. The one in possession of the Way smites the one lacking the Way [i.e., the one that has

---

[79] *Ch'un-ch'iu fan-lu, ch.* 1, "Ch'u Chuang-wang." [*Cf.* Bodde, *op.cit.*, p. 62.]

[80] *Ch'un-ch'iu fan-lu, ch.* 23, "San tai kai-chih chih-wen," establishes a system for the change of institutions. However, the text has lacunae and corrupt passages, and the meaning is unclear at many points. The general sense of it is that: (1) The dominance of black, white, and red alternate in sequence. (2) "A Shang dynasty after a Hsia dynasty [that is, a dynasty emphasizing] simplicity [*chih*] after one [emphasizing] refinement [*wen*]. Shang and simplicity take heaven as the guiding principle; Hsia and refinement take earth as the guiding principle. The age of the *Spring and Autumn Annals* [of mid-Chou, as chronicled by Confucius] take man as their guiding principle." [*Cf.* Bodde, *op.cit.*, p. 61.] (3) "Emphasizing heaven [a dynasty] takes Shang as its model . . . emphasizing earth, it takes Hsia as its model . . . emphasizing heaven, its model is simplicity . . . emphasizing earth, its model is refinement. . . . These four models [i.e., "Shang" and "Hsia" as abstract types, plus "simplicity" and "refinement"] are like the four seasons; when their course has come to its end it starts over again." Tung's biography in *Han Shu, ch.* 56, in his "Examination Essay Number Three," states: "Hsia venerated loyalty, Yin [i.e., Shang] venerated reverence, and Chou venerated refinement," thereby differing from the foregoing statements. [Compare other uses of the *chih-wen* 質文 polarity, and other translations of the term "*chih*": "simplicity," "substance," etc., in Chapter One, Sections One and Two, pp. 33 and 36, above, and *passim*.]

grown tyrannical]; this is the orderly principle of heaven."[81] The ruler's position is granted and taken away by heaven; one who possesses virtue may undertake military measures to punish him. Thus, elevated in veneration though the ruler of men be, he cannot indulge himself in uninhibited behavior. Since the basic element in the state is the servitor of heaven, his power and authority are subject to certain controls.

Heaven not only places limits on the ruler of men by its capacity to grant and take away the ruler's position; it also carries on a constant supervision overseeing the actions of government. In accordance with the successes and failings of those, it displays calamitous or auspicious omens. In the opening passages of Tung's "Examination Essay [Number One," quoted in full in *Han Shu, ch.* 56], he states: "Your servitor respectfully notes that in the *Spring and Autumn Annals* deeds of an earlier time are examined in order to perceive those occasions when the affairs of heaven and man interacted; it is most awesome. Whenever the state was on the verge of failures stemming from a loss of the Way, heaven first would send forth calamities and prodigies as warning. When [the rulers] were incapable of correcting themselves, it again would send forth strange and extraordinary phenomena in order to worry and frighten them. When they still did not change their ways, injury and downfall then came upon them. From this one can see that the mind of heaven holds the ruler of men in benevolent regard and desires to stop him from engaging in acts arousing disorder. Unless it has become an age of total abandonment of the Way, heaven strives to support and secure the ruler. It thus becomes a matter of his vigorous striving, and nothing else."[82]

Tung also drew on the history of the Chou dynasty to illustrate this point. He said that even though King Wu had gained the empire as a consequence of receiving the Mandate, "yet by later ages [the Chou dynasty], debauched and degenerated into insignificance, was incapable of maintaining control over the people. The feudal lords were defiantly rebellious, and they ravaged the population in their struggles over territory, abandoning [proper government through] virtue and instruction in favor of punishments and penalties. The inequities of their punishments and penalties engendered an evil effluvium [*hsieh ch'i* 邪氣]. This evil effluvium accumulated below, while resentments and hatreds converged above. When above and below were no longer harmonious, *Yin* and *Yang* became distorted and irregular so that evil auguries were produced. This is how calamities and prodigies came into being."[83] Where the

---

[81] *Ch'un-ch'iu fan-lu, ch.* 25, "Yao Shun pu shan yi."

[82] *Ibid.,* in *ch.* 30, "Pi jen ch'ieh chih," speaking of "the things of heaven and earth," the meaning there comes close to this passage.

[83] *Han Shu, ch.* 56, "Examination Essay Number One." *Ch'un-ch'iu fan-lu, ch.* 6, "Wang tao," speaking of "the Chou dynasty's decline," lists governmental failures as well as

Spring and Autumn Annals record [prodigies such as] eclipses, falling stars, collapsing mountains and the earth cracking open, fishhawks flying backward and grackles building nests in trees, the purpose in this is "by these signs to show evidence of perversity and depravity [in government], so as to warn the ruler, "Also hoping that he would awaken to heaven's reproaches and fear heaven's majesty; within he would move to a firm resolve, and without he would display attentiveness to affairs; he would cultivate his character and examine his own conduct, manifesting the virtuous mind, so as to return to the Way."[84]

Further, Tung also had a theory about the interactions of the Five Agents. He listed the calamities and prodigies induced by failures of government and the methods of redressing those.[85] His central ideas are compatible with the theories about the "Five Agents" and the "General Verifications" found in the "Great Norm" [*Hung-fan*] chapter of the *Book of Documents*. [Cf. Chan, *Source Book*, pp. 8–11.] Although Tung Chung-shu was once turned over to the law officers because of his discourse on calamities and prodigies [and after being pardoned, is said never again to have dared discuss the subject], from reading the accounts in the "T'ien-wen" and "Wu-hsing" Treatises [*chs.* 26 and 27] in the *History of the Former Han Dynasty*, it becomes quite clear that "heaven's and man's interactions" had already become a dominant branch of learning in the Western Han, and that Tung Chung-shu was its leading master. Nonetheless, it is important to recognize that in Tung's discussions of heaven and man, his purpose in fact always is to stress that the Mandate could be lost, while giving scant attention to acquiring the Mandate, and he is exhaustive on calamities and prodigies while touching only briefly on auspicious omens. On the basis of extant documentation one can demonstrate that such an interpretation is not unfair to him.[86] His learning

---

calamities and prodigies; it is more complete than this passage, and is worth consulting in this connection. [For the latter half of this passage, compare the translation in Fung/Bodde, vol. II, p. 57. For "evil effluvium" the more abstract "deviant force" can also be understood.]

[84] *Ch'un-ch'iu fan-lu, ch.* 15, "Erh tuan."

[85] See: *ch.* 62, "Chih-luan wu-hsing"; *ch.* 63, "Wu-hsing pien-chiu"; and *ch.* 64, "Wu-hsing wu-shih."

[86] Wherever Tung discusses receiving the Mandate he implies a doctrine of the Mandate's impermanence; his references to auspicious omens are no more than one or two in the *Ch'un-ch'iu fan-lu* and in the "Examination Essays" [quoted in his *Han Shu* biography]. Meng Wen-t'ung [the contemporary scholar,] in his article "Ju-chia cheng-chih ssu-hsiang chih fa-chan" ["The development of Confucian political thought"] (Special Study Topic Number Two in his National Szechwan University Syllabus; this article subsequently was published in *Chih-lin*, the Journal of National Northeastern University, No. 2), p. 22, states that Tung Chung-shu altered his teachings in order to accommodate them to the Han dynasty, and was therefore no different from Kung-sun Hung in his sycophancy. This would seem to be a hypercritical view.

perpetuated ideas present in Tsou Yen's "talk about heaven." When compared, however, with [other] Confucian scholars of the Han period who distorted their learning in order to win favor, and who advanced views on the heavenly Mandate merely to please their ruler, Tung's learning may seem superficially similar, but its spirit is entirely different. We must not confuse the two simply because both upheld the Five Agents and *Yin-Yang* theories.

His sense of the relationship between heaven and man being clear, we can proceed to an account of Tung Chung-shu's theories concerning the duties of rulership and methods of ruling. The ruler's duties of office, in simplest terms, are to extend a transforming influence on behalf of heaven, and to carry to completion those tasks which heaven could not itself perform. For although man is of a kind with heaven, ordinary persons are incapable on their own to realize fully the goodness of their natures. "Human nature is of the [unrefined] substance. . . . Therefore man's nature may be compared to the rice stalks and goodness to rice. Rice comes out of the rice stalk, but not all the stalk becomes rice. [Similarly,] goodness comes out of nature but not all nature becomes good. Both goodness and rice are results of human activity in continuing and completing that creative work of heaven which lies beyond heaven's own operation, and are not inherent in what heaven has produced, which is within its operation. The activity of heaven extends to a certain point and then stops. What exists within that stopping-point is called human nature endowed by heaven, and what exists beyond [heaven's] stopping-point is called human activity."[87] "What exists within the stopping point [of heaven's operations] is called human nature endowed by heaven; what exists beyond that stopping point is the king's instruction."[88] "Heaven produces the people, whose nature includes the substance of goodness yet who are [by themselves] incapable of being good; it therefore has established kings in order to realize their goodness. This is heaven's purpose. The people receive from heaven their nature which is [by itself] incapable of goodness, and thereafter receive from the king instruction which fulfills their nature. It is the duty of the king to assume heaven's purpose in bringing the people's natures to fulfillment."[89]

[87] *Ch'un-ch'iu fan-lu*, *ch.* 35, "Shen-ch'a ming-hao." [Translation follows Chan, *Source Book*, pp. 274–75, with modifications.]

[88] *Ibid.*, *ch.* 36, "Shih hsing."

[89] *Ibid.*, *ch.* 35, "Shen-ch'a ming-hao." [Modified from Chan, *Source Book*, p. 276.] The same chapter [of Tung's writings] also states that the "goodness," *shan*, of Mencius' discourse on the goodness of human nature, as in: "And since man is better than animals, this may be called good," is different from what Confucius called goodness, as in: "A good man is not mine to see." [Following the wording adopted by Chan in his translation of *ch.* 35, *Source Book*, especially pp. 277, 278.] However, Tung's theory is not the same as Hsün Tzu's view that human nature is evil.

These theories of Tung Chung-shu are expressed with force and clarity. Yet in fact they elaborate on the standard Confucian concepts of the ruler-as-teacher and governing-as-teaching, and are not original with him. Coming to his methods for disseminating the instruction: these too do not go beyond [the familiar elements of] self-cultivation and establishing one's norms as a starting point, adopting [the canons of] benevolence, righteousness, the rites and music as teaching materials, and assuming the rectification of names and the establishment of political institutions as providing the necessary conditions. Tung wrote: "The ruler is the people's heart; the people are the ruler's body. In what the heart delights, the body will surely be content. With that in which the ruler finds delight, the people will surely comply."[90] And further: "The ruler is the origin of the state. He speaks and he acts, and all things find their pivot in him."[91] And again: "The Way is that via which to proceed along the road toward good government. Benevolence, righteousness, the rites and music are all instruments for that."[92] All these are the well-known Confucian clichés and there is no need to discuss them further.

Tung Chung-shu went beyond previous thinkers in one respect, however, when he declared the rectification of names to be a matter undertaken on behalf of heaven. Also, his discussion on establishing political institutions, aimed as it was at the particular evils of his own time, was still less a mere repetition of vague and empty phrases from the past. Tung wrote: "Ordering well, the state commences with rectifying

[90] *Ibid.*, *ch.* 41, "Wei jen che t'ien."

[91] *Ibid.*, *ch.* 19, "Li yuan sheh." The "Examination Essay Number One" [quoted in Tung's biography] in *ch.* 56 of the *Han Shu*, quotes Confucius' saying [*Analects*, xii/19] that when the wind blows the grass must bend. It then goes on to say: "The superior's transforming influence on inferiors and the inferior's response to the superior can be likened to the clay on the potter's wheel which becomes whatever the potter makes of it, or to the metal in the crucible which becomes whatever the smelter casts of it." This meaning is the same.

[92] *Han Shu*, "Examination Essay Number One." *Ch'un-ch'iu fan-lu*, *ch.* 19, "Li yuan shen" in discussing "the teachings of the Rites and Music" mentions at the same time such matters as "establishing the imperial university and village schools, cultivating filial and fraternal submission, respect and deference." In *ch.* 29, "Jen yi fa," Tung defines benevolence and righteousness as follows: "What the *Spring and Autumn Annals* regulates are others and the self. The principles with which to regulate others and the self are benevolence and righteousness. Benevolence is to give others peace and security and righteousness is to rectify the self. . . . The principle of benevolence consists in loving people and not in loving oneself, and the principle of righteousness consists in rectifying oneself and not in rectifying others. If one is not rectified himself, he cannot be considered righteous even if he can rectify others, and if one loves himself very much but does not apply his love to others, he cannot be considered benevolent." [Translation follows, with minor modification, Chan, *Source Book*, pp. 285–86.]

names."[93] "The standard of correctness for names and [other] appellations is found in heaven and earth; heaven and earth provide the ultimate rightness [*ta yi* 大義] for names and appellations. When the sages of old uttered cries to correspond to [elements observed in] heaven and earth, those utterances are what we call appellations [*hao* 號]; when they called out in giving designations, those are what we call names. . . . 'Name' and 'appellation' differ in sound but share the same basis, for both are cries and calls made to express [the sages' awareness of] heaven's intent. Heaven does not speak, but causes men to express its intent; it does not act, but causes men to carry out its principles. Names thus are that by which the sages expressed heaven's intent, and therefore must be profoundly scrutinized. . . . Thus one whose appellation is 'Son of Heaven' must indeed look upon heaven as upon a father, and must serve heaven in the Way of filial submission. Those whose appellation is 'feudal lord' must deferentially look to the one who is their suzerain, and honor him as the son of heaven. Those whose appellation is Great Officer [literally "big man" or *ta-fu* 大夫] must deepen their loyalty and sincerity, be earnest in their propriety and righteousness, causing their goodness to hold greater import than that of ordinary men [*p'i-fu* 匹夫], and thereby become capable of transforming men. 'Officer' means 'to serve'; 'people' means 'with eyes closed.' The officers may not be qualified for transforming others; they can be assigned to fill their posts and obey their superiors, and no more."[94] Inasmuch as names and appellations are the expression of heaven's intent, the rectification of names in fact is no different from taking heaven as the model. That, then, is precisely the reason why [the rectification of names] is where the Way of governing commences.

The Way of governing ultimately comes down to transforming through teaching, but it requires a framework of institutions. To discuss those in the most comprehensive sense, the one who governs the state should cause all the people of both higher and lower status to "know measure in their food and drink, observe regulation in their clothing and dress, be subject to standards in their palaces and houses, be limited in the amounts of animals and goods, and the numbers of servants and attendants they may possess, and be subject to prohibitions on boats and carts, armor and weapons. While living, there are [prescribed] carriages and caps according to their positions in service, and [limits prescribed for] lands and houses

---

[93] *Ch'un-ch'iu fan-lu*, *ch.* 4, "Yü ying."

[94] *Ibid.*, *ch.* 35, "Shen ch'a ming-hao." [Another translation can be found in E. R. Hughes, *Chinese Philosophy in Classical Times*, pp. 298 ff. Tung's argument depends on phonetic similarities and etymological hypotheses which are not apparent in translation.] The following passages present a theory about the larger import of the appellations *chün* [ruler] and *wang* [king], for each of which he offers a five-part subdivision, moreover differing somewhat from the foregoing.

according to their noble ranks and emoluments. After death, there are standards for coffins and coffin-casings, burial garments and grave mounds. No matter how worthy or talented or handsome a person might be, lacking the rank he would not dare to wear the garments [prescribed for such rank]. No matter how wealthy one's family, not receiving it as official emolument one would not dare to spend his money."[95]

In a narrower sense, the function of institutions is to maintain a balance between rich and poor, preventing the growth of excessive discrepancy. "Confucius said [of the head of a family or state]: 'He is not concerned lest his people should be poor, but only lest what they have should be unevenly-apportioned.' [*Analects*, xvi/1.] For where there is accumulation, there will then also be destitution. Great wealth breeds arrogance, great poverty brings anxiety. Anxiety leads to brigandage, and arrogance to oppression. This is the condition of the masses. The sage discerns the roots of disorder in the condition of the masses. Therefore in governing men, he differentiates the higher and lower statuses, allowing to the rich enough to display their noble rank but not to the point of arrogance, and to the poor sufficient means to maintain life without knowing anxiety. By applying such a standard and gaining equitable apportionment, there will then be no lack of material resources, the upper and lower [levels in society] will be at peace with each other, and readily governed."[96] Tung Chung-shu also held that persons in high positions compete [with common people] for economic gains and the rich annex farm lands [at the expense of small peasants] and that these are the two major causes of inequitable apportionment. His discussion of conflict over interests says: "For heaven also makes distinctions in its gifts: where teeth are given horns are taken away; where wings are attached legs are in one pair. [This observes that animals having horns, such as cattle, lack certain upper teeth that non-horned animals have, and that birds, having wings, have only two legs.] This shows that where a large benefit is granted, some smaller thing must be taken away. In antiquity those who were granted emolument of office did not receive income from the labor of peasants nor did they engage in commerce. That too is a case of receiving the greater [gain] so having to suffer deprivation of the lesser, and, in that, is the same as heaven's intent. Now to have already received the greater and still to take the lesser—even heaven cannot make such provision fully; much less can man do it. This [excessive vested interest now existing among our nobles] is why the people wail in bitterness over their insufficiencies. Those recipients of favor who because of that possess lofty status, living in their warm houses and consuming their generous emoluments, can further utilize the re-

---

[95] *Ibid.*, ch. 26, "Fu chih."
[96] *Ibid.*, ch. 27, "Chih tu" [drawing heavily on Bodde, *op.cit.*, p. 53].

sources of wealth and noble position to compete for gain with the ordinary people below them. How can the ordinary people equal them? That is why they [the privileged] can acquire larger numbers of slaves and servants, increase their herds of cattle and sheep, extend their fields and houses, broaden their property holdings, accumulate their hoarded stores, unrelentingly devoting themselves to these things and, in so doing, oppressing and exploiting the people. The people under constant exactions and harassment gradually become quite impoverished. The rich increase the scale of their luxury, while the poor know ever more pressing misery. When their misery reaches extremes of poverty and those above do not come to their aid, the people no longer find joy in living. When the people have no joy in living, neither do they any longer fear dying, so how can they be expected to avoid breaking the laws? That is why punishments and penalties can be multiplied but still be unable to overcome crime and misconduct."[97]

Tung's discussion of [the evils of] extended land-holdings says that the state of Ch'in "Used the methods of Lord Shang, so the institutions of the emperors and kings [of old] were changed. The well-field system was abolished, and the people were allowed to sell and buy land. The fields of the rich extended far on all sides, while the poor had not even enough land into which to stick an awl. Furthermore, [the rich] alone had possession of the profits of streams and marshes, and controlled the abundant resources of mountains and forests. In profligacy and dissipation they overrode the government institutions, and they overstepped extravagances in order to outdo one another. In the cities there were [persons who enjoyed] honors befitting the ruler of men; in the villages there were [individuals who possessed] riches worthy of feudal lords. How could the lowly people but be held in poverty? . . . When the Han arose, it followed [the Ch'in institutions] without changing them. Although now it would be difficult to act precipitately [to restore] the ancient well-field system, it would be appropriate to draw somewhat closer to the old system. Let the people's ownership of land be limited in order to benefit those who do not have enough, and to block the road toward monopolization. The [profits of] salt and iron should revert to the people. Abolish making slaves and bondservants [of offenders, as punishment] and eliminate the prerogative of killing [servants and slaves] on one's own authority. Reduce taxes and levies and lessen labor services, in order to give freer scope to the people's energies. Thereafter, they can be well governed."[98]

During the pre-imperial ages of feudal government, the nobles all

---

[97] *Han Shu*, ch. 56, "Examination Essay Number Three."

[98] *Han Shu*, ch. 24A, "Shih-huo chih, shang." [Translation draws heavily on Nancy Lee Swann, *Food and Money in Ancient China*, pp. 180–81 and 182–83.]

were landlords and the ordinary people worked for them, tilling the public fields [*kung-t'ien* 公田]. Social conditions therefore were such that: "The family which keeps its stores in ice does not rear cattle or sheep." [*Great Learning*, "Commentary," x/22; Legge, p. 380. That is, privileged families of high status did not themselves engage in the productive activities of the common people.] It was not so much that they did not compete for gains with the common people as that there were in fact no other people in society then who could compete with them. By Tung Chung-shu's time, the feudal order had long disappeared, and the inequalities inherent in the ancient social stratification had long since vanished. However, other kinds of economic difficulties now faced the authoritarian world empire. The Emperor Wu [reigned 140–87 B.C.] was heir to policies of conserving and nurturing instituted under the Emperors Wen and Ching [reigned 179–141 B.C.] so that when he first came to the throne, agricultural production was high and goods were plentiful. "Thereupon, the net [of the law] was slackened, and the people became affluent. They put wealth to work, and grew ever more arrogant, at times resorting to annexation of lands. Followers of the rich and powerful employed force [illegally] to dominate the villages and hamlets. Members of the imperial clan who held princedoms, the great lords of the realm, high officials, and all on down, vied to exceed each other in profligate extravagance."[99] Tung Chung-shu's statements were made with this background in mind. To draw an inference about his intention, he probably did not feel that the realities natural to the long-past feudal world represented an ideal that ought still to prevail in the authoritarian world of his own time. This becomes particularly clear from examining his views on the issue of limiting land-holdings. The [feudal institution of] public lands [*kung-t'ien*] was one in which the noble clans were the proprietors and the common people were their agricultural serfs. Limited land-holding implies that the land is all privately owned but expects that the common man shall acquire and till his own land. Tung Chung-shu clearly stated that the well-field system could not be reinstated,[100] therein recognizing that the system of private ownership of land had become unshakeable.

Section Four
Heaven-Man Correlative Theories
after Tung Chung-shu

Most of those Western Han period masters of classical scholarship who followed the New Text tradition wrote on heaven's and man's interaction,

---

[99] Same as footnote 98, above. [*Cf.* Swann, *op.cit.*, p. 176, for a different version.]

[100] *Ch'un-ch'iu fan-lu*, *ch.* 28, "Chüeh Kuo," discusses the well-field system in order to explain the *Spring and Autumn Annals*, but not in advocacy of a governmental policy.

and on calamities and prodigies. In addition to Tung Chung-shu, others whose doctrines assumed some prominence and whose political thought warrants our discussion, are Sui Hung, who specialized on the *Kung-yang Commentary*, Liu Hsiang on the *Ku-liang Commentary*, Li Hsün on the *Book of Documents*, Ku Yung on the *Book of Changes*, and Yi Feng on the *Odes*. One intent common to all these was to restrain and correct the behavior of their contemporary rulers, and their thought displays some minor discrepancies with the main tenets of Tung Chung-shu's learned views. As for persons who instigated wild talk about prognostication texts [concerning the Mandate] and their auspicious manifestations, in order to curry favor with the ruler, or to arouse the age and deceive the common people, such appeared in considerable number from the reigns of Emperors' Ai and P'ing [6 B.C. to A.D. 5] onward. Following the Sui dynasty's [A.D. 589–617] suppression of prognostication texts and the apocrypha, most of those disappeared.[101] The best we can do today is gain glimpses of them from quotations preserved in old writings.

Sui Hung, whose courtesy name was Meng, studied the *Spring and Autumn Annals* under Ying Kung. During the third year of the *Yüan-feng* reign period of the Emperor Chao [78 B.C.] a large rock on Mt. T'ai stood itself upright; in Ch'ang-yi [princedom, near Mt. T'ai in modern Shantung] a long-dead shrine timber began to grow; in the imperial palace park a dead willow log set itself upright and again commenced to grow; insects eating its leaves ate the outline of characters saying: "The Kung-sun clan's disabilities having ended, they will then ascend the throne." In consequence, Sui Hung "calculating what this meant according to the sense of the *Spring and Autumn*, took it that rocks and willow trees both are of the *Yin* category, and thence were a sign of the humble people. Mt. T'ai also was [known by the name of] the Mountain of Tai-tsung [岱宗, literally, "Mountain of the Superssession," which, according to the *Po-hu t'ung* 白虎通, being in the east, marks the place where things in nature supplant one another with the arrival of spring]. It therefore is the location at which a king who has displaced the [fallen] ruling house an-

---

[101] Hu Ying-lin [1551–1602] has written that the *Ch'an-wei* [prognostication texts and apocrypha] burgeoned toward the end of the Western [Former] Han period, then in consequence of the Emperor Wen [reigned 589–604] of the Sui dynasty having ordered them banned and destroyed, the books have long ceased to exist. One still in existence, the *Ch'ien-k'un tso-tu*, is but the forgery of some unprincipled person, he states, and also lists by name several tens of apocrypha [*wei shu*] to the various classics. Many of the apocrypha were not related to a particular classic [to which they purport to be supplements]; surviving examples of this kind were particularly scarce, but he also lists by name ten of those. For the details consult his "Ssu-pu cheng-o," (quoted in Chang Hsin-ch'eng's *Wei shu t'ung k'ao*, vol. I, pp. 95–99). Nonetheless, the *Yü-han shan-fang chi-yi-shu* [compiled by Ma Kuo-han, 1794–1857] preserves fragments of a large number of apocrypha; quotations from the apocrypha in what follows all are taken from that source.

nounces the succession. Now, a large stone has set itself erect and a fallen willow has stood itself up, things beyond human powers to accomplish. This should be taken to signify that a Son of Heaven will emerge from among the common people. A dead shrine timber is restored to life; a Kung-sun clan, previously reduced to commoner status should now arise again." Subsequently he submitted a communication to the court, saying: "My former teacher, the late Tung Chung-shu, has said that even though a ruler may properly maintain the dynastic tradition and uphold the way of refinement, he cannot succeed in doing harm to a sage who has received the Mandate [to found a new dynasty]. The Han imperial clan, as descendants of [the Sage Emperor] Yao [who abdicated to the Emperor Shun], has the destiny of voluntarily transmitting its rule to another. The Han Emperor should send emissaries throughout the realm to seek out the most worthy person, then abdicate the imperial throne in his favor, thereafter withdrawing to a [small] fief of a hundred *li* chosen by himself such as those granted to the descendants of the [Shang-] Yin and Chou dynasties. In this way he will be complying with heaven's decree."[102] At that time Huo Kuang was in control of the government; he found this insufferable. Sui Hung was charged with the crimes of monstrous talk and great refractoriness, and was executed.

Liu Hsiang, courtesy name Tzu-cheng, originally bore the name Keng-sheng; during the reign of the Emperor Yuan [48–33 B.C.] he was appointed, as a member of the imperial clan, to a position as assistant in government. Concerned that consort clans and eunuchs were improperly manipulating the imperial power, he repeatedly submitted memorials discussing inauspicious occurrences, holding that the essential objective should be to eliminate calumniators and keep apart from perverse doctrines so as to save the state from heaven's anger. During the reign of the Emperor Ch'eng [32–7 B.C.], while Wang Feng was active in government [as a member of a powerful consort clan], "Liu Hsiang noted that the 'Hung Fan' Chapter of the *Book of Documents* tells how the Viscount of Chi had set forth before King Wu the appropriate responses of the Five Agents and the *Yin* and *Yang*—showing good or evil omens [relevant to acts of governing]. Liu Hsiang thereupon assembled all the records of auspicious and inauspicious portents from early antiquity onward, coming through the Spring and Autumn and Warring states eras to the Ch'in and Han dynasties; calculating from the evidence about the conduct of affairs, he made coherent accounts of the occurrences of evil and good fortune,

---

[102] *Han Shu*, ch. 75, from Sui Hung's biography. The third year of the *yuan-feng* reign corresponds to 78 B.C. [A philological comment is omitted.] Note that in *Han Shu*, ch. 88, "Biographies of Confucians," it states that Ying Kung studied under Master Hu-mu, who "was a fellow student" [i.e., in the study of the *Spring and Autumn Annals* and the *Kung-yang Commentary*] of Tung Chung-shu.

with emphasis on the way each fulfilled the prognosis that had been indicated; these were classified according to type, for each of which he supplied descriptive headings, the work totalling eleven sections [*p'ien*], was given the title *Hung-fan wu-hsing chuan*."[103]

Li Hsün, courtesy name Tzu-chang, was a specialist on the *Documents*, in which he was particularly drawn to the chapter "Hung Fan," and to the calamities and prodigies [recorded in it]. He also studied astronomy, the "Monthly Commands" [chapter of the *Li Chi*], and *Yin-yang* doctrines. He served the Chancellor Chai Fang-chin. During the reign of Emperor Ch'eng [32–7 B.C.], a member of a consort clan [the brother of the young emperor's mother] Wang Ken controlled the court; he consulted Li Hsün on the meaning of calamities and prodigies. Li Hsün observed signs indicating that the house of Han was at a perilous juncture of mid-point decline, his view being that there would be a great inundation causing a disaster. He therefore urged Wang Ken to seek out worthy persons [for appointment] and cultivate virtue as a means of seeking the dynasty's preservation.[104] After the Emperor Ai [reigned 6–1 B.C.] ascended the throne, Li Hsün was again consulted on the interpretation of natural calamities. Li referred to unusual movements of sun and moon, stars and constellations, as reason for persuading the emperor to stay away from meddling palace women, dismiss court sycophants, observe the calendrical prescriptions, and restrain the consort clan members [of his empress' clan, from interfering in government]. Subsequently he attached himself to [the faction of] Hsia Ho-liang [executed 5 B.C.] and secretly applied the [prognostication manual written one or two decades earlier by] Kan Chung-k'o called *T'ien kuan li pao yuan t'ai p'ing ching*.[105] This work held

---

[103] *Han Shu*, *ch.* 36, in Liu Hsiang's biography. For the text of his memorials submitted to the throne see this biography.

[104] Li Hsün is quoted saying: "In the *Documents* it states: [Yao commanded his astronomers of the Hsi and Ho clans to examine the Heavens] '. . . to calculate and delineate the movements and appearances of the sun, the moon, the stars and the zodiacal spaces.' [Legge, *Shoo*, "Yao Tien," p. 18.] This means that they looked upward to note the astronomical phenomena, and gazed downward to examine the terrestrial patterns; they observed tidings from sun and moon, attended the movements and groupings of stars and constellations, surveyed changes in mountains and rivers, and considered the folk airs and chants of the masses, on the basis of which to set norms and standards, and to evaluate [possibilities for] good and bad fortune. They pointed out that when actions were bad and perverse, misfortune and decline would be imminent, omens of which would appear in advance. The enlightened ruler thereupon knew fear and cultivated uprightness, turned to all sides and widely solicited advice, thereby turning bad fortune into good."

[105] The general import of the work is "to tell that the Han dynasty had come to one of heaven's and earth's great terminal points, when it was to be expected that it would receive anew the Mandate from heaven. The ruler of heaven has sent the True Man, Ch'ih-ching Tzu, ["the Master of the Red Essence," an oblique reference to the Han Founder] to descend to instruct me in this truth [*Tao*]."

that the Han would pass through a mid-period of decline but then would receive the Mandate anew. He urged the emperor to change the dynastic calendar and use a new dynastic name in response to heaven's warnings. When his predictions failed to materialize he was sentenced to death; the sentence, however, was reduced one degree, banishing him to Tun-huang Commandery [on the Western marches in Inner Asia].[106] That occurred during the sixth moon of the second year of the Chien-p'ing reign period [5 B.C.].

Ku Yung, whose courtesy name was Tzu-yün, responded to an imperial edict of the third year of the Chien-shih reign period [30 B.C.] calling for interpretations of calamities and prodigies. The histories record that: "He commanded the most arcane aspects of the astronomer-official, Ching [Fang's interpretations of] the *Book of Changes*,"[107] thus he was

---

[106] *Han Shu*, *ch.* 75, from Li Hsün's biography.

[107] Ching Fang's courtesy name was Chün-ming. He specialized in the study of the *Book of Changes* under Chiao Yen-shou, and was particularly skilled at interpreting calamities and irregular occurrences. He assigned the days [of the year] separately to one of the sixty-four hexagrams; they controlled affairs according to their successive correspondences to the days. He took wind and rain, cold and warmth, as manifestations, for each of which prognostic omens exist. [*Cf.* Fung/Bodde, vol. II, pp. 109–110.] The Emperor Yüan [reigned 48–33 B.C.] relied heavily on his favorite, Shih Hsien; Ching Fang admonished the emperor and remonstrated against that, even to the point of comparing the emperor [in face-to-face conversation] with Kings Yu and Li, [eighth- and ninth-century B.C. rulers, respectively, of the Chou dynasty, traditionally symbols of misguided and inept rulership]. In the second year of the *Chien-chao* reign period [37 B.C.] Ching Fang fell victim to a trap set by Shih Hsien, and was executed at the age of forty (77–37 B.C.). See his biography in *Han Shu*, *ch.* 75. The extant work called *Ching shih Yi-chuan* ["Mr. Ching's Commentary on the *Book of Changes*] in three *chüan* (reprinted both in the *Ching-tai pi-shu* and *Hsüeh-ching t'ao-yuan* collectanea), discusses divination employing weather phenomena. Meng Wen-t'ung [the contemporary scholar] has written: "Kan Pao [fl. early fourth century A.D.] transmitted the *Ching shih Yi* [text, and tradition of its interpretation], and it displays his response to theories such as the 'Three Bases' and 'Six Feelings', [the former equivalent to the 'Three Bonds' and the latter a theory of the emotions related to the 'Six Rules'; see Fung/Bodde, vol. II, extracts from the *Po Hu T'ung*, pp. 40–45]; this shows that the Ch'i version of the Odes and Ching Fang's *Book of Changes* shared the same school tradition. . . . Sun Sheng [fourth century] based his interpretation of *The Changes* on Kan Pao. His work states: 'Rulers were installed in antiquity in order to oversee and shepherd the common people. Whenever excessive tyranny was indulged in, inflicting great hardships on the people, the agent of heaven then would kill those [leaders], in carrying out its extermination of depraved rulers. Thus when [the Sage Kings] T'ang and Wu took up arms, they were never accused of treason; when the Han founder raised his sword he did not violate moral duty. How is that to be explained? Because [the tyrannical rulers against whom they fought] were in truth bitter enemies of the entire realm and deserved to be cast out by both gods and men.' This shows that Ching Fang's commentary on the *Changes* was close to the views embodied in Mencius, Hsün Tzu, and the Ch'i version of the *Odes*." (Meng's "Ju chia cheng-chih chih fa-chan," p. 20.) [See note 86 above.]

skilled in interpreting calamities and prodigies. He submitted, at one time or another, interpretations of more than forty such happenings; the views embodied in these are somewhat repetitious. He did little more than attack the emperor for his own conduct and express criticisms of doings in the inner palace quarters, from his stance as an adherent of the Wang [consort] clan faction. Yet his response to the Emperor Ch'eng's questions concerning portentous disasters in the first year of the Yüan-yen reign period [12 B.C.] are illumined by, and in turn display the influence of Tung Chung-shu's ideas. In that, Ku Yung wrote: "Heaven produces the masses of common people who are incapable of governing themselves; therefore it establishes kings over them in order to control and order them. Setting out the institutions of the empire is not for the good of the Son of Heaven; dividing off the land and creating fiefs is not for the good of the feudal nobles. Instead, all of those acts are for the good of the people. Revealing the Three Sequences [san t'ung 三統], setting forth the Three Beginnings [san cheng 三正], eradicating the unprincipled, launching the virtuous [these actions] are not done privately for one [ruling] clan, but manifest the fact that the empire [t'ien-hsia] is the empire's empire and is not one man's empire. A [true] king is one who in his own person achieves the moral way and accords with heaven and earth. . . . Thereupon the correspondences of the hexagrams and the days offer a pattern to be followed; the Five Verifications [wu cheng 五徵 of weather phenomena; see Documents, "Hung Fan," Legge, p. 339] maintain a timely sequence. . . . Good signs and omens descend, to show that [heaven] grants its protection. If [the ruler] abandons the Way and acts improperly, opposing heaven and committing violence to things . . . then the correspondence of the seasons with the hexagrams will be thrown into confusion, and ominous portents will become very conspicuous. Heaven above will shake with anger, while calamities and prodigies will descend with frequency. . . . If [the ruler] fails ultimately to reform and come to his senses, evil developments will all occur. There will be no further warnings and reprimands; the Mandate will be transferred to one of virtue. The Odes say: 'He [great heaven] turned his kind regard on the West, and there gave settlement' [to King T'ai. . . . See Legge, p. 449. This allusion is to heaven's providing for the virtuous Chou dynasty to supplant the degenerate Shang.] For, to eradicate evil and displace that which has declined, transferring the Mandate to the sagelike and worthy, that is the regular course of heaven and earth, and such has been the common experience of all the hundred kings."[108]

Among the masters of classical scholarship during the Western [Former] Han period, the one whose political thought probably should be regarded

---

[108] *Han Shu*, *ch*. 85, in Ku Yung's biography.

as that most significantly embodying somewhat new ideas is Yi Feng, a specialist in the Ch'i version of the *Odes*. [The Lu, Ch'i, and Han versions of the text all were current in early Han times, but eventually were supplanted by the extant Mao version, the only one to survive; a traditional view of their history appears in Legge, *She King*, "Prolegomena."] Yi Feng's courtesy name was Shao-chün. He, Hsiao Wang-chih, and K'uang Heng studied together under the same master [i.e., Hou Ts'ang, central figure in the Ch'i tradition of the first century B.C.], but he alone among them was drawn principally to prognostication based on the pitch-pipes, the calendar, and *Yin-yang* theories. [Cf. Fung Yu-lan, Fung/Bodde, II, pp. 118 ff.] He served under the Emperor Yuan [reigned 48–33 B.C.] and submitted numerous memorials interpreting calamities and prodigies and weather period [*hou* 候] prognostications. In the second year of the *Ch'u-yuan* reign period [47 B.C.] an edict was issued in consequence of an earthquake [causing] collapsing mountains; it solicited scholars' frank words and unrestrained remonstrance. Yi Feng responded by submitting a confidential memorial in which he said: "Your servitor has heard from his teachers that heaven and earth have been established in their positions, the sun and moon suspended, the stars and constellations spread out, *Yin* and *Yang* distinguished, the four seasons determined, the Five Agents arranged, so that the Sage [ruler] can observe them; that is called the *Tao*. The Sage perceives the *Tao* and consequently knows the pattern [*hsiang* 象] of kingly government. Thereupon he divides the land into prefectures, establishes [the relationship of] ruler and servitor, ordains the pitch-pipes and the calendar, and sets forth [the principles of] success and failure for the observation of worthy men; that is called the warp [*ching* 經]. The worthy men perceive the warp [of the fabric of society] and consequently know the duties of man's way [*jen tao* 人道], which are [embodied in] the *Documents*, the *Changes*, the *Spring and Autumn Annals*, the *Rites* and the *Music*. The *Changes* have the *Yin* and the *Yang*, the *Odes* have the Five Periods [*wu chi* 五際], the *Spring and Autumn* have the calamities and prodigies. All of them present the sequence of endings and beginnings, inferences about achievement and failure, and investigations of the mind of heaven, thereby to discourse on security and peril to the kingly Way." These statements reflect the basic principle of the heaven-man correlation. Employing that in conjunction with administrative acts, it becomes possible to predict their auspicious or evil consequences, using the evidence manifested in calamities and prodigies. "Your servitor, Yi Feng, has studied the Ch'i version of the *Odes*, knows its sections concerning the Essentials of the Five Periods and the Intersectings of the Ten Months, understands the consequences of solar eclipses and earthquakes; these are clearly evident and explicable. It is as one who lives in nests knows the winds, one who dwells in caves understands the rains."

At that time the power of the consort clans had grown too great. With
that in mind, Yi Feng replied in statements employing an argument that
the *Yin* forces had become overextended, the [cosmic] reaction to that
being the earthquakes. In the following year, during the Emperor Yüan's
consultation with him, Yi Feng further accused the Emperor of the error
of excessive expenditures. He commented that during the Three Dynasties
of antiquity accumulated virtue had led to kingship, yet dynastic succession had not been maintained for more than a few centuries. Even so
worthy a ruler as King Ch'eng [of the early Chou dynasty] had been
admonished by the Duke of Chou with the words:

> "Before the Yin lost the multitudes,
> [Its Kings] could be the counterparts to the
>   ancestral ruler in heaven.
>   Look to Yin as a mirror;
>   The vast Mandate is not easy to keep."

[The *Odes*, iii/i/i, translation based on Legge, *She King*, p. 431, and
Karlgren, *Book of Odes*, p. 186.]

The Han dynasty had gained the empire by force of arms and its
transformation to the way of virtue was still incomplete. By the time of the
Emperor Yüan, the dynasty had already seen "eight generations and nine
rulers"; heaven displayed irregularities and the people were in distress so
there was in fact a basis for fearing the dynasty's fall. "Your servitor hopes
that Your Majesty will, in consequence of these celestial irregularities,
relocate the capital; that would be what is known as making a new beginning along with the whole empire."[109] "The Way of heaven ends, then
again begins, gets used up then returns to the source. Thereby it is able to
endure, and never be exhausted."[110]

The theory that the Ch'i tradition of the *Odes* particularly dwelt upon
is that of the "Five Periods." It is roughly equivalent to the theory of the
"Three Sequences" in the *Kung-yang Commentary* to the *Spring and Autumn
Annals*, for both expound the meaning of a withdrawal of the Mandate.
The Five Periods are [the years, months or hours including in their cyclical
designations five of the twelve "earth branches", *ti-chih* 地支]: *mao, yu, wu,
hsü,* and *hai.* "Those years in which the *Yin* and *Yang*, the endings and
beginnings find periods of conjunction are those when in administrative
matters there should be changes."[111] To proceed with an analysis of this:

---

[109] When Liu Hsüan [a member of the Han imperial clan who attempted a restoration
after Wang Mang's usurpation] adopted the reign period "*Keng-shih*" ["a new beginning,"
A.D. 23–24] he apparently was heeding these theories; this is evidence that they had
spread very widely.

[110] *Han Shu*, ch. 75, from Yi Feng's biography. The second year of the Ch'u-yuan reign
period corresponds to 47 B.C.

[111] The *Han Shu*, ch. 75, from a note in which Meng K'ang [third century A.D.] quotes
from the *Shih nei chuan* [a no longer extant apocryphal work on the *Odes*].

"Thus, *hai* is the time for changing the Mandate. This is the first Period. *Mao* is the point at which *Yin* and *Yang* meet each other. This is the second Period. *Wu* is that in which the *Yang* declines and the *Yin* flourishes. This is the third Period. *Yu* is that in which the *Yin* is fullest and the *Yang* dwindles away. That is the fourth Period. *Hsü* is that in which the *Yin* reaches the apex and *Yang* comes into being. This is the fifth Period. As for the *tzu, ch'ou, yin, ch'en, ssu, wei* and *shen* [the other seven "earth branches"], they do not occur at the periods of conjunction of *Yin* and *Yang*, thus do not constitute Periods."[112]

The *Odes* further identify *hai* with "Great Radiance." [I.e., "Ta ming," *Odes*, III/i/II; Legge, p. 432.] The ode "Great Radiance" has to do with "The field at Mu."[113] [Mu was the open field where the Chou founder made a speech to his forces as the attack on the Shang-Yin commenced, hence is symbolic of the change of Mandate. See *Documents*, Legge, p. 300.] Master Yuan Ku [the fountainhead of Han period Ch'i studies of the *Odes*, died ca. 135 B.C.] had stated: "Chieh and Chou [tyrant last kings of Hsia and Shang] were dissolute and disorderly; the hearts of all in the whole empire had turned from them to Kings T'ang and Wu [the conquering founders of Shang and Chou]. T'ang and Wu were following the hearts of all in the empire when they executed Chieh and Chou. The people who had belonged to Chieh and Chou refused to serve them and

---

[112] [*Huang*] *Ch'ing ching chieh, hsü pien* [compiled by Wang Hsien-ch'ien, published in 1886–88], *ch.* 128, "Ch'i shih Yi shih hsüeh," ["Mr. Yi's studies of the Ch'i version of the *Odes*"].

[113] The *Shih wei fan li shu* [an apocryphal work on the *Odes*] states: "The period between *wu* and *hai* is that for changing the Mandate; the period between *mao* and *yu* is for reforming and rectifying. *Mao* is 'Heaven Protects.' *Yu* is the 'Minister of War.' *Wu* is 'Gathering White Millet'. *Hai* is 'Great Radiance.' " [The four correspondences refer to titles of four of the Lesser and Greater *Odes*, see Legge, pp. 255, 298, 284, 432 respectively.] In addition to these four periods, the period between *hsü* and *hai* "is the 'Gate of Heaven,' where on going out and coming in, there is listening and waiting"; that corresponds to the second Period, it follows after *hai* and before *mao, wu* and *yu*. This all differs from Yi Feng's statements. [*Cf.* variant translation of these and other relevant passages in Fung/Bodde, Vol. II, pp. 124–126.] Note [the warning tone of] the first ode, "Tai ming" ["Great Radiance"] in the "Decade of King Wen," "Major Odes of the Kingdom," in the *Odes*, of which the first stanza is:

"Shedding radiance below,
Majestic on high,
Heaven is difficult to rely on.
It is not easy to be king;
Yin's proper descendant on the heavenly throne
Was not permitted to encompass the four quarters."

The sixth stanza has:

"I shall protect and help you,
To march and attack the great Shang [Yin]."

[Slightly modified from B. Karlgren, *Book of Odes*, p. 188.]

turned [their allegiance] to T'ang and Wu. T'ang and Wu had no course
but to assume the rulership. If that is not receiving the Mandate, what is
it?"[114] That would appear to be an argument based on *"hai* is the time
for changing the Mandate," used to rebut the views of Master Huang
[a Taoist favorite of the Emperor Ching; he argued against the Mandate
theory and denied the ethical relevance of dynastic succession].

Yi Feng stated: "The Way of the Han dynasty has not yet come to its
end"; by moving the capital and making a new beginning, it could pro-
long its possession of the throne. "If in the first month of summer in a
ping-tzu year, we [the Han state] were to go eastward following the T'ai-
yin [star controlling the new year], then later on, during the year following the seventh year, we would be certain to have the accumulation of
five years' surplusses. Thereafter we could carry out in grand style the
rituals of *K'ao-shih* [marking the completion of the new palace]. Not even
the Chou dynasty at its height could have achieved more." When we make
some inferences about Yi Feng's intention, it apparently turned on the
fact that the third year of the *Ch'u-yüan* reign period [46 B.C.] was a year
designated *yi-hai*, thereby falling precisely in the period in which to
change the Mandate. If the Han house were but capable of responding to
this by altering its government, then following the *ping-tzu* year [45 B.C.]
its situation would be no different from one of having received anew the
great Mandate. The Way of heaven would reach a terminus and begin
again. Yet there was no necessity to obtain a different imperial surname
[clan], or replace the ruler, before being qualified to show that it had met
the requirements of changing the Mandate.

Yi Feng also had a "method of knowing subordinates" that is indeed as
curious as it is specious, and it would seem to bear no relation to the Ch'i
tradition of the *Odes*. His confidential memorial says: "An essential aspect
of the Way of governing lies in knowing whether subordinates are wicked
or upright. . . . The method of knowing one's subordinates is no more
than understanding the six feelings and the twelve pitch-pipes." His
theory looked upon [the cyclical characters naming the "earth branches"]
shen and *tzu* as governing desire; their character is covetous and rapacious.
Hai and *mao* govern anger; their character is secretive and crafty. *Wei* and
ch'en govern pleasure; their character is treacherous and degenerate. These
six comprise the *Yin* [陰, of *Yin* and *Yang*] and are the wicked feelings.
Yin [寅, of the 12 earth branches] and *wu* govern abhorrence; their character is chaste and pure. *Chi* and *yu* govern happiness; their character is
tolerant and generous. *Hsü* and *ch'ou* govern sadness; their character is

---

[114] *Han Shu, ch.* 88, "Biographies of Confucians." [For a translation of the variant but
parallel passage, in the context of Yuan Ku's biography, see B. Watson, *Shih Chi,* Vol. ii,
p. 403 ff.]

impartial and upright. These six comprise the *Yang*, and are the upright feelings.

Also, Yi Feng held that: "The [cyclical character for the] hour is that of the guest; [that for] the day is that of the host. When [a subordinate] is received by the enlightened ruler, his attendants are what is referred to as the host. If the hour is upright and the day is wicked, the one being received is upright and the attendants are wicked. When the hour is [governed by a cyclical character indicating] wickedness and the day is [named by an indicator of] uprightness, the one being received in audience is wicked and the attendants are upright. When a loyal and upright person is being received, even though attendants are wicked, the hour and the day both will be upright. When the greatly wicked are being received, even though the attendants are upright, both hour and day will be [under indicators signifying] wickedness. Should the ruler himself know that his attendants are wicked, and the day is wicked though the hour is upright, the one being received will counteract the wickedness. Should the ruler know that his attendants are upright and the day is upright though the hour is wicked, the one being received will counteract the uprightness."[115] Such notions come close to specious ramblings. When set against his theories about the change of Mandate, with their capacity for warning rulers and keeping them alert to the unanticipated, these ideas clearly are not of comparable significance.

The two reigns of the Emperors Yüan and Ch'eng [48–7 B.C.] witnessed the apex, and the beginning of the decline, of the thought centering on the correlations of heaven and man as affecting the change of the Mandate. An investigation into the reasons for this decline in theorizing about the change of the Mandate suggests that it was an inevitable development. The theory of heaven's and man's interaction was designed to impose restrictions on the ruler. Yet, vigorous rulers in the heroic mold frequently were strong-willed and insatiable in their desires, by temperament not inclined toward religion and superstition. Even when credulous they were more apt to cultivate divinities and adepts who could offer them hope of personal immortality rather than to be attracted to the limitations that the Five Agents and related theories of calamities and ominous prodigies placed upon their personal behavior. The First Emperor of the Ch'in and

---

[115] *Han Shu, ch.* 75. Should this method be known to the subordinates, they would then be sure to avoid the wicked [days and hours] and choose the upright ones, and the method would then become ineffective. Therefore Yi Feng held that the only suitable practice would be for "the ruler alone to employ it," and further that he should use methods of prognostication according to the wind, as a supplement. In the [*Huang*] *Ch'ing ching chieh, Hsü pien, ch.* 162, there appear Meng K'ang's explanations of this, under the title *Ch'i shih Yi shih hsüeh shu cheng* ["commentary on and evidence for Mr. Yi's studies of the Ch'i version of the *Odes*"], to which reference can be made.

Emperor Wu of the Han are the most obvious examples. Those rulers who lived in reverential fear of heaven and spirits and who simultaneously always seemed to have the gentler and more generous characters were also the ones most susceptible to manipulation and control by powerful officials and sycophantic courtiers. Though they might indeed accept the inestimable counsels about their uncertain hold on the Mandate, too often and all too unfortunately their imperial power fell into the hands of their associates, and once such patterns were established it was virtually impossible to break free from them.[116] Moreover, those loyal advisors who offered earnest remonstrance, even though they couched that in language expressing heaven's purposes, were quite likely to fall victim to powerful ministers, and to die violently in consequence.[117] One look through the events in the reigns of Emperors Yuan and Ch'eng [48–7 B.C.] is enough to show that this view is well founded. Furthermore, a discourse on withdrawal of the Mandate could offend an [imperial] ear, while one concerning its acquisition might better move the hearer. The advisor submitting his views would hope that by talking about how the Mandate is acquired, he also could make his main points clear concerning the loss of the Mandate; the ruler accepting that advice would, however, buy the jewel casket but return its jewels [i.e., keep the wrong part], happily accept some aspects of the advice without considering its overall import, and find only those portions of the advice dealing with the acquisition of the Mandate acceptable and pleasing.[118] "What the superior loves, his inferiors will be found to love exceedingly." [*Mencius*, III/i/2/4; Legge, p. 238.] People observed that the way to please an emperor was to theorize about [the rightness of] his having acquired the Mandate; in consequence, auspicious omens, signs, and secret writings appeared in great profusion, for such circumstances made that inevitable.

Intellectual thought concerning heaven's and man's interactions degenerated, shifting from its focus on calamities and ominous prodigies warning of the change of Mandate, to one on apocrypha and signs attesting heaven's bestowal of the Mandate. This shift occurred during the

---

[116] Liu Hsiang, observing the peril posed to the Han house by the Wang clan, submitted a confidential memorial discussing calamities and prodigies. The Emperor Ch'eng: "Sighed long, distressed by its import, and said: 'That is enough, sir; I shall ponder the matter.' " *Han Shu, ch.* 36, in Liu Hsiang's biography.

[117] E.g., during the reign of Emperor Yuan, Ching Fang [see footnote 107 above] was brought down by Shih Hsien and was executed; during the reign of Emperor Hsüan, Chai Fang-chin opposed the faction of Wang Feng, so received the imperial command to commit suicide.

[118] The story of Sui Meng is the clearest illustration of this point. The Emperor Chao [86–74 B.C.] had Sui executed for discoursing on the loss of the Mandate; the Emperor Hsüan [73–49 B.C.] rewarded his son with appointment of office because Sui Meng had predicted that Hsüan would succeed to the throne.

age of the Emperors Ai and P'ing [6 B.C. to A.D. 5].[119] Wang Mang followed upon that, eventually succumbing to the ambition to usurp the throne, ushering in a decade or more of governing marked by "chanting the Six Arts [i.e., the Six Classics] in order to embellish treacherous statements."[120] And after he had gained power, his governmental measures did not go beyond the two activities of simulating ideas expressed in the classics and trusting in heavenly signs attesting his possession of the Mandate. We need not take up the issue of whether Wang Mang's reverence for Confucian precepts was sincere. In actual practice, he never failed to initiate all policies strictly in accord with statements found in the classics, as in: the construction of the Hall of Radiance [*Ming t'ang*], the National Academy [*P'i-yung*], and the Office for Astronomical Observations [*Ling-t'ai*] (in the fourth year of the reign period Yüan-shih, A.D. 4) of the Emperor P'ing; storing tablets in a metal-bound coffer [Chin-t'eng; *cf. Documents*, v/6/11; Legge, p. 356], first occupying the regency [in emulation of the Duke of Chou] from which to succeed to the throne (in the fifth year, A.D. 5, of the Yüan-shih reign period); conducting the Spring Sacrifices in the southern suburb of the capital, and the Great Shooting ritual (in the first year of the Chü-she reign period, A.D. 6); restoring the well-field system, and prohibiting slave-owning (in the first year, A.D. 9 of the Shih-chien-kuo reign period); on the basis of the *Documents*, and the *Chou Rituals* [*Chou Li*] and the "Royal Institutes" Chapter ["Wang chih," of the *Li Chi*] he promulgated his system of offices, and of titles and en-fieffments, in establishing his own dynasty (in the first year of the T'ien-feng reign period, A.D. 14).[121] In none of these acts did he fail to respond to meanings indicated in different passages of the classics. In light of these facts, were we to state that the government of Wang Mang's Hsin ["New"] dynasty was the largest-scale experiment in realizing Confucian ideals, but simultaneously was the most inglorious failure in two thousand years, we would not be far wrong.

That comment notwithstanding, our purpose here is not to recount Confucianism's successes and failures, but to describe in general terms the extent to which the prognostication texts and the apocrypha were current. In assisting Wang Mang's Hsin dynasty with portents showing that it should displace the Han house, Meng T'ung's white stone bearing an inscription in vermilion, dating from the fifth year of the Yüan-shih

---

[119] This was noted by Chang Heng [A.D. 78–139]; see his biography in *ch.* 89 of the *Hou Han Shu*. [*Po-na* ed., *ch.* 49, p. 15-b.]

[120] "Encomium" [*tsan*] to Part Two of Wang Mang's biography, *Han Shu, ch.* 99-C. One may also refer to *The Hu Shih wen-ts'un*, second collection, *ch.* 1, "Wang Mang," where Hu Shih discusses Wang Mang from a modern point of view.

[121] For all of these acts, see *Han Shu, ch.* 99-B.

reign period [A.D. 5] was the first harbinger of things to come.[122] Thereafter there appeared to the Bailiff in Lin-tzu a Heavenly Lord bringing
a message in his dream[123] and Ai Chang's golden casket and charter.[124]
Wang Mang believed that these signs truly had been bestowed by heaven.
Thus in the first year of the [newly proclaimed] reign period, Shih-
chien-kuo [A.D. 9] he dispatched the Wu-wei Generals [and others,
twelve in number, throughout the realm,] to distribute the *Fu-ming* in
42 sections; this listed the manifestations of virtue and blessing, the
mysterious commands, the answering omens, and the like. He believed
that he had gained the power of the agent earth, which would succeed to
the Han dynasty's power of fire and would gain the empire for him.[125]
He also enfeoffed the descendants of former kings, stating that the Lius
[the clan of Han emperors] were the descendants of the [Sage Emperor]
Yao, and that the Wangs were descendants of Shun. For the Hsin dynasty
to succeed the Han was, thus, exactly parallel to Yao's having abdicated
in favor of Shun.[126] Examples of fantastic and specious statements like
that one are indeed numerous. "At that time people competed in offering
mysterious commands on the basis of which they might receive noble
rank. Some who did not engage in that sort of thing said jokingly to each
other, 'What? has there not yet been a letter of appointment from the

[122] The wording on it was: "Announcing that the Duke of An-han, [Wang] Mang,
is to be the Emperor." [The stone was said to have been uncovered in the course of digging
a well.]

[123] This occurred in the third year of the Chü-she reign period [A.D. 8]. "The messenger
of the Heavenly Lord" said to the Bailiff of Ch'ang-hsing post station [in Lin-tzu Hsien,
modern Shantung]: "The regent emperor should become the real [emperor]. If you don't
believe me, within this post station there will appear a new well." When he awoke and
looked, it was truly so.

[124] "Ai Chang, a man of Tzu-t'ung [Hsien, in Kuang-han Commandery, in modern
Szechwan], had been doing elementary studies in Ch'ang-an. Heretofore he was a worthless person and loved to boast. When he saw that [Wang] Mang was acting as Regent, he
immediately made a bronze casket with two envelope covers. He wrote on one of them,
"The chart in the golden casket [with] the Seal of the Lord of Heaven." On the other he
wrote, "The golden charter [with] the Seal of the Red Emperor, which a certain person
[i.e., Liu Pang, the Han Founder] transmits now to the Yellow Emperor [i.e., Wang
Mang]. . . . The text [of the "golden charter"] said that Wang Mang should be the actual
Son of Heaven. . . . The text named eight chief officials of Wang Mang, moreover includ-
ing two [unknown persons just for] having auspicious names: Wang Hsing ["Wang
Flourishes"] and Wang Sheng ["Wang Prospers"]. Ai Chang, taking advantage [of this
opportunity, also] inserted his own name, making a total of eleven persons, for all of whom
there were written official titles and noble ranks as principal aides and assistants." *Han
Shu, ch.* 99-a. [Following, with modification, the translation by H. H. Dubs, *History of the
Former Han Dynasty*, Vol. III, pp. 254–56.]

[125] See, Wang's "General Explanation of the Mysterious Commands" ["Fu-ming
tsung shuo"], in *Han Shu, ch.* 99-B. [Translated in de Bary, *Sources*, pp. 196–98.]

[126] For the wording of the patents of enfieffment, see the *Han Shu, ch.* 99-B.

Celestial Emperor?' The Ssu-ming [official title], Ch'eng Ch'ung, spoke to Wang Mang about the matter, 'This opens a way of aggrandizement for treacherous officials, and it throws heaven's commands into confusion; it should be cut off at the point of origin.' Wang Mang also found the matter unpleasant, consequently he ordered the Chancellor, Chao Ping, to investigate and to imprison all persons [whose claims about "mysterious commands" were] not in accord with the work distributed by the Wu-wei General."[127] Just from this one incident one can imagine the true circumstances at that time with regard to the mysterious commands.

Wang Mang's credulity with respect to these auspicious omens brought his own destruction upon him and caused the extermination of his clan; yet to the very end he failed to come to his senses.[128] His simplemindedness was in truth beyond equal. The remarkable part about it all is that even after the fall of the Hsin dynasty, people both at court and away from court still could not give up those vulgar and crude superstitions. During the chaotic period prior to the Emperor Kuang-wu's accession, the rivals for power were all pitting brains and strength against each other, while the literati argued over mysterious commands. The issue at debate among them then was not whether such auspicious omens are to be believed, but, instead, they turned on which person was receiving the signs of the Mandate and should gain the empire.

To generalize, there were two principal theories, the one being that some other clan would displace the imperial line, and the other being that the Liu fortunes would prosper anew. Proponents of the view that a new clan would displace the previous rulers in the main perpetuated the concepts associated earlier with Wang Mang's Hsin era; Kung-sun Shu, and his Grand Minister over the Masses, Li Hsiung, may be taken as conspicuous examples of that. Kung-sun Shu proclaimed himself king from his base area in Shu [in modern Szechwan]. Li Hsiung urged him to claim the imperial title. "Kung-sun Shu said: 'Emperors and Kings possess the Mandate; how can I consider myself adequate to hold that

---

[127] This occurred during the second year of the reign period Shih-chien-kuo, [or A.D. 10].

[128] When the military uprising in Ch'ang-an [the capital city] took place, and fires reached the palace precincts, "Wang Mang, fleeing the flames, went into the palace hall forming the front part of the Great Palace [*Hsüan shih*] . . . he was dressed entirely in robes of indigo shot with a red thread . . . clasping the dagger of the Emperor Yü [i.e., Shun, claimed as his remote ancestor], his astronomer before him consulting his star charts saying: 'This [auspicious] time-juncture favors you.' Wang Mang shifted his seat so always to be facing the handle of the Dipper [constellation]. He said: 'Heaven produced the virtue that is in me. The Han armies—what can they do to me?' " [*Cf. Analects*, VII/22; Legge, p. 202, for the parallel statement by Confucius.] On the following day, Wang Mang was murdered on the garden terrace adjoining the Great Palace. *Han Shu*, *ch.* 99-C.

position?' Li Hsiung replied: 'The Mandate of heaven is inconstant; the
people approve the man of ability [*neng* 能, and are glad to make him
king, quoting *Yi ching*, "Hsi-tz'u," hsia, 12]. A person of ability will
assume the imperial role, so what doubts need Your Highness have?'
Kung-sun Shu had a dream in which a person spoke to him: '*Pa, ssu,
tzu, hsi* [i.e., parts of words that combine to form his surname]; twelve
[Han dynasty reigns] is the limit.' [Or, as later reinterpreted after Kung-
sun Shu died in the twelfth year of his reign, "twelve years are your
limit."] On waking he said to his wife, 'Though one's status be noble, the
royal dignity is short. What can one do?' His wife replied, 'If a man in the
morning hear the right way, he may die in the evening without regret.
[Quoting *Analects*, IV/8.] How much less need one regret twelve!' At that
time a dragon emerged from his palace, and in the night a radiant glow
was seen. Kung-sun Shu looked upon those as auspicious omens, and in
consequence had lines cut on the palm of his hand reading 'Kung-sun
Emperor.' In the fourth month of the first year of the Chien-wu reign
period [A.D. 25] he proclaimed himself The Son of Heaven, and named his
state Ch'eng-chia [from his capital city, Ch'eng-tu]; white was his color
symbol, and he established the new era name of *Lung-hsing*. . . . Kung-sun
Shu also was much given to matters involving mysterious commands,
spirits and divine beings, and the answering omens. He quite brazenly
quoted from the *Ch'an-chi* [a prognostication text] stating that Confucius
in compiling the *Spring and Autumn Annals* prescribed the period of the Red
Sequence, and therefore stopped after [recording the reigns of] twelve
dukes, indicating thereby that the Han dynasty [which also reigned under
the color red] had run its course when it came to the Emperor P'ing
[reigned A.D. 1–5], who was of the twelfth generation [of Han rulers].[129]
[And:] One surname could not receive the Mandate a second time. He
also quoted [a prognostication text,] the [*Ho t'u*] *Lu yün fa* to say 'Depose
the Ch'ang Emperor and enthrone a Kung-sun'; [This could be interpreted to make Ch'ang refer to Wang Mang, or in other favorable ways;
and from another,] the [*Ho t'u*] *Kua ti hsiang*, saying; 'Emperor Hsüan-
yuan [i.e., claimed by Wang Mang as his antecedent] received the Mandate, the Kung-sun clan then grasps it'; [and from] the [*Hsiao ching*]
Yüan shen ch'i, saying, '*Hsi t'ai-shou, yi mao chin*' meaning 'The Grand
Administrator of the West crushes *mao-chin* [卯金 i.e., the Liu clan]. In

---

[129] Wang Mang's charter [*Ts'e wen*] had said that Confucius, compiling the *Spring and
Autumn Annals*, "Came to [Duke] Ai, the Fourteenth [Duke of Lu chronicled therein] at
which time an era ended." [A parallel between the reigns chronicled in the *Spring and
Autumn*, and the reigns of the Han, is explicit there.] From the time the Emperor Ai
ascended the throne [in 6 B.C.] to the third year of the reign period Chü-she [A.D. 8] was
also a period of fourteen years, and "The Red Sequence had reached its final point, from
which there was no way to force its resuscitation." *Han Shu*, ch̞. 99-B.

the Sequence of the Five Agents, yellow succeeds to red, and white follows from yellow. Metal [whose color is white] has a base in the West, from which, representing the power of white, it will be the successor to Wang Mang, obtaining therein the proper sequence [of the Agents]." He sent letters to Central China hoping to arouse feelings sympathetic to his cause among the masses there.[130]

At that time, however, somewhat more broadly current were theories favoring a renewal of the Liu clan's political prosperity. No doubt the people clung in their thought to the Han era, so that these theories more easily gained popular acceptance. Moreover, having relatively more longstanding origins, they were the more readily believed. Such views had already been aired earlier, during the reigns of Emperors Yüan and Ch'eng [48–7 B.C.] by such persons as Yi Feng, Kan Chung-k'e, Hsia Ho-liang, Ku Yung, and others,[131] and later on, during Wang Mang's time, others including the Taoist adept Hsi-men Chün-hui and the classics master Chih Yün continued to maintain this view.[132] During the reign of the Keng-shih Emperor [Liu Hsüan, the first member of the Liu clan who claimed to reign, A.D. 23–24, following Wang Mang's decline], these

[130] The Emperor Kuang-wu was made anxious by this, and on one occasion sent Kung-sun Shu a letter urging that he not emulate Wang Mang's [use of portents]. [The long quotation in the text is from Kung-sun Shu's biography, *Hou Han Shu*, *ch*. 43. The portents are translated, and his use of them discussed, in Hans Bielenstein, *The Restoration of the Han Dynasty*, Vol. II, especially pp. 245–48.]

[131] *Han Shu*, *ch*. 75, "Biography of Yi Feng"; *ch*. 85, "Biography of Ku Yung." The *Hou Han Shu*, in *ch*. 53, "Biography of Tou Jung," speaks of Ku Yung [T. Tzu-yün] and Hsia Ho-liang as "scholars broadly informed about and [skilled practicioners of] the prognostication arts . . . who clearly demonstrated the signs indicating that the Han would receive the Mandate again."

[132] *Han Shu*, *ch*. 99-C, states: "Hsi-men Chün-hui was devoted to astronomy and the [prognostication work] *Ch'an-chi*. . . . He announced that 'a comet has swept in the [Heavenly] Palace. The Liu clan ought to rise again. [The next emperor] will have the surname and given name of the Duke State Master, that is, Liu Hsiu.' " [Translation follows, with some additions, that in Bielenstein, *op.cit*. in note 130, p. 240.] Wang She, Tung Chung and others thereupon [A.D. 23] plotted together to kill Wang Mang; the matter was discovered and all were executed. Also, in the first year of [Wang Mang's] reign period *Ti-huang*, [A.D. 20–21] a fortune-teller by the name of Wang K'uang persuaded [a local official] Li Yen, with the words: "The House of Han should rise again, and a man of the surname Li will assist in that." He also composed a prognostication book of over one-hundred thousand words purporting to emanate from the Emperor Wen [reigned 179–157 B.C.]. Chih Yün understood astronomical and calendrical prognostication. During the reign of Wang Mang he made a prognostication based on astral signs from which he knew that the Han house was destined to receive the Mandate again. Thereupon he traveled westward to Ch'ang-an [the capital], where he submitted a memorial to persuade Wang Mang that he should return the rulership to the Liu clan. Wang Mang was enraged, but he did not dare have Chih Yün executed. (*Hou Han Shu*, *ch*. 59, "Biography of Chih Yün.")

theories achieved especially widespread currency. A number of persons, such as Pan Piao, Cheng Hsing, Wang Ch'ang, Shen-t'u Kang, Feng Yen, and Su Ching[133] held this view and urged it on the competing military upstarts of the time, hoping they would devote themselves to the restoration cause, or turn to the support of Emperor Kuang-wu. This theory varied only in minor detail from one of its spokesmen to another. Pan Piao's "Wang Ming Lun" ["Discussion of the Mandate of Kings"] is more or less representative of all.

Emperor Kuang-wu ascended his throne at Chi-chou [modern Hopei province, on August 5, A.D. 25]; Pan Piao was twenty years old at that time. In responding to Wei Hsiao's inquiry [about political circumstances that might favor his desire to establish himself as founder of a new dynasty], Pan Piao wrote his "Discussion" in order to dispel the doubts of the age. It said, in part: "In antiquity when the Emperor Yao was about to abdicate, he said 'Oh! you, Shun, the heaven-determined order of succession now rests in your person. . . . Shun also used the same words in transmitting his Mandate to Yü.' . . . [*Analects* xx/1, 2.] Subsequently in the eras of T'ang [founder of the Shang dynasty] and Wu [founder of the Chou], they were able to gain sway over the empire. Though they encountered different times and the manner of the successions was different, yet in responding to the will of heaven and according with the people's wishes, they followed the same principle. In the same way the Liu clan [of the Han dynasty] inherited the blessings of Yao, as we see from its family record prominently chronicled in the *Spring and Autumn Annals*. Emperor Yao ruled by the virtue of [the Agent] fire, which was handed down to the Han. When [the future Han founder] first arose in the marshland of P'ei, the spirit of the old woman appeared weeping in the night as a sign from the Red [fire] Emperor. [The old woman, according to the *History of the Former Han Dynasty*, ch. 1, was the mother of the White Emperor's son, who assumed the form of a huge snake and was slain by Liu Pang, the Han Founder, i.e., the Red Emperor.] From all this evidence, we say that in order to be secure in the blessings of rulership, an emperor must possess not only the virtue of radiant sageliness and conspicuous excellence; he must also be heir to a patrimony of abundant merit and favor long accumulated. Only then can his purified sincerity communicate with the spiritual intelligence, and be able to extend the favor of his grace to all the living people. Then he will receive good fortune from spirits and divine beings, and the empire will turn willingly to him. There never has been a case of a man who, the successive generations

---

[133] See, *Han Shu*, ch. 100, "Hsü chuan"; and *Hou Han Shu*, ch. 66, "Biography of Cheng Hsing," ch. 45, "Biography of Wang Ch'ang," ch. 59, "Biography of Shen-t'u Kang," ch. 58-a, "Biography of Feng Yen," and ch. 60, "Biography of Su Ching."

having passed without the evidence of merit being noted, could suddenly rise to the position of great eminence." [Modified from de Bary, *Sources*, p. 193.] From the hearts of the people the Mandate of heaven is to be known, and the indubitable fact that in their hearts the people still clung to the Han,[134] constituted clear evidence that the Liu clan would again flourish; there was need for no trace of doubt on that score.

Pan Piao's composition approaches high standards of refinement and elegance. Yet the omens and prognostications that the Emperor Kuang-wu upheld in order to seize the empire are scarcely if at all different in character from Wang Mang's white stone [with its vermilion inscription] or his golden casket [containing the divine charter]. Kuang-wu's first rise [as a claimant for the Mandate] came about in consequence of the prognostication told him by Li T'ung. His accession to the imperial position was decided when Ch'iang Hua submitted his *Prognostications on the Latent Power of the Red Sequence* [Ch'ih-fu fu].[135] To the end of the Chien-wu and Chung-yuan reign periods [A.D. 25–57], auspicious omens and prognostications virtually constituted a kind of national religion centering on the emperor as defender of legitimacy. In the second year of his Chung-yuan reign period [A.D. 57], the emperor promulgated the *T'u-ch'an* [a book of prognostication texts] throughout his realm; it was an event

---

[134] Ambitious men at that time were extremely conscious of this and contrived ways to benefit from it, hence frequently posed as members of the imperial clan in launching spurious claims to the throne. Examples are Wang Ch'ang (Wang Lang), who pretended to be Tzu-yü, the son of Emperor Ch'eng, and Lu Fang, who pretended to be Wen-po, the grandson of Emperor Wu. (*Hou Han Shu, ch.* 42, "The Biographies of Wang Ch'ang and Lu Fang.") Liu Hsin [the Emperor Kuang-wu] changed his personal name to Hsiu in response to a prognostication, also hoping to receive the Mandate as an imperial clan member.

[135] *Hou Han Shu, ch.* 1-A, "Basic Annals of the Emperor Kuang-wu, Part One"; here it states that a native of Wan County, Li T'ung, in the third year of [Wang Mang's] Ti-huang reign period [A.D. 22], pronounced that "The Liu family will rise again and the Li family will be a support." [Following Bielenstein, *op.cit.*, p. 239; the wording of the original is slightly different from Wang K'uang's prophecy, quoted in footnote 132, above.] During the first year of his Chien-wu reign period [A.D. 25] when Emperor Kuang-wu was at Ch'ang-an, his former study-mate Ch'iang Hua submitted a prognostication that said: "Liu Hsiu will mobilize troops and capture the wicked; barbarians from the four quarters will swarm in while the dragons duel in the wilds; at the junctire of four and seven [i.e., in the twenty-eighth, or two-hundred and twenty-eighth year] fire will reign." [Modified from Bielenstein, *op.cit.*, p. 240.] In his incantation offered upon ascending the throne, Emperor Kuang-wu included the sentence: "The *Ch'an-chi* says, 'Liu Hsiu will mobilize troops and capture the wicked; *mao-chin* [i.e., parts of the character "Liu"] cultivate their powers to become the Sons of Heaven.' " Li Hsien [A.D. 651–684] in his Commentary [to the *Hou Han Shu*] quotes a work called *Ch'un-ch'iu yen K'ung t'u* [a Han apocryphal work on the *Spring and Autumn Annals*] saying, "*Mao-chin-tao* form the name Liu; descendants of the Red Emperor, they will reign second after the Chou."

very similar to Wang Mang's dissemination of his *Fu-ming*. At his most extreme, he even made decisions on appointments to office on the basis of prognostications, and turned his anger against servitors who disparaged the prognostication books.[136]

To found doctrines on the way of spiritual forces, thereby greatly encouraging the role of soothsayers [as Emperor Kuang-wu did] was truly a rare and curious act among founders of dynasties [in all of Chinese history]. The first rise of the heaven-and-man theorizing can be traced roughly to the most prosperous era of Western Han history [i.e., to the reign of Emperor Wu, 140–87 B.C.]. Those theories developed considerably, undergoing various changes throughout more than a century, until the time of Emperor Kuang-wu [A.D. 25–57]. They were applied to a wide variety of ends, and with a steady erosion of their original meaning. To describe that process in most general terms, during the ages of Emperors Wu and Chao [140–74 B.C.], the explication of calamities and prodigies was mainly directed toward warning the ruler and giving peace and

---

[136] Chao Yi [1727–1814] in his *Erh-shih-erh shih cha-chi, ch.* 4, [under the heading "Kuang-wu hsin ch'an shu," or "The Emperor Kuang-wu believed in prognostication books"] states: "Prognostication books and the apocrypha arose at the end of the Western Han. . . . Kuang-wu in particular believed intensely in those arts, even to the point of consulting prognostication books as a guide to making appointments and undertaking administrative actions. While deliberating on the selection of a person to be appointed Grand Minister of Works, a statement was noted in the *Prognostications on the Latent Power of the Red Sequence* saying 'Wang Liang while Lord of Wei shall become the Hsüan-wu.' The Emperor knew that Yeh-wang County had been the place to which the King of Wei had moved [in 241 B.C.], that Hsüan-wu was the name of the Spirit of the Waters, and that the Minister of Works was the official responsible over water and earth. Wang Liang was a native of An-yang [the ancient name for which had been Yeh-wang]. Given name, surname, place name all corresponded; in consequence, he appointed [his long-time supporter, whose name happened to be Wang] Liang to the office of Grand Minister of Works." (*Hou Han Shu, ch.* 52, "Biography of Wang Liang.") ". . . He also noted that a prognostication text included the line 'Sun Hsien subdues the *Ti* barbarians'; consequently, he named Sun Hsien, his General for Pacifying the *Ti* barbarians, to the post of Commander in Chief." (See, *Hou Han Shu, ch.* 52, "Biography of Ching Tan.") ". . . Huan T'an remarked to the Emperor [after being asked to interpret an omen] 'Your servant does not study prognostication books'; moreover, he argued strenuously that the prognostication books are not canonical works. The Emperor was very angry, holding that [Huan T'an] reviled the Sages and defied the laws, and wanted to have him beheaded, [but did not do so]." (*Hou Han Shu, ch.* 58-A, "Biography of Huan T'an.") ". . . The Emperor also consulted Cheng Hsing, saying he wished to consult prognostication texts to determine some matters relevant to the Suburban Sacrifice. Cheng Hsing said 'Your servant does not study prognostication books.' The Emperor, enraged, said 'Are you disparaging them, then?' Cheng Hsing knelt and replied, 'Your servant acknowledges that among books there are those which he has not studied, but there are none which he disparages.' Cheng Hsing memorialized on a number of governmental matters, but the Emperor, holding him ignorant of the prognostication works, did not in the end appoint him to any office." (*Hou Han Shu, ch.* 66, "Biography of Cheng Hsing.")

security to the people [hoping that the errant rulers would mend their ways]. From the reigns of Emperors Yüan and Ch'eng onward [48–7 B.C.] they tended toward the suppression of treachery and the protection of ruler and dynasty. During the time of Emperors Ai and P'ing [6 B.C. to A.D. 5] those who presented their auspicious omens concerning the Mandate were providing pretexts for the usurper. After the collapse of the Hsin rule [of Wang Mang, the usurper], the theories again came to serve as potent weapons for combatting treachery and sedition while supporting the legitimate succession. At the beginning, it was loyal ministers who relied on such theories as foundation for their remonstrations; later, unworthy persons employed them to their personal aggrandizement. In the early phases, servitors applied threats embodied in calamities and prodigies, with their implications for withdrawal of the Mandate, to the correction of governmental failings; at the end, the rulers themselves were drawing on the *Fu-ming* and the *Ch'an-chi* in order to reinforce their status and power. The learning of Tsou Yen and Tung Chung-shu, by this stage of the development, still existed in name but in reality had disappeared.[137]

Nonetheless, that statement that Tung Chung-shu's learning had, in

---

[137] This is to characterize the overall contours of its heyday and decline. During the Eastern Han there still were classics masters and Confucian scholars who discussed administrative actions in relation to calamities and prodigies. Examples are: Cheng Hsing, active during the reign of Kuang-wu (*Hou Han Shu*, ch. 66, "Biography of Cheng Hsing"); Ho Ch'ang, during the reign of Emperor Chang, A.D. 76–88 (*ibid.*, ch. 73); Ting Hung, during the reign of Emperor Ho, A.D. 89–105 (*ibid.*, ch. 67); Lang Yi, during the reign of Emperor An, A.D. 107–125 (*ibid.*, ch. 60-B); Lang Yi and Chou Chü, during the reign of Emperor Shun, A.D. 126–144 (*ibid.*, ch. 91), as well as Li Ku (*ibid.*, ch. 93); and both Hsiang K'ai (*ibid.*, ch. 60-B) and Chu Mu (*ibid.*, ch. 73, "Biography of Chu Hui") during the reign of the Emperor Huan, A.D. 147–167. All of these to some small degree preserved the idea as it had been developed in the Western Han. By the time of the Liu clan's abdication in favor of the Ts'ao rulers [when the Wei dynasty in A.D. 220 displaced the Han], the various documents accompanying the new ruler's accession to the throne more or less imitated those promulgated at the time of the transfer from the Han to [Wang Mang's] Hsin dynasty; (see the *Wei Shu*, ch. 2, commentary on "The Basic Annals of the Emperor Wen"). Thereafter, throughout the Six Dynasties [until 589], instances of usurpation also used the heavenly Mandate terminology to embellish their proclamations. However the phraseology grew ever more ornate and elegantly allusive, no longer striving after efficacy through preserving the rustic crudities of the prognostication texts. Wang Mang and the Emperor Kuang-wu still genuinely believed in the mysterious omens surrounding the Mandate, (or, at the very least they "manipulated the false until it, unintended, acquired a certain reality"). From Wei and Chin times [third century] onward, the various [usurpers assuming the image of] "Emperor Shun of Yü" [Shun, in high antiquity, accepted the throne from the abdicating Yao] were not necessarily in real awe of heaven's Mandate. For an overview, one can read the accounts of dynastic change described in ch. 3 of the *Chin Shu*, ch. 2 of the *Sung Shu*, ch. 1 of the *Liang Shu* and ch. 1 of the *Sui Shu*.

reality, disappeared, is to speak only of that one aspect of it that turned on heaven's and man's interaction at the change of Mandate. To speak more comprehensively about the full range of political thought using the *Kung-yang Commentary* to the *Spring and Autumn Annals*, there was Ho Hsiu, who still was able to expound conspicuously on these doctrines, during the period of the Emperors Huan and Ling [A.D. 147–188]. We must not fail to discuss him in bringing this section to its close.

Ho Hsiu's courtesy name was Shao-kung. "He had expertly mastered the Six Classics; none of the Confucian scholars of his time was his equal. As the son of a high ranking minister of state, he was granted imperial appointment to the office of Palace Attendant, but that in no way attracted him, so he resigned on the excuse of illness and left the court; neither would he serve at the local level in administration. . . . The Grand Guardian, Ch'en Fan, pressed appointment on him to serve as a counsellor to the central administration. Ch'en Fan fell from power [in conflict with the eunuch party of late Han], and Ho Hsiu was implicated, and sentenced to be barred permanently from holding government offices. Thereupon he composed his *Ch'un-ch'iu Kung-yang chieh-ku*, on which he concentrated intently for seventeen years without once glancing beyond his door. . . . Ho Hsiu was skilled at calendrical calculation. He and his teacher, the Erudit Yang Pi, carried on the line of argument adopted by Li Yü [*fl.* ca. A.D. 70–90; in calculating errors in dates, with which] to discredit the other two Commentaries [i.e., the *Tso* and *Ku-liang Commentaries* to the *Spring and Autumn*, in order to demonstrate the superiority of the *Kung-yang Commentary*]; he wrote the *Kung-yang Mo-shou* ['Unyielding defense of the Kung-yang'], the *Tso-shih Kao-huang* ['On Mr. Tso's fatal illness'] and *Ku-liang Fei-chi* ['The *Ku-liang Commentary*'s infirmities']." In his late years he again emerged to hold office, reaching the post of Grand Remonstrant. He died in his fifty-fourth year, in the fifth year of the Kuang-ho reign period.[138]

Ho Hsiu's concept of the heaven-man correlation, generally speaking, is the same as Tung Chung-shu's.[139] He said that the king "Extends

---

[138] *Hou Han Shu, ch.* 109-B, "Biographies of Confucians, Part Two." Calculating on the basis of his death date, Ho. Hsiu was born in the fourth year of the Emperor Shun's Yung-chieh reign period, thus his birth and death dates correspond to A.D. 129–182. However, Ch'en Fan died in the first year of the Chien-ning reign period (168), fifteen years earlier than the death date given for Ho Hsiu, giving rise to suspicion that there may be an error in the text of his biography.

[139] However, Ho Hsiu stated: "The Origin is the material force [*ch'i*, or "ether"]. The formless arises from it; forms separate within it, fashioning and building heaven and earth, that being the beginning of heaven and earth." (*Ch'un-ch'iu Kung-yang chieh ku*, under "First year of Duke Yin, Spring the King's First Month"). This differs slightly from Tung's statements.

heaven's [function], respectfully assuming the Origin's [intent], thereby nourishing and bringing to completion all the myriad things."[140] He received heaven's Mandate in order to gain blessings on his rule, and according to the excellence of his virtue, his name and title are then determined. "The one whose virtue corresponds to the Origin is called *Huang* ["august, imperial"]. Confucius said, '*Huang* is the image of the Origin; his divining powers are unfettered. Even without [mysteriously revealed] writings [to guide his rule], his virtue is brilliantly enshrined. The one whose virtue corresponds to heaven is called *Ti* ["the supreme ruler"]. He has received the *River Chart* and the *Lo Writing*, so the auspicious signs can be matched to it. The one who corresponds to [the standards of] benevolence and righteousness is called *Wang* ["the king"]. He responds to the signs and omens signifying the Mandate's bestowal, and all the realm turns willingly to him."[141] Yao of T'ang and Shun of Yü and the other sovereigns of the Three Dynasties received the Mandate in response to their radiant virtue. Later on, when the Han dynasty gained the realm, that likewise was not accomplished solely by intelligence and force. Ho Hsiu bases these views on theories about Confucius, who, as the "uncrowned king" established the laws and institutions that would prevail throughout the world; he used the [historical incident concerning the] capture of the unicorn [*lin*] by men hunting in the west to demonstrate that the Han Founder was the new king produced in response to the sequence of the dominant cosmic forces. He said: "Confucius had long known from his study of the prognostication charts [*t'u lu*] that a man of the common people, Liu Chi [i.e., Liu Pang, the Han Founder], was destined to succeed the Chou dynasty. When he saw that it was a woodcutter who had captured the unicorn, he knew that this foretold that person's emergence. How is that explained? The unicorn is the spirit of wood; the woodcutter stands for the idea of the commoner making a fire [i.e., red]. This meant that the Red Emperor would in the future succeed to the Chou and occupy its position; therefore the unicorn was captured by a woodcutter. Capturing it while hunting in the west indicates that from the east will come one who will hold sway over the west. The east is under the [cyclical]

---

[140] *Ibid.*, *loc.cit.* Under the line of the *Annals*, which says: "Duke Ch'eng's eighth year [582 B.C.]. In Autumn, in the seventh month, the Son of Heaven sent the Earl of Shao to confer on the Duke the symbol of investiture" [Legge, p. 366], Ho Hsiu comments, "The Sage who receives the Mandate is in all cases given birth by heaven." Under the line: "In Duke Hsüan's third year [605 B.C.], in spring, in the king's first month," he comments, "The way of heaven is dark and obscure, therefore one draws inferences from the way of man in order to extend it." [*Cf.* Legge, p. 292; the passage concerns the Duke of Lu's decision to cancel the border sacrifice after the first sacrificial bull and its replacement both died.]

[141] *Ibid.*, under the line in the eighth year of Duke Ch'eng: "The Duke of Shao comes."

sign *mao*; the west's symbol is *chin* [gold]. To say that it was captured is to indicate a word for weapons [*tao*]; it thus indicates that the Han surname, [Liu, composed of the elements] *mao*, *chin*, and *tao* [卯金刀 equals 劉] will gain the empire by force of arms. Moreover, prior to that there had occurred the [untimely appearance of] locusts hopping in swarms in the winter [Duke Ai 12, 484 B.C.; Legge, p. 828], and of the gold essence [invaded by a] comet, sweeping the morning sky, and placing there the sign of the new. [A comet "sweeping" its tail across the gold star, i.e., of the west, presaging the Ch'in dynasty's fall, construing an event of Ai 13, 483 B.C.; Legge, p. 831.] Confucius knew there would ensue the period in which the Six States would struggle for supremacy, from signs indicating the vertically and horizontally aligned states killing each other, and fore-knowledge of the Ch'in dynasty and Hsiang Yü [rival of the Han founder in the post-Ch'in civil war] being eliminated, amidst bones heaped up and blood flowing, and that thereafter one of the Liu clan would become the Emperor. Deeply grieving that the people would endure such protracted suffering, he therefore wept presciently." [Confucius, on being shown the captured, dead unicorn, covered his face with his sleeve and wept, according to the *Ch'un-ch'iu*, Ai, 14.]

Ho Hsiu also quoted from certain apocrypha to explain such *Kung-yang Commentary* statements about eliminating disorder and restoring the world to good order. "After the unicorn was caught, the heavens rained blood which formed into writing on the main gate of Lu. . . . [Confucius' disciple] Tzu-hsia, next day went to look at this, whereupon the writing flew away as a red bird. This then changed itself into white writing, bearing the title *Expository Chart on Confucius* [*Yen K'ung t'u*]. In it are de-lineated charts for instituting laws. Confucius looked upward to make his deductions about the heavenly Mandate, and looked downward to ex-amine the events of the time; indeed, he could see what was yet to come, understanding completely all things in advance; he knew that the Han dynasty would follow after a great disorder. He therefore made his rules for eliminating disorders, to transmit [to later ages]."[142]

---

[142] From the commentary in the *Ch'un-ch'iu Kung-yang chieh-ku* appended to the line [in the *Ch'un-ch'iu*] under the fourteenth year of Duke Ai [482 B.C.; Legge, p. 833; Fung/Bodde, pp. 71–72], which says: "In the fourteenth year, in spring, hunters in the west captured a *lin*." Note that [an apocryphal work on the *Spring and Autumn Annals*,] the *Ch'un-ch'iu yen K'ung t'u*, says: "The *lin* emerges, so the Chou dynasty will end; therefore [Confucius] wrote the *Spring and Autumn Annals*, ruled as the uncrowned king [*Su-wang*], and transmitted [his ordinances to the rulers] destined to rise in the future." The [apocry-phal work on the *Classic of Filial Piety*, the] *Hsiao-ching yu ch'i*, says: "Confucius dreamed at night that amidst three ash trees [symbol of the Three Lords, the highest officials among an emperor's attendants], in the region of Feng-p'ei [northern Kiangsu, where the Han founder was born], he saw a red smoke vapor rise. He called [his most intimate disciples] Yen Yüan and Tzu-hsia to go with him to look at that. They drove their cart

Throughout, this displays a reliance on the prognostication charts and apocrypha which date from the reigns of Emperors Ai and P'ing [reigned 6 B.C. to A.D. 5] and later, in order to elucidate the meaning of the classic [the *Spring and Autumn Annals*]. Not only were these ideas that Confucius had never held, they also were things Tung Chung-shu had never heard of. From the time that Emperor Kuang-wu placed high value on the prognostication texts, thought and learning had been unable to escape their influence.[143]

Some Confucian scholars who distorted their learning to earn favor, seeing how specious notions could arouse their audience, invented these tales about the Uncrowned King enacting his laws, in profound disservice to the man Confucius. The most crafty among them still further developed a theory of the "subtle meanings" [of the classic], by twisting their inter-

---

to the northwest part of the State of Ch'u, in front of the street where the Fan Family [lived]. There they saw a fuel gatherer carrying [in his cart] a *lin* [unicorn] which had injured its left foreleg. He had made bundles of firewood and covered it over. Confucius said: 'Come here. What is your surname?' The fellow said: 'My surname is Ch'ih-sung, my courtesy name is Shih-ch'iao and my formal name is Shou-chi.' [Intricate allusions to the future Han dynasty are embedded in these names.] Confucius then said: 'Have you not perhaps seen something?' The fellow replied: 'I have seen something. It is a beast resembling an antelope, with a head like a sheep on which there is a horn, fleshy to its tip. It was just going toward the west.' Confucius said: 'The realm now is to have its overlord. He will be the Red [Emperor] Liu; Ch'en [She] and Hsiang [Yü, two other rebels against the Ch'in, ca. 209–202 B.C.] will be his adjuncts. Five stars will enter the constellation *ching*, and will appear in company with the eastern star.' The firewood was taken off and the *lin* unloaded, so as to show it to Confucius. Confucius hastened to that place. The *lin* whispered into his ear, and spit out three rolls of charts three inches wide and eight inches long, each containing twenty-four characters. They stated that the Red [Emperor] Liu would arise, saying, 'The Chou collapses; the red air rises. The great sun rises; Hsüan-ch'iu [i.e., the mysterious Confucius] issues the Mandate to the *mao-chin* [i.e., Liu] Emperor.'" The objective of this is identical with that of the *Kung-yang* specialists, although the phrasing varies somewhat.

[143] The *Hou Han Shu*, ch. 66, in the "Biography of Chia K'uei," says that the Emperor Kuang-wu elevated the *Tso* and *Ku-liang Commentaries* to the *Spring and Autumn Annals* [to the status of canons for which Erudits were appointed], but "since none of the masters in these two academic traditions had ever been versed in the prognostication charts and texts, it was ordered that those posts be allowed to lapse." This makes it clear that during the period from Kuang-wu through the reign of Emperor Chang [A.D. 25–88], the *Kung-yang* scholars alone among those specializing in any of the three *Commentaries*, monopolized the application of prognostication works. Yet, during the Yung-p'ing reign period [A.D. 58–75] of the Emperor Ming, Chia K'uei submitted a memorial stating that the prognostication works and the *Tso Commentary* were compatible, and in the first year of Emperor Chang's Chien-ch'u reign period [A.D. 76] he again submitted a memorial in which he declared that among the Five Classics, only the *Tso Commentary* explicitly declared the Liu [imperial] clan to be descended from the Sage Emperor Yao, and that Yao ruled in response to the power [of the Agent] fire. Thus it appears that the classics masters in the Tso tradition also fell into the trap of imitating their competitors.

pretations and adducing all sorts of bizarre assumptions that they presented as the most essential import of the Confucian teachings. Compared with Kung-sun Hung's sycophancy before the Emperor Wu, the intent here is similar, but their personal character is still further debased. By the end of Han such doctrines had penetrated deeply into the academic sphere and gradually took form in traditions of scholarship. Thus Ho Hsiu's *Ch'un-ch'iu Kung-yang chieh-ku* [i.e., his exegetical work on the *Kung-yang Commentary*] continued to make use of such doctrines. In less than fifty years thereafter, Ts'ao P'ei, [Emperor Wen of Wei, reigned A.D. 220–226] usurped the Han throne. This was an event of which Ho Hsiu definitely had gained no foreknowledge. Otherwise, in light of the prescience attributed to Confucius, why was it that the *Spring and Autumn Annals* would contain no single word pointing out this event to the later students of the classic? Why was Ho Hsiu, although so close in time to the founding of the Wei dynasty, unable to draw upon its subtle meanings to "set forth the conjunctions of heaven and man, record prodigies, and evaluate omens,"[144] and thereby calculate that the "Red Sequence" was close to its end?

In his discussions of calamities and prodigies, Ho Hsiu also to some degree accepted the concepts prevailing in the Western [Former] Han period, while at the same time slightly altering them. For example, Tung Chung-shu had stated that calamities appeared first, then were followed by prodigies [stressing an unvariable sequence of such warnings]. Ho Hsiu, on the other hand, merely spoke of calamities as the less grave and prodigies as the more ominous phenomena [stressing their relative gravity].[145] Also, Tung Chung-shu rarely spoke of auspicious signs, whereas Ho Hsiu discoursed at length on the favorable omens [affecting the Mandate].[146] Here too he reveals the influences emanating from the tone of the Later Han court, and the matter does not warrant lengthy discussion. In its scattered and brief references to the methods of governing, Ho Hsiu's *Ch'un-ch'iu Kung-yang chieh-ku* also merely follows the larger

---

[144] *Ch'un-ch'iu wo-ch'eng t'u* [an apocryphal work].

[145] For Tung's theory, see the items cited in note 82 of this chapter. For Ho Hsiu, see his *Ch'un-ch'iu Kung-yang chieh-ku*, the first year of Duke Ting [508 B.C.; Legge, p. 744], under the line: "In winter, in the tenth month, there fell hoarfrost, which killed the pulse."

[146] For example, see Ho Hsiu's *chieh-ku*, comment appended to the line concerning the capture of the unicorn. Ho Hsiu also held the theory that by correcting errors, calamities could be eliminated; see his comment on the line: "In summer, in the fourth month, it did not rain" under the third year of Duke Hsi [656 B.C.; Legge, p. 137]. The *Hou Han Shu* from the Emperor Chang's Yuan-ho reign period [A.D. 84–86] reports many prodigies manifested in plants, trees, birds, and animals which people of the time all took to be auspicious omens; Ho Ch'ang submitted a memorial rebutting that kind of interpretation, (*ch*. 73, "Biography of Ho Ch'ang"). The history also includes other such records thereafter. Records of such matters are relatively infrequent, however, in the Former Han.

outlines of the Kung-yang school tradition, and those need not be repeated here.

In his explanation of the *Kung-yang Commentary*'s "Three Ages," however, Ho Hsiu offers some ideas not anticipated by Tung Chung-shu. The *Spring and Autumn Annals*, under the First Year of Duke Yin [i.e., 721 B.C., the first year chronicled in the *Annals*], writes: "Kung-tzu Yi-shih died." On this, the *Kung-yang Commentary* adds: "What was directly witnessed is differently stated; what was heard is differently stated; what was known through transmitted records is differently stated." [That is, the wording varies in historical accounts according to the recorder's distance from events.] Ho Hsiu explains that to mean: "What he [Confucius, reputed author of the *Spring and Autumn Annals*], directly witnessed was the period of Dukes Chao, Ting, and Ai, [540–469 B.C.], corresponding to the lifetimes of his father and himself. What was heard about was the period of Dukes Wen, Hsüan, Ch'eng, and Hsiang [625–541 B.C.], corresponding to the time of his grandfather. What was known through transmitted records was the period of Dukes Yin, Huan, Chuang, Min, and Hsi [721–626 B.C.], corresponding to the times of his great grandfather and great-great grandfather." Confucius, "In [chronicling] the age of which he knew through transmitted records, portrayed an order arising amidst decay and disorder, and so directed his mind loosely to the larger outlines. Therefore he looked upon his own state [of Lu] as the center and the states of the other feudal lords as the periphery. He spoke first of the center, and then treated the periphery. He recorded major events and only briefly noted minor ones. He wrote about lesser villainies at the center, but did not write about lesser villainies in the peripheral states. For the larger states he recorded its Great Officers, but [dignitaries of] smaller states are referred to merely as 'persons.' And also, he noted assemblies [of the feudal lords] that failed to reach agreement, but he did not record such fruitless assemblies in the peripheral states.

"In [chronicling] the age of which he heard [by oral reports] he portrayed the order of Ascending Peace. He looked upon all the feudal states comprising China as the center and the various barbarians as the periphery. He thus recorded even those assemblies beyond [his own state] that failed to reach agreement, and noted the names of the Great Officers even in the small states. In the eleventh year of Duke Hsüan, in the autumn [where he records that] the Marquis of Chin had an assembly with the *Ti* [barbarians] at Ts'uan-han, and in the twenty-third year of Duke Hsiang, where Pi-wo of the State of Chu-lou came as a fugitive, are instances of this.

"Coming to the age which he witnessed directly, he made evident the order of Universal Peace. The barbarians are advanced and attain feudal rank; the whole world, far and near, large and small, is as one. He directed his mind with particular profundity to the details. Thus he exalted acts of benevolence and righteousness, while criticizing the use of double personal names; Wei Man-to of the State of Chin and Chung-sun Ho-chi are examples of this." [Following, in part, the translation in Fung-Bodde, Vol. II, p. 83.]

From the point of view of historical study, this theory of Ho Hsiu of course can be granted no credence.[147] But if we view it simply as conveying a particular ideal of political progress, then we probably are justified in describing it as unprecedented. For the "Evolution of the Rites" ["Li Yün," chapter in the *Li Chi*] presents the concept of a "Great Community" [*Ta-t'ung*] that is nothing less than noble, but it provides for an age of "Minor Peace" [*Hsiao-k'ang*] to follow that of the Great Community, implying that there must occur some regression. Tung Chung-shu's "Three Sequences" offers a theoretical foundation that is quite extraordinary, but in its alternation of refinement and simplicity it, together with the doctrine of the "Five Periods" in the Ch'i version of the *Odes*, which indicates that successive endings and beginnings constitute the Way of heaven, assumes a cyclical law of history. Ho Hsiu's Three Ages go from Disorder through Ascending Peace to Universal Peace, therein being unique in their optimism about the ideal of progress. This may have been adopted from his school tradition, but, in any case, if Ho Hsiu had not written about it in his *Ch'un-ch'iu Kung-yang chieh-ku*, later ages would have no way of learning about this remarkably different conception.[148]

---

[147] See Chapter One, Section Six, of this book. Hu Shih, in his *Shuo Ju*, using, as evidence the passage in the *Analects* [IX/8; Waley, p. 140] that says: "The phoenix does not come; the river gives forth no chart. It is all over with me!" along with several items in the *Tso Commentary*, deduces that in the Spring and Autumn period there were persons who looked to Confucius to be the leader of the Yin peoples' restoration [to rule over China, by overturning the Chou], and that this is the basis of his "uncrowned King" appellation. His evidence, however, would seem to be inadequate.

[148] The *Ch'un-ch'iu fan-lu*, Section One, "Ch'u Chuang-wang" says: "The *Spring and Autumn Annals* divides the twelve reigns [chronicled therein] into three categories: that directly witnessed; that heard about; that known through transmitted records. . . . Regarding what he [Confucius] directly witnessed he uses subtle phraseology; regarding what he heard about, he expresses sorrow for calamities; regarding what he knew through transmitted records, he sets his compassion aside. This is to accord with the feelings." [Modified from Fung/Bodde, Vol. II, p. 81.] There is absolutely nothing here of the concept of political progress. K'ang Yu-wei of the Ch'ing dynasty held that the Great Community should constitute the Age of Universal Peace. He also said that the hexagrams of the *Book of Changes* may be either compliant or contrary. The inner hexagrams provide for the three ages in counter sequence, from the Age of Universal Peace (primitive chaos) descending to the Age of Disorder (the Three dynasties of Antiquity). The outer hexagrams provide for compliance with the sequence of the Three Ages, from the Age of Disorder (the Spring and Autumn period on through to the Ch'ing) [to 1911] entering into the era of Universal Peace (the Great Community). He has smelted the past and the

SECTION FIVE
From Huan T'an to Chung-ch'ang T'ung (A.D. 179–219)

FOLLOWING the Emperor Kuang-wu's restoration of the Han dynasty: "There was a bifurcation along higher and lower status lines, forming two factions. The state's official proclamations continued to adhere to the prognostication texts and apocrypha. All major events at the Eastern [Later] Han capital were dealt with according to the prescriptions drawn from the Five Agents theories and the interpretation of calamities and prodigies. Yet, these were looked upon as mere formulas eliciting little genuine faith. When calamities and prodigies occurred, one of the Three Lords [*san kung*, holders of three highest substantive posts in the court] would be retired, but that came to be no more than a convenient means by which consort clan members and eunuchs could manipulate appointments. Scholarly types at the National University all repudiated prognostication theories and the apocryphal works and directed their approval toward other kinds of learning."[149] It would appear that anyone possessing even a modicum of judgment could see through the specious fabrications comprising the *T'u-lu* [texts dealing in particular with portents legitimating the Mandate]. Except for persons whose minds were set on winning imperial favor and personal advantage, not even the awesome authority of the Son of Heaven could compel people to believe and accept those.

Repudiation of the prognostication works was initiated by Huan T'an during the reign of the Emperor Kuang-wu [A.D. 25–57], and that nearly cost him his life. Even more worthy of mention, however, are the critical remonstrances of Yin Min and the clear-minded arguments of Chang Heng. The Emperor Kuang-wu looked upon Yin Min as a person of broad learning, hence commanded him to edit the prognostication texts so as to expurgate all items added to support Wang Mang. Yin Min responded: " 'The prognostication works are not from the hands of the Sages. They contain many passages using vulgar and virtually unintelligible expressions, very close in style to the coarse phrases current among the ignorant people. I would fear that [by retaining these works] we shall only bring doubt and error upon later persons studying them.' The Em-

---

present, China and the outside world in one crucible, leaving Ho Hsiu staring in the dust far behind.

[149] Hsia Tseng-yu [died 1924], *Chung-kuo ku tai shih*, p. 342. Note that the *Hou Han Shu* in *ch*. 89, "Biography of Chang Heng," says: "In the beginning the Emperor Kuang-wu valued prognostication works, and later the Emperors Hsien-Tsung and Su-tsung [i.e., Ming and Chang, reigned A.D. 58–88] followed the ancestral precedent. Thus from the dynasty's restoration onward, Confucians have scrambled to study the prognostication works and the apocrypha."

peror did not heed him. Yin Min filled in the spaces where passages had been expurgated by adding the words: [what follows is an untranslatable riddle in the manner of the prognostication texts, i.e., *chün wu k'ou, wei Han fu* 君無口, 爲漢輔, the import being 'Yin Min is a supporter of the Han dynasty']. On seeing this, the Emperor was mystified, so he summoned Yin Min, to ask him what it meant. Yin Min replied: 'Without weighing my worth, I have dared [to do what they have done] hoping thereby to gain an outside chance [of receiving imperial favor].'"[150]

During the reign of Emperor Shun [A.D. 126–144], Chang Heng submitted a memorial stating that the prognostication works were of recent provenance and were incompatible with the teachings of the ancient Sages. He went on to cite, passage by passage, their incongruities and errors. He commented: "In the *Documents* it states that [the Sage Emperor] Yao sent Kun to bring the flooding waters under control, but that after nine years his efforts had come to naught, so Kun was kept prisoner until his death, and [his son, the Great] Yü then carried on his work with success. Yet the apocryphal work on the *Spring and Autumn Annals* states that Kung-kung [Yao's Minister of Works] was the one who succeeded in controlling the waters. All the prognostication works state that the Yellow Emperor took punitive measures against Ch'ih-yu, except that apocrypha on the *Odes* which alone states that upon the defeat of Ch'ih-yu, Yao [who was] generations later than the Yellow Emperor] then received the Mandate. The [apocryphal work supplementing the *Spring and Autumn Annals* called] *Ch'un-ch'iu yuan ming pao* contains references to Kung-shu Pan and Mo Ti. Yet the contexts in which they are named are from the Warring States era; they do not belong to the Spring and Autumn Period. This work also mentions that there is also an administrative division called Yi-chou, yet the establishment of Yi-chou dates only from the Han dynasty. It uses terms such as the *San Fu* [the three administrative officers of the Han capital] and the various mausolea ["*ling*," names by which Han rulers were posthumously known], so that the era from which these date can be known. As for the charts, they contain references coming down to the reign of the Emperor Ch'eng [32–7 B.C.]. In any chapter of these works there can be found numerous mutually inconsistent items. The words of the Sages certainly admit no such things. These works must have been concocted from thin air by persons deceiving their age for profit. . . . It would be best to call in all the prognostication charts and books, and totally prohibit and eliminate them. Then purple will no longer blind the eye to vermilion [see *Analects*, XVII/17], and the [true] canonical works will be without flaw."[151]

[150] *Hou Han Shu, ch.* 109-A, "Biographies of Confucians, Part One."
[151] *Hou Han Shu, ch.* 89, "Biography of Chang Heng."

Nonetheless, what these Later Han period Confucian scholars decried was that aspect of fabrication in the prognostication charts and books. Heaven-man correlations and theories about calamities and prodigies all were accepted as having canonical import, expressing the views of the Sages. Despite the repudiation of prognostication texts on the part of Cheng Hsing, Yin Min, Chang Heng, and others, those [heaven-man correlations and theories about portents] continued to be employed in urging or warning rulers. Heaven-man correlative theories, in consequence, showed some signs of perhaps regaining the aura they had possessed in Western [Former] Han times. However the rulers of the age, now no longer believing those, limited their responses to formulaic gestures such as quitting [temporarily the comforts of] the palace and assuming the blame [for disasters].[152] This reached the point that every time there occurred some disastrous event, "the Three Lords were severely reprimanded."[153] Compared with presenting a sacrificial sheep at the announcement of each new moon [*Analects*, iii/17, symbolic of a ritual form that had become irrelevant to the conduct of government], this practice was even less beneficial, and far more apt to be harmful. That is, those scholar-officials intent on rectifying the ruler and correcting the administration continued to rely on the same old methods, but those had become self-defeating. They saw their own weapon turned against themselves by treacherous and evil persons taking advantage of the situation.

The Confucians of the Later Han confined themselves to the preexisting ideas not only in the realm of heaven-man correlative thought; their political thought, generally speaking, was similarly deficient in new elements. The more prominent among them for their thought and learning

---

[152] Reference should be made to the "Basic Annals" of the various emperors, in the *Hou Han Shu*.

[153] From a memorial submitted during the reign of the Emperor An [A.D. 107–25], Ch'en Chung, remonstrating against removing the Three Lords from office because of calamities and prodigies. (*Hou Han Shu* 76, "Biography of Ch'en Chung.") At that time, from the first year of the Yung-ch'u reign period [A.D. 114] onward, such dismissals were frequent occurrences. Hsü Fang, who as Grand Commandant [one of the Three Lords] was dismissed because of calamities, prodigies, and bandits, was the first example. After him, in the fifth year of the Yung-ch'u reign period [118], Chang Yü "was dismissed from office because of disharmonies of the *Yin* and *Yang*." (*Hou Han Shu*, ch. 74, from his biography.) Yet this treatment is generous in comparison with that accorded the Chancellor Chai Fang-chin who, during the reign of Emperor Ch'eng [32–7 B.C.] had been ordered to commit suicide. During the Former Han period, Chancellors who were dismissed because of calamities and prodigies include K'ung Kuang, who was manipulated out of office by the consort Fu clan [during the reign of Emperor Ch'eng]. (*Han Shu*, ch. 81, "Biography of K'ung Kuang.") The Emperor Wen of the Wei dynasty, in the second year of the Huang-ch'u reign period [A.D. 221] issued an edict: "Hereafter, when accusations arise from [irregular phenomena of] heaven and earth, it shall no longer be permitted to hold the Three Lords responsible." (*Wei Shu*, ch. 2.)

were Huan T'an, Pan Ku, Wang Fu, Ts'ui Shih, Hsün Yüeh, Chung-ch'ang T'ung, and Hsü Kan.

Pan Ku was a historian; on the basis of his various prefaces and en-comiums [*hsü, tsan*] in his *History of the Former Han Dynasty* [*Han Shu*], it can be seen that his political thought stressed heaven's and man's interac-tions, venerated benevolence and righteousness, and clearly belonged to the mainstream of Confucian orthodoxy.[154]

Huan T'an, Wang Fu, Ts'ui Shih, Hsün Yüeh, and Hsü Kan all had as their intention to apply their lancets to current evils and be rid of them; they had very little that was new to say about the principles of govern-ment as such. If we measure their views on the Confucian scale, Huan T'an's and Ts'ui Shih's thought shows admixtures of strong statist [*pa* 霸] ideas, while the other three are somewhat more purely Confucian. In terms of chronology, only Huan T'an among these was born in the Former Han period; the others all were born during the reigns of Emperors Ho and An [A.D. 89–125] or later, and lived through the final century of the Later Han's gradual decline and fall. Huan T'an, emulating Lu Chia [see footnote 41, above] in the writing of the *Hsin yü* ["New Discourse"], wrote his *Hsin lun* ["New Treatise"] in twenty-nine essays, which he sub-mitted to the Emperor Kuang-wu. The book has long been lost; only fragments remain. One of the important concepts underlying Huan T'an's views on government, it would seem, was that of "according with the times" [*yin shih* 因時]. Thus he wrote: "All the Confucians, having fixed their gaze on the text of the *Spring and Autumn Annals*, record the successes and failings of government as if a Sage, should one again appear, would again produce those same *Annals*. To that I say 'Not so.' Why is that? It is because earlier Sages and later Sages will not necessarily follow in each other's traces."[155] For "One who is skilled in governing observes the

---

[154] Pan Ku's courtesy name was Meng-chien; he was born in the eighth year of the Chien-wu reign period and died in the fourth year of the Yung-yuan reign period (A.D. 32–92). His biography is in *ch.* 75 of the *Hou Han Shu.* See also his "Hsü chuan" ("author's postface"), *ch.* 100, of his *Han Shu.* His discourses on government are scattered among his prefaces to *ch.* 23, "Treatise on Penal Norms," *ch.* 24, "Treaties on Food and Money," *ch.* 26, "Treatise on Astronomy," *ch.* 89, "Biographies of Reasonable Officials," *ch.* 90, "Biographies of Harsh Officials," *ch.* 91, "Biographies of the Money-makers," as well as in the Basic Annals, e.g., *ch.* 4, "Emperor Wen," *ch.* 5, "Emperor Ching," *ch.* 7, "Emperor Chao," and in the Encomiums to *ch.* 48, "Biography of Chia Yi," *ch.* 62, "Biography of Ssu-ma Ch'ien," etc. The *Po-hu t'ung* ["Discussions in the White Tiger Hall"] has in the past carried Pan Ku's name as its author, but in reality it is a pastiche assembled from many hands. (See Hung Yeh, "Preface" to *Index to the Po-hu t'ung.*) [Translations of chap-ter titles follow Hulsewé, Swann and Watson.]

[155] From the fragments as preserved in Sun Feng-yi's *Wen-ching-t'ang ts'ung-shu* [pub-lished in 1797–1802]. The *Hsin lun* was no longer extant [as an integral text] already in the Sung dynasty. Huan T'an was born during the Kan-lu reign period of the Emperor

common practices of the people and then applies his teachings; he examines their failings and then establishes ways of preventing those. Intimidation and benevolent concern prevail alternately; the civil and the military means are employed in turn."[156] The True King [*wang*] and the Powerful Hegemon [*pa*] represent differing methods, yet "both may possess the empire, be the ruler over the myriad people, and transmit their rule to sons and grandsons; in these things they are the same."[157]

Ts'ui Shih advanced views that "clearly indicated the most pressing of current problems, in words that were discerning and hard-hitting." Moreover, he "possessed thorough understanding of the governmental institutions; and had more than ample talent for office-holding"; he was still closer to Legalism than was Huan T'an. His discourses on government were praised by Chung-ch'ang T'ung, who said of them: "Any ruler should copy them out by hand and place them beside his seat."

Fan Yeh's *History of the Later Han Dynasty* records the essential elements in Ts'ui Shih's political thought as follows: "Whenever the empire is in disorder, that must occur when the ruler has long known an era of peace, when the people's practices have gradually grown corrupt but he fails to become aware, when the governing has slipped gradually into decline but he fails to reform it. When the kingly discipline is allowed to grow lax at the top, the wise scholar-official below becomes frustrated and unhappy." If effort is not expended to bring about a midpoint recovery [*chung-hsing* 中興], the pains of peril and collapse cannot be avoided. On the other hand, however, "Why should one presume that methods for saving the times and delivering the age must cling to Yao, imitate Shun, before order can be achieved! If one hopes to patch up the broken dykes, prop up the sagging pillars, one must cut and chop according to real conditions, for the essential task is no more or less than to maneuver these times toward security and stability. Therefore, when the Sages took command in crisis they designed institutions as the times demanded. Step by step they devised their individual ways, neither compelling people to do what they were incapable of, nor ignoring the urgencies at hand while admiring deeds known only by reports of the past. . . . In these present times, since it is not possible to model actions purely on the eight generations [of a golden antiquity, i.e., the reigns of the Three August Rulers and the Five Imperial Rulers, *san-huang wu-ti*], then it is quite appropriate to mix in elements from the Hegemons' governing. Thus it is appropriate to

---

Hsüan, and died during the Chien-wu reign period of the Emperor Kuang-wu, at the age of over seventy. (The Kan-lu reign period included the four years from 53–50 B.C.) His biography is in *Hou Han Shu*, ch. 48-A.

[156] *Hou Han Shu*, ch. 48-A; the quotation is from his "Statement concerning current government," i.e., "Ch'en shih-cheng shu."

[157] [From the text fragments in] *Wen-ching-t'ang ts'ung-shu.*

increase rewards and intensify punishments, thereby gaining control of
the situation; and give prominence to laws and methods, thereby keeping
check on things. . . . The Emperor Hsüan [reigned 73–49 B.C.] profoundly
understood the way of ruling over men, and had examined the principles
underlying governmental measures. In consequence, he made the laws
strict and the punishments severe, thereby demolishing that temerity that
leads to treacherous acts. All within the seas was purified and stilled; all
the empire was tranquil. He contributed achievement at the ancestral
shrine and is favored with the appellation *Chung-tsung* ["the successful
emperor"; this title was granted him posthumously by the Emperor
Kuang-wu in A.D. 43, in respect for his achievements]. His calculations
were efficacious, more so than those of the Emperor Wen [reigned
179–157 B.C., famous for lenient government]. When Emperor Yüan
[reigned 48–33 B.C.] came to the throne he implemented numerous
lenient measures, and in the end he fell victim to them. The imperial
might and awe was first wrested away [in his reign], and he became the
ruler who laid the foundation for the Han dynasty's disaster." When we
look into the administrative actions that characterized the reigns of Emperors Huan and Ling [reigned A.D. 147–188] we can understand Ts'ui
Shih's purpose in expressing such arguments. Nonetheless, he had not
really made a clean break with Confucian governing methods. In fact,
he acknowledged that "To set the norms for the state can be compared
with caring for one's health; in the usual circumstances, just nourish it,
but when there is disease, take active measures against that. The penalties
and fines [*hsing-fa* 刑罰] are medicine for controlling disorder. Benevolent
teachings are as the fine grains and meats of flourishing times. But to use
benevolent teachings wherewith to eradicate violence would be like
using fine grains and meats with which to control disease. To employ
penalties and fines as regulators for ordinary times would be like relying on
medicines to supply one's nourishment."[158]

---

[158] *Hou Han Shu, ch.* 82, "Biography of Ts'ui Shih. Ts'ui Shih's courtesy name was
Tzu-chen. At the beginning of Emperor Huan's reign [A.D. 147–67] he was selected by
provincial authorities for appointment as a court attendant. His *Discourse on Government,
Cheng lun,* contains the phrase: "In the three-hundred and fifty-odd years since the
founding of the Han dynasty"; this work therefore must have been written during the
Chien-ho or Yung-hsing reign periods of the Emperor Huan (147–154). He at one time
joined with the Erudits in preparing definitive texts of the Five Classics. He died during
the *Chien-ning* reign period of Emperor Ling (A.D. 168–71). The *Yü-han shan-fang chi-yi-shu*
[Collectanea of books "restored in fragments," compiled by Ma Kuo-han, 1794–1857]
includes Ts'ui Shih's *Cheng-lun* as the first item under the heading of Legalist works; that
would seem to be somewhat inappropriate. Actually, it is a work of Confucianism combined with Legalism; the fact that it is not purely Confucian does not justify classifying it
as the work of one of Shen Pu-hai's and Lord Shang's later followers.

Surviving writings of Wang Fu, Hsün Yüeh, and Hsü Kan are some-what more numerous, and they occasionally display new ideas. Wang Fu's courtesy name was Chieh-hsin; he was a friend of Ma Jung, Chang Heng, and others. From the reigns of Emperors Ho and An [reigned A.D. 89–125] and onward the age was marked by a great striving for career advancement, but Wang Fu was stubbornly upright; moreover he was looked upon with some contempt because he had no powerful relatives by marriage, thereby lacking that aid to advancement. "With deep feelings of frustrated will and resentment," he lived the life of a recluse and wrote a book in thirty-six sections, but did not attach his name to it; he called it *Ch'ien-fu lun* ["Discourses from an obscure man"].[159] The central purpose of the entire work is to reaffirm the governmental principles of heaven's [cosmic] ordering, and of the basic importance of the people. It expatiates at length upon the governing methods of employing the worthy and vener-ating virtue. In discussing the relationship of heaven and man, and of ruler and people, although his ideas are drawn from the past, his language achieves great precision and force. He states: "In all the ruler of men's governing there is nothing more important than being in harmony with the *Yin* and *Yang*. The *Yin* and *Yang* are rooted in heaven. When the mind of heaven is complied with, then there is harmony with the *Yin* and *Yang*. When the mind of heaven is contravened, then the *Yin* and *Yang* are discordant. Heaven takes the people as its mind. When the people are secure and happy, then heaven's mind has been complied with. When the people are sad and in distress, then heaven's mind has been contravened. The people take the ruler as their overlord. When the ruler's governing is good, then the people are harmonious and orderly. When the ruler's governing is bad, then the people are resentful and disorderly."[160]

Wang Fu also discussed the origins of government as proof of his theo-ries: "In earliest antiquity, when the ordinary people commenced their first activities, there was as yet no [distinction of] superior and inferior, and people nonetheless maintained a natural order. Heaven had not yet taken action and rulers were not yet established. Subsequently, people became somewhat more deceitful and oppressive, whether inflicting in-jury and cruelty, or seeking to take advantage of one another, in those ways bringing great harm to all the ordinary people. Thereupon heaven

---

[159] *Hou Han Shu*, *ch.* 79, "Biography of Wang Fu." His biography quotes from five of the sections: "Kuei chung," "Fou ch'ih," "Shih kung," "Ai jih," and "Shu she"; [i.e., *ch.* 11, 12, 14, 18 and 16; *ch.* 11 is called "Kuei chung" as quoted in the *Hou Han Shu*, but "Chung kuei" in most editions of *Ch'ien-fu lun*.]

[160] *Ch'ien-fu lun*, *ch.* 9, "Pen cheng." This book exists in several editions, e.g., those in the *Ssu-pu ts'ung-kan*, the *Han-Wei ts'ung-shu*, the *Po-tzu ch'üan-shu*, and the *Tzu-shu po-chia*. The quotations in this section all are taken from the edition collated and annotated by Wang Chi-p'ei [preface date 1814], included in the *Hu-hai-lou ts'ung-shu*.

gave its charge [Mandate] to a Sage to act as the superintendent and shepherd of the people, so that they should not lose their proper nature. [See *Tso chuan*, Hsiang 14; Legge, p. 411.] All within the four seas bene-fited; there were none to whom his virtuous concern did not extend, and all in unison supported and acknowledged him [the Sage], calling him the Son of Heaven. Thus heaven's act of establishing the ruler was not biased in favor of this person, to grant him the labor of the people. Rather it was so that he could extirpate violence and eliminate harm, to benefit all the masses of the people."[161] The ruler of men became the Son of Heaven by right of receiving the Mandate; the servitors of the ruler supported him in their capacity as "officers of heaven" [*t'ien-kuan* 天官]. "Hence the en-lightened ruler would not dare bestow [office upon them] for selfish rea-sons, nor would the loyal servitor dare receive it falsely. To take other persons' valuables is what is called being a bandit; how much more [would one deserve to be called that] if he should acquire an office of heaven by theft for his own selfish advantage."[162]

Even though Wang Fu's discussions on the methods of governing some-what lack creative elements, each of his pointed thrusts revealed needs and deficiencies of the time in a way quite unlike the usual empty plati-tudes and vague generalities. To put it briefly, there were problems in appointing personnel, in reforming the penal regulations, and in suppress-ing extravagance. The important issue in appointing persons to office lay in widely listening to advice and in examining records of achievement.[163] In this, his thought is fairly close to Hsün Tzu. Wang also forcefully at-tacked the practice of selecting scholar-officials on the basis of their fame and reputation; Grand Administrators' and Chancellors' [*shou-hsiang* 守相, i.e., governors of provincial units] controlling regions that were too large; and the institution of certain offices and ranks being hereditary. "Factions are moved by private interests; they ignore realities and seek after superificial appearances."[164] This describes the evil of selecting persons for office on the basis of their reputations only.

---

[161] *Ibid.*, *ch.* 15, "Pan lu."

[162] *Ibid.*, *ch.* 11, "Kuei chung." See also in this connection the *Han Shu*, *ch.* 23, "Hsing-fa chih" ["Treatise on Penal Norms"], in the "Introduction" to which Pan Ku gives his "Discourse on the Origins of Government." [Translated by Hulsewé, *Remnants of Han Law*, vol. I, pp. 321–332.]

[163] *Ibid.*, *chs.* 6 and 7, "Ming an" and "K'ao chi."

[164] *Ibid.*, *ch.* 14, "Shih kung." This essay also says: "Those whose minds are set on the Way have few friends, while those who pursue the vulgar ways have numerous compan-ions." And, further: "For, as regards the official, it is his specific abilities that are to be valued; it is not necessary to expect one man to be capable of everything." [*Cf. Analects* XVII/10; also XIII/25; following Waley, pp. 222–23.] And, "The wise person disregards a man's shortcomings and uses his talents in order to produce results. Nowadays one employing those recommended for appointment must by all means investigate the facts;

[They have] "awesome authority and overwhelming power, greater than that of the feudal lords [of antiquity]; yet in shining talent or virtuous uprightness they are not necessarily superior to the men of old. . . . They violate all the laws and regulations, set aside and ignore all the edicts and commands. They devote themselves solely to their own interests and feel no care or concern for their public duties." This describes the evils inherent in regional governors' controlling territories of too great size. "Accomplishing nothing for the Han dynasty; offering no benevolent concern for the people; they monopolize their states, facing the south [in the ceremonial position of the King], and supinely consume their vast revenues."[165] This describes the evils in hereditary office and rank.

When we examine the late Han conditions, the recommendations for official appointment coming from the commanderies and the counties, the hereditary titles granted to the nobles, and the despotic manner adopted by the Regional Inspectors [*Tz'u-shih*; in effect, regional war lords], we must feel that Wang Fu's words are both profoundly discerning and aptly succinct. In his advocacy of the basic importance of agriculture and of suppressing wasteful extravagance[166] he also mercilessly excoriates degenerate customs, and similarly with realistic intent. His theories on reforming penal institutions focused on maintaining law and order in the state, and were particularly appropriate medicine for the age following the reigns of Emperors Ho and An. Wang Fu wrote: "The reason why the people do not become disorderly is that officials are set over them. The reason that the officials do not commit treacheries is that there are laws governing office-holding. The reason that the laws are complied with is that the state has a ruler. The reason that the ruler's status is elevated is that he possesses righteousness in his person. The righteousness that he possesses in his person is [what establishes] the ruler's government. Laws are the ruler's commands. The ruler of men is correct in his thoughts as he issues his commands, therefore no one, be he noble or humble, worthy or ignorant, can violate those; so it is that the ruler occupies the position above, while below the masses of the people are well-governed. If the ruler issues a command with which the noble servitors and proud officials do not comply, then the ruler faces regicide and the people are at the brink of chaos. For the laws and commands are that by which the ruler makes use

---

those who are found to have minor blemishes should not be under compulsion to camouflage those." [The Chinese text here follows the quotations from *ch.* 14 in Wang Fu's biography, *ch.* 79, in the *Hou Han Shu*; Wang Chi-p'ei's text is slightly different.] This anticipates the style by which, under the Ts'ao rulers' Wei dynasty [A.D. 220–264] officials were employed according to standards stressing skills and with little concern for ethical qualities.

[165] *Ibid.*, *ch.* 17, "San shih."
[166] *Ibid.*, *ch.* 12, "Fou ch'ih," and *ch.* 18, "Ai jih."

of his state.· If the ruler issues commands that are not obeyed, it is equivalent to there being no ruler." The ruler's commands are as all-important as that. "In consequence, officials who recklessly violate laws and servitors who recklessly fabricate commands must be executed."[167] These theories favoring the elevation of the ruler and the importance of his commands would seem to be incompatible with the Confucians' principle of transforming through virtuous suasion. Wang Fu explained that: "Critics are certain to hold that punishments and death penalties should not be used and that moral suasion's transforming force can be solely relied upon. This is not the argument of one who understands changing circumstances; it is not the words of one who would deliver the age. For surpassing Sageliness, none exceeded Yao and Shun, yet they banished the four [high officials who failed in their duties; see *Documents*, ii/i/3/12; Legge, p. 40]. In abundance of virtue, none exceeded Kings Wen and Wu, yet they arose majestic in wrath. . . . [*Odes*, iii/i/vii/5; Legge, p. 453.] Thus there are instances of applying the death penalty to stop killings, of using punishments to ward off depredations. For, bringing the world to a state of order is like climbing a hill; it is necessary first to cross over its lower slopes before one can then tread its heights. That is why the world must first be brought into an orderly condition; after that, the government of the Three Kings [of antiquity] can be implemented. When the Way has been brought about, to the level of the Three Kings, the transformation [through moral suasion] of the Five Rulers can then be practiced. When the Way has been brought about, to the level of the Five Rulers, thereafter the great Way of the Three August Emperors can be followed."[168]

Government in the Later Han, in the era from the Emperors Ho and An onward [ca. A.D. 100], rather nicely re-enacted the degeneration of Former Han government from the reigns of Emperors Yuan and Ch'eng onward [from 48 B.C.]. The imperial authority fell into the hands of associates, the ruler's own power became insignificant, consort clans and eunuchs usurped authority and threw government into disorder. These statements of Wang Fu indeed hit the crucial issues, and they resound in tones similar to those of Huan T'an and Ts'ui Shih; this also displays the force of the circumstances under which they wrote.

Hsün Yüeh's courtesy name was Chung-yü; he was a thirteenth-generation lineal descendant of the philosopher Hsün Tzu. At the age of eleven he could lecture on the *Spring and Autumn Annals*. During the reign of Emperor Ling [A.D. 168–188], when eunuchs wielded great power,

---

[167] *Ibid.*, *ch.* 20, "Shuai chih."

[168] *Ibid.*, *ch.* 20, "Shuai chih." [Adopting Wang Chi-p'ei's exegesis of the second translated sentence.] However, *ch.* 33, "Te hua," still firmly maintains the ancient idea that instruction in virtue constitutes the basic method of governing.

Hsün Yüeh used the pretense of illness as excuse for living as a recluse. When Emperor Hsien came to the throne [A.D. 189], Hsün Yüeh was appointed to the staff of Ts'ao Ts'ao, the General of the Eastern Command. His service in office eventually took him to the post of Palace Secretariat Attendant. The actual governing had shifted into Ts'ao Ts'ao's hands; the Son of Heaven reigned in name only. Hsün Yüeh thought deeply about loyal advice to aid the emperor, but that was never adopted. Consequently, he composed the *Shen chien* in five sections and submitted that to the throne. In the fourteenth year of the Chien-an reign period [209] he died, at the age of sixty-one.[169]

Although Hsün Yüeh was a descendant of Hsün Tzu, he did not adhere closely to that family tradition in learning. Hsün Tzu spoke of "the distinction between heaven and man," while Hsün Yüeh adopted from the Han Confucians the theory about "heaven's and man's mutual interactions." Thus in his essay on "The Forms of Government" [*cheng t'i*] he says: "Heaven provides the Way; the Emperor provides the cosmic axis; the servitors provide the supports; the people provide the base." He also says: "Elements comprising the governing of the former wise kings were: one, to acknowledge heaven; two, to make one's person upright; three, to employ the worthy; four, to feel concern for the people; five, to make the institutes of government clearly manifest; and six, to engender accomplishment."[170] Among these six items, it is in his comments on acknowledging heaven that Hsün Yüeh brings forth some rather novel ideas. He states that the ruler of men must acknowledge heaven, because heaven and earth alone produce living beings and "the ruler of men is one who has received heaven's Mandate to sustain and nurture the people."[171] Moreover, in as much as heaven responds to the faults and errors of government with calamities and prodigies, the ruler of men should by all means observe such portentous warnings and change his ways.[172] The essential purport of acknowledging heaven does not go far beyond these ideas.

Yet Hsün Yüeh was able to cast off completely the superstitions that had grown up during the two Han eras concerning *Yin* and *Yang*, prognostica-

---

[169] His biography is in *ch.* 92 of the *Hou Han Shu*. On the basis of his death date it can be known that Hsün Yüeh was born in the second year of the Emperor Huan's Chien-ho reign period (148–209). The *Shen chien*, i.e., "the proffered mirror," exists in such editions as: the *Ssu-pu ts'ung-k'an*, *Po-tzu ch'üan-shu*, *Tzu-shu po-chia*, and the *Han Weit s'ung-shu*. The latter also has his [collected works called] *Hsün Shih-chung chi*. In addition, there also exists a work of Hsün Yüeh's, the *Han Chi*, in thirty sections.

[170] *Shen chien, ch.* 1, "Cheng t'i."

[171] *Ibid., ch.* 4, "Tsa-yen, shang." In this connection, reference should also be made, in Hsün Yüeh's collected works, the *Hsün Shih-chung chi*, to his "Kao-tsu tsan" ["Eulogy of the Emperor Kao-tsu," the Han Founder].

[172] "Discourse on Calamities and Prodigies" ["Tsai-yi lun"], in Hsün's collected works.

tion texts and the apocrypha, and conveyed with great clarity the spirit of "the superior man who quietly and calmly awaits the appointments of heaven." [See *Doctrine of the Mean*, xiv/4; Legge, p. 396.] He explained: "Calamitous and auspicious portents sometimes are borne out, and sometimes not. . . . It is in the nature of things and events that some come about spontaneously, and some come about through human effort (while some) do not come about if they lack human effort, and others, though benefiting from human effort, still in the end cannot be brought about. This is what is called the three potentialities [*san shih* 三勢]. . . . Nowadays when people observe that something is unmoving, they say of that: 'Human effort is irrelevant.' Aware of something in which spiritual forces are flowing, they say of that: 'Heaven and man have combined their efforts and work in conjunction.' In both cases, they have seized upon but one feature and have failed to take note of the entire course of events. . . . The design underlying the three potentialities is always most profoundly difficult to recognize; therefore the superior man exerts his mental and physical efforts to the full [in his undertakings] and relies on heaven's command [*ming*, to decide the outcome]."[173] This theory combines elements from Confucius and Mo Tzu, from Mencius and Hsün Tzu, finding a mid-point among them. Judged by modern standards, even though it may be objected that Hsün Yüeh has not been sufficiently thoroughgoing in his analyses, in terms of disciplining the self while pursuing a career in government, he quite clearly achieves that state in which "the truly good know no anxiety." [See *Analects* xiv/30.] His attitude certainly is healthier than that of Wang Ch'ung with his fatalistic views.

In his discussions of heaven's and man's interactions Hsün Yüeh did not perpetuate the family learning [as established by Hsün Tzu], but in his methods of governing he more or less preserves the earlier views of Hsün Tzu concerning government by the rites [*li*]. He said: "The methods for achieving good government are first to banish the four afflictions, then to uphold the five administrative tasks. The first [of the former] is falsity, the second is selfishness, the third is self-indulgence, and the fourth is extravagance. Falsity throws the people's customs into disorder. Selfishness wreaks damage on the laws. Self-indulgence leads to transgressing the proprieties. Extravagance destroys the institutions. . . . When the people's customs are in disorder, morality will be abandoned. . . . When the laws suffer damage, then the times face decline. . . . When the proprieties are transgressed, then the rites are lost. . . . When the institutions are destroyed, then the desires will have full license. . . . These are called the four afflictions. To promote agriculture and sericulture in order to nourish their [the people's] lives; to investigate the good and the bad in order to

[173] *Op.cit. supra.*

make their customs upright; to disseminate cultivation and instruction in order to encourage their moral transformation; to erect military preparations in order to hold up his [the ruler's] majesty; to make rewards and penalties clear and precise so as to provide control over his laws; these are called the five administrative tasks."[174] Nourishing the people's lives holds the meaning of providing all the state's wants while enriching the people. To make the people's customs upright implies the idea of insisting that the reality correspond to the name. To encourage the people's ethical improvement calls upon the rites and teachings. Holding up the ruler's majesty means having sufficient military strength. Control over the laws means dispensing precise rewards while making penalties invariable and certain. All of these are points that Hsün Tzu had earlier elucidated and that Hsün Yüeh now offers again.

Nonetheless, the political theories embodied in the *Shen chien* are not unrelated to the actualities [of Hsün Yüeh's own experience]. Hsün Tzu's views on governing are by far the strictest and most rigorous within the Confucian fold, and came close to those of the Legalists; they were equal to the task of delineating all the evils springing from dissolution of the bonds and norms, which so characterized the end of the Han. Hsün Yüeh's four afflictions and five administrative tasks thus certainly were not mere high-flown bombast. He also favored a restoration of the feudal [*feng-chien*] order, probably because he hoped to eliminate the danger, in the [directly administered] commandery-county system, of the ruler's isolation, which could so easily lead to usurpation [of his authority, or even his position]. Hsün Yüeh said that the Sage Kings established the institutions with which to provide for the people. As a result, the feudal nobles all possessed their noble status in hereditary succession. "And the king then held unified control over all in supervising his government. Then should any one be guilty of offenses against ritual propriety within his feudal state, the people below would rise in revolt and the king would apply punishment from above. . . . In a situation where the Son of Heaven behaved improperly, the feudal lords would correct him; if the royal court was weak, the great feudal states then would support it. Although the king might lack virtue, he could not inflict cruelties upon the whole realm." This describes the basic great advantage in the feudal order: it could provide the means for giving the people enduring peace. When previous ages had practiced it and faults emerged, those were engendered by mistakes in the size of the feudal territories. During the Hsia and Yin [Shang] dynasties, large states were no larger than one hundred *li* in

---

[174] *Shen chien, ch.* 1, "Cheng t'i." Hsün's collected works include an "essay on establishing institutions" ["Li chih-tu lun"] expounding with particular clarity the essential meaning of government by rites, which might be consulated.

extent; the mistake was in making them too small. "Thus the feudal lords were weak and the Son of Heaven was powerful; [the tyrant last kings of each] Chieh and Chou could practice their cruelties without restraint." The Chou dynasty enfieffed large states up to five-hundred *li* in extent, which was to over-correct, to the extent that the trunk was weak and the branches strong, and they struggled chaotically until all were overthrown and destroyed. The Ch'in dynasty then abruptly introduced sweeping change, replacing the feudal order with the commanderies and the counties. "To unify all authority, to centralize control over the whole empire." The result of that was "When the ruler behaved improperly, then the entire realm uniformly suffered; when the ordinary people revolted then the whole nation crumbled, and there was no means to correct or to save the situation." The Han dynasty was heir to the faults of both the Chou and the Ch'in dynasties, simultaneously establishing both commanderies and princedoms. But its mistake was in making these too strong and too large, in consequence of which it encountered the disastrous revolts of the Six Princes and the Seven States [154 B.C.]. Subsequently, the Han totally eliminated the power of its feudal lords. In this, "the institutions of the present are not necessarily the methods employed by the Hundred Kings [of antiquity]."[175]

Hsün Yüeh's views on this issue are close to those of Chia Yi, and the opposite of Wang Fu's views. Wang Fu's concern was drawn to the actual cases of princes and nobles whose conduct was unrestrained and rapacious. Chia Yi and Hsün Yüeh both expressed their dismay with authoritarian government. Also, Hsün Yüeh, expressing his feelings on the eve of the Later Han's collapse, probably was still more deeply dismayed than Chia Yi had been. Later, during the Wei and Chin eras, Ts'ao Chiung and Lu Chi [during the third century] continued to expand on such views [favoring restoration of certain feudal forms], and in the *Chen-kuan* reign era [of the early T'ang] proposals favoring enfieffing [princes of the imperial line in hereditary] states were again discussed.[176] These kinds of evidence are testimony to the unbounded concern and suspicion that more than four hundred years of authoritarian rule had planted in the minds of some perceptive persons. Yet in offering their theories, they were incapable of breaking out of the cycle of the one king and the five grades [of his feudal lords, as in the idealized Chou dynasty system]. Even though their diagnosis was profoundly clear-minded about the crux of the problem, the prescriptions they prepared were for medicines in no way strong enough to counteract this deep-seated and chronic disease.

---

[175] "Discourse on the Feudal Nobles," i.e., "Lieh hou lun," in Hsün's collected works.
[176] See, [Ts'ao] *Wei Shu, ch.* 20 [Po-na edition, p. 16-b ff.], commentary, [quoting from a memorial of Ts'ao Chiung, "of the imperial clan"]; also, *Chin Shu, ch.* 54, "Biography of Lu Chi"; and the *Chen-kuan cheng-yao,* "Feng-chien p'ien."

Hsü Kan's courtesy name was Wei-ch'ang; he was one of the group who, along with K'ung Jung, Wang Ts'an, and others, were called the Seven Masters of the Chien-an Period. He wrote a book called the *Chung lun* in more than twenty sections.[177] Although this work has received considerable praise, that in fact has been for the classical elegance of its literary style; as for its content, it "advanced the tenets of Confucius and Mencius."[178] It contains virtually no original views of the author, and therefore can be passed over here with no further comment.

Although Chung-ch'ang T'ung's book is no longer in existence, his thought reveals quite a number of unusual elements, and therefore demands some comment. Chung-ch'ang T'ung's courtesy name was Kung-li. As a youth he was strongly drawn to learning; he had no patience for the niceties [of conventional behavior], and people sometimes labelled him an "eccentric fellow" [or "madman" "*k'uang sheng*" 狂生]. At first he lived the life of a recluse, refusing appointment to office; later on, through the introduction of Hsün Yü [Hsün Yüeh's brother], he joined the military advisory staff of the Chancellor, Ts'ao Ts'ao. His discourses ranged through all of past and present, on the customs of the age and on the conduct of affairs; he wrote a work of more than one-hundred thousand characters in length, in thirty-four sections, called the *Ch'ang yen*. He died at the age of forty in the twenty-fourth year of the Chien-an period.[179] In discussions of governing methods, Chung-ch'ang T'ung listed sixteen "administrative objectives"; these do not go beyond the standard kind of Confucian pronouncements.[180] When, however, he came to investigate the causes of social order and disorder, he struck to the very core of the weaknesses of the authoritarian political system, expressing things of which earlier persons had not spoken. He said: "When a mighty leader [*hao-chieh* 豪傑] assumes the Mandate [by dint of sheer ability], he does not at first have legitimate claim [*fen* 分] to the empire. Because he lacks such claim, competing claimants rise to contest his position in war. At such a juncture all of them pretending to have received heaven's authorization, assemble armed forces, occupy various parts of the realm,

---

[177] *Wei Shu, ch.* 21, "Biography of Wang Ts'an." Hsü Kan died in the twenty-second year of the Chien-an reign period [217]. The extant *Chung lun* consists of 20 sections [*p'ien*]; editions include those in the *Ssu-pu ts'ung-k'an* and the *Han-Wei ts'ung-shu.*

[178] *Chung lun,* "Preface" by Tseng Kung [1019–1083].

[179] *Hou Han Shu, ch.* 79, "Biography of Chung-ch'ang T'ung." From the year of his death we can calculate that his birthdate falls in the second year of the Kuang-ho reign period of the Emperor Ling [179–219]. The *Ch'ang yen* ["Straightforward Talk"] by Sung times already had dwindled to only fifteen sections, and subsequently was wholly lost. Fragments can be found in his biography in the *Hou Han Shu* and in the *Yü-han shan-fang chi yi shu.*

[180] *Ch'ang yen,* "Sun Yi p'ien."

and match their wit, cunning, daring, or military strength with his. . . . [Eventually], when those who compete with cunning all become exhausted and those who struggle with force have suffered defeat—when it is no longer feasible for them to resist him—then and only then will they, heads bending and necks leashed, submit to his halter and harness. . . . Then, during the reign of his successor, the people's hearts and minds will settle. Throughout the empire all depend on him for life and livelihood, and receive from him the means to wealth and high station. . . . Impulses of would-be mighty leaders will all have been stilled; ambitions of scholars and commoners will remain in proper bounds. Noble status will reside in certain clans; supreme dignity will inhere in one person [the ruler]. At this time, should even a person of the lowest and dullest talents occupy the throne, he could still be a fount of grace equal to heaven and earth, and would be clothed in awesome majesty matching that of spirits and deities. . . .

"Subsequently [however], a stupid ruler seeing that no one in the empire dare challenge him, regards himself as being perpetual, like heaven and earth. He thereupon indulges in his private passions and rushes to vent his base desires. He abandons all aspects of governing to utter neglect, relegating men and things to destruction. . . . His trusted and cherished appointees are all specious talkers, flatterers, sycophants; those he favors with noble status and great riches are all members of his empresses' and harem women's clans. . . . Eventually he will have decocted the wealth [literally, *chih-kao* 脂膏, the fat and grease] of the whole empire—extracting [figuratively speaking] the people's marrow by smashing their bones while they are still alive. Resentment and hatred will give rise to despair. Unrest and disorder will spread everywhere. The Central Realm [*Chung-kuo* 中國] will be in turmoil; the barbarians on the four sides will rebel and invade. The entire scene will disintegrate and, one morning, all will be lost. Those who until recently were nourished as sons and grandsons at his breast, now all will have become implacable enemies seeking his blood. Is this not proof that wealth and high status engender unkindliness, and that deeply ingrained habits lead to blind foolishness? Thus [dynasties] rise and fall, one after another; order and chaos from now on will move in recurring cycles. This is the constant great design of heaven's Way.

"[Moreover], chaotic periods are long and orderly ones are brief"; the later the time in history, the more severe the disasters. The disorders of the Warring States Period were worse than those of the Spring and Autumn Period, while the atrocities accompanying the fall of Ch'in and the rebellion of Hsiang Yü [in the civil war leading to the Han founding] exceeded those of the Warring States; then the Hsin dynasty of the usurper Wang Mang spread death and destruction in numbers several times those at the fall of Ch'in and the war against Hsiang Yü. "And coming now to our own time, famous capital cities are emptied and untenable, while the inhabitants of extensive areas [*pai li* 百里] are exterminated, the number of whom is beyond reckoning. This then is a still worse age than that witnessing the fall of [Wang Mang's] Hsin dynasty. How sad! In less than five hundred years great disasters have arisen three times, not counting the intermediary disturbances that have occurred on numerous occasions. Upheavals become ever more malicious; the more time passes, the more cruel they are. To infer from this, the future might well see the end of everything. Alas! One wonders what means the Sages of the future may find to deliver the world. One wonders, too, if this [great] design is extended to its bitter end, to what would one wish someday to turn?"[181]

The basic attitude underlying Confucian political thought is one of optimism. Confucius, Mencius, and Hsün Tzu all lived through chaotic times. Yet Confucius stated that if some ruler would but employ him, in three years he could finish off the whole work. [*Analects*, XIII/10.] Hsün Tzu clearly described the efficacy of the Confucians in governing with equity and improving the people's ways. Mencius said that a true king would arise after five hundred years. Though he talked about alternations of order and disorder, the way to achieve order could be known. Among Han Confucians, Chia Yi, Tung Chung-shu, and others all believed that there was great potential for human action in the affairs of the world. Only with Huan T'an, Wang Fu, Ts'ui Shih, and Hsün Yüeh is an element of pessimism gradually exposed. They no longer cling firmly to those lofty ideals of the sagelike ruler and his worthy aides, of the world's turning to benevolence and being transformed to righteousness; instead, these thinkers wanted greater reliance on punishments and on the inclusion of hegemonic rule by force, among the methods for patching up the fabric of government and treating the symptoms [of decline]. Since, however, they still wanted to patch things up and treat symptoms, they still believed that the Way was not exhausted, that the great civilization could be sustained, and, although pessimistic, they did not go to extremes of pessimism. Now we come to Chung-ch'ang T'ung, who not only despaired because the world's disorders were becoming ever harsher, but who also doubted whether there was any way of overcoming disorder and chaos. To draw an inference about the sense underlying his statements, he was virtually announcing the bankruptcy, simultaneously, of both the authoritarian institutions of government and the Confucian methods of governing. This in truth marks a vast transformation quite without precedent in all the history of Confucian thought since its earliest beginnings.

[181] *Ibid.*, "Li luan p'ien."

Examining the reasons why Han dynasty Confucian statements on government went from optimism to pessimism, the largest reason would appear to be the failures in actual practice of the authoritarian forms of government. Confucius had hoped that the feudal order could be made to flourish again; Mencius and Hsün Tzu longed for the unification of the empire. Insofar as they held such hopes, they allowed no room for pessimism. The Ch'in dynasty was overturned during its second reign, and commentators placed all the blame on Ch'in's reliance on the laws; they did not extend any doubts to the authoritarian structure of government or to the Confucian governing methods as such. Followers of the [Taoist] Huang-Lao school, and of [the Legalists] Shen Pu-hai and Lord Shang, made their forceful attacks on benevolence, righteousness, the rites and the music, as factors meaningless to good government. As Confucians viewed that, however, those signified nothing more than the schools' factional quarrels. They were not sufficient to shake their faith in Confucius as the one who had established the norms for all time, or in the unchanging nature of the Way, both that of government and that of heaven. The Han dynasty then implemented its mix of governing methods, drawing for support on the learning of Huang-Lao, Shen Pu-hai and Lord Shang, Confucius and Mencius, and in the end still could not evade chaos and collapse. The weaknesses of the authoritarian political form all were offered up to view, one by one. Consequently, the theoreticians of politics shared an awareness that all the forms of government practiced from past to present and the ways of governing established by all the Sages and Worthies, included no single system capable of maintaining enduring stability and peace throughout the empire. Therefore Chung-ch'ang T'ung's pessimistic theory about degenerating cycles of order and disorder became a quite natural terminus for Confucian political thought of the Ch'in and Han eras.[182]

---

[182] Chung-ch'ang T'ung may have been influenced by Wang Ch'ung.

CHAPTER TEN

From the *Lü-shih Ch'un-chiu* to Wang Ch'ung's *Lun Heng*

SECTION ONE
Taoists and Eclectics

CONFUCIAN political thought in the Ch'in and Han eras turned from optimism to pessimism; we have described the general outlines of that in the preceding chapter. Taoist thought during that span of time also displays a similar tendency. The pre-Ch'in philosophy based on Lao Tzu and Chuang Tzu, however, was negative to begin with. In the belief that the world should not be made the object of action, their doctrines were, therefore, centered on individual self-interest. After the Ch'in-Han unification of the empire, when the entire realm was newly stabilized, Lao-Chuang thought also began to undergo a transformation. There were certain peripheral branches of the Taoist school focusing on divinities and immortals, claiming their authority from the Yellow Emperor or Lao Tzu, which held out hopes for longevity and everlasting youth as their means of gaining favor with rulers; those need not enter our discussions. Beyond those aspects of Taoism, however, there were followers of the Huang-Lao doctrines [i.e., identifying with the Yellow Emperor, or Huang Ti, and with Lao Tzu],* who aspired to apply governing methods based on purity, quiescence, and non-action, to counteract the officious and oppressive modes prevailing throughout the Warring States and Ch'in eras; their basic objective was no longer merely to assure the safety of the individual, but had become the security and stability of the empire. The emperors and empresses, lords and high officials, of the time made very extensive use of these doctrines as "the methods appropriate to one facing south" [i.e., to occupying the throne].[1] Thus even though such Han period Huang-Lao doctrines had ultimate origins in the pre-Ch'in teachings of Lao Tzu and Chuang Tzu, they had come to differ from them in their basic objectives.

---

*Square brackets indicate that the words enclosed were added by the translator.

[1] *Han Shu, ch.* 30, "Journal of Literature" states: "The school of the Taoists emerged from the Office of the Recorders [or "historians," *shih kuan* 史官, which in early contexts may also be translated "office of the astrologers"]; they kept continuous records of the Way of [political] successes and failures, of survivals and extinctions, of bad and good fortune, past and present, in consequence of which they knew how to hold aloft the essentials and grasp the basic issues; they adopted pure and humble ways to discipline themselves, lowly and yielding stances to uphold themselves. These are methods appropriate to the ruler as he faces south [i.e., "as he assumes the throne"].

Nor does that exhaust the matter. For, inasmuch as Taoists now sought to hold political positions, they could no longer rely purely on the doctrine of taking no action. Consequently, they borrowed heavily from other schools to meet the demands introduced by these changed circumstances. Ssu-ma T'an [died 110 B.C.], in his Discussion of the Essentials of the Six Schools, thus says of the Taoists that "they accept the orderly sequence of nature from the *Yin-yang* school, gather the good points of Confucians and Mohists, and combine with these the important features of the Nominalist and Legalist schools."[2] Thus the content of Huang-Lao [politically oriented Taoism] is different again from the methods of Lao-Chuang [Taoism] cited in the *Chuang Tzu, ch.* 33, "T'ien hsia p'ien." However that may be, inasmuch as Taoists now gathered miscellaneously from the various schools, how should their school be distinguished from that school which in Han times people called the "Eclectics" [*tsa-chia* 雜家]? We should note that Ssu-ma T'an's "Essentials" does not mention the Eclectics. Only with the *Han Shu*'s "Journal of Literature" [written by Pan Ku, died A.D. 92] do we first read: "The school of the Eclectics emerged from the office of counsellors of state [*yi-kuan* 議官]. It bridges Confucianism and Mohism, combines Nominalism and Legalism." This seems to make it appear that what the *Han Shu* calls Eclectic [*tsa*] is the same as what the *Shih Chi* [in quoting Ssu-ma T'an's views] calls Taoist; recent scholars have sometimes held that the two are one school under two names, or have believed that the Eclectics did not include the Lao-Chuang tradition,[3] or have said that "The Taoists were the school from which all other schools emerged," or the Eclectics "gained the genuine transmission of Taoism."[4] To arrive at a judgment about the correctness of these various statements, we must first understand the boundaries of the Eclectic School

---

[2] *Shih Chi, ch.* 130, "Author's Postface." [Translation follows Bodde, Fung/Bodde, *History*, Vol. I; pp. 170, with modifications.]

[3] Fung Yu-lan, *Chung-kuo che-hsueh shih*, vol. I, p. 211. [First published in 1931, translated by Derk Bodde as *History of Chinese Philosophy*, Vol. I, p. 170.] A note appended at this point states: "Dr. Hu Shih has said that the Taoist school mentioned in this passage [by Ssu-ma T'an] is merely the Taoist school as it existed at the beginning of the Han dynasty, and hence is the same as what the *Journal of Literature* chapter of the *Han Shu* calls the Eclectic School, rather than the original school of Lao Tzu and Chuang Tzu. Yet in the classification of schools as given in the *Journal of Literature*, there is a Taoist school in addition to the Eclectic school, therefore the Eclectic school does not include the Lao-Chuang thought. When Ssu-ma T'an speaks of the Taoists he includes the Lao-Chuang thought." [A somewhat different translation appears in Fung-Bodde, *History*, Vol. I, p. 171; e.g., for that context, Bodde translates *tsa-chia* as "the Miscellaneous School" instead of "Eclectic School," etc.]

[4] Chiang Ch'üan, *Tu tzu chih yen* [pub. 1917], "Lun Tao-chia" ["On the Taoist School"], states that the Taoist School was that from which all other schools emerged. This view is completely without foundation; Fung Yu-lan in his *History* [*op.cit.* in note 3], p. 211, has pointed this out.

as we encounter it in the *Han Shu* "Treatise." That records and describes twenty Eclectics' works. These include; the *Lü-shih Ch'un-ch'iu*, "composed by the perceptive and broadly informed scholars assembled by Lü Pu-wei"; as well as the *Huai-nan Tzu*, "Inner" and "Outer" texts, the former said to "discourse on the Tao," the latter being composed of "Eclectic theories," [*tsa-shuo* 雜說]. Among works other than those two we also find: the *Shih Tzu*, of which the commentary says "by the teacher of the Prime Minister of Ch'in, Lord Shang"; the *Wei Liao*, "comprising the learning of Lord Shang"; the *Po-shih ch'en-hsien tui*, which was "Han period refutations of Han Fei Tzu and Lord Shang"; the *Tzu-wan Tzu*, by "a man of Ch'i who specialized in military proposals, resembling the [military work called] *Ssu-ma Fa*"; the *Tsa yen*, "discussing the Way of hegemons and kings"; the *Ching K'o lun*, "with discussions [on the would-be assassin of the First Emperor, Ching K'o] by Ssu-ma Hsiang-ju and others"; the writings of *Po Hsiang hsien-sheng*, a recluse, "offering nothing to benefit the government of the empire's overlord"; the *Ch'en Yüeh*, "composed during the reign of the Emperor Wu." From the above, one can see that what Pan Ku labelled Eclectic was of extremely mixed character. Not only is it not just a variant name for Taoist; in no way can this category, as a whole, represent the main lines of transmission of Taoist learning. However, since many of the works included there are no longer extant, the standard that was applied in classifying them cannot be determined. To infer from the *Lü-shih Ch'un-ch'iu* and the *Huai-nan Tzu*, however, it appears that all works were relegated to the Eclectic category that present thought and learning not purely of one tradition, or that as literature does not qualify as *belles lettres*, thereby being eligible for listing neither under the various philosophic school divisions, nor under those for "poetry and rhyme prose" and the like. Therefore, the word *tsa* ["mixed," hence "eclectic"] in the term for the Eclectic School [*tsa-chia*] appears to hold two meanings: the one is a single school development within which there emerged disparate, diverse factions; the second is a single book or work that adopts elements simultaneously from many schools.[5] Moreover, in simultaneously adopting elements of many schools, each work may vary in adopting more from one and less from another. If one work has taken Lord Shang and Han Fei Tzu as its central corpus of thought, another will have taken the Huang-Lao doctrines as its ultimate reference point. The "Taoists" as defined by Ssu-ma T'an [in *Shih Chi, ch*. 130] are an example of the second meaning. The *Lü-shih Ch'un ch'iu* and the *Huai-nan Tzu* are the most important extant representatives [of these two meanings, the *Huai-nan Tzu* of the work encompassing a single school, and the *Lü-shih Ch'un-ch'iu* of the work drawing on many schools].

---

[5] The meaning of the former is close to that of the English words "miscellaneous" or "unclassified"; that of the latter to the English word "eclectic."

If we are not mistaken, then, there were two schools of thought included in what was called "Taoist School" [*tao-chia* 道家] during the Ch'in and early Han times: the first is the "Huang-Lao" school, which had transformed the BASIC OBJECTIVES of pre-Ch'in Lao Tzu-Chuang Tzu thought [from egocentricity to political effectiveness]; the second was the "Taoist" school, which had transformed the CONTENT of pre-Ch'in Lao Tzu-Chuang Tzu thought [from the narrowly Taoist to the broadly eclectic. Emphasis added.] In this chapter each will be described in outline.

SECTION TWO
Han Dynasty Huang-Lao

IN the previous chapter it has been stated that political thought centering on "non-action," *wu-wei*, was widely current in early Han times, and that not even the Confucians escaped its influence. The teachings of Lao Tzu had been transmitted, not suffering extinction during the Ch'in holocaust. Although Li Erh's [the reputed author of the *Tao-Te Ching*] sons and grandsons failed to maintain the family tradition in learning, the lineal descendents of Yüeh Yi [*fl. ca.* 300 B.C.; famous general of the State of Yen] eventually became the revered teachers of Huang-Lao methods in the Ch'in-Han period.[6] From that time onward, those methods were widely applied at the court, to the extent that they virtually forced out Confucian and Legalist doctrines and occupied the powerful position of being the sole doctrine of the state. After sixty or seventy years had passed that influence gradually waned.

Within the imperial clan itself, it was the Emperor Wen [reigned, 179–157 B.C.] and [his consort, d.135] the Empress Tou who particularly

---

[6] *Shih Chi, ch.* 63, "Biographies of Lao Tzu, Chuang Tzu, Shen Pu-hai, and Han Fei Tzu," says: "Lao Tzu's son was named Tsung. Tsung became a general of the State of Wei, and was enfieffed at Tuan-kan. Tsung's son was Chu, and Chu's son was Kung. Kung's great-great-grandson was Chia, who held office under Emperor Wen [reigned 179–157] of the Han dynasty. Chia's son Chieh became grand tutor to An, Prince of Chiao-hsi, and so moved his home to Ch'i." [Following, with minor modification, Bodde, Fung-Bodde, Vol. I, p. 171.] *Shih Chi, ch.* 80, in the "Encomium" to "The Biography of Yüeh I," states: "The Honorable Yüeh Ch'en (*ch.* 104, "Biography of T'ien Shu," writes his name as Yüeh Chü) studied the teachings of Huang-ti [the Yellow Emperor] and Lao Tzu; the original teacher [in the tradition he followed] was styled the Old Man on the River Bank, but we do not know whence the tradition came. The Old Man on the River Bank taught Master An Ch'i, who taught the Honorable Mao Hsi, who taught the Honorable Yüeh Hsia, who taught the Honorable Yüeh Ch'en, who taught the Honorable [Yüeh] Ko. The Honorable Ko taught at Kao-mi and at Chiao-hsi in Ch'i, and was the teacher of Prime Minister Ts'ao [Shen]." [Translation follows, with minor changes, Frank A. Kierman, Jr., *Four Warring States Biographies*, p. 25.]

favored Huang-Lao. "When the Emperor Wen ascended the throne, an office of government submitted an opinion that the ritual forms and the norms of etiquette should be defined. The Emperor Wen was devoted to the learning of the Taoists, and felt that tiresome rituals and superficial adornment were of no benefit to government. He had adopted simple ways in his personal life, and asked what objections there were to that. Consequently, he rejected the matter."[7] Later, the Empress Tou sought even more vigorously to extend the influence [of Huang-Lao doctrines], virtually placing them under her personal protection. In consequence, Tou Ying, T'ien Fen, and others were dismissed from office for upholding Confucianism, and Yuan Ku was made to fight boars for having ridiculed the Tao.[8] "The Emperor Ching, his heir apparent, and all the members of the Tou family were required to study the doctrines of the Yellow Emperor and of Lao Tzu and to learn their methods."[9]

As for devotees of Huang-Lao among the highest officials at court and within the scholar-officialdom generally, the fashion had developed still earlier, and the numbers were considerably greater. In the reigns of Kao-tsu [the dynastic Founder] and the Emperor Hui [his successor], we find Ch'en P'ing and Ts'ao Shen.[10] During the reigns of the Emperors Wen and Ching [179–141 B.C.] there were Teng Chang, Master Wang, T'ien

[7] *Shih Chi*, *ch*. 23, "Li shu" ["Treatise on the Rites"].

[8] *Shih Chi*, *ch*. 107, "Biography of T'ien Fen." The events referred to occurred in the second year of the *chien-yüan* reign period [139 B.C.]. The Imperial Secretary Chao Wan and the Supervisor of Attendants Wang Tsang were thrown into prison, where they committed suicide. For the incident involving Yuan Ku, see *ch*. 121, "Biographies of Confucians."

[9] *Shih Chi*, *ch*. 49, "Wai-ch'i shih chia." [cf. Watson, *Shih Chi*, Vol. I, p. 386.] The *Kuang Hung-ming-chi* [Buddhist anthology dating from the seventh century], *ch*. 1, "Wu chu hsü Fo Tao san tsung," quotes [without specific reference, the history of the Three Kingdoms State of Wu], the *Wu Shu*, where, in the fourth year of Sun Ch'üan's *ch'ih-wu* reign period A.D. 241], K'an Tse says: "The Emperor Ching of the Han dynasty found such profound meaning in Master Huang's [a Taoist teacher active at the court of Emperor Ching; see *Shih Chi*, *ch*. 121] elucidation of the *Lao Tzu* that he changed that from the status of a philosophical work to that of a canonical text; he first established Taoist teachings [as the official doctrine] and commanded that at court and in the provinces everyone should chant those texts." It is not known what basis in fact may have existed for this comment, and these words are not found in the *San Kuo Chih*, *Wu Shu*, "Biography of K'an Tse" [as it now exists. The Emperor was the son of Empress Tou].

[10] *Han Shu*, *ch*. 40, "Biography of Ch'en P'ing." Ch'en P'ing "studied the methods [of governing] of the Yellow Emperor and Lao Tzu." *Ch*. 39, "Biography of Ts'ao Shen." When Ts'ao Shen served as chancellor in the [princely state of] Ch'i, "he heard about the Honorable Ko in Chiao-hsi, who was a skilled interpreter of the Huang-Lao doctrines. He sent messengers bearing a large gift of money to invite Ko, and upon their meeting Ko spoke, to say that the way of governing should prize purity and quiescence, then the people would be settled of themselves." Ts'ao Shen applied his theories and thereafter "in his governing he mainly used Huang-Lao methods." *Vide*, *Shih Chi*, *ch*. 56 and 54.

Shu, Chih Pu-yi, and Ssu-ma T'an.[11] From the period of the Emperor Wu's reign [140–87 B.C.], notable examples are Chi An and Cheng Tang-shih.[12] These persons all carried the idea of governing by purity and quiescence into practice, and some were prominent as students of Huang-Lao doctrines. However, none of these produced writings that have survived, and we might also assume that they made no contribution to theory. However, we must take note of the fact that the single reign of the Emperor Ching [156–141 B.C.] marks the period of the greatest flourishing of the Huang-Lao theories. Thereafter, Confucian learning began to displace it, and "non-action" was no longer looked upon as the method appropriate to rulership. Not merely do the numbers of the Huang-Lao followers recorded in the historical works diminish; most of those who are recorded applied the techniques of purity and quiescence to their own self-cultivation. In the whole period from the Emperors Chao and Hsüan to the Hsin dynasty of Wang Mang [A.D. 9–21], no more than one or two persons active in officialdom were held to be noteworthy because of an identification with Huang-Lao doctrines.[13] Throughout the two hundred years of the Later Han, such persons recorded in the histories, even though more numerous in the late generations of that era than in the Former Han, all are described as belonging to the category of "recluse" or

[11] In the Han Shu, ch. 49, "Biography of Ch'ao Ts'o," it states that Teng Chang was prominent among the court nobles because of his learning in Huang-Lao doctrines. In the biography of Chang Shih-chih, Shih Chi, ch. 102, it says: "Master Wang was expert in the teachings of Huang-Lao; he was a recluse scholar. He once had been summoned to reside at the court. The Three Lords and Nine Senior Ministers all stood during an audience, [except for] Master Wang, who, being old, said: 'My shoe is untied.' Turning to Commandant of Justice Chang Shih-chih, he said: 'Tie my shoe for me!' Chang knelt and tied it." Some persons criticized Master Wang, who commented: "Chang [Shih-chih] is today one of the most eminent men of the empire, so therefore I deliberately humiliated the Commandant of Justice, making him kneel to tie my shoe, desiring that people would value him the more [for being humble of spirit]." In ch. 104, in the biography of T'ien Shu, it states: "T'ien Shu studied the Huang-Lao governing methods at the place of the Honorable Yüeh Ch'en." [Cf. footnote no. 6, above.] In ch. 103, in the biography of Chih Pu-yi, it states: "Chih Pu-yi studied the teachings of Lao Tzu." In ch. 130, in the "Author's Postface," Ssu-ma Ch'ien says [of his father, Ssu-ma T'an]: "T'an studied the Taoist doctrines with Master Huang." [See footnote no. 9, above, for Master Huang.]

[12] Shih Chi, ch. 120, "Biographies of Chi An and Cheng Tang-shih": "Chi An studied Huang-Lao doctrines; in the conduct of his own office and in administering the people, he was devoted to purity and quiescence. . . ." "Cheng Chuang [i.e., Tang-shih] was fond of the Huang-Lao teachings." One of the imperial princes of Emperor Wu's time who admired Huang-Lao was Liu Te; vide, Han Shu, ch. 36, "Biography of Prince Yuan of Ch'u."

[13] One of those was Ts'ai Hsün, of the reign of Emperor P'ing [reigned A.D. 1–5]; see Hou Han Shu, ch. 90-B, "Biography of Ts'ai Yung."

"Taoist adept" [i.e., a practitioner of occult arts];[14] their words and deeds were not directly relevant to politics. At this point, Taoism restored the subjective, egocentric objectives of the pre-Ch'in traditions derived from Lao Tzu and Chuang Tzu, and, in so doing, became the forerunner of the emphasis on metaphysics and mysticism that characterized the [Neo-] Taoism of the Wei and Chin periods.

To locate the basic reasons why the Han dynasty Huang-Lao doctrines, having shifted from nourishing the self to ordering the world, and then again having moved back from engagement with society to the subjective focus upon the self, here again one must look to the historical backgrounds. After undergoing the protracted warfare and disorder of the Warring States period and again that accompanying the collapse of the Ch'in dynasty, the Chinese world had been brought to a nadir through exhaustion and impoverishment. "The Han dynasty was founded in the wake of the evils caused by the Ch'in. Able-bodied men had all gone off with the armies, while the aged and the youths had been forced to transport their supplies. Though people labored bitterly, the goods they could produce were scanty. Not even the Emperor was able to have a matched team of four horses, while generals and chief ministers might be obliged to ride in ox-carts, and the common people had nothing to hold in store."[15] Thus the case of the two Confucian scholars from the State of Lu who were unwilling to associate themselves with Shu-sun T'ung in reviving the rites and music.[16] When the Emperor Wen refused [ca. 179 B.C.] to adopt Chia Yi's proposals concerning changes in the institutional forms, he can be

---

[14] Examples include: *Han Shu*, *ch.* 72-A, "*Fang shu chuan*, or "Biographies of Taoist Adepts," Che Hsiang "prized the Huang-Lao teachings"; in *ch.* 107, "K'u li chuan," i.e., "Biographies of Harsh Officials" tells that in the time of Emperor Ming [A.D. 58–75] there was a person called Fan Jung, who "cherished Huang-Lao and was unwilling to accept appointment as an official"; *ch.* 113, "Yi-min chuan," i.e., "Biographies of Recluses," tells that during the time of Emperor Chang [76–88] there was a [recluse] man named Kao Hui who "as a youth had studied Huang-Lao," and also mentions a contemporary of Ma Jung [79–166] named Chiao Shen, who "when young had been drawn to Lao Tzu." Among those who did not flee the world as recluses there were: a man by the name of Tu Fang, mentioned in Huan T'an's *Hsin lun*, section 8, "Ch'ü pi," as having: "studied Lao Tzu's book, and lectured on Lao Tzu's applicability [to politics]"; during the period of Emperors Ming and Chang [A.D. 58–88] there was Jen Wei who "in his youth had been drawn to Huang-Lao's purity and quiescence and the limitation of desires" (from his biography in *ch.* 51 of the *Hou Han Shu*); active in the reign of Emperor An [107–125] was Ch'eng Yi, who "had profound understanding of Taoist methods" (his biography in *ch.* 81 of *Hou Han Shu*).

[15] *Shih Chi*, *ch.* 30, "P'ing-chun shu." [Cf. complete translation in Watson, *Shih Chi*, Vol. II, pp. 79–106.] *Han Shu*, *ch.* 24-A, "Shih-huo chih," has slightly different wording. [Cf. complete translation in Swann, *Food and Money*, especially p. 148.]

[16] *Shih Chi*, *ch.* 99, "Biography of Shu-sun T'ung." [Cf. Watson, *Shih Chi*, Vol. I, especially pp. 293–94.] *Han Shu*, *ch.* 43, has a more or less parallel account.

said to have been profoundly in harmony with the needs of the times. After the several decades of rest, resuscitation, and restoration of production afforded by the reigns of Emperors Hui, Wen, and Ching,[17] at the beginning of Emperor Wu's reign [in 140 B.C.], conditions of wealth and plenty had again been achieved. The state's resources now being abundantly supplied, its policies naturally tended toward the positive. Moreover, that happened to coincide with the reign of Emperor Wu, a ruler who delighted in expansive and aggressive action, a man "inwardly impelled by many desires though outwardly conveying benevolence and righteousness." [Said to him by his counsellor Chi An; see *Shih Chi, ch.* 120]. Consequently, the followers of Huang-Lao's purity and quiescence "their tasks being completed, then withdrew." [*Tao Te Ching,* 9.] Adoption of Confucian methods centering on the rites and the music also followed the movement of the times, and thus now flourished. From the reigns of Emperors Chao and Hsüan onward [from 86 B.C.], Huang-Lao gradually faded into obscurity, and by the last generations of the Later Han it had again assumed the position of a school of thought and learning quite apart from the court and the government.[18] The principal reasons for that would seem to lie in these historical facts.

Section Three
The *Lü-shih Ch'un-ch'iu* (241 B.C.)

During the "Former" and "Later" halves of the Han dynasty, the Huang-Lao doctrines reverted from the application to governing back to egocentrism, while the Eclectic school of Ch'in and Han times shifted its outlook from optimism to pessimism. The *Lü-shih Ch'un-ch'iu* marks the commencement of that; the *Huai-nan Hung-lieh* [or *Huai-nan Tzu*] continued the development; and Wang Ch'ung's *Lun Heng* embodies the ultimate stage of that transformation. Although the *Lü-shih Ch'un-ch'iu* was composed before the First Emperor accomplished the Ch'in dynasty's

---

[17] The Emperor Hui's mother, the Empress Lü, consort of Kao-tsu, the Founder, already had implemented "non-action" policies: *vide, Shih Chi, ch.* 9, Basic Annals of the Empress Lü." [Cf. Watson, *Shih Chi,* esp. p. 340.]

[18] Emperor Huan [reigned A.D. 147–167] was a believer in Taoism; for example, in the eighth year of the Yen-hsi reign period [A.D. 165] he sent the Palace Attendant, Tso Kuan, to offer sacrifices to Lao Tzu at [his reputed birthplace at] Hu-hsien. Again, in the next year, he conducted the sacrifice in person. (*Vide,* respectively, *Hou Han Shu, ch.* 7, "Basic Annals of Emperor Huan," and *ch.* 18, "Chi ssu chih," "Treatise on the State Sacrifices.") These acts, however, derive from the Emperor Huan's having been "devoted to matters concerning divine beings and immortals" and not from employing Huang-Lao in governing.

unification,[19] the book's influence extended into the Han period, therefore it is discussed here.

Lü Pu-wei was a large-scale merchant of Yang-chai [capital of the State of Han; in modern Honan], who served King Chuang-hsiang [of Ch'in, reigned 250–247 B.C.] as Chancellor, and was enfieffed Marquis of Wen-hsin. After the First Emperor assumed the throne [of Ch'in, as King Cheng, in 247 B.C.], Lü Pu-wei was elevated to the position of Prime Minister, and was addressed as "Uncle" [chung-fu 仲父]. Ten years later [237] he was involved in the affair of Lao Ai [a scandal concerning Lao Ai, a supposed eunuch introduced into the household of the Queen Mother by Lü Pu-wei, with improper intent], and was dismissed from the Prime Ministership. In the twelfth year of King Cheng's reign, he was banished to Szechwan, where he committed suicide [235 B.C.].

There are a number of differing accounts, both ancient and recent, about Lü Pu-wei's objectives in gathering guest scholars to compile and publish this book. The Shih Chi states that during the years he served as Prime Minister to the First Emperor, "the State of Wei had the Lord of Hsin-ling, in Ch'u there was the Lord of Ch'un-shen, in Chao there was the Lord of P'ing-yuan, and in Ch'i there was the Lord of Meng-ch'ang; each of the states displayed condescending cordiality toward scholars and gladly welcomed guest retainers, vying to outstrip one another [in this way to enhance the prestige of their states and themselves]. Lü Pu-wei considered it humiliating, in view of Ch'in's great power, to be inferior to the other states in this; therefore he also recruited scholars and treated them generously, ultimately acquiring three thousand such stipendiaries. At that time the feudal nobles all had many learned debaters, men such as Hsün Tzu, who wrote books that were disseminated throughout the realm. Lü Pu-wei therefore directed each of his guests to write concerning his own learning. He collected these discourses together, forming from them eight lan 覽 or "surveys," six lun 論 or "discourses," and twelve chi 紀 or "chronicles," totaling more than two-hundred thousand characters. Holding that this work could supplement the knowledge of the

---

[19] The "Preface" [Hsü-yi] to the Lü-shih Ch'un-ch'iu says: "In the eighth year of Ch'in, when the year was at [the point in the cycle called] t'un-t'an. . . ." The commentary states that a year with [the cyclical character] shen was called T'un-t'an. Ch'ien Mu, basing his view on the study in Yao Wen-t'ien's Sui-ya-t'ang chi [pub. 1821] called: "Wei Ch'in pa-nien sui tsai t'un-t'an k'ao" [i.e., a study of the line referred to above], calculates the year following the last year of the Eastern Chou [249 B.C.] to be the first year of Ch'in rule, that being the year with the cyclical designation kuei-ch'ou [248]. The eighth year following that would have been the year keng-shen (241 B.C.). That was still twenty years before the First Emperor established the thirty-six commanderies [symbolic of his having imposed unified direct rule over all of China]. It may be noted here that Hsü Wei-yü's Lü-shih Ch'un-ch'iu chi-shih [author's preface dated 1933] edition is the best.

whole world's and all its myriad components' affairs, past and present, he called it *Lü-shih Ch'un-ch'iu*," i.e., "Mr. Lü's Spring and Autumn Annals."[20]

The Sung dynasty scholar Kao Ssu-sun has written: "The First Emperor was not warm towards scholars. Lü Pu-wei therefore beckoned all the most illustrious, assembling the most outstanding. Their hair-clasps and slippers filled the court until they were to be counted in the thousands. The First Emperor had a marked distaste for books. Lü Pu-wei therefore used up all the writing slips, put all the brushes and ink to work, picking out the best items and recording the most unusual matters, and formed them into his own system of thought. Ah, why was it that Lü Pu-wei acted in this manner? Is it not curious? His *Ch'un-ch'iu* says, 'Across a distance of ten *li* the ear cannot hear; beyond the walls around one's house the eyes cannot see; within the space of three *mou* of land, there are things the mind cannot be aware of. Yet one desires to gain the East as far as K'ai-wu, to rule the South as far as To-yen, to make the West submit as far as Shou-mi, and longs for the North as far as Tan-erh [i.e., the names of four mythical lands at the farthest points of the four directions]. How could that ever be achieved!' This expresses his ridicule of the First Emperor."[21] The contemporary scholar Ch'ien Mu has written: "I suspect that this book was the device used by the guest scholars in the Lü household to gather widespread acclaim [for their sponsor, Lü Pu-wei], thereby to gain the empire's allegiance to him. It purports to use the vehicle of one man's *Annals* to justify the models that a new king should adopt, and gives the credit for this to Lü Pu-wei. This resembles earlier instances such as that of the Wei family in Chin and the T'ien family in Ch'i [referring to usurpations from within the courts in question; in 402 in Chin and in 390 in Ch'i]; those who served Lü as his guest retainers could scarcely have failed to hope he would seize the Ch'in King and displace him. When we note that [in his "Preface"] he uses the dating

---

[20] *Shih Chi*, ch. 85, "Biography of Lü Pu-wei." [The "Lords" named here were all scholar-advisors on governing who were granted titles by their princely hosts.]

[21] From [Kao's critical essays on philosophical books] the *Tzu lüeh*. [Kao was a chin-shih of 1184.] The passage headed: "His *Ch'un-ch'iu* says . . ." comes from ch. 17, section 3, "Jen shu," here quoted from the *Ch'un-ch'iu* "Hsü Yi" and "Fu K'ao" ["Preface" and "Critical Appendix," found at the end of most editions of the work]. The Ming scholar Fang Hsiao-ju [1357–1402], elaborating on this view of Kao Ssu-sun's, has stated: "The book's sections on "Frugal Funerals" and "Peaceful Death" ["Chieh sang" and "An ssu," ch. 10, sections 2 and 3] criticize the evils of lavish funerals. Its section called "Not in Person" ["Wu kung," ch. 17, section 4] claims the essential for the ruler lies in employing others. His section on "Utilizing the People" ["Yung min," ch. 19, section 4] states that punishments and penalties are not as useful as virtue and the rites. The sections "Unloosing Repressions" ["Ta yü," ch. 20, section 5] and "Dividing Responsibilities" ["Fen chih," ch. 25, section 4] both discuss the full measure of the ruler's art. These all strike precisely at the First Emperor's faults." Quoted from the "Critical Appendix" [Fu-k'ao, *loc.cit.*].

'in the eighth year of Ch'in'; it is clear that this was written before [the Ch'in King Cheng] had assumed the position of First Emperor. At that time there surely existed a situation of suspicion and of guarding against conflicts between the Ch'in royal court and Lü Pu-wei, about which the historical accounts supply no information. The First Emperor was fortunate to have taken action first, leading to his implicating Lü in the Lao Ai affair."[22]

Of these three views, this last appears to be the most relevant to the elucidation of Lü Pu-wei's motives. Yet the theory, advanced by Kao Ssu-sun, that he wished to ridicule or criticize the First Emperor also can be accepted, the two being mutually supporting theories. For if Lü Pu-wei indeed did hope to displace the Ch'in ruler and make himself emperor, he would have felt compelled to attack the traditional Ch'in policies and promulgate a distinct set of principles for establishing the state. For that reason, Lü Pu-wei as Prime Minister to Ch'in following the demise of the Chou certainly would not have acknowledged the Ch'in as the legitimate successor to the Chou dynasty; thus he continued to say: "The Chou house having been extinguished, the Sons of Heaven are now without successors," and "Ravaging each other by carrying on warfare [the states] can gain no respite or recovery."[23] The book also says: "In this present time the world is extremely murky. The bitter suffering of the common people must not be increased. The Son of Heaven is now without a successor, and worthy men have been cast aside. The world's overlords indulge in unrestrained acts, and alienate themselves from the people." Here Lü Pu-wei's book not only expresses criticism of the First Emperor; it even goes so far as to class the State of Ch'in with the other Six States, and fundamentally repudiates all of Ch'in's enriching and strengthening policies, its wars to absorb adjacent territories, its excessive reliance on laws, and the value granted to utilitarian accomplishment, that had marked Ch'in's policies ever since the reign of Duke Hsiao [whom Lord Shang had served, reigned 361–338].

Knowing that the *Lü-shih Ch'un-ch'iu* is an anti-Ch'in book, then, those elements of its political thought such as "Emphasis upon the Self" ["Chung-chi," 1/3], valuing the people, the essence of Tao, and the usefulness of Confucianism, elements designed specifically to counter the ideas of Lord Shang and Han Fei Tzu, need hold no surprise. Throughout the twelve *Chi* ["chronicles," forming the first half of the book], the line of

---

[22] Ch'ien Mu, *Hsien Ch'in chu-tzu hsi-nien k'ao-pien*, p. 450. Note that in *Shih Chi*, *ch*. 6, it records that when Lü Pu-wei was dismissed from the Prime Ministership in the tenth year [237], at the same time a command was issued to disperse his guest scholars.

[23] *Lü-shih Ch'un-ch'iu*, *ch*. 13, section 5, "Chin t'ing." (The wording in *ch*. 16, section 2, "Kuan shih" is quite similar.)

reasoning adopted there consistently if indirectly rejects Legalism. Pre-Ch'in philosophers, including Confucius, Mo Tzu, Huang Tzu [The Yellow Emperor's doctrines], Lao Tzu, Chuang Tzu, Lieh Tzu, Kuan Tzu, T'ien [P'ien], and Tzu-hua Tzu, all are among those cited with approval, while there is no single such reference to Lord Shang or to Han Fei Tzu. The "Preface" ["*Hsü yi*," originally placed at the end of *ch.* 13], being placed after the twelve *Chi* ["chronicles"], as well as the twelve *Chi* being arranged according to the four seasons, more or less correspond-ing to the model established in the "Spring and Autumn Annals," it is to be assumed that this portion conveys the essentials of the entire book, loosely constituting what in later ages were designated "Inner Chapters." The eight *Lan* ["surveys"] and six *Lun* ["discourses"], although making occasional reference to Shen Pu-hai and Lord Shang[24] nevertheless in their central ideas are quite in conformity with the twelve *Chi*. All of the governing methods involving harshly rigorous supervision and liability to punishment are avoided. Thus it can be concluded that the political import of the *Lü-shih Ch'un-ch'iu* is that of establishing a new king in opposition to Ch'in rule, and the content of its political thought consists of older learning re-examined for the purpose of repudiating Legalism.[25]

The political thought presented in Lü Pu-wei's book is founded on the Pre-Ch'in egocentric philosophy of life.[26] Yang Chu was not willing to harm a single hair of his body even to benefit the world. [*Vide*, Chapter Five, Section One, especially page 531 and footnote 21, above.] The *Lü-shih Ch'un-ch'iu*, taking up that concept, develops it further in the views it offers on the value of life. It says: "Ch'ui was the most skilled of artisans. Yet people do not love Ch'ui's [miraculous] fingers; they love their own [ordinary] fingers. That is because their own are of use to themselves. People are not deeply concerned about the jade in the far-off K'un-lun mountains or the pearls in the Yangtze and Han Rivers as much as they are concerned about their own poor jade and imperfect pearls; that is because their own are of value of themselves. Now, my own life too is something possessed by me, and of great advantage primarily to me; in evaluating noble or humble status, the rank held by the Son of Heaven

---

[24] *Ibid.*, *ch.* 7, section 3, "Chen luan."

[25] Throughout the entire book the number of quotations attributed to Confucius are the most numerous, surpassing the number of attributions to the Taoists or any other school. Within the eight *Lan* or Survey portions, *ch.* 17, section 3, "Jen shu," quotes Shen Pu-hai, and section 6, "Shen shih," quotes Shen Tao; *ch.* 18, section 4, "Li wei," cites anecdotes about Teng Hsi throwing the government into confusion [*vide Ch.* VIII, note 4, above]; and *ch.* 19, section 4, "Yung min," cites the examples of Kuan Tzu and Lord Shang in instituting laws; *ch.* 22, section 2, "Wu yi" uses Lord Shang as an example.

[26] *Vide*, *Hu Shih wen-ts'un*, third collection, "Tu *Lü-shih Ch'un-ch'iu*, i.e., "On Reading the *Lü-shih Ch'un-ch'iu*."

cannot be compared to it in value. In evaluating material worth, the wealth of the empire is not worth exchanging for it. In assessing safety and danger, if tomorrow my life is lost, this person will never regain it." That is why: "The Sage, profoundly contemplating the world's affairs, knows that nothing has a higher value than life."[27] Even be that so, however, what is termed valuing life is not merely a matter of protecting and preserving one's life. In Ch. 2, Section 2, "Kuei sheng," it says: "Tzu-hua Tzu has said: 'The whole life is best; the diminished life is next best, while to be [righteously] moribund is still less good, and the harried life is least good.' Therefore what is termed honoring life is what we call the whole life. In this so-called whole life, the six desires all are appropriately satisfied. In the diminished life, appropriate satisfaction of the six desires is partially achieved . . . what is called moribund ["being committed to death for honor"] designates lacking the means of knowing [the value of life], hence willingly returning to the state of not having been born [a commentary suggests: as in the case of one who "righteously" dies for a vanquished ruler]. In the case of what is termed the harried life, no one of the six desires is appropriately satisfied. . . . Therefore it is said that to lead a harried life is not as good as being dead. How can one know that to be true? When the ears hear a hated sound, it is better not to have heard. When the eyes see a hated sight, it is better not to have seen. So, when there is thunder, people cover their ears, and when there is lightning, they cover their eyes. This is a fitting analogy."[28]

That whole life is the highest ideal of living; likewise, it is the ultimate aim of government. Therefore the *Lü-shih Ch'un-ch'iu* says: "It is heaven ["Nature"] which brings life into being in the first place, and it is man that nurtures life and brings it to fulfillment. Possessing a capacity to nurture what heaven has brought into life and do no violence to it, such a one can be called the Son of Heaven. The Son of Heaven's actions are undertaken to make whole heaven's [bestowal]. This is why official posts subsequently have been instituted; official posts are for the purpose of making life whole."[29]

---

[27] Respectively: *ch.* 1, section 3, "Chung chi"; *ch.* 2, section 2, "Kuei-sheng." Note also *ch.* 21, section 4, "Shen wei." [For the allusion to the artisan Ch'ui, *vide Chuang Tzu, ch.* 19, "Ta-sheng."]

[28] The concept of a "whole life" does not mean giving rein to all desires. *Ch.* 1, section 3, "Chung chi," says: "The growth of all living things is compliant [with life]. That which makes for failure to comply with life is the desires. Therefore the Sages found it necessary first to regulate the desires." Kao Yu's commentary states that *shih* [in the last sentence] is to be interpreted in the sense of "to regulate," 適猶節也. This idea is in sharp contrast with the views of T'o Hsiao and Wei Mou [hedonists castigated by Hsün Tzu, *ch.* 6, "Fei shih-erh tzu"].

[29] *Lü-shih Ch'un-ch'iu, ch.* 1, section 2, "Pen sheng."

The *Lieh Tzu* quotes Yang Chu's statement that if everyone would refuse to take the world as a gain, then the world would be in perfect order. [*Vide*, Chapter Five, esp. p. 567 and footnote 92, above.] The *Lü-shih Ch'un-ch'iu* does not advocate the view, recognizing instead that political organization is a necessary condition for ensuring the beautiful and good life to the individual. For it was felt that in earliest antiquity both China and the barbarian peoples on all four sides had no rulers. Not only was the level of culture low and crude; life also was extremely difficult. "The people lived the uncultivated lives of animals. The young gave orders to their seniors; the aged feared the strong. A man having physical strength was looked upon as a worthy person; a violent and arrogant person was venerated. Day and night people attacked and injured each other; there was no rest from it, and whole clans were exterminated by that violence. The Sages made profound observations of these calamities, and consequently their long-standing concern led them to conclude that the best plan for the long range would be to establish a Son of Heaven for the empire, and the best long-range plan for the states would be to institute kings. . . . Once the way of the ruler was instituted, benefits were extended to the masses of the people, and all the people's preparations [against weather, enemies, etc.] could be made complete."[30] We have remarked earlier that the characteristic of Legalist thought is its focus upon the ruler as the basic element in government.[31] Although the *Lü-shih Ch'un-ch'iu* places much emphasis on the capability of the ruler, throughout it consistently denies that the state exists to serve the ruler's interests, and it repeatedly proclaims this point. Thus it says: "The empire is not one man's empire; it is the empire's empire." Again; "The Kings were not established as a favor to the kings; the Son of Heaven was not installed as a favor to the Son of Heaven. The chief officials were not instituted as a favor to the chief officials. Virtue waned and the world grew disorderly. Subsequently, however, the Sons of Heaven brought benefits to the empire, the kings brought benefits to their princely states, and the chief officials brought benefits to [the localities] of

---

[30] *Ch.* 20, "Shih chün lan," sections 2 and 1. *Ch.* 7, section 2, "Tang ping," says: "Even before the time of Ch'ih-yu [i.e., the reputed first instigator of war and disorder in the ancient world; *vide*: Documents, v/xxvii, "Lü hsing," p. 2; Legge, p. 590], the people surely must already have been stripping the trees in the forests to make weapons for war. Victors were made leaders, but such leaders were incapable of maintaining order. Therefore they installed kings, but, again, kings were not enough to ensure order. So, they instituted a Son of Heaven. The establishment of the Son of Heaven came from the kings; the establishment of kings came from the leaders; the establishment of leaders came about because of warring." This version of the theory is somewhat different, but not necessarily contradictory.

[31] *Vide*, the first paragraphs of Chapter Six, Section Two, above.

their official posts. That is how the state alternately flourishes and languishes."[32]

Inasmuch as the *Lü-shih Ch'un-ch'iu* opposes Legalism and is sympathetic to the Confucian position, it is inevitable that it should accept the concepts of according with the minds and hearts of the people and of executing violent and tyrannical rulers, as advocated by Mencius and Hsün Tzu. In other words, having repudiated the theory of monarchical authoritarianism that was reaching its full development in the last years of the Warring States period, it then reiterated the older theories based on the ancient patterns of kingly rule and of the basic importance of the people. Though there is no creative originality in this, it possesses historical significance that demands our attention. For during the early Han, the Huang-Lao thinkers made their great justification for the governing methods of purity and quiescence, while Chia Yi and others also elucidated the merits of benevolence, righteousness, and ethical principles, in both cases to correct the faults that the First Emperor had engendered by relying heavily on punitive means of governing. Yet Lü Pu-wei and his guest-retainers, even prior to the First Emperor's unification of the empire, had already launched their frontal assault on that kind of thought and theorizing in Shen Pu-hai and in Han Fei Tzu, and against the administrative measures of Lord Shang and Li Ssu. Indeed, it is not too much to say that they anticipated the "faults of Ch'in" [type of anti-Legalist reaction seen in the rebellion] of Ch'en She [in 209 B.C.]. Although Lü's effort failed, and Lü Pu-wei himself was killed, his achievement in having posed such challenges cannot be overlooked.

In his opposition to authoritarian rule, Lü Pu-wei offered very penetrating arguments; indeed, few Han period figures are comparable in this respect. He had high praise for the righteous-minded Shang and Chou founding rulers for having grieved about the people's sufferings and having expelled the evil-doers; the details of all that are so familiar by now that we need not discuss them further.[33] His greatest contribution would appear to

[32] *Vide*, respectively, *Lü-shih Ch'un-ch'iu*, *ch*. 1, section 4, "Kuei kung," and *ch*. 20, "Shih chün."

[33] *Ibid.*, *ch*. 7, section 4, "Chin sai," demolishes [Mo Tzu's] theories against aggressive war as offering encouragement to violent and tyrannical rulers. If [the symbolic tyrants] Kings Chieh and Chou had been led to understand that they could not escape the fall of their dynasties and their own deaths, and that their lines would be exterminated, I do not know whether even they would have persisted in the oppressive pursuit of evil as they did." In *ch*. 7, section 5, "Huai ch'ung," he expresses full approval of the actions of a righteous uprising that exterminates a tyrant, and also advocates undertaking such a punitive campaign; in this, Lü's view is similar to that which Confucians held in their discussions of the events at Mu-yeh. [The reference is to the decisive contest between the armies of the tyrant King Chou of Shang, and the conquering King Wu, who founded the Chou dynasty; *vide Documents*, v/ii, "Mu shih"; Legge, p. 300.]

be his proposals for all kinds of methods by which to restrict the ruler, preventing him from indulging his whims and passions. Those sections of the book in which he speaks of complying with the people's wishes, heeding remonstrance, limiting the desires, and taking no action, are particularly significant. In *Ch.* 9, section 2, "Shun min" ["complying with the people"] it says: "The Former Kings first complied with the hearts of the people; therefore their accomplishments and their fame were consummated."[34] The basic element in complying with the people is having true concern for the people's attitudes, and implementing policies that benefit the people. But, in his desire to know how painful and bitter the life of the ordinary people is, and to know the strengths and weaknesses of the state, the ruler must take it as his urgent duty to heed a broad range of frank admonishment. King Li [of the Chou royal line, reignd 877–842 B.C.; died 828] was universally resented, and the Duke of Shao called him to account for his misdeeds: the "repressed resentments in the state" would lead to its downfall, and in the end, he did not escape banishment.[35] "The ruler of a collapsing state will be one who is arrogant in manner, believes himself to be omniscient and lacks concern for [the value of] things. His arrogance leads him into overbearing treatment of his officials; a belief that he knows all makes him dictatorially arbitrary, and his lack of [practical] concern leaves him ill-prepared. Being ill-prepared invites disaster; arbitrary dictatorship imperils his throne, and overbearing arrogance blocks the channels of information."[36] Moreover, the ruler not only must not believe himself to be all-knowing, neither should he practice unrestrained indulgence. The *Lü-shih Ch'un-ch'iu* quotes: "The Yellow Emperor has said: 'Refrain from immoderate enjoyment of music; refrain from overindulgence in erotic pleasures; refrain from using perfumes to excess; refrain from eating lavish foods; refrain from having extravagant dwellings.' "[37] "The world's kings and nobles, whether they be worthy or good-for-nothings, all desire to live forever." Yet they are incapable of observing the Yellow Emperor's prohibitions, to regulate their desires and to nurture their vitality, so

---

[34] *Ibid.*, *ch.* 9. "Pu erh," in *ch.* 17, states: "Heed all the proposals from the masses of the people, and the state will be in immediate peril." This, however, is said in rejection of the dissident views put forth by recluse scholars; it does not necessarily conflict with the view that the ruler should comply with the popular mind.

[35] *Ibid.*, *ch.* 20, "Ta yü." [This anecdote refers to bad King Li's unrestrained excesses and his efforts to stop all criticism; the repression of popular resentment eventually contributed to his downfall, in a revolt that led to the King's exile in 842 B.C.] In *ch.* 23, all six sections commencing with "Kuei chih lun," i.e., "Discourse on valuing straightforward admonition," set forth the view that the ruler must heed remonstrance.

[36] *Ibid.*, *ch.* 20, "Chiao-tzu."

[37] *Ibid.*, *ch.* 1, "Ch'ü-ssu."

"what benefit to them is their desire [for longevity]?"[38] If the three methods of governing [complying with the people's mind, accepting remonstrance, and regulating the desires] are put into practice, the ruler will be restricted both psychologically and materially and will no longer be able to follow his own arbitrary, self-willed ways, in just that manner which the Second Emperor later was to describe as "indulging his will and extending his desires," or which Li Ssu was later to describe as concentrating on using the empire for [the ruler's] personal whims. [Cf. Chapter Eight, Section Two, above, esp. pp. 439–40.]

The *Lü-shih Ch'un-ch'iu* is concerned that those [three methods] might yet not suffice, and further adopts the theory from Shen Pu-hai and Han Fei Tzu by which the ruler should maintain inaction, hoping in that way to add a further restriction in the area of the ruler's employment of political power. Five of the eight sections comprising the chapter "*Shen fen lan*" are devoted to developing this concept.[39] For one example, it says there: "One who has attained the Way can only be quiescent. The quiescent person is without awareness. To be aware that one is to be without awareness can be spoken of as the Way of the Ruler." It also states: "The ruler regards never being appropriate as appropriate, and never being effective as effective. To be appropriate and effective are not concerns of the ruler but are the concerns of his servitors."[40] For, any one person's "ears and eyes, and his knowing mind, or all his capacities for knowledge, are extremely limited; one's capacities for hearing and seeing are extremely shallow. Should he, with that limitation and that shallowness, try to maintain sway over the empire, and to bring stability despite the varying customs, and order to all the myriad people, there is no way his pronouncements can prevail."[41] Moreover, "When the ruler assumes he is wise, that is to make the others [his courtiers and servitors] stupid; when he assumes he is skilled, that is to make the others clumsy. When this happens, those stupid and clumsy ones make inquiries of him, and that wise and skilled one instructs them. The more he instructs, the more those who inquire. As their inquiries increase, there becomes nothing about which they will not inquire. Though a ruler be truly wise and skilled, he cannot be omniscient. When one who is not omniscient undertakes to respond to an unlimited range of inquiries, his way [*tao*] must fail. If one is the ruler and yet has repeatedly failed before his subordinates, how can he then continue to rule over people? To fail and not to know one's failure is to induce a growing source of trouble. That is called the repeatedly baffled

---

[38] *Ibid., ch.* 1, "Chung-chi."

[39] *Ibid., ch.* 17, "Shen-fen lan," "Chün-shou," "Jen-shu," "Wu-kung," and "Chih-tu."

[40] *Ibid.* [*ch.* 17], "Chün-shou."

[41] *Ibid.* [*ch.* 17], "Jen-shu."

[literally, "stopped"] ruler, the state that cannot survive." Hence the proper way of the ruler is to delegate the governing by "entrusting it to the worthy,"[42] "to rectify the names and examine status and duties"[43] as the means to control the officials; "to engage in no action and to perfect the self so that the empire shall become well-governed of itself."[44] We may note that for the ruler to engage in no action is one of the central components of Shen Pu-hai's discourses on governing methods [*shu* 術], where its function is to guard against the treachery of servitors and to ensure supervision of their accomplishment, in order to protect the powers of the authoritarian ruler's position. The *Lü-shih Ch'un-ch'iu*'s intent is different. As we consider all the various elements, including complying with the people, and accepting remonstrance, together with that of engaging in no action, we become aware that they conceal the intent to promote a "titular monarchy."[45] The spirit of this is all the more strikingly at odds with what Li Ssu was to call the mentality of the one [the ruler] who in solitary splendor can fully indulge his unrestrained passions.[46]

The *Lü-shih Ch'un-ch'iu* not only sets itself in opposition to the authoritarian structure of the Ch'in state; it also opposes its governing methods. It does that the most obviously in its reaffirmation of the ideal of rule by virtue, presented as the corrective for Lord Shang's excesses of harsh penalties and aggressive warfare. "Of old, those rulers of vanquished states considered fault to lie with other persons, so they practiced daily killings without end, to the very downfall of their states, and still they failed to realize their error."[47] The Five Emperors [of legendary antiquity] gave priority to the Way [*Tao*] and only secondary attention to its Power [*te*], with the consequence that its powers [i.e., the practical consequence of its workings] have never been more flourishing than at that time: The Three Kings [the Founders of Hsia, Shang, and Chou] gave priority to teaching and only secondary attention to punishments, with the consequence that service to the state was never more splendid. The Five Hegemons [variously identified, but always including Dukes Huan of Ch'i and Wen of Chin of Ch'un-ch'iu times] gave priority to their service and only secondary attention to military matters, with the consequence

---

[42] *Ibid.* [*ch.* 17], "Chih-tu."

[43] *Ibid.* [*ch.* 17], "Shen-fen lan."

[44] *Ibid.*, *ch.* 3, "Hsien chi."

[45] *Hu Shih wen-ts'un, Third Collection, ch.* 3, "Tu *Lü-shih ch'un-ch'iu.*" However, Hu Shih also states that the rule of law in Legalism was in theory intended to restrict monarchical power, a view that is at best debatable.

[46] *Vide* Chapter Eight, Section Two, of the present work, the passage beginning "The Fourth is implementing systems of supervision and of fixing responsibility," on page 439 above.

[47] *Lü-shih Ch'un-ch'iu, ch.* 3, "Lun jen."

that no armies were stronger than theirs. In this present age, trickery and plotting go hand-in-hand [with governing], sham and chicanery are frequently resorted to, agressive warfare is unceasing, vanquished states and humbled rulers are ever more numerous, and governing has reached the nadir."[48] The attitude of rigorously severe criticism [of the Ch'in] in Chia Yi's "Discourse on the Faults of Ch'in" would seem to be in no sense more extreme than this. Chia Yi was distressed that "Ch'in's customs steadily deteriorated," noting the facts of collapse of family and clan morality. [Cf. Chapter Nine, Section Two, esp. p. 478 above.] The *Lü-shih Ch'un-ch'iu* conveys somewhat analogous views. Thus the book devotes much attention to the doctrines of loyalty and filiality, even going so far as to acknowledge filiality as the very basis of government,[49] which manifests a sharp contrast to the inclinations of Lord Shang and of Han Fei.

When we turn to the book's advocacy of feudalism [*feng-chien*] its views are even more starkly at variance with Li Ssu. The *Lü-shih Ch'un-ch'iu* states: "The kings of antiquity selected the center of the realm [*t'ien hsia chih chung*] at which to establish the state. . . . The territory from which the Son of Heaven formed his state was [only] a thousand *li* square, and within that he achieved the limits of responsibility for good governing. . . . His many feudatories were not established to favor worthy servitors, but were to enhance his power and complete his authority, and were to broaden [the force of] his righteousness. When his righteousness was broadened and the benefits [of his rule] were broadened, he feared no enemies. The state without enemies is tranquil. Thus it can be seen in the past that when the king's feudatories were numerous, his well-being was increased and his fame made resplendent. Shen-nung [one of the legendary Five Emperors] and his heirs held the realm through seventeen generations, and the realm was as one with them."[50] These statements are closely in keeping with the advice offered [to the First Emperor in 213 B.C.] by Ch'un-yü Yüeh.[51] From Li Ssu's point of view, Lü Pu-wei surely should have been declared guilty of "using the past to repudiate the present."

---

[48] *Ibid.*, *ch.* 3, "Hsien chi"; cf. also *ch.* 19, "Shih wei." In *ch.* 2, "Kung-ming," it says: "One can command people to laugh but they may not feel happy, command them to weep but they may not feel sad. So, command as a method may merely achieve the superficial; it cannot bring about the genuine accomplishments."

[49] *Ibid.*, *ch.* 4, "Ch'üan-hsüeh," and *ch.* 14, "Hsiao-hsing lan."

[50] *Ibid.*, *ch.* 17, "Shen shih." (The text is slightly defective; emendation follows Hsü Wei-yü's "*Chi-shih*" edition.)

[51] For Ch'un-yü Yüeh's statement, see *Shih Chi*, *ch.* 87, "Biography of Li Ssu." [Ch'un-yü's arguments in favor of the ancient feudal structure led the First Emperor to burn books containing deviant traditions and unauthorized learning. See Chapter Eight, Section Two, esp. pp. 436–37, above.]

However, the *Lü-shih Ch'un-ch'iu* contains one element, which, although not offered with the intent of serving the Ch'in, nonetheless was shortly thereafter adopted by the First Emperor. This is the theory of the Five Agents and their sequences of interaction [*wu-te chung-shih* 五德終始]. In the "Basic Annals of Ch'in Shih-huang-ti" and in the "Treatise on the Feng and Shan Sacrifices," of the *Shih Chi*, it states that Ch'in had gained its imperial supremacy through the power of the agent water, and took Duke Wen's [reigned 764–714 B.C.] having obtained [a sign from] a black dragon as proof. [Both the color black and the dragon were associated with the agent water. Cf. Watson, *Shih Chi*, vol. I. p. 23.] This in point of detail agrees with what is said in the *Lü-shih Ch'un-ch'iu* [*ch.* 13, section two], "Ying-t'ung" [about the agent water eventually overcoming the Chou dynasty whose agent was fire]; it may even be based directly on the *Lü-shih Ch'un-ch'iu*. There [antiquity's founding rulers] the Yellow Emperor, The Great Yü [Hsia], T'ang the Victorious [Shang], and King Wen [Chou] are assigned the agents of earth, wood, metal, and fire, respectively, for which the prophetic signs were taken to be the appearances of giant earthworms and crickets [earth], the survival of green plants and tree leaves despite the coming of autumn and winter [wood], the vision of metal blades coming forth from water [metal], and a red bird carrying cinnabar script in its beak [fire]. The *Lü-shih Ch'un-ch'iu*, however, does not specify any association of the Ch'in state with the agency of water, merely stating: "That state which succeeds to the power of fire must employ water. Heaven will first reveal that the power of water has triumphed. Water being triumphant, the color that state venerates will be black, and the agent it serves will be water." To make a deduction about the import of that, we may note that in the [author's preface, *ch.* 12, section 6] "Hsü-yi" the [book's completion] date is given as "the eighth year of the Ch'in" [239 B.C.]. Yet after Lü Pu-wei died [235 B.C.] and twenty years after his scholar-guests had been scattered, this passage, contrary to the original intent, was utilized by the First Emperor to serve as a theoretical basis for his political power. The authors of the book could never have anticipated such a thing.

The *Lü-shih Ch'un-ch'iu*'s cycle of the Five Agents theory in fact follows that set forth by Tsou Yen. Tsou's views on the natural alternation through periods of good order and disorder somewhat resemble Mencius' discussions of the heavenly mandate. The *Lü-shih Ch'un-ch'iu* takes the view that although good and bad fortune are called forth by man himself, success and failure [in the state] always develop from unplanned circumstances. "All instances of good government and disorder, of survival and downfall, of tranquility and peril, of strength and weakness, necessarily depend on a chance [combination of circumstances] and only in consequence of that, then take their shape. If the combination is the same on each [of two opposing sides], then the situation [favoring one side over the other] would not present itself. Thus one can say that although [the tyrannical last rulers] Chieh and Chou were unworthy, their [states'] downfalls occurred because they chanced to come up against [the virtuous dynastic founders] Kings T'ang and Wu. That they chanced to encounter Kings T'ang and Wu was from heaven [or, the workings of nature] and not [only] because Chieh and Chou were unworthy. Even though Kings T'ang and Wu were worthy, their rise to overlordship came from their happening to come up against Chieh and Chou. That they encountered Chieh and Chou was heaven, and not [only] a consequence of Kings T'ang's and Wu's having been worthy. If Kings Chieh and Chou had not encountered Kings T'ang and Wu, their downfalls might well not have occurred. If Kings Chieh and Chou had not been vanquished, though they were indeed unworthy, their humiliations might not have led to such an end. If Kings T'ang and Wu had not happened to come up against Kings Chieh and Chou, they might never have become founding kings. If Kings T'ang and Wu had not become kings, despite their worthy qualities, their eminence might never have reached so far. . . . One may use the example of a good farmer. He may be able to ascertain the most suitable conditions of the soil and apply himself arduously to the plowing and the harrowing, but it is not certain that he will harvest a crop. Yet in order to have a harvest anyone must do as this man in the beginning. After that it is the chance of encountering timely rains. Encountering timely rains is a matter of heaven and earth [*t'ien-ti*, or the natural world]; it is not something the good farmer can bring about."[52]

According to what the *Lü-shih Ch'un-ch'iu* says, then, man definitely is incapable of overruling heaven [or, "nature"]; the superior man can only exhaust his own means. What he refers to as "taking heaven and earth as his model" and "acting as father and mother to the people" are no more than the [the ruler's] means of instructing his people to follow moral ways and of hoping for the best possible government to ensue; it does not imply that success is a certainty. Mencius said that success lies with heaven, and that the ruler who seeks to govern well should "be strong to do good; that is all." [*Mencius*, II/ii/14/3; Legge, p. 175.] That tallies very well with the general sense of the *Lü-shih Ch'un-ch'iu*. Mencius, however, believed profoundly that alternating cycles of good order and disorder would prevail throughout the world, and that a true king must arise after five hundred years; therefore he fervently anticipated a new king, and was wholly optimistic. The *Lü-shih Ch'un-ch'iu*, on the other hand, inclines toward a view that rise and decline of governments exhibits a random convergence of cosmic forces. Although it firmly maintains an attitude of

[52] *Lü-shih Ch'un-ch'iu*, *ch.* 14, "Ch'ang-kung." Cf. [in *ch.* 14], "Shen jen" and "Yü ho."

unworried acceptance of fate, nonetheless it cannot compare in optimism with the Mencius. Wang Ch'ung took over its outlook, and carried it a step farther, leading to the writing of his wholly pessimistic discourse "Chih ch'i" [ch. 17, no. 53, "On the Phases of Good Government"]. It is common for people to be startled by [Wang's writings, the *Balanced Essays*, or] the *Lun Heng*, as an "extraordinary book," not realizing that Wang was not entirely apart from all scholarly traditions, and did not create all his ideas by his own mind alone.

Another point that merits our attention is that the *Lü-shih Ch'un-ch'iu* was heavily influenced by the Taoist school, and that its negative elements are not limited to the one just discussed. To value one's life and to stress one's self-interest [loosely translating, "*Kuei-sheng*" and "*Chung-chi*," the names of sections of *chs.* 1 and 2] constitute the basic tenets of the entire book; as expanded and developed, the inescapable conclusion to which they lead is a view of life of escapism and egocentricity. The section called "On Valuing One's Life" ["*Kuei-sheng*," in *ch.* 2] recounts how [the sage-king of legendary antiquity] Yao wished to relinquish his throne to Tzu-chou Chih-fu, and how the people of the State of Yueh tried strenuously to put Prince Sou on their throne, and that the ruler of the State of Lu sent a gift of money to [the recluse worthy] Yen Ho. In all three cases these men were unwilling that any extraneous objects should injure their lives; they each refused, or fled and hid themselves, and rejected what was offered. "Thus it is said: the true Tao lies in maintaining one's self; its superfluities may be applied to serving the state; its bits and scraps may be applied to governing the empire. Accordingly, it can be seen that the accomplishments of emperors and kings are but the sage's secondary affairs; they are not that whereby he perfects himself, and nourishes his life." This looks back to Chuang Tzu's parable about the sacred tortoise that would rather be dragging its tail in the mud [*Chuang Tzu, ch.* 17]. It is quite different in its import from the activisim in politics of the early Han period Huang-Lao Taoism. Instead, here we see preserved the original character of pre-Ch'in egocentric thought. It provides another example of the way the *Lü-shih Ch'un-ch'iu* sets forth the earlier sources of its learning.

Section Four
The *Huai-nan Hung-Lieh* (*ca.* 130 B.C.)

IF we are to label the *Lü-shih Ch'un-ch'iu* the forerunner of the Han Eclectic School, then the *Huai-nan Hung-lieh* [淮南鴻烈, or, more commonly, the *Huai-nan Tzu*] fully merits being designated the orthodox expression of its "Taoist Schools." Liu An was the eldest son of Liu Ch'ang [posthumous title], Prince Li, who had been enfieffed as Prince of Huai-nan. Liu

Ch'ang was banished to Shu [modern Szechwan] for having committed crimes, and en route died by starving himself. The Emperor Wen [reigned 179–157 B.C.] in pity enfieffed his four sons, among whom Liu An was granted the title Marquis of Fu-ling in 172, and Prince of Huai-nan in 164. "He constantly resented the manner of Prince Li's death, longed to revolt, but never found an excuse for that."[53] "He was by nature fond of books and of playing the lute, and did not like hunting and hounds, or racing about on horseback. Moreover, he desired to acquire secret reservoirs of support among the people by pleasing them, and gaining a widespread reputation. He gathered together guest scholars and Taoist adepts to the number of several thousand; they compiled an *Inner Text* [*nei-shu*] of twenty-one essays, and an *Outer Text* [*wai-shu*] of very numerous parts. There was also a *Middle Text* [*chung-shu*] in eight chapters, discussing divine beings and immortals as well as "alchemical arts" [*huang-po chih shu* 黃白之術], which additionally comprised more than two-hundred thousand words."[54] In the first year of the Emperor Wu's *yuan-shou* reign period [122 B.C.] it was discovered that Liu An was plotting to revolt; he committed suicide by cutting his throat.[55]

[53] *Shih Chi*, ch. 118, "Biography of the Princes of Huai-nan and Heng-shan." [Watson, *Shih Chi*, Vol. II, pp. 359–92, "The Biographies of the Kings of Huai-nan and Heng-shan."]

[54] *Han Shu*, ch. 44, "Biography of the Prince of Huai-nan." The "Treatise on Literature" [ch. 30 of the *Han Shu*] lists the *Huai-nan Nei* ["Inner"] in 21 *p'ien* ["chapters"], the *Huai-nan Wai* ["Outer"] in 33 *p'ien*, the *Huai-nan Wang Fu* ["Prose-poems by the Prince of Huai-nan"] in 82 *p'ien*, the *Huai-nan Wang Ch'ün Ch'en Fu* ["Prose-poems by the Prince of Huai-nan's Courtiers"] in 44 *p'ien*, and the *Huai-nan Tsa Tzu Hsing* [under the category of "astronomy"] in 19 *chüan*. The chapter "Yao-lüeh" [the summarizing chapter 21 of the *Huai-nan Tzu*] claims that the book was "composed by Mr. Liu" [i.e., by Liu An himself] and also states that it represents: "the comprehensive elucidation of past and present learning [i.e., "*t'ai tsu* 泰族; also the name of ch. 20] of the *Hung-lieh*." Both Kao Yu's "Preface" [ca. A.D. 212] and the *Hsi-ching Tsa-chi* [attributed to Liu Hsin, d. A.D. 23; assembled by Ko Hung, c. 277–c. 357] state that the "Nei P'ien" ["Inner Sections"] constitute the *Hung-lieh* (*hung* meaning "vast"; *lieh* meaning "radiantly manifest"). Liu Hsiang [77–76 B.C.] changed the name to *Huai-nan Nei-p'ien*. The "Journal of Literature" in the *Sui Shu* [seventh century A.D.] first lists it as the *Huai-nan Tzu*. Among those contributing to its composition were eight persons: Su Fei, Li Shang, Tso Wu, T'ien Yu, Lei Pei, Mao Pei, Wu Pei, and Chin Ch'ang. Liu An in his own right also was "highly skilled in literary composition," and it may be that some portion of the work is actually from his hand. The best edition of the *Huai-nan Hung-lieh* [or, the *Huai-nan Tzu*] today is the *Chi-chieh* edition of Liu Wen-tien [1933].

[55] Note that his *Shih Chi* biography states that in the eighth year of Emperor Hsiao Wen's reign [172 B.C.] the Prince of Li's sons all had reached the age of seven or eight. The *Han Shu*, ch. 14, "Table of the Feudal Princes," has Liu An in possession of his titles for forty-two years. From this we can conclude that he was probably fifty-eight at the time of his death and therefore must have been born in the first year of Emperor Wen's reign (179?–122 B.C.).

The *Huai-nan Tzu* describes its own content, stating: "To discuss the *Tao* but not to discuss men's affairs is to be without relevance for the world's ups and downs; to discuss affairs but not to discuss the *Tao* is to provide no means of joining with the play and rest of the cosmic transformations." Therefore, "we observe the manifestations in heaven and earth and penetrate the affairs of past and present . . . in order to encompass everything within the realm, put all things in order, respond to changes, and comprehend differing species. That is not to pursue the tracks along a single course, or to cling to the tenets of but one corner."[56] In his preface to the book, Kao Yu [*fl.* A.D. 212] has written: "Its import is close to the *Lao Tzu*, [stressing] detached tranquility and avoidance of unnecessary action, pursuing the void and clinging to quiescence, it comes and goes through the web of the *Tao*." Although "there is nothing in all the categories of things and affairs that it does not include, yet its main outlines all hark back to the *Tao*."

As we observe that its [summarizing final chapter, *ch.* 21] "Yao lüeh p'ien" takes up eight schools of thought and learning from the Grand Duke Wang [Lü Shang, of the Chou founding] and Confucius, to Shen Pu-hai and Lord Shang, but never touches upon Huang-Lao, and that within its twenty chapters it offers frequent refutations and corrections of the various teachings of Confucians, Mohists, Nominalists, Legalists, even the divine immortals,[57] but does not include the Taoists, it would appear that the authors privately supported Huang-Lao as the proper core of their learning, and further "adopted the best of the Confucians and Mohists, and pieced together the essentials from Nominalism and Legalism," to achieve the maximum utility. Kao Yu's comments truly are quite apt.

In the past the State of Ch'in had adopted the governing methods devised by Lord Shang and Li Ssu, but Lü Pu-wei, in his desire to overthrow the First Emperor, had forcefully refuted Legalism, founding a distinct new school of learning in which the overall guiding tenets were valuing life and complying with the people's wishes. Liu An's purpose in having his book written also was to overthrow his ruler [the Emperor Wu], and he also adopted the format of drawing simultaneously on various schools. Yet his book's one-sided emphasis on Huang-Lao, and the contrast which that provides with Lü Pu-wei's book, seems to be explained by the fact that the *Huai-nan Tzu* took form just as the Han period burgeoning

---

[56] *Huai-nan Tzu, ch.* 21, "Yao lüeh." [For a translation, see de Bary, *Sources*, pp. 201–205.]

[57] For attacks against Confucianism, see *ch.* 7, "Pen Ching"; against Mohism, *ch.* 13, "Fan lun"; against the Nominalists, *ch.* 11, "Ch'i su"; against Legalism, *ch.* 6, "Lan Ming" and *ch.* 9, "Chu shu"; and against the [teachings based on] divine spirits and immortals, *ch.* 7, "Ching shen."

of Huang-Lao doctrines reached its peak and was on the verge of declining, and as the Confucian school was beginning to win the court's admiration.[58] Therefore it was with a one-sided stress on vacuity and quiescence that he assumed the opposition to one who [as the Emperor Wu had been described] was "inwardly impelled by many desires though outwardly conveying benevolence and righteousness," hoping to arouse support in the minds of scholar-officials as well as of the common people. It is to be regretted that documentary evidence is inadequate to permit us a full examination of the facts.

The *Huai-nan Tzu* accepts from the Lao Tzu the concepts of a universe whose basic substance is the *Tao*, and that all physical things are generated by it.[59] Human beings are among those physical things and therefore also embody the Tao. "The human person [*shen*] is a lodging of the *Tao*; when one acts in accord with his person he thus acts in accord with *Tao*."[60] The way to maintaining accord with one's person lies in practicing the teachings of non-action so as to be aligned with the *Tao* and its workings [*Tao-te*]. "To act according to one's nature is called *Tao*; to conform to one's innate character is called *Te*" (same as note 60) [*Te*, "power," "*virtus*" or virtue; cf. Chapter Five, above]. That is to say, all forced and artifical rites and proprieties are destructive of the *Tao* and are therefore worthless. It appears that "to act according to one's nature" refers back to the pristine stage of human life. In antiquity people were in a state resembling innocent childhood: "They dug wells and drank, they cultivated fields and ate . . . relatives by blood or by marriage neither slandered nor praised each other; among friends there was no issue of kindness or injury. Then when the time came that rites and the idea of righteousness were produced, when goods and belongings were valued,

---

[58] The histories do not provide a clear-cut statement on the date of the *Huai-nan Tzu*'s completion. In Liu An's biography in the *Han Shu*, *ch*. 44, it states: "Previously Liu An had gone to the court where he presented the 'Inner Chapters' composed by himself." It also states that Liu An had visited the court in the second year of the *Chien-yuan* reign period [139 B.C.], where, moved by the words of the Marquis of Wu-an, he returned home and "secretly assembled guest retainers, and made efforts to appeal to the common people, for the purposes of his rebellion." In the second year of the *Yuan-shuo* reign period [127 B.C.], he was granted a stool and a cane [by the Emperor, signifying he was exempted by reason of age] from appearing at court. Presenting his book at court therefore must have occurred prior to this date.

[59] *Huai-nan Tzu*, *ch*. 20, "T'ai tsu": "Now the *Tao* is that from which all tangible things have their origin." In *ch*. 3, "T'ien wen": "The *Tao* is called the compass [i.e., that which circumscribes cosmic cycles]; the beginning is the oneness. Oneness however does not generate, therefore its division into the *Yin* and the *Yang*. The *Yin* and the *Yang* couple harmoniously and all things are generated."

[60] *Ibid*., *ch*. 11, "Ch'i-su." [Cf. *The Huai-nan Tzu, Book Eleven: Behavior, Culture and the Cosmos*, by Benjamin E. Wallacker, which offers a translation of this chapter with full notes.]

cheating and falsity sprang up, slander and dispute were common, acts of kindness and injury went side by side. In consequence, there appeared both the admirable behavior of Tseng Shen and Hsiao-chi, and the depraved acts of the Brigand Chih and Chuang Chiao [for Tseng Shen and Hsiao-chi, paragons of filial conduct, note the reference to them in *Chuang Tzu*, ch. 26; Watson, *Complete Works of Chuang Tzu*, p. 294. For the depraved bandits see *Chuang Tzu*, ch. 29 and *Shih Chi*, 116]. Thus, when there are great carriages and dragon pennants, with feather canopies and hanging curtains, with teams of horses four abreast [symbolic of pompous wealth and splendor], then there are certain to be such treachery as thieves boring through the walls and picking the locks, piling up mounds to climb over the rear walls. When there are fancifully patterned and rich embroideries, delicate silks and finest fabrics, there will also be persons in odd cast-off straw sandals, and ragged short coats (same as note 60). Nevertheless "those wise in the *Tao* will turn back to pure simplicity";[61] that is truly an unvarying principle.

"At birth, men are quiescent"; that is, government and society also are late developments [in response to man's loss of his pristine nature]. Heaven produces the myriad things that are "firmly set by that spontaneous process" (same as note 61). "In ancient times mankind was in the midst of unformed darkness. The dynamic forces [*shen-ch'i*] were not active abroad, and the myriad things were all peacefully silent in blissful serenity. . . . At that time, the myriad peoples were wildly free; they did not know east from west. They walked about chewing on their food, and patted their bellies contentedly [i.e., were well-fed and carefree]. They were enveloped in heaven's harmony, and nourished by earth's bounty. They did not practice deceit, nor engage in disputes with each other. How extensive and pervasive! It can be called the supreme governance. . . . Why would they be willing to stir up troubles among people, and imperil their safety for material things?" Thus it is that "in an age when the powers [of the Tao] are most fully realized, people happily passed their days in that unordered, unbounded region, and put their trust in their vast dwelling place. . . . No attempts were made to control, manage, separate, or segregate things, but hidden and covert, they throve of themselves. Turbid and vast, the pristine simplicity was not yet dispersed; it was all-enfolding in its oneness, and the myriad things were abundant."[62]

Sadly, however, "the primordial great purity" could not be perpetuated. "Coming to the degenerate age," desires became ever more numerous as human affairs became ever more complex. "The people were numerous and goods were scarce; no matter how hard they labored, their sustenance remained inadequate; so quarrels and disputes arose. So it was

---

[61] *Ibid.*, ch. 1, "Yuan tao."
[62] *Ibid.*, ch. 2, "Ch'u chen."

that benevolence came to be venerated. But benevolence and meanness were not in balance. The evil flocked together in cliques to carry on dishonest stratagems, harboring their cunning and deceitful intentions, to the loss of men's pristine natures. So it was that righteousness came to be venerated. But the *Yin* and the *Yang* [female and male] emotions provide that no one is without lusty impulses. Men and women had lived together in groups, intermixed and without separation of the sexes. So it was that the rites came to be venerated. But the emotions of life could well up and inflict themselves on others despite the rites, thereby leading to discord. So it was that [harmonizing] music came to be venerated. [The next sentence adds: "Thus benevolence, righteousness, rites and music could relieve failings, but could not lead to overall good order."] . . . Finally it came to the point where the mountains and rivers, streams and valleys were divided, making fields and boundaries. Reckonings were made of how many people there were, providing allotments and quotas for everyone. Walls were built and moats dug, and mechanical devices and defenses were provided in full. [The state] was embellished with offices and titles, costumes and rankings were instituted, the noble and the common were distinguished, the worthy and the incompetent were set apart, accounts were written of demerit and merit, and rewards and punishments were implemented. Then military preparations waxed strong as hostilities sprang up. The ordinary people suffered decimation, destruction, and disaster. They were ravaged and slaughtered without cause; they were penalized and executed for no crime. Such were the consequences."[63]

The origins of government are laid to the decline of the age. Yet establishing the ruler and instituting leaders were not wholly without benefit and utility. After the *Tao* was dispersed and its powers lost, disasters both of nature and of man brought on their sufferings, whereupon the Sages appeared to relieve those. The Way of the Ruler [*chün tao*] then followed, and was established. "In the past, in the time of Master Jung-ch'eng [reputed advisor to the Yellow Emperor], the people would just take places in file [like wild geese in flight] as they walked, they entrusted their children to birds' nests, stored their excess grain at the edge of the fields. Tigers and leopards might wander near, scorpions and snakes might crawl about [without harming people], and no one gave a thought to why it was so. Subsequently, coming to the time of Emperor Yao, the ten suns came forth simultaneously, scorching the grain in the fields, killing plants and trees, and the people had nothing to eat. The *chieh-yü* [fierce man-eating animal], the *tso-ch'ih* [monster], the *chiu-ying* [harmful apparitions], the Wind God, the giant wild boars, and the giant snake all worked their harm on the people. Therefore Yao sent

---

[63] *Ibid.*, ch. 8, "Pen ching."

[the archer] Yi, who exterminated the *tso-ch'ih* in the wilds of Ch'ou-hua [Southern marshlands] and killed the *chiu-ying* on the River Hsiung [in the northern steppes], and strangled the Wind God in the lake of Ch'ing-ch'iu [in the East] and shot [nine of] the ten suns up overhead as he also shot the *chieh-yü* [predators] down below. He decapitated the giant snakes at the Tung-t'ing Lake and captured the giant wild boars at the Mulberry Grove. The myriad people were all overjoyed. They placed Yao on the throne as Son of Heaven. Consequently throughout the length and breadth of the land, in mountains and plains, far and near, there came for the first time to be roads and hamlets."[64] This is an example of the leader who has relieved the people's calamities thereby being established as the ruler.

"All forms of animal life having passions also have fangs or horns, forefoot claws or hindfoot hooves. Those with horns gore, those with teeth bite, those with venom sting, those with hooves kick. When in good spirits they play with each other, using those; when angered they wound each other. That is their innate nature. Mankind has desires for clothing and food and the materials [supplying those] are insufficient. Hence they live in groups that dwell side-by-side. When things are inequitably divided and their demands are not satisfied, there is conflict. In conflict the strong coerce the weak and the fearless encroach upon the timid. Humans do not have as much strength of sinew and bone, or the sharpness of claw and tooth. Therefore they skin hides to make armor, smelt iron to make blades. Avaricious and greedy persons then ravaged and plundered the realm; the myriad people have been troubled and stirred, unable to find safety wherever they were. Sages rose up in indignation to take punitive action against the strong and violent, pacifying the disorderly age, levelling hazards and eliminating defilement. The turbid was made clear, the imperiled was made secure."[65] Therefore: "In antiquity the establishing of emperors and kings was not done in order to serve and sustain their desires. Sages who mounted the throne did not do so for the sake of their personal ease and pleasure. It was because throughout the realm the strong attacked the weak, the many ran roughshod over the few, the deceitful cheated the ignorant, the fearless encroached upon the timid, those with knowledge did not teach others, those with accumulated goods did not share with others. That is why the Son of Heaven was established to equalize things and make them uniform. Because one person's intelligence is inadequate to reflect on everything within the realm, there were established also the Three Lords and the Nine Ministers to support and assist him. Isolated states with variant customs in remote distances and inaccessible places could not come under the spread of his virtue and

---

[64] *Ibid.*
[65] *Ibid.*, ch. 15, "Ping lüeh."

receive its benefits, so the feudal lords were established to teach and guide them."[66] This offers the theory that the ruler was instituted to ameliorate human calamity.

The *Lao Tzu* says: "When the uncarved block is fragmented and dispersed, one then makes implements. The Sage uses those [instruments of civilization]; he establishes officials and rulers."[67] The *Huai-nan Tzu* praises the ideal of "the great purity," while acknowledging the need for ruler and leaders. This idea is in fact based on the *Lao Tzu*. To state it as the highest ideal, I will not rule others and others will not look to me for rule. Hsü Yu [in whose favor Yao wanted to abdicate; *vide Chuang Tzu*, *ch*. 1, *ch*. 28, etc.] would not accept the empire but "in following along with the world ["*t'ien-hsia*"] I act for the empire [*t'ien-hsia*]. . . . For this thing that is the world is also possessed by me, and I am also possessed by this world. How could there be any separation between me and the world! That is to say, why need the one who possesses the world grasp authority and wield power, hold the control over life and death, and thereby assure obedience to his commands? What I refer to as possessing the world does not mean that. It means only to gain oneself; gaining oneself, the world also acquires me. . . . What I call gaining oneself means making oneself whole, for when one has become whole, he has become one with the *Tao*."[68] In point of the practical necessities, however, when the *Tao* has been lost and the world has degenerated, disaster and disorder press in, one atop the other. "The one who comprehends the *Tao* . . . [also] has ties to the world. . . . When the world is in disorder, the knowing person cannot achieve order for himself alone."[69] Furthermore, the methods to be employed by the ruler on the throne must then be a matter of the utmost urgency.

Seen in this light, the *Huai-nan Tzu's* form is that of the *Tsa-chia*, drawing simultaneously on all the schools; its objective, however, is that of the *Huang-Lao* school, in concern for the governing of the age. For the Han dynasty, it definitely is to be regarded as the principal representative of "Taoism," just as Tung Chung-shu represents the orthodox line of its Confucianism.

In discoursing on the methods of governing, the Huai-nan Tzu holds non-action and spontaneity [or the natural way, *tzu-jan*] to be basic, in that agreeing with Huang-Lao. In including statements about the prominence to be given the laws, and about self-cultivation, it further exhibits the identifying characteristics of the "Taoist School." Since those are all familiar to us, we need merely cite the essential points to display the

[66] *Ibid.*, *ch*. 19, "Hsiu wu."
[67] *Tao Te Ching*, *ch*. 28.
[68] *Huai-nan Tzu*, *ch*. 1, "Yuan tao."
[69] *Ibid.*, *ch*. 2, "Ch'u chen."

outlines of the book. Non-action [or, taking no unnecessary action] is labelled "pure quiescence" [*ch'ing-ching* 清靜]. *Ch.* Eleven, "*Ch'i su*," states: "The *Tao* of governing is for the ruler to have no oppressive commands and for the officials to perform no troublesome governing acts. . . . Thus a disorderly state will seem to be flourishing, while a well-ordered state will appear to be empty. A stable state will present an appearance of deficiency, while a collapsing state will seem to have a surplus." [At the author's suggestion, translation here follows T'ao Hung-ch'ing's emendation of the *Huai-nan Tzu* text, namely, reversing the words *wang*, "collapsing" and *ts'un*, "stable," thus bringing the passage in line with the immediate context. The following lines are: "Surplus does not indicate bountiful wealth; as desires are limited, expenditures will be few. Deficiency does not indicate lack of goods; people being reckless, much will be wasted."] In *ch.* Twenty, "T'ai tsu" it says: "In making achievements one should not disdain limitations. In managing affairs [of governing], one should not disdain reducing them. In seeking to get things, one should not disdain asking for less. Limited achievement is more easily completed. Reduced affairs are more easily controlled. Smaller requests are more easily satisfied."[70] Even though one "decreases and yet further decreases" [*Lao Tzu, ch.* 48], that does not in itself exhaust the quintessential meaning of *wu-wei*, or taking no action. "It is also sometimes said that the one who takes no action is so quiet as to be without a sound, so detached as to be wholly unmoved. When pulled he does not come; when pushed he does not go. Such a one as this, it is thought, has gained the likeness of the *Tao*. I, however, say that is not so." Such as the Divine Agriculturalist, [legendary emperor, and the sage rulers] Yao, Shun, Yü, and T'ang all acted to promote the people's advantages and to eradicate their evils. "One has never heard about a situation in which, from the Son of Heaven all the way down to the common people, no one belabored his four limbs, no one applied his thought, and yet affairs are properly managed and desires satisfied. The circumstances of topography are such that rivers flow eastward, and humans must give attention to them. Having done so, the waters are directed to flow through the valleys. The grains sprout with the coming of spring, and humans must apply their efforts to them; in consequence of which, the five cereals are enabled to mature. If, on the other hand, the waters had been allowed to flow their own way, and the grains

---

[70] *Ibid., ch.* 9, "Chu shu," states: "When the water is murky, the fish turn their heads upward [to the surface, for air]; when governing is oppressive, the people are agitated. . . . Thus also when there are many schemings at the top, there is much deceit below; when there is much busyness at the top, there are many posturings below; when the top vexes and harrasses, below there is uncertainty; when the top demands too much, then below quarrelling ensues. . . . Therefore the Sage's undertakings are few and his governing is made easy; he demands little and is easily satisfied."

had been allowed to grow of themselves, the vast deeds of Kun [and his son, the Great] Yü would never have been accomplished, and the wisdom of Hou-chi [the legendary emperor and patron of millet] would never have been put to use. [Kun and Yü "channeled the rivers"; Hou-chi improved grain culture.] The kind of exemplar of non-action of whom I speak is one whose private purposes would never enter into the public way, and whose personal tastes and desires would never deflect the standard methods. Such a one would undertake matters in accord with principles [of the natural world], and would erect his authority in accord with his inner qualities. The spontaneous forces would prevail, and pretenses would not be tolerated. When undertakings were completed, he would assume no personal credit; when deeds were accomplished, he would claim no fame. That is not to say that he would feel the stimulus but fail to respond, know the need but fail to be moved. Rather, suppose one were to use fire to dry out a well, or to use the waters of the Huai River [which runs through the lower North China Plain] for irrigating the mountains; that would be to exert the self while contradicting spontaneity [Nature], hence that can be called taking action. Suppose instead one were to use boats on water, wagons on sand, sledges on the mud, and baskets [for transporting earth] in the mountains, making ditches in the summer [when the rainfall occurs] and making retaining ponds in the winter; where the land is high, taking it for mountains, and where it lies low using it as ponds. Such would not constitute what I have called taking action."[71]

The meaning of taking no action, therefore, is to let things be what their nature indicates, spontaneously according with their character.[72] The high-pressure control policies of authoritarian government are thus included among those things which are eschewed. That is because the natures of individual things differ one from another, and they express their natural dispositions in their modes of existence. The ruler of the state should, by giving free reign to spontaneity, cause each to achieve what is appropriate to it. "So, when Yao reigned over the empire, Shun was his Chancellor, Hsieh was his Grand Marshall, Yü was his Grand Secretary, Hou-chi was his Grand Master of Agriculture, and Hsi-chung was Minister of Works. [These are fanciful references to semi-legendary sages who usually are said to have lived at widely different times.] In his guidance

[71] *Ibid., ch.* 19, "Hsiu wu."

[72] *Ibid., ch.* 1, "Yuan tao" states: "Silently, taking no action, yet nothing remains undone. Placidly, doing no governing, yet nothing remains ungoverned. That which is called taking no action means not assuming precedence over things when acting. What is called nothing remains undone means according with the actions that things [naturally] do. What is called doing no governing means not altering the spontaneous [developments]; what is called nothing remains ungoverned means going along with the normal interactions among things."

of the myriad people, those who dwelt by the waters practiced fishing, those in the mountains were woodcutters, those in valleys herded, and those on the dry land farmed. Their location was suited to their activities, their activities were suited to their implements, their implements were suited to their uses, and such uses were suited to those persons." In this way, "each thing is used in appropriate ways, applied to what is fitting. Then all things are equal and there is no room for anyone to fault [or infract the individuality] of another. As for clinging to one standard by which to equalize all things, forcing people to conform to oneself, that is totally contrary to the *Tao* of governing, and inevitably will produce chaos. Moreover, the world's ordinary tendencies toward distinguishing as between white and black and fixing one inviolate standard [i.e., *Legalist principles*] or toward venerating one orthodoxy and eradicating variants [i.e., Confucian and other tendencies] all arise from the mistaken belief that there exist clear criteria for right and wrong. They fail to understand that: "The right and wrong of the world cannot be determined. Everyone in the world says right for what he holds right and says wrong for what he holds wrong. What are called right and wrong all differ, each person considering himself right and holding others to be wrong. . . . For that which unifies all right and wrong is the universe. Now when I wish to select what is right and cling to this, while selecting what is wrong and discarding that, I fail to know that what the world calls right and wrong are indeterminate as to who is right and who is wrong. Lao Tzu said: 'Rule a large country as you would cook a small fish.' The broad-minded will say [that means] do not stir it too often; the harsh-minded will say, make it extremely salty and sour, and that is all!"[73]

Taking no action provides the framework of all governing methods, and their major items do not go beyond: employing the right persons; giving prominence to the laws; effecting the transformation [of the governed]; and assuring sufficient food. The *Huai-nan Tzu* fully reflects the facility with which the [Han dynasty] Taoist School accommodated to *Yin-Yang* doctrines, drew from Confucianists and Mohists, and patched together elements of Nominalism and Legalism. Thus, in discussing employing persons, it adopts from Shen Pu-hai and Han Fei Tzu the theories about the ruler being at ease while his servitors labor, and dividing up duties to which clear responsibility for accomplishment attaches.[74] In

[73] *Ibid.*, ch. 11, "Ch'i su."

[74] *Ibid.*, ch. 9, "Chu shu" mostly illustrates this idea. See also *ch.* 6, "Lan ming," and *ch.* 14, "Ch'üan yen." *Ch.* 9, "Chu shu," states: "The method of ruling over the people is to undertake matters of non-action and implement teachings of non-speaking. [The ruler] must be pure and quiescent and refrain from action; he must maintain his stance and avoid wavering. He should follow along with circumstances while giving full rein to [the people] below, demand performance [from servitors] but not belabor himself. . . . Thereby his plans shall never fail, his concerns never go awry. His words shall set the clear

discussing the prominence to be given to the laws, it accepts from the *Kuan Tzu* and *The Book of Lord Shang* the views that the ruler and his servitors must jointly uphold and observe laws, that rewards and punishments must be impartial, and that institutions must change with the times.[75] In discussing how to implement the people's transformation, it agrees with the Confucians on self-cultivation to make the self upright, on the basic importance of benevolence and righteousness, and on punishment and administration being of but superficial importance.[76] Discussions

---

patterns and his deeds the models of comportment for the entire realm. His comings and goings will be in response to the seasons; his activity and rest shall accord with principles. He will not have likes or dislikes for beauty and ugliness; he will not feel pleasure or anger in meting out rewards or punishments. Names will be fixed of themselves, classifications will be determined of themselves; affairs will unfold spontaneously and nothing will ensue from [the ruler] in person."

[75] *Ch.* 9, "Chu shu," states: "The laws are the standards of measure for the realm and the rulers gauge. . . . Of old, offices of government were established through which to interdict the people and to prevent their unrestrained conduct. Consequently, the establishment of the ruler was done so as to have control over the offices of government and assure that they would not act in unauthorized ways. The law codes, the rites and righteousness, were the means of interdicting the ruler, assuring that he would not be self-willed, or arbitrary in judgment. The people being no longer unrestrained in their conduct, the *Tao* triumphed. With the triumph of the *Tao*, orderliness was fully achieved. Thus there was a return to non-action." And, in *ch.* 10, "Miou ch'eng," it states: "The enlightened ruler's rewarding and punishing is not done for his own interests; it is done for the sake of the state. When something meets his personal interests but makes no contribution to the nation, he should not bestow any rewards there. When something is counter to his personal interests but is of advantage to the nation, he should not mete out any punishments there." In *ch.* 13, "Fan lun," it states: "For how could there be any constant laws in this world? Appropriate to the affairs of an age, derived from human principles, in accord with heaven and earth [i.e., the natural world] and in compliance with ghosts and spirits, only then can laws keep governance correct. . . . Of old The Divine Agriculturalist had no institutions or regulations yet the people obeyed. . . . In this present age, when people suffer insult and ignore humiliation, are avaricious and virtually shameless, should one desire to rule according to the Way of the Divine Agriculturalist, it would only produce certain chaos."

[76] *Ibid.*, *ch.* 20, "T'ai tsu," states: "Therefore, even though the laws be in existence, it is necessary to await a Sage before there can be good government; though the pitch pipes be complete, it is necessary to await an ear before they can be heard. Thus what accounts for a state's being preserved is not that it have laws, but that it have worthy persons." It says further: "In ruling a country well, the optimum is to nurture moral influence; next to that is to promulgate just laws." And, "Thus benevolence and righteousness are the basis of good government." Also, "If the people lack integrity and a sense of shame, they are ungovernable; unless the rites and righteousness are cultivated, integrity and the sense of shame cannot be established. . . . Without laws, governing cannot be carried on; if one does not know the rites and righteousness, he cannot implement laws." In *ch.* 12, "Tao ying," it states: "I have never heard of a case where the ruler was well ordered in his own person and yet his state was in disorder; nor have I ever heard of a case where the ruler was disorderly in his own person and yet the state was in good order."

of assuring sufficient food also acknowledge the concepts drawn from Confucius and Mencius about the importance of the people and about the people regarding food as equal in importance to Heaven, as well as their views on keeping taxes low and the ruler's desires limited.[77] None of these points contains the slightest modicum of newness, and they demand no further discussion. As for the book's drawing eclectically upon the Five Agents and *Yin-yang* doctrines and in adjusting those to the naturalism of the *Lao Tzu* and the *Chuang Tzu*, despite displaying in those respects few differences of content with the thought of Tung Chung-shu,[78] in its factional stance the work is indeed quite distinct from his Confucian-oriented *Ch'un-ch'iu fan-lu*. [Cf. Chapter Ten, Section Three, above.]

Section Five
Wang Ch'ung, *Lun Heng* (*circa* A.D. 80)

Wang Ch'ung's courtesy name was Chung-jen; he was born in the third year of the Emperor Kuang-wu's *Chien-wu* reign period [A.D. 27]. As a child he displayed high intelligence. He was not fond of play and games. Early in life he went to the capital as a student in the Imperial Academy [*T'ai hsüeh*], where he studied under Pan Piao. He held office, reaching the post of Inspector in the Metropolitan Prefecture. In the second year of the *Chang-ho* reign period [A.D. 88] of the Emperor Chang he left his post and returned to live at his home. The Emperor ordered a government carriage sent to bring him to the court, but, on the excuse of being elderly and ill, he did not accept that [honor]. He died during the *Yung-yuan* reign period [89–104] of the Emperor Ho. His autobiographical account [*ch.* 30, "Tzu chi," *Lun Heng*] records: "I am poor without one *mou* of land to secure my livelihood; my ambitions are out of place among princes and lords. Lowly indeed, without so much as a peck or a bushel of official stipend, my mind is as expansive as if I enjoyed a princely emolument [literally: ten-thousand bushels]. I obtained official appointment but

---

[77] *Ibid., ch.* 9, "Chu shu," states: "Food is basic to the people; the people are basic to the state; the state is basic to the ruler." *Ch.* 11, "Ch'i su," says: "When the people have a surplus, they are deferent; when they do not have enough, they contend." *Ch.* 14, "Ch'üan yen," says: "The basis of good government lies in devoting full effort to keeping the people tranquil. The basis of keeping the people tranquil lies in there being a sufficiency for their use. The basis of providing that sufficiency for their use lies in avoiding robbing them of their [seasonal agricultural working] time. The basis of avoiding robbing them of their time lies in reducing [the state's] business. The basis of reducing business lies in limiting [the ruler's] desires. The basis of limiting desires lies in restoring the nature. The basis of restoring the nature lies in abandoning all burdens [of the mind]."

[78] *Ibid., ch.* 3, "T'ien wen"; *ch.* 5, "Shih Tze"; *ch.* 6, "Lan ming"; and *ch.* 7, "Ching shen." The ideas set forth there concerning the interactions between heaven and man are in agreement with those of Tung Chung-shu.

found no pleasure there; I lost my position with no regrets. Now, though in circumstances of idle happiness, I do not give rein to desires; living in poverty, my ambitions do not flag. I read ancient writings profligately, and listen with delight to curious conversations. The books of this age and the common views frequently make me uneasy. Dwelling in solitary seclusion, I examine and appraise the true and the false. . . . The common nature is to lust for advance and to disdain retreat, to gather the successful and cast off the failures. When I was raised up and appointed to office, crowds of people swarmed around me; when I was dismissed and went into humble retreat, my former associates turned away and ignored me. To make a record of how the vulgar lack grace, in my idleness I have written twelve essays under the titles "Satires on Vulgar Ways" and "Fidelity and Righteousness" [*Chi-su, Chieh-yi* 譏俗; 節義]. . . . Also, sympathizing with the ruler, whose sole desire is to bring about good order among men, but who cannot find the proper way, who does not understand where the essentials lie, whose spirit grieves, and whose thought is troubled while not perceiving in what direction he should move, I have therefore composed a book on *The Conduct of Government* [*cheng-wu* 政務]. Moreover, distressed by the lack of truth and sincerity in the counterfeit books and vulgar writings, I have written my book of *Balanced Inquiries* [*Lun Heng* 論衡]. . . . It consists of eighty-five essays, totalling more than two-hundred-thousand words. . . . After leaving my prefectural post, as my age approached seventy . . . I have written a book "On Nurturing the Nature" [*Yang hsing* 養性] in sixteen chapters."[79] "Today, only the *Lun Heng* is still in existence."[80]

[79] Based on the *Lun Heng, ch.* 30, "Tzu chi" ["Personal Record"], and *Hou Han Shu, ch.* 79, his biography. [The "Personal Record," written in the third person in accord with convention, is here translated in the first person.] The third year of the *Chien-wu* reign period corresponds with A.D. 27. The *Yung-yuan* reign period lasted sixteen years, from 89 to 104. In the second year of the *Chang-ho* reign period [A.D. 88] Wang Ch'ung's "age approached seventy," so at his death [probably after A.D. 96?] he was over seventy.

[80] *Lun Heng, ch.* 30, "Tzu chi" ["Personal Record"] states: "My book also [i.e., like the writings of Tung Chung-shu referred to by name] has just exceeded a hundred chapters." The *Ssu-k'u t'i-yao* ["Table of Contents with Abstracts" of the Ch'ing Imperial Library, in *ch.* 120], because of this remark, suspects that portions of the *Lun Heng* were already lost in Han times. We should note that this comment is made following Wang Ch'ung's enumeration of his three books, the *Chi-su,* the *Cheng-wu,* and the *Lun Heng.* It may be that he was adding together the 85 chapters with those in the *Chu su* (12 chapters) and the *Cheng-wu* (number not stated), and did not necessarily mean for the remark about "my book(s)" to refer only to the *Lun Heng.* What the histories and biographies record [especially the *Hou Han Shu* biography, which refers to 85 chapters] seems in all likelihood to be the number of chapters in the original work. The extant text contains 84 chapters (the chapter called "*Sheng* pao," whose name appears at the end of no. 84, "Tui tso," has been lost), exists in a number of printings, including that in the *Ssu-pu ts'ung-k'an,* the *Pao ching t'ang* collated edition, and those in the *Han-wei Ts'ung-shu, Po-tzu ch'üan-shu,*

Wang Ch'ung himself said of his *Lun Heng* that its overall purpose, in a single phrase, is "hatred of the false and the preposterous."[81] Throughout all the more than eighty essays, the major portion of them is devoted to dispelling the errors and absurdities in all the thought and practice of past and present.[82] The special feature of the *Lun Heng* of greatest significance, however, is its fatalism grounded in naturalism. Earlier, Mo Tzu had attacked Confucianism on the grounds that it advocated belief in fate, holding that to be one way to destroy the empire. That, however, is based on a misunderstanding of the real meaning of statements that Confucius and Mencius made about fate, and does not warrant acceptance as a definitive critique.[83] That is, although Mencius believed in a heavenly determinism [i.e., *t'ien ming*, in some contexts the "Mandate of Heaven"], his intent was to demonstrate that heaven is the highest power in government. The mind of heaven likes the good and detests the evil; therefore immoral rulers will encounter personal setbacks or overthrow, but if he does good deeds his descendents are sure to reign. Nonetheless, the determination of whether to confer or withhold [rulership] lies with heaven, while the decision to perform good or evil lies with man. Retribution may come earlier or later in individual cases, yet human powers are capable of influencing heaven. Subsequently Tung Chung-shu [c. 179–104 B.C.] and his like discussed calamities and prodigies most earnestly and extensively, also in the desire to make the ruler and people aware that good or bad performance in government can change the course of heaven's

---

Tzu-shu po-chia, *Hu-pei chü-k'e*, and other editions. Of the content of his book *Cheng-wu*, it is said: "It sets forth comprehensively the political matters that should be taken as the most urgent by principal administrators of commanderies and senior officials of the counties. Its intent is to effect the general well-being of the people and to establish transforming influences, and to acknowledge the state's beneficence" (*ch.* 29, no. 84, "Tui tso"). [The 85 essays are designated by number, e.g., "no. 84"; the 30 *chüan* under which those are arranged are indicated by "*ch.*"]

[81] *Lun Heng*, *ch.* 20, no. 61, "Yi wen."

[82] The various essays devoted to the refutation of the counterfeit and the preposterous include no. 25, "Yü tseng," no. 26, "Ju tseng," and no. 27, "Yi tseng." Essays demolishing superstition include the "Nine Essays on Falsity" (from no. 16, "Shu Hsü," to no. 24, "Tao hsü"), as well as the eleven essays from no. 41, "Han wen," to no. 52, "Shih ying," and the nine essays from no. 68, "Ssu hui," to no. 76, "Ssu yi." Essays correcting errors and absurdities in thought and learning include no. 28, "Wen K'ung," no. 29, "Fei Han," no. 30, "Tz'u Meng," no. 31, "T'an t'ien," no. 32, "Shuo jih," no. 81, "Cheng shuo," and no. 83, "An shu." Those condemning elaborate funerals and demonstrating that ghosts do not exist are no. 62, "Lun ssu," no. 63, "Ssu wei," and no. 67, "Po tsang."

[83] The generation of all the myriad things also emerges spontaneously from nature. "They are born from the vital forces [*ch'i* 氣, here *Yin* and *Yang*], those of the various species together giving birth, so that all the myriad things are generated within the natural world [*t'ien-ti chih chien* 天地之間], all together constituting one reality" (*ch.* 3, no. 14, "Wu shih").

mandate. His theories can be seen as the counterpart to those of Mencius. Also, Hsün Tzu had said: "Strengthen the base [i.e., agriculture] and curtail consumption, then heaven will be incapable of impoverishing"; in that way completely rejecting the heaven-man relationship, yet his attitude is notably positive. Wang Ch'ung took up that Confucian optimism that man can prevail over heaven in determining things, and totally demolished it. He relegated to a fate quite beyond man's intervention all issues of human success and failure, and of order and chaos in the state.

At some points Wang Ch'ung's thought bears a superficial resemblance to that of Hsün Tzu. Hsün Tzu had written: "Nature [t'ien] operates with constant regularity" [cf. Chapter Three, Section Seven, p. 349, above] not allowing that man can alter its constancy. The *Lun Heng* goes a step further and rejects the ancient view that heaven has generated mankind and maintains control over human destiny. In its essay no. 14, "Wu shih," it states: "The Confucians' discourses say that heaven and earth by intent gave birth to mankind. This statement is preposterous. For as heaven and earth unite their vital forces [ho ch'i 合氣], inadvertently mankind is spontaneously produced. It is like husband and wife uniting their vital forces and a child thereupon coming by itself to be born. When husband and wife unite their vital forces, it is not that they at that moment have the intent subsequently to produce a child. Their feelings and passions are aroused so they unite; having united, a child is produced. . . . Rather it might be said that mankind's being born within heaven and earth is like fish in the water's depths or fleas on a man" (same as note 83).

The Confucians also said that heaven produced the people and established the ruler over them, so that offices of government were made to shepherd them. Although Wang Ch'ung did not directly refute that, we can infer from the entire corpus of his thought that he would have tended to find that hard to accept. Wang Ch'ung said that heaven's [Nature's] production of the myriad things was wholly spontaneous. There could have been no intent in that to provide mankind with clothing and food. "The blooded creatures are conscious of hunger and cold. Seeing the five grains are edible, they obtain and eat them. And seeing that silk floss and hemp can be worn, they obtain and wear them."[84] Since clothing and food are not produced by heaven, then the ruler and the teacher also must not be established by heaven. The conceptualization of heaven's powers that had developed from earliest antiquity, in Wang Ch'ung's eyes, consisted entirely of groundless statements. Also, then, the theories about heaven's and man's interactions, about calamities and prodigies revealing reprimands and warnings, or about the sequences of producing and of overcoming among the Five Agents, it should go without saying, are all the

---

[84] *Lun Heng*, ch. 18, no. 54, "Tzu jan." [Adapted from Chan, *Source Book*, p. 296.]

more false and preposterous. For: "Heaven has neither mouth nor eyes . . . it is tranquil and without desires . . . it is spontaneous and takes no actions . . . and things act of themselves." The rain and the sunshine appear in their own time, come forth quite definitely with no mindful intent, so "when calamities and strange occurrences occasionally arise, the natural forces have spontaneously produced those; not only are heaven and earth incapable of such acts, they are also incapable of being aware of them."[85]

Wang Ch'ung also adopted the astronomical knowledge of his times and used that to explain the principles underlying calamities and strange occurrences, stating: "One occurrence in the sky is that of solar and lunar eclipses. Every forty-two months there is a solar eclipse, and every fifty-six months there also occurs a lunar eclipse. These eclipses have their constant numbers; they have nothing to do with government. A hundred such strange occurrences or a thousand calamities all share the one [natural] explanation; they are not something that the ruler or the government could bring about."[86] This principle being clear, one must then realize that all those matters which Tung Chung-shu had called heaven's and man's interactions are purely hypothetical deductions about things invented in men's minds. "For, that heaven does not purposely produce the five grains, silk floss, and hemp in order to feed and clothe people is very much like the fact that there are calamities and strange occurrences having no intent to reprimand and warn people. Things are spontaneously produced and man wears and eats them; material forces spontaneously cause strange occurrences and people are afraid of them." Wang Ch'ung is confident that his views "accord with the *Tao* and are not construed to happenings, and although they disagree with the theories of the Confucians, they are in keeping with the meaning of the Yellow Emperor and Lao Tzu [i.e., Huang-Lao]."[87]

Should one insist on maintaining the theory of cosmic interaction, then Wang Ch'ung applied cleverly sophistic argumentation to demonstrate internal inconsistencies, going back and forth to display its contradictions and to show that the theory cannot stand. When the [sage emperor] T'ang encountered a drought, he enumerated the five transgressions in assuming personal blame for it, constituting an example that the heaven-man theorists delighted in citing. Wang shows the falsity of the story thus: "The Sage was pure and perfect; his conduct displayed no deficiencies or mistakes. Why should he charge himself with five transgressions? However, if it was in fact as the *Book of Documents* says, that when T'ang blamed himself, heaven responded with rain, T'ang being without fault even

---

[85] *Ibid.*, "Tzu jan."
[86] *Ibid.*, *ch.* 17, no. 53, "Chih ch'i."
[87] *Ibid.*, "Tzu jan" [in part modified from Chan, *Source Book*, p. 297].

though blaming himself for the five transgressions, for what reason did heaven send rain? If he induced a drought without having committed transgressions, then also he must have known that by blaming himself it was not possible to obtain rain. Explained in this way, the drought was not induced by T'ang, and the rain was not in response to his self-reproach. Instead, the prior drought and the subsequent rain were just the spontaneous acts of nature's forces." And, further: "T'ang encountered seven years of drought. His blaming himself for that, on account of his five transgressions, is said to have taken place at what time? Was it a case of experiencing one drought and immediately blaming himself, or after the drought had recurred for seven years that he then blamed himself? If it is said that on once experiencing drought he immediately blamed himself but it was seven years before the rain fell, why indeed was heaven's response so long delayed? If it is said that he waited seven years before blaming himself, prolonging the misery of the common people, why was he so slow about it?"

Wang Ch'ung has also argued the case told in the "Books of Chou" in the *Documents*, in the document "The Metal-bound Coffer" ["Chint'eng," Legge, p. 351], telling how King Ch'eng believed the slander against the Duke of Chou, and how after lightning and rain and a [miraculously] reversed wind [caused the beaten-down grain to stand up again, showing heaven's pleasure at the ultimately just outcome]. He states: "Lightning is [taken] to signify heaven's anger, while rain is [supposed to be] an expression of its favor. If heaven were truly angered on account of [the slander against] the Duke of Chou, there should only have been lightning, and should not have been rain. On this occasion the rain also came; was heaven simultaneously both angry and pleased?"[88]

Nor is that all. Just as heaven does not reprimand and warn people, neither can people move heaven. There were those who said: "Calamities and prodigies must occur because the ruler's governing moves heaven; heaven moves the material forces in response to his [bad] governing." Wang Ch'ung denied that, saying: "This is also doubtful. For though heaven move things, how can things move heaven? . . . Man, living between heaven and earth, is like fleas living inside a person's clothing or ants occupying holes and cracks. Can fleas or ants by going backward or forward, or now sideways, now ahead, cause the material forces to move or to change within the clothing, or within their holes and cracks?"[89] Heaven and man, moreover, are separated by a vast space, so what could

---

[88] *Ibid., ch.* 18, no. 55, "Kan lei." See also: *ch.* 5, no. 19, "Kan hsü"; *ch.* 6, no 23, "Lei hsü"; *ch.* 14, no. 41, "Han wen" and no. 42, "Ch'ien kao"; *ch.* 15, no. 43, "Pien tung," no. 45, "Ming yü," and no. 46, "Shun ku." [For details of T'ang's act see *Lü-shih Ch'unch'iu, ch.* 9, no. 2, "Shun min."]

[89] *Ibid., ch.* 15, no. 43, "Pien tung" [slightly modified from Chan, *Source Book*, p. 303].

affect the movement of the one by the other? "If we were to speak of heaven as physical body, it must be so high up that it could not hear people's speech. If we were to speak of heaven as breath [or, material force, *ch'i*], how could that breath, there like clouds and mists, hear people's words?"[90] Should it be argued, then, that perfect sincerity can arouse heaven's response and in that way obviate any need for physical ears and eyes, when tested against the nature of things that too proves not to be so. "For perfect sincerity is something that depends on the mind's likes and dislikes. Should there be such a thing as fruits and melons in front of a person, no more than a foot from his mouth, though in his mind he desired to ear them, he could not get them by sucking his breath into his mouth. [I.e., by moving the *ch'i* through his intense desire.] When he uses his hand to pick them up and put them in his mouth he then, however, can get them. Now consider how small those fruits and melons are, and how easily moved if we really want them, and that they are not far from the mouth, yet desiring them in perfect sincerity still does not obtain them. Heaven, moreover, is so high and distant from man, the breath [*ch'i*] comprising that empyrean vastness is without a beginning or an ending point!"[91]

The statements saying that the interactions between man and heaven can cause strange phenomena are thus shown to be lacking credibility. That the rise of such theories occurred so early and that their diffusion has been so widespread finds two explanations. The one is that the ways of spiritual beings had been invoked in establishing moral teachings. "In the texts of the Six Classics the Sages speak frequently of heaven; the reason for doing so is that they desired to transform evil-doers by striking fear into those unenlightened people—by suggesting that [their injunctions against misdeeds] stemmed not merely from their own wish but also from heaven's intent. So when they spoke of heaven [they referred to heaven's will], something analogous to man's mind, they did not refer to the high heaven's vast expanses. The School of Calamity-Response [*Pien-fu chih chia* 變復之家], seeing [the Sages'] deceptive words about heaven, produce statements concerning [heaven's] reprimands and warnings, whenever calamities and prodigies occur." The second explanation is that man has been taken as the analogue of heaven: "In the time of the Three Emperors [of legendary antiquity] people were at ease when sitting, relaxed when walking, now acting as a horse, now serving as an ox. Pure virtues prevailed and the people were simple and unknowing; the knowing, perceptive mentality had not yet taken form. At that time, also, there were no "calamities and prodigies," or, when calamities and prodigies occurred,

<hr />

[90] *Ibid., ch.* 4, no. 17, "Pien hsü."
[91] *Ibid., ch.* 15, no. 43, "Pien tung."

they were not called reprimands and warnings. How is that so? People at that time were simple and ignorant; they did not know enough to judge and criticize each other. In these latest times of decline and degeneracy, with those above and those below making charges against each other, as calamities and prodigies occur from time to time, statements that those are reprimands and warnings are fabricated about them. The heaven of today is the heaven of yesteryear; it is not that the heaven of the past was generous while that today is mean-spirited. Those statements about heaven's warnings and reprimands are made in these times because man has taken his own mind to be analogous to that [of heaven]."[92]

With the theories about heaven's and man's interaction demolished, those other theories about the Five Agents, ominous prodigies and auspicious signs were also readily disposed of. Common belief current at the time concerned the four directions, the five colors, and the twelve beasts [symbols in the Chinese time-sequence systems] as manifestations of the five colors [i.e., the Five Agents] in their conquest of the one by the other. Wang Ch'ung criticized those, saying: "All the myriad things are unfeeling in their mutual depredations, and the blooded creatures impose dominance over each other to the point that they even eat each other, according to the sharpness or clumsiness of teeth and claws, their superiority or inferiority in muscular strength, their agility of movement, or the courage of their temperaments. It is much the same with humans in this world, where inequality of power and unevenness of physical strength causes them to assume dominance or submission, both to impose domination through brute strength and to make depredations against each other by use of swords. . . . People may be courageous or cowardly; hence in battle there are victors and vanquished. The victors do not necessarily possess the material force [ch'i] of metal, and the vanquished have not necessarily been imbued with the essence of wood. [Metal is in the relationship of dominance over Wood, among the Five Agents.] Confucius feared Yang Hu; he hastily left Yang's presence, perspiring. [Cf. commentary on *Analects*, xvii/1 and *Tso Chuan*, Ting ix, x; Legge, pp. 772–77.] Yang Hu was not necessarily of the [symbolic] color white, nor was Confucius' face necessarily green. Hawks attack doves and sparrows, as owls peck at swans and geese; yet hawks and owls are not necessarily produced in the South [Fire], nor are doves, sparrows, swans, and geese necessarily born in the west [Metal; i.e., as the correlation of directions with the dominance succession of the Five Agents would suggest should be so.][93]

[92] *Ibid.*, *ch.* 14, no. 42, "Ch'ien kao," and *ch.* 18, no. 54, "Tzu jan."

[93] *Ibid.*, *ch.* 3, no. 14, "Wu shih." Nonetheless *ch.* 23, no. 66, "Yen tu," draws on *Yin-yang* and the Five Agents in explaining human events, in apparent contradiction with this.

That ominous prodigies are unworthy of belief also is most obvious. "The School of Calamity-Response will say that insects eating the grain is induced by officials in the offices of government. When those commit venality and corruption, the insects in consequence will eat the grain. When their bodies are black and their heads red, it means that the guilty are military officials, but when the insects' heads are black and bodies are red, that indicates civil officials. If punishments are imposed on those officials who are symbolized thereby, the insects will perish and not appear again." Wang Ch'ung disputed that, noting that insects that eat grain "are born on a particular day and likewise die in a certain month; as their time is fulfilled, they undergo their changes, and do not remain insects forever. Should the ruler fail to punish his officials, the insects still would die on their own." Moreover, "among the three hundred naked insects ['creatures'], man is chief. From this point of view, man also thus is to be counted an 'insect.' Man eats what insects eat, and insects also eat what man eats. Both, as insects, eat each other's food, so what is remarkable about that? If insects had knowledge they too would denounce man, saying: 'You are eating what heaven has produced, and I also eat that. You call us a strange phenomenon; you might as well call yourselves a calamity'. . . . For if insects were able to speak and should thus denounce man, man would have no way to refute them."[94]

The auspicious signs that were commonly acknowledged included most prominently such things as the male and female phoenix [*feng huang*], the unicorn [*ch'i-lin*], lucky stars, and the "sweet dew." Wang Ch'ung exhaustively examined all the references to unicorns and phoenixes, past and present, noting all the discrepancies in the descriptions of their feathers and fur, their bones and their horns. Thereby he showed that the real thing would not be easy to identify, and that those sighted were not necessarily genuine.[95] "The *Shang-shu chung-hou* [one of the apocryphal works] states that 'during the reign of the Emperor Yao an auspicious star appeared in the constellation *chen* [軫].' Such auspicious stars may be simply an occasional appearance of one of the five movable stars. The largest of those is T'ai-po, the Year Star. [Wang Ch'ung appears to be confusing T'ai-po, the Metal Star, conventionally identified as Venus, with the Year Star, or Wood Star, identified with Jupiter.] On the reported occasion it may be that the Year Star T'ai-po appeared in the sector of [the asterism] *chen*. The ancient times were unrefined and people did not yet know how to calculate the movements of the five movable stars and did not know how to identify by its appearance the Year Star, T'ai-po. When they observed a large star they just called it an auspicious

---

[94] *Ibid.*, *ch.* 16, no. 49, "Shang ch'ung."
[95] *Ibid.*, *ch.* 16, no. 50, "Chiang jui."

star." The *Erh-ya* [early Han dictionary] states that sweet dew on occasion falls, and gives it the name *Li ch'üan* [醴泉, "the sweet wine spring"]. "These days the Confucians explain it [differently], saying that this spring water comes forth from the middle of the earth, and that its flavor is sweet like sweet wine, therefore it is named the sweet wine spring. Those two explanations vary widely, and in truth there is no way of knowing."[96] Since auspicious signs are so difficult to verify, as these [examples show], the desire to make of them responses to good governing is indeed very close to the ridiculously specious.

We should note, however, that Hsün Tzu's purpose in dispelling the superstitious beliefs in the interactions between heaven and man had been to establish the positive political attitudes of humanism. Wang Ch'ung's objective in eliminating the interaction notion was to demonstrate his own pessimistic fatalism. Wang Ch'ung accepted the idea that every thing and event that emerged within the cosmos was the product of purely fortuitous conjunctions. He called such fortuitous conjunctions "fate" [*ming* 命]; in consequence, he said: "Fate presides over good luck and bad. The way of spontaneity, the factors in happenstance, have no causes in other material forces, or in any process by which other things exert influences and overcome one another, or induce interactions to bring them about."[97] What he calls the fortuitous, however, is seen in relation to the entire cosmos. The heavenly movements are spontaneous, all things are self-generating, and, inasmuch as they occur without intent, so all the less are they purposeful. Consequently, they can be designated fortuitous. In terms of each individual thing and event, its fortuitous conjunctions are not at all self-determined, and once they have become real they are beyond altering. The fortuitous thus acquires the force of necessity.[98]

To discuss this in terms of mankind, at birth one's fate is set. "There are the fates of dying or living, of longevity and of premature death, and there are the fates of being noble or humble, of being poor or rich."[99] Thereafter, all the conjunctions of one's whole life are subject to the control of those alternate fates. "If one's fate is to die young, even though he is disposed toward unusually noteworthy conduct, in the end he will not succeed in living long. If he is set to be a poor and humble person, even though he do good deeds, in the end he will not achieve [eminence and

---

[96] *Ibid.*, *ch.* 17, no. 52, "Shih ying."

[97] *Ibid.*, *ch.* 3, no. 10, "Ou hui."

[98] To speak in terms of each individual thing and event, the fact of being governed by inexorable fate may not always be apparent, so the circumstances of situations appear to be fortuitous. The arguments set forth in *ch.* 1, no. 1, "Feng yü," and no. 2, "Lei hai," etc., all are based on this view.

[99] *Lun Heng*, *ch.* 1, no. 3, "Ming lu."

wealth]."[100] Thus altruistic conduct is not enough to alter one's fated poverty or early death, nor are evil deeds necessarily going to diminish one's fated wealth and long life. "Yen Hui [Confucius' favorite disciple] was often in want, he did not resent coarsest food, and finally he died prematurely. So, what is heaven's reward for one who does good? The brigand Chih repeatedly murdered the innocent, minced the flesh of humans, and gave full license to his violent passions. He assembled a following of several thousand persons and inflicted his depredations on the whole realm, but in the end died of ripe old age. So, what dictated that consequence?"[101] By good deeds one cannot make his own fate; moreover, spiritual beings, immortals, and the arts of the adepts also are powerless to reverse the movement of heaven. "One's body cannot be transformed or altered; one's fate cannot be added to or subtracted from."[102] "There is no road of ascent to the heavens," and in the oceans there is no "drug of immortality."[103] Of what use is it to one's life to do good deeds? To seek immortality is all the less worth the effort. In mankind's life therefore no room is left for hope.

Wang Ch'ung also drew upon this fatalistic view of life to explain order and chaos in government. "It is widely said in these times that in antiquity the rulers were worthy, therefore they implemented virtuous ways, and because they implemented those they were successful in realizing good government and stability. Where rulers were unworthy, virtuous ways were forsaken or abandoned, and because those were forsaken or abandoned, their efforts were unsuccessful and government was disordered. All commentators of past and present say the same. What are their reasons? They observe that [the semi-legendary rulers] Yao and Shun, being worthy and sagelike, brought on eras of great peace, while Chieh and Chou [tyrannically bad last emperors], being immoral, ushered in chaos and were themselves killed. . . . Thus the transition to peril and chaos is blamed on the ruler by all the commentators, who find the fault in the failure of those who rule to observe the Way. Those rulers who bear responsibility in blaming themselves, grieving their spirits, and taxing their minds, exert all the strength of their bodies, yet the transition to peril and disorder in the end cannot be averted. For naught the ruler's indignation is aroused, and a perceptive ruler must hypocritically acknowledge

---

[100] *Ibid.*, *ch.* 2, no. 6, "Ming yi." Note that in *ch.* 3, no. 11, "Ku hsiang," it states that from one's skeletal form one's fate can be known. "Man's fate is imparted by heaven so it is manifested in signs [*piao hou* 表候] in the body. . . . That which is called manifested in signs is the method of bone [physiognomy]." This is quite contrary to Hsün Tzu's [*ch.* Five] "Against Physiognomy."

[101] *Ibid.*, *ch.* 6, no. 21, "Huo hsü."

[102] *Ibid.*, *ch.* 2, no. 7, "Wu hsing."

[103] *Ibid.*, *ch.* 7, no. 24, "Tao hsü."

[undeserved] blame. The accumulated views and current opinion all work to make it so." But if the truth were admitted, order and chaos, stability and peril, are outgrowths, "spontaneously, of the fate-determined time," to which the government's merits and shortcomings are irrelevant. "For a worthy ruler is capable of governing well a people destined to be stable, but he cannot transform an age ready for chaos. A good physician can apply his needles and medicines, and make his prescriptions produce their good effects; it is because he encounters a patient who, not fated to die yet, has contracted a non-fatal disease. If the person's fate has run out and his disease is severe, then even if he had [the services of the eminent physician] Pien Ch'üeh it would do him no good. For when a person's fate has run its course and he is severely ill, it is like the situation of a people in chaos who cannot be brought to stability. . . . Thus, an age of good government is not the achievement of worthies and sages, while decline and chaos are not induced by [the ruler's] immorality. When the state is ready for decline and chaos, worthies and sages cannot make it prosper. When the time is one of order, evil men cannot induce chaos. The order or chaos of an age does not lie with government; the state's stability or peril lies in the workings of destiny and not in [the ruler's] instructing."[104] When the destined time has arrived, the various relevant factors will converge, and either order or chaos will take shape, with no way of altering that. "It was Yao's fate to have to abdicate in favor of Shun; Chu of Tan [Yao's son; cf. *Documents*, ii/iv/8; Legge, p. 84] behaved immorally. The overlordship of the Yü [Shun's clan name] was destined to be transmitted to the Hsia dynasty [in the person of the Great Yü]; Shang Chün [Shun's son] acted in irregular ways. . . . When the Hsia and the [Shang-] Yin dynasties were fated to come to an end, it happened also that the evils of Chieh and Chou [their last rulers] reached a climax; when the times for the destined rise of the Shang and Chou dynasties arrived, it happened also that the virtues of [their founders,] the Emperor T'ang and the King Wu, became abundant."[105] Success and failure, rise and fall, definitely do not occur through man's efforts.

The state and the individual are both under the control of fate. The individual's fate can be seen in his bone structure and physiognomy. The fate of the state is decided according to heaven's time, and calamitous or

---

[104] *Ibid.*, *ch.* 17, no. 53, "Chih ch'i." In *ch.* 5, no. 18, "Yi hsü," it states: "Whether men live or die is a matter of whether their fate holds premature death or high longevity; it does not lie with whether their deeds are good or evil. Whether states survive or perish is a matter of whether their appointed duration is long or short; it does not lie with the successes and failings in governing."

[105] *Ibid.*, *ch.* 3, no. 10, "Ou-hui." This is the view set forth in the *Lü-shih Ch'un-ch'iu*, *ch.* 14, no. 5, "Ch'ang kung," but here offered with a somewhat more fully developed explanation. *Vide*, the passage cited in footnote 52 of this chapter.

auspicious signs will reveal evidence of that. In discussing heaven's time, Wang Ch'ung said: "Is not the reason that an age falls into chaos because bandits grow numerous, warfare flares up, the people cast off the rites and righteousness and rebel against their superiors? Such occurrences are caused by a lack of grain and foodstuffs, and people being unable to bear hunger and destitution. When hunger and destitution appear everywhere, those who can desist from wrong deeds are few, just as when food and plenty are present, those who will not do the good are rare. . . . Seen in this way, the rites and righteousness prevail because grain is plentiful. Now we can observe that the grain crop succeeds or fails according to the [growing conditions of the] year. If the year is one of flood or drought, the five grains will not produce a good harvest."[106] "The occurrences of flood and drought depend on their own timing."[107] Although we cannot precisely foretell occurrences of flood and drought, we nonetheless can observe the evidences for the state's prosperity or decline in calamitous or auspicious signs. When the state is approaching collapse, there are certain to be disasters. Moreover, "When the mandate of heaven [t'ien ming, or, "heaven-appointed fate"] is about to be launched, and a Sage-King is on the point of emerging, the material forces [ch'i], before and after the event, give proofs which will be radiantly manifest." For example, both at the Mang and Tang [wastes, where the future Han founder, Kao-tsu, hid from the First Emperor of Ch'in], and at Ch'ung-ling [where an agent of Wang Mang became suspicious of Kuang-wu, the future restorer of the Han dynasty], there were extraordinary cloudlike emanations [ch'i]. "With the likes of the Emperor Kao-tsu and the Emperor Kuang-wu, would there not be radiant manifestations in heaven and among men, with spiritual beings and strange appearances?"[108]

Wang Ch'ung previously has thoroughly denounced all theories claiming interactions between heaven and man, but here also now acknowledges that calamitous and auspicious events can be taken as signs of good and bad government. Yet these do not represent inconsistencies. For calamitous and auspicious events, like good and bad government, are all products of fortuitous conjunctions. The errors of the School of Prognosticators are not in acknowledging the occurrences of calamities and auspicious happenings, but lie in their erroneous belief that the successes and failings of government bear a cause-and-effect relationship to those. Wang Ch'ung felt that "the accession of a worthy ruler happens to occur in an age that is going to be well governed; his virtues are self-evident above, and the people are automatically good below. The world is at peace and the peo-

---

[106] *Ibid.*, *ch.* 17, no. 53, "Chih ch'i."

[107] *Ibid.*, *ch.* 14, no. 41, "Han wen." Wang Ch'ung, however, has not indicated how their occurrences are to be calculated.

[108] *Ibid.*, *ch.* 2, no. 9, "Chi yen."

ple are secure. Auspicious signs all display themselves and the age speaks of those as induced by the worthy ruler. The immoral ruler happens to be born at a time when chaos is to exist; the empire is thrown into troubles and the people's ways become disorderly, with unending disasters and calamities, leading to the fall of the state, the death of the ruler, and the displacement of his successors. The world all refers to that as having been induced by his evils. Such observations are clear about the external appearance of good and evil, but fail to perceive the internal reality of good and bad fortune. Good and bad fortune have nothing to do with goodness and evil; the proofs of goodness and evil are not found in good and bad fortune. A senior official arrives at his post who has not yet undertaken any actions, where governing and instruction continue as in the past without any changes having been effected, yet bandits may be many or few, and disasters may or may not occur. How is that to be explained? The rank of the senior official is high, and his promotions and appointments depend on peace and stability [in his prefecture]. It may be that his fate is to be humbled so he will lose his appointment by reason of some peril or disorder. If we compare this senior official of today with the emperors of antiquity, we will then have a basis for discussing their states' security and danger, preservation or collapse."[109]

Although there is no cause- and-effect relationship between calamitous and auspicious signs on the one hand, and evil or good on the other, the prosperity and decline, as well as the calamitous and auspicious signs, are all arranged by fate, and similarly reflect the force of necessity. All the actions of the king who is about to flourish will spontaneously accord with the timely factors of destiny. "Followers will come to him unsummoned, and auspicious objects will come to him unsignaled. Invisibly moved, they will all come together as if they have been sent." All such auspicious signs as the red bird and the white fish should be looked upon in this way. In a country on the verge of decline, calamities and prodigies will repeatedly be observed. When the time of chaos is at hand, nothing can bring about its reversal. Calamities and prodigies must occur along with the decline of government, the principle underlying that being precisely analogous to that which explains the matching of auspicious signs to a flourishing age.[110] Therein lies the reason why calamitous and auspicious signs are sufficient evidence for chaos and good government.

[109] *Ibid., ch.* 17, no. 53, "Chih ch'i."

[110] There, however, are also exceptions. In *ch.* 17, no. 51, "Chih jui," it says: "In ages of decline there may also be a harmonious atmosphere [i.e. material force, *ch'i*]. . . . Sages are born in ages of decline. . . . In an age of decline a Sage King will encounter sagelike things, just as a person of a good fate will encounter things belonging to the class of auspicious signs. In fact, these appear together coincidentally; it is not that one comes because of another." Here we see that the individual's verifications of his destiny bear no relation to the fortunes of the age.

Since we know that chaos and good government are determined by the time factors of fate [*shih-shu* 時數], then not only need we not find value in the auspicious signs, neither will we find governing and instructing worth undertaking. "Using non-governing to govern it" becomes the only rational method of governing. "The methods of Huang-Lao are that the person [of the ruler] remains at ease and detached, his governing being accomplished by taking no purposive action. By maintaining his uprightness in himself, the *Yin* and the *Yang* were harmonious of themselves. He gave no thought to any action, and all things were spontaneous in their own transformations. He directed no attention to making things grow, and all things grew of themselves."[111] As for all the other [governing devices], such as the Confucians' benevolence and righteousness, Lord Shang's and Li Ssu's penalties and laws, they represented nothing more than obtuse persons creating trouble for themselves; they contributed nothing to human affairs, and, on the contrary, worked damage. Wang Ch'ung had nothing good to say for them. Yet we should note that Wang Ch'ung's advocacy of Huang-Lao displayed an attitude different from that of the early Han dynasty School of Huang-Lao. Although Ts'ao Shen and Chi An, and their like [cf. Chapter Ten, Section Two, above] opposed action-oriented, positive governing policies, they nonetheless believed that government was capable of turning developments toward or away from prosperity and decline, and their attitude still was close to optimism. Wang Ch'ung's advocacy of non-action was based solely on fatalism. According to his views there exist in the whole world no governing methods capable of bringing about good government or of suppressing disorders. The ruler who can avoid action, on encountering a period of order, can then fold his hands and enjoy an age of great peace, but if he encounters the conjunction of events that will end his state, he might as well have his hands tied as he awaits death. The circumstances they encounter differ as to being fortunate or unfortunate, but they are the same in that both obviate the futile act. Moreover, as both governing and instructing [to guide the people] clearly are useless, rulers and leaders are also functionless ornaments. Even though Wang Ch'ung never expressed the conclusion of eliminating the ruler, yet logically that really is the inevitable conclusion to which his fatalism leads. This also is something not present in Huang-Lao or Taoist thought of Han times.

The *Lun Heng* offers another unexpected point worth noting, and one that demands some discussion. The Confucians looked upon the era of Yao and Shun and the Three Dynasties of Antiquity as an age when government and society had been at their most perfect. The followers of Lao Tzu and Chuang Tzu also held up the [ancient] age of great purity and

---

[111] *Ibid., ch.* 18, no. 54, "Tzu jan."

perfect virtue as their ideal. Wang Ch'ung did not deny the existence of a "golden age," but he denied that such had existed only in the antique past. "The saying goes that people in early ages were of pristine integrity and easily guided into good ways, while people in later ages are of artful duplicity and are difficult to govern." It is also said, "In high antiquity the sages were of superior virtue so achieved extraordinary results in governing." In subsequent eras the rulers gradually declined in quality and achievement, and those rulers tended to become ever more slipshod and superficial. Wang Ch'ung refuted all of those statements, finding them groundless fabrications. To assess the matter in terms of the various rulers' personal virtues, he found that "Rulers of antiquity who achieved good government were Sages, and rulers in recent ages who have achieved good government also are Sages. The virtue of an ancient Sage is no different from that of a later Sage, nor is a well-governed age in itself different whether earlier or later." Speaking of the principles of good government and disorder, he said: "When the material forces [ch'i] of heaven and earth are in harmony, Sages are born, and the governing of such Sages leads to their great accomplishment. But the harmony of the material forces is not found only in early antiquity, so why should only those ancient sages be considered superior?" Speaking in terms of the nature of mankind itself, he said: "Men of high antiquity clung to the five norms of behavior [Wu ch'ang 五常], and men in later ages also have clung to those same five norms. All mankind has adhered to the morality of the five norms, and all have been born in possession of the same material force. Therefore, what would account for humans of early antiquity having pristine integrity and those of later ages having no more than artful duplicity? . . . It is the common nature of this age to praise the past and slander the present, to diminish what is seen and to enlarge what is known by hearing."[112] There lies the cause of all such error.

Wang Ch'ung procedes to discuss the achievements of the Han dynasty, and what he looked upon as the "resplendent virtues of the ten emperors" during the three hundred years from Kao-tsu [the dynastic founder, reigned 206–195 B.C.] to the Emperor Chang [reigned A.D. 76–88, among the seventeen Han rulers to his own time]. They had brought order out of chaos, leading to an age of peace, and auspicious signs had repeatedly appeared. Superficially speaking, "Kao-tsu and Kuang-wu of the Han are as Kings Wen and Wu [i.e., the most glorious] of the Chou. Emperors Wen, Wu, Hsüan, and the present Emperor (the Emperor Chang) surpass the [best of the] Chou Kings, Ch'eng, K'ang, and Hsüan.[113] "Most grandiosely," the Han record for political success vastly exceeded all

---

[112] *Ibid.*, *ch.* 18, no. 56, "Ch'i shih."
[113] *Ibid.*, *ch.* 19, no. 57, "Hsüan Han."

throughout past and present, in "turning peril into security, adversity into success. Of all the Five Emperors and Three Kings [of antiquity], which can equal this?"[114] And, when one comes to speak not of governing but of auspicious manifestations, there too "the Han surpassed the Chou."[115] "The auspicious signs received by the T'ang and the Yü [regimes] must be considered genuine, and thus the virtues of [the rulers of these regimes, namely] Yao and Shun were manifestly glorious. [The Han Emperor] Hsiao-Hsüan [73–49 B.C.] is comparable to Yao and Shun [in the numbers of times phoenixes appeared]; the realm enjoyed great peace, for ten-thousand *li* all turned admiringly to him and were transformed, and the way of benevolence prevailed. All the birds and beasts that are susceptible to benevolence were moved by his influence to come forth. . . . When the successes and failings of government are measured against the mass of auspicious signs, there is no doubt that they were genuine." As for the many occasions during the Yung-p'ing and Chang-ho reign periods [A.D. 58–75 and 87–88] when sweet dew descended auspiciously, every single such occurrence was also genuine and constituted indubitable evidence of the great peace then prevailing.[116]

When we consider Wang Ch'ung's urgent pursuit of "factual knowledge" and his hatred of the false and the preposterous, that he made such statements as the foregoing can only arouse in us the feeling that this is quite unexpected. To draw an inference about the explanation for this, it must lie among the following three possibilities: the first is that he was flattering the Han; the second is that he was satirizing the Han; the third is that he was rectifying the common attitudes. Wang Ch'ung, "as one living under Han rule," praised its good qualities to the utmost, in truth giving rise to the suspicion that he may indeed have been "magnifying the acclaim and exclaiming in praise, seeking to be known as one anxious to please."[117] Yet we can observe how detached Wang Ch'ung was by nature, and that his actions bespeak integrity; there is no trace of sycophancy or lust for gain in his career. If we were to charge him with the crime of fawning on the Han court, it would no doubt lead to an unsolved case of "no apparent motive." The suspicion that he was satirizing the Han looms somewhat larger. The reigns of the Emperors Wu, Hsüan, Ming, and Chang, which Wang extolled, were in fact far distant from the ideal of "great peace." When we note that Wang Ch'ung also wrote works called

---

[114] *Ibid., ch.* 19, no. 58, "Huei kuo."

[115] *Ibid., ch.* 19, no. 57, "Hsüan Han."

[116] *Ibid., ch.* 16, no. 50, "Chiang jui." Note that during the reign of Emperor Hsüan [73–49 B.C.] there had appeared numerous "auspicious signs," leading to the adoption of reign period names such as "Divine Sparrows," "Five Phoenixes," "Sweet Dew," and "Yellow Dragon."

[117] *Ibid., ch.* 19, no. 57, "Hsüan Han."

"Satires of Vulgar Ways" and "The Conduct of Government," we can know that he also had admitted that the age in which he lived was not a splendid era of all sweetness and light, above and below, in which every household merited noble status [as sometimes said about the age of Yao and Shun]. Moreover, the Emperor Wu was given to vain display and pursuit of glory, while the Emperor Ming was "obsessively punctilious," both quite contrary to the government by non-action which Wang Ch'ung valued. Yet Wang Ch'ung enumerated various accomplishments of the Han house, such as founding the dynasty and extending the frontiers of the empire, to serve as evidence that its virtues surpassed those of Wen and Wu [of the Chou]. In so doing, he either fell into self-contradiction or resorted to ridicule through sarcasm. He also noted that the reign of the Emperor Chang witnessed much of disaster and famine. Appropriate relief measures were carried out that, despite the peril, averted chaos. "Although the people were starved for grain, they were replete with virtue."[118] This too is contrary to the theory set forth in the Chapter "The Phases of Good Government" [ch. 17, no. 53, "Chih ch'i"; cf. the passage, page 594 above, to which footnote 106 applies.] Although that essay is enough to make us doubt the sincerity of his chapter, "In Praise of the Han" [ch. 19, no. 57], yet we are quite without factual basis for solidly establishing that he was satirizing with malicious intent.[119] As for the objective of rectifying common attitudes, that is perfectly obvious. Wang Ch'ung wrote: "As the *Spring and Autumn Annals* provided the Han with its institutes and ordinances, so my *Lun Heng* is to provide the Han with critical views."[120] That this presents his sincere intent is beyond any doubt.

Even so, Wang Ch'ung's purpose would seem not to be limited to that. "Ch'i shih" and "Hsüan Han" [no. 56, "The Equality of the Ages" and no. 57, "In Praise of the Han"] on the surface honor the present, but they cloak the reality, i.e., that they depreciate the past. Han government had elements of both the good and the bad, of security and danger, side by side. Wang Ch'ung had to have been profoundly aware of that; it also was common knowledge to his contemporaries. The government of the Three Dynasties of antiquity could not have surpassed that of the Han. Thanks to [the practice as delineated in] "Groundless Records" [no. 16, "Shu hsü"] and "Exaggerated Accounts" [no. 25, "Yü tseng"], these have become known as paragons of perfect government. This was Wang Ch'ung's unique observation, and something all others had failed to

---

[118] *Ibid., ch.* 19, no. 58, "Hui kuo."

[119] *Ibid., ch.* 29, no. 84, "Tui tso," states that the *Lun Heng* "lacks any word of slander . . . can be held to be free from wrong-doing." This declares that its purpose is not to satirize.

[120] *Ibid., ch.* 20, no. 60, "Hsü sung."

perceive. Because of that, Wang Ch'ung persuasively argued his views about "The Equality of the Ages," in which he elevated the in fact not-so-perfect Han dynasty to a parity with the ideally perfect Three Dynasties. With facts that cannot be ignored, therefore, what he said [in the chapter titled] "In Praise of the Han" is tantamount to taking the fantasy of a "golden age" and shattering it completely at one blow. When Wang Ch'ung stated that good government and chaos have nothing to do with human affairs, it was to declare all present effort to be in vain. When he further stated that a flourishing age must revert to decline and disorder, it was to make all future expectations nothing but empty foolishness. This only further proved that antiquity and the Han shared a common character, thereby making the past not worthy of nostalgia. In consequence, throughout all the vast universe there was no horizon worth valuing or seeking, and all human history became nothing more than a cycle of order and chaos, having no goal, no meaning and no resolution.[121] If our assessment does not err, then Wang Ch'ung's thought is the most serious call to despair with regard to political life to have come from any person of the Ch'in-Han era. It not merely implies that Ch'in and Han political policies signified no more than obtuse persons making trouble for themselves; the authoritarian form of government itself also was held up to unconditional reproach. The *Lun Heng*, "lacking any word of slander," in fact has few equals from past or present as a slanderous book. Wang Ch'ung himself may not have been aware of that, but the implicit significance of his thought is extremely clear.

When we come to look into the question of why Wang Ch'ung arrived at so starkly pessimistic a conclusion, that would appear to be derived from the content of Lao-Chuang [i.e., the school of philosophical speculation built upon the *Lao Tzu* and the *Chuang Tzu*] thought, together with the influences from the milieu of the Ch'in-Han epoch. Pre-Ch'in Lao-Chuang learning had tended toward negative political thought. Han dynasty Huang-Lao, however, had turned toward an attitude of personal involvement in the governing of the age, and the "Taoist School" (or the Eclectic School) went further, adopting elements from the various schools to broaden their methods for responding to human affairs. Consequently, the negative stance of the Lao-Chuang followers was led toward a relatively more positive position. The Ch'in dynasty had relied on Legalism and had quickly perished. People of the Han reflected on that, in con-

---

[121] Wang Ch'ung does, however, acknowledge that individual morality as well as cultivation of learning is possible. That is to say, noble and humble rank are determined by fate, but good and evil lie with the individual himself. The average person's nature is such that he can be transformed by instructing so that he will do what is good. See *ch*. 2, no. 8, "Shuai hsing" and *ch*. 3, no. 13, "Pen hsing."

sequence attempting to correct the Ch'in error by adopting Huang-Lao. As we come to the age of the Emperor Wu, material wealth had grown abundant, and the people's lives were sound; people gradually had taken on optimistic attitudes, and government was strongly activist. Confucian thought, riding the crest of the times and accommodating to the scene, was pressed into the position of the "sole eminence." Those involved in Huang-Lao could not escape the powerful currents of this tide, so they also adopted elements of Confucian benevolence and righteousness in support of the Way and its Power, so that Huang-Lao was further transformed into the Taoist School [*Tao-chia*] and as such was the competitor of the Confucian school. The advocates of a relatively activist position and those of a relative non-action, as two factions, subsequently came to constitute the main currents of political thought throughout the Han. But during those several hundred years of trying out their methods they achieved only limited successes and in the end were of no use in averting disorder and collapse. Deeply thoughtful persons could not help becoming doubtful about the governing means of that relative activism as of that relative non-activism. Moreover, since Mohism's development had been broken off, while Legalism had suffered repudiation, and now confidence in Confucianism and Taoism had also been lost, the theories dealing with the governance of the state and the protection of the people that had come down from Pre-Ch'in times were virtually all headed for nullity. The pessimistic thought of absolute non-action, consequently, witnessed a temporary flourishing.[122] Wang Ch'ung initiated this movement, and during the Wei and Chin periods [third and fourth centuries] that current waxed strong.[123] During the one thousand years from the Warring States period to the Chin dynasty, the thought-system of non-action went from "Lao-Chuang" through the phase of "Huang-Lao" and all the way back to "Lao-Chuang," therein constituting a cyclical movement.

[122] Wang Ch'ung was inclined to deny that the relative non-action of the "Taoist School" could bring about good government and to favor absolute non-action. In standpoint as in content his thought differs from Han dynasty "Huang-Lao" thought.

[123] In his *Chung-kuo t'ung-shih hsüan-tu* ["Selected Readings in Chinese History"], Volume III, page 406, Lei Hai-tsung has said that Wang Ch'ung represents "the comprehensive conclusion of ancient thought," and that the *Lun Heng* signifies the denial of value to the ancient culture. Yao Shun-ch'in, in his *Ch'in-Han Che-hsüeh shih* ["History of Ch'in-Han Philosophy"], p. 385, calls the *Lun Heng* the herald of Wei-Chin Taoist metaphysics [*hsüan-hsüeh.*]

CHAPTER ELEVEN
From Wang Pi to Ko Hung

SECTION ONE

The Backgrounds and Sources
of Lao-Chuang Thought in the Wei
and Chin Periods (A.D. 220–419)

IN the preceding two chapters, in the course of relating separately the
political thought of the Confucian and Taoist Schools of the Ch'in-Han
period, we have discovered that both displayed the tendency to turn away
from optimism and toward pessimism. In seeking the causes that induced
that change we have concluded that the failures of authoritarian government, and the disillusionment of the people at the time with the forms of
authoritarian rule, were the principal objective and subjective reasons.
For two bodies of thought so strikingly disparate in content simultaneously
to undergo such analogous transformations certainly could not have been
a fortuitous coincidence. That, however, is to speak only of the Ch'in-
Han period; if we extend the discussion to include the larger contours of
thought throughout the entire six- or seven-hundred-year period from
the Ch'in and Han dynasties through the Wei and Chin dynasties, we
find that the Ch'in-Han situation in which the Confucian and Taoist
Schools vied for supremacy changed with the approach of the Wei-Chin
period to one of Confucian insignificance and Taoist ascendancy. Moreover, among the Taoist factions, the thought currents of naturalism
[*tzu-jan chu-yi* 自然主義, or "spontaneity"]* and of anarchy [*wu-chün
chu-yi* 無君主義, literally, "no ruler-ism," an aspect of anarchism for
which there is no precise English equivalent] to which Wang Ch'ung
had added impetus were, for a time, more widely flourishing than the
[other Taoist] doctrines stressing minimalized rulership and quiescent
detachment. To state the matter differently, the Wei-Chin period was an
age when Lao-Chuang thought achieved sole eminence.[1]

---

*Square brackets indicate that the words enclosed were added by the tanlator.

[1] The "Wei Chih," in the *San-kuo Chih*, the dynastic history of the Three Kingdoms,
ch. 1, in its "Critique" [*p'ing*] of the Emperor Wu [in power *c.* A.D. 196–220], tells that he,
Ts'ao Ts'ao, "seized upon the laws and methods of Shen Pu-hai and Lord Shang." Huan
Fan, [fl. A.D. 250] wrote a "Shih yao lun" or "Discourse on Essentials of the Age" that is
classified as a Legalist work in Ma Kuo-han's *Yü-han shan-fang chi-yi shu* ["collectanea of
lost works restored in fragments" ca. 1850]. The "Shu Chih" in the *San-kuo Chih*, *ch.* 5,
states that Chu-ko Liang in governing the State of Shu "rigidly maintained the laws and
regulations, and made rewards and punishments inflexibly certain," thus also was close to
Shen Pu-hai and Lord Shang. His writings, however, are no longer extant (the compila-

Confucian thought, from its position of sole eminence achieved in the Western or Former Han, veered abruptly toward decline and defeat; that truly constitutes one of the most remarkable phenomena in the history of Chinese thought. The political and historical background that we have discussed above provides the basic if distant reasons. Yet there are two very obvious and more immediate reasons as well. To state the case succinctly, the one reason is the rapid degeneration of Confucian learning itself; the second reason is a wearied repugnance for its proponents, who had held the scene too long. That is, the Confucian learning of the Western Han, in consequence of the Emperor Wu's backing, had achieved a sudden prominence. A student of the classics might attain a marquisate; scholars all competed in reciting the "Six Arts" [i.e. the Confucian classics]. With advantage and official emolument in the offing, motives were at best mixed. As that contaminated the court, Confucian practices came to be deceptive embellishments,[2] for scholars looked upon the *Odes* and the *Documents* as the means with which to press for advantage and advancement. The unscrupulous might even go so far as to alter and corrupt the texts of the classics,[3] while the more inhibited remained mired in superficial textual commentary *ad nauseam*.[4] From the reigns of the

tion of them by Chu Lin in the Ch'ing period, the *Chu-ko ch'eng-hsiang chi*, consisting mainly of spurious writings). The *Chin Shu*, in *ch.* 49, in the biography of Juan Fu, states that the Emperor Yuan [reigned A.D. 317–22] "drew upon Shen Pu-hai and Han Fei by which means to save the world." Thereafter, however further echoes [of Legalism] are rare.

[2] Liu Chih of the T'ang dynasty has stated: "Emperor Kuang-wu [reigned A.D. 25–57] was fond of learning, and although unable to apply that in government, yet he personally lectured on the classics. From the Emperor Su-tsung [reigned 76–88] onward, the rulers occasionally emulated that ancestral example in venerating the Confucian methods, and even when they could not attain the intent they still would contemplate the words. Although the Three Lords and the Imperial Secretaries were appointed from among scholars of classical learning, they failed to implement the Way of that classical learning." From Liu's "Hsüan-chü lun," in the *Ch'üan T'ang wen*.

[3] The *Hou Han Shu*, *ch.* 108, in the biography of Lü Ch'iang, and in *ch.* 109-A, in the "Preface" to the "Biographies of Confucians," states that the Erudits [*Po-shih*] conducting the Class A and B civil service examinations engaged in contention over the rankings, made charges against each other, and went so far as to accept bribes for altering the characters of the "painted texts" in the Lan-t'ai [the palace library, containing the standard version of the classics "painted" on bamboo strips] so that those would agree with [the mistakes] written by their protégés. In the fourth year of the Hsi-p'ing reign period [A.D. 175], the classics were, in consequence, engraved on stone at the T'ai-hsüeh, the Han Imperial Academy. *Ch.* 90, in the biography of Ts'ai Yung, states that he and others proposed that these texts be verified.

[4] *Ibid.*, *ch.* 65, where the "Comment" [*lun*] on the biography of Cheng Hsüan states: "After the Ch'in dynasty's burning of the Six Classics, the Sages' writings were obscured and obliterated. With the rise of the Han dynasty, the Confucians actively cultivated the literary arts. Coming to the time of the Eastern [Later] Han, various scholars came to be counted eminent specialists and their disciples, clinging to the teachings of each of those,

Emperors An and Shun [107–144] onward the rulers no longer gave such matters their serious attention, so that even that name-without-reality situation could be maintained no longer.[5] By the time of the Cheng-shih reign period [240–248] of the Wei dynasty, among more than four-hundred court officials only ten were competent at literary composition.[6] Cultural activity, along with thought and learning as such, came to the verge of extinction; the decline of Confucianism was the inevitable consequence of those conditions. Opinion has always held the burning of the books and burial alive of Confucians by the First Emperor of Ch'in to have been the great disaster of all time, failing to note that "the Sages' writings were obscured and obliterated" at the end of the Han under

---

stubbornly maintained what had been transmitted to them. Variant teaching traditions proliferated, mutually repudiating and attacking, with the consequence that there were many different schools for each classic, each school developing many versions of its learning. Their written commentaries in the cases of the more voluminous ones might reach the length of a million or more words."

[5] *Ibid.*, *ch.* 109-A, "Preface" to the "Biographies of Confucians," states: "From the time when the Emperor An [reigned 107–25] presided over the government, it disdained the arts and literary refinements; the Erudits [in attendance at court] leaned back on their mats and did not expound [the classics, not being called upon]; the factional groups just stared at each other in lax negligence [of their advisory responsibilities]; the halls of the Imperial Academy fell into disrepair, all overplanted with vegetable plots and with herd-boys and grass-cutters and even fuel-gatherers doing their work in its precincts." It also states: "At the beginning [of the Later Han] when the Emperor Kuang-wu returned the capital to Lo-yang, the classical writings and archival records filled over two-thousand carts. Thereafter the books came to number three times what had previously existed. Then, at the juncture when Tung Cho moved the capital (in the first year of the Emperor Hsien's Ch'u-p'ing reign period—A.D. 190), the government employees and people rioted and created disorders, leading to the complete dispersal of the archival records and writings from the Pi-yung [Imperial Academy], Tung-kuan, Lan-t'ai, Shih-shih, Hsüan-ming, and Hung-tu [palace library] collections. Those books and pictures [or, maps?], written on silk rolls, if large, were joined together to make hangings and curtains, while the smaller ones were made into bags and purses. Those which Wang Yün gathered up to transport to the West were reduced to no more than seventy-odd wagon-loads. But the road [to the Western Capital at Ch'ang-an] was long and difficult, so half of those had to be abandoned. Subsequently, in the Ch'ang-an uprising there was a period of burning and looting, so nothing escaped the utter destruction there."

[6] In the biography of Wang Su, *ch.* 13 of the "Wei Chih" of the *San-kuo Chih*, the *Wei Lüeh* is quoted: "During the Cheng-shih reign period a meeting was convened for consultations regarding the Temple of Heaven; all scholars were invited to attend. At that time the officials under the Supervisor of Attendants [*Lang-kuan*] and the Chancellor [*Ssu-t'u*] . . . who were then present in the capital numbered more than ten-thousand; yet those who answered the invitation and took part in the discussion were not more than a scant few. Furthermore, at that time there were more than four-hundred court officials from the ranks of Lords and Chief Ministers on down, among those who could wield a brush [competently, to produce a document or literary composition] were perhaps less than ten."

conditions that must be judged more or less analogous to those at the beginning of the Han era.

Following that Confucian decline, the Taoist School, with its only formidable opponent now removed, could of course flourish as the successor. The great burgeoning of Lao-Chuang thought that took place during the Wei-Chin period, however, also had intrinsic reasons. The thought of the Lao-Chuang school of learning originally had centered on forgetting about the world in egocentric concern for the individual, and its somewhat decadent way of life was, furthermore, a phenomenon regularly accompanying ages of decline and disorder. That the Lao-Chuang thought should have become widely current during the Wei-Chin period is therefore a most natural development and demands no profound or detailed discussion. Throughout the two-hundred years from the Huang-ch'u reign period [220–226] to the Chien-hsing reign period [313–316] the empire was in continuous upheaval. The people's livelihood was subject to severe hardships; the conduct of government was murky and chaotic.[7] The actual circumstances of general dismay and suffering probably were little different from those in the Warring States period. Men of ability and commitment, thus, living amidst those frustrating conditions might well have been unable to escape the recognition that "peril awaits those who now engage in affairs of government" [Analects, xviii/5; Legge, p. 333]; therefore many withdrew and sought stratagems for insuring their personal safety.[8] One might well ask how Chuang Tzu's philosophy of life, with its self-contented "wandering in unfettered bliss" [hsiao-yao], could have failed to posses that age. Additionally, the full flourishing of the Lao-Chuang vogue also was due in part to its promotion by the high officials and scholar-bureaucrats of the Chin era. The Chin Shu, the dynastic history of the Chin, states: "During the Cheng-shih reign period [240–48] of the Wei dynasty, Ho Yen, Wang Pi, and others, taking Lao-Chuang learning as their standard, established the theory that heaven, earth, and all the myriad things have the basis of their existence in non-being [wu]. That which is called non-being is the beginning of things and the conclusion of affairs; it exists everywhere." Wang Yen enthusiastically supported those concepts. He was both greatly talented and of handsome appearance, god-like in his intellectual perceptiveness. He acquired a vast reputation, and his influence dominated the age. "He was marvelously skilled in metaphysical discourse [i.e., "hsüan yen" 玄言, or discourse on the Taoist "Great Mystery"], and felt that discourse on Lao-Chuang thought was the only activity of importance. . . . He oc-

---

[7] See, in the Chin Shu: ch. 26, "Shih-huo chih"; ch. 45, "Biography of Liu Yi"; and, ch. 94, "Biography of Lu Pao."

[8] Juan Chi and Hsiang Hsiu are the most eminent examples; for details, see below.

cupied successively the most eminent official posts, and without exception younger scholars admiringly emulated him. When selected for appointment and given assignments at court, they all accorded him the highest praise. Aristocratic arrogance and high-flown extravagances of utterance subsequently became the custom."[9]

"Pure conversation" [ch'ing-t'an 清談, as the movement represented by Wang Yen was called] drew its norms from Lao-Chuang. In their philosophical foundations all its leading figures were the same, exhibiting no differences worth noting. Nevertheless, in their political thought, on the basis of the intensity of their negativeness, they can be divided into the two groups: those who advocated taking no action, wu-wei; and those who advocated no ruler, wu-chün [or "anarchy," in the sense noted above]. The former are somewhat closer to the Pre-Ch'in Lao Tzu tradition, while the latter expounded the Pre-Ch'in Chuang Tzu tradition. There is a problem in the fact that although the Chin dynasty followers of Lao-Chuang thought were prolific writers, their works are in the main unsystematic. Some produced annotations and commentaries on the *Lao Tzu* and the *Chuang Tzu*,[10] while some wrote essays and discourses. Their language occasionally exhibits a more animated incisiveness than earlier writers but the content does not go beyond the limits set by the Pre-Ch'in thinkers. Thus the Wei-Chin period witnessed a resurgence of the thought of Lao Tzu and Chuang Tzu, but does not justify our speaking of a new level of development in Taoism.

[9] *Chin Shu*, *ch.* 43, "Biography of Wang Yen." Wang Yen was killed in the fifth year of the Yung-chia reign period [311] by Shih Lo, when he was in his fifty-sixth year of age. On that basis it can be calculated that he was born in the first year of the Wei dynasty's *Kan-lu* reign period, (thus his dates are 256–311).

[10] Ch'en Li [1810–1882], in *ch.* 11 of his *Tung-pi tu-shu chi*, quotes Hung Chih-ts'un [Hung Liang-chi, 1746–1809], saying: "From the time of the Han dynasty founding the Huang-Lao learning was widely prevalent; Emperors Wen and Ching [reigned 179–141 B.C.] followed it in ruling the state. By the end of the Han the dominant tendency was to value the mysterious and the vacuous [*hsüan hsü*]; in consequence Huang-Lao at that time first began to undergo a transformation and to be called Lao-Chuang. Ch'en Shou's "Wei Chih" [in the *San-kuo Chih*] at the end of the biography of Wang Ts'an [*ch.* 21] states that Chi K'ang was fond of discussing Lao-Chuang. The linking of Lao Tzu and Chuang Tzu in one term in fact first occurred at this time. In terms of the annotations to the texts of the two [the *Lao Tzu* and the *Chuang Tzu*], those who provided exegesis to the *Lao Tzu* include Lin, Fu, and Hsü [listed in the *Han Shu*, "Journal of Literature," with authors' names incomplete], of Ho-shang Kung, Liu Hsiang, Kuan-ch'iu Wang-chih, and Yen Tsun, all prior to the Western Han. There are no such references to [annotators of] the *Chuang Tzu*. Annotations of the *Chuang Tzu* in fact begin only with the Chin period Court Attendant, Ts'ui Chuan of Ch'ing-ho, after which Hsiang Hsiu, Ssu-ma Piao, Kuo Hsiang, Li Yi, and others followed after him." We should note that the name "Lao-Chuang" became a fixed term during the Chin dynasty, but the tendencies that transformed Huang-Lao into Lao-Chuang were already evident in the late Han. See the last portion of Section Five in Chapter Ten of the present work.

Section Two
"Taking No Action"

THE most prominent of the figures in the Wei-Chin period who promoted the concepts of governing well by taking no purposive action [*wu-wei erh chih* 無爲而治] are Ho Yen, Wang Pi, Chi K'ang, Hsiang Hsiu, Kuo Hsiang, and Chang Chan.

Ho Yen's courtesy name was P'ing-shu; he was the grandson of the Han dynasty Grand General, Ho Chin. His mother, of the surname Yin, subsequently became a consort of the Emperor Wu [i.e., Ts'ao Ts'ao, the T'ai-tsu] of the Wei dynasty. "Ho Yen was reared within the palace, furthermore was married to an imperial princess. As a youth he was noted for his intelligence and cultivation. He greatly admired the Lao-Chuang writings; he composed a "Discourse on *Tao* and *Te*" as well as essays, prose-poems, and other writings, in all several tens in number." In the tenth year of the Cheng-shih reign [249] he was killed by Ssu-ma Yi.[11] Very few of his writings are extant.

Wang Pi's courtesy name was Fu-ssu. When only in his teens he exhibited an attraction for the *Lao Tzu*; he was a master of debate and skilled in speech. "Ho Yen, when Minister of Personnel, was deeply struck by his remarkable qualities, saying, with an exclamation of wonder: 'Confucius said that we must show respect for the young [for who knows but that they will be better than our present? *Analects*, IX/22]. With a person such at this, however, one can discuss the very nexus of Nature's and man's relationship.' [The allusion suggests awe.] Ts'ao Shuang [of the Wei dynasty imperial clan] had him appointed a Vice-Minister; in the tenth year of the Cheng-shih reign period [249] he became ill and

---

11 From the *San-kuo Chih*, "Wei Chih," *ch.* 9; the tenth year of the Cheng-shih reign period corresponds to A.D. 249. Also, a note in the same work quotes the *Wei Lüeh*: "When T'ai-tsu [i.e., Ts'ao Ts'ao] held the post of Ssu-k'ung [i.e., Imperial Secretary, at the Han court] he took Ho Yen's mother as a consort, and also took in [the boy] Ho Yen whom he reared [as a member of his household]." We also note that in *ch.* 1, "Annals of the Emperor Wu," of the "Wei Chih," it states that Ts'ao Ts'ao became Ssu-k'ung in the first year of the Chien-an reign period [196]. In the thirteenth year [208] the posts of the Three Lords [including Ssu-k'ung] were abolished and Ts'ao Ts'ao became Chancellor. It is not clear in which year he took the lady Yin [Ho Yen's mother] as consort; at the very latest Ho Yen was born before 209. As for his writings, in addition to what the biography in the dynastic history lists [in the passage translated here,] there also are the *Lun-yü chi-chieh* [commentary on the *Analects*] in ten *chüan*, *Chou Yi chieh* [commentary on the *Book of Changes*], and *Collected Writings* in eleven *chüan*, of which the *Lun-yü chi-chieh* is extant; it contains no political thought.

died, in his twenty-fourth year of age."[12] His writings include *Lao Tzu chu* in two *chüan*, *Chou Yi chu* in six *chüan*, the *Chou Yi lüeh-li* in one *chüan*, the *Lun-yü shih-yi* in three *chüan*, and *Collected Writings* in five *chüan*. [Except for the last, the others are commentaries on the *Lao Tzu*, the *Book of Changes* or *Yi Ching*, and the *Analects* of Confucius.]

Chi K'ang's courtesy name was Shu-yeh. Orphaned when young, he gave evidence of remarkable intelligence. "By nature calmly detached and subject to few desires, forebearing and willing to overlook others' flaws [cf. *Tso Chuan*, Hsüan 15; Legge, p. 327], magnanimous and un-affected, he possessed great breadth of spirit. In studies he followed no teacher, but read widely, gaining comprehensive knowledge. As he reached maturity he became devoted to Lao-Chuang thought. He was related by marriage to the Wei imperial [Ts'ao] clan, and was appointed a Palace Grandee."[13] In the third year of the Ching-yuan reign period [262] he was killed by Ssu-ma Chao. His collected writings contained fifteen *chüan*, of which ten still exist.

Hsiang Hsiu's courtesy name was Tzu-ch'i; he was a close friend of Chi K'ang. "As a youth he was known to Shan T'ao [with Chi K'ang and others, called the Seven Sages of the Bamboo Grove, a group of individualistic eccentrics]. He greatly valued the learning of Lao-Chuang. Including both its Inner and Outer portions, the book of Chuang Chou [the *Chuang Tzu*] contains several tens of chapters. Despite successive generations of Taoist specialists' [*fang shih* 方士, or adepts'] insights, no one had yet adequately explained the whole work's thought system. Hsiang Hsiu therefore set forth an explanation of its hidden meanings, his discoveries holding quite remarkable fascination and lending strong impetus to the metaphysical vogue [*hsüan feng* 玄風]. His readers gained transcendant enlightenment, none failing to attain for a time the sense of self-contained contentment [that is its message]. During the reign of the Emperor Hui [of the Chin dynasty, *reg.* 290–306], Kuo Hsiang reformu-lated and enlarged the work. The lingering marks of Confucianism and Mohism were scorned, while the sayings of the Taoist School thereafter swelled to dominance." After Chi K'ang's death, Hsiang Hsiu, wishing to avoid similar calamity, sought appointment through the provincial selection and took service under Ssu-ma Chao. He held successive posts, reaching that of Assistant Policy Advisor, Attending Censor, and Policy Advisor [all high-ranking but nominal positions of attendant at the Inner

---

[12] *Ibid.*, *ch.* 28; the commentary quotes Ho Shao's biography of Wang Pi. Calculating from the year of his death, we know that Wang Pi was born in the sixth year of the Huang-ch'u reign period, (thus his dates are 226–249).

[13] *Chin Shu*, *ch.* 49, Chi K'ang's biography. Chi K'ang was born in the fourth year of the Wei dynasty's Huang-ch'u reign period (thus his dates are 223–262). [His name is also spelled "Hsi K'ang."]

Court]. "At court he assumed no responsibilities, putting in an appearance and no more."[14]

Kuo Hsiang's courtesy name was Tzu-hsüan. "As a youth he displayed a thoughtful mentality, was fond of Lao-Chuang learning, and was skilled in 'pure conversation.' The Grand Commandant Wang Yen often remarked: 'Listening to Kuo Hsiang's speech is like listening to a river flowing over a waterfall: it pours out inexhaustibly.' " Kuo served in a succession of offices, rising to the post of Attending Censor. Ssu-ma Yüeh, Prince of Tung-hai, took Kuo into his service, appointing him Grand Tutor and Registrar. In the sixth year of the Yung-chia reign period [312] he died of an illness. "Previously, several score of scholars had produced commentaries on the *Chuang Tzu*, but none had been able to elucidate its thought system. Going beyond the older commentaries Hsiang Hsiu wrote the [*Chuang Tzu*] *Chieh-yi*. Marvelously developed and reaching extraordinary heights, his work greatly stimulated the vogue for metaphysical conversation. But the two chapters "Autumn Floods" and "Perfect Happiness' [*chs*. 17 and 18] had not been completed when he died. Hsiang Hsiu's son was but a young child; the interpretations [of his manuscript commentary] became scattered and lost. Nonetheless, many copies of it were being circulated. Kuo Hsiang was a man of base character, and because Hsiang Hsiu's interpretations were not to be [otherwise] transmitted, he plagiarized them and presented them as his own commentary, adding his commentary to 'Autumn Floods' and 'Perfect Happiness,' and somewhat altering the commentary on [*ch*. 9] 'Horses' Hoofs.' As for the commentaries on all the other chapters he no more than edited the sentences. Subsequently the Hsiang Hsiu interpretation appeared in another edition, so that today there exist both the Hsiang Hsiu and the Kuo Hsiang versions of the *Chuang Tzu*, but the interpretation is identical in the two."[15]

[14] *Ibid., ch.* 49, Hsiang Hsiu's biography.

[15] *Ibid., ch.* 50, Kuo Hsiang's biography. It should be noted that this biography's account of plagiarizing the commentary seems doubtful. Hsiang Hsiu's biography tells that when he had completed his commentary he showed it to Chi K'ang. Chi K'ang said: "This surely will never be surpassed!" (The *Shih-shuo hsin-yü, ch.* 4, "Wen-hsüeh p'ien," quotes Hsiang Hsiu's *pieh-chuan* or "informal biography" in more or less the same sense and adds Lü An's remark: "Chuang Chou has not died!") Yet Kuo Hsiang's biography states that before the two chapters "Autumn Floods" and "Perfect Happiness" had been completed, Hsiang Hsiu died. (Chi K'ang died long before Hsiang Hsiu.) This is the first point of doubt.

Hsiang Hsiu's biography says of his commentary that among "His readers . . . [there were] . . . none failing to attain for a time the sense of self-contained contentment," so those who read it were more than one person. How, then, could Kuo Hsiang have dared to plagiarize it? Would no one have exposed him, but, on the contrary, Taoist discourse be stimulated to flourish by it? This is the second point of doubt.

The five men discussed above all lived during the age of the Ts'ao Wei and the [Ssu-ma] Western Chin dynasties. Only Chang Chan was a man of the Eastern Chin period, and he thus represents a last current of the thought of non-action. His courtesy name was Ch'u-tu; no records remain of his birth and death dates or of his career. According to the biography of Fan Ning in *ch.* 75 of the *Chin Shu*, at some point Chang Chan had held the post of Assistant Privy Councilor, and was a contemporary of Fan Ning, both thus living during the era from the reign of Emperor Ch'eng to that of Emperor An [326–418].[16]

Ho Yen's statement: "Heaven, earth, and all the myriad things have the basis of their existence in non-being," is adequate to sum up the cosmology of the Wei-Chin Taoist school. That is, *wu* or "non-being" is the ontological reality of the cosmos. In the "beginning of things and the completion of affairs" it is *yu* or "being" that is produced by it. Non-being produces [generates], and is being; that concept is not necessarily in conflict with that of *Tao*. Ho Yen explained that: "For *Tao* never possesses anything. But, since the beginning of the universe it has possessed all things. Yet it still is called *Tao*, because it has the further ability not to

---

Kuo Hsiang's biography states that when Hsiang Hsiu died his son was still a young child, and his interpretations became scattered and lost. How does it happen, then, that Kuo Hsiang needed to fill in only the originally uncompleted chapters "Autumn Floods" and "Perfect Happiness"? The biography also states that the other edition containing Hsiang Hsiu's interpretations appeared only after the plagiarized commentary had been issued; that, therefore, definitely could not have provided the basis for Kuo Hsiang's commentary. This is the third point of doubt.

Wang Yen was a profound student of Lao-Chuang learning. Kuo Hsiang's biography states that Wang Yen expressed highest praise of Kuo Hsiang's "pure conversation." Would it, therefore, have been necessary for Kuo to depend on Hsiang Hsiu's interpretations in order to compose his own commentary? Kuo Hsiang also was a specialist on Lao-Chuang learning, so would he not have known that Hsiang Hsiu's work existed in other copies, so he would not be able to produce a plagiarized version based on it? This is the fourth point of doubt.

Hsiang Hsiu's biography says of his interpretations: "Kuo Hsiang rephrased and enlarged the work." That probably is closer to the truth. Ch'ien Tseng's [1629-*ca.* 1700] *Tu-shu min-ch'iu chi* remarks that the time is far in the distant past, the accounts vary among themselves, and that he fears Kuo Hsiang's biography probably is not to be relied upon. That is a most judicious and fair view. The *Ssu-k'u ch'üan-shu tsung-mu t'i-yao* [the Ch'ing imperial catalog, 1781–83] bases an argument on Lu Te-ming's [556–627] *Ching-tien shih-wen* to demonstrate that the Kuo Hsiang commentary is a work of plagiarism; reference may also be made to that. In this chapter all the quotations from the commentary are credited to Kuo Hsiang; that is to adopt that device of men of the ancient past by which the dubious is transmitted [even though known to be dubious]; it also makes for convenience in citing.

[16] Fan Ning was born in the fifth year of the Eastern Chin Emperor Ch'eng's Hsien-k'ang reign period and died in the fifth year of the Emperor An's Lung-an reign period (thus his dates are 339–401).

possess things." On investigating its workings, it is seen to be a matter of complying with the spontaneous [*tzu-jan*, or Nature]. "Hsia-hou Hsüan said: heaven and earth spontaneously move in their cycles; the Sage spontaneously functions. By spontaneity is meant the *Tao*."[17] To speak in terms of heaven's and earth's and the myriad things' spontaneous cycles of movement and of production, heaven and earth do not purposely produce the myriad things, nor do the myriad things know for what they are produced.[18] Heaven and earth "take no purposive action with respect to the myriad things, and each of the myriad things adapts to its own functioning."[19] Since, then, the production of the myriad things is entirely spontaneous, we also can, in view of that, say that "the myriad things all are subject to their fates [*ming* 命]," so man's "intelligence and strength have no application there." For, "The living are not alive because they have the capacity to produce life; the transforming are not transformed because they have the capacity to transform; it is simply that they cannot but generate, cannot but transform."[20] Therefore, "What is called 'of Nature' [*t'ien* 天] is the allotment of spontaneity."[21] "Spontaneity is the unseen cyclic movement." That unseen cyclic movement [*ming yün* 冥運, or "unknown destiny"] is that which is so though we do not know why it is so. "That which is so though we do not know why it is so is fate [*ming* 命]." "Fate is the inexorable appointment, the heretofore-determined allotment."[22]

Holding to that cosmology, and applying it to government, brought about the governing methods of non-action. Although Wang Yen, Ho Yen, and those who followed after in this group were all well-versed in both the *Lao Tzu* and the *Chuang Tzu*, their own thought in fact adhered largely to the character established in the *Tao Te Ching*. The "Yang Chu" chapter of the *Lieh Tzu* contains phrases urging "governing one's own self" [instead of governing the state well], "giving ease to one's nature" [instead of striving], and [happily] "bringing the way of ruler and

---

[17] Chang Chan's commentary to the *Lieh Tzu*, ch. 4, "Chung-ni p'ien," quoting Ho Yen's "Wu-ming lun" or "Treatise on the Nameless." [Translation slightly modified from Chan, *Source Book*, p. 325.] Hsia-hou Hsüan's courtesy name was T'ai-ch'u; he was a contemporary of Ho Yen, and was praised by him. Refer to the quotation in the commentary of P'ei Sung-chih [dated 312] to *ch*. 9 of the "Wei Chih" in the *San-kuo Chih*.

[18] Wang Pi's commentary to Chapters 21 and 24 of the *Lao Tzu*.

[19] *Ibid.*, in Chapter 5.

[20] Chang Chan's commentary to the *Lieh Tzu*, ch. 6, "Li ming p'ien" and *ch*. 1, "T'ien jui p'ien." [The words "living," "alive," "life," and "to generate" all translate "*sheng*" 生, elsewhere also "to produce," "production," etc.; "transforming," "transformed," and "to transform" all translate "*hua* 化, which also is a Taoist word for "death," for "change," etc.]

[21] *Ibid.*, *ch*. 4, "Chung-ni p'ien."

[22] *Ibid.*, *ch*. 6, "Li ming p'ien." This probably is influenced by Wang Ch'ung.

servitor to its end." Chang Chan's commentary here says: "In the force of its language this chapter makes a wholly unreasonable onslaught; it scarcely seems to embody the tone and temper of the superior man." This clearly displays his attitude of advocating non-action yet opposing the no-ruler anarchy. From the point of view of this group of thinkers, humans are involved in political life as one result of all Nature's spontaneous transformations. Since the establishment of the ruler has come about spontaneously, institutions cannot be denied. The one aspect that should arouse caution, however, is the need to prevent their development from approaching levels at which spontaneity would be violated. Wang Pi [in his commentary on the *Lao Tzu, Chapter* 28] explains the lines: "When the uncarved block is fragmented and dispersed one then makes implements. [The Sage uses those; he establishes officials and rulers]" as follows: "The uncarved block [*p'u* 樸, "pristine simplicity"] is that which is genuine. When the genuine is dispersed, all the hundred ways of acting emerge, and the different varieties of things are produced, such as implements. The Sage, accepting that division and dispersal [of the genuine, pristine simplicity, now displaced by civilization], therefore establishes officials and rulers for man; he takes the good to be the teachers of man, and those who are not good to be the lesson material [of his teachings, or, his followers; cf. *Tao Te Ching, Chapter* 27]. He alters manners and changes customs causing all to revert to oneness." And for the line [in *ch.* 32], "When there first were institutions and regulations, there were names," he explains as follows: " 'When first there were institutions and regulations' describes the time when the uncarved block was dispersed and there first were officials and rulers. When institutions and regulations, officials and rulers are initiated, it is impossible not to establish names and statuses by which to determine superior and inferior; therefore when first there are institutions and regulations, there will be names."[23]

Kuo Hsiang's statements are particularly clear and revealing. He wrote: "Whether one is a ruler or a servitor, a superior or an inferior, and whether it is the hand or the foot, the inside or the outside, that follows from the spontaneity of Natural Principle [*t'ien-li chih tzu-jan* 天理之自然]; how could it be thus directly from man's actions? . . . For the one whom the age takes to be worthy becomes the ruler, while those whose talents do not correspond to the demands of the age become servitors. It is analogous to the heavens' being naturally high and earth naturally low, the head being naturally on top and the feet occupying naturally the inferior position."[24] Moreover, not only is the establishment of ruler and servitor a consequence of spontaneous Nature; it also is a

[23] Wang Pi's commentary to the *Lao Tzu*, Chapters 28 and 31.
[24] Kuo Hsiang's commentary to the *Chuang Tzu, ch.* 2, "Ch'i-wu Lun."

consequence of its very needs. For, "Since we are living with men, we cannot get away from them. . . . When a thousand people are collected together, if one is not made their master [*chu* 主, or "ruler"] they must either be disorderly or become scattered. Thus it is that though many may be worthy, there cannot be many masters, and even though none is worthy, yet neither can there be no master. This is the way of heaven and man [or, the natural way of man]; and the appropriate condition to be arrived at. . . ."[25] Nevertheless we would be well advised not to misinterpret this to mean that inasmuch as the empire cannot lack a ruler, the ruler of men should therefore exert himself in purposive action. "For the one who can make the empire be well-governed is the one who does no governing. . . . That is, being well-governed comes from not governing, and action comes from taking no action. . . . Therefore it is he who in every act is with the people who, wherever he may be, can be the world's ruler. To be the ruler in this way is to be innately lofty as are the heavens; that is in truth the virtue of the ruler. . . . Are we to demand that a person sit silently, arms folded, in the midst of an alpine grove before he can claim to be a man of non-action? Such [misapprehension] explains why the sayings of Chuang Tzu and Lao Tzu are cast aside by persons bearing high responsibilities in office. Persons bearing high responsibilities in office must enter into the realms of action without a thought of turning back; that is what explains it."[26]

The methods of non-action have three essential features. The first is for the ruler to follow along with the lead of his servitors in governing, and thus take no action. Wang Pi said: "Heaven and earth [or, the natural process] establish the ruler's position; the Sage achieves [to the limits of] his abilities. People may lay plans, and ghosts may lay plans, but the common people join themselves together with that man of ability. That able one [the Sage] gives to them while his chosen assistants take from them. When the abilities are great, that one then becomes the Great [Sage emperor], and when the assistants are of high value [*kuei* 貴] they are then ennobled [*kuei*]. So material things find their master, and affairs have their ruler. This way a ruler can have strings of beads hanging from his crown [as court ritual prescribes] that cover his eyes and still have no fear of being deceived; he can have cap-flaps covering his ears and still have no worry about being spoken of with disrespect. How much less need he then belabor his intelligence his whole life long in investigating his people's doings! For when one uses one's light to investigate things, those things also will apprehensively respond to that same light. When one in distrust investigates things, things also apprehensively respond

[25] *Ibid.*, *ch.* 4, "Jen-chien-shih."
[26] *Ibid.*, *ch.* 1, "Hsiao-yao Yu." According to this standard, Wang Yen can be said to have possessed the capacity to implement "the virtue of the ruler."

with distrust. For the minds of the [people comprising] the empire must vary; yet they dare not differ in the way they respond because none is willing to show his own feelings. Grave indeed are the greater causes of harm, but none is so great as using one's light [of the discerning mind]."[27] Kuo Hsiang said: "When the king does not make himself useful in the various offices, the various officials will manage their own affairs; those with clear vision will do the seeing, those with sharp ears will do the hearing, and the knowledgeable will do the planning while the valiant will do the protecting. What need is there [for the ruler] to take any action? He remains far away and deeply silent; that is all."[28] Chang Chan also said that the ruler who took himself to be capable would thereby become "isolated and without support, whereas the one who recognizes capabilities in others has the wise ones planning for him, the able ones serving for him. When then, among men, no talent is discarded, the state is easily governed."[29] Kuo Hsiang further extended this idea so as to include the whole society: "The scope of non-action is indeed vast! [When the ruler dwells in it] what in the empire is not fulfilled in non-action? That is why [the best of antiquity's] rulers above did not take upon themselves the tasks of their Chief Ministers, and in consequence [the great Chief Ministers of early Shang and early Chou, respectively] Yi Yin and Lü Shang, quiescently supervised their offices. The Chief Ministers did not take upon themselves those duties of the various offices of government, and in consequence the various officials quiescently dealt with all affairs. The various officials did not engage themselves in the obligations of all the myriad people, and in consequence the myriad people all went peaceably about their work. When among the myriad people no one exchanges his function with that of another, then throughout the realm quiescence prevails in his relations with others. Thus it is that from the Son of Heaven on down to the ordinary people, indeed, even down to the insect and animal creatures, where can one take unnecessary action and accomplish anything? Therefore it can be said that the more there is non-action the more [the ruler] is venerated."[30]

The second of those essential features is not to undertake troublesome and burdensome acts of governing. That the ruler is to achieve his non-

[27] Wang Pi's commentary to the *Lao Tzu*, Chapter 49.

[28] Kuo Hsiang's commentary to the *Chuang Tzu*, ch. 4, "Jen-chien-shih." The commentary on *ch.* 20, "Shan Mu," also states: "Although [Yao] possessed the realm, all was entrusted to the Hundred Officials and left to the myriad things themselves; he did not engage himself with such. That is to say, he did not make the people his. He followed along with the people's inclinations and gave free reign to all things, and did not belabor himself about them. That is, he did not thereby become the possession of the people." [Cf. Chan, *Source Book*, page 335.]

[29] Chan Chan's commentary to the *Lieh Tzu*, ch. 8, "Shuo fu."

[30] Kuo Hsiang's commentary to the *Chuang Tzu*, ch. 13, "T'ien Tao."

action through relying on his servitors is not thereby to say that the servitors should put their knowledge and abilities actively to work. The world's ways of governing actively do not go beyond the two sets of activities: applying punishments and penalties [as in Legalism] and upholding benevolence and righteousness [as in Confucianism]. Wang Pi said that the one who is skilled in governing the state: ". . . merely accords with things' own natures and does not impose punishments to keep things in order. . . . Should he, however, enlarge the net of the law, multiply penalties and punishments, block off paths and roads, and set upon people in their remote dwellings, then all the myriad forms of existence will lose their spontaneity, and the common people will be as if deprived of their hands and feet. The birds overhead will be confused, and the fishes in the deep will be confounded. Therefore the Sage does not establish laws and punishments in order thereby to impose restrictions on things."[31] As for benevolence [jen, or "humanity"] and righteousness [yi], rites and music, which also were all produced after the Tao had declined and its powers [te] had been lost, those all represented the "inferior virtues." [Hsia te; vide Tao Te Ching, Chapter 38]. "The inferior virtues are all gained by seeking them; they are made complete by taking action. In consequence, the Good was established as the means for making all things orderly." However, when one gains by seeking, some loss must be present. When something is completed through purposive action, some failure must also be present. When the names for "the Good" were produced, the bad came into being in response to those."[32]

On pursuing the issue of why benevolence and righteousness are inadequate to achieve good government, we find it is because they are quite contrary to human nature. Chi K'ang explained it as follows: "It is the nature of the people that they like security and detest danger, that they are fond of ease and dislike labor. Thus, when they are not disturbed, that satisfies their desires; when they are not pressed, that accords with their will. In the primeval era the great simplicity still was undiminished. The ruler above lacked the refinements, and below, there were no contentions among the people. Things were complete in themselves and the principles [of nature] prevailed. Nothing failed to achieve its own fulfillment. . . . But, coming to a time when the Perfect Man went out of existence [with the degeneration of the pristine simplicity], the Great Tao was in decline, and only then did men commence to use writing to transmit their ideas, and to make distinctions among the multitudes so that clan affiliations came into being. Benevolence and righteousness were contrived and established as the means to work on people's minds;

---

[31] Wang Pi's commentary to the Lao Tzu, Chapters 36, 49 and 28.
[32] Ibid., Chapter 38.

names and statuses were instituted as the means to circumscribe their outward behavior, while exhortations to learning and instruction in the refinements sought to impart an aura of the supernal [*shen* 神] to their teachings. . . . Thus benevolence and righteousness are directed toward ordering the artificial [cf. Hsün Tzu, as in Chapter Three, Section Five, above]; they are not the essential methods for nurturing the genuine. The [attitudes] of uprightness and deference are born of strife and force; they are not products of spontaneity [Nature]."[33] In this view, then, although the methods employed by Mencius and Hsün Tzu or by Lord Shang and Han Fei were different, they all were as one in damaging life and impairing the nature.

The third element is *laissez-faire*. The *Tao* is present in non-action, and that anticipates that all things will find their own fulfillment [*tzu-te* 自得], not that they will be passively inactive. Kuo Hsiang said: "One must not fail to look carefully into the term non-action. The one who wields the empire [i.e., the ruler] thereby undertakes the action of wielding [political power]. Such action however is that of [the ruler's] own fulfillment for he fully accords with the natures of things, and for that reason it is called non-action."[34] When we understand that the method of non-action lies in "giving free reign so that each thing will obtain its own fulfillment," then the authoritarian monarchy's policies of excessive restraints and demands all should be cast aside. Thus Kuo Hsiang said: "When one imposes himself on things to control them, things then lose their true qualities."[35] And, again: "The individual self achieves its perfection in interaction with the world. If now one person should impose authoritarian control on the world, the world would be obstructed, so how could he himself remain unobstructed? Thereby, not only would that one person [the ruler] suffer frustration, but on all sides there would be unlimited loss."[36]

Nevertheless, a disputant will ask, if the art of governing lies in *laissez-faire* and non-action, why, then, is there the need to establish the ruler in the first place? Kuo Hsiang rebuts this argument with the statement: "If the realm were to lack an enlightened ruler, then nothing would be able to reach its fulfillment. Such fulfillment as there now is must be accounted the achievement of enlightened rulers. Yet that achievement lies in his non-action and in turning responsibility back to the world. All the [constituent parts] of the world having obtained autonomy, the consequence is that their [individual fulfillment] does not appear to be

[33] Chi K'ang, "Nan tzu-ran hao-hsüeh lun" (from the *Chi Chung-san Chi* in the *Han-Wei Lu-ch'ao Po-san Ming-chia-chi*).

[34] Kuo Hsiang's commentary to the *Chuang Tzu*, ch. 13, "T'ien Tao."

[35] *Ibid.*, ch. 7, "Ying ti-wang."

[36] *Ibid.*, ch. 11, "Tsai yu."

the achievement of the enlightened ruler."[37] The enlightened ruler is thus in fact quite necessary.

The people of the empire, if "let alone so that they are under no constraints, will then be well-governed"; once this principle is comprehended, then other than the severe punishments and oppresive governmental measures, there is virtually nothing that may not be compatible with the Way of governing. Kuo Hsiang says: "Indispensable to the nature [of people] are food and clothing; indispensable among their affairs are tilling and weaving. It is these matters which are universally the same and on which the empire is based. Maintaining the Way in these matters is the ultimate of non-action."[38] He states further: "Benevolence and righteousness are, after all, human feelings; but they should be left to free [spontaneous] play. . . . Yet ever since the Three Dynasties [of antiquity] the sounds of strife have been omnipresent; human feelings have been cast aside in feverish pursuit of outward forms. Is that not most sorrowful?"[39] This view would place all such matters as food and drink, relations between men and women, benevolence and righteousness, loyalty and trust, beyond the scope of the enlightened ruler's urgings and restrictings. Benevolence and righteousness [i.e., the hallmarks of the Confucian system] should be left free of interference; the true and the false likewise should be allowed to coexist. Kuo Hsiang said of the myriad things in the world: "Although they differ in their excellence, they are similar in all being somehow excellent. When each is held to be excellent for its [particular] excellence, all things become as one in excellence. When each is held valid for its [particular] validity, all the empire becomes as one in validity." Therefore, "The person who has profound perception of the cosmic flux accepts the world so as to understand the world. When none in the world says: 'I am wrong,' that shows nothing in the world is 'wrong'; when none in the world says: 'He is right,' that shows nothing in the world is 'right'. There is no right, there is no wrong; all merge in the oneness."[40] By this reasoning when the First Emperor of the Ch'in dynasty distinguished [right and wrong as] black and white and established a single standard to be honored, or when the Emperor Wu of the Han raised some to eminence and banished others in disgrace, both were entirely contrary to the concept of letting things alone, [*tsai yu* 在宥; cf. Chapter Five, Section Five, above].

Chi K'ang set forth some ideas relevant to the idealized vision of governing through non-action. He wrote: "The kings of antiquity ac-

---

[37] *Ibid., ch.* 7, "Ying ti-wang."
[38] *Ibid., ch.* 9, "Ma t'i."
[39] *Ibid., ch.* 8, "P'ien mu."
[40] *Ibid., ch.* 5, "Te-ch'ung fu."

knowledged Nature [*t'ien* 天] in setting things in order; they invariably reverenced the teachings of simplicity and ease and they implemented the governance of non-action. The ruler above was quiescent, while his servitors below were agreeably compliant. The mysterious transformations [of Nature] though unseen were pervasive, and the interactions between Nature [*t'ien*] and man were harmonious. All thirsting species were permeated and nourished by the mystical secretions. Within the whole universe [*liu-ho chih nei* 六合之內] the enriching currents flowed grandly, washing away dust and defilement and causing all forms of life to feel contentedly at ease. Turning naturally to the pursuit of all good things, [people] complied with the *Tao* without having to talk about it; they harbored loyalty and clung to righteousness without being aware of their reasons for doing so."[41]

Chi K'ang also described the ideal ruler as follows: "The Sage comes as though inevitably to rule over the empire without intending to do so, hence takes [the mind of] all the myriad things as his own mind. He leaves all the forms of life to themselves, and guides his own person by means of the *Tao*, being therein the same as all the world in gaining his own fulfillment. Effortlessly, he takes the absence of involvement as his work; calmly, he looks upon the empire as a commonality [*t'ien-hsia wei kung* 天下爲公]. Although he occupies the throne and receives the homage of the myriad states, his manner is as gentle as that of an ordinary scholar receiving guests. Although he has implanted his royal standard and wears the ornamented imperial robes, he is as unassuming as though dressed in plainest cloth. Accordingly, the ruler and his servitors are unmindful of each other at the top, while below them the ordinary people have sufficiency in their households. Nor would [such a ruler] ever encourage the common people to venerate himself, nor carve out an empire to make it his personal thing, nor regard wealth and high status as worthy of veneration, nor long for them endlessly in his own heart!"[42]

We have stated earlier that: "Lao Tzu and Chuang Tzu were skeptical about the efficacy of government and affirmed the value of the individual."[43] Chi K'ang's ideas are quite compatible with that. He believed

[41] Chi K'ang, "Sheng wu ai-lo lun."

[42] Chi K'ang, "Ta 'Nan Yang-sheng lun'." Ho Yen's "Ching-fu-tien fu" says: "Embody Nature in enacting the forms of government; accord with the seasons in establishing the acts of governance. . . . At a distance, comply with the spontaneity of *Yin* and *Yang*; near at hand, base oneself on the true natures of men and things. . . . Abolish offices that have no useful function, and eliminate causes that lead to proliferating tasks. Do away with the accumulations of varied custom in the complex rites, and return the people's mentality to the pristine simplicity." From the *Wen Hsüan* [anthology compiled by Hsiao T'ung, 501–531], *ch.* 11. Chi K'ang's thought is close to this.

[43] Chapter Five, last paragraph of Section One, of the present work [p. 282, above].

that the security and well-being of the individual was the ultimate objective in human life. Thus: "The Sage comes as though inevitably to rule over the empire without intending to do so . . . [and is] the same as all the world in gaining his own fulfillment." From this we can know that the governing through inaction is a necessary condition for the ideal life and not the ultimate destination of human life. The section "Kuei sheng" ["On Valuing One's Life," *ch.* 2, section 2] in the *Lü-shih Ch'un-ch'iu*, says: "The true *Tao* lies in maintaining one's self; its superfluities may be applied to serving the state; its bits and scraps may be applied to governing the empire." [Cf. Chapter Ten, Section Three, Page 570, above.] This statement most adequately expresses the attitude of the Lao-Chuang thinkers toward government. Chi K'ang's "Discourse on Nourishing Life" ["Yang-sheng Lun"] in fact belongs to that same tradition, and is particularly close to the *Tao Te Ching*'s doctrines of limiting the desires and being content with what one has.[44]

SECTION THREE
"No Ruler"

WANG Pi, Ho Yen, and those others acknowledging that governmental institutions were products of Nature's transformations therefore advocated that rulers were necessary, yet they adopted non-action as their method of governing. Since there was that prior commitment to non-action, however, of what utility was the ruler? Although Kuo Hsiang had provided an explanation of this, it remained an issue ultimately vulnerable to the suspicion of inconsistency. Juan Chi, T'ao Ch'ien, and Pao Ching-yen went a step further and developed the position that there need be no ruler. The conclusion that the logic of government by non-action made inescapable was in this way finally brought to mature development.

T'ao Ch'ien's courtesy name was Yüan-ming;[45] he was a poet rather

---

[44] The "Ta 'Nan Yang-sheng lun' " ["Reply to 'A Rebuttal of the Discourse on Nourishing Life' " by Chi K'ang] states: "The desires and one's life cannot be sustained together; fame and one's person cannot be preserved simultaneously. . . . That is why the ancients, knowing that wine and meat are sweet poisons, cast them aside as good riddance. Recognizing that fame and status are enticing bait, they passed them by without a backward glance. Actions should only be to supply one's needs, with no excessive use of things. Knowing is for correcting one's self, but not for enterprises going beyond." It also says: "If one is contented, though he has only a small plot to cultivate, a coarse garment to wear, and beans to eat in no case will he not have his own fulfillment. If one is not contented, though the whole world support him and all things serve him, he still would not be gratified." [The second passage is modified from de Bary, *Sources*, pp. 288–89.]

[45] T'ao Ch'ien was born in the third year of the Chin dynasty Emperor Ai's Hsing-ning reign period, and died in the fourth year of the Yuan-chia reign period of the Sung Emperor Wen (365–427). His biography appears in *ch.* 93 of the *Sung Shu* and in *ch.* 94 of the *Chin Shu*.

than a thinker. The outlines of his rulerless ideal society are merely hinted at in his "Story of the Peach-blossom Stream" and in his other poetry. ["*T'ao-hua yüan chi*" is an allegory about a community that escaped from the harsh government of the Ch'in and had lived in perfect happiness without a ruler ever since.] All of this is very well known so it is unnecessary to go into detail here.[46]

Although Juan Chi also offers no systematic body of thought, his statements are somewhat more substantial and more revealing. Juan Chi's courtesy name was Ssu-tsung; he was born in the fifteenth year of the Han dynasty's Chien-an reign period, and died in the fourth year of the Wei's Ching-yuan reign period. "He read widely throughout the various writings, but was particularly fond of the *Chuang Tzu* and the *Lao Tzu.*" The histories record: "Juan Chi originally aspired to be of use to the world. He lived during the transition from the Wei dynasty to the Chin when the empire was subject to numerous vicissitudes and when few notable personages long survived. Juan Chi therefore desisted from involvement in the world's affairs, his regular activity thereafter being drinking." When Kao-kuei Hsiang-kung [i.e., Ts'ao Mao, who reigned 254–259, posthumously the Emperor Shao] ascended the throne, Juan Chi was given the nobiliary rank [designated by the title] of Marquis of Kuan-nei and was then transferred to the post of *San-ch'i ch'ang-shih* [a nominal court-attendant post]. Later, he died at home, of an illness. Among his writings in poetry and prose are his "Ta Chuang Lun" ["On Comprehending Chuang Tzu"] and "Ta-jen Hsien-sheng Chuan" ["Biography of a Great Sage"] which give adequate evidence of his thought.[47] Basing himself on ideas drawn from the *Chuang Tzu*, he held that: "Man lives within heaven and earth and embodies the forms of Nature." There is no separation between things and the self; death and life are of one piece. "The perfect man is one who is vital in life and quiescent toward death."[48] "Thus the perfect man has no residence, being a traveler through heaven and earth. The perfect man has no host, heaven

---

[46] [The "Peach-blossom Stream" consists of the "narrative" or *chi* and a poem reflecting on it.] The poem contains the lines: "From the spring cocoons we take the long silk fibers; from our fall harvests we pay no royal tax." And, further: "Although we have no calendar to record the years [because issuing the calendar was a prerogative of emperors] the four seasons quite naturally make up the year. Content, we know a surplus of happiness, so why need we put clever minds to work [to contrive political institutions]?" This is close to Chuang Tzu.

[47] His birth and death dates correspond to A.D. 210 and 263. His biography is in *ch.* 49 of the *Chin Shu.* The extant *Juan Ssu-tsung Chi* [Juan Chi's collected writings] has two *chüan,* the remnants of a collection the larger portion of which has been lost. Yen K'o-chün's *Ch'üan San-kuo Wen* [in his Ch'üan Shang-ku San-tai Ch'in-Han San-kuo Liu-ch'ao Wen, preface dated 1836] includes some of the missing pieces.

[48] Juan Chi, "Ta Chuan Lun."

and earth providing his lodgment. The perfect man has no undertakings, heaven and earth supplying his involvements. He knows no distinction of true and false, no difference between good and evil."[49] For he takes as natural and invariable principles that: "things gained by seeking are losses, points demonstrated in dispute are errors, the person without desires is self-content, the open empty [i.e., humble] person receives what is real." In the common ways of the world these things cannot be understood, for "everyone believes that a life of a hundred years is difficult to achieve and that the passage of time brings uncertainties. Everyone seeks an abundance of servants and horses, adornments of clothing, brilliant gems, elaborate dwellings. Outside the home they flatter the ruler and superiors; at home they deceive fathers and elder brothers. Vigorously they apply their talent and cleverness in competitive pursuits on all sides. Families are overturned by quick-witted sons; states are extinguished by talented servitors."[50] The desire to gain fortune produces, on the contrary, disaster; that too must be seen as inevitable.

There is a still further dimension to this: such debacles in the day-to-day world are not only the consequence of excessive desires, they also stem from adherence to the ritual norms. The "superior man" [chün-tzu] on whom the world bestows so much honor "chants the teachings bequeathed by the Duke of Chou and Confucius and admiringly sighs over the virtues of Yao and Shun. He is punctilious in cultivating the norms, punctilious in submitting to the rites. In his hands he grasps the jade symbols [of propriety] as his feet tread the straight and narrow line. By his acts he expects to be the model near at hand; by his words he hopes to provide maxims for all time. . . . He accepts the charge from his ruler to shepherd the common people, and when he retires it is to develop his family and personal interests so as to care for and sustain wives and children." He believes himself to have acquired the sure way to enduring happiness and lasting security. He cannot see that in the way he carries on he is no different from "a flea in someone's trousers . . . which does not dare stray away from the seam, fears to go beyond the seat of the trousers, thinking himself thereby to have gained the proper measure [of his security]. When hungry he bites the man, and believes that he has found the inexhaustible food supply. Yet in a torrid land when the heat spreads, scorching towns and consuming cities, the fleas will all die in the trousers because they have no way to get out."[51] When, thus, has behavior that conforms to the methods of the rites ever been able to lead away from disaster and draw nigh to fortune, to keep people safe and whole?

[49] Juan Chi, "Ta-jen Hsien-sheng Chuan."
[50] "Ta Chuang Lun."
[51] "Ta-jen Hsien-sheng Chuan."

Nevertheless it is just those of the vulgar world who seek advantages and emoluments and who maintain the ritualized norms who have presumed to institutionalize the ruler-servitor, superior-inferior relationships, as if those were the unquestioned expression of natural principle, and conveyed the essential truths of human relations. From Juan Chi's view of the matter, however, political life is the consequence of man's degeneracy; not only is it totally without value for mankind itself, it in fact possesses immeasurable harm for him. Juan Chi tells of the perfect, pristine scene he envisioned: "In the ancient past when heaven and earth were just assuming form, all the myriad things together came into existence. The greater delighted in their natures; the lesser placidly accepted their forms. The *Yin* was the reservoir of their material force; the *Yang* put forth their essence. There was no danger from which to flee; nor was there advantage to pursue. Let free, nothing was lost; gathered in, nothing was garnered. Death was not looked upon as premature; survival was not regarded as longevity. There was no good fortune to seek, nor was there misfortune to blame. All accepted their fates, passing their lives together in integrity. Those with clear minds did not use their intelligence to win victories, nor were the obtuse made to lose because they were stupid. The powerful did not exploit their strength, and the weak were not in fear of oppression. For there were no rulers and everything was in order; there were no officials and every matter went well." Coming to that time when the pristine simplicity had become dispersed, the world degenerated and the *Tao* was attenuated. The Sages, the superior men, and their kind: "Have devised the musical notes and thrown sound into confusion; made the colors and distorted form; externally they alter appearances, and internally they conceal their feeling. They harbor desires and seek to acquire more of things; they cheat and falsify in the quest for fame. Once rulers were instituted, oppression arose; once officials were appointed, robbery began. Detached and apart, they instituted the rites and the norms by which to impose the bonds on the common people. Cheating the stupid and defrauding the unsophisticated, they conceal their cleverness and have made themselves appear divine. The powerful squint, unseeing, as they carry on maltreatment and violence; the weak are worn and distressed as they serve others. They feign integrity in order to succeed in their avarice; at heart they are crafty although they offer the appearance of benevolence. . . . Honoring the worthy, they seek to overtop others; vying in their abilities, they endeavor to outstrip others. Through contests of power, they come to lord over others; relishing high status, they intend to outrank others. The empire is driven to pursue the same course; that is why superior and inferior come to inflict harm on each other. The utmost of heaven, earth, and the myriad things are exhausted in order to supply insatiable sensual desires. Such is not the way to nourish the ordinary people. Consequently, fearing that the people would know all that, they resort to granting heavy rewards in order to mollify, and dispensing severe punishments in order to intimidate the people. Treasuries were depleted, but the rewards could not be paid. Punishments reached the extremes and no [further] penalties could be applied. And then commenced the fall of states and the slaughter of rulers, and all the disasters of downfall and defeat." In this view, the ruler-servitor institutions as well as "the ritual norms of the superior man are in truth the very methods for ravaging and plundering the empire, to the point of rebellion, peril, and final demise."[52]

This essay by Juan Chi, if read by Chang Chan, would most surely have been objected to as incongruous and insupportable, not at all resembling the expression of a superior man. Yet Pao Ching-yen's statements about dispensing with rulers are still more strident and must be considered the most extreme expression of anarchistic thought of the Wei-Chin period. Nothing of Pao's life and career can now be documented. His views can be read [as quoted] in the *Pao-p'u Tzu*, in the chapter "Chieh Pao" ["Interrogating Mr. Pao," *Wai-p'ien, ch.* 48].[53] His major purpose is to argue the point that "antiquity, having no rulers, was superior to the present age." Dissecting this, we find his argumentation appears to comprise two issues:

The first is that the establishment of the ruler was not in response to a Heavenly Mandate. "The Confucians say that heaven produced the masses of the people and erected the ruler over them. But is it likely that August Heaven ["Nature"] in its earnest words would have declared such an intent? Rather, the strong coerced the weak, and the weak then submitted to them. The intelligent deceived the simple-minded and in consequence the simple-minded came to serve them. From that submission arose the way of ruler and servitor; from that servitude the people, being devoid of strength, were brought under control. Truly, then, that submission and that servitude result from the contest of strength and the matching of wits [among humans] and have nothing to do with a vast and distant heaven."

The second point is that having the ruler is not in response to the will of the people. That is, freedom and equality are the natural character of mankind *per se.* "At the dawn of time, the nameless was valued, and the various living beings found their pleasures in being let alone to go their

[52] *Ibid.*

[53] [Ko Hung's *Pao-p'u Tzu*,] "Wai-p'ien," *ch.* 48, "Chieh Pao," says: "Mr. Pao, by name Ching-yen, is devoted to the writings of Lao Tzu and *Chuang Tzu*, and has mastered the rhetoric of incisive debate." Pao probably was a contemporary of Ko Hung [early fourth century] or perhaps slightly earlier.

own ways. That is, to peel the bark from the cassia tree and to slit open the lacquer tree are not the wishes of trees. To pluck the pheasants and to strip feathers from the kingfishers are not the wishes of birds. To force on bridles and put bits in their mouths does not reflect the nature of horses. To impose the cart-poles to make them pull heavy loads is not to the happiness of oxen. . . . Thus [rulers] impress the masses of the common people so as to sustain the livelihood of those who hold office; those of high status receive high emoluments while the people bear ever more hardship." The establishment of rulers was contrary to the basic character of freedom, so the "people's acceptance [of their overlordship]" and "heaven's bestowal [of the Mandate]" both are but specious claims; that is too obvious to demand further analysis. But, that is not all. "For as heaven and earth hold their [relative] positions, so the two modal forces provide models for things. Those which delight in the *Yang* may soar in the clouds; those fond of the *Yin* may stay in the streams. They respond to the yielding and to the firm as their natures lead them. They follow the four [seasons] and the eight [annual festivals marking the divisions of solar time] in the transformations that occur in their lives, each attaching itself where it is comfortable, and originally knowing no distinctions of noble and humble. After rulers and officials were instituted, numerous changes ensued. For, where the otters are numerous, the fish are disturbed; where the hawks are many, the birds are in confusion. When offices of government are set up the common people are fettered and where their superiors are lavishly served, the ordinary people below are impoverished." According to this, it was after rulers were established that the people suffered exploitation. Moreover, the acts of exploitation depend on institutions of inequality. Thus it is obvious from the nature of things that mankind would not willingly give up its natural equality to have the suffering caused by having rulers imposed upon it.

Having taken up the major theoretical bases of monarchical authority as found in Confucian thought and demolishing those, Pao Ching-yen then proceded to attack the system of monarchical government as such. On the one hand, he described the joys of being without a ruler, and, on the other hand, he listed all the sorrows that stem from having rulers. As the two are juxtaposed, the joy and the sorrow come forth very clearly. Without his stating the point, which should be rejected and which adopted becomes evident. He described the joys of the rulerless state as follows: "In earliest antiquity there were no rulers and no officials. [People] dug wells and drank, tilled fields and ate. When the sun rose, they went to work; and when it set, they rested. Placidly going their ways with no encumbrances, they grandly achieved their own fulfillment. They neither vied nor strove; they knew neither glory nor disgrace. There were no trails and paths through the mountains, and neither boats nor bridges existed in the waters. When streams and valleys offered no passage, there was no spreading land-ownership encroachment; where knights and hosts could not be assembled there was no warfare afield. . . . Ideas of using power for advantage had not yet burgeoned. Disaster and disorder did not occur. Shields and spears were not used; city walls and moats were not built. The myriad things of existence all knew a mysterious unity and were unconscious of [their separate] existences within the *Tao*. Epidemics and afflictions did not spread abroad, and the people enjoyed long lives. Purity and naïveté resided in all breasts, so calculating thoughts did not arise. People munched their food and disported themselves; they were carefree and contented." At that time, rulers had not yet been instituted, and the people on their own were quite at peace. The situation in which mankind found itself was indeed perfect in all respects and deficient in nothing.

Regrettably, that innocence was readily spoiled and the pristine simplicity could not remain intact. "After rulers and officials were installed, the manifold deceits daily increased." Thereafter, mankind's interminable miseries all arose in their wake. Pao Ching-yen explains that: "Coming to this dernier age, cleverness is employed and trickery arises. Since the Way and its powers declined, the elevated and the humble have assumed rank-ordered places. The rites of ascending and descending [in ceremonial occasions] and the rules of increasing and decreasing [governing the number, size, and height of raiment, paraphernalia and buildings] have proliferated; the [ritually prescribed] beribboned hats and robes of black and gold have become their adornment; their building works rise to scrape the skies, stacked up with painted beams of red and green. They topple the heights in their search for gems and plumb the depths in the quest for pearls. Jade can be gathered in [amounts resembling] forests but not be sufficient to meet all their needs; gold can be piled up like mountains and still not be enough to cover their expenses. They dally in the realm of licentious dissipation, violating the very basis of their Great Beginning [i.e., Nature]. Departing ever farther from their origins, they increasingly do violence to their pristine natures. Because they elevate the worthy, people struggle for fame; because they value goods, thieves and robbers arise. On seeing objects of desire, the true and upright mind is thrown into confusion; when power and its advantages are displayed, the pathway to plunder is opened. As keen weapons are fashioned, the maladies of invasion and annexation grow. . . . The ruler of men trembles in anxiety before his ancestral shrine; the common people suffer in distress amidst troubles and sorrows." Compared with the era of early antiquity when there still was no ruler, the discrepancy between safety and peril, joy and sorrow, cannot be measured in miles.

Attempting to refute all this, one might note that human nature is quite unevenly good and bad, and that any individual can also behave violently. Since that is so, how can the sum total of all violence be attributed to rulers alone? Pao Ching-yen's replies to such questions can be divided into three parts: First, in the age of complete virtue, people's hearts and minds were pure and altruistic, so no reasons for their becoming disorderly existed. Moreover, to draw an inference from ordinary circumstances, when there is no oppressive government interjecting its harrassments, the people's minds will naturally turn to thoughts of good order. "For, when a person is not himself subjected to the overlord's corvee and his household is free of the costs of the transport and textile taxes, he can be secure in his landholding and happy in his work, following the progress of Nature's seasons and taking his share of the earth's bounty, within [his home] adequately supplied with clothing and food, and on the outside unaware of all struggles for power and aggrandizement. For him then to take up arms in attack and plunder would be contrary to human nature."

The fact, however, that thieves and bandits have appeared constantly throughout the realm is because rulers have made it so. . . . "[Rulers] make them [i.e., the people] toil without rest and wrest away things from them endlessly, so that their fields become overgrown with weeds and their grain bins bare, the looms empty, insufficient food to fill the mouths, and not enough clothing to cover the bodies;—even should one desire to make disorders cease, would that be possible? Thus it is that though efforts may be made to relieve disaster, disasters only increase; though prohibitions be made harsher, the prohibited acts are unceasing. Customs barriers at passes and bridges are intended to halt misdeeds, but slippery officials capitalize on them to carry on their misdeeds. Measures of weight and volume are means with which to prevent cheating, but evil persons capitalize on them to cheat. High officials are relied on to support their rulers in crises, but wicked officials only hope that the rulers are in danger. Arms and armor are intended to pacify scenes of trouble, yet bandits steal them for use in making troubles. All these things are brought about because there are rulers." Should people now hold a contrary view, suspecting that people will foment disorders among themselves making rulers desirable in order to bring about good government, they are in fact making the serious error of confusing cause and effect.

His other line of reasoning is that should we fall back one step to admit that individual persons too could have the capacity for generating disorders; compared to the disorders that stem from rulers, those are as night and day, not to be mentioned in the same breath. [paraphrased] "Disputes among the ordinary people are merely trivial matters, for what scope of consequences can a contest of strength between ordinary fellows generate? They have no spreading lands to arouse avarice, they have no walled cities to be taken as useful, they possess no gold and gems that others might covet, and they wield no authority through which to advance their struggle. Their power is not such that they can assemble mass followings, and they command no awe that might quell [such gatherings] by their opponents. How can they compare with a display of the royal anger, which can deploy armies and move battalions, making people who hold no enmities attack states that have done no wrong? At one move, the stiffened corpses may be counted in tens of thousands; as it flows, the spurting blood may be so copious as to float large shields and to color the fields all red. Rulers without morality exist in every age, and as they unleash their oppression and chaos no state in the world [will be spared]. At court, the loyal and good men will be destroyed, and across the land the common people's bones will be strewed. How can that be thought of as no more than the difficulties ensuing from a minor dispute [among the ordinary people]?" That is to say, the quarrels of rulers will assume vast scale and will involve organized military conflict, obviously being beyond comparison with the struggles among private individuals.

A further point is that the ruler holds power over life and death: "He will be able to indulge fully the dictates of his own mind, in solitary splendor, and no one shall dare oppose him."[54] Thus, "The likes of [the tyrant kings] Chieh and Chou could get away with roasting people, and in castigating remonstrators they could slice up feudal lords, pickle the flesh of the Lords of the Marches, cut people's hearts out, and break people's shinbones. They could exhaust all the limits of overbearing and unrestrained evil and employ the cruelest of tortures. Had all such individuals been commoners, despite their cruel and extreme nature they would not have been able to do such things. What enabled such individuals to give vent to their cruelty and unleash all their passions, to butcher and chop up the empire, is that they were rulers and therefore could give free rein to all desires." Thus it follows that only the institutionalization of rulership is what Chieh and Chou relied upon as they indulged their evil natures.

When countered by the rebuttal that the institutionalization of rulers has led to disastrous consequences in the cases of violent rulers, but under such good rulers as Yao and Shun, should it not be noted that the people enjoyed blessings, *ergo* one cannot fail to distinguish good rulers from cruel ones and reject all alike, Pao Ching-yen's response is again very simple. He believed that the origins of government lay in the struggle between the strong and the weak and in the contest of wits between the

[54] The phrase is from Li Ssu's "Tu-tse Shu," ["Memorial on Supervision, and on Fixing Responsibility"; *vide* Chapter Eight, Section Two, page 440, above]. The sufferings caused by the existence of rulers that Pao Ching-yen points out apparently reflect contemporary events of the Three Kingdoms and the two Chin dynasties era. The conditions of hardship and distress recorded in *ch.* 26 of the *Chin Shu* may be taken as corroboration of this.

intelligent and the simple-minded. Government's objectives, therefore, are to control and to plunder, not to benefit all the people. Even though one can make the distinction between the benevolent and the violent among sovereign past and present, in point of actual fact the distinction is as between fifty paces and one hundred paces [i.e., merely relative; *vide Mencius*, 1/i/3/2; Legge, pp. 129–30.] It definitely is not a distinction comparable to that between [the present age] and the age when there were still no rulers. "For though [rulers] were to spread abroad all the gold of Lu-t'ai or distribute all the grain at Chü-ch'iao [as good King Wu did after taking the tyrant King Chou's capital] and there was no one who was not pleased at that, how much more so would they have been pleased if the gold had not been accumulated and the grain collected from the people in the first place! That [King Wu, in his conquest of the Shang tyrant king, cf. *Documents*, "Books of Chou," "Wu ch'eng,"] rested his oxen at T'ao-lin and let loose his horses on Mt. Hua, then called in shields and spears and returned to their cases bows and arrows [cf. *Odes*, no. 273], all are regarded as splendid acts of peace; how much better if there had been no military campaigns, no need to do battle and to guard the frontiers, in the first place! Thatched roofs and mud steps [describing the austere life styles of sage kings Yao and Shun], throwing out the weaving and pulling up the garden vegetables [said of Kung-yi Hsiu, chief minister to Duke Mu of Lu, reigned 408–396 B.C., who because he received official emolument would not allow his family members to engage in productive activity 'in competition with the ordinary people'], or using [discarded cloth to make] bags and bed-hangings [said of the Han Emperor Hsien, after the sack of his capital; cf. footnote 5, above], or using common cloth for quilts and clothing [said of some high Han officials, e.g., Kung-sun Hung], or one's wives not wearing silk and one's horses not being fed on grain [said of the virtuous Sun-shu Ao, chief minister of Ch'u in the sixth century B.C.]; all such examples of frugality [among the high and mighty] suitable for the commonality to follow are taken as exemplary anecdotes. That is as if to say of the Bandit Chih that when dividing up the loot his taking a smaller portion is to be called conciliatory; it is as when fish are stranded on the dry land they spew spittle on each other. [For these allusions see the *Chuang Tzu*, chs. 10 and 6; Watson, pp. 108–09 and 180.]

Although Pao Ching-yen's views have their distant origins in Chuang Tzu and his basic principles display nothing new, the audacity with which he assumes his extreme stance must be described as without precedent.[55] To summarize his views: stating that the establishment of

---

[55] Although the ideal society described in the *Chuang Tzu* is somewhat closer to Nature than Lao Tzu's "small states with few people," yet it never clearly upholds the idea of

the ruler was not accomplished through the heavenly mandate nor by mankind's acceptance of him is to state that the ruler's authority is without foundation. To say that without rulers the people can have peace and security is to say that the governing of the state is not necessary. Stating that the installation of rulers has induced troubles is to state that political acts should not be. Chuang Tzu held in highest value the ideal of wandering in unfettered bliss [hsiao-yao 逍遙] but still observed of the duty of servitor to ruler that "there is no escaping it in heaven or earth."[56] Confucius looked upon the relationship of ruler and servitor, and of father and son, as the eternal and unvarying bonds and norms, and especially since the Ch'in and Han eras that has been the orthodox line in thought. And, as authoritarianism came to be truly established under the Han the ruler's position grew ever more elevated, and he became virtually sacrosanct along with heaven and earth, mountains and rivers.[57] We must note that Wang Ch'ung's Chi-su ["Satires on Vulgar Ways"] still did not dare openly to criticize the ruler as being useless; thus he felt compelled to insinuate it vaguely in "Equating the Ages" and "Glorifying the Han" [i.e., "Ch'i shih" and "Hsüan Han," nos. 56 and 57 of Wang's Lun Heng; cited in footnotes 112, 113, 115, 117, of Chapter Ten, above]. Strictly speaking, therefore, prior to the Wei-Chin era the thought centering on having no ruler did not exist. Juan Chi first started it and Pao Ching-yen then greatly added to the theory. Traditional thought focusing on respect for the ruler, which had held sway for several centuries through the Ch'in and Han dynasties, was at this time subjected to a wholly unprecedented assault.[58] In light of that fact, Juan and Pao in truth

---

having no ruler; moreover, it repeatedly indicates that there were rulers in high antiquity, therein indisputably differing from Juan Chi and Pao Ching-yen. Refer to the footnotes to Chapter Five, Section Five, above.

[56] Chuang Tzu, ch. 4, "Jen-chien-shih."

[57] During the Han dynasty, after the death of an emperor in addition to the erection of funerary shrines and maintenance of offerings at the capital, commands also were issued to the commanderies and the princely states throughout the empire to erect such shrines. (Shih Chi, ch. 8, "Basic Annals of the Emperor Kao Tsu.") [Cf. Watson, Shih Chi, Vol. I., esp. p. 117.] By the time of the Emperor Hsüan [reigned 73–49 B.C.] there were sixty-eight commanderies and princedoms throughout the empire having such imperial ancestral shrines, those numbering one-hundred sixty-seven. When the Emperor Hsüan and his imperial grandfather carried out mourning for the Emperor's father [i.e., the Emperor Chao, reigned 86–74 B.C., had been the grand-uncle of the Emperor Hsüan, whose father had not held the throne] new shrines were built adjoining the imperial tombs, the total number of such shrines now reaching one-hundred seventy-six. (Han Shu, ch. 73, "Biography of Wei Hsüan-ch'eng.")

[58] The Lü-shih Ch'un-ch'iu, ch. 11, Section "Tang wu," says that [the Bandit] Chih: "had comprehensive arguments condemning the six [Sage] Kings and the Five Pa [the Hegemons of Spring and Autumn times], holding that Yao was notoriously unkind, that Shun's behavior was contrary to filial piety, that Yü exemplified the drunkard, that

occupy a position in the history of Chinese political thought that cannot be depreciated.

SECTION FOUR
The *Lieh Tzu*

A book known as the *Lieh Tzu* is recorded in the "Treatise on Literature" of the *Han Shu* [History of the Former Han Dynasty, by Pan Ku, A.D. 32–92] where the commentary states that Lieh Tzu "whose name was Yü-k'ou, was prior to Chuang Tzu; Chuang Tzu praised him." Yet the book [as we know it] appeared quite late, and ever since Liu Tsung-yuan [773–819] scholars have been suspicious of it on the grounds that it contains many spurious later additions.[59] Recent scholars have approved and added to that view, more or less concluding that the book was composed by someone of the Wei-Chin period.[60] Although this matter continues to

---

T'ang and Wu [founders of the Shang and the Chou dynasties, respectively] had been guilty of banishing and of murdering [their sovereigns], and that the Five Hegemons had plotted to commit violence and rebellion. All the world praises them, while all the people avoid speaking frankly about them; this is a case of delusion. [Cf. *Analects*, xii/10/2.] Thus he intended that when he died he should be buried with a bronze axe in his hands, explaining: 'When I go below and encounter those Six Kings and Five Hegemons I want to crack their heads.' " Although this is radical enough it would seem to be a different point of view from that held by Juan Chi and Pao Ching-yen.

[59] In his *Liu Liu-chou Wen-chi*, *ch.* 4, "Pien *Lieh Tzu*" [On identifying the *Lieh Tzu*"]; (This book "contains much interpolated matter"). Kao Ssu-sun [*ca.* 1184] in his *Tzu-lüeh*; ("made up of bits and pieces assembled by a later person"). Huang Chen [1213–80] in his *Jih-ch'ao*; ("Sometime after the Ssu-ma house had moved [the Chin] capital to the south of the Yangtze [A.D. 317] this book emerged from various schools; whether it represents the true *Lieh Tzu* is virtually impossible to ascertain"). Sung Lien [1310–81], in his *Chu Tzu Pien*; ("Most definitely not written by [the historical] Lieh Yü-k'ou himself . . . in larger part is in agreement with Buddhist pronouncements"). Yao Chi-heng [born 1647] in his *Ku-chin Wei-shu K'ao*; ("Probably written by Taoist scholars who made the false attribution. . . . Very little of it, however, is genuine, and the remainder is entirely the interpolations of later persons"). See Chang Hsin-ch'eng, ed., *Wei-shu t'ung-k'ao*, 1939, vol. 2, pp. 700–04.

[60] Liang Ch'i-ch'ao in his "Ku-shu chen-wei chi-ch'i nien-tai," concludes that it was pieced together by Chang Chan of the Eastern Chin period from various Taoist writings. Ma Hsü-lun in his "*Lieh Tzu* wei-shu k'ao" (in the collectanea *T'ien-ma shan-fang ts'ung-shu*) cites twenty points of evidence, on the basis of which he concludes: "Since Wei and Chin times irresponsible persons drawing on the *Kuan Tzu*, the *Yen Tzu*, the *Analects*, *Shan-hai Ching*, the *Mo Tzu*, the *Chuang Tzu*, *Shih Chiao*, *Han Fei Tzu*, *Lü-shih Ch'un-ch'iu*, *Han-shih wai-chuan*, *Huai-nan Tzu*, *Shuo-yüan*, *Hsin-hsü*, and the *Hsin-lun*, and adding later statements, composed these eight chapters and forged the preface by Liu Hsiang [77–6 B.C.] to make it appear more important. When Wang Pi [A.D. 226–49] was annotating the *Book of Changes* he drew heavily on the *Lao Tzu* and the *Chuang Tzu*, and this also has come from Wang Pi; how could it be the work of any of Wang Pi's followers?" (Note that according to Chang Chan's preface Chang's grandfather was the nephew of Wang Pi and had

elude conclusive judgment,[61] we shall follow the majority opinion and include a discussion of the work at this point, taking it to be a representative work of Wei-Chin decadent thought.

During the pre-Ch'in period there had appeared a school of egocentric thought to which belonged T'o Hsiao and Wei Mou who [according to Hsün Tzu]: "fully indulge their feelings and take pleasure in dissolute acts; their behavior is that of birds and beasts." The "Yang Chu" chapter of the *Lieh Tzu* is a distant heir to those ideas, expounding and elucidating them at some length. As we examine the atmosphere prevailing among Wei and Chin scholar-officials, we come to understand the historical factors explaining why that self-indulgent thought was for a time dominant. The century or more corresponding to the Ts'ao Wei dynasty and the Eastern Chin dynasty [roughly 200–320] was marked by the dissolution of Chinese society and at the same time was a period of reaction against the doctrines of [the formalized Confucian] ethics. That movement of repudiation of ethics was combined with a tide of reaction against authoritarian politics; one of the forms it assumed was a personal philosophy of dissolute behavior providing the basis for a political anarchism [literally: "no-ruler theories"]. The *Lieh Tzu* is perhaps the most important documentation of that.

The mid-point restoration [of the Han dynasty] accomplished by the Emperor Kuang-wu [reigned A.D. 25–57] took steps to punish the faults of immorality and loss of integrity that had marked the last phase of Western Han; great attention was devoted to arousing the morale of scholar-officialdom and to commending the upright spirit. Consequently, honor was paid first of all to Yen Kuang as the moral exemplar of the realm.[62] Subsequently, after the decline of the Eastern Han, striking consequences of all that were manifested. "During the reigns of Emperors Huan and Ling [147–188] the rulers were dissolute and their governing

---

acquired a copy of the eight chapters [i.e., the *Lieh Tzu*] from the book collection that had belonged to Wang Ts'an [A.D.177–217; one of the "Seven Masters of the Chien-an period"]. After the [Chin capital's] transfer to the south only the two chapters "Yang Chu" and "Shuo Fu" still existed. Subsequently four chapters were acquired from Liu Cheng-yü's household, and from the family of Wang Yen's son-in-law, Chao Chi-tzu, six chapters were obtained. These parts were assembled to form a complete copy. Liu Cheng-yü also was a nephew of Wang Pi.)

[61] Chiang Hsia-an's *Chou-Ch'in chu-tzu k'ao* and Takeuchi Yoshio's "*Lieh Tzu* yüan-tz'u" both argue against all of Ma's various points, holding the view that the extant text of the eight chapters "... in the main still preserves the features of the work as it existed when Liu Hsiang collated it [in the first century B.C.].

[62] Hsia Tseng-yu [died 1924], *Chung-kuo ku-tai shih*, p. 388. [Yen Kuang had been the intimate friend of the new emperor in the humble years of his obscure youth; he exemplified integrity in refusing to make personal gain from that connection after the emperor's accession, and for becoming a frank, occasionally critical recluse.]

was capricious. The fate of the dynasty was in the hands of eunuchs with whom scholar-officials were ashamed to associate. Ordinary persons expressed resentment, and recluses widely disseminated critical views, arousing attention and drawing prominence to themselves as they reinforced each other. They passed judgments on lords and high ministers and assessed critically those in control of government. A spirit of outspoken probity prevailed from this time onward." Kuo Lin-tsung, Chia Wei-chieh, Li Ying, and Ch'en Fan at the head of some 30,000 Imperial Academy students: "combining threatening words and perceptive argument, gave no ground before the powerful. From the chief lords and high ministers on downward there were none who did not fear their charges of misconduct."[63] Moreover, the "pure critiques" [*ch'ing-yi* 清議] were used not only to pass judgment on those controlling government; they also came to be used for criticizing and correcting the conduct of private persons. Scorn was heaped upon Wang Fu because his mother [a concubine] had no family [of standing]; K'ung Jung was killed because his acts aroused suspicion and he expressed opinions loosely.[64] These cases provide some evidence for the tenor of that age.

Subsequently, under the Ts'ao Wei dynasty, as its "Nine Ranks and Impartial Evaluation" law was put into effect [i.e., the *chiu-p'in chung-cheng* 九品中正 system of evaluating and ranking civil service officials], "pure critiques emanating from the districts" came to assume specially large influence and importance. Whether official careers would be blocked or would be successful all hinged on those. The pure critiques themselves were based largely on the Confucian moral precepts; at their worst they were subject to petty-minded fault-finding and to utilization for making unfounded charges. Among the more notorious examples is that of Ch'en Shou, who, while in mourning for his father, became ill and had a servant women prepare medicine for him; "in his home district this was made the grounds for censorious judgment, and for some years thereafter all advancements in his career were blocked." Later, while in office as Attending Secretary for Drafting Rescripts [at Lo-yang, the capital] he complied with his mother's wish that after death she be buried at Lo-yang and "again was charged with an offense, that of failing to return his mother to the family home for burial, and for that he was sub-

---

[63] *Hou Han Shu, ch.* 97, "Preface" to "Tang-ku chuan" ["Memoir on the suppression of factions"; nonetheless, their eunuch opponents won this engagement, in the years 166–69].

[64] *Ibid., ch.* 79 and 100. [For Wang Fu as the author of the *Ch'ien-fu lun*, see Chapter Nine, Section Five, above. His biography in the *Hou Han Shu* indicates surprise at scorn for the child of a concubine, and explains that it was an attitude peculiar to that region. K'ung Jung was a descendant of Confucius, and an arrogant political schemer. He was executed by Ts'ao Ts'ao in 208.]

jected to adverse criticism." Thus he again was made to suffer expulsion from office and humiliation.[65] Another example is that of Pien K'un's father Pien Ts'ui, who, because his younger brother was charged by a personal enemy with irregularities in his private life, "subsequently was made the butt of scorn and criticism for his failure to admonish [a younger brother], so that for successive years thereafter his career was blocked." When the stepmother of Wang Shih, the *Hsiao-chung-cheng* ["minor referee," or local official in charge of evaluations] at Huai-nan, died, he complied with the petition of her former husband's son to allow her to be buried alongside her former husband. Pien K'un, who then held the post of Assistant Imperial Secretary, impeached him, saying that Wang Shih "had violated ritual propriety and flaunted righteousness." An edict from the throne commanded that he be "turned over to his home district for pure critique, and that he be barred from office-holding for the remainder of his life."[66]

Defamation and praise of these kinds, intended to uphold the social norms and bonds, although somewhat marred by pettiness and harshness, nonetheless if expressing sincere intentions might not fail in the function of keeping people's attitudes upright. When we look even superficially into the historical facts, however, we can see that such was not entirely the case. The Nine Ranks and Impartial Evaluation system ostensibly was to solicit and heed people's opinions, but frequently failed to avoid "arbitrarily putting people up or down, holding the keys to glory or humiliation." It produced situations so extreme that: "There were no men of poor family in the upper ranks and none from powerful clans received the lower rankings."[67] Pure critiques might state thus and so, with the sole consequence that those who observed morality were relegated to difficult circumstances and slanderers were granted convenience in loosing their onslaughts; they hardly produce worthwhile results in correcting debased ways.[68]

When things reach the extreme, they must reverse themselves; that is a natural principle and the pure critiques phenomenon was not immune to its workings. During the Eastern Han [25–220] scholar-officials delighted in siding with the consort clans in attacks on the eunuchs. Emperor Wu of the Wei [i.e., Ts'ao Ts'ao, who held actual power throughout the

[65] *Chin Shu, ch.* 82, "Biography of Ch'en Shou." [Ch'en Shou is best known as the author of the *San Kuo Chih.*]

[66] *Ibid., ch.* 70, in Pien's biography. Other examples are numerous; *vide* Chao Yi, *Erh-shih-erh shih cha-chi, ch.* 8, "Chiu-p'in chung-cheng."

[67] *Ibid., ch.* 45, "Biography of Liu Yi."

[68] The evils of Chin dynasty social custom and government can be deduced in general outline from the "Lun" [the historian's commentary] in *ch.* 5, "Basic Annals of the Emperor Min," and in *ch.* 94, "The Biography of Lu Pao."

last quarter-century of the Han] "was the grandson of the Palace Regular Attendant Ts'ao T'eng [for thirty years a leader of the Inner Court forces], so his family were quite naturally opponents of the great clans; moreover, as a usurper [Ts'ao Ts'ao] was gravely disadvantaged by expressions of moral righteousness, therefore he invariably promoted the tendencies toward knavery and rebuffed moral fervor. . . . [His son] the Emperor Wen, continued in that and was of still less restrained temperament."[69] Wang Yen and others at that point proceeded to launch the interest in Lao Tzu and Chuang Tzu, and in consequence pure conversation [ch'ing-t'an 清談] came greatly into vogue, displacing that of the pure critiques. Juan Chi, Chi K'ang, and their circle, being contemptuous of the hypocricy of conventional proprieties and still more resenting the restrictions imposed by the Confucian ethical norms, banded together to demolish the standard ethics, "bursting through all the restraining bonds" by their words and deeds.

Juan Chi attended his mother in particularly filial devotion. When his mother died, he was in the midst of a chess game with a friend "whom he retained in order to finish the match. After that he drank two liters of wine, cried a loud cry, and vomited several cups of blood. When the time came for her burial, Juan Chi ate steamed dried meat [meat being inappropriate to mourning], drank two liters of wine, after which he went to speak his parting words to her. He simply said, 'How grievous'; then, raising his voice, he let out a loud cry, and again spit up several cups of blood. Grief so consumed him that he became emaciated and was on the

---

[69] Same as footnote 62. The Emperor Wu [posthumous title of Ts'ao Ts'ao] in the nineteenth year of the Han dynasty's Chien-an reign period [214] while still the Duke of Wei, issued a command saying: "Scholar-officials of superior personal conduct are not necessarily inclined to advance and lay hold of opportunities, while those who are capable of advancing and laying hold of opportunities are not necessarily capable of superior conduct. Was Ch'en P'ing [wily Chancellor under the first Han reigns who plotted to restore the Liu clan after the Empress Lü's attempted take-over] a person of punctiliously honest behavior? Was Su Ch'in [suasive strategist of the late Warring States period who designed the anti-Ch'in "vertical alliance"] a man who could always keep his word? Yet, Ch'en P'ing secured the Han dynasty and Su Ch'in saved the weak State of Yen. Seen in this light, even though a scholar-official have some partial shortcoming should he for that be cast aside?" (San Kuo Chih, Wei Chih, ch. 1, "Wu-ti chi.") Further, Fu Hsüan [217–278] said: "Emperor Wu of Wei was fond of Legalist methods, so throughout the empire the doctrines of actualities and names [hsing ming 刑名] were honored. The Emperor Wen of Wei admired the uninhibited and free-spirited, so throughout the empire those who carefully observed the ethical standards were disdained." (Chin Shu, ch. 47, in Fu's biography.) We can observe that among the great lords, ministers, and scholar-officials of the Wei and Chin dynasties, very few were capable of scrupulously observing the Confucian ethics, honestly and sincerely. Some falsified appearances to gain approval and some manipulated circumstances to attack others; such practices also are among the important reasons for the upsurge of antipathy.

point of its extinguishing his life. P'ei K'ai went to condole with Juan Chi and found him, hair unkempt, squatting on the floor, drunk, and staring blankly. . . . Juan Chi's older brother's wife was about to return for a visit to her parents' home; he went to see her and bade her farewell [in violation of the taboo against associating with a brother's wife]. When someone criticized him for that, he replied: 'Were the ritual proprieties established for men like me?' A neighboring household had a daughter-in-law of exceptional beauty who took care of the wine vats where wine was sold. Juan Chi once went there to drink, and when drunk, lay down at her side. Since Juan Chi himself displayed no uneasiness, her husband looking in upon it also had no suspicions. A military man's daughter was both talented and beautiful; she died before being married. Although Juan Chi was not acquainted with her father or brothers, he nonetheless went to mourn at her funeral, displayed extremes of grief, and then went home. Externally observed, he was self-possessed and relaxed; inwardly, he was guileless and sincere; all his doings were of that character.'[70]

In addition to Juan Chi, there were others of the kind represented by the "unfettered eight" [*pa ta* 八達, or, "the eight who have abandoned all restraint"] whose lack of inhibitions exceeded even his.[71] Their mode swept the age, spreading even to women.[72] Noble relatives of the imperial

[70] *Chin Shu*, ch. 49, "Biography of Juan Chi."

[71] Hu-mu Fu-chih, Hsieh K'un, Juan Fang, Pi Cho, Yang Man, Huan Yi, and Juan Fou let their hair hang loose, stripped naked, locked the gates, and drank to inebriation. Kuang Yi arrived later and was refused admission by the gatekeeper. "He thereupon took off his clothing outside the house, stuck his head in through the dogs' entrance [the hole for dogs to come and go through the wall] to spy on them, and shouted aloud." Their contemporaries called them "the unfettered eight." [Cf. Fung/Bodde, Vol. II, p. 190, where *ta* is translated "comprehension." The word is here taken in the sense of "*jen ta*" 任達 or "utter lack of self restraint," as used in the biographies of these figures in *Chin Shu*, ch. 49.] Juan Hsien, while in mourning for his mother, "indulged his emotions beyond the norms of propriety." He borrowed a guest's horses to pursue a serving maid who was leaving to get married, and rode back with her in the same carriage. He also was known to sit on the ground and drink amidst the pigs. Pi Cho while serving in office as Assistant Minister of Personnel stole wine to drink and was trussed up [like an ordinary criminal]. Hsieh K'un who "was completely uninhibited and beyond control," once was making advances to the daughter of a neighbor of the Kao family when she threw a shuttle at him, breaking two of his teeth. Contemporaries had a saying: "Because there's no rule he won't flout, Yu-yü's teeth got knocked out." [Yu-yü was Hsieh's courtesy name.] Unrepentant, Hsieh K'un replied: "It hasn't spoiled my whistling and singing yet." [For all of the above, see *Chin Shu*, ch. 49]

[72] *Chin Shu*, ch. 5, "Lun" to the "Basic Annals of the Emperor Min," says: "With their make-up and hair-dress and clothing finery, they depend entirely on maids and servants to do for them; they know nothing of women's work in the tasks of silk and linen making, nor of the household work of preparing foods and wines. They marry prematurely; they act just as they feel. Consequently they admit no shame for licentious transgressions, and have no compunctions about displaying faults of jealousy. Their fathers and older brothers

household and the wealthy could go still farther in extravagance and dissipation.[73] In the view of Confucians, the spreading tide of sensuality truly warranted deep sighs.

Nevertheless, the freeing of the passions in which such persons indulged was not solely a matter of abandoning inhibitions but had its theoretical grounds. Chapter 6, "Ta tsung-shih," of the *Chuang Tzu* tells of the three friends Tzu Sang-hu, Meng Tzu-fan, and Tzu Ch'in-chang. Tzu Sang-hu died, and the other two composed a melody, played the lute and sang. [Confucius' disciple] Tzu-kung admonished them with the question: "I venture to ask whether it is in accord with propriety to sing in the presence of a corpse?" The two looked at each other, laughed, and replied: "How is he to know the meaning of propriety!"[74] Kuo Hsiang's commentary says: "For the person who knows the meaning of propriety must roam in the transcendental [*yu wai* 遊外] so as to keep order in the mun-

---

do not reproach them, nor does the world condemn them." The *Pao-p'u Tzu* [see Section Five, below], *Wai-p'ien, ch.* 25, "Chi miou," says: "Nowadays ordinary women have given up their tasks in sericulture and have abandoned their duties of household weaving [paraphrased]. They do not spin their hemp, but saunter idly in the markets. Ignoring their household tasks of caring for the food, they are assiduous in their devotion to the social activities. They pay visits back and forth among their relatives. . . . Sometimes they sleep at other houses; sometimes they brave the night to return. They sport and frolic at Buddhist temples, or they go to watch the fishermen and hunters. They climb to high places or visit the riverbanks, make the rounds of celebrations and mournings, ride out in carriages with the curtains raised, traveling all about the town and country." The situation described there suggests analogies to recent times in respect to freedom of marriage and in the openness of social relations.

[73] Shih Ch'ung, along with imperial relatives such as Yang Hsiu, Wang K'ai, and their kind, strove to outdo each other in Sybaritic tastes. Shih Ch'ung once visited the Imperial Academy with Wang Tun, and sighed as they looked at the portraits of Yen Hui and Yüan Hsien [two prominent disciples of Confucius noted for their cheerful acceptance of poverty]. Wang Tun [turning to Shih Ch'ung] said: "[Compared with Yen Hui and Yüan Hsien,] Tzu-kung stood rather closer to you." [*Shih Chi, ch.* 67, "Biographies of Confucius' disciples," tells that Tzu-kung, of noble rank, after a brilliant career in statesmanship and diplomacy, retired to manage the family business, and acquired a large fortune.] Shih Ch'ung [displeased even by that comparison] said with serious demeanor: "The scholar-official should attain the best both in his person and with respect to his fame; what point is there is telling us about [someone whose life style, like Yüan Hsien's, was so shabby that he had to use old broken] jars for windows!" [Cf. the anecdote in *Chuang Tzu, ch.* 28, "Jang Ti-wang"; Watson, *Complete Chuang Tzu*, pp. 315–16.] *Chin Shu, ch.* 33, "Biography of Shih Ch'ung," and Liu Yi-ch'ing, *Shih-shuo hsin-yü, ch.* 10, section 30, "T'ai-ch'ih." At that time however there also were some persons who clung to cautious doctrines of self-preservation; one example is to be found in P'an Ni's "An shen lun," ["Discourse on living safely"]. See his biography in *Chin Shu, ch.* 55. P'an Ni died in the fifth year of the Yung-chia reign period [311] at an age of more than sixty.

[74] *Chuang Tzu, ch.* 6, "Ta tsung-shih"; in reply to Tzu-kung's question about what sort of persons are Meng Tzu-fan and Tzu Ch'in-chang, Confucius said: "They are persons who roam in the transcendental world." [Cf. Chan, *Source Book*, p. 198.]

dane sphere [*ching nei* 經內]; must cling to the mother in order to preserve the son, must acknowledge his feelings and straightaway act accordingly. Should he display anxiety about his reputation or be restricted by the formalities, then his filial piety will not be sincere and his compassion will not be genuine. Father and son, elder brother and younger [as formalized relationships, make one] hold feelings that lead to mutual deceptions. How can that be the larger meaning of propriety!" Juan Chi's behavior precisely matches the principle of "acknowledging the feelings and straightaway acting accordingly." His reasons for looking with scorn on men of conventional propriety, and for comparing the "superior man" to a flea in the trousers, were that he intended thereby to destroy the hypocritical Confucian ethical system; his underlying premises were in fact derived from Chuang Tzu. Therefore also in his "Yung Huai" ["expressing feelings"] poems he satirizes his contemporaries, saying that they: "When out in the world talk loudly of purity and uprightness, but behind their doors virtue and cultivation are sadly diminished. . . . Bending and bowing correctly at every turn; their bearing and manner bring a pain in my bowels." P'ei K'ai praised him as a "scholar who is in the transcendental realm"; that must be judged a most perceptive comment on Juan Chi's mentality.

The "unfettered eight" and others displayed their uninhibited behavior, and Juan Chi made very clear his reasons for wanting to destroy the rites. It was not until the *Lieh Tzu* appeared during the Eastern Chin era, however, that a libertine disregard for restraints and a hedonistic view of life were taken as the basis for political thought. The thought conveyed in its eight chapters is not entirely consistent. Here we shall limit our references to its general features.

The *Lieh Tzu's* cosmology is an elaboration of the *Lao Tzu's* "Heaven and earth are not benevolent" [or, "not humane," *t'ien-ti pu jen* 天地不仁; *Lao Tzu*, Chapter Three]. Further, it is quite consonant with Wang Ch'ung's fatalism. [Cf. Chapter Ten, Section Five, above, especially page 585.] The *Lieh Tzu* in Chapter Eight, "Shuo Fu," states: "The myriad things of heaven and earth constitute the kinds of life generated [*sheng* 生] along with us. Among these kinds there are no distinctions of noble and base; it is only that some may have greater or lesser intelligence and strength by which some control others, some eat others, and not that they were generated for that purpose. Humans take what is edible and eat it; does that mean that heaven originally generated those things for mankind? [No!] Also, mosquitoes and gnats bite our skin, while tigers and wolves eat flesh. Does that mean that heaven originally generated humans for the sake of mosquitoes and gnats, or beings with flesh for the sake of tigers and wolves?" That is to say, the processes of Nature [*t'ien yün* 天運] are spontaneous, and all the myriad categories of things are self-generating.

We do not know how this is so, nor have we any means of stopping it. Long life or short, straightened circumstances or unobstructed success, all are decided by fate [ming 命]. Yet that which is designated fate does not refer to some omnipotent governor whose will controls all things. The *Lieh Tzu* devises answers spoken by Fate to questions posed by Effort [li 力] as follows: [Effort has said that they can agree that he causes nothing; he goes on to ask if then Fate controls things.] "Since you call [what I represent] Fate, how can a question arise about control? As for me, if a thing is straight, that is the way I push it, and if it is crooked I let it be that way. Long life and short, obscurity and success, noble and humble status, wealth and poverty, all occur of themselves. How could I oversee all that?" Yet, although Fate also was in no way able to intervene purposively in the conjunctions of human affairs, the individual through his own Effort was all the less able in any way to forestall a development. Therefore: "P'eng Tsu [the Methuselah whom legend states served the Emperors Yao and Shun] was not superior in wisdom to Yao and Shun, yet he lived to the age of eight hundred. Yen Yüan [Confucius' favorite disciple] was not inferior in talent to ordinary persons, yet he lived to only four times eight years. Confucius was not inferior in virtue to the feudal lords, yet he was caused by them to endure difficulties, between the states of Ch'en and Ts'ai. The [tyrant King] Chou of the Yin [-Shang] dynasty was not in his conduct better than the Three Men of Benevolence [his good advisors, all of whom he banished or executed] yet he occupied the throne. Chi-cha [who declined the throne of Wu in 561 B.C.] held no noble rank in Wu, yet [the infamous] T'ien Heng usurped control over the State of Ch'i [in 386 B.C.]. Po Yi and Shu Ch'i [noble-minded recluses at the time of the Chou founding] starved themselves at Mt. Shou-yang; the Chi family [who held power illicitly in Lu during Confucius' lifetime] were wealthier than Chan-ch'in [a worthy servitor of Lu, also known as Liu-hsia Hui]."[75] All of these circumstances were brought about by fate, their root in Nature, and their manifestation a matter of inevitability.

Once we know that human life is not self-determining, we can then progress a further step to the realization that human beings cannot even claim possession of their own lives. The body "is a form lent by heaven and earth [Nature] . . . one's life is a harmony lent by heaven and earth . . . one's nature and fate follow a course set by heaven and earth . . . one's children and grandchildren are what heaven and earth cause to be metamorphosed from one's self [as an insect from the larva]."[76] Consequently, human life itself truly lacks lofty or profound significance. Except

---

[75] *Lieh Tzu, ch.* 6, "Li ming"; [cf. Chan, *Source Book*, pp. 312–13; Graham, *Lieh-tzu*, translates the chapter title "Endeavor and Destiny."]

[76] *Ibid., ch.* 1, "T'ien jui" [cf. Graham, *Lieh-tzu*, p. 29].

for cultivating pleasure through the five senses, and singlemindedly pursuing enjoyment, there are no further tasks or duties worth the striving. Yet eight or nine times out of ten the events of our lives are not what we would like. Man should realize that even should he devote all his efforts to achieve pleasure, he would still find that he cannot always attain his objective. The ordinary ways of the world fail to recognize that the essential interests must be pursued; therefore people allow success and fame, fortune and status, to interfere with their pleasures. That should be called the great delusion. The *Lieh Tzu*, speaking through the words attributed to Yang Chu, says: "A life of a hundred years is virtually the outside limit and not one person in a thousand achieves that. Suppose one person does. Infancy and senility occupy more or less half of it. Of what remains, a further half is accounted for by what is lost in sleep at night and daytime naps. After that, almost half of what is left is occupied by pain, sickness, grief sorrow, death, loss, and distress.[77] One can estimate that within the space of the decade or more [still not accounted for] a person may scarcely know a moment or two during which he will feel wholly at ease and content, with no intruding concerns. Mankind's life then, —what is it all about? Where is its joy? In beauty and richness, in sound and in color [i.e., in fine clothes and food, music and sex]. Yet the beauty and richness of life cannot always be partaken to the full. Sound and color are not always there to be enjoyed. In addition, we are further intimidated and enticed by penalties and rewards, pushed and pulled by the concern for reputation and the restrictions of law. Pressed and harried, we vie for a brief moment of empty praise, contriving to gain some glory that will outlast life. Anxiously we take care over everything our eyes and ears see and hear, paying heed to those things which our bodies would judge right and wrong [i.e., heeding our inhibitions]. In that way we only lose the supreme joys of those years, being unable to cast aside the restraints for even a moment. How does that differ from bearing heavy fetters and shackles of prison?"[78]

Fame and advantage, that is to say, are external to ourselves; they are

[77] *Ibid.*, *ch.* 3, "Chou Mu-wang," tells that Hua Tzu of Yang-li in the State of Sung suffered a loss of memory while still in middle age. A Confucian of the State of Lu treated and cured him. "When Hua Tzu came to his senses he was in a rage. . . . He said: 'Formerly when I had forgotten everything I was in a state of unspoiled vastness not even aware of whether heaven and earth so much as existed. Now suddenly I am made aware of things past, and of all the lives and deaths, successes and failures, sorrows and joys, likes and dislikes of several decades that rise up with their countless implications to trouble me. I fear that all the lives and deaths, successes and failures, sorrows and joys, likes and dislikes, of the future will now also upset my mind in the same way. Can I ever again possibly gain another moment of forgetfulness?" [Cf. Graham, *Lieh-tzu*, pp. 70–71.]

[78] *Ibid.*, *ch.* 7, "Yang Chu" [cf. the translations of this passage in de Bary, *Sources*, pp. 290–91, and in Graham, *Lieh-tzu*, pp. 139–40].

not things that can be acquired through our efforts and, furthermore, they are things offering absolutely no benefits to human life. "Yang Chu said: 'The myriad things of existence differ in life but are all the same in death. In life they may be wise or stupid, noble or humble, and that is how they differ. In death they rot, smell bad and disintegrate, and that is how they are the same. Nonetheless being wise or stupid, noble or humble, are not things that they are capable of causing, nor are the rotting, the smelling bad, and the disintegrating things that they are capable of causing. Consequently, life is not from their causing life nor death from their causing death. Widsom is not of their doing, nor is stupidity. Noble status comes not from their ennobling, nor humble status from their debasing. Rather, the myriad things are all equal in that they are born and they die, in that they are wise or stupid, in that they are noble or humble. Some die in ten years and some die in a hundred. Benevolent sages die, and the vicious and stupid also die. Living, one may be a Yao or a Shun, but dead he is rotting bones. Living, one may be a Chieh or a Chou, but dead he is rotting bones. Rotting bones are all the same; who can perceive any differences there? So, find pleasure while you are alive; what can trouble one after death?'"[79] Nevertheless, to have scorn for wealth and status does not mean that one should seek poverty and humble station. Yang Chu said: "Yüan Hsien's deprivations harmed his life; Tzu-kung's wealth-producing enterprise was a burden to him. [Cf. footnote 73, above.] Thus neither deprivation nor enterprise is good; where, then, lies the good course? The answer: It lies in the life of enjoyment, it lies in the life of ease. Consequently, those skilled in enjoying life will avoid deprivation; those skilled at finding ease in life will not engage in enterprise."[80] The *Lieh Tzu* also offers an exchange of questions and answers attributed to Kuan Chung and Yen Ying [who were statesmen in Ch'i, in the mid-seventh and mid-sixth centuries, respectively], in order to set forth its doctrines about enjoyment and ease. "Yen Ying asked Kuan Tzu about nourishing life. Kuan Tzu replied: 'Just be free of all restraints. Don't be stopped; don't be blocked.' Yen Ying then asked: 'What specifically does that involve?' Kuan Tzu said: 'Indulge your ears in whatever they desire to hear,

[79] *Ibid.*; the same chapter also says: "From earliest antiquity to the present the number of years that have passed is beyond reckoning. Merely from the time of [the legendary ruler] Fu Hsi onward there have elapsed more than three-hundred thousand years, and there have been none, whether wise or stupid, beautiful or ugly, successful or failures, right or wrong, who have not perished, the only difference being some earlier, some later. Granting importance to ephemeral praise or blame, causing spirit and body to suffer distress and pain for the sake of gaining a fame that might endure for a few hundred years—can one by those means attain anything that will moisten his long-dried dead bones, or match life's joys?" [Cf. Graham, *Lieh-tzu*, p. 153.]

[80] On the basis of this and the following quotation, it is clear that the author of this chapter of the *Lieh Tzu* definitely could not have been from a poor family.

indulge your eyes in whatever they desire to see, indulge your nose in whatever it desires to turn toward, indulge your mouth in whatever it desires to utter, indulge your body in whatever it desires for its comfort, indulge your mind to turn wherever it desires to go. . . . Then, wait serenely and contentedly for death,—whether it be one day or one month, one year or ten years. That describes what I call nourishing.' "[81] In that way, not only are the day-to-day world's ritual norms and its fame and profit no longer objects of concern; even one's own longevity, one's life and death, become matters that no longer stir one's inward feelings.

When one thus becomes clear about the art of nourishing life, then one can grasp the methods for governing the state. Governing the state is a matter of serving one's own interests and not a matter of governing others; thereby others and one's self both get what they wish. The *Lieh Tzu* quotes Yang Chu: "If a man in ancient times by losing one hair could benefit the empire he would not have given it, and if the whole empire were offered to him he would not have taken it. When no one will lose a single hair and no one will benefit the empire, the empire will be well governed." When everyone is concerned about himself only, then political organization loses its function.

The *Lieh Tzu* invents an allegory telling about Tzu-ch'an when governing the State of Cheng [died 522 B.C.; *vide Analects* v/15]; he was greatly worried that his older brother Kung-sun Chao and his younger brother Kung-sun Mu did not heed the teachings. "Chao was addicted to wine, and Mu to women. In his house Chao had collected a thousand jars of wine and had accumulated a mound of yeast [for wine-making]. If one but came within a hundred paces of his gateway, the smell of wine dregs would assault the nose. When he was overcome with wine, he was insensible to issues of safety and peril to the world, to the aggravations of men's ways, to what did or did not exist within his house, to all the degrees of relationship with members of his clan, and to all the sorrows and joys attendant on living and dying. He would be unaware of fire and water, or of the clashing of weapons before his face. In Mu's rear courtyards were several dozen adjoining rooms, all occupied by specially selected young and graceful women. When he was lost in his debauchery there, he gave up all contacts with family and cut off all associations with friends, hiding out in his rear courtyards, his daytime hours supplementing the nights. If he emerged only once after three months, he would still think himself deprived. Any beautiful virgin in his district would be enticed with gifts or procured through matchmakers, and only if all efforts failed to gain her would he then give up." Tzu-ch'an adopted the

---

[81] This appears to contradict the intent of the opening lines of *ch.* 2, "Huang-ti," which advocates limiting the desires.

advice of Teng Hsi, and attempted to change his brothers' ways by reminding them of the rites and righteousness, fame and status. Chao and Mu responded: "The one who is skilled at ordering the externals may not always succeed in putting those in order and yet bring distress upon himself. The one who is skilled at setting his own life in order does not necessarily throw other things into disorder, yet his own nature will be at ease. Such means as yours for governing the externals may be briefly implemented in one state, but not accord with men's minds. Our means of ordering our own lives could be extended throughout the whole empire, and the way of ruler and servitor would then be brought to its end."[82]

Bringing an end to the way of ruler and servitor [i.e., to the basic nexus of government] is the logically inescapable conclusion to which egocentric thought leads, and thus offers no surprise. That which we should note, however, is that not only did the author of the *Lieh Tzu* never advocate any revolutionary methods of bringing down the rulers; the similarly logically necessary corollary to that, anarchism, is never fully maintained. We can infer that the *Lieh Tzu's* idea probably is that conveyed by the statement: "If everyone can govern his own life, it will make no difference whether there is a ruler." The ruler should take utmost care not to bring distress to himself by afflicting the people [with acts of governing] and that is all. When Yao was the emperor, he did not govern and everything was well-governed. That provides the ultimate model for the art of ruling.[83]

Beyond that, [the tyrant kings] Chieh and Chou are not deprecated, nor do Shun and Yü, [the two model sage kings other than Yao] merit praise. "Shun plowed at Ho-yang and labored as a potter at Lei-tze. His four limbs never got a moment's ease; his mouth and stomach never got any decent food. He could not receive the love of his parents, nor share the family ties with his younger brothers and sisters. He was thirty years old when without even having announced it [to his clan elders] he married. By the time Yao abdicated the throne in his favor, he was already of advanced years and of feeble wits. [His son and heir] Shang-chün lacked abilities, so Shun abdicated in favor of Yü. He was a pained and troubled man all the way to his death. He was indeed the dismal and tormented one among heaven's people. . . . As a ruler, Yü was in no wise better than Shun. He labored at controlling the waters until his body was half-paralyzed and his hands and feet were calloused. After ascending the throne, he lived in only a humble palace and used the poorest clothing and food. This was a person made to grieve and suffer by both heaven and

---

[82] *Lieh Tzu, ch.* 7, "Yang Chu." [See the full anecdote as translated in Graham, *Lieh-tzu*, pp. 143–46.] Chao is a disguised portrait of Liu Ling, and Mu seems to be a caricature of Hsieh K'un. [Liu and Hsieh were among the "unfettered eight"; see *Chin Shu, ch.* 49.]

[83] *Ibid., ch.* 3, "Chou Mu-wang."

man. . . . Chieh inherited the accumulated wealth of generations, and occupied the high dignity of the throne. He was smart enough to fend off his underlings, and his majesty was sufficient to make the empire tremble. He indulged to the limit his ears and eyes in pleasures, and exhausted his imagination devising thing he wanted to do, happily and contentedly all the way to his death. He was truly the carefree and unbridled one among heaven's people. Chou also inherited the accumulated wealth of generations, and occupied the high dignity of the throne. His majesty assured the doing of whatever he wished, and obedience to all his plans. In his lofty palaces he indulged all his passions, and let his desires reign through the Long Nights [a name for extended feasting lasting weeks or months]. He did not impose upon himself the vexations of rites and righteousness, but lived happily and contentedly all the way to his execution. He was the self-indulgent, dissolute one among heaven's people."[84] It has been the world's custom for all to praise Shun and Yü and to condemn Chieh and Chou. That fails to recognize that, judged as individuals, the four were indeed poles apart throughout their lifetimes, in terms of sorrows and joys, but after their deaths all had become the same in their desolation and extinction. Which model should be cast aside and which followed; is long thought required to arrive at a decision?

Chi K'ang looked upon the limitation of desires as the key to nourishing life; in that there was retained a transcendent ideal lying beyond man's physical life. Pao Ching-yen advocated doing without rulers, and he strongly condemned the dissolute and licentious ways of violent government; thus, within a nostalgia for the spontaneous life, there lurked the thought that the individual's desires should be limited. Then we come to the *Lieh Tzu*, which advanced the case for fully indulging all desires and which, with respect to the ruler, went so far as to admire Chieh and Chou in the course of disparaging Shun and Yü. That is an extraordinarily novel idea, unknown in all the past. The *Lieh Tzu's* formulations are extreme in their wording and somewhat shallow, not warranting serious consideration. Yet when judged on the single point of its advocacy of hedonism, it is logically consistent and cannot on that ground be faulted. To carry that point one step further, the Bandit Chih regarded the Six Kings and the Five Hegemons as false benefactors so wanted [to be buried holding] a bronze axe with which he could chastize them in the underworld. Even though he shredded Yao's and Shun's reputations as Sages, he still maintained a faith in rulership's exalted virtues. The *Lieh Tzu*, however, demeaned Shun and Yü as pitiably afflicted persons, full of grief and suffering; by the device of ridiculing them despite their genuine benefactions, what he thereby demolished was the virtue of government itself. That

---

[84] *Ibid.*, ch. 7, "Yang Chu."

is a far more radical position than any the Bandit Chih had ever attained. For, the Bandit Chih limited himself to resentment against the world as it was, while the *Lieh Tzu* expresses a fundamental despair about human life. In viewing the *Lieh Tzu* as presenting the extreme of decadent thought, we probably are not far wrong.

SECTION FIVE

Ko Hung

BY Wei and Chin times, Confucian thought was moving into decline but was not totally extinguished. Fu Hsüan, whose life covered the span from the end of the Han to the beginning of the Chin,[85] was a solitary upholder of Mencius and Hsün Tzu just as Lao Tzu and Chuang Tzu were coming into prominence; his writings comprise more than one hundred essays [*p'ien*].[86] He may be seen as an impressive holdover from earlier glories, a vigorous late proponent of the Han era's Confucian learning. His political thought, however, did not go beyond such matters as venerating benevolence and righteousness and advocating the revival of the rites and music, stabilizing institutions and discouraging crafts and commerce. These all being stock items, long familiar, they require no further exposition at this point.[87]

Coming to the Cheng-shih age [the reign period 240–48] and thereafter, when metaphysical studies [*hsüan-hsüeh* 玄學, i.e., the study of the

[85] Fu Hsüan was born in the twenty-second year of the Han dynasty's Chien-an reign period and died in the fourth year of the Chin dynasty's Hsien-ning reign period (217–278). During the reign of the Emperor Wu [of the Chin, reigned 265–89] he served in office as high as Minister of the Imperial Stud [*T'ai-p'u*]; his biography appears in *ch.* 47 of the *Chin Shu.*

[86] The *Chin Shu* says of Fu Hsüan that "he composed discourses on the statecraft of the Nine Schools and events from the Three Histories, making critical judgments on strengths and weaknesses, each case being classified by type. His book is called the *Fu Tzu* ["The Book of Master Fu"] and consists of Inner, Outer, and Central chapters, altogether four *Pu* [divisions] and six *Lu* [records], totalling one hundred and forty essays and several hundred thousand words. Together with his literary collection [*wen-chi*], his writings comprise more than one hundred *chüan*, as extant now." By the time of the Sung dynasty only twenty-three essays [*p'ien*] of the *Fu Tzu* had survived. Later persons, by collecting fragments, have greatly added to that number. One now can count the edition included in the *Wu-ying-tien Chü-chen-pan* Collectanea, the reconstituted edition compiled by Ch'ien Pao-t'ang of Hai-ning, and that compiled by Yen K'o-chün of Wu-ch'eng (in the Kwang-tung printing of the *Ch'üan Shang-ku chih Nan-Pei-ch'ao Wen-pien*). The best edition is that of the *Fu-shih Yen-shen-chai* (compiled by Yen K'o-chün and collated by Sun Hsing-yen). His literary collection also is lost. The *Han-Wei Lu-ch'ao Po-san Ming-chia-chi* [compiled by Chang P'u, 1602–42, consisting of restored collections based on scattered fragments] contains the *Fu Ch'un-ku Chi* [collected writings of Fu Hsüan].

[87] See various essays in the *Fu Tzu* such as "Chih-t'i," "Chiao-kung," "Chien Shang-ku," "Jen-lun," "Li-yueh," "Fa-hsing," "T'ung-chih," and "An-min."

obscure] prevailed, certain figures who were antagonistic to [the focus on the concept of] nothingness [*hsü-wu* 虛無], concentrated their attacks on that. During the Western Chin dynasty [265–316], among those who joined the counterattack on that tide and who became the pillars of a mid-stream position, P'ei Wei probably is the most prominent figure. "P'ei Wei was deeply distressed by the libertine practices of the age and the failure to venerate the Confucian ways. Ho Yen and Juan Chi had long been held in high esteem in that age. Everyone chattered about the transient and the vacuous; no one adhered to the ritual norms. Official appointments were sinecures dependent on favoritism; office-holders ignored their responsibilities and duties. Eventually those of Wang Yen's ilk acquired excessive reputations; they held high position and wielded great influence, yet did not take practical matters seriously. Consequently, as they came to be imitated, moral customs and ethical teachings fell into disarray, leading P'ei to compose his "Treatise on Esteeming the Existent" [*Ch'ung-yu lun* 崇有論] to dispel their errors. . . . A profusion of attacks and rebuttals from the Wang Yen crowd poured in, but they could not force him to yield."[88] The principal points of the "Treatise on Esteeming the Existent" comprise demonstrations that the concerns of government, proper human relations, the ways of the rites, and institutional forms, all are indispensable conditions of social life. Adherents of the Lao-Chuang philosophy esteemed the [values of] vacuity and nothingness and indulged their desires as a means of enriching their lives. They failed to realize that: "As the desires unfold, calamities come apace; as the feelings flow unchecked, resentments multiply. By taking it upon oneself to be dissolute, one gives rise to accusations; when one is concerned only with advantage, it invites plunder. It can be said that in the name of enriching life they in fact lose lives." On the other hand, "Evidence can be adduced that explains [existing] forms and material things, while the significance of emptiness and nothingness is difficult to ascertain. Truly clever speech in debate is something to enjoy, but vague symbolism in speech only brings confusion. . . . Their singing arouses others to make a matching response; many are drawn away to them and few come back. In consequence, those duties which hold the world together are deprecated, and the usefulness of outstanding achievement is debased. The career of frivolous drifting is held up, while the abilities that keep practical matters in order are dis-

---

[88] *Chin Shu*, *ch*. 35, "Biography of P'ei Wei." P'ei's courtesy name was Yi-min. During the reign of the Emperor Hui [290–306] he rose in office to the post of Left Executive Assistant to the Chief Councillor [Shang-shu Tso-p'u-yeh]. In the first year of the Yung-k'ang reign period, in his thirty-fourth year of age, he was killed by Prince Lun of Chao. By this reckoning it would appear that he was born in the third year of the T'ai-shih reign period (267, and died in the year 300). His "Treatise on Esteeming the Existent" is included in his biography.

dained. . . . Those uninhibited ones go along with all that, sometimes perversely rejecting the rites for the auspicious and the inauspicious occasions [e.g., weddings and funerals], and heedless of their demeanor and conduct. They indecorously abandon the ranking of senior and junior, throwing into chaos the gradations from eminent to humble. At their most extreme they go naked, joke and frolic with utter disregard for what is appropriate." When the conduct of the scholar-officialdom is such as that, how can the work of governing then be undertaken? P'ei Wei's conclusions are as follows: "The nurturing of the real elements of present existence is not something that [their ideal of] 'the useless' can guarantee; maintaining order among the people here and now is not something that 'non-action' can bring to pass. . . . That would be as if to rely on the desire to catch a fish in deep water; it is not a deed that supine leisure can accomplish. To bring down a bird from the highest tower is not a victory that hands folded in quiescence can gain. One may thus conclude that such skills as shooting and fishing are not commanded by knowing nothing. From this point of view, all those things which can be of use to the existing are in themselves things which exist; how can vacuous nothingness contribute beneficially to all the beings already in existence?"

Even though P'ei Wei's Treatise is profoundly relevant to the circumstances, his attitudes are nonetheless somewhat milder than those of certain Eastern Chin persons who held pure conversation primarily responsible for the loss of North China. When Huan Wen launched his campaign to recover the North [from the Eastern Chin court at modern Nanking], he passed through the regions of the Huai and the Ssu Rivers, then ascended the P'ing-sheng Tower, and, as he gazed across the North China plain, said with deep emotion: "That this Wondrous Realm [shen chou 神州, or "China"] should have sunk away to become but an empty waste for these hundred years is something for which Wang Yen and those others cannot escape the responsibility."[89] Huan Wen having made such a statement, historians thereafter followed his lead and that virtually became the final judgment.[90] Moreover, the scholar-officialdom in the lower Yangtze

[89] *Chin Shu*, ch. 98, "Biography of Huan Wen." This event occurred in the twelfth year of the Yung-ho reign period (356). Yuan Hung refuted him, saying that the rise and fall [of dynasties] belongs to the workings of destiny, therefore how can the faults of a few individuals decide such matters?

[90] The preface to the "Biographies of Confucians," ch. 91 in the *Chin Shu*, says: "Throughout the Chin dynasty, starting at the court in the North and extending to [the period of its transfer to] the lower Yangtze region, all have valued the ornate and vied in the fanciful, finding their models in vacuous metaphysics. They cast aside the classical works of Confucianism and applied themselves to those doctrines still lingering from the Cheng-shih reign period [240–46]. Pointing to the ritual norms as having become vulgarized, they gave themselves over to all forms of license, calling that the pure and the lofty. The institutes and regulations, consequently, were allowed to fall into disuse, and

region [into which the Eastern Chin was pressed], deeply resentful of the alien incursions and seeking explanations for them, also largely placed the blame on Wang Yen, Ho Yen, and their kind. Wang T'an-chih, Fan Ning, and Sun Sheng are the most prominent exponents of that view.

Fan Ning composed a discourse setting forth the view that: "The crime of Wang Pi and Ho Yen goes deeper than that of [the tyrant kings] Chieh and Chou. For the violence and evil deeds of Chieh and Chou only raised havoc in their own times. They died, and their dynasties fell, but therein they have provided particularly effective lessons to guide later ages. Wang Pi and Ho Yen attracted empire-wide celebrity; that further contributed to their overfed arrogance. They depicted monsters that were taken to be clever; they incited libertine behavior that was taken up as the common practice. How true it is that the [licentious] airs of Cheng can throw music into disorder, the facile tongue can cause the downfall of states! Thus I firmly hold that a disaster afflicting one generation is the lighter and that the crime pervading successive ages is the greater. A conflict costing one his own life is a small matter, but an offense that deludes the people is a large one."[91]

Wang T'an-chih wrote his essay on "Reasons for Abolishing Chuang Tzu" in which he solely attacked Chuangtzian thought and learning while exculpating the Lao Tzu. His principal idea is that the sage, knowing the feelings [ch'ing 情] of the people must not be given free rein, therefore has instituted government and teachings to restrain them. Even though the

---

the moral teachings to decline and be destroyed. The Five Barbarian nations then took advantage of that opportunity to join in the strife, and the two capitals [Ch'ang-an and Loyang] one after the other were invaded and lost." Ku Yen-wu [1613–82] in his *Jih-chih Lu, ch.* 13, under the heading "Cheng-shih" wrote: "At the top, the state was collapsing, while below the ethical teachings were disappearing. The Ch'iang and the Jung [barbarians] by turns engaged in usurpation; rulers and ministers were repeatedly displaced. If this is not to be blamed on those various worthies of the groves [i.e., the recluses advocating Taoist metaphysics] then who is to bear the blame?" Yet, in the *T'ai-yen Wen-lu* [of Chang Ping-lin, 1868–1936], *ch.* 1, under the heading "Hu-ch'ao hsüeh," it states: "The reason why the five dynasties [invaded at this time] did not resist is because they relied on hereditary nobles and also because they made appointments to office on the basis of a person's eloquent speech and good looks; the reason does not lie in Neo-Taoist metaphysics." If the *Chin Shu*, however, is not guilty of a distortion, in Wang Yen's biography Wang himself just before his death also acknowledged his own responsibility. His words there are: "Alas! Although the men of my group were not up to the standards of the men of antiquity, if only we had not so venerated the transient and the vacuous and had devoted full energies to setting the realm in order, things might not have come to this present pass."

[91] During the time that the [future] Emperor Chien-wen [reigned 371–72] served as chief minister he deeply admired Fan Ning. In the reign of the Emperor Hsiao-wu [373–96] Fan Ning served in office with rank as high as Executive Officer of the Central Secretariat [Chung-shu shih-lang]. His biography appears in the *Chin Shu, ch.* 75.

sage is forced in spite of himself to take such action, he has in fact done so
for the sake of the common people. But Chuang Tzu has taught people to
roam [in the mind] beyond this world; "The people have taken that as
license to be evil and irresponsible. The good people of the world however
are few while the bad are many. Master Chuang's benefical contributions to the world have been few and his injuries to the world have been
many." Such were the reasons why Chuang Tzu should be abolished.[92]

Sun Sheng wrote an essay "On Lao Tan Not Being a Major Sage," in
which the sole charge against Lao Tzu [i.e., Lao Tan] is that he advocated
purity and quiescence. Sun states that Lao Tan: "Cast aside the rites and
music to secure his arguments in favor of giving free rein to spontaneity.
How could he have failed to know that when things have reached the last
stage of degeneration they will not again revert to the spontaneity of the
Tao? He wanted to state directly those values which he cherished, but he
could not evade favoring that which he himself delighted in, thus showing
that he was not one who could submerge his own mind in order to aid
other beings. Not only could he not aid them, he encouraged them in
their faults."[93]

The Neo-Taoist metaphysicians [*hsüan-hsüeh chia*] had inclined toward
extremes of uninhibited behavior and thereby had aroused antipathy; it
came close to a reenactment of the early Han Confucian-Taoist struggles
for supremacy. Yet, during the Wei-Chin era there was no dearth of persons who devoted full effort to harmonizing the two schools. Li Ch'ung's
"Hsüeh Chen" [Admonitions for Learning] and Ko Hung's *Pao-p'u Tzu*
are representative of that effort.

Li Ch'ung held that the [Taoist] non-action and the teachings of the
[Confucian] sages each had its own utility. When applied according to the
needs of an age, neither one was superior or inferior to the other. Ruling
through non-action had appeared at the primeval beginnings but, as the
pristine era declined, institutions arose. "The former kings observing that
the Way and its Virtue [*tao te*] were not being practiced thereupon employed benevolence and righteousness to bring about reform. The implementation of benevolence and righteousness grew insincere, so the rites
and the pitchpipes [*lü* 律, i.e., music] were used to bring about corrections.
The correctives grew ever more numerous, but falseness also became the

---

[92] He was born in the first year of the Hsien-ho reign period and died in the third year
of the Ning-k'ang reign period (326–375). In his career he reached the office of Presiding
Minister of the Central Secretariat [Chung-shu-ling]. For his essay "Reasons for Abolishing Chuang Tzu" [Fei Chuang Lun], see his biography in the *Chin Shu*, ch. 75.

[93] *Chin Shu*, ch. 82, "Biography of Sun Sheng." He served in office, rising to the post of
Reviewing Policy Advisor at the Imperial Library [Pi-shu-chien Chi-shih-chung]. He was
a contemporary of Wang Tao. For his essay "On Lao Tan Not Being a Major Sage" see
the compilation by the T'ang Monk Tao-hsüan, the *Kuang Hung Ming Chi*, ch. 5.

more widespread. Lao Tzu and Chuang Tzu noted this in order to demonstrate the benefits of non-action and to block the doorway to strivings after desires. . . . Thus [the Taoists] would transform [mankind's errant ways] by cutting free from the sages and casting off knowledge, and would restrain them by means of the pristine simplicity of the nameless. The sages' teachings can salvage the later stage; Lao Tzu and Chuang Tzu can manifest the beginnings. While the circumstances encountered earlier and later are starkly different, the purposes of the teachings are the same." Those protagonists of vacuity and transience have speciously proclaimed theories that would destroy all moral teachings. They simply do not understand that: "An age may be perilous or secure, and the rotation [of the cosmic forces] may be blocked or unblocked. Decrease and increase are in response to the times; ascent and descent are in accord with principle. The Way [of the Taoists] is not to be abandoned in one day, but neither is it something to be advocated with a new dawn. The rites [of the Confucians] cannot be maintained as the unalterable institutions of a millennium, nor can they be terminated at any one year. Without benevolence there is no means to sustain the growth of things; without righteousness there is no way to limit the shameful. Since benevolence and righteousness cannot be parted from, anything that harms benevolence and righteousness surely should be eliminated, and that is all. One fears that he may not succeed even when he practices [benevolence and righteousness] strenuously; anxiously hoping [for the Way] will not bring him close [to that remote goal]."[94]

This essay of Li Ch'ung's has as its purpose to counteract the advocates of transience and emptiness [or, the Neo-Taoist metaphysicians]. For a more systematic syncretizing effort, we must turn to Ko Hung. His courtesy name was Chih-ch'uan, and his informal nickname was Pao-p'u Tzu ["the Master who Embraces the Pristine"]. As a youth he was orphaned and poor, fond of learning and intense in its pursuit. And, because repeatedly subjected to the effects of warfare and destruction, all the books collected by his forebears had been destroyed, he put his pack on his back to go where he could borrow books; but although he read very widely, he was unable to carry his studies to the point of mastery. At first he had been uninterested in office-holding, but when the [future] Emperor Yuan [reigned 317–323] was serving as Chief Minister, he appointed Ko Hung to his staff. Successful in suppressing banditry, he was awarded the title of Marquis of Kuan-nei. In the first years of the Emperor Ch'eng's Hsien-ho reign period [326–334] the Chief Minister Wang Tao summoned him to the post of prefectural registrar, and he was subsequently promoted to that of Advisory Inspector [Tzu-yi ts'an-chün]. Kan Pao recommended

[94] *Chin Shu*, *ch.* 92, "Biographies of Literary Figures" [Wen-yüan Chuan].

Ko Hung as one whose talent was equal to the duties of State Historian, and he was appointed Policy Advisor, concurrently Chief Historian. Stating that he was of advanced age and wished to undertake spiritual discipline [*lien-tan* 煉丹, literally "smelt cinnabar,"] he firmly declined, and succeeded in refusing those appointments. He then lived as a recluse in the Lo-fu Mountains [in Kwangtung], where he died in his eighty-first year. He wrote the *Pao-p'u Tzu*, consisting of Inner Essays in twenty *chüan* and Outer Essays in fifty *chüan*, with a total of one-hundred sixteen essays. From the time he commenced it in his twenties until its completion during the Chien-wu reign period [317] more than ten years passed. In addition to that he composed stele inscriptions, odes, poems, and prose-poems totalling one-hundred *chüan*, as well as military proclamations, memorials, notes and memoirs of thirty *chüan*, biographies of immortals in ten *chüan*, biographies of recluses in ten *chüan*, as well as copyings concerning adept practices and miscellaneous matters from the classics, the *Shih Chi*, the [two] *Han Shu* and various writers, totalling three hundred and ten *chüan*, the *Chin-kuei Yao-fang* [secret medical formulae] in one-hundred *chüan*, and *Chou-hou Yao* [or *Pei*] *Chi-fang* ["emergency medical treatments"] in four *chüan*. Such a wealth of literary production was quite unprecedented.[95]

Ko Hung's views on harmonizing the differences between the Confucians and the Taoists, in their general purport, are based on the Grand Historian's "Essentials of the Six Schools" [in *ch.* 130 of Ssu-ma Ch'ien's *Shih Chi*; this section usually attributed to his father, Ssu-ma T'an]. Ko Hung states: "The *Tao* is the basis of Confucianism, and Confucianism is the ultimate extension of the *Tao*. . . . Confucianism is very compre-

---

[95] *Chin Shu, ch.* 72, "Biography of Ko Hung," and his "Author's Postface" in *ch.* 50 of his *Pao-p'u Tzu*. Ko Hung's birth and death dates have not yet been firmly established. The *Pao-p'u Tzu* was completed in the initial year of the Chien-wu reign period [317]. On the basis of that fact, one can calculate that he must have been born close to the third year of the Emperor Wu's Hsien-ning reign period and died about the first year of the Emperor Mu's Sheng-p'ing reign period (*c.* 277 to *c.* 357). But if one accepts Yuan Yen-po's *Lo-fu Chi* as quoted in *ch.* 160 of the *Huan-yü Chi*, which states that he died in his sixty-first year, then his death would have occurred in the third year of the Emperor Ch'eng's Hsien-k'ang reign period (337). Ch'ien Ta-hsin's [eighteenth century] *Yi-nien-lu* states that he died during the Hsien-ho reign period [326–34], thus disagreeing with the above. We may note that his biography in the dynastic history states that Ko Hung, in the first year of the Hsien-ho reign period [326] was appointed as acting Prefectural Registrar, and gradually through successive transfers and appointments, subsequently was sought to become governor of Kou-lou [prefecture in modern Kwangsi], but in the end remained at Lo-fu. "He resided in the mountains for many years, delighting in travel and nurturing himself in ease, constantly engaged in writing." Considering the import of those words, it would seem that he was in the mountains for a very long time. One might then suspect that Ch'ien Ta-hsin's view is incorrect. The *Pao-p'u Tzu* today exists in the *Ssu-pu Ts'ung-k'an* edition, in the *Chiao-ching-shan-fang* collectanea, in the *Huai-lu Chia-shu* edition, in the *P'ing-chin-kuan* Collectanea, and in the *Po-tzu ch'üan-shu* and the *Tzu-shu po-chia* editions.

hensive but short on essentials; it belabors one yet produces few results. Mohism is so frugal as to be difficult to follow; it cannot be cultivated to the exclusion of other things. Legalism is severe and lacking in mercy; it is destructive of benevolence and righteousness. Only the Taoists' teachings cause a person's spirit to become focussed, so that his movements all accord with non-action. They encompass the good that is within Confucianism and Mohism, incorporate the essentials of both the Nominalists and the Legalists, shift with the conditions of the times, respond to the transformations of things, offer simple directives that are easily understood, undertake less but accomplish more."[96] That is to say, to steer the world according to the *Tao* is the ultimate rule for governing. The rise of Confucian teachings occurred during the dernier ages; in excellence therefore they cannot be compared with those of governing through non-action. Nonetheless, although Taoist governing is superior to that of benevolence and righteousness in its purity, detachment, and singleness of focus, that is not to say that one can cast aside and abandon all the institutions of ruler and servitor and all the splendor of material civilization. Ko Hung felt that Master Pao's anarchism [i.e., that of Pao Ching-yen; see Section Three, above] was unreasonable and incapable of being practiced, and he carefully considers those views from all angles in refuting them. To summarize, his theory is threefold:

First is his view that the establishment of the ruler has come about spontaneously and naturally [*ch'u yü tzu-jan* 出於自然]. His "Chieh Pao P'ien" [*Wai P'ien, ch.* 48] says: "When the pristine chaos had been opened up, the murky parts descending and the clear ones rising, the empyrean arch now to be gazed upon overhead and the broad earth to be seen below; heaven and earth [*ch'ien k'un* 乾坤] were in their fixed positions, and all things above and below assumed their forms. Drawing on things distant, the noble heavens and the lowly earth were taken to manifest the essence of human relations. Drawing from closer at hand on the human body, the head and the limbs were taken to display the order among ruler and servitors. Hierarchism has its archetype in nature."[97]

Second, the establishment of the ruler has been beneficial to the people. Master Pao said that the rise of rulers and superiors had resulted from the struggle of strong against weak and the contest of the clever against the simple. Ko Hung rebutted that, saying: "The sage ruler received a mandate from heaven to carry on his work. Whether it was to plait nets for hunting and fishing, or to observe the heavenly bodies to

[96] *Pao-p'u Tzu, Nei-p'ien, ch.* 10, "Ming pen." [For a translation of Ssu-ma T'an's "Essentials," see de Bary *et al., Sources*, p. 189–90.]

[97] *Ibid., Wai-p'ien, ch.* 48, "Chieh Pao." The *ch.* 5, "Chün tao," also says: "The sages of the past drew upon the bi-modal pair [i.e., the *Yin* and the *Yang*] and thus the Way of ruler and servitor was established."

make fire with speculum and borer, or to test the plants so as to select the cereal grains, or to construct buildings so as to have cover overhead, all things were provided and put to use, and evils were eradicated, benefits fostered. The common people gladly supported [those culture-hero rulers of mythical antiquity], upheld them and venerated them. How then can one speak of cheating the ignorant or abusing the weak?"[98] Moreover, we need only compare ages with no rulers with those which had them, and we can see all the more clearly that having a ruler is superior. The people of the earliest beginnings "gathered together like birds or scattered like animals, roosted in trees, or slunk away into caves. Feathers and blood were their food; plaited grasses served as their clothing. At home they were without the senior-and-junior relationships among the six classes of kin, while abroad they did not know the grades of authority embodied in official rankings. That was less satisfactory than having spacious buildings to shelter their bodies; grains and delicacies [to eat]; ornamented fine fabrics [to make clothing] for protection against winter's cold and summer's heat; enlightened rulers to govern men, worthy stewards and skilled artisans [to serve them]—with offices instituted and functions assigned, harmony pervades the world." Should those who advocate anarchism still doubt these words, then let them calmly and dispassionately attempt to put themselves in those circumstances, and most carefully think through the question of whether they sincerely would be willing to live the primitive life of savages. "What if instead of your present dwelling one were to revert to the crudeness of tree nests and caves, if the dead were to be merely cast away in the fields, if blocked by water one had to wade or swim across, if in the mountains one had to climb on foot, carrying a load on the back? Throw away the cooking implements and eat raw or rancid foods; abolish the needle and probe and allow diseases to run their natural course. Regard nakedness as being adorned and do away with all upper and lower clothing. On encountering a female take her for your mate, without using the services of a go-between. Then I am sure you would say 'Impossible'! And still more so, if there were no ruler."

Furthermore, when Master Pao pointed out the evils caused by tyrannous rulers in order to demonstrate that the existence of rulers is the source of harm, he was committing an error of logic. That is, rulers of course

---

[98] *Ibid., Wai-p'ien, ch.* 48, "Chieh Pao." It should be noted that the "Inner Chapters" [*Nei-p'ien*] and the "Outer Chapters" [*Wai-p'ien*] frequently are contradictory of each other in the views expressed. For example, where it here states that the sages received their mandate from heaven, *Nei-p'ien, ch.* 7, "Se nan," adopts from Wang Ch'ung the theory that the production of things by heaven and earth is fortuitous, and that heaven and earth lack all knowledge of how that occurs. [The emergence of human civilization through the discoveries and policies of culture-hero kings, alluded to here, more or less follows traditional accounts of the Yellow Emperor, the Divine Agriculturist, etc.]

may be either good or bad. "Now you speak only of the crimes of a degenerate age, yet include no comment on an age when complete order prevails. . . . Because of a [tyrant such as the infamous] Chieh or Chou you would consider having no ruler." Is that any different from "destroying your house from concern that it might catch on fire, or filling in the river because you have a fear of wind and waves?"

Third, instituting the ruler is a matter of necessity. Ko Hung believed that the age of high antiquity was not only unattractive but also unsafe. Those advocating theories about having no ruler mistakenly believed the earliest age to be one of purity and peace, consequently hoped that the way of ruler and servitor might be dispensed with. That view, however, is totally unfounded, and it displays an ignorance of human nature. "If it were possible that in earliest times men were like wood and stones so that even when everything froze they felt no cold, and when all provisions were exhausted they knew no hunger, then perhaps that [vision of purity and peace] might have been possible. But, if concerns about clothing and food were present in their minds, then they too would contend for goods, and not just for gold and jade. They too would strive and contend, and not just for honor and high rank. Fighting and disputes can arise over sticks and straw; attack and plunder may be incited by no more than millet and beans. For, the characteristic of having desires emerged as early as mankind had life; the propensity to enrich oneself was manifested as soon as humans assumed form. To steal, kill, and seize others' belongings come about quite naturally. On what rests the principle that disorder could not have existed?"

Since primitive men thus were certain to engage in injuring and killing each other, there need be no doubt that they could not have governed themselves without rulers. "When between man and man there can be struggles over the miniscule value of some straw or millet, when between families there can be disputes for possession of tree nests and caves, and overhead there are no officers to deal with wrongs while below there are factions formed on clan lines, then the private feuds will be more excessive than public wars, and the clubs and stones sharper than weapons. Corpses will be strewed through the fields and blood will stain the roadways. Were a long time to pass without a ruler, the race of mankind would be exterminated."[99]

As for the reasons why later, degenerate ages are unable to do without rulers, those too are quite obvious. For, "No age will be without violent and treacherous incidents. If let alone with nothing to fear, then [violent men] such as the Brigand Chih will be unopposed in their plundering and killing, while the good will have no recourse but to fold their hands and

[99] This is loosely analogous to the theories of the English philosopher Thomas Hobbes.

await disaster. There will be no overlord to hear complaints, and no power
on which to rely. Then to hope that each household will preserve good
order and that all individuals will be as [saintly as the Brigand Chih's
brother] Liu-hsia Hui,—how does that differ from transporting a pig on
one's back and hoping not to stink, or standing in the river's edge and
hoping not to get damp? Without bridle and reins to ride a galloping
horse, or to throw away the oars and travel by canoe, I have never known
such things to be done."

Ko Hung's theories about having rulers are diametrically opposed to
those of Juan Chi and Pao Ching-yen, but are close to those of Wang Pi
and Kuo Hsiang. To state that differently, roughly one century elapsed
between Wang Pi and Ko Hung during which Taoist political thought
moved from Lao Tzu on into Chuang Tzu, then encountered a reaction
that took it back to Lao Tzu. Yet in this later phase it displays a difference
from Wang Pi and Kuo Hsiang, in that Wang and Kuo still placed great
emphasis on the ruler's personal worthiness and virtue,[100] whereas Ko
Hung solely valued the ruler's position. Ko Hung stated that to merit
service a ruler need not be a Yao or a Shun.[101] and that removing a ruler
and replacing him with another was entirely contrary to the teachings of
the *Spring and Autumn Annals*. As he expressed it: "Removing a ruler
and installing another is a matter of minor compliance [with duty and
virtue] and of major disobedience; it should not be encouraged [i.e.,
allowed to grow]. . . . For the ruler is as heaven, as the father. If the
ruler can be removed then heaven also can be changed, fathers also can
be changed. . . . Everything conveyed in [the early Chou documents],
the wood and bamboo tablets supports the elevation of the ruler and the
subordination of the servitor, the strengthening of the trunk and the weakening of the branches. The meaning of the *Spring and Autumn Annals* is that
heaven must not be taken as one's adversary. The Great Sage [Confucius]
composed the classic to support fathers and serve rulers. The people live
within the three [sustaining relationships, of ruler, father, and teacher];
those are all to be maintained as one. [Cf. the *Kuo Yü, ch.* 7, "Chin Yü," 1.]
To allow that the ruler be removed and replaced is to initiate the beginnings of immorality. Those below engage in *lèse majesté* and the one above
is superseded; that constitutes a matter most difficult to explain [in
instructing the people in morality]."[102] Although he has not stated so, in

[100] *Vide* footnote 24 in this chapter.

[101] *Pao-p'u Tzu, Wai-p'ien, ch.* 12, "Jen neng," states: "Can one imagine that there
would be a servitor who would test to find out how much intelligence his ruler had, and
calculate how impressive his demeanor was, demanding that he locate a Yao or a Shun
before serving him? Whom can one serve if not the ruler? Whom can he employ if not the
people?"

[102] *Ibid., Wai-p'ien, ch.* 7, "Liang kuei."

this view Ko Hung has drawn on the Confucian rectification-of-names theory, for no such thought belongs within the boundaries of Huang-Lao theory. The reason why Ko Hung so stressed this view probably is that he was deeply perturbed by the aggressive usurpations of authority by powerful ministers throughout the Wei and Chin eras, and the relative insignificance of the ruler's powers; thus his concern to try and counteract that.

There is also a further consideration here. Kuo Hsiang had stated: "Inasmuch as benevolence and righteousness are in fact human feelings they can be granted full play."[103] In that earlier time Kuo simply had not felt called upon to devote his attention to upholding the moral teachings. Ko Hung, profoundly distressed by the profligacy and license of Chin dynasty persons, wrote essays "In Ridicule of Delusion" and "In Hatred of Absurdities" [*Wai P'ien*, *ch.* 26, "Chi Huo" and *ch.* 25 "Chi Miu"]. Adopting the traditional Confucian standards for the rites and the proprieties, he criticized the profligacy and excesses of the scholar-officials and of their women in the society of his own time, with an attitude of extreme severity.[104] He did that for a specific purpose, just as had P'ei Wei, Fan Ning, and those others; there is no need therefore to expatiate at length here. As for the governing methods he sets forth in this connection, those are mainly based on Confucian tenets,[105] but with some interpola-

---

[103] *Vide* footnote 39 in this chapter [and Section Two, pp. 607–19 above].

[104] *Pao-p'u Tzu*, *Wai-p'ien*, *ch.* 26, "Chi huo" ["In Ridicule of Delusion"] states: "In the very earliest times there were no rankings among the people. The ancient sages grieved that the primitive conditions were so crude, feeling pity on account of the rusticity of tree nests and caves. Therefore they had buildings constructed so that the people could be separated from the birds and animals, and they instituted ritual proprieties to make distinctions on the basis of rank and authority. They taught [proper conduct to keep people from undisciplined self-indulgence, by] instructing them with rules of etiquette and propriety [literally, "teaching them to walk circuitously, instructing them to bow deferentially"]. . . . For restraint of excesses is a matter of urgent human need. . . . If one occupy the superior position to govern the people he must employ these means or none at all." *Ch.* 25, "Chi miu" ["In Hatred of Absurdities"] says: "With head uncombed and temple-hair in disarray, wearing no hair-clip; they may *en déshabillé* receive guests, they may squat spread-legged and half-naked. . . . When they encounter each other they no longer bother to say farewells or express greetings. A guest may go through the gateway and hail the servants [instead of the master], while a host may gaze toward the guest while talking to the dog. . . . On festive occasions they will gather like foxes and drink like oxen, squabbling over the food and competing to get it, pulling and pushing in disorderly confusion. They no longer have integrity or shame." The same essay has been quoted above for its account of women; see footnote 72 in this chapter.

[105] *Ibid.*, *ch.* 5, "Chün tao," states: "The ruler must cultivate himself as foremost within the four seas; he must eschew favoritism in order equably to uphold the Kingly Way. . . . Persons of capacity should be named for appointment; talented ones must not fail to be granted appointment. . . . Make them skilled through the Six Arts and restrain them through loyalty and faithfulness. Supervise them with compassion and harmony; keep

tion of Taoist purity and simplicity.[106] Such ideas being quite familiar, we may also omit further discussion of them here.

SECTION SIX
Disputes Introduced by Buddhism

BUDDHISM, spreading into China, began to flourish during the Wei-Chin period. Its scriptures multiplied, both *sangha* and believers became increasingly numerous, and the number of its temples and monasteries gradually swelled.[107] Even had there been no offensive acts committed by any of the *śramaṇa*, by reason of its alien thought it inevitably would have aroused the antipathy of some persons.[108] During the two hundred years following the Eastern Chin dynasty [ended 419], in terms of school factionalisms, conflict developed both between Confucians and Buddhists, and between Taoists and Buddhists. In terms of the content of thought, there were disputes over Chinese *versus* alien elements, and over remaining in laity *versus* entering the sangha. Here we shall briefly recount the conflicts in the content of thought by way of concluding this chapter.

The Buddhadharma [or, the Law preached by the Buddha] taught people *"pravrajyā"* [*ch'u-chia* 出家, to abandon the family and society to become a monk or nun, or *śramaṇa*], which struck a fundamental blow precisely at the traditional Chinese concept of *"jen-lun"* [人倫, ethical human relationships]. Opponents of the Buddhadharma, in consequence, developed a theory of the "three destructions" [*san p'o* 三破]. "The first destruction is that it enters the state and destroys the state. Speaking wildly and uttering falsehoods, encouraging building without limits, it imposes bitter hardships on the people. It depletes the state and impoverishes the people, contributing nothing to the state's revenues while [Buddhist celibacy] reduces the birthrate of mankind. It goes even so far that

---

them well-disciplined through ritual and penalty." See, in the *Wai-p'ien*, *ch.* 11, "Kuei hsien," *ch.* 12, "Jen neng," *ch.* 14, "Yung hsing," and *ch.* 15, "Shen chü."

[106] *Ibid.*, *ch.* 31, "Sheng fan."

[107] During the Western Chin [265–317] there were 180 temples, and by the Eastern Chin [317–419] there were 1,768; in Northern Ch'i times [550–77] there were 40,000 temples, and during the Chien-te reign period (572–77) there were about three million monks and nuns. See *Wei Shu*, *ch.* 114, "Treatise on Buddhism and Taoism." [Translated in part by J. R. Ware, *T'oung Pao* 30, 1933; and in full by Leon Hurvitz in *Yün-kang*, Vol. xvi, 1956, supplement to *Yün-kang*, *The Buddhist cave-temples of the fifth century A.D. in North China*, ed. by Mizuno, Seiichi and Nagahiro, Toshio, Kyoto, thirty-two volumes, 1952–56.]

[108] During the seventh year of the T'ai-p'ing-chen-chün reign period (446) of the Northern Wei Emperor T'ai-wu, monks were executed and temples destroyed in consequence of illicit behavior of monks. See *Wei Shu*, *ch.* 114, "Treatise on Buddhism and Taoism." [Cf. footnote 107 of this chapter.]

persons who will not engage in sericulture yet are to be clothed, and who will not work at agriculture yet are to be fed; when the state has been extinguished and its people exterminated, the loss will have stemmed from this."

"The second destruction is that it enters the family and destroys the family. It brings fathers and sons to serve different ends, elder and younger brothers to observe different laws. It abandons parents, terminating the Way of filial piety. It makes [members of one family] differ about joys and sorrows, and not to sing or weep about the same things. It engenders hatreds amongst kith and kin, and its adherents forever forgo their place in their families. It opposes the workings of suasion and disrupts compliance [to parental authority], and does not recompense the debts for vast-as-heaven parental love. The five rebellious acts [against heaven, earth, ruler, parents and teachers] and the failure to show filial submission could be no more excessive than this."

"The third destruction is that it enters the body and destroys the body. First, people's persons suffer the ills of its injuries and wounds; second, they endure the pains of the tonsure; third, they perform rebellious acts of unfiliality; fourth, they are guilty of terminating their clans [through celibacy]; fifth, they give up their bodies in observing the religious commandments. For what kinds of reasons indeed can people be taught to be unfilial! [The religion's commandments order that children shall not kneel before parents, and the people eagerly observe this. If a son should first become a monk, and the mother subsequently become a nun, she will then kneel before her son. Such ideas, contrary to all ritual propriety, have long been eradicated in China; how could we now come to observe such a practice?]"[109] The above charges bring up virtually all the basic issues in the disputes over remaining in laity *versus* entering the sangha.

The *śramaṇas* and their sympathizers relied on the Buddhadharma for the general sense of their rebuttals, but also made use of both Confucian and Taoist ideas at many points.[110] There were some who elucidated the concept of *pravrajyā*, such as the Chin dynasty monk Hui-yuan, who wrote: "Those who leave their families to become monks all live in seclusion, seeking their life's purpose [*chih* 志]; they change away from ordinary ways of life in order to attain their *Tao* ["bodhi," or enlightenment, in its

---

[109] Taoist statements quoted by Liu Hsieh in his "Mieh-huo Lun," in the Liang dynasty monk Seng-yu's compilation, the *Hung Ming Chi*, *ch.* 8. Liu Hsieh was born in the first year of the Ch'i dynasty's Yung-t'ai reign period, and died in the fifth year of the Liang dynasty's Ta-t'ung reign period (498–539), [better: 465–522].

[110] At the time there were many who discussed Buddhism in terms drawn from the *Chuang Tzu*; that process was called "*ko-yi*" [格義, or "matching of terms"]. (See Fung Yu-lan, *History of Chinese Philosophy*, vol. II, pp. 663–666) [translated by Derk Bodde, Vol. II, pp. 240–43]; Taoism, thus, was used not only as a resource for opposing Buddhism.

specific Buddhist sense]. . . . Having done so, they then can save the drowning from the deep waters, and rescue the wayward person from the weight of recurrent *kalpas*. They can unblock the way to that distant ferry of the Three Vehicles [which carry people beyond mortality], and grandly open up the roadway of men and devas. For that reason, within the family they can deviate from the natural relationships, yet not violate filiality; outside the home they can be remiss in offering the ruler the reverence due him and yet not fail in respectfulness."[111] There were those who distorted the meaning of the obligation to care for one's parents, such as Liu Hsieh, who said: "When filial piety is carried to the ultimate, monks and laymen are in accord with each other. Although remaining within or being outside [of the family] sets them on different courses, the spiritual function of each is of the same order."[112] Hui-yüan wrote: "The Confucian classics also say that one should establish himself and practice the *Tao* in order to bring glory to one's parents, and such being [the definition of] filial conduct, what need is there to return to the family?". . . The Buddha also permits monks, in accord with their particular conditioning circumstances, to cultivate the Way of religion through the summer and winter, and in the spring and autumn to return home and attend their parents. Thus [Sakyamuni's disciple] Maudgalyāyana begged for food to offer to his mother, and Tathāgata carried the coffin at [his parents'] funeral. This principle is one of great wisdom, and not one that could have been unilaterally [by Buddhism] abolished."[113] And, there were also those who argued from the facts of history in defending the Buddhist teachings, such as Liu Hsieh, who wrote: "In antiquity when [the legendary Emperor Yü] assembled the feudal lords, there was wealth throughout the myriad states. By the time of the Warring States, only seven kingdoms had survived. In the Keng-shih era [at the end of the Former Han, A.D. 23] the government had abundant wealth and commoner households all enjoyed prosperity. After the warfare and chaos of the Red Eyebrows [of roughly the same time] for a thousand miles no human life was to be seen. In such instances of states being extinguished and people being exterminated, should one seek the reason in this [Buddhism]? At the time of Hu-hai and Tzu-ying [the reference is to the two immediate heirs to the First Emperor, in the years 209–207,] a picul of rice cost ten-thousand cash, while during the reigns of [the early Han Emperors] Ching and Wu, the grain piled up until it rotted. That is not because at the end of the Ch'in there were many monks and in the early Han there was no Buddhism [since

---

[111] "Ta Huan T'ai-wei shu" ["Letter in reply to Grand Marshall Huan Hsüan"], (*Hung Ming Chi, ch.* 12).

[112] In his "Mieh-huo Lun" [see footnote 109, above].

[113] "Ta Chou Wu-ti" ["In reply to Emperor Wu of Chou"], (in the *Kuang Hung Ming Chi*, compiled by the T'ang monk, Tao-hsüan, *ch.* 10).

both antedate the appearance of Buddhism there]. Basing on what we know of the past to judge the present, what injurious consequences for government can it induce?" As for the charge that it would deplete the state and extinguish the human race, that would have to await a time when everyone would leave the family to be monks and nuns before it would stand. But, "Both entering the Way [of the *sangha*] and remaining in the ordinary world would depend entirely on [the laws of] cause and effect ... and it has never been heard of that everyone in the whole would would all at the same time become monks and nuns."[114] The theory of the three destructions was arbitary and shallow, and clearly was incapable of disinclining the minds of Buddhist followers.

Buddhists' abandoning of family life to become monks and nuns was in direct conflict with family ethics; ultimately, also, it led to inevitable conflict in politics. "Within the sea-boundaries of the land, all are the king's servitors." [*Shih, Hsiao-ya*, "Pei-shan"; slightly modified from Legge, *She King*, II/vi/1, p. 360.] There is no place in the world where one can flee from the duties of servitor to the ruler. [Paraphrasing the Taoist ridicule of Confucians; *Chuang Tzu*, ch. 4; cf. Watson, *Complete Works*, pp. 59–60.] Such concepts had long formed the substance of China's political theory. Yet Buddhist scriptures such as the *Bramajāla-sutra*, second chapter; the *Nirvāṇa-sutra*, chapter 6; the *Vinaya in Four Divisions*, and the like, all state explicitly that the *śramaṇa* should not venerate anything worldly.[115] As such teachings were practiced, both rulers and fathers were excluded from being the recipients of reverence and respect. The debate over the appropriate behavior for believers within the family and on abandoning it to become monks and nuns became the more heated over this issue. The immediate cause of the explosion that it induced was an edict of the sixth year of the Chin Emperor Ch'eng's Hsien-k'ang reign period.[116] The Emperor was but a child and the government was under the guidance of Yü Ping. Yü felt that the *śramaṇas* should perform ritual homage to the ruler, so issued an edict that included the following: "The hierarchical order of ruler and servitors derives from the respect shown by sons to fathers. Complying with the institutions, venerating the ritual proprieties and rankings,—can these be for nothing? They have their sound reasons.

---

[114] Liu Hsieh, "Mieh-huo Lun." See also *Hung Ming Chi*, ch. 8, "Shih San-p'o Lun" ["Dispelling the issues raised in the 'Discourse on the Three Destructions' "] by the monk Seng-shun. At that time there was also the theory of the "Five Perversities" ["Wu-heng"]; see *Hung Ming Chi*, ch. 6, the "Shih Po Lun," by the Chin monk, Tao-heng. [For the inexplicable words "*tsung so*" 宗索 in the passage quoted from Liu Hsieh, above, Professor L. S. Yang on the basis of the version of that essay appearing in the Kyoto edition of the *Tripitaka*, suggests emending those words to read "Hai Ying" 亥嬰; the translation follows that suggestion.]

[115] As quoted from the *Kuang Hung Ming Chi*, ch. 25.

[116] The date corresponds to A.D. 340.

Then, can it be said that the Confucian ethical norms [*ming chiao* 名教]
have been established unreasonably? Moreover, does the Buddha now
really exist? Might he not continue to exist in the future? If the Buddha
now exists, his doctrines will in any event prosper. If he does not exist,
what is to be taken as right? Even granting Buddhism's reliability, it per-
tains to matters beyond the mundane. Should matters beyond the mundane provide the forms for this world's affairs? And should one then
mortify the flesh, repudiate the normal obligations, alter the ritual rules,
and cast aside the ethical teachings? This I seriously doubt. The Confucian ethical teachings have their long history, and a hundred generations have not set them aside. . . . All such people [Buddhist converts] are
subjects of the Chin state. Judged by their talent and intelligence, they
are just ordinary persons. Should they then, by virtue of the disputatious
way they argue their views, the prepossessing manner in which they robe
and ornament themselves, the arrogant demeanor with which they impose
their alien practices, be allowed to remain erect in the imperial presence?
This too is something that I cannot accept."[117]

Thereupon a great court debate arose, some taking the one side and
some the other. Subsequently, during the *Yüan-hsing* reign period of the
Emperor An,[118] the Grand Marshall Huan Hsüan further elaborated on
Yü Ping's points, arousing still more heated discussion and refutation.
Huan Hsüan stated that Yü Ping's ". . . Purpose was to elevate the ruler,
but his reasoning was not exhaustive," so he offered further arguments,
as follows: "Lao Tzu included kings and feudal lords among the Three
Great Ones. His reasons for so acknowledging their importance are, in
their entirety, that rulers sustain life, and that they are the vehicle of fate.
It is not merely because the ruler on the throne is to be seen in relation
to the two primal modes [*erh yi*, 二儀; "heaven and earth"]. The great
power of heaven and earth is set forth as that of generating life; [the
complementary capacity] to be in communication with all life and to
maintain order among all things resides in the rulers. To show veneration
and respect to the rulers' authority [*shen ch'i*, 神器, literally, "divine uten-
sil", i.e., the throne] the ritual proprieties are truly important. How can
it be a groundless show of veneration, merely to acknowledge the imperial
dignity? After all, it is the ruler's ministration and ordering that make
possible for *śramaṇas* to exist, generation after generation. How then could
they receive the benefits he bestows upon them and fail to observe the

---

[117] *Hung Ming Chi, ch.* 12; neither the "Basic Annals" of Emperor Ch'eng nor the "Biography of Yü Ping" in the *Chin Shu* includes mention of this. [A translation of all the relevant
documents is found in E. Zürcher, *The Buddhist Conquest of China*, two vols., 1959, Ch.
III, Appendix A, pp. 160–163; note page 160 for another translation of Yü's edict.]

[118] Corresponding to the years 402–04.

propriety, accept his beneficence and yet neglect to pay him homage?"[119]

When the content of the counter arguments from the opposing side is summarized, it does not go beyond the following points: (One) "The *śramaṇas* leave their families and abandon their kin," and regard their bodies as earth or wood, "not placing hope in this one life but desiring blessings through ten-thousand kalpas. Those things which the world values they have all put aside. Those things to which the rites and teachings attach importance all are things that in their minds have ceased to matter." How, then, could they direct any obeisances to any rulers?[120] Moreover, the *sramanas* are "visitors dwelling beyond the mundane," therefore not to be considered the servitors of the Son of Heaven. "The religion that they profess has led them to realize that all sorrows and fetters derive from having a body, and that by not preserving their bodies they can extinguish sorrow. They know that birth and rebirth are caused by remaining subject to the transformations, and that by not complying with transformation they can aspire to the highest principle. . . . Therefore all who have left the family dwell in seclusion, seeking to fulfill their aspirations, and they change away from the ordinary practices so they may realize the Way. Having altered daily practices and standard dress, they cannot share in the institutes and rituals of the ordinary world." Under such circumstances, they cannot submit themselves to the same ritual forms of the laity.

(Two) The *śramaṇas* have their own meritorious achievements by which they are to be considered not necessarily inferior to rulers. "If one [monk] can bring his virtue to perfection, then his enlightenment will imbue his immediate family in the six categories of kinship, and his beneficence will extend to the whole realm. Even though he does not occupy the position of a king or lord he nonetheless is in harmonious union with the Imperial Absolute, providing great aid and protection to the living." By this reasoning, then: "Within the family such a person can deviate from the natural relationships and yet not violate filiality; outside the home he can be remiss in offering the ruler the reverence due him and yet not fail in respect."[121] How, then, could the monk be judged according to the standards for ordinary persons?

---

[119] "Yü pa-tso lun sha-men ching shu" ["Letter to the eight ministers discussing homage by the *śramaṇas*"], (*Hung Ming Chi, ch.* 12). See also the biography of the monk Hui-yüan in Hui-chiao's *Kao Seng Chuan* ["Biographies of Eminent Monks"].

[120] In the "Reply to Huan Hsüan's Letter" by Huan Ch'ien and others, [*Hung Ming Chi, ch.* 12].

[121] See footnote 111, above. [From Hui-yüan's letter in reply to Huan Hsüan, *Hung Ming Chi, ch.* 12. For a partial translation, see E. Zürcher, *op.cit.*, pp. 258–59, where part of it is misidentified as from *HMC, ch.* 11.] Refer also to the monk Tao-heng's "Shih Po Lun" (*Hung Ming Chi, ch.* 6). Tao-heng's discourse was composed during the Yi-hsi reign period (405–418); [translated in part in E. Zürcher, *op.cit.*, p. 262].

(Three) "One of high accomplishment is given no reward. Thanks to one whose bounty has been profound are to be forgotten."[122] The ruler's virtue is as immense as heaven; it cannot be recompensed by a single obeisance. Why then coerce the śramaṇa to "bend his body to perform a rite"?

(Four) It has long been the established custom for śramaṇas not to pay homage. That should not be thrown into confusion by changes, or it will "lead to sorrow and apprehension."[123]

The disputes over the behavior appropriate to Buddhists, whether within the family or after leaving the family to become monks or nuns, represented a conflict between Buddhist doctrine and family and political ethics; the disputes over alien *versus* Chinese ways constituted a conflict between the alien religion and the national culture. In earlier times Mencius had castigated Ch'en Hsiang for having abandoned the learning of China, saying: "I have heard of men using the doctrines of our great land to change barbarians, but I have never yet heard of any being changed by barbarians."[124] During the Six Dynasties the opponents of Buddhism based their arguments in the main on this.[125] Ku Huan's "Treatise on the Barbarians and Chinese" [*Yi Hsia Lun* 夷夏論] may be taken as the most prominent representative of the type. Summarizing his arguments there, we find he makes two points: The first is that Taoism and Buddhism have one source, both having emerged from Lao Tzu. "Lao Tzu went through the Pass [westward from China] and arrived at the State of Wei-wei [Kapilavastu, the Buddha's birthplace] in T'ien-chu [India]. The wife of that state's king was called Ching-miao. Because she napped during the daytime, Lao Tzu used the essence [semen] of the sun to enter Ching-

---

[122] Wang Mi, "Ta Huan T'ai-wei Shu" ["Letter in response to Grand Marshall Huan Hsüan"], (*Hung Ming Chi, ch.* 12). Wang Mi was born in the fourth year of the Chin dynasty's Sheng-p'ing reign period and died in the third year of its Yi-hsi reign period (360–407). [Cf. E. Zürcher, *op.cit.*, pp. 232–36.]

[123] Memorial by Ho Ch'ung and others, "Sha-men pu-ying chin-ching piao" ["*śramaṇas* should not pay homage"], (*Hung Ming Chi, ch.* 12). Subsequently, the proposal submitted by Ho Ch'ung and the others was adopted, permitting monks not to offer homage. Thereafter, the Emperor Te-tsung of the T'ang dynasty, in the second year of the Lung-shuo reign period (622) finally decreed that the *śramaṇas* must do obeisance to their parents but not to the ruler. See *Kuang Hung Ming Chi, ch.* 25.

[124] Mencius, III/i/i/12, "T'eng Wen-kung," Part One [Legge, pp. 253–54].

[125] The Northern and the Southern states reviled each other, the Northern one calling the Southern courts the "usurpers of the Chin" and the "island barbarians" [an ancient name from the *Documents* for primitive peoples living on the South China coast], while the Southern states called the Northern dynasties the "Wei caitiffs" ["Wei" refers to the T'o-pa dynasty] and the "braided heads" [a play on words referring both to the steppe hairdress and to braided ropes by which captives were tied]. (See, respectively, the *Wei Shu, ch.* 96, and the *Nan Ch'i Shu, ch.* 57.) These names imply a measure of racial consciousness.

miao's mouth. In the next year at midnight on the eighth day of the fourth moon, [the Buddha] was born through an incision in her left armpit. As he fell to the ground, he walked seven steps, and from that time Buddhism flourished."

The second point is that although Buddhism and Taoism are identical, the Barbarians and the Chinese have different customs. Therefore we should adopt the *Tao* that belongs to the Chinese culture zone and discard the Barbarians' Buddhism. Ku Huan wrote: "Buddhism and Taoism are comparable in their capacities to transform, but display the differences that exist between Barbarians and Chinese. . . . Now we have come to making the Chinese nature conform to the Western Barbarian ways. . . . That promotes social incivilities and offenses against gentility, without our having so much as become aware. . . . Now to forsake what is Chinese to emulate the Barbarian, what will be the justification? If [the choice be made on account of] doctrine, there is no difference [between Taoism and Buddhism]. Or, if the choice be made on account of customs, there is indeed great discrepancy [between superior Chinese and inferior Barbarian ways]."[126] Further, in taking up the issues of Buddhism's alien social practices, the gentry modes were repeatedly contrasted with shaving the head and wearing the outlandish robes, so that a great discrepancy in values emerged. So the inferiority of Buddhism to Taoism can again be discerned. "Buddhism arose among the Western Barbarians, and is that not because the customs of the Barbarians originally were evil? Taoism arose among the Chinese, and is that not because Chinese ways originally were good?"[127]

The Buddhist refutations were aimed exactly at those two points. Yuan Ts'an rebutted the idea that Buddhism and Taoism had emerged from the same source, saying: "Confucius and Lao Tzu considered ministration of this world as the fundamental duty, while Sakyamuni regarded *pravrajyā* as the highest deed. Their starting points being widely diverse, so are they different in their ultimate goals. The notion of their compatibility stems obviously from groundless speculation. Moreover the incarnation and birth of the Tathāgata occurred prior to the age of Lao Tzu." How therefore can it be claimed that Lao Tzu went out through the Pass and was transformed into him?[128] As for the distinction that the Barbarians were evil and the Chinese good, from a Buddhist believer's

---

[126] *Nan Ch'i Shu, ch.* 54, "Biography of Ku Huan."

[127] "Reply to Yüan Ts'an's Rebuttal of the Treatise on the Barbarians and Chinese" [Ta Yüan Ts'an po Yi-Hsia Lun], (*Nan Ch'i Shu, ch.* 54).

[128] *Ibid.,* "Rebuttal of the Treatise on the Barbarians and Chinese." Yüan Ts'an was born in the first year of the [Liu] Sung dynasty's Yung-ch'u reign period, and died in the first year of the Sheng-ming reign period (420–77). His biography is included in *ch.* 89 of the *Sung Shu.*

point of view this also was lacking any reasonable grounds whatsoever. For, throughout the universe, human beings are all of one kind. Hsieh Chen-chih stated: "Humans are joined with the two primal modes [i.e., heaven and earth] and together they are called the Three Powers [*san ts'ai* 三才]. Is the scope of the Three Powers' relevance divided by [the boundary between] Barbarian and Chinese? We must recognize that human beings must belong to the human kind, just as animals must herd together with animals. To find a proof for this near at hand, the seven precious gems [also to be taken in the sense of the Saptna Ratna of Buddhism] are dear to all human beings, thus Chinese and Barbarians are the same in valuing them. Reverence and respect are things which human beings cherish; therefore they are granted special esteem throughout all the Nine Zones [of the universe]."[129]

If one is to use geography for distinguishing [Barbarian from Chinese], there too it is difficult to establish a criterion. The monk Seng Yu wrote: "Confucius wished to live among the wild tribes of the East, [*Analects* IX/1] while Lao Tan [Lao Tzu] traveled to the region of the Western Barbarians. The *Tao* does not have any geographical preference for its location."[130] Now, as all mankind has the same life, irrespective of place of habitation, so all localities share in one great unity, obliterating boundaries between Chinese and Barbarians. The monk Hui-t'ung said: "The great teaching is without discrimination; the perfect virtue knows no partiality. The same truth leads all to the same destination. Among the Western and the Northern Barbarians [*Jung, Ti*] it has the same resonance; admidst the Tartars and the Chinese [*Hu, Han*] it is still the same sound. Would the Sage wish to go on to divide the regions and provide different doctrines for the inhabitants, or to segregate the places of abode and institute diverse customs? Indeed, is there such a thing as "Barbarian" [*Yi*]? Is there such a thing as "Chinese" [*Hsia*]"?[131]

These statements taken together are more than adequate to rebut Ku Huan's ethnocentric thought. But to the defenders of Buddhism this was still inadequate, so they proceeded to propound theories esteeming the Barbarian and depreciating the Chinese. Ever since the time of the "Yü Kung" [the Tributes of Yü chapter in the *Book of Documents*] the Chinese have taken themselves to be the residents of the "central region," surrounding which were the barbarians of the four quarters. The Buddhist

---

[129] "Letter to Taoist Master Ku Huan, arguing against his Treatise on the Barbarians and Chinese" [Yü Ku Tao-shih shu, che Yi-Hsia Lun], (*Hung Ming Chi, ch. 6*).

[130] "Hou-hsü" [postface] to the *Hung Ming Chi*. Seng Yu was born in the twenty-second year of the Sung dynasty's Chia-yü reign period, and died in the seventeenth year of the T'ien-chien reign period of the Liang dynasty (445–518).

[131] "Refutation of the 'Treatise on the Barbarian and Chinese' " [Po Yi-Hsia Lun], (*Hung Ming Chi, ch. 7*).

believers now overturned that idea, taking India to be the middle region. Seng Yu stated: "The north star is in fact to the northwest [seen from China] so one can know thereby that India occupies the center."[132] The monk Hui-t'ung also wrote: "India occupies the center of heaven and earth; thus it is the place from whence Buddhism has come forth."[133] And, also in terms of culture, China was put on the lower level. Although Ku Huan took it as a defect that India's social customs were not in accord with rites and culture, he simply was ignorant of the fact that India was in accord with some of the ways of high antiquity. "In the beginnings of ancient times the nature of things was still pure. Without recourse to rites and doctrines they could nonetheless maintain their uprightness; without applying punishments or penalties they still could govern themselves. The dead were buried in the fields, without mounds and without planting trees. Mourning periods were not fixed; when grief arose, one wept. These then were the pure ways of high antiquity, and they are well worth emulating." As for: "The ornaments of the gentry elite, the reverence shown by bowing, the rituals for burial, these all date from the time when the Great *Tao* had been cast aside."[134] Moreover, China's degeneration was not only of that measure. "Ever since the Han dynasty the pure ways have become demoralized, and benevolence and righteousness have gradually declined. The learning of the Great *Tao* has not been transmitted, while the study of the *Five Classics* has grown ever more rare. The great principles have been perverted and the subtle meanings [of the ancient Confucian works] also have been lost. No one sojourns to the Door of all Subtleties [*Lao Tzu*, Ch. 1] and no one observes the standard of the Doctrine of the Mean. The ritual proprieties have fallen into decline and the ceremonial music also is in decay. Customs and practices are steadily deteriorating; between rulers and servitors no norms prevail. The true teachings have been utterly debased and human relations have lost their proper order." The rites, which had become necessary after loyalty and trust were attenuated, had now themselves been eroded away. The Chinese state was incapable of achieving its own reformation. "Then the sacred Way [of Buddhism] rectified what was amiss, its celestial fortune spreading from afar, the mystic transformation spreading to the east [China], girding the world in compassion, with benevolence for the multitudinous people. Overcoming all their former ways and hearing the new gospel with joy, they, abandoning their old ways, follow and embrace it, so that the profound truth prevails again."[135] From this one sees that Buddhism

---

[132] "Hou-hsü" to the *Hung Ming Chi*.

[133] "Refutation of the 'Treatise on the Barbarian and Chinese,' " by Hui-t'ung.

[134] *Ibid.*

[135] "Refutation of the 'Treatise on the Barbarian and Chinese,' " by Chu Chao-chih of the [Liu] Sung dynasty (*Hung Ming Chi, ch.* 7).

was China's "savior," so how could it be rejected or vilified? Moreover, since the Buddha was born in India, it constituted proof that that nation's culture was of surpassing excellence. "Thus it can be known that India occupies the central zone of the Sahā [i.e., this present world] and is located at the conjunction of all that is pure and good. Thus it has been able to be sensitive to and respond to the most perfect of Sages, and its land be the center of the Trisahasra [i.e., the three thousand realms of existence]."[136]

It has generally been the case that when there is social disorder and the nation is weak, the scholar-officials have developed a serious and far-reaching skepticism about their traditional customs, institutions, and culture. They may criticize the old order and project new ideals, or they may devote their entire energy to destructiveness, altogether without the intent to be constructive. Among the major figures of the pre-Ch'in era Confucius and Mo Tzu belong to the former category, while Lao Tzu and Chuang Tzu belong to the latter. Nonetheless, despite the attacks that Lao Tzu and Chuang Tzu launched against all governing by positive action, they clearly never advocated abandoning the Chinese and emulating the Barbarian, nor did they disparage Chinese culture *per se*. Their derision was turned against the benevolence and righteousness [claimed for the sage emperors of antiquity,] Yao and Shun, while their ideal of the imperial ruler was the Yellow Emperor, the progenitor of the race. Only since the Later Han era, when Wang Ch'ung satirized vulgar ways and argued against delusions [referring to his *Chi Su* and the chapter "Pien huo" in his *Lun Heng*], had Chinese culture itself come under serious attack. The pure conversation of the Wei and Chin continued that; the "great principles and great norms" that the "successive sages have accepted and upheld" then tended to become all the more insecure. Then the Indian religion, opportunely enough, was brought into China on a large scale. In itself, it included refined and subtle theorizing, and its supra-mundane religious faith held out the attraction of being able to dispel the misery and disillusionment of human life in a chaotic age. Consequently, a portion of the scholar-officialdom as well as the ordinary people could not escape "abandoning completely all that they had learned so as to study this" [*Mencius*, III/i/4/3]. They even went so far as willingly to risk being in the wrong, and loudly advocated relinquishing their own [cultural norms] to follow others, repudiating in its entirety their national culture. This was indeed a vast and unprecedented development in the history of Chinese thought. The adoption of alien cultural elements is in itself a frequently encountered phenomenon in human history and

---

[136] "A Further Letter to the Taoist Master Ku Huan" [Ch'ung yü Ku Tao-shih shu], by Hsieh Chen-chih, (*Hung Ming Chi, ch.* 6).

repeatedly has been the catalytic agent for hastening the process of advance, so is not something to be regretted. That which can be acknowledged as unfortunate, however, is that on this first occasion when China came into contact with a comparatively high alien culture, it happened to be that of Buddhism, and that Buddhism was a pessimistic religion that disavowed governing. The result of the contact was that although it spurred progress in religious and philosophical thought. it made no contribution to social and political life. Moreover, the negative political thought of the Buddhists was something already present in the Lao-Chuang thought. Thus, the monk Tao-an could exclaim: "There is a sage in the Western Regions who does not govern, yet there is no disorder, who does not speak yet is spontaneously trusted, who does not transform yet people spontaneously respond."[137] The monk Tao-heng also said: "The śramaṇa in this life are in truth devoid of any apparent merit in relation to the civil service advancement. However, beyond [advantages of Confucian] ethical teachings, [Buddhism] in fact offers unseen benefits."[138] All such statements merely gather up stale clichés left over from pure conversation; there is here not trace of a contribution to political thought.

Thereafter, under the unification achieved by Sui and T'ang [sixth and seventh centuries], empire-wide conditions were more or less stabilized; the nation's self-confidence was gradually restored; and Confucian power and influence were again ascendant. The scholar-officials came again to rely on the methods and ways "transmitted by the successive sages" with which to repulse "heterodoxies," to order the state and govern the nation. At the time of the Five Dynasties [tenth century] Lao-Chuang thought again flourished for a brief interval. The cyclical development of thought that had progressed through the period of Ch'in and Han, Wei and Chin, by that time had played out its second cycle.[139]

---

[137] The monk Tao-an, "Discourse on the Two Teachings" [Erh-chiao lun], *Kuang Hung Ming Chi, ch.* 8. This quotes the *Lieh Tzu, ch.* 4, "Chung-ni P'ien," with slight changes of wording. [Cf. A. C. Graham, *Lieh-tzu*, p. 78.] Tao-an died in the twenty-first year of the Chien-yuan reign period of the Former Ch'in dynasty of the [Tibetan] Fu Chien (385).

[138] Tao-heng, "Shih Po Lun" (*Hung Ming Chi, ch.* 6).

[139] If the cultural element introduced during the Wei-Chin era, instead of Buddhism, had been Greek philosophy or Roman law, the Chinese of necessity would have undergone an absolutely different course of development in the thousand or more years thereafter. Although one cannot be sure of anything else, one can at least safely conclude that political thought and institutions would have displayed a more positive content, and more rapid change, or advance.

Glossary, Bibliography, and Index

Glossary, Bibliography, and Index: Explanatory Note

The Glossary, Bibliography, and Index are designed to supplement each other in specific ways. The Glossary and Bibliography contain Chinese characters that identify the proper nouns and special terms entered in the Index. All three contain enough supporting information to make correspondences of individual entries from one of the three to the others unambiguous. Note also the following features of each of the three:

The Glossary. Chinese characters identifying extant books and their authors mostly are to be found only in the Bibliography, but in cases where the author or book is important in the body of the work as a topic under discussion, those names will be entered in the Index, with corresponding entries including Chinese characters in the Glossary. Otherwise, Chinese words in transliteration appearing in the body of the work are entered in the Glossary, unless their identification in Chinese is not of great importance to the understanding of the passage or of the topic under discussion. Many proper nouns and special terms are entered in the Glossary that are not included in the Index. Names of all the disciples of Confucius mentioned in any context are entered in the Glossary, because their names present a number of problems of confusion in romanization. Followers of other philosophers, and names of other persons, are entered in the Glossary only when they are important to the discussion, e.g., when their own ideas are cited. Few kings or other rulers are entered, their names presenting few ambiguities of identification. Names of states and dynasties are entered, but not reign-periods. The terms of political thought and discourse are entered in the Glossary, albeit selectively, in the hope that the Glossary will constitute a basic vocabulary of political thought terminology, with standardized English equivalents. The identifications of the words and phrases included here are designed to serve that purpose, as well as to make their correspondence with Index entries unambiguous.

The Bibliography. The Bibliography is the sole location for Chinese equivalents of most extant books cited or quoted throughout the body of the work, including some Western language writings and translations mentioned by the translator, in square brackets. For example, "Pan Ku" appears as a topic heading in the Index, and in the Glossary to provide Chinese character identification for that name, and in the Bibliography as the author of the *Han Shu*, because Pan Ku is both a subject under discussion in political thought and the author of a much-cited historical reference work. On the other hand, "Yao Ssu-lien" appears only in the Bibliography, as the author of one of the cited dynastic histories, the *Liang Shu*. All occurrences in the body of the work of any kind of reference to any work quoted or cited can be located through the Index; in many cases, useful bibliographic information has been provided by the author in his footnotes at those places.

The Index. The Index includes no Chinese characters; it is intended to be supplemented in that respect by the Glossary and the Bibliography. The author's Table of Contents for this work is itself analytical, and should be used as the principal guide to the content of the volume. Where its Chapter and Section titles are included as topics in the Index, no further indexing of that topic for those pages is included here. Beyond indexing proper nouns and special terms in their romanized forms, the Index is analytical for terms and topics in English. It also provides an exhaustive but non-analytical listing under the book title (whether in romanization or in translation, according to "standard usage") of all citations of and translations from Chinese classical works. Later traditional sources and modern scholarly writings are entered under their authors' names. Principal actors on the historical scene are not entered in the Index in most cases; exceptions are those political figures who are directly relevant to political thought as discussed in the body of this work. For example, "Ts'ao Ts'ao" appears as an entry in the Index and in the Glossary; his elder son "Ts'ao P'ei (P'i)" appears in the Glossary, but in the Index he is entered under the heading "Wei dynasty." Other members of the Ts'ao clan are entered by name in the Glossary. None happens to have been cited for his writings, so there are no entries under the names of that clan's eminent literary figures in the Bibliography.

Western language works cited only in square brackets [that is, only cited by the translator] are indexed only at those occurrences where some opinion or further information has been invoked by the translator.

The names of mythical persons, e.g., invented characters or real persons used a-historically in the *Chuang Tzu*, are not entered in the Index unless they have become topics used importantly in political thought. For example, *Chih, Tao Chih,* or "the brigand Chih" is entered in the Index although there is no reason to believe he was not a product of Chuang Tzu's imagination. Real if historically vague figures, whose names are used as symbols for political concepts, e.g., the Sage Rulers Yao and Shun, and the Tyrant Kings Chieh and Chou, are fully indexed. Rulers of pre-Ch'in states mostly are omitted, but references to their states usually are included unless there is no relevance for political circumstances or for political thought. Stock phrases, e.g., "rites and music," are indexed wherever they occur because of their connotations for political thought. Occurrences of official titles are not indexed unless political functions or ideas in connection with them are under discussion.

One may question the utility of including, for example, over one-hundred and twenty page numbers under the entry "*Shih Chi*," showing all the locations where that book has been mentioned, cited as authority, or quoted from. This Index is designed to serve various purposes; therefore those non-analyzed entries have been retained, in the hope that their occasional use by some scholar may justify that.

Glossary, Index, and Bibliography have been prepared by the translator and have not been examined by the author who is, therefore, absolved of all responsibility for their shortcomings.

Glossary

Ai, Duke of Lu 魯哀公

Ai Chang 哀章 sycophant prognosticator at time of Wang Mang

ai-li 愛利 formulaic reference to *chien-ai* and *kung-li*, basic tenets of Mohism.

Ao 羿 mighty warrior of ancient legend (*Analects* XIV/6)

Cha Sacrifice 蜡祭, Chou era sacrifices at end of year

Chai Fang-chin 翟方進, T. Tzu-wei 子威; died 7 B.C., Chancellor at Han court

Chan-kuo 戰國, era, Warring States Period of late Chou, 479–221 B.C.

Ch'an chi 讖記, a Han era prognostication text

ch'an-shu 讖書, prognostication texts, particularly those of Han era

ch'an-wei 讖緯, prognostication texts (*ch'an-shu*) and apocrypha (*wei-shu*), together forming a category of spurious works influential during the Han dynasty

Chang Chan 張湛, T. Ch'u-tu 處度; active ca. A.D. 340–400; Neo-Taoist thinker

Chang Heng 張衡, T. P'ing-tzu 平子; A.D. 78–139, rationalist-inclined intellectual

Chang Hsiang-ju 張相如, prominent senior official during reign of Han Emperor Wen (179–157 B.C.)

Chang Liang 張良, T. Tzu-fang 子房; associate of the Han founder, early Han dynasty official

Chang-hua Terrace 章華之臺, in State of Ch'u, symbol of cultural splendor of Ch'u in Spring and Autumn era

Chang Shih-chih 張釋之, official during reign of Han Emperor Wen (179–157 B.C.), rigorously observed the letter of the law

Chang Shu 張叔, Legalist expert, tutor to the heir-apparent during reign of Han Emperor Wen

Chang T'ang 張湯, died 115 B.C., high official during reign of Emperor Wu of Han (140–87 B.C.)

Chang Ts'ang 張蒼, 256–152 B.C., advisor to Han Founder, Chancellor under Han Emperor Wen

Chang Yi 張儀, died 309 B.C., Diplomatist and professional strategist of Warring States era

Ch'ang Chü 長沮, pre-Ch'in philosopher

Chao 趙, one of three successor states of Chin, in Warring States era

Chao Chi-tzu 趙季子, third century A.D., Wang Yen's son-in-law, important in the transmission of the text of the *Lieh Tzu*

Chao Kao 趙高, eunuch chief minister in Ch'in after death of the First Emperor

Chao Ping 趙並, Chancellor under Wang Mang ca. A.D. 10

Chao Tun 趙盾, T. Hsüan Tzu 宣子; Legalist-minded statesman in Chin in 621 B.C.

Chao Wan 趙綰, died 139 B.C., Imperial Secretary at court of Emperor Wen of Han (179–157 B.C.)

Chao Yü 趙禹, Legalist-minded harsh official, Imperial Secretary under Han Emperor Wu (140–87 B.C.)

Ch'ao Ts'o 晁[鼂]錯, 275–154 B.C., official, Legalist-minded political thinker, active during reigns of Han Emperors Wen and Ching (179–141 B.C.)

Ch'e Ch'ien-ch'iu 車千秋, Chancellor, presided over the Debates on Salt and Iron at Han court, ca. 85 B.C.

chen 貞 or *chen-chieh* 貞節, chastity, "pure and blameless"

chen-jen 眞人, "true man," term for the enlightened Taoist

ch'en 臣, or *ch'en-hsia* 臣下, servitor(s), officials of the state

Ch'en 陳, pre-Ch'in state

Ch'en Chung 陳忠, official during reign of Han Emperor An (A.D. 107–125), opposed dismissals in response to portents

Ch'en Chung Tzu 陳仲子, pre-Ch'in philosopher

Ch'en Ch'ung 陳崇, high official at court of Wang Mang, A.D. 10

Ch'en Fan 陳蕃, T. Chung-chü 仲舉; ca.

95–168, leader of anti-eunuch faction at Han court A.D. 166–68, sponsor of Ho Hsiu

Ch'en Hsiang 陳相, Confucian-minded follower of Ch'en Liang in fourth century B.C. (*Mencius* III/i/4)

Ch'en Hsin 陳辛, Confucian follower of Ch'en Liang (see above)

Ch'en Liang 陳良, pre-Ch'in student of Confucianism in Ch'u, praised by Mencius (III/i/4/12)

Ch'en Liang 陳亮, 1143–94, Neo-Confucian philosopher

Ch'en P'ing 陳平, died 178 B.C., scholarly advisor to early Han emperors

Ch'en She 陳涉 (Ch'en Sheng 陳勝), rebel leader against Ch'in dynasty, 210–206 B.C.

Ch'en Shou 陳壽, T. Ch'eng-tso 承祚; A.D. 233–97, author of the *San Kuo Chih*; intellectual and political figure

Ch'en Yüeh 臣說, title of book listed under "Eclectics" in *Han Shu* 30

Cheng 鄭, pre-Ch'in state

cheng 正, to rectify, rectitude

cheng 政, broadly: politics; narrowly: administrative measures

cheng-chang 正長, officials of the feudal lords (*Mo Tzu*)

cheng-fa 征伐, punitive campaigns, in Chou times, technically the sole prerogative of the Chou kings

Cheng Hsing 鄭興, political figure, supported view during reign of Wang Mang that the house of Liu (of the Han) would be restored to rule

Cheng Hsüan 鄭玄, T. K'ang-ch'eng 康成; A.D. 127–200, pre-eminent exegete of Later Han court

Cheng K'ao-fu 正考父, ancestor of Confucius

cheng-min 正民, in the sense of *cheng-min* 整民 "to rectify the people" (*Tso*, Chuang 23)

cheng ming 正名, the rectification of names, as technique in politics

cheng-pen 政本, the basis of government

Cheng Tang-shih 鄭當時, prominent official at the courts of Emperors Ching and Wu of Han dynasty; expert on Huang-Lao

cheng-t'i 政體, the forms of government; name of essay by Hsün Yüeh

Cheng-yi 正義, designates either of two standard commentaries on classical writings, but as used here, always that of Chang Shou-chieh of the T'ang dynasty, i.e., his *Shih Chi Cheng-yi* (see Bibliography)

Ch'eng 成王, King Ch'eng, son of founding Chou King Wu of twelfth century B.C. for whom Duke of Chou was regent

Ch'eng Yi 程頤, 1033–1108, Neo-Confucian philosopher, "Master Yi-ch'uan" 伊川

Chi 稷 or Hou-chi 后稷, legendary founding ancestor of the Chou royal line; patron of millet and all cereal grains

Chi 姬, royal Chou surname

Chi An 汲黯, died 112 B.C., prominent official at courts of Han Emperors Ching and Wu

Chi-cha 季札, worthy recluse who refused the throne of Wu in 561 B.C.

Chi Ch'ih 己齒, Mohist follower in Warring States era

chi-ch'üan 集權 centralization of authority, or of state's powers; (modern term)

Chi clan 季氏, dominant clan in Lu at time of Confucius; one of Three Great Families of Lu

Chi-hsia 稷下, Academy in State of Ch'i in Warring States era

Chi K'ang 嵇康, T. Shu-yeh 叔夜; 223–262, Neo-Taoist thinker (also spelled Hsi K'ang)

chi shih 嘖室, assembly halls for expressing public opinion (*Kuan Tzu*)

Chi Tzu 箕子, the Viscount of Chi, twelfth century B.C.

ch'i 齊, balance, evenness, regularity; in *Chuang Tzu*, relativity

Ch'i 齊, pre-Ch'in state

Ch'i 杞, state associated with the rise of the Hsia dynasty

Ch'i 岐, ancient state associated with the ancestors of the Chou dynasty

ch'i 氣, material force, ethers, primal matter, breath

"*Ch'i shih Yi shih hsüeh*" 齊詩翼氏學, "Mr. Yi's studies of the Ch'i version of the Odes"; see under Yi Feng. See also, under Meng K'ang

ch'i-shu 七術, seven methods, by which rulers prevent treachery among officials (*Han Fei Tzu*)

Ch'i-tiao K'ai 漆雕開, T. Tzu-k'ai 子開; disciple of Confucius

ch'i-wu 齊物, Taoist relativism; name of Chapter Two of the *Chuang Tzu*

Ch'i-yüan 漆園, the "lacquer Garden," where Chuang Tzu is said to have served as an official

chia-ch'en 家臣, "household servitors," criticized by Confucius

chia-chün 家君, "head of the family," or clan heads (*Mo Tzu*)

chia jen 假仁, "to feign benevolence," to make a pretence of virtue, or a pretence of benevolence

Chia K'uei 賈逵, T. Ching-po 景伯; A.D. 30–101, scholar, *Tso Chuan* specialist who defended compatibility of the *Tso* and Han prognostication texts (HHS 66)

chia t'ien-hsia 家天下, the empire as the property of the ruling dynasty, contrasted with *t'ien-hsia wei-kung* 天下爲公, the empire in which "a common and public spirit prevails" ("Li Yün" chapter of the *Li Chi*)

Chia Wei-chieh 賈偉節, leader of students in anti-eunuch faction at court in A.D. 166–69 (HHS 97, "Preface")

ch'iang 強, to act forcefully, to overcome resistance, e.g., in *Mencius, ch'iang wei shan* 強爲善, "work forcefully to accomplish what is good"

Ch'iang Hua 彊華, associate of the Han Emperor Kuang-wu; submitted the *Ch'ih-fu fu* 赤伏符 prognostication text predicting Han restoration

chiao 教, teaching, education, instructing as political technique

chiao-hua 教化, transforming through teaching

Chiao Yen-shou 焦延壽, active in reign of Emperor Yuan (48–33 B.C.), specialist in *Yi-ching*, teacher of Ching Fang; wrote *Chiao-shih Yi-lin* 焦氏易林

Chieh 桀, tyrant last king of the Hsia dynasty of high antiquity; symbol of political tyranny

Chieh Ni 桀溺, pre-Ch'in philosopher

chieh-tsang 節葬, simplicity in funerals and burials (*Mo Tzu*)

Chieh Tzu 接子, pre-Ch'in philosopher

Chieh-yü, see Ch'u K'uang

chieh-yung 節用, economy of expenditures, economic austerity (*Mo Tzu*)

chien 儉, frugality

chien-ai 兼愛, universal love (*Mo Tzu*)

chien-chün 兼君, "universal ruler" (*Mo Tzu*)

chien-jen 賤人, a "mean person," a person of the lowest stratum of society, as determined by occupation

chien-shih 兼士, "universal man" (*Mo Tzu*)

chien-wei 見微, "perceiving the subtle" (*Lao Tzu*)

ch'ien-hsia 謙下, humility (*Lao Tzu*)

ch'ien-k'un 乾坤, heaven and earth; names of the first two hexagrams in the *Yi-ching*

Ch'ien-k'un tso-tu 乾坤鑿度, Han dynasty prognostication text

Ch'ien Lou Tzu 黔婁子, no longer extant Taoist work (HS 30)

chih 質, simplicity as antonym of *wen* 文, "refinement"; substance, matter

chih 智[知], wisdom, as Confucian virtue; knowledge, as Taoist evil

Chih 跖, or Tao Chih 盜跖, "the brigand Chih," "Robber Chih"; mythical figure in the *Chuang Tzu*, described as brother of Liu-hsia Hui

chih-fa 治法, the methods of governing

chih-jen 至人, "perfect man," enlightened person (*Chuang Tzu*)

chih p'ing 至平, "absolute equity," in the orderly society (*Hsün Tzu*)

Chih Pu-yi 直不疑, prominent official in the reign of Han Emperors Wen, Ching, and Wu; exponent of Huang-Lao

chih shih 志士, or *yu-chih chih shih* 有志之士, "man of principle"; "man of upright ambition"

chih tao 治道, the Way of governing; the art of ruling

chih tsu 知足, contentment (*Lao Tzu*)

Chih Tu 郅都, military commander of the capital during the reign of Han Emperor Ching (156–141 B.C.)

Chih Yün 郅惲, classics master at time of Wang Mang

ch'ih 恥, sense of shame, one of the Confucian virtues

Ch'ih-ching Tzu 赤精子, "Master of the Red Essence," term in Han prognostication texts referring to the Han founder

Ch'ih-fu fu, see Ch'iang Hua

ch'ih-hsien 赤縣, the Red Region (Tsou Yen)

Chin 晉, pre-Ch'in state, subdivided between 453 and 402 B.C. into the Three (successor) States of Chin, i.e., Han, Wei and Chao

chin-ti-li 盡地力, "exploiting natural resources to the fullest extent," Legalist governing principle

chin-wen 今文, New Text tradition; school in classical learning

ch'in 琴, ancient musical instrument

Ch'in 秦, pre-Ch'in state; after 221 B.C. the Ch'in dynasty

ch'in-ch'in 親親, the family is accorded familial regard

Ch'in Ku-li 禽滑釐, disciple of Mo Tzu, Mohist teacher

Ch'in Shih-huang-ti 秦始皇帝, the First Emperor, of the Ch'in dynasty (221–210 B.C.)

ching 經, "warp," also used metaphorically, e.g., the warp of human relationships; the classics, especially of Confucian tradition (the apocryphal pseudo-classics being the wei 緯, or woof)

Ching 荊, region of Central Yangtze; alternate name for the state of Ch'u

ching 敬, reverence, respect, veneration

ching-ch'an 經產, the well-regulated livelihood of the people; a managed production (Kuan Tzu)

ching-ch'en 經臣, the well-regulated bureaucracy; regulating officialdom (Kuan Tzu)

Ching Fang 京房, T. Chün-ming 君明; 77–37 B.C., astronomer-official and specialist in the Yi-ching, teacher of Ku Yung

Ching K'o lun 荆軻論, title of book listed under "Eclectics" in HS 30, attributed to Ssu-ma Hsiang-ju and others

ching-nei 經內, "keep order in the mundane sphere," (Kuo Hsiang)

ching-su 經俗, regulating the people's customs (Kuan Tzu)

ching-t'ien 井田, well-field, ancient social system described in Mencius and other early texts

ch'ing 卿, minister, as in shih-ch'ing 世卿, k'e-ch'ing 客卿, shang-ch'ing 上卿, etc.

ch'ing 清, purity, in political behavior; also detachment (Taoist term)

ch'ing-ching 清靜, "purity and quiescence," formulaic tag for Taoist or Huang-Lao governing methods

ch'ing-chung 輕重, a term for prices, money, commodity controls, from the name of a chapter in the Kuan Tzu

Ch'ing-miao 清廟, the ancestral temple in Chou times; later known as the T'ai-miao 太廟

ch'ing-t'an 清談, "pure conversation," a movement in third century A.D. Neo-Taoism

ch'ing-yi 清議, "pure critiques," a feature of late Han political life

Chiu-chang Lü 九章律, early-Han "Statutes in Nine Sections," a simplified code

chiu-chou 九州, the Nine Divisions comprising the Chinese world, in the Yü-kung chapter of the Documents

chiu fu 九服, Nine Zones of the universe, term used by Yuan Ts'an (fifth century A.D.)

chiu-liu 九流, Nine Categories, classification of pre-Ch'in thought

Chiu-p'in chung-cheng 九品中正, "Nine Ranks and Impartial Evaluation," system of rankings for officials instituted under the Ts'ao Wei dynasty, early third century A.D.

Chou 周, dynasty, the third of the Three Dynasties of antiquity, ca. 1111–249, or 221 B.C.

Chou 紂, tyrant last king of Shang dynasty in twelfth century B.C., symbol of political tyranny

Chou Ch'ang 周昌, the founding King Wen of the Chou dynasty, twelfth century B.C.

Chou Chü 周舉, statesman during reign of Han Emperor Shun, A.D. 126–44

Chou Chung-yung 周仲雍, uncle of King Wen, the Chou dynasty founder

Chou Fa 周發, the founding King Wu of the Chou dynasty, son of King Wen

Chou Kuan 周官, also called *Chou Li*, the *Institutes of Chou*, one of the three classical ritual texts

Chou Li 周禮, the *Institutes of Chou* (see above)

Chou Po 周勃, died 169 B.C., aid to Han dynasty founder, later prominent in the reign of Han Emperor Wen (179–157 B.C.)

Chou T'ai-po 周太伯; uncle of the Chou dynastic founder King Wen, also known as Wu T'ai-po (q.v.)

Chou Yü 周紆; "Harsh Official," favored Legalist methods, during the reign of Han Emperor Ho (A.D. 89–105)

Chu Chao-chih 朱昭之, fifth century A.D., wrote in defense of Buddhism's universality

Chu-fu Yen 主父偃, died 127 B.C., important advisor early in reign of Han Emperor Wu (140–87 B.C.)

chu-hou 諸侯, prince, duke, marquis etc ruler of a state; the feudal lords as a group in Chou political system

Chu Hsi-tsu 朱希祖, born 1879, modern scholar

Chu-hsia-shih 柱下史, title of Archivist at the Chou court

Chu hsing 竹刑, Bamboo Penal Code, law code engraved on bamboo tablets in the State of Cheng, sixth century B.C.

Chu-ko Liang 諸葛亮, T. K'ung-ming 孔明; A.D. 181–234, prime minister of Three Kingdoms state of Shu; Legalist-minded statesman

Chu Mu 朱穆, statesman during reign of Han Emperor Huan, A.D. 147–67

Chu Ssu 洙泗, names of two rivers in State of Lu, symbolic of Confucianism

chu-yün 主運, "dominant cosmic influence," in *Yin-Yang* thought

Ch'u 楚, pre-Ch'in state

ch'u-chia 出家, translation of Sanskrit *pravrajyā*, meaning to abandon family and secular life to become an ordained Buddhist monk or nun

Ch'u K'uang 楚狂, or Chieh Yü 接輿; the "Madman of Ch'u" said to have been of the surname Lu 陸

ch'u-shih 處士, recluse

Chuan-hsü 顓頊, legendary emperor of antiquity

Chuan-sun Shih, see Tuan-sun Shih

Chuang Chiao 莊蹻, "the brigand Chiao," younger brother of King Chuang of Ch'u who became a bandit (*Shih Chi* 116)

Chuang Chou 莊周, the philosopher Chuang Tzu, fourth century B.C.

Ch'un-ch'iu 春秋, era in mid-Chou history, 770–479 B.C.; also *Ch'un-ch'iu*, the *Spring and Autumn Annals*, a chronicle of that period

Ch'un-shen Chün 春申君, Lord of Ch'un-shen, Minister in third century B.C. State of Ch'u

Ch'un-yü Yüeh 淳于越, an Erudit (*Po-shih*) at the court of the First Emperor who defended the Chou feudal order

chung 鍾, pre-Ch'in unit of measure

Chung-ch'ang T'ung 仲長統, T. Kung-li 公理; A.D. 179–219, Confucian thinker, wrote no longer extant book *Ch'ang-yen* 昌言

chung-hsin 忠信, loyalty and good faith (trust), Confucian virtues

chung-hsing 中興, mid-point recovery; restoration of the dynasty and its Mandate

Chung-shan 中山, pre-Ch'in state

Chung-tu 中都, city in Lu in pre-Imperial era

Chung Yu 仲由, T. Tzu-lu 子路, Chi-lu 季路; disciple of Confucius

chung-yung 中庸, the ideal of the "golden mean"; also *Chung-yung*, *The Doctrine of the Mean*, one of the Confucian Four Books

Ch'ung-erh 重耳, prince, later the Duke Wen of Chin 晉文公, ruled 636–628 B.C.

Chü 莒, small state eliminated in Warring States period

chü-chih-lan-ku 鑢枝蘭敔, precise definition unclear, it was a form of symbolic debt repayment of poor farmers to landlords (*Kuan Tzu*)

Chü-fu 莒父, city in Lu in time of Confucius

chü-tzu 巨[鉅]子, the title borne by the Mohist Great Masters, heads of the Mohist organization

Ch'ü Chiang Tzu 屈將子, a Mohist

Great Master in Warring States era

Ch'ü-jen 曲仁里, hamlet, in Li Ward 厲鄉, of Hu Hsien in the State of Ch'u, the reputed birthplace of Lao Tzu

Ch'ü Yuan 屈原, formal name Ch'ü P'ing 屈平; ca. 340–277 B.C., poet, statesman of Ch'u in Warring States era

Ch'ü Yüan 蘧瑗, T. Po-yü 伯玉; associate of Confucius

Chüan Tzu 蜎子, non-extant Taoist book (HS 30)

ch'üan, li 權利, socially disadvantageous "power and profit" (*Debates on Salt and Iron*)

chün-ch'en 君臣, ruler and servitor; the ruler-servitor relationship

chün-chu chuan-chih 君主傳制, monarchic despotism (modern term)

chün-hsien 郡縣, Commanderies and Counties; system of direct, centralized administration of regions instituted fully by the Ch'in dynasty

chün-shu 均輸, "equal distribution" offices for monopoly production, e.g., salt and iron, in Han dynasty

chün Tao 君道, "the Way of the ruler" (*Huai-nan Tzu*)

chün-tzu 君子, "superior man," Confucian term

ch'ün 羣, the social group; the capacity to form social groups (*Hsün Tzu*)

erh-ming 二名, the "two-word name," a technicality of usage, in the *Kung-yang Commentary*

Erh-ya 爾雅, early Han period dictionary; one of the Confucian thirteen canonical works

erh-yi 二儀, "heaven and earth"; the two primal modes

fa 法, laws, norms, models; to emulate; Legalist doctrines

fa-cheng 法政, laws and governmental measures (*Hsün Tzu*)

fa-chih 法治, in Legalism: government by laws; in Western political thought: "the Rule of Law"

fa-kuan 法官, "law officers" (*Book of Lord Shang*)

fa-li 法吏, law enforcing officials, concurrently the "teachers nf the empire" (*Book of Lord Shang*)

fa-shu 法術, laws and (political) methods

fa-tu 法度, laws and standards

fa-yi 法儀, standards (norms) of social behavior (*Mo Tzu*)

fan 反[返], reversal (*Lao Tzu*)

fan-ai 泛愛, "Broad and encompassing love for mankind"; "overflowing love"; term attributed to Confucius ("Li Yün," *Li Chi*)

Fan Ch'ih 樊遲, disciple of Confucius, formal name Fan Hsü

Fan Chü 范睢 (also read Fan Sui); political and military strategist at court of King Chao of Ch'in, reigned 305–250 B.C.

Fan Hsü 樊須, T. Tzu-ch'ih 子遲, also called Fan Ch'ih; disciple of Confucius

Fan K'uai 樊噲, Lord of Lin-wu 臨武; contemporary of Hsün Tzu in service to the State of Chao

Fan Li 范蠡, fifth century B.C. statesman in Yüeh; wealthy man

Fan Ning 范寧, T. Wu-tzu 武子; ca. 326 to ca. 418, Confucian-minded official, contemporary of Chang Chan

fan-tung 反[返]動, the movement of reversal; the all-inclusive transforming process (*Lao Tzu*)

Fan Yeh 樊曄, "Harsh Official" who favored Legalist doctrines as governor during reign of Later Han Emperor Kuang-wu (A.D. 25–57)

Fan Yeh 范曄, T. Wei-tsung 蔚宗; A.D. 398–445, thinker, author of the *Hou Han Shu*

Fang Hsiao-ju 方孝孺, 1357–1402, Confucian scholar and political thinker

fang-po 方伯, Chou dynasty "Earls of the Marches," or senior nobles of a region in Chou political structure; in imperial era, euphemistic form of address for local officials

fang-shih 方士, Taoist adept, magician, fortune teller, etc.

Fang Ta-fu 防大夫, Great Officer of the City of Fang, title borne by Confucius' great-grandfather

fang-ts'e 方策, records on wood and bamboo tablets; the documentation of the early Chou *Institutes*

Fei 費, city in Lu in time of Confucius

fei-kung 非攻, condemnation of offensive warfare (*Mo Tzu*)

fei-ming 非命, anti-fatalism (*Mo Tzu*)

fei-yüeh 非樂, anti-music (*Mo Tzu*)

fen 分, differentiation of social role and status, lot, fate; "allotments and assignments" (*Hsün Tzu*)

feng-chien 封建, political and social system of early Chou, and an ideal social system thereafter; in modern usage, the translation of "feudal"

Feng Ching 馮敬, senior official during reign of Han Emperor Wen (179–157 B.C.)

feng, shan 封禪, sacrifices of state, performed in person by the First Emperor

Feng-su t'ung, see Bibliography, under Ying Shao

Feng Yen 馮衍; during Wang Mang era, supported the view that the Han dynasty would be restored under the house of Liu

Fo-fa 佛法 (*Fu-fa*), Buddhadharma, or the teachings of the Buddha, Buddhism

fu 浮, transcience of all material things (Neo-Taoism); also *hsü-fu* 虛浮 vacuity and transcience

fu 符, or *fu-ming* 符命, auspicious omens of political import

fu 輔, to assist, to support

Fu Ch'ien 服虔, second century A.D. *Ch'un-ch'iu* scholar

fu-ku 復古, "reviving the ancient," restoring antiquity, archaism

fu-kuo ch'iang-ping 富國強兵, or *fu-ch'iang*, "enriching the country and strengthening its military forces," or "enriching and strengthening," statist policies associated with Legalism

Fu-ming tsung-shuo 符命總說, "a complete explanation of the prognostications relevant to our dynasty," a document distributed by Wang Mang in support of his usurpation

Fu Pu-ch'i 宓[虙, 伏]不齊, T. Tzu-chien 子賤; disciple of Confucius

Fu Sheng 伏勝, called Master Fu 伏生; expert on the *Documents*, transmitted the text orally to Ch'ao Ts'o during reign of Han Emperor Wen (179–157 B.C.)

Fu-su 扶蘇, able elder son of the First Emperor

Fu T'un 腹䵍, Mohist Great Master in the State of Ch'in

Han 韓, one of the three successor states of Chin, in Warring States era

Han 漢, dynastic era 206 B.C. to A.D. 220

Han Fei Tzu 韓非子, political philosopher, synthesizer of Legalist theory in late third century B.C.; his book, the *Han Fei Tzu*

Han Hsüan Tzu 韓宣子, Grand Historian in the State of Ch'in

Han Ying 韓嬰, active 157 B.C., scholar, compiler of the *Han Shih Wai-chuan* 韓氏外傳

Han Yü 韓愈, 768–824, T'ang literatus and philosopher

Ho Ch'ang 何敞, died A.D. 105, statesman during reign of Han Emperor Chang, A.D. 76–88

ho-ch'i 和氣, harmony, harmonious

ho-ch'i 合氣, union of vital forces, e.g., of heaven and earth, man and woman, etc., to generate life

Ho Chin 何進, T. Sui-kao 遂高, died A.D. 189, general, grandfather of Neo-Taoist thinker Ho Yen

Ho Ch'ung 何充, T. Tz'u-tao 次道, 292–346, pro-Buddhist statesman who argued successfully that monks and nuns need not render homage to the ruler

Ho Hsiu 何休, T. Shao-kung 邵公, A.D. 129–182, Han scholar and *Kung-yang* theorizer

Ho K'uei 荷蕢, "the man carrying the straw basket," pre-Ch'in philosopher and critic of Confucius

Ho Kung 蓋公, from Chiao-hsi (Shantung), early Han leader of a local Huang-Lao school, also known as the Honorable Ko

Ho-shang Kung 河上公, "the Old Man on the River Bank," early Han (?) founder of a tradition in Taoist studies

Ho Shao 何劭, T. Ching-tsu 敬祖, born A.D. 236, wrote a biography of Wang Pi

Ho-t'u 河圖, the "River Chart" (Yellow River Diagram), a prognostication text

Ho-t'u kua-ti hsiang 河圖括地象, title of a Han prognostication work

[*Ho-t'u*] *Lu yün fa* [河圖]錄運法, title of a Han prognostication text

Ho Yen 何晏, T. P'ing-shu 平叔, born

before A.D. 209–249, Neo-Taoist thinker

hou 候, weather periods, periods of time, and other phases of development, as basis for prognostication

Hou-chi, Lord of Millet, see Chi

Hou Ts'ang 后蒼, T. Chin-chün 近君; central figure in first century B.C. Ch'i tradition of the *Odes*, teacher of Yi Feng and of Tai Te

hou wang 後王, the Later Kings

Hsi-men Chün-hui 西門君惠, Taoist adept at time of Wang Mang

Hsia 夏, dynasty, first of the Three Dynasties of antiquity, ca. 2200 to 1800 B.C.

Hsia 夏, or Chu-hsia 諸夏, "the Chinese," the various tribes of the Hsia; to distinguish the Han Chinese from the "barbarian" peoples of the borders

Hsia Ho-liang 夏賀良, died 5 B.C., leader of court faction opposing the Wang consort clan

Hsia-hou Hsüan 夏侯玄, T. T'ai-ch'u 太初, born A.D. 209, figure in Wei dynasty intellectual circles

hsiang 象, elephant; used abstractly for pattern, image, symbol

hsiang 相, assistant, to assist; assistant at ritual sacrifices; assistant to the ruler, chief minister, etc.

hsiang-ai 相愛, mutual love (*Mo Tzu*)

hsiang-chang 鄉長, village headman, local senior leader of sub-official status

hsiang hsing 象刑, symbolic punishments

Hsiang Hsiu 向秀, T. Tzu-ch'i 子期; active mid-third century A.D., Neo-Taoist thinker, specialist in the text of the *Chuang Tzu*, wrote a work called *Chuang Tzu chieh-yi* 莊子解義

Hsiang Hsü 向戌, sixth-century-B.C. statesman of the State of Sung, pacifist

hsiang, hsü, hsüeh, hsiao 庠序學校, four kinds of local and higher schools emphasized by Mencius

hsiang-hsüeh 鄉學, local schools defined in the *Chou Li*

Hsiang K'ai 襄楷, statesman during reign of Han Emperor Huan, A.D. 147–169

Hsiang Tzu-niu 項子牛, Mohist follower in Warring States era

Hsiang Yü 項羽, formal name Hsiang

Chi 籍; leader of aristocratic restoration forces in civil war at end of Ch'in dynasty, rival of the Han founder

Hsiao Ching 孝經, The Classic of Filial Piety

Hsiao Ching Yu-ch'i 孝經右契, Han apocryphal work

Hsiao Ho 蕭何, died 193 B.C., Chief Minister during first Han reign

hsiao-jen 小人, small, i.e., common man; petty-minded, mean man

hsiao-jen ju 小人儒, petty-minded Confucian (term of reproach used by Confucius, to whom it meant an unworthy man of learning)

hsiao-k'ang 小康, the age of Lesser Tranquility in *Kung-yang* School's Three Ages theory; also translated "Approaching Peace"

Hsiao-po 小白, name by which Duke Huan of Ch'i, whom Kuan Chung served, was known in his youth

hsiao-ti 孝弟, filial piety and fraternal submission, Confucian virtues

hsiao-tz'u 小疵, "minor blemish," term used by Han Yü to characterize faults in Confucianism of Hsün Tzu and Yang Hsiung

Hsiao Wang-chih 蕭望之; fellow student of Ch'i tradition of *odes* with Feng Yi, in early Han

hsiao-yao (*yu*) 逍遙遊, "unfettered roaming," a term for freedom of the individual in *Chuang Tzu*; name of Chapter One in the *Chuang Tzu*

Hsieh 契, ancient worthy, Minister of Education under Emperor Shun

Hsieh Chen-chih 謝鎭之, fifth century A.D. pro-Buddhist writer, argued for universality of human nature

hsieh ch'i 邪氣, "evil effluvium," degenerate influences

Hsieh K'un 謝鯤, T. Yu-yü 幼輿, A.D. 280–322, one of the "unfettered eight"

Hsieh Tzu 謝子, Warring States era Mohist

hsien, hsien jen 賢, 賢人, worthy person, person of wisdom and ability

hsien-liang 賢良, "wisdom and virtue," man of; title given to persons recommended for appointment to civil office in Han and later

hsien sheng chih Tao 先聖之道, the Way of the Former Sages

Hsien Tzu-shih 縣子碩, a Mohist follower

hsien wang chih Tao (or, *fa*) 先王之道(法), the Way of the Former Kings, the Methods of the Ancient Kings

Hsien-yang 咸陽, capital city of the Ch'in dynasty

hsin 信, constancy, faith, trust, belief, trustworthy

hsin chai 心齋, the "fasting of the mind" (*Chuang Tzu*)

hsin-fa 心法, the "true mind" or essence of a teaching or tradition

hsing 刑, punishments, as a method in governing; penal regulations

hsing 性, the nature (of persons or things); the specific character

hsing-ming 刑名, actuality and name, a designation for terminological problems in pre-Ch'in philosophy; in Han and later times, a formulaic tag for Legalist doctrines

hsing-shu 刑書, penal laws, penal codes

hsing Tao 行道, to practice the Way

hsing-ting 刑鼎, penal tripods, bronze vessels with penal codes cast or incised on their surfaces

hsiu-shen 修身, cultivation of one's character, self-cultivation

hsü-chün 虛君 figurehead monarchy, titular monarchy (modern term)

Hsü Fan 許犯, a Mohist

Hsü Hsing 許行, philosopher of Agriculturalist School, in Warring States period

Hsü Kan 徐幹, T. Wei-ch'ang 偉長; A.D. 170–217, one of the Seven Masters of the Chien-an Period 建安七子

hsü-shih 虛實, void and reality (Taoist cosmology); unreal and real

Hsü Yu 許由, lofty recluse at the time of the Sage Emperor Yao

hsüan-hsü 玄虛, "mysterious and vacuous," term used in Neo-Taoism for the *Tao*, or for the object of their learning

hsüan-hsüeh 玄學, Taoist, especially Neo-Taoist metaphysics (third to fifth centuries); an aspect of Neo-Taoism used to designate the movement

hsüan-hsüeh chia 玄學家, Neo-Taoist metaphysicians

hsüan-hsieh 縣[懸]解, "the release of the spirit" (*Chuang Tzu*)

hsüan-yen 玄言, Metaphysical discourse (in the context of Neo-Taoism)

Hsüeh 薛, pre-Ch'in state

hsüeh-shu ssu-hsiang 學術思想, "thought and learning" (learning and thought), modern term for academic and intellectual activity

hsün 訓, admonition; commentary

Hsün K'uang 荀況, T. Ch'ing 卿, ca. 298–238 B.C., the philosopher Hsün Tzu; his surname is also written Sun 孫

hsün-shou 巡狩, Chou era "royal tours of inspection"

Hsün Yüeh 荀悅, T. Chung-yü 仲豫; 148–209, Confucian thinker, author of the *Shen Chien*

Hu Fei Tzu 胡非子, title of no longer extant Mohist work (HS 30)

Hu 苦, modern Hu-hsien 苦縣, reputed birthplace of Lao Tzu

Hu-mu 胡母, Master, or Hu-mu Sheng 胡母生, T. Tzu-tu 子都; early Han Erudit for the *Spring and Autumn Annals*, and fountainhead of *Kung-yang* School traditions

Hu-mu Fu-chih 胡母輔之, T. Yen-kuo 彥國, died at age forty-eight ca. 324 A.D., one of the "unfettered eight"

Hu Shih 胡適, modern scholar

hua 化, to transform, transformation, change

Hua Yuan 華元, sixth-century-B.C. statesman of the State of Sung, pacifist

Huan 桓公, named Yu 友, first Duke of Cheng 鄭, enfeoffed 805 B.C.

Huan 桓公, Duke of Ch'i 齊, reigned 684–642 B.C., first of the Hegemons

Huan Ch'ien 桓謙, active ca. 402–404, rebutted anti-Buddhist arguments of Grand Marshall Huan Hsüan (see below)

Huan Hsüan 桓玄, T. Ching-tao 敬道, A.D. 369–404, Grand Marshall at the Chin court, opponent of Buddhism

Huan T'an 桓譚, T. Chün-shan 君山, 43 B.C. to A.D. 28, Han period thinker, author of the *Hsin Lun* 新論

Huan Wen 桓溫, T. Yuan-tzu 元子, 312–373, a leading general and statesman of

Eastern Chin era

Huan Yi 桓彝, T. Mao-lun 茂倫, 276–328, one of the "unfettered eight"

Huan-yü Chi, or *T'ai-p'ing Huan-yü Chi*, early Sung encyclopedia, see Bibliography, under Yüeh Shih

Huan Yuan 環淵, pre-Ch'in philosopher

Huang, Master 黃生, debater on history from Legalist point of view at court of Han Emperor Ching (156–141 B.C.); teacher of Ssu-ma T'an

Huang-Lao 黃老, Taoist-syncretic school of political theory stressing relative non-action, important in the Han dynasty

huang-po chih shu 黃白之術, alchemical arts, expecially turning base metals into gold

Huang Ti 黃帝, the Yellow Emperor, mythical ruler, supposed progenitor of the Chinese people

Hui Shih 惠施, sophist, statesman, intimate of Chuang Tzu

Hui-t'ung 慧通, died ca. A.D. 478, monk who wrote refutation of Ku Huan's arguments for superiority of Chinese over Barbarians

Hui-yuan 慧遠, 334–416, eminent Buddhist monk of Lu-shan in Kiangsi

hun-hsin 渾心, the "undifferentiating mind" which rulers should adopt (*Lao Tzu*)

Hung Fan Chiu Ch'ou 洪範九疇, "The Great Plan with its Nine Divisions," referring to *Documents*, V/iv/par. 3–4; Legge 323–24

Hung Liang-chi 洪亮吉, T. Chün-chih 君直, Chih-ts'un 稚存, 1746–1809, scholar

Huo Kuang 霍光, T. Tzu-meng 子孟, died 68 B.C., general, statesman

Jan Ch'iu 冉求, T. Tzu-yu 子有; disciple of Confucius

Jan Keng 冉耕, T. Po-niu 白牛, 百牛; disciple of Confucius

Jan Yung 冉雍, T. Chung-kung 仲弓; disciple of Confucius

jen 仁, benevolence, humanity, love

jen 忍, to bear, to suffer; as in *pu jen hsin* 不忍心, "the mind that cannot bear . . . (the suffering of others)," the commiserating mind (*Mencius*)

jen 任, the sense of duty (in political behavior); to appoint; to rely fully on

jen-ai 仁愛, benevolence and love

jen-chih 人治, a government of men, government stressing the human qualities of the governors ahead of the institutional means

jen-chih 仁治, a benevolent government, governing through benevolence

jen-fa 任法, "full reliance on the laws," Legalist political method

jen-hsin 仁心, the benevolent mind

jen-lun 人倫, human relations; the principles of correct human relations in Confucianism; normal, ethical human relations

jen-pen chu-yi 人本主義, "humanism" (modern term)

jen-tao 人道, the Way of mankind, humanity, humaneness

jen-yi 仁義, benevolence and righteousness, formulaic tag for Confucian values, Confucian principles in governing

jen-yi-li-chih 仁義禮智, benevolence, righteousness, propriety and wisdom, the Four (Confucian) Virtues

Jih-sun 日損, daily diminishing, divesting oneself of knowledge and desires day-by-day (*Lao Tzu*)

Ju 儒, the bearers of a tradition in Chou learning; later, "Confucianism" or Confucians

Ju-lai 如來, the Buddha *Tathāgata*

Juan Chi 阮籍, T. Ssu-tsung 嗣宗, 210–263, Neo-Taoist anarchist thinker and literary figure

Juan Fang 阮放, T. Ssu-tu 思度, 280–323, one of the "unfettered eight"

Juan Fou (Fu) 阮孚, T. Yao-chi 遙集, born after 281, active 317–23, son of Juan Hsien 咸, one of the "unfettered eight"

Juan Hsien 阮咸, T. Chung-jung 仲容, nephew of Juan Chi, father of Juan Fou; skilled musician

Jung-ch'eng Shih 容成氏, reputed advisor to the Yellow Emperor of high antiquity

Kan Chung-k'o 甘忠可, author of prognostication manual written about 20 B.C., called *T'ien kuan li pao yuan T'ai-ping Ching* 天官歷包元太平經

Kan Pao 干寶, T. Ling-sheng 令升; fl. early fourth century A.D., writer *kan-ying* 感應, responses (of heaven, i.e. the cosmos, to man); interactions, and theories of, between man's feelings and the cosmos

K'ang-shu 康叔, first Duke of the State of Wei 衞 in early Chou

Kao Ch'ai 高柴, T. Tzu-kao 子羔, disciple of Confucius

Kao Ho 高何, a Mohist follower

Kao Shih Tzu 高石子, a Mohist follower

Kao Yao 皋陶, legendary worthy, Minister of Punishments in the time of Emperor Shun

Kao Yu 高誘, fl. A.D. 205, scholar, annotater of *Huai-nan Tzu* and other works

k'ao-shih, Ritual of 考室之禮, for completion of new royal palace

k'e-ch'ing 客卿, "guest minister"

Keng Chu Tzu 耕柱子, a Mohist follower

keng-shih 更始, a new beginning, institutional new beginnings, Han reign title A.D. 23–24

Ko Hung 葛洪, T. Chih-ch'uan 稚川, ca. 277 to ca. 357, political thinker, author of the *Pao-p'u Tzu*

ko-ming 革命, withdrawal of the Heavenly Mandate; as a modern term, "revolution"

ko-yi 格義, literally, "invoking the meaning"; i.e., matching of terms, a technique used in translating Buddhist works into Chinese

Kou-chien 勾踐, King of the State of Yüeh, fifth century B.C.

ku 孤, orphan, form of the royal "We"

ku 觚, cornered vessel, or four-cornered vessel

ku-fa 骨法, telling a person's fate from signs in the bones of his body; physiognomy

Ku Huan 顧歡, T. Ching-yi 景怡, 420–483, wrote an essay: "Yi-hsia Lun" 夷夏論, "Treatise on the Barbarians and Chinese," maintaining the superiority of Chinese ways over Buddhism

Ku-liang Chuan 穀梁傳, the *Ku-liang Commentary* to the *Spring and Autumn Annals*, written by Ku-liang Ch'ih 赤 of late Warring States era

ku-wen 古文, Old Text tradition, and the school in classical learning based on it

Ku Yung 谷永, T. Tzu-yün 子雲; active 30 B.C., specialist in *Yi-ching* studies and Ching Fang's commentary; prognostication theorist

K'u Huo 苦獲, a Mohist follower

kua 寡, a bereaved person; a form of the royal "We"

Kuan-ch'iu Wang-chih 毌丘望之, commentator on the *Lao Tzu* in Former Han dynasty

Kuan Chung 管仲, reputed author of the *Kuan Tzu*; see under Kuan Yi-wu

kuan-li 冠禮, the rites of capping, for men at about age twenty

Kuan Yen 管嚴, of the surname Chi 姬; father of Kuan Chung

Kuan Yi-wu 管夷吾, better known (by his courtesy name ? as) Kuan Chung 仲, also known as Kuan Ching-chung 管敬中; statesman in service of Duke Huan of Ch'i in the mid-seventh century B.C.; reputed author of the *Kuan Tzu*

Kuan Yin Tzu 關尹子, non-extant Taoist work (HS 30)

Kuan Ying 灌嬰; meritorious official during Han founding, later chief minister to Emperor Wen (179–157 B.C.)

k'uan-jung 寬容, "generous accommodation," in relations with others (*Lao Tzu*)

Kuang Yi 光逸, T. Meng-tsu 孟祖, active 317–322, one of the "unfettered eight"

K'uang Heng 匡衡, fellow student of the Ch'i *Odes* with Yi Feng

k'uang-sheng 狂生, "eccentric" or "madman"; libertarian personality type

kuei 軌, wheeltracks, regulations, to be "on track" or "in order"

kuei-kuei 貴貴, honor and privilege accorded the nobility

kuei-shen 鬼神, spiritual beings, ghosts and spirits

kung 工, craftsmen, artisans, labor, extended effort; one of four ideal occupational categories in society

kung 公, the title of nobility usually translated "duke"; to be just; the realm as commonality; the public interest; (and other derived meanings)

kung 功, merit, accomplishment

Kung-hsi Ai 公皙哀, T. Chi-tz'u 季次, disciple of Confucius

Kung-hsi Ch'ih 公西赤, T. Tzu-hua 子華, disciple of Confucius

kung-li 功利, accomplishment and profit (benefit), utility, utilitarianism

Kung-liang Huan Tzu 公良桓子, man of the state of Wei, with whom Mo Tzu spoke

Kung-shang Kuo 公尙過, a Mohist follower

Kung-shu Pan (P'an) 公輸般[盤], craftsman, builder of attack machinery, against whom Mo Tzu pitted his defensive strategems

Kung-sun Ch'ou 公孫丑, disciple of Mencius

Kung-sun Hung 公孫弘, T. Chi 季, 200–127 B.C., prominent official at Han court

Kung-sun Lung 公孫龍, T. Tzu-shih 子石, third century B.C. (?), philosopher, leader of the School of Dialecticians

Kung-sun Shu 公孫述, died A.D. 36, opponent of the Han Emperor Kuang-wu in the wars of the Han succession

Kung-sun Yang 公孫鞅, better known as Shang Yang 商鞅, or Shang Chün (Lord Shang); died 338 B.C., statesman and Legalist thinker

Kung-sun Yen 公孫衍, professional political advisor of the fourth century B.C.

kung-t'ien 公田, public fields, as element of ancient well-field system

Kung Tzu Mou 公子牟, no longer extant Taoist work (HS 30)

Kung-yang Chuan 公羊傳, the *Kung-yang Commentary* to the *Spring and Autumn Annals*, written by Kung-yang Kao 高 of the Warring States era

Kung-yeh Ch'ang 公冶長, T. Tzu-ch'ang 子長, Tzu-chih 子之, disciple of Confucius

K'ung Chi 孔伋, T. Tzu-ssu 子思, grandson of Confucius

K'ung Ch'iu 孔丘, T. Chung-ni 仲尼, the philosopher Confucius

K'ung Fang-shu 孔防叔, great-grandfather of Confucius

K'ung Fu-chia 孔父嘉, ancestor of Confucius

K'ung Jung 孔融, T. Wen-chü 文舉, A.D. 153–208, twentieth-generation descendant of Confucius; one of the Seven Masters of the Chien-an Period

K'ung-k'uei (yi) 孔悝邑, city in Lu at the time of Confucius

K'ung Shu-liang Ho 孔叔梁紇, father of Confucius

kuo-chün 國君, "Ruler of the state" (*Mo Tzu*)

Kuo Lin-tsung 郭林宗, leader of students in anti-eunuch faction at Later Han court, ca. A.D. 166–169

Kuo Hsiang 郭象, T. Tzu-hsüan 子宣; died A.D. 312, Neo-Taoist thinker, author of a commentary on the *Chuang Tzu*

kuo-tzu 國子, "scions of the realm," sons of noble families in Chou times; later, men admitted to the National University (Imperial Academy) at the capital

Lai Chu 萊朱, also known as Chung-hui 仲虺, worthy assistant of King T'ang, the Shang dynasty founder

Lan-ling 蘭陵, city in northeastern Ch'u (modern Shantung) where Hsün Tzu served as governor

Lang Yi 郎顗, statesman during reigns of Han Emperors An and Shun, A.D. 107–144

Lao Ai 嫪毐, a supposed eunuch, central figure in a scandal at the Ch'in court involving Lü Pu-wei in 237 B.C.

Lao-Chuang 老莊, a movement in philosophical Taoism with anarchistic tendencies, drawing on the *Lao Tzu* and the *Chuang Tzu*

Lao Lai Tzu 老萊子, said by some to be the same as Lao Tzu

Lao P'eng 老彭, or P'eng Tzu 彭祖, the Methusaleh of Chinese legend; sometimes identified with Lao Tzu; Waley calls him "the Chinese Nestor"

Lao Tan 老耼, Lao Tzu (?), also Lao Tan 老儋

Lao Tzu 老子, the reputed founder of Taoism

Lei Hai-tsung 雷海宗, modern historian (see Bibliography)

li 禮, rites, propriety, institutions; *Li*, the ritual classics, esp. the *Li Chi*

li 理, principle, the orderly principles of

the cosmos; reason, rationalism

li 里, "mile"; hamlet

li 利, profit, benefit, advantage; see also *kung-li*, "utilitarianism"

li 力, effort, striving, endeavor (*Lieh Tzu*); force, strength

li 吏, minor official, clerk; in pre-imperial usage often equivalent to later use of *kuan* "official"

li 歷, the calendar, calendrical calculations

Li 厲王, Chou King Li, reigned 878–842 B.C., symbol of Chou decline

li-chang 里長, hamlet chief, neighborhood headman

Li Chi 李季, modern scholar, archeologist and historian

li-chiao 禮敎, "rites and teachings," Confucian normative concepts and methods, Confucian ethical formalism; see also *ming-chiao*

Li Ch'ung 李充, T. Hung-tu 弘度, active early fourth century A.D., scholar, wrote essays opposing Taoist metaphysics but defended Confucian-Taoist values; devised *ssu-pu* 四部 system for Chin imperial library

Li Erh 李耳, T. Po-yang 伯陽, pth. Tan 聃, 耼, names of the philosopher Lao Tzu as given in one account cited in the *Shih Chi*

Li Hsien 李賢, 651–684, T'ang imperial prince, annotator of the *Hou Han Shu*

Li Hsiung 李熊, Grand Minister over the Masses, under Kung-sun Shu at time of Later Han restoration

li-hsüeh 理學, the movement in Confucian thought usually called Neo-Confucian Rationalism, of the eleventh century A.D. and later

Li Hsün 李尋, died 5 B.C., specialist on the *Documents* and prognostication theory

Li K'e (K'o), see Li K'uei

Li Ku 李固, statesman during reign of Later Han Emperor Huan, 147–167

Li K'uei 李悝, also written Li K'e (K'o) 克; late fifth century B.C., legal thinker, author of the *Fa Ching* (*Classic of Law*)

li kung 立功, to achieve merit

Li Shan 李善, died A.D. 689, scholar

Li Shang 酈商, prominent general during the Han dynasty founding

li-shih 吏師, or *yi li wei shih* 以吏爲師, magistrates (i.e., local officials) serving as the only teachers (Legalist principle)

Li Ssu 李斯, ca. 280–208 B.C., Chief Minister of the Ch'in dynasty under the First Emperor

Li T'ung 李通, prognosticator ca. A.D. 20 who favored the Han Emperor Kuang-wu

Li Yi 李頤, Chin dynasty commentator on the *Chuang Tzu*

li-yi 禮義, "rites and righteousness"; Confucian virtues seen as underlying all government

Li Yi-chi 酈食其, Confucian scholar who aided the Han dynasty founder

Li Ying 李膺, T. Yuan-li 元禮, 110–169, leader of students in anti-eunuch faction at Later Han court, ca. 166–169

Li Yü 李育, fl. A.D. 70–90, specialist in calendrical calculations and *Spring and Autumn* studies

li-yüeh 禮樂, "rites and music," basic Confucian institutions; broadly, the institutionalization of Confucian norms

Liang 梁, one of the Three (successor) States of Chin, in the Warring States era, more properly known as Wei 魏

Lieh Yü-k'ou 列禦寇, the pre-Ch'in philosopher Lieh Tzu, to whom the later *Lieh Tzu* is attributed

lien 廉, integrity

Lien P'o 廉頗, third-century-B.C. general and statesman of the State of Chao

lien-tan 煉丹, "smelt cinnabar," used literally and, more commonly, as metaphor for physical and spiritual disciplines associated with Taoism and Neo-Taoism

Lin-tzu 臨淄, capital city of pre-Ch'in State of Ch'i, noted for wealth and commerce

Lin-wu, Lord of, see Fan K'uai

ling 令, commands; as in terms *fa-ling* 法令 and *lü-ling* 律令, laws and regulations in Legalist statecraft

Liu An 劉安, 179?–122 B.C., Prince of Huai-nan, under whose auspices the *Huai-nan Tzu* was written

Liu Cheng-yü 劉正輿, third century A.D., nephew of Wang Pi, important in the transmission of the text of the *Lieh Tzu*

Liu Chi, see Liu Pang

"Liu-chia yao-chih" 六家要旨, "Essentials of the Six Schools," of Ssu-ma T'an (*Shih Chi* 130)

Liu Chih 劉秩, T'ang dynasty scholar

liu-ch'in 六親, "the six relationships" of kinship, in the broadest sense

liu-ch'ing 六情, the six feelings, emotions

Liu-hsia Hui 柳下惠, pre-Ch'in political figure discussed by Mencius and others

Liu Hsiang 劉向, T. Tzu-cheng 子政; 77–6 B.C., scholar, bibliographer, political thinker (see also Bibliography)

Liu Hsieh 劉勰, T. Yen-ho 彥和, 465–522, literary theorist; pro-Buddhist writer

Liu Hsin 劉歆 (Hsiu 秀), died A.D. 23, scholar, son of Liu Hsiang

liu-hsing 六興, the Six Policies, constituting a comprehensive economic order (*Kuan Tzu*)

Liu Hsüan 劉玄, of the Han imperial line, after death of Wang Mang, claimed the restored Han throne as the Keng-shih 更始 Emperor, A.D. 23–24

Liu Ling 劉伶, T. Po-lun 伯倫, third century A.D., Neo-Taoist figure famous as drinker; one of Seven Sages of the Bamboo Grove

Liu Pang 劉邦, formal name Liu Chi 季, founding emperor (Kao-tsu 高祖) of the Han dynasty

liu-shih 六蝨, the Six Parasites of the State, i.e., the Confucian moralistic virtues, according to Lord Shang

Liu T'ao 六韜, ancient work on military subjects

liu te 六德, Six Virtues, as listed in the *Chou Li* ("Ti-kuan Ta-ssu t'u"), i.e., *chih* 知, wisdom; *jen* 仁, benevolence; *sheng* 聖, understanding; *yi* 義, judgment; *chung* 中, 忠, moderation; and *ho* 和, compatibility

liu yi 六儀, Six Ritual Deportments (*Chou Li*)

liu yi 六藝, the Six Disciplines (six arts, or skills); sometimes identified with the Six Classics

liu yü 六欲, the Six Desires, the animal passions

Lo-fu Mountains 羅浮山, scenic mountain range in Kwangtung Province, associated with Ko Hung

Lo Shu 洛書, the Lo Writing, together with the River Chart, important prognostication documents of Han times

Lo-yi 洛邑, the Chou eastern capital, i.e., Lo-yang 洛陽

Lou Ching 婁敬, advisor to the Han Founder

Lu 魯, Chou era state; region in modern Shantung

Lu Chi 陸機, T. Shih-heng 士衡, 261–303, literary and intellectual figure

Lu Chia 陸賈, advisor to the Han founder, reputed author of the *Hsin Yü* 新語 (*New Discourses*)

Lu yün fa, see [*Ho-t'u*] *Lu yün fa*

lü 律, the pitchpipes; regulations, laws

Lü An 呂安, T. Chung-t'i 仲悌, died A.D. 262, Neo-Taoist personage

Lü Liu-liang 呂留良, 1629–1683, scholar, anti-Manchu writer

Lü Pu-shu 呂步舒, student of Tung Chung-shu in Former Han dynasty

Lü Pu-wei 呂不韋, died 237 B.C., Chief Minister to Prince Cheng, the future First Emperor; assembled scholars to write the *Lü-shih Ch'un-ch'iu*

Lü Shang 呂尚, surname Chiang 姜, known also as T'ai-kung Wang 太公望, first Duke of the State of Ch'i at time of Chou founding

luan (*ta*) *lun* 亂[大]倫, to subvert the proper human relations; to subvert the Great Relationship of ruler and servitor

man 蠻 or *man-yi* 蠻夷, "Barbarians of the South"

Mao-men, Law of 茆門之法, a law promulgated in Ch'u, ca. 600 B.C.

Mei Fu 梅福, first-century-B.C. personage

men-fa 門閥, the great clans of the elite in Han and post-Han times

men-hu 門戶, school or other faction; attitudes of factional exclusiveness

Meng 蒙, pre-Ch'in state

Meng clan 孟氏, one of Three Great Families of Lu in the time of Confucius

Meng K'ang 孟康, T. Kung-hsiu 公休; third-century-A.D. scholar, writer, annotator of Yi Feng's and other texts in the Ch'i tradition of the *Odes*

Meng K'o 孟軻, T. Tzu-yü 子輿; 372–279 B.C., the philosopher Mencius

Meng Sheng 孟勝, a Mohist follower

Meng T'ien 蒙恬, able general of Ch'in under the First Emperor

Meng T'ung 孟通, aid to Wang Wang

min kuei lun 民貴論, theory of the value, importance, of the people (*Mencius*)

min-pen 民本, the fundamental importance of the people, political theory of Mencius

Min Sun 閔損, T. Tzu-ch'ien 子騫, disciple of Confucius

min-t'i 民體, the social form of the people (*Kuan Tzu*)

min-tsu ssu-hsiang 民族思想, nationalistic (racist, ethnocentric) thought (modern term)

min wei kuei 民爲貴, the people are the (most) important element in the state—not the ruler (*Mencius*)

min-yüeh 民約, the "social contract" of European political thought

ming 明, light, of the discerning mind (Neo-Taoist term)

ming 命, fate, personal fate, destiny of a dynasty or state; life, life span, an individual's life; the ruler's imperium or power to command, a command, a decree

Ming-chia 名家, the School of Names, or Nominalists

ming-chiao 名教, Confucian moral teachings, often interchangeable with *li-chiao*, Confucian ethical formalism

ming fen 名分, "names and duties," role and responsibility

ming hsüeh 名學, logical theory, especially of the Later Mohists

ming-kuei 明鬼, proving that spirits exist and dominate human affairs (*Mo Tzu*)

ming-shih 名實, "names and realities"; doctrines stressing need for correspondence of, as political method, e.g., Legalists

ming-yün 冥運, the unseen cyclic movement, or unseen destiny, in Neo-Taoist cosmology

Mo-shou 墨守, the Mohist defense, the stubborn defense in war or in rhetoric

Mo Ti 墨翟, the philosopher Mo Tzu 墨子

Mu Ho 穆賀, contemporary of Mo Tzu

Mu, the field at 牧野, important battlefield site in the founding of the Chou dynasty

Nan-kung Ching-shu 南宮敬叔, disciple of Confucius, possibly the same person as Nan-kung K'uo

Nan-kung K'uo 南宮括, T. Tzu-jung 子容, disciple of Confucius

neng 能, *neng-che* 能者, able, ability, "the man of ability will be approved by the masses" (*Yi-ching*, "Hsi-tz'u, hsia" 12)

Ning Ch'eng 寧成, administrator during the reigns of Han Emperors Ching and Wu, late first century B.C.

no-jo 懦弱, "yielding softness' (*Lao Tzu*)

nung 農, farmers, farming; one of four ideal occupational categories

nung-chia 農家, "Agriculturalist School" of pre-Ch'in thought, led by Hsü Hsing

nung-kung 農工, agriculture and the crafts, farmers and artisans

nung-sang 農桑, agriculture and sericulture, i.e., the basic productive activity of man

niu-ting 牛鼎, ox cauldron, classical allusion

pa 霸, also written *pa* 伯, hegemon; force, brute power

pa-cheng 霸政, 伯政 "rule by hegemon"; "rule by force"

pa-kuo 霸國, hegemonic state, i.e., ruled by force, not by benevolence and righteousness

pa shu 八術, Eight Methods, by which officials commit villainies against the ruler (*Han Fei Tzu*)

pa ta 八達, the "unfettered eight," uninhibited Neo-Taoist eccentrics of the third century A.D.

pai, see *po*

Pan Ku 班固, T. Meng-chien 孟堅, A.D. 32–92, Confucian political thinker, historian (see Bibliography)

Pan Piao 班彪, T. Shu-p'i 叔皮, A.D. 3–54, statesman, historian, father of Pan Ku

P'an-keng 盤庚, Yin (Shang) ruler of ca. 1450 B.C., moved the Shang capital to Yin

P'an Ni 潘尼, T. Cheng-shu 正叔, ca. 245–311, author of a political essay: "An-shen lun" 安身論

Pao Ching-yen 鮑敬言, active early fourth

century A.D., anarchist political thinker quoted by Ko Hung in *Pao-p'u Tzu* ("wai-p'ien" *ch.* 48)

pao-min 保民, protect the people

Pao Shu(-ya) 鮑叔牙, a Great Officer in Ch'i in seventh century B.C., friend of Kuan Chung

p'ei-ch'en 陪臣, subsidiary ministers of the Great Officers in Chou era

P'ei K'ai 裴楷, active ca. 260–280, associate of Juan Chi, Neo-Taoist personage

P'ei Wei 裴頠, T. Yi-min 逸民, 267–300, Confucian thinker opposed to Neo-Taoist metaphysics

pen 本, fundamental, the fundamental; in Confucian theory: agriculture and sericulture; in Mencius: the people; in Mo Tzu: historical precedents basic to validation of his "three standards"

P'eng Keng 彭更, disciple of Mencius

P'eng Meng 彭蒙, pre-Ch'in Taoist thinker

P'eng Tsu 彭祖, the mythical Chinese Methuselah; see also Lao P'eng

Pi Cho 畢卓, T. Mao-shih 茂世, active 318–20, one of the "unfettered eight"

Pi-kung 畢公, of Chou royal line, ancestor of the Kings of Wei

p'i-fu 匹夫, an ordinary man, the masses

P'i-lu, the Law of 被廬之法, promulgated in Chin in 633 B.C.

pieh 別, to fix distinctions in society (*Hsün Tzu*); partial, not whole, e.g., partial man, ruler, as opposed to universal man, ruler (*Mo Tzu*)

pieh hei-pai 別黑白, "Separate white from black," i.e., to be arbitrary—an error of rulers (Taoism)

pieh Mo 別墨, the Later Mohists, the Mohist logicians

Pien-che 辯者, the School of debaters or sophists; the Dialecticians

Pien Ch'üeh 扁鵲, physician of legendary skills in Warring States era

Pien-fu chih chia 變復之家, the School of Calamity-Response, a school of thought concerned with interpretation of portents

pien-hei-pai erh ting-yi-tsun 辨黑白而定一尊, "distinguish white from black and estab-

lish one exalted ruler," phrase used to refer to the arbitrary and authoritarian policies of the First Emperor

Pien K'un 卞壼, 281–328, son of Pien Ts'ui 粹; eminent official of the Chin dynasty

p'ien 篇, essays, chapters

pin-shih 賓師, guest teacher (of the state)

p'ing-chun 平準, standardization of prices, and offices for, in early Han era; also translated "the balanced standard" (B. Watson)

po 伯, earl, title of nobility; as hegemon, read *pa*

Po Ch'i 白起, also read Pai Ch'i; commoner chief minister and eminent general in State of Ch'in, fourth century B.C.

Po-chia 百家 (*Pai-chia*), the Hundred Schools of pre-Ch'in thought

Po-ch'in 伯禽, son of the Duke of Chou, enfieffed in Lu, late twelfth century B.C.

Po Hsiang hsien-sheng 伯象先生, title of book listed under "Eclectic School" (HS 30)

po hsing 百姓 (*pai hsing*), the hundred clans, the people

Po-hu t'ung 白虎通, Han scholarly work, see Bibliography under Pan Ku

Po-kung Yi 北宮錡, disciple of Mencius

Po-li Hsi 百里奚[傒], worthy minister of Duke Mu of Ch'in, 658–620 B.C.

Po-shih 博士, Erudit, also translated: scholars of wide learning, an official title in the early empire

Po-shih ch'en-hsien tui 博士臣賢對, title of book listed under the "Eclectic" school (HS 30)

po-shih chi-chung 博施濟衆, "extensive dispensation of succor to the masses," Confucian ideal

Po-yi and Shu-ch'i 伯夷叔齊, suicide recluses of early Chou; symbols of loyalty to the ruler and dynasty

pu-chao chih ch'en 不召之臣, a "servitor who cannot be summoned" (*Mencius*)

pu-jen 不忍, *pu-jen-hsin* 不忍心, "unable to bear," "the mind that is unable to bear" . . . the suffering of others; the commiserating mind (*Mencius*)

pu-ku 不穀, unlucky, unworthy; a form of

the royal "We"

Pu Shang 卜商, T. Tzu-hsia 子夏; disciple of Confucius

pu-yi ch'ing hsiang 布衣卿相, "ministers and premiers of commoner status"

p'u 樸[朴], "the uncarved block," pristine Nature, simplicity (Taoism)

P'u-ku 蒲姑, ancient regional name of Ch'i, in modern Shantung

P'u-ou, Law of 僕區之法, penal code of seventh century B.C. State of Ch'u (Legge, *Tso*, Chao 7, has "Puh-gow," i.e., P'u-kou)

San-chang chih fa 三章之法, the Three Articles, earliest Han dynasty law code

san cheng 三正, the Three Beginnings, term used by Ku Yung of Former Han

san fa 三法, the three methods, used interchangeably with *san piao* three standards (*Mo Tzu*)

san huo 三惑, the three fallacies of the sophists and debaters (*Hsün Tzu*)

san huang 三皇, Three Emperors, of mythical antiquity, variously identified

san-kang 三綱, the Three Bonds, of ruler-servitor, father-son, husband-wife, stressed by Confucians

san kuei 三歸, private diversions of Kuan Chung, variously described (*Analects* III/22)

San Kung 三公, the Three Senior Lords, highest-ranking ministers of early imperial government

San-min Chu-yi 三民主義, the *Three People's Principles*, lectures delivered by Sun Yat-sen (1924)

san piao 三表, the three standards (*Mo Tzu*); cf. *san fa*

san p'o 三破, the Three Destructions (of the individual, the family and the state) caused by Buddhism, according to Six Dynasties critics

san shih 三勢, three potentialities, term of political analysis used by Hsün Yüeh

san ta 三大, the Three Great Ones: heaven, earth, the king (*Lao Tzu*)

san ts'ai 三才, Three Powers, three dynamic elements of the cosmos, usually defined as heaven, earth and man

san t'ung 三統, the Three Systems, also translated Three Sequences (Tung Chung-shu)

San Yi-sheng 散宜生, Minister at the Chou court in the time of King Wen, twelfth century B.C.

Sang Hung-yang 桑弘羊, 152–80 B.C., economic expert at the court of Han Emperor Wu

seh 瑟, ancient musical instrument

seng-ch'ieh 僧伽 (samgha), or *seng-t'u* 僧徒 the Sangha, the Buddhist monastic community; a monk

Seng Shun 僧順, Buddhist monk active ca. 402–404, wrote *Shih San-p'o Lun* 釋三破論, rebutting the theories of the Three Destructions in Buddhism

sha-men 沙門 (Sanskrit *śramaṇa*), monks observing the ascetic regimen; monks in general

shan 善, goodness e.g., of human nature (*Mencius*)

Shan T'ao 山濤, T. Chü-yuan 巨源, 205–283, one of the Seven Sages of the Bamboo Grove

shang 商, merchants, traders, commercial activity; one of four ideal occupational categories of society

Shang 商, second of the Three Dynasties of antiquity, ca. 1750–1111 B.C.; the latter half from about 1450 B.C. also called Shang-Yin 殷, or Yin, from the name of the new capital built at that time

shang chih 尚質, esteem for simplicity, as opposed to refinement, *wen*

shang-ch'ing 上卿, a chief minister, or a minister accorded highest rank and prestige if not substantive authority

shang hsien 尚賢, elevation of the worthy (*Mo Tzu*)

Shang-shu chung-hou 尚書中候, no longer extant Han apocryphal work related to the *Documents*

shang t'ung 尚同, identification with the superior (*Mo Tzu*)

shang wen 尚文, esteem for refinement, as opposed to *shang chih*, esteem for simplicity

Shang Yang 商鞅, i.e., Kung-sun Yang, or Lord Shang

Shang-yen 商奄, an ancient regional name of Lu in modern Shantung

She Chi 社稷, Spirits (or Altars) of Land

and Grain; the principal shrine and symbol of the state and the ruling dynasty

she-hsiang 攝相, or *she-hsing hsiang-shih* 攝行相事, "concurrently chief minister"

shen 身, the body, the physical person, the human person

shen 神, spirits, the spiritual, the divine, spiritual power; the supernal; supreme quality of human experience

shen-ch'i 神氣, "dynamic forces" (*Huai-nan Tzu*); air or manner of a person; imposing qualities

shen-ch'i 神器, the "divine vessel," metaphor for the imperial position and the emperor

shen-chou 神州, China, as the Divine Province (Tsou Yen); the "wondrous realm," euphemism for the ancient center of China in the Yellow River valley, hence China in general

Shen-nung 神農, the Divine Agriculturalist, mythic ruler of high antiquity and culture hero

Shen Pu-hai 申不害, died 337 B.C., thinker of the Legalist tradition; or, of the Statecraft School

Shen Shu-shih 申叔時, statesman of Warring States era State of Ch'u

Shen Tao 慎到, ca. 350 to ca. 275 B.C., Legalist philosopher

Shen-t'u Kang 申屠剛, during the Wang Mang era, supported the view that the Han would be restored

sheng 生, alive, life, to give birth, to generate, to produce

sheng 笙, ancient musical instrument

sheng 聖, the Sage, sageliness, "saint" in Christian usage; profound understanding

"*sheng chih shih che*" 聖之時者, "the Sage whose acts display timeliness," said by Mencius of Confucius

Sheng Ch'o 勝綽, a Mohist follower

sheng-p'ing 升平, the Age of Ascending Peace (Ho Hsiu); in K'ang Yu-wei's interpretation of the Three Ages, also translated "the Age of Approaching Peace"

sheng wang 聖王, the Sage Kings of antiquity

sheng-yung 省用, frugality (*Kuan Tzu*)

Shih 詩, or *Shih-ching* 詩經, the *Odes*, or *Classic of Poetry*

shih 士, knights, officers, in early Chou usage; scholar, literatus, scholar-official, in Warring States and later usage

shih 勢, power, force, as political power; the "compelling force of circumstances," hence, conditions, circumstances, balance of forces

Shih Chiao 尸佼, legal expert at court of Ch'in in fourth century B.C.

Shih Chiao 史角, Chiao the Archivist, person at early Chou court

shih-chih 勢治, governing through overwhelming power (Legalism)

shih-ch'ing 世卿, hereditary chief ministers, in Chou society; inherited official positions in general

Shih Ch'ung 石崇, T. Chi-lun 季倫, 249–300, Chin era sybarite

Shih-fu 師服, eight-century-B.C. person

Shih Hsien 石顯, died 32 B.C., favorite of the Han Emperor Yuan

shih-ju 師儒, "local teacher" (*Chou Li*)

Shih K'uang 師曠, music master of the sixth century B.C. State of Chin

Shih Lo 石勒, founder of Later Chao dynasty of fourth century A.D.

shih-min 石民, the "bedrock people" of the state, i.e., the common people (*Kuan Tzu*)

Shih Nei-chuan 詩內傳, no longer extant Han apocryphal work related to the *Odes*

Shih Po 史伯, Grand Recorder of Chou court, ninth century B.C.

Shih shih 師氏, "Masters of Instruction" (*Li Chi*)

shih-shu 時數, time factors of fate (Wang Ch'ung)

shih ta-fu 士大夫, classes of "officers" and "great officers" in Chou society; scholar-officials and the gentry elite of imperial times

Shih wei fan li shu 詩緯汜歷樞, Han period apocryphal work on the *Odes*

shih-wen 釋文, commentary on a word or passage in exegetical works

Shih Yi 史佚, early Chou personage; name of no-longer extant Mohist book

Shih Yü 史魚, the historian Yü praised by Confucius, an honest minister in State of Wei, ca. 500 B.C., whose name was Shih Ch'iu 史鰌 T. Tzu-yü, 子魚

shih yü erh wen pu-yü 實與而文不與, "Actualities (of history) allow this but the style (of didactic historiography) does not allow it," formula used in Kung-yang and Ku-liang Commentaries

shih-yün 世運, dominant cosmic influence on an age (Tsou Yen)

shou-hei 守黑, "keeping to the black," identifying with the passive or the negative (Lao Tzu)

shou ming 受命, "receiving the Mandate"

Shu 書, or Shang Shu 尙書, Shu-ching 書經, the Documents, or Classic of History

shu 疏 (su), sub-commentary (to chu 注) in classical exegesis

Shu clan 叔氏, one of Three Families dominant in Lu, in time of Confucius

shu 術, methods, an aspect of Legalism, or of statist statecraft, associated with Shen Pu-hai and Han Fei Tzu

shu 數, numbers, numerology, determinant, and many derived meanings

shu-chih 術治, statecraft, in the sense of governing through political methods as contrasted with power, laws, institutions or ethics

Shu Hsiang 叔向, statesman in Chin ca. 536 B.C. who opposed the laws

shu shih 庶士, the "common knight," in Chou social system

Shu-shu-chia 數術家, School of Numerology Diviners; theorists about cosmic process who utilized numerology

Shu-sun T'ung 叔孫通, Confucian scholar who served the First Emperor, then the Han Founder

Shu-yü 叔虞, younger brother of Chou King Ch'eng, eleventh century B.C.

Shun 舜, or Yü-ti Shun 虞帝舜, "Emperor Shun of Yü," ancient emperor and ideal ruler symbol

shun-min 順民, "following the people's wishes" (Kuan Tzu)

ssu-cheng 四政, Four Policies, of Confucians, held to be harmful by the Mohists

Ssu-ch'eng Tzu-han 司城子罕, usurping chief minister in the pre-Ch'in State of Sung

Ssu Chuan 駟歂, chief minister in Cheng, sixth century B.C., who had Teng Hsi put to death

Ssu-k'ou 司寇, "Minister of Crime," or minister of penal matters, in various states during the Chou era

Ssu-k'ung 司空, Minister of Works

Ssu-ma 司馬, "Grand Marshall," or a principal military officer

Ssu-ma Chao 司馬昭, T. Tzu-shang 子上, 211–265, posthumously known as Emperor Wen of the State of Chin, father of Ssu-ma Yen

Ssu-ma Ch'ien 司馬遷, T. Tzu-ch'ang 子長; 145–90 B.C., historian, author of the Shih Chi

Ssu-ma Hsi 司馬喜, courtier of the State of Chung-shan in Warring States era

Ssu-ma Keng 司馬耕, T. Tzu-niu 子牛; disciple of Confucius

Ssu-ma Piao 司馬彪, died A.D. 306, scholar and exegete

Ssu-ma T'an 司馬談, died 110 B.C. (?), father of Ssu-ma Ch'ien; Taoist-inclined thinker and historian of thought

Ssu-ma Yen 司馬炎, 236–290, Emperor Wu of the Chin dynasty

Ssu-ma Yi 司馬懿, T. Chung-ta 仲達; 179–251, chancellor in Three Kingdoms state of Wei; prepared for the usurpation effected for his grandson Ssu-ma Yen, first emperor of the Chin dynasty

Ssu-ma Yüeh 司馬越, fl. ca. A.D. 300, Prince of Tung-hai 東海 of the Chin imperial clan; patron of Kuo Hsiang

ssu-min 四民, the four ideal occupational categories of society: scholar-officials, farmers, craftsmen, and merchants

ssu-tuan 四端, the "Four Beginnings," of virtue, in human nature (Mencius)

ssu-wei 四維, the four cords, of political morality, i.e., li propriety, yi righteousness, lien integrity, and ch'ih the sense of shame (Kuan Tzu)

su, subcommentary, see shu

su 素, unadorned, plain, simple, the ideal of simplicity in Taoism

Su Ch'in 蘇秦, died 317 B.C., leading Diplomatist of Warring States era

Su Ching 蘇竟, during Wang Mang era,

supported the view that the Han dynasty would be restored

su-ming lun 宿命論, fatalism (modern term)

Su-wang 素王, the "Uncrowned King," a term applied to Confucius by certain later Confucians

Sui Fei Tzu 隨非子, title of a lost Mohist work (HS 30)

Sui Hung 眭弘[宏], T. Meng 孟; active 80–70 B.C., New Text scholar, prognostication theorist, *Spring and Autumn Annals* specialist

sun 損, to diminish (desires and activities), a Taoist attitude toward government; see also *jih-sun*

Sun Hsien 孫咸, appointed "general to subdue the *Ti* Barbarians" by the Later Han Emperor Kuang-wu

Sun Pin 孫臏, commoner chief minister and military expert in pre-Ch'in State of Ch'i

Sun Sheng 孫盛, T. An-kuo 安國; ca. 307 to ca. 385, Confucian-minded scholar-official who wrote "*Lao Tan fei ta-sheng lun*" 老聃非大聖論, transmitted Ching Fang's views received via Kan Pao

Sun Wu 孫武, or Sun Tzu 孫子; pre-Ch'in writer on military matters; reputed author of *Sun Tzu Ping-fa* 孫子兵法

Sung 宋, Chou era State, home of Shang-Yin descendants; Southern dynasty (Liu Sung), 420–78; dynasty (Chao Sung) 960–1279

Sung Hsing 宋鈃, see Sung K'eng

Sung K'eng 宋牼, prominent Mohist follower, also called Sung Hsing

ta-chih 大治, the Great Order of good government (*Kuan Tzu*); the "Supreme Governance" (*Huai-nan Tzu*)

ta-fu 大夫, Great Officer, hereditary office in Chou government; an office holder in imperial times

Ta-fu Statute 大府之憲, Code of the State of Wei 魏, possibly long antecedent to fifth century B.C. when first documented

Ta Ssu-nung 大司農, or *Ta Nung*, "Minister of Agriculture" in Han with functions somewhat analogous to later imperial era *Hu Pu* (Ministry of Revenues)

ta-t'ung 大同, the ideal of the Great Community, or Great Unity

ta-yi 大義, the "ultimate rightness," the standard for which is heaven (Tung Chung-shu)

"*ta-yi mieh-ch'in*" 大義滅親, "a higher principle of righteousness supersedes family relationships," said by the Duke of Chou

Tai 代, small state eliminated in Warring States era

Tai Sheng 戴聖, and his nephew Tai Te 戴德; Han period classical scholars, compilers of versions of the *Li Chi*

t'ai-ch'ing 太清, the Great Purity, political ideal in *Huai-nan Tzu*

t'ai-hsüan 太玄, the Great Mystery, Taoist cosmological concept

T'ai-miao 太廟, the Great Temple, ancestral shrine of the rulers

T'ai-kung Wang, see Lü Shang

Tan 儋, the Grand Historian (T'ai-shih 太史) of the State of Chou, sometimes said to have been the same person as Lao Tzu, or Lao Tan

Tan-fu 單父, also read Shan-fu, city in Lu in time of Confucius

T'an 郯, small state eliminated in Warring States period

T'an-t'ai Mieh-ming 澹臺滅明, T. Tzu-yü 子羽, disciple of Confucius who later taught in Ch'u

T'ang 湯 or Ch'eng T'ang 成湯, founder of the Shang dynasty of antiquity, ca. 1750 B.C.

T'ang 唐, fief of Shu-yü in early Chou dynasty, 618–906

T'ang Ku-kuo 唐姑果, a Mohist follower

T'ang-shu 唐叔, founder of Chin ducal line in early Chou

Tao 道, the Way

Tao-an 道安, 312–385, eminent Buddhist monk

Tao-chia 道家, the Taoist school; a Taoist

Tao-heng 道恆, active 405–418, eminent monk and writer on Buddhism

Tao shu 道術, the art of the *Tao*, or the methods of *Tao* (*Chuang Tzu*); "ways and teachings" of antiquity

Tao t'ung 道統, "the transmission of the Way," of the *Tao*, or, of orthodoxy in a line of teachings

T'ao Ch'ien 陶潛, T. Yuan-ming 淵明; 365–427, poet, Neo-Taoist thinker; wrote "T'ao-hua-yuan Chi" 桃花園記 expressing anarchist sentiment

te 德, in Confucianism, ethical nature of man, virtue, the ethical impulse; in Taoism, power, innate capacity of things, *virtus*

te-chih 得志, to realize one's ambitions, to achieve one's will, to succeed

Teng Chang 鄧章, prominent official at courts of Han Emperors Wen and Ching, exponent of Huang-Lao political thought

Teng Hsi 鄧析, pre-Ch'in philosopher and legal expert, to whom is attributed the Nominalist School work the *Teng Hsi Tzu*

Teng Ling Tzu 鄧陵子, a Mohist follower

T'eng 滕, pre-Ch'in state

T'eng Keng 滕更, disciple of Mencius

Ti 翟, name of a Mohist follower, native of Cheng, surname unknown

ti-chih 地支, the set of twelve characters used in the sexagenary cycle

ti-li 地利, earth's benefits, advantages, and ways of exploiting them (*Kuan Tzu*)

t'i 體, body, forms, embodiment, the essentials of something

t'i-yung 體用, "essence and function"

tien-hsing 典刑, laws and penalties, as tools of governing

T'ien, family of 田氏, rulers of the State of Ch'i from their usurpation about 385 B.C. until the Ch'in unification in 221 B.C.

T'ien Ch'ang 田常, or T'ien Ch'eng Tzu 成子; great grandfather of T'ien Ho who gained the ducal throne in Ch'i about 385 B.C.; started the usurpation process

t'ien chen 天眞, the natural reality of things; pristine nature of persons (Taoism); näiveté

T'ien Chi 田忌, general in the State of Ch'i, fourth century B.C.

t'ien chih 天職, the "celestial office," the imperial office (*Hsün Tzu*)

t'ien chih 天志, the will (purpose) of Heaven (*Mo Tzu*)

T'ien Chiu 田鳩, a Mohist follower

T'ien Ch'iu Tzu 田俅子, title of a lost Mohist work

T'ien-chu 天竺, India, as known to Chinese Buddhists in early imperial era

t'ien-ch'üan 天權, "heaven's authority," invoked to restrain rulers in early Han era, an explanation of the cosmic process

t'ien-chüeh 天爵, "natural nobility," innate capacity to achieve nobility through self-cultivation

t'ien-fang 天放, natural freedom, possessed by the ordinary people (*Chuang Tzu*)

T'ien Fen 田蚡, died 131 B.C., prominent Confucian official during reigns of Former Han Emperors Wen, Ching and Wu

t'ien-hsin 天心, "the mind of heaven" (Tung Chung-shu)

T'ien Ho 田和, died 384 B.C., usurper of the Ch'i throne

t'ien-hsia 天下, "all under heaven," "the world," or "the Empire"

t'ien-hsia kuei-jen 天下歸仁, "everything under heaven will revert to benevolence" (*Analects* XII/1), Confucian political ideal based on a sentence of widely varying interpretations

T'ien Hsiang Tzu 田襄子, a Mohist follower

t'ien-hsing 天性, the natural, hence perfect, character of beings (*Chuang Tzu*)

t'ien-kuan 天官, "officers of heaven," officials appointed by the Sage Rulers of antiquity (Wang Fu)

t'ien-li 天理, "heaven's orderly principle" (Tung Chung-shu); cosmic principle

t'ien-li chih tzu-jan 天理之自然, the spontaneity of nature's principles (Neo-Taoism)

t'ien-li 天吏, "heaven's agent" (*Mencius*)

t'ien lo 天樂, heavenly happiness, or sharing the full joy of nature, a state of mind (*Chuang Tzu*)

t'ien-ming 天命, Mandate of Heaven; also, the decrees of heaven, the will of heaven, heaven's (Nature's) wish or disposition, etc.

T'ien P'ien 田駢, pre-Ch'in Taoist

t'ien-shih 天時, the heavenly (natural, or, in accord with cosmic situation) timeliness, as of political actions (*Kuan Tzu*; Wang Ch'ung)

T'ien Shu 田叔, high official at courts of first four Han emperors; exponent of Huang-Lao political thought

t'ien-shu 天數, the inherent potential in things; the "numerical (categories of) heaven" (in Tung Chung-shu); see also *shu*, number

t'ien Tao 天道, the Way of heaven; in Taoism, the Way of Nature

t'ien-ti 天地, heaven and earth, the cosmos, the natural world

t'ien-tse 天則, principles in nature (*Kuan Tzu*)

T'ien-tzu 天子, "Son of Heaven," title of the Chinese Emperor and of pre-imperial kings

T'ien Tzu 田子, title of a lost Mohist work (HS 30)

T'ien Tzu-fang 田子方, pre-Ch'in Confucian statesman

t'ien-yi 天意, "heaven's intent" (*Mencius*, Tung Chung-shu, etc.)

t'ien yün 天運, the processes of Nature (*Lieh Tzu*)

ting fa 定法, clearly establishing the laws, a Legalist principle

Ting Hung 丁鴻, statesman during reign of Later Han Emperor Ho (89–105)

ting yi-tsun 定一尊, "fix a single, highest standard," an error of rulers (Taoism); "establish one exalted ruler" (Legalist principle)

t'ing-chang 亭長, police bailiff, a Ch'in local official (e.g., Liu Pang)

T'o Hsiao 它囂, pre-Ch'in Taoist or hedonist

Tou Ying 竇嬰, died 131 B.C., prominent Confucian statesman at Han court during reigns of Emperors Wen, Ching and Wu, first century B.C.

Tsa-chia 雜家, the Eclectics, School of thought in Han era

Tsa yen 雜言, title of lost work listed under Eclectic School (HS 30)

tsai 宰, steward, or governor of a town, in late Chou usage

tsai-yi 災異, calamities and prodigies, abnormal phenomena, especially when interpreted as political portents

tsai-yu 在宥, "letting people (or the world) alone," political principle central to Chuang Tzu's thought

Tsai Yü 宰予, T. Tzu-wo 子我; disciple of Confucius

Ts'ai 蔡, pre-Ch'in state

Ts'ai K'ung-hsin 蔡孔新, author of a chronological biography of Confucius (cited p. 92n)

ts'ai-neng 才能, or *ts'ai* 才, talent and ability, especially as qualification for office apart from status, from ethics

Ts'ai Tse 蔡澤, commoner chief minister in Ch'in, third century B.C.

Ts'ai Yung 蔡邕, T. Po-chieh 伯喈, 133–192, eminent scholar of the late Han court

Tsang Ts'ang 臧倉, favorite of the Duke of Lu, in time of Mencius

tsao-wu-che 造物者, the "maker of things," or Nature, the cosmogonic force (*Chuang Tzu*)

Ts'ao Chiung 曹冏, third century, A.D., of the Wei imperial clan; political thinker

Ts'ao Kung Tzu 曹公子, a pre-Ch'in Mohist

Ts'ao P'ei (P'i) 曹丕, 187–226, the Emperor Wen of the Wei dynasty

Ts'ao Shen 曹參, died 190 B.C., proponent of Huang-Lao governing methods during the reigns of Han Emperors Kao-tsu and Hui

Ts'ao Shuang 曹爽, died A.D. 249, Prince of Ch'i in Three Kingdoms state of Wei

Ts'ao Ts'ao 曹操, 155–220, posthumously known as Emperor Wu of the Wei dynasty

tse 則, principle, standard, rule

Tseng Ching 曾靜, 1679–1736, scholar

Tseng Kung 曾鞏, 1019–1083, Neo-Confucian writer

Tseng Shen 曾參, T. Tzu-yü 子輿; disciple of Confucius, also known as Tseng Tzu, reputed author of the *Hsiao Ching* 孝經

Tseng Shen 曾申, reputed teacher of Wu Ch'i (died 378 B.C.)

Tseng Tien 曾蒧[點], disciple of Confucius, father of Tseng Shen

Tseng Tzu, reputed author of *Hsiao Ching*, see Tseng Shen

Tsou 鄒, small pre-Ch'in state in modern Shantung, native place of Mencius

Tsou Ta-fu 鄒大夫, Great Officer of the town of Tsou, title of Confucius' father

Tsou Yen 鄒衍, third-century-B.C. thinker, founder of the *Yin-Yang* School

Ts'ui Chuan 崔譔, Chin dynasty commentator on the *Chuang Tzu*

Ts'ui Shih 崔實, T. Tzu-chen 子眞; died ca. A.D. 170, Confucian-Legalist political thinker

tsun-chün 尊君, elevation of the ruler, to venerate the ruler and to institutionalize his elevation in status, dignity and authority

tsun-t'ien 尊天, "reverence for Heaven" (*Mo Tzu*)

tsung-fa 宗法, Clan-law; the basic social institution of early Chou society

Tsung-heng chia 縱橫家, the School of the Diplomatists; the proponents of the Vertical and Horizontal Alliances in Warring States times

tsung-shih 宗師, authoritative teacher; founder of a tradition; any widely venerated person of learning

tsung-tzu 宗子, eldest son of the senior branch in a lineage, in Chou Clan-law society

ts'ung Chou 從周, "following the Chou" (Confucius)

Tu Chou 杜周, Commandant of Justice under Han Emperor Wu (140–87 B.C.)

Tu Yü 杜預, third-century-A.D. exegete

T'u-ch'an 圖讖, prognostication book disseminated by Later Han Emperor Kuang-wu

t'u (tu) fa pu hsing 徒[獨]法不行, "laws cannot function of themselves" (*Hsün Tzu*)

t'u-lu 圖籙[錄], "Heavenly Plan," a particular work, and a class of writings foretelling the future as revealed by divine beings

tuan 端, incipience, innate capacity, e.g., for virtue (Mencius); see *ssu-tuan*

Tuan-kan Mu 段干木, scholar of Chin praised in *Mencius* (III/ii/7/2)

Tuan-mu Ssu (Tz'u) 端木賜, T. Tzu-kung 子貢; disciple of Confucius

Tuan-sun Shih 顓孫師, T. Tzu-chang 子張; disciple of Confucius (also read Chuan-sun Shih)

t'ui-en 推恩, "realization in deeds of one's kindness of heart" (*Mencius*)

Tung Cho 董卓, warlord at end of Later Han

Tung Chung-shu 董仲舒, ca. 179 to ca. 104 B.C., leading Confucian scholar of the Former Han period

Tung Hsüan 董宣, magistrate of Lo-yang during reign of Later Han Emperor Kuang-wu (A.D. 25–57)

Tzu-ch'an 子產, formal name Kung-sun Ch'iao 公孫僑; died 522 B.C., skilled statesman in the State of Cheng

Tzu-chang 子張, disciple of Confucius; see Tuan-sun Shih

Tzu-chih 子之, favorite of King K'uai of Yen, fourth century B.C. (*Mencius* II/ii/8)

Tzu-han 子罕, strategist in State of Sung; see Ssu-ch'eng Tzu-han

Tzu-hsia 子夏, disciple of Confucius; see Pu Shang

tzu-hsiu 自修, self-cultivation

Tzu Hua Tzu 子華子, pre-Ch'in Taoist

tzu-jan 自然, nature, the natural, spontaneity (Taoism)

tzu-jan chu-yi 自然主義, naturalism (modern term based on Taoist usage)

Tzu-kung 子貢, disciple of Confucius; see Tuan-mu Ssu

Tzu-lu 子路, disciple of Confucius; see Chung Yu

Tzu-ssu 子思, grandson of Confucius; see K'ung Chi

tzu-te 自得, self-fulfillment of all things, an active process in Nature (Neo-Taoism)

Tzu-tu 子都, favorite of the King of Cheng (*Mencius* VI/i/7/7)

Tzu-wan Tzu 子晚子, title of book listed under the Eclectic School (HS 30)

Tzu-yu 子游, disciple of Confucius; see Yen Yen

Tzu-yü 子羽, disciple of Confucius; see T'an-t'ai Mieh-ming

tz'u-shih 刺史, "Regional Inspectors," senior regional officials in Later Han

wai-sheng 外生, transcending life (*Chuang Tzu*)

Wan Chang 萬章, disciple of Mencius

wang 王, king, to rule; the ideal of the true ruler, in Confucian political thought; see *wang cheng*

wang 望, ritual observances for the fifteenth of the lunar month

Wang, Master 王生, recluse expert in Huang-Lao teaching, active during reign of Former Han Emperor Ching (156–41 B.C.)

Wang Ch'ang 王常, during Wang Mang era supported the view that the Han dynasty would be restored

wang cheng 王政, Kingly Government, ideal government in Confucian thought; the opposite of *pa-cheng*, rule of force, in Mencius

Wang Chi 王吉, harsh governor in P'ei, under Later Han Emperor Ling (168–188)

Wang Chien 王翦, third-century-B.C. general in State of Ch'in

Wang Ch'ung 王充, T. Chung-jen 仲任; A.D. 27 to ca. 100, thinker, author of *Lun Heng* and other works

Wang Feng 王鳳, member of consort clan; dominated court of Han Emperor Ch'eng (32–7 B.C.)

Wang Fu 王符, T. Chieh-hsin 節信; active ca. 120–160, political thinker, author of *Ch'ien-fu Lun* 潛夫論

Wang K'ai 王愷, Chin dynasty sybarite

Wang Ken 王根, member of consort clan, important court official during reign of Han Emperor Ch'eng (32–7 B.C.)

Wang K'uang 王況, wrote anti-Wang Mang prognostication text

Wang Liang 王梁, supporter of Later Han Emperor Kuang-wu

Wang Ling 王陵, prominent aid to early Han emperors

Wang Mang 王莽, usurper of the Han throne, emperor of so-called Hsin 新 dynasty A.D. 9–23

Wang Mi 王謐, T. Chih-yuan 稚遠; 360–407, wrote in support of Buddhism

Wang Pi 王弼, T. Fu-ssu 輔嗣, 226–249, Neo-Taoist thinker

Wang Shih 王式, local official in early fourth century A.D., involved in "pure critiques"

Wang Shou-jen 王守仁, T. Yang-ming 陽

明; 1472–1529, Neo-Confucian statesman and philosopher

Wang T'an-chih 王坦之, T. Wen-tu 文度; 326–275, wrote essay "Fei Chuang Lun" 廢莊論 ("Reasons for Abolishing *Chuang Tzu*")

Wang Tao 王導, T. Mao-hung 茂弘; 276–339, Chancellor at Eastern Chin court

Wang Ts'an 王粲, T. Chung-hsüan 仲宣, 177–217, one of the Seven Masters of the Chien-an Period

Wang Tsang 王臧, died 139 B.C., high official at court of Han Emperor Wen

Wang Tun 王敦, T. Ch'u-chung 處仲; 266–324, Chin dynasty sybarite

Wang Wen-shu 王溫舒, harsh governor under Han Emperor Wu (140–87 B.C.)

Wang Yang-ming, see Wang Shou-jen

Wang Yen 王衍, T. Yi-fu 夷甫; 256–311, Neo-Taoist thinker

wei 威, majesty, awe of the ruler, an important element of politics in Legalist theory

Wei 魏, also called Liang 梁, one of successor states of Chin, in Warring States era; dynasty founded by Ts'ao Ts'ao, one of the Three Kingdoms of the third century A.D.; Northern dynasty of the T'o-pa alien conquerors, 386–534

Wei 衛, fief of K'ang-shu, of the royal Chou clan; important early Chou state

Wei Chao 韋昭, T. Hung-ssu 弘嗣, 204–273, scholar and statesman, annotator of the *Kuo Yü* 國語

Wei Hsiao (Ao) 隗囂, died A.D. 33, warlord opponent of the Later Han Emperor Kuang-wu during the wars of the restoration

Wei Mou 魏牟 or, Mou of Wei; pre-Ch'in Taoist or hedonist

wei-kuo 爲國, "the administration of the state" (*Hsün Tzu*)

Wei Liao 尉繚, title of book listed under the Eclectic School (HS 30)

Wei Lüeh 魏略, book cited in the *Wei Chih* of the *San Kuo Chih*

wei-shu 緯書, the apocrypha of Han times, spurious counterparts to the *ching*, "classics"

Wei Tzu 微子, named Ch'i 啓, scion of

the Yin royal family, enfieffed in the State of Sung at time of the Chou conquest

Wei Wan 衛綰, active ca. 160–140 B.C., military leader and high official

wei wo 爲我, "for myself," i.e., egocentric; in some contexts, "individualistic; characterizes Taoist thought

wei-yen 微言, "subtle expressions," the "meaning between the lines," an exegetical tradition in classical studies

wen 文, refinement, as opposed to *chih*, "simplicity"; civil, literary

wen-chih 文質, the antithesis of the refined and the simple, or the cultivated and the pristine, identified with the Chou and the Shang dynasties, respectively

Wen Tzu 文子, a no-longer extant early Taoist work, the extant *Wen Tzu* being a forgery

wen-wu 文武, the antithesis of the civil and the military, of intellect and force, etc.

Wen and Wu 文王武王, father and son, the founding kings of the Chou dynasty in the late twelfth century B.C.; symbols of good government

Wo Tzu 我子, title of lost Mohist work (HS 30)

Wu 吳, pre-Ch'in state; the lower Yangtze region

wu 無, nothing, non-being, nothingness; a basic concept in Taoism with various developments of meaning

wu ch'ang 五常, "five norms of behavior," also known as *wu lun* 五倫, i.e., the relationships of the *san-kang* plus those of elder and younger brother, and of friends

wu cheng 五政, the five administrative tasks (*Hsün Yüeh*)

wu cheng 五徵, five verifications, in prognostication theory

wu cheng-fu ssu-hsiang 無政府思想, anarchism, anarchist thought (modern term)

Wu-ch'eng 武城, city in Lu in time of Confucius

wu chi 五際, the Five Periods, or conjunctions of periods, in Han era prognostication theory based on the calendar

Wu Ch'i 吳起, died 378 B.C., chief minister

in Ch'u, Legalist-minded Confucian statesman

wu-chih 無治, non-governing, anarchism (Taoism)

Wu-ching Po-shih 五經博士, Erudits for the Five Classics, government posts established by the Emperor Wu in 136 B.C.

wu-chün chu-yi 無君主義, political theory favoring having no rulers, a formulation of anarchist thought dominant in Wei-Chin era Taoism

wu-heng 五橫, the "five perversities," anti-Buddhist charges against which Monk Tao-heng argued

wu-hsin 無心, purposelessness, of the spontaneous process of nature (*Lao Tzu*)

wu-hsing 無形, the formless, the principle underlying the production of things in nature (*Lao Tzu*)

wu hsing 五刑, the five punishments, as named in the *Documents* (Legge, p. 44)

wu hsing 五行, Five Agents, or Five Elements; a system of thought

Wu K'ang 吳康, modern scholar

Wu-keng 武庚, son of the last Shang-Yin king

Wu Kuang 吳廣, rebel leader against Ch'in dynasty, 210–206 B.C.

Wu Kung 吳公, Lord Wu, Legalist-minded administrator during reign of Former Han Emperor Wen (179–157 B.C.)

Wu Lü 吳慮, rustic in Lu, criticized by Mo Tzu

wu lun, see *wu ch'ang*

wu ni 五逆, the five rebellious acts, crimes defined in Confucian ethical theory

Wu T'ai-po 吳泰伯, uncle of King Wen, the Chou founder; bearer of civilization to the Southern Barbarians

wu Tao 無道, "lacking the Way," i.e. ill-governed (of the state), depraved (of individuals)

wu te 五德, the "five powers" in *Yin-Yang* thought

wu-wei 無爲, non-action, inaction, taking no purposive action (*Lao Tzu*)

wu-wo 物我, the world and the self

Wu-yeh 無射, the bell cast at wasteful expense by Chou King Ching; symbol of royal extravagance *wu-yung* 五壅, the five obstructions, preventing the ruler from controlling his officials (*Han Fei Tzu*)

yang 養, to nourish, to rear; to provide sustenance for

Yang Ch'iu 陽球, administrator who favored Legalist methods during reign of Later Han Emperor Ling (168–188)

Yang Chu 楊朱, T. Tzu-chü 子居, ancient philosopher; title of chapter in the *Lieh Tzu*

Yang Hsiu 羊琇, Chin dynasty sybarite

Yang Hsiung 揚雄, T. Tzu-yün 子雲, 53 B.C. to A.D. 18, thinker and writer

Yang Hu 陽虎, household servitor of the Chi clan, dominated the government of Lu in time of Confucius

Yang Man 羊曼, T. Tsu-yen 祖延, 274–328, one of the "unfettered eight"

Yang Pi 羊弼, second century A.D., Erudit for *Spring and Autumn Annals*, teacher of Ho Hsiu

yang-sheng 養生, nourishing the self, keeping one's own life safe and cultivating one's own powers (Taoism)

yang wu ch'i 養五棊, "cultivating the five extremes," extending civilized man's capacities for satisfaction (*Hsün Tzu*)

Yao 堯, or Emperor Yao of T'ang 唐帝堯, ancient emperor, ideal ruler

Yen 燕, pre-Ch'in state

Yen Hui 顏回, T. Tzu-yüan 子淵, also known as Yen Yüan; favorite disciple of Confucius

Yen Kuang 嚴光, T. Tzu-ling 子陵, 37 B.C. to A.D. 43, recluse, friend of Emperor Kuang-wu, the "moral exemplar" of the Han restoration

Yen K'ung t'u 演孔圖, or *Ch'un-ch'iu Wei Yen K'ung t'u* 春秋徽, "Expository Chart on Confucius," a Han period apocryphal work based on the *Spring and Autumn Annals*

Yen Shih-ku 顏師古, 581–645, compiler of commentary to *Han Shu*

Yen Tsun 嚴遵, Former Han era commentator on the *Lao Tzu*

Yen Yen 言偃, T. Tzu-yu 子游, disciple of Confucius

Yen Yen-nien 嚴延年, infamous harsh official under Former Han Emperor Hsüan (73–49 B.C.)

Yen Ying 晏嬰, T. Chung 仲, P'ing-chung 平仲, sixth century B.C. minister in Ch'i, reputed author of the *Yen Tzu Ch'un-ch'iu* 晏子春秋

Yen Yüan, disciple of Confucius, see Yen Hui

yi 儀, ritual formalities, rites in the narrow sense, deportment; also the *Yi Li* 儀禮, one of the three classics of the rites

yi 義, righteousness, justice, generosity, meaning, etc.

Yi 羿, the mighty archer of legend

Yi Feng 翼奉, T. Shao-chün 少君; first century B.C., scholar and official at the Han court; political thinker

yi-hsia 夷夏, Barbarians and Chinese, term from *Tso Chuan* indicating the cultural or ethnic distinction

yi-hsin 義信, righteousness and good faith, Confucian virtues

yi hsing 壹刑, unification of punishments, meaning the equality of all social ranks before the laws and regulations of the state (Lord Shang)

yi-ku 疑古, skepticism of antiquity, attitude current among modern scholars especially in the 1920's and 1930's

yi min 一民, "unifying the people" by making them uniform through the laws, a Legalist principle

Yi Shih-chen 伊世珍, a Yuan dynasty scholar (see Bibliography)

yi-ti 夷狄, Barbarians of the West and the North

Yi Tsung 義縱, died 117 B.C., important official early in the reign of the Han Emperor Wu

Yi-ya 易牙, expert cook of the seventh century B.C.

Yi-yi 夷逸, recluse in the State of Ch'i mentioned in *Analects* XVIII/8/4

Yi Yin 伊尹, worthy minister of King T'ang, founder of the Shang dynasty

Yin 殷, or Yin-Shang 殷商, the later part of the Shang dynasty from about 1450 to about 1100 B.C., a cultural era; Yin is a site of the capital, modern An-yang, Honan

Yin Hsi 尹喜, "keeper of the Han-ku Pass 函谷關" in the legend about Lao Tzu

Yin-hsü 殷墟, "the Wastes of Yin," site where the Yin cultural remains have been excavated, near An-yang in Honan Province

Yin Min 尹敏, scholar active during reign of Later Han Emperor Kuang-wu, A.D. 25–57

yin shih 因時, to accord with the times (Huan T'an)

Yin-Yang Chia 陰陽家, the *Yin-Yang* School of pre-Ch'in times, led by Tsou Yen, and its continuation in later thought

Yin-yi 尹佚, early Chou official and the book attributed to him

Ying 郢, region of Central Yangtze; capital of the State of Ch'u

Ying Kung 嬴公, "Lord Ying," Former Han era specialist on the *Spring and Autumn Annals*, teacher of Sui Hung

ying-t'ien shun-min 應天順民, "respond to heaven, accord with the people," a cliché of succession claims and theories

Yu 幽王, Chou King, reigned 781–771 B.C.; symbol of Chou decline

Yu 友, brother of Chou King Hsüan, enfieffed Duke Huan of Cheng in 805 B.C.

yu-hsia 遊俠, knights errant

Yu Jo 有若, T. Tzu-jo 子若, disciple of Confucius

yu Tao 有道, "has the Way," i.e., is well-governed (of the state); is virtuous (Confucianism) or is enlightened (Taoism) of the individual

yu-wai 遊外, "roam in the transcendental," Kuo Hsiang's term, adapted from *Chuang Tzu*

yu-wei 有為, purposive action, contrasted with the Taoist "no purposive action" *wu-wei*

yu wu 有無, being and nothing, being and non-being, concepts originally important to Taoism and Neo-Taoism, later to Buddhism

yü 竽, ancient musical instrument

Yü 禹, Emperor Yü, "the Great Yü," first ruler of the Hsia dynasty of antiquity who received the throne from Shun on merit, and transmitted it on the basis of heredity

Yü Chung 虞仲, recluse of Ch'i (*Analects* XVIII/8/4)

yü-min 裕民, *yü-min-sheng* 生, enriching the people, enriching the people's livelihood

Yü Ping 庾冰, T. Chi-chien 季堅; 296–344, leading figure at Chin court, opposed to Buddhism

yü-yen 寓言, "metaphor," typical of Chuang Tzu's language; name of Chapter 27 of the *Chuang Tzu*

yüan 原, to examine into things; one of the Three Standards (*Mo Tzu*)

Yüan Hsien 原憲, T. Tzu-ssu 子思, disciple of Confucius

Yüan Hung 袁宏, T. Yen-po 彥伯, 328–376, writer, served as secretary to Huan Wen

Yüan Jang 原壤, friend of Confucius

Yüan Ku, Master 轅固生, debated history from Confucian point of view at court of Han Emperor Ching (156–141 B.C.)

yüan-shih 元士, "scholars of the first class" (*Mencius* V/ii/2/5)

Yüan Ssu 原思, disciple of Confucius, see Yüan Hsien

Yüan Ts'an 袁粲, T. Ching-ch'ien 景倩, 420–477, rebutted Ku Huan's racial arguments against Buddhism

yüeh 約, restraint, simplicity, austere, limited

yüeh 樂, music; one of the Six Disciplines, Six Classics; as a classical text, lost before Han times

Yüeh 越, pre-Ch'in state in area of modern Chekiang

Yüeh-cheng K'e 樂正克, T. Tzu-ao 子敖, disciple of Mencius

"Yüeh Ling" 月令, "Monthly Commands," chapter in the *Li Chi*

Yüeh T'ai 樂臺, T'ang dynasty scholar, wrote no longer extant *Mo Tzu chu* 墨子注, commentary on the *Mo Tzu*

Yüeh Yi 樂毅 (also Yo Yi, Lao Yi), third-century-B.C. statesman and general in the State of Yen

yün-t'i 雲梯, wall-scaling ladders; attack machinery of warfare

yung 用, practical application of a doctrine, one of the Three Standards (*Mo Tzu*)

Bibliography

(Books cited by the author or by the translator)
Note: Works no longer extant, essays and smaller works, and certain
other writings are entered in the Glossary

I. The Confucian Classics

Lun Yü 論語, *The Analects* of Confucius, translations include: Legge,
1861, 1893, reprint Hong Kong 1960; Waley, 1938

Meng Tzu 孟子, *The Book of Mencius*, translations include Legge, 1861,
1894, reprint Hong Kong 1960; W. A. C. H. Dobson, 1963; D. C.
Lau, 1970

Ta Hsüeh 大學, *The Great Learning*, translations include: Legge, 1861,
1893, reprint Hong Kong 1960

Chung-yung 中庸, *The Doctrine of the Mean*, translations include: Legge,
1861, 1893, reprint Hong Kong 1960

Yi-ching 易經, *The Book of Changes*, translations include: Legge, 1882,
1899, reprint New York 1963; R. Wilhelm, 1924, rendered into
English by Cary F. Baynes, 1950

Shu 書 (*Shang Shu* 尚書, *Shu Ching* 書經), *The Book of Documents* (*The Classic
of History*), translations include Legge, 1865, reprint Hong Kong
1960; B. Karlgren, 1950

Shih 詩 (*Shih Ching* 詩經), *The Book of Odes* (*The Book of Songs, The Classic
of Poetry*, etc.), translations include: Legge, 1872, reprint Hong Kong
1960; Waley, 1937; B. Karlgren, 1950

Chou-li 周禮 (*Chou-kuan* 周官), *The Institutes of Chou*

Yi-li 儀禮, *Ritual Proprieties*, translation: *I-li*, John Steele, 1917

Li-chi 禮記, *The Book of Rites*, translation, Legge, 1885

Ch'un-ch'iu 春秋, *Spring and Autumn Annals*, with its Three
Commentaries: *Tso Chuan* 左傳, *The Commentary of Tso; Kung-yang
Chuan* 公羊傳, *Kung-yang Commentary; Ku-liang Chuan* 穀梁傳, *Ku-liang
Commentary;* translation: Legge, *The Ch'un-ch'iu with the Tso Chuan,*
including sample translations from the other two Commentaries,
1872, reprint Hong Kong 1960

Hsiao Ching 孝經, *The Classic of Filial Piety* attributed to Tseng Shen 曾參,
translation: Legge, 1879

Erh-ya 爾雅 (Dictionary)

II. Dynastic Histories

Shih Chi 史記, by Ssu-ma Ch'ien 司馬遷 (145–90 B.C.), punctuated edition
by Ku Chieh-kang 顧頡剛 and Hsü Wen-shan 徐文珊, three volumes,

Peiping, 1936; translations include: B. Watson, *Records of the Grand Historian of China: Translated from the Shih Chi of Ssu-ma Ch'ien* (partial translation), two volumes, 1961

Han Shu 漢書, by Pan Ku 班固 (32–92)

Hou Han Shu 後漢書, by Fan Yeh 范曄 (398–445)

Wu Chih 吳志 (*Wu Shu* 吳書), *Shu Chih* 蜀志 (*Shu Shu* 蜀書), and *Wei Chih* 魏志 (*Wei Shu* 魏書), together comprising the *San Kuo Chih* 三國志, by Ch'en Shou 陳壽 (233–297)

Chin Shu 晉書, by Fang Hsüan-ling 房玄齡 (578–648) and others

Sung Shu 宋書, by Shen Yüeh 沈約 (441–513)

Nan Ch'i Shu 南齊書, by Hsiao Tzu-hsien 蕭子顯 (489–537)

Liang Shu 梁書, by Yao Ssu-lien 姚思廉 (557–637)

Wei Shu 魏書, by Wei Shou 魏收 (506–572)

Sui Shu 隋書, by Wei Cheng 魏徵 (580–643) and others

Hsin T'ang Shu 新唐書, by Ou-yang Hsiu 歐陽修 (1007–1072), Sung Ch'i 宋祁 (998–1061) and others

Sung Shih 宋史, by T'o-T'o 脫脫 and others (1345)

III. Other Works Cited or Quoted

Adams, George B., *The Origins of the English Constitution* (1912)

Bentham, Jeremy, *An Introduction to the Principles of Morals and Legislation* (1780)

    A Fragment on Government (1776)

Bielenstein, Hans, *The Restoration of the Han Dynasty*, three volumes, 1953, 1959, 1967

Bodde, Derk, *China's First Unifier* (1938)

Carlyle, R. W. and A. J. Carlyle, *A History of Mediaeval Political Theory in the West*, six volumes, 1903–1936

Chan, Wing-tsit, *A Source Book in Chinese Philosophy*, 1963

Chan-kuo Ts'e 戰國策, attributed to Liu Hsiang 劉向 (77–6 B.C.), translation by James Crump: *Intrigues of the Warring States* (1970)

Chang Ch'un-ming 張純明, "Yen-t'ieh-lun chih cheng-chih pei-ching" 鹽鐵論之政治背景, *Ching-chi T'ung-chi Chi-k'an* (Nan-kai University, Tientsin), 2: 1, March, 1933, pp. 1–56

Chang Ch'un-yi 張純一 (modern scholar), "Mo Tzu Lu-jen shuo" 墨子魯人說 (appended to some modern reprintings of Sun Yi-jang's *Mo Tzu Chien-ku*)

Chang Hsin-ch'eng 張心澂, *Wei-shu t'ung-k'ao* (1939) 偽書通考

Chang Hsüeh-ch'eng 張學誠 (1738–1800), *Wen-shih t'ung-yi* 文史通義

Chang Hui-yen 張惠言 (1761–1802), *Ming-k'e Wen-pien* 茗柯文編 contains his "Shu *Mo Tzu* 'ching-shuo chieh' hou" 書墨子經說解後 (also appended to Sun Yi-jang's *Mo Tzu Chien-ku*)

Chang Ping-lin 張炳麟 (1868–1936), *Chang T'ai-yen wen-lu* 張太炎文錄,

containing: *Chien lun, san,* 檢論，三 "Yüan fa" 原法; "Ch'in cheng-chi" 秦政積; "Po chien-li K'ung-chiao yi" 駁建立孔教議; "*She-hui t'ung-ch'üan* shang-tui" 社會通詮商兌; "Shih Tai" 釋戴

Chang P'u 張溥 (1602–1641), compiler, *Han-Wei Lu-ch'ao po-san Ming-chia-chi* 漢魏六朝百三名家集

Chang Shou-chieh 張守節 (T'ang), *Shih Chi Cheng-yi* 史記正義

Chao Yi 趙翼 (1727–1814), *Nien-erh shih cha chi* 廿二史劄記 (*Erh-shih-erh shih cha chi*)

Ch'en Li 陳澧 (1810–1882), *Tung-shu tu-shu chi* 東塾讀書記

Ch'en Li 陳立 (1809–1869), *Kung-yang Yi-shu* 公羊義疏

Ch'en Liang 陳亮 (1143–1194), *Lung-ch'uan Wen-chi* 龍川文集

Ch'eng Fu-hsin 程復心 (Yuan), *Meng Tzu nien-p'u* 孟子年譜

Ch'eng Hsüan-ying 成玄英 (T'ang), *Chuang Tzu Shu* 莊子疏

Ch'i Shao-nan 齊召南 (1706–1768), *Han Shu K'ao-cheng* 漢書考證

Chia Yi 賈誼 (200–168 B.C.), *Hsin Shu* 新書

Chiang Ch'üan 江瑔, *Tu-tzu chih-yen* (1917) 讀子卮言

Chiang Hsia-an 江俠庵 (modern scholar), *Chou-Ch'in chu-tzu k'ao* 周秦諸子考

Chiang Yung 江永 (1681–1762), *Hsiang-tang t'u-k'ao* 鄉黨圖考; *K'ung Tzu nien-p'u* 孔子年譜

Ch'iao Chou 譙周 (201–270), *Ku-shih k'ao* 古史考

Ch'ien Mu 錢穆, *Hsien-Ch'in chu-tzu hsi-nien k'ao-pien* (1936) 先秦諸子繫年考辨; "Chou Kuan chu-tso shih-tai k'ao" 周官著作時代考 *Yen-ching Hsüeh-pao* 11(1932), pp. 2191–2300

Ch'ien Ta-hsin 錢大昕 (1728–1804), *Yi-nien-lu* 疑年錄

Ch'ien Tseng 錢曾 (1629 to ca. 1700), *Tu-shu min-ch'iu chi* 讀書敏求記

Ching Fang 京房 (77–37 B.C.), *Ching-shih Yi-chuan* 京氏易傳

Ch'ing Shih-tsung 清世宗 (the Yung-cheng Emperor, reigned 1723–1735), *Ta-yi chüeh-mi lu* 大義覺迷錄

Chou Ch'uan-ju 周傳儒 (modern scholar), *Chia-ku wen-tzu yü Yin Shang chih-tu* 甲骨文字與殷商制度

Chou Kuang-yeh 周廣業 (1730–1798), *Meng Tzu ssu-k'ao* 孟子四考

Chou Liang-kung 周亮工 (1612–1672), *Yin-shu-wu shu-ying* 因樹屋書影

Chu Hsi 朱熹 (1130–1200), *Chu Tzu yü-lu (-lei)* 朱子語錄 (類); *Lun Yü chi-chu* 論語集註; *Meng Tzu chi-chu* 孟子集註; *Chu Tzu wen-chi* 朱子文集

Chu-ko Liang 諸葛亮 (181–234), *Chu-ko Ch'eng-hsiang chi* 諸葛丞相集, edited by Chu Lin 朱璘 (Ch'ing)

Chu Yu-tseng 朱右曾 (late Ch'ing), *Yi-Chou-shu chi-hsün shih* 逸周書集訓釋, in *Hsü Ch'ing Ching-chieh* 續清經解

Chuang Chou 莊周 (fourth century B.C.), *Chuang Tzu* 莊子, translations include: Legge, 1891, reprint New York 1962; H. A. Giles, 1926; Fung Yu-lan (Chapters One–Seven), 1933; B. Watson, 1968

Ch'ü T'ung-tsu 瞿同祖, *Chung-kuo feng-chien she-hui* (1937) 中國封建社會

Creel, H. G., *Confucius, the Man and the Myth* (1949), republished as *Confucius and the Chinese Way*

Dubs, Homer H.: *Hsüntze, the Moulder of Ancient Confucianism* (1927); *The Works of Hsüntze* (1928); *The History of the Former Han Dynasty* (partial translation of the *Han Shu*, with extensive annotation), three volumes, 1938, 1944, 1955

du Plessis-Mornay (Duplessis-Mornay), Philippe, *Vindiciae contra Tyrannos* (1579)

Duyvendak, J. J. L., *The Book of Lord Shang* (1928)

Fang Shou-ch'u 方授楚 (modern scholar), *Mo-hsüeh yüan-liu* 墨學源流

Fu Hsüan 傅玄 (217–278), *Fu Tzu* 傅子, edition of Ch'ien Pao-t'ang 海寧錢保塘 of Hai-ning; *Fu Ch'un-ku Chi* 傅鶉觚集, in Chang P'u, *Han-Wei Lu-ch'ao po-san Ming-chia chi*

Fu Ssu-nien 傅斯年 (modern scholar), "Chou tung-feng yü Yin yi-min," 周東封與殷遺民 in Hu Shih, *Hu Shih Lun-hsüeh chin-chu*

Fung Yu-lan (Feng Yu-lan) 馮友蘭 (modern scholar), *Chung-kuo che-hsüeh shih* (1931, 1934) 中國哲學史, translated by Derk Bodde as *A History of Chinese Philosophy*, Volume One, 1937, 1952; Volume Two, 1953

Fung Yu-lan, *A Short History of Chinese Philosophy* (1948)

Giles, Herbert A., *Chuang Tzu, Mystic, Moralist and Social Reformer*, second edition, 1926

Graham, A. C., "The Logic of the Mohist *Hsiao-ch'ü*," *T'oung Pao* 51 (1964); *The Book of Lieh Tzu* (1960)

Han Fei 韓非 (died 233 B.C.), *Han Fei Tzu* 韓非子, translation by W. K. Liao, two volumes, 1939, 1959

Han Yü 韓愈 (768–824), *Ch'ang-li Hsien-sheng wen-chi* 昌黎先生文集, contains "Tu *Mo Tzu*" 讀墨子; "Tui Yü wen" 對禹問

Hang Shih-chün 杭世駿, compiler (1969–1773), *Hsü Li-chi chi-shuo* 續禮記集說

Hawkes, David, *Ch'u Tz'u: The Songs of the South* (1959)

Hincmar, Bishop of Rheims (ninth century A.D.), *De Regis Persona*

Ho Hsiu 何休 (129–82 B.C.): *Ch'un-ch'iu Kung-yang chieh-ku* 春秋公羊解詁; *Kung-yang Mo-shou* 公羊墨守; *Tso-shih Kao-huang* 左氏膏肓; *Ku-liang Fei-chi* 穀梁癈疾

Hobbes, Thomas, *Leviathan* (1651)

Hsia Hung-chi 夏洪基 (Ming), *K'ung Tzu nien-p'u kang-mu* 孔子年譜綱目

Hsia Tseng-yu 夏曾佑 (died 1924), *Chung-kuo ku-tai shih* 中國古代史

Hsiao Kung-ch'üan 蕭公權 (K. C. Hsiao, Kung-chuan Hsiao): *Chung-kuo cheng-chih ssu-hsiang-shih ts'an-k'ao tzu-liao* 中國政治思想史參考資料 (Tsing-hua University syllabus, Pei-p'ing, no date); *Chi-yüan Wen-ts'un* 迹園文存, edited by Wang Jung-tsu 汪榮祖, Taipei, 1970; "K'ang Yu-wei and Confucianism," *Monumenta Serica* XVIII (1959), republished with minor changes in *A Modern China and a New World: K'ang Yu-wei, Reformer and Utopian, 1858–1927*, Seattle and London, 1975

Hsü Heng 許衡 (1209–1281), *Lu-chai yi-shu* 魯齋遺書

Hsü Hsieh-chen 徐協貞 (modern scholar), *Yin-ch'i t'ung-shih* 殷契通釋

Hsü Kan 徐幹 (170–217), *Chung lun* 中論

Hsü Wei-yü 許維遹, *Lü-shih Ch'iu-ch'iu chi-shih* (1933) 呂氏春秋集釋

Hsün K'uang 荀況 (ca. 298–238 B.C.), *Hsün Tzu* 荀子, translation: Dubs, 1928

Hsün Yüeh 荀悅 (148–209), *Shen-chien* 申鑒, translation by Chi-yun Chen (forthcoming); *Han Chi* 漢紀; *Hsün Shih-chung chi* 荀侍中集

Hu Shih 胡適 (modern scholar), *Chung-kuo che-hsüeh-shih Ta-kang* (1919) 中國哲學史大綱; "Shuo Ju" 說儒 in *Hu Shih lun-hsüeh chin-chu, ti-yi-chi* (1936) 胡適論學近著, 第一集

Hu Ying-lin 胡應麟 (1551–1602), *Ssu-pu cheng-o* 四部正譌

Huai-nan Hung-lieh 淮南鴻列, *Huai-nan Tzu* 淮南子, see Liu An

Huan Fan 桓範 (third century A.D.), *Shih-yao Lun* 世要論

Huan T'an 桓譚 (43 B.C. to A.D. 28), *Hsin Lun* 新論 translation by Timotheus Pokora, *Hsin Lun (New Treatise) and Other Writings by Huan T'an*, Ann Arbor, 1975

Huang Chen 黃震 (1213–1280), *Huang-shih Jih-ch'ao* 黃氏日鈔

Huang Ch'ing Ching-chieh (1829) 皇清經解, compiled and printed under the direction of Juan Yüan (1764–1849), and its continuation, *Hsü Huang Ch'ing Ching-chieh* 續, or *Huang Ch'ing Ching-chieh, Hsü-pien* (1868–1888) 續編, compiled and published under the editorship of Wang Hsien-ch'ien

Huang Tsung-hsi 黃宗羲 (1610–1695), *Ming-yi tai-fang lu* 明夷待訪錄

Hughes, E. R., *Chinese Philosophy in Classical Times* (1942, revised edition, 1954)

Hui Chiao 惠皎 (sixth century A.D. monk), *Kao Seng Chuan* 高僧傳

Hulsewé, A. F. P., *Remnants of Han Law*, volume one (1955)

Hung-ming Chi 弘明集, Buddhist doctrinal anthology compiled by the Monk Seng Yu 僧佑 [祐] (445–518)

Hurvitz, Leon, translator of "Treatise on Buddhism and Taoism," *ch* 114 of the *Wei Shu* 魏書 of Wei Shou, in Mizuno, S., and Nagahiro, T., eds., *Yün-kang*, Vol. XVI (1956)

Jen Chao-lin 任兆麟 (eighteenth century), *Hsin-chai shih-chung* 心齋十種 containing: "Meng Tzu shih-shih lüeh" 孟子時事略

Jenks, Edward, *A History of Politics* (1900), translated by Yen Fu (*qv*)

Juan Chi 阮籍 (210–263), *Juan Ssu-tsung chi* 阮嗣宗集, containing: "Ta Chuang lun" 達莊論; "Ta-jen Hsien-sheng chuan" 大人先生傳

Juan Yüan 阮元 (1764–1849): *Yen-ching-shih chi* 經室集; compiler, *Huang Ch'ing Ching-chieh*

K'ang Yu-wei 康有為 (1858–1927): *K'ang Nan-hai Hsien-sheng wen-ch'ao*

康南海先生文鈔; *K'ung Tzu kai-chih k'ao* 孔子改制考; *Chung-yung chu* 中庸注; *Meng Tzu wei* 孟子徵; *Ta-hsüeh chu* 大學注; *Ch'un-ch'iu pi-hsüeh ta-yi wei-yen k'ao* 春秋筆削大義徵言考

Kao Heng 高亨 (modern scholar), *Lao Tzu cheng-ku* 老子正詁 (revised edition, 1943)

Kao Ssu-sun 高似孫 (c.s. 1184), *Tzu lüeh* 子略

Karlgren, Bernhard, *The Book of Documents*, translation of the *Shang Shu* 尚書, BMFEA no. 22 (1950)

Kierman, Frank A., Jr., *Four Warring States Biographies* (1962)

Ko Hung 葛洪 (ca. 277 to ca. 357), *Shen-hsien chuan* 神仙傳; *Pao-p'u Tzu* 抱樸子, translation of the "Wai p'ien" 外篇 of *Pao-p'u Tzu* by Jay Sailey (1978)

Krabbe, Hugo, *Modern Ideas of the State* (1915), translation by Wang Chien (*qv*)

Kramers, R. P., *K'ung Tzu Chia Yü*, study and partial translation, 1950

Ku Chieh-kang 顧頡剛, "Wu-te chung-shih shuo hsia ti cheng-chih ho li-shih," 五德絡始說下的政治和歷史 *Tsing-hua Hsüeh-pao* 6: 1, June, 1930, pp. 71–268

Ku Shih 顧實 (modern scholar), *Han Shu Yi-wen-chih chiang-shu* 漢書藝文志講疏

Ku Yen-wu 顧炎武 (1613–1682), *Jih-chih-lu* 日知錄

Kuan Chung 管仲, *Kuan Tzu* 管子 (Warring States era compilation) partial translation by W. A. Rickett (1965)

Kuang Hung-ming-chi 廣弘明集, continuation of Buddhist anthology, by Monk Tao-hsüan 釋道宣 (seventh century A.D.)

Kung-sun Yang 公孫鞅 (died 338 B.C.), *Shang Chün Shu* 商君書 translation by J. J. L. Duyvendak (1928)

K'ung Tzu Chia-yü 孔子家語 (late Chou or Han work); study and partial translation by R. P. Kramers, *K'ung Tzu Chia Yü: The School Sayings of Confucius* (1950)

Kuo Mo-jo 郭末若 (modern scholar), *Chung-kuo ku-tai she-hui yen-chiu* 中國古代社會研究 (1929)

Kuo Yü 國語 (anonymous third-century-B.C. historical work)

Lao Tzu 老子 or *Tao-te Ching* 道德經, translations include: Legge, 1891, reprint New York 1962; Waley, *The Way and Its Power*, 1935; Lin Yutang, 1948; J. J. L. Duyvendak, 1954; Wing-tsit Chan, 1963; D. C. Lau, 1963

Legge, James (1815–1897), *The Chinese Classics*, copyright reissue in five volumes, Hong Kong University Press, 1960; *The Texts of Taoism*, volumes 39, 40 in Max Müller, ed., *The Sacred Books of the East*, 1891; *The Li Ki* (*Li Chi*), volumes 27 and 28 of the above, 1885; the *Hsiao-ching* in volume 3 of the above, 1879; and others

Lei Hai-tsung 雷海宗 (modern historian), *Chung-kuo t'ung-shih hsüan-tu*

中國通史選讀

Li K'uei 李悝, also written Li K'e 李克 (late fifth century B.C.), *Fa Ching* 法經

Li Shan 李善 (died A.D. 689), *Wen-hsüan chu* 文選註 (Commentary on the *Wen Hsüan* anthology)

Liang Ch'i-ch'ao 梁啓超 (1873–1929), *Yin-ping-shih ch'üan-chi* 飲冰室全集, containing: *Ch'ing-tai hsüeh-shu kai-lun* 淸代學術概論, translated by Immanuel C. Y. Hsü as *Intellectual Trends in the Ch'ing Period* (1959); *Hsien-Ch'in cheng-chih ssu-hsiang shih* 先秦政治思想史, translation by L. T. Ch'en, *History of Chinese Political Thought during the Early Tsin Period* (1930); "Hsüeh-wen chih ch'ü-wei" 學問之趣味; *Ju-chia che-hsüeh* 儒家哲學; "Ku-shu chen-wei chi ch'i nien-tai" 古書眞僞及其年代; *Kuan Tzu Chuan* 管子傳; "Lun Chung-kuo hsüeh-shu ssu-hsiang pien-ch'ien chih ta-shih" 論中國學術思想變遷之大勢; *Mo-ching chiao-shih* 墨經校釋; *Mo Tzu hsüeh-an* 墨子學案; "P'ing Hu Shih *Chung-kuo che-hsüeh-shih Ta-kang*" 評胡適中國哲學史大綱; *Shao-nien Chung-kuo shuo* 少年中國說

Liang Yü-sheng 梁玉繩 (1745–1819), *Shih Chi chih-yi* 史記志疑

Liao, W. K., *Han Fei Tzu, Works from the Chinese*, two volumes, 1939, 1959

Lieh Tzu 列子 (post-Han work attributed to pre-Ch'in philosopher Lieh Yü-k'ou), translation by A. C. Graham, *The Book of Lieh Tzu*, 1960

Lin Ch'un-p'u 林春溥 (1775–1861), *Chu-po shan-fang shih-wu-chung* 竹柏山房十五種, containing *K'ung Tzu nien-piao* 孔子年表; *Meng Tzu lieh-chuan tsuan* 孟子列傳纂

Ling T'ing-k'an 凌廷堪 (1757–1809), *Chiao-li-t'ang chi* 校禮堂集

Liu An 劉安 (179?–122 B.C.), *Huai-nan Tzu* 淮南子 or, *Huai-nan Hung-lieh* 淮南鴻烈; for translation of *ch.* 11, see under Wallacker, B. E.

Liu Hsiang 劉向 (77–6 B.C.) of the following titles or sections of works cited, some exist only in fragments: *Hsin Hsü* 新序; *Shuo Yüan* 說苑; *Sun Ch'ing shu lu hsü* 孫卿書錄序; *Pieh-lu* 別錄; *Ch'i-lüeh* 七略; *Shih Pen* 世本; *Hung-fan wu-hsing chuan* 洪範五行傳

Liu Ta-k'uei 劉大櫆 (1697?–1779), *Hai-feng wen-chi* 海峯文集

Liu Tsung-yüan 柳宗元 (773–813): *Liu Ho-tung chi* 柳河東集 containing "Feng-chien lun" 封建論; *Liu Liu-chou wen-chi* 柳柳州文集 containing "Pien Lieh Tzu" 辨墨子

Liu Wen-tien 劉文典 (modern scholar), *Huai-nan Hung-lieh chi-chieh* (1933) 淮南鴻烈集解

Liu Yi-ch'ing 劉義慶 (403–444), *Shih-shuo hsin-yü* 世說新語, translation by Richard B. Mather, *A New Account of Tales of the World* (1976)

Lo Chen-yü 羅振玉 (1866–1940), *Yin-hsü shu-ch'i k'ao-shih* 殷墟書契考釋

Lo Ken-tse 羅根澤 (modern scholar), *Kuan Tzu t'an-yüan* (1931) 管子探源

Lu K'uei-hsün 陸奎勳 (1663–1738), *Tai Chi hsü-yen* 戴記緒言

Lu Sheng 魯勝 (active A.D. 290–306), *Mo Pien chu* 墨辯注

Lü Pu-wei 呂不韋 (died 237 B.C.), assembled scholars who compiled his *Lü-shih Ch'un-ch'iu* 呂氏春秋

Ma Hsü-lun 馬敍倫 (born 1884), *Lao Tzu ho-ku* 老子覈詁; *Lieh Tzu wei-shu k'ao* 列子僞書考

Ma Kuo-han 馬國翰 (1794–1857), compiler, *Yü-han shan-fang chi-yi-shu* 玉函山房輯逸書

Ma Su 馬驌 (1621–1673), *Yi-shih* 繹史

Ma Tsung 馬總 (died 823), *Yi-lin* 意林

Machiavelli, Niccolo, *Il Principe* (1531)

Mao Ch'i-ling 毛奇齡 (1623–1716), *Mao Hsi-ho ho-chi* 毛西河合集, containing: *Ssu-shu sheng-yen* 四書賸言, *Ssu-shu kai-ts'o* 四書改錯

Mariana, Juan de, *De rege et regis institutione* (1559)

McIlwain, Charles H., *The Growth of Political Thought in the West* (1932)

Mei, Y. P., *The Ethical and Political Works of Motze, from the Chinese* (1929)

Meng Wen-t'ung 蒙文通 (modern scholar), "Ju-chia cheng-chih ssu-hsiang chih fa-chan" 儒家政治思想之發展, *Chih-lin* 志林, *Journal of National Northeastern University*, no. 2

Mill, J. S., *On Liberty* (1859)

Mo Ti 墨翟 (ca. 490 to ca. 403 B.C.), *Mo Tzu* 墨子, partial translations by Y. P. Mei (1929); B. Watson (1963)

Ou Tsung-yu 歐宗佑 (modern scholar), "Yen-t'ieh chün-shu chih yu-lai chi hsing-chih" 鹽鐵均輸之由來及性質; Chung-shan University, *Li-shih yü-yen yen-chiu-so chou-k'an*, 1: 7, December, 1927, pp. 159–165

Pan Ku 班固 (A.D. 32–92), *Po-hu t'ung* 白虎通, i.e., *Po-hu t'ung-yi* 白虎通義 or *Po-hu t'ung-te lun* 白虎通德論; Han scholarly work probably wrongly attributed to Pan Ku. Partial translation and study by Tjan Tjoe Som, *Po hu t'ung*, *The Comprehensive Discussions in the White Tiger Hall*, volume one, 1949

Pan Piao 班彪 (A.D. 3–54), "*Wang Ming Lun*" 王命論

Paine, Thomas, *Common Sense* (1776); *The Rights of Man* (1972)

P'ei Yin 裴駰 (fourth century A.D.), *Shih Chi Chi-chieh* 史記集解

Pi Yüan 畢沅 (1745–1799), *Mo Tzu Chu* 墨子注

Plato, *The Republic*

P'u Hsüeh-feng 浦薛鳳 (modern scholar), *Hsi-yang chin-tai cheng-chih ssu-ch'ao* 西洋近代政治思潮

Rickett, W. Allyn, *Kuan-tzu, A Repository of Early Chinese Thought* (study with translation of twelve chapters of the *Kuan Tzu*) (1965)

Rousseau, Jean-Jacques, *Social Contract* (1962)

Sedulius Scotus (Scottus), *De Rectoribus Christianis* (ca. 860)

Shang Chün Shu, The Book of Lord Shang, see Kung-sun Yang

Shao Yung 邵雍 (1011–1077), *Huang chi ching-shih shu* 皇極經世書

Shen Tao 慎到 (ca. 350 to ca. 275 B.C.), *Shen Tzu* 慎子, text preserved in critical editions by: Shen Mou-shang 慎懋賞 (late Ming), and Ch'ien Hsi-tso 錢熙祚 (1801–1844)

Shih Chiao 尸佼[校] (fourth century B.C.), *Shih Tzu* 尸子, cited in edition of Wang Chi-p'ei 汪繼培 (born 1775), in the collectanea *Hu-hai-lou ts'ung-shu* 湖海樓叢書

SKTY, see below

Ssu-k'u ch'üan-shu tsung-mu t'i-yao 四庫全書總目提要 (abbreviated SKTY), "*Abstracts of Works in the Catalog of the Ch'ing Imperial Library*" (1781)

Ssu-ma Chen 司馬貞 (T'ang), *Shih Chi So-yin* 史記索引

Stirner, Max (Kaspar Schmidt), *Der Einzige und sein Eigenthum* (1844)

Stubbs, William, *The Consitutional History of England* (1874)

Su Shih 蘇軾 (1037–1101), *Tung-p'o hsü-chi* 東坡續集; contains the essay "*Ch'un-ch'iu pien Chou*" 春秋變周

Su Yü 蘇輿 (died 1914), *Ch'un-ch'iu Fan-lu yi-cheng* 春秋繁露義證, contains "*Tung Tzu nien-piao*" 董子年表

Sun Feng-yi 孫馮翼 (Ch'ing), *Wen-ching-t'ang ts'ung-shu* (1797–1802) 問經堂叢書

Sun Hsing-yen 孫星衍 (1753–1818): *K'ung Tzu chi-yü shih-p'u* 孔子集語事譜; "*Mo Tzu chu hou-hsü*" 墨子註後序

Sun Yi-jang 孫詒讓 (1848–1908), *Mo Tzu chien-ku* 墨子閒詁; appended to most editions are: *Mo Tzu chuan lüeh* 墨子傳略; *Mo-hsüeh ch'uan-shou k'ao* 墨學傳授考; *Mo-chia chu-tzu kou-ch'en* 墨家諸子鉤沉; *Mo Tzu nien-piao hsü* 墨子年表序

Sung Lien 宋濂 (1310–1381), *Chu Tzu Pien* 諸子辨

Swann, Nancy Lee, *Food and Money in Ancient China; Han Shu Twenty-four with Related Texts*, translated and annotated (1950)

T'ai-p'ing yü-lan 太平御覽, encyclopedic work compiled about A.D. 980, by Li Fang 李昉 and others

Takeuchi, Yoshio 武內義雄 (modern scholar), "*Lieh Tzu yüan-tz'u*" 列子冤詞 (published in Chinese; publication data unavailable)

T'an Ssu-t'ung 譚嗣同 (1865–1898), *Jen-hsüeh* 仁學

Tao-te Ching, see *Lao Tzu*

T'ao Hung-ch'ing 陶鴻慶 (modern scholar), critical notes on the *Huai-nan Tzu*, cited by author's name only

Teng Hsi 鄧析 (pre-Ch'in), *Teng Hsi Tzu* 鄧析子, critical edition by Wang Ch'i-hsiang 王啓湘, in his *Chou-Ch'in Ming-chia san Tzu chiao-ch'üan* 周秦名家三子校詮 (1957)

Ti Tzu-ch'i 狄子奇 (nineteenth century), *Meng Tzu pien-nien* 孟子編年

Tsou Yen 鄒衍 (third century B.C.), the titles cited are known today only in fragments of the originals: *Tsou Tzu* 鄒子; *Chung-shih wu-te* 終始五德; *Ta-sheng* 大聖; *T'an-t'ien* 談天; *Ch'un-ch'iu Tsou-shih chuan* 春秋鄒氏傳

Ts'ui Shih 崔適 (1851–1924), *Shih Chi t'an-yüan* 史記探源

Ts'ui Shu 崔述 (1740–1816): *Chu-Ssu k'ao-hsin lu* 洙泗考信錄; *Meng Tzu shih-shih lu* 孟子事實錄

Tu Yu 杜佑 (735–812), compiler of the *T'ung Tien* 通典

Tung Chung-shu 董仲舒 (ca. 179 to ca. 104 B.C.): *Ch'un-ch'iu fan-lu* 春秋繁露; other works by Tung cited by title or quoted from fragments (most are known only by fragments), include: *Ch'un-ch'iu chüeh-shih pi* 春秋決事比; *Kung-yang Tung Chung-shu chih-yü* 公羊董仲舒 治獄; *Tung Chung-shu pai-erh-shih-san p'ien* 董仲舒百二十三篇

Tung Yüeh 董說 (1620–1686), *Ch'i-kuo-k'ao* 七國考

T'ung Tien, see Tu Yu

Tzu Hua Tzu 子華子 (pre-Ch'in Taoist work; fragments only extant)

Waley, Arthur: *The Analects of Confucius* (1938); *Three Ways of Thought in Ancient China* (1939); *The Way and Its Power* (1935); *The Book of Songs* (1937)

Wallacker, Benjamin E., *The Huai-nan Tzu, Book Eleven: Behavior, Culture and the Cosmos* (1962), a study with translation and annotation of *ch.* 11, "Ch'i su" 齊俗

Wang Chien 王檢 (modern scholar), translator of Hugo Krabbe, *Modern Ideas of the State*, under the title *Chin-tai kuo-chia kuan-nien* 今代國家觀念

Wang Chung 汪中 (1745–1794), *Shu Hsüeh* 述學, containing the following titles cited in the present work: "Lao Tzu k'ao-yi" 老子考異; "*Mo Tzu* hsü" 墨子序; "Hsün Tzu nien-piao" 荀子年表; "Ching-yi hsin-chih chi" 經義新知記

Wang Ch'ung 王充 (A.D. 27 to ca. 100), *Lun Heng* 論橫; translation by Alfred Forke, two volumes, 1907, 1911

Wang Fu 王符 (active ca. A.D. 120–160), *Ch'ien fu lun* 潛夫論; cited in critical edition of Wang Chi-p'ei 汪繼培 (born 1775), in *Hu-hai-lou ts'ung-shu* 湖海樓叢書

Wang Hsien-ch'ien 王先謙 (1842–1918), "[*Yen-t'ieh lun*] chiao-k'an hsiao-chih" [鹽鐵論]校刊小識

Wang Hsien-shen 王先愼 (recent scholar), *Han Fei Tzu chi-chieh* (1895) 韓非子集解

Wang Kuo-wei 王國維 (1877–1927), *Ku-shih Hsin-cheng* 古史新證

Wang T'ung 王通 (583–616), *Yüan ching* 元經

Wei Yüan 魏源 (1794–1856), *Ku-wei-t'ang wai-chi* 古微堂外集; containing "Meng Tzu nien-piao k'ao" 孟子年表考

Wu Yi 武億 (1745–1799), "Pa *Mo Tzu*" 跋墨子 (appended to Sun Yi-jang's *Mo Tzu chien-ku*

Yang Liang 楊倞 (ninth century), *Hsün Tzu chu* 荀子注 (first printed 818)

Yang Yu-chiung 楊幼炯 (modern scholar), *Chung-kuo cheng-chih ssu-hsiang-shih* 中國政治思想史

Yao Chi-heng 姚際恆 (born 1647), *Ku-chin wei-shu k'ao* 古今偽書考

Yao Nai 姚鼐 (1732–1815), *Lao Tzu chang-yi* 老子章義

Yao Shun-ch'in 姚舜欽 (modern scholar), *Ch'in Han che-hsüeh shih* 秦漢哲學史

Yao Wen-t'ien 姚文田 (1758–1827), *Sui-ya-t'ang chi* 邃雅堂集

Yeh Shih 葉適 (1150–1223), *Hsi-hsüeh chi-yen* 習學記言

Yen Fu 嚴復 (1853–1921), translator of Edward Jenks' *A History of Politics* (1900) under the title *She-hui t'ung-ch'üan* (1904) 社會通詮

Yen Jo-chü 嚴若璩 (1636–1704), "*Meng Tzu sheng-tsu nien-yüeh k'ao*" 孟子生卒年月考

Yen K'o-chün 嚴可均 (1762–1843), *T'ieh-ch'iao man-kao* 鐵橋漫稿; *Ch'üan shang-ku san-tai Ch'in-Han San-kuo Liu-ch'ao wen* 全上古三大秦漢三國六朝文 (lost ancient texts assembled from scattered fragments)

Yen Ying 晏嬰 (sixth century B.C.), *Yen Tzu ch'un-ch'iu* 晏子春秋 (traditionally attributed to Yen Ying)

Yi Chou shu 逸周書 (anonymous ancient historical work)

Yi Shih-chen 伊世珍 (Yüan), *Lang-huan chi* 瑯環[嬛]記

Ying Shao 應劭 (ca. 140 to ca. 206), *Feng-su t'ung(-yi)* 風俗通[義]

Yü Cheng-hsieh 俞正燮 (1775–1840), *Kuei-ssu lei-kao* 癸巳類稿

Yü Chia-hsi 余嘉錫 (modern scholar), *Ssu-k'u t'i-yao pien-cheng* (1932) 四庫提要辨證

Yü Yüeh 俞樾 (1821–1907), *Chu Tzu p'ing-yi* (1870) 諸子平議

Yüeh Shih 樂史 (930–1007), (*T'ai-p'ing*) *Huan-yü chi* [太平]寰宇記

Zürcher, Eric, *The Buddhist Conquest of China*, two volumes (1959)

Index

abdication, *see* succession theory

ability, *hsien*; in *Mo Tzu*, *see* worthy, elevation of; in *Kuan Tzu*, 364–65; *neng*, or *ts'ai-neng*, Hsün Tzu's primary criterion, 189, 197–98; the man of *neng* will receive the Mandate (*Yi-ching*), 518

absolute equity, *chih p'ing*, as goal of the orderly society (Hsün Tzu), 186

absolutism, *see* authoritarianism; monarchic despotism

accomplishment and profit, *kung-li*, *see* utilitarianism

according with the times, *yin-shih* (Huan T'an), 534

action, political activism, *see* purposive action; no action, non-action, etc.; *see also* non-action

actuality and name, *see* hsing-ming

"actualities (of history) allow this, but the style (of historiography) does not" (*shih yü erh wen pu yü*), as formulaic element in *Kung-yang* and *Ku-liang* Commentaries, 134–36, 281n

Adams, George B., English constitutional historian, 345n

administration of the state, *wei kuo* (Hsün Tzu), 203

administrative measures, *cheng*, *see* governing

admonition, *hsün*, in *Kuan Tzu*: appropriate for women, 350; form of ruler's guidance over society, 353

advantage, *see* profit, *li*

advisors, political, how to use correctly (in Legalism), 412ff. *See also* political strategists

aggression, aggressive war, *see* war; warfare

agricultural year, work cycles of in re politics, 150n, 154n, 187, 262, 338, 338n, 355, 360n

Agriculturalist School, *Nung-chia*, in pre-Ch'in political thought, 61, 64–65, 69, 71, 75, 220n. *See also* Hsü Hsing

agriculture (and sericulture), *nung* (-*sang*) as mankind's basic activity: in Confucius, 119; in Hsün Tzu, 209; in the *Kuan Tzu*, 351–52; books on exempted from Ch'in ban on private learning, 437; in *Debates on Salt and Iron*, 462–63; stressed by Wang Fu, 539; by Hsün Yüch, 542–43

agriculture, Hou-chi patron of, 119; in re politics, in Confucius, 109–110, in Mencius, 150n, 152, 154n, in Mo Tzu, 220n; stimulating production, in the *Kuan Tzu*, 357–58, in Han era, 454–55; Han Ministry of (*Ta Ssu-nung*) had economic management functions, 455. *See also* taxation, farmers

agriculture and crafts, *nung kung*, as occupations of the masses: in the *Mo Tzu*, 253; in the *Kuan Tzu*, 351–52; interdependence of seen by Sang Hung-yang, 459–62

agriculture and war, Legalist statist means: Chapter Seven, Section Three, 393–97, 423, 443; discussed by Han Legalist-minded thinkers, 454–55

ai, *see* love

alchemy (*huang-po chih shu*), First Emperor's use of, 443; discussed in the *Huai-nan Tzu*, 571

alien intrusions in re political thought, 16–18; Buddhism as alien doctrine, 656, 660, 662–67; as feature of cultural history, 666–67. *See also* Barbarians

alliances, "vertical and horizontal" *tsung-heng*, of Warring States era, 42n, 144, 361n, 415. *See also* diplomacy

allotments and assignments, *fen*, 192, 325. *See also* social differentiation

Altars of the State, *she-chi*, *see* Land and Grain, Altars of

alternating order and chaos, cyclical theory in Mencius: Chapter Three, Section Four, 177–82; random convergences determining, in *Lü-shih Ch'un-ch'iu* (compared with Mencius), 569

Analects of Confucius, *Lun Yü*, mentioned, 52n, 55n, 76n

quoted or cited (quotations and citations in Chapter Two, 79–142, are not individually indexed below):

Book One, I/6: 229–30, 392n

anarchism, comparable to modern "*wu cheng-fu ssu-hsiang*," in *Chuang Tzu*, 20, 317–18, *Chuang Tzu's* compared with European, 318n; in Taoism, 41–42, 161; *Lao Tzu's* "inaction differs from, 298–99; anarchism expressed as "no-rulerism," *wu-chün chu-yi*, in Neo-Taoist thought, 602f, 606, 619–30; opposed by Neo-Taoist "relative non-action," 612; extreme expression of anarchism by Pao Ching-yen, 623–30; Pao Ching-yen refuted by Ko Hung, 651–56

ancestor veneration among the people, 351; in re The Law of the Inner Gate, in State of Ch'in, 402n

ancestral shrines of the ruling house, *T'ai-miao*, *Ch'ing-miao*, 275n, 277, 307, 312, 625

Ancient Kings, *hsien wang*, *see* Former Kings

anti-fatalism, *fei-ming* (*Mo Tzu*), 226, 248–50. *See also* fate

anti-music, *fei-yüeh* (*Mo Tzu*), 226, 257–65. *See also* music

apocrypha, *wei shu*, influence of on Confucian learning during Former Han, 472; in re Mandate theory in Han, 486ff; quoted, *see* portents

apportionment, of material wealth of society, *see* absolute equity; distribution of goods

Approaching Peace, Ascending Peace, *sheng-p'ing*, one of the Three Ages as defined by K'ang Yu-wei, 127–29; in Ho Hsiu's Three Ages Theory, 529–30

archaism, in Confucius and Mencius, 172, 230, 242; in Mencius as contrasted with Confucius,181 ; in Hsün Tzu, 201–02

archives, at courts of Chou era, 269, 281; Lao Tzu said to have been archivist, *chu-hsia-shih* of Chou court, 85, 273n, 275, 281. *See also* records on wood and bamboo tablets

archives, of Han dynasty government, dispersed after A.D. 190, 604n

aristocracy, *in Chou era*: changing status of, 195; decline of, 32, 91, 93; debauchery of, 261, 378; disappearance of, 324, 409;

in terms of excessive *Yin* forces, 510; the Wang clan, late in Former Han, 514n; during Later Han, 531, 633; used portents to obtain dismissals and appointments, 533n; tend to become problem during mid-course of dynasties, according to Chung-ch'ang T'ung, 546

constitutional government in Europe, developed from concepts of the Rule of Law, 420, 445n

constitutional monarch in Europe, compared with China's authoritarian despot, 445

consumption, ideal of increasing, 186n, 262, 262n

consumption, regulation of, *chieh-yung* (*Mo Tzu*), *see* economy of expenditures

consumption, to be restricted, in the *Mo Tzu*, 258; in the *Kuan Tzu*, 357–58; reduced so as to increase wealth, 262; profligate extravagance of in Han times, 502–03; ruler's should avoid extravagance, according to *Lü-shih Ch'un-chiu*, 564. *See also*: economy of expenditure; wealth, material, etc

contentment, *chih tsu* (Taoism), 289, 317, 619a

Continuation (Continuity), Period of (221 B.C. to 1367), 12–16, 425ff

convention, conventional behavior, expressed as Confucian *li-chiao*, rejected by Neo-Taoist anarchists, 630–40

cooks, cooking, in political metaphor, 417n

cooperation, *see* social organization

correlative theories, *see* interactions (between heaven and man), *kan-ying*

correspondence, between physical man and the numerical categories of heaven, 489n

corvée, *see* labor service

cosmology, 62, 292–93; cosmos and human affairs, explained in terms of *chu-yün*, *shih-yün*, the dominant cosmic influences of an age, in the *Yin-Yang* school, 61, 64, 64n, 65, 485, 524n; random convergences of cosmic influences determine order and chaos (*Lü-shih Ch'un-ch'iu*), 569–70; cosmos and human affairs (*Huai-nan Tzu*), 572–74; human events independent of cosmic influences, in Hsün Tzu, 206–11; in Wang Ch'ung, 585ff; cos-

mology of Wei-Chin Taoism, 610–11, relevance for government, 611ff; the *Lieh Tzu's* cosmology derived from *Lao Tzu*, 637–38

crafts and commerce, or craftsmen and merchants, *kung-shang*, the "secondary occupations," in the *Kuan Tzu*, 357–58, 360n; in the *Debates on Salt and Iron*, 458–62; growth of in the mid-Chou State of Ch'i, 361, 362n; to be discouraged, according to Fu Hsüan, 644. *See also* arts and crafts

craftsmen, *kung*, one of four occupational categories of society, Mo Tzu as a craftsman, 215, 258; in the *Kuan Tzu*, 351

creation, intentional act of, not present in Taoist cosmology, 292

Creativity, Period of (551–221 B.C.), 9–12, 28–424

Creel, H. G., modern scholar, cited, 101; his *Confucius, the Man and the Myth*, translator's comments on, 92n, 97–98, 98n

cultivation of character, *hsiu shen*, 164n, 204. *See also* self-cultivation, *tzu-hsiu*

cultural identity, transcending race, 24n

customs, practices of the people, how regulated, *ching-su*, in the *Kuan Tzu*, Chapter Six, Section Four, 347–55; responsibility of government, in Hsün Yüeh, 542–43; those of China and Barbarians differ (anti-Buddhist argument), 663

cycles of cosmic motion, 611

cyclical theories, of government, 62, 177–82; in Mencius, 177–82, 569; of cosmic explanation, 210, in Taoism, 284–91; in re Five Agents, 338n; of historical explanation, 530; of cosmic alternations, 649

Cynics, of ancient Greek thought, 318

cynicism and hypocrisy, in re Hsün Tzu, 193n

Cyrenaic School of ancient Greek thought, 318

Debates on Salt and Iron, *see* Huan K'uan

debts, social problem, solution proposed in the *Kuan Tzu*, 360n, 362

decadence, of elite life from end of Han

dynasty onward, 605

defamation and praise, in political life, *see* Pure Critiques

delegation of authority by ruler, urged by Hsün Tzu, 196–97

democracy, in Chinese past, perceived by K'ang Yu-wei, 128, 128n; in re Mencius, 161; in re Mo Tzu, 242–43; tendencies toward in the *Lao Tzu*, 290–91, 422; why not emergent from the *Chuang Tzu*, 316–18; compared with authoritarianism, 332n; development of in England, 345n, in Europe, 346; law in relation to democracy, 346n

deportment, *yi*, defined, 182. *See also* propriety

desires, limitation of in Taoism, 42, 289, 297, 555n, in Neo-Taoism, 619, 620–21, "divesting onself of desires, day by day, *jih-sun*, 68: gratification of, in Hsün Tzu, 184–85, 186n, in the *Lü-shih Ch'un-ch'iu*, 561, 564; contradictory statements about in the *Lieh Tzu*, 641n; attitudes toward compared, 643; unchecked desires destructive, according to P'ei Wei, 645

despotism, 346n; need for rulers to be despotic (Legalism), 417–18; Confucians' attempts to limit by arousing rulers' fears, 485ff. *See also* monarchic authoritarianism

destiny (of state), *see* fate, *ming*

dialectical pairs, of nature (Taoism), 284–85

diminution, decreasing actions, *sun*, in Taoist political thought, 59, 294, 317–18, 421, 578

diplomacy in pre-Ch'in era, 23–24, 269, 361n; as aid to preventing war (*Mo Tzu*), 270

Diplomatists, School of, *tsung-heng chia*, 42n, 90, 415, 472n, 526

disciplines, spiritual and physical, *lien-tan*, of Taoism, practised by Ko Hung, 650

dismissals from highest offices, as response to portents during Han, 531, 533, 533n

distinctions, to make or to fix, *pieh*, to differentiate, of social role, in Hsün Tzu, 184, 185, 185n, 188–89; in *Mo Tzu* as perceived by Hsün Tzu, 254–55; all distinctions merged, in Chuang Tzu's

relativism, 302–05; invented by Sage Kings of the past, according to Ko Hung, 651–52, 655n

"distinguishing black from white, fixing a single standard" *pien hei-pai erh ting yi-tsun*, phrase describing the absolute and arbitrary policies of the First Emperor of Ch'in, 200, 437, 580, 617

distribution of goods in society, importance of equity in, to Confucians, 110; equity of, in Confucius and Mencius, 154, 154n; in Hsün Tzu, 186–88; evils in inequality of according to *Lao Tzu*, 295; discussed by Tung Chung-shu, 501

divination, noted favorably by Confucius, 208; efficacy of denied by Hsün Tzu, 209; by rulers, described in "Hung Fan" chapter of the *Documents*, 211n; by tortoise and milfoil, works on exempted from Ch'in ban on private learning, 437; prominence of in Former Han, 485; misused by "petty diviners," 485n

Divine Agriculturalist, *shen-nung*, mythical ruler and culture hero of high antiquity, 71, 72, 308n, 567, 578, 581n, 652n

divine authority used by Mo Tzu to reinforce secular authority, 246–50

divine beings, *see* spirits and gods

"Divine Province," i.e., China, see *shen-chou*

division of labor, as social principle in the *Mo Tzu*, 220n, 221n, 253f; in the *Kuan Tzu*, 357, 357n

divorce, men divorcing wives discouraged by *Kuan Tzu*, 350

Doctrine of the Mean, Chung-yung, attributed to Tzu-ssu, quoted: 10, 20, 70, 93, 97, 100, 108, 123, 190, 200, 279, 493, 542; paraphrased, 202, 281, 408; discussed, 129n, 143n, 207–08, 208n, 484n, 665

Documents, Book of, or *Classic of History, shu, shang-shu, shu-ching*, quoted, 44n, 106n, 113, 115n, 117n, 152, 158n, 211n, 246, 249n, 494; cited, 44, 104–05, 115–16, 120n, 131, 160, 175, 179, 180, 180n, 231n, 278n, 484n, 497, 505, 515, 540, 562n, 563n, 586–87, 593, 628, 662n; Erudits for, in Han government, 437, 467, 664; discussed, as a text, 3, 3n, 12, 104–05, 117n, 471, as object of study, 5n, 10, 11, 71, 84, 437, 468n, 472. *See*

302–05; equality before the laws, demanded in Legalist theory, 401–03, 449–50; the natural condition of man according to Pao Ching-yen, 623–24

Erh-ya, early Han period (?) dictionary, 591

Erudit, *po-shih, see* scholars

escapism, in *Lü-shih Ch'un-ch'iu,* 570

essence and function, *t'i-yung,* 156

ethical formalism, Confucian, *li-chiao, ming-chiao,* reactions against in Wei-Chin era, 631, 634ff, 637, 649; Confucian ethical norms, *li-chiao,* in decline in third century A.D., 645; *ming-chiao* upheld by Ko Hung, 655

ethics, in Confucius, *jen* as social ethics, 102–03; ethical issues in Confucius' thought, 107, 110–14, 121–24, in Mencius, 165; consistency between ethics and politics in Confucius and Mencius, 192; to be maintained by the rites, in Hsün Tzu, 182–85; Confucian ethics compared with the *Mo Tzu,* 256–57; in the *Kuan Tzu,* 348–50; placed beyond scope of politics, in Legalism, 386–87; ethics *versus* law as standard for behavior, in Legalism, 401, at issue in *Debates on Salt and Iron,* 464–68; in Chia Yi, 479, 563; in Wang Ch'ung, 588, 600; in re Buddhism, 660ff

　　the material basis of ethics: in Mencius, 152; in the *Mo Tzu,* 234; in the *Kuan Tzu,* 355–56; in Wang Ch'ung, 594

ethics, *te, versus* effectiveness, *kung,* in officialdom, Confucianism and Mohism compared, 256–57; effectiveness the more important according to Ts'ao Ts'ao, 634n

ethnocentric thought, Chinese, 17; denial of ethnic barriers, 24–25, 137–42; in anti-Buddhist arguments of Six Dynasties era, 662–67. *See also:* Barbarians; alien intrusions

eunuchs, at court of Han Emperors Yüan and Ch'eng, 505; at Later Han court, 531, 632

European political thought compared with China's, 7, 7n, 383. *See also* Law, Rule of; democracy; and names of Western political thinkers, e.g. Plato, Bentham, etc. etc.

evaluation of officials' performance, *see* officialdom

evil effluvium, *hsieh ch'i,* or "deviant force," in Tung Chung-shu, 496

"Evolution of the Rites," "Li Yün," chapter in the *Li Chi,* authenticity of discussed, 125–27. *See also Li Chi*

expenditures, control over, in the *Mo Tzu, see* economy of expenditure

exploitation of natural resources, *chin ti-li,* Legalist doctrines concerning, *see* statism

fa, law, laws and norms, models, in Legalist doctrine, 21, 76; as rules of government in Chou times, 95n; in Chia Yi, 477; as methods of the Former Kings, in Mencius, 175, 177; as models, in Tung Chung-shu, 490. *See also: li* and *fa* compared; laws; Legalism; etc.

Fa Ching, the *Classic on Laws, see* Li K'uei

fa kuan, law officers, in Legalist practice, 399

fa li, law-enforcing officials, to serve as teachers of the empire, in Legalist ideal, 399

factions, in learning, *see* school; in politics, 363, 538; of great families, tend to control wealth and power (*Debates on Salt and Iron*), 462; formed on status lines at Later Han court, 531; factional struggles of late Han analyzed, 632ff

faith, *see* trust, *hsin*

fame, desire for as motive for aggressive war, 268–69

family, as basis of Confucian ethics and social order, 102–04, 120, 149n, 195; legal issues of family responsibility, 173; Confucianism compared with Mohist thought, 233, 255; family interests opposed by Mo Tzu, 227–28, 233; Confucian family primacy compared with Legalism, 386–87; in Chia Yi, 480–81; clan heads in re local government, in Mo Tzu, 237–38; family primacy superseded by "higher principle" *ta-yi mieh-ch'in,* 255; family values, in the *Kuan Tzu,* 349, 390; stress on family organization, in the *Kuan Tzu,* 350–51, 354, 365; family values incompatible with goals of Legalism, 405, 413; clan interests, in Ko Hung, 653;

threatened by Buddhism, 657

family relationships in re higher principle of integrity, characterized by Duke of Chou ("*ta-yi mieh-ch'in*"), 255

famine, and rulers' responsibilities, in Mencius, 261; provision against, in the *Kuan Tzu*, 349; in Sang Hung-yang, 460; Legalist views of problem, 405n. *See also* relief measures

fan ai, "broad and encompassing love for mankind," in Confucianism, *see* love

Fan Ch'ih, i.e., Fan Hsü, disciple of Confucius, 80, 83, 87, 137, 207, 230

Fan Chü (also read Fan Sui), the Marquis of Ying, early third-century strategist in Ch'u, 147, 205n, 428n

Fan K'uan, meritorious official of the first reign of Han, 428n

Fan Ning, ca. 326 to ca. 418, scholar-official and Confucian-minded opponent of Buddhism during Eastern Chin, 610, 610n, 647, 655

Fang Hsiao-ju, 1357–1402, scholar, 558n

fang-po, Chou era "Earls of the Marches," 29n

fang-shih, *see* Taoist adepts; magicians

Fang Shou-ch'u, modern scholar, expert on Mohism, 57n, 61n, 214n, 215n, 218n, 222n, 223n, 224n, 226n, 230, 241n, 246n, 256n; views on decline of Mohism, 433n

farmers, *nung*, one of four occupational categories in society, in the *Kuan Tzu*, 351

"fasting of the mind," *hsin-chai*, a state of mind, in Chuang Tzu, 303n

fatalism, *su-ming lun*, in Wang Ch'ung's *Lun Heng*, 584–85, 591–601; in Neo-Taoist cosmology, 611; in the *Lieh Tzu*, 637–38. *See also* fate

fate (personal), or destiny (of the state), *ming*, the Chou dynasty's destiny, 169n; in Mencius, 179; denied by Hsün Tzu, 210; in Mohism, *see* anti-fatalism; in Confucius and Mencius, compared with Mohism, 230, 249–50; unworried acceptance of, in *Lü-shih Ch'un-ch'iu*, 570; views of compared, 584–85; *ming* as fortuitous conjunctions, in Wang Ch'ung, 591ff; all things subject to their own fates, in Neo-Taoism, 611; fate *vs.*

effort, in the *Lieh Tzu*, 638

favorites of the ruler, as an evil of government, 253; wastefulness of, 261; dangers from, 412ff, 453; Han Emperor Yuan warned against, 507

feigned benevolence, *see* pretence to benevolence

female, symbol of the, in Lao Tzu, 287

female infanticide, 389

fen, measure, share, i.e., as the "legitimate claim" to rulership that the upstart lacks according to Chung-ch'ang T'ung, 545. *See also* allotments and assignments, *fen*

Feng-su t'ung, *see* Ying Shao

Feng Yu-lan, *see* Fung Yu-lan

feudal, i.e. *feng-chien* social order and era, term defined, 5; in *Mo Tzu*, 236–37, 240; feudal world, in thought, 19–20, 71, 129, 144; era in social history, 8n, 28–33, 86, 300, 317; geographic factors in re, 42–65; Chou fedual forms in Confucian thought, 86–87, 89–91, 98, 101–04, 120, 134–42, 167, 323, in Mencius, 172–75; personal relationships dominated by, 194; collapse of as background for emergence of Legalism, 375–76; feudal elements in the *Kuan Tzu*, 354–55, 364, 367; feudal law compared with Legalist, 402; feudal decentralization ended in 221 B.C., 427ff, 434; its restoration urged by Chia Yi, 482–83, 483n, by Hsün Yüeh, 543, by various thinkers during third century A.D. and in early T'ang, 544, by *Lü-shih Ch'un-ch'iu*, 567–68

figurehead monarch, *hsü chün*, the ideal of the *Lao Tzu*, 291

filial piety, filial submission, classic of, *see Hsiao Ching*

filial piety, *hsiao* (and fraternal submission, *ti*), doctrine of, in Confucian thought, 102–03, 112, 147, 152, 193n; linked with loyalty, 155n, with self-cultivation and good government, 255; as an issue in the *Mo Tzu*, 227–28, 233, 233n; in the *Kuan Tzu*, 349, 350–51, 364; seen as a vice, in Legalism, 386–87, 404; opposed by Lao Tzu, 421; stressed in Chia Yi, 480–81; father-son relationship seen by Tung Chung-shu on analogy to

Kings

Former Sages, *hsien sheng*, doctrines of, 200

forms, *t'i*, or embodiments, of righteousness, in the *Kuan Tzu*, *see* seven forms; of government, *cheng-t'i*, in Hsün Yüeh, 541

four afflictions, *ssu huan*, of government and society, in Hsün Yüeh, 542–43

four beginnings, of virtue, in the human mind, i.e., the *ssu tuan*, 149n. *See also* incipience, *tuan*

four cords, *ssu wei*, of political morality, in the *Kuan Tzu*, 348–50

four (occupational) categories of people in society, *ssu min*, in the *Kuan Tzu*, 351–55; in Spring and Autumn era writings, 354–55

four policies, *ssu cheng*, by which Confucians harmed the state, according to the *Mo Tzu*, 259

four positions (stances) of authority, which the ruler assumes, in the *Kuan Tzu*, 325

four seasons in cosmological theory, in Tung Chung-shu, 489n, 490, 492–93, 495n; in post Tung Chung-shu prognostication theory, 508, 509

four virtues, in Mencius, 148

freedom, social freedoms, versus restraints, in Hsün Tzu, 189; natural freedom, *t'ien-fang*, in *Chung Tzu*, 309–10; absolute freedom advocated by Chuang Tzu, 314–15; freedom as goal of Taoism contrasted with the goal of control, in Legalism, 422; the natural condition of man, according to Pao Ching-yen, 623–24

frontiers, defenses of, in early Han, 454–55, 457n

frugality, *chien*, or austerity, in Mohism, 257; in *Analects*, quoted by Sang Hung-yang, 461; concept of alien to modes of Ch'in dynasty, 432

frugality, *sheng-yung*, or economizing, in the *Kuan Tzu*, 349

Fruition, Period of, 1924–, 18

Fu Ch'ien, Han scholar, 34n

fu-ch'iang, *see* statism

Fu Hsüan, 217–218, scholar and Confucian thinker, author of the *Fu Tzu*, 320n, 361n, 634n, 644

fu-ku, *see* reviving the old

Fu Pu-ch'i, i.e. Tzu-ch'ien disciple of Confucius, 55

Fu Sheng, Erudit for the *Documents* in Ch'in, transmitter of that text in early Han, 468n, 471

Fu Ssu-nien, modern scholar, 34n

funerals, simplicity in, *chieh-tsang*, in Mohism, 226, 257–65, 430, 431n

funerals and burial rites, extravagance in opposed by Mo Tzu, 66, 216, 255n; burial rites mentioned in various contexts, 69, 82, 96, 96n, 100, 183, 230, 275n, 665; to be regulated by taxation, in the *Kuan Tzu*, 360n; to be subject to status regulations, in Tung Chung-shu, 501; extravagance in condenmed by Wang Ch'ung, 584n; for rulers, Han practices, 629n; subject to Confucian ethical formalism, 632–33; Buddhist, 658. *See also* mourning

Fung Yu-lan, modern scholar, on pre-Ch'in learning and thought, 7n; on the dating of Lao Tzu, 76n; on terms, 101; compares Mo Tzu and Hobbes, 239n–240n; on development of Taoist thought, 283n, 301n, 304n, 306; on people and state, in various schools, 323n; on Lord Shang's theory of "Three Ages," 392n; on *Tsa-chia*, 550n; on "*ko-yi*," 657n

Fung-Bodde, i.e., Fung Yu-lan's *Chung-kuo che-hsüeh shih*, translated by Derk Bodde as *A History of Chinese Philosophy*, *see* Bodde, Derk

genie, genii, *see fang-shih*

Germanic law, in re limitations on rulers, 346n

generous accommodation, *k'uan-jung*, a Taoist practice, 287–88

geography, concepts of, 62, 63, 338–39

ghosts, *see* spirits

gifts, ritual, political significance of, 366n

governance, the supreme, *ta-chih*, in *Huai-nan Tzu*, 574

governing, *cheng*, i.e., administrative measures, defined in re law, 335; the Way of, *chih tao*, described by Tung Chung-shu, 500–01

governing, principles of, Mohism's austerity contradicts, 263–64; Confucian and Mohist compared, 263–65; need

487
heaven's intent, *t'ien yi*, or "the mind of heaven," in Mencius, 179, 584; in Tung Chung-shu, 490, 493; determines bestowal of Mandate, 495; expressed in names and appellations, 500

heaven's time, *t'ien shih*, or the heavenly (natural) timeliness of political acts, in the *Kuan Tzu*, 337–38; in Wang Ch'ung, 593ff

heaven's will:

t'ien ming, meaning heaven's decree, heaven's command, heavenly determinism, etc., 179, 206, 207n, 211–13, 433, 542, 584; for other meanings of this term demanded by other contexts, *see*: Mandate of Heaven; fate

t'ien-chih, the will (purpose) of Heaven, in the *Mo Tzu*, 242, 243–50, 485; in Tung Chung-shu, 489n

hedonism, in Wei-Chin Neo-Taoism, 630–44

hegemon, of Chou dynasty, *see pa*

hereditary employments and privileges, in Chou society, especially the *shih-ch'ing*, or hereditary ministerships, 29n, 31n, 85, 195, 198, 211, 250, 250n, 380, 409, 433; in Confucius' thought, 119–20, 127; in Mencius, 165–66, 172–77, 347; views of Mencius and Hsün Tzu compared, 189; in the *Mo Tzu*, 250n, 252, 255–56. *See also* clan-law

hereditary occupations throughout society, in the *Kuan Tzu*, 351–55, 364; hereditary Han period offices opposed by Wang Fu, 538–40

heterodoxy, widely prevalent in Warring States period, 5, 90, 438; in later imperial period, 667

hexagrams, of the *Yi-ching*, in Han prognostication theory, 507n, 508

hierarchy, social concept and social fact, 62; accepted by Mo Tzu, 253; in the *Kuan Tzu*, 335–36; under Legalism in the Ch'in era, 372; defended by Shu Hsiang and Confucius as superior to laws, 377–78; has its archetype in nature according to Ko Hung, 651; Buddhist monks also subject to, 659–60

Hincmar of Rheims, medieval European political thinker, 345n

historiography, techniques of a conveying judgments in the *Kung-yang* and *Ku-liang* Commentaries, 134–36; office of the historians, 549n, 650

history, uses of, historical precedents as standard of validity in the *Mo Tzu*, 228n–229n

History, the, Shang Shu, see Documents

Ho Ch'ang, died A.D. 105, repudiated auspicious portents during reign of Emperor Chang (76–88), 523n, 528n

Ho Ch'ung, 292–346, pro-Buddhist statesman at Chin court who argued successfully that monks need not render homage to rulers, 662n

Ho Hsiu, T. Shao-kung, 129–182, Han political theorist and exegete, views of Confucius, 101n, 132n, 142; theory of the Three Ages, 127–31, 134; in re K'ang Yu-wei, 136; cited by Ch'ien Mu, 195n; writings of, 266n; cited by Yao Shun-ch'in, 488n; sycophancy of, 494n; in re Later Han *Kung-yang* theory, 524–30

Ho K'uei, "the old man carrying the basket," pre-Ch'in philosopher, 44, 48, 80, 122, 122n

Ho-shang Kung, "the Old Man on the Riverbank," founder of a tradition in Taoist studies, 552n, 606n

Ho-t'u, see River Chart

Ho Yen, before A.D. 209–249, Neo-Taoist thinker, 605, 607, 607n, 610–18, 619, 645, 647

Hobbes, Thomas, compared to Mo Tzu, 239n–240n; compared to Ko Hung, 653n

homage, dispute over monks' obligation to perform ritual homage to fathers and rulers, 659–62

hou, weather periods, *see* weather phenomena

Hou-chi, patron of millet, *see* Chi

Hou Han Shu, History of the Later Han Dynasty, 396n, 447n, 451n, 452n, 515n, 519n, 521n, 522n, 523n, 528n, 531n, 534n, 535, 536n, 537n, 539n, 555n, 556n, 583n, 632n

"household servitors," *see chia-ch'en*

Hsi K'ang, *see* Chi K'ang

Hsi-men Chün-hui, Taoist adept at time

442; "Continuing Strands of Legalist Thought" in the Han dynasty, Chapter Eight, Section Three, 446–55; competition with Confucianism through Han era, 456–68; Chia Yi incorrectly identified with, 474, 477n; Hsün Tzu's rigorous views close to, 543; in Huang-Lao, 550; basic tenets of challenged in *Lü-shih Ch'un-ch'iu*, 559–68; criticized in the *Huai-nan Tzu*, 572, 580; influence of evident in the *Huai-nan Tzu*, 580ff; rejected in Han times, 601; promoted by Ts'ao Ts'ao, 634n; described by Ko Hung, 651. *See also* laws, *fa*, in Legalism; *jen-fa*; etc.

Legge, James, 1815–1897, scholar and translator, 39, 101, 180

legitimacy, dynasty, *see* Mandate, Heavenly; theories establishing the Han dynasty's legitimacy, 484ff

Lei Hai-tsung, modern scholar, 601n

lèse-majesté, event of in 605 B.C., committed by the Fifth Hegemon, 366; discussed in Ko Hung, 654. *See also* ruler

Lesser Tranquility, *hsiao-k'ang*, *see* Three Ages

"letting people alone" ("letting the world alone"), *tsai-yu*, a political principle in Chuang Tzu, Chapter Five, Section Five, 306–18; principle of, not understood by some rulers, 617

li, orderly principle, as in the expression "heaven's orderly principle," *t'ien-li*, in Tung Chung-shu, 489n

li, profit, benefit, advantage, in Mencius, 154; in Mo Tzu, 231–35, 257, 258; the unprofitableness of war, in Mencius and Mo Tzu, 266–67; the advantages to be drawn from the earth, *ti-li*, in the *Kuan Tzu*, 337–38; the profits of commerce and crafts, in the *Kuan Tzu*, 347–59; profits of frontiers and markets, in Lord Shang, 395; material profit an ignoble goal of government, 464. See *also* utilitarianism, *kung-li*

li, rites and *fa*, laws, compared, in re Hsün Tzu, 182–83; in re the *Kuan Tzu*, 333–34

li, ritual, *see* rites; propriety; the *Li Chi, Book of Rites*; etc.

Li Chi, Book of Rites, discussed, 187n,

authenticity of "Li Yün" chapter discussed, 125–27

   quoted: 34n, 56n, 83n, 85, 95n, 96, 96n, 97, 99n, 115n, 125–26, 180–81, 181n, 182, 186n–87n, 189n, 190n, 207, 248n, 288n, 295, 402n

   cited: 18n, 29n, 69, 73, 94n, 143n, 183n, 263n, 274n, 275n, 338n, 431n, 484n, 506, 515, 530

Li Chi, modern scholar, 433n

Li Ch'ung, active early fourth century A.D., Confucian literatus, librarian of Chin court library, syncretizer, 648

Li Hsien, 651–84, T'ang imperial prince, annotator of the *Hou Han Shu*, 521n

Li Hsiung, associated with Kung-sun Shu in civil war at time of Han restoration, 517

li-hsüeh, Neo-Confucian rationalism, 17

Li Hsün, died 5 B.C., specialist in the *Documents*, prognostication theorist, 504, 506–07

Li K'e, pre-Ch'in writer on law, *see* Li K'uei

Li K'uei, also written Li K'e, author of a *Fa Ching*, or "Classic on Law," 10n, 32n, 43, 46, 52–53, 53n, 56, 58, 58n, 59, 66, 71, 72n, 89, 193, 369, 370–71, 373n, 377n

Li Shan, died A.D. 689, scholar, 131, 214n

Li Shang, general prominent in the Han founding, 428n

Li Ssu, ca. 280–208 B.C., Chief Minister to First Emperor of Ch'in, principal discussion of, Chapter Eight, Section Two, 434–46; as student of Hsün Tzu, 52, 66, 147n, 148, 193, 200, 374; practitioner of Legalist statecraft, 21, 59, 200, 321, 369, 447n, 450, 567, 572; responsible for Ch'in suppression of learning, 399n, 428; defined role of Legalist ruler, 432n, 452, 565; repudiated in Han, 473, 563

"Li Yün," *see* "Evolution of the Rites"

Liang Ch'i-ch'ao, 1873–1929, scholar, views on pre-Ch'in thought, 7n, 39n, 52, 180n; on political participation, 26n; on Northern and Southern schools of Chou era thought, 42; on Mohism, 67n, 224n, 226n, 254n, 433, on the dates of Lao Tzu, 76n; on *jen*, 102, 105n; on Hsün Tzu, 146n; on Kuan Tzu, 332n,

403, 415, 417ff; defined by Han Fei Tzu as "the sharp instrument of the state," 417; as tag for Legalist governing in Han usage, 447n; in re remission of penalties, in Han, 454; the power to employ derived from the people, in Chia Yi, 475–76; in Tung Chung-shu, 493; to be made precise, according to Hsün Yüeh, 543; at issue, in *Huai-nan Tzu*, 581n

righteousness, *yi*, in political thought, one of four basic human virtues, in Mencius, 148; made possible by secure livelihood, in Mencius, 153; defined as benefit (*li*) in Mo Tzu, 232; origin of, in Heaven, in Mo Tzu, 243–44; importance of in the *Kuan Tzu*, 348–50; in thought of Chia Yi, 477–78, uses of contrasted with legal penalties, 479; in Tung Chung-shu, 489n. *See also* rites and righteousness; propriety; etc.

righteousness and good faith, *yi-hsin*, Confucian virtues, 147

rights of the individual in society, 185; in the *Mo Tzu*, 260

rise and fall, flourishing and decline of the state, portents of in the *Tso Chuan*, 206–07

rites, *li* (also, ceremonies, ritual proprieties, ritualized behavior, etc.), concept of, in re concept of law, 66–67, 194–95, 195n; Confucian stress on, 74, 79n–80n, 84, 93–95, 100, 109ff, 139, 322, 398; in Mencius, 154n, 177; in Hsün Tzu, 146n, 182–94; his old and new concepts of, 195, 195n, his views on governing according to, 200, 237; rites rejected by Mo Tzu, 216, 255, 255n, 263; in re Taoism, 280, 408n; ceremonies of the court, 194–95; ceremonies of the Suburban Temple (Temple of Heaven), 215; ceremonies preserved in Royal Chou archives, 273n, 274n, 275; place of rites in the *Kuan Tzu*, 321n, 333–34, 348–50; effectiveness of as political instrument weakened, 376; waning of, compared with waning of the laws, 378–79; rites do not extend downward to the common people, 402n, 482; capacity of, for becoming law in clan-law society, 53n, 445n; rites worthless, according to *Huai-*

nan Tzu, 573; Neo-Taoists' desire to destroy, Chapter Eleven, Sections Two and Three, 607–630; rites ignored by Neo-Taoists, 645; strongly reaffirmed by Ko Hung, 655–56. *See also Chou Li; Yi Li; Li Chi; Three Ritual Classics*; rites and music; rites and righteousness; rites and teachings; ritual; ritualization

Rites, Book of, see *Li Chi*

rites and music, *li-yüeh* (also: *Rites* and *Music*; "institutes and music; etc.), instrument of Chou royal government, 29, 74, 98, 105; formulaic reference to Confucian teachings, 17, 22, 53n, 84, 112, 115, 346, 499; high utility of, in Confucian school view, 263–65, 295; rejected, as institutions, by Mo Tzu, 230, by Lao Tzu, 281, 298, by Chuang Tzu, 311–14, by the *Huai-nan Tzu*, 334n, 404, 419–20; restored in early Han, 555–56; devised to regulate human emotions, in view of *Huai-nan Tzu*, 575; in Ko Hung, 644; in Sun Sheng, 648. *See also* rites

rites (or propriety) and (the sense of) righteousness, *li-yi*, in the "Li Yün" chapter of the *Li Chi*, 125–26; in re Hsün Tzu, 148n, 184, 189, 190–91, 256, 314; in the *Kuan Tzu*, 348–50; in Confucian school doctrines, 352; in Chia Yi, 477ff; rejected by Han Emperor Wen, 553; necessary to government, in the *Huai-nan Tzu*, 581n

rites and teachings, *li-chiao*, Confucian ethical formalism, 543. *See also* ethical formalism, etc.

ritual, tendency to degenerate into superficialities decried by Confucius, 115; of the court in early Han, devised by Shu-sun T'ung, 473n; rituals for completion of a new palace, 512. *See also* rites

ritual propriety, *li*, see rites

ritualization, excessive during the early Chou, 280; Chuang Tzu not in favor of, 315; social evils of rejected by Juan Chi, 621–23

River Chart, Ho-t'u, Han dynasty prognostication text, 210, 212, 525

Roman law, compared with pre-Ch'in Legalism, 346; speculation about its possible impact on China if it had be-

Masters of Chien-an Period, 545, 606n, 631n

Wang T'ung, 583–616, defended T'o-pa Wei against slurs as alien conquerors, 25n

Wang Wen-shu, active under Han Emperor Wu, harsh administrator, 451, 464n

Wang Yen, A.D. 256–311, thinker and statesman, defied ghosts, 210; biographical note, 605; his comment on Kuo Hsiang, 609, 610n; sponsored new interest in the *Lao Tzu*, 611–12, 634; relationship to Wang Pi, 631n; blamed for social and political weaknesses, 645–46, admitted his guilt, 647n

war, modes of, 139n; as Legalist policy, 90, 393–97, 458–59; repudiated in *Lü-shih Ch'un-ch'iu*, 559, 562n, 566–67; Yin people's conventions of, 106; countered by pacifism in Confucian thought, 153–54; technology of, 217, 219, 265; in political thought of the *Lao Tzu*, 287, 295, 299; wars of conquest, to establish a new dynasty, 168; frequency of, in Warring States era, 227, 324, 559; tactics, Confucius' views on, 265; Mencius' views on, 266; "punitive action" distinguished from offensive war, in the *Mo Tzu*, 272; origins of, in the *Huai-nan Tzu*, 575; war unknown before there were rulers, according to Pao Ching-yen, 625. *See also* pacifism; warfare; weapons

Ware, James R., modern scholar, 656n

warfare, condemnation of offensive, *fei-kung*, major tenet of Mohism, Chapter Four, Section Seven, 265–72, 226n; Mohism's view refuted in *Lü-shih Ch'un-ch'iu* as encouragement to tyrants, 563; in re Confucianism, 266; concept of, deprived of significance by Ch'in unification, 432

warfare, defensive, need to prepare for, stressed in the *Mo · Tzu*, 259, 270–71; technology for, 265; "armed peace" to prevent war, in Confucius, 271, in Hsün Tzu, 271–72; need for diminished after Ch'in unification, 432

warlords, late Han Regional Inspectors (*tz'u-shih*) equivalent to, 539

warp, *ching*, of society, 509

Warring States Period, *Chan-kuo* 480–221 B.C. (Chapters One through Seven all concern the Warring States Period), dates of, discussed, 4n; transition into, characterized by Ku Yen-wu, 6n; Feng Yu-lan's views on periodization, 392n; flowering of political thought in, 5–6, 31–33, 144, 166, 202, 321n, 376; special conditions of in re emergence of Legalism, 369ff; violence of, 63, 144, 226–27; changing social conditions in, 85, 90, 175–76, 198, 240, 261, 321, 347, 354–55, 658; Confucius' hope to forestall changes of, 100; Chou hegemony waning in, 170, 175, 240; influence of, on Han government, 451n, 486; compared with third century A.D., 605

"wastes of Yin," *see* Yin-hsü

water, symbolic of strength in yielding, in the *Lao Tzu*, 286; environmental impact of, on man, discussed in the *Kuan Tzu*, 338–39

Watson, Burton, contemporary scholar, translator, 455n, 487n

Way of heaven, *t'ien Tao*, *see* heaven, Way of

wealth, material abundance, in re morality, 110, 153, 582, 582n; increase of as a goal of government, in Hsün Tzu, 185–88; material circumstances determine ethical content, according to the *Mo Tzu*, 234, 256–57; ways to increase production of, lacking in Mohism, 265; relation of, to the orderly society, according to the *Kuan Tzu*, 355ff; wealth derived from management, not production *per se*, according to *Debates on Salt and Iron*, 461; extremes of private wealth to be avoided, according to Tung Chung-shu, 501; extracted from the realm by bad rulers, according to Chung-ch'ang T'ung, 546

weapons, in re state policy, in Confucius, 110n, in Mencius, 153; destroyed by Ch'in dynasty, 432

weather phenomena, in re prognostication theory, 507n; Five Verifications of, 508; weather periods, *hou*, in re prognostication theory, 509

Wei, Chou state whose dukes were of royal

Library of Congress Cataloging in Publication Data

Hsiao, Kung-ch'üan, 1897–
    A history of Chinese political thought.
    Translation of Chung-kuo cheng chih ssu hsiang shih.
    Includes index.
    CONTENTS: v. 1, From the beginnings to the sixth
century A.D.
    1, Political science—China—History. 2, Philosophy,
Chinese. I. Title.
JA84.C6H6813   320.5′0951   ·77–85553
ISBN 0–691–03116–9
ISBN 0–691–10061–6 LPE